O9-ABH-224

FOOD AND DRUG LAW AND REGULATION

THIRD EDITION

Edited by

David G. Adams
Partner, Venable LLP
Adjunct Professor, George Washington University Law School

Richard M. Cooper
Partner, Williams & Connolly LLP

Martin J. Hahn
Partner, Hogan Lovells LLP

Jonathan S. Kahan
Partner, Hogan Lovells LLP
Adjunct Professor, George Washington University Law School

FDLI

FDLI

© 2015 FDLI. All rights reserved. ISBN 978-1-935065-73-9

Authorization to photocopy items for internal or personal use of specific clients is granted by the Food and Drug Law Institute, provided that the base fee of US $.75 per page is paid directly to the Copyright Clearance Center (CCC), 222 Rosewood Drive, Danvers, MA 01923, USA. For those organizations that have been granted a photocopy license by CCC, a separate system of payment has been arranged. The fee code for users of the Transactional Reporting Service is: 978-1-935065-73-9/02.75

To order additional copies of this publication, please visit our website at www.fdli.org.

1155 15th St. NW, Suite 910, Washington, DC 20005
Tel: (202) 371-1420 Fax: (202) 371-0649
email: comments@fdli.org
website: www.fdli.org

CONTENTS

PREFACE

Food and drug law occupies a unique position in American jurisprudence: it governs safety, efficacy, labeling, and availability of products that are central to health and well being, and that account for 20 to 25 percent of consumer spending in the United States. From the elegant simplicity of the Pure Food and Drugs Act of 1906 to the technically elaborate Drug Quality and Security Act of 2013, the body of food and drug regulatory law has grown into a vast and complex array of statutes, regulations, interpretive documents, and judicial decisions, for which treatment in an authoritative text is needed. In the last several decades, the Food and Drug Law Institute (FDLI) has met this need by developing texts authored and edited by experts from all areas of food and drug law. This book carries on that important mission in greater scope and depth.

The book's 26 chapters are intended to cover every major aspect of food and drug law and regulation, including five chapters on drugs, four on food, and chapters on dietary supplements, cosmetics, veterinary food and drugs, biologics and biosimilars, medical devices, combination products, and tobacco products. An introductory chapter provides an overview of the subject matter, and five additional chapters describe the purposes, methods, and inner workings of the Food and Drug Administration, including regulation of healthcare professionals; administrative procedures; enforcement authority; the agency's role in emergencies—medical countermeasures, emergency preparedness, and response roles and authorities; and its role at the international level. The final three chapters address the related regulatory missions of other agencies and governmental entities: the Federal Trade Commission's regulation of advertising, the Drug Enforcement Administration's regulation of controlled substances, and federal regulation of reimbursement, fraud, and abuse.

Although the authors are attorneys affiliated with federal agencies, university law schools, pharmaceutical manufacturers, and private law firms, they have sought to be objective in the treatment of their subjects.

The book provides discussions that are practical and supported by citations to guide further research. It is intended as a resource for practicing attorneys who want to learn about food and drug law or gain greater expertise in a particular area. It is also intended to complement law school casebooks and as a general reference for law libraries, practitioners in other fields, and those interested in how food, medical products, cosmetics, and tobacco products are regulated by the U.S. government.

We thank FDLI for its dedication to publishing this book and the authors for their generosity in sharing their expertise with our readers.

David G. Adams
Richard M. Cooper
Martin J. Hahn
Jonathan S. Kahan

ABOUT THE EDITORS

David G. Adams is Chair of the FDA Practice Group at Venable LLP. Mr. Adams previously held senior positions at the Food and Drug Administration (FDA) in the Office of the Commissioner and Office of the Chief Counsel. He has served as Chair of the American Bar Association Food and Drug Law Committee and as Chair of the Editorial Board of the *Food and Drug Law Journal*. Mr. Adams also teaches food and drug law as an adjunct professor at the George Washington University Law School.

Richard M. Cooper is of counsel in the Washington, D.C. law firm of Williams & Connolly LLP. He has written extensively on food and drug law and has taught that subject at Georgetown University Law Center. He was Chief Counsel of the Food and Drug Administration during 1977-1979. Earlier in 1977, he was a special assistant to James R. Schlesinger and a senior member of the Office of Energy Policy and Planning, Executive Office of the President. He was a law clerk to Hon. William J. Brennan, Jr., U.S. Supreme Court, in 1969-70.

Martin J. Hahn is a partner at Hogan Lovells. His practice focuses on a wide variety of regulatory issues affecting the food and dietary supplement industries. Mr. Hahn monitors new developments and has co-authored a manual on the regulation of foods derived from biotechnology and a manual on the issues presented by allergens in foods. He has presented numerous speeches on food labeling and food safety and is a frequent speaker for programs sponsored by the Food and Drug Law Institute and the Food Allergy Research and Resource Program.

Jonathan S. Kahan is a Co-Director of Hogan Lovells' food, drug, medical device, and agriculture group. His practice focuses primarily on assisting medical device companies in navigating the Food and Drug Administration regulatory process. Mr. Kahan is the author of *Medical Device Development: Regulation and Law* (Parexel 2014) and *Medical Devices: Obtaining FDA Market Clearance* (Parexel 1995). He is the Chair Emeritus of the Dean's Advisory Board of the George Washington University Law School and an adjunct professor at the law school teaching medical device law. He is the former Chairman of the Federal Bar Association Section on Health and Human Services. He is a member of Phi Beta Kappa and Order of the Coif.

ABOUT THE AUTHORS

Carolyn Alenci is an associate in the Intellectual Property Group at Duane Morris LLP in Boston. She focuses her practice on the area of intellectual property litigation, with a concentration on the chemical and pharmaceutical industries. She assists generic pharmaceutical companies filing abbreviated new drug applications with the Food and Drug Administration with pre-litigation strategic planning and patent litigation.

Emily Alexander is the Director of External Affairs in the Biologics Strategic Development group at AbbVie, Inc. Emily works with a cross-functional team that is dedicated to ensuring that international, national, and state biosimilar laws and policies are focused on patients and based in sound science. Emily regularly speaks and writes on issues related to the Food and Drug Administration's implementation of its biosimilar authority. Prior to joining AbbVie, she was an attorney in the Food & Drug practice group at Covington & Burling LLP's Washington, D.C. office, where she focused on advising biopharmaceutical companies and related trade associations on the legal and regulatory implications of originator biologic and biosimilar approval pathways around the world. Emily was also involved in the legislative debates surrounding the Biologics Price Competition and Innovation Act and the Biosimilar User Fee Act. She holds a law degree from the University of Virginia School of Law and a Bachelor of Arts from Purdue University.

Deborah C. Attwood is an associate attorney in Keller and Heckman LLP's Food and Drug practice group. She represents businesses and trade associations on global legal and regulatory compliance activities for human and pet food, animal feed, and food and drug packaging. Ms. Attwood assists clients with obtaining essential premarket regulatory approvals from governmental authorities worldwide and responding to regulatory enforcement actions and litigation. Ms. Attwood also collaborates with trade associations and companies to develop responsive strategies to new legislative and regulatory initiatives, particularly in the U.S., EU, China, and MERCOSUR.

Frederick (Rick) R. Ball is Vice-Chair of the White-Collar Criminal Defense division of Duane Morris' Trial Practice Group. Mr. Ball focuses his practice on assisting companies or individuals when they are adverse to state or federal governments, including administrative, civil, and criminal matters, with the Food and Drug Administration, Federal Trade Commission, Drug Enforcement Administration, Centers for Medicare & Medicaid Services, Office of Inspector General, and other federal and state regulatory agencies. Mr. Ball helps generic pharmaceutical companies, biologics manufacturers, food companies (including supplement manufacturers), pharmacies, long-term care providers, and other healthcare providers navigate the complex challenges faced by state and federal regulation of their industries including complying with current Good Manufacturing Practices, price reporting (AMP, AWP, ASP, etc.), the Foreign Corrupt Practices Act, False Claims Act, and

Anti-Kickback Statute, as well as meeting labeling and advertising requirements. Mr. Ball also assists generic manufacturers bring product to market through patent analysis and Hatch-Waxman litigation. Mr. Ball is experienced in conducting internal investigations and advising companies on actions following the investigation. Mr. Ball emphasizes a team approach to client problem solving and manages matters to achieve client goals both financial and legal.

Scott Bass heads Sidley Austin's Global Life Sciences Team, coordinating pharmaceutical, medical device, food, and dietary supplement matters in the United States, Europe, and Asia. Mr. Bass served as an adjunct professor at Georgetown University Graduate School, where he co-taught food safety with the Food and Drug Administration; as Co-Chair of the American Bar Association Food and Drug Law Committee and Chairman of the New York State Bar Association Section on Food, Drug and Cosmetic Law; as an expert in a European Union Commission study and as an advisor on new China drug and device legislation. Mr. Bass has published many articles and books in the pharmaceutical, enforcement, and dietary supplement fields.

Brooke Courtney is Senior Regulatory Counsel in the Office of Counterterrorism and Emerging Threats in the Food and Drug Administration's (FDA) Office of the Commissioner, where she works on domestic and global statutory, regulatory, and policy issues related to FDA-regulated medical products for public health and national security emergencies. Ms. Courtney was previously the Director of the Office of Public Health Preparedness and Response at the Baltimore City Health Department. She is a term member of the Council on Foreign Relations, and a member of the Institute of Medicine Preparedness Forum. She received her JD and Health Law Certificate from the University of Maryland and her MPH from Yale University.

James N. Czaban is the Chairman of the Food & Drug Law Practice at Wiley Rein LLP in Washington, D.C. where his practice broadly encompasses government regulation of pharmaceutical, biotechnology, food, medical device, and other clients involved in the Life Sciences. Under his leadership, the firm represents such clients with respect to complex regulatory strategies, compliance matters, and in administrative and judicial enforcement actions and other proceedings involving the Food and Drug Administration, the Federal Trade Commission, the Drug Enforcement Administration, the Department of Health and Human Services Office of Inspector General, the Department of Justice, and other federal and state agencies. Mr. Czaban has a long history of service to the Food & Drug bar, having served as Chair of the Legal Writing Awards Committee of the Food and Drug Law Institute (FDLI) and regularly publishing on and teaching food and drug law for FDLI and other organizations. He is consistently recognized as a leading lawyer in food and drug law, including by *Chambers USA's America's Leading Lawyers, Washingtonian* magazine, *PLC/ Which Lawyer,* and other publications. In 2011 Mr. Czaban received the Burton Award for Legal Achievement as a result of his work in the field of biosimilars regulation. Mr. Czaban is a graduate of the University of Virginia School of Law and the University of California, Berkeley.

Gail L. Daubert is a member of the Life Sciences Health Industry Group at Reed Smith, practicing in the area of healthcare regulatory law. She provides legal, regulatory, and legislative counsel to a variety of professional associations and manufacturers of pharmaceutical drug products and medical devices. She has creatively resolved issues related to Medicare reimbursement of new medical technology for the firm's clients. Ms. Daubert has assisted clients with Medicare coverage issues, working directly with the Centers for Medicare & Medicaid Services, Coverage and Analysis Group as well as local Medicare Administrative Contractors. She also handles issues related to CPT and HCPCS coding and payment for new medical technologies. She has worked with device manufacturers and specialty societies to obtain CPT codes for new technology procedures. She has also successfully restructured and created new DRGs and APCs to improve Medicare payment for procedures.

Fred H. Degnan joined King & Spalding's food and drug practice in 1988 after an 11-year career in the Food and Drug Administration's Office of General Counsel. He taught food and drug law at the Catholic University of America from 1989 to 2011 where he served as a Distinguished Lecturer. His numerous publications include the book *FDA's Creative Application of the Law*, a focus on FDA's implementation of its regulatory authority to adapt to the practical demands of regulation (2d ed., 2006). While at FDA he received the agency's highest awards and in 2002 received the FDLI Distinguished Leadership award. For years he served as General Counsel to FDLI and as the Chairman of FDLI's Board from 2009–2010. He has consistently been recognized in numerous independently conducted surveys as being among the nation's top food and drug lawyers.

Mel Drozen is a partner at Keller and Heckman LLP. Mr. Drozen advises clients on a broad spectrum of Food and Drug Administration (FDA), Federal Trade Commission, U.S. Department of Agriculture, and Environmental Protection Agency (pesticides) regulatory matters involving food labeling, ingredients, and advertising issues. Prior to joining Keller and Heckman, he was an Assistant District Attorney in Brooklyn, New York, and then an attorney in the General Counsel's Office of FDA for seven years. With his partners, Mr. Drozen regularly teaches seminars on food law, labeling, and advertising. He earned his BA from Georgetown University and graduated from Brooklyn Law School.

Michael N. Druckman is a partner in the Washington, D.C. office of Hogan Lovells US LLP. He counsels pharmaceutical and biotechnology companies on Food and Drug Administration (FDA) law and regulation. Previously Mr. Druckman worked in FDA's Office of Chief Counsel. He served as co-team leader for biologics, advising on legal issues involving vaccines, blood products, cellular and tissue products, and public health emergency and pandemic planning. Prior to joining FDA, he was a litigation partner at a Washington, D.C. law firm. Mr. Druckman clerked for U.S. District Judge John H. Pratt (D.D.C.). He received his AB from Harvard College and his JD from the University of Pennsylvania Law School.

Daniel R. Dwyer is a partner in the law firm of Kleinfeld, Kaplan & Becker LLP of Washington, D.C. His practice concentrates on law and regulation affecting food, drugs, cosmetics, dietary supplements, medical devices, and other products regulated by the Food and Drug Administration (FDA). He frequently advises on regulatory matters, advertising and promotional rules, recalls and safety issues, corporate compliance, clinical trial compliance, and good manufacturing practice. He is a frequent writer and speaker on FDA topics. Mr. Dwyer is a 1984 graduate of Georgetown University Law Center and is admitted to practice in the District of Columbia and Maryland.

Stacy L. Ehrlich is partner in the Washington, D.C. law firm of Kleinfeld, Kaplan & Becker LLP, which specializes in food and drug law. Her practice focuses on representing pharmaceutical, food, dietary supplement, tobacco, cosmetic, and medical device companies on a variety of matters involving the Food and Drug Administration (FDA), the U.S. Department of Agriculture, and the Federal Trade Commission, as well as state agencies. Ms. Ehrlich serves on the FDLI *Update* Editorial Advisory Board and is included in the 20th Edition of *The Best Lawyers in America* (2014) for FDA law. She received her BA with high honors in English from Emory University and her JD, *cum laude*, from Harvard Law School.

Lesley Fair is a Senior Attorney with the Federal Trade Commission's (FTC) Bureau of Consumer Protection, where she has represented the FTC in numerous investigations of deceptive advertising for health-related products. Ms. Fair has been on the adjunct faculty of the Catholic University of America School of Law since 1984 and is a Professorial Lecturer at George Washington University Law School. A graduate of the University of Notre Dame and the University of Texas School of Law, she clerked for U.S. District Judge Fred Shannon and served as a staff counsel to the U.S. Court of Appeals for the Fifth Circuit.

Ciara Farrell's practice focuses on European Union (EU) and national regulatory law governing pharmaceutical law, medical devices, food law, and the environment. Ms. Farrell's experience includes advising on marketing authorization procedures, promotional and marketing activities in the pharmaceutical sector, conduct compliance, anti-bribery investigation for life sciences companies, and food labeling regulatory compliance, including health and nutrition claims. Ms. Farrell joined Hogan Lovells in 2013. She was admitted as a Solicitor (Republic of Ireland) in 2013 and as an Attorney & Counsellor of Law (New York State) in 2010. Ms. Farrell is also a member of the Brussels Bar (E-list).

John A. Gilbert, Jr. is a Director at Hyman, Phelps & McNamara, P.C. in Washington, D.C. Mr. Gilbert advises clients on the regulation of controlled substances, prescription drugs, and chemicals in the United States and under the international drug control treaties. Prior to joining HPM, Mr. Gilbert was an attorney in the Drug Enforcement Administration's (DEA) Office of Chief Counsel and served as a law clerk in the DEA Office of Administrative Law Judges. Mr. Gilbert graduated from Westfield State College and received his law degree from the Catholic University of America, where he was an associate editor of the *Catholic University Law Review*.

Abeba Habtemariam is an associate in the FDA and Healthcare Practice at Arnold & Porter LLP where she provides advice and strategic guidance to pharmaceutical, biotechnology, and medical device companies on a range of regulatory matters under the Federal Food, Drug, and Cosmetic Act and the Public Health Service Act. Abeba counsels clients on Food and Drug Administration (FDA) regulatory issues throughout the product life cycle, including on the regulation of clinical research, product approval strategies, cGMP compliance, advertising and promotion, compliance with postmarket requirements, and responses to FDA inspections and government investigations. At present, her practice focuses on, among other things, the regulation of medical device software and healthcare IT products, the regulation of biologics and biosimilars, and promotional compliance matters. Abeba received a bachelor's degree in natural sciences public health from Johns Hopkins University, a master's degree in biotechnology also from Johns Hopkins University, and her law degree from Yale Law School.

Michael S. Heyl, Catholic University, Columbus School of Law (*magna cum laude*), is a partner in the Washington, D.C. office of the law firm of Hogan Lovells US LLP. His practice is in the medical device area with an emphasis on postmarket enforcement matters. He focuses extensively on postmarket compliance issues, including the Quality System Regulation (QSR), adverse event reporting, and recalls. Mr. Heyl is a frequent speaker at medical device seminars and has authored articles on device regulations. Prior to joining Hogan & Hartson (the predecessor to Hogan Lovells), he represented the interests of specialty chemical producers before the U.S. Congress and numerous administrative agencies.

Devon Wm. Hill is a partner in the Food and Drug practice group at Keller and Heckman LLP where he has worked since 1996. Mr. Hill represents clients and trade associations on compliance and testing issues surrounding the regulation of food, animal feed, cosmetics, and food and drug packaging materials in various jurisdictions around the world. Mr. Hill is a frequent speaker on the regulation of food contact materials in the United States, Canada, Europe, South America, and Asia. Prior to attending law school, Mr. Hill obtained his master's degree in chemistry and worked as a university research chemist and in industry.

Daniel A. Kracov is Co-Chair of Arnold & Porter, LLP's FDA and Healthcare Practice. He assists clients, including start-up companies, trade associations, and large manufacturing companies, in negotiating the challenges relating to the development, approval, and marketing of drugs, biologics, and medical devices. Mr. Kracov regularly handles product and compliance-related investigations, the development of regulatory corporate compliance programs, and due diligence in financings, mergers, and acquisitions. He has a widely recognized experience in biomedical product-related public policy matters, including congressional investigations and FDA-related legislative strategies.

Geoffrey M. Levitt is Senior Vice President and Associate General Counsel for Regulatory Law at Pfizer, where he is responsible for managing global legal support for regulatory, safety, manufacturing, clinical development, and environmental operations. Prior to joining

Pfizer in October 2009, Mr. Levitt served as Vice President and Chief Regulatory Counsel at Wyeth. He has published and lectured extensively on regulatory law, and is a past member of the editorial board of the *Food and Drug Law Journal* and a current member of the editorial board of the *FDA Advertising and Promotion Manual*. Mr. Levitt has served as Chairman of the Board of the Food and Drug Law Institute and received the Institute's 2009 Distinguished Service and Leadership Award. His publications include the book *Competitive Challenges in the Drug Approval Process: Generics, Hybrids and Follow-on Biologics* (2005) and the chapter "The Drugs/Biologics Approval Process" in *A Practical Guide to Food and Drug Law and Regulation* (5th ed. 2014). He earned his JD from Harvard Law School and his BA from Columbia University.

Erika Lietzan is an Associate Professor of Law at the University of Missouri School of Law. She joined the Missouri faculty from Covington & Burling, LLP, in Washington, D.C., where she was a partner. Professor Lietzan teaches and writes primarily in the areas of drug and device regulation, intellectual property, and administrative law. She has published law journal articles on, among other things, the release of safety and effectiveness data in drug marketing applications, generic drug exclusivity under the Hatch-Waxman Act, preemption of failure to warn suits against biopharmaceutical manufacturers, conflicts of interest on advisory committees serving the Food and Drug Administration (FDA), and the disgorgement remedy theory for violations of the Federal Food, Drug, and Cosmetic Act. She has written several monographs and book chapters, including on the law and policy of biosimilar biological products, federal regulation of clinical trials, and the application of First Amendment principles to health claims on foods and dietary supplements. Professor Lietzan is an elected member of the American Law Institute. She also serves in the leadership of the Science and Technology Section of the American Bar Association, now chairing its Life Sciences Division, which includes the Biotechnology Committee (which she chaired for many years), Medical Device Committee, and several other committees. She serves as an editor of the American Bar Association's treatise, *Biotechnology and the Law*, and she has written more than a dozen shorter pieces for a variety of other publications, including two empirical pieces on judicial review of FDA decisions for FDLI *Update*.

Anne V. Maher is a partner at Kleinfeld, Kaplan & Becker LLP, a food and drug law firm. She specializes in Advertising Law. Her expertise includes health, environmental, children's, online, and social media marketing claims, including advertisement meaning and substantiation issues. She represents clients before the Federal Trade Commission (FTC), the state Attorneys General, and the National Advertising Division. She was Chairman of the Editorial Advisory Board of the *Food and Drug Law Journal*. Ms. Maher was formerly Assistant Director of Advertising Practices at the FTC, where she was the designated Food and Drug Administration and U.S. Department of Agriculture liaison. She frequently speaks at conferences involving advertising law and policy. Ms. Maher received her BA from Boston University and her JD from Northeastern University School of Law.

Stephen Paul Mahinka is the chair of Morgan Lewis' global Life Sciences industry group, and a partner resident in the firm's Washington, D.C. office. He is the founder of the firm's

FDA practice and a former leader of its Antitrust practice. His practice focuses on both Food and Drug Administration regulatory and antitrust issues throughout the product life cycle, concerning pharmaceuticals, biologics, medical devices, and food additives, and Federal Trade Commission and state consumer protection matters. Mr. Mahinka is widely published, is a co-author of *Life Sciences Mergers and Acquisitions* (2008) and *Winning Antitrust Strategies* (2004), a contributing author of the *Pharmaceutical Industry Antitrust Handbook* (2009), and is a past member of the Editorial Advisory Board of the *Food and Drug Law Journal*. He was selected to the Legal Media Group's Life Sciences Hall of Fame in 2013, and is a member of the Editorial Advisory Board of *Life Sciences Law360*. He is a graduate of Johns Hopkins University, Phi Beta Kappa, and of the Harvard Law School.

Christina M. Markus serves as Deputy Chair of the FDA & Life Sciences practice group and is a partner in King & Spalding's Washington, D.C. office. Her practice focuses on the regulation of foods, drugs, and related products by the Food and Drug Administration (FDA), the U.S. Drug Enforcement Administration, and related state agencies (e.g., food and drug agencies, boards of pharmacy). She represents companies and institutions in a range of regulatory compliance, enforcement, licensing, and business transactions involving product development and approval, safety, labeling, marketing and advertising, competition strategy, and supply chain. Ms. Markus is recognized as a leading FDA and Life Sciences counselor in the United States. She received her JD from the University of Virginia, where she was an FDLI Food and Drug Law Scholar; she received her AB degree from the College of William and Mary.

William McConagha is a partner in Sidley Austin's Food and Drug practice, which he joined after working for more than 17 years at the Food and Drug Administration (FDA). During his tenure at FDA, Mr. McConagha served in the Office of Chief Counsel, as an Assistant Commissioner, and as a Health Policy Advisor to the Senate Committee on Health, Education, Labor and Pensions (HELP). At Sidley, Mr. McConagha advises clients on a range of FDA-related regulatory and enforcement issues, and he has helped a number of clients navigate FDA-initiated civil and criminal investigations. He also co-teaches a seminar on Health Law at American University's Washington College of Law.

Joseph W. Metro is a partner in the Washington, D.C. office of Reed Smith LLP. Mr. Metro is a member of the firm's Life Sciences and Health Industry group, and represents pharmaceutical, biologic, and medical device industry clients on matters relating to reimbursement, fraud, and abuse and government pricing. His practice includes transactional, counseling, and investigational aspects, and he is a frequent speaker on matters relating to the Medicaid rebate program and the Veterans Health Care Act. Mr. Metro is a 1986 graduate of Dickinson College and received his law degree in 1989 from the George Washington University National Law Center.

Suzan Onel is a partner at the global law firm K&L Gates LLP and chairs the firm's FDA practice. Ms. Onel advises on all aspects of Food and Drug Administration (FDA) law and regulatory compliance across cosmetics, over-the-counter drug products, medical devices, food, and supplement industries. Ms. Onel has extensive experience representing companies on market entry strategies, labeling and promotional activities, regulatory compliance, adverse event reporting, recalls, and enforcement defense. She also regularly advises clients on the development of corporate compliance programs and regulatory strategy and conducts executive training sessions. Her transactional work includes conducting regulatory due diligence for life science companies and investors, drafting supplier and distributor contracts, and drafting clinical trial and investigator agreements. Ms. Onel is a frequent author and lecturer on FDA-related topics, including contributing a chapter to Aspatore's 2014 Inside the Minds series, "Recent Developments in Food and Drug Law" and co-editing the PLI treatise, *Medical Devices Law and Regulation Answer Book 2015* (4th edition). Ms. Onel received her BA with honors in neurobiology and history from the University of Pennsylvania and her JD from the University of Virginia School of Law.

Joseph A. Page is a professor at the Georgetown University Law Center, where he has been teaching food and drug law since 1980. He currently serves as the Georgetown Law faculty advisor to the student staff of the *Food and Drug Law Journal*. He has written about aspects of food and drug law in the *UCLA Law Review,* the *Food and Drug Law Journal,* Books-on-Line, the *Washington Monthly, The New Republic,* and *Commonweal.* He has also served on the Drug Effects Study Advisory Panel of the Office of Technology Assessment of the U.S. Congress, and was a member of the Board of Directors of Public Citizen from 1972 to 2009. A 1955 graduate of Harvard College (*magna cum laude*), where he majored in classics, Professor Page holds both an LLB and an LLM from the Harvard Law School.

Karla L. Palmer is a Director at Hyman, Phelps & McNamara, P.C. in Washington, D.C. Ms. Palmer focuses on Drug Enforcement Administration (DEA) and Food and Drug Administration (FDA) enforcement and litigation matters, with particular emphasis on Controlled Substances Act (CSA) issues. Before joining Hyman, Phelps & McNamara, Ms. Palmer was a partner at a large international law firm where she was head of the Washington, D.C. trial department. Following law school, Ms. Palmer clerked for the Honorable Claude M. Hilton, former Chief Judge of the U.S. District Court for the Eastern District of Virginia, Alexandria Division. Ms. Palmer graduated from the College of William and Mary and received her law degree from the University of Richmond School of Law where she was an associate editor of the *University of Richmond Law Review.*

Eve C. Pelonis is a Food and Drug Counsel at Keller and Heckman LLP. Ms. Pelonis' practice focuses on all regulatory and compliance matters of the U.S. Food and Drug Administration and the U.S. Department of Agriculture. Ms. Pelonis graduated from the Johns Hopkins University with a BA in international studies in 1999 and received her JD from the Catholic University of America in 2003.

William Pendergast is a retired partner and founding member of the Food and Drug Group of Arent Fox LLP. While serving as a trial attorney with the Food and Drug Administration

(FDA) in the mid-1960s, Mr. Pendergast was responsible for the conduct of some 100 trials and adjudicatory hearings involving principally the pharmaceutical, cosmetic, and food additive industries. Following his work at FDA, Mr. Pendergast worked in private practice, serving as lead counsel in more than 40 litigated cases involving FDA, including the representation of leading manufacturers of human and animal drugs, cosmetics, and food ingredients. Mr. Pendergast is the author of more than 20 articles published in FDA-related professional journals.

Jeannie Perron, JD, DVM, is a partner at the law firm of Covington & Burling LLP in Washington, D.C. Her practice emphasis is food and drug law, particularly animal food and drug law, and animal welfare cases. She has authored or co-authored numerous articles and chapters in various publications. She is a member of a number of state and federal bars and the U.S. Patent and Trademark Office. Dr. Perron received her JD from George Washington University and her DVM from Texas A&M University.

Fabien Roy's practice focuses on European Union (EU) and national regulatory matters involving pharmaceutical and medical device laws and guidelines. He has developed close contact with relevant government authorities in these sectors. Fabien focuses particularly on the different stages of the medical device CE marking process. He advises on a wide variety of topics which include the following: determination of the appropriate classification of individual products; clinical investigation procedure, review of Instruction For Use, products' labeling and promotional material including websites; postmarketing surveillance activities including the notification of adverse event, product recall, or product withdrawal; reimbursement; and conduct of compliance and anti-bribery investigations for life sciences companies. Fabien also advises on questions regarding marketing authorization procedures, variation procedures, clinical trials, and promotional and marketing activities in the pharmaceutical sector.

Elizabeth Sadove is Director, Medical Countermeasure Regulatory Policy, in the Office of Counterterrorism and Emerging Threats in the Food and Drug Administration's (FDA) Office of the Commissioner. She is responsible for advancing FDA's statutory, regulatory, and policy framework to support the development and availability of FDA-regulated medical products for public health and national security emergencies. Ms. Sadove joined FDA in 2003 as Regulatory Counsel in the Center for Drug Evaluation and Research. Prior to joining FDA, she handled public policy issues and legislative affairs both in private practice law and for a Subcommittee of the U.S. House of Representatives. She earned her BA from Franklin & Marshall College and her JD from George Washington University, National Law Center.

Kathleen M. Sanzo is a partner in and leader of Morgan Lewis' FDA Practice, representing drug, device, food, and cosmetic manufacturers in regulatory, transactional, enforcement, and compliance matters. She graduated from Duke University, Emory Law School and received her LLM from the George Washington University National Law Center, as the Food and Drug Law Institute Fellow. Ms. Sanzo is the author or co-author of numerous speeches and publications, including for the last four years FDLI's *Top 20 Food and Drug Cases, & Cases to Watch*. She was named "US Regulatory Attorney of the Year," "FDA Pharmaceutical Industry Lawyer of the Year," and a "Life Sciences Star" by Legal Media Group Life Sciences. Ms. Sanzo is also listed in *America's Leading Lawyers for Business* by Chambers USA.

Gordon Schatz is a partner in Reed Smith's Life Sciences Health Industry group, specializing in reimbursement for devices, diagnostics, and drugs. He has obtained new billing codes, improved hospital DRG and APC payment, and expanded coverage for innovative medical technologies. Mr. Schatz represents manufacturers of cardiovascular, orthopedic, neurology, oncology, diagnostic imaging, clinical laboratory, surgery, and other specialty products. His reimbursement counseling enables companies to integrate reimbursement with clinical trials, regulatory approvals, product promotion, and customer support. He also advises clients on pricing, marketing, and sales programs to comply with the Medicare fraud and abuse laws. Mr. Schatz served as Reed Smith's Life Science Integration partner in China. An honors graduate of Haverford College, he received his JD and the Barristers Award from Temple University School of Law. Mr. Schatz has lectured at the Georgetown Law Center O'Neill Institute for Global Health, and Tsinghua Health Law Research Center in Beijing, China. In 2014, he was recognized as a "Life Sciences Star" in the *LMG Definitive Guide to the Leading Life Science Attorneys in North America*.

Brett T. Schwemer is a principal at Olsson Frank Weeda Terman Bode Matz PC and head of the firm's USDA practice group. His primary specialty is food safety and labeling law, representing meat and poultry companies and trade associations before the U.S. Department of Agriculture's (USDA) Food Safety and Inspection Service, and in the case of dual jurisdiction establishments and other food companies, before the Food and Drug Administration. He also specializes in regulatory, compliance, and enforcement matters before other USDA agencies, such as the Grain Inspection, Packers and Stockyards Administration. He received his BBA in 1989 from the James Madison University and his JD from Ohio Northern University School of Law in 1992, graduating with distinction.

Jeffrey K. Shapiro has represented healthcare companies on Food and Drug Administration (FDA) related matters since 1994. He advises companies in the areas of medical devices, combination products, and human tissue products, including product approvals, marketing, clinical studies, jurisdictional issues, recalls, and enforcement. Mr. Shapiro has written and lectured extensively on FDA-related topics. He is co-editor of *Promotion of Biomedical Products* (FDLI 2006) and co-author of *Combination Products: How to Develop the Optimal Strategic Path for Approval* (FDA News 2005). He is a Director in the law firm of Hyman, Phelps, & McNamara, a firm focused exclusively on FDA law and regulation.

Laura E. Sim is a Special Counsel in the food and drug group in the Washington, D.C. office of Covington & Burling LLP. She advises drug and biologic manufacturers and trade associations on a range of regulatory and consumer protection issues, with a focus on domestic and international regulation of biosimilars, drug and biologic life cycle development, Hatch-

Waxman Act and Biologics Price Competition and Innovation Act implementation, and drug safety. She has published articles and given speeches concerning biosimilar regulation in the United States and abroad.

Smitha G. Stansbury is a partner in King & Spalding's FDA & Life Sciences practice group in Washington, D.C. She assists clients with regulatory matters before the Food and Drug Administration (FDA), the U.S. Department of Agriculture, the Federal Trade Commission, and other health and safety regulatory agencies at the federal and state levels. Ms. Stansbury has particular expertise in food law, and has worked extensively with various food and beverage manufacturers and distributors, food industry trade associations, equipment suppliers, retailers, and restaurants on issues related to food safety, ingredients and product formulation, and food labeling and advertising. She has published many articles and given speeches on food-related issues such as FDA's implementation of the Food Safety Modernization Act. Ms. Stansbury received her JD from the University of Virginia School of Law and her BA from the University of Virginia.

Jolyda O. Swaim is a principal in the Washington, D.C. law firm of Olsson Frank Weeda Terman Matz PC, focusing on Food and Drug Administration (FDA) and U.S. Department of Agriculture Food Safety and Inspection Service regulatory matters related to production of various FDA ready-to-eat products and meat and poultry production, respectively. Prior to becoming an attorney, she had extensive experience in the food industry. Her last position was with Sara Lee Corporation as Corporate Food Safety Director with oversight of meat and poultry plants and high-risk bakery and cheese plants in the United States and Mexico. Ms. Swaim received her BS from Mercyhurst University in Erie, Pennsylvania, and her JD *cum laude* from Western Michigan University Thomas M. Cooley Law School in Lansing, Michigan.

Brian P. Waldman is a member of Arent Fox LLP's Executive Committee, and co-manager of the firm's Regulatory Department. Mr. Waldman concentrates his practice in the area of food and drug law and advertising law, counseling manufacturers and distributors of pharmaceuticals, medical devices, foods (including dietary supplements and medical foods), and cosmetics, with particular emphasis on developing effective strategies for introducing and promoting new products. He received his JD degree from the University of California at Los Angeles and his MBA and BA from the University of Chicago.

Marsha Wertzberger is the senior food and dietary supplement attorney at Arent Fox. Ms. Wertzberger practices in the areas of food and drug law and biotechnology, with a focus on regulatory and enforcement matters, advertising and marketing issues, and product development. She is active in mentoring activities within the firm and is a founding member of the women in food and drug law group of the Food and Drug Law Institute. She is a pharmacist and is a graduate of Georgetown Law Center.

Edward C. Wilson, Jr. ("Ted"), JD, University of Virginia School of Law, AB, Davidson College (*cum laude*, Phi Beta Kappa), is a partner at Hogan Lovells US LLP in Washington, D.C. His practice focuses on a wide variety of regulatory and enforcement issues affecting the medical device industry. Mr. Wilson is a certified quality systems auditor who helps companies worldwide attain regulatory compliance. He has taught numerous courses on FDA's premarket and postmarket requirements. His experience includes assisting in the defense of government investigations, conducting internal investigations of alleged company misconduct, and providing legal advice on a variety of device-related issues.

Ann H. Wion is Senior Advisor to the Chief Counsel in the Office of the General Counsel, Department of Health and Human Services (DHHS), Food and Drug Division. She received a PhD from Cornell University and a JD from Stanford Law School. After joining the DHHS Office of General Counsel in 1979, she specialized primarily in drug and biologics law. From 1993-2013 she was Deputy Chief Counsel for Program Review and oversaw the attorneys providing legal counsel in DHHS on FDA-related matters. The views expressed in Chapter 20 are the author's and do not necessarily represent those of DHHS/FDA.

Elisabethann Wright focuses on European Union (EU) law relating to life sciences, with particular emphasis on pharmaceutical law, medical devices, food law, and the environment. This includes assisting clients in classification of their products, establishment of a pathway to authorization and marketing of their products in the EU (including related regulatory obligations), pharmacovigilance obligations, promotion and marketing of products, sales agreements, clinical trial agreements, adverse event reporting, product withdrawals, and challenges to national authority and EU Institution decisions concerning classification and marketing of medicinal products and medical devices. Prior to joining Hogan & Hartson (now Hogan Lovells), she served as Senior Legal Officer and Hearing Officer at the EFTA Surveillance Authority.

Gary L. Yingling is a senior attorney in Morgan Lewis' FDA Practice in Washington, D.C. He focuses his practice on issues involving the U.S. Food and Drug Administration and has also represented clients in matters involving the Drug Enforcement Administration, the Federal Trade Commission, and various states. His clients have included corporations, partnerships, and individuals in matters involving pre-IND, IND, and end of Phase II meetings, NDA submissions, ANDA applications, paragraph IV filings, REMS, OTC Monographs, labeling, importation, regulatory marketing strategy, recalls, seizures, and criminal matters. He is a co-editor of *Good Clinical Practice*, which focuses on FDA-regulated clinical trials. He has also counseled on FDA pre-approval manufacturing and clinical site inspections, assisted with 483 responses, and been involved in all aspects of drug regulation. Mr. Yingling earned his JD from Emory University School of Law in 1968. Prior to attending law school, he practiced community pharmacy and is a registered pharmacist in Maryland and D.C. He earned his MS from Purdue University in 1966 and his BS from University of North Carolina in 1962. He served in the FDA Office of General Counsel for a number of years and received FDA's Award of Merit for his work on the OTC Review.

CHAPTER 1
INTRODUCTION

....

RICHARD M. COOPER

The Focus of the Law

Food and drug law is about certain types of physical things. Most of these things are put into or onto, or are used with, the bodies of humans or animals—foods, drugs, medical devices, cosmetics, and, since June 22, 2009, tobacco products. Food and drug law also concerns aspects of radiation-emitting products (e.g., microwave ovens, laser lights) that relate to safety. The principal requirements and prohibitions of the law are about things: they shall not be adulterated or misbranded; they shall be manufactured and tested in accordance with certain standards; on their labels and in their labeling, certain disclosures shall be made, and certain kinds of claims shall not be made; certain kinds of things shall not be introduced into interstate commerce until their distribution has been authorized by the regulatory agency; and so on.

During the first few decades of modern food and drug law, the law's characteristic form of enforcement action was an *in rem* seizure action against physical objects that were in violation of the law.[1] The purpose of this type of action was to protect patients or other consumers from things that might harm or deceive them. In recent decades, seizure actions have largely (though not completely) been replaced by recalls, which serve the same purpose without intervention by a court. To the extent food and drug law regulates people and what they do, it regulates them only in relation to the physical things that are within the jurisdiction of the law, through injunctive, criminal, debarment, civil-penalty or certain other types of proceedings.

Some products within the jurisdiction of the Food and Drug Administration (FDA)—e.g., drugs and medical devices—are discovered or invented after substantial research. Generally, such a product undergoes a developmental process that includes testing in a laboratory and then in animals and humans; creation and validation of processes for manufacturing

---

[1] Federal Food, Drug, and Cosmetic Act (FDCA) § 304, 21 U.S.C. § 334 (2012).

and quality control on a commercial scale; and development of labeling that sets forth conditions of use. It then goes through some form of review by FDA and is approved, cleared, or otherwise permitted to be distributed in interstate commerce. Next, the product is manufactured in packaged and labeled form, is advertised and promoted, and is shipped commercially. During its life on the market, the product is from time to time the subject of reports of adverse events experienced by consumers and of complaints by consumers, which are reviewed by the product's manufacturer and possibly by FDA. Medical devices may undergo engineering changes. The labeling of drugs and medical devices changes as information on how to use them most effectively and safely accumulates. Additional uses for such products may be discovered, tested, and included in product labeling. Food and drug law addresses most stages of this product life cycle.

This focus on physical things sets the framework for regulation by FDA. The agency's most labor-intensive activities include: 1) review of applications to test potential new medical products in human subjects; 2) review of applications for permission for commercial marketing of new products or ingredients for use in products, and for changes in already marketed products; 3) review of reports and other data bearing on the safety of marketed products; 4) inspections of factories and of goods offered for importation, and testing of samples obtained in such inspections; 5) review of advertising and marketing of products; 6) regulatory and enforcement actions that result from such inspections and reviews; and 7) development and publication of regulations and guidance documents relating to products and activities within its jurisdiction.

FDA regulates products that account for more than 20 percent of consumer spending in the United States.[2] Whereas other administrative agencies have gone through periods of deregulation, in recent years Congress has expanded FDA's jurisdiction and its regulatory authorities.

A Little History

Although there were antecedents in the 19th century in America and even earlier in England,[3] the modern history of food and drug regulation begins with the Pure Food and Drugs Act of 1906.[4] That legislation, which had long been championed by Dr. Harvey W. Wiley, Chief Chemist of the U.S. Department of Agriculture (USDA), finally resulted from the sensational disclosures by the muckrakers of corruption, fraud, and improper conditions in many areas

---

[2]   Margaret A. Hamburg, M.D., Commissioner of Food and Drugs, Remarks at Generic Pharmaceutical Association Annual Meeting (Feb. 18, 2010), *available at* http://www.fda.gov/NewsEvents/Speeches/ucm201833.htm. *See also* Sean Silverthorne, *The FDA: What Will the Next 100 Years Bring?*, HARVARD BUS. SCH. WORKING KNOWLEDGE (Sept. 24, 2007), *available at* http://hbswk.hbs.edu/item/5753.html; Alastair J.J. Wood, M.D., *Playing "Kick the FDA"—Risk-free to Players But Hazardous to Public Health*, 358 N. ENG. J. MED. 1774, 1774-75 (Apr. 24, 2008), *available at* http://www.nejm.org/doi/full/10.1056/NEJMp0802227.

[3]   *See, e.g.*, Peter Barton Hutt, *The Basis and Purpose of Government Regulation of Adulteration and Misbranding of Food*, 33 FOOD DRUG COSM. L.J. 505, 506-09 (1978).

[4]   Pub. L. No. 59-384, 34 Stat. 768 (1906). Congress previously had enacted legislation to regulate products of biological origin. Pub. L. No. 57-244, 32 Stat. 728 (1902).

of economic activity, including food processing and the manufacture and marketing of patent medicines.[5]

The law specified conditions under which foods and drugs would be considered adulterated or misbranded (and therefore barred from interstate commerce), and authorized USDA's Bureau of Chemistry to recommend enforcement actions to the U.S. Department of Justice (DOJ). The law did not provide for governmental review of products prior to their marketing, and was limited in other ways.

Many of the recognized defects in the 1906 act were remedied by the FDCA of 1938, FDA's organic statute and the principal authority for its regulatory activities.[6] This statute greatly expanded FDA's authority by providing for premarket review of drugs under a requirement of safety, for standards of identity and quality for food, for regulation of medical devices and cosmetics, and for inspections by FDA employees of factories, warehouses, and other places where regulated products are made, tested, or held. This statute remains the basic food and drug law; and it has been amended many, many times, in most instances in ways that expand and strengthen the regulatory scheme. The principal amendments (some of which have been subsequently amended) have included the following:

- A series of amendments providing for regulation of insulin and various antibiotics;[7]

- Miller Act, which added to the FDCA section 301(k) (adulterating or misbranding a regulated product after it has been shipped in interstate commerce) and correspondingly amended section 304(a) (relating to seizure);[8]

- Durham-Humphrey Amendment (providing a statutory basis for a prescription requirement);[9]

- Pub. L. No. 83-217 (strengthening FDA's inspectional authority);[10]

- Food Additives Amendment of 1958;[11]

- Color Additive Amendments of 1960;[12]

---

[5]   See generally Richard M. Cooper, The Struggle for the 1906 Act, in FDA: A CENTURY OF CONSUMER PROTECTION 25-69 (Wayne Pines ed., FDLI 2006). The phenomenon of enacting food and drug legislation in response to harm, or a perceived threat of harm, to the public health (perceived as resulting from a lack of adequate regulation) was repeated, e.g., in 1938, when the modern food and drug statute was enacted; in 1962, when major amendments to the drug law were enacted; in 1976, when major amendments to the medical device law were enacted; in 2007, when further major amendments to the drug law and other parts of the Federal Food, Drug, and Cosmetic Act were enacted; and in 2013, when further amendments as to drugs were enacted.

[6]   Pub. L. No. 75-717, 52 Stat. 1040 (1938) (codified as amended at 21 U.S.C. §§ 301-399f (2012)). Section 408 of the FDCA, 21 U.S.C. § 346a, relating to tolerances and exemptions for pesticide chemical residues, is administered by the Environmental Protection Agency.

[7]   Pub. L. No. 77-366, 55 Stat. 851 (1941) (insulin); Pub. L. No. 79-139, 59 Stat. 463 (1945) (penicillin); Pub. L. No. 80-16, 61 Stat. 11 (1947) (streptomycin); Pub. L. No. 81-164, 63 Stat. 409 (1949) (aureomycin, chloramphenicol, bacitracin); Pub. L. No. 83-201, 67 Stat. 389 (1953) (chlortetracycline).

[8]   Pub. L. No. 80-749, 62 Stat. 582 (1948).

[9]   Pub. L. No. 82-215, 65 Stat. 648 (1951).

[10] 67 Stat. 476 (1953).

[11] Pub. L. No. 85-929, 72 Stat. 1784 (1958).

[12] Pub. L. No. 86-618, 74 Stat. 397 (1960).

- Drug Amendments of 1962;[13]
- Animal Drug Amendments of 1968;[14]
- Drug Listing Act of 1972;[15]
- Medical Device Amendments of 1976;[16]
- Vitamins and Minerals Amendments;[17]
- Infant Formula Act of 1980;[18]
- Orphan Drug Act;[19]
- Drug Price Competition and Patent Term Restoration Act of 1984 (Hatch-Waxman Act);[20]
- Drug Export Amendments Act of 1986;[21]
- Prescription Drug Marketing Act of 1987;[22]
- Food and Drug Administration Act of 1988 (statutory establishment of FDA);[23]
- Generic Animal Drug and Patent Term Restoration Act;[24]
- Nutrition Labeling and Education Act of 1990;[25]
- Safe Medical Devices Act of 1990;[26]
- Food and Drug Administration Revitalization Act;[27]
- Generic Drug Enforcement Act of 1992;[28]
- Prescription Drug Amendments of 1992;[29]
- Medical Device Amendments of 1992;[30]
- Prescription Drug User Fee Act of 1992;[31]
- Animal Medicinal Drug Use Clarification Act of 1994;[32]
- Dietary Supplement Health and Education Act of 1994;[33]

---

[13]   Pub. L. No. 87-781, 76 Stat. 780 (1962).
[14]   Pub. L. No. 90-399, 82 Stat. 342 (1968).
[15]   Pub. L. No. 92-387, 86 Stat. 559 (1972).
[16]   Pub. L. No. 94-295, 90 Stat. 539 (1976).
[17]   Pub. L. No. 94-278, 90 Stat. 410 (1976).
[18]   Pub. L. No. 96-359, 94 Stat. 1190 (1980).
[19]   Pub. L. No. 97-414, 96 Stat. 2049 (1983).
[20]   Pub. L. No. 98-417, 98 Stat. 1585 (1984).
[21]   Pub. L. No. 99-660, 100 Stat. 3743 (1986).
[22]   Pub. L. No. 100-293, 102 Stat. 95 (1988).
[23]   Health Omnibus Programs Extension of 1988, Pub. L. No. 100-607, tit. V, 102 Stat. 3048, 3120-22 (1988).
[24]   Pub. L. No. 100-670, 102 Stat. 3971 (1988).
[25]   Pub. L. No. 101-535, 104 Stat. 2353 (1990).
[26]   Pub. L. No. 101-629, 104 Stat. 4511 (1990).
[27]   Pub. L. No. 101-635, 104 Stat. 4583 (1990).
[28]   Pub. L. No. 102-282, 106 Stat. 149 (1992).
[29]   Pub. L. No. 102-353, 106 Stat. 941 (1992).
[30]   Pub. L. No. 102-300, 106 Stat. 238 (1992).
[31]   Pub. L. No. 102-571, 106 Stat. 4491 (1992).
[32]   Pub. L. No. 103-396, 108 Stat. 4153 (1994).
[33]   Pub. L. No. 103-417, 108 Stat. 4325 (1994).

- FDA Export Reform and Enhancement Act of 1996;[34]

- Food Quality Protection Act of 1996;[35]

- Animal Drug Availability Act of 1996;[36]

- Food and Drug Administration Modernization Act of 1997;[37]

- Best Pharmaceuticals for Children Act;[38]

- Public Health Security and Bioterrorism Preparedness and Response Act of 2002;[39]

- Medical Device User Fee and Modernization Act of 2002;[40]

- Animal Drug User Fee Act of 2003;[41]

- Pediatric Research Equity Act of 2003;[42]

- Title XI of the Medicare Prescription Drug, Improvement, and Modernization Act of 2003 (relating to generic drugs);[43]

- Minor Use and Minor Species Animal Health Act of 2004;[44]

- Food Allergen Labeling and Consumer Protection Act of 2004;[45]

- Dietary Supplement and Nonprescription Drug Consumer Protection Act;[46]

- Food and Drug Administration Amendments Act of 2007;[47]

- QI Program Supplemental Funding Act of 2008 (section relating to certain antibiotic drugs);[48]

- Family Smoking Prevention and Tobacco Control Act;[49]

- Patient Protection and Affordable Care Act of 2010 (section relating to nutrition labeling of standard menu items at chain restaurants);[50]

- FDA Food Safety Modernization Act[51];

- Food and Drug Administration Safety and Innovation Act;[52] and

- Drug Quality and Security Act.[53]

---

[34] Pub. L. No. 104-134, tit. II, ch. 1A, 110 Stat. 1321-313 through 1321-320 (1996).
[35] Pub. L. No. 104-170, 110 Stat. 1489 (1996).
[36] Pub. L. No. 104-250, 110 Stat. 3151 (1996).
[37] Pub. L. No. 105-115, 111 Stat. 2296 (1997).
[38] Pub. L. No. 107-109, 115 Stat. 1408 (2002).
[39] Pub. L. No. 107-188, 116 Stat. 594 (2002).
[40] Pub. L. No. 107-250, 116 Stat. 1588 (2002).
[41] Pub. L. No. 108-130, 117 Stat. 1361 (2003).
[42] Pub. L. No. 108-155, 117 Stat. 1936 (2003).
[43] Pub. L. No. 108-173, 117 Stat. 2066, 2448 (2003).
[44] Pub. L. No. 108-282, tit. I, 118 Stat. 891, 891-905 (2004).
[45] Pub. L. No. 108-282, tit. II, 118 Stat. 905, 905-11 (2004).
[46] Pub. L. No. 109-462, 120 Stat. 3469 (2006).
[47] Pub. L. No. 110-85, 121 Stat. 823 (2007).
[48] Pub. L. No. 110-379, § 4, 122 Stat. 4075, 4076 (2008).
[49] Pub. L. No. 111-31, 123 Stat. 1776 (2009).
[50] Pub. L. No. 111-148, § 4205, 124 Stat. 119, 573 (2010).
[51] Pub. L. No. 111-353, 124 Stat. 3885 (2011).
[52] Pub. L. No. 112-144, 126 Stat. 993 (2012).
[53] Pub. L. No. 113-54, 127 Stat. 587 (2013).

Although FDA is the agency principally responsible for regulation of foods, drugs, medical devices, cosmetics, and tobacco products, certain regulatory functions relating to some of those products are also performed by USDA, the Drug Enforcement Administration in DOJ, the Federal Trade Commission, and the states. In addition, the system for federal reimbursement for therapeutic products is administered by the Centers for Medicare & Medicaid Services in the Department of Health and Human Services (DHHS).

FDA's Place in the Executive Branch

FDA is, and always has been, an agency in the executive branch of the federal government.[54] Therefore, its budget, legislative proposals, congressional testimony, and major regulatory proposals are subject to approval by the Office of Management and Budget (OMB) on behalf of the President.

Like other executive branch agencies, FDA is subject to a wide variety of executive orders issued by the President. It is also subject to general statutes that bear on its regulatory activities.[55]

Also like other agencies in the executive branch, FDA has no authority to represent itself in court, but is represented by DOJ.[56] All litigation—civil and criminal—involving the agency, and including litigation brought against the agency, is supervised on behalf of the agency by the Consumer Protection Branch (CPB) (formerly known as the Office of Consumer Litigation) in the Civil Division of DOJ. In practice, responsibility for the actual conduct of litigation on behalf of the agency is divided between the CPB and the Offices of the United States Attorneys throughout the country. In general, DOJ permits lawyers in FDA's Office of the Chief Counsel to assist in the representation of the agency in litigation.

FDA originated as the Bureau of Chemistry in USDA before the enactment of the Pure Food and Drugs Act of 1906.[57] The agency remained part of USDA (under various names) until 1940, when it was transferred to the Federal Security Agency, which later became the

---

54   By contrast, the Federal Trade Commission and the Consumer Product Safety Commission, for example, are independent agencies.

55   E.g., Administrative Procedure Act, Pub. L. No. 79-404, 60 Stat. 237 (1946) (codified as amended at 5 U.S.C. §§ 551, 553-559, 701-706 (2012)); Freedom of Information Act, Pub. L. No. 89-554, 80 Stat. 383 (1966) (codified as amended at 5 U.S.C. § 552 (2012)); Federal Advisory Committee Act, Pub. L. No. 92-463, 86 Stat. 770 (1972) (codified as amended at 5 U.S.C. app. 2 (2012)); National Environmental Policy Act of 1969, Pub. L. No. 91-190, 83 Stat. 852 (1970) (codified as amended at 42 U.S.C. §§ 4321, 4331-4335 (2012)); Regulatory Flexibility Act, Pub. L. No. 96-354, 94 Stat. 1164 (1980) (codified as amended at 5 U.S.C. §§ 601-612 (2012)); Government Performance and Results Act of 1993, Pub. L. No. 103-62, 107 Stat. 285 (1993); Unfunded Mandates Reform Act of 1995, Pub. L. No. 104-4, 109 Stat. 48 (1995) (codified as amended at 2 U.S.C. §§ 1501-1504, 1511-1616, 1531-1538, 1551-1556, 1571 (2012)); Paperwork Reduction Act of 1995, Pub. L. No. 104-13, 109 Stat. 163 (1995) (codified at 44 U.S.C. §§ 3501-3520 (2012)). These statutes have been amended from time to time.

56   See 28 U.S.C. §§ 516, 519 (2012). The agency is also bound by opinions of the Attorney General.

57   The Bureau of Chemistry began in 1862 with President Lincoln's appointment of a chemist in the USDA. U.S. Department of Health and Human Services, Historical Highlights, available at http://www.hhs.gov/about/hhshist.html (last reviewed June 6, 2014). The name "Food and Drug Administration" first officially appeared in the Agricultural Appropriation Act of 1931, Pub. L. No. 71-272, 46 Stat. 392 (1930).

Department of Health, Education and Welfare, and then DHHS.[58] The agency was formally established by law in 1988.[59]

As part of DHHS, FDA is subject to oversight by the department on the same matters as to which it is subject to oversight by OMB. FDA is subject to review by DHHS of other important actions, including certain types of regulatory actions,[60] internal reorganizations, and important personnel actions. Issues of integrity or efficiency with respect to FDA are investigated by DHHS's Office of Inspector General.

Although not legally independent, FDA is culturally independent of DHHS. FDA's principal offices are located on a campus in White Oak, Maryland—a substantial distance from DHHS's headquarters which are near the U.S. Capitol in Washington, D.C. The agency perceives its statutory and regulatory systems as complex and highly technical, and its expertise in administering them as unmatched by any group outside the agency. FDA has a long history of deferring to superior legal authority only to the extent necessary, and of acting as independently as circumstances permit.

FDA and Congress

Despite the movement of FDA from USDA to DHHS, FDA's annual appropriation is still part of the agricultural appropriations process, and is reviewed and determined by the Subcommittees on Agriculture of the House of Representatives and Senate Appropriations Committees. FDA's authorizing committees are the Senate Committee on Health, Education, Labor, and Pensions and the House Committee on Energy and Commerce. Within the latter, the Subcommittee on Oversight and Investigations and the Subcommittee on Health historically have taken a strong interest in the agency. The House Committee on Oversight and Government Reform also has responsibilities with respect to FDA. From time to time, other committees also have conducted investigations and hearings relating to FDA.

FDA frequently has been the subject of reports issued by congressional committees and by the Government Accountability Office (formerly known as the General Accounting Office).[61]

FDA's Internal Organization and Budget

FDA's internal organization is set forth in Part 5 of Title 21 of the *Code of Federal Regulations*. The head of the agency is a single Commissioner,[62] who, under a statute enacted in 1988,

---

58 *See generally* Michael Brannon, *Organizing and Reorganizing FDA, in* FOOD AND DRUG LAW 113-63 (Richard M. Cooper ed., FDLI 1991).

59 *See supra* note 23.

60 *See infra* notes 85-86 and accompanying text.

61 *See* Peter Barton Hutt, *Investigations and Reports on the Food and Drug Administration, in* FOOD AND DRUG LAW 41-60 (Richard M. Cooper ed., FDLI 1991).

62 There is no corresponding commission.

is appointed by the President with the advice and consent of the Senate.[63] Under the Commissioner, FDA units with agency-wide responsibilities are:

- Office of the Commissioner (including Chief of Staff)
  - Office of the Chief Counsel[64]
  - Office of the Executive Secretariat
  - Office of the Counselor to the Commissioner
    - Office of Legislation
    - Office of External Affairs
    - Office of Policy and Planning
  - Office of the Chief Scientist
    - National Center for Toxicological Research
    - Office of Women's Health
    - Office of Minority Health
- Office of Operations
  - Office of Equal Employment Opportunity
  - Office of Finance, Budget and Acquisitions
  - Office of Facilities Engineering & Mission Support Services
  - Office of Information Management and Technology
  - Office of Human Resources
  - Office of Security Operations
- Office of Food and Veterinary Medicine
  - Office of Resource Planning and Strategic Management
  - Office of Coordinated Outbreak Response and Evaluation Network
  - Center for Veterinary Medicine
  - Center for Food Safety and Applied Nutrition
- Office of Medical Products and Tobacco
  - Office of Special Medical Programs
  - Center for Devices and Radiological Health
  - Center for Biologics Evaluation and Research

---

[63] FDCA § 1003, 21 U.S.C. § 393(d); *see supra* note 23. Previously, the Commissioner had been appointed by the Secretary without Senate confirmation.

[64] FDA's Office of the Chief Counsel is, technically, part of the Office of the General Counsel of DHHS, which, in turn, is part of the Office of the Secretary. The FDA Chief Counsel is officially an Associate General Counsel of DHHS, and as such reports to the General Counsel of DHHS. *See* DHHS, Office of the General Counsel, Key Personnel, Food and Drug Division, *available at* http://www.hhs.gov/ogc/personnel/index. html#FoodandDrugDivisionStaffContactInformation (last updated Apr. 23, 2014). For a description of the Office of the Chief Counsel, *see* Office of the Chief Counsel, http://www.fda.gov/AboutFDA/CentersOffices/OC/OfficeoftheChiefCounsel/default.htm (last updated Feb. 24, 2010).

- Center for Drug Evaluation and Research
- Center for Tobacco Products

- Office of Global Regulatory Operations and Policy
  - Office of International Programs
  - Office of Regulatory Affairs.[65]

FDA also has an agency-wide ombudsman and ombudsmen in the Centers for Drugs, Devices, Biologics, Tobacco, and Veterinary Medicine.[66]

The organization of the Office of the Commissioner changes from time to time to suit the preferences of particular Commissioners.

FDA's principal regulatory programs are administered by six Centers:

- Center for Biologics Evaluation and Research;
- Center for Devices and Radiological Health;
- Center for Drug Evaluation and Research;
- Center for Food Safety and Applied Nutrition;
- Center for Tobacco Products; and
- Center for Veterinary Medicine.

As of January 2015, FDA had numerous advisory committees, principally for drugs, biological products, and devices.[67]

FDA's total appropriated program funding in fiscal 2014 (ending September 30, 2014) was $4.4 billion, which included $2.561 billion in appropriated budget authority and $1.826 billion in user fees.[68] For fiscal 2015, the President requested a total of $4.7 billion in program funding, of which $2.584 billion is budget authority and $2.161 billion is user fees.[69]

---

[65] Information about these offices is available at www.fda.gov/AboutFDA/CentersOffices/ (last visited Jan. 18, 2015).

[66] *See generally* the description of the Office of the Ombudsman, *available at* http://www.fda.gov/AboutFDA/CentersOffices/OC/OfficeofScientificandMedicalPrograms/ucm197508.htm (last updated Dec. 4, 2014); FDA's Office of the Ombudsman, Consultation[,] Dispute Resolution[,] Mediation (undated), http://www.fda.gov/downloads/aboutfda/contactfda/resolveadispute/ucm164330.pdf (last visited Jan. 18, 2015).

[67] *See* http://www.fda.gov/AdvisoryCommittees/default.htm (last updated Feb. 25, 2015) (for lists of committees, click on individual subject matter areas).

[68] FY 2015 FDA Justification of Estimates for Appropriations Committees, Overview of the Budget Request, *available at* http://www.fda.gov/downloads/AboutFDA/ReportsManualsForms/Reports/BudgetReports/UCM 394601.pdf (last visited Jan. 18, 2015).

[69] *Id.*

In fiscal 2014, FDA's estimated staffing of full-time-equivalent positions was as follows:

Center for Food Safety and Applied Nutrition	948
Center for Drug Evaluation and Research	4,245
Center for Biologics Evaluation and Research	1,138
Center for Veterinary Medicine	521
Center for Devices and Radiological Health	1,666
National Center for Toxicological Research	281
Office of Regulatory Affairs	4,970
Headquarters and Office of the Commissioner	1,307
Export Certification	22
Color Certification	37
Family Smoking Prevention and Tobacco Control Act	570
TOTAL	15,705[70]

Although FDA has received budget increases in recent years, there is reason to believe that the resources provided by Congress to FDA chronically have been, and remain, inadequate to enable the agency to fulfill its statutory responsibilities.[71]

FDA's Statutory Authorities

All authority exercised by FDA is derived from congressional delegations to the Secretary of Health and Human Services (the Secretary), and redelegations by the Secretary to the Commissioner of Food and Drugs.[72] FDA has no independent regulatory authority delegated directly to it by Congress.[73]

FDA administers the FDCA, and certain other statutes, including the Mammography Quality Standards Act of 1992,[74] certain provisions of the Public Health Service Act,[75]

---

[70]   *Id.*, Detail of Full-Time Equivalent (FTE) Employment, *available at* http://www.fda.gov/downloads/ AboutFDA/ReportsManualsForms/Reports/BudgetReports/UCM394944.pdf (last visited Jan. 18, 2015).

[71]   *See, e.g.*, FDA SCIENCE AND MISSION AT RISK, REPORT OF THE SUBCOMMITTEE ON SCIENCE AND TECHNOLOGY (Nov. 2007), *available at* http://www.fda.gov/ohrms/dockets/ac/07/briefing/2007-4329b_02_01_FDA%20 Report%20on%20Science%20and%20Technology.pdf.

[72]   The delegations are set forth in FDA STAFF MANUAL GUIDES VOLUME II – DELEGATIONS OF AUTHORITY, REGULATORY, DELEGATIONS OF AUTHORITY TO THE COMMISSIONER FOOD AND DRUGS § 1410.10 (2014), *available at* http://www.fda.gov/downloads/AboutFDA/ReportsManualsForms/StaffManualGuides/UCM273771.pdf. *See also* Removal of Delegations of Authority and Conforming Changes to Regulations, 69 Fed. Reg. 17,285 (Apr. 2, 2004) (removing list of delegated authorities from the *Code of Federal Regulations*).

[73]   The Commissioner is directly authorized by FDCA § 1004, 21 U.S.C. § 394, to establish technical and scientific review groups and to appoint and pay their members.

[74]   Pub. L. No. 102-539, 106 Stat. 3547 (1992).

[75]   *See* FDA STAFF MANUAL GUIDES VOLUME II – DELEGATIONS OF AUTHORITY, REGULATORY, DELEGATIONS OF AUTHORITY TO THE COMMISSIONER FOOD AND DRUGS § 1410.10, ¶ 1, *supra* note 72.

the Filled Milk Act,[76] the Federal Import Milk Act,[77] the Saccharin Study and Labeling Act,[78] and certain provisions of laws relating to controlled substances and drug abuse,[79] and has important functions under the Federal Caustic Poison Act,[80] the Lead-Based Paint Poisoning Prevention Act,[81] and the Fair Packaging and Labeling Act.[82] The agency also has certain functions under statutes administered principally by USDA.[83] The functions that FDA performs under statutes other than the FDCA are ancillary to its functions under the FDCA.[84]

Moreover, despite the broad delegations by the Secretary to the Commissioner, the Secretary in 1982[85] reserved, and continues to reserve, authority to approve regulations promulgated by FDA that:

(1) Establish procedural rules applicable to a general class of foods, drugs, cosmetics, medical devices, or other subjects of regulation; or

(2) Present highly significant public issues involving the quality, availability, marketability, or cost of one or more foods, drugs, cosmetics, medical devices, or other subjects of regulation.[86]

This reservation of authority was not intended to create any private right or benefit,[87] although, as a practical matter, it does invite lobbying at the department with respect to regulations to which it applies.

FDA's internal redelegations of authority are available at http://www.fda.gov/AboutFDA/ReportsManualsForms/StaffManualGuides/ucm136380.htm (last updated Oct. 22, 2014).

---

[76]   21 U.S.C. §§ 61-64.

[77]   *Id.* §§ 141-149.

[78]   Pub. L. No. 95-203, 91 Stat. 1451 (1977). This statute subsequently has been amended.

[79]   Comprehensive Drug Abuse Prevention and Control Act of 1970, Pub. L. No. 91-513, tit. I, § 4, 84 Stat. 1236, 1241 (1970); Controlled Substances Act, Pub. L. No. 91-513, tit. II, § 303(f), 84 Stat. 1242, 1253, 1255 (1970) (codified as amended at 21 U.S.C. § 823(f) (2012)).

[80]   Pub. L. No. 69-783, 44 Stat. 1406 (1927).

[81]   Pub. L. No. 91-695, tit. IV, § 401, 84 Stat. 2078, 2079 (1971), *as amended by* Pub. L. No. 94-317, tit. II, 90 Stat. 695, 705 (1976) (codified as amended at 42 U.S.C. § 4831(a) (2012)).

[82]   15 U.S.C. §§ 1451-1461 (2012).

[83]   Federal Meat Inspection Act § 409(b) (codified as amended at 21 U.S.C. § 679(b) (2012)); Poultry Products Inspection Act § 24(b) (codified as amended at 21 U.S.C. § 467(b) (2012)); Egg Products Inspection Act (codified as amended at 21 U.S.C. § 1031-1056) (2012)).

[84]   For a list of other statutes FDA considers itself affected by, *see* http://www.fda.gov/RegulatoryInformation/Legislation/ucm153119.htm (last updated June 18, 2009).

[85]   Reservation of Rulemaking Authority of the Food and Drug Administration in Matters Involving Significant Public Policy; Revision, 47 Fed. Reg. 16,318 (Apr. 16, 1982).

[86]   *See* FDA Staff Manual Guides Volume II – Delegations of Authority, Regulatory, Delegations of Authority to the Commissioner Food and Drugs § 1410.10 at 10, § 2 (Reservation of Authority), *supra* note 72.

[87]   *Id.* § 2.C.

An Overview of the Federal Food, Drug, and Cosmetic Act

The FDCA is organized into 10 chapters:

- Short Title;
- Definitions;
- Prohibited Acts and Penalties;
- Food;
- Drugs and Devices;[88]
- Cosmetics;
- General Authority;
- Imports and Exports;
- Tobacco Products; and
- Miscellaneous.

The statute is codified in Title 21 of the *United States Code*. The critical terms of the statute are defined in section 201.[89] Among the terms defined are the jurisdictional terms ("food," "drug," "device" (the term "device" refers to a medical device), "cosmetic," and "tobacco product"), and other terms critical to the operation of the statute (e.g., "interstate commerce," "label" and "labeling," "new drug," "food additive," and "color additive"). Section 201(u) specifies that, for purposes of food additives, new animal drugs, and color additives, the term "safe" refers to "the health of man or animal";[90] but the statute contains no general definition of "safe" or "safety," and consequently the definitions of those terms for particular regulatory purposes must be derived from other legal and regulatory materials.

The general strategy of the statute consists of three steps. First, the statute specifies circumstances in which an article (food, drug, device, cosmetic, or tobacco product) is "adulterated" or "misbranded,"[91] or lacks required permission to be marketed.[92] Second, the

---

[88]   The provisions relating to electronic products, including definitions, substantive, administrative, and enforcement provisions, and a list of prohibited acts, appear in FDCA sections 531-542, 21 U.S.C. §§ 360hh-360ss. FDA originally regulated radiation-emitting electronic products under the Radiation Control for Health and Safety Act of 1968, Pub. L. No. 90-602, 82 Stat. 1173 (1968), which originally was codified as part of the Public Health Service Act. Responsibility for administration of this statute was transferred to FDA by Redelegation of Authority, 36 Fed. Reg. 12,803 (July 7, 1971); and the statute, itself, was recodified in the FDCA by Pub. L. No. 101-629, § 19(a)(3), (4), 104 Stat. 4511, 4529-4530 (1990).

[89]   21 U.S.C. § 321.

[90]   21 U.S.C. § 321(u).

[91]   *See* FDCA §§ 402 (adulterated food), 403 (misbranded food), 501 (adulterated drugs and devices), 502 (misbranded drugs and devices), 601 (adulterated cosmetics), 602 (misbranded cosmetics), 902 (adulterated tobacco products) & 903 (misbranded tobacco products), 21 U.S.C. §§ 342, 343, 351, 352, 361, 362, 387b & 387c.

[92]   *See id.* §§ 404 (emergency permit control for certain foods), 505 (new drugs for human use), 21 U.S.C. §§ 344, 355. Other requirements for authorization for distribution, including *id.* §§ 409 (food additives), 512 (new animal drugs), 515 (Class III devices), 721 (color additives), & 910 (tobacco products), 21 U.S.C. §§ 348, 360b, 360e, 379e, & 387j, operate through the adulteration provisions, *id.* §§ 402(a)(2)(C)(i) (food additives), 402(a)(2)(C)(ii) (foods containing a new animal drug), 501(a)(5)-(6) (new animal drugs), 351(f)

statute defines a set of prohibited acts with respect to such an article.[93] Third, the statute authorizes a set of enforcement actions in response to a prohibited act.[94]

With respect to food, drugs, devices, cosmetics, and tobacco products, the adulteration and misbranding provisions use terms elaborated on in other substantive provisions of the statute, located in Chapter IV (Food), Chapter V (Drugs and Devices), Chapter VI (Cosmetics), and Chapter IX (Tobacco Products). Under FDCA section 701(a),[95] FDA has exercised general authority to elaborate by regulation the statutory standards for adulteration and misbranding, and those for approvals and other authorizations for marketing of products.[96] Section 301 prohibits certain acts with respect to an article that is adulterated or misbranded.[97] For example, section 301(a) declares it a prohibited act to introduce such an article into interstate commerce.[98] Similarly, section 301(d)[99] directly (i.e., without reference to adulteration or misbranding) prohibits the introduction into interstate commerce of any new drug for which an approval required by section 505(a)[100] is lacking and of any food subject to section 404[101] for which a permit required under that section is lacking.

Under section 304, an article that was adulterated or misbranded when introduced into interstate commerce or while in interstate commerce or while held for sale after shipment in interstate commerce, or that lacks a required authorization for distribution, is subject to seizure.[102] Commission of acts prohibited by section 301 may be enjoined under section

---

(Class III medical devices), 402(c) (food containing a color additive), 501(a)(4)(A) (drug or device containing a color additive), 501(a)(4)(B) (color additive for use on a drug or device), 601(e) (cosmetic containing a color additive), 902(6) (tobacco product), 21 U.S.C. §§ 342(a)(2)(C)(i), 342(a)(2)(C)(ii), 351(a)(5)-(6), 342(c), 351(a)(4)(A), 351(a)(4)(B), 361(e), 402(c), & 387b(6).

Food and drug law uses varying terminology to refer to actions by FDA to permit the distribution of different kinds of products in interstate commerce. For example, FDA may "approve" a new drug application under FDCA § 505(c)(1)(A), 21 U.S.C. § 355(c)(1)(A); and it may "approve" a device premarket approval application under section 515(d)(1), 21 U.S.C. § 360e(d)(1). FDA may "clear" a device to enter the market by means of a notification under section 510(k), 21 U.S.C. § 360(k). *See, e.g.*, FDA, 510(k) Clearances, *available at* http://www.fda.gov/MedicalDevices/ProductsandMedicalProcedures/DeviceApprovalsandClearances/510kClearances/default.htm (last updated Jan. 13, 2015). Under section 404, 21 U.S.C. § 344, FDA issues "permits" for interstate distribution of certain foods. With respect to a new tobacco product reviewed under FDCA § 910, 21 U.S.C. § 387j, FDA may, under section 910(c)(1)(A)(i), 21 U.S.C. § 387j(c)(1)(A)(i), "issue an order that the new product may be introduced or delivered for introduction into interstate commerce . . . ." Most authorizations for marketing are by letter (which constitutes an "order" for purposes of the Administrative Procedure Act, 5 U.S.C. § 551(6)), but an authorization for the marketing and use of a food additive or color additive is in the form of a regulation, *see* FDCA § 409(c), 21 U.S.C. § 348(c) (food additives); FDCA § 721(b)(1), 21 U.S.C. § 379e(b)(1) (color additives).

[93] FDCA § 301, 21 U.S.C. § 331.

[94] FDCA §§ 302-310, 21 U.S.C. §§ 332-337. Certain additional, administrative enforcement actions are authorized in substantive provisions of the statute. For example, FDCA § 505(e), 21 U.S.C. § 355(e), authorizes withdrawal of approval of a new drug application on certain specified grounds.

[95] 21 U.S.C. § 371(a).

[96] *See, e.g.*, 21 C.F.R. pts. 101 (food labeling), 110 (current good manufacturing practices for human food), 201 (drug labeling), 210-211 (good manufacturing practices for drugs), 314 (premarket approvals of new drugs), 801 (device labeling), 814 (premarket approvals of devices), and 820 (quality system regulation for devices).

[97] 21 U.S.C. § 331.

[98] *Id.* § 331(a).

[99] *Id.* § 331(d).

[100] *Id.* § 355(a).

[101] *Id.* § 344.

[102] *Id.* § 334.

302,[103] and may be the basis for a criminal prosecution and/or, in certain circumstances, an action for civil penalties under section 303.[104] Other remedies for certain kinds of prohibited acts are available to FDA under other provisions of the statute.[105]

FDA's Mission

FDA's mission is stated in section 1003(b) of the FDCA:

The Administration shall—

(1) promote the public health by promptly and efficiently reviewing clinical research and taking appropriate action on the marketing of regulated products in a timely manner;

(2) with respect to such products, protect the public health by ensuring that—

(A) foods are safe, wholesome, sanitary, and properly labeled;

(B) human and veterinary drugs are safe and effective;

(C) there is reasonable assurance of the safety and effectiveness of devices intended for human use;

(D) cosmetics are safe and properly labeled; and

(E) public health and safety are protected from electronic product radiation;

(3) participate through appropriate processes with representatives of other countries to reduce the burden of regulation, harmonize regulatory requirements, and achieve appropriate reciprocal arrangements; and

(4) as determined to be appropriate by the Secretary, carry out paragraphs (1) through (3) in consultation with experts in science, medicine, and public health, and in cooperation with consumers, users, manufacturers, importers, packers, distributors, and retailers of regulated products.[106]

Here is FDA's statement of what it does:

FDA is responsible for protecting the public health by assuring the safety, efficacy and security of human and veterinary drugs, biological products, medical devices, our nation's food supply, cosmetics, and products that emit radiation.

---

[103]   *Id.* § 332.
[104]   *Id.* § 333.
[105]   *See generally* Chapter 21, *infra.*
[106]   21 U.S.C. § 393(b).

FDA is also responsible for advancing the public health by helping to speed innovations that make medicines more effective, safer, and more affordable and by helping the public get the accurate, science-based information they need to use medicines and foods to maintain and improve their health. FDA also has responsibility for regulating the manufacturing, marketing and distribution of tobacco products to protect the public health and to reduce tobacco use by minors.

FDA plays a significant role in the Nation's counterterrorism capability. FDA fulfills this responsibility by ensuring the security of the food supply and by fostering development of medical products to respond to deliberate and naturally emerging public health threats.[107]

FDA states that it strives to:

- Enforce FDA laws and regulations, using all appropriate legal means.

- Base regulatory decisions on a strong scientific and analytical base and the law; and understand, conduct, and apply excellent science and research.

- Be a positive force in making safe and effective products available to the consumer, and focus special attention on rare and life-threatening diseases.

- Provide clear standards of compliance to regulated industry, and advise industry on how to meet those standards.

- Identify and effectively address critical public health problems arising from use of FDA-regulated products.

- Increase FDA's effectiveness through collaboration and cooperation with state and local governments; domestic, foreign, and international agencies; industry; and academia.

- Assist the media, consumer groups, and health professionals in providing accurate, current information about regulated products to the public.

- Work consistently toward effective and efficient application of resources to our responsibilities.

- Provide superior public service by developing, maintaining, and supporting a high-quality, diverse workforce.

- Be honest, fair, and accountable in all of our actions and decisions.[108]

---

[107] Statement of FDA Mission, *available at* http://www.fda.gov/downloads/aboutfda/reportsmanualsforms/reports/budgetreports/ucm298331.pdf (last visited Jan. 18, 2015).

[108] FDA INVESTIGATIONS OPERATIONS MANUAL, FDA Principles § 1.8.1, *available at* http://www.fda.gov/ICECI/Inspections/IOM/ucm122507.htm (last updated Dec. 18, 2014).

FDA's International Activities

Under Chapter VIII of the FDCA, FDA long has had responsibilities with respect to import and export of articles within its jurisdiction. In connection with imports, FDA, in cooperation with the U.S. Customs and Border Protection, conducts inspections of foreign goods presented for entry into the United States;[109] the agency also has responsibility to inspect, or arrange for inspection of, foreign facilities that manufacture or process goods for importation into the United States.[110] In connection with exports, the agency reviews applications for export approval where required,[111] and provides export certificates.[112] The agency also has active programs to achieve harmonization of its regulatory requirements with those of other countries with sophisticated regulatory systems.[113]

Food and Drug Law and Regulation, and the Practice of the Healing Arts

Although the food and drug laws and FDA's regulations apply to articles that affect health and to articles that are used to protect, promote, and restore health, they do not apply directly to the practice of medicine or other healing arts. In general, physicians, dentists, pharmacists, and other providers of healthcare are regulated by their respective professional societies and by state governmental agencies; and, in general, FDA does not regulate medical professionals except when they engage in clinical research, and when they manufacture, prepare, dispense, or market products within FDA's jurisdiction.[114]

Food and drug laws and regulations do directly affect the practice of the healing arts. FDA's regulation of drugs (including biological products), medical devices, and medical foods determines their availability to practitioners and patients. The FDA-approved labeling for such products influences the ways they are used. As a matter of food and drug law and regulation, practitioners are free to use such products outside the conditions stated in their labeling,[115] but they are responsible for such use under state law. Thus, for example, FDA regulates devices used in surgical and other medical procedures, but does not regulate the procedures, themselves; and physicians are free to use such devices in ways not recommended in their FDA-approved labeling.

---

[109] *See* FDCA § 801(a)-(d), 21 U.S.C. § 381(a)-(d).

[110] *See* FDCA § 510(i)(3), 21 U.S.C. § 360(i)(3); ORA Field Management Directive No. 13A: Foreign Inspection Program (rev. Oct. 5, 2010), *available at* http://www.fda.gov/ICECI/Inspections/FieldManagementDirectives/UCM056644 (last updated May 2, 2011).

[111] *See* FDCA §§ 801(e)(2), (4), 802, 21 U.S.C. §§ 381(e)(2), (4), 382.

[112] FDA, Guidance for Industry: FDA Export Certificates (July 2004) (Corr. copy Apr. 2005), *available at* http://www.fda.gov/regulatoryinformation/guidances/ucm125789.htm (last visited Jan. 18, 2015). *See also* Export Certificates, http://www.fda.gov/InternationalPrograms/ExportsandExportCertificates/ucm130041.htm (last updated Feb. 13, 2014).

[113] *See generally* Chapter 23, *infra*.

[114] *See generally* Chapter 19, *infra*.

[115] FDCA § 1006, 21 U.S.C. § 396; Proposed New Drug, Antibiotic, and Biologic Drug Product Regulations, 48 Fed. Reg. 26,720, 26,733 (June 9, 1983); *Use of Approved Drugs for Unlabeled Indications*, 12 FDA Drug Bull. 4 (1982); Legal Status of Approved Labeling for Prescription Drugs; Prescribing for Uses Unapproved by the Food and Drug Administration, 37 Fed. Reg. 16,503 (Aug. 15, 1972).

FDA does regulate clinical trials of unapproved drugs and devices conducted in the United States, and clinical trials on approved drugs and devices (including clinical trials on unapproved drugs and devices outside the United States) where the sponsors of the trials intend to submit data from them to the agency in support of applications for approval or other authorization for distribution in interstate commerce.[116] When practitioners participate in such trials, their participation is regulated by FDA.[117] Moreover, when medical professionals step outside their normal therapeutic roles and misbrand or adulterate drugs or devices or engage in what FDA considers regulated activities indistinguishable from manufacturing and marketing drugs or devices, the agency may take regulatory action against them.[118]

Physicians and other healthcare practitioners play significant roles in FDA's activities. In recent decades, FDA Commissioners have been physicians or have had related academic credentials. Many senior and other officials of FDA, particularly those responsible for reviews of new medical products, are physicians. FDA's advisory committees, whose advice the agency usually accepts, consist principally of physicians, most with academic appointments. Moreover, physicians design, oversee, and conduct virtually all of the clinical research on which FDA regulatory decisions about specific products are based.

State Regulation of Foods and Drugs

Most states have food and drug laws that are similar to the FDCA. States regulate intrastate products and activities, and work cooperatively with FDA on matters of mutual interest. State Attorneys General, from time to time, also have taken enforcement action with respect to matters within the general area of food and drug law and regulation.

Additional Sources of Information About FDA

FDA's website address is www.fda.gov. FDA regulatory documents are posted at www.regulations.gov. Other governmental agencies and congressional committees that interact with FDA have their own websites, on which materials relevant to FDA can be found.

The Food and Drug Law Institute publishes the *Food and Drug Law Journal*, a magazine, books, and an e-mail newsletter; conducts conferences and educational programs relating to

---

[116]   *See generally* FDCA §§ 505(i), 520(g), 21 U.S.C. §§ 355(i), 360j(g).

[117]   *See generally* 21 C.F.R. pts. 50, 54, 56, 312, 812 (2014).

[118]   *See, e.g.,* United States v. Sullivan, 332 U.S. 689 (1948) (criminal prosecution of retail pharmacist for misbranding drug after it had been shipped in interstate commerce); United States v. Regenerative Services, LLC, 741 F.3d 1314, 1320 (D.C. Cir. 2014) (affirming injunction against two physicians, their laboratory director, and a related corporation for producing and administering, as part of their medical practice, a substance consisting of a mixture of a patient's stem cells and an antibiotic); United States v. Diapulse Corp. of America, 514 F.2d 1097, 1098 (2d Cir. 1975) (per curiam) (devices in offices of medical practitioners for use in treatment of patients are "held for sale" within the meaning of FDCA § 301(k), 21 U.S.C. § 331(k)); United States v. Kaadt, 171 F.2d 600 (7th Cir. 1948) (prosecution of physicians for distributing misbranded drugs); United States v. Sene X Eleemosynary Corp., 479 F. Supp. 970 (S.D. Fla. 1979) (enjoining compounding, promotion, and distribution of certain drugs by pharmacist and others).

food and drug regulation; maintains a directory of professional services; and provides other educational services. Its activities cover the full range of products regulated by FDA. Its website is www.fdli.org. The Drug Information Association provides similar services with respect to drugs, medical devices, and related products. Its website is http://www.diahome.org/DIAHome/Home.aspx. Both organizations are neutral and not-for-profit.

Many trade publications report on FDA's activities, including:

- CCH (reporters on food, drugs, devices, cosmetics), http://health.cch.com/news/food-drug-devices/041211.asp;
- FDA Week, http://insidehealthpolicy.com;
- FDANews (a variety of newsletters), http://www.fdanews.com/newsletters;
- FDC Reports (a variety of newsletters), http://www.pharmamedtechbi.com/;
- Food Chemical News, http://www.agra-net.com/portal2/fcn/home.jsp;
- Supermarket News (has a legislation/regulation section), http://supermarketnews.com/news/laws-regulations;
- NewsRx (has a news section on food and drug law; offers pay-as-you-go and some free news stories/alerts), http://www.newsrx.com/NewsRxCorp/;
- Rx Compliance Report, http://www.rxcompliancereport.com/;
- FDA Enforcement Manual, http://www.thompson.com/public/offerpage.jsp?prod=FEDS; and
- Dickinson's FDA Review, http://www.fdareview.com/.

FDA lists trade publications relating to cosmetics at http://www.fda.gov/cosmetics/resourcesforyou/industry/ucm077674.htm. Many medical journals also publish, in addition to scientific reports, editorials and comments relating to food and drug law and regulation.

Blogs relating to food and drug law include:

- FDA Law Blog, www.fdalawblog.net;
- Drug and Device Law, druganddevicelaw.blogspot.com;
- Orange Book Blog, www.orangebookblog.com;
- The Rest of the Story, http://tobaccoanalysis.blogspot.com; and
- WSJ Health Blog, http://blogs.wsj.com/health/ (from the *Wall Street Journal*—general health/industry).

Many trade associations, public interest groups, and other organizations interact frequently with FDA or are otherwise involved in food and drug regulation, and thus may be useful sources of information on some matters relating to FDA. Here is a partial list (excluding, *inter alia*, the numerous medical professional colleges and societies and also organizations focused on particular medical conditions):

- Abigail Alliance for Better Access to Developmental Drugs, www.abigail-alliance.org;
- AdvaMed, www.advamed.org;
- Alliance for a Stronger FDA, http://strengthenfda.org;
- American Clinical Laboratories Association, www.acla.com;
- American Herbal Products Association, www.ahpa.org;
- American Hospital Association, www.aha.org;
- American Public Health Association, www.apha.org;
- Association for the Advancement of Medical Instrumentation, www.aami.org;
- Association of Food and Drug Officials, http://www.afdo.org;
- Association of Food Industries, Inc., www.afius.org;
- Association of Health Care Journalists, www.healthjournalism.org;
- Association of Medical Diagnostics Manufacturers, www.amdm.org;
- Campaign for Tobacco-Free Kids, www.tobaccofreekids.org;
- Center for Public Integrity, www.publicintegrity.org;
- Center for Regulatory Effectiveness, www.thecre.com;
- Center for Science in the Public Interest, www.cspinet.org;
- Center for Tobacco Control Research & Education, http://www.ucsf.edu;
- Consumer Healthcare Products Association, www.chpa-info.org;
- Consumers Union, www.consumersunion.org;
- Council for Responsible Nutrition, www.crnusa.org;
- ECRI Institute, www.ecri.org;
- European Public Health Alliance, www.epha.org;
- Food Animals Concerns Trust, www.foodanimalconcerns.org;
- Generic Pharmaceutical Association, www.gphaonline.org;
- Grocery Manufacturers of America, www.gmaonline.org;
- Healthcare Distribution Management Association, www.healthcaredistribution.org;
- Institute for Agriculture & Trade Policy, www.iatp.org;
- Medical Device Manufacturers Association, www.medicaldevices.org;
- National Community Pharmacists Association, www.ncpanet.org;
- Natural Products Association, www.npainfo.org;
- Personalized Medicine Coalition, www.personalizedmedicinecoalition.org;
- Pharmaceutical Research and Manufacturers of America, www.phrma.org;
- Physicians for Social Responsibility, www.psr.org;
- Public Citizen Health Research Group, www.citizen.org;

- Regulatory Affairs Professionals Society, www.raps.org;
- Research! America, www.researchamerica.org;
- Union of Concerned Scientists, www.ucsusa.org;
- Utah Natural Products Alliance, www.unpa.com; and
- World Watch Institute, Global Resources Action Center for the Environment, http://www.worldwatch.org/node/1458.

A list by FDA of trade and professional associations of interest to the cosmetics industry is available at http://www.fda.gov/cosmetics/resourcesforyou/industry/ucm077669.htm (last updated June 23, 2014).

CHAPTER 2
FOOD SAFETY

FRED H. DEGNAN, CHRISTINA M. MARKUS,
AND SMITHA G. STANSBURY

Introduction

The food supply is diverse. The regulatory authority the Food and Drug Administration (FDA) relies upon to ensure the safety of food reflects this diversity. The Federal Food, Drug, and Cosmetic Act (FDCA)[1] contains a variety of standards for the regulation of food safety and, particularly upon the enactment of the FDA Food Safety Modernization Act (FSMA),[2] invests FDA with the authority to provide comprehensive and practical public health protection.

Legislation like FSMA can have a dramatic effect on FDA's and a manufacturer's respective responsibilities in assuring food safety. For example, FSMA confronts FDA with the enormous challenge of developing and substantiating more than 50 regulations and/or guidances on a diverse, demanding array of subjects ranging from preventive controls designed to ensure the safety of food to standards for accrediting auditors of the practices followed at foreign facilities. For manufacturers, the challenges presented by FSMA are no less demanding and include, for example, implementing compliant preventive controls in domestic food facilities *and* crafting programs of sufficient rigor and flexibility to meaningfully certify that foreign ingredient suppliers employ food safety systems and practices that conform with those required in the United States. Simply put, FSMA, like the FDCA itself, places the highest of expectations on FDA and on the food industry, thus rendering the study of modern food safety, in part at least, a study of the capacity, commitment, and talent of government and industry alike.

---

[1]   Pub. L. No. 75-717, 52 Stat. 1040 (1938), as amended 21 U.S.C. §§ 301 *et seq.* (2011).
[2]   Pub. L. No. 111-353, 124 Stat. 3885 (2011).

From time to time, developments in modern science have created challenges of a different nature—challenges that have forced FDA to interpret and apply its regulatory authority in ways never contemplated by Congress. Thus, the study of food safety also involves not only an understanding and appreciation of the guiding legal standards and their implementation but also the recognition that food safety decisions often are the result of a necessary amalgam of legal, scientific, and policy considerations.

Rather than being an exhaustive treatise on food safety regulation, this chapter is intended to focus on FDA's current regulation of food safety, the key historical bases for that program, and a number of the important issues that have challenged it.[3] The history of food safety regulation is, thus, presented as central to appreciating the current legal geography. The resulting picture, at times, is one of a dynamic process hallmarked by efforts to accommodate the public health protection goals of the law with scientific advancements in detection of and modern understanding about the hazards presented by the food supply. Unfortunately, however, at other times the picture is incomplete, a victim of the intractable problem of resources: FDA's efforts to achieve its goals being constrained by the available resources allocated to the agency for such purposes.

Although the impact of FSMA on food safety regulation is likely to be profound, key regulations have yet to be implemented, critical policies have yet to be finalized, and likely problems of implementation have yet to be encountered or acknowledged. Thus, with respect to FSMA, this chapter necessarily focuses on the present, avoids extensive speculation about the future, and attempts to describe key, but by no means all, elements of the legislation and place them in their proper context.

Overview: Historical and Current Statutory Bases for Food Safety Regulation

Food Adulteration and the "May Render Injurious to Health" Standard

In 1879, a bill was introduced in the House of Representatives for the purpose of "preventing the adulteration of articles of food and drink."[4] This initiative was the first federal effort to provide a standard of safety for domestically produced and marketed food that found its way to the table of the American consumer. Twenty-seven years later, this effort culminated in the enactment of the Pure Food and Drugs Act of 1906 (the 1906 act).[5]

The 1906 act possessed a certain symmetry: it addressed two products, foods and drugs; prohibited two acts, "adulteration" and "misbranding"; and provided two remedies, criminal prosecution and product seizure and condemnation. Under the act, foods were adulterated

---

[3]   Although this chapter deals with aspects of the Environmental Protection Agency's (EPA) regulation of pesticide residues in food, it does not address in detail this issue or the one presented by the U.S. Department of Agriculture's (USDA) regulation of meat, poultry, and eggs.

[4]   H.R. REP. No. 346, 46th Cong., 2d Sess. (1880).

[5]   Pub. L. No. 59-384, § 7, 34 Stat. 768, 769 (1906).

if they were prepared in ways that reduced quality, permitted passing off, rendered them injurious to health, or resulted in contamination with filth. The act also authorized regulations for "the collection and examination of specimens" (the sampling of food). Upon detecting an adulterant in food, the burden was placed on the government to initiate legal action against such food.

One adulteration provision, in particular, merits attention. Section 7 of the 1906 act provided that a food was adulterated if it "contained an added poisonous or other deleterious ingredient which may render [the food] injurious to health." This standard was interpreted in 1914 by the Supreme Court in *U.S. v. Lexington Mill & Elevator Co.*[6] In that case, the government detained 625 sacks of flour that had been shipped from Nebraska to Missouri, and charged that the flour had been treated with nitrogen peroxide gas, a recognized toxic substance. The government contended that the flour contained an "added poisonous or other added deleterious" substance and, as a result, was adulterated. The Lexington Mill & Elevator Company claimed an interest in the flour and defended the proceeding by denying that the flour had become adulterated. The trial court instructed the jury that the addition of a poisonous substance in any quantity would adulterate the product. Lexington Mill objected, arguing that a food would not be adulterated under section 7 by the mere presence of a poisonous or deleterious added substance unless that substance were present in such quantity that it could reasonably render the food injurious to health.

Although unsuccessful in the lower courts, Lexington Mill's argument was accepted by the Supreme Court. The Court found that if Congress had intended to condemn a food that contained any amount of a poisonous or deleterious substance, it would not have included the phrase "which may render such article injurious to health."[7] The Court went on to observe that if the seized flour could not "by any possibility, when the facts are reasonably considered," injure the health of a consumer, it could not be condemned under the act, even though it did contain a small amount of a poisonous or deleterious ingredient.[8] The Court's interpretation of the statutory standard (now found in section 402(a)(1) of the FDCA)[9] continues to this day to be controlling.

The *Lexington Mill* decision placed an unwanted evidentiary burden on the government: unless the amount of the added poisonous or deleterious ingredient in the particular food was enough to render it possibly injurious, the government could not take action against the food. Moreover, in any individual case the government had no authority to take into account the fact that several different foods other than the seized food might contain the same or similar added poisonous or deleterious ingredients. Thus, the government had no realistic way to protect the public from the cumulative exposure to potentially harmful ingredients in the diet.

The Court's interpretation of the adulteration provisions of the 1906 act not only made sense in light of the words selected by Congress but also in light of the fact that the act had been

---

[6]   232 U.S. 399 (1914).

[7]   *Id.* at 411.

[8]   *Id.*

[9]   21 U.S.C. § 342(a)(1).

enacted largely in response to obvious, and often outrageous, episodes of food adulteration.[10] The new act gave the government the tools to detect and condemn foods so adulterated. In fact, the government not only could take action against added substances present at clearly toxic levels but also against foods rendered unfit by filth, microbiological contamination, or other forms of spoilage. The *Lexington Mill* decision, however, left industry otherwise unconstrained in its use of new substances and technologies.

The 1938 Act and Section 406 Tolerances

For many, the 1906 act's relatively limited authority over the use of new substances was viewed as a weakness. As a result, when Congress adopted the FDCA in 1938, it included a *per se* rule against all unnecessary and avoidable poisonous and deleterious substances added to food. Section 406 of the act provides:

> any poisonous or deleterious substance added to any food, except when such substance is required in the production thereof or cannot be avoided by good manufacturing practice, shall be deemed to be unsafe and, thus, adulterated within the meaning of section 402(a)(2)(A).[11]

Congress went on to provide that when a poisonous or deleterious substance, in fact, is required in the production of food or could not be avoided by good manufacturing practices (GMPs), the government could establish a "safe" tolerance for the food.

Section 406 provides that a tolerance is to be set at a level that is not only deemed necessary to protect the public health but also that takes into account the extent to which a substance is unavoidable or necessary. This new authority gave FDA more flexibility in responding to the practicalities of agricultural and processing practices, including the then-novel use of agricultural pesticides and the resulting safety problem posed by residues of such pesticides in food. More important, the section permitted the agency, when setting a tolerance, to

---

[10] In 1906, Upton Sinclair described the meat industry at the turn of the 20th century in his book *The Jungle*:

> There was never the least attention paid to what was cut up for sausage; there would come all the way back from Europe old sausage that had been rejected, and that was moldy and white—it would be dosed with borax and glycerine, and dumped into the hoppers, and made over again for home consumption. There would be meat that had tumbled out on the floor, in the dirt and sawdust, where the workers had tramped and spit uncounted billions of consumption germs. There would be meat stored in great piles in rooms; and the water from leaky roofs would drip over it, and thousands of rats would race about on it. It was too dark in these storage places to see well but a man could run his hand over these piles of meat and sweep off handfuls of dried dung of rats. These rats were nuisances, and the packers would put poisoned bread out for them, and they would die, and then the rats, bread and meat would go into the hoppers together.

Sinclair went on to describe the steam rooms in which men processed the meat:

> There were open vats upon the level of the floor and the peculiar trouble of these workers was that they fell into the vats; and when they were fished out, there was never enough of them to be worth exhibiting. Sometimes they would be overlooked for days, till all but the bones of them had gone out to the world as Anderson's Pure Leaf Lard.

UPTON SINCLAIR, THE JUNGLE (Signet Classic Ed. 1960).

[11] FDCA § 406, 21 U.S.C. § 346.

consider cumulative dietary exposure to a substance. This characteristic continues to be a critical component of modern food safety risk assessment techniques.

Traditional Foods and the "Ordinarily Injurious to Health" Standard

The 1938 act not only retained the prohibitions in the 1906 act against potentially injurious added substances, but also established a new standard for the adulteration of food caused by naturally occurring substances.[12] Under this standard, naturally occurring substances can cause a food to be adulterated only if their presence renders the food "ordinarily" injurious to the consumer. This was intended and has proven to be a far less rigorous safety standard than that which applies to added substances.[13] The provision was designed to distinguish between those products that could be injurious to health "in a mild way" and those "unquestionably dangerous in a very definite way."[14] The legislative history reveals that the ordinarily injurious language was crafted to limit the ability of the government to consider traditional foods to be adulterated unless they, like poisonous mushrooms or mussels, presented a situation unquestionably dangerous to health.[15]

Section 408, Pesticide Residues and Further Reliance on Safety Tolerances

In 1954, Congress focused attention on pesticide residues in food and, with the passage of the Pesticide Residues Amendment,[16] added an entirely new section, section 408, to the 1938 act dealing exclusively with such residues.[17] Under section 408, pesticide residues were deemed, as a matter of law, to adulterate food unless a tolerance or tolerance exemption for the residues was promulgated.

A tolerance under section 408 was to be set at levels "necessary to protect the public health." In establishing whether the tolerance was appropriate, the government was given the authority under section 408 to consider the need for an adequate, wholesome, and economical food supply. As in the case of section 406 tolerances, section 408 authorized the government to consider factors other than safety in determining an appropriate tolerance for food.

In 1996, Congress passed landmark pesticide food safety legislation, the Food Quality Protection Act (FQPA).[18] The FQPA revised section 408 by strengthening the tolerance-setting standards for pesticide residues. The FQPA included chemical pesticide residues in processed food within its scope, thereby eliminating FDA's ability to control the safety of

---

[12]   FDCA § 402(a)(1), 21 U.S.C. § 342(a)(1).

[13]   S. REP. No. 2139, 75th Cong., 3d Sess. 6 (1938); see United States v. 1232 Cases American Beauty Oysters, 43 F. Supp. 749 (W.D. Mo. 1942).

[14]   S. REP. No. 2139, supra note 13, at 6.

[15]   H.R. REP. No. 2284, 85th Cong., 2d Sess. 4-5 (1958).

[16]   Pub. L. No. 518, 68 Stat. 511 (1954) (codified at 21 U.S.C. § 346a).

[17]   FDCA § 408(a), 21 U.S.C. § 346a(a).

[18]   Pub. L. No. 104-170, 110 Stat. 1489 (1996).

such residues and vesting the Environmental Protection Agency (EPA) with comprehensive authority to evaluate the safety of all pesticide uses.[19]

The Food Additives Amendment and a Comprehensive Scheme for the Safety of Food Ingredients

In 1950, 1951, and 1952, Congressman James J. Delaney chaired a House select committee investigating the use of chemicals in foods and cosmetics. After extended hearings, the committee filed a report on June 30, 1952, urging that the then-existing law be amended to provide that chemicals used in or on food be subject to essentially the same safety requirements as those for "new drugs."[20] According to the report, approximately 840 chemicals were thought to be used in food in the early 1950s. Of this total, only 420 were considered to be safe.[21]

Although the 1938 act included a preclearance provision for new drugs, no similar provision existed for additives in food. Thus, FDA had no way of ensuring that chemicals used in food were safe before the chemicals actually were added to food and people were exposed to them. To take action against a product containing a chemical of questionable safety, FDA first had to find the product and then prove under section 402 of the act that the chemical was toxic and that its presence in food might be injurious to health. More often than not, making these showings required testing, creating a slow, relatively unresponsive regulatory system.[22]

Regulation of added ingredients under the FDCA also posed problems for manufacturers. Although toxic at high levels, many chemicals added to food could be safely used at low levels. Section 406 of the act, however, deemed the use of such a chemical unlawful unless it could be shown that it was "required" in the production of the food or could not be "avoided."[23] Thus, certain additives that manufacturers desired to use in food could be prohibited from use even at levels acknowledged to be safe.

By 1958, there was general agreement among industry, government, and Congress that a more workable, specific mechanism was necessary for regulating the safety of chemicals added to food. The result was the Food Additives Amendment.[24] The objectives of the Food Additives Amendment were 1) safety, "to protect the health of consumers" by requiring manufacturers of food additives to "pretest any potentially unsafe substances added to food"; and 2) innovation, "to advance food technology by permitting the use of food additives at safe levels."[25]

---

[19]   A discussion of the FQPA and its impact on pesticide regulation is contained elsewhere in this chapter.

[20]   H.R. REP. No. 2356, 82d Cong., 2d Sess. (1952).

[21]   Id.

[22]   For an in-depth discussion of section 402, its history and the role it has played in the regulation of added substances, *see* Richard Merrill, *Regulatory Carcinogens in Food*, 77 MICH. L. REV. 171, 184-204 (1978).

[23]   Id. at 192-94.

[24]   Pub. L. No. 85-929, § 4, 72 Stat. 1784, 1785 (1958) (codified at 21 U.S.C. §§ 321(s), 348).

[25]   H.R. REP. No. 795, 86th Cong., 1st Sess. 9 (1959).

These dual goals of safety and innovation were to be achieved in part through a premarket approval system that subjected substances satisfying the statutory definition of "food additive" to a rigorous yet practical, nonabsolute safety standard. Congress explained in legislative history that the manufacturer's burden to prove safety would be met on presentation of evidence establishing to FDA's satisfaction a "reasonable certainty" that "no harm" would result from the intended use of the additive.[26] Congress expressly acknowledged that safety is dose dependent (i.e., that substances toxic at high doses might be safe at low doses) and that proof of absolute safety under all circumstances is a scientific impossibility.[27] In short, Congress sought to ensure safety and advance food technology by permitting the reasonable exercise of sound scientific judgment by FDA when evaluating the safety of food ingredients.

Congress also sought to balance safety with the practical needs of not disrupting the food supply and knowledgeably allocating scientific and regulatory resources. Balance was achieved through the definition of the term "food additive." By excluding from the definition (and thus from the premarket approval scheme) substances that are either generally recognized as safe (GRAS) or prior-sanctioned, Congress revealed its willingness to accept means for ensuring the safety of certain food ingredients other than formal premarket approval.

Another Safety Standard: The Delaney Clause

The Food Additives Amendment contained one additional food safety standard that bears the name of its proponent, Congressman Delaney. The Delaney Clause provides that "no additive shall be deemed to be safe if it is found to induce cancer when ingested by man or animal, or if it is found after tests which are appropriate for the evaluation of the safety of food additives, to induce cancer in man or animal . . . ."[28] Although the Delaney Clause highlights cancer as a public health concern, the effort to regulate is largely redundant in light of the general safety standard in section 409, which provides FDA with authority for regulating the use of suspected (as well as proven) carcinogens in food.[29]

---

[26] *Id.* at 4; S. REP. No. 795, 86th Cong., 1st Sess. 9 (1959).

[27] The House committee primarily responsible for developing the Food Additives Amendment stated in its report on the bill, "[S]afety requires proof of a reasonable certainty that no harm will result from the proposed use of an additive. It does not—and cannot—require proof beyond any possible doubt that no harm will result under any conceivable circumstance." This was emphasized particularly by the scientific panel that testified before the subcommittee. The scientists pointed out that "it is impossible in the present state of scientific knowledge to establish with complete certainty the absolute harmlessness of any chemical substance . . . . Reasonable certainty determined in this fashion that an additive will be safe, will protect the public health from harm and will permit sound progress in food technology." H.R. REP. No. 2284, *supra* note 15, at 4-5. Relying upon this congressional guidance, FDA codified a conforming definition of the term "safe" as the term appears in the Food Additives Amendment. *See* 21 C.F.R. § 170.3(i).

[28] FDCA § 409(c)(3)(A), 21 U.S.C. § 348(c)(3)(A). There are, in fact, three Delaney clauses in the act. The two other clauses apply to color additives (section 721(b)(5)(B)) and compounds for food-producing animals (section 512(d)(1)(I)). The clauses do not significantly differ.

[29] Elliot Richardson, Assistant Secretary of the Department of Health, Education and Welfare, made this point clear in written testimony on pending food additive legislation in 1958. 104 CONG. REC. 17,415 (Aug. 15, 1958). Mr. Richardson reasoned that the Delaney Clause was unnecessary in light of the strong safety standard contained in the food additives bill.

Conforming Standards: Color Additives and Substances Administered to Food-Producing Animals

Although the Food Additives Amendment of 1958 applied to food colors, the act was further amended in 1960 by the Color Additive Amendments to subject all colorants used in food, drugs, and cosmetics to a uniform system of regulation comparable to that adopted for food additives.[30] These amendments established a comprehensive premarket approval system and a rigorous safety standard (including the Delaney Clause). The legislation was designed to repeal the "harmless per se" standard found then in section 406(b) of the FDCA which permitted the use of "harmless" coal tar colors.[31] A 1958 interpretation of this standard by the U.S. Supreme Court had threatened the availability of many food, drug, and cosmetic colors by questioning FDA's use of tolerances to establish the safe use in food of otherwise harmful—and thus not "harmless"—coal tar colors.[32]

In 1962, Congress again amended the food safety provisions of the statute by adding a new provision to the Delaney Clause.[33] The provision relaxed the rigidity of the clause as it could be construed to apply to compounds administered to food-producing animals. The DES proviso allowed the use of carcinogenic animal feed additives, provided they would not adversely affect the animals and would leave "no residue" in edible tissue as determined by a government-approved analytical method. In the Animal Drug Amendments of 1968, the DES proviso was made applicable to the residues of animal drugs, whether administered in feed or otherwise.[34]

Standards for Specific Types of Product: Infant Formulas and Dietary Supplements

Infant Formula. In the Infant Formula Act of 1980, Congress amended the FDCA to ensure the nutritional quality of infant formulas.[35] The agency subsequently promulgated regulations establishing infant formula quality control procedures designed to ensure that infant formula products contain the nutrients specified by the statute.[36] The statutory requirements and FDA's implementing quality control procedures for infant formula fall within the realm of food safety: sustained consumption of a nutritionally deficient formula can seriously impair the health of an infant.

In 1986, Congress amended the Infant Formula Act to make the quality control procedures even more stringent and to vest FDA with the express authority to require that infant formulas are produced according to GMPs.[37] The philosophy of the statute (and FDA's implementing regulations) is that there should be no margin for error in the manufacture of

---

30   Pub. L. No. 86-618, tit. I, § 103(b), 74 Stat. 397, 399 (1960) (codified at 21 U.S.C. §§ 321(t), 379e); note, however, that Congress did not include a GRAS exception to the definition and regulation of color additives.

31   S. REP. No. 795, *supra* note 26, at 1-2.

32   Flemming v. Florida Citrus Exch., 358 U.S. 153 (1958).

33   Drug Amendments of 1962, Pub. L. No. 87-781, § 104(x)(1), 76 Stat. 780, 785 (codified at 21 U.S.C. §§ 348(c)(3)(A), 379e(b)(5)(B), 360b(d)(1)(I)).

34   Pub. L. No. 90-399, § 101(b), 82 Stat. 342, 343 (1968) (codified at 21 U.S.C. § 360b).

35   Pub. L. No. 96-359, 94 Stat. 1190 (1980) (codified at 21 U.S.C. § 350a).

36   *See* 21 C.F.R. pt. 106 (2008).

37   Pub. L. No. 99-570, tit. IV, § 4014(a), (b)(1), 100 Stat. 3207-120 (1986) (codified at 21 U.S.C. § 350a); *see also* 21 C.F.R. pt. 106.

infant formula products, and that redundancy should be built into the system to ensure that no infant will be exposed on a sustained basis to a product that does not meet the statutory nutritional requirements.

Dietary Supplements. In 1994, Congress passed the Dietary Supplement Health and Education Act (DSHEA),[38] which excluded dietary supplement ingredients from the definition of food additive (and, thus, from the compass of the food additive premarket approval system, the Delaney Clause, and the GRAS concept). Moreover, the legislation increases FDA's burden in taking action against such substances by providing that supplements may be deemed to be adulterated only if the government can establish that they, when used according to their labeling and under the recommended conditions of use, present a "significant or unreasonable risk" of injury or illness to the consumer.[39] For dietary supplements containing a "new" dietary ingredient (one not marketed before October 15, 1994), DSHEA required a manufacturer to notify FDA before marketing and ensure that the supplement is "reasonably expected to be safe" for its labeled use.[40] The amendment also provided the Secretary of the Department of Health and Human Services (DHHS) with the power to remove a dietary supplement immediately from the market if it is shown to "pose an imminent hazard to public health or safety."[41] And, DSHEA vested FDA with the authority to impose mandatory GMP requirements on dietary supplement producers.[42]

In December 2006, the Dietary Supplement and Nonprescription Drug Consumer Protection Act was signed into law and amended the FDCA to include adverse event reporting and recordkeeping requirements for dietary supplements (and for nonprescription drugs marketed without FDA approval).[43] The legislation required manufacturers to report to FDA "serious adverse events" and to maintain records related to each report for a period of six years.

Prevention-Based Controls and Standards: "Modernizing" Food Safety Authorities

For decades a key aspect of FDA's food safety regulation has involved the combined approach of relying on GMP criteria and regulatory inspections in an effort to reduce the potential for the contamination, in particular microbial contamination, of food. As discussed at some length in the pages to come, FDA's efforts to impose standards for good manufacturing practice required creativity on the agency's part in light of the fact that, unlike the case with drugs and medical devices, the FDCA provided the agency no express authority to require GMPs for the general food industry.[44] Recognizing the critical need for such practices, FDA inferred from the general food adulteration provisions of the FDCA the authority to require

---

[38]   Pub. L. No. 103-417, 108 Stat. 4325 (1994).

[39]   FDCA § 402(f)(1)(B), 21 U.S.C. § 342(f)(1)(B).

[40]   FDCA § 413(a), 21 U.S.C. § 350b(a).

[41]   FDCA § 402(f)(1)(C), 21 U.S.C. § 342(f)(1)(C).

[42]   After years of delay, FDA in 2007 promulgated final regulations implementing these requirements (72 Fed. Reg. 34,751 (June 25, 2007) (21 C.F.R. pt. 111)).

[43]   Pub. L. No. 109-462, 120 Stat. 3469 (2006) (codified at 21 U.S.C. § 379aa-1(e)(1)).

[44]   As noted earlier in this text, with respect to two special classes of food, "infant formula" and "dietary supplements," Congress, in 1986 and 1994, respectively, granted FDA express authority to require GMPs. *See* FDCA §§ 412(a)(3) and 402(g), 21 U.S.C. §§ 350a(a)(3) and 342(g).

specific GMPs for certain other foods (e.g., low-acid canned foods, acidified foods, and bottled water)[45] and general GMP requirements for all foods.[46] Nonetheless, FDA's regulations did not provide specific prevention-based controls for the bulk of the food industry.

During the course of the first decade of the 21st century, the development and refinement of epidemiological investigation techniques and DNA-based detection methodologies facilitated FDA's ability to associate various foods with major disease outbreaks. In the wake of these outbreaks, FDA became to be viewed as being better equipped to react to a foodborne disease outbreak than to prevent the outbreak from occurring. Faced with the reality that such outbreaks are largely preventable, Congress was spurred to consider comprehensive food safety reform and, after nearly two years of deliberation and debate, enacted the Food Safety Modernization Act. President Obama signed the legislation into law on January 4, 2011.

The fundamental purpose of FSMA is to help enable FDA to better protect the public health by empowering the agency to strengthen its food safety systems *and* to demand broad compliance with these systems. The key new authorities and mandates granted by the statute may be divided into five categories: prevention, inspections and compliance, regulatory response, control over imports, and governmental collaboration.

Prevention. FSMA empowers FDA to require science-based preventive controls across the food supply.[47] This new authority applies to all domestic facilities and, by way of import supplier certification requirements, to all foreign facilities.[48] Moreover, FSMA grants FDA specific authority to establish science-based, minimum standards for the safe production and harvesting of produce.[49] And, FSMA requires FDA, in the context of intentional contamination, to develop regulations establishing science-based mitigation strategies to strengthen food safety practices at problematic and vulnerable links along the food supply chain.[50] These and related enhancements to FDA's ability to help prevent food safety problems from occurring are placed in context and discussed in more detail later in this chapter.

Inspections and Compliance. As also discussed more fully later in this chapter, FSMA reflects not just a commitment to establishing preventive standards but also to enforcing compliance with them. To this end, the legislation requires FDA to identify not only "high-risk" foods[51] but also "high-risk" facilities.[52] FSMA proceeds to set goals for the frequency of FDA inspections of such high-risk facilities[53] as well as non-high-risk facilities[54] and foreign facilities from which food is imported into the United States.

---

[45]   21 C.F.R. pts. 108, 113, 114, and 129.
[46]   21 C.F.R. pt. 110.
[47]   FDCA § 418, 21 U.S.C. § 350g.
[48]   *Id.*, *see also* FDCA § 805, 21 U.S.C. § 384a.
[49]   FDCA § 419, 21 U.S.C. § 350h.
[50]   FDCA § 420, 21 U.S.C. § 350i.
[51]   21 U.S.C. § 2223(d)(2)(B).
[52]   FDCA § 421(a), 21 U.S.C. § 350j(a).
[53]   FDCA § 421(a)(2)(B), 21 U.S.C. § 350j(a)(2)(B).
[54]   FDCA § 421(a)(2)(C), 21 U.S.C. § 350j(a)(2)(C).

FSMA also attempts to address what has generally been perceived as a gap in the statutory authority with respect to agency access to food-related records. Whereas FDA for decades has been entitled to almost all records involving the production, manufacture, and distribution of drugs and medical devices, FDA's authority with respect to food has been much more limited with FDA access being the exception, not the rule. In an effort to remedy this dichotomy, FSMA provides FDA with access to records regarding food safety plans and foreign supplier certifications.[55] Moreover, FSMA modifies existing law that grants FDA access to records if the agency has a reasonable belief that there is a "reasonable probability" that a food will cause "serious adverse health consequences or death to humans or animals."[56] Where such a "belief" is established, senior agency staff will issue an "FDA 482c Notice of Inspection – Request for Records," authorizing the inspector to review "all records" that relate to *any* food "likely to be affected in a similar manner," provided the records are "needed to assist" the agency in determining whether there is, in fact, a reasonable probability that the use of or exposure to the food at issue will cause "serious adverse health consequences or death to humans or animals."[57]

Regulatory Response. FSMA also enhances FDA's ability to respond effectively to food safety problems and/or emergencies as they arise. The legislation empowers FDA to *require* a company to recall a food.[58] New section 423 of the FDCA imposes an empirical burden upon the agency that must be met before a recall can be ordered. To that end, FDA must establish that there is a "reasonable probability" that an article of food (other than an infant formula—a product category for which recall requirements were already in place when FSMA was enacted) is adulterated under section 402 or misbranded under section 403(w) *and* that the use of or exposure to the article "will" cause "serious adverse health consequences or death."[59] Under such circumstances, FDA may issue an "order" requiring a company to immediately cease distribution of the food and, as applicable, immediately notify all parties in the distribution and use chain. A party may object within a two-day period to any recall order. The authority to issue an order cannot be delegated below the Commissioner. The new section makes clear that nothing in the authority granted FDA limits the agency's ability to request a "voluntary recall" or to issue an order to cease distribution or to recall under any other provision of the FDCA or the Public Health Service Act.[60]

---

[55]   FDCA § 418(h), 21 U.S.C. § 350g(h) (health plans); FDCA § 805(d), 21 U.S.C. § 384a(d) (foreign supplier certifications).

[56]   FDCA § 414(a), 21 U.S.C. § 350c(a).

[57]   *Id.* FDA published an interim final rule and a final rule amending FDA's record availability regulation to incorporate the changes made by FSMA. 77 Fed. Reg. 10,658 (Feb. 23, 2012); 79 Fed. Reg. 18,799 (Apr. 4, 2014). The revised regulation provides that "[w]hen FDA has a reasonable belief that an article of food, and any other article of food that FDA reasonably believes is likely to be affected in a similar manner, is adulterated and presents a threat of serious adverse health consequences or death to humans or animals, or when FDA believes that there is a reasonable probability that the use of or exposure to an article of food, and any other article of food that FDA reasonably believes is likely to be affected in a similar manner, will cause serious adverse health consequences or death to humans or animals, any records and other information accessible to FDA under section 414 or 704(a) of the Federal Food, Drug, and Cosmetic Act (21 U.S.C. 350c and 374(a)) must be made readily available for inspection and photocopying or other means of reproduction. Such records and other information must be made available as soon as possible, not to exceed 24 hours from the time of receipt of the official request, from an officer or employee duly designated by the Secretary of Health and Human Services who presents appropriate credentials and a written notice." 21 C.F.R. § 1.361.

[58]   FDCA § 423, 21 U.S.C. § 350l.

[59]   *Id.*

[60]   Pub. L. No. 99-660, 100 Stat. 3751 (1986).

FSMA also enhances FDA's existing administrative detention authority. Prior to the legislation, section 304 authorized an FDA investigator to detain an article of food for which the investigator had "credible evidence or information indicating" that the food presented a threat of serious adverse health consequences or death. The new legislation replaces the credible evidence requirement with the less burdensome requirement that the investigator need only have a "reason to believe" that the food is "adulterated" or "misbranded."[61] This provision, in effect, provides FDA with the type of embargo authority the agency has always lacked and that, as a result, has had to rely on state authorities to impose.

Perhaps the most powerful new compliance tool FSMA grants FDA is the ability to suspend a food facility's registration should the agency conclude that food manufactured, processed, packed, received, or held in the registered facility carries, to a "reasonable probability," the potential of causing "serious adverse health consequences."[62] Under such circumstances, FDA can issue an order suspending the registration of the facility "responsible" for creating the potential or that had reason to know of that potential. This power, although wholly administrative, is nonetheless injunctive in nature. The legislation provides a procedure for seeking an opportunity for a hearing before the agency on a suspension order and for a post-hearing corrective action plan for addressing problematic conditions. The effect of a suspension of registration is profound: food from a facility whose registration has been suspended cannot be introduced into interstate or intrastate commerce and cannot be imported or exported. FDA is required to promulgate regulations to implement the suspension provisions but may issue them on "an interim final basis."[63] As of December 2014, FDA has yet to issue such regulations. The agency's authority to suspend a food facility's registration, however, became effective on July 3, 2011, and registered facilities are currently subject to the suspension of registration provisions.[64]

FDA first used its registration suspension authority on November 26, 2012, when it suspended the food facility registration of Sunland, Inc. (Sunland) due to the company's history of violations and the fact that peanut butter made by the company had been linked to a widespread outbreak of *Salmonella* Bredeney.[65] FDA did not fully authorize Sunland to resume receiving, preparing, processing, packing, holding, and distributing food at or from its peanut butter facility until May 17, 2013.[66] The suspension of a food facility registration, particularly for such an extended period of time, can result in significant financial and reputational consequences for the owner of the facility.

---

[61]   FDCA § 304(h)(1)(A), 21 U.S.C. § 334(h)(1)(A). FDA published an interim final rule and a final rule amending FDA's administrative detention regulations to incorporate the changes made by FSMA. 76 Fed. Reg. 25,538 (May 5, 2011); 78 Fed. Reg. 7994 (Feb. 5, 2013). The revised regulations provide, among other things, that "[a]n officer or qualified employee of FDA may order the detention of any article of food that is found during an inspection, examination, or investigation under the act if the officer or qualified employee has reason to believe that the article of food is adulterated or misbranded." 21 C.F.R. § 1.378.

[62]   FDCA § 415(b), 21 U.S.C. § 350d(b).

[63]   FDCA § 415(b)(5), 21 U.S.C. § 350d(b)(5).

[64]   FDCA § 415(b)(6), 21 U.S.C. § 350d(b)(6); FDA Guidance for Industry: Questions and Answers Regarding Food Facility Registration (Fifth Edition) (Dec. 2012), at 8-9.

[65]   FDA Letter to Sunland Inc. Concerning Suspension of Food Facility Registration; Notice of Opportunity for Hearing (Nov. 26, 2012).

[66]   FDA Letter to Sunland Inc. Regarding *United States of America v. Sunland Inc., and Jimmie D. Shearer*, Civil No. 2:12-cv-01312 (D.N.M.) (May 17, 2013).

Under FSMA, FDA is also empowered to establish a product tracing system to receive information and improve the capacity of the agency to "rapidly and effectively" track and trace food that is in the United States when it is offered for import.[67] FDA may not establish such a system until pilot projects for identifying effective "decision technologies" for such tracking have been completed. Moreover, recognizing the value of sound, reliable data to various disciplines related to preventing, controlling, and reacting to disease outbreaks, FSMA requires certain food testing to be carried out by accredited laboratories and instructs the agency to establish a program for laboratory accreditation.[68]

Imported Food and Food Ingredients. With respect to imports, FSMA grants FDA unprecedented authority to help ensure that imported food products comply with all domestic food safety standards. These requirements, which are discussed later in this chapter, include a foreign supplier verification program, third-party certification for high-risk foods, and broad authority to deny entry into domestic commerce of any food of questionable or noncompliant origin.[69]

Governmental Collaboration. The fifth general area of focus and new authority provided in FSMA involves one of the more aspirational aspects of the legislation. The legislation embodies the view that ensuring food safety is a shared enterprise and that all food safety agencies, both domestic and international, need to combine their forces in an integrated way if the public health goals of the statute are to be achieved. Examples of such collaboration include state and local "capacity building" (e.g., FSMA provides FDA with a multiyear grant system designed to encourage investment in state food safety programs),[70] foreign capacity building (e.g., FSMA commands FDA to develop training programs for foreign governments and food producers in U.S. food safety requirements),[71] and reliance on inspections by domestic governmental agencies, as need be, to create a web of preventive control and oversight.[72]

Moreover, FSMA provides explicit direction to the Centers for Disease Control and Prevention (CDC) to take a lead role in food safety surveillance of foodborne illness outbreaks.[73] Section 205(a) of FSMA defines "food-borne illness outbreak" in as broad terms as possible: "the occurrence of two or more cases of a similar illness resulting from the ingestion of a certain food." Paragraph (b) requires CDC to "enhance food-borne illness surveillance systems"[74] and to improve the collection, analysis, reporting, and usefulness of data on foodborne illnesses. As a practical matter, CDC has performed these functions for years without the specific authorization FSMA now provides. CDC is now statutorily empowered to take the lead in coordinating federal, state, and local foodborne surveillance systems, including complaint systems, and increasing participation in national networks of public health and food regulatory agencies and laboratories. CDC is also required to facilitate the sharing of surveillance information, develop improved epidemiological tools, obtain quality exposure

---

67   21 U.S.C. § 2223.
68   FDCA § 422, 21 U.S.C. § 350k.
69   *Infra* at text associated with footnotes 363 through 384.
70   FDCA § 1009, 21 U.S.C. § 399.
71   FSMA § 305.
72   FDCA § 421(a)(2)(E), 21 U.S.C. § 350j(a)(2)(E).
73   21 U.S.C. § 2224.
74   *Id.*

data and microbiological methods for classifying cases, augment such systems to improve attribution of a foodborne illness outbreak to a specific food, and expand the capacity of such systems to identify new or rarely documented cases of foodborne illness.

Summary

The foregoing history and runup to the present and brief overview of FSMA, although by no means exhaustive, illustrates the proposition articulated at the outset of this chapter: the food supply is diverse, and the legislative scheme for regulating food has evolved and must continue to evolve to reflect that diversity. The safety of food is clearly the statutory goal. Nevertheless, Congress over the years in granting FDA authority has recognized that a determination of safety may be situational and, as a result, can often be assessed against a background of social and economic values, depending on the nature of the food and the nature of the risk. Standards for assessing food safety, therefore, are not uniform; some foods are held to higher standards of safety than others. Science has had a critical impact on how these diverse statutory standards have been interpreted and applied. As the following sections reveal, the result has been, and appears likely to continue to be, meaningful progress in the regulation of food safety.

FDA's Regulation of Contaminants and Other "Adulterants"

Introduction

Until the early 1970s, FDA relied on its enforcement authority, particularly its litigation powers, to implement the food safety laws. Although highly successful, this approach was limited in focus and impact. Violative products could be removed from the channels of distribution, but the agency's response was limited only to those violations that it could find and prove. Gradually, the agency became convinced that litigation alone was not a sufficient food safety tool and that the safety of the food supply could be improved by providing guidance to industry in both agency criteria and interpretations of the legal requirements. By the 1970s, in an effort to more efficiently use its resources, as well as to encourage voluntary compliance, FDA had engaged in setting prospective standards, designed to generally inform the industry of the steps necessary to produce a safe food.

This dual approach of "standards plus enforcement" to regulation became a hallmark of FDA food safety policy. Agency standards provide critical guidance to the food industry, and in many cases became the basis for the most common form of FDA enforcement activity through 2010: the "voluntary" recall of food.[75] FDA's standards include promulgating tolerances and

---

[75]   Until the passage of the Food Safety Modernization Act, FDA lacked statutory authority to compel the recall of adulterated food (other than infant formula) that had been determined by the agency to present a risk to health. *See* United States v. K-N Enterprises, Inc., 461 F. Supp. 988 (N.D. Ill. 1978); FDCA § 412(e) (1), 21 U.S.C. § 350a(e)(1). Even though FDA now has such authority, in many cases, especially where a statutory violation or safety problem is clearly present, companies will recall products voluntarily and often in cooperation with FDA pursuant to guidelines governing voluntary recalls. 21 C.F.R. § 7.40-.59. These guidelines detail the considerations, decision points, and procedures that have come to characterize recall

action levels for added poisonous or deleterious substances; defect action levels for filth; specific good manufacturing regulations for a few types of food, most notably, low-acid canned foods; "umbrella" GMP regulations for the industry; quality control requirements for infant formula; and Hazard Analysis and Critical Control Point (HACCP) requirements for seafood and juice products. FDA supplemented these efforts with less formal mechanisms to provide suggested standards. Chief among these mechanisms is the "guidance document."

FSMA builds upon FDA's "standards plus enforcement" approach by vesting FDA with new prevention-focused tools and a clearer regulatory framework to require food and food ingredient producers to implement comprehensive, preventive-based practices across the food supply chain. The legislation also significantly enhances FDA's ability to oversee, understand and police the millions of food products not only in interstate commerce but also being imported into the country. For perspective, this chapter focuses on FDA's historical approach to food safety and then explores how aspects of the agency's broad new authorities are designed to enhance the agency's effectiveness in helping to ensure the safety of food.

Tolerances and Action Levels for Added Poisonous or Deleterious Substances

As noted earlier, section 402(a)(1) of the FDCA provides that a food is adulterated if it contains any added "poisonous or deleterious substance which may render . . . it injurious to health."[76] The similarly worded predecessor provision in the 1906 act applied to all potentially harmful added substances, including those that had been added *intentionally*.

Section 402(a)(1)'s exclusive hold on added substances was broken with the new addition of section 406, which gave FDA authority to promulgate tolerances for a major subcomponent of the universe of food contaminants: *unavoidable* added, poisonous, or deleterious substances (including pesticide residues). Subsequent enactments, including the Pesticide Residues Amendment of 1954, the Food Additives Amendment of 1958 and the Color Additive Amendments of 1960, subjected other specific categories of added substances to their own systems of regulation, sharply limiting the types of substances to which section 402(a)(1) and section 406, in practice, would apply.

As a result of these statutory developments, sections 402(a)(1) and 406 have been used almost entirely to regulate unavoidable "added" contaminants in food, such as polychlorinated biphenyls (PCBs) in fish; polybrominated biphenyls (PBBs) in animal feed; aflatoxin in corn, peanuts, and other food crops; mercury in fish; and lead and cadmium in food contact pottery.[77]

---

determinations and conduct. The guidelines provide an excellent example of how nonbinding, voluntary standards can become operative, guiding norms for an entire industry.

76   See *supra* discussion in text accompanying notes 5-8.

77   FDA considers a substance "added" unless it is an "inherent natural constituent" of the food. 21 C.F.R. § 109.3(d). The courts generally have supported this broad reading. Merrill, *supra* note 22, at 194. One court has held that demonstrable human intervention is required to render a substance "added." United States v. Anderson Seafoods, Inc., 622 F.2d 157, 159-61 (5th Cir. 1980). Of course, section 402(a)(1) has been, and continues to be, relied upon by FDA for the enforcement of "adulteration" acts arising from an array of possible contaminants other than "unavoidable" contaminants.

Once FDA establishes a section 406 tolerance for a contaminant in a particular food, the tolerance is a legally enforceable limit. In a court enforcement action, FDA need only show that the contaminant is present in an amount exceeding the tolerance; the agency does not have to prove in court the actual or potential health effects of the substance in question. Tolerance setting under section 406, however, is not a simple matter: it is subject to the formal rulemaking requirements of section 701(e) of the FDCA.[78] This involves not only publication of a proposal, consideration of comments, and issuance of a regulation, but also a formal evidentiary hearing at which the factual basis for the regulation can be challenged in a trial-like setting. These proceedings are extremely time consuming and resource intensive for FDA, and result in the establishment of tolerance levels that can be changed only through lengthy proceedings as described above, despite the fact that the circumstances affecting the propriety of a particular tolerance level vary over time. As a result, FDA has promulgated formal tolerances under section 406 for only *one* environmental contaminant: PCBs.[79] The agency has proposed, but never finalized, tolerances for lead in milk[80] and aflatoxin in shelled peanuts and peanut products.[81]

In order to create a more flexible mechanism for regulating unavoidable contaminants in food, FDA developed informal guides, commonly referred to as "action levels," as an exercise of its enforcement discretion under section 402(a)(1). Action levels are set using the substantive criteria for promulgation of tolerances under section 406 (i.e., they are set at a level sufficient for the protection of the public health, taking into account the extent to which the presence of the substance cannot be avoided).[82] Action levels are not set, however, through the formal rulemaking procedures applicable to tolerances; in fact, action levels are set without any rulemaking at all.[83] As a result, action levels do not have the force and effect of law. Action levels identify the level of contamination at which FDA may take enforcement action under section 402(a)(1); in such an action, FDA must prove that the "may render injurious" standard has been violated.

In practice, action levels are commonly relied on by FDA and industry as defining the line between the foods that may lawfully enter commerce and those that may not. Thus, when FDA or industry detects that a food contains a contaminant greater than the applicable action level, the food is often voluntarily removed from commerce by industry for reconditioning or other action to avoid violation of the action level. Action levels have come to play a key role as an important guide as to how FDA balances safety and other factors in regulating environmental contaminants.[84]

In 1987, FDA's authority to establish action levels without following notice-and-comment rulemaking procedures was challenged.[85] The court found that action levels had all the appearances of binding regulations, and held that they must be established through

---

[78]　21 U.S.C. § 371(e).

[79]　*See* 21 C.F.R. § 109.30.

[80]　39 Fed. Reg. 42,740 (Dec. 6, 1974).

[81]　*Id.* at 42,748.

[82]　21 C.F.R. § 109.6(b), (c).

[83]　FDA publishes a notice announcing the action level and inviting comments. 21 C.F.R. § 109.4(c)(2). The action levels are codified in FDA's *Compliance Policy Guides Manual* (CPG).

[84]　*See* 21 C.F.R. § 109.6(d).

[85]　Community Nutrition Inst. (CNI) v. Young, 818 F.2d 943 (D.C. Cir. 1987).

rulemaking procedures. In response, FDA published a notice in the *Federal Register* emphasizing that action levels do not have the force of law and that FDA is not bound by them.[86] FDA explained that it retains the flexibility to take action against a product that is contaminated below the action level, and to refrain from action against products that exceed action levels, depending on the circumstances of each case.

Defect Action Levels for Filth

Section 402(a)(3) of the act deems food to be adulterated if "it consists in whole or in part of any filthy, putrid or decomposed substance, or if it is otherwise unfit for food." This prohibition against any "filth" is related only indirectly to food safety. Violations of section 402(a)(3) are often said to be aesthetic in nature because consumption of substances that qualify as "filth" rarely present any health hazard. Protection of food against filth, however, is important in maintaining the basic integrity of the food supply and food manufacturing practices as well as avoiding conditions that could develop into safety problems.

FDA's implementation of section 402(a)(3) is also an example of the agency's efforts to balance the goal of cleanliness against other essentially economic factors. It is well established as a matter of law that the statute prohibits any amount of filth in food except in the occasional circumstance where courts have found the level of contamination to be below the *de minimis* (i.e., trivial) amount required to trigger the act.[87] FDA has recognized, however, that small amounts of filth (typically in the form of insect parts or excreta) in many food crops are unavoidable. Rather than enforcing section 402(a)(3) to its full literal extent, FDA has exercised its enforcement discretion through informal standard setting similar to the adoption of action levels for poisonous or deleterious substances. In the 1970s, FDA adopted the practice of developing "defect action levels" for insect and rodent filth, mold, rot, and other forms of filth in a wide variety of raw and processed food products.[88] The defect action levels are set at tolerances that can be achieved practicably by firms applying GMPs, especially in the area of sanitation, and reflect a workable accommodation between the ideal of filth-free food and the realities of crop production, food processing, and handling.[89]

FDA has recognized that defect action levels are set because it is not feasible for farmers to grow, harvest, and process crops that are totally free of natural defects. The agency also has recognized that the alternative to establishing defect levels in some foods might be to insist on increased utilization of chemical substances to control insects, rodents, and other natural sources of contamination.[90] Unfortunately, it is expensive to sponsor and collect data necessary to establish defect action levels. In recent years, funding has not been available for the development of up-to-date defect action levels for all foods. Developing a defect action level involves researching the possible sources of contamination and reliable methods of

---

[86]   53 Fed. Reg. 5043 (Feb. 19, 1988).

[87]   *See, e.g.*, United States v. General Foods Corp., 446 F. Supp. 740 (N.D.N.Y. 1978), *aff'd*, 591 F.2d 1332 (2d Cir. 1979).

[88]   FDA's defect action levels for filth are published in the agency's *Compliance Policy Guides Manual*.

[89]   For example, FDA typically will not take action under section 402(a)(3) against wheat flour contaminated with insect filth unless the flour contains an average of 75 or more insect fragments per 50 grams. CPG 7104.06.

[90]   For a discussion of FDA's role in setting defect action levels, the procedures followed, the history of the practice, and current problems of enforcement based on action levels, *see* K.L. Harris & F.H. Degnan, *Sanitation Law Enforcement for Foods with Defect Action Levels,* 40 CEREAL FOODS WORLD 592 (1995).

analysis capable to assess whether GMPs have been followed. Moreover, surveys must be conducted to establish background levels of defects that are present when GMPs are, in fact, employed. Thus, current defect action level guidelines are neither as extensive as the food supply they purport to cover, nor as contemporary as they should be to reflect the dynamics of the modern food production industry.

"Unfit" Food

The second distinctive prong of section 402(a)(3) deems food to be adulterated if it is "otherwise unfit for food." The legislative history of the act fails to provide a concrete interpretation of what constitutes being "unfit" for food. In light of the fact no standard of "fitness" is suggested in either the act or its history, a wide variety of possible interpretations exists. Interestingly, a counterpart provision is included in section 601(m)(3) of the Federal Meat Inspection Act and provides that a meat or meat product is adulterated if it is "unsound, unhealthful, unwholesome, or otherwise unfit for human food."[91] This distinction suggests that the reach of "otherwise unfit for food" in section 402(a)(3) does not extend to foods that may be unfit by virtue of their unhealthfulness.

Consistent with this observation, courts and FDA in the past tended to narrowly interpret "unfit for food" in a manner consistent with the concern about the aesthetic quality of food. One court, for example, held that "in order for a product to be subject to condemnation as unfit for food on account of its tough and rubbery consistency, the product must be proved to be so tough and rubbery that the average, normal person, under ordinary conditions, would not chew and swallow it."[92] In recent years, however, FDA has applied the provision to foods that are "unfit" because they present a safety concern. In fact, in an era in which threats to the food supply may not always be identified with the precision necessary to successfully invoke the safety provisions of the FDCA, the broad language of "otherwise unfit for food" provides arguable support for regulatory actions and decisionmaking involving unconventional hazards not specifically covered by other provisions. As a result, a statutory provision that on its face seems intended to be—and for most of its history has been—limited to regulating food on the basis of its aesthetic or edible nature may serve as a modern food safety tool. Some examples are instructive.

In a 1990 Warning Letter, FDA considered the grease byproduct of a food processing operation to be "unfit" for both human food and animal feed because the grease possibly contained harmful contaminants[93] and was, thus, "unfit" for food. FDA deemed the grease unfit for food even though neither the presence nor the identity of the contaminants could be ascertained with any certainty.

In December 1988, FDA issued an automatic import detention of candy pacifiers on the ground that the pacifiers were "unfit" under section 402(a)(3) in light of the fact that their "size and shape . . . tended to increase the likelihood of . . . [their] lodging in the upper airway and producing partial or complete obstruction."[94] Similarly, beginning in October

---

[91]   21 U.S.C. § 601(m)(3).

[92]   United States v. 24 Cases, More or Less, 87 F. Supp. 826, 828 (1949).

[93]   Daniel G. McChesney, *FDA's View on the Use of Non-traditional Products in Animal Feed* (Jan. 1996).

[94]   FDA Import Alert 33-04.

2001, FDA issued a series of import alerts with respect to "mini-cup" gel candies that, by virtue of their size and consistency, posed a choking hazard.[95] The candies had, in fact, been implicated in a series of suffocation deaths and near-deaths in children and elderly persons. Citing section 402(a)(3), FDA concluded that such candies were, because of the risks they presented, "unfit for food."

In 2004, confronted with concerns arising from the possible presence of bovine spongiform encephalopathy (BSE)-causing prions in food derived from bovines, FDA proposed to require manufacturers and processors of human food to document that food is not manufactured from, processed with, or does not otherwise contain "prohibited cattle materials."[96] FDA reasoned that it was important for such records to be kept so that the agency could ensure that products on the market were not "adulterated." Although the agency relied on several provisions in section 402 of the Act as authority for the proposed requirement, the agency placed primary reliance on section 402(a)(3) explaining its view that a food can be "otherwise unfit for food" based on health risks. The agency concluded that the discovery of a BSE positive cow in the United States presented the possibility of disease transmission to humans from exposure to material from a non-ambulatory, disabled cow. As a result, any edible products from such an animal were "unfit for food" within the meaning of section 402(a)(3). No comments objected either to the agency's rationale or its reliance on section 402(a)(3).

Following on the type of reasoning upon which the BSE recordkeeping regulation was based, FDA in November 2008 once again relied on section 402(a)(3) as a regulatory tool for exercising regulatory authority over foods that might be contaminated. At issue were—and continue to be—Chinese dairy products (as well as food and food products made from dairy ingredients from such Chinese dairy products) offered for import into the United States.[97] Concerned about the possible presence of the contaminant melamine in such foods, FDA issued a broad import alert that authorized agency investigators to detain any such food and prohibit its being offered for entry into domestic commerce until the food is shown to be free from melamine contamination. So interpreted and coupled with the expansive authority granted FDA under section 801 of the Act (a section that permits the detention of imported food that "appears" to be adulterated), section 402(a)(3), when used in the face of suspicious but not confirmable public health concerns presented by a given food, serves as a potent tool for preventing importation of a product that may not otherwise fall within the strictures of the Act but nevertheless raises a possible safety concern.

FDA has been cautious in its use of section 402(a)(3)'s "otherwise unfit for food" standard as a safety tool. Moreover, in the BSE and melamine examples, FDA has not relied exclusively on section 402(a)(3) and has also incorporated paragraphs (a)(1) and (a)(4) of section 402 to further support its position. Nevertheless, the agency's extension of the "unfit" concept to include products presenting merely possible safety risks raises legal questions that have not been tested in court—including not only the propriety of the section as a safety tool but also as to the evidentiary burden the agency would have to meet in proving that a *possibly* unsafe food is "unfit."

---

95   *See*, for example, FDA Import Alert 33-15.
96   69 Fed. Reg. 42,275, 42,277 (July 14, 2004).
97   FDA Import Alert 99-31.

Low-Acid Canned Food Regulations

Canned foods are a staple of the American diet made possible by a technology that provides for all-season availability through long shelf life for basic foods, and permits transportation of such foods over long distances. It is critical that canned foods, especially those naturally low in acid, be properly prepared and canned to prevent the growth (under anaerobic conditions) of the organism capable of producing the often fatal botulinum toxin.

Under section 402(a)(4) of the Act, food is deemed adulterated "if it has been prepared, packed or held under insanitary conditions whereby it may have become contaminated with filth, or whereby it may have been rendered injurious to health." Section 404 of the act further provides that, in order to prevent the distribution of food that may be injurious due to contamination by microorganisms, FDA can require a manufacturer to obtain and comply with the terms of an "emergency permit" to remain in operation.[98]

FDA has used these authorities to set rigorous standards for the preparation of low-acid canned foods.[99] These regulations prescribe in detail the personnel, equipment, procedures, controls, and records required for the safe processing and packaging of low-acid foods in hermetically sealed containers. The regulations also require manufacturers to register their facilities with FDA and file a description of their canning processes before commencing operations.[100] Manufacturers who do not meet these criteria may be required by FDA to obtain and operate under an emergency permit as a condition to make further shipments of products in interstate commerce.[101]

These regulations have the force and effect of law. No responsible canner would consider producing a product that does not comply with agency requirements. FDA's low-acid canned food regulations and similar regulations related to "acidified" foods,[102] although invisible to the public-at-large, may have enhanced food safety in the United States more than any other single FDA decision or activity.

Good Manufacturing Practices

As mentioned earlier, although in the case of pharmaceuticals, medical devices, infant formulas, and dietary supplements, the FDCA expressly adopted the concept of GMPs, giving FDA authority to promulgate legally binding GMP regulations and to deem products unlawful if their manufacturer violates the GMP standards,[103] no such explicit statutory authority existed requiring preventive GMP controls on food production until the passage of the Food Safety Modernization Act. The food industry, nevertheless, has developed, refined,

---

[98] FDCA § 404, 21 U.S.C. § 344.

[99] 21 C.F.R. pt. 113. FDA also has promulgated standards for avoiding harmful contamination by microorganisms in the manufacture of acidified foods. *Id.* at 114. Both sets of standards in part were precipitated by a botulin toxin episode (involving a New York banker who died after consuming a poisonous can of Bon Vivant vichyssoise soup) and by botulism scares involving other national brand soups. *See* PETER BARTON HUTT & RICHARD A. MERRILL, FOOD AND DRUG LAW: CASES AND MATERIALS 277-79 (2d ed. 1991).

[100] 21 C.F.R. § 108.35.

[101] 21 C.F.R. § 108.5.

[102] 21 C.F.R. pt. 114.

[103] *See* FDCA § 501(a)(2)(B), 21 U.S.C. § 351(a)(2)(B), *and* 21 C.F.R. pts. 210, 211 (regarding drug GMPs); FDCA §§ 501(h), 520(f), 21 U.S.C. §§ 351(h), 360j(f), *and* 21 C.F.R. pt. 820 (regarding medical device GMPs).

and observed the concept of GMPs. And FDA promulgated regulations setting forth current GMPs in the manufacturing, packing, or holding of human food.[104] These GMPs were issued under the general authority of section 402(a), and represent general standards of food processing and handling deemed necessary to avoid contamination of food with poisonous or deleterious substances, filth, or potentially harmful microorganisms. The regulations address layout and maintenance of facilities, personnel qualifications, equipment and utensils, processes and controls, and other measures required to ensure basic sanitation and cleanliness. Because the regulations represent general standards covering all food, they are commonly referred to as the "umbrella" food GMPs.

In enforcement cases, FDA has never exclusively relied on the umbrella food GMP regulations as creating legally binding requirements, but instead uses the evidence gathered during factory inspections to prove a direct violation of section 402(a)(4). Nevertheless, the umbrella GMPs are another example of an FDA standard that as a matter of practice has become at least a minimum standard in the food processing industry. And, of course, evidence of clear violations of the general principles in the regulations would bolster the contention that section 402(a)(4) has been violated.

As noted earlier, FDA augmented its umbrella GMPs with binding GMPs covering acidified and low-acid foods and, as discussed hereafter, with binding HACCP requirements for juice products and seafood. These initiatives stretched the reasonable limits of section 402 and set the stage for the comprehensive changes in agency authority ushered in by the Food Safety Modernization Act.

Microbial Contamination

In 1986, former Director of FDA's Center for Food Safety and Applied Nutrition, Dr. Sanford A. Miller, concluded that "the most perplexing and hazardous problems of food safety remain today as they always have been—problems of assuring microbiological safety."[105] The conclusion is just as true today, decades later. Simply put, foodborne pathogens present complicated regulatory problems. Unlike chemical contaminants or additives, pathogens grow. Moreover, they are difficult to investigate, control, and prevent. Pathogens constantly adapt and find new hosts, and have the ability to mutate over time.

The problem presented by pathogens in food is not the remote possibility of harm that becomes evident years after exposure, but rather immediate illness ranging from stomach discomfort to death (particularly death among the very young, the elderly, and others whose health status or immune system is compromised). Examples of pathogens include *Listeria monocytogenes* in dairy products (including milk, cheese, and ice cream); *Vibrio vulnificus* in seafood; and *Escherichia coli* O157:H7 in meat and produce. These pathogens have the potential to mutate into organisms of even greater public health concern. Unlike chemical and pesticide contaminants, the amount of a pathogenic organism required to cause harm can be exceedingly small, and the resulting infection can be transmitted from one person to another.

---

[104] 21 C.F.R. pt. 110.
[105] Sanford A. Miller & John E. Kvenberg, *Reflections on Food Safety*, Paper presented at the Nat'l Food Processors Ass'n Annual Convention, Atlanta, GA (Feb. 3, 1986).

Until the passage of the Food Safety Modernization Act, FDA's statutory tools for addressing microbiological contamination were primarily those found in the original 1906 act pertaining to "added, poisonous or deleterious substances" and insanitation. Because pathogens grow, it was difficult to rely on tolerances, action levels, or defect action levels as a means of protecting the public health. FDA's approach became to employ a combination of its authorities (sections 402(a)(1), 402(a)(3), and 402(a)(4)) to establish food-processing standards designed to avoid contamination in the first place. A significant exception to this approach involves FDA's 20-plus-year-long effort to assess the relative risks presented to the public from various possible sources of foodborne *Listeria monocytogenes*. In November 2003, FDA announced it would rely upon the results of the risk assessment to "redirect and revise enforcement and regulatory strategies."[106] In effect, the risk assessment results have provided a reliable empirical basis upon which FDA can prioritize its public health protection activities toward those foodborne events presenting meaningful public health risks. In April 2011, FDA announced its desire to update the risk assessment and called for scientific data and information capable of assisting and informing that enterprise.[107]

The *Food Code*

A unique component in FDA's food safety toolkit has been the U.S. Public Health Service's (PHS) *Food Code*.[108] According to FDA, the *Food Code* is neither federal law nor federal regulation. It simply represents FDA's best advice for a uniform system of regulation to ensure that food is safe and properly protected and presented at the retail level. The *Food Code* finds its origins in model food code provisions developed by FDA and adopted by the states. As of January 2009, 49 of 50 states have retail food codes patterned after previous editions of the *Food Code*. Although not federal law, these codes are consistent with the laws and regulations FDA administers.

In 1993, FDA combined the model codes into a new *Food Code* that emphasizes the importance of time and temperature controls in safe food-handling practices, and incorporates HACCP as a framework for the application of principles at retail. Although the *Food Code* does not have the force and effect of law, it does provide a basis for a contention in an FDA enforcement action that products processed or handled in clear violation of such accepted practices create a reasonable possibility of microbial contamination and, as a result, are adulterated within the meaning of section 402(a)(4).

---

[106]   Reducing the Risk of *Listeria monocytogenes*, Update of the Listeria Action Plan, Nov. 2003, *available at* http://www.cfsan.fda.gov/%20~dms/lmrwplan.html.

[107]   67 Fed. Reg. 19,311 (April 7, 2011).

[108]   Public Health Serv., Food Code (2009). The Public Health Service's authority for providing assistance to state and local governments is derived from the Public Health Service Act (PHSA), 42 U.S.C. § 243 (1994). Responsibility for carrying out the provisions of the PHSA relating to food have been delegated to FDA (specifically, the Commissioner of Food and Drugs). 21 C.F.R. § 5.1(a)(2), (4).

HACCP

As briefly noted earlier in this text, HACCP is a system for identifying and monitoring potential specific foodborne hazards. HACCP was developed in the 1960s by the Pillsbury Company in an effort to ensure that food used in the U.S. space program would not be contaminated with pathogens and would thus be incapable of causing illness or injury to astronauts.[109] HACCP is designed to replace end-product testing as the primary means for ensuring the safety of food using a quality control system designed to prevent the conditions that create the possibility of a hazard. Two key elements of HACCP include hazard analysis[110] and the establishment of critical control points.[111] HACCP has gained acceptance in the international food safety community as a state-of-the-art means to ensure the safety of food.[112] Domestically, both FDA and the U.S. Department of Agriculture's Food Safety Inspection Service have come to recognize the value of the HACCP system.

Regardless of how beneficial HACCP standards may be, as noted above, until the enactment of FSMA, FDA did not have express regulatory authority to impose the standards.[113] Nonetheless, general support for HACCP-based regulations was found in sections 402 and 404 of the FDCA. Accordingly, in December 1995, FDA issued its final regulations imposing HACCP on the seafood industry.[114] Section 402(a)(4) was the key statutory basis for the final rule.[115] To solidify its conviction that section 402(a)(4) was the only reasonable statutory authority upon which to rely, the agency concluded that seafood was not in an "overall state of emergency" from a public health standpoint. Thus, seafood was not an appropriate candidate for the "extreme" emergency situations contemplated by section 404 and, as a result, the formal rulemaking requirements that attend agency action under section 404 did not apply.

---

[109] For a thorough discussion of HACCP, see *Implementation of HACCP in a Food Processing Plant*, 56 J. Food Protection 548-54 (1993).

[110] In initial efforts to apply HACCP, FDA has relied on the National Advisory Committee on Microbial Criteria for Foods' (NACMCF's) definition of hazard: "a biological chemical or physical property that may cause a food to be unsafe for consumption." NACMCF, *National Advisory Committee on Microbiological Criteria for Foods, Hazard Analysis and Critical Control Point System Adopted March 20, 1992*, in HACCP: Principles and Applications (Van Nostrand Reinhold 1992). According to NACMCF, in assessing the likelihood that such a hazard accompanies a food process or practice, it is important to consider not only the likelihood that the hazard will occur, but also the severity of harm that will result. 59 Fed. Reg. at 39,889. A hazard analysis also must address and define the preventative steps or controls available for combating the identified hazards. *Id.*

[111] FDA also has relied on NACMCF's definition of "critical control points" as those aspects of a food process or practice that must be controlled to ensure the safety of food. *Id.* at 39,890. The HACCP system contemplates that "critical limits" or "critical criteria" be developed to document the procedures that should be followed at each critical control point. Monitoring and verification steps are incorporated at each critical control point to ensure that potential risks are controlled.

[112] In particular, the Committee on Food Hygiene of the United States' Codex Alimentarius Commission (Codex) has endorsed the HACCP concept in a worldwide guideline. Principles and Application of the HACCP System, ALINORM 93/13, app. vi.

[113] 59 Fed. Reg. at 39,890.

[114] 60 Fed. Reg. 65,096 (Dec. 18, 1995). In addition to this final rule, FDA published in the *Federal Register* on April 7, 1994, a notice of availability of draft guidelines, primarily directed toward processors, on how to develop HACCP controls for specific types of processing operations. 59 Fed. Reg. 16,655 (Apr. 7, 1994).

[115] The agency also relied upon section 402(a)(1) but not nearly, for obvious reasons, to the extent it relied on section 402(a)(4).

In contrast with this rather narrow reading of section 404, FDA, in its final rule implementing the seafood HACCP requirements, broadly interpreted its authority under section 402(a)(4) to require HACCP-based processing practices and, in conjunction with section 701(a), record maintenance and record access.[116] The agency emphasized that section 402(a)(4) addresses "conditions" that may render a food injurious to health rather than conditions that actually have caused the food to be injurious. As a result, according to the agency's analysis, the question presented by section 402(a)(4) is whether the "conditions" in a plant are such that it is reasonably possible that food may be rendered injurious to health; if a seafood processor did not incorporate certain basic controls into its procedures for preparing, packing, and holding food, it would be "reasonably possible" under such "conditions" that the food may be rendered injurious to health and, therefore, at odds with section 402(a)(4).

The agency proceeded to also broadly interpret the delimiting, antecedent term "insanitary" to cover a wide set of circumstances necessary to ensure that food is not produced under "conditions" that may render it injurious to health. The agency reasoned that given the risks inherent in many seafood operations, if a processor does not identify critical control points in its process and monitor what goes on at those points, there is a real possibility that the failure to implement such practices will result in food that will be "injurious to health." Thus, the failure on a manufacturer's part to analyze its processes, to identify the points at which problems may occur, and to establish the parameters that must be met if those problems are to be avoided would constitute "insanitary conditions." The agency rationalized that this modern parsing of a 50-year-old provision is consistent with the underlying purpose of section 402(a)(4): ensuring "the observance of those precautions which consciousness of the obligation imposed upon producers of perishable food products should require in the preparation of food for consumption by human beings."[117]

In finalizing its seafood HACCP requirements, FDA once again interpreted section 402(a)(4) as providing it the authority to issue recordkeeping requirements. Relying on past litigation upholding FDA's claimed access under specific confectionery GMP regulations to secure coding and distribution records, FDA noted the essentiality of records to the agency's ability to verify compliance with the overall HACCP program. Acknowledging that specific record access authority is provided it in very narrow terms only under sections 703 and 704 of the act, FDA posited the view that the lack of an explicitly delegated authority does not invalidate agency regulations as long as the regulations are consistent with the act's overriding purpose—broad public health protection. Moreover, relying on section 701(a), the agency argued that recordkeeping assists in the "efficient enforcement of the Act" and is essential to FDA's ability to confirm compliance with HACCP procedures. This reasoning is controversial.[118] Admittedly, in areas where real hazards are shown to exist that HACCP systems can prevent or significantly limit, it would not be surprising for a court to find agency access to HACCP records to be logically related to section 402(a)(4) control over insanitary conditions. In cases presenting less than true hazards, however, an unresolved question

---

[116]   60 Fed. Reg. at 65,098-101.

[117]   *Id.* at 65,100 (citing *Hearings on S. 2800 Before the Senate Comm. on Commerce*, 73d Cong., 2d Sess. (Mar. 1934)).

[118]   Edward Dunkelberger, *The Statutory Basis for FDA's Food Safety Assurance Programs; From GMP, to Emergency Permit Control, to HACCP*, 50 FOOD & DRUG L.J. 357, 379-383 (1995). In proposing records access authority as a key element of current GMPs for dietary supplements, FDA used the same rationale as it did for access to HACCP records. *See* 49 Fed. Reg. 12,158, 12,168 (Mar. 13, 2003).

exists as to whether access to food records is outside the scope of protection authorized by the section. Nevertheless, as staked out, the agency's position serves to emphasize the importance of recordkeeping to a successful HACCP program and encourages voluntary grants of access to key HACCP records.

In the wake of its success in establishing binding HACCP principles for seafood, FDA once again turned to HACCP to address the concerns presented by the microbial contamination of food. In late October 1996, an outbreak of E. coli O157:H7 infections was associated with the consumption of unpasteurized apple juice. Sixty-six people became ill, of whom 14 suffered from hemolytic uremic syndrome. One child died.

The outbreak attracted a great deal of publicity and media attention. In response, FDA prepared a comprehensive review of the safety of vegetable and fruit juices documenting a long history of cases where such juices served as vehicles for serious disease outbreaks.[119] The agency's carefully assembled dossier of evidence revealed that juice and juice beverages are very susceptible to microbiological contamination.[120]

As a result, in April 1998 FDA proposed the implementation of mandatory HACCP procedures and principles to processing vegetable and fruit juices.[121] The proposal was not accompanied by any extensive legal discussion—a far cry from the detailed analyses of section 402(a)(4) accompanying the seafood HACCP proposal as well as the agency's GMP initiatives throughout the 1970s. A simple discussion of section 402(a)(4) (and to a lesser extent section 402(a)(1)) as the controlling statutory authority was deemed all that was necessary by the agency in proposing the requirement.[122] In spite of the limitations of its literal language, section 402(a)(4) had become synonymous for FDA with HACCP authority.

The response of the food industry to the concept of HACCP-based controls over food processing has been consistently positive. Industry is familiar with HACCP principles—principles that represent the application of good common sense to the production of safe food. Industry has been following these practices for decades. Nonetheless, industry has from time to time differed with FDA over the nature of the criteria to be applied in any HACCP program as well as the scope of programs attempting to impose mandatory HACCP requirements. Although differences are likely to continue, many are resolved in FDA's favor by FSMA.

Requiring Hazard Analysis and Risk-Based Preventive Controls

Preventive Controls. The centerpiece of FSMA is its vesting FDA with the express authority to require that risk-based preventive controls be observed by the majority of food producers. New section 418[123] requires that "the owner, operator, or agent in charge of a facility" identify and evaluate known or reasonably foreseeable hazards, develop a written

---

[119] Notice of Intent, 62 Fed. Reg. 45,593 (Aug. 28, 1997).

[120] Id.

[121] 63 Fed. Reg. 20,450 (Apr. 24, 1998).

[122] Id. at 20,457.

[123] FDCA § 418, 21 U.S.C. § 350g.

analysis of the hazards, and implement a plan containing preventive controls designed to significantly minimize or prevent the identified hazard (including hazards intentionally introduced) from being present in food. Classic HACCP components (e.g., effectiveness monitoring, corrective action, verification, recordkeeping, etc.) are not only required but also identified in detail. Moreover, subsection 418(i)[124] requires the re-analysis of the propriety of preventive controls whenever a change at the facility creates a reasonable potential for a new food hazard or significantly increases the potential of a previously identified hazard. Even if no such changes occur, a re-analysis of possible food hazards must be conducted at least once every three years. The upshot: now, as a general rule, "food," like "drugs" and "medical devices," is subject to statutorily mandated production controls.

Facilities operating under currently existing seafood HACCP and juice HACCP controls are exempted from the requirements of section 418.[125] Similarly, companies following agency requirements for thermally processed low-acid foods are exempt from the requirements of the section—but only to the extent that the facilities' practices focus on microbiological hazards regulated under the low-acid or acidified food regulations.

Also exempted from FSMA preventive controls requirements are "qualified facilities." A "qualified facility" is either a "very small business"[126] or a facility for which the average annual monetary value of food sold is less than $500,000 and the value of food manufactured, processed, packed, or held at the facility that is sold directly to consumers or retail restaurants exceeds the value of all other food sold by the facility to other purchasers. Although not subject to the requirements of section 418(b)-(h), a "qualified facility" must submit to the agency documentation that the company does, in fact, implement preventive controls to address identified hazards and that the company is monitoring the propriety of such controls. A "qualified facility" must also "prominently and conspicuously" label its products with the name and business address of the facility where the food was manufactured or processed. With respect to a food for which labeling is not required, the name and address of the qualified facility must be prominently and conspicuously displayed at point of purchase.

Section 418(n) required FDA to promulgate, within 18 months after the enactment of the legislation, "regulations" establishing "science-based minimum standards" for preventive controls compliance and defining the terms "small business" and "very small business."[127] FDA issued two long-awaited proposed rules on preventive controls for human and animal food in 2013, and issued supplemental proposals in September 2014,[128] but as of December 2014, had yet to publish the final rules.[129] FSMA requires the preventive controls regulations

---

[124]   FDCA § 418(i), 21 U.S.C. § 350g(i).

[125]   FDCA § 418(j), 21 U.S.C. § 350g(j).

[126]   FDCA § 418(l), 21 U.S.C. § 350g(l). If the facility is a subsidiary or affiliate of another entity, all subsidiaries and affiliates must "collectively" meet the definition of a "very small business."

[127]   FDCA § 418(n), 21 U.S.C. § 350g(n).

[128]   FDA's proposed rules on preventive controls are entitled "Current Good Manufacturing Practice and Hazard Analysis and Risk-Based Preventive Controls for Human Food," and "Current Good Manufacturing Practice and Hazard Analysis and Risk-Based Preventive Controls for Food for Animals." 78 Fed. Reg. 3646 (Jan. 16, 2013); 78 Fed. Reg. 64,736 (Oct. 29, 2013). FDA issued supplemental proposals on September 29, 2014. 79 Fed. Reg. 58,523 (Sept. 29, 2014); 79 Fed. Reg. 58,475 (Sept. 29, 2014).

[129]   The Center for Food Safety and the Center for Environmental Health brought suit against FDA for the agency's failure to meet the statutory deadline for promulgating these and certain other rules mandated by FSMA. Under a 2014 consent decree, FDA agreed to make every effort to issue the final rules on: 1)

to "provide sufficient flexibility" for all sizes and types of facilities.[130] Providing "sufficient flexibility" while at the same time providing the rigor that FSMA implicitly demands has proven to be a challenge for FDA. Making FDA's task even more difficult is the fact that the regulations must also "acknowledge" differences in risk and, accordingly and to the extent possible, "minimize" the number of separate standards.[131]

As noted above, dramatic FSMA-initiated change in agency authority with respect to preventive controls involves records access. FDA investigators may request and are entitled to have access to not only a facility's food safety plan but also the facility's records, including records documenting the monitoring of the preventive controls implemented, instances of non-conformance material to food safety, and the results of testing and other means of verification.[132]

The failure to operate a facility in a manner consistent with the requirements of section 418 is a prohibited act under section 301 of the FDCA.[133]

Performance Standards. Section 104 of FSMA[134] requires the agency, after appropriate review and consideration, to issue "contaminant specific and science-based" guidance documents, including guidance documents regarding action levels or regulations for specific products or product classes. There is no amendment to the FDCA that reflects this requirement.

Standards for Produce Safety. New section 419[135] of the FDCA reflects the recognition that fruits and vegetables that are raw agricultural commodities merit special attention. Accordingly, FDA was required to propose within one year after the enactment of the legislation "science-based minimum standards for the safe production and harvesting of those types of fruits and vegetables . . . that are raw agricultural commodities" and for which FDA has determined that such standards will minimize the risk of "serious adverse health consequences."[136] FDA issued a proposed rule on produce safety on January 16, 2013, and a supplemental proposal on September 29, 2014,[137] but as of December 2014, had yet to publish the final rule.[138]

---

preventive controls for human and animal food by August 30, 2015; 2) the foreign supplier verification program, produce safety standards, and the accreditation of third-party auditors by October 31, 2015; 3) the sanitary transportation of food by March 31, 2016; and 4) the intentional adulteration of food by May 31, 2016. Center for Food Safety v. Hamburg, Consent Decree, Case No.: 12-cv-04529-PJH (Feb. 20, 2014).

[130]   FDCA § 418(n)(3)(A), 21 U.S.C. § 350g(n)(3)(A).

[131]   FDCA § 418(n)(3)(C), 21 U.S.C. § 350g(n)(3)(C).

[132]   FDCA §§ 418(g) and (h), 21 U.S.C. §§ 350g(g) and (h).

[133]   FDCA § 301(uu), 21 U.S.C. § 331(uu).

[134]   21 U.S.C. § 2201.

[135]   FDCA § 419, 21 U.S.C. § 350h.

[136]   FDCA § 419(a)(1)(A), 21 U.S.C. § 350h(a)(1)(A).

[137]   FDA's proposed rule on produce safety is entitled "Standards for the Growing, Harvesting, Packing, and Holding of Produce for Human Consumption." 78 Fed. Reg. 3504 (Jan. 16, 2013). FDA published a supplemental proposal on September 29, 2014. 79 Fed. Reg. 58,433 (Sept. 29, 2014).

[138]   Under a 2014 consent decree, FDA has agreed to make every effort to issue the final produce safety rule by October 31, 2015. Center for Food Safety v. Hamburg, Consent Decree, Case No.: 12-cv-04529-PJH (Feb. 20, 2014).

In light of the inherent difficulties in policing the safety of such raw agricultural commodities, the legislation requires that any final regulation "provide sufficient flexibility to be applicable to various types of entities engaged in the production and harvesting of fruits and vegetables." As is the case with respect to regulations to be issued under section 418(n), no guidance is provided on what safety factors or considerations may influence "sufficient flexibility."[139] Section 419(a)(4), however, requires FDA to prioritize the implementation of regulations based on the known risks accompanying certain types of raw agricultural commodities.[140] Past foodborne outbreaks and their severity are suggested as valuable touchstones to consider in any effort at prioritization.[141] The criteria to be employed in developing the regulations must focus on minimizing the risk of serious adverse health consequences and include procedures, processes and practices reasonably necessary to prevent the introduction of known or reasonably foreseeable biological, chemical, and physical hazards.[142]

For "small businesses" and "very small businesses" (terms, as noted above, to be defined by FDA by regulation), the effective date of any regulation is to be delayed by one year and two years, respectively. A state or foreign country from which food is imported may request a variance from FDA from any of the regulation-based requirements. The grant of a variance hinges on whether the requested variance increases the likelihood that the food for which the variance is requested will be adulterated under section 402 and whether the variance provides the same level of public health protection as the requirements of the regulations adopted under section 419.[143]

Farms that sell directly to consumers are exempt from the requirements of section 419 and any implementing regulations as long as the average monetary value of food sold by such farm to consumers or restaurants exceeds the average annual value of food sold to all other buyers *and* the average annual monetary value of all food sold is less than $500,000.[144] Such foods (as is the case with foods similarly exempt from the requirements of section 418) must bear either labeling or be accompanied by placarding "prominently and conspicuously" displaying the name and business address of the farm.[145]

Improving FDA's Capacity to Respond to Food Safety Problems

High-Risk Facilities. New section 421 of the FDCA requires that FDA identify "high-risk" facilities based upon safety risks, compliance histories, the rigor and effectiveness of a facility's preventive controls, etc.[146] FDA is required to increase the frequency of its inspections of domestic facilities identified as "high-risk." "High-risk" facilities must be inspected not less often than once in a five-year period following enactment and not less often than once every three years thereafter.[147] Non-high-risk food facilities must be inspected "not less than" once

---

139   FDCA § 419(c)(1)(B), 21 U.S.C. § 350h(c)(1)(B).
140   FDCA § 419(a)(4), 21 U.S.C. § 350h(a)(4).
141   FDCA § 419(b)(1), 21 U.S.C. § 350h(b)(1).
142   FDCA § 419(c)(1)(A), 21 U.S.C. § 350h(c)(1)(A).
143   FDCA § 419(c)(2), 21 U.S.C. § 350h(c)(2).
144   FDCA § 419(f), 21 U.S.C. § 350h(f).
145   FDCA § 419(f)(2)(A), 21 U.S.C. § 350h(f)(2)(A).
146   FDCA § 421(a), 21 U.S.C. § 350j(a).
147   FDCA § 421(a)(2)(B), 21 U.S.C. § 350j(a)(2)(B).

in the seven-year period following enactment of FSMA and not less than once every five years thereafter.[148] The extent to which these aspirational inspection frequency goals are achievable will largely depend on congressional funding for FDA.

Enhancing Tracking and Tracing of Food and Recordkeeping. Section 204 of FSMA requires FDA to establish a product tracing system to receive information and improve the capacity of the agency to "rapidly and effectively" track and trace food that is in the United States or that is offered for import.[149] FDA may not establish such a system until pilot projects for identifying effective "decision technologies" for such tracking have been completed.[150] Moreover, FDA, within two years of the enactment of the legislation, was required to publish a notice of proposed rulemaking focused on establishing recordkeeping requirements (in addition to those required under section 414 of the FDCA) for those facilities that manufacture, process, pack or hold "high-risk" foods.[151] FDA did not meet this two-year statutory deadline, and as of December 2014, had yet to issue a proposed rule.

FDA is required to publish, once the aforesaid regulations are finalized, a list identifying "high-risk" foods.[152] In arriving at such a designation, FDA must consider a number of factors including the known safety risks of the particular food, the history of outbreaks attributed to the food, the likelihood that a particular food has a high potential risk for microbiological or chemical contamination, etc.[153] Limitations on this requirement exist for fishing vessels, for "comingled raw agricultural commodities" (any commodity that is combined or mixed after harvesting and before processing, but not including the types of fruits and vegetables determined under section 419 to be subject to special produce standards), and for foods expressly exempted by FDA for cause.[154] A facility that handles any "high-risk" food that is so limited or exempted must, nevertheless, be required to maintain records that identify the immediate previous source of such food and the immediate subsequent recipient of the food.[155] Farms selling directly to consumers, however, are exempt from any such recordkeeping requirement.[156]

In recognition of the importance of being able to trace and track high-risk foods, section 204(f) of FSMA[157] empowers FDA to require that a farm identify potential immediate recipients (other than consumers) of any article of food that is the subject of such an investigation and that FDA "reasonably believes" is adulterated under section 402 of the Act,

---

[148] FDCA § 421(a)(2)(C), 21 U.S.C. § 350j(a)(2)(C).

[149] 21 U.S.C. § 2223.

[150] In March 2013, FDA released a final report on two product tracing pilot projects conducted by the Institute of Food Technologists under an existing contract with FDA. The final report, entitled "Pilot Projects for Improving Product Tracing Along the Food Supply System," can be found at http://www.fda.gov/downloads/Food/GuidanceRegulation/UCM341810.pdf.

[151] 21 U.S.C. § 2223(d).

[152] 21 U.S.C. § 2223(d)(2)(B). On February 4, 2014, FDA published a *Federal Register* Notice to seek comments and scientific data to help the agency refine its draft methodological approach to identifying high-risk foods. 79 Fed. Reg. 6596 (Feb. 4, 2014). FDA has indicated that it will develop the list of high-risk foods after its draft methodological approach is finalized.

[153] 21 U.S.C. § 2223(d)(2)(A).

[154] 21 U.S.C. § 2223(d)(6).

[155] 21 U.S.C. § 2223(d)(6)(F).

[156] 21 U.S.C. § 2223(d)(6)(H).

[157] 21 U.S.C. § 2223(f).

was so adulterated at the subject farm, and that presents a threat of serious adverse health consequences or death.

Failure to abide by any recordkeeping requirement established under section 204 of the legislation is a prohibited act under section 301(e).[158] Failure of a foreign company to maintain such records is a basis for refusal of food produced at such facility when the food is offered for import.

Protection Against Intentional Adulteration. In a FSMA-related enhancement of FDA's bioterrorism authorities, section 420[159] of the FDCA empowers FDA to promulgate, in consultation with the Department of Homeland Security (DHS) and USDA, regulations regarding food the agency determines carries a "high risk" of "intentional contamination" that could cause "serious adverse health consequences."[160] The section also requires that the agency issue guidance documents related to protecting consumers against the intentional adulteration of food and develop mitigation/litigation strategies and/or measures to guard against such adulteration. The regulations and guidances must be periodically reviewed and updated by the agency. The failure to comply with a regulation adopted under section 420 is a prohibited act under section 301(ww) of the Act.[161] These new authorities are complimented by the requirement in FSMA that DHHS, in conjunction with USDA and DHS, develop a "food defense strategy" hallmarked by the key goals of enhancing the "preparedness" of the agriculture and food systems and ensuring an "efficient response" to a food "emergency."[162]

Mandatory Reporting of Potentially Serious Food-related Risks: The Reportable Food Registry

Finding that, with respect to food safety, there had been a loss of public confidence in the American food supply, Congress in 2007 amended the FDCA to include section 417.[163] Section 417 is patterned after the requirements noted earlier that Congress passed in 2006 with respect to dietary supplements and governing the establishment of a reporting system for serious adverse events for supplements and nonprescription drugs. Prior to the enactment of section 417, the only "foods" subject to any form of mandatory product safety-related reporting requirements were infant formulas and dietary supplements. In enacting section 417, Congress expressly sought to provide a "reliable mechanism to track patterns of adulteration in food [which] would support efforts by the Food and Drug Administration to target limited inspection resources to protect the public health."[164] To facilitate the Reportable Food Registry, Congress required that FDA establish an electronic portal by which instances of "reportable food" must be submitted to FDA by "responsible parties."[165]

---

[158]   21 U.S.C. § 2223(j).

[159]   FDCA § 420, 21 U.S.C. § 350i.

[160]   *Id.* On December 24, 2013, FDA published a proposed rule on "Focused Mitigation Strategies To Protect Food Against Intentional Adulteration." 78 Fed. Reg. 78,014 (Dec. 24, 2013). Under a 2014 consent decree, FDA has agreed to make every effort to issue the final rule on intentional adulteration by May 31, 2016. Center for Food Safety v. Hamburg, Consent Decree, Case No.: 12-cv-04529-PJH (Feb. 20, 2014).

[161]   21 U.S.C. § 331(ww).

[162]   21 U.S.C. § 2202.

[163]   21 U.S.C. § 350f; Food and Drug Administration Amendments Act, Pub. L. No. 110-85, 121 Stat. 832 (2007).

[164]   Pub. L. No. 110-085, § 1005(a)(4).

[165]   FDCA § 417(a) and (b), 21 U.S.C. § 350f(a) and (b).

Moreover, after receiving a report under section 417, FDA is required to review and assess the information and issue an alert or notification as the agency deems necessary to protect the public health.[166]

The basics of the reporting requirement appear to be straightforward. Any "responsible party" (defined as that person who submits a facility registration to FDA under section 415 of the Act) must notify FDA within 24 hours after the party "determines" that an article of food it has distributed presents a "reasonable probability" that exposure to the food "will cause serious adverse health consequences or death to humans or animals."[167] If the adulteration originated with the responsible party, the party must also investigate the cause of the adulteration.[168] For each report, a responsible party must maintain records related to the report for two years and must permit FDA inspection of such records.[169] The failure to submit a report, the falsification of a report and the refusal to permit access to required records each constitute a "prohibited act" under section 301 of the FDCA, thereby exposing the responsible party to the relevant penalties of the FDCA, including prosecution.[170] A responsible party is not required to submit a reportable food report to FDA only if *all* of the following criteria are met:

- The adulteration originated with the responsible party;

- The responsible party detected the adulteration prior to any transfer of the food to another person; *and*

- The responsible party corrected the adulteration or destroyed or caused the destruction of such article of food.[171]

FSMA amended section 417 to provide FDA with the authority to require a responsible party to submit to the agency consumer-oriented information regarding a reportable food (e.g., a description of the article of food), implicated product identification codes (such as UPC, SKU, or lot or batch numbers), contact information for the responsible party, and any other information FDA determines to be necessary to help a consumer accurately identify whether the consumer is in possession of a reportable food.[172] FDA must prepare for each reportable food event a one-page summary containing critical information capable of enabling a consumer to identify the food.[173] Moreover, FDA must publish the summary on the agency's website and any grocery stores that are a part of chain establishments with 15 or more physical locations must within 24 hours of the posting of such a summary prominently display the summary in conspicuous locations in grocery stores.[174]

---

166   FDCA § 417(c), 21 U.S.C. § 350f(c).
167   FDCA § 417(a) and (b), 21 U.S.C. § 350f(a) and (b).
168   FDCA § 417(d)(1)(B), 21 U.S.C. § 350f(d)(1)(B).
169   FDCA § 417(j), 21 U.S.C. § 350f(j).
170   FDCA § 301(e), 21 U.S.C. § 331(e).
171   FDCA § 417(d)(2), 21 U.S.C. § 350f(d)(2).
172   FDCA § 417(f), 21 U.S.C. § 350f(f). On March 26, 2014, FDA published an advance notice of proposed rulemaking related to this new authority entitled "Implementation of the Food and Drug Administration Food Safety Modernization Act Amendments to the Reportable Food Registry Provisions of the Federal Food, Drug, and Cosmetic Act." 79 Fed. Reg. 16,698 (Mar. 26, 2014).
173   FDCA § 417(g), 21 U.S.C. § 350f(g).
174   FDCA § 417(h), 21 U.S.C. § 350f(h).

In spite of the apparent straightforwardness of the reporting requirements, a number of questions of interpretation have arisen. As a result, FDA has issued two editions of a guidance designed to clarify the scope and effect of the reporting requirement.[175] Notably, the scope and meaning of the term "transfer" in section 417(d)(2)(B) has proven particularly controversial—and, as a result, FDA in 2010 asked for comment on the meaning of the term.[176] As FDA explained:

> Section 417(d)(2) of the act provides an exemption from the requirement that a responsible party submit a reportable food report. In order for the exemption to apply, the adulteration must have originated with the responsible party, the responsible party must have detected the adulteration prior to any transfer to another person of the article of food, and the responsible party must have corrected the adulteration or destroyed the food. However, Congress did not provide a definition for the term "transfer" as it is used in section 417(d)(2)(B) of the act. In Edition 1 of the guidance at Question and Answer numbers 27 and 28, and in the draft Edition 2 guidance at Question and Answer numbers E.4 and E.5, FDA said that a transfer to another person occurs when the responsible person releases the food to another person. In this document, FDA is asking for comment on whether this interpretation of the term "transfer" is appropriate, and if not, what other interpretations of the term "transfer" as it is used in section 417(d)(B)(2) of the act would be more appropriate. Specifically, we are requesting comment on whether the interpretation of the term "transfer" should be dependent upon possession of the food, whether the interpretation should be dependent on ownership of the food, or whether there are other interpretations we should consider, such as a combination of possession and/or ownership.[177]

Obviously, a broad interpretation of the term "transfer" severely limits the applicability of the lone statutory exception to the reporting requirement.

Although subject to less commentary, the definition of "reportable food"—"an article of food . . . for which there is a reasonable probability that the use of, or exposure to, such article of food will cause serious adverse health consequences or death to humans or animals"—is also subject to interpretation. The definition is nearly identical to the regulatory definition for a Class I recall.[178] The difference, though, between the statutory definition of "reportable food" and the regulatory definition of a Class I recall is potentially significant. The definition of a Class I recall focuses on the use of or exposure to "a violative product." By not including the language "violative product," Congress, in effect, removed from consideration of a "reportable food" a key empirical statutory standard or basis for adulteration. This, in turn, would seem to make the standard for determining a "reportable food" even broader than

---

[175] Questions and Answers regarding the Reportable Food Registry as Established by the Food and Drug Administration Amendments Act of 2007 (Edition 2), 75 Fed. Reg. 29,350 (May 25, 2010). At the time this chapter went to press, FDA had yet to offer any conclusions regarding any of the questions of interpretation on which it sought comment.

[176] *Id.* at 29,351.

[177] *Id.*

[178] *See* 21 C.F.R. § 7.3(m)(1).

that attending a Class I recall, i.e., finding a food to be a reportable food does not require as a predicate the application of the facts to an objective statutory standard for adulteration. Perhaps a broad interpretation of "reportable food" is the only way to ensure comprehensive reporting. Consider, for example, that there are more than 400,000 "registered" food facilities (and, thus, numerous "responsible parties").

Summary

The historical standard-setting and criteria-establishing activities discussed initially in this section were critical to FDA's food safety program and helped clear the path for general acceptance throughout the food industry for the extensive preventive controls and related requirements provided by the Food Safety Modernization Act and the reporting requirements of the Reportable Food Registry. In terms of actual impact on the public health and consumer confidence in the food supply, FDA's historical efforts have arguably been the agency's most important long-term food safety activities. In any event, FDA's historical efforts also reflect the value of providing guidance and standards to industry and the willingness to follow through with litigation as an enforcement tool should guidance and direction not be followed. Moreover, they reflect FDA's tendency to use, if not stretch, its existing statutory tools to creatively and effectively enhance the safety of the food supply. The agency's efforts to implement new statutory authorities will likely be consistent with this legacy. Nonetheless, the nature and extent of the broad new authorities FSMA gives FDA prompt at least one pragmatic concern. The heavy reliance FSMA places on preventive controls as the key mechanism for helping to assure food safety may, by so channeling FDA's and industry's focus and efforts, serve to discourage agency and industry research and investigation into alternative or complimentary initiatives and innovations possessing the potential to achieve even greater improvements in our modern ability to consistently provide consumers with safe food.

FDA's Regulation of Food Ingredients

Introduction

The Food Additives Amendment of 1958 was a necessary measure designed to ensure the safety of food ingredients and to promote public confidence in the processed food supply.[179] The amendment replaced existing *ad hoc* arrangements (whereby new ingredients had been tested to varying degrees by their manufacturers or users) and represented a significant congressional attempt to regulate the process used to determine the safety of food ingredients. At the core of the process was the shift from voluntary testing and informal review of such ingredients to mandatory testing and formal regulatory review of food additives. The amendment continues to present an approval system designed to balance safety and innovation.

The food additive approval process can be burdensome on those seeking approval of food additives. As a result, a key aspect of modern regulation of food safety involves the threshold

---

[179]   *See supra* text accompanying notes 20-27.

question of whether a substance is, by definition, a "food additive." Rephrasing the question reveals its significance: is the substance subject to time-consuming and costly premarket review, or is the ingredient exempt from that regulatory rubric and capable of being marketed pursuant to less formal mechanisms of review?

An Overview of Food Additive Regulation

Focusing on the definition of a food additive is critical to understanding how FDA regulates intentional food ingredients. As stated in section 201(s) of the FDCA:

> The term "food additive" means any substance the intended use of which results or may reasonably be expected to result, directly or indirectly, in its becoming a component or otherwise affecting the characteristics of any food (including any substance intended for use in producing, manufacturing, packing, processing, preparing, treating, packaging, transporting or holding food; and including any source of radiation intended for any such use), if such substance is not generally recognized, among experts qualified by scientific training and experience to evaluate its safety, as having been adequately shown through scientific procedures (or, in the case of a substance used in food prior to January 1, 1958, through either scientific procedures or experience based on common use in food) to be safe under the conditions of its intended use; except that such term does not include—
>
> (1) a pesticide chemical in or on a raw agricultural commodity or processed food; or
>
> (2) a pesticide chemical; or
>
> (3) a color additive; or
>
> (4) any substance used in accordance with a sanction or approval granted prior to September 6, 1958 pursuant to this chapter, the Poultry Products Inspection Act (21 U.S.C. 451 and the following) or the Meat Inspection Act of March 4, 1907 (34 Stat. 1260), as amended and extended (21 U.S.C. 71 and the following); or
>
> (5) a new animal drug; or
>
> (6) an ingredient described in paragraph (ff) in, or intended for use in, a dietary supplement.

Note that the definition applies to "any" substance the "intended use" of which may reasonably be expected to result in its becoming "a component of food." This definition reflects a notable shift in the statute's focus. The 1906 act (as interpreted in the *Lexington Mill* decision) focused on the food to which a substance is added; the 1938 act (with the addition of section 406) focused on the substance itself. By focusing on the *intended use of* the additive, the Food Additives Amendment and the definition of "food additive" reveal a concern regarding how a substance is used (in fact, under the Food Additives Amendment, a substance can, theoretically, be safe for some uses and not for others).

Note, too, that the definition is broad: it covers "any" substance "directly" or "indirectly" becoming a "component" of food. By examining the food additive definition in context, it becomes clear that Congress was concerned that substances that are used in making food should be shown to be safe. It follows that Congress excluded or made exception for those uses of substances whose safety could be assured in other ways: general recognition among qualified experts about safety; prior sanctioning by FDA or USDA have found to be safe; or, as in the case of pesticides, color additives, and dietary supplements, separate, distinct statutory-based systems to assure safety.

The Food Additive Approval Process

Section 409 establishes a system in which substances meeting the definition of food additive must receive premarket clearance for their intended use. Until a food additive is tested and shown to FDA's satisfaction to be safe for such a use, it is deemed to be unsafe.[180] If a food additive is added to a food prior to approval, its presence renders that food adulterated and subject to regulatory action.[181]

Clearance for the use of a food additive is granted by FDA only on issuance of a regulation prescribing a set of conditions under which the substance may be safely added or applied to food. The agency issues such a regulation in response to a sponsor's petition, as long as it finds that the use of the ingredient is safe.[182] Because Congress has established a "safe for intended use" system, information about how the ingredient is to be used and the amount of the substance (or its by-products) that will be consumed must be provided to the agency in addition to the results of toxicological testing on the safety of the ingredient.

Section 409 of the act provides that the review of a food additive petition should be completed by FDA within 180 days of petition submission.[183] Once the agency acts on a petition (by either approving or denying it), interested parties have a right to object to the action and to request a hearing. A hearing request must demonstrate that a material and substantial issue of fact exists. Without such a demonstration, no hearing will be granted. The agency's final decision, either after holding a public hearing or not, is subject to review in any U.S. court of appeals. The standard of judicial review is the substantial evidence test.[184]

---

[180] FDCA §§ 402(a)(2)(C), 409(a), 21 U.S.C. §§ 342(a)(2)(C), 348(a).

[181] *Id. See also* FDCA § 301, 21 U.S.C. § 331.

[182] The requirements for petition for the use of a food additive are set forth in section 409(b) of the FDCA and in 21 C.F.R. pt. 171.

[183] FDA came close to meeting this statutory directive between 1959 and 1971. Nevertheless, over the last three decades, the agency's track record in meeting section 409's timeframes has been inconsistent. For example, of those petitions approved in 1990, the average time to approval was nearly 80 months. From 1985 to 1995, the average time for a food additive petition to secure approval was approximately 40 months. Alan M. Rulis, *Reinventing Food Ingredient Evaluations*, Remarks at The Food & Drug L. Inst.'s Seminar (Sept. 15, 1995). FDA currently advises that the average time between submission of a food additive petition and approval is 24 months. FDA, Guidance for Industry: Questions and Answers About the Food Additive Petition Process (Apr. 2006).

[184] The agency's proceedings with regard to the artificial sweetener aspartame offer a good example of how the food additive approval process works. FDA approved the sweetener in soft drinks (48 Fed. Reg. 31,376 (July 8, 1983)), denied requests for a hearing (49 Fed. Reg. 6672 (Feb. 22, 1984)), and had its decision endorsed by the court of appeals in *Community Nutrition Institute v. Young*, 773 F.2d 1356 (D.C. Cir. 1985).

Determining the Safety of Food Additives

Section 409 establishes a two-part safety standard for food additives (the second part of the standard is the Delaney Clause, discussed later in this chapter). The fundamental safety standard in section 409 is found in what is commonly referred to as the "general food safety clause." This clause provides that a food additive regulation cannot be issued unless the petition establishes that the proposed use of the additive is "safe"; the statute, however, does not define in any detail what "safe" means or entails in this context. Nevertheless, section 201(u) and, as noted earlier, the legislative history, instruct that the concept of safety used in the legislation involves the question of whether a substance is hazardous to the health of man or animal.[185] The legislative history further provides that safety under section 409 requires proof of a "reasonable certainty" that no harm will result from the proposed use of the additive.[186] The legislative history is clear that this "does not—and cannot—require proof beyond any possible doubt that no harm will result under any conceivable circumstances."[187] As noted earlier, in 21 C.F.R. § 170.3(i) FDA has codified a definition of "safe" that captures the guidance offered by the legislative history.

As interpreted and applied by FDA, the safety of the given additive involves informed judgments based on educated estimates by scientists and experts regarding the anticipated ingestion of an additive and its likely patterns of use.[188] Determining "reasonable certainty" that an additive will be safe protects the public health from harm and provides an opportunity for progress in food technology.

FDA has outlined in its *Redbook* the types of testing in animals that may be required to show that a particular use by people of a food additive is safe (testing in laboratory animals is the primary means of developing data upon which food safety assessments are made).[189] Assuming that the testing does not show that the additive "induce[s] cancer" (thereby invoking the Delaney Clause), FDA reviews safety data from the required tests and determines the level at which the additive does not cause an adverse effect. The agency then applies a safety factor to that number.[190] The level of the safety factor will depend on the nature of the observed effects. Although FDA will apply as much as a thousand-fold safety factor if the ingredient is a teratogen, it normally will apply a one hundred-fold safety factor. In other words, in calculating the acceptable daily intake (ADI) for humans of a food additive, FDA, in an effort to assure safety in people, sets the level of intake at least 100 times below the level found to be safe in animals. Then, based on information in the petition about the conditions of use of the additive, FDA calculates the estimated daily intake (EDI) of the additive arising from the proposed use. If the EDI is less than the ADI, FDA can find the use of the food additive to be safe within the meaning of the general food safety clause. In this

---

[185]   FDCA § 201(u), 21 U.S.C. § 321(u); H.R. REP. No. 2284, *supra* note 15, at 4.

[186]   *Id.*

[187]   *Id.*; *see also supra* text accompanying notes 24-27.

[188]   For a detailed discussion of how FDA has implemented the general food safety clause, *see* Frederick H. Degnan & W. Gary Flamm, *Living With and Reforming the Delaney Clause*, 50 FOOD & DRUG L.J. 235, 239-43 (1995).

[189]   *See* FOOD & DRUG ADMIN., TOXICOLOGICAL PRINCIPLES FOR THE SAFETY ASSESSMENT OF DIRECT FOOD ADDITIVES AND COLOR ADDITIVES IN FOOD (for shorthand purposes referred to as the *Redbook* because the 1982 edition bore a red cover). The public availability of the *Redbook* was first announced in 47 Fed. Reg. 46,141 (Oct. 11, 1982). The availability of an updated, revised draft was announced in 58 Fed. Reg. 16,536 (Mar. 29, 1993).

[190]   21 C.F.R. § 170.22.

fashion, FDA takes into account—albeit with an apparent measure of conservatism—the cumulative effect of the additive in the diet.

FDA takes no function more seriously than judging whether substances offered for human ingestion are safe. Thus, when questions arise concerning the safety of an additive (even after FDA scientists have reviewed available data), the agency sees it as the sponsor's responsibility to resolve the issues by developing new data or further analyzing existing data. As the agency charged with and held accountable for ensuring safety, FDA has a natural tendency to be conservative in its evaluations when the public perceives a threat from unsafe additives. Gaps in available data or insufficient understanding of an apparently relevant biological phenomenon observed in a toxicity study inevitably tend to operate against the sponsor of the additive. Lack of knowledge or understanding on FDA's part is a petitioner's worst enemy. Petitioners often resort to reminding the agency of not only the legislative history of the act, but also the agency's regulations that recognize what Congress made clear in 1958: "it is impossible in the present state of scientific knowledge to establish, with complete certainty, the absolute harmlessness of the use of any substance."[191] Nevertheless, the agency's ultimate decision making regarding the safety of food additives is likely to be guarded and conservative.

Food Ingredients and Substances That Are Not Food Additives

FDA has been criticized for its conservatism and perceived inability to efficiently and promptly evaluate food additive petitions and their approvability.[192] This debate serves to highlight the fact, noted earlier, that substances that do not meet the definition of food additive are attractive to the food industry because their use does not entail or require the formal agency involvement provided under the Food Additives Amendment. A consequence of FDA's implementation of the food additive definition and food additive approval process has been the development of a hierarchy of food substances, ranging from foods to food additives, with various subcategories of GRAS, prior sanctioned, and other substances in between. This hierarchy has great practical importance because the level on which a substance is categorized determines the regulatory basis and attending safety substantiation standard governing market entry.

Traditional Foods as Ingredients

According to a literal reading of the food additive definition, whole foods can be food additives when used as components of prepared foods. Congress, however, never intended to require FDA premarket approval of traditional foods, and FDA never has considered it necessary to examine, for example, whether potatoes, carrots, coffee or beef are, in fact,

---

[191] 21 C.F.R. § 170.3(i).
[192] *See Food Additive Petitions, Hearings Before the Subcomm. on Human Resources and Intergovernmental Relations of the House Government Reform and Oversight Comm.,* 97th Cong., 1st Sess. (1995). Criticism has included allegations of agency delay in approvals, adherence to a compendium of required (but not necessarily appropriate) tests, reliance on redundant review procedures, and the failure to consistently exercise sound scientific judgment. For a "gloves off" discussion of the agency's food additive approval process, *see* Peter Barton Hutt, *Approval of Food Additives in the United States: A Bankrupt System,* Paper presented at the Annual Meeting of the Institute of Food Technologists, Washington, D.C. (June 5, 1995).

GRAS. When questions occasionally have arisen about the safety of a naturally occurring substance in a food, such as the toxin in a poisonous mushroom, FDA has dealt with the substance as a poisonous or deleterious substance under section 402(a)(1) of the FDCA. This approach disregards the fact that a poisonous mushroom found to be adulterated under section 402(a)(1) could not be considered GRAS and technically could be a food additive when combined with other foods. In disregarding this fact, FDA has exercised common sense. Another example of the agency's pragmatic reading of the statute in this context is its approach regarding nonrecombinant DNA food crops. Traditional plant breeders produce new strains and varieties of food crops to make them resistant to heat, drought, disease, or insects to improve their nutritional profile, handling characteristics, etc. These techniques alter the genetic makeup and, to varying degrees, the composition of established foods, but FDA has not attempted to regulate them on a routine basis. Thus, new food crops have for years entered the market without any FDA safety review. In the event that a problem arises (e.g., increased levels of solanine in a new strain of potatoes), FDA addresses it under section 402(a)(1). As discussed later in this chapter, FDA has largely relied on a similar "common sense approach" in developing procedures for evaluating the safety of crops produced with recombinant DNA techniques (i.e., biotechnology).

Prior-Sanctioned Substances

The statutory definition of "food additive" excludes "any substance used in accordance with a sanction or approval granted prior to enactment of this paragraph [September 6, 1958] pursuant to this Act . . . ."[193] By enacting the Food Additives Amendment, Congress was aware of the informal pre-1958 practice by food processors to, on occasion, request FDA to consider the safety of a food ingredient. For ingredients previously so reviewed and passed on by FDA, Congress decided that an additional review under the amendment was not necessary to ensure safety, thereby "grandfathering" these substances by excluding them from the food additive definition. Prior-sanctioned substances, however, are not exempt from all regulation. They are treated as added substances and if found "poisonous or deleterious" can be excluded from commerce if, under section 402(a)(1), FDA can show that the added substance "may render" food injurious.[194]

There is no recorded account for the total number of prior-sanctioned substances. In the early 1970s, FDA attempted to identify the number of prior-sanctioned substances by publishing a regulation that established criteria for prior-sanction status and listed a number of substances used in food packaging that FDA knew prior-sanctioned substances existed for, and by stating the agency's intention to publish a list of all known prior sanctions in the regulation.[195] This goal has yet to be achieved. Sodium, potassium nitrate, and nitrite are the only direct food ingredients to be so listed, although it is known that numerous other ingredients received FDA or USDA sanction or approval prior to 1958.

Prior sanctions tend to emerge at times of crisis, especially when a safety question arises and the continued marketing of a substance as a food additive or GRAS substance is being challenged. For example, the prior sanctions for sodium nitrite and nitrate were documented

---

[193]   FDCA § 201(s)(4), 21 U.S.C. § 321(s)(4).
[194]   FDCA § 402(a)(1), 21 U.S.C. § 342(a)(1).
[195]   21 C.F.R. pt. 181.

and subsequently codified in response to a consumer group's effort (based on a concern about the substance's possible carcinogenicity) to ban the use of nitrite in bacon.[196]

GRAS Substances

Background. From the perspective of the regulated food industry, no exception to the food additive definition is as significant as the GRAS exception. The GRAS exception embodies the early congressional recognition that an exclusion-less definition of "food additive" would not be the best way to ensure the safety and integrity of the entire food supply. Any such reading would fail to take into account the fact that food safety questions differ in public health significance and in the extent and nature of substantiation needed to answer them. Between 1958 and 1969, the GRAS exception provided FDA with the means to prioritize food safety issues and efficiently address them.[197]

In 1958, shortly after passage of the Food Additives Amendment, FDA proposed regulations to implement the new law.[198] The proposal included an initial list of approximately 180 substances the agency considered to be "generally recognized as safe."[199] As a condition to some of the listed ingredients maintaining their GRAS status, the agency proposed that the ingredients could only be used for certain designated purposes and in accordance with GMPs. The agency also took the position that any substance added to food and having no history of common use as a food ingredient should be regarded as a substance that is not GRAS.

On November 20, 1959, FDA finalized its initial list of GRAS substances.[200] The agency did not identify the data, information, or opinions on which it based its determinations. Scientific proof of safety was not the issue the agency wanted to address in the first GRAS list. Rather, the issue was "general recognition" of safety based on some unexplained amalgam of scientific opinion and common use of a compound in food prior to January 1, 1958. The agency continued to publish revised GRAS lists in 1959 and 1960.[201] By February 1961, the agency had listed more than 718 substances as GRAS.[202] These early years reflect significant agency decision making in ruling on what was and was not GRAS.

This basic approach to dealing with the GRAS exception lasted for nearly 11 years, until 1969, when the safety of the GRAS substance cyclamate was called into question.[203] Cyclamate was a widely used artificial sweetener. Data suggested the compound created an increased rate of bladder tumors in laboratory animals. For the first time, it became apparent that a substance widely used and uniformly considered to be safe could, overnight, have its safety

---

[196]   *See* Public Citizen v. Foreman, 631 F.2d 969 (D.C. Cir. 1980).

[197]   For an analysis of the history of GRAS and FDA's implementation of it, *see* Frederick H. Degnan, *Rethinking the Applicability and Usefulness of the GRAS Concept*, 46 FOOD DRUG COSM. L.J. 553 (1991).

[198]   23 Fed. Reg. 9512 (1958).

[199]   Among the substances listed were common emulsifiers, stabilizers, nutrients, preservatives, antioxidants, and anti-mycotics.

[200]   24 Fed. Reg. 9368 (1959).

[201]   *See FDA Questions and Answers*, 15 FOOD DRUG COSM. L.J. 222 (1960).

[202]   *See Food Additives—Extension of Traditional Provisions of the Food Additives Amendment, Hearings on H.R. 3980 Before the House Comm. on Interstate and Foreign Commerce*, 87th Cong., 1st Sess. 3 (1961).

[203]   *See* Degnan, *supra note* 197, at 567-68.

questioned. As a result, the agency set out to reevaluate and affirm the GRAS status of all substances on its published GRAS lists.[204]

The first steps toward establishing FDA's review of GRAS substances were to set forth criteria for determining which substances would or would not be classified as GRAS and to establish a general administrative process for assessing the GRAS status of substances.[205] The latter took the form of regulations governing how to petition the agency to affirm the GRAS status of a substance.[206]

The period immediately following the cyclamate episode also saw an increase in FDA enforcement actions levied against the use of unapproved food additives. These actions helped refine and reinforce the legal criteria for determining a lack of "general recognition" (i.e., a lack of GRAS status).[207] The resulting judicial holdings establish that unanimity among experts is not necessary to show that a substance is, in fact, GRAS.[208] The cases also instruct that the focus of an inquiry regarding a product's GRAS status is "not to determine actual safety . . . but to ascertain . . . the product's general reputation in the scientific community for such characteristics."[209] Accordingly, where the agency successfully established that a genuine dispute among experts existed, the courts rarely found there to be a lack of general recognition.[210] Moreover, cases established that a product's reputation for safety must be documented by at least the same amount of evidence necessary to obtain approval of a product in the first instance,[211] and the evidence must be public and available to the scientific community.[212] In summary, the case law confirmed that before a food ingredient (whose safety cannot be established based on pre-1958 use in food) can avoid FDA premarket clearance procedures, the ingredient must be GRAS, and that recognition must be based on scientific procedures and publicly available studies.

The combined impact of these developments (GRAS review, GRAS affirmation process, and the judicial support for the agency's interpretation of the meaning of the GRAS exception) was felt immediately. FDA no longer interpreted or applied the GRAS concept flexibly. Fewer substances were regarded by FDA as GRAS. And, for those that were, an emphasis on categorization served to differentiate among substances that were GRAS (i.e., those that were GRAS by virtue of their common use in food, by virtue of scientific procedures, or by virtue of their status as traditional foods).

---

[204]   *Id.*

[205]   *Id.* The first step was a proposal published in 1970. 35 Fed. Reg. 18,623 (Dec. 8, 1970).

[206]   The agency characterized these procedures as "necessary to establish a general administrative plan for establishing substances as GRAS." 35 Fed. Reg. 12,093 (June 25, 1971).

[207]   *See* Degnan, *supra note* 197, at 573-76.

[208]   *See, e.g.,* United States v. An Article of Drug...Furrestrol, 294 F. Supp. 1307, 1311 (N.D. Ga. 1968), *aff'd,* 415 F.2d 390 (5th Cir. 1969).

[209]   United States v. Articles of Food and Drug...Coli-trol 80, 372 F. Supp. 915, 920 (N.D. Ga. 1974), *aff'd,* 513 F.2d 743 (5th Cir. 1975).

[210]   *Furrestrol,* 294 F. Supp. at 1311. For a listing of more than 30 reported cases during this period addressing these issues *see* Degnan, *supra* note 197, at 573, n. 94-99.

[211]   *See* Weinberger v. Bentex Pharmaceuticals, Inc., 412 U.S. 645, 652 (1973).

[212]   *See* United States v. Article of Drug...Bentex Ulcerine, 469 F.2d 875, 880 (5th Cir. 1972), *cert. denied,* 412 U.S. 938 (1973).

Traditional Foods. As discussed above, traditional foods, when combined with other ingredients, could theoretically be food additives, except for their GRAS status.[213] The FDCA provides no other explicit legal category for such foods; thus, they can be considered the first subcategory of GRAS substances, although FDA has not regulated most traditional foods on this basis.

Traditional, "Unlisted" GRAS Ingredients. Following passage of the Food Additives Amendment in 1958, FDA sought to advise the food industry on the ingredients or additives that would be considered "food additives" (and therefore subject to the requirement of review and approval by FDA), and which ingredients or additives would be deemed GRAS (and escape the requirement). To this end, as discussed above, FDA published by regulation a list of substances regarded as GRAS.[214] In so doing, however, FDA acknowledged that the list was incomplete: "[I]t is impracticable to list all substances that are generally recognized as safe for their intended use. However, by way of illustration the Commissioner regards such common food ingredients as salt, pepper, sugar, vinegar, baking powder and monosodium glutamate as safe for the intended use."[215] Consequently, there is a category of "common food ingredients" that does not appear in FDA's GRAS regulations list but that the agency regards as GRAS.

The "Old GRAS List."[216] The third subcategory of GRAS substances consists of the substances that FDA included on its original GRAS list now codified in Part 182 of FDA's regulations. One of the striking features of this list is that it consists almost entirely of substances that might, at first, appear to be food additives. Among the substances on the original list were hydrochloric acid,[217] caffeine,[218] sodium tripolyphosphate,[219] tricalcium silicate,[220] the preservatives BHA and BHT,[221] and the artificial sweeteners cyclamate and saccharin.[222] These substances all perform classic food additive functions, but were placed on the original GRAS list. At the time, FDA believed itself knowledgeable enough of the substances to be confident of safety, and that requiring food additive petitions for them would waste the efforts of both FDA and industry. FDA reached this conclusion despite the fact that the agency lacked scientific data for many of these substances that was required to gain their approval as food additives. The old GRAS list is another example of FDA taking practical considerations into account when making safety-related decisions. The old list also demonstrates that the term food additive is a very specialized term of art: a substance can resemble and function as a food additive and yet still, for purposes of regulation, escape the definition.

---

[213] See *supra* text between notes 192 and 193.

[214] See *supra* text accompanying notes 198-200. *See also* 23 Fed. Reg. 9511, 9516 (1958); 24 Fed. Reg. 9368, 9639 (1959) (codified at 21 C.F.R. pt. 182).

[215] 21 C.F.R. § 182.1(a).

[216] 21 C.F.R. § 182.

[217] 21 C.F.R. § 182.1057.

[218] 21 C.F.R. § 182.1180.

[219] 21 C.F.R. § 182.1810.

[220] 21 C.F.R. § 182.2906.

[221] 21 C.F.R. §§ 182.3169-182.3173, respectively.

[222] See 24 Fed. Reg. at 9369. Cyclamate and saccharin have been removed from the Part 182 GRAS list. Cyclamate is listed by FDA among the substances prohibited from food in 21 C.F.R. § 189.135, although a petition seeking its approval as a food additive is pending before FDA. Saccharin is listed by FDA as an "interim food additive." 21 C.F.R. § 180.37.

Substances "Affirmed" as GRAS. As a result of the FDA-created GRAS review and the petition process, there is now a distinct category of GRAS substances listed in Part 184 of FDA's regulations whose safety has been affirmed by FDA based on a systematic review of available scientific evidence.[223] The original GRAS status of many of these substances was based heavily on the experience gained through their common use in food prior to 1958; the criteria required for GRAS affirmation were far more stringent.

"Self"-Affirmed GRAS Substances. Adding to the web of GRAS substances "listed" as GRAS and those "affirmed" as GRAS are those independently determined by manufacturers to be GRAS. The sponsor or user of a substance is free to make an independent determination that a substance is GRAS and market it on that basis without any prior approval or affirmation by FDA. The risk in doing so is that FDA may disagree after the fact, and if the agency can convince a court that the substance is not GRAS, the substance and foods containing it immediately become unlawful. Even without court action, FDA can often prevent the use of a substance believed to be an unapproved food additive through various informal means, including correspondence and publicity.

Gene Transfers and the Presumption of GRAS Status. In the mid-1980s, scientific developments led to the ability to produce or enhance traditional plant crop foods and ingredients using genetically altered organisms. In light of these developments in molecular biology, food technologists gained the ability to select a piece of DNA from one source and attach it to the DNA from another sexually noncompatible organism, and in the process confer a desirable trait. This new "biotechnology" differs from traditional plant breeding in its precision; i.e., in its ability to consistently and predictably impart a specific trait. For example, the gene in the flounder that permits the fish to withstand near-freezing water may be introduced into a tomato to reduce freezing damage; a gene from a giant silk moth can be introduced into a potato to increase resistance to disease; a gene from a bacterium may be introduced into soybeans to improve herbicide resistance. Many other less dramatic transfers may be accomplished by moving genes from one strain of plant to another.

The rigid reading of the GRAS concept that had evolved by 1992 created a regulatory climate in which transferred specific DNA constructs could easily be treated as food additives and, thus, subject to premarket approval. Lengthy premarket review of the safety of every transferred gene had the potential to cripple the usefulness of the technology and, perhaps more important, the willingness of industry to invest resources and interest in the use and development of the technology. Moreover, to treat all such products as either candidates for food additive petitions or GRAS affirmation petitions would create an enormous strain on the agency's resources.

Anxious to foster the use and development of the innovative new technology, several science-based organizations suggested that FDA affirm the practice of making independent GRAS determinations with respect to specific types of biotechnology-derived food products, and that it establish an informal procedure for notifying an agency about these determinations.[224]

---

[223]   21 C.F.R. pt. 184.

[224]   *See, e.g., Biotechnologies and Food: Assuring the Safety of Foods Produced by Genetic Modification* (pt. 2), 12 J. Reg. Toxicology & Pharmacology (Dec. 1990).

A narrow interpretation of the GRAS provisions would, clearly, be an obstacle to following through on these recommendations.

In an exercise of flexibility similar to that employed in the late 1950s and 1960s to implement the GRAS concept, in May 1992 the agency announced its policy for new plant varieties derived from innovative technologies, and summarily concluded that the transferred genetic materials (which are primarily nucleic acids) should be "presumed" to be GRAS and exempt from premarket approval.[225] This was in large part based on the fact that these genetic materials are present in the cells of every living organism, including plants.

In one exercise, the agency shifted its scrutiny from the source of a transferred organism to the effects of the organism in food and, thus, to the safety of the food itself. FDA did not rule out the possibility that transferred materials ultimately might be regulated as food additives but, as a general rule, concluded that the postmarket protections provided by section 402 of the FDCA generally would be sufficient to ensure the protection of the public health from any possible risks presented by modified foods. Should section 402 not prove sufficiently protective, the agency noted that it would reconsider its presumption of GRAS status and focus on food additive status as the reasonable alternative.[226]

The agency's first formal authorization of a genetically engineered plant product reflected the diversity of this approach. In May 1994, the agency, under the postmarketing rubric of section 402, permitted a tomato that had been inserted with a delayed ripening gene to be marketed.[227] FDA concluded that the tomato had not been altered significantly when compared to tomatoes with a history of safe use. On the same day, however, the agency approved, as a food additive, the "marker gene" that encoded the enzyme used in developing the tomato and that helped scientists ensure that the modified plant expressed the desired genes.[228] In considering the marker gene not GRAS and thus a food additive requiring food additive approval, FDA was able to rigorously assess the possible effects of the antibiotic-resistant gene on human health.

GRAS Notifications. The success of the agency's regulation of biotechnology food products and its according the presumption of GRAS status to transferred DNA prompted the agency, in a formal, open way to reconsider the advantages a flexible interpretation of the GRAS provisions provided in an age of scientific and technological advancement. By the mid-1990s, FDA let it be known that it was working on a proposed regulation that would clarify the criteria for determining whether a substance was GRAS and thereby exempt from regulation as a food additive. In April 1997, the agency published its proposal.[229] Building on the positive experience and feedback resulting from its plant biotechnology policy, the agency proposed to amend existing regulations to clarify that general recognition of safety requires that there be "common knowledge" among the qualified expert community that there is reasonable certainty the substance is not harmful under its intended conditions of use.

---

[225] *See* Statement of Policy for Regulating New Plant Varieties, 57 Fed. Reg. 22,984, 22,990 (May 29, 1992).

[226] *Id.* at 22,990.

[227] 59 Fed. Reg. 26,647 (May 23, 1994).

[228] *Id.* at 26,700.

[229] 62 Fed. Reg. 18,938 (Apr. 17, 1997).

To this end, the agency proposed to clarify the types of technical evidence of safety that ordinarily would constitute "common knowledge" about a substance that is GRAS through scientific procedures, and to clarify the role of publication in satisfying the "common knowledge" element of the GRAS standard. Moreover, the agency proposed to replace the GRAS affirmation process with a procedure whereby any person might notify FDA of a GRAS determination. In response to such a notification, FDA promised to evaluate in a timely manner whether the notice provided a sufficient basis for a GRAS determination, and whether information in the notice or otherwise available to FDA raised issues that prompt the agency to question whether the use of the substance is GRAS. Under the proposal, all GRAS affirmation petitions filed prior to the effective date of the notification would be "presumptively converted" to GRAS notifications.

Although FDA has never finalized the proposal, the agency has implemented as policy the key components of the proposal. The proposal remains a remarkable document that has changed fundamental agency decision making. The agency's reliance on the terminology "common knowledge" in the document has become the means of making more intelligible the "general recognition" standard. At the heart of the common knowledge concept is the need for technical evidence of safety, and a basis to conclude that this technical evidence is generally known and accepted. Thus, a GRAS substance is distinguished from a food additive precisely on the basis of the "common knowledge" about the safety of the substance for its intended use. In considering the basis for such common knowledge—the data and information generally available—the agency, in deference to precedent, noted in the proposal that information published in a peer-reviewed scientific journal is the "usual mechanism" to establish that scientific information is generally available. FDA was quick to acknowledge in word and practice, however—and thereby diverge from the case law of the early 1990s—that other mechanisms exist in addition to publication in a peer-reviewed journal and, to that end, that 1) publication of data and information in secondary scientific literature, such as scientific review articles and textbooks; 2) documentation of the opinion of an independent expert panel specifically convened for assessing the GRAS status of the ingredient; and 3) the opinion or recommendations of an authoritative body, such as the National Academy of Sciences, all help establish "common knowledge."[230]

In February 2010, the Government Accountability Office (GAO) issued a report concluding that FDA should reconsider its GRAS notification program and practices.[231] GAO recommended several reforms, including that FDA develop a strategy to minimize the potential for conflicts of interest of experts who assist companies in developing GRAS determinations for submission in a GRAS notification. GAO also suggested that FDA develop a strategy to monitor the propriety of the processes companies follow in developing GRAS notifications and for the agency to develop criteria to trigger a reconsideration of the conclusions reached by the agency upon review of a GRAS notification. On December 28, 2010, largely in response to questions raised by GAO, FDA reopened the comment period on its 1997 proposed rule concerning its GRAS notification policy.[232] This initiative would

---

[230]   *Id.* at 18,942.
[231]   U.S. GOV'T ACCOUNTABILITY OFFICE, REPORT TO CONGRESSIONAL REQUESTERS: FOOD SAFETY, FDA SHOULD STRENGTHEN ITS OVERSIGHT OF FOOD INGREDIENTS DETERMINED TO BE GENERALLY RECOGNIZED AS SAFE (GRAS) (Feb. 2010).
[232]   71 Fed. Reg. 81536.

seem to reflect a commitment on FDA's part to continuing but nonetheless enhancing the GRAS notification process.

Reopening the comment period served to foster additional in-depth review and commentary with respect to not only the agency's GRAS notification program but also the agency's overall handling of GRAS-related issues. Critics included the Pew Charitable Trusts (Pew). Pew undertook a public and visible role in exploring the history of FDA's interpretation and application of the GRAS concept. Pew officials ultimately concluded that "in many cases, FDA has not kept pace with scientific developments" related to ensuring the safety of food ingredients and recommended "a comprehensive review of FDA's science and decision making—as well as the 'modernization' of food ingredient safety assessments."[233] The officials noted that areas of concern included "toxicology test guidelines, tools used to predict health outcomes, conflict of interest in manufacturers' decisions, lack of a reassessment strategy, and lack of a definition of harm."[234] As of February 2015, FDA has not issued a formal response to the concerns voiced by Pew and others. FDA employees, however, participated in workshops and panel discussions and questioned the accuracy and significance of many of the expressed concerns. The relatively high-profile nature of the criticisms, particularly involving GRAS assessments, could lead to legislative focus on the issues and suggested amendments along the lines of eliminating the "self-GRAS" option for manufacturers and making the notification process mandatory.

Dietary Supplements

With the passage of DSHEA, dietary ingredients intended for use in dietary supplements joined prior-sanctioned and GRAS substances as a category exempt from the definition of food additive.[235] FDA's regulation of dietary supplements has been long and contentious.[236] DSHEA was the result of a large grass-roots effort by consumers and small industries, and reflects the dual realities that dietary and nutritional supplements are desired by consumers and are profitable to manufacturers. DSHEA, in addition to exempting dietary ingredients

---

[233] Maffini, M. et al., *Looking Back to Look Forward: A Review of FDA's Food Additive Safety Assessment and Recommendations for Modernizing Its Program*, COMPREHENSIVE REVIEWS IN FOOD SCIENCE AND FOOD SAFETY, Vol. 12 (2013).

[234] *Id.*

[235] *See supra* text accompanying notes 38-42. For a concise and informative explanation of the key provisions of DSHEA, *see* Anthony L. Young & I. Scott Bass, *The Dietary Supplement Health and Education Act,* 50 FOOD & DRUG L.J. 285 (1995).

[236] Upon ruling on procedural issues accompanying agency efforts in the mid-1970s to publish regulations relating to vitamin and mineral supplements, the Second Circuit Court characterized the differences of opinion between FDA and the manufacturers and vendors of dietary supplements as a "bitter battle." National Nutritional Foods Assn. v. Kennedy, 572 F. Supp. 377 (2d Cir. 1978). The court explained:

> While the manufacturers and vendors have obvious private interests as well, the battle reflects what appears to be a sincere sentiment on the part of many citizens that daily ingestion of a substantial quantity and variety of vitamins and minerals in the form of pills or liquids in addition to those furnished by ordinary diet, is needed for good health, especially because of the increasing consumption of modern food fads…and the FDA's equally sincere belief that the promotion of what, on a previous review, this court called a "dazzling array" of recommended daily doses and combinations, is causing consumers to waste millions of dollars annually in the purchase of vitamin and mineral preparations which they either do not need at all or do not need in the potencies or combinations that are being bought.

intended for use in supplements from the definition of food additive, established "dietary supplements" as a new category of food and did not limit such substances to wholly nutritional products (i.e., traditional vitamins and minerals) but rather extended the scope of the term to "herbs or other botanicals, amino acids or other dietary substances for use by man to supplement the diet by increasing the total dietary intake."[237] As a result, all such products are in large part beyond the reach of the food additive premarket approval requirements and the Delaney Clause and are not subject to assessments as to whether they meet the elements of a GRAS substance.[238] A discussion of a sampling of safety issues presented by the regulation of dietary supplements appears later in this chapter.

Color Additives

Section 201(t) of the act defines "color additive," in relevant part, as a dye, pigment, or other substance that when added or applied to a food "is capable (alone or through reaction with other substances) of imparting color thereto."[239] The definition goes on to provide that an ingredient that is used for purposes other than coloring, but that nevertheless imparts color, is exempt from the color additive definition (e.g., chocolate in chocolate milk).

The 1906 act permitted, or more accurately "listed," seven color additives for use in food. Under that act, a rather barebones voluntary certification program was established for "man made" colors and for years was administered by USDA. As a result of this program, color additives became known as "certifiable" color additives. With the passage of the 1938 act, the certification of color additives for use in food became mandatory and the authority for regulating such additives was transferred from USDA to FDA.

In 1960, Congress passed the Color Additive Amendments to the FDCA.[240] These amendments placed all color additives on a "provisional" list and required that the additives be shown to be safe and, for new color additives, imposed a premarket clearance requirement comparable to that for food additives. Moreover, like food additives, the amendments contained a Delaney Clause for color additives. Interestingly, though, Congress opted not to enact identical requirements for the regulation of color additives and food additives. Perhaps the most important distinction between color additives and food additives is that there is no comparable exemption for color additives to the GRAS exemption for food additive status. Moreover, there is no provision exempting "prior sanctioned" color additives from premarket testing requirements.

Classifications Related to Food Additive Status
Interim Food Additives

As a general proposition, the FDCA does not preclude creativity in attempting to deal with safety issues that for scientific or commonsense reasons should not be subject to rigid categorization. "Interim food additives" and "threshold" indirect additives are administrative

---

[237]   FDCA § 201(ff), 21 U.S.C. § 321(ff).
[238]   Of course, if a dietary ingredient is used not to supplement the diet except for a functional use (e.g., a dough conditioner), the exception from food additive status would not apply.
[239]   21 U.S.C. § 321(t).
[240]   Pub. L. No. 94-295, 74 Stat. 397.

creations designed by FDA to ensure reasonable regulation without sacrificing public health goals. The interim food additive category was created in 1972, following FDA's removal of cyclamate from the GRAS list (and, possibly, in anticipation of the possible need to act on saccharin).[241] When FDA declared cyclamate no longer GRAS, the substance immediately became an unapproved (and thus illegal) food additive. The interim food additive category provides an intermediate step for substances for which a substantial question of safety has been raised, but for which there remains a reasonable certainty that the substance will not cause harm during the time required to resolve the question.[242]

The interim food additive category requires a creative reading of the FDCA, due to the conceptual difficulty of reconciling the existence of a substantial question deserving study with the finding of a reasonable certainty of no harm that is required to maintain approval of a food additive.[243] FDA's creativity, however, served the worthwhile cause of giving the agency flexibility to deal in a practical way with safety questions that should be addressed but that do not justify disrupting the marketplace.

FDA formally has listed only four interim food additives[244] and proposed interim listing for only a few others.[245] The availability of this authority can serve to encourage sponsors of additives whose safety is questioned to conduct needed tests that can resolve the safety question promptly.

"Threshold" Indirect Additives

The food additive definition includes any substance that reasonably may be expected to result "directly or indirectly" in its becoming a component of food.[246] This aspect of the food additive definition presented FDA with a unique challenge. If interpreted broadly, the definition would include any food contact surface (e.g., plastic packaging materials, Styrofoam cups) or material, as well as their individual elements, that could possibly migrate into food. The challenge was complicated by the fact that analytical methodologies have become increasingly sensitive and precise, and have the ability to identify migrating molecules of a compound at levels as tiny as the low parts per trillion or parts per quadrillion.[247]

As a result, in the 1980s FDA began focusing on whether certain specific uses of substances in food contact materials did not require regulation under the food additive provisions. This approach was supported in the opinion of the U.S. Court of Appeals for the District

---

[241] *See* Richard Merrill & Michael Taylor, *Saccharin: A Case Study of Government Regulation of Environmental Carcinogens*, 5 VA. J. NAT. RESOURCE L. 1 (1985).

[242] 21 C.F.R. § 180.1(a).

[243] The "interim food additive" construct nevertheless has been upheld by the courts. Jacobson v. Edwards [1971 Transfer Binder] Food Drug Cosm. L. Rep. (CCH) ¶ 56.059.10, (D.D.C. 1971), *aff'd*, No. 71-2046 (D.C. Cir. 1972).

[244] The other substances placed on the interim list are acrylonitrile copolymers, mannitol, and brominated vegetable oil. *See* 21 C.F.R. §§ 180.22, 180.25, 180.30, respectively.

[245] *See, e.g.*, 42 Fed. Reg. 27,603 (May 31, 1977) (butylatedhydroxytoluene (BHT)); 45 Fed. Reg. 69,817 (Oct. 21, 1980) (caffeine).

[246] *See supra* text between notes 179-180.

[247] Alan M. Rulis, *Establishing a Threshold of Regulation*, in RISK ASSESSMENT IN SETTING NATIONAL PRIORITIES 271-78 (1989); Alan M. Rulis, *Threshold of Regulation: Options for Handling Minimal Risk Situations*, in FOOD SAFETY ASSESSMENT 484, 237-329 (Am. Chem. Soc. Symposium Series 1992).

of Columbia in *Monsanto v. Kennedy*.[248] In *Monsanto*, the court found that before FDA could determine that an indirect additive became a component of food within the meaning of the food additive definition, the agency was obligated to determine "with a fair degree of confidence that a substance migrates into the food in more than insignificant amounts."[249] The court went on to find that FDA may determine that a given level of migration into food of a particular substance is so negligible as to present no public health concerns; furthermore, in such cases, FDA has the inherent discretion to decline to define the substance as a food additive even though the substance comes within the strictly literal terms of the statutory definition.[250]

With the ability to lawfully exclude such indirect components of food from the definition of food additive, FDA is able to direct its limited resources more responsibly, and industry is able to avoid unnecessary and costly efforts to justify the marketability of many food contact products. In 1993, FDA proposed a regulation to establish a process for determining the turning point at which a substance does not require regulation as a food additive, based on the possibility (or extent) of migration to food of a substance used in a food contact article.[251] The agency's initiative, finalized in 1995, is commonly referred to as the "threshold of regulation."[252] The threshold of regulation final rule permits substances to be exempt from the food additive definition *provided* that the substance is not a known carcinogen; does not migrate or is not expected to migrate into food at levels that result in dietary concentrations above 0.5 parts per billion; has no technical effect in or on food to which it migrates; and, when used in the food contact article, does not have a significant adverse impact on the environment.[253] The threshold of regulation final rule also permits the use of a regulated direct additive in a food contact article where the resulting dietary concentration is negligibly small compared to the dietary concentration resulting from those uses in which it is added directly to food.[254]

"Food Contact Substances"

In 1997 the Food and Drug Administration Modernization Act (FDAMA)[255] amended the FDCA by defining "food contact substance" as "any substance intended for use as a component of materials used in manufacturing, packing, packaging, transporting, or holding food if such use is not intended to have a technical effect in such food."[256] The 1997 amendment also established a notification process for food contact substances with the intent that this process would serve as the primary method of authorizing new uses of food additives that meet the definition of food contact substance.[257] FDA has publicly expressed its expectation that most new uses of food contact substances that previously would have been regulated by the issuance of a food additive regulation in response to a food additive

---

[248]   613 F.2d 947 (D.C. Cir. 1979).
[249]   *Id.* at 955.
[250]   *Id.*
[251]   58 Fed. Reg. 52,719 (Oct. 12, 1993).
[252]   60 Fed. Reg. 36,582 (July 17, 1995).
[253]   *See* 21 C.F.R. § 170.39(a).
[254]   21 C.F.R. § 170.39(a)(2)(ii).
[255]   Pub. L. No. 105-115, 111 Stat. 2295 (1997).
[256]   21 U.S.C. § 349(h)(6).
[257]   21 U.S.C. § 349(h).

petition or would have been exempted from such a requirement under the "threshold of regulation" process, should be the subject of food contact notifications.[258]

Under section 409(h) of the act, a manufacturer may file its food contact substance notification with FDA 120 days before introducing the substance into interstate commerce. Included in the information required in the notification is a comprehensive discussion of the data and information forming the basis for the conclusion that the intended use of the substance is safe. A notification becomes effective 120 days after receipt by FDA unless the agency concludes 1) that the data and information submitted do not establish safety and 2) that, accordingly, the sponsor must submit a food additive petition and secure food additive approval prior to being able to lawfully market the substance. The issuance of such an objection by FDA constitutes final action and is subject to judicial review as such.

Summary

By interpreting the food additive definition to allow the concepts of interim additives and threshold of regulation, FDA creatively and pragmatically has developed flexible mechanisms for permitting the rational allocation of its resources and for making reasonable regulatory decisions regarding hundreds of substances. This approach is consistent with how the agency, during the late 1950s and throughout the 1960s, handled GRAS substances; it does not appear to have lessened the agency's ability to ensure the safety of the food supply.

FDA's Regulation of Carcinogens in Food

Background: The Role of Sound Science

As discussed earlier, section 409 contains two food safety standards for food additives. The standards are premised on the use of scientific judgment and discretion[259]: the general food safety clause and the Delaney Clause.[260] In the case of the Delaney Clause, once judgment and discretion are employed and a substance has been found to induce cancer, the clause operates to preclude the agency's discretion to approve the substance.[261]

For years, a plausible argument has been made that there is no scientific public health safety basis to single out cancer for special regulatory treatment.[262] Nevertheless, the rigidity of the Delaney Clause has contributed to an emphasis on whether a food ingredient may be a carcinogen. For example, a disproportionate number of the most visible food safety issues

---

[258] Guidance for Industry on Preparation of Food Contact Notifications, 98 Fed. Reg. 35,826 (May 21, 2002).

[259] *See supra* text accompanying notes 185-191.

[260] *See supra* text accompanying notes 25-29.

[261] Public Citizen v. Young, 831 F.2d 1108, 1117 (D.C. Cir. 1987), *cert. denied*, 108 S. Ct. 1470 (1988). (The Delaney Clause can be characterized as imposing a "rigid" policy once FDA has found that an additive "induces cancer," it does not, however, prescribe how the FDA must arrive at such a finding.)

[262] In fact, even in 1958 FDA argued against special statutory attention for cancer. *See* 104 CONG. REC. 17,415 (1958). For an extended discussion of FDA's assessment in 1958 of the need for the Delaney Clause, *see* Richard A. Merrill, Robert Z. Bohan, Frederick H. Degnan & Stuart M. Pape, *The FDA's Authority Under the Delaney Clause to Consider Mechanisms of Action in Determining Whether Additives "Induce Cancer,"* 47 FOOD & DRUG L.J. 77, 79-83 (1992).

FDA confronted the last third of the 20th century involved substances known or suspected (based on animal feeding studies) to cause cancer.[263] These cases were complicated by advances in the scientific understanding of cancer and the likely risks presented even by substances unequivocally identified in animal studies as carcinogens.

By the 1980s, scientific understanding had advanced through dramatic improvements in analytical chemistry. And, by the 1990s, the parts-per-million measurement range used in 1958 had become an even more precise parts-per-trillion (or parts-per-quadrillion) range, resulting in a greater number of possible carcinogens that may be found in the food supply. Furthermore, scientists came to recognize that the natural food supply contains an abundance of substances known or suspected to be carcinogens. As a result of these developments, FDA, in interpreting and applying the Delaney Clause, generally has not accepted or acted on less than compelling scientific proof that a substance "induces cancer."[264] Importantly, FDA has interpreted the clause as providing that the mere association between the administration of an additive to test animals and an elevation in tumor incidence neither justifies nor requires a finding that the additive induces cancer. As a result, before the Delaney Clause can be found to apply, FDA scientists critically evaluate study results that suggest such an association, and any conclusion made is the product of a thorough, far-ranging scientific assessment of numerous scientific endpoints and considerations drawn from the most up-to-date data available.

An example of the evaluation FDA traditionally has undertaken in assessing whether a substance induces cancer is found in the case of FD&C Yellow No. 6, a dye for direct use in food. In the early 1980s, results from a two-year study in rodent experiments strongly implicated the dye as capable of inducing adrenal tumors.[265] A key observation at issue involved a statistically significant increase in adrenal medullary tumors in female rats. On review, FDA scientists identified a number of scientific reasons that precluded a "finding" that the tumors could be considered related to exposure to the dye and, thus, why the dye should not be found to induce cancer.[266] FDA reasoned that there was a lack of confirmation

---

263   These include the controversies over cyclamate, saccharin, nitrate, methylene chloride (used to decaffeinate coffee), PCBs, aflatoxin, and a number of pesticides present both as residues in processed forms of target crops (such as ethylene dibromide in food grains) and as inadvertent contaminants of nontarget crops or commodities (such as DDT in fish). These controversies capture public attention for diverse reasons. In some cases, the public is alarmed by the potential removal of familiar and valued products, such as bacon and hot dogs (nitrite) and diet soft drinks (saccharin). In other cases, the public and media are concerned that FDA is not adequately protecting consumers from foodborne carcinogens, such as PCBs in fish.

264   See Merrill, et al., *supra note* 262, at 83-91.

265   See 51 Fed. Reg. 41,765 (Nov. 19, 1986).

266   Id. at 41,769-70. The reasons were as follows:

- there was only a small increase in the number of treated animals with a type of tumor that occurs spontaneously with a high and variable incidence;

- there was a lack of morphological or other support for a treatment-induced carcinogenic process, including the lack of any effect on the latency period for the observed tumors;

- there was an absence of a dose response relationship between the incidence and severity of effects normally accompanying compound induced tumors;

- male rats, although more susceptible than female rats to the effect of renal carcinogens, showed no treatment-related effects; and

- the affected animals suffered from an underlying kidney disease that could have been affected by the feeding regimen in the test.

of the effect from other studies of the compound.[267] The scientific implausibility and lack of confirmation, in the agency's view, "reduce[d] the possibility that feeding FD&C Yellow No. 6 resulted in a carcinogenic process . . ." and precluded an "induce cancer" finding.[268] To confirm its assessments, the agency took the additional step of subjecting the conclusion to peer review: the panel of experts supported the agency's conclusions.

Consideration of this precedent reveals the basic elements of FDA's weight-of-the-evidence analysis performed in evaluating the potential carcinogenicity of a substance.[269] Such an evaluation includes considering whether there is corroborative evidence of carcinogenicity from other studies, and whether there is evidence that the putative carcinogen has a direct role in tumor production or whether its administration simply makes tumor occurrence by some other possible mechanism.[270] Moreover, biological considerations have to be taken into account in determining whether the observed results are, in fact, evidence of a real association between the administration of the substance and the induction of cancer.

Other aspects of FDA's weight-of-the-evidence analysis of carcinogenicity data involve the evaluation of benign and malignant tumors, the appropriateness of particular test species as models for drawing conclusions as to the risk to humans presented by exposure to a substance, and the interaction of the substance with DNA or its action through broad physiological processes that may be resisted by the body's inherent defense mechanisms.[271] Numerous examples of FDA's consideration of these and other endpoints have been detailed.[272] Suffice it to say, any finding that a substance induces cancer requires, at a minimum, a full biological, pathological, and statistical evaluation.

Administrative Efforts to Limit the Impact of the Delaney Clause

Viewing the issue of whether a substance induces cancer as, above all, a question of science, it should not be surprising that FDA, where possible, has opted to avoid premature and legalistic applications of the Delaney Clause. In the process, FDA has pioneered the use of risk assessment techniques and the careful consideration of how best to balance and accomplish the dual goals of the Food Additives Amendment: safety and innovation. Thus, a common theme throughout the agency's decision making is an effort to make sound and defensible public health decisions that ensure the safety of the consuming public without unnecessarily removing from the food supply substances and products that can perform a useful function or convey value to consumers.

---

[267]   *See* 51 Fed. Reg. at 41,773.

[268]   *Id.*

[269]   For a review of the basic scientific concepts and standard practices governing the safety evaluation of putative carcinogens, *see* Joseph Rodricks, Thomas Starr & Michael Taylor, *Evaluating the Safety of Carcinogens in Food—Current Practices and Emerging Developments,* 46 Food Drug Cosm. L.J. 513 (1991).

[270]   In a proceeding before FDA involving the use of butylated hydroxyanisole (BHA) in food, the question has been raised whether, in determining whether BHA "induces cancer" within the meaning of the Delaney Clause, FDA may continue to rely on mechanistic evidence (as it traditionally has). *See* 55 Fed. Reg. 49,576 (Nov. 29, 1990). For a discussion of the legal issues presented, *see* Merrill, et al., *supra note 262.*

[271]   *See* Merrill, et al., *supra note 262,* at 85-90.

[272]   *See, e.g.,* Degnan & Flamm, *supra note 188,* at 246-54.

Sensitivity of the Method

The federal government's first formal effort to incorporate quantitative carcinogenic risk assessment in decision making about food ingredients began in the early 1970s and involved the DES proviso to the Delaney Clause.[273] This proviso permits carcinogenic animal drugs, animal feed, and color additives to be approved, notwithstanding the Delaney Clause, if "no residue" of the carcinogen will be found in any edible portion of the animal when tested by an analytical method approved by FDA.[274] After the enactment of the DES proviso in 1962, FDA worked hard to implement it against a background of rapidly advancing analytical chemistry that ensured that residues undetectable one day would be detectable the next. FDA focused on the then-nascent use of quantitative risk assessment and refined existing risk assessment techniques until the agency had an acceptable tool for calculating conservative upper bounds on the likely human risk from exposure to substances found carcinogenic in animal studies. These techniques formed the scientific basis for implementing the DES proviso in a manner that would achieve its public health purpose: the assurance that no meaningful risk of cancer would accompany the use of compounds in food-producing animals.

Previously, FDA had required use of either the best available detection method or a uniformly low detection capability of two parts per billion for all substances subject to the DES proviso.[275] These approaches had the potential, however, to permit substances posing unacceptably high risks or to prohibit ones posing acceptably low risks (as determined by using quantitative risk assessment). The agency attempted to resolve this problem by developing the sensitivity of the method (SOM) approach. Under SOM, the agency equated "no residue" with the notion of "no significant risk." Instead of using the required analytical method as a means to verify that no residue was present, the SOM approach used the method for detecting that level of residue judged by use of risk assessment to pose no real or meaningful risk of cancer. Carcinogenic animal drugs and feed additives whose residues were undetectable at this level could be approved because they were not only safe but also presented, at most, only a theoretical risk of cancer.[276]

FDA originally set the acceptable risk level under SOM at 1/100,000,000 but this level was later changed to 1/1,000,000.[277] FDA's final regulation in 1977 on SOM was challenged successfully in court on procedural grounds.[278] FDA subsequently published two revised proposals refining the SOM criteria and, in 1987, the agency issued a final regulation that prescribes the bases on which carcinogenic residues in animals currently are regulated.[279]

---

[273]   FDCA §§ 409(c)(3)(A), 721(b)(5)(B), 512(d)(1)(I), 21 U.S.C. §§ 348(c)(3)(A), 379e(b)(5)(B), 360b(d)(1)(I).

[274]   Id.

[275]   See Richard A. Merrill, *FDA's Implementation of the Delaney Clause: Repudiation of Congressional Choice or Reasoned Adaptation to Scientific Progress,* 5 YALE J. ON REG. 1, 25-29 (1988).

[276]   38 Fed. Reg. 19,226 (1973).

[277]   Id. at 19,227. Confusion often accompanies this figure. It does not mean that 1 in every 1,000,000 people will, by virtue of a product approval, be at risk of developing cancer. The level of risk is an upper-bound level and not an actuarial risk. 50 Fed. Reg. 51,551, 51,557 (Dec. 18, 1985). An actuarial risk is determined by the actual incidence of an event. In contrast, the upper-bound level of risk is based on a projection that results in an estimated risk that is actually too small to be measured. Id. The 1/1,000,000 level of risk, according to FDA, "imposes no additional risk of cancer to the public." 44 Fed. Reg. 17,070, 17,093 (Mar. 20, 1979).

[278]   Animal Health Inst. v. FDA [1977-1978 Transfer Binder] Food Drug Cosm. L. Rep. (CCH) ¶ 38,154 (D.D.C. 1978).

[279]   44 Fed. Reg. at 71,070; 50 Fed. Reg. 45,530 (1985); 52 Fed. Reg. 49,572 (1987).

In 2002, FDA published a final rule revising the definition of "no residue" to give the language its "ordinary meaning."[280] The action was taken in response to an unsolicited opinion from the Office of Legal Counsel at the Department of Justice. In its opinion, the Office of Legal Counsel emphasized that FDA remained authorized to use the "no significant risk" level as the benchmark for assessing the propriety of analytical methods implementing the DES proviso. As a result, the revision worked no meaningful change with respect to the procedures FDA had developed for accepting or rejecting analytical methods implementing the proviso. The practical effect of the change was the possibility of an increase in the time prior to slaughter that an animal must not be administered a particular drug.[281] The agency's early reliance on its "operational definition" had served the same level of public health protection regardless of what practical definition was accorded to the definition of "no residue."

Constituents Policy

The SOM policy implements language in the statute that creates an express exception to the absolute bar of the Delaney Clause. Another major step for FDA required a new interpretation of existing statutory language to create another exception to the Delaney Clause. This step addressed other common problems under the clause: carcinogenic trace constituents and manufacturing impurities in food and color additives, and low-level migrants from food packaging materials.

Historically, FDA regarded carcinogenic constituents of additives and carcinogenic migrants from packaging materials as within the scope of the Delaney Clause. By the late 1970s, however, increasingly sensitive analytical methodologies greatly improved detection of trace constituents of food and color additives and low-level migrants from packaging materials. Once again, FDA decided that quantitative risk assessment could solve the "problem" of constituents (which could not implement the DES proviso).[282] Using risk assessment, FDA could determine whether a trace carcinogenic constituent or migrant posed a risk below the agency's 1/1,000,000 benchmark level of risk. If it did, the agency was prepared to judge that constituent "safe."

FDA re-interpreted the term "additive" in the Delaney Clause ("no additive shall be deemed to be safe if it is found to induce cancer") to mean the additive as a whole and not its unavoidable, nonfunctional constituents.[283] Under this interpretation, the Delaney Clause would be invoked only if the additive as a whole had been found to induce cancer. If carcinogenic constituents were detected, FDA would evaluate them under the general safety clause for food additives and, using risk assessment and taking into account the carcinogenic constituent, determine whether the additive as a whole could be judged safe.

In 1982, FDA first applied the constituents policy by approving the listing of Green No. 6, a color additive that contains the carcinogenic contaminant n-toluene.[284] The policy has been applied on numerous occasions since then, including approving the acrylonitrile

---

[280]   67 Fed. Reg. 7812, 7813 (Dec. 23, 2002).

[281]   Id.

[282]   47 Fed. Reg. 14,464 (1982).

[283]   Id.

[284]   47 Fed. Reg. 14,138 (1982).

beverage bottle originally denied approval in 1977.[285] The policy and the underlying legal interpretation have been challenged in court and upheld.[286]

The *De Minimis* Policy

The scientific issues presented by a different set of color additives forced FDA to consider yet another re-interpretation of the Delaney Clause. FDA found that, when individually tested, the color additives Orange No. 17 and Red No. 19 were carcinogenic in animal studies but, due to their usage, posed extremely low estimated risks (well below FDA's 1/1,000,000 benchmark for safety).[287] Orange No. 17, for example, posed an increased risk of cancer of 1 in 19 billion. To put this risk in perspective, compare it with the risk attributed to cigarette smoking. For purposes of background, each 1/1,000,000 risk amounts to less than 1/200,000 the lifetime risk so attributed.[288] Thus, at the 1/1,000,000 risk level, a person would have to be exposed to more than 2,000 chemicals bearing the 1/1,000,000 lifetime risk, at the rates assumed in the risk assessment, in order to reach one hundredth the risk reported with smoking. To reach that level of risk with chemicals equivalent to Orange No. 17, the consumer would have to be exposed to more than 40,000,000 such chemicals.[289] Clearly, the risk of cancer presented by Orange No. 17 was exceedingly small.

These cases forced FDA to grapple with the essence of the Delaney Clause because they involved situations in which the additives as a whole had been found to induce cancer. FDA responded by invoking the judicial doctrine of *de minimis non curat lex*, which (when roughly translated) means "the law does not concern itself with trifles." FDA used this doctrine to contend that, despite its seemingly absolute language, the Delaney Clause was not intended to preclude the use of carcinogenic food and color additives that posed no real risk of cancer and that could easily be judged to be safe. And, so contending, FDA approved the two colors.[290]

These actions provoked controversy and criticism. Some contended that the policy was an appropriate response to advances in science, was fully protective of the public health, and was a lawful exercise of FDA's broad authority to interpret the statute in a manner consistent with modern circumstances.[291] Others questioned the prudence of approving even *de minimis* risks and attacked the policy as an unlawful usurpation by FDA of the congressional prerogative to amend the law.[292] Still others accepted FDA's policy goal but questioned the wisdom and legality of its *de minimis* interpretation given the rigid language of the Delaney Clause.[293]

---

[285]   49 Fed. Reg. 36,635 (1984).

[286]   Scott v. FDA, 728 F.2d 322 (6th Cir. 1984).

[287]   51 Fed. Reg. 28,331, 28,346 (Aug. 7, 1986).

[288]   Crouch & Wilson, *Inter-Risk Comparison*, in Merrill, Assessment and Management of Chemical Risks 97, 105, 108 (Rodricks & Tardiff eds. 1984); *see also supra* note 188.

[289]   Crouch & Wilson, *supra* note 288; *see also Public Citizen*, 831 F.2d at 1111.

[290]   *Public Citizen*, 831 F.2d at 1111.

[291]   See Michael Taylor, *The De Minimis Interpretation of the Delaney Clause, Legal and Policy Rationale*, 7 J. Am. C. Toxicology 529 (1988).

[292]   See William B. Schultz, *Why the FDA's De Minimis Interpretation of the Delaney Clause is a Violation of Law*, 7 J. Am. C. Toxicology 521 (1988).

[293]   *See* Richard M. Cooper, *Stretching Delaney 'Til It Breaks*, Regulation, Nov.-Dec. 1985, at 11.

Public Citizen, a consumer group, challenged the *de minimis* policy in court. In *Public Citizen v. Young*, the U.S. Court of Appeals for the District of Columbia Circuit expressed sympathy for FDA's policy objective and agreed that the risks of cancer presented by the additives were trivial, but unanimously rejected FDA's *de minimis* interpretation of the Delaney Clause.[294] The absolute language of the clause and its legislative history suggested to the court that Congress meant exactly what it said: *no additive* shall be deemed safe if it has been found to induce cancer when ingested by man or animals. The government declined to seek Supreme Court review of the decision. Private parties sought review unsuccessfully.

The decision in *Public Citizen* does not preclude FDA from applying its constituents policy. Nor does the decision affect FDA's considerable scientific judgment and legal discretion in interpreting and applying the phrase "induce cancer" within the meaning of the Delaney Clause. Although the impact of the *Public Citizen* decision is limited to color additives, its message is clear: once FDA concludes that a substance induces cancer within the meaning of the clause, the agency has no choice and may not resort to the dictates of sound science over responsible policymaking. Under such circumstances, the only legally acceptable consequence is that the additive be prohibited from food.

Les v. Reilly: **Broadening the Impact of the Delaney Clause**

In light of how strictly FDA has interpreted and applied the Delaney Clause, it is not surprising that the agency explicitly has invoked the clause and found it applicable in only a handful of instances since 1958.[295] In the early 1990s, however, developments in the federal regulation of pesticide residues dramatically changed the potential regulatory impact of the clause.

The Delaney Clause was just one element of a complex statutory scheme for the regulation of pesticides and pesticide residues found in food. The regulation of food-use pesticides (and their safety) is accomplished not only under the FDCA, but also the Federal Insecticide, Fungicide, and Rodenticide Act (FIFRA).[296] FIFRA governs the registration of pesticides.

Registration addresses specific uses of a pesticide; without such registration, a pesticide cannot be sold lawfully for that use in the United States.

A major part of the registration process for food-use pesticides involves tolerance setting. A tolerance is the maximum residue level of a pesticide that legally may be present in or on raw agricultural commodities, food, or feed. In general, tolerances must be established under the FDCA for all raw agricultural commodities, processed commodities, rotational crops, and livestock in which residues of a pesticide are expected to occur. EPA will not

---

[294] *Supra note* 261; 831 F.2d at 1108.

[295] *See, e.g.*, Flectol-H, 32 Fed. Reg. 5675 (Apr. 7, 1967); 4,4-methylenebis 2-choroanaline, 34 Fed. Reg. 19,073 (Dec. 2, 1969); Cinnamyl Anthranilate, 50 Fed. Reg. 42,932 (Oct. 23, 1985); Orange No. 17, 51 Fed. Reg. 28,331 (Aug. 7, 1986); Red No. 19, 51 Fed. Reg. 28,346 (Aug. 7, 1986); Red No. 8 & 9, 53 Fed. Reg. 26,766 (July 15, 1988).

[296] Pub. L. No. 100-532, 102 Stat. 2654 (codified at 7 U.S.C. § 136 *et seq.* (1994)).

register a new pesticide or pesticide use under FIFRA unless the necessary tolerances or exemptions first have been granted to cover the anticipated pesticide residues.[297]

There were two types of relevant tolerances that could be granted under the FDCA: section 408 tolerances permitting the presence of pesticide residues in or on raw agricultural commodities, and section 409 tolerances (i.e., food additive regulations) permitting such residues in or on processed foods.[298] Section 409 did not apply automatically to pesticide residues present in processed foods. If the residue was present in the processed food (e.g., apple juice) as a result of pesticide use on the "parent" raw agricultural commodity (e.g., apples), section 402(a)(2)(C) provided that a section 409 tolerance was necessary only where the concentration of the residue in the processed food when "ready to eat" exceeded the section 408 tolerance established for that pesticide in the parent commodity.[299] A section 409 tolerance was required if the pesticide residue in the processed food results from the application of a pesticide during or after processing.

Although FDA has always had primary responsibility for implementing the FDCA, EPA had responsibility for evaluating the safety of pesticide residues in raw agricultural commodities under section 408, as well as the safety of pesticide residues that were food additives under section 409.[300] FDA retained authority under section 409 to evaluate the safety of food additives other than pesticides.

In *Les v. Reilly*, the Natural Resources Defense Council (NRDC) and other parties challenged the refusal of EPA to revoke 14 food additive tolerances.[301] NRDC alleged that the tolerances were inconsistent with the Delaney Clause. EPA had denied the revocation of the section 409 tolerances, even though the agency conceded that the pesticides subject to the tolerances did, in fact, induce cancer. Specifically, EPA had determined that its review of the available data supported application of the *de minimis* exception to the substances.[302] The U.S. Court of Appeals for the Ninth Circuit upheld the challenge and, relying on *Public Citizen*, found that the Delaney Clause prohibits the establishment of food additive tolerances for pesticides that induce cancer, no matter how trivial or infinitesimal the risk of cancer may be.[303]

As a result of the decision in *Les v. Reilly*, EPA began proceedings in 1993 to revoke food additive tolerances for a number of pesticides that induced cancer within the meaning of the Delaney Clause.[304] The agency predicted revocation actions against a multitude of pesticides on the same grounds. Never before had the Delaney Clause been used to jeopardize so many substances, and the force of the clause was fully realized: substances that EPA previously had concluded "presented no meaningful risk to consumers" had to be banned as a matter of law.

---

[297]   *See* 40 C.F.R. § 152.112(g) (1996).

[298]   *See supra* discussion in text accompanying notes 15-24.

[299]   *See* FDCA § 402(a)(2)(C), 21 U.S.C. § 342(a)(2)(C).

[300]   EPA was vested with this authority pursuant to Reorganization Plan No. 3, 84 Stat. 2086 (1970).

[301]   986 F.2d 985 (9th Cir. 1992), *cert. denied*, 113 S. Ct. 1361 (1993).

[302]   *See* 55 Fed. Reg. 17,560 (Apr. 25, 1990); 56 Fed. Reg. 7750 (Feb. 25, 1991). EPA first announced its *de minimis* policy in a notice published in October 1988. 53 Fed. Reg. 41,104 (Oct. 19, 1988).

[303]   986 F.2d at 985.

[304]   58 Fed. Reg. 27,862 (July 14, 1993).

Reforming the Regulation of Pesticide Residues

These developments prompted legislative efforts to determine how best to regulate potentially carcinogenic pesticide residues on raw agricultural commodities and in processed foods.[305] These legislative initiatives culminated, in 1996, in the passage of the Food Quality Protection Act (FQPA).[306]

The FQPA amended the FDCA by removing chemical pesticides in processed foods from the definition of "food additive." This, in turn, removed chemical pesticide residues from the reach of the Delaney Clause. The FQPA did not amend the Delaney Clause itself. The clause remains untouched and continues to apply, with full vigor, to food additives, color additives, and compounds administered to food-producing animals. The FQPA significantly amended the tolerance-setting standards for pesticide residues formerly contained in section 408 of the FDCA. As amended, section 408 applies to pesticide residues in both raw and processed foods, and requires that a tolerance for a pesticide chemical can be established only if the residue is "safe." The FQPA also defined "safe" to mean "that there is a reasonable certainty that no harm will result from aggregate exposure to the pesticide chemical residue, including all anticipated dietary exposures and other exposures for which there is reliable information." This fully comports with the risk-based general food safety standard FDA has used for years for noncarcinogenic food additives and incorporates into its regulations defining "safe."[307]

The FQPA provided that in establishing a tolerance, specific considerations concerning the exposures of infants and children must be made. The act further required that a number of "other relevant factors," including the cumulative effects of pesticide residues and other substances that have a common mechanism of toxicity, be considered in establishing a tolerance. Moreover, the FQPA required that all existing tolerances be evaluated by EPA within 10 years to ensure that the tolerances meet the act's new health-based standards.

The FQPA also strictly limited the ability of the government to consider factors other than safety (i.e., benefits) in determining an appropriate pesticide tolerance for food. This authority is now confined to "eligible pesticide chemical residues." An eligible pesticide residue, as defined in the FQPA, must have been the subject of a tolerance at the time FQPA was enacted and must be associated with a nonthreshold effect that can be reliably characterized by quantitative risk assessment procedures (if the eligible pesticide residue also has a threshold effect, the risk associated with the threshold effect must meet the section's new safety standard). A pre-FQPA tolerance for an eligible pesticide chemical residue may remain in effect if the use protects consumers from health effects posing a greater risk or if the use is necessary to avoid significant disruption of the food supply, and if 1) the yearly risk associated with the nonthreshold effect from aggregate exposure to the pesticide residue is not greater than 10 times the yearly risk that would meet the new general section 408 safety standard; 2) the lifetime risk is not greater than two times the risk that would meet the general safety standard; and 3) the tolerance meets the act's requirements concerning the protection of infants and children.

---

[305] See Degnan & Flamm, *supra note* 188, at 255-56.

[306] Pub. L. No. 104-170, 110 Stat. 1489 (1996).

[307] See 21 C.F.R. § 170.3(1).

The FQPA represents a major breakthrough in federal efforts to update and resolve inconsistencies between pesticide-related provisions of the FIFRA and the FDCA. By compelling what in practice is a single health-based standard for all pesticides in foods, it also replaced the complicated interplay between former section 408 and existing section 409. By eliminating differences in the standards applicable to tolerances set for raw and processed foods, the act permits coordination with standards and actions under FIFRA and a more consistent regulatory scheme. At the heart of this landmark compromise legislation is the implicit recognition of the need for pesticides in producing an abundant, wholesome, and economic food supply.

Applying the Safety Standards of the FDCA to Advancements in Technology

FDA has been a leader in developing sound scientific criteria and employing a flexible interpretation of the statutory requirements to ensure that this new technology does not pose a risk to consumers, while at the same time not burdening the technology with unnecessarily rigorous premarket approval requirements. In regulating biotechnology products, FDA has not sought any additional statutory authority and has persuasively contended that its existing statutory authority for regulating the safety of food is sufficient to ensure the safe use of food from plant varieties derived from biotechnology.[308]

FDA's Regulation of Plant Biotechnology. In 1992, the agency issued a policy statement that provided scientific criteria to help determine whether a new plant or crop variety is as safe and nutritious as its parental variety.[309] The safety procedures focused on the characteristics of the host and the donor species, the nature of the genetic change, the identity and function of newly introduced substances, and the unintended effects that may accompany the genetic change.

FDA's policy is based largely on section 402(a)(1). As discussed earlier, FDA has relied on this section for years in regulating new strains and varieties of food crops.[310] Such products enter the market without any FDA safety review. Logically, FDA's biotechnology policy provides that new plant varieties will be considered violative of section 402(a)(1) if the levels of genetic material in the new food "may render" the food injurious to health.[311]

In FDA's view, section 402 provides ample authority to address a problem (should one arise postmarketing), and thus provides the lion's share of the agency's authority in regulating plant products of biotechnology. Nevertheless, FDA has stated that it will apply the food additive and GRAS rubrics as necessary to ensure the protection of the public health.[312]

---

[308] *See* Statement of Policy for Regulating Products of Biotechnology, 51 Fed. Reg. 23,309 (June 26, 1986). This agency position regarding the adequacy of its existing statutory authority to deal with the issues raised by biotechnology is longstanding and applies with equal force to the application of biotechnology to all FDA-regulated products, not just to foods.

[309] 57 Fed. Reg. 22,984 (May 29, 1992).

[310] *See supra* discussion in text between notes 192 and 193.

[311] 57 Fed. Reg. at 22,940.

[312] For an extensive science-based consideration of the propriety of relying primarily on section 402 *see Biotechnologies and Food: Assuring the Safety of Foods Produced by Genetic Modification* (pt. 2), 12 J. Reg. Toxicology & Pharmacology, Dec. 1990. This publication was the culmination of two years of research

The agency's decision on how best to regulate plant products of biotechnology reflects the recognition that reliance on one statutory provision to serve as the exclusive basis for regulating plant products of biotechnology is not reasonable.

As also discussed earlier, the agency's first formal authorization of a genetically engineered plant product—a delayed ripening tomato—reflects the diversity of this approach. In May 1994, the agency permitted, under section 402(a)(1), the marketing of a tomato that had been inserted with a delayed ripening gene[313] and on the same day the agency approved the kanamycin-resistant "marker gene" (which encoded the enzyme used in developing the tomato and helped scientists ensure that the modified plant expressed the desired genes) as a food additive.[314] In many ways, resorting to an amalgam of regulatory authorities to regulate products of biotechnology is merely a continuation of a process begun decades ago by FDA to practically address the complicated safety questions presented by the food supply. The agency continues to balance the broad goals contained in the statutory provisions and to recognize that proof of absolute safety is scientifically impossible. In the spirit of the dual purposes of the Food Additives Amendment, the agency has taken seriously the charge to ensure safety and promote innovation and food technology by relying on the use of sound scientific judgment based on good science.

FDA has adopted a policy of holding consultations with the industry sponsor of a plant product of biotechnology. In each case, the sponsor provides FDA with conclusions based on extensive studies designed to help determine whether the new plant variety is as safe and nutritious as its parental variety. After reviewing the sponsor's conclusions, FDA decides whether the new modified food differs significantly in structure, function or composition from substances found in the traditional counterpart food, and whether any public health value would be served by subjecting the product to more rigorous review.

As the number and diversity of field tests for bioengineered plants increase, the possibility arises that cross-pollination may become a problem due to 1) pollen drift from field tests to commercial fields or 2) commingling of seeds produced during field tests with commercial seeds or grain. Concerned about this possibility, FDA in 2004 issued a draft guidance[315] stressing FDA's expectation that developers should provide the agency with information about the safety of a new protein at an early stage of development of the crop. This early communication with the agency is designed to help ensure that any potential food safety issues regarding a new protein in a new plant variety are resolved well in advance of any possible inadvertent introduction into the food supply of material from the new plant variety. Once a developer decides to commercialize a particular crop, FDA still expects the developer to participate in the agency's voluntary premarket consultation process.

---

by a multidisciplinary team of scientific experts from academia and industry, and was peer-reviewed by approximately 150 experts from industry, academia, and government. *See also* discussion in text accompanying notes 224 through 230.

[313]   59 Fed. Reg. 26,647 (May 23, 1994); *see* discussion in text accompanying notes 227 and 228.

[314]   *Id.* at 26,700.

[315]   FDA, Guidance for Industry: Recommendations for the Early Food Safety Evaluation of New Non-Pesticidal Proteins Produced by New Plant Varieties Intended for Food Use, *available at* http://www.cfsan.fda. gov/~dms/bioprgui.html.

FDA's Regulation of Animal Biotechnology. Researchers today are developing genetically engineered food-producing animals. The genetic modifications being perfected may be divided into several broad categories. With respect to food-producing animals, these categories include genetic modifications to enhance food quality or agronomic traits (fish that grow faster, pigs that produce less environmentally deleterious waste products) and genetic modifications to improve animal health (e.g., disease resistance). Other classifications generally apply to genetic modifications in non-food-producing animals, e.g., genetic modifications to produce products intended for human therapeutic use ("biopharm" animals), genetic modifications to produce industrial or consumer products (e.g., fibers for multiple uses), and genetic modifications to enhance a given animal species interaction with human (e.g., hypoallergenic pets).

In January 2009, FDA issued a guidance in which the agency defined "genetically engineered animals" as those animals modified by rDNA techniques, including all progeny that contain the modification.[316] In FDA's view, the term "genetically engineered" animal can refer both to animals with a heritable rDNA construct and to an animal with a non-heritable rDNA construct (e.g., a construct intended as therapy for a disease in that animal).[317]

FDA regulates GE animals under the new animal drug provisions of the FDCA.[318] In light of the fact that section 201(g)[319] of the FDCA defines "drugs," in part, as "articles (other than food) intended to affect the structure or any function of the body of man or other animals," FDA has concluded that any rDNA construct in the resulting GE animal meets this definition.[320] Thus, the GE animal itself is not a drug, the animal is just "along for the ride" with the rDNA construct, the "drug."

With respect to food-producing animals, the safety of the food from a GE animal must be evaluated just like the safety from any food-producing animal on the receiving end of a new animal drug must be evaluated. The food safety evaluation FDA employs focuses on whether the food from the GE animal poses any risk to humans or animals consuming edible products from the GE animal compared to the edible products from appropriate non-transgenic comparators. FDA divides the food safety risk questions into two overall categories. First, FDA asks whether there is any direct toxicity, including allergenicity, associated with the expression product of the construct or components of the construct. Second, FDA focuses on potential indirect toxicity associated with both the transgene and its expression product (i.e., will the expression of the transgene affect the physiological processes and the resulting animal so that unintended food consumption hazards are created or existing food consumption risks are exacerbated or increased). Natural adverse outcomes are identified by determining whether there are any biologically relevant changes to physiology in the animal and whether reasons for toxicological concern are suggested by any biologically relevant changes in the composition of edible products from the GE animal compared with those from the appropriate non-transgenic comparator.

---

[316]   FDA, Guidance for Industry: Regulation of Genetically Engineered Animals Containing Heritable Recombinant DNA Constructs, *available at* www.fda.gov/downloads/AnimalVeterinary/GuidanceComplianceEnforcement/GuidanceforIndustry/UCM113903.pdf.

[317]   *Id.*

[318]   FDCA § 512, 21 U.S.C. § 360b.

[319]   FDCA § 201(g)(1)(C), 21 U.S.C. § 321(g)(1)(C).

[320]   21 U.S.C. § 321(g).

FDA has yet to approve under section 512 a new animal drug application (NADA) for a food-producing GE animal. That said, FDA has convened its Veterinary Medicine Advisory Committee to discuss approval issues related to an NADA for a genetically engineered Atlantic salmon modified to grow faster than conventionally bred Atlantic salmon.[321] The possibility that FDA might be close to approving an NADA for a genetically engineered food-producing animal attracted significant product attention and comment.[322] It is expected that when the agency does, in fact, for the first time approve such an NADA, other authorizations will soon follow.

FDA's Regulation of Nanotechnology

Nanotechnology is a burgeoning technology that enables scientists and product developers to create and manipulate matter on the size scale of molecules. It is now possible to employ nano-size materials in the manufacture of FDA-regulated products, notably and for our purposes in this chapter foods, food ingredients, and food packaging.

To put nanotechnology in context, consider the fact that a nanometer is 1-billionth of a meter. In comparison, the page upon which this print appears is about 100,000 nanometers thick. Although the potential benefits of applying nanotechnology to food production appear numerous and significant, concerns understandably accompany the development and use of the technology with respect to food and food-related products. The Institute of Medicine (IOM) has aptly summarized several of the key concerns:

> . . . How do the properties of nanomaterials change when introduced to different types of food matrices or migrate from packaging materials into foods? What happens when nanomaterials interact with a unique biological system such as the human gut? And what is required for evaluating and balancing the potential benefits and risks of introducing nano-size materials into foods and via the foods, into the human body?[323]

Recognizing that nanotechnology poses questions regarding the adequacy and application of its regulatory authorities, FDA commissioned its Nanotechnology Technology Task Force in 2006 to help assess the scope and adequacy of FDA's regulatory authorities to deal with products of nanotechnology. In July 2007, the task force issued its report.[324] The task force made various recommendations to augment FDA's regulatory authority. FDA's informal response to the task force report and, in general, to the use of nanotechnology in food has

---

321   *See* 75 Fed. Reg. 52,605 (Aug. 26, 2010) announcing a meeting of FDA's Veterinary Medicine Advisory Committee.

322   Marion Nestle, *The GM Salmon Saga Continues*, FoodPolitics.com, Sept. 21, 2010; Lyndsey Layton, *Fears over modified salmon voiced*, WASH. POST, Sept. 21, 2010; Andrew Pollack, *Panel Leans in Favor of Engineered Salmon*, N.Y. TIMES, Sept. 20, 2010; FrankenFish: *How Genetically Engineered Salmon Could Hurt Our Health and Environment*, FOOD AND WATER WATCH, Sept. 2010.

323   Leslie Pray & Ann Yaktine, Nanotechnology in Food Products, Institute of Medicine, National Academies Press, Washington, DC (2009).

324   Nanotechnology Task Force Report 2007, *available at* www.fda.gov./ScienceResearch/SpecialTopics/Nanotechnology/NanotechnologyTaskForceReport2007/default.htm.

been to suggest that the agency's statutory authorities provide FDA with adequate tools for evaluating and regulating the food uses of nanotechnology.[325] To that end, FDA has encouraged manufacturers who wish to employ nanotechnology in any food application to consult with agency experts in an effort to understand the data collection and substantiation expectations for a given use.[326]

In June 2014, FDA issued a series of guidance documents regarding nanotechnology. One guidance provided FDA's overarching framework for determining whether an FDA-regulated product involves the application of nanotechnology,[327] and the other three provided more particularized guidance for approaching the use of nanotechnology in product-specific areas, including food.[328] In its food-specific guidance, FDA, among other things: 1) alerts manufacturers to the potential impact of any significant manufacturing process change, including those involving nanotechnology, on the identity, safety, and regulatory status of food substances; and 2) expressly recommends that manufacturers consult with the agency regarding a significant manufacturing process change for any food substances currently being marketed, even when they conclude that the change does not affect the substance's safety or regulatory status.[329] FDA notes that such consultation with the agency is particularly "prudent" when "the manufacturing process change involves emerging technologies, such as nanotechnology."[330]

In its nanotechnology guidance documents, FDA also reiterates that it will regulate nanotechnology products under existing statutory authorities, in accordance with the specific legal standards applicable to each type of product under its jurisdiction. In the food context, FDA's regulatory authorities, particularly those authorities over food additives, GRAS substances, food contact substances, and food adulterants, provide a framework for regulation. Whether this framework may be made more efficient by tailored legislative change is not resolved.

---

[325]   *Supra* note 323, Nanotechnology in Food Products, p. 7.

[326]   *Id.*

[327]   FDA, Final Guidance for Industry: Considering Whether an FDA-Regulated Product Involves the Application of Nanotechnology (June 2014). This FDA guidance identifies two points to consider when determining if an FDA-regulated product involves the application of nanotechnology: 1) whether a material or end product is engineered to have at least one external dimension, or an internal or surface structure, in the nanoscale range (approximately 1 nm to 100 nm); and 2) whether a material or end product is engineered to exhibit properties or phenomena, including chemical or physical properties or biological effects, that are attributable to its dimension(s), even if these dimensions fall outside the nanoscale range, up to one micrometer (1,000 nm). *Id.* at 6. FDA notes that an affirmative finding to either of these points might "suggest the need for particular attention by the [a]gency and/or industry to the product to identify and address potential implications for safety, effectiveness, public health impact, or regulatory status of the product." *Id.* at 4.

[328]   FDA, Final Guidance for Industry: Assessing the Effects of Significant Manufacturing Process Changes, Including Emerging Technologies, on the Safety and Regulatory Status of Food Ingredients and Food Contact Substances, Including Food Ingredients that are Color Additives (June 2014); FDA, Final Guidance for Industry: Safety of Nanomaterials in Cosmetic Products (June 2014); FDA, Draft Guidance for Industry: Use of Nanomaterials in Food for Animals (June 2014).

[329]   FDA, Final Guidance for Industry: Assessing the Effects of Significant Manufacturing Process Changes, Including Emerging Technologies, on the Safety and Regulatory Status of Food Ingredients and Food Contact Substances, Including Food Ingredients that are Color Additives, at 4-5.

[330]   *Id.* at 5.

FDA's Regulation of the Safety of Dietary Supplements

In passing DSHEA, Congress chose new, unique safety standards for dietary supplements. Congress first provided that a dietary supplement will be considered adulterated if it "presents a significant or unreasonable risk of illness or injury" under its ordinary conditions of use.[331] The burden of proving that a substance does not measure up to this standard is placed squarely on FDA.

The standard is slightly different if the supplement contains a "new" dietary ingredient. A new ingredient is defined as one "not marketed in the United States before October 15, 1994."[332] A dietary supplement containing a new ingredient is considered adulterated unless one of two conditions applies: 1) the supplement contains "only dietary ingredients which have been present in the food supply as an article used for food in a form which the food has not been chemically altered," or 2) there is a "history of use or other evidence of safety establishing that the dietary ingredient when used under the conditions recommended or suggested in the labeling . . . will reasonably be expected to be safe."[333] If the latter applies, a manufacturer or distributor of the ingredient or dietary supplement must file a premarket notification with the agency at least 75 days before marketing the product.[334] The notification must bear all information, including citations to published articles, on which the basis for the conclusion that the dietary supplement containing the new ingredient "will reasonably be expected to be safe."[335] In light of persistent questions regarding whether a dietary ingredient is a new dietary ingredient and under what circumstances a 75-day notification must be submitted, FSMA required FDA to issue guidance clarifying both issues.[336]

DSHEA reflects the congressional value judgment that dietary supplements are sufficiently safe to merit regulation comparable to that governing traditional whole foods. By removing dietary ingredients from the premarket approval strictures of the food additive rubric,[337] and by placing the burden on proving that a supplement either presents "a significant or unreasonable risk of illness or injury" or poses an "imminent hazard," DSHEA, in effect, embodies the rebuttable presumption that most supplements are safe. In response to the new statutory standards, FDA, for all practical purposes, limited its safety and enforcement focus to a few botanical products of concern. Among these were ephedrine alkaloids.

Ephedrine alkaloids are chemical stimulants that occur naturally in some botanicals. They also can be synthetically derived. Dietary supplements containing ephedrine alkaloids were widely sold in the United States prior to 2004. In the 1990s, in particular, dietary supplements containing ephedrine were labeled and used primarily for weight loss, energy, or to enhance athletic performance. A growing body of scientific evidence and reports of serious adverse events, including death, following consumption of dietary supplements

---

[331]   FDCA § 402(f)(1)(A), 21 U.S.C. § 342(f)(1)(A).

[332]   FDCA § 413(c), 21 U.S.C. § 350b(c).

[333]   FDCA § 413(a), 21 U.S.C. § 350b(a).

[334]   Id.

[335]   Id.

[336]   FDCA § 413 note, 21 U.S.C. § 350b note. In July 2011, FDA issued a draft guidance document addressing these new dietary ingredient issues. FDA, Draft Guidance for Industry: Dietary Supplements - New Dietary Ingredient Notifications and Related Issues (July 2011).

[337]   But see supra note 238.

containing ephedrine alkaloids raised concerns about the safety of ephedrine alkaloids and dietary supplements containing them.

In June 1997, FDA proposed to make a finding that any dietary supplement containing eight milligrams or more of ephedrine alkaloids per serving was "adulterated" within the meaning of DSHEA's adulteration provisions.[338] During the comment period on the proposal, the government-sponsored Commission on Dietary Supplement Labels published a report addressing the ephedrine alkaloid issue and encouraging FDA to take swift enforcement action against the substances.[339] However, before FDA could finalize its proposal, the U.S. General Accounting Office (GAO) (since renamed the Government Accountability Office) began a study 1) of the safety issues presented by the use of ephedrine alkaloids and 2) of the agency's proposal. GAO did not complete its work until July 1999.[340] GAO concluded that the evidence supported concern about the safety of ephedrine alkaloid dietary supplements but criticized FDA's reliance on adverse event reports as the basis for proposing restrictions on dosage, frequency, and duration of use.

In April 2000, FDA withdrew its proposed finding that a dietary supplement would be adulterated if it contained eight milligrams or more of ephedrine alkaloids per serving as well as other related requirements the agency had wished to impose.[341] The agency emphasized that withdrawal of the proposal did not limit its discretion to initiate enforcement actions with respect to dietary supplements containing ephedrine alkaloids. At the same time, the agency announced the availability of certain new documents updating the administrative record with respect to the adverse event reports associated with ephedrine alkaloid use.[342]

In March 2003, FDA issued a notice making available for comment additional new evidence related to the safety of ephedrine alkaloids.[343] Among this information was a report by the Southern California Evidence Based Practice Center and commissioned by the National Institutes of Health. This report identified 21 "sentinel events" among the ephedrine alkaloids-related adverse event reports it reviewed.[344] The sentinel events included stroke, heart attack and death. The report defined a "sentinel event" as a case that met all three of the following criteria: 1) documentation of an adverse event that met the selection criteria; 2) documentation that the person having the adverse event took an ephedra containing supplement within 24 hours prior to the event; and 3) documentation that alternative explanations for the adverse event were investigated and were excluded with reasonable certainty. The report also found limited evidence that ephedrine alkaloid supplements have any effect on short-term weight loss or athletic performance.

---

[338]   62 Fed. Reg. 30,678 (June 4, 1997).

[339]   Final Report of the Commission on Dietary Supplement Labels (Nov. 24, 1997).

[340]   U.S. General Accounting Office, Dietary Supplements: Uncertainties in Analyses Underlying FDA's Proposed Rule on Ephedrine Alkaloids, GAO/Health, Education, and Human Services Division (HEHS)/General Government Division (GGD)-99-90 (July 1999).

[341]   65 Fed. Reg. 17,474 (Apr. 3, 2000).

[342]   Id. at 17,509.

[343]   68 Fed. Reg. 10,417 (Mar. 5, 2003).

[344]   P. Shekelle et al., Ephedra and Ephedrine for Weight Loss and Athletic Performance Enhancement: Clinical Efficacy and Side Effects, Evidence/Technical Assessment, No. 76, AHRQ Publication No. 03-E022, Rockville, MD, Agency for Healthcare Research and Quality, Docket No. 1995 N-0304, BKG, vol. 30. See also P. Shekelle et al., Efficacy and Safety of Ephedra and Ephedrine for Weight Loss and Athletic Performance: A Meta-Analysis, 289 JAMA 1537-1545 (2003).

In July 2003, GAO representatives testified at a House subcommittee hearing on issues relating to dietary supplements containing ephedrine alkaloids.[345] In their testimony, the GAO representatives discussed and updated some of the findings of the 1999 GAO report. The testimony focused on 92 serious events that included heart attacks, strokes, seizures and deaths associated with the use of ephedrine alkaloid dietary supplements.

On February 11, 2004, FDA issued a final rule in which the agency concluded that dietary supplements containing ephedrine alkaloids were adulterated under the DSHEA adulteration standard (section 402(f)(1)(A) of the act) because they presented an "unreasonable risk of illness or injury" under the conditions of use recommended or suggested in labeling.[346] Debate had preceded the final rule with respect to whether the evidence concerning the safety of ephedrine alkaloid supplements, even though troubling, was of sufficient weight and merit to meet the demanding standard apparently presented by the "significant or unreasonable risk of illness or injury" standard.

FDA, focusing on the language "significant or unreasonable risk," concluded that the standard does not require that there be evidence *proving* that the supplement has caused actual harm to specific individuals. FDA reasoned that if scientific evidence supports the *existence* of risk, the burden of proof for "unreasonable risk" is met when the risk presented by a product outweighs the benefits of using the product according to the claims and directions for use in the product's labeling (or if the labeling is silent, under ordinary conditions of use).[347] Under this interpretation, the statutory standard of "unreasonable risk" calls for merely a weighing of the product's known and reasonably likely risks against its known and reasonably likely benefits. In the absence of a sufficient benefit, the presence of even a relatively small risk of a significant adverse health effect to a user may lawfully be characterized as "unreasonable."

Legislative materials leading up to the passage of DSHEA suggest that such a reading of section 402(f)(1)(A) is inconsistent with congressional intent—an intent not only to raise the standard for taking regulatory action to an affirmative showing of lack of safety but also to place the burden of meeting that standard on FDA.[348] Although the agency's creative reading of the provision temporarily allowed it to prohibit the marketing of dietary supplements that had seriously called into question the adequacy of the safety provisions of DSHEA, the first court to consider the agency's interpretation of authority rejected it.[349] The Tenth Circuit Court of Appeals, however, ruled in favor of FDA, finding that the agency correctly followed the congressional directive to analyze the risks and benefits of substances like ephedrine alkaloids.[350]

---

[345] U.S. General Accounting Office, "Dietary Supplements Containing Ephedra, Health Risks and FDA Oversight," Testimony: Before the Subcommittee on Oversight and Investigations, Committee on Energy and Commerce, U.S. House of Representatives, GAO-03-1042T, 2003.

[346] 69 Fed. Reg. 6788 (Feb. 11, 2004).

[347] Id.

[348] *See, e.g.*, REP. No. 103-410, Dietary Supplement Health and Education Act of 1994, 103d Cong., 2d Sess. 21-22.

[349] Nutraceutical Corp. v. Crawford, et al., 364 F. Supp. 2d 1310 (D. Utah 2005). The court ruled that under DSHEA dietary supplements are presumed to be safe. The court held that FDA's interpretation of the "unreasonable risk" language was inconsistent with the burden Congress placed squarely on the government to establish the existence of such an unreasonable risk.

[350] Nutraceutical Corp, et al. v. von Eschenbach, et al., 459 F.3d 1033 (10th Cir. 2006).

In November 2004—ten years after the passage of DSHEA—FDA issued a new "regulatory strategy" for the "further" implementation and enforcement of DSHEA.[351] The agency candidly stated that the safety of "new dietary ingredients" had become a concern and, as a result, a regulatory priority. Fearful that many products available to consumers might contain new dietary ingredients for which notifications had not been submitted or for which the information submitted in the notification did not establish a reasonable expectation of safety, FDA announced its plans to improve the evidentiary base for safety and decision making concerning new dietary ingredients.

In the process, the agency suggested it would adopt a framework for evaluating the safety of dietary supplements developed by the IOM and the National Research Council of the National Academies.[352] At the heart of this approach is a "transparent and systematic process" for evaluating safety concerns about dietary ingredients and dietary supplements.[353] The process is designed to begin with "signal detection"; i.e., the identification of possible safety concerns as evidenced from a variety of sources including federal, state and local counterparts; adverse events reports; foreign regulatory actions; media reports; information from consumer groups; and consultation with experts. If a concern proves to be real, the regulatory strategy would not be limited to enforcement litigation. In fact, in a clear departure from its post-1938 disposition to rely upon enforcement litigation to police the dietary supplement industry, FDA advised that it would consider relying on publicity and educational outreach efforts to provide consumers access to reliable scientific information about the safety of specific dietary ingredients and supplements. Included in this public outreach effort would be efforts to educate healthcare providers as well as consumers.

A Special Problem: Assuring the Safety of Imported Food

Traditional Agency Authority. For decades FDA has had broad authority to secure the detention of imported regulated articles on the mere appearance that they are violative.[354] The scope of this authority is understandable in light of the extraordinary task confronted by import officials of attempting to control the volume of products being offered for import. FDA exercises its import authority in conjunction with and in cooperation with the U.S. Customs Service. Section 801(a) of the FDCA permits FDA to refuse admission to an imported article if "it appears" that the article is in violation of the Act.[355] Thus, the fundamental test for refusal rests merely upon the "appearance" of a violation—a standard that, when considered literally, is almost impossible for the agency not to meet should it believe a product to be violative. The Customs Service's authority over imports also arises, in part, under section 801, which vests the U.S. Secretary of the Treasury with the authority to deliver samples of imported products to FDA for analysis. In actual practice, FDA personnel

351   69 Fed. Reg. 64,957 (Nov. 9, 2004); Regulatory Strategy for the Further Implementation and Enforcement of Dietary Supplement Health and Education Act of 1994 ("Regulatory Strategy"), *at* http://www.cfsan.fda. gov/~ dms/ds3strat.html.

352   COMMITTEE ON THE FRAMEWORK FOR EVALUATING THE SAFETY OF DIETARY SUPPLEMENTS, NATIONAL RESEARCH COUNCIL, DIETARY SUPPLEMENTS: A FRAMEWORK FOR EVALUATING SAFETY, Institute of Medicine of the National Academies. National Academy Press, Washington, D.C. (Apr. 2004).

353   Regulatory Strategy, *supra* note 351.

354   FDCA § 801, 21 U.S.C. § 381.

355   21 U.S.C. § 381(a).

collect the samples at most ports, issue the appropriate notice of sampling and, where applicable, having determined that an article is in violation and may not be brought into compliance, issue a refusal notice.

Policing the safety of imported food is perhaps FDA's most daunting job. More than $65 billion worth of food products are imported annually.[356] The sheer volume precludes inspection of every imported product and, as a practical matter, demands the cooperation forged by FDA and the Customs Service. And, the problems presented by potentially violative products being introduced through import regularly invite congressional scrutiny of FDA actions and consideration of ways, usually through greater resources, to augment FDA's and the Customs Service's abilities to protect the public from risks presented by imported products. Notably, in 2002 Congress passed legislation designed to help reduce the ability of international terrorists to contaminate foods imported into the United States.[357] The legislation requires food importers to provide FDA with advance notice of shipments of human and animal food imported or offered for import into the United States. This advance information permits FDA, in conjunction with U.S. Customs, to channel resources and target inspections—a necessity in light of the fact that every day FDA receives approximately 25,000 notifications with respect to incoming shipments of food. The legislation authorizes FDA to ask Customs to institute a temporary hold for 24 hours on any food offered for import if FDA has credible evidence or information indicating that the food presents a threat of serious adverse harm and FDA is unable to immediately inspect or examine the food.[358]

Adding to the complexity of regulating imported food is the fact that more than 150 countries export food into over 300 U.S. ports.[359] Approximately 60 percent of fresh fruits and vegetables consumed in the United States are imported.[360] Moreover, the type of imported foods has changed in recent years from unprocessed food ingredients (whose subsequent processing would be covered by FDA domestic oversight) to foods inherently more likely to pose risks, e.g., ready-to-eat food products, seafood, and fresh produce).[361] Although FDA "screens" all import entries using an automated system designed to identify those products posing the greatest safety risk, FDA resources permit only a small percentage of imported food to actually be inspected.

Concerns over FDA's ability to protect the American public from unsafe imported foods heightened as a result of a spate of recalls (notably contaminated pet food from China).[362] The episodes giving rise to the contamination revealed the relative ease with which harmful food could be imported and make its way into the domestic food supply. Several congressional

---

[356] Nora Brooks, "U.S. Agriculture Ends Calendar Year with Record Trade; Exports at $71 billion, Imports at $65 billion," U.S. Agricultural Trade update, ECONOMIC RESEARCH SERVICE, Feb. 15, 2007 at 1.

[357] The Public Health Security and Bioterrorism Act of 2002 ("The Bioterrorism Act"), Pub. L. No. 107-188; § 307 of the Bioterrorism Act. FDA has promulgated regulations governing import notifications, 21 C.F.R. §§ 1.287 - 1.285.

[358] Section 303 of the Bioterrorism Act; FDCA § 801(j)(1), 21 U.S.C. § 381(j)(1).

[359] FDA, Food Protection Plan: An Integrated Strategy for Protecting the Nation's Food Supply (Nov. 2007), available at www.fda.gov/oc/initiatives/advance/food/plan.html.

[360] Id.

[361] Id.

[362] Pet Food Recall (Melamine)/Tainted Animal Feed, July 23, 2007, available at www.fda.gov/oc/opacom/hottopics/petfood.html.

initiatives to reform the FDCA to enhance FDA's ability to police food imports coalesced to yield several key provisions of the Food Safety Modernization Act.

Foreign Supplier Verification. New section 805[363] of the FDCA defines "importer" as "the United States owner or consignee" of an article of food "at the time of entry of such article into the United States." In the case where there is no U.S. owner or consignee as so defined, the United States agent or representative of a foreign owner or consignee of the article of food is considered to be an "importer" for purposes of section 805. The definition is important because the section requires[364] every "importer" to perform risk-based foreign supplier verification activities for the purpose of assuring that imported food is produced in compliance with the requirements of section 418, 419, or both as applicable, and is not adulterated under section 402 or misbranded within the meaning of the allergen declaration requirements of section 403(w).[365]

Section 805 required FDA, within one year after the enactment of the legislation, to "promulgate" regulations governing the content of foreign supplier verification programs.[366] FDA issued a long-awaited proposed rule on foreign supplier verification programs on July 29, 2013, and issued a supplemental proposal on September 29, 2014,[367] but as of December 2014, had yet to publish final regulations.[368] The regulations must require that a verification program be adequate to provide assurances that each foreign supplier complies with the aforesaid requirements. FDA may, in its discretion, impose additional requirements. Moreover, as already noted elsewhere in this chapter, section 805 expressly authorizes FDA to require the importer to maintain, for not less than two years, records confirming the importer's verification program. The records must be made available "promptly" to a duly authorized agent of FDA. It is a prohibited act to import and even to "offer" for import a food for which an importer does not have a compliant foreign supplier verification program in place.[369] Moreover, FDA is empowered to refuse import of a food if it appears that the importer has not complied with the foreign supplier verification requirement.[370]

For obvious reasons, seafood HACCP, juice HACCP, and thermally processed low-acid foods facilities are exempt from the recordkeeping requirement (except with respect to thermally processed low-acid foods facilities, exemption extends only to systems applying to microbiological hazards). FDA is also empowered to exempt food imported in small

---

[363]   FDCA § 805(a)(2), 21 U.S.C. § 384a(a)(2).

[364]   FDCA § 805(a)(1), 21 U.S.C. § 384a(a)(1).

[365]   21 U.S.C. § 343(w).

[366]   FDCA § 805(c), 21 U.S.C. § 384a(c).

[367]   FDA's proposed rule on foreign supplier verification is entitled "Foreign Supplier Verification Programs for Importers of Food for Humans and Animals." 78 Fed. Reg. 45,730 (July 29, 2013). FDA issued a supplemental proposal on September 29, 2014. 79 Fed. Reg. 58,573 (Sept. 29, 2014).

[368]   Under a 2014 consent decree, FDA agreed to make every effort to issue the final rule on foreign supplier verification programs by October 31, 2015. Center for Food Safety v. Hamburg, Consent Decree, Case No.: 12-cv-04529-PJH (Feb. 20, 2014).

[369]   FDCA § 801(a), 21 U.S.C. § 381(a).

[370]   *Id.* In a further effort to help strengthen FDA's authority over the safety of imported food, section 801(n)(1) of the FDCA now authorizes FDA to require, by regulation, that the agency be notified prior to import of any food, if the food has been refused entry into any other country and, in such a case, that FDA be informed of the identity of the country refusing entry. 21 U.S.C. § 381(n)(1).

quantities for research or for personal consumption provided such foods are not intended for retail sale or public distribution.

Importer Certification. In cases where FDA concludes that an imported food is "high-risk" or that the food safety programs in a country or territory are inadequate to ensure that the food at issue is as safe as a similar article of food manufactured in the United States, FSMA amends section 801(a) of the FDCA to authorize FDA to require, as a condition of granting admission to a food offered for import, a certification assuring compliance with all "applicable requirements"[371] of the FDCA. Such certification may be obtained from either 1) an agency or representative of the government of the country from which the food is being imported or 2) an accredited third-party auditor.[372]

FSMA also mandated that FDA, within two years from the date of enactment, establish a system for recognizing accreditation bodies that accredit third-party auditors to issue certifications.[373] The concept behind the requirement is that FDA establish criteria recognizing "accreditation bodies" which bodies, in turn, would be responsible for accrediting third-party auditors. On July 29, 2013, FDA issued a proposed rule regarding the accreditation of third-party auditors,[374] but as of December 2014, had yet to publish a final rule establishing a third-party accreditation system.[375] Since FDA failed to establish an accreditation system within the required two-year period, the agency is technically permitted to accredit third-party auditors on its own initiative.[376] A third-party auditor may not be accredited by an accreditation body without first agreeing to certify each shipment of food offered for import by an entity the third-party auditor is eligible to certify. Moreover, with respect to a third-party auditor, FDA has the singular authority to require the auditor to provide FDA with the regulatory audit and any other documents and reports relating to the audit process for any entity the auditor has certified.[377] Moreover, an accredited third-party auditor must warn FDA if the auditor discovers at any time during an audit a condition that could cause or contribute to a serious risk to the public health.[378] FSMA also provides FDA with the authority to withdraw accreditation and re-instate accreditation.[379] The importer certification and the accreditation provisions in FSMA present FDA with perhaps its most difficult FSMA implementation challenges.

---

[371] 21 U.S.C. § 381(a).

[372] 21 U.S.C. § 381(n)(1).

[373] FDCA § 808, 21 U.S.C. § 384d.

[374] FDA's proposed rule on third-party accreditation is entitled "Accreditation of Third-Party Auditors/ Certification Bodies to Conduct Food Safety Audits and to Issue Certifications." 78 Fed. Reg. 45,782 (July 29, 2013).

[375] Under a 2014 consent decree, FDA agreed to make every effort to issue the final rule on the accreditation of third-party auditors by October 31, 2015. Center for Food Safety v. Hamburg, Consent Decree, Case No.: 12-cv-04529-PJH (Feb. 20, 2014).

[376] FDCA § 808b(1)(A)(ii), 21 U.S.C. § 384d(b)(1)(A)(ii).

[377] FDA is not entitled to access an auditor's "consultative" audit of an eligible entity. A consultative audit assesses whether the entity is in compliance with the requirements of the FDCA and the results of such audit are for internal entity use and purposes only. FDA, nevertheless, can gain access even to such consultative audits if pursuant to section 414, FDA has a reasonable belief that an article of food is adulterated and presents a threat of adverse health consequences or death to humans or animals. FDCA § 414(a), 21 U.S.C. § 350c(a).

[378] FDCA § 808(c)(4), 21 U.S.C. § 384d(c)(4).

[379] FDCA § 808(c)(6) and (7), 21 U.S.C. § 384d(c)(6) and (7).

Inspection of Foreign Food Facilities. Section 201 of the Food Safety Modernization Act, new section 421 of the FDCA, requires that, with respect to foreign facilities, FDA must inspect no fewer than 600 facilities in the initial one-year period following enactment.[380] In each of the subsequent five years, FDA must inspect "not fewer" than twice the number of foreign facilities inspected during the previous year.[381]

New section 807 of the FDCA authorizes FDA to enter into "arrangements" or "agreements" with foreign governments in an effort to facilitate the inspection of foreign facilities registered under section 415 of the FDCA.[382] Tellingly, FDA may refuse admission of imported food from a foreign factory, warehouse or other establishment that has refused an FDA request to inspect.[383]

Many of the import provisions of FSMA were outlined in FDA's 2007 "Food Protection Plan"[384] as desirable enhancements to FDA's authority over imported food. To this end, the plan revealed that FDA recognized that there were legal limits to its current ability to pursue creative regulatory responses to the imported food safety challenges it faces. Although it is rare for FDA to request new legislative authority, the agency's plan revealed that FDA decided that it needed to play an active, leading role in identifying and defining the contours of the problems it faces and the tools it needs to craft empirically sound, informed, and forward-looking responses to imported food safety concerns. New tools now in hand, FDA has the option of choosing how to use them most efficiently and meaningfully in dealing with one of the agency's most complex and longstanding regulatory problem areas.

Conclusion

A review of the course of food safety regulation since 1906 reveals that the scientific, legal, and policy issues that accompany food safety considerations have been and continue to be complex. A result of this complexity is change: change in the legislative authority and change in the administrative policy, criteria, and rubrics used to implement that authority. The legislative changes generally have been borne from the need to keep up with technology and innovation, as well as current scientific understanding, thought and developments, and to respond to catastrophes and political realities. In general, these legislative changes have provided FDA with the flexibility it requires to make meaningful food safety decisions. When legislation has failed to materialize, FDA consistently has sought ways to interpret the statute so as to foster and continue its ability to make meaningful food safety decisions. In part, this agency willingness to be creative is based on the recognition that science is an open-ended process that eventually can question past decisions and precedent. On balance, the processes and structures put into place by both Congress and FDA have provided regulation that is commensurate with the risk to be prevented.

---

[380]   FDCA § 421(a)(2)(D), 21 U.S.C. § 350j(a)(2)(D).
[381]   *Id.*
[382]   FDCA § 807(a)(1), 21 U.S.C. § 384c(a)(1).
[383]   FDCA § 807(b), 21 U.S.C. § 384c(b).
[384]   *Supra* note 359.

There are exceptions to the foregoing generalizations, the Delaney Clause being arguably the most obvious. Nevertheless, in light of the practical problems that confront the federal regulation of food, an openness toward flexibility is essential if meaningful decision making is to be accomplished. For example, FDA's willingness in the context of plant products of biotechnology to dust off a GRAS concept that it had interpreted narrowly for nearly two decades (and, in the process, "presume" genetic material to be GRAS) reveals how the agency successfully can adapt its available legal tools and administrative processes to address new times and new challenges.

FDA is faced with new and numerous challenges in implementing the Food Safety Modernization Act. The legislation carries with it high expectations that FDA will be able to efficiently issue required regulations and guidances, to increase domestic inspections, to forge a program of foreign facility inspections, to coordinate safety-related activities with other federal agencies, to oversee the safety of imported food, to establish and enforce import and laboratory accreditation criteria, to help increase the capacity of state and local food safety authorities, etc. In order to be successful, the agency will need to prioritize its activities and reach out across government and, to a large extent, across industry for expert input, assistance, and cooperation. More than ever, resources will continue to be an intractable problem that risks hindering the agency's ability to address and resolve the complex food safety issues it is confronted by and is charged by FSMA to address and resolve. As a result, "food safety" will, also more than ever, be a shared enterprise between the regulator and the regulated. The precedent set by FDA in more than 100 years of regulating the food supply is the foundation for meeting the current regulatory changes and for how scientific data will be taken into account, how innovation will be accommodated, and how the public health goals of the law will be applied and, hopefully, achieved.

CHAPTER 3
FOOD LABELING

....

MEL DROZEN AND EVE PELONIS

Introduction

The Federal Food, Drug, and Cosmetic Act (FDCA)[1] and the Fair Packaging and Labeling Act (FPLA)[2] are primarily responsible for setting forth federal food[3] labeling[4] requirements. The Food and Drug Administration (FDA), an agency of the U.S. Department of Health and Human Services (DHHS), enforces these acts with respect to food.[5]

---

[1]   Pub. L. No. 75-717, 52 Stat. 1040 (1938) (codified as amended at 21 U.S.C. §§ 301-904 (2000 and Supp. V 2005)).

[2]   15 U.S.C. §§ 1451-61 (1994).

[3]   Section 201(f) of the FDCA defines "food" as "(1) articles used for food or drink for man or other animals, (2) chewing gum, and (3) articles used for components of any such article." 21 U.S.C. § 321(f). This definition is incorporated by reference into the FPLA. 15 U.S.C. § 1459(a).

[4]   Section 201(m) of the FDCA defines "labeling" as "all labels and other written, printed, or graphic matter (1) on any article or any of its containers or wrappers, or (2) accompanying such article." 21 U.S.C. § 321(m). Section 201(k) of the FDCA defines "label" as "a display of written, printed, or graphic matter upon the immediate container" of a food. *Id.* § 321(k). For a discussion of the placement requirements for food labeling information *see discussion infra* Format and Placement Requirements.

[5]   This chapter does not apply to the labeling of dietary supplements (*see* Chapter 6), the labeling of meat or poultry products, which are the subjects of separate laws enforced by the U.S. Department of Agriculture (USDA), or to the labeling of alcoholic beverages, which are subject to separate legislation enforced by the Alcohol, Tobacco Tax and Trade Bureau (TTB) of the U.S. Department of the Treasury. *See, e.g.,* 21 U.S.C. § 607 (labeling of meat or meat food products); *id.* § 457 (labeling of poultry products); 27 U.S.C. § 205(e) (1994) (labeling of alcoholic beverages). For a discussion of the regulation of meat and poultry by USDA, *see* Chapter 5. In addition, this chapter does not address labeling of organic products, which are regulated by USDA's Agricultural Marketing Service (AMS), National Organic Program (NOP) pursuant to the passage of the Organic Foods Production Act of 1990.

Labeling Requirements

Pursuant to the FDCA, the FPLA and related FDA regulations in the *Code of Federal Regulations*, food labels must generally provide the following information:

- product name/statement of identity;
- quantity of contents;
- name and place of business of manufacturer, packer, or distributor;
- listing of ingredients, including allergen information; and
- nutrition information.

Supplementing these basic requirements, FDA has issued regulations that impose additional requirements, usually under the agency's general authority to promulgate regulations for "the efficient enforcement" of the FDCA.[6] All of these requirements are discussed below.

Importantly, these basic mandatory food-labeling requirements generally apply to food in "packaged form." FDA defines a "package" to mean "any container or wrapping in which any food, drug, device, or cosmetic is enclosed for use in the delivery or display of such commodities to retail purchasers . . . ."[7] This definition does not include: 1) bulk shipping containers or wrappings used to ship bulk quantities of commodities; 2) shipping containers and outer wrap used by retailers to deliver products to their retail customers, so long as the wrap bears no printed information on any particular commodity; 3) retail display trays; and 4) transparent wrappers or containers that bear no written or graphic matter obscuring required label information.[8] This section also provides that FDA's labeling requirements will not be considered to be satisfied unless the required information appears on the outer container or wrapper of a retail package or can be easily seen through a transparent outer container or wrap.

Further, there is a distinction between label requirements imposed pursuant to the FDCA and requirements imposed pursuant to the FPLA. Generally, requirements imposed pursuant to the FDCA apply both to the immediate container of a product and to the outside container or wrapper of the retail package, if any. This result derives from the act's definition of the term "label":

> The term "label" means a display of written, printed, or graphic matter *upon the immediate container of any article;* and a requirement made by or under the authority of this [Act] that any word, statement, or other information appear on the label shall not be considered to be complied with unless such word, statement, or other information *also appears on the outside container or wrapper,* if any there be, of the retail package of such article, or is easily legible through the outside container or wrapper.[9]

---

6   FDCA § 701(a), 21 U.S.C. § 371(a).

7   21 C.F.R. § 1.20.

8   *See* 21 C.F.R. § 1.20(a)-(e).

9   FDCA § 201(k), 21 U.S.C. § 321(k) (emphasis added).

In contrast, label requirements imposed pursuant to the FPLA apply only to the outside container or wrapper of the retail package.[10] FDA has published a list of regulations premised solely on the FPLA.[11]

Product Name/Statement of Identity

Section 401 of the FDCA authorizes FDA to publish "regulations fixing and establishing for any food, under its common or usual name so far as practicable, a reasonable definition and standard of identity . . . ."[12] Standards of identity are set forth by product category in 21 C.F.R. Parts 131 through 169. If FDA has published a definition and standard of identity for a food, section 403(g) of the FDCA requires that the label of the food bear "the name of the food specified in the definition and standard."[13] In addition, if a food product bears the name of a food specified in a standard of identity, the food product is misbranded if it does not conform to the standard.[14] For example, a product represented as "mayonnaise" must comply with FDA's standard of identity for mayonnaise.[15] The standards of identity were intended to prevent economic deception—to "protect consumers from receiving debased or watered down food products in which water or other fillers had been substituted for more valuable constituents."[16] If FDA has not published a definition and standard of identity for a particular food, section 403(i)(1) of the FDCA requires that its label bear "the common or usual name of the food, if any there be."[17]

Building on these basic identity-labeling requirements appearing in the FDCA, the FPLA provides for FDA to establish regulations requiring retail food packages to "bear a label specifying the identity of the commodity."

In regulations premised on both the FDCA and the FPLA, FDA has applied these separate statutory requirements by stating that "[t]he principal display panel of a food in package form shall bear as one of its principal features a statement of the identity of the commodity."[18]

The product identity statement shall be in terms of:

(1) The name specified and/or required by an applicable federal law or regulation (usually, a standard of identity); or

(2) If no such required name exists, the "common or usual name" of the food; or

---

[10] 15 U.S.C. § 1459(b).

[11] 21 C.F.R. § 1.1(c).

[12] 21 U.S.C. § 341. Such regulations usually establish detailed recipes with mandatory and optional ingredients. *See* Richard A. Merrill & Earl M. Collier, Jr., *Like Mother Used to Make: An Analysis of the FDA Food Standards of Identity,* 74 COLUM. L. REV. 561 (1974).

[13] 21 U.S.C. § 343(g).

[14] *Id.*

[15] 21 C.F.R. § 169.140.

[16] 60 Fed. Reg. 67,492, 67,494 (Dec. 29, 1995).

[17] 21 U.S.C. § 343(i)(1).

[18] 21 C.F.R. § 101.3(a).

(3) In the absence of either of the above, an "appropriately descriptive term." When the nature of the food is obvious, a fanciful name commonly used by the public may also be used for such food.[19]

This fundamental requirement of a prominent label product identity statement is rooted in common sense. Consumers need to be able to determine, easily and accurately, what they are buying, and manufacturers need and want to inform consumers of the identity of their products. Occasionally, however, controversy arises over the proper statement of identity for a particular food.

For example, FDA once attempted to stop manufacturers of frozen fish products from describing uniform rectangular pieces of fish (cut from pressed frozen blocks of fish fillets) as fish "fillets." In response, a leading manufacturer of these products, which had been using the statement of identity "frozen fish fillets" for many years without objection from the government, consumers, or competitors, brought an action for declaratory judgment and obtained a court ruling that the "fillet" terminology was a proper statement of identity for its frozen fish product.[20]

Disputes over the appropriate statement of identity for a product also arise between competitors. For example, when manufacturers of traditional potato chip products found themselves competing with new, fabricated food products shaped to resemble traditional potato chips but formulated from processed, dehydrated potatoes, the manufacturers of the traditional potato chip products asked FDA to take enforcement action against the new, fabricated products on the premise that the new products were not true "potato chips" and instead should be identified as "imitation potato chips." FDA ultimately resolved the controversy by issuing a regulation that states that "[t]he common or usual name of the food product that resembles and is of the same composition as potato chips, except that it is composed of dehydrated potatoes . . ., shall be 'potato chips made from dried potatoes.'"[21]

Relying on section 701(a) of the FDCA to issue regulations for the "efficient enforcement" of section 403(i)(1), which requires a label statement of "the common or usual name of the food, if any there be,"[22] FDA has published several regulations establishing specific "common or usual names" for particular foods.[23] These regulations sometimes require, as part of the name to appear on the label of a food, additional information about the nature of the food that would not commonly be regarded as part of a traditional "name." For example, onion rings made from diced onions (instead of whole rings) are required to reveal that information as part of the name of the food;[24] the fish sticks or portions made from minced fish (instead of whole pieces of fish) are required to declare that information as part of the name of the food.[25]

---

[19]   *Id.* § 101.3(b).
[20]   Mrs. Paul's Kitchens, Inc. v. Califano, Food Drug Cosm. L. Rep. (CCH) ¶ 50,154.13 (E.D. Pa. 1978).
[21]   21 C.F.R. § 102.41.
[22]   21 U.S.C. § 343(i)(1).
[23]   21 C.F.R. pt. 102.
[24]   *Id.* § 102.39.
[25]   *Id.* § 102.45.

Some industry attorneys have argued that FDA's use of an expanded "common or usual name" concept—to require by regulation a name that provides additional information not customarily thought to be part of a name—exceeds FDA's authority. Nevertheless, in a test case brought by an industry trade association challenging two of FDA's most novel common or usual name regulations, the U.S. District Court for the District of Columbia and the U.S. Court of Appeals for the District of Columbia Circuit ruled that FDA regulations establishing names for frozen heat-and-serve dinners and for seafood cocktails are authorized, reasonable and proper.[26] The regulation concerning frozen heat-and-serve dinners requires that said dinners include a protein component and at least two other courses from a designated list, and that all courses be identified on the label in descending order of predominance by weight as a part of the name.[27] The regulation concerning seafood cocktails requires declaration of the percentage by weight of seafood in the product as a part of the name.[28]

FDA's regulations include several technical requirements regarding the format for the label declaration of the statement of identity;[29] sometimes the technicalities of these format requirements cause difficulties. For example, the regulations provide that the statement of identity "shall be in lines generally parallel to the base on which the package rests as it is designed to be displayed."[30] When soft drink manufacturers wanted to declare product names prominently but vertically on soft drink cans, a second regulation was needed to create a limited "exemption" for soft drink cans from the general requirement that identity declarations be parallel to the base.[31]

Quantity of Contents

Section 403(e)(2) of the FDCA requires that a food in package form bear a label containing "an accurate statement of the quantity of the contents in terms of weight, measure, or numerical count."[32] The FPLA provides for FDA to issue regulations requiring "[t]he separate label statement of net quantity of contents" on retail food packages.[33] Relying on the FDCA and the FPLA, FDA has published regulations requiring that "[t]he principal display panel of a food in package form shall bear a declaration of the net quantity of contents."[34]

FDA's regulations currently mandate declaration of the quantity of contents in terms of traditional U.S. units of measure—avoirdupois pounds and ounces, gallons, quarts, pints, and fluid ounces.[35] Due to the 1992 amendments to the FPLA,[36] however, in 1993 FDA issued a proposed amendment to this regulation to require declaration of the quantity of contents in terms of traditional U.S. units of measure *and* metric units—kilograms, grams, liters, and

---

[26]   American Frozen Food Inst. v. Mathews, 413 F. Supp. 548 (D.D.C. 1976), *aff'd sub nom.*, American Frozen Food Inst. v. Califano, 555 F.2d 1059 (D.C. Cir. 1977).

[27]   21 C.F.R. § 102.26.

[28]   *Id.* § 102.54.

[29]   *Id.* §§ 101.3, 101.15, 102.5.

[30]   *Id.* § 101.3(d)

[31]   *Id.* § 1.24(a)(5)(iv).

[32]   21 U.S.C. § 343(e)(2).

[33]   FPLA § 4(a)(3), 15 U.S.C. § 1453(a)(3).

[34]   21 C.F.R. § 101.105(a).

[35]   *Id.* § 101.105(b)(1)-(2).

[36]   Pub. L. No. 102-329, 106 Stat. 847 (1992).

milliliters.[37] Although the final rule has not yet been issued, FDA expects manufacturers to use both the U.S. units of measure and metric units.

FDA's regulations provide that the quantity of contents of solid, semisolid, or viscous, or a mixture of solid and liquid products generally should be expressed in terms of weight, and the quantity of contents of liquid products generally should be expressed in terms of fluid measure.[38] The regulations also recognize, however, that a different "firmly established general consumer usage and trade custom" may be used instead.[39] Thus, ice cream, for example, although solid, is labeled customarily with a quantity of contents declaration expressed in terms of fluid measure (gallon, quart, or pint) instead of weight.

FDA has issued extensive, detailed regulations governing the declaration of quantity of contents.[40] For example, if the area of the principal display panel (PDP) exceeds five square inches the quantity of contents must appear in the lower 30 percent of the PDP and a declaration of quantity of contents must be separated from other printed label information appearing above or below the declaration "by at least a space equal to the height of the lettering used in the declaration."[41] This is designed to create a degree of consistency in the placement of these statements so that consumers will know where to look to find the information. The regulation should be consulted when designing any label to be certain that all technical requirements are met.

Name and Place of Business of Manufacturer, Packer, or Distributor

Section 403(e)(1) of the FDCA requires that a food in package form bear a label containing "the name and place of business of the manufacturer, packer, or distributor."[42] In an analogous provision, the FPLA provides for FDA to issue regulations requiring retail food packages to "bear a label specifying . . . the name and place of business of the manufacturer, packer, or distributor . . . ."[43] Pursuant to these statutory provisions, FDA has issued regulations providing that "[t]he label of a food in packaged form shall specify conspicuously the name and place of business of the manufacturer, packer, or distributor."[44]

It is not necessary for the label of a food to identify the actual manufacturer; it is equally satisfactory to identify the packer or distributor. For example, when a distributor of a food employs the services of a contract manufacturer, the label of the food may identify the distributor only, without also identifying the contract manufacturer. This often is an important concern of distributors who may not want the labels of their products to identify companies other than their own.

---

[37]   58 Fed. Reg. 29,716 (May 21, 1993). FDA proposed also to recodify the net quantity of contents regulation to 21 C.F.R. § 101.7. *See also* 58 Fed. Reg. 67,444 (Dec. 21, 1993).

[38]   21 C.F.R. § 101.105(a).

[39]   *Id.*

[40]   *Id.* § 101.105.

[41]   *Id.* § 101.105(f).

[42]   21 U.S.C. § 343(e)(1).

[43]   FPLA § 4(a)(1), 15 U.S.C. § 1453(a)(1).

[44]   21 C.F.R. § 101.5(a).

FDA regulations provide that "[w]here the food is not manufactured by the person whose name appears on the label, the name shall be qualified by a phrase that reveals the connection such person has with such food; such as 'Manufactured for _____ ,' 'Distributed by _____,' or any other wording that expresses the facts."[45]

Listing of Ingredients

Section 403(i) of the FDCA provides that a food shall be deemed to be misbranded:

> [u]nless its label bears . . . in case it is fabricated from two or more ingredients, the common or usual name of each such ingredient . . .; except that spices, flavorings, and colors not required to be certified under section 721(c) of this title, unless sold as spices, flavorings, or such colors, may be designated as spices, flavorings, and colorings without naming each.[46]

In addition, section 403(k) of the act provides that if a food "bears or contains any artificial flavoring, artificial coloring, or chemical preservative," it must bear labeling stating that fact.[47] FDA has published regulations interpreting the meanings of these terms and the status of particular ingredients, and describing the appropriate labeling for certain products.[48]

For example, the regulations provide that "[a] food to which a chemical preservative(s) is added shall . . . bear a label declaration stating both the common or usual name of the [preservative] ingredient(s) *and* a separate description of its function (e.g., 'to retard spoilage' or 'to help protect flavor')."[49]

Any color additive added to a food is considered by FDA to be an artificial color. While in other contexts FDA distinguishes between "natural" and "artificial" substances (e.g., "natural flavor" and "artificial flavor"),[50] the agency makes *no* such regulatory distinction for colors added to food. FDA's color additive ingredient labeling regulations for foods define artificial color as "*any* 'color additive' as defined in § 70.3(f)" of the agency's regulations.[51] Section 70.3(f) states that a color additive is:

> any material . . . that is a dye, pigment, or other substance made by a process of synthesis or similar artifice, *or extracted, isolated, or otherwise derived . . . from a vegetable, animal, mineral, or other source* and that . . . is capable . . . of imparting a color.[52]

Thus, a color additive added to a food is an artificial color regardless of whether the color is synthetic (artificial) or natural. FDA does not use the word "artificial" to denote a synthetic

---

45   *Id.* § 101.5(c).
46   21 U.S.C. § 343(i).
47   *Id.* § 343(k).
48   21 C.F.R. § 101.22.
49   *Id.* § 101.22(j) (emphasis added).
50   *Id.* §§ 101.22(a)(1), (a)(3).
51   *Id.* § 101.22(a)(4) (emphasis added).
52   *Id.* § 70.3(f) (emphasis added).

substance. Rather, a substance is artificial to a food because it is not normally present in the food (i.e., the food is artificially colored). Thus, even caramel and beet juice are considered "artificial colors" when used in a food although they are natural substances. FDA has stated in a compliance policy guide:

> The use of the words "food color added," "natural color," or similar words containing the term "food" or "natural" may be erroneously interpreted to mean the color is a naturally occurring constituent in the food. Since all added colors result in an artificially colored food, we would object to the declaration of any added color as "food" or "natural."[53]

This does not mean that all colors added to food must be identified on the label as artificial colors. The regulations provide that:

> Color additives not subject to certification may be declared as "Artificial Color," "Artificial Color Added," or "*Color Added*" (or by an equally informative term that makes clear that a color additive has been used in the food). *Alternatively*, such color additive may be declared as "Colored with _____" or "_____color," the blank to be filled with the name of the color additive.[54]

A color additive subject to certification also is not required to be identified as "artificial color" and must be identified by its proper name (e.g., FD&C Yellow No. 5).[55]

Section 403(w) requires more complete labeling of foods that contain the eight most common food allergens or ingredients containing protein derived from them.[56] The label must either:

- use the word "contains" followed by the name of the food source from which the major food allergen is derived (e.g., "Contains peanuts") or

- bear the common or usual name of the major food allergen in the ingredient list followed by the name of the food source from which the major food allergen is derived (e.g., "semolina (wheat)," "whey (milk)").

The name of the food source from which the major food allergen is derived is not required in parentheses next to the common or usual name of the food allergen in the ingredient list when the common or usual name uses the name of the food source or the name of the food source appears elsewhere in the ingredient list.

The eight major food allergen groups, as defined by section 201(qq)(1) of the FDCA, are: 1) milk; 2) eggs; 3) fish (e.g., bass, flounder, or cod); 4) crustacean shellfish (e.g., crab, lobster, or shrimp); 5) tree nuts (e.g., almonds, pecans, or walnuts); 6) wheat; 7) peanuts; and 8) soybeans. The term "major food allergen" also includes food ingredients that contain protein

---

[53]   FDA, Compliance Policy Guide No. 7127.01.

[54]   21 C.F.R. § 101.22(k)(2) (emphasis added).

[55]   *Id.* § 101.22(k)(1).

[56]   The Food Allergen Labeling and Consumer Protection Act of 2004 (FALCPA) amended the FDCA by adding sections 403(w) and 201(qq); *see* Pub. L. No. 108-282, tit. II, 118 Stat. 905, 905-11.

derived from one of the eight. The term "name of the food source from which the major food allergen is derived" refers to these major food allergen groups. In the case of tree nuts, fish, or crustacean shellfish, however, the specific type must be included in the declaration (e.g., almond, salmon, shrimp). Spices, flavoring, colorings, or incidental additives that are or that bear or contain a major food allergen must also adhere to the above outlined labeling requirements (e.g., "natural flavor (almond)").

Highly refined oils that are derived from any of the major allergen groups and ingredients from these highly refined oils are exempt from the labeling requirements. In addition, there is a petition and notification process to exempt certain food ingredients. Both exemption procedures involve submitting scientific evidence (including analytical method used) to demonstrate that there is no allergenic concern attributable to the substances.

Nutrition Labeling

The Nutrition Labeling and Education Act of 1990 (NLEA)[57] amended the FDCA to require standard-format nutrition labeling for most food products. NLEA added section 403(q)(1) to the FDCA, which provides that a food shall be deemed to be misbranded "if it is a food intended for human consumption and is offered for sale, unless its label or labeling bears nutrition information."[58] FDA has published regulations implementing this requirement, and describing the information that must be provided in nutrition labeling and the format that must be used to present this information.

Nutrition information must be provided on the basis of a "serving size" that is determined from the "reference amounts customarily consumed per eating occasion" that FDA has established for numerous categories of foods.[59] Nutrition labeling also must indicate the serving size on the basis of which the information is being provided.[60] The serving size declared in nutrition labeling and the reference amount established by FDA need not always agree. For example, although the reference amount for beverages is 240 milliliters (8 fluid ounces),[61] if a can of soda contains 12 fluid ounces, the manufacturer must use 12 fluid ounces as the serving size (e.g., one can (12 fluid ounces))[62] and provide the nutrition information on that basis.

In general, declaration of the following substances is mandatory in nutrition labeling: calories, calories from fat, total fat, saturated fat, trans fat,[63] cholesterol, sodium, total carbohydrate, dietary fiber, sugars, protein, vitamin A, vitamin C, calcium, and iron.[64] Other nutrients such as potassium and soluble fiber may be declared voluntarily, except that their declaration is mandatory if a claim is made in the labeling about the nutrient.[65] In addition, vitamins and minerals that are added as a nutrient supplement to a food must be

---

[57] Pub. L. No. 101-535, 104 Stat. 2353.

[58] 21 U.S.C. § 343(q)(1).

[59] 21 C.F.R. § 101.9(b)(1), 101.12.

[60] Id. § 101.9(d)(3)(i).

[61] Id. § 101.12(b) (table 2).

[62] Id. § 101.9(b)(6).

[63] Trans fat became a mandatory element of the Nutrition Facts box beginning on January 1, 2006. See 68 Fed. Reg. 41,433 (July 11, 2003).

[64] 21 C.F.R. § 101.9(c)(1)-(8).

[65] Id. § 101.9(c)(5), (c)(6)(i)(A).

declared.[66] No nutrients or food components other than those specifically authorized to be declared may appear in nutrition labeling.[67]

The amount of the nutrient (except for vitamins and minerals) and the percentage of the "Daily Value" of that nutrient provided by the food, when established,[68] must be included in the nutrition labeling.[69] The percentage of the "Daily Value" of a nutrient provided by a food is determined from the Daily Reference Values (DRVs) that FDA has established for macronutrients such as carbohydrates and fat, and the Reference Daily Intakes (RDIs) that the agency has established for micronutrients such as vitamins and minerals.[70] FDA used a 2,000-calorie per day diet as the basis in establishing DRVs and RDIs.[71]

There are several exemptions from the nutrition labeling requirements (e.g., small businesses, foods of no nutritional significance, and medical foods).[72]

Section 403(q)(5)(i)-(ii) of the FDCA requires the disclosure of calorie information on menus or menu boards for foods sold by restaurants and other retail food establishments with 20 or more locations. In addition, the restaurant or retail food establishment must inform the consumer about the availability of (and have available to the consumer upon request) additional nutrition information. Section 403(q)(5)(iii) requires the disclosure of calorie information for foods sold in a vending machine that is operated by a person who owns or operates 20 or more vending machines. FDA has published regulations to clarify these requirements.

The nutrition labeling regulations are detailed and complicated. They should be consulted to be certain that all requirements are met.

Nutrient Content Claims and Health Claims

NLEA added new sections to the FDCA to govern the use of nutrient content claims and health claims in food labeling. The Food and Drug Administration Modernization Act of 1997 (FDAMA) created additional mechanisms for notifying FDA of nutrient content and health claims. Prior to FDAMA, nutrient content and health claims could be used only if FDA, following a lengthy petition process, issued a regulation authorizing the claim. Under new procedures set forth in FDAMA, manufacturers may use a claim that is based on an "authoritative statement" of an appropriate governmental scientific body if the manufacturer

---

[66]   *Id.* § 101.9(c)(8)(ii).

[67]   *Id.* § 101.9(c).

[68]   *Id.* For example, FDA has not established daily values for trans fat or sugars.

[69]   *Id.* § 101.9(d)(7)-(8). Declaration of the percentage of the Daily Value of protein is voluntary, unless the labeling bears a claim about protein. *Id.* § 101.9(c)(7)(i). FDA exempted protein from this requirement because protein deficiency is not a concern in the U.S. diet and the analytical tests needed to determine the protein digestibility-corrected amino acid score of the protein in a food are very expensive. 58 Fed. Reg. 2079, 2102 (Jan. 6, 1993).

[70]   21 C.F.R. §§ 101.9(c)(9), (c)(8)(iv).

[71]   *Id.* § 101.9(c)(9).

[72]   *Id.* § 101.9(j)(1), (j)(4), (j)(8).

notifies FDA of the claim at least 120 days before marketing and FDA fails to object to the claim.

Nutrition Content Claims

Section 403(r)(1)(A) of the FDCA provides that any claim in the label or labeling of a food "which expressly or by implication . . . characterizes the level of any nutrient which is of the type required . . . to be [in nutrition labeling]" may be made only if the characterization of the level made in the claim uses terms that have been defined by FDA in a regulation.[73] This section of the FDCA was intended to address food-labeling claims such as "high in fiber" and "low fat." For example, based on this authority, FDA has published regulations establishing the conditions under which a food may claim to be a "good source" of a nutrient, "low in fat," "sodium free," "lite," and "low calorie." Section 206 of the Food Allergen Labeling and Consumer Protection Act of 2004 (FALCPA) required FDA to establish a definition for "gluten free" and as a result, FDA published a regulation to define the term.[74]

For example, the label of a food may state "fat free," "free of fat," "no fat," "zero fat," "without fat," "nonfat," "trivial source of fat," "negligible source of fat" or "dietarily insignificant source of fat" if

- (i) [t]he food contains less than 0.5 grams (g) of fat per reference amount . . . and per labeled serving . . .;
- (ii) [t]he food contains no added ingredient that is a fat or is generally understood by consumers to contain fat unless the listing of the ingredient in the ingredient statement is followed by an asterisk that refers to the statement below the list of ingredients, which states "adds a trivial amount of fat," "adds a negligible amount of fat," or "adds a dietarily insignificant amount of fat;" and
- (iii) [i]f the food meets these conditions without the benefit of special processing, alteration, formulation, or reformulation to lower fat content, it is labeled to disclose that fat is not usually present in the food (e.g., "broccoli, a fat free food").[75]

FDA also has established "general principles" applicable to nutrient content claims.[76] For example, if the food contains more than 13 grams of fat, 4 grams of saturated fat, 60 milligrams of cholesterol or 480 milligrams of sodium per reference amount and per labeled serving, the food must disclose, as part of the referral statement, that the nutrient exceeding the specified level is present in the food as follows: "See nutrition information for _____ content."[77]

FDA has defined some nutrient content claims in relation to the RDIs and DRVs established by the agency. For example, the terms "high," "rich in," or "excellent source of" may be used if the food contains 20 percent or more of the RDI or the DRV of the nutrient per reference

---

[73] 21 U.S.C. § 343(r)(1)(A).

[74] See FALCPA, *supra* note 56; 21 C.F.R. § 101.91.

[75] 21 C.F.R. §§ 101.62(b)(1)(i)-(iii).

[76] *See id.* § 101.13.

[77] *Id.* § 101.13(h)(1).

amount; the terms "good source," "contains," and "provides" may be used if the food contains 10 percent to 19 percent of the RDI or the DRV of the nutrient per reference amount.[78] Thus, FDA has taken the position that if there is no RDI or DRV for a nutrient, the label for a food that contains the nutrient may not claim that the product "contains [nutrient]" or "provides [nutrient]."[79] In such cases, the defined term may be used only if the specific amount of the nutrient is stated in the claim (e.g., provides [amount] of [nutrient] per serving).[80]

FDAMA nutrient content claim notifications have been submitted without FDA objection for choline and linoleic acid.[81]

Health Claims

Section 403(r)(1)(B) of the FDCA provides that any claim in the label or labeling of a food that "expressly or by implication . . . characterizes the relationship of any nutrient which is of the type required . . . to be [in nutrition labeling] to a disease or a health-related condition" may be made only if the claim has been authorized by FDA in a regulation.[82] In the regulations implementing this provision, FDA has named this type of claim a "health claim" and has defined it as:

> any claim made on the label or in labeling of a food . . . that expressly or by implication, including "third party" references, written statements (e.g., a brand name including a term such as "heart"), symbols (e.g., a heart symbol), or vignettes, characterizes the relationship of any substance to a disease or health-related condition.[83]

FDA defines "disease or health-related condition" as:

> damage to an organ, part, structure, or system of the body such that it does not function properly (e.g., cardiovascular disease), or a state of health leading to such dysfunctioning (e.g., hypertension); except that diseases resulting from essential nutrient deficiencies (e.g., scurvy, pellagra) are not included in this definition).[84]

Because the FDCA defines "drug," in part, as an article "intended for use in the diagnosis, cure, mitigation, treatment, or prevention of disease,"[85] the FDCA also provides that a food

---

[78]   *Id.* § 101.54(b) and (c).
[79]   *See Center for Food Safety and Applied Nutrition, FDA, Food Labeling Questions & Answers*, 37 (1993).
[80]   *Id.*
[81]   FDA also published a final rule regarding nutrient content claims for omega-3 fatty acids alpha-linoleic acid (ALA), eicosapentaenoic acid (EPA), and docosahexaenoic acid (DHA). See 79 Fed. Reg. 23,262 (Apr. 28, 2014). The rule prohibits the use of DHA- and EPA-related nutrient content claims and some ALA-related nutrient content claims that had been the subject of FDAMA notifications. The rule also explains that FDA will not take action against certain ALA claims at this time. Of course, quantitative statements relating to all three of these substances would be permitted.
[82]   21 U.S.C. § 343(r)(1)(B).
[83]   21 C.F.R. § 101.14(a)(1).
[84]   *Id.* § 101.14(a)(6).
[85]   FDCA § 201(g)(1)(B), 21 U.S.C. § 321(g)(1)(B).

for which a health claim is made in accordance with FDA's regulations "is not a drug . . . solely because the label or labeling contains such a claim."[86]

Certain foods are disqualified from bearing health claims, unless specifically authorized in the regulations:

* Foods that contain more than 13 grams of fat, 4 grams of saturated fat, 60 milligrams of cholesterol, 480 milligrams of sodium per reference amount and per labeled serving size (and per 50 grams for foods with a RACC of 30 grams or 2 tablespoons or less).[87]

* Foods represented or purported for consumption by infants and toddlers less than two years of age.[88]

* Foods that do not provide, prior to any nutrient additions, 10 percent or more of the RDI or DRV for vitamin A, vitamin C, iron, calcium, protein, or fiber per reference amount.[89]

A substance in food is eligible for consideration as the subject of a health claim:

* if the substance is "associated with a disease or health-related condition for which the general U.S. population, or an identified U.S. population subgroup, is at risk";[90]

* if the substance is to be consumed as a component of a conventional food at decreased dietary levels, the substance is a fat, a saturated fat, cholesterol, sodium, a carbohydrate, a sugar, dietary fiber, or protein, or one that FDA has required to be included in nutrition labeling;[91] and

* if the substance is to be consumed at other than decreased dietary levels, a) the substance contributes taste, aroma or nutritive value, or has other technical effect in the food, and retains that attribute when consumed at levels that are necessary to justify the claim, and b) the substance is a food or food ingredient or component of a food ingredient whose use at the levels necessary to justify the claim has been demonstrated to be safe and lawful under the food safety provisions of the FDCA.[92]

FDA may authorize a health claim if the agency determines, based on the totality of publicly available scientific evidence, that there is "significant scientific agreement" (SSA) among experts qualified by scientific training and experience to evaluate such claims that the claim is supported by such evidence.[93] To date, FDA has authorized 12 SSA health claims concerning the relationship between: 1) calcium and osteoporosis, 2) fat and cancer, 3) sodium and hypertension, 4) saturated fat/cholesterol and heart disease, 5) fiber-containing grains/fruits/vegetables and cancer, 6) fiber-containing grains/fruits/vegetables and heart disease, 7) fruits/vegetables containing antioxidant vitamins or fiber and cancer, 8) folate and neural tube defects, 9) dietary noncariogenic carbohydrate sweeteners and dental caries, 10) soluble fiber from certain foods and heart disease, 11) soy protein and

---

[86] FDCA § 201(g)(1), 21 U.S.C. § 321(g)(1).
[87] 21 C.F.R. § 101.14(a)(5), (e)(3).
[88] Id. § 101.14(e)(5).
[89] Id. § 101.14(e)(6).
[90] 21 C.F.R. § 101.14(b)(1).
[91] Id. § 101.14(b)(2).
[92] Id. § 101.14(b)(3).
[93] Id. § 101.14(c).

heart disease, and 12) plant sterol/stanol esters and heart disease.[94] FDA considered, but did not authorize, health claims concerning the relationship between fiber and heart disease, and zinc and immune function in the elderly.[95]

FDAMA health claim notifications have been submitted without FDA objection for 1) whole grain foods and reduced risk of heart disease and certain cancers, 2) whole grain foods with moderate fat content and reduced risk of heart disease, 3) potassium and reduced risk of high blood pressure and stroke, 4) fluoridated water and reduced risk of dental caries, 5) saturated fat, cholesterol, and trans fat and reduced risk of heart disease and 6) substitute of saturated fat with unsaturated fat and reduced risk of heart disease.

The continuing viability of the SSA standard was called into question in the case of *Pearson, et al. v. Shalala, et al.*[96] In short, the *Pearson* court indicated FDA's application of NLEA's significant scientific standard to dietary supplements to be unconstitutionally vague. While the court limited its holding to dietary supplements, the standard is also unconstitutional when applied to conventional foods.[97] Indeed, FDA decided to apply *Pearson* through the *Interim Procedures for Qualified Health Claims in the Labeling of Conventional Human Food and Human Dietary Supplements*. FDA currently permits qualified health claims that are supported by adequate scientific evidence if the use of disclaimers would remove the possibility that the claims may otherwise be misleading.

Pearson, at first blush, appears to be a significant blow to FDA's ability to regulate "health claims." While the court's decision does place some limitations on FDA's ability to prohibit outright a particular health claim, the decision leaves FDA's basic authority to regulate health claims intact. Yet, the decision does signal a willingness among the courts to scrutinize FDA's decision to restrict the type of health claims that may appear on product labels and labeling if there is some reasonable scientific basis for the claim. More specifically, the court suggested, without concluding, that FDA may be required under the First Amendment to allow health claims if the quality of scientific evidence in support of the claim is at least equal to the quality of scientific evidence against the claim; i.e., the scientific evidence is inconclusive. The court further stated, however, that FDA could require that an equally prominent disclaimer appear as part of the claim if prohibiting the claim outright would violate the commercial speech doctrine of the First Amendment.

On October 6, 2000, FDA issued an interim enforcement strategy for dietary supplement health claims under which claims would be permitted if they are supported by—to borrow a legal phrase—a preponderance of evidence.[98] Under the interim standard, FDA denied the folic acid and fiber claims at issue in *Pearson*. Moreover, where FDA deemed a qualified claim to meet the lower "preponderance" threshold, the versions suggested by FDA are of such little value that they constitute a denial of the requested claim as a practical matter.

---

[94]   *Id.* §§ 101.72-101.83.
[95]   *Id.* § 101.71.
[96]   164 F.3d 650 (D.C. Cir. 1999).
[97]   67 Fed. Reg. 78,003 (Dec. 18, 2002).
[98]   65 Fed. Reg. 59,855 (Oct. 6, 2000).

In July 2003, FDA issued Guidance on the Interim Evidence-Based Ranking System for Scientific Data. The interim guidance, which has since been withdrawn, describes a process the agency uses to evaluate and rank the scientific evidence in support of a substance/disease relationship that is the subject of a qualified health claim petition. The system provided a means by which the totality of the publicly available scientific evidence relevant to a substance/disease relationship could be assigned to one of four ranked levels. In particular, the guidance established a process whereby FDA could categorize the qualified health claim into one of three levels (i.e., a "B," "C," or "D" level) based on the strength of the scientific evidence being used to support the health claims:

- Level B . . . "although there is scientific evidence supporting the claim, the evidence is not conclusive.",

- Level C "Some scientific evidence suggests . . . however, FDA has determined that this evidence is limited and not conclusive." and

- Level D "Very limited and preliminary scientific research suggests . . . FDA concludes that there is little scientific evidence supporting this claim."

In January 2009, FDA replaced the interim guidance with its Guidance on the Evidence-Based Review System for the Scientific Evaluation of Health Claims.[99] The final guidance identifies the type of studies that FDA will consider in its assessment of health claims and the criteria the agency will use in evaluating the studies. FDA replaced the standard qualifying language used for Level B, C and D claims found in the interim guidance stating, "[w]hen the evidence for a substance-disease relationship is credible but does not meet the SSA standard, then the proposed claim for the relationship should include qualifying language that identifies limits to the level of scientific evidence to support the relationship."[100]

FDA has issued numerous letters of enforcement discretion and letters of denial for qualified health claims, some of which are applicable exclusively to dietary supplements and others exclusively to conventional foods.

In addition to qualified health claims, FDA has also taken the position that "structure/function" claims, which were permitted under legislation for dietary supplements, would also be permitted for conventional foods. "Structure/function" claims are claims that describe the effect of a food or nutrient on the structure or function of the body. FDA has not issued regulations that identify the type of structure/function claims that may be made for conventional foods. The agency has issued a regulation for the use of such claims on dietary supplements at 21 C.F.R. § 101.93(f). While the final regulation is limited to the claims that may be made for dietary supplements, FDA acknowledges that it is likely "to interpret the dividing line between structure/function claims and disease claims in a similar manner for conventional foods as for dietary supplements."[101]

For foods, it appears that the claim must be based on the nutritive value of the food or nutrient (e.g., "cranberry products help maintain urinary tract health." or "calcium builds

99   FDA, Guidance for Industry: Evidence-Based Review System for the Scientific Evaluation of Health Claims - Final (Jan. 2009).

100   Id.

101   65 Fed. Reg. 1000, 1034 (Jan. 6, 2000).

strong bones and teeth.").[102] FDA has not objected to the use of "helps maintain cholesterol levels within the normal range" and similar claims on the label of some conventional foods containing stanol and sterol esters, which function by blocking the body's absorption of cholesterol. With regard to the health claims for stanol and sterol esters, FDA concluded these substances had nutritive value because they have an effect on the digestive process, which is a function of the body.[103] Structure/function claims must not suggest that food is useful in the diagnosis, cure, treatment, or prevention or mitigation of a disease or health-related condition. For example, FDA would likely take issue with the claim "folic acid helps reduce the accumulation of plaque on arterial walls" because the buildup of plaque on arterial walls is an indicator of arteriosclerosis, a disease condition.

Other Labeling Issues

"Imitation" Foods

Section 403(c) of the FDCA provides that a food that is an "imitation" of another shall be clearly labeled as such and a product is misbranded "if it is an imitation of another food, unless its label bears, in type of uniform size and prominence, the word 'imitation' and, immediately thereafter, the name of the food imitated."[104] The agency intends the imitation regulations to encourage new substitute foods to be formulated as nutritionally equivalent to their traditional counterparts.[105] The act does not define the term "imitation" but by regulation has provided that a food will be subject to this labeling requirement "if it is a substitute for and resembles another food but is nutritionally inferior to that food."[106] Conversely, the regulations provide that a food that is a substitute for and resembles another food shall not be deemed to be an imitation if: 1) the new food is not nutritionally inferior to the food for which it substitutes and that it resembles; and 2) the new food bears a distinctive common or usual name that accurately identifies or describes its basic nature.[107]

If the product is not nutritionally inferior to the product imitated, the word "imitation" does not need to be used as part of the product name. Of course, the standardized name may not be used, but a "common or usual name" or "an appropriately descriptive term" may be used. For example, products that substitute for and resemble mayonnaise or eggs may be identified as "mayonnaise substitute" or "egg substitute."

Fresh Descriptor

FDA regulates the use of the descriptor "fresh" and its related terms (e.g., "fresh frozen").[108] FDA's regulation includes the use of the term in a brand name or as a sensory modifier (e.g., to describe the food's texture, color, flavor, or taste) whenever the term suggests or

---

[102]   62 Fed. Reg. 49,859, 49,860 (Sept. 23, 1997).

[103]   65 Fed. Reg. 54,685, 54,688 (Sept. 8, 2000).

[104]   21 U.S.C. § 343(c).

[105]   Stephen McNamara, *Some Legal Aspects of Providing a Sufficient Food Supply for a Hungry Population,* 30 Food Drug Cosm. L.J. 527, 530-31 (1975).

[106]   21 C.F.R. § 101.3; *see also* United States v. 651 Cases Chil-Zeri, 114 F. Supp. 430 (N.D.N.Y 1953).

[107]   21 C.F.R. § 101.3(e)(2).

[108]   21 C.F.R. § 101.95.

implies that the food is unprocessed or unpreserved. Uses of the term that do not suggest that the food is unprocessed—such as "fresh bread" and "fresh milk"—are not subject to the definition.

The term "fresh" is generally limited to use on foods that have not been subject to freezing, thermal processing, or any kind of chemical processing. The addition of approved waxes or coatings, the post-harvest use of pesticides, the application of a mild chlorine or mild acid wash on raw produce, and the treatment of raw foods with ionizing radiation at a level less than or equal to 1 kilogray do not preclude the use of the term "fresh." Similarly, refrigeration does not preclude the use of the term "fresh." A food made with concentrated or processed ingredients, however, is not considered fresh and may not bear the term. It is not clear how FDA will view the use of the term "fresh" on foods made with processed ingredients, such as bleached flour in bread.

The terms "fresh frozen" and "frozen fresh" may be used to describe a food that is "quickly frozen" while still fresh or when recently harvested. FDA has determined that a food is "quickly frozen" if it is frozen by a method such as blast-freezing that ensures quick freezing of the entire food portion with virtually no deterioration.

Regarding the use of the term "fresh" to describe ingredients in a processed food, FDA indicates that it will regulate this practice on a case-by-case basis and take action under section 403(a) of the FDCA if such use is misleading. The agency noted, however, that "consumers generally are not misled when such statements are made . . . provided that the statements clearly refer to the ingredients and do not imply that the food itself is unprocessed."[109]

FDA has not specifically defined the term "freshly" when used to modify such terms as prepared, baked, roasted, etc., and it apparently intends to regulate the use of these phrases on a case-by-case basis (e.g., how recently the food was prepared before being offered for sale). The agency has, however, provided guidance on its appropriate use. To qualify as being freshly prepared or made, the food must actually have been prepared from a recipe. Simply opening a can and emptying the contents into a display container does not qualify.[110] The presence of processed ingredients in a food does not prohibit the use of the term "freshly."[111] Further, as with foods described as "fresh," refrigeration is allowed for foods bearing the term "freshly."

Natural Claims

Although FDA has not issued a specific regulation defining the term "natural," as used to describe food, the agency has adopted an informal policy regarding use of the term. This policy states that the term "natural" means:

---

[109]   58 Fed. Reg. 2405 (Jan. 6, 1993).
[110]   56 Fed. Reg. 60,464 (Nov. 27, 1991).
[111]   56 Fed. Reg. at 60,465.

nothing artificial or synthetic has been included in, or has been added to, a food that would not normally be expected to be in the food.[112]

Except as to "flavors" and "colors," FDA has not defined or issued guidance on the terms "synthetic" or "artificial." Additional guidance regarding the use of the term "natural" can be found in FDA's regulation defining the term "natural flavor."[113] This regulation states that the term "natural flavor" means:

> the essential oil, oleoresin, essence or extractive, protein hydrolysate, distillate, or any product of roasting, heating or enzymolysis . . . of a spice, fruit or fruit juice, vegetable or vegetable juice, edible yeast, herb, bark, bud, root, leaf or similar plant material . . . or fermentation products thereof.

Importantly, FDA interprets its "natural flavor" regulation as strictly limiting the chemical reactions that may be used to produce natural flavors; specifically, FDA considers that only the products of "roasting, heating, or enzymolysis" reactions are "natural flavors."[114] With regard to colors, it is FDA's position that any added color is an artificial color, even if the added color is from a source considered to be "natural" (e.g., beet juice).[115] FDA's rationale for this position is that a color must inherently exist in the food to be natural; if the color is added to the food, it cannot be natural.[116] FDA also has indicated that it is false and misleading for a food containing added color to be labeled as "natural" or "all natural." The agency has issued several Warning Letters to food manufacturers for describing finished products as "natural" or "all natural" when the food contains added color. Finally, we note that a lack of a formal definition from FDA has resulted in numerous consumer class action lawsuits. Thus, it is important to assure that use of a "natural" claim does not otherwise render the label false or misleading.

Country of Origin Labeling

Section 304 of the Tariff Act of 1930, as amended, provides that all articles of foreign origin, or their containers, imported into the United States shall be legibly and conspicuously marked to indicate the English name of the country of origin to the ultimate purchaser in the United States, unless specifically exempted. The purpose of the country of origin labeling requirements, set forth in 19 C.F.R. Part 134, is to ensure that consumers are aware of the country of origin of articles so they may choose between buying domestic or foreign products.[117] Under these rules, country of origin is determined on the basis of one of two tests, depending on the country from which the product is being imported—the traditional "substantial transformation" test, or the relatively new "tariff shift" test. Under

---

[112]   58 Fed. Reg. at 2407.

[113]   21 C.F.R. § 101.22(a)(3).

[114]   *See* April 1, 1992 Warning Letter issued to Fries & Fries, Inc.

[115]   *Accord* 21 C.F.R. 101.22(a)(4); *see also* COMPLIANCE POLICY GUIDE No. 7127.01.

[116]   *See* COMPLIANCE POLICY GUIDE No. 7127.01.

[117]   We note that "Made in the USA" claims are regulated by the Federal Trade Commission (FTC); *see* FTC's Enforcement Policy Statement on U.S. Origin Claims *available at* http://www.ftc.gov/public-statements/1997/12/enforcement-policy-statement-us-origin-claims; *see also* 62 Fed. Reg. 63,755 (Dec. 2, 1997).

the "substantial transformation" test, an article that is not wholly grown or manufactured in one country will be considered to be the product of the country in which it last underwent a substantial transformation. A "substantial transformation" has traditionally been defined as a change that results in a new or different article of commerce with a new name, character, or use. The "substantial transformation" test currently applies to all goods imported into the United States from countries not part of the North American Free Trade Agreement (NAFTA). For imports from NAFTA countries—i.e., Canada and Mexico—Customs applies the "tariff shift" test, where a good is deemed transformed if it has undergone a sufficient change in tariff classification. There are specific tariff shift rules for each category of goods.

In addition, the 2002 Farm Bill, which was signed into law on May 13, 2002, contained a provision requiring mandatory country of origin labeling for fresh fruits and vegetables, peanuts, fish, and meat (e.g., beef, lamb, and pork). The law, which is implemented by USDA's Agricultural Marketing Service (AMS), requires retailers to inform consumers, at the final point of purchase, of the commodity's country of origin. Commodities that are ingredients in processed products are not subject to the labeling requirements. After some legislative delays, the requirements went into effect for beef, pork, lamb, chicken, goat, perishable agricultural commodities (fresh and frozen fruits and vegetables), peanuts, pecans, ginseng, and macadamia nuts on September 30, 2008 (they had already gone into effect for fish and shellfish on April 4, 2005).[118]

Label Warnings

The FDCA does not explicitly authorize FDA to require label warnings on food products. Nevertheless, perceiving risks to consumers from improper use of certain self-pressurized products, FDA has published regulations requiring several label warnings. The most general warning applies to most food products in self-pressurized containers: "**Warning**—Avoid spraying in eyes. Contents under pressure. Do not puncture or incinerate. Do not store at temperature above 120°F. Keep out of reach of children."[119]

Although these food label warning requirements were not challenged in court, the cosmetics industry challenged companion warnings for cosmetics in self-pressurized containers, which had been issued by FDA at the same time and under analogous statutory authority. In judicial decisions that would appear to be applicable also to FDA's food label warning regulations, the U.S. District Court for the District of Columbia and the U.S. Court of Appeals for the District of Columbia Circuit ruled that FDA's cosmetic label warning requirements for products in self-pressurized containers were a proper exercise of the agency's authority.[120]

FDA also has promulgated another food label warning regulation. In response to reports of illnesses and deaths associated with the use of protein products in very low-calorie diets for rapid weight loss, FDA required several alternative warnings cautioning consumers about these potential consequences. A trade association whose membership included manufacturers of dry, whole protein products challenged the regulation in court. The U.S.

[118] 73 Fed. Reg. 45,106 (Aug. 1, 2008) and 69 Fed. Reg. 59,708 (Oct. 5, 2004).
[119] 21 C.F.R. § 101.17(a)(1).
[120] Cosmetic, Toiletry and Fragrance Ass'n v. Schmidt, 409 F. Supp. 57 (D.D.C. 1976), *aff'd mem. sub. nom.*, Cosmetic Toiletry and Fragrance Ass'n v. Kennedy, No. 76-1242 (D.C. Cir. Aug. 19, 1977).

District Court for the District of Columbia held that FDA had the authority to impose the label requirements.[121]

Foods for Special Dietary Uses

Section 403(j) of the FDCA provides that if a food "purports to be or is represented for special dietary uses," FDA may issue regulations requiring declaration on the label of "such information concerning its vitamin, mineral, and other dietary properties as [FDA] determines to be . . . necessary in order fully to inform purchasers as to its value for such uses."[122]

Relying on this authority, FDA has published regulations that require additional information on the labels of certain foods for special dietary use, included hypoallergenic foods,[123] infant foods,[124] and foods represented to have "usefulness in reducing or maintaining body weight.[125]

Special dietary food-labeling regulations are subject to the procedural requirements of section 701(e) of the FDCA, including the requirement that FDA provide an opportunity for a formal evidentiary hearing.[126] These procedures have been criticized as unwieldy and extremely time-consuming. In recent years, FDA generally has been reluctant to undertake section 701(e) rulemaking proceedings, at least when there is a likelihood of substantial controversy in a proceeding.[127]

Nutritional Quality Guidelines

A nutritional quality guideline prescribes the minimum level or range of nutrient composition (nutritional quality) appropriate for a given class of food.[128] A food product that complies with all requirements of an applicable nutritional quality guideline is permitted to bear the label statement, "This product provides nutrients in amounts appropriate for this class of food as determined by the U.S. Government."[129]

A nutritional quality guideline also operates to deter nutritional fortification that FDA believes is inappropriate (e.g., "overloading" a food product with excessive added vitamins).

---

[121]   Council for Responsible Nutrition v. Goyan, Food Drug Cosm. L. Rep. (CCH) § 50,208.151 (D.D.C. 1980). FDA eventually withdrew the regulation because the court questioned whether there was sufficient evidence to require some of the alternative warnings. The final regulation was again promulgated in 1984. 49 Fed. Reg. 13,679 (Apr. 6, 1984) (codified at 21 C.F.R. § 101.17(d)). Challenges to the 1984 final regulation were unsuccessful. Council for Responsible Nutrition v. Novitch, Food Drug Cosm. L. Rep. (CCH) § 50,208.20 (D.D.C. 1984); National Nutritional Foods Ass'n v. Novitch, 589 F. Supp. 798 (S.D.N.Y. 1984).

[122]   21 U.S.C. § 343(j).

[123]   21 C.F.R. § 105.62.

[124]   *Id.* § 105.65.

[125]   *Id.* § 105.66.

[126]   21 U.S.C. § 371(e).

[127]   *See* discussion of the procedural requirements of 21 U.S.C. § 371(e) in Robert W. Hamilton, *Rulemaking on a Record by the Food and Drug Administration,* 50 Tex. L. Rev. 1132 (1972); Robert W. Hamilton, *Procedures for the Adoption of Rules of General Applicability: The Need for Procedural Innovation in Administrative Rulemaking,* 60 Cal. L. Rev. 1276, 1283-93 (1972); Merrill & Collier, *supra* note 12, at 81-84.

[128]   21 C.F.R. § 104.5(a).

[129]   *Id.* § 104.5(b).

The general principles governing nutritional quality guidelines provide that if a product is within a class of food for which a guideline has been established, and a nutrient has been added to the product that is not within the guideline, the product is required to bear the label statement, "The addition of _____ to (or 'The addition of _____ at the level contained in') this product has been determined by the U.S. Government to be unnecessary and inappropriate and does not increase the dietary value of the food."[130]

Only one nutritional quality guideline has become final—the guideline for frozen "heat and serve" dinners.[131] FDA appears to have little interest in issuing additional nutritional quality guidelines.

Requirements for Particular Products

In addition to the requirements discussed above, both FDA and Congress have established other labeling requirements for particular foods.

Salt. In an effort to encourage the addition of iodide to salt, and to advise consumers when iodide has not been added, FDA has issued a regulation requiring the statement, "This salt supplies iodide, a necessary nutrient" on iodized salt for human use, and the statement, "This salt does not supply iodide, a necessary nutrient" on salt for human food use to which iodide has not been added.[132]

Aspartame. FDA's food additive regulation that authorizes the use of the sweetener aspartame provides that food products sweetened with this ingredient must carry a special cautionary statement for persons suffering from phenylketonuria: "Phenylketonurics: Contains Phenylalanime."[133]

Saccharin. In 1978, Congress amended the FDCA to require a label warning on food products containing the artificial sweetener saccharin. The required warning reads: "Use Of This Product May Be Hazardous To Your Health. This Product Contains Saccharin Which Has Been Determined to Cause Cancer In Laboratory Animals."[134]

Juice-Containing Beverages. Section 403(i)(2) of the FDCA provides that a food purporting to be a beverage containing vegetable or fruit juice must state "with appropriate prominence on the information panel . . . the total percentage of such fruit or vegetable juice contained in the food."[135] FDA has promulgated regulations implementing this requirement.[136]

---

[130]   *Id.* § 104.5(f).
[131]   *Id.* § 104.47.
[132]   *Id.* § 100.155(a)-(b).
[133]   *Id.* § 172.804(e)(2).
[134]   21 U.S.C. § 343(o)(1).
[135]   *Id.* § 343(i)(2).
[136]   21 C.F.R. § 101.30. *See also id.* § 102.33, which is FDA's common or usual name regulation for beverages that contain fruit or vegetable juice.

General Prohibition Against False or Misleading Labeling

In addition to the basic label requirements discussed above, there is a basic prohibition against false or misleading labeling. Section 403(a) of the FDCA provides that a food shall be deemed to be misbranded if "its labeling [is] false or misleading in any particular."[137] Over the years, FDA has taken regulatory action against numerous food products that the agency concluded bore false or misleading labels, or that were accompanied by false or misleading labeling. Generally, the courts have upheld a high standard of consumer protection in interpreting this section of the act.[138]

Expanding on section 403(a), section 201(n) of the act provides that:

> If an article is alleged to be misbranded because the labeling . . . is misleading, then in determining whether the labeling . . . is misleading there shall be taken into account (among other things) not only representations made or suggested by statement, word, design, device, or any combination thereof, but also the extent to which the labeling . . . fails to reveal facts material in the light of such representations or material with respect to consequences which may result from the use of the article to which the labeling . . . relates under the conditions of use prescribed in the labeling . . . thereof or under such conditions of use as are customary or usual.[139]

Thus, food labeling may be false or misleading not only for what it affirmatively states, but also for what it fails to state in the light of those affirmative statements.

Format and Placement Requirements

The Principal Display Panel and the Information Panel

The FPLA defines "principal display panel" (PDP) as "that part of a label that is most likely to be displayed, presented, shown, or examined under normal and customary conditions of display for retail sale."[140] FDA regulations repeat this basic definition and provide further details.[141]

---

[137] 21 U.S.C. § 343(a).

[138] *E.g.*, United States v. Ninety-Five Barrels . . . Apple Cider Vinegar, 265 U.S. 438 (1924) (construing language, including prohibition of labeling that was "false or misleading in any particular," in the Pure Food and Drugs Act of 1906, Pub. L. No. 59-384, § 8, 34 Stat. 768 (1906), the predecessor statute to the FDCA); United States v. An Article of Food . . . Nuclomin, 482 F.2d 581 (8th Cir. 1973); United States v. An Article of Food . . . "Manischewitz . . . Diet Thins," 377 F. Supp. 746 (E.D.N.Y. 1974); United States v. An Article of Food . . . 432 Cartons . . . Candy Lollipops, 292 F. Supp. 839 (S.D.N.Y. 1968).

[139] 21 U.S.C. § 321(n).

[140] 15 U.S.C. § 1459(f).

[141] 21 C.F.R. § 101.1.

In addition to the PDP, FDA regulations have created an "information panel,"[142] defined (with certain exceptions) as "that part of the label immediately contiguous and to the right of the principal display panel as observed by an individual facing the principal display panel."[143]

The FPLA provides that the quantity of contents shall be required by regulation to appear on the PDP,[144] and FDA has so required.[145] In the exercise of its discretion, FDA also has required that the statement of identity appear on the PDP.[146] Other mandatory labeling usually may be placed "either on the principal display panel or on the information panel."[147]

Conclusion

In general, food labeling is governed by the FDCA, the FPLA, and related FDA regulations. Most foods are required to bear informative labeling, including a product statement of identity; information about the quantity of contents; a statement of the name and place of business of the manufacturer, packer, or distributor; list of ingredients, including allergen information; and nutrition information. Additional information may be required for certain foods. Moreover, false or misleading information is prohibited.

---

[142]   *Id.* § 101.2.
[143]   *Id.* § 101.2(a).
[144]   15 U.S.C. § 1453(a)(2).
[145]   21 C.F.R. § 101.105(a).
[146]   *Id.* § 101.3(a).
[147]   *Id.* § 101.2(b).

CHAPTER 4
FOOD AND DRUG PACKAGING

....

DEVON WM. HILL AND DEBORAH C. ATTWOOD

Introduction

Each year FDA receives nearly ten times the number of requests to approve the use of new food contact materials as it does for additives used directly in food. Over the past several years, there has been an increase in the awareness and scrutiny of the safety of these materials. Even though there has not been a food safety issue attributable to a food contact material, the growing concern over exposure to chemicals generally, accompanied by focused media attention to certain specific chemicals, has highlighted these products for food companies and consumers. As this chapter will explain, the U.S. Food and Drug Administration (FDA) administers a comprehensive premarket approval program for food contact materials to ensure that materials in contact with food are just as safe as substances directly added to food.

This chapter provides an overview of the regulation of food contact materials and drug packaging materials in the United States. The term "food contact material" encompasses, most commonly, food packaging, but it also includes many other articles that contact food during processing, storage, and shipping.

In 1958, Congress established a premarket approval system for food additives that encompassed food packaging and other types of food contact materials. From this point on, many food contact materials needed to be approved by FDA and the subject of a food additive regulation prior to use. This system remained in place and unchanged for nearly four decades, until a 1997 amendment to the Federal Food, Drug, and Cosmetic Act (FDCA)[1] established a new, administratively simpler, clearance mechanism, known as the Food Contact Notification (FCN) program.

---

[1]   Pub. L. No. 75-717, 52 Stat. 1040 (1938), as amended 21 U.S.C. §§ 301 *et seq.*

Although FDA approves many new and new uses of food contact materials through the FCN program, there are many important exceptions from the need to obtain premarket approval from FDA, and it benefits manufacturers and marketers to understand all the available regulatory options for legally marketing these products. This chapter discusses not only the ways to obtain explicit FDA sanction, but also the circumstances under which it is not necessary to obtain an explicit premarket clearance from FDA.

Manufacturers also should be aware of the regulatory and legislative initiatives underway in the United States that could potentially restrict the use of certain chemicals in the manufacture of food packaging. Certain food contact materials continue to receive a lot of attention by the media, consumers, and legislators. The most notable example is bisphenol A (BPA), which, despite favorable safety assessments by respected regulatory authorities worldwide, has been the subject of pervasive news coverage alleging safety concerns. These reports have fueled numerous legislative proposals at both the federal and state level to ban the use of BPA in food contact plastic materials, and led to widespread deselection in the marketplace. The situation with BPA also illustrates a growing trend of enhanced scrutiny of chemicals, which has manifested in a growing number of state green chemistry laws. These state laws typically aim to create comprehensive lists of toxic chemicals used in consumer products and encourage companies to replace them with "safer" alternatives. The implications of this legal patchwork include detailed reporting requirements, chemical-by-chemical bans (notwithstanding the safety of a final product), product deselection in the marketplace, and repetitive, redundant, or conflicting compliance requirements.

Lastly, this chapter provides a brief discussion of FDA's regulation of drug packaging. Pharmaceutical packaging materials are regulated in relation to the requirements for the drugs that they hold. In most cases, the packaging is evaluated as part of FDA's review of the drug product. While a suitable status for use in contact with food is not a requirement for clearance of a material for use in drug packaging, it is often viewed by FDA and pharmaceutical companies as initial evidence that a material will be suitable and not pose any health or safety concerns.

Legislative Framework for Food Contact Materials

The Evolution of FDA's Statutory Authority Over Food Packaging

FDA regulates food packaging under the FDCA in a very similar manner as substances intentionally added directly to food. The same general safety requirement that applies to food and substances added to food is equally applicable to food packaging, namely that the packaging must not adulterate food.[2] Food contact materials, to the extent they are reasonably expected to become a component of food, require premarket clearance from FDA. The 1938 version of the FDCA established that food would be considered adulterated

---

[2]   FDCA §§ 301 *et seq.*, 21 U.S.C. §§ 331 *et seq.*

if it contained a quantity of an added substance that may render it injurious to health,[3] but there were no specific legal requirements established for food additives, including packaging and other food contact materials. Beginning in the 1950s, however, Congress began to take notice of the increasing amount of new substances being added to food. In response to consumer concerns as to the safety of these additives, Congress initiated investigative hearings, forming the Select Committee to Investigate the Use of Chemicals in Food and Cosmetics, chaired by New York Representative James Delaney. This committee held hearings from 1950-1952, with its findings and recommendations presented in a series of reports ultimately concluding that legislation was needed to ensure that new additives were tested to demonstrate their safety prior to being placed on the market. The first bill to amend the FDCA to provide "for the regulation of chemical additives in food" was introduced in the House on March 15, 1951 by Representative Miller of Nebraska.

Many iterations of this bill were introduced in subsequent comments, and Congress again held hearings, beginning in 1956, on the proposed legislation. Finally, on September 6, 1958, President Eisenhower signed the Food Additives Amendment of 1958 into law, thereby establishing a broad new premarket approval scheme for substances directly or indirectly added to food.[4]

Under the premarket approval scheme, manufacturers were required to file a food additive petition (FAP), which resulted in FDA promulgating a new food additive regulation clearing a substance for its intended use. This process was cumbersome and time-consuming, due in part to the legal requirement for FDA to undertake a notice-and-comment rulemaking procedure that resulted in publication in the *Federal Register* and *Code of Federal Regulations*. As a result, new clearances often took between two and four years to obtain and, in a number of cases, substantially longer. Industry and FDA became increasingly frustrated with the lengthy reviews and burdensome procedural requirements. Finally, in 1997 Congress passed legislation, as part of the Food and Drug Administration Modernization Act of 1997 (FDAMA), authorizing a new and administratively simpler procedure known as a Food Contact Notification (FCN).[5] FDA implemented the FCN program on January 18, 2000, and this program is now the method by which virtually all food contact substances, unless otherwise exempt from the need for premarket clearance by the agency, obtain approval from FDA.

Impact of the Food Additives Amendment and FDAMA on Food Packaging

The Food Additives Amendment in 1958 made many significant changes to the existing law.[6] Most notably for our purposes, the law made three significant amendments to the FDCA: 1) added section 201(s), which provided a definition of the term "food additive"; 2) amended section 402 to state that food is adulterated per se if it contains an uncleared food additive; and 3) added section 409 to establish the requirements and criteria for obtaining premarket approval for new food additives.

---

3   FDCA § 402(a)(1), 21 U.S.C. § 342(a)(1).
4   *Food Additives: Hearings on Bills to Amend the Federal Food, Drug, and Cosmetic Act with Respect to Chemical Additives in Food Before a Subcomm. of the House Comm. on Interstate & Foreign Commerce*, 85th Cong. 44 (1958).
5   Food and Drug Administration Modernization Act of 1997 (FDAMA), Pub. L. No. 105-115, 111 Stat. 2296.
6   Pub. L. No. 85-929, 72 Stat. 1784 (1958).

Despite many objections at the time, the new definition of food additive was drafted in such a way that food contact materials were subject to the same regulatory standards as additives intentionally used in food.[7] Section 201(s) defines a food additive, in relevant part, as:

> . . . any substance the intended use of which results or may reasonably be expected to result, directly or indirectly, in its becoming a component or otherwise affecting the characteristics of any food (including any substance intended for use in producing, manufacturing, packing, processing, preparing, treating, packaging, transporting, or holding food; and including any source of radiation intended for such use), if such substance is not generally recognized, among experts qualified by scientific training and experience to evaluate its safety, as having been adequately shown through scientific procedures (or, in the case of a substance used in food prior to January 1, 1958, through either scientific procedures or experience based on common use in food) to be safe under the conditions of its intended use . . . .[8]

This is a long and complicated definition, but understanding it is key to determining whether a new substance used in food packaging needs premarket approval from FDA. The changes made by the 1958 Food Additives Amendment resulted in food being considered adulterated if it bears or contains any food additive which is unsafe. Food is considered "unsafe" if it bears or contains a food additive that is not the subject of a food additive regulation (i.e., approved by FDA).[9]

Consequently, under the Food Additives Amendment, if a food contact substance falls within the definition of a food additive, and it is not the subject of a regulation permitting its use in food, then the food is adulterated. The government need not show that the substance is poisonous or deleterious, or that it may render the food injurious to health. Moreover, from a practical standpoint, whether a substance fits the food additive definition can be crucial in terms of a manufacturer's decision to use it. If a manufacturer determines that a substance falls within the food additive definition, then it cannot be used without premarket approval by FDA.

When Congress passed FDAMA in 1997, this legislation added section 409(h) to the FDCA creating the FCN program as an alternative method for permitting the use of food contact substances.[10] Now, a food contact substance that is a food additive is not considered "unsafe" if it is the subject of either a food additive regulation or effective FCN. FDAMA also

---

[7]   Legislators, in fact, treated what came to be called "indirect additives" (food packaging products) almost as an afterthought.

[8]   FDCA § 201(s), 21 U.S.C. § 321(s).

[9]   Section 402(a)(2)(C) states that a food is adulterated "if it is, or if it bears or contains" any food additive that is unsafe within the meaning of section 409. Section 409(a)(2)-(3) states that a food additive shall be deemed to be unsafe unless: "(2) there is in effect, and it and its use or intended use are in conformity with, a regulation issued under this section prescribing the conditions under which such additive may be safely used; or (3) in the case of a food additive as defined in this Act that is also a food contact substance, there is—(A) in effect, and such substance and the use of such substance are in conformity with, a regulation issued under this section prescribing the conditions under which such additive may be safely used; or (B) a notification submitted under subsection (h) that is effective."

[10]   FDCA § 409(h), 21 U.S.C. § 348(h).

introduced a new definition for food contact substance, as "any substance intended for use as a component of materials used in manufacturing, packing, packaging, transporting or holding food if such use is not intended to have any technical effect in such food."[11] This definition established the boundaries of what FDA would consider under an FCN.

Carcinogens and the Constituents Policy

During the legislative development of the what became the Food Additives Amendment, Representative Delaney championed the inclusion of an "anticancer" clause, which prohibited FDA from authorizing the use of a food additive "if it is found to induce cancer when ingested by man or animal, or if it is found, after tests which are appropriate for the evaluation of the safety of food additives, to induce cancer in man or animal."[12] This became known as the Delaney Clause.

Although well-intentioned, the implementation of the Delaney Clause created many issues for FDA, and particularly for its treatment of food contact materials. Many monomers used to manufacture polymers exhibit toxicity concerns, but those monomers are present in the finished article only at extremely low levels. Other impurities may be unintentionally present in a substance, such as reaction products created during polymerization or breakdown products. Recognizing this, FDA developed a policy to deal with substances that pose a negligible toxicological risk by distinguishing between an additive, itself, and its individual constituents (i.e., impurities and carcinogenic monomers used to make polymers).[13] Under FDA's Constituents Policy, if an additive as a whole is not carcinogenic, the presence of *unavoidable* low levels of carcinogenic constituents does not automatically trigger the anticancer clause barring the use of the additive. Instead, the safety of the constituents may be evaluated under the general safety provisions of the FDCA. Thus, noncarcinogenic additives that contain "safe" levels of carcinogenic constituents remain suitable for use in food packaging.[14] The use of the Constituents Policy as a means of avoiding application of the anticancer clause in appropriate instances was judicially upheld in *Scott v. FDA*.[15]

FDA considers any potential dietary exposure to a carcinogenic constituent to be safe if there is a reasonable certainty that no harm will result from the proposed use of the additive that contains the constituent.[16] To determine whether a constituent meets this safety standard FDA assesses the risk, using data from animal carcinogenicity studies, that the potential dietary exposure could result in the occurrence of one additional tumor in a population of one million. If the risk level over a 70-year lifetime, based on the cumulative

---

[11]   FDCA § 409(h)(6), 21 U.S.C. § 348(h)(6).

[12]   FDCA § 409(c)(3)(A), 21 U.S.C. § 348(c)(3)(A).

[13]   47 Fed. Reg. 14,464 (Apr. 2, 1982). Although this advance notice of proposed rulemaking was withdrawn by the agency in a November 26, 2004 *Federal Register* notice (69 Fed. Reg. 68,831, 68,836), the impetus of the withdrawal was administrative only and FDA has since made clear that the Constituents Policy remains a valid means by which to evaluate minor carcinogenic constituents of food additives.

[14]   *Id.* at 14,468.

[15]   Scott v. FDA, 728 F.2d 322 (6th Cir. 1984) (upholding FDA's conclusion that the Delaney Clause was inapplicable where a color additive itself did not cause cancer and finding that FDA did not abuse its discretion in determining that trace levels of a carcinogenic impurity created no reasonable risk of harm to exposure to the additive).

[16]   47 Fed. Reg. at 14,468.

daily exposure to the substance, is less than or equal to 1 in 1 million, FDA considers the risk to be negligible.

The FDA Food Safety Modernization Act (FSMA)

In January 2011, President Obama signed into law the FDA Food Safety Modernization Act (FSMA), broadly sweeping legislation designed to implement policies toward the prevention of foodborne illness. The focus of FSMA is on food that is consumed, rather than food packaging. Nevertheless, some provisions of FSMA apply, or could be considered to apply, to food contact substances.[17]

Most notably, FDA can order a mandatory recall of a food contact material if there is a reasonable probability that it is adulterated or misbranded, and may cause serious adverse health consequences or death (i.e., a "Class I recall" situation).[18] Similarly, FDA may administratively detain a food contact material for which the agency has "reason to believe" is "adulterated or misbranded."[19]

Two other important new requirements imposed by FSMA are the Foreign Supplier Verification Program (FSVP) for imported food, and best practices for the sanitary transportation of food. Under the FSVP, an importer must verify that imported "food" is not adulterated, or misbranded due to improper allergen labeling, and was produced in compliance with the newly added hazard analysis and risk-based preventative controls. Both of these provisions potentially could apply to food contact substances; at the time of this writing, FDA is only now promulgating implementing regulations, and the agency may conclude that food contact materials will be exempt from these provisions.

One other minor requirement relates to new recordkeeping requirements. Manufacturers of food contact substances (other than the finished container) are exempt from any requirements to establish and maintain records for such substances, but any existing records that are generated must be made available to FDA upon request if the agency has a reasonable belief that the product is adulterated and presents a threat of serious adverse health consequences or death to humans or animals.[20] FSMA expanded FDA's record access authority to permit the agency to access records of products related to the food at issue, which could include food packaging, and not just the food, itself.

---

[17]   Many of FSMA's requirements apply only to a "food facility" that is required to register with FDA pursuant to section 415 of the FDCA. FDA regulations implementing section 415 explicitly exempt food contact substances, as defined in section 409(h)(6) of the FDCA, from the definition of food and, thus, from the section 415 registration requirement. *See* 21 C.F.R. § 1.227(b)(4)(i)(A).

[18]   FDCA § 423, 21 U.S.C. § 350l.

[19]   FDCA § 304(h)(1)(A), 21 U.S.C. § 334(h)(1)(A).

[20]   *See* 21 C.F.R. § 1.361 ("What are the record availability requirements?").

FDA's Regulatory Framework for Food Contact Materials

The remainder of this chapter describes the regulatory framework that manufacturers use to establish that their food contact materials comply with the FDCA. We begin with the statutory premarket approval mechanisms, namely FDA's food additive regulations and the FCN program. We then discuss several important exceptions and exemptions from the need for either type of specific premarket clearance under specific circumstances.

Food Additive Regulations

Prior to the implementation of the FCN program, any "food additive" used in contact with food was required to be the subject of a regulation covering its intended use (unless it was exempt from regulation under FDA's Threshold of Regulation process, discussed later). Because a food additive petition was the only regulatory clearance mechanism, a large number of regulations have been issued since the passage of the 1958 Food Additives Amendment, covering the use of hundreds of food contact substances.

FDA's food additive regulations are found in Title 21, Parts 170 through 189 of the *Code of Federal Regulations*. These regulations cover both substances that are directly added to food to perform a technical effect in the food and those substances that may become components of food because they are used in contact with food (e.g., food packaging, processing equipment, etc.).

The regulations can be classified into three general types: 1) regulations covering the use of substances in particular types of packaging applications (e.g., components of paper and paperboard in section 176.170 or coatings on metal substrates or repeated use articles in section 175.300); 2) regulations covering specific polymers (generally found in Part 177, such as polyethylene terephthalate in section 177.1630 or various nylons in section 177.1500); and 3) regulations covering the use of substances by their technological function (e.g., emulsifiers in section 178.3400 or antioxidants in section 178.2010). All three types of regulations list the permitted substances, any applicable specifications that must be met, and the conditions under which the particular substance may be used. Importantly however, with formulated food contact articles, rarely will a reference to one regulation sufficiently portray all the applicable clearances, as a complex system of regulation over 50 years has led to a large amount of overlap among different regulations and a confusing mix of clearances.

Due to the complexity of many food packaging materials, a manufacturer must closely review a regulation to determine whether it provides a sufficient clearance. If the regulation covers a specific type of packaging application or use of a substance for a specific technological function, then the clearance only applies to the use of that substance in that application or for that function. For example, the listing of a substance in section 175.300, which covers coatings on metal substrates and repeated use articles, does not permit its use in coatings on paper or single-use plastic films. By contrast, there are a number of regulations that provide a broad clearance for a particular type of polymer, which may then be used in food contact applications generally, provided that any other limitations, such as use level or purity specifications, are met. Likewise, a number of substances are permitted for use in a wide range of food contact applications, such as calcium stearate and silica.[21]

These regulations also may limit the use of a substance to certain food types or conditions of use. Frequently, such limitations are expressed by cross-reference to FDA's Food Types and Conditions of Use. The most common cross-reference in the regulations is to the table of food types provided in 21 C.F.R. § 176.170(c), "Table 1—Types of Raw and Processed Foods."[22] Some of the food types listed in Table 1 are based on gross physical characteristics (e.g., dry solid food or aqueous food), whereas others are based on "grocery" classifications (e.g., beverages or bakery products). However, because foods are not always easily matched to the listed food types or may appear to fit within more than one category, it is important to evaluate food type limitations on a case-by-case basis.

Also provided in section 176.170(c) is a table, "Table 2," of FDA's Conditions of Use. "Conditions of Use" represent the time and temperature for which a food contact material is permitted for use. It is important to note, however, that this table does not represent FDA's current list of Conditions of Use. Table 2 only describes Conditions of Use A ("High temperature heat-sterilized (e.g., over 212 deg. F)") through H ("Frozen or refrigerated storage: Ready-prepared foods intended to be reheated in container at time of use"). The current list can be found on FDA's website, and includes two additional conditions of use—I ("Irradiation") and J ("Cooking at temperatures exceeding 250 deg. F").[23] Other limitations may also appear in a regulation concerning specifications the substance must meet, limitations on the types of polymers in which the substance may be used, or on the use level of the substance in the finished article.

Scope of a Regulatory Clearance and Method of Manufacture

A significant characteristic of the food additive regulations is that FDA clears substances on a generic rather than a proprietary basis. In other words, FDA generally does not include manufacturing parameters in a food additive regulation. Where it does, it is often an artifact of the wording of a food additive petition as opposed to a stricture on how the substance should be made.

An outgrowth of the generic nature of polymer clearances is the basic resin doctrine. FDA considers the "basic resin" to be the product that results when the polymerization process has been carried to commercial completion.[24] In the case of resins and polymers, as long as the basic polymer is listed in a regulation, is manufactured in accordance with good manufacturing practices and complies with applicable limitations such as stated extraction

---

21   For calcium carbonate, see e.g., 21 C.F.R. § 173.340 ("Defoaming agents"); 21 C.F.R. § 176.170 ("Components of paper and paperboard in contact with aqueous and fatty foods"); 21 C.F.R. § 177.2410 ("Phenolic resins in molded articles"). For silica, see e.g., 21 C.F.R. § 176.210 ("Defoaming agents used in the manufacture of paper and paperboard"); 21 C.F.R. § 177.1550 ("Perfluorocarbon resins"); 21 C.F.R. § 177.2600 ("Rubber articles intended for repeated use").

22   Similar tables of Food Types and Conditions of Use are set forth in 21 C.F.R. § 175.300(d), Tables 1 and 2, respectively.

23   The most current Conditions of Use are available on FDA's website at http://www.fda.gov/Food/IngredientsPackagingLabeling/PackagingFCS/FoodTypesConditionsofUse/ucm109358.htm.

24   Although not articulated in the FDCA or its implementing regulations, the basic resin doctrine is a longstanding policy employed by FDA in its review of food contact materials.

requirements, it is covered by that regulation even though different manufacturers may make the polymer by different processes and employ different catalysts, reaction control agents, and the like.

Although it is a case-by-case analysis, substances typically considered to fall under the basic resin doctrine are necessary to the commercial manufacture of the polymer, used at low levels (normally less than 0.5 percent), incorporated into the polymer backbone or washed out of the polymer, and do not render the polymer and the final food product, unsafe.

It is common for manufacturers to want to use multiple substances to produce a new food contact product. The mixture doctrine permits a manufacturer to physically blend two different polymers or other combinations of substances, without further FDA approval, if all components are cleared by FDA (regulation or FCN) or are exempt in some way (generally recognized as safe (GRAS), prior sanctioned, not expected to migrate to food, or deemed exempt under the Threshold of Regulation rules) for their intended use. Each individual substance in the mixture must comply with any application limitations described in its clearance, and the mixture must be used in accordance with the most restrictive end-use limitation applicable to any component. Importantly, the mixture doctrine refers only to physical blends. If there is a chemical reaction between any of the combined substances, then the result of the reaction is considered to be a new substance requiring its own regulatory clearance, and the mixture doctrine does not apply.

Regardless of the manner in which a food contact material is made, a manufacturer must ensure that that all materials are "safe and suitable" for their intended use. This standard derives from FDA's regulation at 21 C.F.R. § 174.5. Paragraph (a)(2) of that section requires that food-contact materials be of a "purity suitable for [their] intended use." For a product to be suitably pure, any impurities remaining in the product, such as solvents and residual monomers, or products of side reactions and chemical degradation, must be evaluated to ensure that the potential dietary exposure to these substances does not present a public health or safety concern.

End Test Requirements

Some regulations include compliance testing to serve as a quality control measure. These "end tests" or "extraction tests" verify whether a particular product is equivalent to the material that served as the basis for the regulation, and thus do not necessarily reflect actual use conditions or use food-simulating solvents. The tests may need to be performed either on a polymer (for example, there are end tests for chlorinated polyethylene cleared under section 177.1610) or on the finished food contact material (such as closures with sealing gaskets for food containers cleared under section 177.1210). These end tests are usually of short duration (mainly 30 minutes or 2 hours, or occasionally as long as 24 or 48 hours), and typically only require gravimetric analysis for total migration. The results are used to determine whether the material or article passes the given specification.

Importantly, end tests are not intended for assessing migration to an unregulated compound for purposes of determining whether a substance is properly considered a food additive or to obtain premarket clearance from FDA.[25]

Obtaining a Food Additive Regulation

From 1958 until the implementation of the FCN process, if a substance used in food contact applications was not regulated or exempt from the need for premarket approval, manufacturers were required to file a food additive petition (FAP) to establish a food additive regulation for the intended use of the substance. As stated above, this is because the FDCA requires FDA to treat food contact materials in the same manner as direct food additives, including the need under section 409 of the FDCA for a petition to promulgate a new food additive regulation. Although it now is rarely used, the food additive petition process is still a valid procedure for the clearing of some food contact substances and, in some rare cases, FDA may still require an FAP instead of an FCN. For example, if for marketing reasons a company wished to revise an existing clearance in the food additive regulations, a petition may be appropriate. The data requirements for an FAP are generally the same as for FCNs, but a company interested in filing a petition must discuss this alternative with FDA first, as FDA would need to agree to accept an FAP in most situations. Once an FAP has been submitted to FDA, the agency must publish notification of the filing in the *Federal Register*. Upon completion of its review, FDA must then publish a final rule in the *Federal Register* and the new regulation in the *Code of Federal Regulations*. Importantly, once the rule is final, the clearance for the new substance is not proprietary and may be generally relied upon by any company that wishes to manufacture or distribute the food contact substance.

The Food Contact Notification Program

Certainly the most important manner by which manufacturers now obtain an official sanction from FDA for the use of new food contact materials is through the FCN process. Since the program's inception in 2000, FDA has received an average of approximately 80 to 100 FCNs a year to permit the use of new food contact substances and new uses of food contact substances. Most of the approved FCNs have become effective within a 120-day time period—a dramatic and remarkable improvement over the two to four years that it previously took to obtain a clearance under the food additive petition process. The impact of the new notification program established by FDAMA cannot be understated. Instead of a multiyear FAP review process, FDA now has 120 days to review a submission and, if the agency does not object in writing within that time frame, the FCN automatically becomes effective.[26] Thus, if at the end of the 120-day review period FDA has not objected to an FCN, the notifier can begin using the substance under the terms and limitations specified in the submission.

---

[25]   FDA's migration testing for supporting either a "no migration" position or a food contact notification is intended to simulate the actual intended conditions of use of the package. This type of testing is typically conducted over a longer period (10 days or longer) in contrast to compliance testing, and virtually always requires analysis for one or more specific potential migrants. The results are used to determine whether the substance under examination (either resin or adjuvant) is expected to become a component of food and, thus, subject to FDA's jurisdiction as a "food additive." If the substance is found to migrate, the results can be used to ascertain the potential contribution of the substance to the human diet.

[26]   FDCA § 409(h)(2)(A), 21 U.S.C. § 348(h)(2)(A).

One very important feature of FCNs is that they are unique to the notifer. Consequently, only the notifier and its customers may rely upon the clearance provided by an FCN.[27] Interestingly, FDA has indicated that it prefers FCNs to be company-specific because by requiring each company to submit its own FCN, the agency has a better understanding of the potential dietary exposures to chemicals on the market. Although FCNs are proprietary, it is possible for notifiers to file a "me too" FCN that covers the same substance and applications as an already effective FCN. "Me too" submissions have reduced data requirements if the substance is substantially similar to the previously notified substance, and FDA can rely on its prior evaluation of safety conducted for the already effective FCN. A "me too" notifier must still submit its own chemical identity, manufacturing, and impurity information, and must address the safety of any new impurities or higher level of impurities that were not considered previously by FDA.

The FCN Process

FDA's regulations implementing the FCN program and describing the information that must be submitted in a notification appear in the *Code of Federal Regulations* at 21 C.F.R. §§ 170.100 through 170.106. For the substantive content, notifiers must include information related to the identity and intended use of a substance, its potential dietary exposure, and support for the safety of the substance when used as intended. In addition to its regulations in Part 170, FDA has issued three guidance documents on the administrative, chemistry, and toxicology requirements to assist companies in determining what information and data must be included in their submissions.[28] At the time of this writing, FDA also is in the process of implementing a program for notifiers to submit FCNs electronically, and has issued guidance on these electronic submissions.[29]

The agency has provided a standard form for use in submitting an FCN to FDA. This document, known as Form 3480, is discussed in the agency's administrative guidance document.[30] FDA is also very receptive to answering questions concerning the FCN process and the types and extent of data that will be needed to evaluate the safety of a specific food contact substance. The agency encourages the use of Prenotification Conferences (PNCs) to clarify questions and issues with notifiers prior to the submission of their FCN. A PNC can take the form of a meeting at FDA, a teleconference, or written communication.

Once FDA receives an FCN, it begins by conducting its "Phase 1" review. Upon completion of the Phase 1 review, the agency provides feedback to the notifier concerning any questions

---

[27]   FCNs are proprietary as a result of compromises that were reached during the drafting and legislative history of the FDCA. Originally, FDA would only agree to the legislation if it included user fees to fund the program, and industry believed it appropriate that the FCN should be proprietary if a filing fee was necessary. Ultimately, the user fee proposal was struck from the proposed legislation during its passage through Congress, but the proprietary nature of the FCNs was maintained.

[28]   *See infra* notes 30, 35 and 38.

[29]   FDA, Guidance for Industry: Providing Regulatory Submissions in Electronic or Paper Format to the Office of Food Additive Safety Part V: Food Contact Substance Submissions (March 2010), *available at* http://www.fda.gov/Food/GuidanceRegulation/GuidanceDocumentsRegulatoryInformation/Ingredients AdditivesGRASPackaging/ucm195854.htm.

[30]   FDA, Guidance for Industry: Preparation of Food Contact Notifications: Administrative (May 2002), *available at* http://www.fda.gov/Food/GuidanceComplianceRegulatoryInformation/GuidanceDocuments/ FoodIngredientsandPackaging/ucm081807.htm.

or deficiencies it identifies in the submission. FDA generally provides this feedback within four to six weeks of the filing of the FCN. If FDA has no initial questions, the agency provides a letter acknowledging receipt of the submission. This acknowledgment letter will provide information on the description of the substance, the uses that will be covered, as well as any specifications or limitations on the use of the substance and the date the FCN will become effective if FDA does not raise additional questions or concerns.

If FDA does have questions during its Phase 1 review of the substance, the agency will issue a deficiency letter to the notifier identifying its concerns. In its deficiency letters, FDA generally states that the notifier should respond to all questions within 10 business days or withdraw the FCN. If FDA considers the notifier's response to its questions not substantive (i.e., only administrative or clarifying in nature), then the agency will provide the notifier with a letter acknowledging receipt, and the 120-day review period will start from the original filing date of the FCN. If FDA considers the information provided in the response substantive to its review, the agency will restart the 120-day notification period from the time answers to all of its questions were received. In the case of questions for which the response will require longer than 10 days to complete, FDA will request that the notifier withdraw the submission. The withdrawal of an FCN does not adversely impact any future submissions, and a notifier is free to resubmit the FCN at a later time with the information or data requested by FDA. If an FCN is withdrawn, FDA will maintain as confidential the existence of, and all information included in, the filing.[31]

FDA conducts a Phase 2 evaluation during the remaining notification period. In the authors' experience, while new questions sometimes arise during the course of FDA's Phase 2 review, FDA does a good job of raising the significant issues in its Phase 1 response to the notifier. It is unusual for questions or concerns to arise in the second evaluation that would necessitate an FCN to be withdrawn or change the effective date of the filing, but this does occasionally occur.

Once an FCN becomes effective, FDA will issue a letter to the notifier confirming the same information provided in the acknowledgment letter regarding the substance, any limitations, and the effective date of the FCN. FDA will then post this information on the agency's Inventory of Effective FCNs on its website. Like the letter, the online listing will identify the food contact substance, the uses for which it is permitted, any specifications or limitations on its use, as well as the notifier and manufacturer of the substance. The website listing and the confirmation letters are important tools that companies use to assure their customers of the suitable regulatory status of their products.

Administrative Requirements

FDA's administrative guidance document provides general information on FCN submissions, including, for example, the scope of an effective FCN and the proper format of a submission, and details regarding the overall process, such as the timing of FDA's review.[32]

---

[31]   21 C.F.R. § 170.102 ("Confidentiality of information in a premarket notification for a food contact substance").

[32]   FDA, Guidance for Industry: Preparation of Food Contact Notifications: Administrative (May 2002), *available at* http://www.fda.gov/Food/GuidanceComplianceRegulatoryInformation/GuidanceDocuments/FoodIngredientsandPackaging/ucm081807.htm.

Notably, by law, confidential business information contained in the FCN may be claimed as confidential and, provided it is appropriately marked, it will be maintained as confidential by the agency and will be exempt from public disclosure under the Freedom of Information Act (FOIA).[33]

The data requirements for an FCN are substantially similar to those required for a food additive petition. The notifier must provide adequate information to identify the substance and its potential dietary exposure, and sufficient toxicology data must be provided to determine that the proposed use is safe. Of course, specific issues arise on a case-by-case basis, and the data requirements summarized below may sometimes not be necessary or, in other cases, additional data may be required.[34] The following illustrates the basic information and data that generally must be included in an FCN.

Chemistry Data

The chemistry data requirements are discussed in detail in FDA's guidance document entitled "Guidance for Industry: Preparation of Premarket Submissions for Food Contact Substances: Chemistry Recommendations."[35] As discussed in this document, notifiers must provide complete information on the identity of the proposed food contact substance, its manufacturing process, manufacturing specifications, and impurity profile. Analytical data must be provided to identify the substance (such as an infrared spectrum) and the level of impurities.

Notifiers must also provide detailed information on the intended conditions of use for the food contact substance, including its technical purpose and the types of food and temperatures at which the substance will contact food. The FCN must then adequately demonstrate the potential dietary exposure that would result when the food contact substance is used under the clearance requested. The dietary exposure can be determined using several different methods, all of which are discussed in the guidance. One method is to calculate the worst-case potential migration of a substance to food under the intended conditions of use. Such calculations assume that 100 percent of the food contact substance would migrate. Alternatively, modeling based on the principles of diffusion can sometimes be used to develop a more realistic estimate of migration.[36] The final option is to conduct migration testing on the product under the intended conditions of use. This type of testing provides a more accurate estimate of how much of a substance will migrate to food.

---

[33] 5 U.S.C. § 552(b)(4) (implemented by 21 C.F.R. § 20.61(c)).

[34] In particular, if a food contact material is intended for contact with infant formula or in other infant applications, additional considerations apply with regard to calculating dietary exposure and establishing what toxicity data is needed to support those exposures.

[35] FDA, Guidance for Industry: Preparation of Premarket Submissions for Food Contact Substances: Chemistry Recommendations (Apr. 2002; Dec. 2007).

[36] For more information on diffusion theory and methodology, see A. Baner, J. Brandisch, R. Franz & O.G. Piringer, The Applications of a Predictive Migration Model for Evaluating the Compliance of Plastic Materials with European Food Regulations, 13 FOOD ADDITIVES AND CONTAMINANTS 5, 587-601 (1996); W. Limm & H.C. Hollifield, Modeling of Additive Diffusion in Polyolefins, 13 FOOD ADDITIVES AND CONTAMINANTS 8, 949-967 (1996); T. D. Lickly, C.V. Breder & M.L. Rainey, A Model for Estimating the Daily Dietary Intake of a Substance from Food-Contact Articles: Styrene from Polystyrene Food-Contact Polymers, 21 REGULATORY TOXICOLOGY AND PHARMACOLOGY 3, 406-417 (1995).

Once the notifier has determined, either by calculation or testing, how much of the food substance will get into food, that value is converted to the concentration of the substance in the diet utilizing information available on how much and what types of food are packaged in a given material. FDA has developed "consumption factors" and "food type distribution factors" for manufacturers to use—a consumption factor (CF) describes the fraction of an individual's daily diet that is expected to contact a specific packaging material, while a food type distribution factor (f_T) reflects the fraction of all food contacting a packaging material that is aqueous, acidic, alcoholic, and fatty.[37] Finally, if a substance already is regulated for other uses, either by regulation, effective FCN, or under a Threshold of Regulation exemption, the notifier must estimate the cumulative exposure to the substance. The existing cumulative estimated dietary intake (CEDI) is available from FDA upon request.

Toxicology Data

Once the potential dietary exposure from the intended use has been calculated, toxicology data must be submitted to demonstrate the safety of that exposure. The type and extent of data required is outlined in FDA's toxicology guidance document.[38] All relevant toxicology data that are available to the notifier on the food contact substance must be submitted with an FCN. In addition, FDA has established a tiered system for the minimum amount of data needed to evaluate a substance based on the potential dietary exposure, as follows:

- For substances with a potential dietary exposure below 0.5 parts per billion (ppb), no additional data are required unless the substance exhibits a structural alert or some other physicochemical property indicating that there is a toxicity concern at this level of dietary exposure.

- For substances with a potential dietary exposure between 0.5 ppb and 50 ppb, two genotoxicity studies indicating that the substance is not mutagenic or genotoxic must be included.

- For substances with a dietary exposure above 50 ppb and up to 1 part per million (ppm), a third genotoxicity study in the form of an in vivo chromosomal aberration study and two subchronic feeding studies (generally in a rodent and in a non-rodent animal) also are required.

Substances with a potential dietary exposure above 1 ppm are a special case. Although FDA has indicated that a full range of toxicity studies would be required, including a chronic (two-year) carcinogenicity study in rats and mice, a one-year study in a non-rodent species, and a multigeneration reproductive toxicity study in addition to the data identified above, FDA's regulations state that a food additive petition is necessary to permit the use of a food contact substance at this level of dietary exposure.[39] Notifiers anticipating the filing of a submission for this type of substance should meet with FDA to discuss what regulatory path is most appropriate and the necessary data requirements.

---

[37]   *See supra* note 35.

[38]   FDA, Guidance for Industry: Preparation of Food Contact Notifications for Food Contact Substances: Toxicology Recommendations (Apr. 2002), *available at* http://www.fda.gov/Food/ GuidanceComplianceRegulatoryInformation/GuidanceDocuments/FoodIngredientsandPackaging/ ucm081825.htm.

[39]   21 C.F.R. § 170.100(c)(1).

An FCN also may not be appropriate when a bioassay exists for the substance that FDA has not reviewed and that is not clearly negative for carcinogenic effects.[40] In that case, potential notifiers should consult with FDA prior to submitting the FCN.

Environmental Requirements

In addition to chemistry and toxicology data, FCNs must include an environmental assessment (EA) evaluating the environmental impact of the use, manufacture, and disposal of a substance, unless a categorical exemption from the need to prepare an EA applies. The EA requirement is imposed by the National Environmental Policy Act (NEPA), which requires federal agencies to assess the environmental impact of major federal actions.[41] FDA interprets this requirement to apply to its promulgation of a regulation clearing a food additive, and the agency believes that these requirements also apply to its review of FCNs.[42] Section 25.32 of FDA's regulations sets forth the categorical exclusions from the need to prepare an EA for food additive petitions and FCNs. If none of the exclusions apply, then an EA must be prepared. Guidance for the data and information that must be included in an EA is available in an FDA document entitled "Guidance for Industry: Preparing a Claim of Categorical Exclusion or an Environmental Assessment for Submission to the Center for Food Safety and Applied Nutrition."[43]

Statutory Exemptions From the Need for Premarket Approval

As highlighted above, the statutory definition of a food additive in section 201(s) of the FDCA provides several important exemptions from the need to obtain premarket approval from FDA for a new food contact material.[44] Whether a substance qualifies for one of these exemptions requires a case-by-case evaluation of the intended use of the particular substance.

Not Reasonably Expected to Become a Component of Food or the "No Migration" Exemption

Food packaging is designed to be inert and not to transfer its components or have an effect on food. Substances used in food-contact materials often are trapped within a matrix (e.g., a polymer, coating, or paper) and are designed not to leach from the product. As stated above, only those substances that are reasonably expected to become components of food fall under the definition of a food additive that requires premarket clearance by FDA. The question of whether a particular substance has the potential to migrate is one of fact. If a manufacturer can demonstrate that a substance will not become part of the food, then there would be no subsequent dietary exposure to the substance and no approval from FDA is necessary.

---

[40]   21 C.F.R. § 170.100(c) (1) and (2).
[41]   42 U.S.C. §§ 4321 et seq. (1998).
[42]   21 C.F.R. § 25.20(i).
[43]   FDA, Guidance for Industry: Preparing a Claim of Categorical Exclusion or an Environmental Assessment for Submission to the Center for Food Safety and Applied Nutrition (May 2006), available at http://www.fda.gov/Food/GuidanceComplianceRegulatoryInformation/GuidanceDocuments/FoodIngredientsandPackaging/ucm081049.htm.
[44]   FDCA § 201(s), 21 U.S.C. § 321(s).

In some cases, it is easy to determine that a substance will not become a component of food because there is a "functional barrier" preventing migration. The U.S. Court of Appeals for the First Circuit[45] affirmed this position when it concluded that a packaging material would not be a food additive if the food to be placed in the food contact article "will be insulated from . . . migration by a barrier impermeable to such migration, so that contamination cannot reasonably be expected to occur . . . ."[46] There are well-known functional barriers, such as aluminum foil, steel, or glass, but other materials may also act as a functional barrier, depending on the type and thickness of the material, as well as the intended conditions of use. Guidance on what constitutes an effective barrier is available in FDA's guidance on the use of recycled plastics in food packaging.[47] Diffusion modeling or migration testing also may be used to support a conclusion that a specific material acts as a functional barrier.

In other cases, a "no migration" position can be supported by either calculations or extraction studies. The calculations assume that 100 percent of a material would migrate to food under its intended conditions of use, while extraction studies quantitatively measure how much of a substance will migrate under the intended conditions of use.[48] The key to the "no migration" position is the determination of an appropriate level of analytical sensitivity for either the calculations or to set a limit of detection for the extraction studies. FDA has never promulgated definitive criteria for determining at what level of sensitivity a material would not be considered to be a food additive; however, the courts and FDA officials have provided useful guidance. In 1979, in *Monsanto v. Kennedy*, the D.C. Court of Appeals concluded that "Congress did not intend that the component requirement of a 'food additive' would be satisfied by . . . a mere finding of any contact whatever with food."[49] In rejecting FDA's argument that contact alone would necessarily result in some migration, the court reasoned that Congress must have intended for FDA to "determine with a fair degree of confidence that a substance migrates into food in more than insignificant amounts."[50] The court stopped short of opining at what level migration is sufficiently low to be considered insignificant.

Nonetheless, a 1969 draft notice of proposed rulemaking circulated by FDA lends support to the position that substances which do not pose special toxicological concerns and migrate to food at levels no more than 50 ppb would not reasonably be expected to migrate to food within the meaning of the food additive definition.[51] A lower analytical sensitivity may be needed for substances of toxicological concern, such as carcinogenic impurities, which must be evaluated on a case-by-case basis using risk assessment procedures.

---

[45]   Natick Paperboard v. Weinberger, 525 F.2d 1103 (1st Cir. 1975), *cert. denied*, 429 U.S. 819 (1976).

[46]   *Id.* at 1107-08.

[47]   FDA, Guidance for Industry: Use of Recycled Plastics in Food Packaging: Chemistry Considerations (Aug. 2006), Chapter VII, *available at* http://www.fda.gov/food/guidancecomplianceregulatoryinformation/GuidanceDocuments/FoodIngredientsandPackaging/ucm120762.htm.

[48]   The design of these studies is generally similar to those described in FDA's Chemistry Recommendations, *supra* note 35.

[49]   Monsanto v. Kennedy, 613 F.2d 947, 955 (D.C. Cir. 1979).

[50]   *Id.*

[51]   Lessel L. Ramsey, The Food Additive Problem of Plastics Used in Food Packaging, Paper presented at the meeting of the Society of Plastics Engineers (Nov. 1969).

The GRAS Exemption

Another exemption from the need for premarket approval that comes from the definition of a food additive in section 201(s) is the exception for materials that are generally recognized as safe (GRAS). Manufacturers may rely upon the GRAS exemption for a substance in one of two cases: 1) it was commonly used in food prior to January 1, 1958; or 2) experts qualified by scientific training and experience have adequately shown through scientific procedures that the intended use of the substance is safe.[52]

Regardless of which basis is used, general recognition of safety requires "common knowledge about the substance throughout the scientific community knowledgeable about the safety of substances directly or indirectly added to food."[53] From a food packaging perspective, it is extremely rare for a manufacturer to be able to rely on the "common use in food" prong of the GRAS exemption. Thus, manufacturers almost always rely on the scientific procedures component to demonstrate general recognition of safety.

Before turning to the GRAS exemption, a manufacturer should first review FDA's regulations as the agency has listed or affirmed some materials as GRAS in 21 C.F.R. Parts 182, 184, and 186. Substances affirmed as GRAS as "direct additives" (i.e., substances directly added to food) in these regulations are also GRAS as "indirect additives" (i.e., additives used in packaging materials that indirectly become components of food), provided any applicable limitations on use are met and it is apparent that the indirect additive application will not lead to any significant increase in the level of dietary exposure.[54] These regulations also make clear, however, that they are a non-exhaustive list of substances FDA considers GRAS.[55]

If there is no existing GRAS regulation for a substance, a manufacturer may determine, without FDA's review, that a substance is GRAS provided that sufficient published toxicological data exist to establish the general scientific recognition component.[56] The standards for such a self-determined GRAS assessment are robust. As stated by two former FDA officials, Drs. Alan Rulis and Joseph Levitt, "many people mistakenly associate GRAS with a sort of 'second' tier of safety protection based on a less-than rigorous standard compared to petitioned food additives. This is not true. In fact, the safety standard applicable to GRAS food ingredients is the same as for food additives; namely reasonable certainty of no harm."[57] Indeed, FDA has clarified that "scientific procedures shall require the same quantity and quality of scientific evidence as is required to obtain approval of a food additive

---

[52]   See FDCA § 201(s), 21 U.S.C. § 321(s).

[53]   21 C.F.R. § 170.30(a)(2).

[54]   21 C.F.R. § 184.1(a).

[55]   See 21 C.F.R. § 182.1, in which FDA states that "[i]t is impracticable to list all substances that are generally recognized as safe for their intended use."

[56]   In a question as to whether or not a substance is a food additive requiring premarket review, FDA has the burden of proving that the substance is not GRAS. This conclusion was confirmed in a 1974 statement from the Office of the General Counsel, whereby FDA acknowledged that FDA has "the burden of proving two things: first, that the ingredient may reasonably be expected to become a component of the food, and, second, that the amount of migration involved is not generally recognized as safe." Memorandum from Peter Barton Hutt, General Counsel, FDA, to Sam D. Fine (Oct. 31, 1974).

[57]   See A.M. Rulis & J. Levitt, FDA's Food Ingredient Approval Process - Safety Assurance Based on Scientific Assessment, 53 Regulatory Toxicology and Pharmacology 20 at 26 (2009).

regulation."[58] General recognition of safety is ordinarily based on published studies which may be corroborated by unpublished studies and other data and information.

Of particular relevance to food packaging manufacturers are several papers published in the public literature that lend support to the conclusion that at extremely low levels of dietary exposure a substance may be considered to be GRAS even in the absence of published toxicity data specifically on the particular substance.[59] These papers set forth a tiered threshold scheme by which manufacturers can evaluate whether a substance may qualify as GRAS at a particular dietary exposure based on its chemical structure and the available toxicity data.

Prior Sanction

A third statutory exemption from the definition of a food additive in section 201(s) applies to those substances that were prior sanctioned by FDA or the U.S. Department of Agriculture (USDA) prior to the enactment of the Food Additives Amendment. Before 1958, FDA and USDA would respond to individual requests by manufacturers as to the suitability of a substance for food packaging. When Congress enacted the Food Additives Amendment, it grandfathered the approval provided by such letters into the FDCA by exempting these materials from the need to go through FDA's approval process anew.[60]

The prior-sanctioned status of a substance is a question of fact depending solely on the existence of an appropriate pre-1958 letter or other indication of acceptance. There is no complete list of the prior sanction letters issued by FDA and USDA, and many of these letters have been lost over time. Nevertheless, a manufacturer or marketer may use any material prior sanctioned for its intended application without further FDA clearance.

FDA has attempted to limit the scope of the exclusion by consistently construing prior sanctions as narrowly as possible.[61] In addition, FDA can take action against prior sanctioned materials under the adulteration provisions of section 402 of the FDCA if the agency has reason to believe that the substance is a carcinogen or would render food injurious to

---

[58]   21 C.F.R. § 170.30(b).

[59]   This *de minimis* principle for determining that a substance is GRAS is supported by 1) FDA's Threshold of Regulation policy and 2) a 1989 Canadian Centre for Toxicology panel of independent experts, which concluded that substances present at dietary concentrations below 1.0 ppb may be considered safe even if no toxicity testing has been performed on the specific chemical, provided there is no reason to believe that it demonstrates unusual toxicological properties. *See* 60 Fed. Reg. 36,582 (July 17, 1995) and I.C. Munro, *Safety Assessment Procedures for Indirect Food Additives: An Overview*, 12 REGULATORY TOXICOLOGY AND PHARMACOLOGY 2 (Aug. 1990). *See also* M.A. Cheeseman et al., *A Tiered Approach to Threshold of Regulation*, 37 FOOD & CHEMICAL TOXICOLOGY 387 (1999); R. Kroes, et al., *Structure-Based Thresholds of Toxicological Concern (TTC): Guidance for Application to Substances Present at Low Levels in the Diet*, 42 FOOD & CHEMICAL TOXICOLOGY 65 (2004); EFSA Scientific Committee, Scientific Opinion on Exploring Options for Providing Advice About Possible Human Health Risks Based on the Concept of Threshold of Toxicological Concern (TTC), 10 EFSA JOURNAL 7, 2750 (2012), *available at*: http://www.efsa.europa.eu/en/efsajournal/doc/2750.pdf.

[60]   FDCA § 201(s)(4), 21 U.S.C. § 321(s)(4).

[61]   *See* United States v. Articles of Food ... Buffalo Jerky, 456 F. Supp. 207, 209 (D. Neb. 1978), *aff'd sub nom.* United States v. Nielsen (8th Cir. 1979), cert. denied, 444 U.S. 832 (1979) (upholding FDA's decision that a food substance consisting partly of buffalo meat did not conform to a prior sanction for meat products under the Federal Meat Inspection Act because its definition for meat products did not specifically include buffalo meat).

health.[62] This is an important consideration as a considerable amount of toxicology data has been generated since FDA began issuing such letters. Of course, manufacturers have an ongoing obligation to ensure that substances used pursuant to a prior sanction are safe and suitable for their intended use.

Non-Statutory Exemptions
Threshold of Regulation

In 1995, before the FCN program came into existence, FDA adopted a regulatory procedure for pre-approving qualifying food contact materials based on low dietary exposures.[63] The program, known as the Threshold of Regulation (TOR) procedure, avoided the administrative burdens of the food additive petition process by exempting from regulation as food additives food contact substances that may migrate to food at very low, or de minimis, levels, provided that certain criteria are met. FDA adopted the TOR process based on studies published in the late 1980s that indicated that there was little toxicological concern from exposure to noncarcinogenic substances at levels below 0.5 ppb in the diet.[64] Under the TOR, substances that are not known to be carcinogens and do not contain known carcinogenic constituents that have a TD_{50} value less than 6.25 mg/kg body weight per day are eligible for exemption from regulation as food additives under the following circumstances: 1) either the *dietary* concentration of the substance is 0.5 ppb or below, or the substance is currently regulated for direct addition to food and the dietary exposure to the substance resulting from the proposed use is less than 1 percent of the acceptable dietary intake established for the direct additive uses; 2) the substance has no technical effect in food; and 3) the substance has no significant impact on the environment.

To obtain this exemption, companies submit a request to FDA with the corresponding data demonstrating that the substance meets the requirements set forth in 21 C.F.R. § 170.39. If FDA concludes that the given use of a substance meets the above-listed criteria, FDA will confirm in writing that it has no objection to the use of the substance for a particular application. FDA maintains a list of substances that are the subject of such letters, which is available to the public on FDA's website.[65] Notably, Threshold of Regulation letters may be relied upon by any company that can meet the parameters of FDA's clearing letter, i.e., they are not proprietary to the company submitting the TOR request to FDA (unlike FCNs).

While the TOR procedure provided an important route toward a shorter approval of food contact materials in the mid-1990s, it has largely been supplanted by the FCN process. Although existing threshold exemptions are still valid, and FDA will issue letters under this rule upon request, they typically fall towards the bottom of FDA's priorities as no statutory review period is mandated under the law.

---

[62] FDCA § 402(a)(1), 21 U.S.C. § 342(a)(1). In such cases, however, FDA has the burden of proof in demonstrating that the substance meets the adulteration standard (21 C.F.R. pt. 181).

[63] 60 Fed. Reg. 36,582 (July 17, 1995). FDA's implementing regulations appear at 21 C.F.R. § 170.39.

[64] The full report and all of the individual papers written as part of the study were published in the August 1990 issue of *Regulatory Toxicology and Pharmacology*, the Journal of the International Society of Regulatory Toxicology and Pharmacology (ISRTP). *See* Munro, *supra note 59*.

[65] Threshold of Regulation (TOR) Exemptions Database, *available at* http://www.accessdata.fda.gov/scripts/fdcc/?set=TOR.

Housewares Exemption

Memorialized in the legislative history of the Food Additives Amendment of 1958, substances that are properly characterized as "housewares" are considered to be exempt from the requirement for premarket clearance applicable to food additives generally.[66] Basically, a houseware is an article that is sold empty (not containing food) and is intended for use by consumers, or commercial food service establishments (but not food processing facilities) to prepare, hold, or serve food. Household dinnerware and utensils, napkins, paper towels, clam shells, cups, and eating utensils for use in restaurants are examples of products that are considered to be "housewares."

Although the "housewares exemption" was never formally written into law or regulations, during the congressional hearings that preceded passage of the 1958 Food Additives Amendment, the Chairman of the House Subcommittee on Health and Science and the floor manager of the bill, Honorable John Bell Williams, specifically stated that the legislation was "not intended to give the Food and Drug Administration authority to regulate the use of components in dinnerware or ordinary eating utensils."[67]

No further question was ever raised about the exemption's validity until 1974 when FDA surprisingly proposed a new rule to "revoke" the exemption. FDA obliquely recognized the exemption in the proposal's preamble, saying, "Since the enactment of the Food Additives Amendment . . . letters and oral opinions have at times been issued by [FDA] advising that ordinary houseware articles such as cutting boards, pots and pans, and eating utensils . . . are not subject to regulations under section 409 of the [FDCA]."[68] FDA then indicated that it was basing its proposed rule on a U.S. District Court case, *United States v. Articles of Food Consisting of Pottery Labeled Cathy Rose* (the *Cathy Rose* case),[69] which upheld FDA's authority to seize adulterated food products under the FDCA. FDA's reliance on this case, however, appeared tenuous at best; the court in the *Cathy Rose* case specifically noted that "ordinary packaging or food holding devices from which there is no migration are not subject to the Act,"[70] and did not mention or discuss the housewares exemption at all, let alone indicate judicial rejection of it. Similarly, in a 1975 case, the First Circuit upheld FDA's seizure of allegedly polychlorinated biphenyl (PCB)-contaminated paper food packaging material on the basis of potential migration, but did not discuss the housewares exemption.[71] In fact, there appears to be no case law discussing the housewares exemption, giving FDA no specific judicial basis for its revocation.

Industry vigorously opposed the 1974 proposal and it was finalized. Instead, FDA withdrew the proposal in a November 26, 2004 *Federal Register* notice, along with approximately 80 other proposed actions and rules that were no longer considered viable candidates for final action, largely in part due to a regulatory backlog and the lack of a public health concern.[72]

---

[66]   104 CONG. REC. 17,418 (Aug. 13, 1958).

[67]   *Id.*

[68]   39 Fed. Reg. 13,285 (Apr. 12, 1974).

[69]   370 F. Supp. 371 (1974).

[70]   *Id.* at 373.

[71]   Natick Paperboard Corp., *supra* note 45.

[72]   69 Fed. Reg. 68,831, 68,836 (Nov. 26, 2004). The notice states that, "withdrawal of a proposal is not intended to affect whatever utility the preamble statements may currently have as indications of FDA's position on a matter at the time the proposal was published," and further that, "in some cases the preambles

Indeed, the aberration of the 1974 proposal notwithstanding, FDA has continued to acknowledge the exemption through publications, letters, and presentations. In an April 2005 guidance document on submitting requests under the Threshold of Regulation, FDA provided the following explanation of the Housewares Exemption:

> In the past, FDA typically has not required food additive petitions containing the data described in item 5 above for food-contact articles used exclusively in the home or in restaurants. Although components of houseware articles that are reasonably expected to become components of food are food additives subject to premarket approval, in most cases, the use of such articles results in trivial levels of migration to food either because of short contact times or because the articles are manufactured using materials (e.g., alloys and ceramics) that pose little likelihood of migration to food. Therefore, the agency, because of limited resources, has not enforced the food additive provisions of the FD&C Act for such cases unless there is evidence of a potential health hazard. However, FDA cannot issue a binding "exemption from regulation" under 21 CFR 170.39 for houseware articles in the absence of information to show that the use of such articles would result in, or would reasonably be expected to result in, dietary concentrations below the "threshold."[73]

While housewares require no premarket approval, FDA still has ample power to take action against housewares that present a public health hazard under section 402 of the FDCA. As the FDCA's general prohibition against the adulteration of food extends to any potential source of contaminants, including "housewares," FDA has the power to seize or condemn foods that are adulterated or equipment and products that, when used as intended, will contaminate food. For this reason, it remains the responsibility of producers of housewares to take every reasonable action to assure that their products are suitable for use with food and will not create a health hazard under the intended conditions of use.

FDA's Good Manufacturing Practices Requirement

Good manufacturing practices (GMP) are necessary to prevent the adulteration of food contact materials. FDA's GMP standard for food contact materials is found in 21 C.F.R. § 174.5(a)(2), which provides that "[a]ny substance used as a component of articles that contact food shall be of a purity suitable for its intended use."

The suitable purity requirement is understood to have two aspects. First, the food contact material must not transfer substances to food that may render the food injurious to health and thus adulterated under section 402(a)(4) of the FDCA because it was prepared, packed, or held under unsanitary conditions whereby it may have become contaminated with filth or rendered injurious to health. Second, the food contact material must not impart a taste

---

of these proposals may still reflect the current position of FDA on the matter addressed." Despite this caveat, however, the fact that FDA ever tried to revoke the exemption is good evidence that it exists.

73   FDA, Guidance for Industry: Submitting Requests Under 21 CFR 170.39 Threshold of Regulation For Substances Used in Food-Contact Articles (Apr. 2005) *available at* http://www.fda.gov/Food/ GuidanceComplianceRegulatoryInformation/GuidanceDocuments/FoodIngredientsandPackaging/ ucm081833.htm.

or odor to the food that causes it to be unfit for consumption and thus adulterated under section 402(a)(3) of the FDCA because it was manufactured under conditions that render it unfit for food.

Importantly, the "suitable purity" requirement is in addition to compliance with the terms of any food additive regulation, FCN, or TOR exemption. Also, the requirement applies even to food contact materials that are not food additives and do not require FDA clearance, such as materials that are not reasonably expected to become a component of food because they do not migrate, are GRAS, or are components of housewares. Further, one facet of assuring suitable purity that may easily be overlooked is that the obligation is continuing, and the standard may change with additional toxicological data; e.g., if new data indicate a lower level of acceptable exposure to a substance that needs to be taken into consideration in evaluating even a material with longstanding FDA clearance.

Regulation of Recycled Content in Food Packaging

More and more, localities are looking to increase the recycling of materials used for food packaging. From a regulatory perspective, FDA handles recycled materials in the same manner as virgin materials. As with any packaging component, the recycled material must meet the suitable purity standard set forth in 21 C.F.R. § 174.5, as well as any compositional requirements and specifications in the food additive regulations for the polymer being produced. Moreover, the same exemptions applicable to a virgin material, such as no migration, are applicable to the recycled material.

For plastics, FDA has issued guidance as to how to demonstrate that the recycled plastic resin is sufficiently free of contaminants and suitably pure for use in contact with food.[74] In particular, FDA advises that the adequacy of a recycling process to remove contaminants can be demonstrated by "challenge" testing to ensure that potential contaminants do not migrate to food at levels resulting in dietary exposures greater than 0.5 ppb.[75] Other factors that manufacturers can use to show that recycled materials will not contaminate food include:

- Control over the source of material for recycling to avoid the use of contaminated feedstock;

- The presence of a functional barrier between the recycled material and food; and

- The imposition of limitations on the conditions of use (e.g., contact with dry foods only).

Although pre-approval of a recycling process or recycled material by FDA is not required, as a practical matter, many companies will voluntarily request an opinion letter (formerly referred to as a "no-objection letter") from the agency to provide assurance to their customers that the recycled material is acceptable for use in food packaging. FDA's responses, with confidential information redacted, are posted on FDA's website.[76]

---

[74]   See *supra* note 47.

[75]   FDA no longer recommends challenge testing for tertiary recycling processes (i.e., chemical reprocessing) of polyethylene terephthalate and polyethylene naphthalate, as existing surrogate testing data indicate that such processes produce suitably pure monomers and oligomers.

[76]   *See* FDA, Recycled Plastics in Food Packaging, *available at* http://www.fda.gov/food/foodingredientspackaging/foodcontactsubstancesfcs/ucm093435.htm.

For paper, 21 C.F.R. § 176.260 clears the use of pulp from reclaimed fiber if certain conditions are met. The conditions mirror the GMP requirements applicable to all food contact materials generally. In summary, recycled paper must not contain poisonous or deleterious substances that may migrate to food so as to render the food injurious to health.

Unlike for recycled plastics, FDA has not issued a final guidance document outlining the manner in which to demonstrate the suitable purity of recycled paper. However, a paper published by FDA in 1998 indicates that FDA would need to review the results of challenge testing similar to testing conducted for plastics demonstrating that a particular paper recycling process can adequately remove contaminants to issue a no-objection letter.[77]

Developments Contributing to the Enhanced Scrutiny of Food Contact Materials

As noted in the introduction to this chapter, the use of BPA in food packaging has received considerable attention by consumers and the media and been the subject of numerous federal and state legislative initiatives. BPA is an industrial chemical that has been used for decades in a variety of applications, including polycarbonate bottles and epoxy liners for metal food and beverage cans. The current controversy regarding its safety stems from the fact that studies employing standardized toxicity tests (the type commonly used for regulatory decision making in the U.S. and other countries around the world) have thus far supported the safety of current low levels of human exposure to BPA, while more recent studies may show some effects using novel approaches and different endpoints to describe neurological or developmental effects in laboratory animals at very low doses compared to estimated human exposures. Notably, global regulatory bodies such as FDA and the European Food Safety Authority have identified flaws in the design and execution of many of these studies making them, in the view of the officials, unsuitable for assessing human health risks from a regulatory standpoint.

In the U.S., FDA has not taken any action to rescind existing clearances for BPA. The industry, however, submitted a petition asking FDA to withdraw the authorized uses of BPA in baby bottles and sippy cups because these uses have been abandoned.[78] Moreover, the agency has not altered its conclusion that current dietary exposures to BPA meet the regulatory standard for food additives—the use of the material meets the criteria for a reasonable certainty of no harm. Indeed, in 2014 FDA reviewed the results of very comprehensive studies it sponsored and concluded that the existing exposures to BPA from food contact materials are safe.[79] To address uncertainties about the safety of BPA at low exposures, however, regulatory officials at FDA presently are monitoring the ongoing studies being conducted on the chemical,

---

[77]   Kristina Paquette, *FDA Regulation of Paper Products for Food Contact*, FOOD, COSMETICS, AND DRUG PACKAGING 35-39 (Feb. 1998).

[78]   77 Fed. Reg. 41,899 (July 17, 2012) (FDA amended the food additive regulations to no longer provide for the use of polycarbonate resins in infant feeding bottles and spill-proof cups in responding to a petition filed by the American Chemistry Council.).

[79]   Memorandum from Jason Aungst, Ph.D., Division of Food Contact Notifications, "2014 Updated safety assessment of Bisphenol A (BPA) for use in food contact applications," June 17, 2014, *available at* http://www.fda.gov/downloads/NewsEvents/PublicHealthFocus/UCM424266.pdf.

and the agency is sponsoring additional research on BPA. FDA also has requested that manufacturers voluntarily submit FCNs for their currently marketed uses of BPA-containing materials as a means to obtain clearer usage information.

Nevertheless, some legislators and consumer advocacy groups perceive FDA's regulatory response on BPA as inadequate to protect the public health and have pushed for legislative bans. Several bans have been enacted in various states restricting the manufacture and sale of baby bottles and sippy cups containing BPA or broader plastic containers used to store baby food, and similar measures have been proposed in the U.S. Congress.

BPA, however, is just one example of a chemical used in food packaging being more heavily scrutinized due to concerns regarding potential low-dose effects. Although it does not appear that the increased emphasis on low-dose effects will significantly impact the manner in which a food contact material is evaluated for purposes of establishing a suitable FDA status, as all available toxicology data should be considered to the extent that they are relevant to the proposed use, FDA has indicated that the agency is considering requiring additional information to evaluate the potential health impacts of endocrine-active chemicals. FDA's plans in this area are consistent with a much larger initiative launched in February 2010 by the agency to advance regulatory science, one aspect of which is to modernize toxicology safety testing.[80]

Potential endocrine disruptors are not the only chemicals being targeted by state chemical control initiatives, which more broadly apply to chemicals used in consumer products. California has been leading the way with its Green Chemistry Initiative (GCI), which aims to create a comprehensive list of toxic chemicals used in consumer products and replace them with supposedly less harmful alternatives, and many other states have passed similar initiatives (Connecticut, Maine, Minnesota, and Washington) or have green chemistry laws in various stages of implementation (Illinois, Massachusetts, Michigan, New York, Oregon, and Vermont). Although the landscape is evolving, these initiatives generally focus on the presence of chemicals in products rather than potential risk of exposure to chemicals from finished products, which could result in the ban of products that do not pose a real safety concern or a *de facto* ban in cases where either the approval process for the chemical is sufficiently onerous that withdrawal from the market is the only commercially feasible option or consumers and retailers drive deselection. Significantly for the food-packaging industry, of the states that have passed green chemistry initiatives, only Washington has provided for a specific exemption for food packaging.[81] As such, food contact materials will potentially be subject to the onerous and burdensome assessment and reporting requirements established by many of the initiatives. Thus, companies manufacturing or marketing food contact materials should consider state laws that may affect their product.

---

[80]   More information regarding FDA's Advancing Regulatory Science Initiative is available on FDA's website at http://www.fda.gov/ScienceResearch/SpecialTopics/RegulatoryScience/default.htm.

[81]   *See* definition of "Children's product" in the Washington Administrative Code (WAC) 173-334-040.

FDA's Regulation of Drug Packaging

FDA's regulatory requirements for drug packaging materials depend upon whether the package will be used to hold a drug that is the subject of a new drug application (NDA), or whether it will hold a drug that is considered to be a generally recognized as safe and effective (GRASE) over-the-counter (OTC) drug.[82] Unlike new drugs, GRASE OTC drugs are not required to be the subject of an NDA prior to marketing. Nevertheless, packaging for both types of drugs must comply with FDA's current Good Manufacturing Practice (cGMP) requirements for drugs. Under 21 C.F.R. § 211.94, drug product containers "shall not be reactive, additive, or absorptive, so as to alter the safety, identity, strength, quality, or purity of the drug beyond the official or established requirements." In addition, drug containers must be clean and, where appropriate, sterilized and processed to remove pyrogenic properties, and the containers must provide adequate protection against deterioration or contamination of the packaged drug.

As mentioned above, in addition to meeting the cGMP requirements, new drugs require the submission and approval of an NDA prior to marketing.[83] Packaging materials used for new drugs must be reviewed by FDA as part of the overall review of the NDA in which FDA will consider whether the packaging is safe and whether it will alter the efficacy of the drug. To preserve the confidentiality of their drug packaging formulations, companies that supply drug packaging components or finished drug packages can submit a drug master file (DMF) to FDA.[84] The agency does not review the DMF upon submission, but rather, only as part of its review of the customer's drug product in an NDA. While the confidential information in the DMF is not disclosed to any third party, the fact that a specific DMF exists and the identity of the owner of the DMF are not confidential, and are included on FDA's website of DMFs.[85]

Guidance on DMFs is available on FDAs website.[86] In general, DMFs used to provide information on drug packaging materials, referred to as Type III DMFs, should contain 1) administrative information on the DMF holder; 2) a list of companies authorized to reference the DMF; and 3) confidential information regarding the product(s), including the generic formulation, specifications for the finished product(s), and testing methods used to determine compliance with those specifications. Because DMF holders are required to notify all customers authorized to reference the DMF if any information is added, changed, or

---

[82] New drugs are defined under section 201(p) of the FDCA as drugs that are *not* "generally recognized . . . as safe and effective [GRASE] for use under the conditions prescribed, recommended, or suggested in the labeling thereof." GRASE OTC drugs are defined in 21 C.F.R. § 330.1 as OTC drugs that meet the requirements of an applicable monograph, are manufactured in accordance with current Good Manufacturing Practice (cGMP), and are not misbranded.

[83] Once an NDA has been approved by FDA, the agency must be notified if any changes are made to the information submitted in the NDA, including changes to information submitted with respect to the drug's packaging.

[84] 21 C.F.R. § 314.420.

[85] 21 C.F.R. § 314.430.

[86] *See* http://www.fda.gov/Drugs/DevelopmentApprovalProcess/FormsSubmissionRequirements/DrugMaster FilesDMFs/default.htm.

deleted,[87] it is not advisable to be too specific and instead to simply provide only information that is essential to assuring a safe and suitable product.

DMFs must be updated annually to assure FDA that the information contained in the file is current. If no changes have been made, this should be noted; however, the annual report is not the appropriate vehicle to submit changes to the DMF. Rather, an amendment must be submitted separately, followed by an annual update summarizing the changes to the DMF. In all cases, the annual update should also provide FDA with an updated list of customers authorized to reference the DMF.

---

[87] 21 C.F.R. § 314.420. Personnel within FDA's Center for Drug Evaluation and Research interpret this regulation in a practical manner, and have indicated that only substantive product modifications require that the DMF holder's customers be notified. In essence, DMF holders are required to notify customers authorized to reference the DMF of any amendment that alters the chemical composition, specifications, quality control procedures, or manufacturing methodologies for the products described in the file (even changes that affect only the non-drug contact surface).

CHAPTER 5

FOOD: MEAT AND POULTRY INSPECTION

....

BRETT T. SCHWEMER AND JOLYDA O. SWAIM

Introduction

The Food Safety and Inspection Service (FSIS) within the U.S. Department of Agriculture (USDA)[1] can trace the origin of its meat and poultry inspection programs[2] to the Meat Inspection Act of 1907.[3] Spurred by Upton Sinclair's book, *The Jungle*,[4] which depicted filthy and diseased conditions in Chicago stockyards, the Meat Inspection Act of 1907 was enacted to require a careful examination of every animal carcass to eliminate diseased meat. When the Poultry Products Inspection Act was enacted half a century later,[5] it also followed this carcass-by-carcass inspection model. However, over time, meat and poultry inspection also began focusing on the sanitary conditions of establishments that slaughter and process meat or poultry, as well as how well these establishments control chemical residues and microbial pathogens.

Historically, FSIS programs have been more expensive and labor intensive than those of the Food and Drug Administration (FDA). This is largely because FSIS, unlike FDA, requires continuous government inspection. In slaughter establishments, this means that a government inspector examines every animal carcass. In further processing plants, this means that inspectors regulate such things as sanitation, cooking procedures, equipment, and product labels, but do not examine each package or batch of product. FSIS has interpreted its inspection statutes as requiring only a daily presence in processing establishments. Accordingly, one inspector may cover several processing plants in what is

---

[1] Since the beginning of federal regulation of meat and poultry, principal jurisdiction has been granted to USDA. Over time, however, various agencies within USDA have administered the regulatory programs. Unless otherwise noted, the current agency, FSIS, will be used.

[2] Egg products (excluding shell eggs) and more recently, catfish, are also subject to FSIS inspection. However, this chapter will focus primarily on FSIS's inspection programs for meat and poultry.

[3] Pub. L. No. 59-242, 34 Stat. 1260 (1907).

[4] THE JUNGLE (Signet Classic Ed. 1960).

[5] Pub. L. No. 85-172, 71 Stat. 441 (1957) (codified as amended 21 U.S.C. §§ 451-470 (2012)).

referred to as "patrol inspection." However, this is still considered continuous inspection. The only difference between processing and slaughter inspection is the actual intensity of continuous inspection.

As food-processing technology has improved over the last 20 years, the most sophisticated manufacturers have developed process control programs to ensure the integrity of their process and products. Such company-originated efforts have become much more sophisticated than the oversight of an inspector, who typically uses his or her eyes and nose to ensure the operations are conducted in a sanitary manner and to evaluate whether the building and equipment appear to be clean and sanitary. Where processors have sophisticated controls, inspection is arguably more effective and less costly by monitoring the processor's control programs, rather than by using a duplicative system of sensory inspection.

In conjunction with the improvements in control programs, a new method for improving food safety was created—Hazard Analysis and Critical Control Points (HACCP) systems. In essence, a HACCP system is designed to anticipate potential food safety risks and control them in the process. The development of a HACCP system begins with a thorough review of the process, focusing on identifying all significant hazards that could pose a risk to health or safety. Once the risks are identified, the company selects those points in the process where the risks can be eliminated. Once these "critical control points" are selected, critical limits are adopted—the dividing line between safe and unsafe products. The critical control points are monitored by the facility, with periodic verification (by the company or the government) to ensure the system is working.

The emergence of HACCP coincided with the growing concern that traditional inspection may be inadequate for controlling microbiological pathogens. As early as 1985, the National Research Council (NRC), noting that traditional inspection cannot detect or control microbiological contamination, urged FSIS to adopt a HACCP model. For almost 10 years, FSIS did little to respond to this recommendation. In large part, this inactivity was caused by reluctance to proceed in modernizing inspection, primarily because there was no agreement on what modernized inspection should be.

Eventually, an increase in foodborne illnesses prompted FSIS to adopt the HACCP model for inspection. The most infamous outbreak was the *Escherichia coli* (E. coli) O157:H7 outbreak in the Northwest in January 1993, in which hundreds of people became ill and several died due to the apparent undercooking of hamburgers at a fast-food chain. Two years later, FSIS promulgated a proposed regulation mandating certain pathogen reduction procedures and making HACCP mandatory at all inspected establishments. This proposed pathogen reduction/HACCP regulation became final in 1996.

The pathogen reduction/HACCP regulation seemed to effectively address concerns with foodborne illnesses with numbers dropping. However, the numbers of foodborne illnesses leveled off or actually started to rise a bit beginning in 2002.[6] This was true for listeriosis as well as a rise in issues caused by *E. coli* O157:H7 and *Salmonella*. As a result, FSIS began implementing initiatives to ensure that inspected establishments adequately address and

---

[6]   *See* http://www.cdc.gov/mmwr/preview/mmwrhtml/mm5553a1.htm.

control pathogens and other food safety risks as part of their HACCP and related programs. For example, in October 2002, FSIS issued a notice requiring all establishments that produce raw beef products to reassess their HACCP plans for *E. coli* O157:H7 and to adopt one or more controls if the pathogen was determined reasonably likely to occur.[7] In June 2003, FSIS issued an interim final rule requiring establishments that manufacture ready-to-eat (RTE) meat and poultry products to adopt controls for *Listeria monocytogenes*. Beginning in 2006 and continuing today, FSIS has implemented incentive-based programs to encourage establishments to improve controls for *Salmonella* and *Campylobacter* in raw meat and poultry.[8]

FSIS also realized that it needed to focus more effort on effective use of its inspection time and on using the data available to better address public health risks. As a key component of this effort, in 2013 FSIS began implementing the Public Health Information System (PHIS), which is a Web-based system allowing inspection program personnel in the field to easily report inspection activities, access data and information about the establishments to which they are assigned, and take actions based on inspection findings. The system ties together all parts of the agency, including imports, exports, in-commerce, and laboratory activities.[9]

In August 2014, FSIS also published a final rule to modernize its poultry slaughter inspection.[10] As part of this controversial rule, young chicken and turkey slaughter establishments have the option to chose an inspection system in which they are permitted to sort carcasses for quality and other defects prior to a final carcass inspection by an FSIS inspector on each line (called the "New Poultry Inspection System" (NPIS)), or to chose an existing inspection system where multiple FSIS inspectors are conducting on-line carcass-by-carcass inspection. Regardless of which inspection system is chosen, all establishments would be required to implement written programs to address contamination during the slaughter process, and test carcasses to demonstrate the program's effectiveness.

FSIS believes that most young chicken and turkey establishments will opt to chose the NPIS. FSIS claims that this will free up inspection personnel so that they can focus less on quality issues and more on issues that present food safety concerns, ultimately resulting in a decrease in foodborne illness. Consumer and labor critics have complained that the rule allows establishments the option to replace inspectors with their own employees—presenting food safety, worker safety, and other issues.

Where these recent changes will lead for meat and poultry inspection is hard to predict. FSIS must continue to maintain public confidence in the wholesomeness of meat and poultry and the integrity of inspection, while at the same time implementing more efficient, less costly inspection programs that incorporate scientific and technical procedures needed to control emerging food safety concerns. To fully understand where changes could occur and where

---

[7]   In 2011, FSIS also declared certain other Shiga-toxin-producing *E. coli* to be adulterants and required establishments to re-assess their HACCP plans in light of these adulterants.

[8]   While FSIS has not declared these organisms to be adulterants in raw meat and poultry products, if an outbreak occurs and can be linked to a specific establishment and a specific production lot of product that is still in commerce, FSIS will ask for a voluntary recall of that specific production of product.

[9]   *See* http://www.fsis.usda.gov/phis.

[10]   79 Fed. Reg. 49,565 (Aug. 21, 2014).

the system could remain the same, it is necessary to review the history of USDA meat and poultry inspections.

The Development of the Meat and Poultry Inspection Acts

Meat Inspection

The first federal meat inspection statute, the Meat Inspection Act of 1890, was enacted to restore European confidence in meat exports.[11] The Europeans had come to regard the U.S. meat inspection system as inadequate, and had restricted imports of American beef and pork. The act was intended to preserve and expand U.S. export markets. However, the act was very limited—only antemortem inspection of animals intended for export was authorized[12]—and was not successful in accomplishing its goal. Many foreign governments still refused to recognize U.S. inspection certificates.

In response, the U.S. Congress made further attempts to strengthen meat export inspection. In 1891, it enacted legislation that included both antemortem and postmortem inspection. The inspection, however, was voluntary.[13] In 1896, Congress determined that the various meat inspection laws "should be brought together in a harmonious statute having a distinct purpose and covering certain details that have been omitted from statutes now in force."[14] The 1896 legislation did not require mandatory antemortem inspection, but merely provided that any exporter could obtain inspection and export certificates on request. Perhaps the major breakthrough in the 1896 statute was a provision allowing inspectors to retain control of condemned meat until it was disposed of by the manufacturer "in a legitimate manner into inedible products."[15]

Notwithstanding these initial federal inspection statutes, meat inspection remained largely ineffectual. Three major defects prevented adequate inspections. First, federal inspectors had no authority to require destruction of animals rejected upon antemortem inspection. Second, the statute did not prohibit the sale of meat in interstate commerce that was not federally inspected. Third, the Bureau of Animal Industry (BAI), which conducted the inspections, was limited by lack of funds and insufficient personnel. A stronger meat inspection law was necessary.

The 1906 Meat Inspection Act

Even before *The Jungle*, problems in the meatpacking industry had been the subject of public discussion. The "embalmed beef" scandals of 1899 raised questions about the quality

---

11   26 Stat. 414 (1890).
12   The Bureau of Animal Industry (BAI) was given authority to conduct the meat inspection. BAI was organized within the Department of Agriculture in 1884, and its first efforts concerned research on the control of animal diseases.
13   26 Stat. 1089 (1891).
14   *Id.*
15   *Id.*

of canned meat provided to American troops in the Spanish-American War. In 1905, a series of articles in *Lancet*, a distinguished English medical journal, attacked the practices of packing houses, and in an article in *Success Magazine*, asked, "Are Packers, as is Often Charged, Deliberately Selling Diseased Meat?"[16] The impact of these expositions, however, was insignificant compared to the outrage created by *The Jungle*.

Sinclair wrote *The Jungle* to protest the exploitation of workers in a capitalist economy and set his story in the stockyards of Chicago. Even though Sinclair's description of filth and disease in the stockyards occupies only 12 pages of the book, the power of his description more than compensates for its brevity. Sinclair's description was so powerful and alarming that many readers thought he was exaggerating. Book publishers initially rejected his manuscript, until President Theodore Roosevelt sent two investigators, Charles P. Neill and James Bronson Reynolds, to Chicago to investigate. Their report documented Sinclair's allegations.[17]

During this time, the meatpacking industry had stalled inspection reform legislation in the House of Representatives. To break the logjam, President Roosevelt released part of the Neill-Reynolds report. Roosevelt's ploy worked, and the House yielded to new federal meat inspection legislation, the Beveridge Amendment.[18] According to the House report, there was no disagreement that "the most rigid inspection of meat and meat food products" was necessary.[19] Moreover, the House strongly recommended that the cost of inspection be borne by appropriated funds. President Roosevelt, in contrast, had recommended that packers bear the cost of inspection. The House rejected Roosevelt's recommendation and appropriated funds for the new program, basing their rationale on the fact that the legislation was designed to restore public confidence in the quality of American meat. Allowing the packers to pay the inspectors would contravene this purpose by creating a doubt whether the inspectors worked for the public or the packers.[20]

The Beveridge Amendment to the 1906 Agricultural Appropriations Bill was ultimately reenacted as the Meat Inspection Act of 1907.[21] These acts required postmortem inspection of all animals and meat prepared for human consumption and transported in interstate commerce. Furthermore, the legislation gave USDA supervisory authority over processing and labeling. For the most part, the legislation addressed the obvious and egregious problems of misleading labeling and insanitary conditions (e.g., standing water, inadequate toilets, rotted wood facilities). Concerns over hazardous residues and other dangers were not expressed at that time.[22]

---

[16] *See* J. BRAEMAN, CHANGE AND CONTINUITY IN TWENTIETH-CENTURY AMERICA 46 (1964).

[17] *Id*. at 45.

[18] Pub. L. No. 59-382, 34 Stat. 669 (1906).

[19] H.R. REP. No. 4953, 59th Cong., 1st Sess. 5 (1906).

[20] *Id*. at 7.

[21] Pub. L. No. 59-242, 34 Stat. 1260 (1907).

[22] CONGRESSIONAL RESEARCH SERVICE, MEAT AND POULTRY INSPECTION PROGRAMS (prepared for Senate Comm. on Agriculture, Nutrition and Forestry, 96th Cong.), reprinted in FOOD SAFETY: WHERE ARE WE? 30 (Comm. Print 1979).

As a result of the 1906 and 1907 Meat Inspection Acts, as well as the 1906 Pure Food and Drugs Act,[23] BAI became responsible for administering new food laws. Given its veterinary science orientation, BAI became responsible for the meat inspection programs, while administration of the new Pure Food and Drugs Act was delegated to the Department's Bureau of Chemistry, headed by Dr. Harvey W. Wiley and his famous "poison squad."[24] Although the scope and authority of the food and drug statute continued to be a subject of great contention, the administration of federal meat inspection proceeded with relatively little legislative attention or controversy for the next 60 years.

1907-1967

The period from 1907 to 1967 was a quiet one with Congress slightly expanding USDA's subject matter jurisdiction and powers. The Horse Meat Act of 1919[25] provided for the inspection of horse meat by the same procedures established in the Meat Inspection Act of 1907, and required special labeling for horse meat and horse meat products. In 1930, section 6 of the Cattle Inspection Act of 1890[26] was amended to prohibit importation of livestock affected by any disease.[27]

Congress also tightened the exemptions from inspection for farmers and retailers. The Act of June 29, 1938,[28] prohibited farmers from slaughtering animals not of their own production, and limited the definition of retail butchers and retail dealers to those persons exclusively engaging in consumer sales, except as otherwise specifically authorized by the Secretary of Agriculture.[29]

During World War II, the Meat Inspection Act again was amended to allow plants operating only in intrastate commerce to obtain federal meat inspection necessary to bid on government procurements.[30] As the House Committee Report explained, this feature was to aid small businesses that otherwise would be foreclosed from the government market, as well as the two- to four-cent per pound differential on government orders.[31] The wartime authority for intrastate inspection of meat terminated with other war emergency powers on July 25, 1947.[32]

The 1967 Wholesome Meat Act

Congressional interest in federal inspection was rekindled in 1967 by concern about the quality of state inspection of slaughter and processing plants engaged only in intrastate commerce.[33] Although some states, notably California and New York, had excellent intrastate inspection systems for meat and poultry, 22 states had no mandatory inspection, and seven

---

[23]   34 Stat. 768 (1906).

[24]   BAI was responsible for research on animal health and meat inspection. The Bureau of Chemistry was responsible for administering the 1906 Pure Food and Drugs Act and eventually became FDA.

[25]   Pub. L. No. 66-22, 41 Stat. 241 (1919), *repealed by* Pub. L. No. 90-201, § 9, 81 Stat. 584, 590 (1967).

[26]   26 Stat. 414 (1890).

[27]   46 Stat. 1460 (1930).

[28]   Pub. L. No. 75-21, 52 Stat. 1235 (1938) (codified as amended at 21 U.S.C. § 623).

[29]   S. Rep. No. 2182, 75th Cong., 2d. Sess. 2-4 (1938).

[30]   Pub. L. No. 77-601, 56 Stat. 351 (1942), *repealed by* S.J. Res. 123, 80th Cong., 1st Sess., 61 Stat. 449 (1947).

[31]   H.R. Rep. No. 2144, 77th Cong., 2d Sess. 1 (1942).

[32]   S.J. Res. 123, *supra* note 30.

[33]   For a more detailed discussion of the 1967 amendments, *see* H. Wellford, Sowing the Wind 5-26 (1972).

had no system at all.[34] At least 25 percent of commercially processed meat was prepared without any federal inspection and without adequate local inspection.[35] As early as 1963, USDA surveys of state plants had highlighted deficiencies in the intrastate plants.[36]

The packing industry and the National Association of State Departments of Agriculture, whose members administered intrastate inspection, responded by attempting to stiffen state inspection laws. Before this objective could be accomplished, however, a new group of writers, the heirs of Upton Sinclair, fueled the demand for new federal legislation. The new activists were consumer advocate Ralph Nader and Nick Kotz, a reporter for the *Des Moines Register*.

Nader wrote an article published in the *New Republic* entitled, "We're Still in the Jungle." Whereas Sinclair was concerned over insanitary conditions and diseased livestock, Nader focused on the use of chemicals and new technologies[37]:

> It would be misleading to compare such intrastate operations today with those conditions prevailing at the turn of the century: As far as impact on human health is concerned, the likelihood is that the current situation is worse! . . . It took some doing to cover up meat from tubercular cows, lump-jawed steers, and scabby pigs in the old days. Now the wonders of chemistry and quick-freezing techniques provide the cosmetics of camouflaging the products and deceiving the eyes, nostrils, and taste buds of the consumer. It takes specialists to detect the deception. What is more, these chemicals themselves introduce new and complicated hazards unheard of sixty years ago.[38]

At the same time, Kotz was publishing a series of Pulitzer Prize winning articles outlining the deficiencies in state meatpacking plants. Congressman Graham Purcell, Chairman of the Agriculture Subcommittee on Livestock and Grain, initially introduced a modest reform bill that would have allowed those states meeting federal inspection standards to obtain a 50 percent cost reimbursement.[39] A much tougher bill would have required mandatory federal inspection in intrastate plants grossing $250,000 or more per year.[40] The House rejected the latter and passed Purcell's bill by a vote of 403 to 1.

The battle was renewed in the Senate.[41] The final result was a compromise allowing states to maintain their own meat inspection programs, provided that within two years each state

---

[34] H.R. REP. No. 653, 90th Cong., 1st Sess. 4-5 (1967); S. REP. No. 79, 90th Cong., 1st Sess. 5 (1967). In addition, 12 states had only voluntary meat inspection statutes, 27 states had mandatory processing inspection and 29 states had mandatory antemortem and postmortem inspection. H.R. REP. No. 653, 90th Cong., 1st Sess. at 5.

[35] H.R. REP. No. 653, *supra* note 34, at 5.

[36] H. WELLFORD, *supra* note 33, at 5-6.

[37] *Id.*

[38] Ralph Nader, *We're Still in the Jungle*, 157 NEW REPUBLIC, July 15, 1967, at 11.

[39] H.R. 12,144, 90th Cong., 1st Sess. reprinted in H.R. REP. No. 653, *supra* note 34, at 29-51.

[40] H.R. 12,145, 90th Cong., 1st Sess. (1967), reprinted in 113 CONG. REC. 21,584.

[41] The bills before the Senate included H.R. 12,144, *supra* note 39; S. 2218, 90th Cong., 1st Sess. (1967) introduced by Senator Montoya.

program was certified to be "at least equal to" federal standards.[42] The federal government would provide 50 percent of the funding to states conducting their own inspection programs; alternatively, federal inspection would be provided at no cost. Thus, while the legislation reflected a compromise by allowing the continuation of state-operated and administered meat inspection programs, it also extended USDA inspection standards to cover all of the commercially processed red meat in the United States.[43]

The terms of the legislation reflected congressional concern that many state plants would have difficulty meeting federal standards. States were given a maximum of three years to make their inspection programs equal to federal standards. Federal requirements of a technical nature, such as blueprint approvals and construction requirements, were not to be applied arbitrarily to smaller facilities. Practical accommodations toward smaller businesses were not to compromise "the requirements in wholesomeness, additives, labeling and the other federal regulations . . . ."[44] The new Wholesome Meat Act was passed in the House and Senate on December 6, 1967, and was signed into law on December 15, 1967. (Upton Sinclair, 89 years old, attended the signing in a wheelchair.[45])

The Federal Meat Inspection Act and Amendments

Today, the meat inspection system is substantially federalized. Indeed, the inspection was "federal" even in the statute's new name; when the Wholesome Meat Act was combined with the Meat Inspection Act of 1907, the statute became the Federal Meat Inspection Act (FMIA).[46] Even states that have continued to operate their own programs must continually review whether there is any point in paying half the cost of running a state meat inspection program when the federal government will take over the program and pay the entire cost.[47] Thus far, 23 states have opted for federal inspection for budgetary reasons, including many larger states such as California, New York, and Pennsylvania.[48]

State-inspected establishments did benefit in 2008 with the passage of Title XI of the Food, Conservation, and Energy Act of 2008 (2008 Farm Bill). The 2008 Farm Bill amended both the FMIA and the Poultry Products Inspection Act (PPIA) to establish a new cooperative state program under which certain state-inspected establishments would be permitted to ship meat and poultry products, bearing a federal mark of inspection, in interstate commerce. Under this law, FSIS, in coordination with the appropriate state agency, can select state-inspected establishments that employ 25 or fewer employees, on average, to ship meat and poultry products across state lines. Establishments with more than 25 employees but less than 35 employees could also be selected to participate, but would be required to transition

---

[42]   If a state was well on its way to developing an "equal" inspection program by December 15, 1969, it was allowed an additional year to comply. Pub. L. No. 90-201, § 15, 81 Stat. at 595 (codified at 21 U.S.C. § 661).

[43]   The legislation contained exemptions for "custom slaughter." When a farmer brings an animal to a meat locker plant, the animal is to be slaughtered for the farmer's own use. *Id.* § 11, 81 Stat. at 591 (codified at 21 U.S.C. § 623).

[44]   S. Rep. No. 799, 90th Cong., 1st Sess. 5 (1967) (accompanying S. 2147).

[45]   H. Wellford, *supra* note 33, at 24.

[46]   Pub. L. No. 90-201, § 1, 81 Stat. at 584.

[47]   Federal inspection also will be imposed at the request of a governor who waives the application of state law, or if the Secretary finds any plant distributing adulterated products dangerous to the public health. 21 U.S.C. § 661(c)(1).

[48]   9 C.F.R. § 331.2 (2014).

to federal inspection after three years if they consistently employed, on average, more than 25 employees. A final rule implementing this program was promulgated on April 21, 2011, and became effective July 1, 2011.[49] Currently, Ohio, Indiana, North Dakota, and Wisconsin participate in this program.

The 2008 Farm Bill[50] also amended the FMIA to make "catfish, as defined by the Secretary," an amenable species.[51] This amendment had the effect of transferring regulatory jurisdiction over catfish from FDA to FSIS and subjecting catfish to continuous inspection. At the same time, the bill recognized the difference in slaughter and processing as compared to other amenable species and added section 21 U.S.C. 625 to the FMIA to exempt catfish from the sections dealing with antemortem and postmortem inspection and humane slaughter,[52] inspection of carcasses and parts before their entry into establishments or further processing departments,[53] and exemptions from inspection for custom and farm slaughter and processing and other exemptions.[54] The bill instructed FSIS to consult with FDA when promulgating rules to implement these amendments.[55]

In February 2011, FSIS issued a proposed rule requesting comments on the definition of "catfish" and other inspection parameters.[56] FSIS proposed two possible definitions for "catfish": 1) fish belonging to the family Ictaluridae, commonly known as the North American Catfish family and includes the fork-tailed channel catfish, blue catfish, and the flathead catfish,[57] or 2) a broader definition of all fish of the order Siluriformes, which would include 36 families of fish, including the Ictaluridae family and other families of catfish commonly raised in Asia, such as the family Pangasiidae or giant catfish. It has been the definition of catfish that has been the most controversial aspect of the proposed rule.

Since 2011, FSIS has been working with FDA to promulgate a final rule, while cognizant of efforts by some lawmakers to repeal the law. However, on February 7, 2014, Congress passed the Agricultural Act of 2014 (2014 Farm Bill) which, among other things, directed FSIS to publish a final rule on mandatory inspection of catfish within 60 days and for FSIS and FDA to enter into a Memorandum of Understanding (MOU) to improve interagency cooperation and prevent duplication regarding inspection of Siluriformes fish and fish products.[58]

The requirement for the MOU made it clear that the broader definition of catfish set forth in the proposed rule should be finalized and that FSIS is to be the primary regulatory authority for all fish of the order Siluriformes. Although the final rule has yet to be published, it has been reported that it was sent to the Office of Management and Budget on May 30, 2014.

---

[49]   76 Fed. Reg. 24,714 (May 2, 2011).

[50]   Pub. L. No. 110-246, § 10016(b).

[51]   21 U.S.C. § 601(w)(2).

[52]   21 U.S.C. §§ 603, 604.

[53]   21 U.S.C. § 605.

[54]   21 U.S.C. § 623.

[55]   See Pub. L. No. 110-246, § 10016(b).

[56]   76 Fed. Reg. 10,434 (Feb. 24, 2011).

[57]   The 2002 Farm Bill had amended the FDCA by adding a section declaring that the term "catfish" was the common or usual name (or part thereof) of only those fish classified in the family Ictaluridae and permitted the labeling or advertising only for those fish classified in this family to include the term "catfish." 21 U.S.C. §§ 321d(a), 343(t); Pub. L. No. 107-171, tit. X, § 10806, 116 Stat. 526.

[58]   Pub. L. No. 113-79, § 12106.

Poultry Inspection

In contrast to meat and meat food products under comprehensive USDA regulation in 1906, poultry remained subject to the Federal Food, Drug and Cosmetic Act (FDCA)[59] until the passage of the Poultry Products Inspection Act in 1957.[60] Prior to 1957, FDA had the same legal jurisdiction over poultry slaughter and processing that it continues to have over fish (other than catfish) and game. Despite FDA's statutory authority, however, USDA was induced to initiate voluntary poultry inspection programs as early as the mid-1920s. This voluntary inspection was conceptually the same as the voluntary, continuous inspection program that USDA's Agricultural Marketing Service (AMS) makes available to fruit and vegetable processors.[61]

Over the years, USDA poultry inspections grew to national proportions as more and more local jurisdictions passed laws prohibiting sales of all but USDA-inspected poultry. While USDA was beginning poultry inspection in the 1920s, New York, Chicago, and several other larger cities passed ordinances requiring that ready-to-cook or further-processed poultry products sold in these cities must be federally inspected. A similar requirement was imposed for export of poultry products to Canada.[62] At that time, most interstate commerce in poultry involved the shipment of live poultry, which was slaughtered in the locality where it would be marketed.[63] Thus, the largest cities were able to inspect and regulate the slaughter of poultry within their city limits, but could not regulate the wholesomeness of poultry products prepared elsewhere. USDA's voluntary inspection program responded to this need by inspecting chicken carcasses, turkey carcasses, and the canning of whole chickens and boned chicken and turkey meat.[64]

Originally, USDA claimed no statutory authority for its poultry inspections. After the enactment of the Agricultural Marketing Act of 1946,[65] the department relied on the general authority of that statute to offer voluntary inspection services at the processor's expense.[66] By the end of World War II, the integrated growing and slaughter of broiler chickens rapidly supplanted the shipment of live poultry for slaughter in the marketplace. At the same time, USDA's poultry inspection program was ready to provide inspection for the vastly larger quantities of poultry products moving in interstate commerce.

The voluntary poultry inspection program developed in USDA's AMS was separate from the BAI, which administered mandatory meat inspection, and the Bureau of Chemistry, which administered the Pure Food and Drugs Act. By the late 1940s, administration of the Pure Food and Drugs Act had been moved out of the jurisdiction of USDA into the Federal Security Agency. USDA's Poultry Division, while still separate from the red meat inspection

---

[59]   Pub. L. No. 75-717, 52 Stat. 1040 (1938) (codified as amended 21 U.S.C. §§ 301 *et seq.*).

[60]   Pub. L. No. 85-172, 71 Stat. 441 (1957) (codified as amended 21 U.S.C. §§ 451-470).

[61]   7 C.F.R. § 353.6.

[62]   Deposition of Dr. Daniel deKamp, *in Tyson's Foods, Inc.* v. USDA, Civ. No. F-77 5059 app. C (W.D. Ark. Feb. 23, 1977).

[63]   7 U.S.C. §§ 218-218d (1994). For this reason, the Packers and Stockyards Act, enacted in 1921, applies to live-poultry dealers and handlers, not to poultry packers or processors.

[64]   Deposition of Dr. Daniel deKamp, in Tyson's Foods, Inc., Civ. No. F-77 5059 app. C, at 13.

[65]   60 Stat. 1087 (1946).

[66]   7 U.S.C. § 1621(h). This statute authorizes USDA to provide voluntary inspection services to processors of a wide variety of agricultural commodities.

program at BAI, made its regulations and standards as close as possible to those used for red meat inspection. This similarity apparently was based on the practical assumption that what was sanitary for red meat processing also would be sanitary for poultry processing, and that the amount of any added substance acceptable for red meat also generally would be acceptable for poultry.[67]

From 1926 until the passage of the PPIA in 1957, USDA provided voluntary, fee-paid inspection for poultry processing, promulgated regulations for poultry slaughter and sanitation, and approved additives and labeling for poultry. During this time, the law regulating use of additives, labeling, and wholesomeness of poultry and poultry products was the Pure Food and Drugs Act, administered first by USDA's Bureau of Chemistry and later by FDA. Finally, in 1957, the PPIA was enacted,[68] not only providing authority for mandatory postmortem inspection of each carcass and antemortem inspection of poultry in interstate commerce "when necessary," but also requiring that the federal government bear the cost of inspection.[69]

The new statute acknowledged the existence of a new, centralized poultry industry. The hearings during the Eighty-Fifth Congress recognized this change:

> Poultry was a "Sunday dinner" specialty in 1906 when the Meat Inspection Act was passed and poultry was not covered by that Act. It continued to be a minor meat product for many years. Until recently, the bulk of poultry was bought by the consumer either live from the farmer-producer or from a produce house, or New York dressed (only blood and feathers removed). The housewife eviscerated and finally prepared the product for cooking observing firsthand if there were abnormalities, spoilage, or evidence of unwholesomeness.[70]

After passage of the Wholesome Meat Act of 1967, there was great pressure in the 1968 election year to extend to poultry the requirement that state inspection programs be at least "equal to" the federal program. Ralph Nader's attention had been directed to the poultry industry even before he became involved in the 1967 meat inspection debate.[71] Only four states had active poultry inspection programs.[72] The PPIA was duly expanded[73] with the clear intent to emulate, as closely as possible, the 1967 Meat Act.[74]

---

67   Deposition of Daniel deKamp, in *Tyson's Food, Inc.*, Civ. No. F-77 5059 app. C, at 9.
68   Pub. L. No. 85-172, 71 Stat. 441 (1957) (codified at 21 U.S.C. §§ 451-470).
69   H.R. REP. No. 465, 85th Cong., 1st Sess. 1 (1957).
70   *Quoted in* CONGRESSIONAL RESEARCH SERVICE, *supra* note 22, at 30.
71   H. WELLFORD, *supra* note 33, at 9.
72   H.R. REP. No. 1333, 90th Cong., 2d Sess. 1 (1967).
73   Wholesome Poultry Products Act, Pub. L. No. 90-492, 82 Stat. 791 (1967).
74   "[V]ariance from the pattern set by the Federal Meat Inspection Act was considered as fraught with possible problems in compliance on the part of industry. The decision was made to adhere, insofar as the subject permitted, as closely to the newly enacted meat legislation as possible." H.R. REP. No. 1333, *supra* note 72, at 1.

The Distinctive Features of USDA Programs—Continuous Inspection: Its Cost and Scope, USDA's Enforcement Powers, and Labeling Requirements

Continuous inspection of each meat and poultry carcass slaughtered and a daily inspection of processing is a vast activity requiring an agency budget substantially more than the FDA budget for food regulation. As constraints on federal spending grow, there will be more and more pressure to use technological advances to streamline inspection. With streamlining, however, will come an increasing use of FSIS enforcement powers. Among other powers, FSIS has summary powers to withdraw inspection,[75] condemn foods,[76] stop processing operations[77] and obtain records.

Cost of Continuous Inspection

For fiscal year 2009, FSIS received $975 million for the direct costs of meat and poultry inspection.[78] Additional reimbursable costs for overtime work of inspectors and laboratory work were estimated to be $125 million. Thus, the budget of FSIS for meat and poultry inspection alone was $1.100 billion.[79] In 2010, this number went to $1.167 billion,[80] 2011 — $1.175 billion,[81] 2012 — $1.160 billion,[82] and for 2013 — $1.151 billion.[83] For a similar period, FDA's funding requests for food regulations, including publication of approvals for food additives, development of food standards and good manufacturing regulations, inspection of processing plants and marketing establishments, and research did not pass the billion mark until fiscal 2011, when $1.041 billion was requested.[84] However, the actual amount received for fiscal year 2011 was $836.24 million, up from $783.2 million in 2010.[85] The budget increased to $866.9 million in 2012 and then decreased to $796.6 million in 2013.[86] Not only is the FSIS budget for meat and poultry inspection significantly larger than the FDA budget for food and cosmetic regulation but also some of the activities in the FDA budget, such as the approval of food additives, are performed for the benefit of meat and poultry inspection.

---

[75]   21 U.S.C. §§ 371 (meat), 455 (poultry).

[76]   Id. §§ 604 (meat), 455 (poultry).

[77]   Id. §§ 604, 605 (meat), 456 (poultry).

[78]   Office of Management and Budget, Budget of the United States Government, Fiscal Year 2011 app. 90 (2010).

[79]   Id.

[80]   Office of Management and Budget, Budget of the United States Government, Fiscal Year 2012 app. 84 (2011).

[81]   Office of Management and Budget, Budget of the United States Government, Fiscal Year 2013 app. 89 (2012).

[82]   Office of Management and Budget, Budget of the United States Government, Fiscal Year 2014 app. 86 (2013).

[83]   Office of Management and Budget, Budget of the United States Government, Fiscal Year 2015 app. 88 (2014).

[84]   Health and Human Services, Food and Drug Administration, Justification of Estimates for Appropriations Committees FY 2011 at 65.

[85]   Health and Human Services, Food and Drug Administration, Justification of Estimates for Appropriations Committees FY2015 at 31.

[86]   Id.

Meat and poultry inspection is expensive because it is continuous. In fiscal year 2013, there were 10 federally inspected slaughter plants, 3,998 federally inspected processing plants, and 1,076 combination slaughter and processing plants.[87] FSIS accumulated 9,158 compensable work years, almost entirely directed to meat and poultry inspection.[88] In addition to this extensive federal activity, 27 states still maintained intrastate meat and poultry inspection, covering an additional 1,641 meat and poultry slaughter and processing plants.[89] Now that FSIS has assumed greater national responsibility for intrastate inspection as detailed in the 2008 Farm Bill, its expenditures will be even larger.

Scope of FSIS Authority

Between the two food regulatory agencies, FSIS by far has the most extensive enforcement authority. FSIS inspectors have summary authority to condemn, and can order the immediate destruction in their presence of, any product determined to be adulterated.[90] Products may not move from an establishment until they have been marked "inspected and passed" by FSIS.[91] Whenever FSIS has reason to believe that meat or poultry is adulterated or misbranded in commerce, the agency may detain the product administratively for 20 days, regardless of whether the product poses a food safety risk.[92] When an inspector challenges, in any part, the sanitary conditions of an establishment or whether an establishment can produce safe and wholesome products, the inspector may suspend inspection—effectively shutting down the plant—until the sanitation or other alleged defect is corrected to the inspector's satisfaction. [93]

The most sweeping grant of regulatory authority in the inspection acts may be the incorporation by reference of the Federal Trade Commission's (FTC) authority to use subpoenas, obtain access to records, and compel reports. This authority (granted to FTC by sections 46, 48, 49, and 50 of Title 15 of the *United States Code*) is extended to the Secretary of Agriculture in section 677 of Title 21.[94] The grant of these FTC powers to the Secretary of Agriculture means that packers and processors may be required to produce records to FSIS almost without limit.

The pervasive presence of meat and poultry inspectors and the extensive powers granted under the statutes have compelled meat and poultry establishments to cooperate with

---

[87] OFFICE OF MANAGEMENT AND BUDGET, BUDGET OF THE UNITED STATES GOVERNMENT, FISCAL YEAR 2015 app. 88 (2014).

[88] *Id.* at 89.

[89] *Id.* at 88.

[90] 21 U.S.C. §§ 604 (meat), 455(c) (poultry).

[91] *Id.* § 606 (meat).

[92] *Id.* §§ 672 (meat), 467a (poultry).

[93] *Id.* §§ 604, 606 (meat), 456 (poultry).

[94] *Id.* § 677 provides in pertinent part:

> For the efficient administration and enforcement of this Chapter, the provisions (including penalties) of Sections 46, 48, 49, and 50 of Title 15 (except paragraphs (c) through (h) of Section 46 and the last paragraph of Section 49 of Title 15), and the provisions of subsection 409 (1) of Title 47 are made applicable to the jurisdiction, powers, and duties of the Secretary in administering and enforcing the provisions of this chapter and to any person, firm, or corporation with respect to whom such authority is exercised . . . .

See also id. § 457c (poultry).

inspectors. Consequently, the number of meat and poultry inspection cases litigated in federal court during the 100-plus years this inspection has been carried out is a small fraction of those litigated under the FDCA. Although FSIS has the authority to institute seizure and condemnation proceedings in federal courts,[95] this authority is seldom used because adulterated meat and poultry can be condemned or retained administratively before leaving the processing plant.

FSIS Enforcement Powers

Separate and apart from FSIS' huge inspection staff is its nationwide compliance staff, consisting of Program Investigators (PIs) and Enforcement Investigation Analysis Officers (EIAOs). Both the PIs and the EIAOs investigate alleged violations of the meat and poultry inspection acts. The PIs focus primarily on violations that could result in criminal prosecution whereas EIAOs focus primarily on violations that could result in administrative sanctions, such as plant suspensions. In this regard, inspection personnel are the "cops on the beat"; PIs and EIAOs are the "detectives." When either inspection or FSIS compliance staff discover violations of the inspection acts, a variety of administrative and judicial actions and sanctions are available to FSIS.

Authority Over Product

FSIS can use four principal regulatory tools against an adulterated or misbranded product. First, although not expressly mentioned in the statutes, FSIS has the authority to prohibit the shipment of product from an inspected establishment. This authority is referred to as a "regulatory control action" and is taken by the inspector placing a "retained tag" on the product. The failure to destroy condemned product is cause to withdraw inspection under the FMIA (but not under the PPIA). Second, FSIS can detain the product in the field.[96] Detention occurs when a compliance officer places a product within the custody of the agency. The product cannot be moved without permission from FSIS. Usually, the processor of the product will negotiate with FSIS for permission to return the product to its inspected establishment, where it will be tagged and held by the resident inspector. Third, if a plant refuses to return a detained product for reworking or destruction, FSIS can institute a "seizure" action,[97] requesting a federal district court to direct a U.S. Marshal to take custody of the product. The agency will then seek a court order condemning the product and authorizing its destruction. Fourth, FSIS can act against a product by requesting its "recall."[98] Although recalls are theoretically "voluntary," they actually are compulsory.[99] If a company refuses to recall, FSIS will issue a press release and a public warning (worse than any recall notice), and may then proceed to detain and seize the product.[100]

---

[95]   *Id.* §§ 673 (meat), 467b (poultry).

[96]   *Id.* §§ 672 (meat), 467a (poultry).

[97]   *Id.* §§ 673 (meat), 467b (poultry).

[98]   FSIS Directive No. 8080.1 Rev. 6 (2010).

[99]   Although FDA now has the statutory authority to order a recall pursuant to the FDA Food Safety Modernization Act of 2010 (H.R. Rep. No. 2751), this authority was not granted to FSIS.

[100]   The 2008 Farm Bill required establishments to "promptly" notify the Secretary of Agriculture if there is any reason to believe adulterated or misbranded product has entered commerce. See H.R. REP. No. 2419, 110th Cong., 1st Sess. (2008). On May 8, 2012, FSIS published a final rule to implement this provision of the Farm Bill. 77 Fed. Reg. 26,929 (2012).

Authority Over Inspected Establishments

In addition to its authority to take action against a product, FSIS can seek other sanctions against inspected establishments through administrative or judicial means.

Administrative Action. The simplest administrative action is to intensify inspection in establishments that are not meeting regulatory requirements or where there might be public health concerns. Until recently, this was accomplished through the Performance Based Inspection System (PBIS), whereby verification of regulatory requirements was mostly conducted through a set of 48 pre-scheduled task codes. The inspector reported in the PBIS the results of these tasks and FSIS would later determine how a plant was performing and direct subsequent procedure assignments accordingly. FSIS is now completing the process of implementing a new integrated data system, called the Public Health Inspection System (PHIS).[101] Under PHIS, rather than be provided with "scheduled" inspection tasks, inspectors are given a prioritized list of tasks to perform within a certain time frame, based on the plant's profile[102] and the results of previous inspection tasks. Inspectors then manage their own inspection calendars based on their knowledge of establishments' operations and their workload. Results of tasks, as well as other data regarding the plant, are entered into PHIS and follow-up tasks are then scheduled based on this data. Electronic messages (alerts) and reports are also provided to inspectors to notify them of "important information" available in the system that may need to be addressed, such as repetitive noncompliances or positive laboratory test results for pathogens. FSIS believes that this system allows inspectors to make more informed decisions and respond more quickly to issues that could present food safety threats.

If an establishment fails a particular procedure, the inspector will issue a Noncompliance Record (NR) to the establishment. The NR will describe the noncompliance in specific detail and will indicate whether there was a previous noncompliance for the same cause. The NR will also identify whether a regulatory control action was taken, which may include the retention of product (as discussed above) or a related action called "rejection." A rejection occurs when the inspector determines that either equipment or an area of the facility is insanitary, and therefore cannot be used again until the issue is resolved and the rejection is terminated. The inspector can also take the immediate action of withholding the mark of inspection on product, without which product cannot be distributed in commerce. Although not expressly permitted by the statutes, FSIS has interpreted the inspection acts to allow it to withhold the mark of inspection if it cannot affirmatively conclude that the product is not adulterated.[103]

Should an inspector document a failure of the establishment's food safety systems (often through multiple NRs depicting repetitive noncompliances for the same cause), the inspector

---

[101] PHIS has four system modules: domestic inspection, import inspection, export inspection, and predictive analytics.

[102] The plant profile would be based on numerous factors, including the volume of production, the types of meat and/or poultry products produced at the plant, and the food safety controls implemented in the plant. *See* http://www.fsis.usda.gov/phis.

[103] On December 10, 2012, FSIS issued a notice indicating that it would withhold the mark of inspection when the agency samples products for pathogens. 77 Fed. Reg. 73,401 (2012). The mark would be withheld until negative results from the tests are received. The agency issued the notice in response to recalls that occurred because inspected establishments failed to voluntarily hold products tested by the agency.

may recommend to the appropriate FSIS District Office that it take enforcement action against the establishment. Prior to conducting such action, the District Office may send an EIAO to the establishment to conduct a "comprehensive food safety assessment." The EIAOs would review the establishment's food safety systems to ensure they meet regulatory requirements and are supported by science. They would also review the establishment's recent compliance history, including NRs. Based on the findings of the inspector and/or the EIAO, the District Office could determine that there is an imminent threat to public health or to inspection personnel and suspend inspection immediately. This action would effectively close the establishment until it could demonstrate or achieve compliance. Alternatively, if the District Office determines the establishment's food safety systems have failed, but there is no imminent threat to public health or inspection personnel, the District Office could issue a Notice of Intended Enforcement Action (NOIE). The NOIE would give the establishment three days to submit a written response, demonstrating either that a systems failure did not occur or that the establishment has implemented preventive actions to achieve compliance. Until the District Office makes a decision on the matter, the establishment would continue to operate.

In cases where establishments continue to demonstrate an inability or unwillingness to comply with regulatory requirements, the District Office may recommend that a complaint be filed before an administrative law judge to withdraw inspection. This permanent enforcement action is discussed further below.

Judicial Sanction. Both the meat and poultry statutes authorize FSIS to seek both injunctions[104] and criminal penalties.[105] An injunction is a court order prohibiting some specific act that the court agrees would violate the law. The department rarely seeks injunctions because it has very broad administrative powers over product and processors that make injunctions unnecessary. Criminal penalties are a much more effective deterrent against covert conduct.

FSIS initiates criminal prosecutions in its meat and poultry inspection programs. In the last 20 years, FSIS compliance has offered establishments the opportunity to present their views prior to referring a matter for prosecution. Although FSIS generally will refer every felony violation of the acts for prosecution, the agency does allow the establishment the opportunity to defend its case orally and in writing and include the establishment's written submission in its file when the matter is referred to an assistant U.S. attorney.

Under the inspection statutes, adulteration (regardless of intent) or a violation of the statute with the intent to defraud (e.g., using nitrate to make meat look fresher, adding water to ground beef) can be charged as a felony.[106] A felony conviction can carry a jail term of up to three years. In addition, because the Criminal Fine Enforcement Act of 1984[107] applies to the FMIA as well as the PPIA, a felony conviction can expose a company to a fine of up to $500,000 and an individual to a fine of up to $250,000. Violations not involving adulteration or intent to defraud are deemed to be misdemeanors, with a maximum fine of

---

[104]   21 U.S.C. §§ 674 (meat), 467c (poultry).
[105]   *Id.* §§ 676 (meat), 461 (poultry).
[106]   *Id.* §§ 676 (meat), 461 (poultry).
[107]   18 U.S.C. § 3571.

$100,000 for either a company or an individual (under the Criminal Fine Enforcement Act) plus a jail term of up to one year.[108]

Withdrawal of Inspection. As noted above, FSIS may seek to withdraw inspection from an establishment permanently if there is a history of noncompliance which demonstrates that the establishment is either unwilling or unable to comply with regulatory requirements. Criminal convictions also provide the opportunity for FSIS to seek withdrawal of inspection from any establishment that has been convicted of any felony or more than one violation not considered a felony.[109] This authority also may be exercised if a "responsibly-connected person"[110] has been convicted. Because federal inspection is needed to slaughter/process meat or poultry for sale, loss of inspection puts a company out of business.

For both meat and poultry establishments, repeated suspension actions for the same cause or convictions almost automatically will trigger a proceeding for withdrawal of inspection, which is covered by an administrative law judge. In this proceeding, FSIS seeks to establish that the repeated noncompliances or the conviction has rendered the company and/or the convicted individuals "unfit" to receive federal inspection.[111] In all but one instance, the agency has been able to meet this burden and withdraw inspection.[112] Nevertheless, FSIS routinely negotiates settlement agreements that allow companies to remain in business. However, if the withdrawal action was the result of a conviction, FSIS could seek to sever any convicted individual from ownership or control of the inspected establishment.

The administrative and judicial sanctions, when coupled with the ability to withdraw inspection, are powerful enforcement tools at FSIS's disposal. Furthermore, as science increases its ability to detect violative products, FSIS has shown a stronger proclivity to use its sanction authority. For example, in the late 1980s when FSIS first developed its testing methodology to detect the presence of poultry or pork in cooked beef products, the agency instituted a large number of recalls whenever an establishment was found to have undeclared pork or poultry in the products. FSIS referred many of these cases for prosecution, even without evidence of intent to substitute the less expensive ingredients. Within a year after developing the testing methodology, FSIS adopted a more practical approach to these matters, only referring for prosecution those cases for which there was corroborating evidence of an intent to defraud.

Labeling

Part of FSIS's broad authority includes its authority to review and approve all labels for meat and poultry products before use.[113] Prior to 1995, this required that all companies prepare a preliminary label, known as a "sketch," and submit the sketch along with the product's formula and processing procedures to an FSIS official in the agency's Labeling and Program Delivery Staff. The official would then review the label to determine whether all required

---

[108]   21 U.S.C. §§ 676 (meat), 461 (poultry).

[109]   *Id.* §§ 671 (meat), 467 (poultry).

[110]   A "responsibly connected person" is an officer, director, or a stock owner with more than 10 percent of the voting stock or an employee in a managerial capacity. *Id.*

[111]   *Id.*

[112]   The singular exception was Utica Packing Co. v. Bergland, Civ. No. 80-72742 (E.D. Mich. Apr. 14, 1981).

[113]   9 C.F.R. §§ 317.4, 381.132.

features are present,[114] the formulation to determine whether the product name comports with any appropriate standard, any claims to ensure they were not false or misleading, and the processing to ensure the product complies with any regulatory requirements.[115]

However, in 1995, FSIS published a final rule to set forth certain types of labels and modifications to labels that were deemed to be approved by FSIS without formal submission to the agency, otherwise known as "generically approved" labels.[116] This category of generically approved labels significantly expanded in November 2013.[117] FSIS now considers all labels generically approved unless they fall under one of the following categories: 1) labels for temporary label approval, 2) labels for products produced under a religious exemption, 3) labels for products for export with labeling deviations, and 4) labels with "special statements and claims," generally defined as natural claims, negative claims, and additional claims, logos, trademarks, or other symbols that are not defined in the FSIS meat and poultry regulations or the FSIS Standards and Labeling Policy Book.[118]

Because FSIS still reviews hundreds of labels every year,[119] the agency must make countless rulings every day on labeling issues that arise. Accordingly, FSIS has adopted a variety of informal policies to provide guidance to officials who are reviewing labels, as well as to industry.[120] In such a dynamic situation, establishing regulatory criteria for all issues is impractical.

In 1993, however, FSIS adopted regulations mandating nutrition labeling of meat and poultry products.[121] These regulations substantially mirror those adopted by FDA under the Nutrition Labeling and Education Act.[122] Under these regulations, meat and poultry products (except raw single-ingredient products and other products specifically exempted) must bear nutrition information, the information must be presented in a manner identical to that required by FDA,[123] and nutrient content claims (such as "low fat" or "high in protein") are governed by substantially the same criteria as those applicable to foods regulated by FDA.

When FSIS promulgated its nutrition labeling regulations, raw meat and poultry single-ingredient products were exempt from mandatory nutritional labeling requirements and were instead subject to voluntary labeling. However, on December 29, 2010, FSIS published

---

[114] This includes the product name, net weight, inspection legend, ingredients statement (if made from two or more ingredients), signature line, nutrition information (if other than a raw single-ingredient product), and handling instructions.

[115] FSIS has adopted certain processing requirements, such as cooking temperatures for roast beef and patties.

[116] 60 Fed. Reg. 67,455 (Dec. 29, 1995).

[117] 78 Fed. Reg. 66,826 (Nov. 7, 2013).

[118] 9 C.F.R. pt. 412.

[119] Even if a label is considered "generically approved," a company may choose to voluntarily submit the label to FSIS for review and approval.

[120] Most of the informal policies are contained in FSIS's *Standards and Labeling Policy Book*, available on FSIS's website. However, when FSIS issued the final rule expanding the categories of generic label approval in November 2013, it announced that it would not add new policies to this book. New labeling policy developed by the agency would be conveyed through the use of other means, such as compliance policy guides posted on the agency's website.

[121] 9 C.F.R. pt. 317, subpt. B and pt. 381, subpt. Y.

[122] Pub. L. No. 101-535, 104 Stat. 2353 (1990).

[123] FSIS does permit use of a simplified format in more cases than would be permitted by FDA.

a final rule to require nutritional labeling on 1) all major cuts of single-ingredient, raw meat and poultry products, unless exempted, and 2) all ground and chopped meat and poultry products, with or without seasoning, unless exempted.[124] For major cuts of single-ingredient products, the nutrition information can appear either on the label or in point of purchase (POP) material. For ground and chopped products, the nutritional information must be provided on the label. The final rule became effective January 1, 2012.

Impact of Technological Developments

In the first 60 years of inspection, the system performed well. Given the initial public health concerns of diseased, insanitary, or economically adulterated meat and poultry, a visual examination was the optimum inspection system. The technological developments of the past 30 years, however, have made the traditional system obsolete. Microbiological contaminants, many of which were unknown 30 years ago, have replaced animal disease as the principal public health concern, and this concern cannot be addressed by an inspection system developed 100 years ago.

Moreover, the last 30 years have been years of change for both the meat industry and the federal inspection program. During this time, more and more plants came under inspection. Much of this program growth was due to the emergence of prepared convenience foods, such as frozen dinners and entrees, which created a new generation of meat processing establishments. Some of this growth was the result of phasing out state meat inspection systems due to state budgetary constraints.

The expansion of prepared-food processing and the inclusion of state plants imposed serious strains on the department's resources. As the meat and poultry industry expanded, there was no proportionate increase in the agency's inspection budget,[125] approximately 79 percent of which is consumed by employee salaries and benefits.[126] To do more with less, the agency had to reshape its traditional inspection system, but with no extra resources to implement such a change.

To meet the challenge, FSIS relied on technological innovations that have resulted in improved animal health and the ability to control process instead of product. These changes enabled both processors and regulators to be more efficient and productive. The agency's attempts at maximizing inspection coverage, however, proved controversial. Efforts to reduce the number of inspector positions generated opposition from the inspectors' union, the American Federation of Government Employees. Consumer activist organizations questioned whether fewer inspectors would result in greater risk to public health.

---

[124]   75 Fed. Reg. 82,147 (Dec. 29, 2010).

[125]   In the years 1980 through 1988, an additional 5 percent meat and 120 percent poultry were inspected while departmental resources were cut by 10 percent. EXECUTIVE OFFICE OF THE PRESIDENT, BUDGET OF THE UNITED STATES GOVERNMENT: FISCAL YEAR 1982 app. I-E95; EXECUTIVE OFFICE OF THE PRESIDENT, BUDGET OF THE UNITED STATES GOVERNMENT: FISCAL YEAR 1990 app. I-E84.

[126]   In fiscal year 1994, outlays for FSIS were $558,000,000, of which $446,000,000 (79 percent), goes to personnel expenses. EXECUTIVE OFFICE OF THE PRESIDENT, BUDGET OF THE UNITED STATES GOVERNMENT: FISCAL YEAR 1996 app. 137.

Consumer activists also were concerned that the system simply was not controlling pathogens, which were attributing to more human illnesses. Yet in large part, FSIS was unable to achieve meaningful change to deal with microbial pathogens due to the lack of funding and the opposition to change within its ranks. The forced inactivity in light of increasing concern over pathogens began to generate adverse press coverage for the meat and poultry industry and the inspection program, exacerbating the public perception that FSIS simply was not doing its job.

In 1986, Congress enacted the Processed Products Inspection Improvement Act (PPIIA),[127] which authorized FSIS to vary inspection frequency at processing establishments when it determined that the plant had adequate control and a good compliance history. The authority would allow FSIS to modernize the system and take advantage of industry's control programs, at least for processing establishments. Due to almost universal opposition to the regulations proposed under the act, however, it was never implemented. Moreover, in 1992, the act was sunsetted.[128]

Meanwhile, FSIS attempted to modernize inspection by restructuring the inspection process through the Inspector System Work Plan and the PBIS. While such systems added efficiency, they still did not address the pathogen issue. It was not until the 1993 *E. coli* O157:H7 outbreak in the Pacific Northwest that the agency truly began to come to grips with the problem. In spite of FSIS's efforts to reform its inspection process, the agency also had to consider the concerns of the inspectors' union, industry, consumer activists, and the press.

The Emergence of Microbiological Contaminants as the Number One Food Safety Concern

The risks of bacterial contamination of food and water have been well known since the middle of the 19th century. The name "Louis Pasteur" is a household word around the world because of the heat treatment process that he invented to control pathogens in raw milk. The *Salmonella* family of organisms (including *Salmonella* typhosa, which causes typhoid fever, and other species, which cause salmonellosis) were also initially discovered in the 19th century. Various coliform organisms, which are generally of fecal origin, have been known and controlled for all of the past century.

Foods of natural origin, whether animal or vegetable, are particularly susceptible to bacterial contamination. Traditional controls have included good sanitation and proper handling (to minimize bacteria levels in raw foods), and effective cooking and/or heat treatment (to eliminate bacteria in RTE foods). During the past decade, it has become evident that these traditional controls provide less than perfect protection against pathogens in food.

While there have been major food poisoning outbreaks associated with *Listeria monocytogenes* in ethnic cheese and *Cryptosporidium* parasite resis in the drinking water supply of Milwaukee, the event that brought new focus to bacterial risk with meat and poultry products occurred in January 1993 with the outbreak of *E. coli* O157:H7 illness. More than 400 people became ill from consumption of hamburgers from Jack-in-the-Box restaurants, particularly in the

---

[127]   Pub. L. No. 99-641, §§ 401-408, 100 Stat. 3556, 3567-72 (1986).
[128]   The PPIIA also expanded FSIS enforcement authority, but these provisions sunsetted as well.

Seattle area. Four children died: three had eaten at Jack-in-the-Box and one had been in contact with a child who had eaten there. The response of USDA to this incident was to institute zero tolerance for fecal contamination on beef carcasses at slaughter, and to require product handling labels on raw meat and poultry products.

Prior to the *E. coli* O157:H7 outbreak in Seattle, FSIS made a clear demarcation between RTE products (e.g., frankfurters and luncheon meats) and raw products (e.g., hamburger and fresh poultry). The agency mandated that RTE products be cooked at temperatures sufficient to kill pathogens,[129] and required Class I recalls where a RTE product tested positive for a pathogen.[130] On the other hand, the agency took the position that consumers could be expected to understand that raw meat and poultry must be cooked before eating. In 1974, this assumption was tested in court when the American Public Health Association (APHA) sought to have the USDA inspection legend on poultry modified to delete any reference to "wholesomeness."[131] The APHA suit was rejected by the U.S. district court, which determined that consumers can be expected to know that raw meat and poultry have to be cooked.

In October 1988, FSIS identified precooked beef patties served in a school cafeteria as a source of an *E. coli* O157:H7 outbreak in Minnesota. This finding led to extensive research by USDA, meat processors, and national fast-food restaurant chains directed at finding the proper cooking temperature necessary to kill the *E. coli* O157:H7 bacteria as well as to develop cooking procedures that would eliminate the risk of this particular bacterium. On December 27, 1988, FSIS first published a proposal to establish minimum cooking temperatures for precooked beef patties[132] making it final on August 2, 1993.[133]

The emerging concern and knowledge about *E. coli* O157:H7 was made possible by advances in science that allowed laboratories to isolate pathogens previously regarded as laboratory curiosities. These new tests and procedures made it possible to identify the O157:H7 strain of *E. coli*, a coliform subtype unknown in the 1970s. Similarly, new methods allowed the identification of *Campylobacter* in poultry, now believed to be more prevalent than *Salmonella* in raw poultry and poultry processing.

FSIS's initial work with *E. coli* O157:H7 in precooked beef patties illustrated the difficulty of drawing a clear line between raw products and cooked products. Prior to 1988, the precooked patty was cooked partially at the processing plant and then again at the restaurant or school cafeteria. FSIS required the cooking temperature at the processing plant to be adequate to control pathogens, because there was no way to ensure that every restaurant or cafeteria would do more than simply rewarm beef patties that appeared RTE.

The Seattle *E. coli* O157:H7 outbreak demonstrated that even a large regional restaurant chain might not thoroughly cook ground meat products to inactivate this pathogen. Following the outbreak, FSIS proceeded on two tracks: instituting tighter slaughter inspection

---

[129]   9 C.F.R. § 318.17.
[130]   For example, the agency has undertaken recalls where hot dogs have been found contaminated with *Listeria monocytogenes*, and fermented sausage with *E. coli* O157:H7.
[131]   American Pub. Health Ass'n v. Butz, 511 F.2d 331 (D.C. Cir. 1974).
[132]   53 Fed. Reg. 52,179 (Dec. 27, 1988).
[133]   58 Fed. Reg. 41,138 (Aug. 2, 1993).

requirements to reduce the chance of fecal contamination of beef carcasses, and requiring safe handling labels for ground meat products to advise both consumers and food service workers of the need to thoroughly cook fresh meat (particularly ground meat).

In March 1993, FSIS imposed zero tolerance standards for fecal contamination on carcasses at slaughter plants. This meant that anything that might be fecal material had to be trimmed from a carcass prior to the final carcass inspection—if it was not trimmed, the line would be stopped for re-examination of the carcasses to be reworked and re-inspected. Alternately, plants could include a rail-out loop to rework the carcasses off-line.

FSIS's next initiative to deal with the risk of pathogenic bacteria was to require the labels of raw products (particularly ground products) to bear safe handling instructions, designed to inform both consumers and food service handlers of the proper methods of handling and preparing products. In August 1993, FSIS proposed that these labels be placed on all raw meat and poultry products within 60 days.[134] While processors and distributors did not object to the substance of the proposed labels, they successfully challenged the lack of an opportunity for notice and comment and a phased implementation period. A federal court in Austin, Texas, required the agency to proceed by notice-and-comment rulemaking[135] and a final rule, virtually identical to the emergency interim regulation, became effective on March 28, 1994.[136]

In August 1994, the new administrator of FSIS responded to criticism from consumer activists and the media by announcing a program to test raw ground meat products for *E. coli* O157:H7. Departing from law established in *American Public Health Association v. Butz*, FSIS announced that *E. coli* O157:H7 would be deemed an adulterant in raw ground meat products. The new proposal generated great consternation among processors and distributors, who were concerned that they would receive FSIS's test results, together with recall notices, for fresh ground beef that had been prepared and shipped two or three weeks earlier. This concern led to new litigation against FSIS, but this time FSIS prevailed and proceeded with its testing program.[137]

During the first year of the FSIS testing program, only three of 4,800 samples were confirmed as positive for *E. coli* O157:H7. However, over the next seven years, the numbers of positives increased, with only a slight increase in testing. As a result of this increase as well as some highly publicized recalls for *E. coli* O157:H7, FSIS began implementing additional initiatives to encourage the beef industry to reduce the prevalence of *E. coli* O157:H7 in its products. FSIS also expanded its definition of adulteration to include other beef products contaminated with *E. coli* O157:H7. These initiatives will be discussed in more detail in the section on *E. coli* O157:H7 later in this chapter.

During the late 1980s and early 1990s, *E. coli* O157:H7 was not the only pathogen that had garnered FSIS's attention. In 1985, listeriosis was linked to the consumption of a "pasteurized" soft cheese that had been contaminated with raw, unpasteurized milk during

---

[134]   58 Fed. Reg. 58,918 (Aug. 16, 1993).
[135]   Texas Food Indus. Ass'n v. USDA, 842 F. Supp. 254 (W.D. Tex. 1993).
[136]   59 Fed. Reg. 14,528 (Mar. 28, 1994).
[137]   Texas Food Indus. Ass'n v. Espy, 870 F. Supp. 143 (W.D. Tex. 1994).

manufacturing, resulting in 142 illnesses with 18 adult deaths as well as 30 fetuses or newborn infants.[138] As a result, FDA and FSIS, which had identified *Listeria monocytogenes* (*Lm*) as an emerging issue with several types of processed meats such as delicatessen meats, began working with processing plants to improve procedures and both agencies emphasized the "zero" tolerance (no detectable level permitted) for the pathogen in RTE products.[139] In 1987 FSIS also initiated a program to test RTE meat and poultry products for *Lm*. Between 1989 and 1993, the rate of illness from *Lm* declined 44 percent.[140]

FSIS took additional action in 1989 when poultry frankfurters were linked to an outbreak of listeriosis in Texas. With this, FSIS issued its first FSIS Directive specifically on *Lm*: FSIS Directive 10,240.1, "Listeria monocytogenes: Testing Procedures and Sanitation Information," and declared *Lm* to be an adulterant in RTE meat and poultry products.[141] In addition, it revised its testing procedures: increasing sample size; focusing on highest risk items; recalling product lots that tested positive on the initial sampling; and pulling and holding products for the stated shelf life before again testing for *Lm*.[142] In August and December 1998 FSIS again updated its *Lm* Directive to provide sampling directions for establishments now under the HACCP system.[143]

Then, in the fall of 1998, a major *Lm* outbreak was associated with hot dogs and delicatessen meats, resulting in a recall of six months of products from one facility. The Centers for Disease Control and Prevention (CDC) reported 101 illnesses, 15 deaths, and six stillbirths or miscarriages.[144] After the 1998 outbreak, FSIS held several public meetings to garner information from experts in academia and the industry. It also updated its sampling plans and worked in consultation with FDA on a risk assessment to determine the prevalence and extent of exposure consumers have to foodborne *Lm* and its public health impact.[145] In the interim, several more major *Lm* outbreaks were linked to poultry with numerous illnesses and deaths.[146]

In 2000, FSIS published a proposed rule with several new requirements for processing RTE meat and poultry products, such as food safety performance standards for all RTE and partially heat-treated products and allowing the use of customized plant-specific processing procedures. In addition, environmental testing requirements were proposed to verify the

---

[138]   Kenneth Todar, *Listeria monocytogenes and Listeriosis*, in TODAR'S ONLINE TEXTBOOK OF BACTERIOLOGY (2008), http://textbookofbacteriology.net/Listeria.html.

[139]   Food Safety and Inspection Service, FSIS Announces Strategy To Control *Listeria monocytogenes* In Ready-To-Eat Meat And Poultry Products (1999), http://www.fsis.usda.gov/Frame/FrameRedirect.asp?main=http://www.fsis.usda.gov/OA/news/1999/lm_haccp.htm.

[140]   *Id.*

[141]   U.S. Department of Agriculture, Economic Research Service, Weighing Incentives for Food Safety in Meat and Poultry (April 2003), http://www.ers.usda.gov/amber-waves/2003-april/weighing-incentives-for-food-safety-in-meat-and-poultry.aspx#.U_St-NKmd-A.

[142]   Presentation by the Microbiology Division, Science, FSIS, USDA (1989).

[143]   FSIS Directive 10,240.2, "Microbial Sampling of Ready-To-Eat Products Produced by Establishments Operating Under a HACCP System" (Aug. 6, 1998).

[144]   USDA-FSIS, Timeline of Events Related to *Listeria monocytogenes* (*Lm*), http://www.fsis.usda.gov/wps/portal/fsis/topics/regulatory-compliance/haccp/updates-and-memos/timeline-of-events-related-to-listeria-monocytogenes/lm-timeline.

[145]   64 Fed. Reg. 24,661 (May 7, 1999).

[146]   USDA-FSIS, Timeline of Events Related to *Listeria monocytogenes*, *supra* note 144.

effectiveness of an establishment's measures to reduce the incidence of *Lm* in RTE meat and poultry.[147] This included testing food contact surfaces for *Listeria* species.

The completed draft "Risk Assessment for *Listeria monocytogenes* in Deli Meat" was released in May 2003 with the "Final Assessment of the Relative Risk to Public Health from Foodborne *Listeria monocytogenes* Among Selected Categories of Ready-to-Eat Foods" released jointly with FDA in September 2003.[148] In between, FSIS published an interim final rule addressing *Lm* control.[149] This rule set the standard for controlling *Lm* in RTE establishments. This will also be discussed in more detail below in the section on *Lm*.

Ultimately, the progress of science has enabled both FSIS and processors to identify a broader range of pathogens and to do so more quickly. Testing, however, has not advanced to the point where it can provide statistically valid assurance that a product is pathogen-free, at least on a cost-effective basis. As faster and less expensive technologies develop, however, these tests increasingly have been used to the extent that USDA defers to them as evidence of good practice and due care, and to the extent that they help protect producers against product liability claims.

Physical Inspection to Science-Based Process Control

From the 1967 and 1968 amendments to the inspection acts, FSIS continued its efforts to change the inspection program from the traditional (but costly) visual inspection to a more scientifically based approach. The National Academy of Sciences (NAS) issued a report in 1985 calling for a more scientifically based, objective inspection system,[150] and emphasized the need for a scientifically based inspection system "not only to reduce the number of occurrences of bacterial infection but also to reduce chemical contamination and ensure the general safety and wholesomeness of meat."[151] NAS issued another similar report in 1987.[152] Both the 1985 and 1987 reports recommended that FSIS replace continuous inspection with sampling and monitoring, and utilize a scientifically based HACCP system.

The move to more reliance on a science-based approach was attempted when the PPIIA was passed in 1986, which permitted FSIS to vary the intensity of inspection by relying on control programs rather than on-site visual inspection. This act, however, was never implemented. Following the 1986 amendments, FSIS took a first step toward a scientifically based HACCP-type system by establishing an Inspection System Work Plan. Under this program, the in-plant inspector and the circuit supervisor reviewed the operations of

---

[147]   66 Fed. Reg. 12,590 (Feb. 27, 2001).

[148]   *See* Quantitative Assessment of the Relative Risk to Public Health from Foodborne *Listeria monocytogenes* Among Selected Categories of Ready-to-Eat Foods, http://www.fda.gov/Food/FoodScienceResearch/RiskSafetyAssessment/ucm183966.htm.

[149]   68 Fed. Reg. 34,208 (June 6, 2003).

[150]   National Academy of Sciences, Meat and Poultry Inspection 116 (1985) [hereinafter 1985 NAS Report].

[151]   *Id.*

[152]   National Academy of Sciences, Poultry Inspection, The Basis for a Risk-Assessment Approach (1987).

each individual establishment that did not have an approved Total Quality Control (TQC) program and identified critical control points in the establishment. FSIS then determined what activities the inspector should monitor as well as the frequency of inspections.[153] Fully implemented by 1987, this system was well received by both inspectors and establishments.

In 1988, FSIS announced a two-part revision of processing inspection designed to respond to the 1986 amendments. The first part, PBIS, dealt with how the agency would inspect. The second part, known as Improved Processing Inspection (IPI), dealt with when the agency would inspect. However, inspection methodology was never made part of the IPI proposed regulations and in response to strong opposition by the industry, the inspectors' union, consumer advocates, and the press, the agency withdrew the IPI proposal in 1989.[154]

It was not until some of the foodborne illness outbreaks discussed above that FSIS had the impetus to make further changes to its inspection system. The agency's response was to turn to the HACCP concepts recommended by the 1985 and 1987 NAS/NRC reports and incorporated in the 1987 Inspection System Work Plan program.

In 1995, FSIS published a proposal to modernize the inspection program and specifically to address microbiological contamination, which was finalized in 1996. This regulation, entitled "Pathogen Reduction: Hazard Analysis and Critical Control Point Systems," was commonly referred to as the "Mega Reg," and later as "PR/HACCP," and included both interim pathogen reduction measures and a mandatory HACCP requirement. The HACCP requirements became effective on January 26, 1998, for large establishments of 500 or more employees, on January 25, 1999, for plants with between 10 and 500 employees, and on January 25, 2000, for plants with less than 10 employees or annual sales below $2.5 million.[155] With the PR/HACCP, FSIS addressed its need to change its system not only to improve food safety and reduce foodborne illness but also to make better use of its resources.[156]

The PR/HACCP

The final rule or PR/HACCP included four new requirements: 1) the development and implementation of sanitation standard operating procedures (SSOPs) or a checklist of measures a plant would undertake daily to assure proper sanitation under inspector oversight; 2) mandatory plant testing of carcasses for generic E. coli, with required corrective action if the plant exceeds a target incident rate to verify the adequacy of the establishment's process controls for the prevention and removal of fecal contamination and associated bacteria; 3) established pathogen reduction performance standards for Salmonella that slaughter establishments and establishments producing raw ground products had to meet; and 4) a requirement for all meat and poultry establishments to develop and implement a system of preventive controls designed to improve the safety of their products: HACCP.[157]

---

[153] FSIS Background, Inspectional System Work Plan (Oct. 1987).
[154] 54 Fed. Reg. 22,300 (May 23, 1989).
[155] 61 Fed. Reg. 38,806 (July 25, 1996).
[156] Id. at 38,807.
[157] 61 Fed. Reg. at 38,806.

SSOP

Sanitation standard operating procedures (SSOPs) were required in all meat and poultry establishments by January 27, 1997, as set forth in the SSOP regulations.[158] These regulations required establishments to develop, implement, and maintain written SSOPs addressing the daily sanitation procedures an establishment would take before and during operations to prevent direct product contamination or adulteration. FSIS inspection program personnel are then required to "verify the adequacy and effectiveness . . . ."[159]

FSIS provided general guidelines and model SSOPs in Appendix A and B of the PR/HACCP.[160] SSOPs may be as general or specific as an establishment chooses to make them as long as the SSOPs are effective in preventing direct product contamination. Even though there is no requirement for microbiological testing to be a part of establishments' SSOPs, they have the option to incorporate these types of testing programs (e.g., *Listeria* species environmental testing in RTE establishments).[161]

Generic *E. Coli* Testing

As an indicator of process control for fecal contamination, the PR/HACCP required all slaughterers to test carcasses for *Escherichia coli* Biotype 1 (generic *E. coli*).[162] This was an important part of the PR/HACCP with the preamble noting that this testing was considered an essential element in a slaughterer's HACCP verification activities.[163] Frequency of testing varies by species and is set so that 80 percent of the samples analyzed should be less than the lower permitted level (m) and 98 percent of the samples analyzed should be below the upper permitted level (M).[164]

Furthermore, the preamble to the PR/HACCP also made it clear that FSIS intended to update the criteria and acceptable levels to ensure it represented the appropriate level of control attainable by slaughtering establishments as results improved.[165]

Salmonella Performance Standards

FSIS conducted baseline studies to determine the prevalence of *Salmonella* on various raw products such as carcasses, ground products, and fresh pork sausage. It periodically tests products to determine whether an establishment is producing products having levels above or below the published baseline percents.[166] Initially, if an establishment had an incident rate higher than that in the published baseline, the plant was subjected to increased compliance activities, which could include withdrawal of inspection for "insanitary" conditions after

---

[158]   9 C.F.R. pt. 416.

[159]   9 C.F.R. § 416.17.

[160]   61 Fed. Reg. 38,871 (July 25, 1996).

[161]   *See* 69 Fed. Reg. 70,052 (Dec. 2, 2004).

[162]   61 Fed. Reg. 38,811 (July 25, 1996). As discussed below, FSIS rescinded this regulation as it applies to chicken broilers and turkeys in August of 2014 in lieu of new carcass testing requirements.

[163]   *Id.*

[164]   *See* 9 C.F.R. § 310.25 or 381.94 (2006).

[165]   61 Fed. Reg. 38,812 (July 25, 1996).

[166]   FSIS Baseline Data for various raw products *at:* http://www.fsis.usda.gov/wps/portal/fsis/topics/data-collection-and-reports/microbiology/baseline/baseline.

failing three consecutive *Salmonella* sets.[167] However, the use of high *Salmonella* numbers to support withdrawal of inspection was challenged by industry.

In 2001, the Court of Appeals for the Fifth Circuit held that FSIS could not suspend inspection at grinding establishments based on the failure of the *Salmonella* performance standard alone.[168] The court found that finished product testing did not necessarily represent the sanitary conditions at a grinding facility. This finding was based on the fact that there was no other evidence that the grinding establishment was "insanitary" and, as the establishment purchased raw meat to grind, *Salmonella* could be introduced into the establishment through no fault of its own (e.g., on raw meat).

Section 8 of the FMIA contains the statutory provision dealing with "insanitary conditions."[169] As FSIS did not claim that the HACCP regulations were violated, its action could only be justified if, in fact, it had demonstrated insanitary conditions existed. In the FSIS appeal, it argued that the term "sanitation" can cover all food safety controls at an establishment, but the Fifth Circuit saw otherwise and indicated that the *Salmonella* performance standard did not fit in the statutory provision dealing with sanitation.[170]

The court said that the *Salmonella* performance standard "regulates the procurement of raw materials," not the conditions existing at an establishment which is what the term "rendered" in the sanitary conditions provision requires.[171] Moreover, the presence of *Salmonella*, which is not an adulterant in raw ground beef or an indicator of adulterating pathogens, does not render product adulterated.[172]

After this decision, FSIS immediately modified its enforcement procedures to focus less on an establishment's failure to meet the *Salmonella* performance standard and more on the establishment's overall compliance with food safety requirements. However, in recent years, the agency has adopted several incentive-based programs intended to ensure that establishments continue to operate well within the *Salmonella* performance standards. The agency also recently revised its *Salmonella* performance guidelines for broilers and turkey, as well as issued new performance guidelines for *Campylobacter* in such products. These initiatives are discussed more fully below in the section on *Salmonella* and *Campylobacter*.

HACCP

The goal of the PR/HACCP was to improve food safety practices by setting public health standards that all meat and poultry establishments had to meet. HACCP was a key part of this concept that was meant to reduce the risk from all foodborne hazards—biological, chemical, and physical—while also providing a means by which to hold establishments accountable for achieving acceptable levels. Moreover, HACCP was touted as being a "farm

---

[167]   *See* 9 C.F.R. § 310.25(b)(3)(iii).

[168]   *See* Supreme Beef Processors, Inc. v. USDA, 275 F.3d 432 (5th Cir. 2001).

[169]   21 U.S.C. § 608 (1999).

[170]   *Supreme Beef Processors* at 443.

[171]   *Id.* at 441.

[172]   *Id.* at 442-43.

to fork" program with references to this phrase in the PR/HACCP and continuing in later speeches and presentations.[173]

HACCP represents a food safety approach that seeks to prevent, rather than to react, to problems in finished products. HACCP uses a "systemic approach" to identify and control foodborne hazards with the use of documentation to support that the processing of meat and poultry is under control and establishments are producing safe and wholesome products. This is done using seven principles:

- Conduct a hazard analysis—identifies the biological, chemical, and physical hazards posed by a product/process and any associated preventive or control measures;

- Identify critical control points (CCPs)—points in the process where identified hazards can be controlled;

- Establish critical limits—limits for control measures associated with each CCP;

- Establish monitoring procedures—procedures to ensure continuous compliance with critical limits;

- Establish corrective actions—actions taken if a critical limit is exceeded;

- Establish recordkeeping and documentation procedures—development, implementation, and maintenance procedures needed for effective documentation of HACCP system; and

- Establish verification procedures to ensure the system works—validation and verification procedures to ensure the HACCP system is working as intended.

These seven principles were developed by the National Advisory Committee on Microbiological Criteria for Foods (NACMCF)[174] based on the HACCP system presented by Pillsbury Company at the U.S. National Conference on Food Protection in 1971. Pillsbury developed HACCP as a means of assuring the safety of foods it was producing for the space program.[175]

Regulatory HACCP

While the above represents "scientific" HACCP, the actual implementation in meat and poultry establishments has also included "regulatory" HACCP. Many believe that HACCP has morphed into more regulatory than scientific HACCP with significant negative consequences for the meat and poultry industry. And the negative effect on small and very small establishments is much greater because of their limited resources.[176]

Examples of what is now considered more "regulatory" than "scientific" include the performance standards in the PR/HACCP that FSIS had indicated would be the most effective way to minimize regulatory burdens on industry while providing a consistent means for that industry to produce safe, unadulterated products. Unfortunately, these

---

[173]   61 Fed. Reg. 38,960 (July 25, 1996); be FoodSafe, The FSIS MAGAZINE, Winter/Spring 2007, at 16. (2007).

[174]   Karen L. Hulebak & Wayne Schlosser, Hazard Analysis and Critical Control Point (HACCP) History and Conceptual Overview, 22 RISK ANALYSIS 547–52 (2002) doi:10.1111/0272-4332.00038.

[175]   Id.

[176]   American Meat Institute comments on Notice of a Section 610 Regulatory Flexibility Act Review of the Pathogen Reduction/Hazard Analysis Critical Control Point (HACCP) Systems Final Rule, Docket No. 05-024N (Oct. 31, 2005).

performance standards are not necessarily based on scientific principles as represented by the requirement that establishments have a CCP even when there is no scientifically validated CCP available.

Pathogen Reduction and Other Food Safety Initiatives Under HACCP

Since the PR/HACCP rule became final in 1996, FSIS has implemented certain initiatives intended to encourage inspected establishments to address pathogens and other food safety issues in their HACCP, SSOP, and other food safety programs. Some of these initiatives are discussed below.

E. coli O157:H7

As noted above, when FSIS initiated its testing program for E. coli O157:H7 in ground beef in 1994, there were only a handful of positives for the first few years. The implementation of HACCP was thought to contribute to this success. However, beginning in 1997 and lasting through 2002, there was an increase in positives, in addition to several recalls for E. coli O157:H7.

In response to this increase in positives and recalls, in October 2002, FSIS published a notice in the Federal Register directing all establishments producing raw beef to reassess their HACCP plans to determine whether E. coli O157:H7 is a food safety hazard reasonably likely to occur. Although FSIS did not mandate a CCP for E. coli O157:H7, it stated that it was issuing the notice based on new studies showing that E. coli O157:H7 was more prevalent than previously thought. If slaughter establishments implemented controls to address E. coli O157:H7, they must deem the pathogen to be a food safety hazard reasonably likely to occur and include the validated intervention controls in the HACCP plan.[177]

For fabricators and grinders, FSIS allows establishments to address E. coli O157:H7 through the use of purchase specifications.[178] However, if there is a positive E. coli O157:H7 finding, the establishment must treat this as an unforeseen hazard and take corrective/preventive measures and reassess its HACCP plan. FSIS expects that there will be some verification testing for O157:H7, whether conducted by the supplier or purchaser. If the supplier conducts the verification testing, the supplier will usually give the purchaser a Certificate of Analysis (COA) demonstrating that a particular lot tested negative for O157:H7.

---

[177]   "Validation" requires the following: 1) there must be scientific support/study for the interventions (use of peer-reviewed articles to validate a critical limit is acceptable); 2) the intervention must be operated at the establishment under the same parameters as were used in the supporting study; and 3) a challenge study must be conducted in-plant using surrogate organisms (FSIS does not expect nor want the use of E. coli O157:H7 for in-plant studies).

[178]   FSIS also expects grinders to consider growth of E. coli O157:H7 and cross-contamination issues in their hazard analyses.

FSIS does not currently sample fabricated, formed, or comminuted raw beef products for *E. coli* O157:H7. FSIS will, however, sample the raw source material for these products. Moreover, the final product—the "non-intact beef" products—would be adulterated if contaminated with *E. coli* O157:H7.[179] This determination was made after several recalls for *E. coli* O157:H7 in non-intact beef products occurred in 2003.[180] A notice in the *Federal Register* in 2005 responded to these recalls by requiring that establishments that process mechanically tenderized beef products (non-intact beef) account for *E. coli* O157:H7 in their next annual HACCP assessment.[181]

On April 8, 2004, the updated revision of *E. coli* Directive 10,010.1, Rev. 1 was released along with "Compliance Guidelines for Establishments on the FSIS Microbiological Testing Program and Verification Activities for *Escherichia coli* O157:H7."[182] The Directive was again revised in 2010.[183] In essence, the Directive and Guidelines describe the procedures FSIS will use in conducting verification sampling for *E. coli* O157:H7 in ground beef products.

All establishments that handle raw beef are subject to FSIS sampling for *E. coli* O157:H7.[184] If a product is presumptive or confirmed positive for *E. coli* O157:H7, the product may be sent to a landfill under documented company control or sent to another official establishment for a lethality treatment either under documented company control or under USDA control. FSIS will conduct a follow-up sampling consisting of a 16-sample set. Suppliers of products to grinders or fabricators whose product is tested positive will also be subject to this follow-up sampling.[185]

Additionally, FSIS will conduct traceback investigations to each supplier (at the time a test is determined to be presumptive) and make a determination with regards to the process control at the slaughter facility. FSIS will evaluate whether the supplier had a "high event period" that could signal a systemic breakdown or a single event that led to the spread of the pathogen. If the sample confirms positive, FSIS will also conduct traceforward to determine all grinders that received the same product.[186]

In 2012, FSIS declared six additional Shiga Toxin-Producing *Escherichia coli* (STECs) (O26, O45, O103, O111, 121, and O145), in raw beef manufacturing trimmings (domestic or imported) as adulterants and began testing.[187] FSIS indicated that literature supports that

[179] *See* FSIS Directive 10,010.1 *at*: http://www.fsis.usda.gov/wps/wcm/connect/c100dd64-e2e7-408a-8b27-ebb378959071/10010.1Rev3.pdf?MOD=AJPERES.

[180] *See* Recall Case Archive 2003 *at*: http://www.fsis.usda.gov/wps/portal/fsis/topics/recalls-and-public-health-alerts/recall-case-archive/recall-case-archive-2003.

[181] *See* 70 Fed. Reg. 30,331 (May 26, 2005).

[182] *See* Compliance Guidelines for Establishments on the FSIS Microbiological Testing Program & Other Verification Activities for *Escherichia coli* O157:H7 *at*: http://www.fsis.usda.gov/wps/wcm/connect/f5001b3d-defa-4db8-a510-881ca90415ff/ecoli o157h7dirguid4-13-04.pdf?MOD=AJPERES.

[183] *See* FSIS Directive 10,010.1 *at*: http://www.fsis.usda.gov/wps/wcm/connect/c100dd64-e2e7-408a-8b27-ebb378959071/10010.1Rev3.pdf?MOD=AJPERES.

[184] All raw ground beef products (except those that include another species and beef sausage products) are subject to sampling.

[185] *See* FSIS Directive 10,010.1 *at*: http://www.fsis.usda.gov/wps/wcm/connect/c100dd64-e2e7-408a-8b27-ebb378959071/10010.1Rev3.pdf?MOD=AJPERES.

[186] *See* 79 Fed. Reg. 47,417 (Aug. 13, 2014).

[187] *See* 77 Fed. Reg. 31,975 (May 31, 2012).

interventions effective for *E. coli* O157:H7 have been demonstrated as effective for the other serotypes of STEC. Individual establishments are expected to validate that this is true in their processing environments.

Listeria monocytogenes (Lm)
The *Listeria* Regulation—9 C.F.R. Part 430

As noted above, in response to several listeriosis outbreaks in the late 1990s and early 2000s due to consumption of RTE meat and poultry, FSIS issued an interim final rule in 2003 to require establishments that produce such products to implement effective *Lm* controls and address *Lm* in their food safety systems.[188] Pursuant to the rule, *Lm* control may be addressed in a HACCP program, SSOPs, or prerequisite program, with one exception. Establishments using a post-lethality treatment on RTE products have to address the post-lethality treatment in their HACCP plan.

How an establishment chooses to control *Lm* in its RTE products determines the degree of verification testing by the establishment and by FSIS. In this regard, FSIS has established three alternatives:

- Alternative 1—*Lm* is controlled by using a post-lethality treatment and an antimicrobial agent or process that suppresses or limits the growth of *Lm*. The post-lethality treatment must be included in the HACCP plan and must be validated as being effective in reducing or eliminating *Lm*. *This alternative requires the least amount of verification testing by the establishment or FSIS;*

- Alternative 2—*Lm* is controlled by using a post-lethality treatment OR an antimicrobial agent or process that suppresses or limits the growth of *Lm*. If the establishment uses a post-lethality treatment, as with Alternative 1, it must be included in the establishment's HACCP plan. In addition, if an establishment only uses the antimicrobial agent or process, it must also provide for testing of food contact surfaces in the post-lethality environment;

- Alternative 3—*Lm* is controlled only through the use of sanitation procedures. Establishments choosing this alternative must also test food contact surfaces in the post-lethality environment as well as identify the conditions under which they will implement hold and test procedures for product to ensure it is not contaminated with *Lm* or Listeria species. Establishments producing products in this alternative will be subjected to the highest verification frequency by FSIS.[189]

If a food contact surface tests positive for *Listeria* species by the establishment, the establishment is expected to take corrective and preventive actions. The positive surface will be retested to verify the actions taken were effective. Depending on the establishment's plan, product would normally be held to determine whether corrective and preventive measures are effective if a second positive was received from the same surface.[190]

---

[188]   68 Fed. Reg. 34,208 (June 6, 2003).
[189]   68 Fed. Reg. 34,219 (June 6, 2003).
[190]   *Id.* at 34,220.

If an establishment tests food contact surfaces for *Lm* and not *Listeria* species and has a positive result, appropriate corrective measures regarding products that came in contact with the positive surface must be taken. FSIS considers a surface positive for *Lm* to be evidence of an insanitary condition that may render product injurious to health.[191] If an establishment did not hold the product in question, that product will be subject to recall and/or must be properly disposed of or treated with a validated lethality process.[192]

Beginning in February 2013, if FSIS tests an establishment's food contact surfaces or product for *Lm* (or other pathogens or adulterants), an establishment is required to hold all affected product as it is considered not to bear the mark of inspection until negative results are received.[193]

FSIS Moves to Risk-Based *Lm* Sampling

As indicated above, FSIS stated it would conduct verification activities at establishments based on the alternative classification of the products being produced. While establishments will have routine product samples pulled by the local FSIS inspection program personnel, establishments may also be scheduled for Intensified Verification Testing (IVT).

Routine *Lm* Sampling

FSIS sends notification to local inspection program personnel to pull RTE product either randomly or based on risk[194] using information provided to the agency by each establishment producing RTE products.[195] If a product sample is *Lm* positive, corrective and preventive measures must be taken as well as a recall if product was not held.[196] The establishment must also reassess its HACCP plan.[197] An establishment or FSIS product positive for *Lm* indicates the potential for possible product contamination, which means FSIS may schedule a Comprehensive Food Safety Assessment that includes an Intensified Verification Testing.[198]

IVT

An IVT may be scheduled as part of the FSIS routine schedule based on the alternative classifications or it may be "for cause" as a result of an earlier *Lm* positive product sample. Establishments will be made aware of when the Food Safety Assessment and the sampling will be conducted. Notification is usually received from the EIAO by the facility about a week prior to the scheduled visit.[199]

---

[191]   *Id.* at 34,214.

[192]   *See* Resource 4, FSIS Compliance Guideline: Controlling Listeria monocytogenes in Post-lethality Exposed Ready-to-Eat Meat and Poultry Products at: http://www.fsis.usda.gov/wps/wcm/connect/d3373299-50e6-47d6-a577-e74a1e549fde/Controlling-Lm-RTE-Guideline.pdf?MOD=AJPERES.

[193]   77 Fed. Reg. 73,401 (Dec. 10, 2012).

[194]   *See* FSIS Compliance Guideline: Controlling *Listeria monocytogenes* in Post-lethality Exposed Ready-to-Eat Meat and Poultry Products *at*: http://www.fsis.usda.gov/wps/wcm/connect/d3373299-50e6-47d6-a577-e74a1e549fde/Controlling-Lm-RTE-Guideline.pdf?MOD=AJPERES *at* 103.

[195]   *See* FSIS Directive 10,240.4 *at*: http://www.fsis.usda.gov/wps/wcm/connect/b8cd03ed-222c-4cef-ad92-3647e3be6c53/10240.4.pdf?MOD=AJPERES.

[196]   *Id.*

[197]   *See* 9 C.F.R. pt. 430.

[198]   *See* FSIS Directive10,240.5 *at*: http://www.fsis.usda.gov/wps/wcm/connect/398d4b7b-56fc-4bd9-af0e-379edcd9274d/10240.5.pdf?MOD=AJPERES.

[199]   *Id.*

All samples taken during the IVT will be analyzed for *Lm* by FSIS.[200] Establishments are always provided the opportunity to arrange product scheduling to allow any products affected by this sampling to be held until results are received.[201]

Based on the results from the sampling, FSIS may take further actions including the issuance of a Notice of Intended Enforcement requesting the establishment provide FSIS with information as to why its food safety program should be considered effective and/or changes it will immediately implement which it believes will make its food safety program effective so that it is not producing potentially adulterated products. After an establishment has successfully completed either of these actions; another IVT will be scheduled by FSIS as verification of the establishment's corrective and preventive measures.[202]

Salmonella and *Campylobacter*

Since the PR/HACCP rule was promulgated, FSIS has also implemented initiatives to encourage slaughter plants to improve their controls for addressing *Salmonella* and *Campylobacter*.

2006 Update to *Salmonella* Reporting

In 2006, when it appeared that the *Salmonella* positives at various slaughter establishments were rising, FSIS published a *Federal Register* notice updating its policy[203] as a way to address the increasing positive trend—especially in broiler plants.[204] FSIS indicated it now intended to publicly report sample results from its *Salmonella* verification sampling program.[205] It also began typing isolates of *Salmonella*-positive samples to determine species[206] and matching these with subtype information associated with human illness.[207]

Under the PR/HACCP, establishments were to be evaluated based on sample set results (51 samples make up a sample set for broilers).[208] Process control was demonstrated when 12 or fewer samples in the set are positive.[209] The updated policy indicated that establishments demonstrating consistent process control by having two *Salmonella* sample sets in a row at or below 50 percent of the performance standard (six or fewer positive samples in a set for

---

[200]   Product samples are also analyzed for *Salmonella*.

[201]   *See* FSIS Directive 10,240.5 *at:* http://www.fsis.usda.gov/wps/wcm/connect/398d4b7b-56fc-4b-d9-af0e-379edcd9274d/10240.5.pdf?MOD=AJPERES.

[202]   *See id.* and FSIS Directive 5000.1 *at:* http://www.fsis.usda.gov/wps/wcm/connect/e8133c3c-d9b8-4a58-ab14-859e3e9c8a52/5000.1.pdf?MOD=AJPERES.

[203]   71 Fed. Reg. 9772 (Feb. 27, 2006).

[204]   A "broiler" is defined as a young chicken, usually less than 13 weeks of age. 9 C.F.R. § 381170(a)(1)(iii).

[205]   While FSIS had a strong focus on broilers, all of the product classes were included. *See* FSIS Establishment Eligibility Criteria and Scheduling Algorithm for the Salmonella Verification Sampling Program for Raw Meat and Poultry *at* http://www.fsis.usda.gov/wps/wcm/connect/f759693b-2fa9-46ee-8564-825ab4584859/Salmonella_Scheduling_Algorithm_Functions.pdf?MOD=AJPERES.

[206]   73 Fed. Reg. 4769 (Jan. 28, 2008).

[207]   *Id.*

[208]   61 Fed. Reg. 38,847 (July 25, 1996).

[209]   *Id.*

broilers) would be placed in the "Category 1" classification.[210] Category 1 plants would be tested for *Salmonella* less often than plants having less consistent process control.[211]

"Category 2" establishments would be those having sample set results at or above 50 percent of the performance standard without exceeding it (7 to 12 positive samples in a set) and have variable process control.[212] Establishments failing the performance standard would be considered as having highly variable process control and would be classified as "Category 3" plants.[213] These establishments (Category 2 and 3) would be subject to an increased frequency of testing by FSIS compared to those plants in Category 1.[214]

Along with the above, the notice also announced the FSIS goal of having 90 percent of all meat and poultry establishments subject to *Salmonella* testing in Category 1 by October 1, 2010.[215]

2008 *Salmonella* Initiative Program (SIP)

New policies for FSIS's *Salmonella* program were again published in January 2008.[216] FSIS indicated that it intended to post results of completed verification sample sets for those establishments showing "inconsistency in their ability to meet *Salmonella* performance standards, beginning with those from young chicken establishments, but including pork and turkey as well."[217] Moreover, it also set forth a "voluntary incentive-based program" for establishments that FSIS believed would provide "significant data on attribution of human illness to FSIS-regulated products."[218]

FSIS took these actions because it was still concerned that policies in the 2006 notice were not robust enough to encourage the industry to continue to improve *Salmonella* control and thus improve public health.[219] With SIP, however, if FSIS found that industry-wide *Salmonella* results were consistently at half or below the current baseline,[220] then FSIS would consider allowing an increase in line speed above the current regulatory speeds.[221] This would be done by waivers for those establishments in Category 1 that have already met the current FSIS *Salmonella* goals. FSIS believed industry would work toward greater *Salmonella* control and improved public health because industry had the opportunity to increase productivity—if positive *Salmonella* results decreased.

---

[210]   71 Fed. Reg. 9774 (Feb. 27, 2006).

[211]   *Id.* at 9775.

[212]   *Id.* at 9774.

[213]   *Id.*

[214]   *Id.* at 9775.

[215]   73 Fed. Reg. 4769 (Jan. 28, 2008).

[216]   *Id.* at 4767.

[217]   *Id.*

[218]   *Id.*

[219]   *Id.* at 4769.

[220]   FSIS has completed a "new" baseline for young chickens and is beginning one on turkeys. *See* http://www. fsis.usda.gov/wps/portal/fsis/topics/data-collection-and-reports/microbiology/baseline/baseline.

[221]   73 Fed. Reg. 4770 (Jan. 28, 2008).

New *Salmonella* and *Campylobacter* Standards

In 2010, FSIS published new proposed standards for young chickens (broilers) and turkeys for *Salmonella* and, for the first time, *Campylobacter*.[222] These were based on a baseline study completed in 2009.[223] The standards were published in March 2011[224] with an effective date of July 1, 2011. While FSIS will continue to track results in terms of categories,[225] the levels for each are as follows:[226]

Salmonella

- For broilers, the standard is 7.5 percent, which translates to no more than five positives per 51-sample set.

- For turkeys, the standard is 1.7 percent, which translates to no more than four positives per 56-sample set.

Campylobacter

- For broilers, the standard is 10.4 percent, which translates to no more than eight positives in the 51-sample set.

- For turkey carcasses, the standard is 1.1 percent, which translates to no more than three positives in the 56-sample set.

As it did previously, FSIS said it would post the establishment names of those that fail the standard for *Salmonella* (Category 3). At the time, FSIS stated that it did not intend to post establishments failing the new *Campylobacter* standards until it has gathered more data.[227] However, FSIS did reserve the right to change these posting parameters "in response to adverse trends."[228] FSIS also made clear that failing either performance standard will trigger a follow-up sample set for both pathogens as well as automatically triggering a comprehensive Food Safety Assessment if the *Salmonella* set is failed and an establishment fails the *Campylobacter* standard twice in a row or has what FSIS would consider an egregious *Campylobacter* failure.[229] While FSIS did not define "egregious" for turkeys, it was defined at 15 positives in a 51-sample set for broilers.[230]

In January 2014, FSIS published a Notice in the *Federal Register* to propose new *Salmonella* and *Campylobacter* performance standards for comminuted poultry and chicken parts and to announce certain changes to the agency's approach to *Salmonella* and *Campylobacter*

---

[222] 75 Fed. Reg. 27,288 (May 14, 2010).

[223] *See*   http://www.fsis.usda.gov/wps/portal/fsis/topics/data-collection-and-reports/microbiology/baseline/baseline.

[224] 76 Fed. Reg. 15,282 (Mar. 21, 2011).

[225] Category 1 is 50 percent or less of the standard rounding down, so for broilers, Category 1 is two or less positives per 51-sample set and for turkeys, Category 1 would be two positives or less per 56-sample set. Category 2 is more than 50 percent of the standard but still passing the standard. Category 3 is failure of the standard.

[226] 76 Fed. Reg. at 15,282.

[227] *Id.* at 15,284.

[228] *Id.* at 15,285.

[229] *Id.* at 15,287.

[230] *Id.*

verification testing for all raw products subject to a performance standard (beginning in March 2015).[231] With regard to the new performance standards, they would be as follows:

Product	*Salmonella* Standard	*Campylobacter* Standard
Comminuted Chicken	13/52 or 25.0%	1/52 or 1/9%
Comminuted Turkey	7/52 or 13.5%	1/52 or 1/9%
Chicken Parts	8/52 or 15.4%	4/52 or 7.7%

With regard to changes to verification sampling, the agency stated that it would no longer use a discrete sample set to determine compliance with the performance standard, but would take samples based on factors such as the size of an establishment or production volume and determine compliance based on a moving window. It also indicated that it would determine an establishment's category status (i.e., Category 1, 2, or 3) based on the moving window and post the category of all establishments on its website, not just Category 3 establishments.

2014 Modernization of Poultry Slaughter Inspection Final Rule

The current poultry slaughter regulations were developed after the introduction of automatic evisceration equipment, but before the adoption of the HACCP. Shortly after adopting HACCP, FSIS instituted the HACCP-Based Inspection Models Program (HIMP).[232] Under HIMP, establishments took over the sorting operations and FSIS reduced the number of on-line inspectors while increasing off-line inspection activity.[233] Although the project was not designed to measure the effectiveness of this inspection system in reducing pathogens of concern, the data generated under HIMP did demonstrate a reduction in these organisms.

In 2011, FSIS updated a risk assessment to determine the public health impact of an inspection system that dedicated more agency resources to off-line activities in lieu of on-line inspection. According to the risk assessment modeling, such a re-allocation would result in approximately 4,286 less *Salmonellosis* cases and 986 less *Campylobacter* cases.[234] On this basis and other support,[235] FSIS developed the proposed New Inspection System. The final rule differs in some respects from that of the proposed rule[236] and includes the following:

---

[231]   80 Fed. Reg. 3940 (Jan. 26, 2015).

[232]   *See* http://www.fsis.usda.gov/wps/portal/fsis/topics/regulatory-compliance/haccp/haccp-based-inspection-models-project/history-HIMP.

[233]   *Id.*

[234]   *See* http://www.fsis.usda.gov/wps/wcm/connect/60885028-48fa-4e9f-9839-d02ea9fbd215/Poultry_Slaughter_Risk_Assess_Nov2011.pdf?MOD=AJPERES.

[235]   For example, the National Advisory Committee on Microbiological Criteria for Food suggested that generic *E. coli* may not be useful to measure process control of pathogens.

[236]   77 Fed. Reg. 4,408 (Jan. 27, 2012).

- Creation of a New Poultry Inspection System (NPIS). This system will be in addition to existing systems.[237] Poultry establishments (broilers and turkey) will have the option to transition to NPIS.[238] In other words, the new system is voluntary. Unlike the proposal, there is no requirement that an establishment transition to NPIS.

- If an establishment opts into NPIS:

  - It must conduct sorting of carcasses prior to FSIS carcass inspection;

  - Line speed is limited to 140 birds per minute (bpm) for broilers (down from the 175 proposed[239]) and 55 bpm for turkeys (as was proposed); and

  - The establishment must expressly comply with Occupational Safety and Health Administration (OSHA) regulations and annually attest to a program addressing worker injury and illness.

- All establishments, regardless of the inspection system at the establishment, must:

  - Develop and implement written procedures to address fecal and other contamination during the slaughter/dressing process, and

  - Test carcasses pre- and post-chill to demonstrate the program's effectiveness.[240]

- Other modifications to existing regulations for all poultry establishments include:

  - Elimination of the mandatory, specific time temperature requirements for product,

  - Elimination of generic E. coli sampling,

  - Elimination of the codified Salmonella Performance Standards,

  - Permission to use of on-line reprocessing without a waiver,

  - Increasing the amount of chlorine that can be used in off-line reprocessing (20 to 20–50 ppm) along with the use of other antimicrobials, and

  - Definition of "air chilling" (modified from the proposal).

- A "severability provision" so that invalidation of one regulation will not automatically invalidate any others.

FSIS proposes to implement the transition to NPIS using a phase-in approach. For the requirements applicable to all plants, this will be implemented by establishment size. It remains to be seen how many poultry slaughter establishments will voluntarily opt into this new inspection option.

---

[237] The five other systems are Streamlined Inspection System (SIS), The New Line Speed Inspection System (NELS), the New Turkey Inspection System (NTIS), Traditional Inspection, and Ratite Inspection.

[238] Other classes of poultry can opt into a NPIS system through a Salmonella Initiative Program (SIP) waiver. FSIS will consider data collected in such poultry establishments operating under a SIP waiver to determine whether to expand NPIS to additional classes of poultry.

[239] For HIMP plants, the broiler establishments can continue to run at 175 bpm, though the HIMP waiver will be modified to comport with the other requirements applicable to NPIS.

[240] FSIS has not defined what the establishment must test for at these locations. FSIS will continue testing for Salmonella and Campylobacter. Establishments are provided the flexibility to use organisms that will provide information related to process control.

Bovine Spongiform Encephalopathy (BSE)
Background

BSE or "mad cow disease" is a progressive, degenerative disease affecting the nervous system of cattle, which belongs to the family of diseases known as "transmissible spongiform encephalopathies" (TSEs).[241] Other diseases in this family include scrapie in sheep and goats, chronic wasting disease in deer and elk, and new variant Creutzfeldt-Jakob disease (nvCJD) in humans.[242] Scientific and epidemiological studies have linked human nvCJD to the consumption of cattle products contaminated with the BSE agent.

It is believed that BSE arose from feeding meat and bone meal made from scrapie-infected sheep to cattle. The spread of BSE is believed to have been amplified by the practice of then rendering cattle tissue and re-feeding. The United Kingdom imposed a ruminant-to-ruminant feeding ban in 1988 that was expanded to a ban against using any animal protein in any livestock feed.[243] The number of confirmed cases in cattle after enactment of the feed bans fell drastically in those cattle born after the feed ban enactments.[244]

Control of BSE in the United States

BSE in cattle is controlled through regulations promulgated by USDA's Animal and Plant Health Inspection Service (APHIS) while FSIS controls the use of cattle parts that are available for the mark of inspection and considered edible. Use of animal proteins in feed is regulated by FDA.

The United States began control of BSE by attempting to keep it out. In 1989, the import of live ruminants was banned from the United Kingdom as well as ruminant products (e.g., beef products, meat, and bone meal). This ban was expanded in 1991 to include products from countries known to have BSE. Later, all live ruminants and most edible products from all of Europe as well as other countries with reported or suspected BSE were included in the ban.[245]

In addition to the import bans, in 1997, FDA issued regulations banning the use of mammalian proteins in ruminant feeds.[246] This ban was strengthened in 2008 when FDA prohibited the tissues having the highest risk for carrying the agent thought to cause BSE in any animal feed.[247] These high-risk cattle materials or Specified Risk Materials (SRMs) are the brains and spinal cords from cattle 30 months of age and older. In addition, the use of the entire carcass of cattle not inspected and passed for human consumption is also prohibited unless the cattle are less than 30 months of age, or the brains and spinal cords have been removed.[248]

---

[241]　70 Fed. Reg. 461 (Jan. 4, 2005).
[242]　Id.
[243]　Id. at 462.
[244]　Id.
[245]　70 Fed. Reg. at 462.
[246]　62 Fed. Reg. 30,936 (June 5, 1997).
[247]　See 81 Fed. Reg. 22,720 (Apr. 25, 2008).
[248]　Id.

Surveillance for BSE began in 1990 with APHIS working in conjunction with FSIS in the collection and analysis of samples from cattle.[249] This program expanded to not only those cattle exhibiting signs of a central nervous system disorder, but also to any nonambulatory or "downer" cattle. After finding a positive sample from a cow imported from Canada in December 2003, sampling was expanded.[250]

The "enhanced" BSE surveillance program began on June 1, 2004, and by July 2006 more than 759,000 animals were sampled with only two found positive. Since that time, sampling has transitioned to testing approximately 40,000 animals per year, which is considered a statistically valid level "consistent with science-based internationally accepted standards."[251]

Included in the control and prevention of BSE were the FSIS regulations that began with the 2001 Harvard Center for Risk Analysis assessment, which studied the effectiveness of the U.S. regulatory measures currently in place.[252] When the risk assessment was initially released in 2002, the conclusion—even though there were recommendations for improvement—was that the United States was "highly resistant" to BSE. With that assessment, no changes were made in regulations controlling the possible introduction of BSE-infected materials into the food chain.[253]

Regulations, however, were quickly put in place with the announcement of the positive test in December 2003. Three interim final rules and directions to the FSIS inspection program personnel were published and made effective on January 12, 2004.[254] With these, FSIS:

- Prohibited SRMs from use as human food (depending on cattle's age), which included central nervous system tissues and related bones; dorsal root ganglia and tonsils and distal ileum;

- Required an accurate determination of cattle's age;

- Prohibited use of nonambulatory cattle for human food;

- Prohibited use of mechanically separated beef for human food;

- Amended the Advanced Meat Recovery rule's definition of meat;

- Prohibited the use of penetrative captive bolt stunning devices that inject air; and

---

[249] *See* 7 C.F.R. pts. 71 and 161.

[250] *See* "BSE Surveillance in the United States" *available at* http://www.aphis.usda.gov/wps/portal/footer/topicsofinterest/applyingforpermit?1dmy&urile=wcm%3apath%3a%2Faphis_content_library%2Fsa_our_focus%2Fsa_animal_health%2Fsa_animal_disease_information%2Fsa_cattle_health%2Fsa_bse%2Fct_surv_in_usa.

[251] *Id.*

[252] This risk assessment has since been updated several times as new information has become available. The latest update may be viewed at http://www.fsis.usda.gov/wps/portal/fsis/topics/science/risk-assessments/!ut/p/a1/04_Sj9CPykssy0xPLMnMz0vMAfGjzOJNAyxdDU28Dbz8g91dDTzdzF2dPUL8jP29DYEKIoEKDAINzAwtnYEKLA3dDDz9wgL9vZ2dDSz8jInUjwM4GhDS70WEBUZFvs6-6fpRBYklGbqZeWn5-hFFmcXZuonFxanFxbmpeSXF-uH6UWCT4D4xMARCTz_jYBMPLz9jA38TdAVYvApRgNsvBbmhE-VU-acGe6YqKAIENNTo!/#BSE.

[253] *See* THE MAD COW DISEASE PRIMER, Olsson, Frank & Weeda, PC (The Food Institute Press 2004).

[254] *See* http://www.fsis.usda.gov/wps/portal/fsis/topics/regulations/federal-register/interim-and-final-rules/interim-and-final-rules-2004.

- Required that FSIS inspection program personnel not apply the mark of inspection to a carcass sampled for BSE until negative results are received.

Since that positive BSE test in December 2003, two additional positive tests occurred: one in Texas in 2005 and one in Alabama in 2006.[255] FSIS finalized and amended its interim regulations on BSE in 2007.[256] It continues to update FSIS directives and/or notices that provide instructions as well as interpretations of the regulations regarding BSE.[257]

Conclusion

With HACCP, meat and poultry inspection started its move away from continuous inspection (based on the physical observations of an inspector) toward more sophisticated inspection techniques that rely on the processor's own controls and records to ensure sanitation and product wholesomeness. It is still not yet clear whether processors, inspectors, or consumer advocates agree that these new, highly technical controls can reduce the need for labor-intensive, sensory inspection. This tension will continue as FSIS implements its data-driven PHIS program.

Processors like the move toward a more sophisticated system because it is more efficient and will enhance public safety. FSIS likes the move away from inspection procedures based on manual labor toward those for reducing risks (which can be measured by scientific procedures). Processors, however, will not support changes perceived to compromise consumer confidence in meat and poultry. Inspectors' unions will continue to oppose more sophisticated systems that might eliminate jobs. Consumer advocates may well determine the extent to which future new technology is substituted for the old.

An important issue still to be resolved is whether FSIS can meet its current inspection obligations through monitoring a processor's control systems rather than establishing and imposing government systems of process control. Processors continue to be reluctant to have FSIS mandate the exact dimensions of their control programs because controls such as a HACCP system should be individualized to each processing plant. In addition, processors continue to be apprehensive that material most consider commercial, and/or confidential from their quality control programs, prerequisite programs, SSOPs, and HACCP plans will be releasable under the federal Freedom of Information Act.[258]

---

[255]   See http://www.fsis.usda.gov/wps/portal/fsis/topics/food-safety-education/get-answers/food-safety-fact-she ets/production-and-inspection/bovine-spongiform-encephalopathy-bse/bse-resources.

[256]   See 72 Fed. Reg. 38,700 (July 13, 2007).

[257]   See various directives and notices at http://www.fsis.usda.gov/wps/portal/fsis/topics/food-safety-edu-cation/get-answers/food-safety-fact-sheets/production-and-inspection/bovine-spongiform-encepha-lopathy-bse/bse-resources/!ut/p/a1/jVFhT8IwEP0144sp7RiSYbIYsmgAZUiIMvbFlO26NWHr7HXo_ PUWiB80oPTS5O76Xu7dK01oTJOK72TOjVQV3-7rZPDKFmzgDkM2nQ_dezaJXhbzhzBk_vLaAtZ_ ACLvQv6ZM2L_8acXDOjpWTjLaVJzUxBZCUXjHAzhFb6DRhoLpTKCXIBpieCpIVgAGP tQa5U16d4KC84sFWs4lDTeqJ2sgGCtqlwKpUsCVQp1wbdqP6YlGwSLQiAaUDU6BaQrmvxUy-1wbk8hb9sfTyGPz_m_ACTuPgPN-WUPyrdoc_m49qjaebzfXIECD7jbatgtj6huHOazBjCNwnRbdf-drN1c5hx8ZtY4QfOO5dz7FC7PU6XAi5ldxAIFBi560B3QZ2waumzmwXO6kqS2m6HwH7TtuAn-VJRKDQ0PjGd1uVz_Pk4GjP5VK58HH0BxK0dyw!!/?1dmy&urile=wcm%3apath%3a%2FFSIS-Cont ent%2Finternet%2Fmain%2Ftopics%2Fregulations.

[258]   5 U.S.C. § 552 (1994).

The traditional animal health and wholesomeness concerns that have justified FSIS's continuous inspection in the past took on new importance with BSE, but is still less significant as concerns over microbiological contamination (such as *Salmonella, Listeria monocytogenes* and *E. Coli* O157:H7) continue to be the much larger issue.

The challenge facing FSIS is to continue to update its inspection system, such as it is attempting to do with its just-released final rule entitled "Modernization of Poultry Slaughter Inspection,"[259] to be more efficient while increasing public health protection.

To succeed, the agency needs supporting consensus from industry, consumer advocates, and inspectors. A change not supported with consensus could undermine consumer confidence in the wholesomeness of the meat and poultry supply, but no change will leave in place an antiquated, costly system that is ill-designed to meet technological problems and new threats ahead. How FSIS faces this challenge in the next five years will affect the inspection system throughout the century.

---

[259]   79 Fed. Reg. 49,565 (Aug. 21, 2014).

CHAPTER 6
DIETARY SUPPLEMENTS

....

WILLIAM R. PENDERGAST, BRIAN P. WALDMAN, AND MARSHA C. WERTZBERGER

Introduction

In 1994, Congress enacted legislation providing a scheme of regulation applicable solely to a class of foods coming within the rubric "dietary supplement," defined as products in tablet, capsule, droplet, softgel, or gelcap form or products in conventional food form that are not represented as conventional foods. Supplement ingredients include vitamins, minerals, herbs, or other substances intended to supplement the diet.[1]

"Vitamin pills" had a long and checkered history at the Food and Drug Administration (FDA) dating to the 1940s—a history marked by extensive litigation and mutual distrust between FDA and the companies that sell such products. It is particularly remarkable, therefore, that Congress chose, in the Dietary Supplement Health and Education Act of 1994 (DSHEA), to carve out a unique and unprecedented legal niche for these nostrums, freeing them from many of the FDA statutory and judicial precedents under which they had been marketed for more than 40 years. DSHEA is even more remarkable when one realizes that it represents the second time that Congress loosened federal controls over this type of product, something done for no other class of FDA-regulated products. Anyone familiar with the history of the products, and their difficulties in court and at FDA, would have expected Congress to tighten FDA's control over them but, instead, the opposite occurred. As a result, there is now a new legal class of food products, uniquely exempt from a wide pattern of legislative and judicial restrictions that nonetheless remain in place for all other FDA-regulated products, including traditional foods, drugs, and medical devices. How this came about, what DSHEA does and, more than 15 years later, how the law has been implemented merits examination.

---

[1]   Dietary Supplement Health and Education Act of 1994 (DSHEA), Pub. L. No. 103-417, 108 Stat. 4325 (Oct. 25, 1994).

The Pattern of Regulation of Vitamin, Mineral and Herbal Products from 1938 to 1994

The 1938 Act

The Federal Food, Drug, and Cosmetic Act of 1938 (FDCA),[2] and the many amendments to it, set up a complex and pervasive pattern of federal regulation for foods, drugs, cosmetics, and medical devices. Under this scheme, any product containing any vitamin, mineral, or herbal ingredient was subject to various provisions of the act either as a food, drug, or combination of these categories, according to the facts in any particular case. A product containing a vitamin, for example, could be a food, or a drug, or both—depending on the particular way it was labeled, marketed, or what other ingredients the product contained. With but one exception, the act contained no provision uniquely applicable to vitamin, herbal, or mineral products; all were regulated the same. The sole exception was section 403(j), enacted in 1938, which provides that a food is misbranded if it purports to be "for special dietary uses" unless its label contains such information about its vitamin, mineral, "and other dietary properties" as FDA may, by regulation, require.[3] We begin our review here.

The legislative history of section 403(j) is virtually nonexistent. When the first version of what became the 1938 act was introduced in 1933, it contained no provision uniquely applicable to herbals, vitamins, or minerals. One section did authorize the Secretary of Agriculture to prescribe such information on the label of foods "as he may deem necessary to protect the public from deception," an authorization that, if enacted, would have permitted the government to require the information later contemplated by section 403(j), but would have also covered all foods as well.[4] It died in Congress.

When the next version (S. 2000) was introduced in 1934, it contained a new subsection specifically referring to vitamins and minerals and other dietary "properties." This provided that a food was misbranded if 1) it were "for special dietary uses, such as by infants or invalids or for other special nutritional requirements" and 2) its label failed to bear any statements, required by regulations, "concerning its vitamin, mineral, and other dietary properties which fully inform the purchaser as to its nutritional value."[5] The earlier proviso, applicable to all foods, was dropped. There is no indication as to why this new, specific, section was added while the older, more general one, was deleted, other than the plainly incorrect observation that the new section "made clearer and more definite" what the earlier proposal would have done "without the sacrifice of any provision essential to public welfare."[6] Subsequently, although there were frequent references to section 403(j) over the following five years, there was no new information of substance so that, in 1939, section 403(j) (as enacted) read that a food is misbranded:

---

2   Federal Food, Drug, and Cosmetic Act of 1938, Pub. L. No. 75-717, 52 Stat. 1040 (1938), as amended 21 U.S.C. §§ 301 *et seq.* (2014).

3   *Id.* § 403(j), 21 U.S.C. § 343(j).

4   S. 1944, 73d Cong., 1st Sess., § 7(f) (1933). A similar provision was introduced in the House of Representatives, H.R. 6110, 73d Cong., 1st Sess. § 8 (1933).

5   S. REP. No. 2000, 73d Cong., 2d Sess., § 7(g) (1934).

6   *Hearings on S. 1944 Before a Subcomm. of the Comm. on Commerce*, 73d Cong., 2d Sess. 494 (1934).

If it purports to be or is represented for special dietary uses, unless its label bears such information concerning its vitamin, mineral, and other dietary properties as the Secretary determines to be, and by regulations prescribes as, necessary in order fully to inform purchasers as to its value for such uses.[7]

One authority did state that the broad grant of authority that S. 1944 would have given to FDA, to require label information on all foods to protect the public from deception, was indeed specifically narrowed by section 403(j) "and directed against the specific field where the need for it was the greatest: foods offered for special dietary uses."[8] Apparently there were those who then believed that products promoted for their vitamin-mineral-herbal content bore watching, while foods generally did not.[9] In any event, Congress certainly expected that vitamin-mineral products would be closely regulated and that FDA should use section 403(j) as the statutory mechanism to see to it that the consumer was fully informed about their true nutritional properties. Section 403(j) regulations were to be the key.

FDA's Response: The Section 403(j) Regulations (1941)

Shortly after the passage of the 1938 act, FDA set about determining what regulations it needed to implement section 403(j). Surprisingly, given the above history, the driving force behind FDA's thinking was not the issue of fraudulent claims but rather a recognition that the real food problem facing the United States was nutritional deficiency and the general inadequacy of the diet.[10] Thus the need to fortify foods with vitamins and minerals was the basic concern, while any need to control health claims became, to FDA, secondary. The question was also raised whether new high-potency vitamin-mineral concentrates, in pill or similar form, should be regulated as foods or should they be regulated as drugs. Those supporting regulation as foods argued that, because vitamins and minerals were nutrients, any product in which they appeared, regardless of form, was a food. Those arguing for drug status argued that such products were "produced by artifact" and, because they were

---

[7]   FDCA § 403(j), 21 U.S.C. § 343(j). The only legislative statement about section 403(j) states that it dealt with "articles offered for special dietary uses, such as infant foods, invalid foods, slenderizing foods, and other dietary products intended for special nutritional requirements . . . . The science of nutrition is rapidly extending the field of its usefulness. In order to keep abreast of these developments, it is necessary that regulation-making power be given here." S. REP. No. 493, 73d Cong., 2d Sess. 12 (1934).

[8]   David F. Cavers, *The Food, Drug, and Cosmetic Act: Its Legislative History and Its Substantive Provisions*, 6 LAW & CONTEMP. PROBS. 2, 30 (1939). Professor Cavers was one of the drafters of the act.

[9]   One FDA official, writing years later, gives us a more candid glimpse of what was of concern:

> At that time [1939], the marketing of special dietary products was confined largely to so-called "health-food stores." Many of the products then distributed were designed to meet the whims and fancies of food faddists which had been cultured by the unscientific teachings of nutritional quacks. There were, of course, a few bona-fide foods for special dietary uses intended for diabetics and others having special dietary needs. These, however, were few in number and were generally characterized by a tastelessness or lack of palatability which discouraged their purchase and use by others than those having a genuine need for them.

Ralph F. Kneeland, Jr., *Foods for Special Dietary Uses Under the Federal Law*, 11 FOOD DRUG COSM. L.J. 41 (1956).

[10] Michael F. Markel, *Foods for Special Dietary Uses—An Historical Outline of Regulatory Aspects*, 22 FOOD DRUG COSM. L.J. 110, 114 (1967).

packaged and marketed as drugs, they were drugs.[11] FDA chose not to resolve this issue.[12] Because the drug provisions of the act gave FDA much more control over drugs than it had over foods, a decision in favor of drug regulation would have drastically altered the legal scene. The final section 403(j) regulations were published in 1940 and 1941 without addressing the drug-food dichotomy.[13]

Because the focus was on the inadequacies of diet, these regulations also did not address the issue of what were acceptable claims for foods for special dietary use; they did not define what were appropriate maximum levels for vitamins or minerals; and they did not even discuss what types of other ingredients (e.g., herbs) might qualify as "nutritional properties" and so come within the ambit of section 403(j). Thus, little was accomplished in enacting the section 403(j) regulations to protect the public from deception, the ostensible reason for the enactment of that section.[14] Instead the regulations were content to define the term "special dietary uses" in the broadest possible way, to include, initially, three classes of products: 1) those that supply a particular dietary need "which exist[s] by reason of a physical, physiological, pathological or other condition," with some examples given (e.g., diseases, pregnancy, allergy, underweight, and overweight[15]); 2) those that supply a special dietary need "by reason of age";[16] 3) those intended to supplement the diet with vitamins, minerals, "or other dietary property";[17] and, later, a final class, 4) any product containing an artificial sweetener unless present only to achieve a food characteristic not available with sugar.[18] Obviously, with such a broad range of "classes," any food, no matter what form it was in, could be subject to section 403(j). The regulations ended up being broad, rather than narrow. Virtually any product could be subject to section 403(j). The regulations then set a minimum daily requirement (MDR) for certain vitamins and minerals and stated that all section 403(j) labels had to list each such MDR.[19] If there were no MDR for a given ingredient, the label had to state "The need for _____ in human nutrition has not been established."[20] Nothing more was required. There were no limits on ingredients or what could be said about them. This was all that was done to meet the congressional directive to regulate vitamin-mineral-herbal foods more closely than conventional foods.

Obviously these regulations were sparse, and over the next several decades they played little part in the day-to-day regulation of dietary supplements. Instead, to police this industry, FDA resorted to extensive litigation directed at claims rather than product content.

---

[11]   *Id.* at 118.

[12]   *Id.* at 119. No findings of fact as to the food-drug distinction were made at the section 403(j) hearings. 6 Fed. Reg. 3304 (1941), 6 Fed. Reg. 5921 (1941).

[13]   5 Fed. Reg. 3565 (1940); 6 Fed. Reg. at 3304; 6 Fed. Reg. at 5921. These regulations remained in force for the next four decades.

[14]   Cavers, *supra* note 8.

[15]   6 Fed. Reg. at 5921, 21 C.F.R. § 2.10a, currently 21 C.F.R. § 105.3(a)(1)(i) (2014).

[16]   *Id.*, currently 21 C.F.R. § 105.3(a)(1)(ii) (2014).

[17]   *Id.*, currently 21 C.F.R. § 105.3(a)(1)(iii) (2014). There is no discussion as to what could be a non-vitamin/mineral "dietary property."

[18]   *Id.*, currently 21 C.F.R. § 105.3(a)(2) (2014). Ever since 1906, artificial sweeteners, specifically saccharin, had been of concern to FDA, because they did not provide the "energy" that sugar provided and thus were needful of regulation. Kneeland, *supra*, note 9, at 46.

[19]   6 Fed. Reg. 5925 (1941), 21 C.F.R. §§ 125.03(b), 125.04(b) (1942).

[20]   *Id.*, 21 C.F.R. § 125.03(a)(2) (1942).

Judicial Issues 1940–1968

Introduction

There is no need to examine all the reported decisions between 1940 and 1968 involving dietary supplement-type products. It is sufficient to examine three issues: 1) the judicial classification of vitamin-mineral-herbal products as foods or drugs; 2) the role of third-party literature (e.g., books and pamphlets), both in that classification process and in determining whether illegal claims are made for them; and 3) the later classification of some ingredients under the Food Additives Amendment, and the consequences thereof.[21] An understanding of these three interrelated issues helps to clarify what Congress wanted to address in enacting DSHEA.

Vitamin, Mineral, Herbal Products as Foods and Drugs

As noted earlier, FDA, in publishing its section 403(j) regulations, avoided the question of whether vitamin and mineral products, in tablet or pill form, were drugs or foods under the act. A product is a drug, *inter alia*, if intended, by its vendor, for the treatment, prevention, or mitigation of any disease.[22] Therefore, depending on the intent of the vendor (however discovered), any product can be a drug. It is not surprising, then, that there are a number of drug cases involving ingredients that are, in ordinary parlance, food ingredients; e.g., fennel,[23] water,[24] ginseng, and sage.[25]

What is of interest in the developing case law (and DSHEA) is that many of the ingredients in offending products were herbs; herbs that were either commonly used as foods (e.g., as spices), or non-spice herbs that had a long history of medicinal use (frequently dismissed as quackery).[26] And it certainly did not help the cause of these herbs that they too often appeared in products in bitterly fought battles such as the many *Hoxsey* cancer cases.[27] Clearly herbs were a serious source of concern to FDA. Perhaps because of this, some cases were brought where the claims actually made for the herbs were innocuous. For example, in 1947, garlic tablets were held to be drugs when all that was claimed for them was that they were recommended for those persons who wished to include garlic in their diet and that "two or three tablets taken three times a day offer a convenient easy method" for doing

---

21   Food Additives Amendment of 1958, Pub. L. No. 85-929, 72 Stat. 1748 (1958), 21 U.S.C. § 348.

22   FDCA § 201(g)(1)(B), 21 U.S.C. § 321(g)(1)(B). This intent can be determined in any number of ways, by examining any promotional materials for the product and by looking at any "other relevant source of information." United States v. Storage Spaces ..., 777 F.2d 1363, 1366 (9th Cir. 1985), *cert. denied*, 107 S. Ct. 1291 (1987). Seemingly, then, "intent" could be found, for example, in marketing a product, without any claims made for it, where there is wide public belief that it has a specific curative benefit. Taking advantage of market demand is surely a form of "intent."

23   United States v. Six Dozen Bottles, 55 F. Supp. 458 (D. Wis. 1944).

24   United States v. Five Cases ... of Capon Springs Water, 62 F. Supp. 736 (S.D.N.Y. 1945), *rev'd on other grounds*, 156 F.2d 493 (2d Cir. 1946).

25   Research Laboratories, Inc. v. United States, 167 F.2d 410 (9th Cir. 1948), *cert. denied*, 335 U.S. 843 (1948).

26   For example, the court in *Research Laboratories* noted a statement made in a then-current pharmacological text that the medicinal properties ascribed to ginseng "had no other existence than in the imagination of the Chinese." *Id.* at 418.

27   *See, e.g.*, United States v. Hoxsey Cancer Clinic, 198 F.2d 273 (5th Cir. 1952).

so.[28] This hardly seems to be a medicinal claim, but FDA took it to court—and won. Garlic tablets are now widely sold.

Herbal products thus faced a history that made them, as a class, suspect. Many had a tradition of both medicinal and food use—a tradition difficult to apply under the act because it was not always clear where a legitimate food use ended and an inappropriate medicinal use began. Many herbs were also promoted, doubtless because of their often exotic history, by charlatans for inappropriate purposes (e.g., curing cancer), placing them, in the minds of many government officials, in the unfortunate category of fraudulent ingredients.[29] These problems were only compounded by the fact that FDA did not, in its 1941 section 403(j) regulations, address the status of herbs as possible "dietary properties" under section 403(j). Had FDA clearly done so, a great deal of confusion—and litigation—could have been avoided. The section 403(j) regulations should have been—but were not—the method by which FDA directly addressed the herbal industry. That FDA did not, led to decades of needless litigation. More traditional supplement ingredients—vitamins and minerals—faced similar drug-food classification problems.

FDA began to deal with the drug-food issue with a tactic that, if pressed, would have dramatically changed history. Another definition of a drug under the act, in addition to the "intended uses" section already discussed, provides that a product is a drug if it is "recognized in [the] official United States Pharmacopeia, official Homeopathic Pharmacopeia of the United States, or official National Formulary, or any supplement to any of them."[30] In a 1944 case, certain vitamin capsules were alleged to be misbranded, as both foods and as drugs (in separate counts), in that their vitamin B potency was misrepresented. The court dismissed each food count because vitamin B was listed in the United States Pharmacopeia (USP) and, therefore, the capsules were drugs.[31] This decision thus gave FDA a potentially valuable tool in controlling the marketing of vitamin-mineral and even herbal preparations in tablet or capsule form, because virtually all vitamins and minerals were in the USP and many herbal preparations appear in the homeopathic dictionary.[32]

Had FDA pursued this reasoning with vigor, and been successful in doing so, its enforcement power over vitamin, mineral, and herbal products would have been greatly enhanced. If dietary supplements had been regulated as drugs since the 1940s, they doubtless would be marketed today in a fashion far different than they are now—if at all. This is especially true

---

[28]   United States v. 150 Packages ... Bush Mulso Tablets, 83 F. Supp. 875 (E.D. Mo. 1947).

[29]   *See, e.g.*, William W. Goodrich, *Challenging Quackery With Truth*, 16 FOOD DRUG COSM. L.J. 684 (1961).

[30]   FDCA § 201(g)(1)(A), 21 U.S.C. § 321(g)(1)(A).

[31]   United States v. Hain (S.D. Ca. 1943); V. KLEINFELD & C. DUNN, FEDERAL FOOD, DRUG AND COSMETIC ACT, JUDICIAL AND ADMINISTRATIVE RECORD 1938-1949 at 265 (1950).

[32]   *See, e.g.*, 1 HOMEOPATHIC PHARMACOPEIA OF THE UNITED STATES, 92 (ginseng), 550 (comfrey) (8th ed. 1979). The consequence of a listing in USP as determining drug status that the court in *Hain* accepted so easily in 1943 became, in 1968, more troublesome. One court held that such a listing, while not conclusive of drug status, was some evidence of it. AMP, Inc. v. Gardner, 275 F. Supp. 410 (S.D.N.Y. 1967), *aff'd*, 389 F.2d 825 (2d Cir. 1968) (sutures). The Second Circuit later refined this, in a vitamin-mineral case, by ruling that mere inclusion in USP was insufficient to confer drug status. NNFA v. FDA, 504 F.2d 761 (2d Cir. 1974). *Accord,* United States v. An Article of Drug ... Ova II, 414 F. Supp. 660 (D.N.J. 1975), *aff'd without op.* 535 F.2d 1248 (3d Cir. 1976) (pregnancy test kit). *Contra,* United States v. Beuthanasia-D Regular, Food Drug Cosm. Rep. (CCH) ¶ 38,265 (D. Neb. 1979), V. KLEINFELD & A. KAPLAN, FEDERAL FOOD, DRUG AND COSMETIC ACT 1978-1980 at 83 (1983) (product to be used in euthanasia of animals).

when one notes the "new drug" provisions of the law. Space does not permit a discussion of these provisions,[33] but the Drug Amendments of 1962 required the purveyors of pre-1962 drugs to demonstrate their efficacy to FDA's satisfaction. Had the vendors of these vitamin and herbal products been required to do so, surely many would have long ago disappeared.

FDA, however, did not pursue the offer in *Hain* and instead chose to confront the use of vitamins and minerals head on—as misbranded drugs for which therapeutic claims were made, and as misbranded foods for special dietary uses when that tactic seemed advantageous. There is no public statement from FDA about why it never pursued *Hain*, but one should note that at about this time, vitamin-fortified breakfast cereals were very popular and any across-the-board application of *Hain* would have been politically unwise.

The Drug-Food Classification and the Role of Books and Pamphlets in Determining Drug Status and the Existence of Misleading Claims for Vitamin-, Mineral- and Herbal-Containing Products

As noted above, a product is a drug if, among other things, it is "intended" for use in the diagnosis or treatment of any disease, and a product, be it food or drug, is misbranded if any false or misleading statements are made about it in "labeling."[34] Therefore, a product containing a vitamin, mineral, or herbal substance could first avoid drug classification if there were no "intended" therapeutic uses for it, and, second could avoid misbranding if there were no misleading or false claims in its labeling. Such seemingly simple tasks pose two questions: one, how is drug "intent" determined and two, what is "labeling"; for, if there are written materials that are not "labeling," then any claims made in such materials would be beyond FDA's reach and, if there were no drug "intent," there would be no need to meet the law's requirements for drugs. When these twin possibilities were coupled with the enthusiasm for popular self-help books, a possible way to avoid FDA was soon devised.

The theory ran this way. Books, magazines, and pamphlets, together with their authors and publishers, enjoy First Amendment rights. Thus, anyone could write a book about, for example, the therapeutic value of molasses, without government interference, even though such a book, the reasoning ran, would logically cause an increase in the public's desire to buy molasses. The molasses industry would benefit as a class. But astute molasses vendors might do even better, in terms of sales, if they put up signs in their stores reminding customers of what the book had to say about the wonders of molasses. They might do better still if the book itself were sold at their stores. Surely, the reasoning went, such books would not be "labeling" because any store selling molasses did not write or publish the book. The molasses vendor would simply be the beneficiary of the fact that someone else wrote a book.

---

[33] *See* Chapter 10.
[34] FDCA § 201(g)(1)(B), 21 U.S.C. § 321(g)(1)(B); FDCA § 403(a)(1), 21 U.S.C. § 343(a)(1); FDCA § 502(a), 21 U.S.C. § 352(a).

Increased sales of molasses would be the innocent result of the First Amendment right to publish. This is exactly what happened. Books and pamphlets were published about various dietary ingredients. It is not surprising that vendors of such supplements took varying steps to take advantage of that happy event. FDA soon responded.[35] First there was the question: are such books "labeling?"

The act defines "labeling" *inter alia* as any written material that accompanies a food.[36] The Supreme Court held that the term "accompany" did not restrict labeling to written materials on or shipped with the food, but rather was broad enough so that any written material is "labeling" if it is designed for use in the promotion of the food. It is not how the material is distributed; instead "[i]t is the textual relationship that is significant."[37] "Labeling" could be anything that accompanied a food and promoted it. Based on this reasoning, FDA instituted an *in rem* action against a retail store's supply of molasses on the charge that that molasses was misbranded by claims made about molasses in general, in a book entitled *Look Younger Live Longer* by Gaylord Hauser, also sold in that store. Both the books and the molasses were seized. The seller of the molasses was not the publisher of the book. The publisher intervened and sought dismissal as to its books only, asserting that the books it published as an independent business could not be labeling for an unrelated company's food products. The court initially granted the motion, pointing out that before any book could be labeling it had to have some relationship to the seized molasses. The publisher had no such relationship to any molasses and because this book had been independently published by another and was generally available, it was not "labeling."[38]

The government amended the libel to allege additional facts showing just how the book was used to promote sales of the molasses, including an article by the author, Gaylord Hauser, announcing that one could obtain molasses from the store; the fact that copies of the book were given with any purchase of molasses in that store; and that the store displayed advertisements referring to both the book and the availability of molasses there. The court then denied a renewed motion to dismiss filed by the publisher, concluding that the amended libel did not interfere with the publisher's right to sell the book generally, in that the lawsuit reached only those copies of the book, in the store, actually used to promote the sale of molasses.[39]

The few subsequent decisions in this area generally followed this fact-bound reasoning, but no court ever drew a clear line between the legitimate sale of books—as to which a food vendor could be an innocent beneficiary—and an illegal use of books as "labeling" to promote such good fortune.[40] The cases do suggest some areas of inquiry. Was the book displayed with the food? Was it jointly promoted with the food or drug or was it

---

[35]   One FDA attorney stated at least his views about such practices in rather vivid terms: "It is common knowledge that many drugs could not be sold at all except upon false and misleading representations directed to the credulous and the ignorant . . . The obvious dodge of the unscrupulous promoter is to try to keep the labeling 'clean' and to make his representations through collateral means outside the labeling." Arthur A. Dickerman, *Adequate Directions for Use*, 7 FOOD DRUG COSM. L.J. 738 (1952).

[36]   FDCA § 201(m), 21 U.S.C. § 321(m).

[37]   Kordel v. United States, 335 U.S. 345, 350 (1948).

[38]   United States v. 8 Cartons of Blackstrap Molasses, 97 F. Supp. 313 (W.D.N.Y. 1951).

[39]   United States v. 8 Cartons of Blackstrap Molasses, 103 F. Supp. 626 (W.D.N.Y. 1951).

[40]   United States v. 24 Bottles, Sterling Vinegar and Honey, 338 F.2d 157 (2d Cir. 1964); United States v. Articles of Drug ... Carlton Fredericks, Intervenor, 32 F.R.D. 32 (S.D. Ill. 1963).

happenstance that both the book and the product were in the same store?[41] Did a vendor in any way refer to the book in any promotional materials? Each case depended on its own facts and one could not see a simple path to compliance. Clearly a store could sell both books and foods, but could a store tell customers about the relationship between the two? Uncertainty here led to confusion and concern about the right of persons to freely sell books. As will be explained, DSHEA attempted to respond to this problem.

Having broadened the scope of "labeling" to include books and pamphlets, FDA, with the help of the judiciary, was also able to do away with even the need to restrict itself to "labeling." The act provides that a drug is misbranded if its labeling does not have "adequate directions" for its "intended" uses.[42] Courts soon ruled that, in determining such "adequate directions" and "intended" use, one could look at whatever was said about a product by its vendor without restriction to labeling.[43] Any statement any time could be examined to determine drug—and therefore new drug—status. If, anywhere, a drug claim were made for a product, even one labeled simply as a food, the product was a drug and had to have adequate directions for its use in labeling. But if it had such adequate directions for use then it had to be a drug. This back-door approach to drug status gave FDA an almost invincible power over all therapeutic claims for dietary supplements; a power, which when coupled with the already broad reach of the term "labeling," allowed FDA to proceed at will against dietary supplements as drugs, based on what was said in lectures,[44] pamphlets,[45] newsletters,[46] and even radio broadcasts.[47] There was no safe harbor where a dietary supplement vendor could sell such products if there were any reasonable way one could conclude that, in fact, the product was being sold for some therapeutic purpose. For example, if an herbal product were widely described in lectures by health professionals as useful in connection with some disease state, and FDA had never approved it for that purpose, a vendor of the herb sold its product solely at the sufferance of FDA. There was no clear way for the vendor to be assured that it complied with the law. DSHEA attempted to clarify the status of such claims when made by such persons.

Other Issues in Developing Appropriate Nutritional and Health Claims for Dietary Supplements, 1939–1968

FDA's apparent policy position between 1939 and the 1980s was that the only true role for vitamins and minerals in the diet was to prevent nutritional deficiency conditions and

---

[41] The court in *Sterling Vinegar* did find that the fact that the two products, the book and the food, were only five feet apart in the store not determinative of the book's labeling status—at least in a store only 20 feet by 25 feet. 338 F.2d at 159. This led many store owners over the years to adopt a "five-foot" rule.

[42] FDCA § 502(f)(1), 21 U.S.C. § 352(f)(1).

[43] Alberty Food Products v. United States, 194 F.2d 463 (9th Cir. 1952) (product labeled simply as garlic tablets, advertised for use in wide range of diseases including heart failure and cholera). See Dickerman, *supra*, note 35 at 740.

[44] United States v. Hohensee, 243 F.2d 367 (3d Cir. 1957), *cert. denied*, 353 U.S. 976 (1957).

[45] United States v. 47 Bottles ... Jenasol, 320 F.2d 564 (3d Cir. 1963).

[46] V.E. Irons, Inc. v. United States, 244 F.2d 34 (1st Cir. 1957).

[47] United States v. Articles of Drug, Foods Plus, Inc., 239 F. Supp. 465 (D.N.J. 1965).

that traditional foods provided what was needed; processing methods caused no nutritional detriments to food; and there were no "subclinical" nutritional deficiencies that could lead to serious health problems.[48] The many cases FDA brought against dietary supplements over the years were based on such premises, but the way some were decided caused confusion. Two cases reveal the problem.

After years of bitter litigation, the government entered into a consent decree of injunction involving a dietary supplement called Nutrilite.[49] Its prohibitory terms are unexceptional, but what FDA, the vendor, and the court agreed could be said was startling. The decree allowed the vendor to represent that subclinical deficiencies do exist in the United States; that vitamin B1 tends to relieve the neuritis of alcoholism and pregnancy; and that calcium is an essential factor in the proper coagulation of blood—all surely drug claims[50] and all claims seemingly at odds with the above FDA premises. This decree, often referred to in the industry as the Bill of Rights, was thus at odds with FDA's enforcement posture both before and after the decree, and the fact that FDA agreed to it sent a confusing message to the industry. Nutrilite, although subject to a decree of injunction, was apparently free to make some drug claims, without complying with drug laws, that the rest of the dietary supplement industry could not.[51]

In another case, FDA made the argument that a vitamin-fortified sugar was misbranded, *ipso facto*, solely because the particular vitamins added to the seized sugar were already in adequate supply in the American diet. In other words, "fortified" sugar is misbranded because there was no need for a fortified sugar. This argument was promptly rejected.[52] FDA's position is especially strange because it seems to argue that no food could be "fortified" since no vitamins or minerals were (or are) lacking in our food supply. This position was totally at odds with what was actually taking place in the food industry generally (e.g., cereals and milk) and totally at odds with what the government agreed could be said about the Nutrilite product. FDA was not sending a clear, consistent signal to vendors of supplements.

The Problem of the Food Additive Law and Herbal Ingredients

In 1958, Congress passed the "food additive" amendments to the act; amendments which provide that FDA approval is required for all ingredients added to foods if they are not

---

[48]   William Goodrich, *The Coming Struggle Over Vitamin-Mineral Pills*, 20 BUS. LAW. 145 (1964).

[49]   United States v. Mytinger & Casselberry, Inc. (S.D. Cal. 1951), reported in V. KLEINFELD & C. DUNN, FEDERAL FOOD, DRUG & COSMETIC ACT 1951-1952 at 204 (1953). The majority and dissenting opinions in an earlier case, Ewing v. Mytinger & Casselberry, Inc., 339 U.S. 594 (1950), reveal just how bitter this battle was.

[50]   *Id.* V, pars 6, 18, and 21.

[51]   This is especially ironic when one notes other cases where the mere listing of vitamins and minerals on the labeling was found offensive. *See, e.g.*, United States v. Vitasafe, Etc. Civ. No. 875-60 (D.N.J. 1964) in V. KLEINFELD & A. KAPLAN, FEDERAL FOOD, DRUG AND COSMETIC ACT 1961-1964 at 779 (1965). There is no way to reconcile these results.

[52]   United States v. 119 Cases New Dextra ... Sugar (S.D. Fl., No. 101-62M-Civ. E.C.), *id.* at 64.

generally recognized as safe.[53] FDA's enforcement of these amendments as to herbal ingredients led to two problems.

First, there was the fact of foreign-origin herbal ingredients. Under these amendments, if an ingredient was commonly used in food before 1958, FDA approval of it was not required.[54] In an effort to implement this proviso, FDA published a regulation stating that the pre-1958 exemption was available only for ingredients commonly used in food in the United States prior to 1958.[55] Substances used only abroad would, therefore, need FDA approval no matter what the facts may be as to their "common use" prior to 1958. But many herbs come from countries other than the United States and, while they were commonly used in foods there, they were not so used here. The FDA regulation, therefore, effectively barred them from use in dietary supplements in this country. On challenge, a court declared the FDA regulation invalid, thus allowing foreign-origin herbs equal access to U.S. markets.[56]

The second and more pervasive problem for herbs under these amendments has to do with the scope of the food additive definition itself. The act defines a food additive as something that is either a component of a food or is otherwise added to it. FDA, in an apparent effort to keep various herbal preparations from the marketplace, argued that a single herbal ingredient food in capsule form was an "additive" even though it was not added to anything. The courts ruled against FDA, one characterizing the FDA argument as "absurd."[57] This effort by FDA to control the sale of herbal supplements by such a strained interpretation of the definition of a "food additive" is the single most important event that brought about DSHEA. The reason is simple for, if FDA's position were upheld, FDA could effectively ban most, if not all, herbs from the marketplace—no matter how truthfully they were labeled or promoted. All FDA had to do was to find witnesses who could testify that these herbs were not generally recognized as safe. FDA would not have to prove that the herbs were unsafe or that anyone had ever been harmed. Given the paucity of data on at least some herbs this task would not have been difficult. DSHEA simply removed herbs, when used in dietary supplements, from the definition of a food additive, thus solving both of the above problems—at least when the herb is used in a dietary supplement. But even before DSHEA, there was earlier legislation designed to address some of these issues.

The Proxmire Amendments

By the 1960s it became apparent to all concerned, FDA, the industry, and to many consumers alike, that the patchwork of judicial decisions and inconsistent enforcement

---

[53]   Food Additive Amendments of 1958, Pub. L. No. 85-929, 71 Stat. 1784 (1958).

[54]   FDCA § 201(s), 21 U.S.C. § 321(s).

[55]   36 Fed. Reg. 12,093 (1971).

[56]   Fmali v. Heckler, 713 F.2d 1568 (9th Cir. 1983). But, while FDA now acknowledges that the common use in food exemption is available for food ingredients from any country, its regulations nonetheless impose restrictions on foreign-origin herbs that are not imposed on domestic products. 21 C.F.R. § 170.30(c)(2) (2014).

[57]   United States v. Two Plastic Drums ... Black Currant Oil, 984 F.2d 814, 819 (7th Cir. 1993); United States v. An Article of Food, 792 F. Supp. 139 (D. Mass. 1992).

postures directed at the supplement industry was intolerable.[58] To address this, FDA proposed a set of regulations that were all encompassing, setting standards, upper limits for vitamin and mineral ingredients, and even mandatory labeling statements about the need— or lack of it—for vitamin and mineral supplementation.[59] The regulations were detailed, lengthy, and all encompassing, and they were not well received; "idiotic regulations" and "antediluvian ideas of FDA" were just some of the critical terms used.[60] While everyone agreed there was a problem, no one agreed to any solution. Some segments of the industry agreed that regulation was needed while others felt that any intrusion into their business was unwarranted. Unfortunately, FDA's proposal was inconsistent, and both too broad and too narrow. FDA tried to do too much and in doing so alienated everyone.

To move these proposals forward, FDA held a rulemaking hearing that, charitably, was a disaster,[61] which was in turn followed by a series of appeals and further hearings, the net result a group of decisions that affirmed some of the regulations but invalidated others.[62] Because these regulations were soon revoked and so are no longer at issue, they need not detain us here.[63] For our purposes, the most important result of this hearing process was that it spawned the first legislation directed solely to dietary supplement problems, the so-called Proxmire Amendments.[64]

The Proxmire Amendments applied to products containing vitamins and minerals, fabricated in nonconventional food forms (e.g., pill, tablet, capsule, or liquid (so long as only drops)), and marketed for "special dietary uses," a term broadly defined to include supplying a dietary need that exists by reason of a physical, physiological, pathological, "or other condition," with examples given (e.g., disease, overweight, or pregnancy).[65] Under these amendments, such products could not be defined as drugs solely because of their vitamin-mineral potency, and no upper limit on their potency could be established, other than under the food additive law. FDA could not limit the combinations of safe vitamins, minerals, and "other ingredients" that could be put in a single product thus allowing herbs and other "non-nutrients" to be combined with vitamins and minerals.[66] These amendments, then, while they set limits on FDA's authority to classify vitamin-mineral products as drugs, did not fully include herbs as exempt ingredients, did not address the question of food additive

---

58   "Our own out-dated regulations have contributed to the confusion . . . ." Goodrich, *supra* note 48 at 146. Mr. Goodrich was then FDA's Chief Counsel.

59   31 Fed. Reg. 8621 *et seq.* (1966).

60   William W. Goodrich, Address to Division of Food, Drug and Cosmetic Law, Sec. on Corporation, Banking and Business Law, ABA (Aug. 12, 1964) *in* [1963-1967 Transfer Binder] Food Drug Cosm. L. Rep. (CCH) ¶ 60,079.

61   *See, e.g.,* Robert W. Hamilton, *Rulemaking on a Record by the Food and Drug Administration*, 50 TEXAS L. REV. 1132 (1972); William K. Pendergast, *Have the FDA Hearing Regulations Failed Us?*, 23 FOOD DRUG COSM. L.J. 524 (1968). The hearing problems were compounded by the appointment of a presiding officer with little experience in litigation and none in FDA matters.

62   NNFA v. FDA, 491 F.2d 1141 (2d Cir. 1974); NNFA v. FDA, 504 F.2d 761 (2d Cir. 1965), *cert. denied,* 420 U.S. 946; NNFA v. Kennedy, 572 F.2d 364 (2d Cir. 1978).

63   The formal revocation appears at 44 Fed. Reg. 16,005 (1979). During these same years FDA had also been considering a legally binding monograph for over-the-counter drugs consisting of vitamins and minerals. This too was revoked. 46 Fed. Reg. 57,914 (1981).

64   Title V, Health Research and Health Services Amendments of 1976, Pub. L. No. 94-278, 90 Stat. 401, 410 (1976).

65   FDCA § 411(e), 21 U.S.C. § 350(e).

66   H.R. CONF. REP. No. 94-1005, 94th Cong., 2d Sess. (1976).

status, and did not alter the law as it related to the role of books, etc. in the promotion of these products.[67]

These amendments, while they surely did not settle all matters, nonetheless had an effect on FDA enforcement. In the following years, while there were the food additive efforts and other litigation directed at herbal products, there was little FDA activity vis-à-vis vitamin-mineral preparations.[68] By now, other events, not just Proxmire, were taking place that radically altered the scene and began to turn FDA's policy against health claims in foods, if not in dietary supplements, in a new direction.

A Change in Philosophy and Public Demand

In 1969, the White House held a widely publicized Conference on Food, Nutrition and Health. The report that followed concluded that what was needed was more, not less, information about both the nutritional value of foods and the central role of sound nutrition practices in public health.[69] This was contrary to FDA's 1938–1969 posture about nutritional and health information, but Congress and then FDA responded to this "new" thinking.

Congress began by considering (but not enacting) a number of bills that would have either mandated greater nutritional information on the labels of foods[70] or given FDA new authority to require such nutritional information.[71] FDA also began, slowly, to loosen its grip on the use of health claims for foods. FDA soon considered percent ingredient labeling for the "characterizing" ingredients in foods; changed the requirements for standardized foods in the direction of greater nutritional labeling and, by inaction at least, generally acquiesced in allowing food vendors to provide more public information about the real value of foods and food ingredients.[72] But none of these initiatives related clearly to health claims and certainly did nothing to change the status of dietary supplements. It took the marketplace to force FDA to finally abandon its old position restricting the use of claims that were other than straight content claims—at least as to traditional foods.

---

[67]   The Proxmire Amendments did give FDA new authority over the advertising of such supplements. If the products' advertising were false or misleading, the products were misbranded and FDA—not FTC—could proceed against the offender, but only after notifying FTC, which then had the opportunity to proceed first. 90 Stat. 412, amending the act by adding section 707 thereto, 21 U.S.C. § 378. FDA never exercised this power. Proxmire is discussed in NNFA v. Kennedy, 572 F.2d 377 (2d Cir. 1978).

[68]   At least one criminal case was brought against an herbal vendor, United States v. General Nutrition, Inc., No. Cr-84-174E (W.D.N.Y. 1984), and a number of FDA Warning Letters were issued to other herbal companies. See Peter Barton Hutt, *Government Regulation of Health Claims in Food Labeling and Advertising*, 41 FOOD DRUG COSM. L.J. 366, 394 (1986).

[69]   WHITE HOUSE CONFERENCE ON FOOD, NUTRITION & HEALTH, FINAL REPORT (1970).

[70]   *See, e.g.,* H.R. 16,638, 91st Cong., 2d Sess. (1970).

[71]   *See, e.g.,* S. 2373, 92d Cong., 1st Sess. (1974). See P. Hutt, *Food Legislation in Perspective*, 34 FOOD DRUG COSM. L.J. 590, 593-96 (1979).

[72]   There is a large body of literature on the history of these changes, *see, e.g.,* Richard M. Cooper et al., *History of Health Claims Regulation*, 45 FOOD DRUG COSM. L.J. 655 (1990); J.B. Cordaro, *The Food-Drug Dilemma: Communicating Disease-Related Claims for Foods*, 40 FOOD DRUG COSM. L.J. 13 (1985); Hutt, *supra* note 71; and Ralph A. Davis, *The New FDA Position on Health-Related Messages for Food Products and Constitutionally Protected Free Speech*, 42 FOOD DRUG COSM. L.J. 365 (1987).

By the mid-1980s several food companies, notwithstanding the long history of FDA opposition, began to promote their products for their role in preventing various diseases—e.g., fiber-containing foods to help reduce the risk of cancer—claims that were well-supported in the scientific literature but which were nonetheless claims that FDA had traditionally opined were drug claims and so could only be made in the context of an approved (by FDA) new drug application (NDA). At first FDA did nothing to stop this trend and FTC actually endorsed it, as did Congress.[73] Furthermore, while the food industry was taking these initiatives, the public was also turning, in ever-increasing numbers, to the use of dietary supplements as a part of its diet—up, for example, from 26 percent in 1977 to 45 percent in 1985 for one group.[74] The public was becoming more health-conscious and the marketplace soon responded. The tide of public opinion, congressional concern, and the science of nutrition were running against the older FDA ethic. FDA responded in a positive way as to health claims in foods, but, and in spite of this sea-change in public opinion and usage, it did not do so with respect to dietary supplements. FDA's position remained strict as to these products.

In 1987 FDA published a statement of policy on health claims in foods.[75] After noting that such claims "may raise complex legal and procedural concerns," FDA nonetheless declared that it "now believes that health-related messages . . . may provide valuable information to health-conscious consumers."[76] FDA announced that it would allow such claims—i.e., not invoke the new drug law—if 1) the claims were true; 2) they were supported by valid, publicly available scientific evidence; 3) they were consistent with generally recognized medical and nutritional principles for a sound diet; and 4) any product involved would bear full "nutritional" labeling.[77] FDA then stated that the same criteria would be applicable to dietary supplements, but added, somewhat ominously, that the "extent to which the criteria can be met [with respect to dietary supplements] may be limited."[78] In other words, according to FDA foods and dietary supplements are not the same and while it may be appropriate to allow claims for foods, FDA did not agree that this meant that claims were appropriate for supplements. This FDA suspicion, that dietary supplements would not measure up, was soon reflected in other areas, for although FDA said it would treat both the food industry and the dietary supplement industry the same, it did not do so. FDA continued to pursue dietary supplements in litigation as unapproved drugs because of alleged claims made for them, something it was not doing for foods generally. As a result, FDA seemed to be taking inconsistent positions—allowing the food industry a liberty it did not bestow on the dietary supplement industry. Thus when FDA seized a supplement on charges that drug claims were made for it, the court dismissed the case pointing out that the government "must govern with an even hand" and was not doing so when it enforced the drug law against dietary supplements but not as to traditional foods.[79]

---

73   See Cooper, supra note 72, at 662.
74   NATIONAL RESEARCH COUNCIL, DIET AND HEALTH IMPLICATIONS FOR REDUCING CHRONIC DISEASE RISK, 18 (1989).
75   52 Fed. Reg. 28,843 (1987).
76   52 Fed. Reg. at 28,845.
77   Id.
78   52 Fed. Reg. at 28,846. FDA concluded that any scientific findings about traditional foods may not be applicable to their specific components. Id. As to the legality of the broader decision that health claims did not cause a product to be a drug, see Cooper, supra, note 72, at 682 ff.
79   United States v. Undetermined Quantities of Article of Drug...Exachol, 716 F. Supp. 787, 795 (S.D.N.Y. 1989).

The health claim proposal generated a considerable amount of comment pro and con. Its one concrete result was the Nutrition Labeling and Education Act (NLEA) of 1990,[80] an act that leads directly to DSHEA.

NLEA, FDA, and Dietary Supplements: The Health Claim Issue[81]

Under NLEA, food health claims—i.e., claims about the relationship of a nutrient to a disease or health-related condition—are allowed, but only in accord with FDA regulations.[82] In proposing implementing regulations, FDA announced its criteria for approving health claims and stated that these criteria would be applied to both traditional foods and dietary supplements.[83] This particular conclusion was controversial because NLEA specifies that FDA must establish separate health claim procedures and standards for dietary supplements apart from those it specifies for traditional foods.[84] There were those who thought this meant something and that FDA's off-hand statement that it could use just one standard was too dismissive of the congressional directive. The legislative history, however, is mixed. On the House of Representatives side a statement was made that, while FDA did indeed have to publish separate regulations for supplements, FDA, in doing so, could adopt the same standards it requires for foods—or even more stringent ones.[85] On the Senate side, Senator Orrin Hatch stated that because of the differences between dietary supplement and traditional foods in their marketing and utility, the standards for health claims must necessarily differ and thus, he concluded, separate and "more lenient" criteria, were in order.[86] FDA chose to accept the House's interpretation, doubtless on the reasonable assumption that, with such a direct split in legislative history, no court would hold FDA wrong in choosing one over the other. Clearly FDA's philosophy and history would also incline it to accept the House version because it was consistent with FDA's earlier proposals on health claims.[87] DSHEA, which rejects FDA's view, was sponsored by Senator Hatch.

The proposed health claim standards for approval were stringent and it was not long before the dietary supplement industry objected both to their stringency and to their applicability to dietary supplements.[88] Congress then sided with the dietary supplement industry and enacted legislation imposing a 14-month moratorium on any FDA implementation of NLEA

---

80 Pub. L. No. 101-635, 104 Stat. 2353, 101st Cong., 2d Sess. (1990).
81 NLEA sweeps across the entire field of labeling for foods, including nutritional content, nutritional descriptors (e.g., high fiber), and "health" claims. Subjects other than health claims are beyond the scope of this chapter. *See* Chapter 3.
82 FDCA § 403(r)(1)(B), 21 U.S.C. § 343(r)(1)(B). An FDA official described this new provision as "a sweeping reversal of the agency's previous policy. Until the mid-1980's, the FDA regarded all health claims as attributes . . . subject to premarket approval . . . ." Fred R. Shank, *The Nutrition Labeling and Education Act of 1990*, 47 FOOD & DRUG L.J. 247, 251 (1992).
83 56 Fed. Reg. 60,537, 60,539 (1991).
84 FDCA § 403(r)(5)(D), 21 U.S.C. § 343(r)(5)(D).
85 103 CONG. REC. H12,953 (daily ed. Oct. 26, 1990) (Statement of House Floor Managers).
86 103 CONG. REC. S16,611 (daily ed. Oct. 24, 1990).
87 52 Fed. Reg. 28,843, 28,846 (1987).
88 *See, e.g.*, Anthony J. Iannacrone, *Scientific Basis for Health Claims for Dietary Supplements*, 47 FOOD & DRUG L.J. 665 (1992).

with respect to supplements in nonconventional food form, certainly a strong signal that Congress wanted the entire matter of allowable health claims for dietary supplements carefully reconsidered by FDA.[89] FDA did so and, after an extended discussion of the wisdom of a more lenient standard for dietary supplement health claims, including herbal health claims, FDA nonetheless again concluded that the scientific criteria for all food health claims should be the same.[90] FDA's arguments were reasonable and probably would have carried the day, but they lost some of their force when other events took place indicating that FDA's decades-long distrust of the dietary supplement industry had not abated—something Congress did not want to hear.

First of all, in response to this legislative turmoil, FDA published a document purporting to detail the many unsubstantiated claims and hazards associated with dietary supplements,[91] and, at the same time, another document calling for comments on the manner in which FDA regulates dietary supplements, posing a number of provocative questions about the safety of the ingredients in dietary supplements.[92] This FDA request for comments noted the agency's concern that the safety data on herbs were scant and that there had been safety problems with herbs in the past. FDA allowed that, based on any comments it received, it would consider either new regulations or further enforcement actions against supplements and the supplement industry.[93] This second document, because of its tone and specific threats, struck both the dietary supplement industry and some in Congress as evidence that FDA had no intention of ever letting up its enforcement actions toward dietary supplements— particularly herbal ones, and their manufacture. Finally, and perhaps most dramatically, the first document—the one dealing with unsubstantiated claims in the marketplace— turned out to be seriously flawed in its facts, further eroding congressional support for FDA.[94] These two documents, therefore, demonstrated, at least to some in Congress, that, although FDA was altering its opinions about health claims for foods, its antagonism toward dietary supplements continued. The result was DSHEA. Extensive litigation in the late 1990s changed the landscape of health claims for dietary supplements irrevocably when the courts forced FDA to allow qualified health claims for dietary supplements (see Chapter 3).

---

[89]   Dietary Supplement Act of 1992, Pub. L. No. 102-571, 106 Stat. 4500 (1992).

[90]   Reproposal, 58 Fed. Reg. 33,700 (1993); final regulations, 59 Fed. Reg. 395 (1994).

[91]   DEP'T OF HEALTH & HUMAN SERVICES, FOOD & DRUG ADMIN., UNSUBSTANTIATED CLAIMS AND DOCUMENTED HEALTH HAZARDS IN THE DIETARY SUPPLEMENT MARKETPLACE (1993).

[92]   58 Fed. Reg. 33,690 (1993).

[93]   Id. at 33,699.

[94]   A Senate staff review of this "unsubstantiated claims" document concluded that the FDA document itself was false and misleading and that FDA should apologize to Congress and to the public for releasing it. Dietary Supplement Legislation Debated [1992-1993 Transfer Binder] Food Drug Cosm. Law Rep. (CCH) ¶ 43,622. Apparently the data used were hurriedly accumulated, put together and printed, with the usual mistakes that such haste guarantees. Politically, it was not FDA's happiest moment.

The Dietary Supplement Health and Education Act

The Definition and Problems Associated With It

Within one year of these events, and with few hearings and virtually no debate, Congress passed the Dietary Supplement Health and Education Act,[95] an act that seeks to address many of the issues discussed earlier in an effort to legislatively direct FDA to take a new and more lenient line with the dietary supplement industry. In doing so, some sections of DSHEA take authority away from FDA, while in other sections its direction is less clear.[96]

DSHEA begins with a series of congressional findings that must guide all readings of this law. Congress finds that consumers should be empowered to make choices about their own preventive healthcare programs based on data from scientific studies of health benefits of particular dietary supplements; that the government should not impose unreasonable barriers on the flow of such information; and that safety problems with supplements are relatively rare.[97] These findings are far different, both in the scientific and public policy viewpoints, from the long history of FDA enforcement against supplements. Their tenor reflects a new (to the government) conclusion that supplements are important, safe, and should be accorded a favored place in FDA policy.

DSHEA then defines the products subject to it. Because this definition is so central and complex, and because of the poor draftsmanship it evidences, it is set out here in full:

> (ff) The term "dietary supplement"—
>> (1) means a product (other than tobacco) intended to supplement the diet that bears or contains one or more of the following dietary ingredients:
>>> (A) a vitamin;
>>> (B) a mineral;
>>> (C) an herb or other botanical;
>>> (D) an amino acid;
>>> (E) A dietary substance for use by man to supplement the diet by increasing the total dietary intake; or
>>> (F) A concentrate, metabolite, constituent, extract, or combination of any ingredient described in clause (A), (B), (C), (D), or (E);
>> (2) means a product that—
>>> (A)(i) is intended for ingestion in a form described in section 350(c)(1)(B)(i) of this title; or

---

[95] See *supra* note 1.
[96] The legislative history is sparse. In fact, there is but one statement which Congress specifically stated would be the entire legislative history of DSHEA. See 108 CONG. REC. H11,179 (daily ed. Oct. 6, 1994) and S14,801 (daily ed. Oct. 7, 1994).
[97] Pub. L. No. 103-417, § 1, ¶¶ 8, 13, and 14.

(ii) complies with section 350(c)(1)(B)(ii) of this title;

(B) is not represented for use as a conventional food or as a sole item of a meal or the diet; and

(C) is labeled as a dietary supplement; and

(3) does—

(A) include an article that is approved as a new drug under section 355 of this title, certified as an antibiotic under section 357 of this title, or licensed as a biologic under section 262 Title 42, and was, prior to such approval, certification, or license, marketed as a dietary supplement or as a food unless the Secretary has issued a regulation, after notice and comment, finding that the article, when used as or in a dietary supplement under the conditions of use and dosages set forth in the labeling for such dietary supplement, is unlawful under section 342(f) of this title; and

(B) not include—

(i) an article that is approved as a new drug under section 355 of this title, certified as an antibiotic under section 357 of this title, or licensed as a biologic under section 262 of Title 42, or

(ii) an article authorized for investigation as a new drug, antibiotic, or biological for which substantial clinical investigations have been instituted and for which the existence of such investigations has been made public,

which was not before such approval, certification, licensing, or authorization marketed as a dietary supplement or as a food unless the Secretary, in the Secretary's discretion, has issued a regulation, after notice and comment, finding that the article would be lawful under this chapter.

Except for purposes of paragraph (g), a dietary supplement shall be deemed to be a food within the meaning of this chapter.[98]

The definition is divided into three sections. Under section 201(ff)(1), a dietary supplement is a food that contains at least one of the following ingredients: a vitamin, mineral, herb, amino acid, or any "dietary substance" used to supplement the human diet by increasing total dietary intake, or any metabolite of any of these.[99]

The term "dietary substance" in section 201(ff)(1)(E), 21 U.S.C. § 321(ff)(1)(E) is unclear and was probably added as a catchall so that DSHEA would reach all possible ingredients that

---

[98]   FDCA § 201(ff), 21 U.S.C. § 321(ff). The paragraph (g) referred to in the last sentence is the definition of a food additive which, by DSHEA, now excludes dietary supplements and thus frees them from the requirements of FDCA § 409, 21 U.S.C. § 349.

[99]   FDCA § 201(ff)(1), 21 U.S.C. § 321(ff)(1).

had ever been used in dietary supplements. In Subparts (A) through (D), Congress identified those classes of ingredients known to it to be used in dietary supplements (e.g., herbs, minerals). To be thorough, Congress then added (E) which does not deal with a particular type of substance, but instead reaches any and all other substances, so long as they are used to "supplement" the diet. Thus Subpart (E) brings within the protection of the act an unidentified category of ingredients that have been used to add to the diet. The "use" will not be easy to determine because doing so also requires a determination that the substance was used to supplement the diet, not as a drug but as a dietary supplement—a task which will bring back all the older case law on "intended uses," "food," and "drug" use, placing such substances in an equivocal position, dependent on a wide range of older judicial opinions, FDA policies, and often unavailable marketing data. This exercise in determining dietary supplement status for DSHEA would involve the very case law that DSHEA was designed to eliminate.[100] Clearly, Subpart (E) was meant to bring some ingredients into DSHEA, but only future decisions can reveal what.[101]

In the second section of the definition, under section 201(ff)(2), a dietary supplement must be fabricated in tablet, capsule, liquid (but only droplets) or powder, softgel or gelcap form[102] or, if not in such a form, it must not be represented to be a conventional food and must be labeled as a dietary supplement.

Section 201(ff)(2) of the definition deleted from section 411(c)(1)(B)(ii), 21 U.S.C. § 350(c)(1)(B)(ii), the phrase, "does not simulate and." The effect is anomalous. It seems to say that a product meets the definition of a dietary supplement even though it "simulates" a conventional food so long as it is not "represented" to be one. Thus, presumably, one could fabricate an herb-containing product that looked like a cookie (i.e., simulates one), but would nonetheless be a dietary supplement so long as it was not represented to be a cookie

---

[100] For example, in the early 1990s, FDA argued that hydrogen peroxide and licorice root tea are drugs, United States v. Vital Health Products, No. C-91-1332 (N.D. Cal. 1993). That was probably correct in that case, but does that mean that neither can now be a dietary supplement under a totally different fact situation? If a court once said an ingredient was a drug, is it forever a drug—in spite of DSHEA?

[101] Perhaps not surprisingly, FDA's interpretation of subpt. (E) has been quite narrow. In response to a Citizen Petition requesting FDA confirmation that homotaurine may be considered a dietary ingredient for use in dietary supplements, FDA concluded that the ingredient was not a dietary ingredient under the statutory definition. See Letter from Michael Landa (CFSAN/FDA) to Marc Ullman, Ullman, Shapiro & Ullman, LLP (representing OVOS Natural Health Inc.) (Feb. 23, 2011). First, FDA determined that homotaurine was not an amino acid based on the agency's understanding of the appropriate definition of "amino acid," in part because the petitioner's ingredient was synthetically made. Second, FDA determined that there was no "evidence that it had ever been a dietary substance for use by man to increase the total dietary intake." Thus, under FDA's interpretation of subpt. (E), the absence of prior use of a substance by man to increase total dietary intake forever precludes its consideration as a dietary ingredient under this subpart of the definition. This is a very narrow reading of subpt. (E) and one that does not appear to be supported by the legislative history.

[102] The first three forms are set out in section 411(c)(1)(B)(i); the last two are added by DSHEA, see Pub. L. No. 103-417, § 3(c)(1), amending FDCA § 411(c)(1)(B). The restriction of liquids to droplets arises by reason of section 411(c)(2) which states that "for purposes of paragraph (1)(B)(i)" a food in liquid form is eligible, only if intended for ingestion in drops or similar small units. Id. It seems sound statutory construction to incorporate this restriction here as well, since to do so avoids the anomaly that conventional liquid foods could be dietary supplements while all other conventional food forms could not. If the term "liquid" is not limited by section 411(c)(2) to droplets, then a soft drink could be sold as a dietary supplement while no other conventional food form could. Of course, under subsection (2)A(ii) any form of a food can be a dietary supplement so long as it is not represented to be a food and is labeled as a "dietary supplement."

(called a "cookie?") and it is labeled as a dietary supplement. Given the restrictions in the rest of section 201(ff)(2), this result is odd.

FDA has never been comfortable with this part of the dietary supplement definition. On the one hand, FDA has acknowledged that products of similar composition may be marketed as either dietary supplements or conventional foods, depending on how the products are promoted.[103] On the other hand, FDA has issued numerous Warning Letters and courtesy letters in which the agency has objected to the promotion of a dietary supplement in conventional food form on the grounds that the form necessitates its regulation as a conventional food.[104] In such cases, once the agency has objected to the promotion of the product as a dietary supplement, the agency also holds the ingredients in the product to conventional food standards, thus requiring the ingredients in the product to be approved food additives or GRAS ingredients.

In one of its most telling actions, in 1998, the agency objected to McNeil Consumer Products' proposed introduction of Benecol®, a margarine-like spread (developed by Raisio Group of Finland) containing plant stanol esters, which had been conclusively shown to lower serum cholesterol levels. McNeil intended to introduce the product as a dietary supplement in spread form, with numerous label declarations (indeed, more than 10 specific statements) that would make clear to consumers that the product was positioned as a dietary supplement. Despite what would appear to have been unmistakable representation as a dietary supplement, FDA cautioned McNeil that "through statements that the product replaces butter or margarine, vignettes picturing the product in common butter or margarine uses, statements promoting the flavor and texture of the product, . . . represents this product as conventional food. Therefore, the product is not a dietary supplement."[105] Although McNeil disagreed with the agency's views—which, on their face, do not seem to be supported by the plain meaning of the dietary supplement definition—the company chose to modify its labeling and position the product as a conventional food.

Section 201(ff)(2) also requires dietary supplements to be "intended for ingestion . . . ." Shortly after enactment of DSHEA, a court found a nasal gel promoted as a dietary supplement to be violative because this provision of the dietary supplement definition required a product to be taken "into the stomach and gastrointestinal tract by means of enteral administration."[106]

---

[103]   See, e.g., 62 Fed. Reg. 49,826, 49,937 (Sept. 23, 1997). "Section 201(ff)(2) of the act further states that dietary supplements are intended for ingestion in a form described in section 411(c)(1)(B)(i) of the act (21 U.S.C. 350 (c)(1)(B)(i)) or in compliance with section 411(c)(1)(B)(ii) of the act, are not represented as conventional food or as a sole item of a meal or the diet, and are labeled as a dietary supplement. Thus, dietary supplements may be similar to conventional foods in composition and form. Whether a product is a dietary supplement or a conventional food, however, will depend on how it is represented. To be a dietary supplement, a product must bear the term 'dietary supplement' as part of its common or usual name."

[104]   See, e.g., Letter from Susan Walker (CFSAN/FDA) to Ira Berman, CCA Industries (Aug. 4, 2004), regarding promotion of Mega-T Chewing Gum; Letter from Susan Walker to John Morley, Natural Factors Nutritional Products, Inc. (Aug. 4, 2004), regarding promotion of SlimStyles Weight Loss Drink Mix with PGX; Letter from Joseph Baca (CFSAN/FDA) to Erwin Simon, The Hain Celestial Group, Inc. (Aug. 17, 2007), regarding promotion of Celestial Seasonings Zinger to Go Tangerine Orange Wave Herb Tea; Letter from Michael Roosevelt (CFSAN/FDA) to Terry Harris, HBB, LLC (July 28, 2011), regarding promotion of Lazy Cakes; Letter from Emma Singleton (FDA Florida District Office) to Joseph Buenconsejo, Natures Health Options (Apr. 2, 2013), regarding promotion of Charautea Ampalaya tea.

[105]   Letter from Joseph Levitt (CFSAN/FDA) to Brian Perkins, McNeil Consumer Products (Oct. 28, 1998).

[106]   United States v. Ten Cartons...Ener-B Nasal Gel, 888 F. Supp. 381, 395 (E.D.N.Y. 1995).

FDA has since applied this limitation in objecting to the promotion of dietary supplements in a variety of other forms, including in the form of lozenge,[107] an oral spray,[108] ear drops[109] and a skin cream.[110] For products intended for oral administration, regardless of the form, as long as the product labeling makes clear that the product must be swallowed in order to achieve its intended affect, FDA would not have a valid basis to object to the product's marketing, at least on the grounds of the form of the product.[111] For example, a product in lozenge form is not inherently objectionable as long as the directions make clear that the lozenge should be allowed to dissolve in the mouth and then swallowed, whereupon the ingredients will be absorbed through the intestinal lining. Of course, FDA may raise safety concerns associated with the form of the supplement.[112]

The third section of the dietary supplement definition, section 201(ff)(3), addresses the problem of the scope of the definition when a dietary supplement ingredient (e.g., an herb or a vitamin) appears in an FDA-approved pharmaceutical. If such an ingredient is present in a product already approved by FDA as a drug, then its presence in a food does not mean that that food is a dietary supplement unless the ingredient had been marketed as a dietary supplement before FDA approved its use in a drug.[113] To be a dietary supplement, a food must contain one of the named ingredients and that ingredient had to have been a dietary supplement ingredient before it was a drug ingredient. This reading of subsections (A) and (B) to section 201(ff)(3) does not jump off the page, but it is the only reading possible.[114]

This part of the dietary supplement definition also excludes from consideration as a permitted dietary ingredient any substance that has been the subject of an investigational new drug (IND) application, for which substantial clinical investigations have been instituted and

---

[107] *See, e.g.,* Letter from Lynn Larson (CFSAN/FDA) to R. Doug Metz, American Specialty Health & Wellness (Oct. 1, 1999), regarding its Melatonin Lozenges intended for sublingual absorption.

[108] *See, e.g.,* Letter from John Foret (CFSAN/FDA) to R. Elliott Dunn, Strictly Supplements, Inc. (Aug. 21, 2000), regarding its Silvicidal GS Oral Spray intended for absorption through the mouth; Letter from Susan Walker (CFSAN/FDA) to Anna Tucci, Aboca USA, Inc. (Oct. 15, 2003), regarding its Planta Medica - Propal Pure Oral Throat Spray intended for absorption through the throat.

[109] See Letter from Vasilios Frankos (CFSAN/FDA) to Sarah McGarvey, Botanical Laboratories (Jan. 29, 2007), regarding its Willow Garlic Ear Oil intended to be absorbed through the ear.

[110] *See, e.g.,* Letter from Barbara Cassens (FDA San Francisco District Office) to Dale Fowkes, Health Freedom Nutrition, LLC (Oct. 18, 2007), regarding its Linolenic Ester Cream intended for topical absorption. See also, United States v. Lane Labs-USA, Inc., 324 F. Supp. 2d 547, 569 (D.N.J. 2004).

[111] However, in January 2014, FDA issued its long-awaited final guidance document, Distinguishing Liquid Dietary Supplements from Beverages. The guidance describes the factors the agency considers when determining whether a liquid product may be marketed as a dietary supplement versus as a conventional food. The factors include, *inter alia,* i) claims made on labeling and in advertising (e.g., claims about a product's ability to "refresh" or "rehydrate" would indicate that the product is represented as a conventional food), ii) the product name (e.g., "beverage," "drink," or "water" would represent the product as a conventional food), iii) product packaging (e.g., the larger the container size, the more likely the product may be viewed as a beverage/conventional food) and iv) serving size and recommended daily intake (e.g., again, the larger the volume recommended, the more likely it is to be viewed as a beverage). As a result of this guidance and the views FDA expressed leading to its issuance, almost all mainstream energy drink products are now marketed as conventional foods.

[112] *See, e.g.,* Letter from Michael Roosevelt (CFSAN/FDA) to Thomas Hadfield, Breathable Foods, Inc. (Mar. 5, 2012), regarding Aeroshot caffeine spray promoted in part for inhalation.

[113] FDCA § 201(ff)(3)(A) and (B), 21 U.S.C. § 321(ff)(3)(A) and (B).

[114] FDA can, nonetheless, issue a regulation authorizing the use of such an ingredient as a dietary supplement. *Id.*

made public, prior to the ingredient's use as a dietary supplement.[115] Accordingly, any person or company conducting such an investigation has a significant motivation to make the fact of its testing public because the effect of doing so would be to assure such a company with valuable property rights to the substance (as a drug) as no one else could market it as a dietary supplement. Whether this protection extends to ingredients tested as a drug before DSHEA but only made public after DSHEA is unclear. Of course, if a company's IND studies and associated drug development program are unsuccessful, the company would have eliminated its ability to then develop the ingredient for dietary supplement use.[116]

Companies formulating new dietary supplements would be well advised to research 1) whether a potential ingredient has been approved by FDA as an active drug ingredient and, if so, whether the ingredient was first marketed as a dietary supplement, and 2) for ingredients that are not FDA-approved active drug ingredients, whether the ingredient is the subject of an IND (which FDA cannot disclose, but the drug sponsor may voluntarily disclose) and, if so, whether substantial clinical investigations have been instituted. In either case, an ingredient may be precluded from use in the dietary supplement.

The new statutory definition leaves unanswered a number of important questions. The most important deals with section 201(ff)(3). According to the terms of the definition, if a particular dietary ingredient was "approved" by FDA under any one of the drug sections of the act, and was not "marketed" prior thereto as a dietary supplement, then the product may not be a dietary supplement under DSHEA unless FDA issues a regulation authorizing its marketing as a dietary supplement. But drugs approved by FDA contain many ingredients and so a threshold question is whether section 201(ff)(3) reaches any ingredient appearing in an approved drug, be it "active" or "inactive." Generally, the "active" ingredients in drugs are those that cause the desired physiological effect, while the "inactives" are those that either perform some other function (e.g., a nutritional) or have a technical manufacturing role (e.g., an excipient or binder).[117] Logic would favor a reading that the section 201(ff) (3) exclusion deals only with vitamins, minerals, or herbs when they appear in drugs as active ingredients—for those are the ingredients in drugs that make them unique. But the language in DSHEA is not specific and FDA might view the matter otherwise,[118] because one

---

[115]   In a Warning Letter issued to Deseo Rebajar Inc. (Mar. 7, 2014), the agency considered the date that the IND was granted as the triggering date for the exclusion even though the clinical investigations were not made public for another 10 years after the IND was granted. Because FDA does not disclose the existence of INDs (although a company may voluntarily make that information public), FDA's interpretation could lead to an odd result—a company might market a dietary supplement for years only to later discover that it is precluded from continuing to market the product if a second company's previously undisclosed IND becomes public.

[116]   See also FDA, Guidance for Clinical Investigators, Sponsors, and IRBs: Investigational New Drug Applications (INDs) – Determining Whether Human Research Studies Can Be Conducted Without an IND (Sept. 2013). In this guidance, FDA states that for dietary supplements, clinical studies of structure/function claims would not require an IND; but a study to evaluate a supplement's effect on a disease endpoint (even if the research is intended to support a structure/function claim) would require an IND. Study sponsors would be well-advised to consider this guidance prior to finalizing their study design in order to avoid the onerous requirements and implications of an IND.

[117]   FDCA § 502(e)(1)(A)(ii), 21 U.S.C. § 352(e)(1)(A)(ii), requires a separate label statement of "active" ingredients.

[118]   Of relevance is that FDA defines a "new drug substance" broadly as any substance that when used in making a drug causes it to be a new drug "whether it be an active substance or a menstruum, excipient . . . or other component," 21 C.F.R. § 310.3(h)(1) (2011).

could probably find almost all the vitamins and minerals in drugs.[119] To date, FDA has not sought to interpret section 201(ff)(3) so broadly.

FDA did, however, rely upon this exclusion from the dietary supplement definition to challenge Pharmanex, Inc.'s marketing of its dietary supplement (Cholestin™) containing Chinese red yeast rice, which contained the same biologically active component—lovastatin—as Merck's NDA-approved Mevacor®.[120] FDA has continued to issue Warning Letters to companies promoting dietary supplements that contain more than trace amounts of lovastatin.[121] FDA similarly has objected to the marketing of dietary supplements that contain other active drug ingredients.[122] For example, after FDA issued a Warning Letter requesting that a company cease the manufacture and distribution of a dietary supplement containing hydroxyhomosildenafil (an analog of sildenafil, the active ingredient in the prescription drug Viagra®), FDA seized the manufacturer's inventory because the company did not immediately remove the product from the market.[123] Indeed, the marketing of dietary supplements containing undeclared active drug ingredients presents a significant problem because the primary method of detection is product sampling by FDA. As part of the agency's GMP enforcement efforts (discussed below), many products have been found to contain active drug ingredients.[124] In 2013, FDA found almost 100 products marketed as dietary supplements with undeclared drug ingredients. From 2007 through June 2014, the agency issued 546 recalls and public notifications about tainted supplements, with the vast majority of such product being promoted for sexual enhancement, weight loss, and muscle building.[125]

Another problem is that section 201(ff)(3) does not deal at all with over-the-counter (OTC) drugs. Most OTC drugs are not the subject of any FDA statutory approval. They are generally marketed pursuant to FDA monographs, and it is FDA's position that drugs meeting the requirements of a monograph are not new drugs.[126] Because of this omission, the fact that

[119] Unless one could show that it had been "marketed" earlier as a dietary supplement. But who decides that question and on what standard, and what evidence would suffice?

[120] Pharmanex, Inc. v. Shalala, 221 F.3d 1151 (10th Cir. 2000), rev'g 35 F. Supp. 2d 1341 (D. Utah 1999).

[121] See, e.g., Letter from W. Charles Becoat (FDA Minneapolis District Office) to Lee Swanson, Swanson Health Products, Inc. (Aug. 8, 2007); Letter from Otto Vitillo (FDA New York District Office) to Sunburst Biorganics (Aug. 7, 2007); Letter from Susan J. Miller (FDA Denver District Office) to Dirk Reischig, Nature's Way Products, Inc. (Jan. 25, 2008); Letter from Ruth Dixon (FDA Florida District Office) to Thomas Sokoloff, iP-6 International Inc. (Apr. 23, 2014).

[122] See, e.g., Press Release, FDA, Tainted Products Marketed as Dietary Supplements Potentially Dangerous (Dec. 15, 2010), citing the three most common categories of illegal products as weight loss products, bodybuilding products, and sexual enhancement products.

[123] See, e.g., Warning Letters issued to and seizure of products distributed by SEI Pharmaceuticals, Inc. and Shangai Distributors (2008). See also Letter from H. Thomas Warwick, Jr. (FDA Denver District Office) to Jason Brailow, Prolatis (Dec. 2, 2010), for dietary supplement found to contain sulfoaildenafil, also an analog of sildenafil.

[124] See, e.g., Letter from Elizabeth Ormond (FDA Florida District Office) to Lenard deMontagnac, Black International Enterprises LLC (July 10, 2014), regarding dietary supplements containing undeclared active drug ingredients approved for erectile dysfunction; Letter from Randy Pack (FDA Baltimore District Office) to Tarra Desmond, Descor, LLC (Aug. 19, 2014), regarding dietary supplement containing undeclared active drug ingredient approved for weight loss; Letter from Alonza Cruse (FDA Los Angeles District Office) to Maurice and Ronnie Ovadia, West Coast Laboratories, Inc. (Sept. 15, 2014), regarding dietary supplements containing undeclared active drug ingredients approved for analgesic use.

[125] Industry Suggests Increase in Spiked Supplements Reflects FDA Investment in Testing, Targeted Selection, F-D-C REP. ("The Tan Sheet"), July 14, 2014 at 1, 4-6.

[126] 21 C.F.R. § 330.10 (2014).

an amino acid was, or is, in an OTC drug is irrelevant to its status as a dietary supplement. Such reading is consistent with the logic of confining the ingredient issue to "active" ingredients because this best implements the DSHEA findings about the broad need for dietary supplements.

Finally, on a related note, DSHEA does not specifically address whether a dietary supplement may be combined with a nonprescription drug, but FDA has long recognized the lawful combination of other product categories including cosmetics/nonprescription drugs (e.g., moisturizing sunscreens, breath freshening anticaries toothpastes) and medical devices/prescription drugs (e.g., drug-eluting stents, spermicide-coated condoms). Despite this, in 2001, in Warning Letters to two manufacturers, FDA took the position that combinations of dietary supplements and nonprescription drugs are unlawful on the grounds that the dietary ingredients are somehow transformed into active drug ingredients (the dietary ingredients are components of the finished drug product—21 C.F.R. § 210.3(b)(3)— for which claims are made, causing them to become active drug ingredients (21 C.F.R. § 201.66(b)(2)). The products then also become "new drugs" (under 21 U.S.C. § 201(p)) for which the companies have not secured approval.[127] Both of those companies appear to have withdrawn the subject products from the market. Several years later, Bayer Healthcare introduced a combination product, Bayer Aspirin with Heart Advantage, promoted as an analgesic and phytosterol supplement (81 mg aspirin/400 mg phytosterols). In October 2008, however, FDA issued a Warning Letter to Bayer Healthcare, objecting to the product on the same grounds as above.[128] It appears that Bayer Healthcare discontinued the product, but later introduced a reformulated version that did not contain aspirin. Despite the FDA Warning Letters and company responses, combination products that are clearly labeled to present both the required drug labeling and the required supplement labeling should have a valid basis for marketing. Certainly one challenge to designing compliant labeling is to ensure that the directions for use for the two components not only comply with the individual recommendations/restrictions imposed upon each ingredient, but that the dosage recommendations and directions are consistent with one another.

The Status of Ingredients in DSHEA Products

Having defined the ingredients subject to it, DSHEA goes on to enact special provisions dealing with their safety. As to existing dietary supplement ingredients, DSHEA liberalized the act by removing the food additive requirement, but in doing so may have increased other standards for safety by adding a new section for determining the adulteration of a dietary supplement. DSHEA also imposed somewhat more onerous requirements on "new" dietary ingredients. Each class is dealt with in turn.

First, dietary ingredients are excluded from the definition of a food additive,[129] thus prohibiting FDA from taking action against a dietary supplement on the grounds that one or

---

[127]   See Letter from David Horowitz (CFSAN/FDA) to James Ascher, Sr., B.F. Ascher & Company (Oct. 16, 2001), regarding its Melagesic PM product, a combination of melatonin and acetaminophen, promoted for "natural, restful sleep" and pain relief; Letter from David Horowitz to Klee Irwin, Omni Nutraceuticals, Inc. (Oct. 16, 2001), regarding its Inholtra Joint Pain Caplets, a combination of glucosamine sulfate and acetaminophen, promoted for relief of joint pain and "long term joint health."

[128]   Letter from Deborah Autor (CDER/FDA) to Gary Balkema, Bayer Healthcare LLC (Oct. 27, 2008).

[129]   FDCA § 201(s)(6), 21 U.S.C. § 321(s)(6).

more of its ingredients are not food additives or generally recognized as safe. This is doubtless the most dramatic change effected by DSHEA. The Food Additive Amendments of 1958 were enacted in order to close safety loopholes in the act as it then existed, and it is surely accurate to say that in the ensuing decades these food additive provisions constituted FDA's most powerful weapon in assuring the safety of the food supply.[130] No longer did FDA have to prove that an ingredient was unsafe. Under the food additive law, FDA preclearance was required if the ingredient was not generally recognized as safe (GRAS). But these provisions no longer apply to dietary ingredients in dietary supplements.[131] While this change corrects the absurd actions taken in the *Black Currant* cases,[132] it also frees the dietary supplement industry from ever confronting the Food Additive Amendments no matter what the facts may be, at least as to existing dietary ingredients. Because the food additive law remains in effect for ingredients in conventional foods, the anomalous result is that an ingredient is not a food additive in a dietary supplement but may be one in a food. This has already happened.

In 1991 FDA issued an import alert instructing FDA field officers to detain all lots of a natural flavoring agent known as stevia as an unapproved food additive. As a result of DSHEA, that alert was amended to allow stevia into the United States when intended for use in a dietary supplement, but not when intended for use in a conventional food.[133] This leads to a discussion of the other safety change effected by DSHEA.

In order to provide additional safety authority to replace that lost in the food additive definition, DSHEA added a new subparagraph to the section on food adulteration in the act.[134] This provision, applicable only to dietary supplements, provides that such supplements are adulterated, and thus illegal, if any one of four conditions occur. This new section then specifies that in any enforcement proceeding, either civil and criminal, the government shall bear the burden of proof as "to each element" of the offense and the court shall hear any issue under this provision "de novo,"[135] and, before FDA can refer any civil matter involving this section to a United States Attorney, it must give the person against whom such proceeding would be initiated "appropriate notice and the opportunity to present views,

---

[130] As to the reasons for the Food Additive Amendments, *see* S. REP. No. 2422, 85th Cong., 2d Sess. (1958).

[131] Oddly enough, they do apply—even to the same ingredients—if used in conventional foods, and they do apply to "nondietary ingredients" in dietary supplements.

[132] See *supra* note 57 and accompanying text.

[133] Import Alert No. 45-06 as amended (Sept. 18, 1995). Oddly enough, FDA asserts that this dietary supplement exemption is *not* available if the *purpose* of the stevia in the product is stated (e.g., as a flavor). There is no support in DSHEA for this. *See also* Letter from Joseph Baca (CFSAN/FDA) to Erwin Simon, The Hain Celestial Group, Inc. (Aug. 17, 2007), objecting to inclusion of stevia in a conventional food. FDA has since "not objected" to the GRAS status of a number of stevia products that have been the subject of GRAS notifications. FDA has taken a similar position regarding the use of ginkgo biloba leaf extract, which is widely used in dietary supplements but not permitted by FDA for use in conventional food. See Letter from Patricia Schafer (FDA New Orleans District Office) to Russell Weiner, Rockstar, Inc. (May 23, 2012), regarding the use of ginkgo biloba leaf extract in coffee and energy drink products; Letter from Charles Breen (FDA Seattle District Office) to Cheryl, James, and Ron Stewart, Stewart Brothers, Inc. (Mar. 28, 2013), regarding the use of ginkgo biloba leaf extract in a juice drink blend product.

[134] Pub. L. No. 103-417, 103 Cong., 2d Sess. § 4, amending section 402 of the act by adding thereto a new subparagraph (f).

[135] FDCA § 402(f)(1), 21 U.S.C. § 342(f)(1).

orally and in writing" about what FDA intends to do.[136] These provisions are designed to control how FDA uses this new authority.

As to the four new substantive adulteration grounds, one represents a significant departure from older adulteration provisions. Under older statutory provisions (still applicable to dietary supplements), a food was adulterated if it contained any poisonous or deleterious substance that "may render it injurious to health."[137] The new provision provides that a dietary supplement is also adulterated if it, or any ingredient in it, "presents a significant or unreasonable risk of illness or injury" either under the conditions of use recommended in its labeling, or if no such conditions are recommended, then "under ordinary conditions of use."[138] Clearly, this is a standard different from the older "poisonous or deleterious" one.

The older provision, that a poisonous or deleterious substance "may" render a food injurious to health, dates, in part, to the first Food and Drugs Act in 1906. Early on, the Supreme Court interpreted this language to mean that the government does not have to prove that the so-called deleterious ingredient "must affect the public health"; it is sufficient that it "may possibly injure the health . . ." of any reasonably identified group of humans.[139] This does not seem to be a particularly heavy burden for the government to bear, and so the question is whether the DSHEA standard is an even lighter one.[140] Certainly, the new standard turns the focus away from the toxic nature of an ingredient to an evaluation of the total risk of ingesting that ingredient in light of the intended uses of the final product in which it appears. This reading has consequences.

Under the DSHEA standard, one would, in determining whether a particular ingredient poses an unacceptable risk, compare its known toxic effect with the intended use of a dietary supplement in which it appears. Under such a comparison, an ingredient could pose an unacceptable risk if a claim made for the dietary supplement in which it appears is one that may be affected by the known hazard. For example, if a dietary supplement is recommended for improved athletic performance and the known toxicity for an ingredient in it concerns cardiovascular incidents that could be exacerbated by exercise, then that product could be adulterated where it would not be if the claim were not made. An ingredient could thus be an adulterant in one product but not in another depending on claims and usage. If such reasoning is what the industry must follow, then a determination that a product is not adulterated under the new standard could be difficult and problematic.[141] In such a

---

[136] FDCA § 402(f)(2), 21 U.S.C. § 342(f)(2). The timing of this notice requirement is tangled in clumsy language. This section speaks of FDA giving the affected persons "appropriate notice and the opportunity to present their views" at least 10 days before such "notice"—an obvious impossibility. Apparently Congress meant that the notice had to be at least 10 days before the matter was "referred" to a United States Attorney. It may be pertinent to note that DSHEA was approved by the House at 3:00 a.m., and the Senate at 12:30 a.m. "The sleep of a laboring man is sweet" (Ecclesiastes 5:12)—but not necessarily productive.

[137] FDCA § 402(a)(1), 21 U.S.C. § 342(a)(1).

[138] FDCA § 402(f)(1)(A), 21 U.S.C. § 342(f)(1)(A).

[139] United States v. Lexington Mill & Elevator Co., 232 U.S. 399, 411 (1914). This reasoning was adopted by the 1938 act, Flemming v. Florida Citrus Exchange, 358 U.S. 153 (1958).

[140] As to the older standard in practice, see, e.g., United States v. Boston Farm Center, Inc., 590 F.2d 149 (5th Cir. 1979).

[141] "Drug" language, comparable to section 402(f), appears in section 505(e), 21 U.S.C. § 355(e), which permits FDA to withdraw an approved NDA if it is unsafe for use under the conditions upon which the NDA was approved.

situation, not only would the safety of ingredients have to be evaluated, but also each claim as well. Further, a manufacturer of an ingredient could well find its risk beyond its control because of claims made (by others) for products in which the ingredient is used.

FDA applied this new safety standard in issuing a final rule banning the use of ephedra in dietary supplements.[142] According to the preamble to that final rule, FDA based its decision on a 133,000-page administrative record that led the agency to conclude that dietary supplements containing ephedrine alkaloids pose an unreasonable risk of illness or injury, especially for those suffering from heart disease and high blood pressure. FDA determined that no dosage of dietary supplements containing ephedrine alkaloids is safe and, therefore, that sale of such products in the United States, regardless of the claimed use, is illegal and subject to enforcement action.[143] After a series of challenges to FDA's regulation, the 10th Circuit Court of Appeals upheld FDA's final rule, reversing a decision by the District Court of Utah.[144] The Supreme Court denied petitioner's writ of certiori, leaving the ruling and regulations in place.

Cynics, including the authors of this chapter, have suggested that the agency waited for years to accumulate a large body of adverse event reports with the hope of 1) demonstrating to Congress that it needed to grant the agency even greater control over the safety of dietary supplements; and 2) at a minimum, strengthening its position that ephedra supplements should be banned. Certainly, the agency declined to take enforcement action in the face of extensive adverse event reports. Finally, FDA relied on those same adverse event reports to conclude that ephedra did not meet the DSHEA safety standard; that is, that the ingredient presented an unreasonable risk of illness or injury. In applying this standard, FDA engaged in a risk-benefit analysis that previously had not been applied to dietary ingredients. Chapter 2 *supra* discusses further food safety issues, including the implications of FDA's risk-benefit approach to evaluating dietary ingredient safety.

DSHEA imposes still further safety restrictions on "new" dietary ingredients; i.e., those not marketed in the United States prior to October 15, 1994. A dietary supplement containing such an ingredient is adulterated if there is inadequate information to provide a reasonable assurance that the ingredient "does not present a significant or unreasonable risk of illness or injury . . . ."[145] This differs from the standard for "old" dietary ingredients in that it focuses on the nature of the data rather than a factual finding of "unreasonable risk." Standing alone, this "new" requirement would probably not be onerous.

But it does not stand alone, because DSHEA states that any such new dietary ingredient is also adulterated unless one of two conditions are met: First, the ingredient is one which has

---

[142]   69 Fed. Reg. 6788 (Feb. 11, 2004) (codified at 21 C.F.R. § 119.1 (2014)).

[143]   Interestingly, the rule did not affect traditional Chinese herbal remedies or products like herbal teas that are regulated as conventional foods, although FDA has stated that ephedra is not GRAS for use in foods or an approved food additive. *See* Letter from Joseph Baca (CFSAN/FDA) to Life Enhancement Products, Inc. (Dec. 1, 2005).

[144]   Nutraceutical Corp. v. Von Eschenbach, 459 F.3d 1033 (10th Cir. 2006), *cert. denied*, 127 S. Ct. 2295 (2007). For a more detailed discussion of the history of this rulemaking and the legal challenges to it, *see* PETER BARTON HUTT, RICHARD A. MERRILL & LEWIS A. GROSSMAN, FOOD AND DRUG LAW: CASES AND MATERIALS (3d ed. 2007), at 452.

[145]   FDCA § 402(f)(1)(B), 21 U.S.C. § 342(f)(1)(B).

been present "in the food supply as an article used for food in a form in which the food has not been chemically altered."[146] As to this language, both Houses agreed that a food was not "chemically altered" under any of several conditions, including dehydration, freeze drying or milling.[147] This proviso is thus designed to allow new dietary ingredients in dietary supplements so long as they can be found as substances in traditional foods with only minor modifications for incorporation into a capsule, etc. form. Herbs are the most likely beneficiary of this proviso. Second, such a "new" ingredient also is not adulterated if there is a history of its use establishing that the ingredient "will reasonably be expected to be safe" when incorporated into a dietary supplement and the person using it notifies FDA at least 75 days before a product incorporating the ingredient is shipped in interstate commerce, supplying the agency with the data on the basis of which this safety determination was made.[148] Prior FDA approval is not required before the sale of the new dietary ingredient under the second provision, but certainly FDA is free to express its views on a "75-day" notice, potentially putting a marketer on the spot if FDA disagrees with it about the data. Any company following this process must realize that by doing so it may be opening itself to lengthy negotiations with FDA, and even a total inability to market the product at all.

Shortly after enactment of DSHEA, a number of trade associations—including the American Herbal Products Association, Council for Responsible Nutrition, and National Nutritional Foods Association—prepared lists of "old dietary ingredients" that had been marketed prior to DSHEA. Although FDA has not endorsed these lists, the agency has not objected to the marketing of ingredients on these lists.

FDA's regulations provide very little detail regarding the desired content of new dietary ingredient (NDI) notifications.[149] The regulations require submitters to include the following information:

- the name and address of the submitter;
- the name of the new dietary ingredient;
- a description of the dietary supplement(s) that contains the new dietary ingredient, including:
  - the level of the dietary ingredient in the dietary supplement; and
  - the conditions of use recommended or suggested in the labeling of the dietary supplement, or if no conditions are recommended or suggested, the ordinary conditions of use of the supplement; and

---

[146]   FDCA § 413(a)(1), 21 U.S.C. § 350b(a)(1). A question here is whether this food use must be use in the United States, especially since the definition of a new dietary ingredient is so limited.

[147]   Neither DSHEA nor FDA regulations define "chemically altered," although the legislative history included the following discussion: "[T]he term 'chemically altered' does not include the following physical modifications: minor loss of volatile components, dehydration, lyophilization, milling, tincture or solution in water, slurry, powder, or solid in suspension." 140 CONG. REC. H11,173 (daily ed. Oct. 6, 1994) (statement of Rep. Waxman). This list is clearly incomplete and any determinations as to whether an ingredient qualifies for this exemption will be made on a case-by-case basis.

[148]   FDCA § 413(a)(2), 21 U.S.C. § 350b(a)(2). FDA is to keep this information confidential for 90 days, thus giving the person submitting it at least some competitive advantage.

[149]   21 C.F.R. § 190.6 (2014).

- the history of use or other evidence of safety establishing that the dietary ingredient, when used under the conditions recommended or suggested in the labeling of the dietary supplement, will reasonably be expected to be safe, including any citation to published articles or other evidence that is the basis for concluding that the dietary supplement will reasonably be expected to be safe.

In November 2004, FDA held a public meeting to solicit comments on how to improve guidance regarding the content of NDI notifications.[150] In January 2009, the Government Accountability Office (GAO) issued a report recommending that FDA issue guidance clarifying when an ingredient would be considered a new dietary ingredient and the type of information that would be necessary to establish its safety.[151] Because FDA had not issued such guidance by the end of 2010, Congress included a provision within the FDA Food Safety Modernization Act that required FDA to issue a guidance within 180 days of enactment.[152] Finally, on July 5, 2011, FDA issued a draft guidance document entitled "Dietary Supplements: New Dietary Ingredient Notifications and Related Issues."

The draft guidance, set up in the form of questions and answers, generated considerable objection from the regulated industry almost immediately after its release. Perhaps not surprisingly given its historical actions against supplements, the agency expressed a number of views that, if followed through to enforcement action, could have a chilling effect on the dietary supplement industry generally, and on innovation in particular. Some of the more controversial positions expressed by FDA include[153]:

- A narrow view of the scope of "old dietary ingredients" (those marketed prior to October 15, 1994). FDA explained that to establish that a dietary supplement was marketed prior to October 15, 1994, a company would need to possess specific documentation, including, for example, sales records, manufacturing records, commercial invoices, magazine advertisements, catalogues or sales brochures (affidavits unsupported by documents would not be acceptable). Further, an ingredient's status as an old dietary ingredient might be forfeited if the method of manufacture had changed. As a consequence of FDA's interpretation, ingredients that have long been considered by industry as old dietary ingredients might suddenly require submission of an NDI notification.

- A narrow view of DSHEA's exemption from the NDI notification requirement. As noted above, a new dietary ingredient is exempt from the notification requirement if it was "present in the food supply as an article used for food in a form in which the food has not been chemically altered." FDA interpreted the "food supply" as being limited to conventional foods (not including dietary supplements), and "chemically altered" as essentially any process other than treatment with water or ethanol to which a supplement is subjected. If FDA were to enforce this view, most new dietary ingredients would need to be the subject of notifications.

- The position that an NDI notification is specific to the submitter, and that changes in use or the manufacturing process would trigger the need for a new notification.

---

[150]   69 Fed. Reg. 61,680 (Oct. 20, 2004).

[151]   U.S. GOV'T ACCOUNTABILITY OFFICE, DIETARY SUPPLEMENTS: FDA SHOULD TAKE FURTHER ACTIONS TO IMPROVE OVERSIGHT AND CONSUMER UNDERSTANDING (Jan. 2009).

[152]   FDA Food Safety Modernization Act § 113; 21 U.S.C. § 350b.

[153]   See e.g., FDA's NDI Guidance and the 18-Year Cycle of Correcting Regulatory Overreach, FDA Law Blog, Hyman, Phelps & McNamara, P.C. (July 14, 2011).

- The position that synthetic versions of botanical constituents cannot be dietary ingredients.

In releasing the draft guidance, FDA insisted that it was merely interpreting DSHEA in a way that is necessary to ensure the safety of dietary supplements and their ingredients, particularly in an environment in which, according to the agency, so many new dietary ingredients are marketed without having been the subject of a required notification.

As noted above, industry reaction to the draft guidance was swift and loud. Further, echoing industry concerns, Senators Hatch and Harkin, principal authors of DSHEA, urged the agency to withdraw the draft guidance.[154] In October 2012, in response to mounting pressure, FDA announced that it would not withdraw the draft guidance, but would revise it based on feedback provided. As of September 2014, the revised guidance had not been issued.

In advance of issuing a final guidance, FDA has taken enforcement action against manufacturers that market products with certain ingredients determined by the agency to be new dietary ingredients for which the manufacturers have not submitted NDI notifications. The ingredient that has drawn the most severe enforcement action is DMAA, also known as 1,3-dimethylamylamine or geranium extract, an ingredient touted as a "natural" stimulant. FDA has issued numerous Warning Letters after receiving more than 20 adverse event reports that raised concern about the ingredient's effect on the cardiovascular system. FDA argued that naturally derived DMAA was a new dietary ingredient (disagreeing with manufacturers that it was an old dietary ingredient present as a constituent of the geranium plant) and that synthetically derived DMAA did not qualify as a dietary ingredient. While most manufacturers voluntarily removed their products from the market, one company, Hi-Tech Pharmaceuticals Inc., did not, resulting in an administrative detention order and a product seizure. By challenging the NDI status of an ingredient, the agency appears to have found a way to effectively remove from the market products that it believes are unsafe without having to meet the regulatory burden of proving that the product or ingredient is unsafe.

Import alerts are another effective enforcement tool used by the agency. For example, FDA has issued an import alert for kratom or Mitragyna speciosa, a botanical associated with numerous adverse health effects.[155] The agency has taken the position that kratom is a new dietary ingredient for which no one has submitted an NDI notification. Imports of the ingredient or products containing the ingredient may be detained at the port of entry.

Between 1995 and June 2014, FDA received just over 700 NDI notifications, accepting approximately 25 percent.[156] In the same period, 40 percent of the 139 notifications that were resubmitted were accepted for filing by the agency once the notifier addressed the agency's initial concerns.[157]

---

[154]   *See* Letter from Senators Hatch and Harkin to FDA Commissioner Hamburg (Dec. 22, 2011).

[155]   FDA Import Alert 54-15.

[156]   Data compiled by American Herbal Products Association as reported in FDA New Dietary Ingredient Rejections Draw 'Roadmap' for Successful Notifications, F-D-C Rep. ("The Tan Sheet"), June 30, 2014 at 5-6.

[157]   *Id. See also* M. McGuffin & A. Young, *Premarket Notifications of New Dietary Ingredients—A Ten-Year Review*, 59 Food & Drug L.J. 229 (2004); A. Talati, *New Dietary Ingredient Notifications: A Comprehensive Review and*

Common bases for rejection may be generally characterized as falling into four categories:

- the ingredient is not properly considered to be a dietary ingredient;[158]
- the notification was incomplete;[159]
- inadequate evidence to establish safety;[160] and
- the ingredient is unsafe.[161]

It remains to be seen whether FDA's final guidance, whenever issued, will improve the quality of NDI notifications and the likelihood of successful reviews, and/or discourage submission of notifications.

Chapter 2 further discusses the new dietary ingredient safety standard. Other authors also have addressed FDA's application of the DSHEA safety standard.[162]

New Promotional Opportunities Under DSHEA

DSHEA also altered the landscape for the promotion of dietary supplements. First DSHEA attacked the problem of the use of books and other periodicals that discuss the use of vitamins, minerals, herbs, and dietary supplements in general. Second, DSHEA carved out a new category of claims—so-called "Statements of Nutritional Support"—that previously had served as the basis for FDA challenges. We address each of these developments in turn.

"Third-Party Literature"

DSHEA excludes from the definition of labeling any publication "used in connection with the sale of a dietary supplement" to consumers if five conditions are met.[163] *One,* the book etc. must not be false or misleading. *Two,* it must not promote a particular company or brand. *Three,* it must be displayed with other publications so as to present a balanced view of the scientific issues at hand. *Four,* it must be physically separate from dietary supplements for sale in the store. *Five,* no stickers or other information can be attached to it. DSHEA

Strategies for Avoiding FDA Objections, 62 Food & Drug L.J. 387 (2007).

[158] *See, e.g.,* Letter from Felicia Satchell (CFSAN/FDA) to Keith Chan, GloboAsia LLC (May 10, 2001), regarding porcine relaxin, an ingredient not considered to be a dietary ingredient and an article authorized for investigation as a biological; Letter from Felicia Satchell (CFSAN/FDA) to Philip Wolfson, PHYTOS (Apr. 30, 2002), regarding *Heliopsis longipes* root extract, because the form of the product (lozenge/gum) was not intended for ingestion.

[159] *See, e.g.,* Letter from Susan Walker (CFSAN/FDA) to Ted Kottcamp, OYC International, Inc. (Aug. 9, 2005), regarding Pancreatopeptidose, for failure to describe the dietary supplement, the level of the dietary ingredient in the supplement, or the recommended conditions of use.

[160] *See, e.g.,* Letter from Linda Pellicore (CFSAN/FDA) to Mark Underwood, Quincy Bioscience Manufacturing, Inc. (Dec. 7, 2007), regarding Aequorin; Letter from Susan Walker (CFSAN/FDA) to Brent Burningham, Albion Laboratories, Inc. (Nov. 10, 2005), regarding Manganese Glucosamine Gluconate.

[161] *See, e.g.,* Letter from James Tanner (CFSAN/FDA) to Sam Berkowitz, Advanced Plant Pharmaceuticals, Inc. (Sept. 24, 1997), regarding Pokeweed Lectins from *Phytolacca americana*; Letter from Lynn Larsen (CFSAN/FDA) to Joseph Nester, Ozelle Pharmaceuticals, Inc. (Jan. 4, 1999), regarding *Nerium oleander* extract.

[162] *See, e.g.,* S. Bass & M. Marden, *The New Dietary Ingredient Safety Provision of DSHEA: A Return to Congressional Intent,* 31 Am. J.L. & Med. 285 (2005); Peter Barton Hutt, *FDA Statutory Authority to Regulate the Safety of Dietary Supplements,* 31 Am. J.L. & Med. 155 (2005), arguing that DSHEA provides FDA greater regulatory authority over dietary supplements than over conventional foods.

[163] FDCA § 403B(a), 21 U.S.C. § 343-2(a).

also emphasizes that these five conditions do not restrict any retailer or wholesaler "in any way whatsoever" in the sale of books or other publications as part of their business.[164] The five conditions for the book exemption, then, apply when a company selling a dietary supplement specifically uses a book to promote sales. But none of these restrictions apply to a retailer in its free and independent sale of books.

A comparison of this section of DSHEA with the case law on books as labeling discussed earlier reveals that the former is firmly grounded in the latter and that it at least sets down better guidelines than there were prior to DSHEA. It lays to rest many older matters of confusion and concern and sets up a basis for assuring that the use of books is not abused.

First, it makes clear that such literature can be used to promote sales,[165] thus allowing vendors to do just that, and eliminating any need to feign ignorance about the obvious fact that the books they sell discuss the supplements they sell. Second, DSHEA provides a mechanism that the older case law did not—a mechanism to assure that any use of books by a dietary supplement manufacturer is balanced. One concern over the years was that stores too often had on display only those books that reflected one side of the argument about the value of an ingredient. Now, given condition *three*, that concern should abate. Finally, by prohibiting the use of trade names etc., at least the most blatant forms of promotion are avoided.

One serious concern does remain. Many books and pamphlets assert that some of the ingredients used in dietary supplements also have value in treating serious diseases, a value that is either not widely accepted or not approved by FDA. Such claims, if unfounded, could have dire consequences for a user who then fails to seek available medical care.

This law seems to allow a field of promotion not available for traditional foods and, indeed, not even available for drugs. For example, one cannot, under present law, promote a drug for any condition for which it is not approved, but, under DSHEA, one could "promote" a dietary supplement, by use of books, for an unapproved drug use. This presents an opportunity for abuse.

There may be an answer to that concern. Earlier we noted that the courts have long been able to determine whether a product was a food or a drug by examining its "intended uses" and, in doing so, was not in any way restricted as to the evidence it could examine. *Anything* can be considered—books, speeches, radio shows, and pamphlets. There is nothing in DSHEA that prohibits a similar evaluation today. Under the case law, courts can still look at books—anywhere—to determine the true "intended uses" of a product and, therefore, whether it is a drug and whether the labeling for that product has adequate directions for use for those uses.[166] Moreover, if one promotes an herb for cancer, then its label must have "adequate directions for use" in treating cancer—but if it did, it would be an unapproved

---

[164]   FDCA § 403B(b), 21 U.S.C. § 343-2(b).

[165]   The statutory phrase "when used in connection with the sale . . ." mandates the concept of promotion.

[166]   One case noted that if the materials at issue do not qualify as third-party literature for dietary supplements, they may cause the article to become an unapproved new drug, based on its objective intended use as shown in the circumstances surrounding the distribution of the article. U.S. v. Lane Labs-USA, Inc., 324 F. Supp. 2d 547 (D.N.J. 2004), *aff'd sub nom.* U.S. v. Lane Labs-USA, Inc., 427 F.3d 219 (3d Cir. 2005).

drug. Either way the product is illegal. While Congress, in DSHEA, clearly contemplated that books could be widely used to promote dietary supplements, it seems to have left the courts with some vestige of this old mechanism to deal with inappropriate promotions about the treatment of diseases.[167]

"Statements of Nutritional Support"/"Structure-Function Claims"

DSHEA also provides a new category of claims that can be made for dietary supplements, called "Statements of Nutritional Support."[168] There are four such statements and they may be made, without running afoul of the drug sections of the act, if certain conditions are met. The statements are:

- a statement of benefit relating to classical nutritional deficiency diseases (e.g., scurvy) so long as the prevalence of that disease in the United States is disclosed;

- a statement that describes the role of a nutrient intended "to affect the structure or function in humans";

- a statement that characterizes how a nutrient acts to "maintain such structure or function"; and

- a statement that describes "general well-being from consumption" of a nutrient.[169]

The conditions that must be met before any of these statements can be made are: 1) the manufacturer of such supplement must be able to substantiate the claim; 2) the claim must be accompanied by a disclaimer, prominently displayed, that "This statement has not been evaluated by the Food and Drug Administration. This product is not intended to diagnose, treat, cure, or prevent any disease."; and 3) notice must be given to FDA (by the manufacturer) no later than 30 days after first marketing of a supplement with the statement.[170]

There are a number of problems here. First, just what is a "structure or function" claim? Its origin is the definition of a drug, "articles (other than food) intended to affect the structure or any function of the body . . . ,"[171] but just what is meant by the term is unclear, especially in light of the statute's prohibition against any reference to a disease or illness.

In April 1998, FDA published proposed regulations to implement the structure/function claim provisions of DSHEA.[172] As noted above, DSHEA permits structure/function claims, but prohibits any such claims that the product will diagnose, mitigate, treat, cure, or prevent a specific disease or class of diseases (so-called "disease claims"). In its proposal, rather than defining those claims that would be permitted structure/function claims, FDA

---

[167] Section 7(a) of DSHEA amends the act to provide that a dietary supplement is not a drug if an approved *health* claim is made for it. But, at least for now, a claim such as the above cancer claim, is not an approved health claim so this exemption is not available here. Section 10(a) of DSHEA states that a dietary supplement is not misbranded solely because it bears directions for use—e.g., take three a day. This provision was added because such directions for use are more like those for drugs than foods and FDA had on occasion so argued. It has nothing to do with the above "back-door" tactic.

[168] Pub. L. No. 103-417, § 6, 103 Cong., 2d Sess. (1994).

[169] FDCA § 403(r)(6), 21 U.S.C. § 343(r)(6); *and see id.*§ 201(g)(1), 21 U.S.C. § 321(g)(1).

[170] *Id.* This section also reiterates that no statement can be made to diagnose, treat, etc. "a specific disease or class of diseases."

[171] FDCA § 201(g)(1)(C), 21 U.S.C. § 321(g)(1)(C).

[172] 63 Fed. Reg. 23,624 (Apr. 29, 1998).

identified a number of categories of disease claims that would not qualify as permissible structure/function claims. Not only did FDA make clear that explicit disease claims would be prohibited but it also extended the proposed prohibition to implied disease claims. Many of the types of claims that FDA proposed to consider implied disease claims far exceeded industry's understanding of congressional intent in passing DSHEA.

In January 2000, after receiving more than 235,000 submissions in response to the proposed rule—most of which "objected to all or part of the proposed rule, arguing that it inappropriately restricted the structure/function claims that could be made for dietary supplements"—FDA issued a final rule on structure/function claims, codified at 21 C.F.R. § 101.93(f),(g).[173] The regulation includes 10 categories of claims that will be considered to be disease claims, even if the claims describe how the dietary supplement affects the structure or function of the body.[174] The lengthy preamble discussion to the final rule includes numerous examples of claims that the agency would consider to be permissible structure/function claims and examples of structure/function claims the agency would consider to be prohibited. The list of disease claims, with examples of permitted and prohibited claims, appears below:

> (i)   Has an effect on a specific disease or class of diseases [*Permitted*: "Helps support cartilage and joint function," "Helps promote urinary health," "Helps maintain cardiovascular function"; *Prohibited*: "Reduces the pain and stiffness associated with arthritis," "Deters bacteria from adhering to the wall of the bladder and urinary tract" (implies prevention of bacterial infections), "Prevents irregular heart beat"]

> (ii)   Has an effect on the characteristic signs or symptoms of a specific disease or class of diseases, using scientific or lay terminology [*Permitted*: "Helps maintain cholesterol levels that are already within the normal range," "Reduces stress and frustration," "Helps maintain regularity"; *Prohibited*: "Lowers cholesterol" (a sign of hypercholesterolemia), "Relieves headache" (a sign of migraine), "Reduces joint pain" (a sign of arthritis)]

> (iii)   Has an effect on an abnormal condition associated with a natural state or process, if the abnormal condition is uncommon or can cause significant or permanent harm [*Permitted*: "Improves absentmindedness," "noncystic acne," "for men over 50"; *Prohibited*: "Alzheimer's disease, and other senile dementias," "cystic acne," "To relieve the symptoms of benign prostatic hypertrophy"]

> (iv)   Has an effect on a disease or diseases through one or more of the following factors:

> A)   The name of the product [*Permitted*: "Cardio Health," "Heart Tabs"; *Prohibited*: "CircuCure," "HepataCare"]

---

[173]   65 Fed. Reg. 1000 (Jan. 6, 2000).
[174]   21 C.F.R. § 101.93(g)(2) (2014).

B) A statement about the formulation of the product, including a claim that the product contains an ingredient that has been regulated by FDA as a drug and is well known to consumers for its use or claimed use in preventing or treating a disease [*Prohibited*: "Digoxin," "Aspirin"]

C) Citation of a publication or reference, if the citation refers to a disease use, and if, in the context of the labeling as a whole, the citation implies treatment or prevention of a disease, e.g., through placement on the immediate product label or packaging, inappropriate prominence, or lack of relationship to the product's express claims

D) Use of the term "disease" or "diseased," except in general statements about disease prevention that do not refer explicitly or implicitly to a specific disease or class of diseases or to a specific product or ingredient [*Permitted*: "A good diet promotes good health and prevents the onset of disease"; *Prohibited*: "Promotes good health and prevents the onset of disease"]

E) Use of pictures, vignettes, symbols, or other means [*Permitted*: Picture of the human body, Picture of a healthy organ (as long as does not imply disease treatment or prevention); *Prohibited*: Electrocardiogram tracings, heart symbol (widely recognized as symbol for disease treatment or prevention)]

(v)   Belongs to a class of products that is intended to diagnose, mitigate, treat, cure, or prevent a disease [*Permitted*: "Energizer," "Tonic," "Appetite suppressant"; *Prohibited*: "Antibiotic," "Antidepressant," "Anti-inflammatory"]

(vi)   Is a substitute for a product that is a therapy for a disease [*Permitted*: "Use as part of your diet to help maintain a healthy blood sugar level"; *Prohibited*: "Use as part of your diet when taking insulin to help maintain a healthy blood sugar level," "Herbal Prozac"]

(vii)   Augments a particular therapy or drug action that is intended to diagnose, mitigate, treat, cure, or prevent a disease or class of diseases [*Permitted*: "Helps maintain intestinal flora"; *Prohibited*: "Helps individuals using antibiotics to maintain normal intestinal flora"]

(viii)   Has a role in the body's response to a disease or to a vector of disease [*Permitted*: "Supports the immune system"; *Prohibited*: "Supports the body's antiviral capabilities"]

(ix)   Treats, prevents, or mitigates adverse events associated with a therapy for a disease, if the adverse events constitute diseases

[*Permitted*: "Upset stomach"; *Prohibited*: "Reduces nausea associated with chemotherapy"]

(x)   Otherwise suggests an effect on a disease or diseases.[175]

Among its more interesting interpretations, FDA permits claims that describe the treatment of common, nonserious conditions associated with life stages, including hot flashes, presbyopia, mild memory problems associated with aging, and noncystic acne. On the other hand, claims regarding serious conditions associated with life stages, such as osteoporosis, Alzheimer's disease, glaucoma, and cystic acne would be considered disease claims. FDA also decided to permit supplements to be promoted with some symptomatic relief claims for certain OTC drug classes, including claims under the following monographs[176]:

- Antacids: "Occasional heartburn," "Relief of sour stomach" (as long as the claim makes clear that it refers to occasional heartburn or acid indigestion)
- Antiflatulents: "Alleviates bloating and pressure"
- Antiemetics: "For the prevention and treatment of the nausea, vomiting or dizziness associated with motion"
- Nighttime sleep-aids: "For relief of occasional sleeplessness" (as long as the claim makes clear that it is not for the treatment of insomnia)

Considering the regulation and FDA's preamble comments as a whole, a rule of thumb governing structure/function claims might be that claims describing the treatment of transient, nonserious conditions are permitted, while claims describing an effect on permanent or serious conditions are prohibited.

FDA regularly issues Warning Letters objecting to claims that go beyond the scope permitted under DSHEA. For example, in July 2013, FDA issued a press release announcing that it had issued Warning Letters to 15 companies objecting to their illegally marketed diabetes products. In August 2014, FDA issued a press release describing the Warning Letters that it had issued to companies unlawfully promoting supplements for treatment of concussions. Beyond issuing Warning Letters, on occasion the agency has sought permanent injunctions to prevent companies from continuing to promote their supplements with claims that go well beyond those permitted under DSHEA.[177]

With respect to the FDA's substantiation standard for structure/function claims, during the rulemaking process the agency received many comments requesting that it articulate the

---

[175]   For a complete list of the permitted and prohibited structure/function claims identified in the preamble to the proposed rule, *see* F-D-C Rep. ("The Tan Sheet"), Jan. 17, 2000 at 12-13, reproduced in Peter Barton Hutt, Richard A. Merrill & Lewis A. Grossman, Food and Drug Law: Cases and Materials (3d ed. 2007), at 282.

[176]   65 Fed. Reg. at 1011-1012.

[177]   *See, e.g.*, Order of Summ. J. and Permanent Inj., United States v. Berst, No. 11-cv-6370-TC (D. Or. Sept. 20, 2012), ECF No. 36, FDA objected to the company's promotion of its supplement products for the treatment of serious disease conditions, such as cataracts, viral and bacterial infections, and cancer; Compl. for Permanent Inj., United States v. Cole, No. 13-cv-1606-SI (D. Or. Sept. 12, 2013), ECF No. 1, FDA objected to the company's promotion of its supplement products for treatment of Alzheimer's disease, autism, and fibromyalgia.

standard. In the preamble to the final rule, FDA declined to provide a specific standard, but noted that claims should be "supported by adequate scientific evidence," a possible nod to the FTC standard of "competent and reliable scientific evidence."[178] In November 2004, FDA issued a draft guidance document and in December 2008 a final guidance document entitled "Substantiation for Dietary Supplement Claims Made Under Section 403(r)(6) of the Federal Food, Drug, and Cosmetic Act." In the draft and final guidance, FDA stated that it intended to apply a standard for substantiation that is consistent with the FTC approach, indicating that while "there is no pre-established formula as to how many or what type of studies are needed to substantiate a claim, [FDA], like the FTC, will consider what the accepted norms are in the relevant research fields and consult experts from various disciplines." FDA recommended that companies consider the following issues in their assessment of the adequacy of their substantiation:

- the meaning of the claim(s) being made;
- the relationship of the evidence to the claim;
- the quality of the evidence; and
- the totality of the evidence.

The guidance describes examples of each of these considerations.

In January 2011, GAO issued a report that recommended that FDA provide additional guidance regarding the type and strength of scientific support necessary to prevent false or misleading structure/function claims.[179] The GAO report also recommended that FDA seek statutory authority to access a company's claim substantiation files and provide direction to FDA inspectors to better identify false or misleading claims. FDA generally agreed with the first two recommendations, but found the third recommendation "impractical" because it would be impossible to provide agency inspectors with the knowledge necessary to make such an assessment of substantiation in the field.

Following the GAO report and concerns raised by public interest groups, the Department of Health and Human Services' Office of Inspector General (DHHS OIG) conducted a study to evaluate compliance of structure/function claims made for a sample of 127 dietary supplement products marketed for weight loss or immune support.[180] The OIG found that substantiation documents were inconsistent with FDA's guidance on competent and reliable scientific evidence and that FDA could not easily determine whether manufacturers had submitted the required claims notification for their claims. Further, the OIG observed that 7 percent of the supplements lacked the required label disclaimer, and 20 percent included prohibited disease claims. The OIG recommended that FDA i) seek statutory authority to review substantiation files for structure/function claims, ii) improve its notification system for claims and iii) expand its market surveillance to enforce the use of disclaimers and to root out unlawful disease claims. FDA did not comment on the first recommendation, but agreed with the second and third recommendations.

---

[178] 65 Fed. Reg. 1000, 1032 (Jan. 6, 2000).

[179] U.S. GOV'T ACCOUNTABILITY OFFICE, GAO-11-102, FOOD LABELING: FDA NEEDS TO REASSESS ITS APPROACH TO PROTECTING CONSUMERS FROM FALSE OR MISLEADING CLAIMS (2011).

[180] DEP'T OF HEALTH AND HUMAN SERVICES, OFFICE OF INSPECTOR GENERAL, OEI-01011-00210, DIETARY SUPPLEMENTS: STRUCTURE/FUNCTION CLAIMS FAIL TO MEET FEDERAL REQUIREMENTS (Oct. 2012).

FDA has challenged relatively few claims that would otherwise be permitted under DSHEA on the basis of inadequate substantiation. The lone area of exception may be claims for weight loss. FDA has issued numerous Warning Letters to manufacturers of weight loss supplements, citing manufacturers for making claims "that are not supported by competent and reliable scientific evidence."[181] Those Warning Letters did not result in court action, however. FDA left that to FTC. FTC has been more aggressive than FDA, challenging dietary supplement products with overblown and unsubstantiated claims, based on the traditional FTC actions under sections 5, 12, 13, and 19 of the Federal Trade Commission Act which prohibit false, misleading, or unsubstantiated claims. These dietary supplement cases follow FTC's traditional interest in products purporting to provide health-related benefits. Many of these cases involve weight loss products,[182] children's products,[183] or those claiming to benefit serious diseases like cancer, AIDS, heart disease, diabetes, or Alzheimer's.[184]

FDA and FTC, through the efforts of a joint working group, also have collaborated and taken joint enforcement action in a number of cases. In such matters, the subject claims have been cited both as being drug claims and as being unsubstantiated.[185]

Dietary Supplements Under NLEA After DSHEA

DSHEA amends various portions of NLEA in order to harmonize the two and to provide certain provisions unique to dietary supplements. FDA issued implementing regulations requiring that dietary ingredients appear in a specific order, first by setting out those dietary ingredients that are in the product in significant amounts and for which the agency has recognized a recommendation for daily consumption, and then listing the rest of the dietary

---

[181]   *See, e.g.*, Letter from Joseph Baca (CFSAN/FDA) to Advanced Pharmaceutical Research, Inc. (Feb. 28, 2003); more than 20 other letters issued the same day. Letter from Joseph Baca to Bionutricals International Inc. (Oct. 25, 2004); almost 10 other Warning Letters issued the same day.

[182]   *See, e.g.*, FTC v. Diet Coffee, Inc., 08 CV 0094 (S.D.N.Y. Jan. 4, 2008); FTC v. Sili Neutraceuticals, LLC, 07 C. 4541 (N.D. Ill. Jan. 23, 2008). See also, Press Release, Federal Trade Commission, FTC Seeks to Halt 10 Operators of Fake News Sites from Making Deceptive Claims about Acai Berry Weight Loss Products (Apr. 19, 2011).

[183]   See e.g., *In the Matter of* NBTY, Inc., a corporation, Naturesmart LLC, a limited liability company, and Rexall Sundown, Inc., a corporation, FTC File No. 1023080 (Mar. 29, 2011). FTC concluded that the advertisers lacked substantiation for the claims made for their DHA-containing children's vitamins. Specifically, the products were found to contain insufficient quantities of DHA to support claims that the product promoted healthy brain and eye development.

[184]   *See, e.g.*, FTC v. Direct Mktg. Concepts, Inc., 624 F.3d 1, 5 (1st Cir. 2010); FTC v. Prophet 3H, Inc., Civ. Act. No. 06-CV 1692 (N.D. Ga. Dec. 13, 2007); and FTC v. Pacific Herbal Sciences, Inc., CV 05-7247 CJC (RZ) (C.D. Cal. Apr. 27, 2007). See also, FTC Consent Order (FTC File No. 112 30935 (May 14, 2014)) with GeneLink, Inc., following unsubstantiated claims that their personalized supplements treat diabetes, heart disease, arthritis, and other ailments; FTC Consent Order (FTC File No. 132-3067 (Aug. 21, 2014)), with i-Health, Inc. and Martek Bioscience following unsubstantiated claims regarding their product's ability to prevent cognitive decline and improve memory.

[185]   *See, e.g.*, Letter from Mary K. Engle (FTC) and Jennifer A. Thomas (CFSAN/FDA) to Apurve Mehra, Telledant LLC (Sept. 28, 2010), objecting to products promoted for treating sexually transmitted diseases; Press Release, Food and Drug Administration, FDA, FTC Act to Remove Fraudulent STD Products from the Market (May 3, 2011); Letter from Howard Sklamberg (CDER/FDA) and Mary Engle (FTC) to Todd Whidden, Flu and Cold Defense LLC (Jan. 24, 2013), objecting to promotion of supplements for ability to kill flu and cold viruses; Letter from Mary Engle (FTC), William Correll (CFSAN/FDA), and Diana Amador Toro (FDA New Jersey District Office) to Rima Laibow and Ralph Fucetola, Natural Solutions Foundation (Sept. 23, 2014), objecting to promotion of supplements for the ability to kill the Ebola virus.

ingredients, if any, in it.[186] Further, DSHEA permitted, and FDA regulations describe, the use of a percentage level claim for a dietary ingredient even if FDA has not established a reference amount for it.[187] The term "dietary supplement" must appear on the label or labeling and, if the product contains an herb or other botanical, the part of the plant from which it is derived must be stated.[188] However, the most significant change was court-ordered. As described in Chapter 3 *supra*, NLEA prescribed the "significant scientific agreement" (SSA) standard for health claims made for conventional foods, but left the standard for dietary supplements to the development of FDA.[189] After several rounds of notice and comment, FDA concluded that the same evidentiary standard should apply to both. The health claim litigations provided resounding defeats for FDA in its efforts to limit the claims for dietary supplements.

Health Claims for Dietary Supplements—*Pearson* and the Rise of Qualified Health Claims

As has been noted before, FDA had solidly opposed any claims for dietary supplements that linked a dietary ingredient to a disease or health-related condition.[190] Indeed, FDA had litigated extensively to prevent such an eventuality and had shown great reluctance to confront the fact that the NLEA-permitted claims were actually "disease claims."[191]

Following NLEA passage, FDA approved only two health claims for dietary supplements— calcium and osteoporosis[192] and folate and neural tube defects.[193] A third claim for dietary supplements containing stanol esters and sterol esters[194] and risk of coronary heart disease was approved in September 2000. Each of these regulations required the demonstration of SSA. Critics denounced the SSA standard as virtually impossible to meet, and as stringent as standards for drug approval.

In 1993, FDA declined to approve four health claims for dietary supplements: dietary fiber and cancer,[195] antioxidant vitamins and cancer,[196] omega-3 fatty acids and coronary heart disease,[197] and folic acid and neural tube defects.[198]

Several manufacturers and marketers of dietary supplements filed suit raising Administrative Procedure Act and constitutional claims, and the district court ruled for FDA.[199] FDA

---

[186] FDCA § 403(g)(5)(F)(i)(iii), 21 U.S.C. § 343(g)(5)(i)(iii); 21 C.F.R. § 101.36 (2014).

[187] FDCA § 403(r)(2)(F), 21 U.S.C. § 343(r)(2)(F); 21 C.F.R. § 101.13(q) (2014).

[188] *FDCA* § 403(s)(2)(B) and (C), 21 U.S.C. § 343(s)(2)(B) and (C); 21 C.F.R. § 101.3(g) (2014).

[189] FDCA § 403(r)(5), 21 U.S.C. § 343(r)(5).

[190] 21 C.F.R. § 101.14(a)(1) (2014).

[191] See, generally PETER BARTON HUTT, RICHARD A. MERRILL, & LEWIS A. GROSSMAN, FOOD AND DRUG LAW: CASES AND MATERIALS 268-275 (3d ed. 2007).

[192] 21 C.F.R. § 101.72 (2014).

[193] 21 C.F.R. § 101.79 (2014).

[194] 21 C.F.R. § 101.83 (2014).

[195] 58 Fed. Reg. 2537 (Jan 6, 1993).

[196] 58 Fed. Reg. 2622 (Jan 6, 1993).

[197] 58 Fed. Reg. 2682 (Jan 6, 1993).

[198] 58 Fed. Reg. 2606 (Jan 6, 1993). FDA subsequently authorized a health claim for folate, but declined to allow such a claim to state that 0.8 mg folate from a dietary supplement is more effective than a lower amount in conventional food form. 58 Fed. Reg. 53,254 (Oct. 14, 1993).

[199] Pearson v. Shalala, 14 F. Supp. 2d 10 (D.D.C. 1998).

recognized that some data for the claims existed but that the data did not meet the rigorous SSA standard and were therefore inherently misleading. The plaintiffs argued that some data existed; therefore, the claims were only potentially misleading and could be cured by an appropriate disclaimer. The D.C. Circuit Court of Appeals reversed that decision, holding that FDA's denial of the claims violated the First Amendment. The court concluded that the claims were not inherently misleading and that *banning* the claims was not necessary, where an appropriate disclaimer would adequately inform consumers and negate potentially misleading claims.[200]

In response to the litigation, FDA announced that it would adopt a new "weight of the scientific evidence" standard for the evaluation of a claim that does not reach the "significant scientific agreement" standard.[201] For such a claim, FDA would not issue a regulation permitting the claim, but would decline to initiate regulatory action provided the claim is adequately qualified.[202] This weight of the evidence approach was not acceptable to industry, which promptly returned to court. The District Court for the District of Columbia then ruled that FDA's decision denying the antioxidant vitamin/cancer claim violated the First Amendment in that "if a health claim is not inherently misleading, the balance tilts in favor of disclaimers rather than suppression."[203]

These cases established the basis for the development of so-called qualified health claims, which would be based on "credible scientific evidence."[204] FDA subsequently issued first an interim guidance on Evidence-Based Ranking System for Scientific Data,[205] and then replacing that with a final guidance on Evidence-Based Review System for the Scientific Evaluation of Health Claims.[206] This system establishes levels of certainty for the claim and suggests appropriate disclaimers for each certainty level.[207]

FDA retains the authority to preclear even qualified health claims under procedures designed to implement *Pearson* and other court decisions. FDA will exercise enforcement discretion for a health claim that has not been authorized by a regulation in certain circumstances.[208] Depending on the amount and quality of the data, FDA will select appropriate qualifying language for the qualified health claim.[209]

---

[200]   Pearson v. Shalala, 164 F.3d 650 (D.C. Cir. 1999).

[201]   67 Fed. Reg. 78,002, 78,003 (Dec. 20, 2002).

[202]   *Id.*

[203]   Whitaker v. Thompson, 248 F. Supp. 2d 1 (D.D.C. 2002).

[204]   68 Fed. Reg. 66,040 (Nov. 25, 2003).

[205]   Guidance for Industry and FDA (July 10, 2003).

[206]   Guidance for Industry (Jan. 2009).

[207]   FDA, Guidance for Industry: Interim Procedures for Qualified Health Claims in the Labeling of Conventional Human Food and Human Dietary Supplements (July 10, 2003).

[208]   The claim is the subject of a health claim petition that meets the requirements of 21 C.F.R. § 101.70 and has been filed for comprehensive review: 1) the scientific evidence in support of the claim outweighs the scientific evidence against the claim; 2) the claim is appropriately qualified, and all statements in the claim are consistent with the weight of the scientific evidence; 3) consumer health and safety are not threatened; and 4) the claim meets the general requirements for health claims in 21 C.F.R. § 101.14 except for the degree of certainty of the evidence. FDA, Guidance for Industry: Qualified Health Claims in the Labeling of Conventional Food and Dietary Supplements (Dec. 18, 2002).

[209]   FDA, Guidance for Industry: Interim Procedures for Qualified Health Claims in the Labeling of Conventional Foods and Human Dietary Supplements (July 10, 2003).

Unfortunately, the disclaimers and cumbersome language in the claim make them consumer unfriendly. For example, a Second Level (B) qualified claim would bear a qualifier to the general effect that "although there is scientific evidence supporting the claim, the evidence is not conclusive."[210] FDA continues to search for ways to improve the qualified health claim process.

Specifically, FDA is considering whether it would be possible to abbreviate the claims to make them more comprehensible,[211] or use another method for communicating confidence in the supporting data. Cynics might observe that the agency's drawn-out implementation of *Pearson* may well have accomplished the FDA goals of making the disease-related health claims rare in the marketplace.

Good Manufacturing Practices

DSHEA authorized the issuance, by FDA, of good manufacturing practice (GMP) regulations to specify the conditions under which dietary supplements are to be manufactured, packed, and held, and these regulations are to be modeled on those for foods generally.[212]

Almost 13 years after being given statutory authority to promulgate GMP regulations, in June 2007, FDA issued final regulations.[213] Although DSHEA explicitly provides that the dietary supplement GMP regulations should be modeled after current GMP regulations for foods, the requirements imposed upon dietary supplement manufacturers by the dietary supplement GMP regulations appear to be more similar with drug GMP requirements than with conventional food GMP requirements.

Under the final rule, dietary supplement manufacturers are required to evaluate the identity, purity, strength, and composition of their supplements. As part of this effort, supplement manufacturers must conduct an identity test on 100 percent of incoming dietary ingredients, although no specific testing program is prescribed; that is, FDA will accept scientifically valid testing systems that may include a mix of in-process testing and finished product testing to ensure that the finished product meets specifications. The agency provided for a little flexibility from the 100 percent identity testing requirement by simultaneously publishing an interim final rule that allows manufacturers to petition for an exemption from this requirement.[214] The petition must set forth the scientific rationale (together with supporting data and information) for proposed alternate testing that would demonstrate no material diminution of assurance. It likely will be difficult for dietary supplement manufacturers to meet this standard.

Interestingly, the final regulation changed the approach set forth in the proposed regulation by making its requirements applicable to dietary supplement manufacturers only, and not to dietary ingredient suppliers. The result, of course, is that dietary supplement manufacturers

---

[210] *Id.*
[211] 69 Fed. Reg. 24,541, 24,546-47 (May 4, 2004).
[212] FDCA § 402(g), 21 U.S.C. § 342(g).
[213] 72 Fed. Reg. 34,752 (June 25, 2007); codified at 21 C.F.R. pt. 111 (2014).
[214] 72 Fed. Reg. 34,959 (June 25, 2007).

now shoulder the ultimate responsibility for ensuring the quality of the ingredients used in dietary supplements.

The rule became effective August 24, 2007, but provided for a three-year phase-in period, depending on the number of full-time-equivalent (FTE) employees employed by the manufacturer. By June 2010, all dietary supplement manufacturers, regardless of size, were required to comply.[215] Since that time, FDA has increasingly been issuing Warning Letters to dietary supplement manufacturers following agency inspections.[216] Warning Letters have focused on a variety of noncompliance issues, including failure to have adequate written procedures, failure to test all components of supplements, failure to include each step in the manufacturing process in the master manufacturing records, and inadequate testing of dietary ingredients or finished products. The agency has reported that about half of the facilities inspected fall short of regulatory expectations, with nearly a quarter committing serious GMP violations.[217] While enforcement action for GMP violations may drive some companies to use contract manufacturers, such companies must remember that FDA will hold them ultimately responsible for ensuring that the products they place into commerce (or cause to be placed into commerce) are not adulterated for failure to comply with GMPs.[218]

Safety Reporting

DSHEA created a voluntary reporting system for adverse events associated with the use of dietary supplements. This system proved to be largely ineffective, with concerns raised due to the dearth of reports, the lack of complete information, and difficulty in follow-up.[219] The system's failure was highlighted by FDA's difficulty in obtaining adverse event reports from Metabolife International, Inc., regarding its ephedra-containing supplements. In part to address these concerns, President Bush signed into law the Dietary Supplement and Nonprescription Drug Consumer Protection Act in December 2006.[220] Among its provisions, this act requires the manufacturer, packer, or distributor whose name appears on the supplement label:

---

[215]   To assist companies in ensuring compliance, in December 2010, FDA issued a Small Entity Compliance Guide entitled, "Current Food Manufacturing Practice in Manufacturing, Packaging, or Holding Operations for Dietary Supplements."

[216]   *See, e.g.,* Letter from H. Thomas Warwich, Jr. (FDA Denver District Office) to John Carroll, Hain North America (Dec. 3, 2010); Letter from Charles Breen (FDA Seattle District Office) to Jeffrey Gollini, All American Pharmaceutical & Natural Foods Corp. (Jan. 14, 2011); Letter from Alonza Cruse (FDA Los Angeles District Office) to Christopher Reed, Reed's Inc. (May 19, 2011); Letter from Alonza Cruse (FDA Los Angeles District Office to Maurice and Connie Ovadia, West Coast Laboratories, Inc. (Sept. 15, 2014).

[217]   *See* GMPs Send Smaller Supplement Firms Into Contract Manufacturers' Arms, F-D-C Rep. ("The Tan Sheet"), Sept. 24, 2012 at 1, 4-5.

[218]   *See, e.g.,* Letter from Elizabeth Ormond (FDA Florida District Office) to Ralph Albrecht, M.D. Science Lab (July 15, 2014).

[219]   Testimony of Michael Mangano, Principal Inspector General for the Department of Health and Human Services, before the Subcomm. on Oversight of Government Management, Restructuring and the District of Columbia (July 31, 2002) at 1-6.

[220]   Pub. L. No. 109-462, 120 Stat. 3469 (2006).

- to submit to FDA, within 15 business days of receipt, any report received of a serious adverse event[221] associated with such supplement when used in the United States, accompanied by a copy of the label;[222]

- to submit updated reports if new medical information regarding the initial report is received within a year of the initial report;[223]

- to submit the reports using FDA's MedWatch form (Form FDA 3500A);[224]

- to maintain records related to each such report for six years and to make those records available to FDA during an inspection;[225] and

- to include on labels a domestic address or domestic phone number through which the company may receive reports of serious adverse events.[226]

The law makes clear that any such report does not constitute an admission that the product caused or contributed to the adverse event.[227]

FDA has issued two guidances to facilitate industry compliance with the law.[228] Although the statute merely requires supplement labels to include the domestic address or phone number through which consumers may report serious adverse events, in FDA's draft guidance on labeling, FDA recommends including a clear, prominent statement informing consumers that the contact information is for reporting serious adverse events.

Failure to comply with the new statutory requirement is a prohibited act under section 301(e), 21 U.S.C. § 331(e), subjecting the violator and its goods to the injunction provisions (section 302, 21 U.S.C. § 332), penalty provisions (section 303, 21 U.S.C. § 333) and seizure provisions (section 304, 21 U.S.C. § 334) of the FDCA. Of the 156 Warning Letters issued to supplement companies between 2011 and June 2014, 20 (13 percent) cite failures to report serious adverse events or not including the required label information.[229] In January 2009, GAO issued a report in which it concluded that there was significant underreporting of serious adverse events, and raised concerns about FDA's ability to adequately protect the public from unsafe products under the current statutory and regulatory scheme.[230] Among

---

[221] "Serious adverse event" is defined as an adverse event that results in death, a life-threatening experience, inpatient hospitalization, a persistent or significant disability or incapacity, or a congenital anomaly or birth defect, or requires a medical or surgical intervention to prevent such an outcome. FDCA § 761(a)(2), 21 U.S.C. § 379aa-1(a)(2).

[222] FDCA § 761(b)(1), (c), 21 U.S.C. § 379aa-1(b)(1), (c).

[223] FDCA § 761(c)(2), 21 U.S.C. § 379aa-1(c)(2).

[224] FDCA § 761(d), 21 U.S.C. § 379aa-1(d).

[225] FDCA § 761(e), 21 U.S.C. § 379aa-1(e).

[226] FDCA § 403(y), 21 U.S.C. § 343(y).

[227] FDCA § 761(g), 21 U.S.C. § 379aa-1(g).

[228] "Questions and Answers Regarding the Labeling of Dietary Supplements as Required by the Dietary Supplement and Nonprescription Drug Consumer Protection Act" (Sept. 2009); "Questions and Answers Regarding Adverse Event Reporting and Recordkeeping for Dietary Supplements as Required by the Dietary Supplement and Nonprescription Drug Consumer Protection Act" (June 2009).

[229] Supplement GMP Inspections Reveal Adverse Event Reports, Prompting Warning Letters, F-D-C Rep. ("The Tan Sheet"), July 21, 2014 at 1, 4-5. See also, Dep't of Health and Human Services, Office of Inspector General, Dietary Supplements: Companies May Be Difficult to Locate in An Emergency, OEI-01-11-00211 (Oct. 2012). OIG found that 20 percent of the 127 dietary supplement product labels reviewed failed to include the required label information.

[230] U.S. Gov't Accountability Office, GAO-09-250, Dietary Supplements: FDA Should Take Further Actions to Improve Oversight and Consumer Understanding (2009).

its recommendations, GAO called for statutory authority to require reporting of all adverse events. FDA generally supported the recommendation, but raised concerns about its ability to efficiently and effectively analyze the information to identify unsafe supplements.

In March 2013, the GAO issued another report on the dietary supplement industry, this one addressing FDA's use of adverse event reports in overseeing dietary supplements.[231] GAO examined the number, source and types of dietary supplements identified in adverse event reports, the actions FDA has taken to help ensure companies are complying with the reporting requirements, and the extent to which FDA is utilizing the adverse event reports to initiate and support its consumer protection actions. GAO recommended, *inter alia*, that FDA explore the possibility of securing access to poison center data (another potential source of adverse event information), of making public the adverse event reports it receives, and of increasing enforcement activity based on adverse event reports. The agency generally agreed with the GAO's recommendations, but clarified that most adverse event reports do not result in enforcement action because the agency receives relatively few adverse event reports and it is very difficult to determine causality based on the limited information received.

The value of the enhanced reporting requirement remains to be seen. While FDA certainly should see an increase in the number of serious adverse event reports received, it is likely that even these reports will represent a relatively small percentage of the adverse events actually experienced. Further, because the new law does not require the inclusion of medical records of the injured party, FDA will have difficulty drawing any conclusions regarding causality or relatedness.[232]

Conclusion

For the 50 years prior to DSHEA, dietary supplements had been aggressively regulated by FDA. The agency historically regarded them as largely bogus, subject to excesses in claims and content, and needful of close regulation. In contrast, industry and, increasingly, scientists and consumers viewed them as products serving a useful, indeed essential, role in enabling the consumer to care for his or her health. With DSHEA, Congress tried to strike a balance between these poles, but DSHEA has not yet eliminated the antipathy. FDA eschewed enforcement in most areas except for health claims, leaving the field to FTC. Because FTC can initiate actions only against violative claims, the question of dietary supplement safety has gone largely unchallenged. It remains to be seen how FDA proceeds and how the agency and industry deal with future safety issues. The GMP regulations offer increased reliability of purity and quality, and the NDI notifications give FDA the ability to protect consumers from unsafe new ingredients. If FDA and industry do not work together, however, then we shall surely hear from Congress again.

---

[231]   U.S. Gov't Accountability Office, GAO-13-244, FDA May Have Opportunities to Expand Its Use of Reported Health Problems to Oversee Products (2013).

[232]   For a general discussion of the new law and concerns regarding its value, *see* K. Wang, *New Mandatory Reporting Requirements for Dietary Supplements and Nonprescription Drugs Solve Very Little*, 35 J.L. Med. & Ethics 336 (2007).

CHAPTER 7
VETERINARY FOOD AND DRUGS

....

JEANNIE PERRON[*]

Introduction

The regulation of foods and drugs for animal use replicates the regulation of human foods and drugs, but in each instance adds additional regulation: proportionately, a greater number of individual animal food and drug products are subject to licensing than human food and drug products; and the regulation systems each contain a twist that results in more extensive regulation of the animal-use product than its human-use counterpart. For example, in the regulation of food, many states premarket license each separate animal food recipe and flavor; in the regulation of drugs, the Delaney anticancer clause applies in all new animal drug approvals; in both foods and drugs, the variety of species and the potential for some of those species ending up as human or animal food adds a dimension to regulation beyond safety and utility to the animal itself. As a result, in many areas, the regulation of animal foods and drugs is on the cutting edge of the issues of regulation involving human health and safety that are being addressed in Congress and other public forums. The animal drug area also presents a major legislative dichotomy between the Food and Drug Administration (FDA) and the U.S. Department of Agriculture (USDA) in which most animal drugs fall under the jurisdiction of FDA, except for veterinary biologicals, which fall under the exclusive jurisdiction of USDA.

Nonbiological animal drugs, as well as animal foods, are regulated by FDA under the Federal Food, Drug, and Cosmetic Act (FDCA).[1] Regulation of these products can be traced back to the 1906 Pure Food and Drugs Act,[2] which first introduced the concept of regulating articles for use by man "or other animals"[3] that remains with us: both foods and drugs for animal

[*]   Eugene I. Lambert, Esq. (1935-2013), the co-author of the first two editions of this chapter, was a leading authority on animal food and drug law, a respected lawyer, generous mentor, gifted teacher, and cherished friend. We miss him every day.
[1]   Pub. L. No. 75-717, 52 Stat. 1040 (1938), as amended by 21 U.S.C. §§ 301 *et seq.* (1994) [hereinafter FDCA].
[2]   Ch. 3915, 34 Stat. 768 (1906).
[3]   *Id.* § 6, 34 Stat. at 769.

use come within the statutory definitions of "foods" and "drugs," and thus are subject to the various controls applicable to each category under Chapters IV and V of the FDCA.[4] These include statutory prohibitions against adulteration and misbranding, statutory provisions for rulemaking programs, and general and specific licensing provisions.

Although there are foods and drugs for fish, birds, amphibians, reptiles, and large and small mammals, the major categories of animal foods and drugs are 1) those used in nonfood-producing animals, such as pet foods and drugs generally used for therapeutic purposes, and 2) those used in food-producing animals, often to improve food production. The major regulatory issues in animal drugs concern the drugs used in food-producing animals; it is here that drug regulation and human safety come together. Prior to January 1983, FDA had divided the responsibility for the review and approval of animal drugs used in food-producing animals between two different bureaus within the agency.[5] The animal area is the only one in which FDA licenses both food processing plants and the presence of animal drugs in those foods.[6]

Biological drugs (i.e., drugs generally characterized by their interaction with the animal's immune system) are regulated by USDA under the 1913 Virus-Serum-Toxin Act as expanded in scope and jurisdiction by amendments in 1985.[7] The act directs USDA to license establishments producing biological drugs for animal use, and to ensure that those biologicals are safe, pure, and potent. Until 1985, the Virus-Serum-Toxin Act only regulated finished products that moved from one state to another. (FDA asserted jurisdiction over biological drugs that did not move in interstate commerce, but that contained components that did.[8]) The 1985 amendments resolved this "split jurisdiction" by giving USDA exclusive jurisdiction over all veterinary biologicals, regardless of interstate movement.[9] USDA exercises its authority through the Animal and Plant Health Inspection Service that, relying on the few paragraphs that comprise the operative authority in the Virus-Serum-Toxin Act, has devised a complex licensing system for both the producing establishments and the products.[10]

In reviewing FDA's extensive authority, this chapter focuses first on the unusual interrelation between federal and state authority in the regulation of food for "other animals," and second on the novel and complex problems that FDA faces in seeking to regulate drugs for these "other animals." For veterinary biologicals, this chapter will explore the problems in expanding USDA's regulatory system to cover products with the least prior regulation.

---

[4]   FDCA §§ 201(f)(1), (g)(1), 401-411, 501-510; 21 U.S.C. §§ 321(f)(1), (g)(1), 341-350, 351-360.

[5]   Full responsibility was finally given to the Bureau of (now Center for) Veterinary Medicine. FDA Statement of Organization, Functions, and Delegations of Authority, 48 Fed. Reg. 337-01 (Jan. 4, 1983).

[6]   FDCA § 512(m), 21 U.S.C. § 360b(m).

[7]   21 U.S.C. §§ 151-159, codifying the Act of March 4, 1913, relating to virus, serum, toxin, and analogous products for domestic animals, ch. 145, 37 Stat. 828, 832, as amended by Pub. L. No. 99-198, § 1768, 99 Stat. 1354, 1654 (1985).

[8]   Animal Health Inst. v. USDA, 487 F. Supp. 376 (D. Colo. 1980); Grand Laboratories, Inc. v. Harris, 660 F.2d 1288 (8th Cir. 1981) (en banc).

[9]   Pub. L. No. 99-198, § 1768(a), 99 Stat. at 1654 (USDA jurisdiction extends to "any place under the jurisdiction of the United States"); see 21 U.S.C. § 392(b) (as interpreted in Grand Laboratories v. Harris, 660 F.2d 1288).

[10]   See 9 C.F.R. pts. 101-123 (1996).

Animal Food

Food and drink for "other animals" were regulated under the Pure Food and Drugs Act of 1906.[11] The FDCA continued this scope of regulation by defining "food" as including "food and drink for man or other animals."[12] Consequently, FDA has the (as yet unexercised) authority to adopt standards of identity, quality, and fill of the containers for animal food, as with human food.[13] FDA can regulate animal food labeling and animal food adulteration in the same manner as human foods; only the areas of nutrition labeling, nutrient content claims, health claims, and special dietary foods explicitly or implicitly have been limited to products for human use.[14] FDA's Bioterrorism Act requirements also apply to animal foods to the same extent and in the same way that they apply to human foods, except that the records required to be maintained for animal feed, including pet food, need only be maintained for one year instead of the two years required for nonperishable human food.[15] FDA, however, has not expended the resources to develop the kind of comprehensive standards and labeling schemes that exist for human foods, largely because that effort has been undertaken by the states in a unique cooperative venture.

Pet foods, nonmedicated livestock feed, and medicated feeds with drug levels below the FDA licensing requirements primarily are regulated by the states through the use of a model act and regulations, covering labeling, and individual state registrations, with FDA backup.[16] Medicated feeds that fall within FDA licensing concentrations are dealt with by the agency (including plant registration and licensing, and mandatory FDA inspection) and followed by state controls.[17] With the exception of infant formulas (which share the "singular" use with animal feeds as the sole item in the diet),[18] no human foods are subject to the detail of control applicable to food for "other animals."

All of the states regulate the composition and sale of livestock feed; such regulation is considered an integral part of the protection and promotion of agriculture. Most of the states have adopted the Model Commercial Feed Law Act developed by the Association of American Feed Control Officials (AAFCO) in cooperation with industry.[19] There are separate sets of AAFCO model regulations to implement the Model Act for livestock feed and pet food (companion animals falling within the definition of the animals covered by the Model Act).[20]

---

[11]   Ch. 3915, § 6, 34 Stat. at 769.

[12]   FDCA § 201(f)(1), 21 U.S.C. § 321(f)(1).

[13]   FDCA § 401, 21 U.S.C. § 341; see 21 C.F.R. pts. 130-169.

[14]   FDCA §§ 402(a)-(c), 403, 21 U.S.C. §§ 342(a)-(c), 343; see Id. §§ 403(j), (q), (r), 411(c)(3), 21 U.S.C. §§ 343(j), (q), (r), 350(c)(3).

[15]   21 C.F.R. § 1.360(d), (e).

[16]   State regulators, commonly part of state departments of agriculture, have organized as the Association of American Feed Control Officials, Inc. (AAFCO). This group is composed of representatives from the United States and Canada. Its annual *Official Publication* contains not only a guide to association activities, but also information on individual state feed law requirements, and the text of the Model Feed Bill and feed and pet food regulations. States that adopt the Model Feed Bill and regulations often adopt subsequent amendments to the regulations automatically. Thus, the AAFCO process is important to both the states and industry in the development of feed regulation. Unless otherwise noted, all citations to the *Official Publication* [hereinafter O.P.] are to the 2014 print edition.

[17]   See FDCA § 512(m), 21 U.S.C. § 360b(m).

[18]   See FDCA § 412, 21 U.S.C. § 350a.

[19]   O.P. 105-16.

[20]   Id. 117-33, 136-47; see also AAFCO, Model Feed Bill § 3(r)-(s), O.P. 106.

In addition to similar information required under the FDCA (e.g., the name of the food, its ingredients, the name and address of the packer or distributor and net weight), the Model Act and corresponding state laws, where they exist, require compositional information—guarantees—intended to permit knowledgeable purchasers of livestock feed and pet food to monitor the nutritional status of animals.[21]

To provide pet owners with additional information, the model pet food regulations require that the label of a pet food state the nutritional use of the food, e.g., "for all life stages" or for "maintenance."[22] There also exists an AAFCO system for substantiating these claims, which takes into account whether the marketer conducted feeding trials of the food, utilizing AAFCO-specified protocols designed to ensure reproducible results, or relied on AAFCO tables establishing the levels of nutrients required for adequate dog and cat nutrition at various life stages.[23] The system is intended to permit pet owners to purchase foods with confidence that the foods will meet the nutritional needs of companion animals. As explained above, label guarantees can provide information about specific nutrients as well. While not establishing nutrient levels, a related system lists the nutrients for a wide range of livestock and poultry for which levels must be provided to the purchasing animal producer.[24]

AAFCO has developed labeling rules, and defined and named the multitude of ingredients used in animal food.[25] This state-federal-industry process of defining feed ingredients has largely taken the place of any federal program for determining whether human food ingredients meet the statutory criterion of being generally recognized as safe (GRAS) and thus not in need of federal approval. Industry proposes ingredient names and definitions to a designated AAFCO coordinator, called an "investigator," who solicits comments from industry and state and federal regulators. The proposed definition is submitted to FDA's Center for Veterinary Medicine (CVM) for a safety evaluation before it can be considered for approval by AAFCO. If CVM is comfortable that the ingredient is safe for the proposed use, it issues a "no objections" letter stating that it has no objection to the proposed ingredient under the proposed conditions of use using the sponsor's proposed labeling. Once an FDA no objections letter is issued, then the ingredient can be voted on by the AAFCO Ingredient Definitions Committee at one of the semi-annual AAFCO meetings. If that committee approves the proposed ingredient, then it is presented for a vote to the AAFCO Board of Directors and annual convention delegates. If both bodies approve the ingredient, then it is listed in the AAFCO *Official Publication* as a "tentative definition." Before it can receive final approval, the AAFCO investigator must recommend that the definition be moved to official status.[26] The final approval process proceeds the same way, requiring successive approval votes by the AAFCO Ingredient Definitions Committee, Board, and membership. The participation of FDA personnel in the AAFCO review process gives an informal sanction

---

[21]   Model Feed Bill § 5(a), O.P. 108-09. Until passage and implementation of the Nutrition Labeling and Education Act, Pub. L. No. 101-535, 104 Stat. 2353 (1990) (principally codified in 21 U.S.C. § 343(q)-(r)) made nutrition labeling in a uniform format almost universally available on human food, animal food labeling was unique in uniformly providing the purchaser with nutritional information useful to ensure proper feeding of the target animal. *See also* 21 C.F.R. pt. 101.

[22]   Pet Food Reg. PF7, O.P. 142-43.

[23]   O.P. 165-94 (feeding protocols), 149-64 (nutrient profile tables).

[24]   *See id.* 120-27, 233.

[25]   *Id.* 353-462.

[26]   *See id.* 337-41 (procedure), 528-38 (action on proposals).

to the ingredients that are reviewed, and permits FDA to identify those ingredients that should undergo the more detailed scrutiny of food additive approval.[27] FDA has recognized for federal labeling purposes the AAFCO-developed feed ingredient definitions.[28] FDA also has sanctioned certain AAFCO-created generic or "collective" feed terms for use in labeling livestock, but not pet, food.[29]

The AAFCO ingredients definition process has proven unwieldy over the last decade, especially with the explosion in the marketplace of functional food ingredients, dietary supplements, and so-called "nutraceuticals" for human use. FDA took the position in a 1996 *Federal Register* notice[30] that the Dietary Supplement Health and Education Act of 1994 (DSHEA), which governs the composition and marketing of dietary supplements, does not apply to supplements for animals. It announced that such products for animals would be regulated as animal feed. Because the AAFCO ingredient definition process is nearly always an expensive, multiyear undertaking requiring the generation of significant safety and other data and because the sponsor of the definition is given no proprietary rights in the definition itself, few sponsors have come forward to seek approval for functional ingredients. As a result, a number of animal feed products containing functional ingredients have been marketed in an extra-regulatory fashion, often with mixed success.

For this reason, in the summer of 2010, CVM began to accept notifications from feed ingredient sponsors advising that the sponsors had determined through expert review that specific animal feed ingredients were GRAS for specified intended uses. Under the federal GRAS notification process, an animal feed ingredient manufacturer or supplier underwrites an independent expert review of publicly available safety data on a specified use of an ingredient, usually in one or more named species. If the expert review culminates in a determination that the animal feed ingredient is "generally recognized" by qualified experts as safe for the specified intended uses, the sponsor then notifies CVM of the expert determination. CVM publishes on its website a copy of the letter it generates reflecting its conclusion with respect to each notification. The Center's publication of a letter stating that it has no questions regarding the notification serves as public notice that FDA has raised no objection to the notification. If CVM does have questions or objections to the notification, it publishes a letter reflecting those issues. That letter serves as public notice that CVM is not comfortable with the GRAS notification as filed. The sponsor has the opportunity to file additional information with FDA in response to any objections or questions the agency raised, and that additional information may result in the issuance by FDA of a letter stating that it has no questions regarding the notification. At the time this publication is going to press four years after CVM launched its GRAS notification program, only 18 GRAS notifications have been filed with CVM, of which three were still undergoing review. The Center has ceased to evaluate five of the notifiers' requests and has issued letters stating it has no questions about the notification in response to only five of the remaining 10.

---

[27]   On November 20, 2012, a new Memorandum of Understanding between AAFCO and FDA went into effect that described each entity's role in the existing AAFCO Ingredient Definitions process. The 2012 MOU can be found at O.P. 102-04.

[28]   Food & Drug Admin., Compliance Policy Guide No. 7126.08 (Oct. 1, 1980); Compliance Policy Guides Manual § 665.100 (1995) (revised).

[29]   21 C.F.R. § 501.110; *see* 51 Fed. Reg. 11,456 (1986) for the decision rejecting collective terms for pet food. AAFCO adopted collective terms are found at O.P. 368-71.

[30]   61 Fed. Reg. 17,706 (1996).

In most states, the CVM GRAS notification process is a recognized alternative to the AAFCO feed ingredient definition approval process, although some states don't yet accept a CVM "no questions" letter issued in response to a GRAS notification as rendering an ingredient "legal" for use in animal feed. As of this writing, CVM and AAFCO are reconsidering FDA's role in the AAFCO feed ingredient approval process.

AAFCO member states keep a close check on animal feed because most states require producers to register feed products on a yearly basis and often review labels for compliance with federal and state (usually AAFCO) requirements.[31] In cooperation with FDA, member states also conduct inspections of feed mills. These inspections take the place of possible federal inspections, thus freeing FDA resources for inspection of human food and drug establishments.[32]

On September 27, 2007, the President signed into law the Food and Drug Administration Amendments Act of 2007 (FDAAA). At least partially in response to a series of high-profile recalls of pet food products as a result of contamination with melamine, a chemical found in plastic plates and other items, Article X of the FDAAA contains provisions specifically directed toward ensuring the safety of pet food. Section 1002 requires FDA, working in conjunction with AAFCO and stakeholders, to promulgate within two years of the law's passage regulations for pet food establishing ingredient standards and definitions; processing standards; and updated standards for labeling that include nutritional and ingredient information. The same section also requires, within one year of enactment, the establishment of an early warning and surveillance system to identify adulteration of pet food and outbreaks of illnesses associated with pet food. Section 1003 requires FDA to establish efficient and effective communication during pet food recalls. As of this writing, FDA has not enacted any of these measures. Article X also requires mandatory reporting to FDA within 24 hours for certain types of recall-triggering events, the establishment of a Reportable Food Registry, and the provision of certain notices to others in the manufacturing and distribution chain as a result of such events.

The Reportable Food Registry went live in September 2009 for both human food and animal feed, although FDA allowed a 90-day period of enforcement discretion to allow reporters time to become used to the new reporting requirements. Food facilities holding Bioterrorism Act food facility registrations under section 415(a) of the FDCA[33] that manufacture, process, pack, or hold food for human or animal consumption in the United States are required to file a report within 24 hours of determining that there is a reasonable probability that the use of, or exposure to, an article of food will cause serious adverse health consequences or death to humans or animals. FDA has established a database to capture this filing. The failure to file a required report is a prohibited act under section 301(mm) of the FDCA[34]

In the fall of 2010, Congress passed the Food Safety Modernization Act (FSMA), which was signed into law on January 4, 2011. That law requires manufacturers of human food and animal feed to conduct a hazard evaluation to identify hazards that are reasonably

---

[31]   State law requirements are summarized in O.P. 81-87.
[32]   *See* Model Feed Bill § 11; O.P. 113-14; 24 C.F.R. § 225.120-.202.
[33]   21 U.S.C. § 350d.
[34]   21 U.S.C. § 331(mm).

foreseeable, including biological, chemical, physical, and radiological hazards, natural toxins, pesticides, drug residues, decomposition, parasites, and unapproved food or color additives.[35] The facility must identify and implement preventive controls to provide assurances that the identified hazards will be significantly minimized and that food will not be adulterated or misbranded. Not later than 18 months after enactment of FSMA, FDA is charged with promulgating regulations that establish science-based minimum standards for conducting a hazard analysis and implementing preventive controls.

Under FSMA, FDA has promulgated regulations directed to preventive controls and hazard analysis for animal feed (including pet food), sanitary transportation, intentional adulteration, and foreign supplier verification, among others. The hazard analysis and preventative controls proposed rule contained the first-ever proposal to establish Good Manufacturing Practice requirements for non-medicated animal feed. That rule is due to be finalized in 2015, as are the other FSMA proposed regulations except the sanitary transportation and intentional adulteration rules, which are expected by 2016.[36]

Section 206 of FSMA also gave FDA mandatory recall authority over food when there is a reasonable probability that the food is adulterated or misbranded and that the use of or exposure to the food will cause serious adverse health consequences or death to humans or animals. Although it remains to be seen how often FDA will exercise this authority, the first time the agency did so was in 2013 for pet food products.[37]

Livestock feed is not only a source of nutrients for the animal but also a carrier for animal drugs. When it has this dual purpose, it is regulated both as a food and as a drug. Drug regulation has been primarily in the hands of FDA, which has tried a number of different forms of controls.

Since the mid-1940s, when drugs were first being added to animal feed, the agency has taken the position that the person who added a drug to feed to be fed to an animal was preparing the finished dosage form of a drug; thus, the person assumed the role of the drug's manufacturer and could be regulated under the new drug (and other drug) provisions of the act.[38] The supplier of the drug ingredient, although the innovator of its use, had no statutorily defined rights. The drug supplier was merely the supplier of information (in a form called a

---

[35]   See FSMA § 103.

[36]   See http://www.foodsafetynews.com/2014/02/fsma-gets-new-deadlines-for-final-rules/.

[37]   See http://www.fda.gov/downloads/aboutfda/centersoffices/officeoffoods/cvm/cvmfoiaelectronicreadingroom/u cm341491.pdf; http://www.fda.gov/newsevents/newsroom/pressannouncements/ucm340513.htm; http://www.foodsafetynews.com/2014/01/fda-reports-on-singular-instance-of-mandatory-recall-authority/.

[38]   The history of the regulation of animal feed as a carrier of animal drugs principally can be found in the hearings on the bills that eventually became the Animal Drug Amendments of 1968, Pub. L. No. 90-399, 82 Stat. 342 (1968) (principally codified in 21 U.S.C. § 360b): *Hearing on the Animal Drug Amendments of 1965 Before the Subcomm. on Public Health and Welfare of the House Comm. on Interstate and Foreign Commerce*, 89th Cong., 2d Sess. (1966) [hereinafter *1966 House Hearing*]; *Hearing on the Animal Drug Amendments of 1967 Before the Subcomm. on Public Health and Welfare of the House Comm. on Interstate and Foreign Commerce*, 90th Cong., 1st Sess. (1967) [hereinafter *1967 House Hearing*]. It also can be found in FDA proposals to restructure the medicated feed licensing system, *see, e.g.,* 46 Fed. Reg. 2456 (1981). Some of this material has also been collected in Eugene I. Lambert, *The Animal Drug Amendments of 1968: War Stories,* 43 FOOD DRUG COSM. L.J. 781 (1988).

"master file") needed by the feed manufacturer to obtain new drug approval.[39] The process used by FDA involved a fiction, for the feed manufacturer did not have the primary interest in the drug approval; the drug manufacturer did. As a result, the drug manufacturer solicited applications from interested feed manufacturers and took full responsibility for pressing the application through to approval.

In other instances, the drug manufacturer had a statutory right of participation in the approval process. In the case of the five antibiotics subject to certification prior to 1962, drug manufacturers sought exemptions from certification to permit use of the drugs in animal feed.[40] These exempting regulations spelled out the permitted conditions of use, and controlled combinations of antibiotics and non-antibiotic drugs in animal feed. After passage of the Food Additives Amendment in 1958, drugs added to feed also were regulated as food additives.[41] The food additive petition was submitted by the drug manufacturer and the resulting regulation spelled out the permitted uses. The food additive process did not substitute for either the new drug or antibiotic procedure; it was superimposed on both.[42]

FDA recognized that the continued issuance of new drug approvals to feed mills required a significant expenditure of manpower and prevented the agency from reviewing new products. Before 1962, the agency would advise the drug manufacturer (after a few years of supervised use) that the drug was no longer deemed a "new drug," and that no additional new drug applications would be required; that practice ceased after 1962 when FDA revoked the validity of prior "old drug" letters.[43]

The Animal Drug Amendments of 1968 were the first step in rationalizing regulatory controls over animal food that contained drugs. Animal drug manufacturers obtained new animal drug approvals, and feed manufacturers were required to obtain a different license for medicated feeds.[44] The medicated feed application still treated the feed manufacturer as a drug manufacturer, but one that obtained its approval by automatic cross-reference to the published regulation codifying the drug approval conditions.[45] The new amendments also continued to assume that every feed manufacturer would obtain an approval for each drug used. Administratively, the requirement remained too demanding and was unnecessary from a public health standpoint.

FDA's first reform, therefore, was to grant "waivers of ministerial requirements" (i.e., waivers of the approval of medicated feed applications) to drugs that met tests of three years' use without major complaints, together with a wide margin of safety.[46] FDA also did not automatically require medicated feed applications for the use of drugs previously treated as old drugs.[47] Finally, an internal FDA study group recommended that the agency make

---

[39]   *1966 House Hearing, supra* note 38, at 28, 39-44; *1967 House Hearing, supra* note 38, at 46-53.
[40]   *See* FDCA § 507, 21 U.S.C. § 357; 21 C.F.R. § 144.25-26.
[41]   *See* FDCA § 409, 21 U.S.C. § 348; *see, e.g.,* 21 C.F.R. § 121.292 (erythromycin).
[42]   *1966 House Hearing, supra* note 38, at 40-41.
[43]   21 C.F.R. § 310.100.
[44]   *Compare* FDCA § 512(b)(1), 21 U.S.C. § 360b(b)(1), *with id.* § 512(m), 21 U.S.C. § 360b(m).
[45]   *See* FDCA § 512(m)(1)(B), 21 U.S.C. § 360b(m)(1)(B).
[46]   40 Fed. Reg. 58,132 (1975) (grant of ministerial waiver for lincomycin); 48 Fed. Reg. 34,574, 34,576-77 (1983) (discussion of practice in Second Generation tentative final rule).
[47]   48 Fed. Reg. at 34,576.

a fresh start and determine whether a medicated feed application would be required based on a single, readily understood criterion: whether the drug had a specified withdrawal period, which is the time between last feeding of the drug and when the animal may be slaughtered.[48] During this period, the drug would pass out of the animal's system to ensure that only a safe residue remained.

FDA called this new program the Second Generation of Medicated Feed Controls.[49] If no withdrawal time was required for the drug, the concentrated mixtures of the drug with other ingredients to facilitate mixing into feed (called "premixes" prior to the new regulation and now called "Type A Medicated Articles") could be sold by drug manufacturers directly to feed manufacturers (including farmers and ranchers mixing for their own animals) without the need for a medicated feed application, or sold to the feed producer complying with other drug requirements, such as plant registration and biennial federal inspection.[50] State officials would pick up the inspection of these facilities as part of their routine of feed mill inspections.

Where there was a withdrawal period requirement, the first purchaser of a premix was required to obtain an approved medicated feed application, and FDA undertook a rigorous preapproval inspection of the facility to ensure compliance with good manufacturing procedures that spelled out necessary quality control processes. Failing that inspection not only put a hold on the pending and subsequent medicated feed applications, but put all prior approvals at risk.[51] If the licensed feed mill diluted the premix sufficiently, subsequent purchasers were not required to obtain approved medicated feed applications.[52]

The Second Generation program had two interrelated goals.[53] The first was to reduce the number of registered mills that the agency had to inspect biennially that submitted medicated feed applications requiring FDA approval. This would permit FDA to concentrate on drugs deemed more likely to present a residue threat if improperly mixed. Second, those mills desiring not to undergo the more extensive inspection that licensing required were to shift to using drug mixtures where the potential for illegal residues from misuse was diminished, either by prior dilution by a licensed mill or the inherent greater margin of safety reflected in lack of any withdrawal period.

The FDA task force report was released in 1978. Rulemaking was undertaken in 1981, reproposed in 1983, revised late in that year and the final rule was issued in 1986, to be finally effective in 1987.[54] Despite an apparent statutory command that all medicated feeds be licensed, FDA created a class of medicated feeds that required no licensing. The Supreme Court has recognized FDA's unreviewable discretion in deciding when to enforce the act.[55]

---

48   *See* 43 Fed. Reg. 58,634 (1978) (announcing conclusions of the FDA Medicated Feed Task Force).

49   *See* 46 Fed. Reg. 2456 (1981).

50   21 C.F.R. § 558.3-4; *see* 51 Fed. Reg. 7382 (1986) (adoption of final rule).

51   51 Fed. Reg. at 7388.

52   21 C.F.R. § 558.3(b)(3)-(4).

53   46 Fed. Reg. at 2457; 48 Fed. Reg. at 34,581-82.

54   43 Fed. Reg. 58,634 (1978); 46 Fed. Reg. 2456 (1981); 48 Fed. Reg. 34,574 (1983); 48 Fed. Reg. 50,358 (1983); 51 Fed. Reg. 7382 (1986).

55   Heckler v. Chaney, 470 U.S. 821 (1985).

In effect, the Second Generation regulation codifies FDA's determination not to enforce the act with respect to certain medicated feeds.[56]

In the 1996 Animal Drug Availability Act (ADAA), the entire medicated feed application system was repealed, and replaced with a simpler system of licensing feed mills, on the basis of their compliance with good manufacturing practices, to mix medicated feeds.[57] The ADAA also implicitly endorses the "Second Generation" program by authorizing exemptions from feed mill licensing. Thus, FDA will be licensing only those mills first mixing animal drugs with withdrawal times into a feed form, i.e., those mills previously required to obtain approved medicated feed applications; mills performing subsequent dilutions or mixing drugs without withdrawal times will require no licenses, just as they required no approved applications.

Veterinary Drugs

Drugs used in animals have been regulated for as long as human drugs. Section 6 of the Pure Food and Drugs Act of 1906 defined the term "drug" to include "any substance or mixture of substances intended to be used for the cure, mitigation, or prevention of disease of either man or other animals."[58] The regulation of drugs at that time, however, was quite simple, and primarily addressed the prevention of adulteration and the use of adequate labeling to disclose the presence of habit-forming or potentially poisonous ingredients.

As in the case of human drugs, the FDCA considerably strengthened and broadened all of the public health provisions applicable to veterinary drugs. The term "drug" was still defined to include articles "intended for use in the diagnosis, cure, mitigation, treatment, or prevention of disease in man or other animals."[59] Veterinary drugs, as drugs, became subject to the general adulteration and misbranding provisions of the act, and also to the new drug provision of the act that required the licensing of veterinary products that were not GRAS for their labeled uses.[60] This statutory structure thus focused on the labeling of drugs and whether they were intended specifically for human or veterinary use.[61]

In the mid-1940s, Congress added a series of provisions to the act explicitly regulating five antibiotic drugs by requiring batch certification.[62] Again, as a result of the general definition of the term "drug," those antibiotics, when intended for veterinary use, were brought within

---

56   Two animal drug manufacturers challenged FDA's final regulation, urging that the rule in effect amended their licenses—the approved new animal drug applications they held—without the opportunity for a hearing ostensibly required by the FDCA. The U.S. Court of Appeals for the District of Columbia rejected the challenge, approving this use of rulemaking. Upjohn Co. v. FDA, 811 F.2d 1583 (D.C. Cir. 1987) (including appeal decision in *Hess & Clark, Inc. v. FDA*).

57   21 U.S.C. § 360b(m).

58   Ch. 3915, § 6, 34 Stat. at 769.

59   FDCA § 201(g)(1)(B), 21 U.S.C. § 321(g)(1)(B).

60   FDCA §§ 501, 502, 505; 21 U.S.C. §§ 351, 352, 355.

61   When a company developed a drug specifically for veterinary use, or separate veterinary uses for an existing drug, that drug was scrutinized by FDA as a separate entity under all of the provisions of the FDCA, including the "new drug" provision.

62   FDCA § 507, 21 U.S.C. § 357.

the new provisions. When the provisions were expanded in 1962 to encompass all antibiotic substances, the expansion was limited to drugs for human use.[63] When used for veterinary purposes, all antibiotic substances (other than the five specifically named in the act)[64] were regulated under the new drug provisions of the act.

Thus, prior to 1968, drugs for nonfood-producing animals fell within one of two regulatory schemes. If they were not one of the five aforementioned antibiotic drugs and were "new drugs," then they were regulated under section 505 of the act and were subject to the same standards as human-use drugs.[65] The five antibiotics, when prepared in dosage form for animal use, remained subject to batch certification requirements, like their human-use counterparts.

Under the 1962 Drug Amendments, the new efficacy requirement of the FDCA, including the requirement for adequate and well-controlled studies as proof of efficacy, became applicable to drugs for animal use.[66] Dosage-form animal drugs were subject to the same labeling requirements as human-use drugs and to the same requirements for compliance with current Good Manufacturing Practices (cGMPs).[67] FDA contracted with the National Academy of Sciences to set up a drug efficacy review program for animal drugs that was comparable in many ways to review for human-use drugs. The implementation, however, has not progressed in the same manner as with human-use drugs because FDA never implemented a formal abbreviated drug application program for animal drugs approved between 1938 and 1962 as it did for human drugs.[68] A series of footnotes scattered through the animal drug regulations identify those pre-1962 products for which FDA will accept abbreviated applications.[69]

The Animal Drug Amendments of 1968 consolidated the regulatory programs applicable to animal drugs.[70] In the case of drugs for nonfood-producing animals, only three changes were significant. First, the five named antibiotics became, by statutory definition, "new animal drugs"; the batch certification requirements were superimposed on the new drug requirements, rather than being set up as an alternative regulatory system.[71] Second, each approval had to appear in the *Federal Register* as a regulation identifying the drug, the applicant, and the intended conditions of use. Thus, information for human drugs found

---

[63]   Pub. L. No. 87-781, 76 Stat. 780, 785-87 (1962).

[64]   FDCA § 507, 21 U.S.C. § 357 (penicillin, streptomycin, chlortetracycline, chlortamphenicol, and bacitracin). FDA ended the routine requirement for the batch certification of "certifiable" human and veterinary antibiotics. 47 Fed. Reg. 39,155 (1982). The authority for the batch certification of the five named antibiotics as animal drugs was repealed as part of the Generic Animal Drug and Patent Term Restoration Act, Pub. L. No. 100-670, §§ 101(b), 107(a), 102 Stat. 3971, 3984 (1988).

[65]   21 U.S.C § 355. Included in the "new drug" category were all antibiotics for veterinary use that were excluded from the five-drug scope of section 507.

[66]   *See* Pub. L. No. 87-781, 76 Stat. at 781-94 (codified at 21 U.S.C. § 355).

[67]   *See* Pub. L. No. 87-781, 76 Stat. at 780, 785, 790-92, 795 (codified at 21 U.S.C. §§ 351(a)(2)(B); 352(e),(g),(l),(n),(o)); 21 C.F.R. pt. 211.

[68]   There was no counterpart in 21 C.F.R. pt. 514 to 21 C.F.R. § 314.55; *see* 21 C.F.R § 314.92-.99 for current abbreviated new drug application regulations implementing 21 U.S.C. § 355(j), added by the Drug Price Competition and Patent Term Restoration Act of 1984.

[69]   *See, e.g.*, 21 C.F.R. § 520.44 & n.1.

[70]   Pub. L. No. 90-399, 82 Stat. 342 (1968) (codified principally at 21 U.S.C. § 360b). The regulatory programs that were pulled together are described *infra* in this chapter dealing with food production drugs.

[71]   21 U.S.C. §§ 321(w)(3), 360b(n) (repealed, *see supra* note 63).

initially only in approved labeling was covered for veterinary drugs by a regulation codified in the *Code of Federal Regulations*.[72] Finally, the anticancer Delaney Clause became applicable to all animal drugs and not simply those incorporated into animal food.[73] Similarly, the DES Proviso, adopted in 1962 to permit the use of carcinogenic animal drugs such as diethylstilbestrol (DES) in the feed of food-producing animals on a "no found residue" basis,[74] also became applicable to all animal drugs. This negated the Delaney Clause for drugs having short-term therapeutic use in nonfood-producing animals; in the case of these animals, there was no "residue" in human food.[75]

Many of the other problems and issues that have been judicially and legislatively resolved for human drugs also exist for veterinary drugs. The Supreme Court decisions involving the transitional provisions of the FDCA,[76] the grandfather clause in the 1962 Drug Amendments,[77] and the definition of "new drug"[78] are equally applicable to animal drugs due to the virtually identical statutory language.[79] Indeed, some provisions, such as the transitional and grandfather provisions, deliberately were copied to preserve whatever rights might exist under those provisions rather than create a difference between human and animal drug regulation arising from the Drug Amendments of 1962.[80] Decisions on the scope of the definition of "new animal drug" were drawn on decisions involving the term "new drug" and thus buttressed FDA's ability to control drugs used in animals.[81]

There remain, however, important differences in the political background and pressures relating to, for example, the new drug/old drug issue. For veterinary drugs, there are no Medicare and Medicaid programs funding drug purchases to provide an incentive to produce new competitive products or to spur the government to seek to reduce the cost of funding animal drugs. As a result, FDA programs concerning veterinary drugs were not as straightforward in adopting the abbreviated new drug application for pre-1962 drugs that have been found effective,[82] nor did the "paper NDA" become a factor in the approval of post-1962 veterinary drugs.[83] Yet, for veterinary drugs, the presence of a published regulation affirming the safety and efficacy of a drug raised questions whether new competitors could avoid replicating the work of the original applicant or whether the published approval itself provided a basis for approving each subsequent applicant. Until 1988, when generic animal drug legislation mooted the issue, the courts answered these questions in the negative.[84]

---

[72]   21 U.S.C. § 360b(i). These regulations serve a function similar to food additive regulations in identifying drugs permitted to be used in animal feed. *See id.* § 360b(m)(1)(B). They serve no comparable function for other animal drugs.

[73]   *Compare id.* § 348(c)(3)(A) *with id.* § 360b(d)(1)(I).

[74]   Pub. L. No. 87-781, 76 Stat. at 785 (codified at 21 U.S.C. § 348(c)(3)(A)).

[75]   21 U.S.C. § 360b(d)(1)(I).

[76]   USV Pharmaceutical Corp. v. Weinberger, 412 U.S. 655 (1973); Weinberger v. Bentex Pharmaceuticals, Inc., 412 U.S. 645 (1973).

[77]   Weinberger v. Hynson, Wescott & Dunning, Inc., 412 U.S. 609 (1973).

[78]   United States. v. Generix Drug Corp., 460 U.S. 453 (1983).

[79]   *Compare* 21 U.S.C. § 321(p) *with id.* § 321(w).

[80]   *Compare* Pub. L. No. 87-781, § 107, 76 Stat. at 788, *with* Pub. L. No. 90-399, § 108, 82 Stat. at 353.

[81]   *See, e.g.,* Tri-Bio Lab. v. United States, 836 F.2d 135 (3d Cir. 1987).

[82]   *See* 21 C.F.R. § 314.55. There was no comparable new animal drug regulation.

[83]   *See* Upjohn Mfg. Co. v. Schweiker, 681 F.2d 480 (6th Cir. 1982), *aff'd,* 520 F. Supp. 58 (W.D. Mich. 1981).

[84]   *See* Tri-Bio Lab., 836 F.2d 135.

Animal drugs were omitted from the 1984 Drug Price Competition and Patent Term Restoration Act,[85] but that did not end FDA, competitive and congressional interests in legislative symmetry between human and animal drugs on the availability of abbreviated applications and patent term restoration. It was recognized, however, that there were important differences between the human drug and animal drug approval systems, with the human food safety requirements superimposed on the drug safety and efficacy requirements in the case of animal drugs. These differences gave an added dimension to the task of demonstrating generic equivalence without replicating food safety studies and to the regulatory burden (in time and money) undertaken by the pioneer drug sponsor to be "compensated" by patent term restoration.

Following unsuccessful efforts by Senator Orrin G. Hatch (R-Utah) and Congressman Henry A. Waxman (D-Cal.) (the principal sponsors of the 1984 legislation) in the 99th Congress,[86] Congressman Waxman[87] and Congressman Tauke[88] introduced bills in the 100th Congress to apply the abbreviated approval process and patent term restoration to animal drugs. A variety of issues that had been glossed over previously rose to the surface, and under the pressure of House action[89] and the impending congressional adjournment, various coalitions of companies sought to resolve problems involving the adequacy of patent protection for products produced using new biotechnology processes, the standards FDA was to apply in judging the safety of antibiotics that were not isolated from their fermentation mass, and the special protection, if any, to be given to recently approved products that might face immediate generic competition. The resulting revised bill passed the House in the waning days of the 100th Congress.[90] An identical bill was then introduced in the Senate, and in a single day, October 13, 1988, the bill passed in both the Senate and the House.[91]

The Generic Animal Drug and Patent Term Restoration (GADPTR) Act differs in a number of respects from the 1984 human drug legislation. The principal differences recognized the human food safety concerns inherent in using drugs in food-producing animals, as well as the greater expenditure of time normally required to obtain the initial approval of such drugs. This led to changes in both the FDA approval process for abbreviated applications as well as the availability of additional options for patent term restoration. In the case of the

---

[85]   Pub. L. No. 98-417, 98 Stat. 1585 (1984).

[86]   H.R. 5069, 99th Cong., 2d Sess. (1986); S. 2407, 99th Cong., 2d Sess. (1986); see *Animal Drug Amendments and Patent Term Restoration Act of 1986: Hearing on S. 2407 Before the Senate Labor and Human Resources Comm.*, 99th Cong., 2d Sess. 20-50 (1986); *Generic Animal Drugs: Hearing on H.R. 5069 Before the Subcomm. on Health and the Environment of the House Energy and Commerce Comm.*, 99th Cong., 2d Sess. 52-84 (1986).

[87]   *Drug Issues: Hearing on H.R. 3120 Before the Subcomm. on Health and the Environment of the House Energy and Commerce Comm.*, 100th Cong., 1st Sess. (1987).

[88]   H.R. 4714, 100th Cong., 2d Sess. (1988).

[89]   H.R. REP. No. 100-972, 100th Cong., 2d Sess. pt. 1 (1988); *Generic Animal Drug and Patent Term Restoration Act: Hearing on H.R. 4982 Before the Subcomm. on Courts, Civil Liberties, and the Administration of Justice of the House Judiciary Comm.*, 100th Cong., 2d Sess. (1988).

[90]   H.R. REP. No. 100-972, 100th Cong.. 2d Sess. pt. 2 (1988); 134 CONG. REC. H9779-87 (daily ed. Oct. 6, 1988). Biotechnology products were excluded from the scope of the legislation, see *infra* text accompanying note 94. FDA was authorized to request data beyond bioequivalence to establish safety and efficacy, see Pub. L. No. 100-670, § 101(c), 102 Stat. at 3976, 3980 (codified at 21 U.S.C. § 360b(c)(2)(A)(viii)(II)-(III), (H)), and no approvals of abbreviated applications were to be made effective prior to January 1, 1991, *id.* § 108, 102 Stat. at 3984.

[91]   S. 2843, 100th Cong., 2d Sess. (1988); see 134 CONG. REC. S15,730-01, S15,854-60, H10,252-59 (daily ed. Oct. 13, 1988).

approval process, for example, FDA was authorized to go beyond requiring bioavailability and bioequivalence data to demonstrate that a generic applicant's product was equivalent to the pioneer drug it was emulating.[92] Under the patent term restoration provisions, a company could choose between an initial companion animal approval and a subsequent food animal approval in seeking a patent term extension.[93]

There also was a total exclusion from both the generic approval process and the patent extension process of animal drugs produced by biotechnology.[94] This exclusion was to permit the biotechnology industry to demonstrate that patents in its area did not provide the same protection, and thus different incentives, as patents on chemically defined drugs. Finally, no abbreviated application would be approved prior to January 1, 1991, although these applications could be submitted any time after 60 days from enactment. The patent extension provisions became effective upon enactment.[95]

The GADPTR Act also contained a special provision dealing with the release of data on the safety and efficacy of drugs that are eligible for abbreviated applications; both the initial requester and any person to whom the data are transferred must submit verified statements to FDA that the data will not be used to market the drug outside the United States.[96] In addition, as discussed earlier, the GADPTR Act repealed provisions that provided authority for the (already obsolete) certification procedures for five named antibiotics; those animal drugs now were regulated with all other animal antibiotics, solely under the general provisions of section 512.[97]

Additionally, controls on the use of animal drugs were altered by the new act. Until its passage, there had been no parallel to section 503(b)[98] to set standards for "prescription" animal drugs. Rather, FDA successfully relied on its regulations exempting those drugs

---

[92]   FDCA section 512(c)(2)(H), as added by Pub. L. No. 100-670, § 101(c), 102 Stat. at 3980 (codified at 21 U.S.C. § 360b(c)(2)(H)), authorizes FDA to require (as scientific principles dictate) bioequivalence studies in each species for which the drug is approved, tissue residue studies in each such species, "or such other data or studies as (FDA) considers appropriate based on scientific principles." *Id.*

[93]   Under the 1984 human drug legislation, patent term restoration had to be sought, if at all, at the time of the first approval for the use of the drug. 35 U.S.C. § 156(a)(5)(A) (1994). In contrast, under the 1988 legislation, the new animal drug applicant can proceed at the time of first approval or, if that approval is for use with nonfood-producing animals, the applicant can wait until the first approval for use in food-producing animals. Pub. L. No. 100-670, § 201(a), 102 Stat. at 3984-85 (codified at 35 U.S.C. § 156(a)(5) (C)). This should grant a longer extension for the more important use in food-producing animals, although coverage of use in nonfood-producing animals ends on the original expiration date of the patent.

[94]   Pub. L. No. 100-670, §§ 106, 201(g), 102 Stat. at 3984, 3987 (codified at 35 U.S.C. § 156(f)(2)(B)). Similarly, the statutory provision that permits a nonpatent-holder to use a patented drug solely in pursuit of federal marketing approval was extended to all animal drugs except those produced by biotechnology, *id.* § 201(i), 102 Stat. at 3988 (codified at 35 U.S.C. § 271(e)(l)), thus reversing Roche Products, Inc. v. Bolar Pharmaceuticals Co., 733 F.2d 858 (Fed. Cir. 1984).

[95]   Pub. L. No. 100-670, § 108, 102 Stat. at 3984; in contrast to the rush for approvals for generic human drugs, it was not until more than a year after the 1991 date that FDA approved the first animal generic drug. *See* 57 Fed. Reg. 26,604 (1992) (codifying in 21 C.F.R. § 520.1484, the May 15, 1992, approval of Pfizer's abbreviated application). Even at the end of 1991, almost a year after the permitted first approval date, FDA reported that only 30 abbreviated applications were under review (and none had been approved). *Lack of Generic Approvals Blamed on Tougher Requirements*, FOOD CHEM. NEWS, Dec. 16, 1991, at 53-55.

[96]   FDCA § 512(p), 21 U.S.C. § 360b(p) (as added by Pub. L. No. § 104, 102 Stat. at 3982-83). The comparable human drug provision enacted in 1984, 21 U.S.C. § 355(l), contains no such requirement.

[97]   *See supra* note 64.

[98]   21 U.S.C. § 353(b).

for which directions for safe and effective lay use could not be written from the statutory requirement for "adequate directions for use;"[99] the effect was to limit such drugs "to use by or on the order of a licensed veterinarian."[100] The GADPTR Act codified FDA practice in a new statutory provision that draws, as is the case with human drugs, an obvious line between those drugs limited to use by or on the order of a veterinarian, and those available without such an order.[101] Even under the codification, the variety of products available over-the-counter (OTC) will continue to be broader in the case of veterinary drugs than in the case of human drugs because the expertise of ranchers, farmers, and other animal husbandry professionals permits drugs to be used safely in the care of animals in ways that are not permitted for human OTC drugs.[102]

Another aspect of veterinary drug controls that differs from human drug controls arises from the somewhat different statutory base for imposing sanctions for the illegal movement of new animal drugs, and thus the different statutory prohibitions attending the misuse of human and animal drugs. Under section 505(a) of the act, it is directly illegal only to introduce an unapproved new drug into interstate commerce.[103] FDA acknowledges that a physician may choose to use a drug based on the physician's judgment of the patient's best interests. Thus, drugs may be used by physicians outside of the scope of approved new drug indications or other limitations on the uses that can be promoted by the new drug sponsor.[104] When FDA finds that a physician is promoting drugs for novel uses, the agency must resort to declaring the drugs to be misbranded because of a lack of adequate directions for those uses to challenge the physician's actions.[105] This approach is codified in FDA regulations, rather than in the act.[106]

In the case of new animal drugs, however, the statutory scheme differs. An unapproved new animal drug is "unsafe," and thus deemed adulterated,[107] and its use adulterates the food

---

[99]   FDCA § 502(f)(1), 21 U.S.C. § 352(f)(1); see United States v. Colahan, 635 F.2d 564 (6th Cir. 1980), cert. denied, 454 U.S. 831 (1981).

[100] 21 C.F.R. § 201.105(b)(l). Partly as a result of the limitation of the preexisting prescription drug provision, 21 U.S.C. § 353(b), to drugs for human use, it is unclear whether the other statutory references to "prescription drugs," such as 21 U.S.C. § 352(n), encompass veterinary drugs; this was not resolved in the adoption of the new provision for animal drugs. See H.R. REP. No. 100-972 (pt. 1), supra note 89, at 8.

[101] Pub. L. No. 100-670, § 105, 102 Stat. at 3983-84 (codified at 21 U.S.C. § 353(f)); although the act states that the new provision is paragraph (c) to section 503, Congress shortly before had passed the Prescription Drug Marketing Act, Pub. L. No. 100-293, 102 Stat. 95 (1988), which added sections 503(c)-(e) to the basic act, so that the veterinary prescription provision had to be treated as paragraph (f). A technical correction to conform the citation was contained in Pub. L. No. 102-108, § 2(d)(3), 105 Stat. 549, 550 (1991).

[102] See discussion text accompanying notes 186-91, infra (concerning the application of the "veterinary prescription drug" standard and the problems posed by the desire to control the use of certain new products).

[103] 21 U.S.C. § 355(a); this is a prohibited act under section 331(d). Because this violation is neither misbranding nor adulteration, "new drugs" do not come within the scope of the export exemption (id. § 381(d)(l)); to maintain symmetry, unapproved new animal drugs were barred from export in the New Animal Drug Amendments, id. Section 802 (id. § 382) authorizes limited administrative grants of export rights for unapproved new drugs and new animal drugs that remain relevant for animal drugs despite the 1996 export amendment. See text at notes 221-22, infra.

[104] 37 Fed. Reg. 16,503 (1972); although never issued as a regulation, this proposal is an advisory opinion binding on FDA, 21 C.F.R. § 10.85(d)(1).

[105] United States v. Evers, 453 F. Supp. 1141 (M.D. Ala. 1978).

[106] See 21 C.F.R. § 201.115.

[107] 21 U.S.C. §§ 351(a)(5), 360b(a)(1).

derived from the treated animal (or even the animal itself).[108] FDA can take action against such "adulteration" at any point in the chain of distribution of the drug or the animal.[109] Prior to the Animal Drug Amendments of 1968, veterinarians routinely used drugs in their practice that had been developed and were offered for human use, and used animal drugs in ways not provided for in the drugs' labeling.

Over the years, FDA did not take exception to this approach to veterinary medicine. The Animal Drug Amendments, however, borrowing from a Food Additives Amendment provision, required that a drug "and [its] use conform" to its FDA approval,[110] thus creating a legal dichotomy between veterinary and human medicine practice. While FDA continued to condone the availability of human drugs in veterinary medicine as long as veterinarians took responsibility for the decision to use these agents,[111] in recent years, the agency has taken the position that the statutory admonition applies directly to veterinarians treating food-producing animals, unless the veterinarian meets a series of tests designed to give an assurance that an "extra-label use" will not result in unsafe residues in meat, milk, or eggs.[112] The requirements include establishing what the American Veterinary Medical Association refers to as a valid veterinarian-client-patient relationship (requiring actual and continued attendance to the animal), determining that the unapproved usage is medically necessary, and ensuring that a prolonged withdrawal time is observed to protect against residues.

The ostensible illegality of extra-label drug use, even in companion and exotic animals where there were limited approvals, and the risk of per se malpractice exposure from "violating" the act sparked concern among veterinarians. This led to the passage of the Animal Medicinal Drug Use Clarification Act of 1994,[113] which largely established the lawfulness of the practices FDA permitted under existing policies[114] but also provided FDA with new authority, when justified by safety concerns, to inspect veterinarian records of extra-label drug use.[115] Thus, the 1994 amendments leave veterinarians regulated differently under the food and drug act than physicians in their respective practices.

The availability of veterinary drugs remains in a state of tension. While the passage of the Animal Medicinal Drug Use Clarification Act largely eliminated the constraints imposed by the Animal Drug Amendments, veterinarians still must vie for clientele with knowledgeable laymen who have considerable experience in animal husbandry, and for whom adequate

---

[108]   *See* United States v. Jacobs, Food Drug Cosm. L. Rep. (CCH) ¶ 38,113 (E.D. Cal. 1989).

[109]   21 U.S.C. § 331(k).

[110]   *Id.* 1360b(a)(I)(B); *see* United States v. Gordon A. Riley, Inc., Civ. No. C86-5086 (N.D. Ohio Jan. 23, 1987), FDA CONSUMER, Apr. 1989, at 43; *see* 21 U.S.C. § 348(a)(2); *see also* Eugene I. Lambert, *Federal Laws Relating to New Animal Drugs*, 161 JAVMA 1376 (1972).

[111]   *See* FOOD & DRUG ADMIN., COMPLIANCE POLICY GUIDE No. 7125.35 (Mar. 19, 1991); FOOD & DRUG ADMIN., COMPLIANCE POLICY GUIDES MANUAL, *supra* note 28, § 608.100; *see also* FOOD & DRUG ADMIN., COMPLIANCE POLICY GUIDE No. 7125.05 (July 1, 1982); FOOD & DRUG ADMIN., COMPLIANCE POLICY GUIDES MANUAL, *supra* note 28, § 615.300.

[112]   FOOD & DRUG ADMIN., COMPLIANCE POLICY GUIDE No. 7125.06 (Mar. 8, 1984); FOOD & DRUG ADMIN., COMPLIANCE POLICY GUIDES MANUAL, *supra* note 28, § 608.100 (1995) (revised). FDA's position became increasingly strict in part due to congressional criticism in light of the statutory prohibition on extra-label use, *see, e.g., Hearings on the Regulation of Animal Drugs by the Food and Drug Administration Before a Subcomm. of the House Comm. on Government Operations*, 99th Cong., 1st Sess. 221-75 (1985).

[113]   Pub. L. No. 103-396, 108 Stat. 4153 (1994) (principally codified as 21 U.S.C. § 1360b(a)(4)-(5)).

[114]   *See supra* notes 110-11.

[115]   21 U.S.C. § 360b(a)(4)(D).

directions for use can be written for a wide variety of drugs. It can be expected that, as food animal production becomes more professional and integrated, there will be increasing tension over the right of animal care professionals who are not veterinarians to make therapeutic drug choices. This is rarely an issue in small animal practice, where a veterinarian stands in much the same relationship to the owner of a dog or cat as a physician dealing with a parent of an ill child. Even in the case of nonfood-producing animals, however, dog breeders and horse trainers are knowledgeable concerning animal diseases, their signs and symptoms, and their appropriate treatment, in a way that consumers simply are not with respect to most human diseases.

Another area of constant confrontation between FDA and regulated industry involves the standard of proof of safety and efficacy. The ADAA made two changes with respect to the efficacy standard. First, the ADAA redefines the term "substantial evidence" that is the basis for evaluating whether a new animal drug has been shown to be effective. Previously, substantial evidence had been defined as consisting of "adequate and well-controlled studies, including field investigation . . . ."[116] The ADAA changes that to "one or more adequate and well-controlled studies, such as—(A) a study in a target species; (B) a study in laboratory animals; (C) any field investigation that may be required under this section . . .; (D) a bioequivalence study; or (E) an in vitro study . . . ." No longer are two studies, one of which must be a field investigation, required; in theory (although unlikely in practice), one laboratory animal study, which could be in the target species, could suffice.

Second, the ADAA sets up a separate set of criteria for evaluating the safety and efficacy of combinations of two or more previously approved animal drugs.[117] These criteria apply both to dosage form combinations and to combinations mixed into feed or water. Because each of the drugs already have been approved separately as safe and effective for their individual use, the new criteria focus solely on the issues that are applicable to their use in combination, such as interfering with assay methods, altering residue patterns, contributing to total efficacy (where the indications for each of the drugs are the same), or providing appropriate concurrent therapy (where the indications differ). In deference to the concerns that continue to be raised about the use of antibacterial drugs in animals, the new rules do not apply to dosage form combinations of nontopical antibacterials, and add additional criteria to feed and water combinations containing more than one antibacterial drug.

Unlike the statutory standard of proof of efficacy that requires that there be adequate and well-controlled studies, the standard with respect to safety simply requires "all . . . reasonably applicable" studies.[118] This formulation leaves greater discretion in FDA's hands and thus also means that there is a greater likelihood of conflict between FDA and industry. FDA, responding in part to a decision pointing out the difficulties posed by the lack of agreement regarding standards, has announced its intention to articulate its standards for proof of safety.[119]

---

[116] *Id.* § 360b(d)(3).
[117] *Id.* § 360b(d)(4).
[118] *Compare id.* § 360b(d)(3) *with id.* § 360b(d)(1)(A).
[119] American Cyanamid Co. v. FDA, 606 F.2d 1307 (D.C. Cir. 1979).

Originally, the statutory standard for efficacy was elaborated in detail for new drugs and then directly applied to new animal drugs.[120] In many instances, however, this standard fails to take into account the difference between the physician-patient relationship and the veterinarian-herd relationship, particularly for food-producing animals. In the former case, a single individual's welfare is paramount; in the latter, the predominant concern is obtaining the best overall performance from the herd, not a particular animal.[121]

Another issue that Congress addressed legislatively in the early 2000s was the lack of approved drugs for "minor species"—i.e., animals other than dogs, cats, horses, cows, pigs, chickens, and turkeys—and for limited or "minor" uses. These drugs, like orphan drugs for humans, provided a very limited return on investment, making it impractical to expect animal pharmaceutical companies to conduct the trials and absorb the other significant costs inherent in securing a drug approval. The Minor Use and Minor Species Act of 2004 (MUMS) provided two mechanisms to make it easier and more cost effective for sponsors of such drugs to obtain FDA sanction of their products. The first mechanism, called "conditional approval" provided that a product for a minor species or minor use could be "conditionally approved" for periods of one year, up to a maximum of five years upon a showing that the drug is safe and that there is a reasonable expectation that the drug will have the effect it purports or is represented to have under the conditions of use prescribed, recommended, or suggested in the proposed labeling. The product could then be marketed while the sponsor performed whatever work was necessary to complete the application process. At the end of five years, the sponsor is supposed to have completed the application process. Under the "conditional approval" system, the sponsor must still obtain a regular new animal drug application (NADA) approval, but the product can be marketed during this process to recoup some of the costs incurred.

The other procedure established by MUMS whereby a sponsor can have its drugs "sanctioned" by FDA is the "indexing" process. The index is a list of drugs for use in minor species or in the non-food life stages of major species. Indexed drugs are not "approved," but are instead accepted for indexing by FDA and are then legal to sell for the purpose listed in the index. Under this process, a sponsor first seeks FDA concurrence that a drug is eligible for indexing. If FDA agrees, the sponsor empanels three or more experts to opine on whether the drug is expected to be safe and effective for a particular minor use or for use in a minor species. The experts compile a report reflecting their opinion of the safety and efficacy of the drug for the proposed use and the report is submitted to FDA. If FDA accepts the report, then the drug is entered on the index and is legal to sell for the listed conditions of use. The MUMS law also provides for exclusivity periods for approved drugs for minor uses or minor species.

Even several years after MUMS approval, CVM acknowledged that there were a number of veterinary drugs on the market that were neither approved nor subject to an alternative oversight route, such as MUMS indexing. In 2010, CVM published a *Federal Register* notice requesting comments on alternative means for increasing the number of marketed animal

---

[120]   *Compare* 21 C.F.R. § 314.126(b) *with id.* § 514.111(a)(5)(ii).
[121]   Some of these issues are addressed in the Animal Drug Availability Act of 1995, S. 773, 104th Cong., 1st Sess. (1995), and its counterpart in the House, H.R. 2508, 104th Cong., 1st Sess. (1995).

drugs having legal marketing status.[122] FDA explained that it was concerned that the safety and effectiveness of such products has not been demonstrated, although it recognized that the continued availability of many of these products was important to address animals' health needs. The comment period ended in 2011 and, as of the time of this writing, FDA has not yet published any proposals as a result of its comment solicitation.

Industry is concerned not only with the standards for approval of new animal drugs, but also with the process the agency follows and the time required to navigate the process. To address the time lag in the review of pioneering new animal drugs, CVM developed the "phased review" system. Under this system, most or essentially all parts of the NADA are submitted for CVM review while the application is still in the investigational new animal drug (INAD) phase. A sponsor can complete and submit for FDA review various required sections of the NADA, such as the Chemistry, Manufacturing and Controls section or the Target Animal Safety section, before the remaining sections are completed. That way, CVM can be reviewing these sections as they are submitted. When all of the sections have been submitted and accepted by CVM, the sponsor need only file the remaining formal parts of the application and, after 2003, pay the application fee, as discussed below.

Although the phased review process can speed up review of a particular application to some extent, there were growing delays in the review of NADAs in the late 1990s and early 2000s. In response to delays in the review of human drugs, the human pharmaceutical industry acquiesced to the imposition of application fees dedicated to the review process in return for process improvement goals that, if not met, could lead to the repeal of the fees.[123] The Prescription Drug User Fee Act (PDUFA) was originally enacted in 1992 and has been reauthorized several times since. User fees for animal drugs were established for the first time by the Animal Drug User Fee Act of 2003 (ADUFA). The animal pharmaceutical industry was generally in favor of the imposition of these fees because they provide funds for CVM to hire additional, much-needed reviewers to review pending NADAs and because they establish a response time that CVM is required to meet in the review of such applications.

ADUFA set the same types of fees PDUFA did; i.e., application, establishment, and product fees. Because of the "phased submission" process for NADAs described above, whereby a sponsor could file and FDA was obligated to review most of the NADA sections while the product was still in the INAD phase and the sponsor thus would not be obliged to pay an application fee until CVM has performed a majority of the necessary work on the application, ADUFA also established a sponsor fee payable by any sponsor of an active INAD or a pending or approved NADA. The sponsor fee is a set annual payment that is the same for all sponsors regardless of how many applications they have. A sponsor can, however, seek reduction or waiver of the fees on various bases.

Besides the existence of a sponsor fee, there are two other key differences between the PDUFA and ADUFA fees. First, PDUFA fees apply only to prescription human drugs, while

---

[122]   75 Fed. Reg. 79,383 (Dec. 20, 2010).

[123]   Prescription Drug User Fee Act, Pub. L. No. 102-571, 106 Stat. 4491 (1992) (principally codified in 21 U.S.C. § 379g-h). The process improvement commitment is referred to in the congressional findings, *id.* § 102(3), 106 Stat. at 4491 (codified at 21 U.S.C. § 379g note). The "sunset" provision is section 105, 106 Stat. at 4498 (codified at 21 U.S.C. § 379g note).

ADUFA fees apply to both veterinary prescription and OTC drugs. Secondly, because the return on investment is frequently much lower for animal drugs, the ADUFA fees are much lower than the corresponding PDUFA fees.

In the first reauthorization of ADUFA in 2008, in addition to reauthorizing the fees associated with pioneer drugs, an Animal Generic Drug User Fee Act was passed. Unlike on the human side, where generic drugs have not been subject to user fees, the generic animal drug industry saw the benefit of additional funding for the review process. Generic drug applicants may be subject to an application fee, a product maintenance fee, or a sponsor fee. FDA is still working out the details of the fee system, which (like the pioneer system) is dependent on congressional appropriations covering the anticipated fee income. As with pioneer applicants, there is an exemption from fees for products covered by the MUMS Act. Both ADUFA and AGDUFA were reauthorized in 2013 and will sunset in 2018 unless reauthorized again.

In summary, the regulation of veterinary drugs used to treat nonfood-producing animals has posed essentially the same issues as the regulation of human drugs. For example, prior to 1988 there were old drug/new drug issues and issues of handling both pre-1962 and post-1962 approvals without complete applications that include clinical trial experience. The resolution of some of these matters in the GADPTR Act depended on the normal array of political forces; unlike the situation with human drugs, there was no need to seek a resolution consistent with other social programs (although there was pressure for statutory symmetry). User fee legislation applied more broadly to "prescription" and nonprescription products, and now to generic animal drugs. Another "twist" of added regulation involves veterinary medical practitioners who, due to the congressional concern over unsafe drug residues in the food supply, are subject to statutory intrusions inapplicable to physicians.

Food Production Drugs

FDA's regulation of animal drugs whose principal utility is promoting more efficient food production by treated animals presents all of the issues involved in human food safety.[124] The influx of human food safety issues into animal drug regulation largely has been due to developments in analytical chemistry. Where once it might have been possible to detect a fraction of one percent of a compound fed to an animal that remained in the muscle, eggs, or milk to be used as human food, it is now possible to trace animal drugs in the food supply in parts per billion and, in some cases, even fractions of a part per trillion. This sudden increase in sophistication of analytical techniques, coupled with changes in law, has shifted the burden of proof of safety from the government to the applicant, and posed serious questions of human food safety and food safety theory.

Animal drugs used in increasing food animal production generally are administered in the feed of the animal, in contrast with most veterinary drugs, which are administered in a specific dosage form (such as a syringe). Animal production drugs usually are sold by

---

[124]   "More efficient production" means that animals grow to market weight faster and require less food for each pound of weight gain.

the drug manufacturer in a very concentrated form that must be substantially diluted with regular feed to be safely administered. Dilution may be done by the feeder, or one or more dilutions may be done by feed mills selling medicated feeds to end users.[125]

Under the FDCA, if one could detect an animal drug residue in meat, milk, or eggs, the basic test was whether or not the residue was a "poisonous or deleterious substance" that might render the food "injurious to health."[126] Even under the construction of the language in *Lexington Mills,* requiring only a reasonable possibility of harm, the burden nonetheless remained on the government to establish the reasonable possibility of injury based on the residue found.[127] In theory, FDA could create certainty or limit unsafe practices by using section 406 of the FDCA, under which the agency was able to establish a tolerance for such residues using elaborate rulemaking procedures on the record.[128] This mechanism was not used in the early development of animal drugs and with the development of other statutory provisions proved to be unnecessary.[129]

The first major animal drugs for food production were antibiotics specifically regulated under section 507 of the FDCA.[130] It was found that when certain antibiotics were fed to animals at levels below those effective to combat specific diseases, many of these drugs, for reasons not wholly understood, improved food production.[131] FDA, through the procedure of exempting such drugs from certification requirements, established requirements for their use in food-producing animals.[132] Some of these uses antedated the passage of the Food Additives Amendment of 1958, and thus were covered by a "prior sanction" under section 201(s)(4) of the FDCA.[133]

The passage of the Food Additives Amendment of 1958 was a major turning point in FDA's regulation of food production drugs.[134] Because most of these drugs were administered to animals through their feed, they fell within the ambit of the amendment in a dual fashion. First, the drugs became direct food additives by being added to the animal feed.[135] Second, FDA asserted jurisdiction over the potential drug residues in edible material (i.e., food for human consumption) so that the agency controlled the indirect or consequential additive effects.[136] Moreover, the Food Additives Amendment contained the anticancer Delaney Clause, which in its original form precluded the approval of an animal production drug that

---

[125] See *supra* text accompanying notes 38-57; 21 C.F.R. § 558.3(b)(4).

[126] FDCA § 402(a)(1), 21 U.S.C. § 342(a)(1).

[127] United States v. Lexington Mill & Elevator Co., 232 U.S. 399 (1914) (interpreting the same language in section 7 of the Pure Food and Drugs Act of 1906, 34 Stat. at 770).

[128] 21 U.S.C. § 346; *see id.* § 371(e). A residue is "unavoidable" when the lawful use of an article (such as a pesticide approved under the pesticide law or a drug approved under the new drug provision) leaves a detectable amount in food, thus violating 21 U.S.C. § 342(a)(2)(A) in the absence of a regulation under section 406.

[129] Originally expected to be applied to pesticides, even this use was superseded by section 408. *See id.* § 346a.

[130] *Id.* § 357.

[131] National Research Council, The Effects of Human Health on Subtherapeutic Use of Antimicrobials in Animal Feed, 319-76 (1980).

[132] *See generally* 21 C.F.R. §§ 510.5, 558.15.

[133] 21 U.S.C. § 321(s)(4).

[134] Pub. L. No. 85-929, 72 Stat. 1784 (1958) (principally codified at 21 U.S.C. §§ 321(s), 348).

[135] 21 U.S.C. § 321(s) ("the intended use . . . results . . . in its becoming a component . . . of any food").

[136] *Id.* § 321(s) ("the intended use . . . may reasonably be expected to result . . . indirectly, in its becoming a component . . . of any food.").

was a food additive if it were found to induce cancer in experimental animals.[137] This bar existed even if the drug could not conceivably cause harm to the animal during its life span, and if no residues of toxicological concern could be found in the resulting edible tissue.

Both the route of administration of a drug and the date of its initial approval became important factors in determining the controls FDA could exercise under the amendment, the end result being significant anomalies in the regulation of animal drug products. Drugs that were not administered through feed, such as implants, did not overtly fall under the Food Additives Amendment; FDA had to assess the potential for residues to see if the drug met the statutory test for food additives (i.e., whether residues were reasonably expected to be present).[138] Conversely, an animal drug added to feed was immediately a potential food additive without regard to whether residues reasonably might be expected to occur.[139] Thus, diethylstilbestrol (DES) in the form of implants raised the question of whether residues reasonably might be expected to occur in animal tissues, while DES administered through feed was a direct food additive. Once FDA asserted that DES caused cancer in various animal species, it was important to determine whether or not DES was a food additive. The answer varied depending on whether the DES was in the form of an implant (no) or in feed (yes); and, in the latter case, whether the drug had been approved prior to 1958 so that it had a "prior sanction" and thus exempt from food additive controls (no), or was proposed for marketing after that date (yes).

Animal drugs in feed were subject to controls for safety under both the new drug and food additive provisions of the FDCA; such drugs also were subject to an efficacy review even before the passage of the Drug Amendments of 1962. The controls occurred under the food additive provision requiring proof that no greater quantity of the drug was proposed for use than was necessary to achieve its intended effect; this required evidence that the drug actually had its intended (claimed) effect.[140] Moreover, in the time between passage of the Food Additives Amendment and the Animal Drug Amendments, the practical controls were exercised by three different organizations within FDA: the Bureau of Medicine (drug approvals), the Bureau of Scientific Standards (food additive approvals), and the Antibiotic Certification Staff (antibiotic combinations with nonantibiotic drugs).

During hearings on what were to become the Drug Amendments of 1962, the animal drug industry complained about the multiple layers of control to which animal drugs were subject and the conflicts between various bureaus of FDA.[141] As noted earlier, FDA took the position that the drug to be approved was the drug-containing feed, rather than the more concentrated mixture made by the drug manufacturer. Thus, the drug manufacturer often did not obtain the actual drug approval; rather, approval was granted to the feed manufacturer based on data (called a "master file") supplied to FDA by the drug manufacturer. The case was different, however, when the drug was an implant produced in final form by the drug manufacturer. For antibiotics, approval took the form of an exemption from certification coupled with an

---

[137]   *Id.* § 348(c)(3)(A).

[138]   *See supra* note 136.

[139]   *See supra* note 135.

[140]   21 U.S.C. § 348(c)(4); FDA required proof that no more was being used than produced the desired production increase.

[141]   *Hearings on H.R. 11581 Before the House Comm. on Interstate and Foreign Commerce,* 87th Cong., 2d Sess. 388-413 (1962) (statement of D. L. Bruner, Animal Health Inst.).

application for manufacturing rights that only required meeting a regulatory standard of purity instead of proof of either safety or efficacy.

In 1962, these industry complaints led to a six-year effort to coalesce the food additive, new drug, and antibiotic provisions of the FDCA into a single approval system for new animal drugs, culminating in the passage of the Animal Drug Amendments of 1968.[142] Built into this approval system was the Delaney Clause of 1958,[143] as well as an exception adopted as part of the Drug Amendments of 1962 known as the DES Proviso, named after diethylstilbestrol, which was used in the course of the 1962 enactment as an example of how the exception would work.[144] The 1962 Proviso permits the approval of a cancer-causing food additive if it will not harm the food-producing animal to which it is fed, and if "no residues [of the additive]…will be found" in edible tissues when tested by a method approved by FDA. The 1968 version applied both the Delaney Clause and the DES Proviso to all animal drugs, including those in feed and other dosage forms.

Similarly, in creating the remaining new animal drug provisions rather than starting anew, Congress searched each of the existing statutory provisions for the relevant controls on safety and efficacy, and melded these into a single statutory section. The new drug provisions of the FDCA contributed the requirement that all reasonably applicable test methods be used to determine safety, as well as the standard of adequate and well-controlled studies to provide "substantial evidence" of effectiveness.[145] The food additive provisions of the FDCA contributed the requirement that drugs only be used in conformity with their approvals, as well as the explicit recognition of safety factors and the presence of the modified Delaney Clause.[146] The antibiotic provisions contributed the requirement (now repealed) for batch certification of five named antibiotics (as a practical matter only applied to dosage form animal drugs and not to those antibiotics when used in animal feed).[147] The transitional provisions of the Animal Drug Amendments specifically provided that all antecedent approvals, even those in the form of master files that were not subject to specific approval, were deemed to be new animal drug approvals carrying with them all the protections of the FDCA.[148]

At the same time, the provisions caused a major change in the relationship between drugs used in feed and feed itself. It was made clear that the more stringent controls were to be applied directly to the manufacturer of a concentrated form of drug to be mixed into feed.[149] The feed manufacturers were to obtain their own licenses after demonstrating their capability to properly mix the concentrated products into animal feed.[150] It was made an act of adulteration to ship a drug intended for feed use to anyone other than a wholesaler or a

---

[142]   Pub. L. No. 90-399, 82 Stat. 342 (1968) (principally codified at 21 U.S.C. §§ 321(w),(x); 360b).

[143]   *See* 21 U.S.C. §§ 348(c)(3)(A), 360b(d)(1)(I).

[144]   Pub. L. No. 87-781, § 104(f), 76 Stat. at 785.

[145]   *Compare* 21 U.S.C. § 355(c),(d)(1), *with id.* § 360b(d)(1)(A),(3).

[146]   *Compare id.* § 348(a),(c)(5), *with id.* § 360b(a)(1),(d)(2).

[147]   *Compare id.* § 357 *with id.* § 360b(n).

[148]   Pub. L. No. 90-399, § 108, 82 Stat. at 353; the principal protection is the right to notice and an opportunity for an evidentiary hearing prior to withdrawal of approval. 21 U.S.C. § 360b(e).

[149]   21 U.S.C. § 360b(b).

[150]   *Id.* § 360b(m).

person holding a medicated feed approval.[151] Thus, animal food manufacturers became the only users of food additives that had to be licensed to use additives.

Just as veterinary drugs used in nonfood-producing animals recapitulate all of the issues presented in the regulation of drugs for human use, food production animal drugs present all of the issues in the human food safety debate, plus a number of problems unique to the regulation of drugs administered through food that may become a part of another food.

Production drugs are administered to animals to achieve specific metabolic or other changes in the animals. Thus, they are active metabolic compounds that can be expected to undergo changes within the animal's body and are excreted unchanged in a limited number of instances. The safety testing of these compounds raises issues concerning metabolic pathways, metabolic inactivation, and the reactivity of compounds when passed through a second species (i.e., when humans eat the original recipient species or its edible products).

This two-phase edible route creates problems in designing testing protocols. When direct food additives are tested in nonhuman species, the rationale for giving very large doses is to challenge the test animal that is the surrogate for humans, and compensate for interspecies differences and the inadequate sample population of most test systems as compared to the exposure of the entire human population. For animal drugs, where a biological "filter" of consumption by the edible animal is involved, the use of high-dose levels in laboratory animals affects the proper interpretation of results by altering the metabolic pathways of excretion and the pattern of metabolites, both in kind and in distribution. Thus, even more complex and controversial issues exist in safety testing of animal drugs than in the case of additives directly ingested by humans.

Animal drugs also implicate the unique issues of the DES exception to the Delaney Clause.[152] FDA consistently has interpreted the exception as a "no found residue" requirement instead of a "no residue" requirement.[153] This raises the question of how hard residues should be looked for (i.e., the required level of sensitivity of the methodology used to detect the presence of a residue of the drug, whether the original compound or some metabolite). In the early years, FDA used a rule of thumb of two parts per billion as being an insignificant level from the standpoint of potential carcinogenic risk. This was the sensitivity of the original bioassay for DES, and was also the sensitivity of the test method for carcinogenic components applied by FDA to petroleum-derived direct food additives.[154] Both the march of technology and increasing knowledge concerning various mechanisms of carcinogenesis made continued adherence to this approach untenable.

This "fixed level" approach was discarded by FDA, both in the regulation of food packaging migrants and in the regulation of animal drugs; yet, only in the case of animal drugs has there been a final regulatory explanation of the agency's policy. FDA proposed the adoption

---

[151]   *Id.* § 360b(a)(1).

[152]   *Id.* § 360b(d)(1)(I) (patterned after *id.* § 348(c)(3)(A)).

[153]   The history of FDA's interpretation of the Delaney Clause and the DES Proviso is summarized in FDA's 1979 proposal to establish procedures for implementing the statute. 44 Fed. Reg. 17,070 (1979); *see also* Hess & Clark v. FDA, 495 F.2d 975.

[154]   *See, e.g.,* 21 C.F.R. § 172.886 (petroleum wax).

of a test scheme under which animal test data would be projected to a "virtually safe" dose, and a residue monitoring system would be required to detect any residues present in excess of that allowable level.[155] In theory the system, known as SOM (sensitivity of [test] method), was simple and elegant. In practice, it has been difficult to articulate and implement.[156] Problems have arisen both in concept and in practical application.

The conceptual issue is that the Delaney Clause, and the DES exception, only apply to a drug that FDA "finds…induces cancer."[157] At what point is a drug found to induce cancer, and thus subject to the Delaney Clause and within the boundaries of the DES Proviso? FDA has attempted a series of guidelines on this issue—called "Threshold Assessment"— that rely less on demonstrated proof of carcinogenicity and more on the risk of unknown exposure to cancer.[158] Depending on whether the drug structurally is related to compounds believed to be of carcinogenic concern and the level at which the drug is to be administered to animals, the drug is put through a series of tests that escalate in duration and expense; a drug to be administered routinely in feed will be required to undergo lifetime feeding trials in rodents as the ultimate test of carcinogenic potential regardless of earlier testing that may or may not have suggested a carcinogenic concern.

The question first posed—"how hard does one search for residues?"—is not so much a scientific issue as one of judgment reflecting societal acceptance. What is determined is the degree of risk of cancer that is "acceptable;" this determination is required because Congress made a major shift in focus with respect to animal drugs from excluding carcinogens from the food supply (the original Delaney Clause) to permitting a negligible risk of cancer in the food supply (the DES Proviso). FDA has expressed this "negligible risk" in a variety of ways. In the final SOM documents, FDA expressed it as the risk of no more than one additional cancer in a million lifetimes.[159] The practical effect of this kind of risk level, according to FDA, is essentially a "no risk" situation.

The difficult practical questions concern the kinds of data needed to make this "no risk" projection. Scientifically rigorous requirements can burden or exceed the practical ability of industry to develop useful and reproducible data. If pushed too far, the data requirements can be so onerous as to vitiate the practical availability of the congressionally mandated exemption. Similarly, if the number of drugs for which data are demanded is expanded, the overall burden on industry may hinder the development and retention of drug products as well.

Questions of overt toxicity and carcinogenicity also must be resolved in the human food additive area; the issue of the transfer of antibiotic resistance from animal to man is unique to animal drugs. The failure of antibiotics in some instances to treat human disease is a

---

155 The first proposal was made in 1973, 38 Fed. Reg. 19,226 (1973). The history of subsequent orders and litigation is summarized in a second proposal in 1979, 44 Fed. Reg. 17,070 (1979).

156 The final order adopting SOM was published December 31, 1987, 52 Fed. Reg. 49,572 (1987). At the same time, FDA released a series of guidelines that provide the working rules on implementation of the procedure, Id. at 49,589.

157 21 U.S.C. § 360b(d)(l)(I).

158 See, e.g., 47 Fed. Reg. 4972 (1982).

159 52 Fed. Reg. at 49,578-79; see also 47 Fed. Reg. 14,464 (1982) (seeking preliminary comments on a new policy to regulate carcinogenic "constituents" of food and color additives).

well-recognized phenomenon. The failure results from the survival of small numbers of organisms with a natural immunity to the antibiotic, which proliferate unchecked by the original drug. Some diseases are becoming untreatable by certain antibiotics. To preserve the effectiveness of some new antibiotics, there is pressure to hold them in reserve rather than to use them routinely.[160]

In the case of antibiotics fed to animals, and particularly those fed routinely at less than therapeutic levels to obtain food production benefits, a variety of issues have been raised that are perhaps impossible to answer. For example, does the use of low levels of antibiotics render similar antibiotics ineffective in treating animal diseases? Does the use of these low levels of antibiotics create antibiotic resistant strains of organisms that can be transferred from animals to man? Can the resistance "carrier" be transferred between organisms, either within the animal or in man? Would this transfer affect not only the antibiotic that has been fed to the animal, but also other antibiotics that are used solely in human medicine? Is there any difference in the virulence of resistant and nonresistant organisms, or those to which the resistance factor has been transferred?[161]

These issues first were clearly articulated by the Swann Committee Report in Great Britain, which led to the imposition of certain distribution controls on the use of veterinary antibiotics in the United Kingdom.[162] These issues, such as resistance-bearing plasmids, transferred to the United States and have been debated for more than two decades. FDA has conducted administrative investigations,[163] demanded that companies conduct additional testing,[164] proposed to withdraw the approval of certain antibiotics,[165] and seen those activities effectively halted by Congress. Responding to demands from the agricultural sector, successive congressional appropriations committees have demanded that FDA conduct further studies outside the agency before proceeding with the NADA withdrawal proceedings.[166] The National Research Council review contracted by FDA concluded that "the postulated hazards to human health...were neither proven nor disproved. The lack of data...must not be equated with proof that the proposed hazards do not exist."[167]

Opponents of the continued use of these antibiotics petitioned the Secretary of Health and Human Services to invoke nondelegable authority under section 512(e)(1) of the FDCA to

---

[160]   *See., e.g.,* the concerns raised in a letter from Dr. David Satcher, Director, Centers for Disease Control and Prevention (CDC), to Dr. David Kessler, Commissioner of Food and Drugs, over the potential approval of new antimicrobial agents for use in food-producing animals. FOOD CHEMICAL NEWS, Sept. 4, 1995, at 25-26. Both CDC and FDA are part of the Public Health Service within the Department of Health and Human Services.

[161]   The difficulty of these questions can be seen in the two reports of the National Academy of Sciences trying to resolve these issues. *See supra* note 130 and *infra* note 170.

[162]   REPORT OF THE JOINT COMMITTEE ON THE USE OF ANTIBIOTICS IN ANIMAL HUSBANDRY AND VETERINARY MEDICINE No. 4190 (1969).

[163]   BUREAU OF VETERINARY MEDICINE, FOOD & DRUG ADMIN., REPORT TO THE COMMISSIONER ON THE USE OF ANTIBIOTICS IN ANIMAL FEEDS (1972).

[164]   *See* 21 C.F.R. § 558.15.

[165]   42 Fed. Reg. 29,999 (1977); 42 Fed. Reg. 43,772 (1977); 42 Fed. Reg. 56,264 (1977).

[166]   *See, e.g.,* H.R. REP. No. 97-172, 97th Cong., 1st Sess. 105 (1981) (summarizing Appropriation Committee actions since 1978).

[167]   NAT'L RESEARCH COUNCIL, *supra* note 130, at xv-xvi.

suspend the approvals on the ground that continued use presented an imminent hazard.[168] Although the petition was denied,[169] FDA decided to seek another review by the National Academy of Sciences through the Institute of Medicine (IOM) and focused on the risk of increased virulence from resistant organisms. This review concluded, as had the earlier one, that the evidence was insufficient to reach a firm conclusion; it then used the inadequate data to project potential added human deaths from the unproven effects of resistance transfer.[170] One important shift that took place in the debate was away from just the "low-level" antibiotics to look at therapeutic products as well. FDA crafted a new framework for regulation that looked at a range of human health affects, including prolonged hospitalization as well as acute effects of resistant organism. The new human antibiotics became the battleground in evaluating human risks from organisms resistant to these newer compounds. FDA eventually proposed the revocation of approval of fluoroquinolone drugs used in the drinking water of poultry. While one manufacturer accepted the withdrawal, another contested the proposed withdrawal, leading to one of the few "on the record" withdrawal proceedings FDA has held for either human or animal drugs. FDA was successful in the hearing, removing the product from the market.

In 1977, FDA issued Notices of Opportunity for Hearing (NOOHs) to withdraw approval of several antibiotics approved for subtherapeutic use in food animals, including tetracycline and penicillin.[171] The agency never held hearings in either case. In 1999, public interest organizations petitioned FDA to withdraw approval for the subtherapeutic use of antibiotics including tetracycline and penicillin, and some of the same groups as well as others repeated the request in 2005 petitions.[172] FDA never issued substantive responses to any of the petitions, and a group of advocacy organizations sued the agency in 2011.[173] Later that year, FDA withdrew the 1977 NOOHs.[174] The United States District Court for the Southern District of New York ordered FDA to institute withdrawal proceedings discussed in the 1977 NOOHs and, if the manufacturers could not rebut the finding that the drug uses at issue were not safe, withdraw approval for those uses.[175] The Second Circuit reversed, concluding that the FDCA does not compel FDA to hold the hearings contemplated when FDA issues an NOOH to withdraw a drug approval if the agency later decides not to pursue that withdrawal.[176]

In late 2013, CVM announced the implementation of a plan to phase out the food production uses of what the agency deemed to be important antimicrobials for human medical use.[177] The announcement followed the June 28, 2010 publication of draft Guidance for Industry

---

168 21 U.S.C. § 360(e)(1); see 49 Fed. Reg. 49,645 (1984) (giving notice of a public hearing to be held by FDA to provide a basis for advising the Secretary on the petition).

169 Decision of the Secretary Denying Petition, Dkt. No. 84P-0399 (Nov. 13, 1985).

170 Institute of Medicine, Human Health Risks With the Subtherapeutic Use of Penicillin or Tetracyclines in Animal Feed 2, 7-11 (1989). FDA solicited comments on the report. 54 Fed. Reg. 5549 (1989).

171 42 Fed. Reg. 43,772 (1977); 42 Fed. Reg. 56,264 (1977).

172 Natural Resources Defense Council, Inc. v. FDA, 760 F.3D 151 (2d Cir. 2014).

173 Id.

174 Withdrawal of Notices of Opportunity for a Hearing: Penicillin and Tetracycline Used in Animal Feed, 76 Fed. Reg. 79,697 (Dec. 22, 2011).

175 Supra note 172.

176 Id.

177 Http://www.fda.gov/AnimalVeterinary/SafetyHealth/AntimicrobialResistance/Judicious UseofAntimicrobials/ucm390738.htm.

209, which described CVM's recommendations on how to avoid all antibiotic uses that could not be considered "judicious."[178] CVM asked the 26 sponsors of such drugs, encompassing 283 applications, to agree 1) to the withdrawal of their approvals for the drugs' production indications and 2) that each drug would be limited to use under the supervision of a veterinarian for any remaining therapeutic indications. All 26 sponsors agreed to make the requested changes by late 2016.[179]

Both the application of the Delaney Clause and FDA's actions responding to the concern about transfer of antibiotic resistance raise an additional, and not yet fully explored, issue of the cost of "safety." For any given direct food additives, the costs usually are easy to isolate and there are often alternative additives that can perform the same function. In one instance when there was no alternative, Congress responded with a judgment that the additive was to be retained.[180] In the case of food production animal drugs, the costs often translate into questions concerning the availability of food and increased food costs for consumers. FDA's estimates in this area have raised the potential of billions of dollars of additional costs to consumers resulting from the removal of certain animal drugs from the marketplace.[181] These issues create almost insoluble conflicts for consumers as well as regulators in trying to balance the unquantifiable risks with the equally unquantifiable economic costs.[182] The congressional actions on saccharin and antibiotics in feed represent two temporary political resolutions of the cost issue, but not actions that ultimately precluded FDA action to remove an antibiotic from animal use.[183]

The problems of food safety—the standards of proof, the burden of proof, and the balancing of safety against the cost of the food supply—hardly exhaust the current and prospective issues involving food production animal drugs. Another major area that remains unresolved involves the controls over the distribution and use of these animal drugs. The issues include who shall decide what drugs are to be used and when, and what controls are to be placed directly on the users of these drugs to prevent misuse.

Food production animal drugs mixed into feed are subject to the restriction on distribution to holders of approved applications to mix these drugs into feeds,[184] although as noted earlier, FDA has sought in the Second Generation of Medicated Feed Controls to reduce the number of products and plants actually subject to licensure.[185] Moreover, implants and

---

178   Http://www.fda.gov/downloads/animalveterinary/guidancecomplianceenforcement/guidanceforindustry/ucm216936.pdf.

179   Http://www.fda.gov/AnimalVeterinary/NewsEvents/CVMUpdates/ucm403285.htm.

180   Saccharin Study and Labeling Act, Pub. L. No. 95-203. 91 Stat. 1451 (1977). The original 18-month moratorium has since been extended a number of times, most recently until May 1, 1997. Pub. L. No. 102-142, tit. VI, 105 Stat. 910 (1991). Subsequent research cleared saccharin, which has been removed from various "cancer" listings. 21 U.S.C. § 343(o) repealed by Pub. L. 106-554, app. A, § 517, 114 Stat. 2763, 2763A-73 (2000).

181   For example, costs would map over $4 billion in 1976 dollars for furazolidone. 41 Fed. Reg. 19,906 (1976) (FDA economic impact analysis in conjunction with a proposal to withdraw furazolidone approvals).

182   Similar problems are posed in FDA's regulation of unavoidable environmental contaminants, such as aflatoxin in cottonseed meal used as animal feed and PCBs in fish. See 21 C.F.R. § 1109.30 (PCB); 47 Fed. Reg. 33,007 (1982) (aflatoxin).

183   See supra notes 165, 170.

184   See 21 U.S.C. § 360b(a)(1)-(2), (m).

185   See supra text accompanying note 53.

injectibles are not subject to these controls. The distribution controls now at issue would be in addition to these current statutory controls.

The first type of additional distribution control would require the intervention of veterinarians in the distribution system for food production animal drugs. Animal drugs, similar to human drugs, are available either OTC or only pursuant to a practitioner's order.[186] Unlike prescription human drugs, prescription animal drugs normally are not dispensed in pharmacies; rather, the veterinarian commonly does both the prescribing and dispensing. The prescription animal drug provision added to the FDCA in 1988 permits certain other locations to fill veterinary orders, but such locations are few in number.[187] Because legitimate prescribing requires a veterinarian-client-patient relationship, there are significant costs to the animal owner in obtaining prescription drugs as compared to those available OTC at a feed store.

There are few drugs intended for herd administration that currently require a veterinarian's order. While FDA proposed such a prescription system as part of its proposed controls on the use and distribution of certain antibiotics,[188] the agency retreated from this approach in the face of severe criticism on both statutory and practical grounds.[189] The ADAA essentially resolved this issue by creating a new class of animal drugs and feeds containing them: those subject to veterinary feed directives (VFDs).[190] Feeds containing VFD drugs, which are, by definition, nonprescription, can be fed to animals only pursuant to a VFD issued by a licensed veterinarian in the course of the veterinarian's professional practice involving a veterinarian-client-patient relationship. Unlike drugs that have to be stored by veterinarians or other establishments authorized to dispense such drugs,[191] VFD drugs and feeds containing them can be distributed for mixing and storage much like other animal drugs and medicated feeds. A cautionary label will set them apart, and they cannot be purchased for use without the requisite veterinary feed directive. The ADAA specifically provides that VFD drugs and feeds are not prescription drugs under either federal or state law.

Veterinary Biological Drugs

In contrast to the complicated, evolutionary pattern of amendments to and developments under the FDCA, the Virus-Serum-Toxin Act of 1913 (before its 1985 amendment) was a surprising remnant from a prior age in form, construction, and reach.[192] Adopted as part of an agricultural program to ensure the reliability of the hog cholera vaccine, the Virus-Serum-Toxin Act was administered by the Bureau of Animal Industry in USDA.[193] The act

---

[186]   21 U.S.C. § 353(f); 21 C.F.R. § 201.105.

[187]   21 U.S.C. § 353(f). The Association of Food and Drug Officials has drafted a model bill for state-by-state adoption dealing with the issues of distribution of veterinary prescription drugs.

[188]   43 Fed. Reg. 3032 (1978).

[189]   See 43 Fed. Reg. 35,059 (1978); 43 Fed. Reg. 4554 (1983).

[190]   Id. § 354.

[191]   Id. § 353(f).

[192]   Act of March 4, 1913, ch. 145, 37 Stat. 832 (codified before 1985 at 21 U.S.C. §§ 151-158).

[193]   Id. The original act was incorporated into the appropriations for the Bureau of Animal Industry for fiscal 1914. In contrast, the 1906 Pure Food and Drugs Act was entrusted to that Department's Bureau of

directs USDA to license establishments producing veterinary vaccines and related products, and ensure that those products are safe, pure, and potent.[194] The difference between the administrative implementation and the structure of this law developed an intriguing dichotomy between regulation and enforcement.

By regulation, USDA constructed a process that in essence parallels the drug approval process used by FDA, complete with experimental permits, licensing requirements, product standards, and standardized test procedures.[195] Establishments as well as individual products are licensed.[196] A USDA laboratory monitors biologics manufacturing in much the same way as FDA once monitored antibiotic production through batch certification procedures.[197] Thus, despite the spare statutory language, the USDA operating system is modern in approach and requirements.

Contrasting with the definition of interstate commerce in the FDCA,[198] the Virus-Serum-Toxin Act's original jurisdictional reach was severely limited.[199] Indeed, a decision interpreting the language upon which the Virus-Serum-Toxin Act was modeled concluded that only finished products shipped from one state and coming to rest in another were covered by the jurisdictional language; products being shipped between two points in one state that pass through other states in the journey were not in interstate commerce within the meaning of that language, and thus were outside the control of USDA.[200]

Because the facilities needed to produce veterinary biologic drugs often are not extensive; some firms chose to set up facilities in numerous states, with each facility serving local clientele. These enterprises were not subject to USDA regulations if the products produced in a state were marketed within the boundaries of that state. As USDA regulation grew in sophistication and complexity, these multiple intrastate marketers avoided the costs and delays of regulation in developing and marketing their products.

FDA responded to this regulatory vacuum. Relying on the expansive concept of interstate commerce in the FDCA, particularly section 301(k),[201] FDA asserted jurisdiction to inspect intrastate facilities, consistent with the biennial inspection requirements in section 510[202] and the congressional findings in 1962 that underlie that provision.[203] FDA's authority to take this action was challenged, but the agency ultimately prevailed.[204] This decision raised

---

Chemistry. This bureaucratic allocation essentially fixed the course of subsequent divergent development of the FDA and Animal and Plant Health Inspection Service.

[194]   See 21 U.S.C. § 151.

[195]   See 9 C.F.R. §§ 102.3, 103.1, pt. 113.

[196]   Id. § 102.4.

[197]   Id. § 113.3.

[198]   21 U.S.C. § 321 (b) ("commerce between any State…and any place outside thereof").

[199]   Id. § 151 ("from one state…to any other State").

[200]   United States v. Powers-Weightman-Rosengarten Co., 211 Fed. 169 (S.D.N.Y. 1913), relied on in Op. Solicitor, U.S.D.A. (Aug. 16, 1915), (construing the Virus-Serum-Toxin Act); see also Animal Health Inst. v. USDA, 487 F. Supp. 376 (D. Colo. 1980).

[201]   21 U.S.C. § 331(k).

[202]   Id. § 360.

[203]   Pub. L. No. 87-781, § 301, 76 Stat. at 793.

[204]   Grand Laboratories, Inc. v. Harris, 660 F.2d 1288 (8th Cir. 1981) (en banc).

the possibility that FDA might try to apply the new animal drug provisions[205] to intrastate biologics, leaving interstate biologics for USDA regulation. The incongruity of this result spurred a search for a legislative solution, in which USDA and both intrastate and interstate producers joined, resulting in a series of amendments to the 1913 act that were a small part of the omnibus spending legislation enacted December 23, 1985.[206]

This legislative solution reflected in part the understanding of all producers that the small size of the regulated industry and the need to proceed by regulatory processes in light of the rather sparse statutory provisions, had led over the years to good working relations between industry and USDA. The pattern of biologics regulation is straightforward and without the complexities arising on the animal drug side at FDA due to the variety of statutory sources that were joined in the Animal Drug Amendments of 1968. Thus, the entire regulatory system at USDA is easier to administer and more amenable to a closer working relationship between industry and government. The users of biologics as well as consumers have benefited from the less confrontational regulatory process that has seen the development of a variety of new products within a fully formed system of licensing, product standards, laboratory oversight, and inspection.

The 1985 legislation did more than bring intrastate biologics under USDA control (although it did that in a comprehensive fashion). Based on statutory findings, the revised act reaches all biological products, regardless of production location or whether the products physically move between states.[207] USDA was given explicit rulemaking authority for its well-developed regulatory program,[208] and the enforcement tools of the Federal Meat Inspection Act, including product detention and seizure (as well as injunctive relief), were made applicable to violations of the Virus-Serum-Toxin Act.[209]

The added provisions accounted for the interests of intrastate producers as well as other persons interested in biologics production. Intrastate products marketed during the year preceding enactment were covered by a four-year transition to permit producers and products to become licensed (if their producers decided to take advantage of the offer).[210] In addition, all producers could apply for special licenses to cover emergency or special local problems.[211] Persons producing for self-use were permitted to operate without obtaining a license, as were veterinarians acting within the scope of a veterinarian-client-patient relationship.[212] Both veterinarians and self-use producers were subjected to USDA inspection and to the statutory proscription on the manufacture of unsafe (harmful) or ineffective (worthless) products.[213] Finally, state licensing programs found to be equivalent to the federal program were permitted to continue; to date, only California has such a program.[214]

---

[205] 21 U.S.C. § 360b.
[206] Pub. L. No. 99-198, § 1768, 99 Stat. at 1654.
[207] *Id.* § 1768(a),(3), 99 Stat. at 1654-55 (codified at 21 U.S.C. §§ 151, 159).
[208] *Id.* § 1768(b), 99 Stat. at 1654 (codified at 21 U.S.C. § 154).
[209] *Id.* § 1768(e), 99 Stat. at 1655 (codified at 21 U.S.C. § 159).
[210] *Id.* § 1768(f),(2), 99 Stat. at 1655.
[211] *Id.* § 1768(c), 99 Stat. at 1654 (codified at 21 U.S.C. § 154a).
[212] *Id.*
[213] *See* 21 U.S.C. §§ 151, 157, as amended by Pub. L. No. 99-198, § 1768(a), (d), 99 Stat. at 1654-55.
[214] Pub. L. No. 99-198, § 1768(c), 99 Stat. at 1654 (codified at 21 U.S.C. § 154a).

The transitional exemption claim period expired on January 1, 1987; the transitional period generally expired on that date in 1990, although individual applicants could obtain up to an additional year upon a showing of a "good faith effort to comply . . . with due diligence."[215] USDA has issued regulations implementing some aspects of the amendments, but a question remains as to the department's diligence in exercising its expanded enforcement authority to ensure that all producers come under USDA regulatory controls.[216] USDA, in ensuring that all commercial products are subject to licensing, may experience problems similar to those that FDA has encountered in monitoring the extent to which veterinarians act solely within a documented veterinarian-client-patient relationship.

Federalism

State regulatory programs generally have been a strong complement to the federal regulation of animal feed and drugs. State inspection of feed plants allows FDA to concentrate its resources on animal drugs and those feeds that warrant closer FDA scrutiny due to their greater risk of leaving residues in edible products. Similarly, new state legislation defining the persons who may deal in prescription animal drugs may assist FDA in controlling the unsupervised use of this class of products.[217] A few state initiatives are of dubious value and legality. These are the ones that attempt to superimpose distribution or labeling requirements on federally licensed products either by duplicating federal decisions or countermanding them. Thus, state attempts to ban federally approved products, to require veterinarian distribution of nonprescription products, or to impose labeling warnings that have been rejected during federal licensing[218] raise serious constitutional questions.

The 1985 amendments to the Virus-Serum-Toxin Act may indicate a congressional intent to have federal programs occupy the field of vaccine regulation, with federal licensing and inspection reaching all producers.[219] The situation under the FDCA is unclear, although the Supreme Court has recognized the need to avoid state interference with FDA regulatory programs implementing the Act's requirements.[220] How these state-federal tensions are resolved will have important consequences for the future of a vigorous animal drug industry; a balkanized domestic market not only will be a disincentive to investment and innovation, but could shift the locus of discovery and production for international markets to the harmonized European Economic Community or the developed Pacific Rim nations.

---

[215]   *Id.* § 1768(f)(2)(B), 99 Stat. at 1655.

[216]   *See* 9 C.F.R. §§ 102.6, 107.1-2.2, 114.2, 118.1-.4.

[217]   *See* 21 U.S.C. § 353(f).

[218]   *See* N.J. Dep't Agric., N.J.A.C. 2:6 (1988).

[219]   *See* 21 U.S.C. § 159 (congressional findings that all veterinary biologics are in or substantially affect interstate commerce, and federal regulation is necessary to prevent or eliminate burdens on interstate commerce).

[220]   Rath Packing Co. v. Jones, 430 U.S. 519 (1977) (including a decision involving goods regulated under the FDCA, *id.* at 533-43); but *see* Hillsborough County v. Automated Med. Laboratories, 471 U.S. 707 (1985) (refusing to find preemption in FDA licensing of blood products). In the area of food labeling, Congress has opted for extensive federal preemption by the adoption of section 403A, 21 U.S.C. § 343-1, as part of the Nutrition Labeling and Education Act, Pub. L. No. 101-535, § 6, 104 Stat. 2353, 2362-64 (1990).

Export and Import Issues

Because section 505 dealing with new drugs was never integrated into the adulteration and misbranding provisions of the act, the export exemption for adulterated and misbranded products did not apply to unapproved new drugs. The new animal drug provisions were tied to adulteration, but the 1968 Animal Drug Amendments retained a prohibition on exporting unapproved new animal drugs. The FDA Export Reform and Enhancement Act of 1996,[221] with the clarification contained in the Agricultural Appropriations Act for Fiscal Year 1997,[222] repealed the last sentence of 21 U.S.C. § 381(e)(1), which had precluded the export of unapproved new animal drugs under the general criteria of that provision. By repealing the limitation, unapproved animal drugs (like unapproved human antibiotics, and food and color additives) now can be exported anywhere in the world as long as the drug accords with the specifications of the foreign purchaser, is not in conflict with foreign law, is labeled for export, and is not sold in domestic commerce. "Unapproved" includes both novel compounds and deviations from FDA-approved labeling to conform to foreign marketing practices. The prior export provision,[223] also substantially modified by the FDA export reform act, no longer applies to animal drugs.

New animal drugs may be approved in foreign countries prior to U.S. approval, and their use in food-producing animals can result in animal drug residues that have no authorization under U.S. law. The ADAA created a new system under which animal drug residue tolerances can be established for drugs approved other than in the United States, where the residues might appear in imported meat, milk, or eggs.[224] FDA had taken the position that a full new animal drug application was required to establish tolerances, even though the sponsor was uninterested in domestic marketing. Under the new authorized procedure, the human food safety tolerance can be adopted, based on data used for the foreign approval, or international evaluations of that safety information, such as those conducted by the Joint Expert Committee on Food Additives (sponsored by the World Health Organization and the Food and Agriculture Organization of the United Nations) that advises the Codex Alimentarius Commission's Committee on Residues of Animal Drugs in Food. While the new procedure has not been used, its existence has led FDA to act by enforcement discretion in the few instances where import residues of drugs unapproved in the United States has been an issue.

---

[221] Pub. L. No. 104-134, 110 Stat. 1321 (1996).
[222] Pub. L. No. 104-180, § 603, 110 Stat. 1569, 1594-95 (1996).
[223] 21 U.S.C. § 382.
[224] Id. § 360b(a)(6).

CHAPTER 8
COSMETIC REGULATION REVISITED

....

GARY L. YINGLING AND SUZAN ONEL

Introduction

Federal control of cosmetics reflects a tangled web of definitions and changing policy applied to a large and diverse industry.[1] While the term "cosmetic" in the Federal Food, Drug, and Cosmetic Act (FDCA or the Act)[2] has remained unchanged since 1938, the range of products that meet that definition has expanded and includes both traditionally regarded cosmetics[3] and products that, in a strict sense, also meet the definition of "drug" under the Act.[4] Indeed, the tension between the "cosmetic" and "drug" definitions is a prime focus of the law of cosmetics.

---

[1]   Estimates place consumer spending on cosmetics at more than $35 billion annually. There are more than 1,400 domestic manufacturing and repacking establishments, which in the aggregate use more than 12,500 different cosmetic ingredients and a corresponding number of fragrance ingredients to make more than 25,000 product formulations. *See* FDA COMPLIANCE PROGRAM GUIDANCE MANUAL 7329.001, pt. I, at 1 (Dec. 2006).

[2]   Pub. L. No. 75-717, 52 Stat. 1040 (1938), as amended, 21 U.S.C. §§ 301 *et seq.* (1994).

[3]   The term "cosmetic" is defined as a product designed to beautify the skin, hair, nails, lips, eyes or teeth. WEBSTER'S THIRD NEW INTERNATIONAL DICTIONARY (Merriam-Webster, Inc. 1981).

[4]   The Federal Food, Drug, and Cosmetic Act (FDCA) defines the term "drug" in section 201(g)(1) as follows:

> (A) articles recognized in the official United States Pharmacopeia, official Homeopathic Pharmacopeia of the United States, or official National Formulary, or any supplement to any of them; (B) articles intended for use in the diagnosis, cure, mitigation, treatment, or prevention of disease in man or other animals; (C) articles (other than food) intended to affect the structure or any function of the body of man or other animals; and (D) articles intended for use as a component of any article specified in clause (A), (B), or (C).

21 U.S.C. § 321(g)(1).

The Evolution of the Federal Law of Cosmetics

The 1906 Act

The current regulation of cosmetics developed from early efforts in the 20th century to extend formal federal controls over foods, drugs, and cosmetics, which culminated in the Pure Food and Drugs Act of 1906 (1906 Act).[5] Congress enacted the 1906 Act to prevent the "manufacture, sale, or transportation of adulterated or misbranded or poisonous or deleterious foods, drugs, medicines, and liquors."[6] Although the 1906 Act did not address cosmetics, the regulatory techniques adopted in the 1906 Act provided the basis for the later emergence of formal cosmetic legislation in 1938.

The 1906 Act applied to a cosmetic only if it also could be brought under the definition of a "drug."[7] A cosmetic met the "drug" definition if it contained an ingredient listed in one of the official compendia of medicinal drugs or if its label claims went so far as to address medicinal attributes of the product. The ability to regulate a cosmetic product as a drug, however, was quite limited. This is because unlike the present statute, the definition of "drug" in the 1906 Act did not include products intended to affect the structure or function of the human body, and instead, only addressed disease claims.[8] Thus, products such as weight loss aids, sunburn prevention creams, and hair-loss talcs fell outside the 1906 Act because they addressed conditions that were not viewed as diseases.

The Federal Food, Drug, and Cosmetic Act of 1938

The FDCA[9] was the first formalized federal effort to regulate cosmetics. The 1938 law addressed the need to bring cosmetics within the purview of federal regulation. It was precipitated by reports of a number of products such as eyelash and eyebrow dyes, hair dyes, and complexion bleaches that caused blindness and other injuries due to the presence of extremely toxic substances such as coal tar dyes,[10] and metals such as lead, arsenic, mercury, and thallium.[11] The 1938 law provides, in brief compass,[12] the basic framework for the Food and Drug Administration's (FDA) regulation of cosmetics today.

---

[5]   Pub. L. No. 59-384, 34 Stat. 768 (1906).

[6]   *Id.*

[7]   Section 6 of the 1906 Act defined the term "drug" to include: "all medicines and preparations recognized in the United States Pharmacopoeia or National Formulary for internal or external use, and any substance or mixture of substances intended to be used for the cure, mitigation, or prevention of disease of either man or other animals."

[8]   The 1906 Act's "drug" definition also did not include remedies recognized in the Homeopathic Pharmacopoeia of the United States, which are covered under section 201(g)(1)(A) of the FDCA, 21 U.S.C. § 321(g)(1)(A).

[9]   The Federal Food, Drug, and Cosmetic Act of 1938 was signed into law by President Franklin Roosevelt on June 25, 1938. *See* 83 CONG. REC. 13,183.

[10]   The Cosmetic, Toiletry and Fragrance Association (CTFA) (now known as the Personal Care Products Council) *Cosmetic Ingredient Dictionary* defines coal tar as "a thick liquid or semi-solid obtained as a by-product in the destructive distillation of bituminous coal."

[11]   *See* S. REP. NO. 493, 73d Cong., 2d Sess. (1934), *reprinted in* 2 DEP'T OF HEALTH, EDUC. & WELFARE, A LEGISLATIVE HISTORY OF THE FEDERAL FOOD, DRUG, AND COSMETIC ACT AND ITS AMENDMENTS 720 (1979).

[12]   A review of a reprint of the FDCA indicates that Chapter IV (Food) covers 40 pages and Chapter V (Drugs and Devices) covers 125 pages, while Chapter VI (Cosmetics) covers less than two pages. *See* COMPILATION OF SELECTED ACTS WITHIN THE JURISDICTION OF THE COMMITTEE ON COMMERCE (U.S. Gov't Printing Off. 1995). FDA's promulgated regulations on food cover more than 1,200 pages (21 C.F.R. pts. 100-199 (2013));

Statutory Controls on Cosmetics

The layman understandably equates "cosmetics" with products such as lipstick, face cream, face powder, nail polish, and other items designed to beautify the body. The definition of "cosmetic" found in the FDCA, however, is broader than the popular definition, and encompasses not only beauty items but also issues of safety and intended use. The FDCA defines the term "cosmetic" as:

(1) articles intended to be rubbed, poured, sprinkled, or sprayed on, introduced into, or otherwise applied to the human body or any part thereof for cleansing, beautifying, promoting attractiveness, or altering the appearance, and

(2) articles intended for use as a component of any such articles; except that such term shall not include soap.[13]

In addition to defining the term "cosmetic," the Act creates statutory provisions to ensure that only safe and properly labeled cosmetics reach the American consumer. The Act accomplishes this objective by prohibiting various actions that relate to the adulteration or misbranding of a cosmetic. Violating these prohibitions subjects the violator[14] to the various remedies available to FDA under the Act, including seizure,[15] injunction,[16] and criminal prosecutions.[17]

The following actions relating to cosmetics are prohibited by the Act:

- the introduction or delivery for introduction into interstate commerce of any adulterated or misbranded cosmetic;

- the adulteration or misbranding of any cosmetic in interstate commerce;

- the receipt in interstate commerce of any cosmetic that is adulterated or misbranded, and the delivery or proffered delivery thereof for pay or otherwise;

- the manufacture within any territory of any cosmetic that is adulterated or misbranded;

- the giving of a false guarantee or undertaking[18] relative to a cosmetic;

- the alteration, mutilation, destruction, obliteration, or removal of the whole or any part of the labeling of, or the doing of any other act with respect to, a cosmetic, if such act is done while such article is held for sale after shipment in interstate commerce and results in such article being adulterated or misbranded.[19]

All of the prohibited acts relating to cosmetics, with the exception of the ban on false cosmetic guarantees, relate to situations when the cosmetic is either adulterated or misbranded.

---

human drug regulations take up more than 500 pages (*id.* pts. 200-499), and device regulations more than 550 pages (*id.* pts. 800-895). Cosmetic regulations, in contrast, cover only 30 pages (*id.* pts. 700-740).

13   FDCA § 201(i), 21 U.S.C. § 321(i).

14   If the violator is a person, his/her corporation also may face the same penalties because the FDCA definition of "person" is defined as including an individual, partnership, corporation and association. FDCA § 201(e), 21 U.S.C. §321(e).

15   FDCA § 304, 21 U.S.C. § 334.

16   FDCA § 302, 21 U.S.C. § 332.

17   FDCA § 303, 21 U.S.C. § 333.

18   On guarantees, *see* FDCA § 303(c)(2), 21 U.S.C. § 333(c)(2).

19   *See* FDCA § 301(a)-(c), (g), (h), (k), 21 U.S.C. § 331(a)-(c), (g), (h), (k).

Unlike drugs, devices, biologics, and food ingredients, there are no premarket approval requirements for cosmetics, no duty to register a cosmetic establishment, and no duty to list a marketed cosmetic with FDA.[20]

Restrictions on the Adulteration of Cosmetics

The Statutory Provisions. Section 601 of the Act sets forth five situations where a cosmetic is "deemed to be adulterated":

(a) If it bears or contains any poisonous or deleterious substance which may render it injurious to users under the conditions of use prescribed in the labeling thereof, or, under such conditions of use as are customary or usual, except that this provision shall not apply to coal-tar hair dye.

(b) If it consists in whole or in part of any filthy, putrid, or decomposed substance.

(c) If it has been prepared, packed, or held under insanitary [sic] conditions whereby it may have become contaminated with filth, or whereby it may have been rendered injurious to health.

(d) If its container is composed, in whole or in part, of any poisonous or deleterious substance which may render the contents injurious to health.

(e) If it is not a hair dye and it is, or it bears or contains, a color additive which is unsafe within the meaning of section 379e of this title.[21]

These adulteration provisions closely track the language of the adulteration clauses that are applicable to foods,[22] drugs, and devices.[23]

Litigation on Adulteration of Cosmetics. Not only is the cosmetic adulteration statutory language brief, but FDA enforcement activity under these provisions is also infrequent. In an average year, FDA engages in approximately 10,600 enforcement activities (seizure, injunction, prosecution, Warning Letters, and recall events).[24] In recent years, the number of these enforcement activities that relate to cosmetics average between one and two, most of which are Warning Letters.[25] Because FDA enforcement activity in the cosmetic area is low, the body of case law is also low with regard to adulteration and misbranding. Indeed, several of the primary cosmetic adulteration cases are significant for other reasons.

---

20   FDA has promulgated regulations that allow a cosmetic establishment to register voluntarily. *See* 21 C.F.R. pt. 710; *see also infra* text accompanying note 91.

21   21 U.S.C. § 361. Clause (e) of the adulteration provisions was amended by the Color Additive Amendments of 1960. *See* Pub. L. No. 86-618, 74 Stat. 397 (1960) (codified at FDCA § 721, 21 U.S.C. § 379e).

22   FDCA § 402, 21 U.S.C. § 342.

23   FDCA § 501, 21 U.S.C. § 351.

24   *See* U.S. Food & Drug Admin., *FDA Enforcement Statistics Summary Fiscal Year 2013*, FDA.gov, http://www.fda.gov/downloads/ICECI/EnforcementActions/UCM384647.pdf (last visited May 30, 2014).

25   *See* Food & Drug Admin., The Enforcement Story Fiscal Year 2006 (Mar. 2007), The Enforcement Story Fiscal Year 2007 (Mar. 2008), and The Enforcement Story Fiscal Year 2008 (Mar. 2009); U.S. Food & Drug Admin., Warning Letters Related to Cosmetics (Apr. 10, 2014), http://www.fda.gov/Cosmetics/ComplianceEnforcement/WarningLetters/default.htm.

In *United States v. Parfait Powder Puff Company,*[26] perhaps the most well-known cosmetic adulteration case, there was no dispute that the cosmetics, hair lacquer pads, were adulterated under section 601(a) because they contained a deleterious substance.[27] Rather, the crucial issue was whether the defendant corporation, a distributor, could be held criminally liable for the injurious acts of its contract manufacturer, even though the defendant had no knowledge that its manufacturer had adulterated the hair pads distributed under defendant's name. The Seventh Circuit found the defendant responsible, and upheld the conviction because the defendant had acted to further the distribution of the adulterated pads.

Another adulteration case, *United States v. C.E.B. Products,*[28] also is significant for reasons unrelated to the law of cosmetics. In 1974, FDA sought to enjoin C.E.B. Products from distributing its product "Long Nails." The agency alleged that the product contained a "poisonous or deleterious substance [methyl methacrylate monomer] which may render it injurious to users" in violation of section 601(a).[29] Although the court found the product to be adulterated, the primary issue was that the court lacked authority to order a recall of the adulterated product.

In *United States v. An Article of Cosmetic...Beacon Castile Shampoo,*[30] the government claimed that a castile shampoo was adulterated because it contained deleterious substances, potassium oleate and Neutronyx 600, that could cause ocular injury at full strength. The court noted, however, that a shampoo is not normally used in the eye, and is seldom, if ever, present in full strength in the eye. The court found that the government studies, which used half strength and less of the shampoo, demonstrated that the product caused nothing but a mild irritation, with no lasting injury to the eye. Therefore, the court concluded that the shampoo was not adulterated because the government failed to show that a full concentration of the shampoo would get into the eye during customary and usual use so as to cause injury.

Color Additives and Cosmetic Adulteration. Because the use of colors pervades the cosmetic industry, the regulation of color additives is an important aspect of cosmetic law. In the early 1900s, the U.S. Department of Agriculture commissioned Dr. Bernard Hess, a German dye expert, to investigate the relationship between food colors and health. Because little was known about the safety of marketed coal tar colors,[31] Dr. Hess suggested that only those colors that were harmless and necessary be used. Later, certification of colors, which had been voluntary under the 1906 act, became mandatory under the 1938 act with the inclusion of section 604: "The Secretary shall promulgate regulations providing for the listing of coal-tar colors which are harmless and suitable for use in cosmetics and for the certification of such colors, with or without dilutants."[32]

---

[26]   163 F.2d 1008 (7th Cir. 1947), *cert. denied,* 322 U.S. 851 (1948).

[27]   *Id.* at 1009.

[28]   380 F. Supp. 664 (N.D. Ill. 1974).

[29]   *Id.* at 666. In a later case, the same court held that the court had jurisdiction to order a recall in a matter relating to misbranded drugs. United States v. K-N Enterprises, Inc., 461 F. Supp. 988 (N.D. Ill. 1978).

[30]   No. C71-53 (N.D. Ohio 1973), *reprinted in* Federal Food, Drug, and Cosmetic Act 1969-1974, at 149 (FDLI 1976).

[31]   *See* coal tar definition, *supra* note 10.

[32]   Pub. L. No. 75-717, § 604, 52 Stat. at 1055.

The status of colors did not change significantly until 1955, when the Secretary of Health, Education, and Welfare[33] ordered that a red coal-tar color (Red No. 32) be removed from the certified list for use in Florida citrus fruit. In seeking to delist Red No. 32, the agency redefined the term "harmless" in the statute to mean that the substance was incapable of causing harm to test animals in any quantity under any conditions. The Supreme Court upheld FDA's position on "harmless" colors in *Fleming v. Florida Citrus Exchange*.[34]

After *Fleming,* Congress pushed to change the law to allow colors that were not purely harmless to reach the market. The Color Additive Amendments of 1960, which applied not only to cosmetics, but also to drugs, devices, and foods, were enacted to address these concerns.[35]

The Color Additive Amendments distinguished between colors that were conclusively safe and those that were questionable, by creating separate "permanent"[36] and "provisional"[37] listings for color additives. The Amendments revised section 706 of the 1938 Act to set standards for testing the safety of colors, the types of listings authorized by the application of the Delaney anticancer clause, and the procedural requirements for regulatory actions and responses on color additives. With respect to specific cosmetics, the Amendments repealed section 604 of the Act because the new version of section 706 addressed the prior requirement to promulgate regulations on color additives that had been mandated by section 604. During the transitional period created by Title II of the Color Additive Amendments, it was the responsibility of industry to perform adequate tests to prove that their colors were safe. If the safety of a color was proven, it would be added to the permanent list.[38]

FDA decided that any substance that "when applied to the human body results in coloring," is a color additive.[39] This interpretation included "lipsticks, rouge, eye makeup colors and

---

[33] The powers granted to the "Secretary" by the Act now are vested in the Secretary of Health and Human Services, who, in turn, has redelegated his or her authority to the Commissioner of Food and Drugs, Food and Drug Administration. FDCA § 201(d), 21 U.S.C. § 321(d); 21 C.F.R. § 5.10.

[34] 358 U.S. 153 (1958).

[35] Pub. L. No. 86-618, 74 Stat. 397 (1960).

[36] *Id.* tit. 1, at 397.

[37] *Id.* tit. 11, at 404.

[38] *Id.*

[39] "Color additive" is defined in section 201(t)(1) of the Act as:

a material which—

(A) is a dye, pigment, or other substance made by a process of synthesis or similar artifice, or extracted, isolated, or otherwise derived, with or without intermediate or final change of identity, from a vegetable, animal, mineral, or other source, and

(B) when added or applied to a food, drug, or cosmetic, or to the human body or any part thereof, is capable (alone or through reaction with other substance) of imparting color thereto;

except that such term does not include any material which the Secretary, by regulation, determines is used (or intended to be used) solely for a purpose or purposes other than coloring.

(2) the term "color" includes black, white, and intermediate grays.

related cosmetics."[40] Because a cosmetic is adulterated under section 601(e) of the Act if it contains any unlisted—or unsafe—color additive,[41] the Color Additive Amendments gave FDA a form of indirect premarket clearance over finished cosmetic products.[42]

The anticancer clause of the Amendments also gives FDA some discretion in making the scientific judgments that may lead to a ban of a cosmetic as carcinogenic. The clause deems "non-ingested colors to be unsafe only if the positive cancer finding is based upon 'appropriate' or 'relevant' evidence."[43] Thus, if a color additive is harmful when ingested, but demonstrably safe if used as a cosmetic ingredient, the color most likely would be approved.

In the years following 1960, debate arose as to whether a risk is presented by extremely low levels of a substance that is toxic at high levels. Some colors are carcinogenic at high levels, but human exposure occurs only at trivial levels. The first cosmetic substance the agency evaluated was lead acetate, a hair dye coloring agent that was found to cause cancer in animals, and which posed a human cancer risk of 2 in 10,000,000 lifetimes. In October 1980, FDA chose to put this substance on the permanent (i.e., approved) list.[44] The agency concluded that the carcinogenicity testing did not yield "appropriate" or "relevant" evidence for exclusion from permanent listing. Prior to this decision, FDA had followed a zero-risk policy, whereby if a color was at all toxic, it would be denied permanent inclusion even for cosmetic use.[45] The permanent listing of lead acetate thus introduced the concept of "risk assessment" or *de minimis* risk to the construction of the anticancer clause of section 706.

FDA continued with the risk assessment approach to colors and the anticancer clause when it permanently listed D&C Green No. 5 for use in externally applied drugs and cosmetics in 1982. The agency stated that the clause did not apply to a color that did not induce cancer when tested regardless of whether it contained *a contaminant* that caused cancer. The agency also concluded that because the lifetime risk from the presence of the contaminant in the color was so low, the test of reasonable certainty of no harm was satisfied.[46] FDA's decision was upheld in *Scott v. Food and Drug Administration*.[47] Risk assessment has continued to be an important aspect of construing the anticancer clauses of the Act.

---

[40]   21 U.S.C. § 321(t). Michael R. Taylor, *History of Cosmetic Color Additive Regulation: Creative Maneuvering by FDA Bodes Well for the Future*, 37 FOOD DRUG COSM. L.J. 152, 157 (1982) (quoting 28 Fed. Reg. 6439 (June 22, 1963) (codified at 21 C.F.R. § 70.3-71.37)).

[41]   A color additive is unsafe if not permanently or provisionally listed. *See* FDCA § 721, 21 U.S.C. § 379e; *see also* United States v. Eight Unlabeled Cases…of "French Bronze Tablets," 888 F.2d 945 (2d Cir. 1989) (use of color additive, which had been approved for use in food and drugs but not for use in cosmetics, caused cosmetic tablets to be adulterated).

[42]   FDA's other policies relating to colors and color additives are found in its Compliance Policy Guides. These guides provide information regarding label declaration of artificial colors, delisted colors in foods for export (e.g., FD&C Red No. 2) and the status of color additives. *See* FDA COMPLIANCE POLICY GUIDES MANUAL §§ 587.100 (Nov. 2005), 587.200 (Mar. 1995), 587.300 (Nov. 2005).

[43]   Taylor, *supra* note 40, at 156.

[44]   45 Fed. Reg. 72,112 (Oct. 31, 1980).

[45]   *Color-Additive Amendments of 1960*, 15 FOOD DRUG COSM. L.J. 432, 440 (1960).

[46]   47 Fed. Reg. 24,278 (June 4, 1982).

[47]   728 F.2d 322 (6th Cir. 1984) (*per curiam*); but note, in *Public Citizen v. Young*, 831 F.2d 1108 (D.C. Cir. 1987), the D.C. Circuit rejected the *de minimis* risk assessment doctrine as applied to color additives. The court distinguished *Scott,* however, by concluding that the latter dealt with chemical constituents of a color additive, not the color additive itself.

Misbranding

Under section 602 of the Act,[48] a cosmetic is deemed to be "misbranded" under the following circumstances:

(a) If its labeling[49] is false or misleading in any particular.

(b) If in package form unless it bears a label containing (1) the name and place of business of the manufacturer, packer, or distributor; and (2) an accurate statement of the quantity of the contents in terms of weight, measure, or numerical count: *Provided*, That under clause (2) of this paragraph reasonable variations shall be permitted, and exemptions as to small packages shall be established, by regulations prescribed by the Secretary.

(c) If any word, statement, or other information required by or under authority of this act to appear on the label or labeling is not prominently placed thereon with such conspicuousness (as compared with other words, statements, designs, or devices in the labeling) and in such terms as to render it likely to be read and understood by the ordinary individual under customary conditions of purchase and use.

(d) If its container is so made, formed, or filled as to be misleading.

(e) If it is a color additive, unless its packaging and labeling are in conformity with such packaging and labeling requirements, applicable to such color additive, as may be contained in regulations issued under section 706. This paragraph shall not apply to packages of color additives which, with respect to their use for cosmetics, are marketed and intended for use only in or on hair dyes (as defined in the last sentence of section 601(a)).

(f) If its packaging or labeling is in violation of an applicable regulation issued pursuant to section 3 or 4 of the Poison Prevention Packaging Act of 1970.[50]

These cosmetic misbranding provisions have generated almost no litigation. One of the few misbranding cases of interest, *Almay, Inc. v. Califano*, involved not a cosmetic, but a proposed FDA regulation that would have defined the term "hypoallergenic" for cosmetic products. In 1974, FDA proposed that, in order for a cosmetic company to use the terms "hypoallergenic," "allergy tested," or "dermatologist tested," the firm must prove by "scientific studies that the relative frequency of adverse reactions in human subjects from the test product [was] significantly less than the relative frequency of such reactions from each reference product(s)."[51] The proposal required "comparison testing" of the labeled product against "reference products," which were defined in the regulation as "similar-use competitive products in the same cosmetic product category," representing a market share of at least 10 percent.

---

[48] 21 U.S.C. § 362.

[49] Section 201(m) of the Act defines "labeling" to mean "all labels and other written, printed, or graphic matter (1) upon any article or any of its containers or wrappers, or (2) accompanying such article." *Id.* § 321(m). Section 201(k) of the Act defines "label" to mean "a display of written, printed, or graphic matter upon the immediate container of any article . . . ." *Id.* § 321(k).

[50] Section 602(f) was added by Pub. L. No. 91-601, § 7, 84 Stat. 1670, 1673 (1970).

[51] 39 Fed. Reg. 7288, 7291 (Feb. 25, 1974).

Major manufacturers sued the agency on the ground that any standard adopted should be objective rather than comparative. The District Court held for the agency, but the Court of Appeals set aside the regulation as arbitrary and capricious.[52]

United States v. Pinaud, Inc.[53] was a criminal misbranding action in which the government alleged a product that was labeled "Eau de Quinine" was misbranded because it contained only a minute amount of quinine. The company defended the product's name based on long use, and argued that the quinine level was insignificant to the consumer who purchased the product for many years and was aware of its intended use. The jury found for the manufacturer.

The relative scarcity of cases in which misbranding cosmetics was the major issue should not be construed as meaning that FDA is not interested in the accuracy of cosmetic labeling. Indeed, misbranding issues are presented by a number of the cases, but the prime concern in these cases is whether the product is a cosmetic or a drug.[54]

Cosmetics can also be misbranded if they are not labeled in compliance with the requirements of the Fair Packaging and Labeling Act (FPLA). The FPLA was enacted by Congress "to ensure that packages and their labels enable consumers to obtain accurate information as to the quantity of the contents and … facilitate value comparisons."[55] Under the FPLA, a "packaged consumer commodity" label must include 1) the identity of the commodity, 2) the name and place of business of the manufacturer, packer or distributor, 3) the net quantity of contents and 4) the net quantity of contents of each serving if the package label includes the number of servings.[56]

False Advertising

The Act proscribes misbranding of cosmetic labeling, but does not address cosmetic advertising. Responsibility for regulating false or misleading advertising of cosmetics rests with the Federal Trade Commission (FTC) pursuant to the Federal Trade Commission Act (FTCA).[57]

Under the FTCA, it is unlawful to disseminate or cause to be disseminated any false advertisement that is likely to induce the purchase of a cosmetic or have an effect on commerce in cosmetics.[58] A person disseminating a false advertisement commits an unfair method of competition or deceptive act,[59] and is subject to injunction[60] or even criminal

---

52 569 F.2d 674 (D.C. Cir. 1977), *rev'd* Almay, Inc. v. Weinberger, 417 F. Supp. 758 (D.D.C. 1976).
53 Unreported case (S.D.N.Y. 1947), *reprinted in* Federal Food, Drug, and Cosmetic Act 1938-1964, at 526 (FDLI 1978).
54 *See infra* text accompanying notes 126-201.
55 15 U.S.C. § 1451.
56 15 U.S.C. § 1453(a).
57 15 U.S.C. §§ 41-58 (1994).
58 *Id.* § 52(a).
59 *Id.* § 52(b).
60 *Id.* § 53.

sanctions.[61] Persons committing deceptive acts also may become subject to FTC proceedings or private lawsuits under the Lanham Act.[62]

Controlling Cosmetics Through Regulation

Enforcement of the Act's cosmetic provisions through litigation has not produced the clear policy mandates that have been generated from drug and device litigation. Instead, FDA has achieved greater compliance with the law through its cosmetic regulations.[63] These regulations provide more detailed information on how to comply with the statutory prohibitions regarding adulteration and misbranding, as well as the statutory requirements set forth by the FPLA.

General Definitions and Special Requirements for Cosmetic Products

Part 700 of Title 21 of the *Code of Federal Regulations* establishes the general definitions applicable to cosmetic regulations,[64] and a number of requirements specific to particular types of products. Separate regulations apply to specific cosmetic products under Part 700. These rules render adulterated any cosmetic containing bithionol;[65] restrict the use of mercury compounds in skin-bleaching cosmetics;[66] ban the use of vinyl chloride[67] and zirconium[68] in aerosol cosmetics; forbid the use of certain halogenated salicylanilides,[69] chloroform,[70] and methylene chloride[71] as cosmetic ingredients; ban chlorofluorocarbon propellants from self-pressurized containers;[72] and establish certain tamper-resistant packaging requirements.[73] Each of these specific requirements addresses a safety concern related to the use or contents of a particular cosmetic when the agency views the general controls provided by the cosmetic provisions of the statute to be inadequate.[74]

---

[61]   *Id.* § 54.

[62]   *Id.* § 1125(a). *See, e.g.,* Thomas C. Morrison, *The Regulation of Cosmetic Advertising Under the Lanham Act,* 44 FOOD DRUG COSM. L.J. 49 (1989).

[63]   21 C.F.R. pts. 700-740.

[64]   *Id.* § 700.3.

[65]   *Id.* § 700.11.

[66]   *Id.* § 700.13. See also *infra* text accompanying note 179, regarding FDA's regulation of skin-bleaching creams prior to the promulgation of 21 C.F.R. § 700.13.

[67]   *Id.* § 700.14.

[68]   *Id.* § 700.16.

[69]   *Id.* § 700.15.

[70]   *Id.* § 700.18.

[71]   *Id.* § 700.19.

[72]   *Id.* § 700.23.

[73]   *Id.* § 700.25.

[74]   Although the cosmetic provisions of the Act do not authorize FDA to issue regulations dealing with individual formulation or ingredient concerns, the agency, under section 701(a) of the Act, 21 U.S.C. § 371(a), has the authority to "promulgate regulations for the efficient enforcement" of the statute.

Cosmetic Labeling

Part 701 sets forth the basic requirements for labeling cosmetic products. For the most part, these regulations impose requirements that are similar to those applicable to foods,[75] drugs,[76] and medical devices.[77] They also serve to implement the misbranding provisions of section 602.

Part 701 contains both general and specific provisions. The general provisions (Subpart A) establish broad principles as to when a cosmetic's labeling is false or misleading, and thus, misbranded.[78] Subpart A also addresses the correct way to format labeling under section 602(c).[79]

Although the cosmetic labeling rules resemble those governing drugs, some differences exist. For example, section 701.3(a) provides that the label of a cosmetic "shall bear a declaration of the name of each ingredient in descending order of predominance, except that fragrance or flavor may be listed as fragrance or flavor."[80] While the cosmetic regulations require ingredient labeling, they also allow manufacturers to ask FDA to grant "trade secret" status for a particular ingredient. This status is granted under very limited circumstances.[81]

A limited exemption from the statutory cosmetic adulteration and misbranding provisions also exists in section 701.9. This regulation, which is required by section 603 of the Act,[82] allows a person, under certain circumstances, to ship a cosmetic without having to comply with the cosmetic labeling requirements if the cosmetic is processed, labeled, or repacked in substantial quantity at another establishment.[83]

Subpart B of Part 701 sets forth the labeling requirements for all cosmetics sold in package form. The outer container (e.g., box, folding carton, wrapper holding the immediate (inner) container) label must include the following information on the principal display panel (PDP)[84]: a statement of the identity of the cosmetic, which is normally the common or usual

---

[75]   The general food labeling provisions appear at 21 C.F.R. pt. 101.

[76]   The general drug labeling provisions appear at *id.* pt. 201.

[77]   The device labeling provisions appear at *id.* pt. 801.

[78]   *Id.* § 701.1.

[79]   *Id.* § 701.2.

[80]   *Id.* § 701.3(a). The drug labeling regulations require that the label of a drug bear the established name and quantity of each active ingredient, together without any intervening written, printed or graphic matter. *See id.* § 201.10(a).

[81]   The manufacturer must prove that the ingredient imparts some unique property to a product and that the ingredient is not well known in the industry. If trade secret status is granted, the ingredient does not have to be listed on the label, but the list must end with the phrase "and other ingredients."

[82]   21 U.S.C. § 363:

> The Secretary shall promulgate regulations exempting from any labeling requirement of this Act cosmetics which are, in accordance with the practice of the trade, to be processed, labeled, or repacked in substantial quantities at establishments other than those where originally processed or packed, on condition that such cosmetics are not adulterated or misbranded under the provisions of this Act upon removal from such processing, labeling, or repacking establishment.

[83]   21 C.F.R. § 701.9.

[84]   The term "principal display panel" for cosmetics is defined at *id.* § 701.10 as "the part of a label that is most likely to be displayed, presented, shown, or examined under customary conditions of display for retail sale."

name for the cosmetic (e.g., nail polish),[85] net quantity of contents,[86] and the 21 C.F.R. § 740.10 warning, if applicable.[87] The label also must include on the information panel the name and place of business of the product's manufacturer, packer, or distributor,[88] the ingredient declaration,[89] any applicable warnings, and any other required information. The immediate (inner) container label is only required to include the name of the product on the front panel and the following information on the information panel: any applicable warnings, the name and place of business, the net quantity of contents, and any other required information.[90]

Voluntary Approach to Cosmetic Regulation

In Part 710 of the regulations, FDA requests owners and operators of cosmetic establishments to register their facilities with FDA. Registration is voluntary because the cosmetic provisions of the Act (unlike those applicable to drugs and devices) do not require registration. The Voluntary Cosmetic Registration Program (VCRP) was established in 1972, and the online VCRP system was established in 2005.[91] Since 1972, there have been 2,929 active cosmetic establishment registrations.[92] Part 720 provides for voluntary filing of cosmetic product ingredient and cosmetic raw material composition statements. Voluntary filing is designed to provide information to FDA about the ingredients and the composition of products. Part 730 provides for voluntary filing of cosmetic product experience reports by foreign and domestic manufacturers, packers, and distributors of cosmetic products. Such reports give FDA information to determine whether certain products or product categories cause injuries or other problems.[93]

These regulations that invite voluntary compliance are supported by the cosmetics industry in the hope that compliance will obviate the need for cosmetic legislation mandating registration, pre-notification, and approval of ingredients, and experience reporting. Similarly, in lieu of regulations for cosmetic good manufacturing practices (GMPs), FDA has issued a draft guidance discussing FDA's current thinking of what constitutes GMPs for cosmetics to assist industry in identifying the standards and issues that can affect the quality of cosmetic products.[94] The draft guidance provides suggested or recommended practices on topics including documentation, records, buildings and facilities, raw materials, production,

---

[85]   *Id.* § 710.11.

[86]   *Id.* § 701.13.

[87]   *Id.* § 740(1), (2).

[88]   *Id.* § 701.12.

[89]   *Id.* § 701.3.

[90]   U.S. FOOD & DRUG ADMIN., FDA COSMETIC LABELING GUIDE (May 6, 2014), http://www.fda.gov/cosmetics/ labeling/regulations/ucm126444.htm. While the FDA guidance identifies "directions for safe use" as information that must appear on the information panel of the inner and outer label, there is no requirement in the FDCA or FPLA for cosmetics to bear directions for use.

[91]   U.S. Food & Drug Admin., Registration Reports: VCRP Monthly Status Reports (May 7, 2014), http://www. fda.gov/Cosmetics/RegistrationProgram/RegistrationReports/default.htm.

[92]   *Id.*

[93]   An example of the effectiveness of this program is FDA's reissuance of its long-standing warning against "permanent" eyebrow and eyelash dyeing in response to a report of an injury possibly associated with eyebrow and eyelash tinting. *See* Talk Paper T92-31 (July 14, 1992).

[94]   *See* FDA, Draft Guidance for Industry: Cosmetic Good Manufacturing Practices (June 2013), *available at* http:// www.fda.gov/downloads/Cosmetics/GuidanceComplianceRegulatoryInformation/GuidanceDocuments/ UCM358287.pdf.

laboratory controls, and recalls. Although these voluntary programs appear to have helped the agency protect the public health, some observers suggest that voluntary programs are inadequate and that mandatory controls are needed to ensure cosmetic safety.[95]

Cosmetic Product Warning Statements

General and specific cosmetic warning statements are required under Part 740 of Title 21 of the *Code of Federal Regulations*. The general provisions mandate that a cosmetic label bear a warning statement "whenever necessary or appropriate to prevent a health hazard that may be associated with the product."[96] Requirements for specific warning statements may be promulgated by FDA on its initiative or in response to a citizen petition.[97]

The regulation that may be the most effective of all current agency cosmetic rules in protecting the public from injurious cosmetics[98] is the regulation requiring that a product containing cosmetic ingredients not proven to be safe bear the following warning on its principal display panel (PDP): "*Warning*—The safety of this product has not been determined."[99] This rule also provides that each cosmetic ingredient or finished product "shall be adequately substantiated for safety prior to marketing."[100]

The substantiation-of-safety requirement does not require FDA preclearance of ingredients or formulas. It does impose, however, a duty on the cosmetic marketer to take appropriate measures to assure that the product is safe.[101] Although FDA apparently has never taken action on this requirement, it remains a potential regulatory weapon. Other specific warning statements include those for self-pressurized containers,[102] feminine deodorant sprays,[103] foaming detergent bath products,[104] and coal-tar hair dyes that pose a risk of cancer.[105]

---

[95]   *See* Margaret Gilhooley, *Cosmetic Regulation: Going Beyond Appearance*, in Seventy-Fifth Anniversary Commemorative Volume of Food and Drug Law 323-49 (FDLI 1984). Periodically legislation is proposed to this effect. For example, on June 24, 2011, Reps. Jan Schakowsky (D-Ill.), Ed Markey (D-Mass.), and Tammy Baldwin (D-Wisc.), introduced a bill entitled the "Safe Cosmetics Act of 2011" (H.R. 2359). The bill would amend the FDCA to provide FDA with authority to require that cosmetic firms register their establishments and ensure that cosmetic ingredients are not harmful and are fully disclosed on a product's labeling. *See* The Safe Cosmetics Act of 2011, H.R. 2359, *available at* http://thomas.loc.gov/cgi-bin/query/z?c112:H.R.2359.

[96]   21 C.F.R. § 740.1(a).

[97]   *Id.* § 740.1(b).

[98]   Gilhooley, *supra* note 95.

[99]   21 C.F.R. § 740.10(a).

[100]   *Id.*

[101]   The actual testing methods employed to establish safety may vary considerably from one company to another. While animal testing is an industry norm, there is considerable pressure on the cosmetic industry from various consumer groups to eliminate the use of animals in safety testing. Industry frequently has responded by changing its approach to safety substantiation.

[102]   21 C.F.R. § 740.11.

[103]   *Id.* § 740.12.

[104]   *Id.* § 740.17.

[105]   *Id.* § 740.18. The effectiveness of this regulation has been stayed until further notice. *See* 47 Fed. Reg. 7829 (Feb. 23, 1982).

Regulating Cosmetic Ingredients

A true cosmetic ingredient,[106] other than a color additive, requires no prior approval by FDA before it may be used. The only enforceable limits on use of such a substance are the adulteration and misbranding provisions. Since new cosmetic ingredients are being developed at a fast pace,[107] we discuss below how FDA handles the entry into the market of new cosmetic ingredients and the controls that are in place.

Agency Actions With Respect to New Ingredients

As with many aspects of cosmetic regulation, the statute and regulations are silent on clearing cosmetic ingredients for entry into the market.[108] Thus, understanding how FDA approaches new ingredients requires reference to the drug provisions of the FDCA and to FDA's Over-the-Counter Drug Review (OTC Drug Review).[109]

For example, during the 10 years since the OTC Drug Review last formally considered sunscreens, a number of new sunscreen agents have been developed and marketed in several countries. FDA has taken the position that these new agents may not be marketed in the United States except pursuant to an approved new drug application.[110] Indeed, the agency has held that sunscreen agents that have not been reviewed by the OTC process must be treated as "new drugs."[111] FDA also has regarded sunscreen agents in cosmetic products as drugs, even when they are not promoted for the prevention of sunburn. In a 1986 letter, FDA took the position that the ingredient, and not the claim, makes the chemical subject to the new drug regulations.[112] FDA's guidance to its field investigators also takes this position; it states that a product should only be treated as a cosmetic "if no 'active ingredient' is declared *and* there are no indications of intended drug use (i.e., labeling claims, promotional statements, etc.)."[113]

---

[106]   A "true" cosmetic ingredient is a substance that has no uses as a drug ingredient, is not claimed to have a drug effect, and is not contained in an official drug compendium.

[107]   In 1995, approximately 2,000 new ingredients had been added to the Cosmetic, Toiletry and Fragrance Association *Cosmetic Ingredient Dictionary* during the last two years. *See* speech by John E. Bailey, Dir., Off. of Colors & Cosmetics, *Cosmeceuticals,* 1995 Annual Winter Meeting of the Toxicology Forum (Feb. 20, 1995). The current edition of the *International Cosmetic Ingredient Dictionary and Handbook* contains more than 17,000 International Nomenclature Cosmetic Ingredient (INCI) labeling names for the United States, the European Union and other countries. *See* http://webdictionary.personalcarecouncil.org/jsp/Home.jsp.

[108]   In 1974, an unsuccessful effort was made to amend the act to require preclearance of cosmetic ingredients. *See Cosmetic Safety Act of 1974: Hearings on S. 863 and S. 3012 Before the Subcomm. on Health of the Senate Comm. on Labor and Public Works,* 93d Cong., 2d Sess. (1974).

[109]   A more comprehensive discussion of the OTC Drug Review's impact on cosmetic regulation appears *infra* in the section titled "Controversies and Issues in the Regulation of Cosmetics: The Cosmetic/Drug Distinction" in this chapter.

[110]   Memorandum of Meeting between Estée Lauder and FDA re: sunscreen ingredients (Apr. 22, 1986); *see also* Citizen Petition, FDA Dkt. No. 78N-0038 (May 25, 1989) (on behalf of BASF AG to consider inclusion of PEG-25 PABA in the sunscreen monograph).

[111]   43 Fed. Reg. 38,206 (Aug. 25, 1978) (proposed rule). *See also* 58 Fed. Reg. 28,194, 28,195 (May 12, 1993) (tentative final monograph); 59 Fed. Reg. 29,706 (June 8, 1994) (notice of proposed rulemaking reopening of comment period).

[112]   Regulatory Letter 87HFN-312-28 to Rachael Perry, Inc. (June 15, 1987). A more lengthy discussion of FDA's handling of sunscreens appears *infra* text accompanying notes 194-198.

[113]   FDA Compliance Program Guidance Manual 7329.001, Part III, at 1 (Mar. 2010).

The agency also has attempted to draw a line between "drug ingredients" reviewed in the OTC Drug Review, and those used in cosmetics at a low or inactive level for technical, nondrug purposes. In the preamble to the tentative final monograph for OTC topical antimicrobial products, FDA stated that substances with drug properties can occur in a cosmetic without the cosmetic becoming a "drug" if the drug-like substance: 1) occurs at a low level—that is, below that specified in the OTC monograph; 2) is employed for nondrug or technical purposes; and 3) the labeling of the product makes no drug claims for the substance.[114]

The Cosmetic Ingredient Review: More Voluntary Compliance

Currently industry conducts a voluntary Cosmetic Ingredient Review (CIR) in which panels of non-industry scientific experts review the safety of cosmetic ingredients in a procedure closely modeled after the OTC Drug Review. CIR findings are reported to members of the industry, who are not specifically bound to follow the review's findings.[115]

FDA's Enforcement of the Law of Cosmetics

How FDA Is Organized to Regulate Cosmetics

Cosmetics constitute the only major product group governed by the FDCA that is not subject to its own separate center at FDA. Instead, the FDA office responsible for regulating cosmetics falls within the Center for Food Safety and Applied Nutrition (CFSAN). This office is known as the Office of Cosmetics and Colors.[116] The Office is divided into the Division of Color Certification and Technology and the Cosmetics Staff.

Within the Division of Color Certification and Technology is the Color Certification Branch, which analyzes color samples that are manufactured for use in foods, drugs, and cosmetics. If the color sample meets the branch's specifications, the color is certified for use.

Also within the Office of Cosmetics and Colors is the Cosmetics Activities Team, which maintains the voluntary registration program for cosmetic establishments and formulations (ingredients). In addition, the Cosmetics Staff is responsible for compliance actions,[117] developing regulations, policy, and guidance, and advising companies on proper product

---

[114] 43 Fed. Reg. 1210 (Jan. 6, 1978).

[115] From 1976 to 2012, the CIR Expert Panel conducted safety assessments for 3,156 ingredients. Of the 3,156 ingredients reviewed, 2,060 (65.3 percent) were rated as "safe in the present practices of use and concentration" or some equivalent variation thereof. COSMETIC INGREDIENT REVIEW, ANNUAL REPORT (2012).

[116] The office is physically housed at the Center for Food Safety and Applied Nutrition in College Park, Maryland.

[117] If FDA contends that a cosmetic is actually a drug, then the Office of Compliance in the Center for Drug Evaluation and Research will take the lead in initiating any regulatory action.

labeling.[118] In all, the Office of Cosmetics and Colors employs approximately 50 persons and was organized into its present structure in December 2007.[119]

FDA Enforcement Policies Regarding Cosmetics

The agency's enforcement policies with respect to cosmetics can be gleaned from several sources. In FDA's *Compliance Program Guidance Manual* (CPGM), one section is devoted to cosmetics. This manual is designed to provide information to FDA field staff as to priorities and policies for handling enforcement activities relating to any FDA-regulated product, including cosmetics. The cosmetic provisions appear at Chapter 29.[120] Under this manual, FDA enforcement priority is devoted to products that may present a health hazard (e.g., bacterial contamination of eye cosmetics) whether produced domestically[121] or imported.[122]

In addition to the *Compliance Program Guidance Manual*, FDA provides two other kinds of guidance to its officials. The *Investigations Operations Manual* (IOM) contains specific instructions to guide FDA inspectors during inspections of cosmetic establishments.[123] FDA also has several *Compliance Policy Guides* (CPGs) that provide specific guidance to FDA inspectors as to how to respond to specific problems, including natural bristle brushes[124] and packaging technologies and tamper-resistant packaging requirements for cosmetics.[125]

Controversies and Issues in the Regulation of Cosmetics: The Cosmetic/Drug Distinction

Since 1938, the cosmetic provisions of the FDCA have generated only limited enforcement activity under both the adulteration and misbranding provisions and the color additive provisions.[126] Instead, FDA's enforcement of the 1938 Act has concentrated principally on resolving the tension that exists between the "drug" and "cosmetic" definitions of the statute. This tension is the primary result of Congress' failure to clearly differentiate between a cosmetic and a drug and FDA's judicial successes in drug litigation.[127]

---

[118]   Email from Don Havery, Voluntary Cosmetic Reporting Program Administrator, Cosmetics Staff, Off. of Cosmetics & Colors, Center for Food Safety & Applied Nutrition, Food & Drug Admin., to Carolina Heavner, Associate (Feb. 4, 2008) (on file with author).

[119]   Email from Don Havery, Voluntary Cosmetic Reporting Program Administrator, Cosmetics Staff, Off. of Cosmetics & Colors, Center for Food Safety & Applied Nutrition, Food & Drug Admin., to Carolina Heavner, Associate (April 4, 2011) (on file with author). *See also* Email from Don Havery to Carolina Heavner, Associate, dated Feb. 4, 2008.

[120]   *Cosmetics Program; Import and Domestic,* FDA COMPLIANCE PROGRAM GUIDANCE MANUAL 7329.001 (Mar. 2010).

[121]   *Id.* at pt. II, 1.

[122]   *Id.*

[123]   *Establishment Inspection,* FDA INVESTIGATIONS OPERATIONS MANUAL ch. 5 (2014).

[124]   FDA COMPLIANCE POLICY GUIDE § 590.400 (Nov. 29, 2005).

[125]   *Id.* § 590.500 (Nov. 29, 2005).

[126]   *See supra* text accompanying notes 9-125.

[127]   The cosmetic/drug distinction has been the source of numerous comments. *See* Stephen H. McNamara, *The Food and Drug Administration Over-the-Counter Drug* Review—*Concerns of the Cosmetic Industry,* 38 FOOD DRUG COSM. L.J. 289 (1983); Morrison, *supra* note 62; Emalee G. Murphy, *Cosmeceuticals—The Regulatory Environment or the Cosmetic Wars and Other Phenomena,* 44 FOOD DRUG COSM. L.J. 41 (1989); Gary L. Yingling, *Cosmetic Regulation, in* FOOD AND DRUG LAW 344-70 (FDLI 1991); Jacqueline A. Greff, *Regulation of Cosmetics*

The Role of Intent in Resolving the Cosmetic/Drug Distinction

It is easy to imagine instances when an article used for cleansing, beautifying or altering the appearance of the human body also would affect the structure or function of the body, and even prevent or cure disease, and thereby satisfy both the definition of "drug"[128] and the definition of "cosmetic."[129] Similarly, chemicals described in an official compendium could have cosmetic uses even though not so promoted. A significant portion of the debate leading to the 1938 Act focused on definitional issues. Congress provided that the manufacturer's "intended use" of the product should determine whether it is a drug. A 1935 Senate report stated:

> The use to which the product is to be put will determine the category into which it will fall. If it is to be used only as a food it will come within the definition of food and none other. If it contains nutritive ingredients but is sold for drug use only, as clearly shown by the labeling and advertising, it will come within the definition of drug, but not that of food. If it is sold to be used both as a food and for the prevention or treatment of disease it would satisfy both definitions and be subject to the substantive requirements for both. The manufacturer of the article, through his representations in connection with its sale, can determine the use to which the article is to be put.[130]

Thus, the drafters of the legislation saw the intended use of the article as dispositive regarding whether it should be regulated as a "drug" or "cosmetic." However, in some instances, determining intent has proven difficult.

Early FDA Attempts to Resolve the Drug Versus Cosmetic Distinction: The Trade Correspondence

After passage of the 1938 Act, the agency issued a series of informal opinions, known as Trade Correspondence (TC).[131] The early TCs applied the statute to specific problems that faced the agency. In later years, TCs were issued more formally and published in the *Federal Register* as "Statements of General Policy or Interpretation." Some of these earlier TCs, however, are still relied upon as support for FDA regulatory policy.

The TCs dealt with many problems pertaining to a cosmetic's intended use. For example, TC-10, issued in August 1939, notified manufacturers, packers, and distributors of cosmetics of "typical examples of claims that are regarded as false or misleading."[132] TC-10 stated that "a survey . . . indicate[d] the probability that a substantial proportion of the cosmetic industry has not realized that certain names and statements which have long been employed in

---

That Are Also Drugs, 51 FOOD DRUG COSM. L.J. 243-272 (1996); Lauren A. Heymann, *The Cosmetic/Drug Dilemma: FDA Regulation of Alpha-Hydroxy Acids,* 52 FOOD DRUG. COSM. L.J. 357 (1997).

128   *See* 21 U.S.C. § 321(g)(1).
129   *See supra* text accompanying note 13.
130   S. REP. No. 361, 74th Cong., 1st Sess. 201 (1935).
131   FEDERAL FOOD, DRUG, AND COSMETIC ACT, *supra* note 53 at 561-753.
132   *Id.* at 566.

the labeling of cosmetics may contravene requirements of the [new] statute."[133] The claims the agency found contrary to law included "contour cream," "crow's foot cream," "eyelash grower," "hair grower," "skin food," and "wrinkle eradicator."[134]

In February 1940, the agency attempted to explain how to classify deodorant products in TC-26 by stating: "[i]f the action of [a deodorant powder was] to stop perspiration, such a product would . . . be a drug; if, however, the only action of the deodorant powder [was] to absorb the perspiration or to mask its odor, it would *probably* be a cosmetic."[135]

In TC-42, issued three days after TC-26, the agency declared that a product containing gum camphor, beeswax, paraffin, and mineral oil would be classified as a cosmetic if the claim was for "softening the lips, hands, and roughened skin."[136] Apparently, the impact on the body was not sufficient to warrant drug classification under the "affect the body" clause of the drug definition.

Also in 1940, in TC-61, FDA said that a product that referred to sunburn or any other disease condition was a drug. Articles that were represented exclusively for the production of an "even tan," however, were cosmetics.

In April 1940, in TC-229, the agency stated that the word "healthful," contained in the labeling of a tooth powder, would "bring the product within the classification of the term 'drug.'"[137] In TC-245 (1940), the agency determined that cuticle removers were cosmetics rather than drugs.[138]

In some instances, FDA's guidance was unenlightening. TC-9 (1939) is particularly noteworthy because it was one of the first "Notices to Manufacturers" regarding a product classified as both a cosmetic and a drug. Regarding the status of mercury bleach creams, the agency stated: "These articles are cosmetics within the meaning of the statute because they are intended to promote the attractiveness and to alter the appearance of the person. They are also drugs because they are intended to affect the structure and function of the body."[139] FDA did not explain, however, what factors would differentiate a "cosmetic" mercury bleach cream from a "drug" mercury bleach cream.

The Wrinkle Remover Cases

The cosmetic/drug distinction has been addressed directly in only three judicial decisions, known as the "Wrinkle Remover cases" or "Bovine Albumin cases."[140] All three cases turned

---

133   *Id.*

134   *Id.* at 566-67.

135   *Id.* at 581 (emphasis added). The use of "probably" may indicate that FDA was merely being cautious or that it found the "drug/cosmetic" dilemma difficult to resolve even during the early years of the Act.

136   *Id.* at 586.

137   *Id.* at 659.

138   *Id.* at 665.

139   *Id.* at 565. In 1973, the FDA withdrew TC-9 because it determined that mercury-containing skin-bleaching beauty and facial preparations posed safety problems. 38 Fed. Reg. 853 (Jan. 5, 1973).

140   United States v. An Article ... Line Away, 284 F. Supp. 107 (D. Del. 1968), *aff'd*, 415 F.2d 369 (3d Cir. 1969); United States v. An Article ... Sudden Change, 288 F. Supp. 29 (E.D.N.Y. 1968), *rev'd*, 409 F.2d 734 (2d Cir. 1969); United States v. An Article ... Magic Secret, 331 F. Supp. 912 (D. Md. 1971).

on the application of clause (c) of the "drug" definition in section 201(g) of the Act—the "affect the body of man" provision.[141]

The first to be decided was *Line Away,* in which FDA seized 36 bottles of "Line Away Temporary Wrinkle Smoother." The agency alleged that the product was a "drug" because it was intended to "smooth, firm and tighten the skin."[142] The court agreed; it found the product to be a drug under the "affect the body of man" clause, and rejected claimant's arguments that the wrinkle effect was so insignificant and of such temporary duration so as not to be subject to drug regulation.

Shortly thereafter, the Federal District Court in Brooklyn addressed a similar issue in another seizure action, this time involving a product known as "Sudden Change." The product's labeling claims in the *Sudden Change* litigation were even more medicinal than those in *Line Away.* The lotion was advertised as providing a "Face Lift Without Surgery." FDA cited the recent *Line Away* decision to support its assertion that the product was a drug. The lower court disagreed, however, and refused to apply the "affect the body of man" clause, partially out of the belief that invoking that clause would render virtually any cosmetic a drug, and also out of recognition that, because of the amount of puffery in cosmetic advertising, it was impossible to regard these as drug claims.

On appeal by FDA, the Second Circuit reversed. It held that the lower court had applied an incorrect standard when it had held that consumers would not interpret the product's claims as promising a structural change. Rather, the "Act will best be affected by postulating a consuming public which includes 'the ignorant, the unthinking and the credulous.'"[143] The Court ruled that the labeling claims "to lift out puffs" and to provide a "face lift without surgery" were distinctly physiological, and suggested to the consumer that the product would "affect the structure . . . of the body"; and therefore, the product was a drug.[144]

Shortly after the appellate decision in *Sudden Change,* the Third Circuit heard the appeal of the claimant, Charles Pfizer & Co., from the decree of condemnation handed down in *Line Away.* In affirming that the product was a drug, the Court of Appeals ruled that, regardless of the actual physical effect of a product, the labeling claims could make it a drug: "Some 'puffery' may not amount to representation of a cosmetic as a drug, but when 'puffery' contains the strong therapeutic implications we find in the Line Away promotional material, we think the dividing line has been crossed."[145] The appellate court's decision seemed to rest more on the fact that the product was promoted as made in a "pharmaceutical laboratory" and packaged under "biologically aseptic conditions," rather than on any specific aspect of the labeling that represented that the product "affected the body of man" or was used to treat disease.[146]

---

[141] *See* 21 U.S.C. § 321(g)(1).

[142] 284 F. Supp. at 109. FDA specifically charged that Line Away was an unapproved new drug in violation of section 505(a) of the Act, 21 U.S.C. § 355(a), and misbranded under section 502(a), *id.* § 352(a), due to lack of adequate directions for use and misleading statements as to its effectiveness in eliminating wrinkles.

[143] 409 F.2d at 740.

[144] *Id.* at 741.

[145] 415 F.2d at 372-73.

[146] *Id.*

The final case in the Wrinkle Remover series involved a Helene Curtis product: "Magic Secret." FDA instituted a seizure action against this product in 1968, but the action was placed in abeyance pending the decisions in *Line Away* and *Sudden Change*. The Court held that because the labeling claims in *Magic Secret* did not approach those made in the prior two cases, the product was a cosmetic. In so doing, it applied the test articulated in *Sudden Change*:

> [T]he question of whether a product is "intended to affect the structure . .
> . of the body of man . . . 'is to be answered by considering, first, how the
> claim might be understood by the' ignorant, unthinking or credulous"
> consumer, and second, whether the claim as so understood may fairly be
> said to constitute a representation that the product will affect the structure
> of the body in some medical—or drug-type fashion, i.e., in some way
> other than merely "altering the appearance."[147]

The result of these cases is that there remains no clear FDA rule regarding the cosmetic/drug distinction and each product needs to be reviewed based on the manufacturer's claims. Since the courts did not accept FDA's argument that any "drug" statement makes the product a drug, both the cosmetics industry and the agency showed greater restraint. In the decade following these cases, industry toned down its claims and FDA took no noteworthy enforcement actions based on the cosmetic/drug distinction.

Reviving the Wrinkle Remover Cases: "Cell Renewal" and "Anti-Aging" Claims

Restraint was short-lived. In a 1983 speech, then FDA Commissioner Arthur Hull Hayes Jr. observed that industry had reverted to "drug" language reminiscent of the Wrinkle Remover cases of the 1960s. He stated that the agency had "seen an increasing number of cosmetics making claims that go far beyond what is generally considered—if you will excuse the phrase 'cosmetic puffery.'"[148]

Two years later, a leading member of the cosmetic bar noted that the situation had not changed noticeably and that, if anything, cosmetic labeling claims were becoming even more "daring."[149] Indeed, by late 1986, numerous companies had introduced aggressive labeling claims on cosmetics that included "anti-aging" and "cell renewal."

Faced with a tumultuous cosmetic marketplace that was replete with drug claims, one anonymous firm, through its counsel, asked FDA to clarify the limits of the label claims dilemma. In a January 1987 citizen petition,[150] FDA was requested to decide whether many of the newly popular claims properly fell under the definition of a "cosmetic" or a "drug."

---

[147]   331 F. Supp. at 917 (quoting *Sudden Change,* 409 F.2d at 741-42).

[148]   Remarks by Arthur Hull Hayes, Jr., M.D., Comm'r. of Food and Drugs, Food & Drug Admin., before the Annual Meeting of the Cosmetic, Toiletry and Fragrance Ass'n, Boca Raton, Fla. (Mar. 2, 1983).

[149]   Stephen H. McNamara, *Performance Claims for Skin Care Cosmetics or How Far May You Go in Claiming to Provide Eternal Youthfulness,* 41 FOOD DRUG COSM. L.J. 151, 152 (1986).

[150]   Citizen Petition of McCutchen, Doyle, Brown & Enersen Re: Bio Advance, FDA Dkt. No. 87P-0006 (Jan. 6, 1987).

In the spring of 1987, the agency issued regulatory letters, now known as "Warning Letters," to 23 firms pertaining to their cosmetic products. The letters alleged that the use of claims such as "cell renewal," "cell recovery," "cell repair," "anti-aging," "reverse facial aging," "increased collagen production," "increase the available oxygen in the cells," and "restructuring the deepest epidermal layers" were drug, not cosmetic, claims. FDA contended that the products were not generally recognized as safe and effective for their labeled claims and were unapproved new drugs that required FDA approval prior to marketing.[151]

In addition to alleging that the products were unapproved new drugs, FDA asserted that almost every one of them was a misbranded drug under either section 502(f)(1) (lack of adequate directions for use), section 502(e) (failure to declare active ingredients on immediate container label), or section 502(o) (failure to list the article with FDA under section 510(j) of the Act and 21 C.F.R. Part 207).

In one response to the agency,[152] the companies attempted to distinguish "physical"[153] effects (cosmetic) from "physiological"[154] effects (drug). FDA rejected this approach and stated:

> We consider a claim that a product will affect the body in some physiological way to be a drug claim, even if the claim is that the effect is only temporary. Such a claim constitutes a representation that the product is intended to affect the structure or function of the body and thus makes the product a drug under 21 U.S.C. 321(g)(1)(c). Therefore, we consider most of the anti-aging and skin physiology claims . . . to be drug claims.[155]

The agency's letter offered the cosmetic houses guidance on what would be an acceptable cosmetic claim:

> [W]e would not object to claims that products will temporarily improve the appearance of such outward signs of aging [i.e., wrinkles]. The label of such products should state that the product is intended to cover up the signs of aging, to improve the appearance by adding color or luster to skin, or otherwise to affect the appearance through physical means.[156]

---

151   *See, e.g.,* FDA Regulatory Letter No. 87-HFN-312-08 to Leonard Lauder, Pres., Estée Lauder (Apr. 17, 1987); FDA Regulatory Letter No. 87-HFN-312-12 to William Slater, Sr., Vice Pres., Christian Dior Perfumes, Inc. (Apr. 24, 1987); FDA Regulatory Letter No. 87-HFN-312-22 to Catherine D'Alessio, Chanel, Inc. (May 15, 1987).

152   *See, e.g.,* letter to John M. Taylor, Associate Comm'r, Regulatory Aff., Food & Drug Admin., from Counsel for Avon Prods., Inc.; Clarins USA, Inc.; Chanel Inc.; Orlane Inc.; Estée Lauder, Inc.; Frances Denney, Inc.; Shiseido Cosmetics (Am.) Ltd.; Christian Dior Perfumes, Inc.; Elizabeth Arden, Inc.; Adrien Arpel; La Prairie, Inc.; and Jacqueline Cochran, Inc. (Sept. 11, 1986).

153   "[E]ffects created through mechanical processes (e.g., exfoliation or massage), the application of products that 'cover' the skin (e.g., lipstick or makeup), or other similar sorts of effects that are associated primarily with the outermost layers of the skin (the stratum corneum) (e.g., 'softening,' 'moisturizing')."

154   "[E]ffects of a biochemical nature or that influence the functioning of cells or tissue beneath the stratum corneum."

155   Letter from John M. Taylor, Associate Comm'r, Regulatory Aff., Food & Drug Admin., to Stuart Lee Friedel, Davis & Gilbert, re: Cosmetic Regulatory Letters 1 (Nov. 18, 1987).

156   *Id.* at 2.

FDA also reiterated its view that sunscreen products are drugs, as were products known as "skin protectants" designed to protect the skin from harmful stimuli. In contrast, products claiming to improve or temporarily maintain the appearance or the feel of skin (e.g., moisturizers and softeners) were cosmetics.[157]

In the only court decision touching on this subject, the court dismissed a declaratory judgment action filed by Estée Lauder in which Estée Lauder sought to uphold the viability of the claims challenged by FDA. The Court ruled that judicial review was improper due to the lack of final agency action.[158] Other than the FDA-initiated wave of regulatory activity in 1987 in the form of Warning Letters, FDA took no significant legal action to address the drug/cosmetic distinction. Thus, while the 1987 revival of the issues first adjudicated in the Wrinkle Remover cases shows that the agency still is interested in cosmetic labeling and drug claims, little new light has fallen on the distinction between the "drug" and "cosmetic" definitions. In fact, based on the limited enforcement activity that followed after the 1987 letters, industry quickly returned to the aggressive claims FDA sought to control in 1987.

Wrinkle Reduction and Anti-Aging Redux

In 2012, the "sleeping giant" appeared to awaken when FDA issued Warning Letters to six companies over a 30-day period. The Warning Letters were directed to both boutique cosmetic houses and established institutions.[159] According to FDA, the companies were making "extreme" anti-aging claims that crossed the line into drug territory. Examples of claims at issue included the following:

- "Boosts the activity of genes."

- "See significant deep wrinkle reduction in UV damaged skin, clinically proven."

- "Start rebuilding collagen in just 48 hours."

- "Stimulate elastin to help improve elasticity and resilience."

- "Help tighten the connections between skin's layers."

- "[R]epairs the structural damage that actually causes those wrinkles."

- "Damaged skin cells repair themselves and then replicate, creating healthier replacement cells."

- "Stimulate cell regeneration."

- "Activates . . . fibroblast stem cells."

- "[A]ccelerate skin regeneration."

---

[157] *Id.*

[158] Estée Lauder, Inc. v. FDA, 727 F. Supp. 1 (D.D.C. 1989).

[159] *See* Warning Letters Address Drug Claims Made for Products Marketed as Cosmetics (FDA), *available at* http://www.fda.gov/cosmetics/complianceenforcement/warningletters/ucm081086.htm.   Independently, the FTC has pursued actions against cosmetic companies for similar anti-aging claims in advertising, alleging that the claims are false and misleading. *See, e.g.,* L'Oreal Settles FTC Charges Alleging Deceptive Advertising for Anti-Aging Cosmetics (FTC June 2014), *available at* http://www.ftc.gov/news-events/press-releases/2014/06/loreal-settles-ftc-charges-alleging-deceptive-advertising-anti.

FDA concluded that these and other identified claims indicate that the products are intended to affect the structure or function of the body, thereby rendering them drugs under the FDCA.

Since that 30-day "blitz," enforcement activity has once again slowed. As a result, it is difficult to assess whether FDA is preparing to take a more active stance against these product claims. Nevertheless, intentionally or not, the enforcement spike has had a corollary effect of prompting an increase in consumer class actions alleging violations under false advertising and consumer protection laws.

The New Wave: Alpha Hydroxy Acids, Thigh Thinners, and Eyelash Growth Products

A number of products currently on the market are labeled as exerting an effect on the structure and function of the body. They often list "active" ingredients typically associated with drugs, but carefully craft their claims to avoid overt statements that, have attracted the attention of FDA in the past.[160] Some believe these products raise interesting questions about the marketing practices of the cosmetic industry, product safety, and whether the law as currently written can address these "new cosmetics." Others are concerned that if FDA were to determine these products were new drugs, a user fee of more than a million dollars and years of review would be disproportionate to their use as cosmetics.

For example, a wide range of "cosmetic" products are formulated using alpha hydroxy acid (AHA) ingredients. AHAs are organic acids that, when applied to the body, are capable of causing exfoliation of the outer layers of the skin. Virtually every major cosmetic manufacturer now offers an AHA product and, by some accounts, AHAs are single-handedly responsible for the recent growth observed in the cosmetic industry. AHA products are being marketed as cosmetics directly to the consumer or for salon use only. None have been shown to be safe and effective for any drug application. These products affect the barrier properties of the skin and are being promoted for preventative and therapeutic benefits such as to treat dry and severely dry skin, unblock and cleanse pores, improve skin texture and tone, help manage oil/acne skin problems, and reduce skin discoloration and age spots. FDA has taken no action against AHA cosmetic products claiming to provide a treatment benefit.

In December 1996, the CIR Expert Panel issued a tentative final report on the safety of two AHAs, glycolic and lactic acids. The panel concluded, after reviewing the Cosmetic, Toiletry, and Fragrance Association's (CTFA)[161] sunburn cell test, and other data, that these acids, their common salts, and their simple esters, are safe for retail and professional use in cosmetic products when limited to specific concentration and pH ranges if they are formulated to avoid increasing the skin's sensitivity to sun or are accompanied by directions for the daily use of sun protection.[162]

---

[160]   These products have been referred to as "cosmeceuticals" by some because, through their promotional claims, they promise to deliver some type of beneficial effect beyond that which is normally associated with "traditional" cosmetics, but they are being marketed under the cosmetic statutory scheme.

[161]   The Cosmetic, Toiletry, and Fragrance Association (CTFA) is now known as the Personal Care Products Council (PCPC). *See* Personal Care Products Council, About Us: A Centennial History of the Personal Care Products Council, http://www.personalcarecouncil.org/about-us/history (last visited May 30, 2014).

[162]   F-D-C Rep. ("The Rose Sheet"), Dec. 23, 1996, at 1-3.

In January 2005, as a result of studies performed by CTFA and FDA on the safety of topically applied AHAs in cosmetic products, FDA issued a guidance[163] recommending a "sunburn alert" labeling statement on AHA-containing products in order to inform consumers about the potential for increased skin sensitivity to the sun, and particularly the increased possibility of sunburn.[164] According to the guidance, the human clinical studies conducted by CTFA and FDA showed that topically applied AHAs increase skin sensitivity to UV radiation. This conclusion was supported by adverse experience reports filed by consumers reporting increased sunburn after using AHA-containing products. FDA noted that the recommended labeling statement was an "interim" measure pending the results of an ongoing study on the long-term exposure to AHAs.

Another category of products that has appeared on the market are the "Thigh Creams" that are formulated using aminophylline and theophylline. These products typically promise to reduce the appearance of fat (cellulite) from the body, "smooth" hips and thighs, and reduce inches from the waist and thigh areas. FDA stated that marketing these products could lead to Warning Letters or product recalls if the products are found to pose health risks to consumers. In February 2000, FDA's Office of Cosmetics and Colors published a fact sheet expressing continued concern over the use of these ingredients and noting that "Thigh Creams" may be more appropriately classified as drugs since the removal or reduction of cellulite affects the "structure or function" of the body.[165] As of May 2014, there had only been three reported actions taken by FDA against companies marketing anti-cellulite thigh cream that claimed to significantly reduce thigh circumference.[166]

More recently, "eyelash enhancement" products have entered the marketplace in large numbers. Many of these products are marketed with claims indicating an intended use as a cosmetic to alter or enhance the appearance of eyelashes (e.g., "longer looking," "appear thicker"). However, others make explicit growth claims (e.g., "lengthening" or "thickening" eyelashes).[167] Some of these eyelash products contain peptides and others contain prostaglandins, ingredients that have been approved as active drug ingredients.[168] These products raise issues similar to the AHA products and bring back into stark relief

---

[163] FDA, Guidance for Industry: Labeling for Topically Applied Cosmetic Products Containing Alpha Hydroxy Acids as Ingredients (Jan. 10, 2005), *available at* http://www.fda.gov/Cosmetics/GuidanceComplianceRegulatoryInformation/GuidanceDocuments/ucm090816.htm.

[164] FDA recommended the following statement should appear on the cosmetic product label: "Sunburn Alert: This product contains an alpha hydroxy acid (AHA) that may increase your skin's sensitivity to the sun and particularly the possibility of sunburn. Use a sunscreen, wear protective clothing and limit sun exposure while using this product and for a week afterwards."

[165] U.S. Food & Drug Admin. THIGH CREAMS (Feb. 24, 2000), http://www.fda.gov/cosmetics/productsingredients/products/ucm127641.htm.

[166] *See* Warning Letter from Alonzo E. Cruse, Director, Los Angeles District, Food & Drug Admin., to Raymond J. Francis, President & CEO, University Medical Products USA, Inc. (Jan. 22, 2004), *available at* http://www.fda.gov/ICECI/EnforcementActions/WarningLetters/2004/ucm146174.htm.; Warning Letter from John Kuerbert for Joseph R. Baca, Director, Office of Compliance, Ctr for Food Safety & Applied Nutrition, to Randy Moss, President, Hydroderm Beverly Hills (Sept. 26, 2005), *available at* http://www.fda.gov/ICECI/EnforcementActions/WarningLetters/2005/ucm075572.htm; Warning Letter from Emma R. Singleton, Director, Florida District, Food & Drug Admin, to Stephan D. Karian, President, Great American Products, Inc. (Apr. 18, 2005), *available at* http://www.fda.gov/ICECI/EnforcementActions/WarningLetters/2005/ucm075374.htm.

[167] F-D-C REP. ("The Rose Sheet"), Sept. 28, 2009, at 1-3.

[168] *See* Approval Letter dated December 24, 2008 for Latisse™ (bimatoprost ophthalmic solution) 0.03%, NDA # 22-369.

the question of whether a product's claims or ingredients ultimately determine a product's intended use.

In 2007, FDA seized more than 12,000 tubes of an eyelash product marketed by Jan Marini Skin Research due to the presence of bimatoprost, a prostaglandin that is the active ingredient in an FDA-approved drug to treat elevated intraocular pressure in glaucoma.[169] According to the FDA press release, the Jan Marini products were both adulterated cosmetics due to the presence of the prostaglandin and unapproved and misbranded drugs because they were being promoted to increase eyelash growth.[170]

In April 2011, FDA issued a Warning Letter to Lifetech Resources LLC (Lifetech) regarding its eyelash and eyebrow growth products.[171] In that Warning Letter, FDA concluded that the products were drugs because "they are articles intended to affect the structure function of the body by inducing eyelash . . . growth."[172] FDA also stated that the "presence of the prostaglandin analog . . . along with the appearance of claims such as 'enhance the appearance of your lashes and brows,' 'fuller healthier-looking lashes' . . . indicate that your products are intended to affect the structure or function of the body."[173]

The FDA Warning Letter raises interesting issues regarding FDA's distinction between cosmetics and drugs. FDA appears to be taking the position that the presence of certain ingredients can make a product a drug even if the marketing claims indicate an intended use as a cosmetic. Moreover, the Warning Letter implies that the ingredient does not have to be an approved drug ingredient—it can be enough for the ingredient to be in the same family of compounds as an approved drug ingredient for FDA to conclude that the product is a drug irrespective of the product's claims. This position, as noted above, is highly controversial and reopens questions that cut to the crux of the cosmetic-drug distinction.

Ingredients and the Cosmetic/Drug Distinction: The OTC Review

In 1972, FDA began to review OTC drugs to determine which ingredients are safe, effective and appropriately labeled.[174] Within that OTC Drug Review were five drug monograph categories involving products that could be classified as drugs or cosmetics, depending on their labeling claims. These categories were topical antimicrobial products,[175] skin protectant

---

[169]   See Press Release, Food & Drug Admin., Approximately $2 Million of Potentially Harmful "Cosmetic" Eye Product Seized; Product contains drug ingredient, makes unapproved drug claims, could damage eye (Nov. 16, 2007), available at http://www.fda.gov/NewsEvents/Newsroom/PressAnnouncements/2007/ucm109028.htm.

[170]   Id.

[171]   See FDA Warning Letter dated April 18, 2011 issued against Lifetech Resources LLC; see also FDA Warning Letter dated May 24, 2011 issued against Allure Laboratories, Inc.

[172]   Id. Lifetech Resources LLC Warning Letter.

[173]   Id.

[174]   37 Fed. Reg. 9464, 9473 (May 11, 1972).

[175]   39 Fed. Reg. 33,103 (Sept. 13, 1974); see also 43 Fed. Reg. 1210 (Jan. 6, 1978); 60 Fed. Reg. 23,304 (May 8, 1995); 64 Fed. Reg. 27,666 (May 21, 1999); 72 Fed. Reg. 49,070 (Aug. 27, 2007).

products,[176] sunscreen products,[177] antiperspirant products,[178] skin-bleaching products,[179] and nasal moisturizers.[180] Over the years, FDA has addressed the cosmetic/drug dichotomy in other OTC monograph categories as well.[181]

Several advisory panels that prepared the OTC proposed monographs recommended that the agency abandon the "intent" test articulated in the TCs and the Wrinkle Remover cases, and adopt an ingredient criterion for resolving the cosmetic/drug distinction.[182] To date, FDA has not articulated an ingredient versus intended use test in the final monographs, and even though it is not complete, it is not likely that FDA will follow the advisory panels' recommendations.

At its inception in 1972, the OTC Drug Review was expected to take less than five years. Some 40 years later, the OTC Monograph Review is still not complete. Because so little progress has been made in the last few years, on February 24, 2014, FDA published a notice of a public hearing to obtain comments on the strengths and weaknesses of the current OTC Monograph Review process and to obtain ideas for modifications or alternatives to the process. A number of people believe the hearing, held on March 25 and 26, 2014, will be the foundation to make major changes in the process. Indeed, many believe the agency is interested in abandoning the notice and comment rulemaking in favor of publishing guidances stating FDA's position on ingredients and labeling. A decision to walk away from the Review will raise a number of issues going forward for the cosmetic and pharmaceutical industry. As will be discussed later in the chapter, many of the difficult cosmetic vs. drug labeling and ingredient issues have been topics of significant discussion in the monograph system, which has included notice and comment rulemaking. A guidance review process would remove the checks and balances that assure adequate and complete agency review. Of equal concern is whether the agency has the time and resources to invest in creating guidances. Without sufficient resources, one wonders if the cosmetic/OTC monograph drugs will become a historical artifact with little or no innovations in ingredients, labeling, or formulations for cosmetics in the future. Since the agency will not be publishing OTC drug monographs defining what is generally recognized as safe and effective in relationship to ingredients and labeling for OTC drug products, the drug/cosmetic issue surely will not be subject to a single definitive resolution. The following are several examples of the differing approaches FDA has taken on this issue over the years.

---

[176]   48 Fed. Reg. 6820 (Feb. 15, 1983). The Tentative Final Monograph for this OTC category has been amended several times to include astringent drug products, poison ivy and insect bite treatment drug products, fever blister and cold sore treatment drug products, and diaper rash treatment drug products. *See* 54 Fed. Reg. 13,490 (Apr. 3, 1989); 54 Fed. Reg. 40,808 (Oct. 3, 1989); 54 Fed. Reg. 40,818 (Oct. 3, 1989); 55 Fed. Reg. 3362 (Jan. 31, 1990); 55 Fed. Reg. 25,204 (June 20, 1990). Final rules have been issued for several of these subcategories.

[177]   43 Fed. Reg. 38,206 (Aug. 25, 1978); *see also* 58 Fed. Reg. 28,194 (May 12, 1993); 64 Fed. Reg. 27,666 (May 21, 1999); 72 Fed. Reg. 49,070 (Aug. 27, 2007); 76 Fed. Reg. 35,619 (June 17, 2011).

[178]   43 Fed. Reg. 46,694 (Oct. 10, 1978); *see also* 67 Fed. Reg. 36,492 (Aug. 20, 1982); 68 Fed. Reg. 34,273 (June 9, 2003).

[179]   47 Fed. Reg. 39,108 (Sept. 3, 1982).

[180]   68 Fed. Reg. 75,585 (Dec. 31, 2003).

[181]   For example, Vaginal Drug Products, 59 Fed. Reg. 5226 (Feb. 3, 1994); Nailbiting and Thumbsucking Deterrent Drug Products, 58 Fed. Reg. 46,749 (Sept. 2, 1993); Acne Drug Products, 56 Fed. Reg. 41,008 (Aug. 16, 1991); and Hair Grower and Hair Loss Prevention Products, 54 Fed. Reg. 28,772 (July 7, 1989). *See also* United States v. Kasz Enterprises, Inc., 1994 U.S. Dist. LEXIS 8597 (D.R.I. 1994).

[182]   *See* 39 Fed. Reg. 33,109 (Aug. 13, 1974); 43 Fed. Reg. 46,694 (Oct. 10, 1978).

Antimicrobial Products

The antimicrobial OTC rulemaking illustrates the range of views on the role of ingredients in determining whether a product is a cosmetic or drug. That proceeding produced two entirely different positions concerning the classification of antimicrobial ingredients. The Antimicrobial Advisory Panel took the position that, if an ingredient was listed in an OTC monograph for drug use and the use was for the purpose recognized in the monograph, any product containing the ingredient would be classified as a drug, regardless of the claims.[183] For example, the Antimicrobial Advisory Panel was reluctant to accept the view that two bar soaps containing the same ingredient (i.e., triclosan) could be classified either as a drug or cosmetic based on whether the product 1) had a drug claim of being an antibacterial soap that killed odor-producing bacteria or 2) had a cosmetic claim of being a deodorant soap. To the advisory panel, both soaps were effective because the active ingredient, triclosan, was a bactericidal agent; the specific claims on the product therefore were irrelevant to the issue of classification as a drug or cosmetic. In the panel's view, both products should be regulated as drugs.[184]

In contrast, in 1983, when a soap manufacturer asked FDA officials whether an antimicrobial soap could be classified as a cosmetic if the product made no drug claims and listed the antimicrobial as an ingredient, the agency "concluded that the mere presence of an antimicrobial ingredient in a product labeled for deodorant use, with the ingredient identified only in the ingredient list and no reference to the antimicrobial anywhere in the labeling, would not cause the product to be considered a drug."[185] FDA repeated this position in the Tentative Final Monograph for OTC First Aid Antiseptic Drug Products.[186] Thus, contrary to the approach recommended by the advisory panel, the agency continues to rely on the labeling claims as the basis for classification of antimicrobial soaps.[187]

Vaginal Drug Products

FDA's statements with respect to its withdrawal of the advance notice of proposed rulemaking (ANPR) for OTC vaginal drug products offer yet another view on the cosmetic/drug distinction.[188] In this proceeding, the advisory panel report recommended that if an active ingredient was present in a therapeutic concentration, the product should be classified as a drug, even if the product does not claim to produce the effect resulting from the action of the therapeutically effective ingredient.[189] In FDA's withdrawal of the ANPR, the agency agreed with a comment that argued that the drug status of a product is

---

[183]   39 Fed. Reg. 33,109 (Sept. 13, 1974).

[184]   Id.

[185]   Memorandum of Meeting between the FDA and Armour Dial, Inc. re: Drug v. Cosmetic Status of Antimicrobial ("Deodorant") Soaps (Mar. 9, 1983).

[186]   56 Fed. Reg. 33,644 (Aug. 16, 1991). FDA stated that the presence of an antimicrobial ingredient in a product does not, in and of itself, make the product a drug provided that no drug claim is made. FDA qualified this conclusion, however, by stating that an antimicrobial ingredient included in a cosmetic product may not exceed the concentration provided in the applicable monograph.

[187]   Similarly, in the Final Monograph for OTC Topical Acne Drug Products, FDA acknowledged that the monograph only covers the drug use of active ingredients and does not apply to the use of the same ingredients for nondrug effects in products intended solely as cosmetics. 56 Fed. Reg. 41,008 (Aug. 16, 1991). See also Tentative Final Monograph for Oral Antiseptics, 59 Fed. Reg. 6084 (Feb. 9, 1994).

[188]   59 Fed. Reg. 5226 (Feb. 3, 1994).

[189]   48 Fed. Reg. 46,694, 46,701 (Oct. 13, 1983).

determined by its intended use, as indicated by its labeling. FDA noted, however, that the type and amount of ingredient(s) present in a product, even if that product does not make explicit drug claims, must be considered in determining its regulatory status. Therefore, the presence of a pharmacologically active ingredient could make a product a drug even in the absence of explicit drug claims, because the intended use would be implied by the known or recognized drug effects of the ingredient.[190] While these comments are of importance, one must separate word from deed. For instance, FDA did not find any ingredients under review for OTC vaginal drug products to be active. Therefore, the practical effect of the ANPR was to convert vaginal drug products to cosmetics.

In the most recent *Federal Register* notice discussing vaginal products, FDA stated its intent to categorize vaginal lubricants that make vaginal dryness and discomfort relief claims as drug products. FDA noted that these products are not cosmetics because the products and their claims do not relate to "cleansing, beautifying, promoting attractiveness, or altering appearance."[191] There has been significant pushback from the industry defending the marketing of vaginal lubricants as cosmetics.[192] As of July 2014, FDA had not issued an OTC drug monograph for vaginal lubricants so, for the time being, these products continue to be regulated as cosmetic products.[193]

Sunscreen Products

Sunscreen ingredients present a different picture. In its report regarding sunscreen drug products, the Sunscreen Advisory Panel rejected the agency's traditional Trade Correspondence cosmetic classification of products whose claims were for "tanning" or "fast tanning." The advisory panel report stated that, "regardless of claims, products intended to be used for prevention of sunburn or any other such similar condition should be regarded

---

[190]   FDA reached a similar conclusion in its 1993 Final Rule on Topically Applied Hormone-Containing Drug Products for OTC Use, 58 Fed. Reg. 47,608 (Sept. 9, 1993), and its Proposed Rule for Cosmetic Products Containing Certain Hormone Ingredients, 58 Fed. Reg. 47,611 (Sept. 9, 1993). The latter limits the amount of the specified hormones to levels that are safe but not effective as drugs. The proposed rule also states that any cosmetic product using the word "hormone" in the text of its labeling or ingredient statement is considered to be making an implied drug claim. In this respect, the proposed rule enunciates a position that is similar to that taken in the OTC sunscreen and dentifrice monographs.

[191]   68 Fed. Reg. 75,585, 75,589 (Dec. 31, 2003) (notice of FDA's request for data and information for certain categories of ingredients in OTC products that are eligible for the original OTC drug review but have not been reviewed by FDA as of 2003). *See also*, 72 Fed. Reg. 71,769 (Dec. 19, 2007) (FDA reiterating that vaginal moisturizers and vaginal sexual lubricants are currently being evaluated under the OTC review process and stating that it will publish its finding in a future *Federal Register* notice).

[192]   See representative sample of comments to Docket 2003N-0539 regarding vaginal lubricants and moisturizers, *available at* http://www.fda.gov/ohrms/dockets/dailys/04/June04/062804/062804.htm.

[193]   Interestingly, on June 25, 2014, the U.S. Department of Justice, at the request of FDA, filed a complaint for permanent injunction against Laclede, Inc., claiming that Laclede was illegally distributing over-the-counter vaginal drug products without the required FDA approval. *See* FDA Seeks Permanent Injunction Against California Pharmaceutical Company (FDA News Release) (July 1, 2014). Two of the four products at issue were vaginal moisturizers and lubricants. *Id.* According to the complaint, FDA had previously told Laclede that it must obtain FDA's approval before selling these products based on product claims and formulation. *Id.* While the OTC drug policy is still in development, it appears that the Center for Devices and Radiological Health is beginning to claim oversight of vaginal lubricants (with or without condom compatibility claims) as devices that require 510(k) clearance to be imported into the United States. Clearly, this remains an area to watch closely.

as drugs."[194] In other words, the advisory panel regarded tanning and sunburn prevention as equivalents.

Three years later, the agency told a cosmetic manufacturer that the use of an unapproved sunscreen ingredient in a cosmetic product could make the product a drug. FDA stated that "the intended use of the ingredient as a UVA sunscreen agent has been well-established through labeling, promotion, and advertising by the *manufacturer of the ingredient*, as well as through the expression of its intended use in the *labeling of other recently marketed sunscreen drug products*."[195] Interestingly, FDA advanced this position of intent by the ingredient manufacturer even though the manufacturer of the finished cosmetic made no claims, direct or indirect, that might promote the product for a drug use.

In 1993, FDA issued a Tentative Final Monograph for OTC Sunscreen Drug Products in which the agency stated that, when an ingredient is used for either drug or cosmetic purposes, its regulatory status can be determined by objective evidence of the distributor's intent. Such intent may be derived from labeling, promotional material, advertising, and any other relevant source, including the consumer's intent in using the product.[196] Because consumers expect protection from such products, irrespective of the way the products are promoted, FDA stated that sunscreen products could be regarded as drugs.

In the preamble of the Final Monograph for OTC Sunscreen Drug Products issued in 1999[197] FDA returned to its long-standing position that any product containing one or more active sunscreen ingredients that is represented as intended to protect the skin from the sun would be regulated as drugs. Furthermore, the agency stated that products (i.e., shampoos, hair conditioners, hair sprays, nail polishes and other similar products) that contain a sunscreen for a nontherapeutic purpose would not be regulated as drugs as long as the labeling clearly describes the nontherapeutic use of the sunscreen ingredient.[198]

Tooth-Whitening Products

FDA's approach to tooth-whitening products containing hydrogen peroxide is another example of where FDA has taken contradictory positions. In 1992, FDA issued Warning Letters to approximately 20 firms manufacturing tooth-whitening products containing hydrogen peroxide. The letters indicated that FDA considered all tooth whiteners that used a bleaching process to be drugs. However, in its April 2014 response to a citizen petition, FDA stated that insufficient data exists to determine whether all peroxide-containing

[194] 43 Fed. Reg. 38,206, 38,209 (Aug. 25, 1978).

[195] Memorandum of Meeting between the FDA and Estée Lauder, Inc. (Apr. 22, 1981) (emphasis added).

[196] 58 Fed. Reg. 28,194, 28,204 (May 12, 1993). Similarly, FDA has stated that the mere presence of fluoride in a dentifrice is sufficient to make a product a drug product, regardless of the claims being made. *See* 59 Fed. Reg. 6084, 6088 (Feb. 9, 1994); 50 Fed. Reg. 39,854 (Sept. 30, 1985).

[197] 64 Fed. Reg. 27,666 (May 21, 1999). On December 31, 2001, FDA published a final rule staying until further notice the final rule for OTC sunscreen drug products that would be regulated under 21 C.F.R. pt. 352. The agency took this action because it plans to amend pt. 352 to address formulation, labeling, and testing requirements for both ultraviolet A (UVA) and ultraviolet B radiation protection in the future. *See* 66 Fed. Reg. 67,485 (Dec. 21, 2001).

[198] 66 Fed. Reg. 67,485 (Dec. 21, 2001). The Sunscreen Final Monograph also identified the permitted active ingredients and combinations, addressed uniform labeling of sunscreens, clarified permitted performance claims, and discussed the test methods available in determining the sunscreen's effectiveness against radiation in the UVB range.

tooth-whitening preparations meet the definition of a drug.[199] According to FDA's response letter, "most peroxide-containing tooth whiteners would meet the definition of a cosmetic in the FD&C Act because they generally 'are intended to be . . . applied to the human body or any part thereof for cleansing, beautifying, promoting attractiveness, or altering the appearance.'"[200] Thus, FDA returned to a case-by-case review of intended use stating that more information would be needed regarding each specific peroxide-containing tooth whitener product to determine whether the products also meet the definition of a drug.[201]

Issues surrounding the drug/cosmetic distinction are further complicated by internal relations between FDA Centers. Drug decisions are made by the Center for Drug Evaluation and Research, which administers the OTC Drug Review, while cosmetic decisions are made by CFSAN.

To date, the OTC Drug Review has left several issues unresolved that the agency will need to grapple with as it confronts the cosmetic/drug distinction in future final monographs. For example, will any of the final OTC monographs decide that certain ingredients, which historically have been cosmetics, are drugs solely based on the nature of the ingredients? How will FDA treat the introduction of new cosmetic ingredients in the future if the new cosmetic ingredient also has the potential to support "drug" claims? Will cosmetic manufacturers be required to submit a new drug application, pay more than a million dollars and wait eight to ten years for approval? Will FDA's regulation of new cosmetic ingredients be handled differently if the OTC Drug Review is ever completed? Will FDA revisit and overturn some of its earlier decisions as it is proposing for vaginal products?

The Future of FDA Regulation

Nanotechnology

An emerging area that presents new challenges to FDA involves the use of nanotechnology. Nanotechnology can be used in, or to make, almost any FDA-regulated product, including cosmetics. In fact, nanotechnology is currently most commonly found in cosmetic products.[202] Although FDA has not established its own formal definition of nanotechnology, the agency recognizes that the term is commonly used in relation to the "engineering (i.e., deliberate manipulation, manufacture or selection) of materials that have at least one dimension in the size range of approximately 1 nanometers (nm) to 100 nm."[203] FDA has acknowledged that nanotechnology poses many questions about the adequacy and application of its regulatory authority.[204]

---

[199] *See* FDA Denial Response to Citizen Petition from American Dental Association (Apr. 22, 2014), *available at* http://www.regulations.gov/#!documentDetail;D=FDA-2009-P-0566-0005.

[200] *Id.* at 3.

[201] *Id.*

[202] Estimated at 58 products. F-D-C Rep. ("The Tan Sheet"), Oct. 26, 2006.

[203] *See* Guidance for Industry Considering Whether an FDA-Regulated Product Involves the Application of Nanotechnology at 5 (June 2014), *available at* http://www.fda.gov/RegulatoryInformation/Guidances/ucm257698.htm [hereinafter Product Involves Application of Nanotechnology Guidance].

[204] In August 2006, FDA formed the Nanotechnology Task Force (Task Force) to help assess these questions. The Task Force issued a report in July 2007 making various recommendations, including suggesting that

In June 2014, FDA issued two final guidance documents relevant to the use of nanomaterials in cosmetic products.[205] In both documents, FDA states that it will continue to regulate nanotechnology products under existing statutory authorities in line with the specific legal standards applicable to each type of product under its jurisdiction.[206] Any technical assessments will be product-specific.[207] In determining whether an FDA-regulated product involves the application of nanotechnology, FDA provides two "points to consider":

- Whether a material or end product is engineered to have at least one external dimension, or an internal or surface structure, in the nanoscale range (approximately 1 nm to 100 nm); and

- Whether a material or end product is engineered to exhibit properties or phenomena, including physical or chemical properties or biological effects, that are attributable to its dimension(s), even if these dimensions fall outside the nanoscale range, up to one micrometer (1,000 nm).[208]

FDA explains that an affirmative finding that a product involves nanotechnology "might suggest the need for particular attention to the product by FDA and/or industry."[209] Specific to cosmetic products involving nanotechnology, FDA states that cosmetic manufacturers should evaluate data needs and testing methods to address any unique properties and function of the nanomaterials used.[210] FDA further recommends that cosmetic manufacturers evaluate several factors in their safety assessments for such cosmetic products, including the physicochemical characteristics, agglomeration and size distribution of nanomaterials under the conditions of toxicity testing and as expected in the final product, impurities, potential routes of exposure, and in vitro and in vivo toxicological data.[211] FDA encourages manufacturers using a nanomaterial in a cosmetic product as a new material or an altered version of an already marketed ingredient to meet with the agency to discuss the test methods and data needed to substantiate the product's safety.[212]

A source of recent controversy has been the use of nanoscale particles in sunscreen drug products. In a May 16, 2006 citizen petition[213] a coalition of public interest groups urged

---

FDA consider issuing guidance that would clarify what, if any, information manufacturers should give FDA about products that contain nanoscale materials and when the use of such materials may change the regulatory status of particular products. As discussed herein, in June 2014, FDA issued final guidance documents as part of the agency's efforts to implement the Task Force's recommendations.

[205] See Product Involves Application of Nanotechnology Guidance; Guidance for Industry Safety of Nanomaterials in Cosmetic Products (June 2014), available at http://www.fda.gov/Cosmetics/GuidanceRegulation/GuidanceDocuments/ucm300886.htm [hereinafter Cosmetic Nanomaterials Guidance]. On the same day, FDA also issued a third final guidance regarding nanotechnology titled "Guidance for Industry: Assessing the Effects of Significant Manufacturing Process Changes, Including Emerging Technologies, on the Safety and Regulatory Status of Food Ingredients and Food Contact Substances, Including Food Ingredients that are Color Additives" (June 2014), available at http://www.fda.gov/Food/GuidanceRegulation/GuidanceDocumentsRegulatoryInformation/ucm300661.htm.

[206] See Product Involves Application of Nanotechnology Guidance at 4.

[207] Id.

[208] Id. at 6.

[209] Id. at 10.

[210] See Cosmetic Nanomaterials Guidance at 13.

[211] Id.

[212] Id. at 13-14.

[213] Citizen Petition of International Center for Technology Assessment, FDA Dkt. No. 2006P-210 (May 16, 2006).

FDA to amend the Sunscreen Final Monograph to exclude products that contain engineered nanoparticles and to designate such formulas as new drugs. According to the petition, nanoparticles pose a health risk because of their small size, which allows them increased mobility in the human body.[214] The use of nanoscale particles of ingredients in sunscreen, however, was recognized by FDA in the preamble to the Sunscreen Final Monograph.[215] In the preamble, the agency addressed comments about the use of "micronized" titanium dioxide, concluding that it did not consider it to be a new ingredient, but a specific grade of the same ingredient.[216] Nevertheless, FDA has asked for comments on the safety and effectiveness of these ingredients, noting that at the time of publication of the Final Monograph it was not aware of any evidence demonstrating a safety concern.[217] At this time, nanoscale particles do not present safety issues in cosmetics, but controversy regarding their use in other categories could impact this area at a future date.[218]

Organic Cosmetics

Cosmetic firms have begun to market "organic cosmetics" due to increasing consumer interest in natural and environmentally friendly products. These products have been a source of controversy because the term "organic" is not defined in the FDCA or any other law or regulation that FDA enforces. The use of the term "organic" is regulated by the U.S. Department of Agriculture (USDA) as it applies to agricultural products through the National Organic Program (NOP) regulation.[219] While the NOP was originally designed to address concerns over organic foods, it was "broadened" to include cosmetics in 2005.[220]

Under the NOP, if a cosmetic, body care product, or personal care product "contains or is made up of agricultural ingredients, and can meet the USDA/NOP organic production, handling, processing and labeling standards, it may be eligible to be certified under the NOP regulations."[221] While a cosmetic product can be certified as "USDA-organic," USDA has stated that it has "no authority over the production and labeling of cosmetics, body care products and personal-care products that are not made up or organic ingredients, or do not make any claims [about] meeting USDA organic standards."[222] Thus, a cosmetic product will only be subject to regulation by USDA if it bears the USDA-organic label, otherwise the NOP standards would not apply. Organic cosmetics certified by other "private standards" may be marketed to meet those standards, but they will not be regulated by USDA.[223]

---

[214]   F-D-C Rep. ("The Rose Sheet"), May 22, 2006.

[215]   *See* 64 Fed. Reg. 27,666, 27,671-72 (May 21, 1999)

[216]   *Id.*

[217]   72 Fed. Reg. 49,070, 49,110 (Aug. 27, 2007).

[218]   The International Cooperation on Cosmetics Regulation (ICCR), an international group of regulatory authorities from Canada, the European Union, Japan, and the United States, has prioritized the review of the use of nanotechnology and nanomaterials in cosmetics as an agenda item. ICCR has issued reports on the issue, including a report addressing safety approaches to nanomaterials in cosmetics. *See* Report of the ICCR Working Group: Safety Approaches to Nanomaterials in Cosmetics (Nov. 2013), *available at* http://www.fda.gov/downloads/Cosmetics/InternationalActivities/ICCR/UCM386543.pdf

[219]   *See* 7 C.F.R pt. 205.

[220]   See USDA Memorandum to "All USDA Accredited Certifying Agents" dated August 23, 2005, *available at* http://www.ams.usda.gov/AMSv1.0/getfile?dDocName=STELPRDC5088947.

[221]   *See* NOP, Cosmetic, Body Care Products, and Personal Care Products, *available at* http://www.ams.usda.gov/AMSv1.0/getfile?dDocName=STELPRDC5068442.

[222]   *Id.*

[223]   *Id.*

The lack of specific guidance for manufacturers of "organic cosmetics" has created confusion among the regulated industry as to what standards to follow. Organizations such as the Organic and Sustainable Industry Standards (OASIS) have "sprung up" offering "private standards" for manufacturers of organic cosmetics.[224] Aside from lack of regulatory standards for these products, the cosmetic industry has also been concerned over deceptive labeling practices calling for the FTC to "investigate . . . . misleading organic personal care product claims."[225] However, even the FTC has refused to address issues related to "organic cosmetics." On October 1, 2012, FTC issued proposed revisions to its Green Guides, but did not address these types of products. In a press release the FTC stated that:

> either because the FTC lacks a sufficient basis to provide meaningful guidance or because the FTC wants to avoid proposing guidance that duplicates rules or guidance of other agencies, the proposed Guides do not address use of the terms "sustainable," "natural," and "organic." Organic claims made for textiles and other products derived from agricultural products are currently covered by the U.S. Department of Agriculture's National Organic Program.[226]

At this time, there does not appear to be a clear answer from the regulatory agencies as to what standards organic cosmetic manufacturers must follow or which agency will take the lead in patrolling this new industry segment. Thus, for now, it will be left to the cosmetic industry to continue to attempt to self-regulate to maintain consumers' confidence in these types of products.

Conclusion

Cosmetics are the least regulated of all the products subject to the FDCA. FDA's control of these products is limited to the plain language of the statutory prohibitions on adulteration and misbranding. There are no preapproval requirements for cosmetic ingredients or finished products, no mandatory inspections of cosmetic establishments, no duty to list cosmetics with the agency, and no obligation to report adverse experiences associated with cosmetics. In view of the relative paucity of statutory and regulatory controls, it is not surprising that the most significant regulatory efforts taken by FDA against cosmetic products have been agency attempts, largely successful, to treat as "drugs" certain products that the layman (and the cosmetic house) might view as cosmetics. By bringing a product under the "drug" provisions of the law, FDA increases its ability to control the marketing of the product and thereby arguably to protect the public health. While that has worked in the past, with user fees and greater controls over new drug applications, FDA may face new challenges in the future.

---

224 F-D-C Rep. ("The Rose Sheet"), Aug. 10, 2009, at 5-6.
225 F-D-C Rep. ("The Rose Sheet"), April 5, 2010 at 4-5.
226 *See* Press Release, Federal Trade Commission, FTC Issues Revised "Green Guidelines," (Oct. 1, 2012), http://www.ftc.gov/news-events/press-releases/2012/10/ftc-issues-revised-green-guides.

The primary challenge for the cosmetic industry since the Act was enacted in 1938 has been to avoid classification of its products as "drugs." The temptation to push cosmetic products and their labeling to the outer edges of the "cosmetic" definition, however, sometimes has proven overly enticing and has led to a strong, almost reflexive, response by FDA. Absent significant tightening of the general controls on cosmetics, it is likely that the tension created by the cosmetic/drug distinction will continue in the future to be the primary feature of the regulation of cosmetics.

CHAPTER 9
DRUGS: GENERAL REQUIREMENTS

DANIEL KRACOV AND ABEBA HABTEMARIAM[*]

Introduction

The Federal Food, Drug, and Cosmetic Act (FDCA) establishes two distinct, parallel and, to some extent overlapping, schemes for regulating drugs.

One scheme permits free entry of products and claims to the market, subject to standards to control the integrity and quality of products and to prohibit deceptive practices. The federal government (acting through the Food and Drug Administration (FDA)) monitors the market and, when it finds violations of the standards, brings enforcement actions, usually in federal courts, where the burden of proof rests on the government. This scheme is reflected in the adulteration and misbranding provisions of the FDCA, which date back to earlier federal laws in the 19th and early 20th centuries. Today, most of the requirements applicable to all drugs for human use are found embedded in the adulteration and misbranding sections of the act, although a few exist in freestanding provisions.

The second scheme puts FDA in the role of gatekeeper to the marketplace, through a rigorous approval process designed to assure product quality and integrity and the safety and effectiveness of ingredients and claims. This scheme began for biologics products in 1902 via what is today the biologic license application (BLA) and was extended to "new drugs" in 1938 via the new drug application (NDA) provisions. This scheme applies, however, only to biologics and to "new drugs."

Congress has never fully integrated the two approaches. When seeking to adopt a new, broadly applicable requirement, Congress has often inserted requirements within the adulteration and misbranding scheme rather than creating freestanding provisions or expanding the licensing scheme. As a result, the adulteration/misbranding requirements

---

[*] The authors wish to acknowledge the role of William Vodra in preparing the prior version of this chapter.

extend to activities that have little or nothing to do with "adulteration" or "misbranding" as these terms are commonly understood by laypersons.

Notwithstanding Congress' dual but separate regulatory schemes under the statutory adulteration/misbranding and NDA/BLA provisions, FDA has taken steps to impose parallel or similar requirements to reach all classes of drug products, often by using different authorities to accomplish that result. For example, FDA initially required adverse event reporting only for "new drugs" by using its authority under section 505 of the FDCA.[1] Then, relying on adulteration provisions, it promulgated similar requirements for prescription drug products that were marketed without approved NDAs.[2] Finally, Congress enacted separate authority for adverse event reporting for nonprescription drugs marketed without approved NDAs.[3] Thus, today, adverse event reporting is required for all drug products, but under three different statutory provisions using conceptually distinct regulatory approaches. Yet functionally, the system is harmonized and integrated, so that the regulated industry is hardly aware that it derives from such disparate sources.[4]

Approval through the NDA process has become FDA's preferred mechanism for regulation of prescription drugs. Since 1975, the agency has opposed virtually all attempts to recognize any prescription drug as other than a "new drug." On the other hand, with nonprescription or over-the-counter (OTC) drug products, FDA has utilized both schemes, but has relied more on the adulteration/misbranding provisions, so that most OTC products are accepted as being not "new drugs" and exempt from approval requirements, while others are still subject to individual product approval under the "new drug" scheme.[5]

This chapter reviews the adulteration and misbranding provisions in the FDCA that are applicable to all drugs and drug products. Other chapters will cover the approval and licensing schemes for new drugs[6] and biological products,[7] respectively. It also addresses certain new statutory frameworks governing aspects of drug regulation: regulation of traditional compounding and drugs produced in "outsourcing facilities," and the tracking and tracing of finished drug products in interstate commerce.

---

[1]   New Drugs: Applications and Experience Reporting, 31 Fed. Reg. 13,347 (Oct. 14, 1966); 21 C.F.R. § 314.80 (2014).

[2]   *Id.* § 310.305 (2014); Adverse Drug Experience Reporting Requirements for Marketed Prescription Drugs Without Approved New Drug or Abbreviated New Drug Applications: Final Rule, 51 Fed. Reg. 24,476 (July 3, 1986).

[3]   Dietary Supplement and Nonprescription Drug Consumer Protection Act, Pub. L. No. 109-462, 120 Stat. 3469 (Dec. 22, 2006); FDCA § 760, 21 U.S.C. § 379aa. Violation of this provision is a prohibited act but not related to the adulteration or misbranding of the product. FDCA § 301(e), 21 U.S.C. § 331(e).

[4]   *See* Chapter 10 *infra* for more information on adverse event reporting.

[5]   *See* Chapter 13 *infra* for more information on the regulation of OTC drug products.

[6]   *See* Chapter 10 *infra* for more information on the regulation of "new drugs" under the NDA approval system.

[7]   *See* Chapter 14 *infra* for more information on the regulation of "biologics" under the biological licensure system.

Jurisdiction and Definitions

What Is a "Drug"?

The FDCA authority to regulate drugs starts with statutory definitions. FDA has no jurisdiction to regulate a product or a component as a "drug" unless it first meets the requirements for being a "drug." The act creates various categories of "articles," such as foods, cosmetics, and drugs.

The boundaries separating these categories have been the focus of numerous disputes over the years, as the agency and private parties have fought over whether FDA has jurisdiction over a product at all, and, if so, whether the product is a drug, a medical device, a food, a dietary supplement, a cosmetic, or is within some other category of regulated article. With regard to the category of "drugs," the FDCA provides:

> The term "drug" means
>
> (a) articles recognized in the official United States Pharmacopeia, official Homeopathic Pharmacopeia of the United States, or official National Formulary, or any supplement to any of them; and
>
> (b) articles intended for use in the diagnosis, cure, mitigation, treatment, or prevention of disease in man or other animals; and
>
> (c) articles (other than food) intended to affect the structure or any function of the body of man or other animals; and
>
> (d) articles intended for use as a component of any article specified in clause (A), (B), or (C).[8]

Compendial Status

The first element of the definition of "drug" relates to the so-called official compendia. The statute identifies three. When the FDCA was enacted in 1938, the United States Pharmacopeia (USP) was issued by the United States Pharmacopeial Convention (USPC), a private nonprofit organization established in 1820 by physicians and pharmaceutical chemists to standardize the quality of medicaments. The National Formulary was issued by the American Pharmaceutical Association, a professional organization of pharmacists. Today, the USPC issues both compendia. The Homeopathic Pharmacopeial Convention of the United States is responsible for the third reference book.[9] Each compendium contains

---

[8]   FDCA § 201(g)(1), 21 U.S.C. § 321(g)(1).

[9]   Inclusion of the Homeopathic Pharmacopeia of the United States (HPUS) in the 1938 FDCA has been attributed to Senator Royal Copeland, sponsor of the legislation in the Senate and a homeopathic physician. Homeopathy is based upon a principle of treating patients with extreme dilutions of substances associated with symptoms similar to those of the targeted illness or condition. It may be doubted that homeopathic drugs could supply the controlled clinical trial data necessary to meet current standards for proof of effectiveness. Thus, the explicit reference to HPUS continues to be an important basis for the legality of these alternative medicines. Homeopathy today plays a tangential role in American practice of medicine, although it continues to have devoted followers among proponents of complementary and alternative medicine. FDA has long regulated these products pursuant to a compliance policy guide that provides specific parameters for homeopathic status, including compliance with the recognized or customary practice of homeopathy,

numerous individual sections, called "monographs," that define the chemical identity and standards or specifications for an ingredient or finished drug product, as well as test methods to determine whether the standard or specification has been met.

Under a literal reading of the statute, the mere listing of a substance in one of the compendia should be adequate to establish jurisdiction, but the compendia include substances that, while used in the making or storage of drugs, also have many other nondrug applications (e.g., sodium chloride, cotton). Moreover, substances such as common vitamins and minerals are also included. When FDA attempted to assert drug jurisdiction over high doses of vitamins A and D sold in capsule form due to concerns about toxicity, it initially relied on the simple fact that these vitamins were listed in the USP. In a series of cases, however, the courts held that a greater justification was required[10] and FDA ultimately conceded that the simple fact that a substance was included in a compendium was insufficient to classify it as a drug.

Thus, the compendial component of the "drug" definition has diminished in importance as an independent basis for drug jurisdiction. Nevertheless, substances found in a compendium may be drugs, depending upon the labeling for the products that contain the substances. If the labeling of an article specifically refers to the USP, for example, it must comply with the referenced monograph,[11] and the citation to the compendium would provide compelling, and possibly dispositive, evidence of statutory drug status, because there would be no reason to refer to a compendium for a nondrug substance. More generally, however, FDA seeks to show that, regardless of its presence in a compendium (or in addition to its inclusion there), an article in issue meets one of the other three elements of the statutory definition of "drug."

Intended Use

Under the broad authority of the FDCA "drug" definition, virtually any substance can be transformed into a drug if the marketer of the product conveys to the market an intent that it be used in one of three ways: to diagnose or treat disease, to affect a bodily function, or to be a component of a product that otherwise is a drug.

While aspects of FDA's broad interpretation have not been tested in court, FDA generally interprets the phrase "intended use" to refer:

> to the objective intent of the persons legally responsible for the labeling of drugs. The intent is determined by such persons' expressions or may be shown by the circumstances surrounding the distribution of the article. This objective intent may, for example, be shown by labeling claims, advertising matter, or oral or written statements by such persons or their representatives. It may be shown by the circumstances that the article is,

---

and appropriate labeling. *See* FDA COMPLIANCE POLICY GUIDE ch. 7132.15: Conditions Under Which Homoeopathic Drugs May Be Marketed (issued May 31, 1988; revised Mar. 1995), http://www.fda.gov/ICECI/ComplianceManuals/CompliancePolicyGuidanceManual/ucm074360.htm. *See* Chapter 13 *infra* for more information on FDA regulation of homeopathic drugs.

[10]   *See* National Nutritional Food Ass'n v. FDA, 504 F.2d 761 (2d Cir. 1974) and National Nutritional Food Ass'n v. Mathews, 557 F.2d 325 (2d Cir. 1977).

[11]   *See* FDCA §§ 501(b), 502(g), 21 U.S.C. §§ 351(b), 352(g).

with the knowledge of such persons or their representatives, offered and
used for a purpose for which it is neither labeled nor advertised.[12]

The usual source of "objective intent" is the label with the product itself or the materials
promoting it (i.e., the uses suggested explicitly or implicitly to potential consumers or
purchasers). The agency has also looked to other public statements of marketers for evidence
of objective intent, such as filings with the Securities and Exchange Commission describing
the potential market for the product for a particular use[13] or patents secured for the product
and claiming exclusive rights to sales for certain uses.[14] A 2013 Warning Letter even cited
statements made by a pharmaceutical company chief executive officer on a cable business
channel.[15]

FDA's interpretation of "intended use" contains two additional points of interest. First:

> The intended uses of an article may change after it has been introduced
> into interstate commerce by its manufacturer. If, for example, a packer,
> distributor, or seller intends an article for different uses than those
> intended by the person from whom he received the drug, such packer,
> distributor, or seller is required to supply adequate labeling in accordance
> with the new intended uses.[16]

In short, the objective intent of a distributor or other seller, not just that of the original
manufacturer, can be used to determine jurisdiction over the product. If Company A sells
bottled water for refreshment (a food use), and Retailer B puts up next to the bottles of water
a display sign promoting the product to treat obesity or cure infections, the bottled water—
in Retailer B's store—has become a "drug" because of the new intended use.

Second:

> [I]f a manufacturer knows, or has knowledge of facts that would give him
> notice, that a drug introduced into interstate commerce by him is to be
> used for conditions, purposes, or other uses than the ones for which he
> offers it, he is required to provide adequate labeling for such a drug which
> accords with such other uses to which the article is to be put.[17]

While FDA has long put forward this interpretation, it has in fact rarely relied upon it
alone to assert jurisdiction. If the policy were rigorously applied, serious issues would be

---

[12]   21 C.F.R. § 201.128.

[13]   Regulatory Letter regarding Favor Smokeless Cigarettes (1984) cited in PETER BARTON HUTT & RICHARD A.
       MERRILL, FOOD AND DRUG LAW: CASES AND MATERIALS 384 (2d ed. 1991).

[14]   Nicotine in Cigarettes and Smokeless Tobacco Is a Drug …: Jurisdictional Statements, 61 Fed. Reg. 44,619 at
       44,924, 44,937 (Aug. 28, 1996). Note that the Supreme Court later held that FDA did not have jurisdiction
       over tobacco products. FDA v. Brown & Williamson Tobacco Co., 529 U.S. 120 (2000).

[15]   FDA Warning Letter to Aegerion Pharmaceuticals, Inc. (Nov. 8, 2013) available at http://www.fda.
       gov/downloads/Drugs/GuidanceComplianceRegulatoryInformation/EnforcementActivitiesbyFDA/
       WarningLettersandNoticeofViolationLetterstoPharmaceuticalCompanies/UCM374338.pdf.

[16]   21 C.F.R. § 201.128.

[17]   Id. § 201.128.

created. Most drugs are used, to greater or lesser degrees, for uses other than those set forth in the manufacturer's labeling; many of these uses are recognized in medical treatises or journals, and are reimbursed by health insurers; they are also identified in market research reports that are widely available to drug companies. Moreover, manufacturers oftentimes have knowledge that their products are intended to be used for such unapproved uses. Thus, arguably, every manufacturer could be shown to have facts that would lead to an obligation to amend the labeling of many of its drug products. FDA has avoided applying its interpretation in such a sweeping manner, however, typically seeking more concrete evidence of intent under FDA's expansive conception of the term.

On the other hand, the agency did assert this interpretation when it sought to regulate nicotine as a "drug" and tobacco products as "medical devices" to deliver the nicotine. Specifically, FDA found that manufacturers of tobacco products "intended" these products to be used to sustain nicotine addiction, and thereby to affect the structure or function of the body. The finding was based on several different rationales: a reasonable manufacturer would foresee such use and therefore, must have intended that result; consumers actually use the products to satisfy addiction; manufacturers were aware that consumers used the products for their pharmacological effects; and manufacturers designed their products to deliver active doses of nicotine to users.[18] FDA's assertion of jurisdiction was challenged in the courts. The district court allowed FDA to proceed on the first and second rationales, without ruling on the others.[19] The Fourth Circuit Court of Appeals reversed on other grounds (i.e., that Congress never granted FDA authority to regulate tobacco), although the dissenting judge would have upheld the district court's ruling.[20] The Supreme Court affirmed the circuit court ruling, in a 5-4 decision.[21] Of significance, the minority would also have upheld FDA's broad interpretation of "intended use,"[22] but the majority in both the Supreme Court and the court of appeals never addressed the issue.[23] This history suggests that, in a case not confounded by the other legislative intent issues raised by tobacco regulation, courts may give FDA great deference in making such jurisdictional determinations.

Diagnosis, Cure, Mitigation, Treatment, or Prevention of Disease

The definitional category of articles "intended for use in the diagnosis, cure, mitigation, treatment, or prevention of disease" has generated considerable jurisdictional controversy and confusion. FDA has interpreted claims as related to disease, even when consumers might not intuitively recognize them as such. For example, an antimicrobial deodorant soap is a drug because it fights bacteria that can cause infections on the skin, and a fluoride toothpaste is a drug because it prevents dental caries. Sometimes, there are disputes over whether a

---

18   Regulations Restricting the Sale and Distribution of Cigarettes and Smokeless Tobacco to Protect Children and Adolescents; Final Rule, 61 Fed. Reg. 44,396 (Aug. 28, 1996) (preamble introduction) (codifying 21 C.F.R. pt. 801, et al.).

19   Coyne Beahm, Inc. v. FDA, 966 F. Supp. 1374, 1390-92 (M.D.N.C. 1997) (observing that no court had ever found that a product is "intended" for a use absent manufacturer's claims as to that use or held that "intended use" could only be established by such claims).

20   Brown & Williamson Tobacco Corp. v. FDA, 153 F.3d 155 (4th Cir. 1998).

21   FDA v. Brown & Williamson Tobacco Corp., 529 U.S. 120 (2000).

22   Id. (J. Breyer, dissenting).

23   More than a decade later, FDA gained jurisdiction over tobacco products with the enactment of the Family Smoking Prevention and Tobacco Control Act, Pub. L. No. 111-31, 123 Stat. 1776 (2009).

particular condition is even a disease. Prior to the passage of specific device authorities, when FDA attempted to block the marketing of a home test kit to detect pregnancy, the court held that pregnancy was not a disease.[24] Occasionally there are disagreements over whether a claim relates to "diagnosis, cure, mitigation, treatment, or prevention." Although FDA considers maintenance of narcotic addiction to be a treatment of a disease,[25] it did not seek to argue that nicotine, used to sustain that addiction, was being used to treat a disease; it elected to argue that it affected the function of the body instead.

Affect the Structure or Function of the Body

Perhaps the most difficult delineation of drug status has been defining the category of "articles (other than food) intended to affect the structure or any function of the body of man or other animals." FDA has long struggled to distinguish those products claimed to have a drug structure/function effect from those articles that have such effects but are more properly regulated as foods or cosmetics. In particular, dietary supplements have presented recurring issues for the agency.[26]

FDA has also, however, relied on this provision to address situations in which the product in question arguably is not treating a disease. The agency has applied this element of the definition to products to induce euthanasia, to aid digestion, to promote hair growth, to remove cellulite, and to supply oxygen for use by athletes.[27]

Component of a Drug

Finally, an article intended to be a component of any article that meets any of the other three elements under the definition of a "drug" is also a "drug." FDA has long relied on this element to meet the statutory requirement that the article be in interstate commerce for FDA to have jurisdiction over it. Thus, if the agency demonstrates that a component of a product moved in interstate commerce, even though the final product did not, it can still regulate the final product. Of course, FDA must still establish that the final product meets one of the other criteria of the definition of "drug" to regulate the product as a drug. (This approach is sometimes called "component jurisdiction.")

The term "component" is not necessarily limited to active and inactive ingredients. FDA has defined "component" to mean "any ingredient intended for use in the manufacture of a drug product, including those that may not appear in such drug product."[28]

---

[24] U.S. v. Ova II, 414 F. Supp. 660 (D.N.J. 1975), *aff'd* 535 F.2d 1248 (3d Cir. 1976).

[25] *See* Approved New Drugs Requiring Continuation of Long-Term Studies, Records, and Reports; Listing of Methadone With Special Requirements for Use, 37 Fed. Reg. 26,790 (Dec. 15, 1972).

[26] *See* Chapter 6 *supra* for more information on the historical regulation of dietary supplements.

[27] *See, e.g.,* U.S. v. Beuthanasia-D Regular, Food Drug Cosm. L. Rep. (CCH) ¶ 38,265 (D. Neb. 1979) (cessation of all bodily functions is an effect on structure or function of body); U.S. v. Zymaferm, Food Drug Cosm. L. Rep. (CCH) ¶ 38,087 (D. Neb. 1976) (digestive aid); U.S. v. Kasz Euters, Inc., 855 F. Supp. 534 (D. R.I. 1994) (hair growth aid); Am. Health Prod., Inc. v. Hayes, 574 F. Supp. 1498 (S.D.N.Y. 1963), *aff'd* 744 F.2d 912 (2d Cir. 1984) (starch blockers to aid in weight reduction); U.S. v. Article ... Consisting of 216 Cartoned Bottles, More or Less, Sudden Change, 409 F.2d 734 (2d Cir. 1969) (skin lotion referring to face lifts); U.S. v. Personal Size PR-O2 Oxygen, Food Drug Cosm. L. Rep. (CCH) ¶ 38,248 (W.D.N.Y. 1991) (oxygen).

[28] 21 C.F.R. § 210.3(b)(3) (2014).

Biologics as "Drugs"

Federal regulation of biologics dates from 1902;[29] it was carried out by the Public Health Service (PHS) apart from FDA until 1972, when responsibility was transferred to the agency.[30] The Public Health Service Act (PHSA) defines the term "biological product" as a "virus, therapeutic serum, toxin, antitoxin, vaccine, blood, blood component or derivative, allergenic product, or analogous product . . . applicable to the prevention, treatment, or cure of a disease or condition of human beings."[31] When the PHSA was recodified in 1944—just six years after enactment of the FDCA—the question arose about the applicability of the FDCA to biologics. FDA acknowledged that many biologics did meet the definition of "drug" in the FDCA. Accordingly, Congress affirmed that, in recodifying the PHSA, it did not limit or supersede the applicability of the FDCA to biologics.[32]

When regulation of biologics was transferred to FDA in 1972, the agency began a long, slow process of integrating biological products not previously regulated as drugs into the standards and processes applicable to other drugs. Today, therapeutic biologics are generally subject to drug requirements (other than the requirement for new drug approval), as well as review of BLAs (in lieu of NDAs) by the Center for Drug Evaluation and Research.[33]

For historical reasons, some articles that arguably meet the PHSA definition of "biological product" were never regulated as biologics, but always treated solely as "drugs" under the FDCA.[34] These include certain therapeutic protein products, such as insulin, human growth hormone, and male and female sex hormones (e.g., estrogen, testosterone).[35] A provision enacted as part of the biosimilars statutory framework will eliminate that anomaly in the coming years. Absent a licensed biologic that could serve as a reference product for a biosimilar application for approval to distribute in interstate commerce, drugs in these classes may continue to be submitted as NDAs until March 2020. Thereafter, applications in these drug classes must be submitted as BLAs, and previously approved products will be deemed licensed under the PHSA.[36]

Distinguishing "Drugs" From Other Regulated Articles

As noted above, the line between "drug" and other categories of regulated products, initially seemingly clear, is often murky, and causes much difficulty for FDA and for regulated industry.

---

[29] Pub. L. No. 59-384, 34 Stat. 768 (1902).

[30] Statement of Organization, Functions, and Delegation of Authority, 37 Fed. Reg. 12,865 (June 29, 1972).

[31] PHSA § 351(i), 42 U.S.C. § 262(i).

[32] PHSA § 351(g), 42 U.S.C. § 262(g); Public Health Service Act, Pub. L. No. 78-410, 58 Stat. 682 (1944).

[33] See Chapter 14 infra for more information on the regulation of biologics.

[34] See Congressional Research Service, FDA Regulation of Follow-on Biologics, at 6 (Apr. 26, 2010), available at https://primaryimmune.org/advocacy_center/pdfs/health_care_reform/Biosimilars_Congressional_Research_Service_Report.pdf.

[35] Id. at 7; Janet Woodcock, Deputy Commissioner, Chief Medical Officer, FDA, testimony before the House Committee on Oversight and Government Reform, March 26, 2007, available at http://www.fda.gov/NewsEvents/Testimony/ucm154070.htm.

[36] Pub. L. No. 111-148, § 7002(e), 124 Stat. 119, tit. VII, subtit. A, "Biologics Price Competition and Innovation Act of 2009" (2010).

Drugs and Cosmetics

The line between cosmetic appearance claims and drug claims has been a source of periodic controversy, particularly as cosmetics and drugs have vied to address the public's concerns about wrinkles.[37] The FDCA defines "cosmetic" as "(1) articles intended to be rubbed, poured, sprinkled, or sprayed on, introduced into, or otherwise applied to the human body or any part thereof for cleansing, beautifying, promoting attractiveness, or altering the appearance, and (2) articles intended for use as a component of any such articles; except that such term shall not include soap."[38] Although this definition appears predicated on a superficial impact on appearance, there can be no doubt that cosmetic products may also have an incremental impact on bodily structure or function—such as moisturization of the skin—without being considered drugs. FDA has limited resources to police promotion in the cosmetic market, but more aggressive claims that go beyond mere appearance to suggest intrusive effects on the structure or function of the body—such as the removal of wrinkles as opposed to creating a youthful, smooth appearance—can properly be regulated as "drugs" because of the intended uses.[39]

Certain products may meet both definitions and bear commingled cosmetic and drug claims. For example, dentifrice, sunscreen, and acne drugs often bear cosmetic appearance claims. Contrary to popular belief, however, the FDCA does not recognize "cosmeceuticals" as a separate category, and such products must comply with the requirements for both cosmetics and drugs.

Drugs and Foods and Dietary Supplements

FDA has long recognized, as necessitated by the "(other than food)" parenthetical in the "drug" definition, that conventional foods necessarily affect the structure or function of the body, albeit in terms of taste, aroma, or nutritive value. Nevertheless, the agency has also had a concern about both toxicity and consumer fraud in the marketing of products as part of the food supply. This concern has led to periodic enforcement actions that proved very controversial and politically charged.

After many years of disputes over the line between drugs and foods, in the 1990s Congress passed amendments to the FDCA—the Nutrition Labeling and Education Act of 1990 (NLEA)[40] and Dietary Supplement Health and Education Act (DSHEA)[41]—that carved out a framework for truthful and non-misleading structure/function claims and disease-related health claims for conventional foods and dietary supplements.[42] Due to the provisions of the

---

[37] *See e.g.* FDA, Warning Letter to Cell Vitals (Nov. 24, 2014), *available at* http://www.fda.gov/ICECI/EnforcementActions/WarningLetters/2014/ucm424920.htm; FDA, Warning Letter to Avon Products Inc., (Sept. 6, 2012), *available at* http://www.fda.gov/ICECI/EnforcementActions/WarningLetters/2012/ucm323738.htm; FDA, Warning Letter to Lancome USA (Sept. 7, 2012), *available at* http://www.fda.gov/ICECI/EnforcementActions/WarningLetters/2012/ucm318809.htm.

[38] FDCA § 201(i), 21 U.S.C. § 321(i).

[39] U.S. v. Article ... Consisting of 36 Boxes, More or Less, Labeled "Line Away Temporary Wrinkle Smoother, Coty," 415 F.2d 369 (3d Cir. 1969); U.S. v. Article ... Consisting of 216 Cartoned Bottles, More or Less, Sudden Change, 409 F.2d 734 (2d Cir. 1969).

[40] Pub. L. No. 101-535, 104 Stat. 2353 (1990).

[41] Pub. L. No. 103-417, 108 Stat. 4325 (1994).

[42] *See* Chapters 2 and 6, respectively, *supra* for more information on regulation of foods and of dietary supplements.

DSHEA—which recognizes the lawful status of structure/function claims for such products that do not relate to any traditionally recognized nutritive value—certain products that are clearly intended to affect the structure or function of the body, such as those labeled for non-disease conditions such as losing or maintaining weight (as opposed to treating obesity or wasting), may fall within drug or dietary supplement authorities, depending on their composition and labeling.

Drugs and Medical Devices

Prior to the Medical Device Amendments of 1976[43] and the Safe Medical Devices Act,[44] there were regular controversies over whether particular articles were drugs or medical devices.[45] The passage of those amendments of the FDCA created a comprehensive medical-device-specific regulatory framework that is independent of drug regulation. This framework includes a clearer statutory distinction between devices, which primarily act through physical or mechanical device means, and drugs, which achieve an effect through chemical means on or within the body. Under the FDCA, the term "device" means:

> an instrument, apparatus, implement, machine, contrivance, implant, in vitro reagent, or other similar or related article, including any component, part, or accessory, which is—
>
> (1) recognized in the official National Formulary, or the United States Pharmacopeia, or any supplement to them,
>
> (2) intended for use in the diagnosis of disease or other conditions, or in the cure, mitigation, treatment, or prevention of disease, in man or other animals, or
>
> (3) intended to affect the structure or any function of the body of man or other animals, and
>
> which does not achieve its primary intended purposes through chemical action within or on the body of man or other animals and which is not dependent upon being metabolized for the achievement of its primary intended purposes.[46]

Combination Products

Products having components or attributes of both a drug and a device, or a drug and a biologic, may be regulated as combination products under applicable sets of statutory authority.[47]

---

[43]   Pub. L. No. 94-295, 90 Stat. 539 (1976).

[44]   Pub. L. No. 101-629, 104 Stat. 4511 (1990).

[45]   See Chapter 16 infra for more information on the history of the regulation of medical devices.

[46]   FDCA § 201(h), 21 U.S.C § 321(h).

[47]   21 C.F.R. § 3 (2014); see Chapter 17 infra for more information on regulation of combination products.

Enforceability of the Drug Adulteration and Misbranding Provisions

Congress enacted a series of mandatory requirements and explicit prohibitions in the FDCA. Tracing these provisions to the enforcement authority of FDA is somewhat challenging because of the statutory framework.

First, the substantive standards are embodied in FDCA sections 501 (defining "adulteration") and 502 (defining "misbranding").[48] In these sections, a drug is "deemed" to be adulterated or misbranded if it fails to meet a regulatory requirement or violates a prohibition. Thus, "adulteration" and "misbranding" are terms of art, removed slightly from the layperson's understanding of these words. Noncompliance that might seem "technical"—or at least not directly affecting the safety, effectiveness, or quality of a product sitting in a bottle on a shelf—nevertheless can "adulterate" or "misbrand" the product. The events triggering adulteration or misbranding can even occur long after the product has been made and shipped. To illustrate, the failure of a manufacturer to investigate complaints about a product causes all the related units of the product still in the marketplace to be "adulterated"; similarly, violative advertising in a medical journal will "misbrand" a prescription drug product that is already in the possession of a pharmacy with the labeling approved by FDA.[49]

The next element of the statutory structure consists of the listing of "prohibited acts" in FDCA section 301.[50] The acts—and the causing of those acts—are forbidden by the FDCA. Among the prohibited acts are:

- the introduction into interstate commerce of a drug that is adulterated or misbranded;[51]

- the adulteration or misbranding of a drug in interstate commerce;[52]

- the delivery or receipt in interstate commerce of a drug that is adulterated or misbranded;[53] and

- doing anything to a drug while it is being held for sale after shipment in interstate commerce that results in its becoming adulterated or misbranded.[54]

Having defined the prohibited acts, the FDCA then authorizes a series of judicial or administrative sanctions that may be invoked when a prohibited act can be proven to have occurred.[55]

---

[48]   21 U.S.C. §§ 351-352.
[49]   A prescription drug distributed or offered for sale in any state is misbranded, unless the manufacturer, packer, or distributor includes in all advertisements and other descriptive printed matter issued or caused to be issued by the manufacturer, packer, or distributor with respect to that drug information specified in section 502(n) of the FDCA. FDCA § 502(n), 21 U.S.C. § 352(n).
[50]   *Id.* § 331.
[51]   FDCA § 301(a), 21 U.S.C. § 331(a).
[52]   FDCA § 301(b), 21 U.S.C. § 331(b).
[53]   FDCA § 301(c), 21 U.S.C. § 331(c).
[54]   FDCA § 301(k), 21 U.S.C. § 331(k).
[55]   *See* Chapter 21 *infra* for more information on FDA's enforcement authorities and how they are used in practice.

Adulteration

Introduction and Overview

The general public understands "adulteration" to involve the mixing of something impure or spurious or of lower value into something that is pure and genuine, resulting in an inferior product, perhaps even tainted by a dangerous substance. That is certainly the origin of the concept in the FDCA.[56] Over time, however, the statute has been amended and interpreted to embrace other situations that do not result in a product that is, in fact, less than or different from what it purports to be. The consequence is that people easily can be confused when FDA alleges that a drug that meets its specifications, contains no detectable impurities, and is both safe and effective for use, is, nevertheless, "adulterated."

Under the FDCA, a drug may be adulterated for any of several reasons:

- If the drug consists in whole or part of any filthy, putrid, or decomposed substance,[57] or if any substance has been mixed or packed with the drug to reduce its quality or strength or a substance has been substituted for any of the drug.[58] These standards reflect the traditional meaning of "adulteration."

- If the drug has been prepared, packed, or held under unsanitary conditions whereby it may have been contaminated with filth, or whereby it may have been rendered injurious to health.[59] The key words here are "may have been." It is not necessary for FDA to demonstrate that the drug actually has been contaminated or will cause injury.

- If the container holding the drug is composed, in whole, or in part, of any poisonous or deleterious substance which may render the contents injurious to health.[60] This provision allows FDA to regulate components of containers that may leach into a product. Again, note the key phrase is "may render"; proof of actual damage to the contents or injury to health is not required.

- If the drug contains a color additive which is unsafe.[61] This provision effectively limits color additives in drugs to those approved for such use by FDA under the FDCA.[62]

- If the drug is represented to be one recognized in an official compendium and it fails to meet the standards set forth in that compendium.[63] Alternatively, if the drug is not recognized in such a compendium and its strength differs from, or its purity or quality fall below, that which it is represented to possess.[64]

---

[56]   H.R. REP. No. 75-2139 (1938).

[57]   FDCA § 501(a)(1), 21 U.S.C. § 351(a)(1).

[58]   FDCA § 501(d), 21 U.S.C. § 351(d).

[59]   FDCA § 501(a)(2)(A), 21 U.S.C. § 351(a)(2)(A). The FDCA uses the word "insanitary" rather than "unsanitary."

[60]   FDCA § 501(a)(3), 21 U.S.C. § 351(a)(3).

[61]   FDCA § 501(a)(4)(A), 21 U.S.C. § 351(a)(4)(A).

[62]   FDCA § 721, 21 U.S.C. § 379e.

[63]   FDCA § 501(b), 21 U.S.C. § 351(b).

[64]   FDCA § 501(c), 21 U.S.C. § 351(c).

- If the methods used in, or the facilities used for, manufacturing the drug do not conform to current good manufacturing practice.[65] In practice, this provision has become the most significant one on this list, and has generated more enforcement actions than all of the others combined, by far.

Current Good Manufacturing Practice

"Quality should be built into the product, and testing alone cannot be relied on to ensure product quality."[66] This philosophy permeates FDA's interpretation and application of the drug "current good manufacturing practice" (cGMP; alternatively called cGMP or simply GMP) requirements. The FDCA was amended in 1962 to add the following language to the adulteration provisions:

> A drug . . . shall be deemed to be adulterated—if . . . the methods used in, or the facilities or controls used for, its manufacture, processing, packing or holding do not conform to or are not operated or administered in conformity with current good manufacturing practice to assure that such drug meets the requirements of this Act as to safety and has the identity and strength, and meets the quality and purity characteristics, which it purports or is represented to possess . . . .[67]

As the word "current" implies, the cGMP requirements are not static, but evolve over time. Moreover, the reference point is not government-imposed standards, but, rather, the practices in use by various manufacturers. The role of FDA is simply to assess which practices in actual use are "good" and enforce those. Thus, cGMPs continuously advance the state of the art within the pharmaceutical industry. The practices "need not be widely prevalent. Congress did not require that a majority or any other percentage of manufacturers already be following" a particular practice for it to become the standard.[68]

The public sources for cGMP standards include academic and technical courses and programs, scientific and engineering journals, speeches and papers of industry experts and consultants, a myriad of FDA materials (such as speeches, guidance documents, inspection observations by FDA investigators, and Warning Letters), and court actions. As a matter of law, FDA does not have to adopt regulations particularizing the cGMP requirements in order to enforce them. Instead, it need only prove to a court in an enforcement action that a) the manufacturer of the product in question did not follow a particular practice and b) that practice is a current good manufacturing practice. This approach has some perils for FDA, because the courts may not always agree.

---

65 FDCA § 501(a)(2)(B), 21 U.S.C. § 351(a)(2)(B). In addition, special rules govern compounded positron emission tomography (PET) drugs, which must adhere to the standards for such compounding and to the official monographs of the United States Pharmacopeia. FDCA § 501(a)(2)(C), 21 U.S.C. § 351(a)(2)(C).

66 FDA, Guidance for Industry: Quality Systems Approach to Pharmaceutical cGMP Regulations at 3 (Sept. 2006) *available at* http://www.fda.gov/downloads/Drugs/.../Guidances/UCM070337.pdf.

67 Pub. L. No. 87-781, 76 Stat. 780 (1962); FDCA § 501(a)(2)(B), 21 U.S.C. § 351(a)(2)(B).

68 Human and Veterinary Drugs; Current Good Manufacturing Practice in Manufacture, Processing, Packing, or Holding; Final Rule; 43 Fed. Reg. 45,014, 45,018 (Sept. 29, 1978) (preamble to final order adopting cGMP regulations for finished pharmaceuticals) (codifying 21 C.F.R. pts. 201 and 211, and other provisions).

Although regulations are not required, in 1978 FDA promulgated a detailed set of them applicable to finished pharmaceuticals for human use.[69] A purpose of the 1978 rulemaking was to make the cGMP regulations binding, so that FDA would not have to prove in individual enforcement actions that a particular practice was a current good manufacturing practice.[70] Thus, a violation of the regulations in the manufacture of a product to which they are applicable can be enforced without expert testimony on the currency or goodness of the manufacturing practice.

Although the regulations are not directly applicable to some drugs (such as active pharmaceutical ingredients), the principles embedded in the regulations provide valuable guidance to FDA's approach to cGMPs in general. First, FDA's view is comprehensive, and covers all aspects of the manufacturing process, including organization and personnel, building and facilities, equipment, control of components and drug product containers and closures, production and process controls, packaging and labeling controls, warehousing and distribution, laboratory controls, records and reports, and returned and salvaged drug products. Second, each manufacturer is permitted to develop its own practices in each area to assure product quality and consistency. FDA does not attempt to be prescriptive in "how to" make products, but requires the manufacturers to do so. A company must establish in writing the specifications for a drug product, then the procedures by which it can assure that the drug is manufactured in a way to meet those specifications. Third, the manufacturer must adhere to its procedures and specifications, and document that it is doing so. It is a maxim of FDA inspectors that, "If it is not documented, it did not happen." Finally, the company must monitor its processes and products, investigate deviations or failures, and take appropriate corrective and preventive actions to preclude similar deviations or failures in the future.

A critical concept in FDA's approach to cGMP is that processes must be operated in a "state of control," even if not always in a "state of compliance." On any given day, there can be—and for most firms probably is—actual noncompliance; humans err, machines malfunction, records are lost. What FDA expects is that the processes are sustainable and capable of self-correction, so that errors and malfunctions are detected quickly, corrective actions are taken to address the damage (if any) to the product, and preventive measures are implemented to reduce the chance of repetition. Seeking to operate in a state of control reflects a corporate culture favoring quality.

It must be emphasized that it is not a defense to a cGMP enforcement proceeding that the drug is actually safe and effective, or even that the drug actually meets applicable standards of strength, quality, and purity. If the operations were not properly performed in accordance with written procedures, or even if the company merely lacks adequate documentation that

---

[69]   21 C.F.R. pt. 211. Although these have been amended in parts, there has not been a comprehensive revision of these regulations in more than 30 years. At the time, the agency contemplated a series of additional regulations, covering a variety of specialized product types such as large-volume parenterals (sterile drugs for injection), small-volume parenterals, medical gases, and bulk pharmaceuticals (now called "active pharmaceutical ingredients"); this project was soon abandoned, however, leaving only one set of regulations in final form.

[70]   See National Ass'n of Pharm. Manufacturers v. FDA, 637 F.2d 877 (2d Cir. 1981) (FDA has authority to issue binding cGMP regulations); Human and Veterinary Drugs: Current Good Manufacturing Practice in Manufacture, Processing, Packing, or Holding, 43 Fed. Reg. 45,013, 45,921 (Sept. 29, 1978).

the operations were so performed, cGMP requirements have been violated and the product is deemed to be "adulterated." Note, also, that cGMP obligations persist long after a product has been made and shipped. For example, stability studies must be performed throughout the labeled shelf life of the product to substantiate continuing compliance with product specifications;[71] complaints about product failures must be investigated;[72] and batch records must be maintained throughout and after the shelf life of the product.[73] Failure to meet these duties causes all products remaining in the market to become legally "adulterated."

Because of the evolving nature and uncertainty surrounding specific practices as "current" and "good," the constitutionality of the cGMP provision of the FDCA has been challenged in courts. Courts have consistently rejected the claims that the cGMPs are unconstitutionally vague; they have held that the standards are sufficiently definite to provide notice of what is legally required.[74] Judges have also said that the regulations provide flexibility to manufacturers in complying with them,[75] but are specific enough to assure that a particular drug is safe and reliable.[76] Finally, they have also opined that the FDA regulations contain adequate substance to guide a judge when making a determination as to whether cGMPs were followed.[77]

Very few companies choose to litigate a cGMP case against FDA in court. In significant part, the lack of litigation may reflect a reluctance by any major healthcare product manufacturer to undergo a public trial on the question of whether its products are "adulterated." The adverse publicity may be damaging, because FDA will always try to convince the judge that the alleged noncompliance is not merely technical but affects the safety of the product. In the cases that have been litigated, courts have generally been deferential to FDA, and have found that the drugs in question were adulterated due to failure to comply with cGMP.[78] Occasionally, however, FDA is not a clear winner. In one hard-fought litigation, the court described the situation as a "confrontation between a humorless warden and its uncooperative prisoner" and the product of "an industry mired in uncertainty and conflict, guided by vague regulations which produce tugs-of-war of varying intensity."[79] The decision analyzed various aspects of the cGMP regulations in much more detail than is typical. After considerable expert testimony on both sides, the court rejected FDA's view that each individual test result falling outside of specifications constituted a "batch failure," triggering a need for a full investigation; instead, the court accepted a "sliding-scale approach" proposed by the manufacturer whereby the nature of the failure governed the intensity of the failure investigation required under the cGMP regulations. On the other hand, FDA did succeed on the argument that, if manufacturing firms either adopt methods that the USP does not recognize or modify USP procedures, they must validate these methods or modified procedures and provide FDA with the raw data from the validation studies. This

---

[71]   See 21 C.F.R. § 211.166 (2014).

[72]   See id. § 211.198 (2014).

[73]   See id. §§ 211.180, 211.188 (2014).

[74]   United States v. Bel-Mar Laboratories, Inc., 284 F. Supp. 875 (E.D.N.Y. 1968); United States v. An Article of Drug Labeled "White Quadrisect," 484 F.2d 748, 751 (7th Cir. 1973).

[75]   United States v. An Article of Drug Labeled "White Quadrisect," 484 F.2d 748, 760 (7th Cir. 1973); National Ass'n of Pharm. Manufacturers v. DHHS, 586 F. Supp. 740 (S.D.N.Y. 1984).

[76]   United States v. Bel-Mar Laboratories, Inc., 284 F. Supp. 875 (E.D.N.Y. 1968).

[77]   National Ass'n of Pharm. Manufacturers v. DHHS, 586 F. Supp. 740 (S.D.N.Y. 1984).

[78]   See, e.g., United States v. Sage Pharm., Inc., 210 F.3d 475 (5th Cir. 2000).

[79]   United States v. Barr Laboratories, 812 F. Supp. 458, 464 (D.N.J. 1993).

case represents the most thorough judicial evaluation of specific FDA positions on cGMP requirements to date.

Most cGMP enforcement actions are resolved either through voluntary actions in response to an FDA Warning Letter or consent decrees for permanent injunction. Consent decrees can be useful sources of information regarding the elements that FDA believes are part of the cGMP, as well as the gravity of problems that will lead to action in court to enforce the law. Over the past several years, there has been an increase in cGMP-related enforcement actions, with FDA entering into consent decrees with several manufacturers, including Ben Venue Laboratories, Inc. and Ranbaxy Laboratories, Inc. This trend is likely to continue as the Department of Justice has identified compliance with cGMP requirements as a "top area of focus" for the Department.[80]

Separate from the drug cGMPs, FDA has also codified manufacturing standards for biological products in 21 C.F.R. Parts 600-680.[81] In July 2013, FDA promulgated a regulation on the cGMPs for combination products, intended to clarify which cGMP requirements apply when drugs, devices, and biologics are combined to create combination products.[82] Under the framework established in the regulation, the cGMP requirements that apply to each of the constituent parts continue to apply when the constituents are combined to make a combination product.

Compendial Requirements

Through the FDCA, FDA also enforces standards adopted by nongovernment entities under the "adulteration" provision. The law states that a drug shall be deemed to be adulterated if it "purports to be or is represented as a drug the name of which is recognized in an official compendium, and its strength differs from, or its quality or purity falls below, the standards set forth in such compendium . . . ."[83]

The USP contains individual sections called "monographs" covering active pharmaceutical ingredients (APIs) and finished dosage forms. An API monograph establishes the chemical standards for identity and specifications for purity and quality that must be met, and the test methods to be used, to qualify as being that API. A finished dosage form monograph contains similar standards for identity, quality, strength, purity, packaging, and labeling for a drug product. Monographs are developed by USP by a public process that involves input from industry, academia, and FDA.[84]

---

[80]   DOJ, Deputy Assistant Attorney General Maame Ewusi-Mensah Frimpong Speaks At the 2013 CBI Pharmaceutical Compliance Congress (Jan. 29, 2013), *available at* http://www.justice.gov/iso/opa/civil/speeches/2013/civ-speech-130129.html.

[81]   For biological products that are also regulated as drugs, the biological product standards may apply in addition to the drug cGMPs.

[82]   Final Rule: 21 C.F.R. Part 4 Current Good Manufacturing Practice Requirements for Combination Products; 78 Fed. Reg. 4307 (Jan. 22, 2013).

[83]   FDCA § 501(b), 21 U.S.C. § 351(b).

[84]   U.S. Pharmacopeia, "USP Standards: Monographs (Written Standards)," *available at* http://www.usp.org/sites/default/files/usp_pdf/EN/regulator/monograph_backgrounder_dec_2011.pdf.

For determinations of strength, purity, and quality, the USP sets forth specific testing requirements for drug products. A manufacturer need not use a USP method to analyze a compendial product if it uses another method that is of equivalent or higher accuracy.[85] For example, an alternative method may be faster or cheaper to run, and would be preferable for routine batch release testing of a product. The manufacturer must validate the alternative method and provide the supporting data to FDA.[86]

In the event of a dispute about conformity with a USP standard, however, the product must meet compendial requirements when tested using the USP method as the "referee test."[87]

Misbranding

Introduction and Definitions

The FDCA prohibits the introduction into interstate commerce of any drug that is misbranded.[88] This section will provide an overview of the acts that may cause FDA to deem a drug "misbranded" under the FDCA. Like "adulteration," the term "misbranding" is a legal term of art, having meanings well beyond common conceptions of the term involving false or deceptive statements on a product container. First, the act contains a long list of discrete items of information required to be included on the container or in accompanying materials, the omission of any of which can misbrand a drug. Second, the law also includes under the heading of misbranding special rules for the physical packaging apart from the labels and labeling. Third, the misbranding provisions can apply to materials that are physically distant from the product container. To illustrate, an advertisement in the *New England Journal of Medicine* can result in misbranding a prescription drug.[89] Consequently, acts or omissions can misbrand a product long after it has actually been manufactured and shipped, even though at the time of shipment it was not misbranded. Finally, some of the acts or omissions have literally nothing to do with the product container or related materials; for example, a drug is misbranded if it was manufactured in an establishment that was not registered with FDA.[90]

Before turning to these detailed provisions, it is critical to note that the statute creates distinct but often overlapping rules for "labels," "labeling," and "advertising." These terms therefore need definition.

A "label" is "a display of written, printed, or graphic matter upon the immediate container of any article."[91] The term "immediate container" does not encompass "package liners,"[92] and

---

85 FDA COMPLIANCE POLICY GUIDES MANUAL, sec. 420.400, CPG 7132.05 (Oct. 1, 1980), *available at* http://www. fda.gov/ICECI/ComplianceManuals/CompliancePolicyGuidanceManual/ucm074360.htm.

86 United States v. Barr Laboratories, 812 F. Supp. at 482.

87 FDA COMPLIANCE POLICY GUIDES MANUAL, sec. 420.400, CPG 7132.05 (Oct. 1, 1980), *available at* http://www. fda.gov/ICECI/ComplianceManuals/CompliancePolicyGuidanceManual/ucm074360.htm.

88 FDCA § 301(a), 21 U.S.C. § 331(a).

89 FDCA § 502(n), 21 U.S.C. § 352(n).

90 FDCA § 502(o), 21 U.S.C. § 352(o).

91 FDCA § 201(k), 21 U.S.C. § 321(k).

92 FDCA § 201(l), 21 U.S.C. § 321(l).

the statute also makes clear that the "immediate container" does not include the "outside container or wrapper of a retail package."[93] In other words, the "immediate container" is the bottle that contains tablets, or the vial containing an injectable, but not the box into which the bottle or vial is packaged for shipping and handling. Nevertheless, any requirement under the FDCA applicable to a "label" must also be satisfied by the outer container (i.e., the box holding the bottle or vial).[94] This container is referred to by FDA as the "package": "any container or wrapping in which [a drug] is enclosed for use in delivery or display of such commodities to retail purchasers."[95]

"Labeling" is a much more expansive term, and includes "all labels and other written, printed or graphic matter (1) upon any article or any of its containers or wrappers, or (2) accompanying such article."[96] Federal courts have broadly read the "accompanying" provision to extend the scope of labeling to materials that supplement or explain the article, even if they are not physically attached.[97] As a result, the definition of "labeling" encompasses any type of written materials, including brochures, reprints of scientific articles, and pamphlets that are used by a product's manufacturer, distributor, or other seller to provide supplemental information relating to the use of the drug.[98]

"Advertising" is not defined in the FDCA, but is subject to rules separate from those applicable to "labels" and "labeling" under the statute. The fact that the act created different sets of requirements for "labeling" and "advertising" implies that the two categories are distinct, but the line between them is hardly clear. In 1963, FDA promulgated the following definitions to draw some a line:

(1)   Advertisements . . . include advertisements in published journals, magazines, other periodicals, and newspapers, and advertisements broadcast through media such as radio, television, and telephone communications.

(2)   Brochures, booklets, mailing pieces, detailing pieces, file cards, bulletins, calendars, price lists, catalogs, house organs, letters, motion picture films, film strips, lantern slides, sound recordings, exhibits, literature, and reprints and similar pieces of printed, audio, or visual matter descriptive of a drug and references published (for example, the "Physicians Desk Reference") for use by medical practitioners, pharmacists, or nurses, containing drug information supplied by the manufacturer, packer, or distributor of the drug and which are disseminated by or on behalf of its manufacturer, packer, or distributor are hereby determined to be labeling as defined in section 201(m) of the [FDCA].[99]

The reference to "lantern slides" demonstrates how dated this regulation is. The most notable omission from this list in the second decade of the 21st century is any reference to

---

93   FDCA § 201(k), 21 U.S.C. § 321(k).
94   *Id.*
95   21 C.F.R. § 1.20 (2014).
96   FDCA § 201(m), 21 U.S.C. § 321(m).
97   *See, e.g.,* Kordel v. United States, 335 U.S. 345, 350 (1948); V.E. Irons, Inc. v. U.S., 244 F.2d 34, 39 (1st Cir. 1957).
98   *Kordel,* 335 U.S. at 348.
99   21 C.F.R. § 202.1(l)(2) (2014); Regulations for the Enforcement of the Federal Food, Drug, and Cosmetic Act and the Fair Packaging and Labeling Act: Prescription Drug Advertisements, 33 Fed. Reg. 9393 (June 17, 1968).

the Internet, which has forced FDA and other agencies (e.g., the Federal Trade Commission (FTC)) to grapple with new classification issues. For example, is information posted on a drug manufacturer's website "advertising" or "labeling"? The FDCA does not give FDA legal authority over the advertising of most nonprescription or OTC drugs, only prescription drugs.[100] Thus, if FDA classifies the materials on the Internet as "advertising," it would lose jurisdiction over some aspects of the promotion of OTC drugs. Were a website classified as "labeling," however, FDA would have authority. But its jurisdictional reach would extend not only to websites for all drug products but also to those for foods, cosmetics, and many other products, the promotion of which has traditionally been under the purview of the FTC. At the time of this writing, FDA and FTC have not fully resolved this definitional and jurisdictional issue, although both agencies continue to assert jurisdiction over promotional materials found on the Internet, and FDA recently issued a series of draft guidance documents addressing promotion in social media.[101]

FDA has subdivided "labeling" for prescription drugs into two categories: formal product labeling and promotional labeling. The first is called by a variety of unofficial names such as the "package insert," "physician prescribing information," "full product information," and "FDA-approved labeling." It is approved by FDA, accompanies the drug in its final package, is reprinted in the *Physicians' Desk Reference* and is posted on the manufacturer's website. FDA takes the position that "promotional labeling" is everything else under the definition of "labeling." The reason for this distinction is that, for new drugs being approved by FDA, the agency must also approve the final "labeling" for the drug product.[102] Because FDA could not possibly review and approve promotional materials that fall within the ambit of the broader definition of "labeling," it has carved out what it will preclear as the formal labeling of the product, and treated the rest in the same manner as "advertising" that need only be submitted at time of use and thereafter subject to FDA's enforcement authority.[103]

General Requirements for Format and Content of Labels and Labeling; Preemption of State Law

The FDCA contains a very broad requirement that drug products have adequate directions for their intended use in the labeling. This core concept has become crucial to FDA's approach to numerous issues in the regulation of drug labeling.

---

[100]   FDCA § 502(n), 21 U.S.C. § 352(n).
[101]   FDA, Draft Guidance for Industry: Internet/Social Media Platforms With Character Space Limitations: Presenting Risk and Benefit Information for Prescription Drugs and Medical Devices (June 2014), *available at* http://www.fda.gov/downloads/drugs/guidancecomplianceregulatoryinformation/guidances/ucm401087. pdf; FDA, Draft Guidance for Industry: Internet/Social Media Platforms: Correcting Independent Third-Party Misinformation About Prescription Drugs and Medical Devices (June 2014), *available at* http:// www.fda.gov/downloads/drugs/guidancecomplianceregulatoryinformation/guidances/ucm401079.pdf; FDA, Draft Guidance for Industry: Fulfilling Regulatory Requirements for Postmarketing Submissions of Interactive Promotional Media for Prescription Human and Animal Drugs and Biologics (January 2014), *available at* http://www.fda.gov/downloads/Drugs/GuidanceComplianceRegulatoryInformation/Guidances/ UCM381352.pdf.
[102]   FDCA § 505(d)(7), 21 U.S.C. § 355(d)(7).
[103]   *See, e.g.*, 21 C.F.R. 314.81(b)(3)(i) (2014).

Requirement for "Adequate Directions for Use"

Perhaps the most significant single provision in the misbranding provisions of the act—certainly for prescription drugs—is the requirement in section 502(f) that the labeling of a drug contain "adequate directions for use" and adequate warnings about unsafe use, for all uses intended by the manufacturer or marketer, unless exempted by FDA.[104]

In regulations promulgated after this requirement became law in 1938, FDA interpreted it to mean that the information had to be "adequate" to a layperson, not simply a healthcare professional.[105] As reflected in the agency's labeling regulations and enforcement posture, the agency also concluded that no labeling would be adequate for laypersons, if the drug could be used safely only under the supervision of a physician.[106] Thus, FDA promulgated a regulation exempting from this requirement drugs that were available only by prescription, as long as the labeling had sufficient information for the healthcare professional.[107] The logic behind exempting prescription drugs from the requirement to have adequate directions for use (by laypeople) lies in the assumption that physicians will inform their patients about the appropriate use of prescription drugs, and thus the manufacturer need not be responsible for assuring that patients understand the complexities associated with use of prescription drugs.[108] Moreover, since by definition prescription drugs can only be used upon the advice of a physician, it is impossible to write adequate directions for lay use of a prescription drug.

FDA has applied the "adequate directions for use" requirement in section 502(f)(1) as a legal theory to attack the promotion of foods or dietary supplements for use as drugs, as well as promotion of approved drug products for unapproved or "off-label" uses. In a tactic known as the "squeeze play," the agency alleges that a product's labeling lacks adequate directions for use and could not contain any because the product has not been shown to be safe or effective for the intended use. If the marketer were to attempt to correct its lack of adequate directions, FDA could then bring an action contending that the directions would violate section 502(a) as "false or misleading."[109] Another litigation option utilized by FDA is called the "back-door new-drug charge": the agency contends that promotional claims going beyond FDA-approved labeling for an approved new drug product provide a new "intended

---

[104] FDCA § 502(f), 21 U.S.C. 352(f); Enforcement of Federal Food, Drug, and Cosmetic Act; New Drugs, 21 Fed. Reg. 3690 (May 30, 1956).

[105] 21 C.F.R. § 201.5 (2014); Alberty Food Products Co. v. U.S., 185 F.2d 321 (9th Cir. 1950); U.S. v. Articles of Drug, 625 F.2d 665 (5th Cir. 1980).

[106] U.S. v. El-O-Pathic Pharmacy, et al., 192 F.2d 62 (9th Cir. 1951); U.S. v. Articles of Drug, 625 F.2d 665 (5th Cir. 1980).

[107] 21 C.F.R. § 201.100; Changes in Labeling Requirements for Drugs, 27 Fed. Reg. 1317 (Feb. 13, 1962). The choice to market the product as prescription only, however, was originally made by the manufacturer, not FDA. By 1951, there was sufficient confusion in the market about the prescription or OTC status of competing products that Congress amended the FDCA to give FDA authority to impose uniform standards for all drugs, deciding which were prescription and which OTC. Durham-Humphrey Amendment, Pub. L. No. 82-215, 65 Stat. 648 (1951); FDCA § 503(b), 21 U.S.C. 353(b). *See* Temin, *Origin of Compulsory Drug Prescriptions*, 22 J. Law & Econ. 91 (1979); Temin, Taking Your Medicine: Drug Regulation in the United States (1980). *See* Chapter 13 *infra* for more information on the classification of drug products as prescription only or OTC.

[108] United States v. Evers, 643 F.2d 1043, 1051-52 (5th Cir. 1981).

[109] *Consider* Alberty Food Prod. Co. v. U.S., 185 F2d 321 (9th Cir. 1950); V. E. Irons, Inc. v. U.S., 244 F.2d 34 (1st Cir. 1957); and U.S. v. Hohensee, 243 F.2d 367 (3d. Cir. 1957), all brought under section 502(f)(1), and the implications if the defendants had sought to argue that the labeling in each case was adequate for laypersons to use the products to treat the diseases described.

use" for which the product fails to contain adequate directions. FDA may then bring an enforcement action alleging that the product is, in effect, with respect to that new intended use not an approved new drug, without having to establish jurisdiction over the product under the new drug provisions of the act.[110]

FDA promulgated regulations exempting certain other types of drug products from the adequate directions for use requirements: bulk drugs intended for processing, repacking or use in the manufacture of another drug;[111] animal drugs to be used only under the supervision of a licensed veterinarian;[112] drugs for which the directions for use are commonly known;[113] in vitro diagnostic products;[114] drugs prepared, packaged and primarily sold as a prescription chemical or component for use by pharmacists in drug compounding;[115] drugs for use in teaching, law enforcement, research, and analysis;[116] and radioactive drugs intended for research use.[117]

General Requirements for Format and Content of Labels and Labeling

FDA has also used the statutory authority in section 502(f)(1) to exempt a drug product from the requirement for "adequate directions for use" on the condition that the product's formal labeling comply with the agency's standards for the format and content of prescription drug labeling.[118] Creation of a consistent format for prescription drug labeling, and imposition of consistent criteria for the quantum of evidence to justify inclusion of information in this labeling, has long been an agency priority.[119] In 2006, FDA promulgated a complete overhaul of the prescription drug labeling requirements,[120] and in 2014, the agency issued a proposed rule requiring electronic distribution of the prescribing information intended for healthcare professionals.[121]

Language required by the FDCA to appear on the label must be prominently placed and must be conspicuous as compared to other language on the label, and must be easily read and understood "by the ordinary individual under customary conditions of purchase and

---

[110] 21 C.F.R. § 201.128 (2014). *See* U.S. v. Articles of Drug, 625 F.2d 665 (5th Cir. 1980). The "back-door new-drug" charge also creates the theoretical possibility, in a seizure action, that the goods may be reconditioned, an option not available for products seized as new drugs in violation of section 505. FDCA § 304(d)(1), 21 U.S.C. § 334(d)(1).

[111] 21 C.F.R. § 201.122 (2014).

[112] *Id.* § 201.105 (2014).

[113] *Id.* § 201.116 (2014).

[114] *Id.* § 201.119 (2014).

[115] *Id.* § 201.120 (2014).

[116] *Id.* § 201.125 (2014).

[117] *Id.* § 201.129 (2014).

[118] *Id.* § 201.100(d)(3) (2014).

[119] Until implementation of the Drug Amendments of 1962, FDA had not routinely approved the complete text of "package inserts." As a result, wide variations existed in format and content; in addition, they were often promotional in tone and rarely a neutral, balanced, and authoritative statement of what was known about the product. Starting in the early 1970s, the agency began exerting much more control over prescription drug labeling through the NDA review process.

[120] 21 C.F.R. §§ 201.56-57 (2014); Requirements on Content and Format of Labeling for Human Prescription Drug and Biological Products: Final Rule, 71 Fed. Reg. 3922 (Jan, 24, 2006).

[121] Electronic Distribution of Prescribing Information for Human Prescription Drugs, Including Biological Products: Proposed Rule, 79 Fed. Reg. 75,506 (Dec. 18, 2014).

use."[122] This provision provides the legal basis for the FDA regulation establishing the format and content requirements for labeling for OTC drug products.[123]

FDA has established special rules for certain special situations:

- **Spanish language.** If a drug is distributed solely in Puerto Rico, the language required on the label and labeling may be in Spanish, rather than English.[124] If the label or labeling contains *any* information in Spanish, then *all* required information must appear in Spanish.[125]

- **Prominence requirements** for display at point of purchase. If required language would not usually "appear on the part or panel of the label that is presented or displayed under customary conditions of purchase," it need not comply with the usual rules for placement of mandatory information.[126]

- **Insufficient label space.** FDA permits exceptions from some label requirements due to insufficiency of label space.[127]

- **Exemptions.** FDA has authority to exempt from the labeling requirements drugs that are "to be processed, labeled, or repacked in substantial quantities at establishments other than those where originally processed or packed, on condition that such drugs . . . are not adulterated or misbranded . . . upon removal from such processing, labeling, or repacking establishment."[128] Using this power, the agency exempts manufacturers of drugs for further processing if certain conditions are met.[129]

These requirements apply up to the point that the drug product is dispensed to the patient, at which point different rules apply. Essentially, when given to a patient or caregiver, a prescription drug container need only have a label that identifies the prescriber (e.g., a physician), and the dispenser (e.g., a pharmacy), the date of filling and the serial number of the prescription, as well as the name of the patient, if stated in the prescription, and any directions for use and precautions the prescriber included in the prescription.[130] FDA also has by regulation required patient-directed labeling for selected prescription drug products; a broader program, under the name "Patient Package Inserts," was proposed but later revoked.[131] For certain prescription drug products that the agency determines pose a serious and significant public health concern, the agency requires distribution of FDA-approved patient labeling in the form of "Medication Guides," which while generally limited in scope, are a common element of REMS programs.[132]

---

[122]   FDCA § 502(c), 21 U.S.C. § 352(c).
[123]   21 C.F.R. § 201.66 (2014).
[124]   *Id.* § 201.15(c)(1) (2014).
[125]   *Id.* §§ 201.15(c)(2)-(3), 201.16 (2014).
[126]   *Id.* § 201.15(a)(1) (2014).
[127]   *Id.* § 201.15(b) (2014).
[128]   FDCA § 503(a), 21 U.S.C. § 353(a).
[129]   21 C.F.R. § 201.150(a) (2014).
[130]   FDCA § 503(b)(2), 21 U.S.C. § 353(b)(2).
[131]   *See, e.g.,* 21 C.F.R. §§ 201.305 (2014) (isoproterenol inhalation products), 310.501 (2014) (oral contraceptives), and 310.516 (estrogenic drug products). Regarding patient package inserts, *see* Prescription Drug Products Patient Package Inserts Requirements Final Rule, 45 Fed. Reg. 60,754 (Sept. 12, 1980) (promulgating the program), Pharmaceutical Mfrs. Ass'n v. FDA, 634 F.2d 106 (3d Cir. 1980) (upholding FDA's authority), and 47 Fed. Reg. 39,147 (Sept. 7, 1982) (revoking the program).
[132]   21 C.F.R. pt. 208 (2014).

Preemption of State Tort Law on Duty to Warn and Other State Laws

Congress enacted a broad express preemption of state law that might establish any requirement for the label or labeling of an OTC drug product, with limited exceptions.[133] No comparable express preemption provision exists for prescription drugs. In 2006, however, FDA formally announced what it characterized as a statement of its longstanding policy regarding preemption; relying on theories of implied preemption, FDA stated that the agency approval process for prescription drug labeling preempts conflicting or contrary state law, including most state product liability claims.[134] However, in 2009, the Supreme Court in *Wyeth v. Levine*,[135] rejected federal preemption of a failure-to-warn product liability claim involving a prescription drug. The Court ruled 6-3 that the state tort claim at issue did not conflict with the FDCA, and affirmed that through the many amendments to the FDCA over the years "it has remained a central premise . . . that the manufacturer bears responsibility for the content of its label at all times." Although the decision leaves a narrow opening for mounting a preemption defense in certain contexts, it is generally seen as a strong rejection of FDA's stated position on preemption, and it has changed the calculus with respect to the submission and implementation of safety-related changes to labeling.[136]

In another landmark decision, in *PLIVA v. Mensing*, the Supreme Court held that the FDCA prevents plaintiffs from bringing state tort claims against generic drug manufacturers for failure to warn because the statute requires generic manufacturers to use the same FDA-approved labeling required for the branded versions of the drugs.[137] The Court found that it would be impossible for a generic manufacturer to comply with state tort laws that would require a stronger warning label, and, to the extent state laws required generic manufacturers to include such warnings, the state law was preempted. As a result, many product liability suits involving generic products—representing 80 percent or more of prescriptions[138]—are preempted. This outcome prompted FDA to propose a new regulatory framework for labeling changes that would allow generic companies to initiate changes in warnings in labeling, negating the outcome of *Mensing*.[139] To date the proposal, which has been highly controversial, has not been finalized.

Specific Requirements for Content of Labels and Labeling

In addition to the general requirements discussed above, the FDCA imposes a number of specific content requirements on drug labels and/or labeling:

---

[133]   FDCA § 751, 21 U.S.C. § 379r.

[134]   *See* Requirements on Content and Format of Labeling for Human Prescription Drug and Biological Products Final Rule, 71 Fed. Reg. 3922, 3933-36 (Jan. 24, 2006).

[135]   555 U.S. 555 (Mar. 4, 2009).

[136]   555 U.S. at 570-571.

[137]   113 S.Ct. 2567 (2011).

[138]   IMS INSTITUTE FOR HEALTHCARE INFORMATICS, THE USE OF MEDICINES IN THE UNITED STATES: REVIEW OF 2011 (revised May 30, 2012), *available at* https://www.imshealth.com/ims/Global/Content/Insights/IMS%20 Institute%20for%20Healthcare%20Informatics/IHII_Medicines_in_U.S_Report_2011.pdf.

[139]   Supplemental Applications Proposing Labeling Changes for Approved Drugs and Biological Products, 78 Fed. Reg. 67,985, 67,989, 67,995 (Nov. 13, 2013) (proposed rule).

- **Name and address of manufacturer, packer, or distributor.** Either the manufacturer, the packer, or the distributor (or a combination of the three) must be identified.[140] FDA has defined the activities of manufacturing that must be done by a company in order to identify that company as the "manufacturer."[141] This policy was adopted to avoid situations in which a company would outsource work to another firm, but claim that it was the manufacturer.[142] Misrepresenting oneself as the manufacturer will cause the drug product to be misbranded.[143]

- **Quantity of the contents.** The label must disclose the net contents, expressed by weight, measure, or numerical count.[144]

- **Generic name and quantity of ingredients.** The "label must contain the established name" of the drug product, if such a name exists; the "established name" and quantity or proportion of each *active* ingredient; and the "established name" of each *inactive* ingredient listed in alphabetical order on the outside container of the retail package and, "if determined to be appropriate by [FDA], on the immediate container . . . ."[145] In addition, for a prescription drug, the established names of the ingredients must be in the labeling of the product.[146] Moreover, for prescription drugs, the "established name" must appear "prominently and in type at least half as large as that used thereon for any proprietary name or designation for such drug" on labels and labeling.[147]

  The FDCA defines "established name" (popularly called the "generic name") as that name designated by FDA under section 508;[148] or, if none, the name recognized in an official compendium, such as the United States Pharmacopeia; or if neither, then the common or usual name of the drug.[149]

  The labeling of a drug product may be misleading, and cause it to be misbranded, by reason of: 1) the order of listed ingredients; 2) the failure to reveal the proportion of drug ingredients "when such proportion or other fact is material in the light of the representation that such ingredient is present in such drug"; 3) the use of a name that implies the drug or ingredient has traits or characteristics that it does not have; 4) the listing of inactive ingredients in a way that implies they are of greater value than they actually are; or 5) the use of a name that may be easily confused with that of another drug or ingredient.[150]

- **Bar codes and NDC numbers.** Under an early regulation, FDA requested (but did not require) the National Drug Code (NDC) number for the product to appear on the label in Arabic numeral form.[151] In 2004, FDA adopted another rule that requires virtually all

---

[140] FDCA § 502(b)(1), 21 U.S.C. § 352(b)(1).
[141] 21 C.F.R. § 201.1 (2014).
[142] *See* Requirements for Designating a Manufacturer's Name on a Drug Product Label Final Rule, 45 Fed. Reg. 25,760 (Apr. 15, 1980).
[143] 21 C.F.R. § 201.1(l) (2014).
[144] FDCA § 502(b)(2), 21 U.S.C. § 352(b)(2).
[145] FDCA § 502(e)(1)(A), 21 U.S.C. § 352(e)(1)(A).
[146] FDCA § 502(e)(1)(B), 21 U.S.C. § 352(e)(1)(B).
[147] *Id.*
[148] FDCA § 508, 21 U.S.C. § 358. FDA does not routinely designate official names, however, so that the compendial authorities generally choose the generic name for a drug ingredient. 21 C.F.R. § 299.4(e) (2014).
[149] FDCA § 502(e)(3), 21 U.S.C. § 352(e)(3).
[150] FDCA § 502.
[151] *Id.* § 201.2. This regulation was based on FDCA § 502(c) (21 U.S.C. § 352(c)). Drug Listing Act of 1972: Revision of Implementing Regulations, 40 Fed. Reg. 52,000, 52,002 (Nov. 7, 1975).

prescription and OTC drugs to include on the label a bar code that must contain, at a minimum, the NDC number for the product embedded in the linear bar code.[152] If the NDC is presented as a number, any representation that the NDC number denotes FDA approval of either the manufacturer or the drug product is misleading and constitutes misbranding.[153] As discussed more fully below, new track and trace requirements that will be implemented in the coming years, include new serialization requirements at the package level, and ultimately an interoperable electronic pedigree system.

- **Expiration dating and storage requirements.** The FDCA authorizes FDA to require that a drug that is liable to deterioration carry on its label precautionary statements specified by the agency.[154] Under its cGMP authority through the adulteration provisions, FDA has separately required stability testing of all drugs to determine appropriate storage conditions and expiration dates.[155] If the stability testing determines that an expiration date is warranted to assure that the drug has not deteriorated prior to use, the expiration date must "appear on the immediate container and also the outer package," unless it is a single-dose container packed in an individual carton, in which case the expiration date may "appear on the individual carton instead of the immediate product container."[156] In addition to the expiration date, the labels of drugs subject to deterioration must indicate appropriate storage conditions.[157]

- **Rx symbol.** A prescription drug is misbranded unless its label bears, prior to dispensing, the symbol "Rx only."[158] Similarly, if a nonprescription drug bears the symbol "Rx only," it will be deemed misbranded.[159]

- **Telephone number for adverse event reporting.** In 2002, Congress directed FDA to promulgate a final rule requiring the labeling for new drugs approved under section 505 of the FDCA to "include the toll-free number maintained by [FDA] for the purpose of receiving reports of adverse events regarding drugs and a statement that such number is to be used for reporting purposes only, not to receive medical advice."[160] In 2004, FDA published in the *Federal Register* a proposed rule regarding the toll-free number.[161] FDA proposed the following conforming statement to be included on the labeling of drug products: "Call your doctor for medical advice about side effects. You may report side effects to FDA at 1-800-FDA-1088."[162] FDA proposed a slightly modified statement for OTC drugs.[163] Despite receiving few comments, FDA did not promulgate a final rule. Therefore, in 2007, Congress enacted a provision that the 2004 proposed rule would

---

[152] 21 C.F.R. § 201.25(a) (2014). This regulation was based on FDCA §§ 502(a) and (f) (21 U.S.C. §§ 352(a) and (f)). 69 Fed. Reg. 9120 (Feb. 26, 2014).

[153] *Id.* § 207.39 (2014).

[154] FDCA § 502(h), 21 U.S.C. § 352(h).

[155] 21 C.F.R. § 211.166(a) (2014).

[156] *Id.* § 201.17 (2014).

[157] *Id.* § 211.137(b) (2014).

[158] FDCA § 503(b)(4)(A), 21 U.S.C. § 353(b)(4)(A). The requirement that the label and labeling for a controlled substance contain the symbol "C" followed by the Roman numeral of the schedule in which the controlled substance has been placed is imposed and enforced by the Drug Enforcement Administration. 21 U.S.C. § 825, 21 C.F.R. § 1302.03 (2014).

[159] FDCA § 503(b)(4)(B), 21 U.S.C. § 353(b)(4)(B).

[160] Pub L. No. 107-377, 116 Stat. 3115 (2002); 21 U.S.C. § 355b(a).

[161] Toll-Free Number for Reporting Adverse Events on Labeling for Human Drug Products Proposed Rule, 69 Fed. Reg. 21,778 (Apr. 22, 2004).

[162] *Id.* at 21,780.

[163] *Id.* at 21,781.

go into effect January 1, 2008, unless FDA promulgated a final rule before that date.[164] Congress clarified that the proposed rule taking effect or a final rule promulgated by FDA shall not apply to an OTC drug as long as the packaging of the OTC product contains "a toll-free number through which consumers can report complaints to the manufacturer or distributor of the drug."[165] FDA did not promulgate a final rule by the deadline, so the statute now requires that prescription drug labeling contain the statement from the 2004 proposed rule.

- **Other FDA-mandated specific disclosures and warnings.** FDA has issued regulations requiring disclosure of certain information in particular instances.[166] For example, the label must reveal that the drug product contains a named allergenic component (e.g., Yellow No. 5,[167] Yellow No. 6,[168] aspartame,[169] and sulfites[170]). The labeling of systemic antibacterial drug products is required to caution against the risk of development of drug-resistant bacteria.[171] FDA also promulgated unique labeling requirements for specific drug products based on concerns about potential negative health effects of those products. To illustrate, the label for drugs containing mineral oil must include the following or similar statement: "Caution: To be taken only at bedtime. Do not use at any other time or administer to infants, except upon the advice of a physician."[172]

- **Conformity to compendial labeling requirements.** If a drug product claims to be or to contain a drug that is recognized in an official compendium, the labeling and packaging must comply with any requirements applicable to it in the compendium.[173]

Prohibitions Regarding Labels and Labeling

In addition to the general and specific disclosure requirements affecting labels and labeling, the FDCA includes a number of broad prohibitions, the violation of which will result in the drug product being misbranded.

- **False or misleading statements about one's own product.** A drug "shall be deemed to be misbranded if its labeling is false or misleading in any particular."[174] Because Congress used the word "or," the act provides that labeling, even if literally true, can still be misleading.[175] Moreover, the statute explicitly provides that, in determining whether

---

164   Food and Drug Administration Amendments Act (FDAAA), Pub. L. No. 110-85, § 502(f), 121 Stat. 823, 890 (2007).

165   FDAAA § 502(f)(2).

166   *See* 21 C.F.R. §§ 201.300-201.323 (2014) for a complete list of all drugs for which FDA requires similar warnings.

167   21 C.F.R. § 201.20(a)-(b) (2014).

168   *Id.* § 201.20(c) (2014).

169   *Id.* § 201.21(b)-(c) (2014).

170   *Id.* § 201.22(b)-(c) (2014).

171   *Id.* § 201.24 (2014).

172   *Id.* § 201.302(d). A statutory requirement that certain drugs carry a warning that they are "habit-forming" was repealed in 1997. Food and Drug Administration Modernization Act of 1997, Pub. L. No. 105–115, 111 Stat 2296 (1997).

173   FDCA § 502(g), 21 U.S.C. § 352(g).

174   FDCA § 502(a), 21 U.S.C. § 352(a).

175   U.S. v. Ninety-Five Barrels…Alleged Apple Cider Vinegar, 265 U.S. 438, 442-43 (1924). This case arose under sections 7 and 8 of the Food and Drugs Act of 1906. Section 7 provided in relevant part that no drug shall be deemed adulterated if "its strength or purity fall below the professed standard or quality under which it is sold," and section 8 provided, in relevant part, that the term "misbranding" applies to a drug

labeling is misleading, FDA and the courts are to consider not only the affirmative statements made but also the omission or failure to reveal facts material in the light of the representations made, or otherwise material with respect to consequences that may result from the use of the drug under the conditions recommended in the labeling or under such conditions of use as are customary or usual.[176]

Whether a product's labeling is misleading is a question of fact. Case law indicates several considerations in determining whether the labeling of a product is misleading. Thus, the statements and representations in labeling should be considered in their entirety.[177] Moreover, the claims should be assessed from the perspective of what effect they would have on the prospective purchaser or the person to whom the information is addressed.[178] A single misleading statement or representation (or material omission) may be sufficient to misbrand the product.[179] Obviously, this broad standard vests considerable latitude in FDA and the courts to find labeling to be misleading and a product to be misbranded.

- **False or misleading statements about other products or ingredients.** FDA's regulations deem a drug to be misbranded if its labeling contains a false or misleading representation with respect to another drug,[180] or if the labeling of a drug containing two or more ingredients designates the drug by a name that does not suggest the presence of all ingredients, even if those ingredients may be listed elsewhere in the labeling.[181]

- **Prohibition against dangerous directions for use.** If a drug is dangerous to health when used as prescribed, recommended, or suggested in the labeling, it is misbranded.[182] Only a few reported cases bear on this provision of the FDCA.[183]

Requirements for Drug Product Packaging

Apart from the rules relating to the labels on and labeling associated with packages containing drug products, the FDCA imposes standards on the packages, themselves.

- **Compendial requirements.** If a drug is labeled to indicate that it is recognized in an official compendium, it will be misbranded unless its packaging complies with any applicable requirements in that compendium.[184] Thus, a product containing vitamin K for injection was ruled misbranded because vitamin K was recognized in the National Formulary, which required that sterile ampules for injection be packed in such a manner

---

"the package or label of which shall bear any statement, design, or device regarding such article, or the ingredients or substances contained therein which shall be false or misleading in any particular."

[176] FDCA § 201(n), 21 U.S.C. § 321(n); *see also* 21 C.F.R. § 1.21 (2014).
[177] *See, e.g.,* V.E. Irons, Inc. v. U.S., 244 F.2d 34 (1st Cir. 1957); U.S. v. 47 Bottles, More or Less, Jenasol RJ Formula "60," 320 F.2d 564, 571 (3d Cir. 1963); U.S. v. Six Dozen Bottles ... of Dr. Peter's Kuriko, 158 F.2d 667, 669 (7th Cir. 1947); Research Laboratories v. U.S., 167 F.2d 410, 422 (9th Cir. 1948).
[178] V.E. Irons, Inc v. U.S., 244 F.2d 34.
[179] U.S. v. One Device Intended for Use as a Colonic Irrigator, 160 F.2d 194, 200 (10th Cir. 1947); *see also* U.S. v. Sene X Eleemosynary Corp., Inc., 479 F. Supp. 970, 980 (S.D. Fla. 1979); U.S. v. An Article of Food ... Manischewitz ... Diet Thins, 377 F. Supp. 746, 749 (E.D.N.Y. 1974).
[180] 21 C.F.R. § 201.6(a) (2014).
[181] *Id.* § 201.6(b) (2014).
[182] FDCA § 502(j), 21 U.S.C. § 352(j).
[183] *See, e.g.,* United States v. 62 Packages ... Marmola Prescription Tablets, 48 F. Supp. 878, 887 (W.D. Wis. 1943), *aff'd* 142 F.2d 107 (7th Cir.) (tablets for the treatment of obesity determined to be dangerous to health when used in the dosage, frequency, and for the duration suggested by their labels).
[184] FDCA § 502(g), 21 U.S.C. § 352(g).

as to prevent contamination or loss of contents, and certain ampules of this product were not completely sealed.[185]

- **Poison prevention packaging requirements.** If a drug product is subject to packaging regulations under the Poison Prevention Packaging Act of 1970,[186] failure to comply will result in the product being misbranded under the FDCA.[187] The regulations under that statute, issued by the Consumer Product Safety Commission, establish special packaging and labeling requirements for drugs found to be hazardous to children, and also provide for noncompliant packaging of certain of those products to enable elderly or handicapped individuals to have access to the products.[188]

- **Prohibition against misleading containers and fills.** A drug is misbranded if "its container is so made, formed, or filled as to be misleading."[189] For example, if a container for a liquid drug product were shaped to suggest that its volume is greater than its actual contents, it would be misbranded.

- **Exemptions.** As noted earlier with respect to labeling, FDA has authority to exempt from packaging requirements drugs that are intended for further processing and packing, and it has used this power to exempt packages of drugs being shipped to another site for processing, labeling, or repacking.[190]

Other Requirements Enforced Through the FDCA's Misbranding Authority

The last element of FDA's authority under the misbranding section of the FDCA involves a variety of disparate matters that are very remote from labels, labeling, and packaging.

Requirements for Registration of Manufacturing Facilities and Listing of Drugs

Each facility in which a drug is manufactured or processed for distribution in the United States (even such facilities located outside the U.S.) must be registered with FDA under section 510 of the FDCA.[191] A drug manufactured in an unregistered facility is deemed to be misbranded.[192]

Each drug or drug product manufactured in a registered facility for distribution in the United States must be listed with FDA.[193] A drug not so listed is deemed to be misbranded.[194]

---

185   United States v. Dianovin Pharmaceuticals, Inc., 342 F. Supp. 724 (D. P.R. 1972).
186   Pub. L. No. 91-601, 84 Stat. 1670-74 (1970).
187   FDCA § 502(p), 21 U.S.C. § 352(p).
188   38 Fed. Reg. 21,247 (Aug. 7, 1973); 16 C.F.R. pt. 1700 (2014).
189   FDCA § 502(i)(1), 21 U.S.C. § 352(i)(1).
190   21 C.F.R. § 201.150(a)(1) (2014).
191   FDCA § 510(b)-(d), (i), 21 U.S.C. § 360(b)-(d), (i).
192   FDCA § 502(o), 21 U.S.C. § 352(o).
193   FDCA § 510(j), 21 U.S.C. § 360(j).
194   FDCA § 502(o), 21 U.S.C. § 352(o).

Requirements for Prescription Drug Advertising

In 1962, the FDCA was amended to give FDA jurisdiction to regulate prescription drug advertising.[195] Congress provided that a prescription drug would be misbranded if its advertising failed to include 1) the established name of the drug, "printed prominently and in type at least half as large as that used for any trade or brand name thereof," 2) the quantitative amount of each active ingredient, and 3) a "brief summary" of side effects, contraindications, and effectiveness.[196] FDA promulgated regulations that greatly expand on the advertising requirements for prescription drugs.[197] The body of administrative precedent, guidance, and case law is now quite extensive.[198]

Requirements for Imprinting on Solid Oral Dosage Forms

Using an array of legal authorities, including the adulteration and misbranding provisions of the FDCA, the agency requires that, with some exceptions, all drug products in solid oral dosage form (i.e., capsules, tablets, or similar products intended for oral use) be clearly marked with a code or imprint that identifies the drug product and the manufacturer or distributor of the product.[199] Identification of the drug's active ingredients and dosage strength is also required.[200] FDA encourages use of a letter or number in the imprint, rather than an individual symbol or logo.[201] A solid oral dosage form drug product that does not contain the required code or imprint may result in the product being declared adulterated, misbranded, or an unapproved new drug.[202]

Prohibition Against Imitations and Counterfeit Products

A drug is misbranded "if it is an imitation of another drug; or . . . if it is offered for sale under the name of another drug."[203] The word "imitation" is not defined in the statute, and was challenged in one case, on the argument that the term was either synonymous with the word "counterfeit" (defined in the FDCA as being a drug bearing, without authorization, the identifying marks of another manufacturer or distributor[204]) or else constitutionally void for vagueness.[205] FDA prevailed. The appellate court held that the term "imitation" is generally understood to mean "resembling something else that is genuine and of better quality: not real. Resemblance alone is not enough to constitute imitation," and that, "before an imitation exists, clearly the imitation product must be identical or similar in general appearance, color, texture, smell, or other physical properties to the 'real product.'"[206]

---

[195] Pub. L. No. 87-781, § 131, 52 Stat. 780, 791-792 (1962).

[196] FDCA § 502(n), 21 U.S.C. § 352(n).

[197] 21 C.F.R. § 202.1 (2014).

[198] *See* Chapter 12 *infra* for more information on regulation of prescription drug advertising.

[199] 21 C.F.R. §§ 206.7, 206.10(a) (2014).

[200] *Id.* § 206.10(a).

[201] *Id.*

[202] *Id.* § 206.10(c) (2014).

[203] FDCA § 502(i)(2)-(3), 21 U.S.C. § 352(i)(2)-(3).

[204] FDCA § 201(g)(2), 21 U.S.C. § 321(g)(2).

[205] United States v. Articles of Drug, 601 F. Supp. 392 (D. Neb. 1984), *aff'd in part, rev'd in part, remanded*, 825 F.2d 1238 (8th Cir. 1987).

[206] United States v. Articles of Drug, 825 F.2d 1238, 1244-45 (8th Cir. 1987) (internal citations omitted).

New FDA Safety Authorities

Under section 901 of FDAAA, which amended the FDCA, a new statutory framework was provided for FDA to require a risk evaluation and mitigation strategy (REMS) for certain drugs and biologics. This provision has profoundly changed the scope of FDA's authority to regulate the use of drugs and biologics as actually prescribed and dispensed.[207]

FDA may now require applicants for approval of a new drug to submit a proposed REMS as part of the application, prior to approval, if the agency determines that it is "necessary to ensure that the benefits of the drug outweigh the risks of the drug."[208] The agency may also require a REMS after approval if FDA "becomes aware of new safety information and makes a determination that such a strategy is necessary to ensure that the benefits of the drug outweigh the risks of the drug."[209] Drugs and biologics approved prior to the effective date of FDAAA were deemed to have a REMS in effect if the risk management programs for such products included elements to assure safe use. A REMS may include various risk management tools (e.g., Medication Guides, communication plans), but the most extensive are known as "elements to assure safe use" (ETASU). The ETASU provisions apply to a drug that has been shown to be effective but is associated with one or more serious adverse effects, and consequently can be approved for marketing only if such elements are required as part of a strategy to mitigate a specific serious risk disclosed in labeling.[210] ETASU may encompass restrictions such as requiring that healthcare providers who prescribe the drug have particular training, experience, or certifications; limiting dispensing of the drug to certain healthcare settings; restricting dispensing to patients only with evidence of safe use conditions or monitoring; or creation and maintenance of a patient registry.

In 2012, Congress slightly modified the REMS framework established by FDAAA through enactment of the Food and Drug Administration Safety and Innovation Act (FDASIA).[211] Section § 1132(a)(4) of FDASIA amended section 505-1(g)(4) of the FDCA to require an assessment strategy to determine whether a REMS is effective or needs modifications made so that the benefits of the drug continue to outweigh the risks and the associated burden on the healthcare delivery system is minimized. An applicant may propose modifications to any component of the REMS at any time.[212]

FDAAA also added provisions giving FDA the authority to require postapproval studies, trials, and labeling changes, subject to specific standards.[213] FDCA section 505(o)(3), added by FDAAA, authorizes FDA to require certain postmarketing studies and clinical trials for prescription drugs and biologics.[214] Postmarketing studies and clinical trials may be

---

[207]   A federal court had previously held that FDA could not dictate which medical providers could prescribe particular drugs. *See e.g.,* American Pharmaceutical Ass'n v. Weinberger, 377 F. Supp. 824 (D.D.C. 1974), *aff'd,* 530 F.2d 1054 (D.C. Cir. 1976). FDA's authority to regulate the actual use of drugs beyond labeling was generally thought to be quite limited absent an accelerated approval based upon surrogate markers or a voluntary agreement to such restrictions by the applicant.

[208]   FDCA § 505-1(a)(1), 21 U.S.C. § 355-1(a)(1)

[209]   FDCA § 505-1(a)(2), 21 U.S.C. § 355-1(a)(2).

[210]   FDCA § 505-1(f), 21 U.S.C. § 355-1(f).

[211]   Food and Drug Administration Safety and Innovation Act, Pub. L. No.112-144, 126 Stat. 993 (2012).

[212]   *Id.* at 1120.

[213]   FDCA § 901.

[214]   21 U.S. C § 355(o)(3).

required to assess a known serious risk related to the use of a drug, to assess signals of serious risk related to the use of a drug, or to identify an unexpected serious risk when available data indicate the potential for a serious risk. Under FDCA section 505(o)(3)(D)(i), before requiring a postmarketing study, FDA must find that other pharmacovigilance measures will not be sufficient. Under FDCA section 505(o)(3)(D)(ii), before requiring a postmarketing clinical trial, FDA must find that a postmarketing study other than a clinical trial will not be sufficient to obtain the required safety information.

FDCA section 505(o)(4), added by section 901 of FDAAA, also authorizes FDA to order labeling changes if FDA becomes aware of new safety information that FDA believes should be included in the labeling of the drug. Section 505(o)(4) imposes time frames for application holders to submit, and for FDA staff to review, such changes, and gives FDA new enforcement tools to ensure timely safety labeling changes.

Tracking and Tracing Drug Products

In 2013, rather than allowing the continued development of a patchwork of potentially conflicting state laws governing "pedigree" requirements for the distribution of drugs in commerce, Congress enacted the Drug Quality and Security Act (DQSA), preempting such state laws.[215] Title II of the DQSA, referred to as the Drug Supply Chain Security Act (DSCSA), creates a national system for tracing prescription drugs through the supply chain, and preempts analogous state requirements.

The DSCSA creates a national uniform approach to tracking, tracing, and verifying the identity and validity of prescription drugs in the domestic supply chain by imposing a number of common requirements on manufacturers, repackagers, wholesale distributors, and dispensers, as well as unique requirements for each respective category of entities engaged in the distribution of drugs. Beginning January 1, 2015, these entities were required to provide subsequent drug product owners with certain transaction data, and manufacturers may distribute only to authorized trading entities.[216]

By November 2017, manufacturers must affix or imprint a product identifier to each package and homogenous case of a product intended to be introduced into commerce in a transaction with another entity and must maintain the product identifier information for such product for at least six years after the date of the transaction.[217] Congress specified that product identifiers must include, unless FDA allows otherwise through guidance the use of other technologies, a two-dimensional data matrix barcode affixed to, or imprinted upon, a package, and a linear or two-dimensional data matrix barcode when affixed to, or imprinted upon, a homogeneous case.[218] Verification of the product identifier may occur by using

---

[215]   Pub. L. No. 113-54, 127 Stat. 587 (2013).

[216]   "In order to minimize possible disruptions in the distribution of prescription drugs in the United States," FDA recently issued guidance indicating that it does "not intend to take action against trading partners who do not, prior to May 1, 2015, provide or capture the product tracing information required by section 582(b)(1), (c)(1), and (e)(1) of the FD&C Act." DSCSA Implementation: Product Tracing Requirements — Compliance Policy Guidance for Industry (December 2014), *available at* http://www.fda.gov/downloads/Drugs/GuidanceComplianceRegulatoryInformation/Guidances/UCM427867.pdf.

[217]   FDCA § 582(b)(2)(A), 21 U.S.C. § 360eee–1(b)(2)(A).

[218]   FDCA § 582(a)(9)(A), 21 U.S.C. § 360eee–1(a)(9)(A).

human-readable or machine-readable methods.[219] Drugs that fail to bear a product identifier are deemed misbranded,[220] and failure to comply with section 582 is a prohibited act.[221]

By November 2023, transaction information and statements must be exchanged in a secure, interoperable, electronic manner in accordance with the standards established under FDA's future guidance.[222] The transaction information must include the product identifier at the package level for each package included in the transaction.[223] Stakeholders must establish systems and processes to 1) verify product at the package level; 2) promptly respond to requests for transaction information and statements for a product in the event of a recall or investigation of a suspect or illegitimate product; and 3) promptly facilitate fact gathering information to respond to a request from FDA, state or federal official, or an authorized trading partner.[224]

As noted, the DSCSA establishes a uniform national policy by prohibiting any state or political subdivision of a state from establishing or continuing in effect any requirements for tracing products through the distribution system that are inconsistent with or more stringent than the DSCSA.[225] States are also prohibited from establishing or continuing in effect any standards, requirements, or regulations with respect to wholesale distributor or third-party logistics provider licensure that are inconsistent with, less stringent than, directly related to, or covered by the standards and requirements of the DSCSA.[226]

Applicability to Drugs to Be Imported to or Exported From the United States

Imported Drugs

As a general proposition, the legal requirements that apply to drugs manufactured within the United States are also applicable to imported drugs. FDA can stop importation at the border by refusing admission of any drug that appears to be misbranded, adulterated or an unapproved new drug.[227] Because the agency need only show that the drug "appears" to be violative, its burden is less than would be the case in an enforcement action brought with respect to a domestically manufactured drug. A drug may also be denied entry if there is a ban or a restriction on the sale of the drug in the country in which it was produced or from which it was exported, even if it otherwise satisfies U.S. laws,[228] although it is unclear how often that authority is utilized.

---

219   FDCA § 582(a)(9)(B), 21 U.S.C. § 360eee–1(a)(9)(B).
220   FDCA § 502(c), 21 U.S.C. § 352(c).
221   FDCA § 301(t), 21 U.S.C. § 331(t).
222   FDCA § 582(g)(1), 21 U.S.C. § 360eee–1(g)(1).
223   Id.
224   FDCA § 582(g), 21 U.S.C. § 360eee–1(g).
225   FDCA § 585(a), 21 U.S.C. § 360eee-4(a).
226   FDCA § 585(b), 21 U.S.C. § 360eee-4(b).
227   FDCA § 801(a)(1), (3), 21 U.S.C. § 381(a)(1), (3).
228   FDCA § 801(a)(2), 21 U.S.C. § 381(a)(2).

There is also, under current law, a prohibition against the re-importation of a prescription drug that was manufactured in the United States and exported, unless the re-importation is by the manufacturer of the drug.[229] FDA may, however, authorize such re-importation if required for emergency medical care.[230]

The ban on re-importation of drugs manufactured in the United States has become controversial, because—largely due to price controls in some countries outside the United States—the drugs are often available at prices lower than Americans pay at home. This situation led to enactment of an amendment to the FDCA that would permit the importation of prescription drugs that would not otherwise satisfy U.S. law.[231] This amendment has not become effective, however. It requires, as a precondition to effectiveness, certification from the Secretary of the Department of Health and Human Services that its implementation will pose no additional risk to the public health and safety and will result in a significant reduction in the cost of drug products to American consumers.[232] To date, the Secretary has refused to make that certification. Nevertheless, there has been considerable resistance to the import prohibition, including acts by state and local governments that promote importation.[233]

FDA does permit the importation of drugs in bulk packages, with the exception of tablets, capsules or other dosage unit forms, to be processed or repacked or used in the manufacture of drugs not yet approved, as long as the final product is held until FDA approval.[234] The FDCA permits the importation of unfinished drugs to the United States for processing and re-export, as long as the importer complies with requirements designed to assure that products not complying with U.S. law are not distributed in this country.[235]

The manufacture of drugs for the U.S. market has become largely globalized, and concerns regarding imported drug products have grown after various incidents, including a 2008 public health crisis caused by adulterated heparin from China. To address these concerns, FDA has established a new Drug Integrity and Security Program to focus on drug quality issues such as economically motivated adulteration, cargo theft, counterfeiting, and other supply chain threats and vulnerabilities. The agency has opened offices in various jurisdictions around the world, and worked to strengthen its partnerships with other regulatory authorities to ensure the quality and integrity of the drug supply chain.[236] In addition, FDA's expectations regarding manufacturer controls over global drug supply chains have increased, and the agency generally expects drug manufacturing quality systems to include risk-based auditing of the supply chain, quality agreements with suppliers, and other risk management measures.[237]

---

[229]   FDCA § 801(d)(1), 21 U.S.C. § 381(d)(1).

[230]   FDCA § 801(d)(2), 21 U.S.C. § 381(d)(2).

[231]   FDCA § 804, 21 U.S.C. § 384.

[232]   FDCA § 804(l)(1), 21 U.S.C. § 384(l)(1).

[233]   See. e.g., An Act To Facilitate the Personal Importation of Prescription Drugs from International Mail Order Prescription Pharmacies, 2013 Me. Legis. Serv. Ch. 373 (S.P. 60) (L.D. 171) (West) (effective Oct. 9, 2013).

[234]   21 C.F.R. §§ 201.122(c), 314(a)(2) (2014).

[235]   FDCA § 801(d)(3), 21 U.S.C. § 381(d)(3).

[236]   See FDA, Global Engagement, available at http://www.fda.gov/downloads/AboutFDA/ReportsManualsForms/Reports/UCM298578.pdf.

[237]   Id.; FDA, Guidance for Industry: Quality Systems Approach to Pharmaceutical cGMP Regulations (Sept. 2006); FDA, Draft Guidance for Industry: Contract Manufacturing Arrangement for Drugs: Quality

Exported Drugs

In certain circumstances, drugs that are manufactured in the United States may be exported, even though those drugs do not comply with FDCA requirements applicable to domestic distribution. The rules differ somewhat between drugs that are approved in the United States for at least one use and those that are not approved at all domestically.

Export of Approved Drugs

The law does not prohibit the export of a drug that complies fully with its approval in the United States. In many cases, however, the country to which the drug is to be exported will have its own labeling requirements, so that the labeling to be placed on the exported drug will not comply with that approved in the United States. Thus, such a drug would be both misbranded and unapproved at the time it is being exported.

As is the case for other FDA-regulated products, a drug may lawfully be exported even though it is misbranded or adulterated under U.S. law if it meets four criteria:

- It must accord to the specification of the foreign purchaser.

- It must not be in conflict with the laws of the country to which it is intended to be exported.

- It must be labeled on the outside of the shipping package as intended for export.

- It must not be sold or offered for sale in the United States.[238]

The use of labeling different from that approved by FDA is permitted only if the drug is also labeled in accordance with the requirements of the FDCA.[239] FDA has interpreted this requirement as permitting export as long as the FDA-approved label is included in the export shipment, without being affixed to each individual exported product.[240]

It will sometimes happen that a drug is approved in the importing country for indications not approved in the United States. In that case, labeling addressing the medication not approved by FDA is permitted, but the labeling must also state that the conditions for use have not been approved under the FDCA.[241] FDA's view is that this permission to include an indication not approved in the United States requires the disclaimer to appear in the foreign labeling.[242]

Agreements (May 2013); 21 C.F.R. 211 (2014).

[238]   FDCA § 801(e)(1), 21 U.S.C. § 381(e)(1).

[239]   FDCA § 801(f)(1), 21 U.S.C. § 381(f)(1). *See* Exports: Notification and Recordkeeping Requirements Final Rule, 66 Fed. Reg. 65,429, 65,437 (Dec. 19, 2001).

[240]   FDA, Guidance for Industry: Exports Under the FDA Export Reform and Enhancement Act of 1996 Guidance for Industry – Exports Under the FDA Export Reform and Enhancement Act of 1996 (July 23 2007), *available at* http://www.fda.gov/downloads/RegulatoryInformation/Guidances/ucm125898.pdf.

[241]   FDCA § 801(f)(2), 21 U.S.C. § 381(f)(2).

[242]   Draft Guidance for Industry: Exports and Imports under the FDA Export Reform and Enhancement Act of 1996, 63 Fed. Reg. 32,219, 32,222 (June 12, 1998).

Export of Unapproved Drugs

For export of drugs that are not approved for any use in the United States, two different rules apply, depending on whether the unapproved drug has been approved in certain countries with advanced drug regulatory systems. The distinction will be discussed below.

In the absence of compliance with certain requirements, the unapproved drug may not be exported at all if any of the following criteria applies:

- The drug is not manufactured in compliance with cGMPs or international analogues acceptable to FDA.[243]

- The drug is adulterated under specified provisions of the statute.[244]

- The drug does not comply with the specifications of the foreign purchaser.[245]

- Sale of the drug is in conflict with the laws of the country for which it is intended to be exported.[246]

- The drug is not labeled on the outside of the shipping packages as intended for export.

- The drug is sold or offered for sale in commerce in the United States.[247]

- FDA issues a notice that the probability of re-importation of the exported drug would present an imminent hazard to public health and safety in the United States, and that the only way to prevent that hazard is to prohibit the export.[248]

- FDA concludes that export would present an imminent hazard of public health to the country to which it would be exported. [249]

- The labeling does not accord with the requirements and conditions for use in the country in which it is approved and/or the country into which it would be exported.[250]

- It is not labeled in languages and units required in the country to which it would be exported.[251]

- The drug is not promoted in accordance with the labeling requirements of the approval by a country with an advanced regulatory system and by the importing country.[252]

Exports if the drug is approved in a country with an advanced regulatory system. If an unapproved drug is eligible for export under the above criteria, its export from the United States is considerably easier if the drug has been approved in one or more of certain countries that are considered, by statute, to have advanced regulatory systems.[253]

---

[243]   FDCA § 802(f)(1), 21 U.S.C. § 382(f)(1).

[244]   FDCA § 802(f)(2), 21 U.S.C. § 382(f)(2). The specified types of adulteration are those described in FDCA § 501(a)(1), (a)(2)(A), (a)(3), (c), (d), 21 U.S.C. § 351(a)(1), (a)(2)(A), (a)(3), (c), (d).

[245]   FDCA § 801(e)(1)(A), 21 U.S.C. § 381(e)(1)(A).

[246]   FDCA § 801(e)(1)(B), 21 U.S.C. § 381(e)(1)(B).

[247]   FDCA § 802(f)(3), 21 U.S.C. § 382(f)(3), cross-referencing FDCA § 801(e)(1)(A)-(D), 21 U.S.C. § 381(e)(1)(A)-(D).

[248]   FDCA § 802(f)(4), 21 U.S.C. § 382(f)(4).

[249]   FDCA § 801(e)(2)(C), 21 U.S.C. § 381(e)(2)(C).

[250]   FDCA § 802(f)(5), 21 U.S.C. § 382(f)(5).

[251]   FDCA § 802(f)(5)(B), 21 U.S.C. § 382(f)(5)(B).

[252]   FDCA § 802(f)(4)(A), (B), (f)(5)(A), (B), (f)(6), 21 U.S.C. § 382(f)(4)(A), (B), (f)(5)(A), (B), (f)(6).

[253]   These countries include those that are members of the European Union (EU) or the European Economic Area (which includes not only the EU, but also the European Free Trade Association) and certain named

The required marketing authorization of the approving country must be for the particular composition of the drug to be exported, and that drug must be sold only for a use that is so authorized.

Once such an authorization has been obtained, and if the drug complies with the other preconditions discussed above, the drug may be exported without FDA approval, either to the country that has granted the authorization or to another country that has authorized the marketing of the product but is not on the list. There is, however, a required notification to FDA if the product is to be re-exported to a country that is not on the list.[254]

When no approval by any listed country has been obtained. The statute also authorizes FDA to permit the export of a drug that has not obtained approval either in the United States or in any of the listed countries, under any of three different approaches:

- In one, the exporter must establish that the drug complies with the laws of the country to which the drug would be exported, and obtains an FDA determination that that country meets statutory criteria to show that it has an advanced regulatory system.[255]

- In the second approach, the exporter must submit scientific evidence acceptable to FDA that the drug would be safe and effective under the conditions of use in the country into which it would be exported. Under this approach, the health authority in the country receiving the export would also have to request U.S. approval of the export.[256]

- The third approach applies to drugs for diseases that are not of significant prevalence in the United States and requires that FDA find that the drug will not expose patients in the importing country to an unreasonable risk of illness or injury, and that the probable health benefit from use of the drug outweighs the risks from its use.[257]

Drug Compounding and Outsourcing Facilities

As noted, on November 27, 2013, President Obama signed the Drug Quality and Security Act,[258] which included title I, the Compounding Quality Act (CQA). After years of confusion over the legal framework governing drug compounding, including arguments over the boundaries between FDA and state activities, the CQA institutes major changes to FDA authorities with respect to both traditional and large-scale drug compounding. The

---

countries. The current list thus includes Australia, Austria, Belgium, Canada, Cypress, Czech Republic, Denmark, Estonia, Finland, France, Germany, Hungary, Iceland, Ireland, Israel, Italy, Japan, Latvia, Lithuania, Luxembourg, Malta, The Netherlands, New Zealand, Norway, Poland, Portugal, Slovakia, Slovenia, South Africa, Spain, Sweden, Switzerland, and the United Kingdom. FDA, Guidance for Industry: Exports Under the FDA Export Reform and Enhancement Act of 1996 Guidance for Industry – Exports Under the FDA Export Reform and Enhancement Act of 1996 (July 23, 2007). FDA is authorized to add additional countries to the list. FDCA § 802(b)(1)(B), 21 U.S.C. § 382(b)(1)(B).

[254] FDCA § 802(g), 21 U.S.C. § 382(g). FDA requires notification of the first shipment to any listed country and requires a separate notice for each nonlisted country. 21 C.F.R. § 1.101(d)(iv) (2014). Recordkeeping is required to demonstrate compliance. 21 C.F.R. § 1.101(e) (2014).

[255] FDCA § 802(b)(2), 21 U.S.C. § 382(b)(2).

[256] FDCA § 802(b)(3), 21 U.S.C. § 382(b)(3).

[257] FDCA § 802(e), 21 U.S.C. § 382(e).

[258] Pub. L. No. 113-54, 127 Stat. 587 (2013).

CQA, is, in significant part, a response to concerns raised by a 2012 outbreak of fungal meningitis, which resulted in more than 64 deaths[259] and was believed to have been caused by contaminated compounded steroid injections.[260]

The CQA made specific changes to section 503A of the FDCA[261] to address challenges FDA experienced in regulating "traditional compounding," where pharmacists compound a drug for an individual patient pursuant to a prescription written by a licensed healthcare provider. Although FDA retains significant authority over traditional compounding, the objective of the statute is to leave much of the day-to-day oversight of such compounding to the states, allowing FDA to focus primarily on large-scale compounding activities. Thus, the CQA also added section 503B,[262] which creates a distinction between traditional compounding and a new statutory category of "outsourcing facilities"—facilities that compound certain sterile drugs in commercial-scale quantities. This new category is a hybrid entity between the categories of traditional compounding pharmacies and drug manufacturers.

Section 503B exempts outsourcing facilities from sections of the FDCA that apply to drug manufacturers, including labeling with adequate directions for use (section 502(f)(1)); prior approval before marketing (section 505); and track and trace requirements under Title II of the DQSA (section 582). In order to secure an exemption from the above requirements, an outsourcing facility must register with FDA annually.[263] Upon initial registration, and twice each year (June and December), outsourcing facilities must submit a report identifying specified information about the compounded drugs the facility produced.[264]

Additionally, outsourcing facilities must comply with adverse event reporting requirements of 21 C.F.R. § 310.305, and will be inspected according to a "risk-based schedule."[265] FDA intends to focus its inspectional and enforcement efforts on those aspects of outsourcing facility compounding operations that pose the highest risk to patient safety, such as sterility assurance. The CQA also establishes user fees for outsourcing facilities, which FDA has outlined in guidance.[266] In addition to the facility requirements, products compounded in outsourcing facilities must meet the following conditions:

(1) The compounded drug cannot be made from a bulk substance unless the bulk substance(s) meet certain established requirements, including appearing on a list of approved bulk substances promulgated by FDA.[267]

---

[259] CDC, Multistate Outbreak of Fungal Meningitis and Other Infections – Case Count (updated Oct. 23, 2013), *available at* http://www.cdc.gov/hai/outbreaks/meningitis-map-large.html#casecount_table.

[260] FDA, Multistate Outbreak of Fungal Meningitis and Other Infections, *available at* http://www.fda.gov/%20Drugs/DrugSafety/FungalMeningitis/default.htm.

[261] 21 U.S.C. § 353a.

[262] 21 U.S.C. § 353b.

[263] FDCA § 503B(b)(1)(a), 21 U.S.C. § 353b(b)(1)(a).

[264] FDCA § 503B(b)(2), 21 U.S.C. § 353b(b)(2).

[265] FDCA § 503B(b)(4), 21 U.S.C. § 353b(b)(4).

[266] FDCA § 503B(a)(9), 21 U.S.C. § 353b(a)(9); FDA, Draft Guidance for Industry: Fees for Human Drug Compounding Outsourcing Facilities Under Sections 503B and 744K of the FD&C Act (November 2014), *available at* http://www.fda.gov/downloads/drugs/guidancecomplianceregulatoryinformation/guidances/ucm39 1102.pdf.

[267] FDCA § 503B(a)(2), 21 U.S.C. § 353b(a)(2).

(2) Any non-bulk ingredients that are used in compounding the drug must comply with the standards of applicable United States Pharmacopeia (USP) and National Formulary (NF) monographs.[268]

(3) The drug compounded cannot appear on a list of drugs that have been withdrawn or removed from the market because of issues regarding safety or effectiveness.

(4) The compounded drug cannot be one that is "essentially a copy of one or more approved drugs."[269]

(5) The compounded drug cannot be on FDA's list of drugs that present "demonstrable difficulties" for compounding, that are reasonably likely to lead to an adverse effect on the safety or effectiveness of the drug or category of drugs, unless it has been compounded in accordance with all applicable conditions identified by FDA as conditions that are necessary to prevent the drug from presenting such demonstrable difficulties.[270]

(6) In the case of a drug compounded from a drug that is subject to a REMS approved with ETASU, the outsourcing facility must show FDA, prior to beginning compounding, that such facility will utilize controls comparable to those under the REMS.[271]

At the time of this writing, FDA is in the process of developing regulations and guidance to clarify and implement the above requirements.[272]

The CQA also establishes requirements for packaging, labeling, and selling compounded drugs. Section 503B(a)(10) requires that compounded drugs be "prominently" labeled with the statement, "This is a compounded drug" or a reasonable comparable alterative, along with: 1) the lot or batch number; 2) the established drug name; 3) dosage form and strength; 4) the date the drug was compounded; 5) storage and handling instructions; and 6) the statement "Not for resale."[273] Additionally, the drug's container must include all the information required on the labeling, as well as information to facilitate adverse event reporting, such as FDA's website and phone number, in addition to directions for use and any other information the Secretary deems necessary.[274]

Additionally, the CQA requires that outsourcing facilities comply with cGMP requirements under section 501(a)(2)(B).[275] In July 2014, FDA issued draft guidance that describes FDA's expectations regarding outsourcing facilities and the cGMP requirements.[276] As expressed

---

[268]　FDCA § 503B(3), 21 U.S.C. § 353b(3).

[269]　FDCA § 503B(d)(2), 21 U.S.C. § 353b(d)(2).

[270]　FDCA § 503B(a)(6), 21 U.S.C. § 353b(a)(6).

[271]　FDCA § 503B(a)(7), 21 U.S.C. § 353b(a)(7).

[272]　FDA, Drug Supply Chain Security Act, *available at* http://www.fda.gov/drugs/drugsafety/drugintegrityand supplychainsecurity/drugsupplychainsecurityact/. (The law requires FDA to develop standards, guidance documents, and pilot programs and to conduct public meetings, in addition to other efforts necessary to support efficient and effective implementation. At the time of this writing, FDA is developing a schedule for implementing the law's requirements.)

[273]　21 U.S.C. § 353b(a)(10).

[274]　FDCA § 503B, 21 U.S.C. § 353b.

[275]　FDCA § 503B, 21 U.S.C. § 353b.

[276]　FDA, Guidance for Industry: Current Good Manufacturing Practice – Interim Guidance for Human Drug Compounding Outsourcing Facilities Under section 503B of the FD&C Act (July 2014), *available at* http://

in the guidance, the agency also intends to promulgate specific cGMP regulations for outsourcing facilities.[277]

Finally, the CQA prohibits the sale or transfer of a compounded drug by any entity other than the outsourcing facility, except when dispensed in a healthcare setting or dispensed pursuant to a prescription under section 503(b)(1).[278] The legislation amends section 301 of the FDCA to make the following activities prohibited acts: 1) reselling a compounded drug that is labeled "not for resale";[279] 2) intentionally falsifying a prescription for a compounded drug; and 3) failing to report drugs or adverse events.[280] The CQA also establishes false or misleading advertising or promotion of a compounded drug as a misbranding violation under section 502 of the FDCA.[281]

Summary

As stated at the outset of this chapter, the FDCA creates two different but overlapping regulatory frameworks for regulating drugs. The scheme relying on the adulteration and misbranding provisions hearkens back to the mid-19th century, and it has evolved considerably, even since the 1906 Pure Food and Drugs Act[282] and the 1938 FDCA.[283] It permits free entry of products and claims to the market, subject to standards to control the integrity and quality of products and to prohibit deceptive practices. FDA polices the market and, when violations of the standards are found, brings enforcement actions, in which the burden of proof rests on the government.

Because the scheme relies heavily on both surveillance and careful preparation of cases, the lack of increases in FDA resources relative to the growth in its responsibilities has strained the agency's ability to rely on the approach, and has caused it to put increasing emphasis on the other scheme, under which FDA acts as gatekeeper to the marketplace. This approach, which has been funded by user fees since 1992, has not suffered from a drop in resources. In addition, it provides FDA with considerable leverage and independence from judicial involvement in most decisions. Nevertheless, the adulteration and misbranding regulatory scheme remains a viable and critical aspect of drug regulation.

As has been the case historically, the statutory framework governing the regulation of drug products will remain a work in progress. In addition to recent changes relating to compounding and tracking and tracing drugs, new proposals continue to emerge, most notably a developing effort in the House of Representatives—entitled the 21st Century Cures Initiative—seeking to accelerate the drug development and approval processes. Moreover,

---

www.fda.gov/downloads/Drugs/GuidanceComplianceRegulatoryInformation/Guidances/UCM403496. pdf.

277   *Id.*

278   CQA § 102; FDCA § 503B(a)(8), 21 U.S.C. § 353b(A)(8).

279   FDCA § 301(ccc)(1), 21 U.S.C. § 331(ccc)(1).

280   FDCA § 301(ccc)(3), 21 U.S.C. § 331(ccc)(3).

281   CQA § 102; FDCA § 502(bb), 21 U.S.C. § 352(bb).

282   Pub. L. No. 59-384, 34 Stat. 768 (1906).

283   Pub. L. No. 75-717, 52 Stat. 1040 (1938).

the five-year cycle of user fee reauthorization now provides a regular opportunity for a reexamination of the regulation of drug products.

CHAPTER 10
DRUGS: INDS AND FULL NDAS

....

JAMES N. CZABAN AND GEOFFREY M. LEVITT[*]

Introduction

Genomic research by a pharmaceutical company identifies a targeted genetic mutation leading to the development of a powerful new cancer drug.[1] High-throughput molecular screening at an academic research institution identifies a promising treatment for multiple sclerosis.[2] An ancient local custom of rubbing a white flower on the forehead leads to a new therapy for Alzheimer's disease.[3] What do these diverse discoveries have in common? Before American patients could benefit from the resulting treatments, a sponsor must have successfully navigated the gauntlet of the Food and Drug Administration's (FDA) new drug development and application process.

Indeed, from the moment a new drug compound enters preclinical testing, it is comprehensively regulated by FDA at every step of the way. The agency not only decides when and whether the drug has met the substantive standards required for marketing approval but also establishes and enforces the rules governing virtually every aspect of the drug's life cycle, including testing, manufacturing, labeling, marketing, and safety monitoring.

[*]   The authors gratefully acknowledge the contributions of Claire Frezza, J.D., Pharm.D. in updating and expanding this chapter.
[1]   *See* Leslie A. Pray, *Gleevec: the Breakthrough in Cancer Treatment*, 1 NATURE EDUCATION 37 (2008), *available at* http://www.nature.com/scitable/topicpage/gleevec-the-breakthrough-in-cancer-treatment-565.
[2]   *See* Joanne Kotz, *Small (Molecule) Thinking in Academia*, SciBX 4(22); doi:10.1038/scibx.2011.617 (June 2, 2011), *available at* http://www.nature.com/scibx/journal/v4/n22/full/scibx.2011.617.html.
[3]   *See Chemistry in its element: compounds*, Royal Society of Chemistry (2014), *available at* http://www.rsc.org/chemistryworld/podcast/CIIEcompounds/transcripts/galantamine.asp; M. J. Balunas & A.D. Kinghorn, *Drug Discovery From Medicinal Plants*, 78 LIFE SCIENCES 431-441 (2005), *available at* http://www.google.com/url?sa=t&rct=j&q=&esrc=s&frm=1&source=web&cd=2&cad=rja&uact=8&ved=0CCsQFjAB&url=http%3A%2F%2Fwww.snupharm.ac.kr%2Fshsung%2Ferp%2Ferpmenus%2Flesson_pds%2FupLoadFiles%2Fdrugdiscoveryfromplant2005.pdf&ei=d6sYVLXJN5ORyATTuoKwBg&usg=AFQjCNGrSxNwjrXtbZ3d1g8ZADsZapMdsw&bvm=bv.75097201,d.aWw.

In short, FDA holds literally life-and-death power over a new drug. And that power is exercised in an arena populated by influential players with vital interests at stake—drug companies, patient groups, doctors, pharmacists, managed care organizations, healthcare payors, and others. It is no wonder that FDA's regulation of human drugs is a perennial target of criticism and proposals for reform.

For many years—from the 1980s into the early 2000s—the debate focused on the issue of speeding up the drug review process. The result was a series of regulatory and legislative initiatives aimed at making drugs available to patients sooner, ranging from user fees to accelerated approval.

The picture changed dramatically in the mid-2000s with the withdrawal of several prominent drugs from the market for safety reasons. Almost overnight it seemed that criticism of FDA's failure to review new drugs fast enough gave way to concerns that the agency was moving too fast to allow new drugs onto the market before their safety risks were adequately understood. These concerns—fueled by allegations that drug sponsors had not always been fully forthcoming in their handling of safety data—triggered intense congressional interest in legislative reform, aimed in large part at bolstering FDA's drug safety oversight powers. The result was the Food and Drug Administration Amendments Act of 2007 (FDAAA),[4] which notwithstanding its prosaic name was widely viewed as the most significant piece of food and drug legislation in many years. While the FDAAA covered a great deal of ground, for purposes of this chapter its most important contributions are in the areas of safety evaluation in the drug review process and management of postmarketing safety issues.

In 2012, Congress expanded on the FDAAA by passing the Food and Drug Administration Safety and Innovation Act (FDASIA).[5] In addition to re-authorizing and amending several provisions of the FDAAA that were scheduled to sunset, FDASIA aimed to expedite the development and review of innovative medicines.

It is safe to say that both the FDAAA and FDASIA have had a major impact on new drug review and oversight in the United States. But the FDAAA and FDASIA will not be the last word in the debate, as drug review user fees must be legislatively re-authorized every five years. Ongoing congressional scrutiny of FDA's oversight of new drugs is inevitable.

This chapter should therefore be viewed as a snapshot of a regulatory system in a state of continuing evolution. At each phase the discussion will address both the fundamental constants of the FDA regulatory process and the more important and enduring of the recent changes to that process. The chapter tracks the key regulatory phases through which the typical new drug must pass, from preclinical testing to clinical investigation to new drug application review to postmarketing oversight.

---

[4]   Pub. L. No. 110-85, 121 Stat. 823 (2007). The FDAAA was enacted in the course of the legislative re-authorization of prescription drug user fees, which occurs on a five-year cycle that began with the enactment of the Prescription Drug User Fee Act in 1992. See *infra* for a discussion of the user fee authority.

[5]   Pub. L. No. 112-144, 126 Stat. 993 (2012).

The New Drug Approval Requirement

The Federal Food, Drug, and Cosmetic Act (FDCA) requires that all "new drugs" be approved before marketing.[6] As described more fully in Chapter 9 *supra*, the act defines the term "drug" broadly[7] and differentiates between prescription and over-the-counter (OTC) drugs. Today, virtually all prescription drugs, and some OTC drugs, are deemed by FDA to be "new drugs" within the meaning of the act.[8]

The two exceptions to the "new drug" category are drugs that are "generally recognized as safe and effective" (a category whose main practical importance is in the context of OTC drugs, discussed in Chapter 13), and "grandfathered" drugs, a historically anomalous category that FDA has essentially interpreted out of the statute.

The "generally recognized as safe/effective" (GRAS/E) standard is in practical terms almost impossible for a company to establish for a prescription drug outside the context of full clinical studies, in part because FDA and the courts have essentially incorporated the new drug approval requirement—that the safety and effectiveness be shown by "substantial evidence" from adequate and well-controlled clinical trials[9]—into the "new drug" definition itself.[10] Moreover, the courts have agreed with FDA that the clinical trials must be published in the scientific literature to support a GRAS/E determination.[11]

Both the 1938 and 1962 acts included grandfather clauses that would exempt pre-existing drugs from the "new drug" classification of the 1938 act, and from the effectiveness requirement of the 1962 act, under limited circumstances. FDA, however, has taken the position that "there are very few drugs on the market that are actually entitled to grandfather status because the drugs currently on the market likely differ from the previous versions in some respect, such as formulation, dosage or strength, dosage form, route of administration,

---

[6]   FDCA §§ 301(d), 505 (a), 21 U.S.C. §§ 331(d), 355(a).

[7]   The definition includes 1) articles recognized in the U.S. Pharmacopeia, the U.S. Homeopathic Pharmacopeia or the National Formulary; 2) articles "intended for use in the diagnosis, cure, mitigation, treatment, or prevention of disease"; 3) articles (other than food) "intended to affect the structure or any function of the body"; and (4) articles intended for use as a component of any of the above. FDCA § 201(g)(1), 21 U.S.C. § 321(g)(1). This definition explicitly excludes foods and dietary supplements for which certain kinds of health-related claims are made, FDCA § 201(g)(1)(D), 21 U.S.C. § 321(g)(1)(D).

[8]   This outcome is not readily apparent from the "new drug" definition, which refers to drugs that are "not generally recognized, among experts qualified by scientific training and experience to evaluate the safety and effectiveness of drugs, as safe and effective for use under the conditions prescribed, recommended, or suggested in the labeling thereof . . . ." FDCA § 201(p)(1), 21 U.S.C. § 321(p)(1). *See also,* FDA, Guidance for FDA Staff and Industry: Marketed Unapproved Drugs—Compliance Policy Guide, § 440.100 Marketed New Drugs Without Approved NDAs or ANDAs (revised, Sept. 2011) *available at* http://www.fda.gov/downloads/Drugs/GuidanceComplianceRegulatoryInformation/Guidances/ucm070290.pdf ("the Agency believes it is not likely that any currently marketed prescription drug product is grandfathered or is otherwise not a *new drug*.").

[9]   *See* FDCA §§ 505(b)(1)(A), 505(d)(1), 505(e)(3), 21 U.S.C. §§ 355(b)(1)(A), 355(d)(1), 355(e)(3), and 21 C.F.R. § 314.126.

[10]   *See* Weinberger v. Hynson, Wescott & Dunning Inc., 412 U.S. 609, 632 (1973) ("a drug can be 'generally recognized' by experts as effective [and thus escape 'new drug' status] . . . only when that expert consensus is founded upon 'substantial evidence' as defined in § [355(d)]."

[11]   Weinberger v. Bentex Pharmaceutical, Inc., 412 U.S. 645, 652 (1973).

indications, or intended patient population. If a firm claims that its product is grandfathered, it is that firm's burden to prove that assertion."[12]

Thus "new drug" status is essentially just a legal "hook" that gives FDA its extensive regulatory oversight authority. The term has nothing to do with the novelty of the drug, nor the length of time it has been on the market. Drugs approved 50 years ago are still legally "new drugs," as are equivalent generic versions of previously approved drugs.[13]

The "Full NDA"

The statute requires that each new drug be the subject of an approved new drug application (NDA) or abbreviated new drug application (ANDA) prior to marketing. As described more fully below, an NDA must be approved based on, *inter alia*, clinical studies. In a traditional, or "full" NDA, the NDA applicant must have rights to the data in the studies. As described more fully in Chapter 11, NDA applicants can also rely on studies in the public domain and on NDAs submitted by others, by submitting applications known as 505(b)(2) NDAs.[14] Applicants seeking to market similar or identical "generic" versions of approved drugs based on bioequivalence to the approved drug can submit an ANDA, which will not involve submission or review of clinical safety and efficacy data.

This chapter addresses the "full NDA," including the clinical development process, standards and processes for approval, and postapproval requirements.

Preclinical and Clinical Testing

The process of bringing a new therapeutic compound onto the market through the submission of a "full NDA" generally follows a clinical development program involving preclinical investigations and human clinical trials.

Preclinical Investigation and Good Laboratory Practices

The first stage in a drug's regulatory life cycle is preclinical (nonhuman) investigation, which can include in vitro experiments and animal testing. The basic goals of preclinical investigation are 1) to identify reasons to believe that a compound may have beneficial effects in humans, through the use of both in vitro experimentation and animal testing, and 2) to gather sufficient data regarding the pharmacology and toxicology of the potential new drug to conclude that it is reasonably safe to begin preliminary testing in humans.[15]

FDA's regulatory interest in preclinical investigations arises largely after the fact. No FDA approval is required to commence a preclinical investigation, and unapproved drugs

---

[12]   FDA COMPLIANCE POLICY GUIDE § 440.100, *supra* note 8.
[13]   *See* United States v. Generix Drug Corp., 460 U.S. 453 (1983).
[14]   *See* Chapter 11.
[15]   21 C.F.R. § 312.23(a)(8).

shipped interstate as part of such an investigation are exempted from the FDCA's general prohibition of such shipment, as long as the drugs are appropriately labeled and adequate records of shipment and receipt are maintained.[16] FDA, however, may terminate a preclinical investigator's ability to ship unapproved drugs if the agency determines that continuing the investigation is "unsafe or otherwise contrary to the public interest" or that the drugs are being used for purposes other than "bona fide scientific investigation."[17]

FDA involvement in preclinical investigations ordinarily comes only after the investigation is done, when the agency reviews the investigational new drug application (IND) that a drug sponsor must submit before beginning human clinical trials.[18] At that point, FDA evaluates the soundness and integrity of the relevant preclinical data and practices, as well as the investigational methodologies used. This evaluation focuses upon the preclinical pharmacological and toxicological data that the sponsor relied upon to reach the required conclusion that it was "reasonably safe to conduct the proposed clinical investigations."[19] The sponsor must also provide information on the identity and qualifications of the individuals who evaluated the preclinical studies and determined that clinical trials could reasonably commence.[20]

FDA has promulgated regulations on preclinical testing that are commonly referred to as the Good Laboratory Practices (GLP) regulations.[21] The GLP regulations govern the laboratory work and facilities associated with any preclinical study intended to support a marketing application for an FDA-regulated product, including all human and animal drugs, medical devices and biologics, as well as food and color additives, animal food additives, and FDA-regulated electronic products.[22] These regulations are intended to assure the quality and integrity of data to be submitted to FDA in support of marketing applications, and do so by establishing certain minimum requirements for different aspects of a testing laboratory's practices, subjecting the testing laboratory to FDA inspectional oversight and providing penalties for noncompliance.

In general, the GLP regulations operate by specifying minimum standards in such areas as personnel, facilities, equipment, and operations. As with the regulations pertaining to current Good Manufacturing Practices (cGMPs) (discussed elsewhere in this treatise), the GLP regulations typically set these standards through procedural and structural safeguards, rather than through specific substantive requirements.[23]

For example, in the area of personnel, the GLP regulations require that individuals involved in preclinical studies be sufficiently trained to conduct the study appropriately, but do not specify what such training must encompass.[24] The personnel controls also require

---

16   *Id.* §§ 312.160, 312.2(b)(3).
17   *Id.* § 312.160(b)(2).
18   FDA regulation of clinical trials is discussed in detail later in this chapter.
19   21 C.F.R § 312.23(a)(8).
20   *Id.*
21   21 C.F.R. pt. 58.
22   *Id.* § 58.1.
23   FDA's Good Laboratory Practices Guidance has remained in essentially unaltered form since 1981.
24   21 C.F.R. § 58.29.

the designation of a study director to oversee, monitor and certify the study,[25] and the establishment of a separate quality assurance unit charged with independently monitoring the progress and scientific soundness of any study being conducted.[26] This quality assurance unit must, among other tasks, maintain copies of study schedules and written protocols, conduct periodic inspections to ensure compliance with all regulations and specifications, submit regular status reports to the management of the testing facility, and prepare and sign a written statement outlining quality assurance efforts, to be included in the final study report.[27]

The GLP regulations also require facilities of suitable size and construction, the appropriate separation of various types of materials, and proper animal care facilities, as applicable.[28] Under the GLP regimen, any study to be submitted to FDA must proceed by way of a detailed protocol specifying the study's objectives and methodologies,[29] and all relevant records and data from the study must be retained for various specified periods.[30] In addition, FDA may inspect any GLP-covered facility to determine that facility's compliance with applicable standards.[31] The regulations give the FDA inspector authority to inspect the records and facilities of the laboratory itself, and to review the inspection procedures that the institution's quality assurance unit is required to maintain.[32]

A testing facility's failure to conform with applicable GLP requirements can result in its disqualification if the nonconformance "adversely affected the validity of the nonclinical laboratory studies" and "[o]ther lesser regulatory actions" are inadequate.[33] Any studies undertaken at a disqualified testing facility that are submitted in support of a subsequent FDA application may be excluded from consideration in the evaluation of that application.[34] Indeed, FDA may disregard a preclinical laboratory study from a nonconforming facility even if the facility's nonconformance with GLP regulations would not warrant a formal disqualification.[35] In addition, if studies performed at a particular facility were submitted as part of a marketing application, and that facility later becomes disqualified, the corresponding study data must be eliminated from consideration (unless the data are determined to be either not essential to the application or otherwise acceptable). This may lead to the termination or withdrawal of approval of the application in question.[36]

In sum, the direct burden of GLP compliance is on the testing facility itself.[37] Yet the GLP regulations create strong incentives for sponsors who plan to rely on preclinical studies for subsequent FDA applications to take an active role in ensuring their proper execution.

---

[25]   *Id.* § 58.33.
[26]   *Id.* § 58.35.
[27]   *Id.*
[28]   *Id.* §§ 58.41-51.
[29]   *Id.* §§ 58.120-130.
[30]   *Id.* §§ 58.185-195.
[31]   *Id.* § 58.15.
[32]   *Id.* § 58.35(d).
[33]   *Id.* § 58.202.
[34]   *Id.* § 58.200.
[35]   *Id.* § 58.215(b).
[36]   *Id.* § 58.210(a).
[37]   *Id.* § 58.219.

Clinical Investigation

As discussed above, a primary purpose of the preclinical investigation is to gather sufficient evidence about the proposed new drug to proceed to the next regulatory stage; i.e. clinical investigation. The primary goal of a clinical investigation, in turn, is to gather sufficient information about the safety and efficacy of the drug to support advancing to the next investigational or regulatory stage; i.e., to support the next phase of expanded human studies, and ultimately to support a new drug application. Clinical investigations may also be conducted to answer questions related to an approved application or to support claims in product promotion. In contrast to the preclinical stage, clinical trials involve significant contemporaneous FDA oversight, designed both to protect the health and safety of the human test subjects and to ensure the integrity and usefulness of the data derived therefrom.

The Investigational New Drug Application

Unlike the preclinical stage, commencement of clinical trials requires formal notification to FDA. At least 30 days before the drug's sponsor wishes to begin such trials, the sponsor must submit an IND to the agency.[38] Although FDA does not "approve" an IND, it can object to the IND and place the proposed studies on "clinical hold" until the problem is resolved to the agency's satisfaction.[39] While a clinical hold can occur at any time during an investigation, the critical juncture for applicants is the first 30 days after IND submission. If FDA does not object within those 30 days, the IND becomes "effective" and the proposed clinical trials may begin.[40]

The specific contents of an IND depend both upon the nature of the drug and the scope of the proposed trials. However, all INDs must include the following basic elements: 1) a detailed cover sheet; 2) a table of contents; 3) an introductory statement and general investigative plan; 4) an investigator's brochure (except in the case of sponsor-investigator INDs; i.e., where the individual investigator is also the sponsor); 5) a set of comprehensive investigative protocols; 6) information on the proposed drug's chemistry, manufacturing, and controls; 7) pharmacology and toxicology information from preclinical studies; 8) a summary of previous human experience with the drug; and 9) such additional information as FDA deems necessary.[41]

Thus, the IND covers two basic categories of information: information on the study drug itself, and information on the proposed clinical investigation. As to the drug itself, the sponsor must provide the pharmacological and toxicological data from preclinical studies upon which the sponsor concluded it was reasonably safe to propose clinical trials involving humans.[42] The IND must also include information describing the manufacturing and control

---

[38] *Id.* § 312.40. In 2013, FDA released a guidance document to help clarify whether an IND is needed. *See* FDA, Guidance: Investigational New Drug Applications (INDs) — Determining Whether Human Research Studies Can Be Conducted Without an IND (Sept. 2013), *available at* http://www.fda.gov/downloads/Drugs/Guidances/UCM229175.pdf.

[39] *Id.* § 312.42. Clinical holds are discussed in more detail later in this chapter.

[40] *Id.* In practice, FDA often communicates informally with the sponsor to indicate that clinical trials may proceed.

[41] 21 C.F.R. § 312.23.

[42] *Id.* § 312.23(a)(8).

of the study drug,[43] as well as comprehensive details on the drug's chemical composition, structural formula, proposed dosage form, and proposed route of administration. Information on any prior human experience with the drug is also required, including any relevant foreign experience,[44] as well as any prior history of the drug's being withdrawn from investigation or marketing.

As to the information on the proposed investigation, the IND must include proposed study protocols, with varying levels of detail depending upon the phase of the clinical trial concerned.[45] Generally, protocols must identify the objectives and purpose of the study, names and qualifications of investigators, patient selection criteria, study design and methodologies, and the study's measurement criteria, including clinical or laboratory monitoring.[46] The IND must also identify the person(s) with overall responsibility for monitoring the study, as well as any participating contract research organizations.[47]

In addition, the IND must include an "investigative plan" containing, among other things, a detailed plan for the drug's investigation, including the rationale behind the research, an outline of the proposed approach, the types of clinical trials to be conducted, an estimate as to the number of patients involved, and a discussion of any significant anticipated patient risks, based upon prior toxicological data.[48] Further, the IND must contain a commitment from the sponsor to conduct clinical trials under the supervision of an Institutional Review Board (IRB), and to follow all applicable rules and regulations, including those pertaining to informed consent.

Informed Consent and Institutional Review Boards

A fundamental goal of FDA regulations on informed consent[49] and IRBs[50] is to assure the protection of the rights and welfare of human subjects.[51] FDA investigators regularly check for compliance with these regulations, and an institution's or sponsor's noncompliance can result in the temporary suspension or formal termination of a clinical study, as well as other administrative sanctions or legal proceedings.

The thrust of the informed consent regulations is to ensure that the subjects' participation in clinical trials is voluntary and knowing. Potential participants must be adequately informed about risks, possible benefits, alternative courses of treatment, and other relevant information before making the decision to participate in the experimental research.[52] Such consent must

---

43   *Id.* § 312.23(a)(7).
44   *Id.* § 312.23(a)(9).
45   *Id.* § 312.23(a)(6). The phases of a clinical investigation are discussed later in this chapter.
46   21 C.F.R. § 312.23(a)(6)(iii).
47   *Id.* § 312.23(a)(1).
48   *Id.* § 312.23(a)(3).
49   *Id.* pt. 50.
50   *Id.* pt. 56.
51   *See id.* § 56.102(g).
52   *Id.* § 50.25. The informed consent regulations, however, provide a narrow exception to the informed consent requirement in cases where a subject is in a life-threatening situation for which available treatments are unproven or unsatisfactory, the subject cannot provide effective consent due to his or her medical condition, and treatment must be administered before consent from a legal representative is feasible. This exception is also subject to additional substantive requirements including that the use of the experimental drug holds

be documented,[53] and research subjects cannot be forced to waive any potential future claims for negligence against the study's investigator, sponsor or institution.[54] Moreover, the patient may withdraw his or her consent at any time for any reason without penalty or loss of benefit.[55] Furthermore, in the case of prisoners used as research subjects, additional restrictions and requirements exist to ensure truly voluntary participation in light of the inherently more coercive penal environment.[56]

The regulations pertaining to IRBs obligate the institution under whose auspices a clinical study is conducted to take a sufficiently active role in the conduct of that study to ensure that the rights of the human test subjects are adequately protected, while, at the same time, rigorous scientific and medical standards are maintained.[57] The IRB itself is essentially a committee designated by the respective institution to review biomedical research involving human subjects.[58] The responsible IRB must review and approve any proposed clinical study before the study commences, and must continue to monitor the research as it progresses.[59] An IRB may approve a proposed clinical study only after determining that certain conditions are met, including that the proposed research appropriately minimizes patient risks, and that such risks are reasonable in relation to anticipated benefits.[60]

The IRB regulations also set up relatively detailed requirements for an IRB's internal "housekeeping." Thus, the IRB must establish written procedures detailing, among other things, its review processes and criteria and its procedures designed to ensure the prompt reporting of changes in ongoing clinical research or in informed consent documents.[61] Moreover, the IRB members must come from sufficiently diverse disciplines to enable the board to review the study not only in terms of specific research issues but also in terms of the study's acceptability under existing community and legal standards, as well as professional conduct and practice norms.[62] The IRB must also keep detailed records of its activities, which are subject to FDA inspection.[63]

The Phases of a Clinical Investigation

Clinical investigations are typically divided into three pre-approval phases,[64] and possible postapproval "Phase 4" studies. Although these phases are analytically distinct, in practice they often overlap, with significant FDA involvement throughout.

Phase 1 studies involve the initial administration of the drug to a small number (typically 20 to 80) of healthy test subjects. Such studies are designed "to determine the metabolism and

---

the potential to benefit the patient, the investigation could not practicably be carried out without the waiver, and additional patient protections are provided. 21 C.F.R. § 50.24.

[53]   21 C.F.R. § 50.27.
[54]   *Id.* § 50.20.
[55]   *Id.* § 50.25(a)(8).
[56]   *Id.* pt. 50, subpt. C.
[57]   *Id.* pt. 56.
[58]   *Id.* § 56.102(g).
[59]   *Id.* pt. 56, subpt. C.
[60]   *Id.* § 56.111.
[61]   *Id.* pt. 56, subpt. C.
[62]   *Id.* § 56.107.
[63]   *Id.* § 56.115.
[64]   *Id.* § 312.21.

pharmacologic actions of the drug in humans, the side effects associated with increasing doses, and, if possible, to gain early evidence on effectiveness."[65] The drug's sponsor must also derive sufficient pharmacokinetic and general pharmacological data from Phase 1 trials to devise appropriate Phase 2 studies.

Phase 2 investigations involve an expanded patient group (up to several hundred patients) afflicted with the disease or condition being studied. The thrust of Phase 2 trials is to obtain evidence of the drug's effectiveness against the targeted disease, to explore further risk and side effect issues, and to confirm preliminary data regarding optimal dosage ranges.[66]

Phase 3 clinical trials may commence, with FDA clearance, once the drug's sponsor has gathered "preliminary evidence suggesting effectiveness of the drug."[67] Such studies may involve up to several thousand patients.[68] They frequently take place at multiple locations and involve more clinical investigators than in earlier phases. The primary goal of a Phase 3 clinical trial is to collect the data necessary to meet the safety and efficacy standards required for FDA approval.

In many cases, a sponsor will also conduct Phase 4 studies after initial approval. As discussed *infra*, Phase 4 studies may be mandated under the accelerated approval provisions of 21 C.F.R. § 314 Subpart H; may be agreed to between FDA and the sponsor to further address safety issues or to comply with deferred pediatric study requirements; may be voluntarily conducted by the sponsor to expand the labeling for the drug; or may be required by FDA under the authority of the FDAAA.

Collaboration With FDA Regarding Clinical Investigations

The Food and Drug Administration Modernization Act of 1997[69] sought to formalize opportunities for sponsors of clinical trials to meet and seek agreement with relevant FDA review divisions on drug development approaches and the design, scope, and adequacy of proposed clinical trials.[70] The policy goal was to reduce the cost and time needed for drug development and approval by allowing sponsors to obtain binding FDA advice for designing and conducting clinical trials in support of product approval.[71] More recently, under FDASIA, FDA implemented "the Program," a new review model aimed at "promot[ing] greater transparency and improve[ing] communication between the FDA review team and the applicant."[72] The Program recommends that sponsors request pre-submission meetings, a mid-cycle communication, and a late-cycle meeting.[73] The three most common and

---

[65]   *Id.* § 312.21(a)(1).

[66]   *Id.* § 312.21(b).

[67]   *Id.* § 312.21(c).

[68]   *Id.*

[69]   Pub. L. No. 105-115, 111 Stat. 2296 (1997).

[70]   21 U.S.C. § 355(b)(5)(B).

[71]   *See* 21 C.F.R. § 312.47(b).

[72]   *See* PDUFA Performance Goals Fiscal Years 2013-2017, at 5, *available at* http://www.fda.gov/downloads/forindustry/userfees/prescriptiondruguserfee/ucm270412.pdf.

[73]   *Id.* at 6-8.

important types of FDA meetings are the Pre-IND meeting, the End-of-Phase 2 (EOP-2) meeting, and Special Protocol Assessment (SPA) meetings.[74]

Pre-IND meetings are typically available in connection with drugs for life-threatening or severely debilitating diseases. These meetings are designed primarily to discuss and reach agreement on the design of preclinical animal studies necessary to support initial human testing, and may also be used to address the scope and design of Phase 1 studies.[75] Under the Program, sponsors may additionally request a written response to its pre-IND questions.[76]

EOP-2 meetings are perhaps the most useful and important type of FDA meeting, as they are conducted with the purposes of "minimizing wasteful expenditures of time and money and thus in speeding the drug development and evaluation process." To achieve this goal sponsors are encouraged to request and conduct EOP-2 meetings "before major commitments of effort and resources to specific phase 3 tests are made."[77] While primarily intended for sponsors developing new molecular entities or major new uses of approved drugs, EOP-2 meetings are available to sponsors of any IND upon request.[78] Sponsors must submit a meeting package at least one month prior to the scheduled meeting date. Such meeting packages should include, among other things, summaries of Phase 1 and Phase 2 data, specific proposed protocols for Phase 3 studies or additional nonclinical studies and, if available, tentative proposed labeling for the drug.[79] The significance of a well-planned and well-conducted EOP-2 meeting is that agreements reached between FDA and the sponsor with respect to the overall Phase 3 plan and the design of particular studies will generally preclude FDA from later questioning the agreed design or demanding new or additional studies.[80]

SPA meetings are a more focused variation of an EOP-2 meeting, and are intended to reach specific agreements on detailed fully developed proposed protocols submitted by a sponsor for FDA review. Like EOP-2 meetings, SPA meetings can focus on Phase 3 pivotal safety and efficacy studies, but may also be used to seek agreement on protocols for carcinogenicity and stability protocols.[81] Because SPA meetings focus closely on specific protocol questions for a drug, prior agency understanding of the drug's overall development context is considered an essential prerequisite for an SPA meeting. Thus in most cases SPA meetings will follow and build upon, rather than substitute for, EOP-2 meetings.[82] Like agreements reached in EOP-2 meetings, SPA agreements are generally considered binding upon FDA and preclude

---

[74]   Other types of clinical-stage meetings include End-of-Phase 1 meetings (21 C.F.R. § 312.82(b)), "Pre-NDA" meetings (21 C.F.R. § 312.47(b)(2)), "Critical Path" meetings, and issue-specific meetings not encompassed by any of the enumerated meeting types.

[75]   21 C.F.R. § 312.82(a).

[76]   See PDUFA Performance Goals, *supra* note 72, at 17.

[77]   21 C.F.R. § 312.47(b), (b)(1)(iii).

[78]   *Id.* § 312.47(b)(1)(ii).

[79]   Additional background and procedural instructions for most FDA-sponsor meetings are provided in FDA, Guidance for Industry: Formal Meetings Between the FDA and Sponsors or Applicants (May 2009), *available at* http://www.fda.gov/downloads/Drugs/Guidances/ucm153222.pdf.

[80]   FDCA § 505(b)(5)(C)-(F), 21 U.S.C. § 355(b)(5)(C)-(F); 21 C.F.R. § 312.47(b)(1)(iv) ("Barring a significant scientific development that requires otherwise, studies conducted in accordance with the agreement shall be presumed to be sufficient in objective and design for the purpose of obtaining marketing approval for the drug").

[81]   FDA, Guidance for Industry: Special Protocol Assessment (May 2002), *available at* http://www.fda.gov/downloads/Drugs/Guidances/ucm080571.pdf [hereinafter the SPA Guidance].

[82]   *Id.* at 5-7.

the agency from later altering its perspective on issues of design, execution, or analysis of the studies, absent compelling public health concerns.[83]

Obligations of Clinical Sponsors and Investigators

Throughout all phases of a clinical investigation, both the sponsor of the study and the individual investigators have responsibilities and duties designed to ensure patient safety as well as the integrity and soundness of the data derived from the investigation. Noncompliance with these requirements may provoke FDA regulatory actions including Warning Letters, exclusion of a disqualified individual investigator's study results, suspension of an IND or new drug approval predicated upon discredited study data or, in the case of serious violations, civil or criminal proceedings.

The study sponsor is responsible for ensuring patient safety and appropriate scientific conduct, and has the primary responsibility to keep FDA informed of the progress of the study and of any significant safety-related events.[84] The sponsor also has numerous specific obligations regarding such matters as selecting appropriate investigators, adherence to proper protocols and practices, recordkeeping, and shipping and handling of investigational product.[85] In addition, sponsors are responsible for compliance with applicable regulations on informed consent and IRBs.[86]

The sponsor also bears responsibility for reporting to FDA and to clinical investigators any adverse safety events that occur during clinical trials.[87] If the adverse event is serious and unexpected—e.g., it suggests a significant life-threatening hazard or side effect that is not sufficiently identified in the written investigative materials accompanying the study—the sponsor must make such a report within 15 calendar days of receiving the information.[88] Moreover, a sponsor "must also notify FDA of any unexpected fatal or life-threatening suspected adverse reaction as soon as possible but in no case later than 7 calendar days after the sponsor's initial receipt of the information."[89]

In September 2010, FDA issued a final rule and in December 2012, issued a final guidance document on safety reporting requirements for human drugs and biological products being investigated under an IND and for drugs that are the subjects of bioavailability and bioequivalence studies.[90] The 2010 rule requires, *inter alia*, that adverse events be reported in INDs in the aggregate rather than as individual cases in an effort to eliminate sponsor

---

83   *Id.* at 9.

84   21 C.F.R. §§ 312.32, 312.50-70. Under the regulations, a sponsor may have either an investigating or non-investigating role, in addition to its role of shouldering primary responsibility for and initiating the clinical investigation. *Id.* § 312.3(b).

85   21 C.F.R. § 312.50-70.

86   *Id.*

87   *Id.* § 312.32.

88   *Id.* § 312.32(a), (c)(i).

89   *Id.* § 312.32(c)(2).

90   *See* 75 Fed. Reg. 59,935 (Sept. 29, 2010), amending 21 C.F.R. pts. 312 and 320; FDA, Guidance for Industry and Investigators: Safety Reporting Requirements for INDs and BA/BE Studies (Dec. 2012), *available at* http://www.fda.gov/downloads/Drugs/GuidanceComplianceRegulatoryInformation/Guidances/UCM227351.pdf.

reporting of individual cases with serious adverse experiences that have little correlation to the drug itself.[91]

Increasingly, sponsors establish independent Data Safety Committees, also known as Data Safety Monitoring Boards (DSMBs), to review on a regular basis the data accumulating from clinical trials, and to advise the sponsor regarding the continuation or discontinuation of the trial based on subject safety and any changes to the scientific validity of the clinical trial in light of the developing data. Although sponsors are in all cases required to monitor the ongoing safety of their clinical trials,[92] formal establishment of DSMBs is not required except in emergency research where informed consent has been waived.[93] Nevertheless, the use of DSMBs has increased significantly in recent years, and FDA has issued guidance on the establishment and use of DSMBs.[94]

For their part, investigators are required, among other things, to obtain valid informed consent from any participating subjects,[95] to follow study protocols, to ensure that other study personnel follow the required protocols, and to report significant adverse events.[96] An investigator may be disqualified from participation in a study for repeated violations of the regulations or be subject to further administrative, civil, or criminal proceedings.[97] If an investigator disqualification occurs, the study's sponsor will be required to establish that the study's overall viability is not threatened by the investigator's misconduct.[98] Investigator misconduct may also result in an FDA determination that the IND can no longer remain in effect, or that a new drug approval predicated upon the data must be withdrawn.[99]

Public Disclosure Requirements for Clinical Trials

Under the FDAAA, the sponsor is required to post on a public registry certain summary information about any clinical trial for a serious or life-threatening disease, other than a Phase 1 investigation, that was underway as of December 26, 2007 (the effective date of the requirement), no later than that date.[100] For any such trial started after that date, the sponsor is required to post the summary information within 21 days after the first patient is enrolled in the trial. For clinical trials that are not for a serious or life-threatening disease and that were underway as of September 27, 2007 (the date of enactment of the FDAAA), the posting requirement went into effect on September 27, 2008. Sponsors are required to certify to FDA that they have complied with these requirements at the time they submit any "application"

---

91 *Id.* at 2-3. The guidance provides significant clarification in introducing new terms and definitions in an effort to harmonize safety reporting internationally. *Id.* at 3-7. The guidance also reminds sponsors to review safety information from a variety of sources during drug development and to notify FDA of any potentially serious risks from clinical trials, cognizant of the further requirement of reporting serious and unexpected suspected adverse reactions. *Id.* at 8-13. FDA also provides guidance on the format and time frame for reporting. *Id.* at 21-24.

92 21 C.F.R. § 312.50.

93 *Id.* § 50.24(a)(7)(iv).

94 FDA, Guidance for Clinical Trial Sponsors: Establishment and Operation of Clinical Trial Data Monitoring Committees (Mar. 2006).

95 21 C.F.R. § 312.60.

96 *Id.*

97 *Id.* § 312.70.

98 *Id.*

99 *Id.*

100 *See generally* 42 U.S.C. § 282(j) (added by FDAAA § 801(a)).

under section 505 of the FDCA (for drugs) or section 351 of the Public Health Service Act (for biologics). In 2009 FDA issued a guidance setting forth a broad interpretation of the statutory term "application" for purposes of requiring clinical trial registration.[101] Finally, the registry database was expanded to include certain basic information about clinical trial results for approved drugs and biologics; some, but far from all, clinical trial entries include results.

Expanded Access to Investigational Drugs

Notwithstanding the availability of accelerated approval processes (discussed below), drugs that show promise for serious diseases often are not available to patients until many years after the drug's potential benefit has been identified. This has long created patient-generated pressure on FDA and pharmaceutical companies to make promising experimental drugs available to patients other than those enrolled in clinical trials for the drug. This dynamic was dramatically portrayed in the 2013 Academy Award-nominated film, *Dallas Buyers Club*, which portrayed the struggles of acquired immune deficiency syndrome (AIDS) patients and FDA to quickly provide access to treatments for that then-emerging, and previously untreatable disease.

Since 1987 the "treatment IND" mechanism has been available to allow an investigational drug to be provided outside controlled clinical trials to treat patients with serious or immediately life-threatening diseases for which no comparable or satisfactory alternative therapy is available.[102] The treatment IND program, however, became widely viewed as inadequate and underutilized, with FDA itself noting that "the existing regulations did not adequately describe the full range of [expanded access] programs available,"[103] and raising the concern that "the lack of specific criteria and submission requirements results in disparate access to treatment use for different types of patients and diseases."[104]

In 2009 FDA revised its regulations to make it easier for patients with serious or life-threatening diseases to gain access to experimental drugs prior to approval.[105] The final rules created three categories of expanded access situations: 1) individual patients, including for emergency use (essentially the former categories known as "single patient INDs" or,

---

[101]   FDA, Guidance for Sponsors, Industry, Researchers, Investigators, and Food and Drug Administration Staff – Certifications To Accompany Drug, Biological Product, and Device Applications/Submissions: Compliance with Section 402(j) of The Public Health Service Act, added by Title VIII of The Food and Drug Administration Amendments Act of 2007 (Jan. 2009) *available at* http://www.fda.gov/RegulatoryInformation/Guidances/ucm125335.htm.

[102]   21 C.F.R. § 312.34.

[103]   FDA, Speeding Access to Important Therapeutic Agents, *available at* http://www.fda.gov/ForConsumers/ByAudience/ForPatientAdvocates/SpeedingAccesstoImportantNewTherapies/default.htm.

[104]   71 Fed. Reg. 75,147, 75,149 (Dec. 14, 2006).

[105]   74 Fed. Reg. 40,872 (charging for drugs under INDs) and 40,900 (expanded access) (Aug. 13, 2009), amending 21 C.F.R. pts. 312 and 316. In 2013, FDA issued a draft guidance discussing the controversial issue of when it is appropriate to charge for the use of an investigational drug. *See* FDA, Draft Guidance: Charging for Investigational Drugs Under an IND — Qs & As (May 2013), *available at* http://www.fda.gov/downloads/Drugs/GuidanceComplianceRegulatoryInformation/Guidances/UCM351264.pdf.

depending on the context, either "compassionate use" or "emergency use" INDs[106]); 2) intermediate-size patient populations;[107] and 3) Treatment INDs or Treatment Protocols.[108]

The baseline criteria for allowing expanded access to investigational drugs are 1) that the drug is intended to treat a "serious or immediately life-threatening disease or condition" for which there is "no comparable or satisfactory alternative therapy to diagnose, monitor, or treat the disease or condition"; 2) that the potential patient benefit outweighs the potential risks; and 3) that providing the drug for treatment uses will not interfere with the clinical investigations that could support marketing approval.[109] Under the 2009 rule, FDA evaluates the operative criteria on a sliding scale, which in some cases could provide access to drugs based on as little as early Phase 1 safety data.[110] The 2009 rule applies "not only to the use of investigational new drugs but also to approved drugs whose availability is limited because the drugs are subject to a risk evaluation and mitigation strategy (REMS)," and clarifies that eligible patients must have a serious disease or condition but do not need to be currently considered seriously ill with that disease or condition. In 2013, FDA issued a draft guidance to answer questions about its 2009 rule.[111]

In addition, under section 564 of the act, as amended by the Project BioShield Act of 2004,[112] FDA may authorize widespread use of an unapproved drug or other medical product "during a declared emergency involving a heightened risk of attack on the public or U.S. military forces, or a significant potential to affect national security."[113]

The issue of early access (or rather the relative lack thereof) also spawned constitutional litigation against FDA by the Abigail Alliance for Better Access to Developmental Drugs, a nonprofit advocacy group, which challenged FDA's refusal to allow general access to investigational drugs by dying patients. In 2006 the U.S. Court of Appeals for the D.C. Circuit issued a surprising 2-to-1 decision finding a constitutional right to access to unapproved investigational drugs. As the court stated, "where there are no alternative government-approved treatment options, a terminally ill, mentally competent adult patient's informed access to potentially life-saving investigational new drugs determined by the FDA after Phase I trials to be sufficiently safe for expanded human trials, warrants protection under the Due Process Clause."[114] FDA sought en banc reconsideration of this decision and on August 7, 2007, the full court rejected the panel's constitutional analysis and held that "there is no fundamental right . . . of access to experimental drugs for the terminally ill."[115] The Supreme Court declined to consider the case further.

---

[106]   See 21 C.F.R. § 312.310.

[107]   See id. § 312.315.

[108]   See id. § 312.320.

[109]   See 71 Fed. Reg. at 75,150-51.

[110]   See id. at 75,151.

[111]   See FDA, Draft Guidance: Expanded Access to Investigational Drugs for Treatment Use — Qs & As (May 2013), available at http://www.fda.gov/downloads/Drugs/GuidanceComplianceRegulatoryInformation/Guidances/UCM351261.pdf.

[112]   Pub. L. No. 108-276, 118 Stat. 835 (2004).

[113]   See, FDCA § 561, 21 U.S.C. § 360bbb; 21 C.F.R. § 312.36; and Guidance: Emergency Use Authorization of Medical Products (July 2007) available at http://www.fda.gov/RegulatoryInformation/Guidances/ucm125127.htm.

[114]   Abigail Alliance v. von Eschenbach, 445 F.3d 470, 486 (D.C. Cir. 2007).

[115]   Id. at 697 (D.C. Cir. 2007).

FDA Oversight: Clinical Holds

Through the imposition of a "clinical hold," FDA may delay a proposed clinical investigation or suspend an existing one.[116] A clinical hold can be imposed for a number of reasons, including an unreasonable and significant risk to patients, the use of improperly qualified investigators, a deficient or disregarded investigative protocol, or any other serious deficiency in the IND or a particular clinical trial.[117] FDA must communicate the imposition of a clinical hold by telephone or other form of rapid communication, and must provide the drug sponsor, within 30 days, with a written explanation of the basis for the clinical hold.[118] As a general rule, until the agency's consent to lift a clinical hold is obtained, any clinical trial or trials subject to the hold cannot commence or resume.[119]

Starting in the early 1990s, FDA undertook various initiatives to evaluate whether clinical holds traditionally had been imposed in a consistent and fair manner, ultimately concluding that the regulations had generally been followed.[120] A committee was also established within the Center for Drug Evaluation and Research (CDER) "to review selected clinical holds for scientific and procedural quality."[121] This committee meets semi-annually to review both randomly chosen clinical hold orders and those orders forwarded by drug sponsors who disagree with the agency's grounds for imposing the hold.[122] In 2008, CDER revised the *Manual of Policies and Procedures* (MAPP) for the Clinical Hold/Refuse to File Committee to, among other things, call for continued meetings of the committee and expand the scope of its inquiry to also specifically evaluate cases where a clinical hold was considered but not imposed.[123]

IND Termination and Suspension

As with the imposition of a clinical hold, FDA can halt further use or distribution of an investigational drug through termination or suspension of an IND.[124] Similar concerns, such as undue patient risk or serious deficiencies in the IND or the clinical protocol, trigger both types of agency action, with IND withdrawal obviously reserved for the more serious cases.

Where the continuation of a clinical study poses, in FDA's judgment, an immediate and substantial danger to human subjects, the agency may order immediate termination of an IND, subject to possible reinstatement.[125] Where no such immediate risk is present, however, if FDA proposes to withdraw an IND, the agency will notify the sponsor in writing and "invite correction or explanation within a period of 30 days."[126] The sponsor's failure

---

[116]   21 C.F.R. § 312.42.

[117]   *Id.*

[118]   *Id.* § 312.42(d).

[119]   *See generally*, FDA, MANUAL OF STANDARD OPERATING PROCEDURES AND POLICIES, Issuance of and Response to Clinical Hold Letters for Investigational New Drug Applications, SOPP 8201 (1999).

[120]   *See* Investigational New Drugs; Procedure to Monitor Clinical Hold Process; Meeting of Review Committee and Request for Submissions, Notice, 60 Fed. Reg. 43,804 (1995).

[121]   *Id.* at 43,805.

[122]   Investigational Biological Product Trials; Procedure to Monitor Clinical Hold Process; Meeting of Review Committee and Request for Submissions, Notice, 61 Fed. Reg. 1032 (1996).

[123]   CDER MAPP 6010.7 (Jan. 2008).

[124]   21 C.F.R. § 312.44.

[125]   *Id.* § 312.44(d).

[126]   *Id.* § 312.44(c)(1).

to respond within the specified time frame results in the termination of the IND.[127] The sponsor may, however, request a formal hearing if FDA refuses to accept the submitted correction or explanation.[128]

The New Drug Application: Standards and Procedures

Once Phase 3 clinical trials are completed, with satisfactory results, the applicant prepares to submit its new drug application.[129] This preparation process ordinarily includes a pre-NDA meeting with appropriate FDA staff, with the goal of helping to ensure that the NDA will be submitted in the proper format and will contain all required data. After this consultation, the applicant formally submits its NDA.

Contents of the NDA

The regulatory requirements that govern the contents of an NDA are intended to give FDA sufficient information to meaningfully evaluate the drug for which the applicant seeks approval.[130] Although the specific data requirements are lengthy and detailed, there are seven broad categories into which the required data fall: 1) preclinical data, such as animal and in vitro studies, evaluating the drug's pharmacology and toxicology;[131] 2) human pharmacokinetic and bioavailability data;[132] 3) clinical data—i.e., data obtained from administering the drug to humans,[133] which must include "adequate tests" to demonstrate that the drug is safe for use under the proposed conditions of use,[134] as well as "substantial evidence" that the drug is effective under the proposed conditions;[135] 4) a description of proposed methods by which the drug will be manufactured, processed, and packed;[136] 5) a description of the drug product and drug substance;[137] 6) a list of each patent claiming the drug, drug product, or method of use, or a statement that there are no relevant patents making such claims;[138] and 7) the drug's proposed labeling.[139]

In addition to these requirements, the applicant also must provide a summary of the application "in enough detail that the reader may gain a good general understanding of the

---

[127] Id. § 312.44(c)(2).

[128] Id. § 312.44(c)(3).

[129] In some cases, Phase 3 trials may continue after submission of the NDA (the so-called "Phase 3B" trial).

[130] FDCA § 505(b), 21 U.S.C. § 355(b); 21 C.F.R. § 314.50.

[131] FDCA § 505(b)(1)(A), 21 U.S.C. § 355(b)(1)(A); 21 C.F.R. § 314.50(d)(2).

[132] 21 C.F.R. § 314.50(d)(3).

[133] Id. § 314.50(d)(5).

[134] FDCA § 505(d)(1), 21 U.S.C. § 355(d)(1).

[135] FDCA § 505(d)(5), 21 U.S.C. § 355(d)(5); 21 C.F.R. § 314.50(d)(5)(iv).

[136] FDCA § 505(b)(1)(D), 21 U.S.C. § 355(b)(1)(D); 21 C.F.R. § 314.50(d)(1)(i)-(d)(1)(ii).

[137] FDCA § 505(b)(1)(B)-(b)(1)(C), 21 U.S.C. § 355(b)(1)(B)-(b)(1)(C); 21 C.F.R. § 314.50(d)(1)(i)-(d)(1)(ii).

[138] 21 C.F.R. § 314.50(h)-(i).

[139] FDCA § 505(b)(1)(F), 21 U.S.C. § 355(b)(1)(F); 21 C.F.R. § 314.50(e). NDA applications also must contain a certification that the applicant has not and will not use the services of any person who has been debarred by the Secretary of the Department of Health and Human Services (DHHS) due to a conviction for conduct related to drug approval, or for conspiring, aiding, or abetting with respect to such an offense. FDCA § 306(k), 21 U.S.C. § 335a(k).

data and information in the application, including an understanding of the quantitative aspects of the data."[140] The summary must conclude with a presentation of both the risks and benefits of the new drug.[141]

Unless an application is publicly disclosed or acknowledged by the sponsor, FDA may not disclose the contents of an application or even its existence until the agency sends an approval letter.[142] The FDAAA requires FDA to publish on its website the action package for approval of any biologics license application (BLA) or any NDA for a new chemical entity within 30 days of approval; for any other new drug or biologic, the action package must be published within 30 days of receipt of the third Freedom of Information Act request for the package.[143] FDA must also publish on its website within 48 hours of approval a summary review documenting conclusions about the drug from all reviewing disciplines and noting any critical issues or disagreements that arose during the review and how they were resolved.[144] The FDAAA further provides that the scientific review of an application "is considered the work of the reviewer and shall not be altered by management or the reviewer once final."[145]

Risk Evaluation and Mitigation Strategy

An additional element that may be required as part of an NDA is the risk evaluation and mitigation strategy (REMS), as provided under the FDAAA.[146] FDA may require a sponsor to include a REMS in its NDA when the agency deems it "necessary to ensure that the benefits of the drug outweigh the risks of the drug."[147]

A REMS must contain, at a minimum, a timetable for submission by the sponsor to FDA of assessments of the REMS 18 months, three years, and in the seventh year after approval, subject to possible variations in frequency within those time frames and to possible elimination of the assessment requirement altogether after the initial three-year period if FDA determines that the drug's serious risks have been adequately identified and are being adequately managed.[148] A sponsor may also submit an assessment of an existing REMS to FDA at any time, along with a proposed modification of the REMS.[149] A proposal to modify

---

[140]   21 C.F.R. § 314.50(c).

[141]   Id. § 314.50(c)(2)(ix).

[142]   Id. § 314.430(b), (d). If an application has been publicly acknowledged, however, FDA may, in its discretion, disclose a summary of selected portions of safety and efficacy data that are appropriate for public consideration. For instance, data to be considered at an open session of an advisory committee that is evaluating the drug could be released in summary form.

[143]   FDCA § 505(l)(2)(A), 21 U.S.C. § 355(l)(2)(A) (added by FDAAA § 916).

[144]   FDCA § 505(l)(2)(B), (C), 21 U.S.C. § 355(l)(2)(B), (C).

[145]   FDCA § 505(l)(2)(D), 21 U.S.C. § 355(l)(2)(D).

[146]   See generally FDCA § 505-1, 21 U.S.C. § 355-1 (added by Pub. L. No. 110-85, tit. IX).

[147]   FDCA § 505-1(a)(1), 21 U.S.C. § 355-1(a)(1). A REMS may also be required for an approved NDA at any time after approval if FDA becomes aware of new safety information and determines that a REMS is necessary to ensure that a drug's benefits outweigh its risks. FDCA § 505-1(a)(2), 21 U.S.C. § 355-1(a)(2).

[148]   FDCA § 505-1(d), 21 U.S.C. § 355-1(d).

[149]   In addition, a sponsor must submit a REMS assessment (which may include a proposal for modification of the strategy) when submitting a supplemental application for a new indication; if the agency determines that new safety or efficacy information indicates that any REMS element should be modified or added; or if the DHHS Secretary determines there may be cause to withdraw the drug's NDA under section 505(e) (21 U.S.C. § 355(e)) of the act. FDCA § 505-1(g), 21 U.S.C. § 355-1(g). For a discussion of NDA withdrawal see infra.

a REMS strategy is not, however, required to be included with an assessment and also can be submitted to FDA at any time.[150]

In addition to the required periodic assessments, a REMS may also be required to provide for the distribution of a Medication Guide[151] or a patient package insert to each patient when the drug is dispensed if FDA determines that such a requirement may help "mitigate a serious risk of the drug."[152] A communication plan aimed at healthcare professionals may also be required if FDA determines that such a plan may support implementation of an element of the REMS.[153]

A more stringent set of REMS elements may be required if FDA determines that it is necessary to "assure safe use of the drug, because of its inherent toxicity or potential harmfulness." These Elements to Assure Safe Use (ETASU) may require that healthcare professionals who prescribe or dispense the drug have particular training or experience or are specially certified; the drug be dispensed only in specified settings such as hospitals; or patient testing, monitoring, and/or enrollment in a registry be required in connection with dispensing the drug.[154]

Whenever a REMS assessment is submitted, FDA must initiate discussion with the sponsor within 60 days, except for assessments required because the Secretary of the Department of Health and Human Services (DHHS) has determined there may be cause to withdraw the NDA, in which case such discussions must begin within 30 days after submission.[155] For proposed REMS modifications submitted as part of an NDA or supplement, FDA must describe the final REMS or any modification to the REMS, as applicable, in the action letter on the application.[156] For proposed REMS modifications submitted as part of a REMS assessment, FDA must describe the final REMS, in most cases, within 90 days of the beginning of the required discussions with the sponsor.[157] Detailed dispute resolution processes apply if FDA and the sponsor disagree on a REMS or REMS modification.[158] Use of the REMS dispute resolution processes, however, "shall not be the sole source of delay of action on an NDA or supplement."[159] Existing REMS also apply to generic versions of the innovator drug, with special procedures and limitations.[160]

---

[150]   See FDCA § 505-1(g) (as amended by FDASIA § 1132(a)(4)). For information on how to propose a REMS modification, see FDA, Draft Guidance: Format and Content of Proposed Risk Evaluation and Mitigation Strategies (REMS), REMS Assessments, and Proposed REMS Modifications (Sept. 2009), available at http://www.fda.gov/downloads/Drugs/GuidanceComplianceRegulatoryInformation/Guidances/UCM184128.pdf.

[151]   See 21 C.F.R. pt. 208.

[152]   FDCA § 505-1(e)(2), 21 U.S.C. § 355-1(e)(2).

[153]   FDCA § 505-1(e)(3), 21 U.S.C. § 355-1(e)(3).

[154]   FDCA § 505-1(f), 21 U.S.C. § 355-1(f).

[155]   FDCA § 505-1(h)(2), 21 U.S.C. § 355-1(h)(2).

[156]   FDCA § 505-1(h)(3), 21 U.S.C. § 355-1(h)(3).

[157]   Id.

[158]   FDCA § 505-1(h)(4)-(5), 21 U.S.C. § 355-1(h)(4)-(5).

[159]   FDCA § 505-1(h)(9), 21 U.S.C. § 355-1(h)(9).

[160]   Drugs approved under ANDAs or 505(b)(2) NDAs that reference an approved drug with a REMS are subject to all elements of the REMS except the requirement to submit assessments and proposed modifications. For those REMS elements involving restrictions on distribution and use, the generic drug applicant and the reference drug applicant are to use a single, shared system, unless FDA determines that the burdens of such a system outweigh the benefits, or that any aspect of the REMS elements in question is patent-protected or

When the REMS authority was enacted as part of FDAAA there were concerns that FDA would overuse this new tool in ways that would overburden sponsors, delay approvals, and dilute the safety messages for drugs generally by overwarning doctors and patients with excessive, but marginally important, safety information. Once FDA created its REMS infrastructure there was indeed an increasing number of REMS required, including many REMS that went beyond just a medication guide by requiring ETASUs of various degrees of complexity. And, there were several examples of NDAs that were delayed beyond their PDUFA action dates due to unresolved REMS issues.

More recently, however, FDA has begun to realize that the burdens of REMS are greater than it imagined, and that they may not be commensurate with the potential safety improvements. Indeed, the agency has received strong criticism from unexpected quarters about the burden of REMS. For example, major health insurance plans and integrated wholesale pharmacy companies have been critical of the burdens some ETASUs, such as physician, patient, and pharmacist registration and recordkeeping requirements, place on their ability to serve their customers and patients. FDA for its part has responded to these concerns with public meetings, an apparent reduction in the percentage of REMS required, and a focus on establishing class-wide and standardized REMS where feasible.[161] Under its PDUFA V Commitment Letter, FDA further stated it "will continue to use user fees to enhance and modernize the current U.S. drug safety system."[162]

Filing of the NDA

When an NDA arrives at FDA, the agency considers it to be "received," not "filed." The application is considered "filed" when FDA formally accepts it for filing. FDA must determine whether or not to file an application within 60 days of its receipt.[163] If no grounds for refusing to file the application exist, FDA must file it; the filing date will be 60 days after the date of receipt.[164]

FDA will accept an application for filing only if the application is "sufficiently complete to permit a substantive review."[165] FDA has the authority to refuse to file an application on several grounds, such as 1) if the application is incomplete or in improper form or omits data

---

proprietary and the ANDA applicant is not able to obtain a license. In this connection, the law prohibits an NDA sponsor from using any REMS element to "block or delay" approval of an ANDA. FDCA § 505-1(i), 21 U.S.C. § 355-1(i).

[161]   The establishment of class-wide REMS has not, however, been any easier than the imposition of individual-product REMS. For example, FDA has struggled to establish a class-wide REMS for extended-release opioid products, starting with a notice in February 2009. After at least seven formal meetings with sponsors and interested parties, in April 2011 FDA finally issued a notice of the required REMS, but has given the industry working group (consisting of 21 different companies) an initial 120-day period to propose a system whereby all sponsors would collaborate in implementing a shared implementation system for the REMS. See generally http://www.fda.gov/Drugs/DrugSafety/InformationbyDrugClass/ucm163647.htm for details on FDA's opioid REMS programs.

[162]   See PDUFA Performance Goals, supra note 72, at 25.

[163]   21 C.F.R. § 314.101(a)(1).

[164]   Id. § 314.101(a)(2). FDA uses confusingly different terminology for ANDAs, which are considered "submitted" upon physical delivery to FDA, and "received" after FDA has determined that the ANDA is sufficiently complete to permit a substantive review. See 21 C.F.R. § 314.101(b).

[165]   Id. § 314.101(a)(1).

critical to assessing safety, efficacy, or adequate directions for use;[166] 2) if the application fails to make required certifications regarding how the preclinical and clinical trials were conducted;[167] or 3) if the application covers a drug product that is already covered by another application.[168]

Although its refusal to file (RTF) authority sounds quite broad, FDA typically uses that authority only for obvious deficiencies in the application, not in cases that involve "matters of subtle judgment."[169] As the agency's 1993 RTF guideline states: "It is important . . . that [RTF] be reserved for applications . . . plainly inadequate, non-reviewable without major repair, or that make review unreasonably difficult."[170] Applications that contain deficiencies this severe will be subject to refusal, because FDA believes that accepting applications in need of extensive repair is unfair to new drug sponsors whose submissions were complete and properly formatted.[171]

There are three circumstances in particular where FDA is especially likely to use its RTF power: 1) omission of a required section of the NDA, or presentation of a section in so haphazard a manner as to render it incomplete on its face; 2) clear failure to include evidence of effectiveness that can meet the statutory and regulatory standards; and 3) omission of critical data, information, or analyses needed to evaluate safety and effectiveness, or to provide adequate directions for use.[172] Because the agency's RTF power is discretionary, however, FDA can choose not to use the RTF procedure for particularly critical drugs even if specific grounds for invoking it are present.[173] In practice, potential RTF issues are usually addressed and resolved before the NDA is submitted. The pre-NDA meeting often provides a forum for this process.

In 2013, FDA sought to clarify its RTF practice in a new *Manual of Policies and Procedures*.[174] Among other reasons, the MAPP specifies that FDA will RTF applications that are "[m]aterially incomplete or inadequately organized," or "contain inadequate information for one or more indications."[175] If FDA chooses to use its RTF authority, it will notify the applicant, which can then request an informal conference on the issue of whether its application should be filed.[176] After the conference, the applicant can request that FDA file the application, with or without amendments to correct the deficiencies. The agency will then file the application "over protest."[177] As a practical matter, however, an applicant has little or no incentive to ask

---

[166]   *Id.* § 314.101(d)(1)-(2).

[167]   *Id.* § 314.101(d)(6)-(7). For instance, an application that fails to state that preclinical studies were conducted in conformity with GLPs can be refused. Similarly, FDA may refuse to file an application that does not state that clinical studies were conducted in accordance with informed consent and IRB requirements.

[168]   *Id.* § 314.101(d)(8).

[169]   Center for Drug Evaluation and Research, Food and Drug Administration, New Drug Evaluation Guidance Document: Refusal to File (July 12, 1993), at 3.

[170]   *Id.*

[171]   *Id.* at 1.

[172]   *Id.* at 4-5.

[173]   *Id.* at 3.

[174]   *See* MAPP Good Review Practice: Refuse to File (Oct. 11, 2013), *available at* http://www.fda.gov/downloads/AboutFDA/CentersOffices/OfficeofMedicalProductsandTobacco/CDER/ManualofPoliciesProcedures/UCM370948.pdf.

[175]   *Id.* at 5.

[176]   21 C.F.R. § 314.101(a)(3). Such a meeting must be requested within 30 days of FDA's notification.

[177]   *Id.*

the agency to do this. If FDA believes the application contains deficiencies egregious enough to warrant an RTF response, there is little chance of subsequent favorable FDA action on the application.[178] Therefore, requests to file an application "over protest" are a rarity.[179]

Substantive Standards for Review

FDA reviewers must find that an application meets several substantive requirements before the agency will approve the NDA. The most basic requirements are that the drug be "safe" and "effective." These words have specialized meanings in the new drug approval context.

The FDCA, as enacted in 1938, did not require a showing of efficacy as a condition for marketing a new drug—only proof of safety. The Drug Amendments of 1962[180] added the requirement that a new drug must be supported by "substantial evidence" that the drug will have the effect it purports to have under the indicated conditions of use.[181] "Substantial evidence" means evidence from adequate and well-controlled clinical studies.[182] Normally, FDA requires two independent studies to demonstrate efficacy.[183] In 1995, however, the agency issued a statement memorializing a practice it had begun to follow in recent years: namely, that if it is possible to replicate efficacy results within one large, well-designed, multicenter study and those study results are strong,[184] a single study may suffice for approval.[185] This policy clearly remains the exception rather than the rule, however. In addition to this policy, the Act was later amended by FDAMA to provide expressly that FDA may accept a single study as "substantial evidence" of efficacy "[i]f the [agency] determines, based on relevant science, that data from one adequate and well-controlled clinical investigation and confirmatory evidence (obtained prior to or after such investigation) are sufficient to establish effectiveness."[186]

---

[178]   In one instance, after FDA determined that an application for the drug deprenyl was insufficiently complete for substantive review, the applicant requested that FDA file the application over protest. FDA reviewed the application as filed and then proposed to disapprove it because it had numerous problems and deficiencies. See Discovery Experimental and Development, Inc.; Deprenyl Gelatin Capsules and Liquid (Deprenyl Citrate); Proposal to Refuse to Approve a New Drug Application; Opportunity for a Hearing, Notice, 59 Fed. Reg. 26,239 (1994).

[179]   In the event that an application is filed over protest, the review clock (see discussion *infra*) will begin on the date the applicant requested the conference rather than on the day the application was received (New Drug and Antibiotic Regulations, Final Rule, 50 Fed. Reg. 7452, 7479 (1985)), and the filing clock will begin 60 days after the applicant's conference request (21 C.F.R. § 314.101(a)(3)). The triggering dates are moved back in this fashion because the hearing on whether the application should be filed consumes part of the review and filing periods. Review and filing clocks are discussed in more detail later in this chapter.

[180]   Pub. L. No. 87-781, 76 Stat. 780 (1962).

[181]   FDCA § 505(d), 21 U.S.C. § 355(d); 21 C.F.R. § 314.105(c).

[182]   FDCA § 505(d), 21 U.S.C. § 355(d).

[183]   Statement Regarding the Demonstrations of Effectiveness of Human Drug Products and Devices, Notice, 60 Fed. Reg. 39,180, 39,181 (1995).

[184]   "Strong" results are those that are not "statistically marginal." *Id.*

[185]   *Id.*

[186]   FDCA § 505(e), 21 U.S.C. § 355(e).

FDA has a special Combination Drug Policy[187] governing how an applicant must demonstrate effectiveness of a drug that contains more than one active ingredient.[188] Although this regulation on its face reads as a permissive policy, it was actually promulgated in order to require additional evidence of efficacy for many fixed combination drug products already on the market.[189] For an NDA for a combination drug containing two (or more) active ingredients, the combination policy means that evidence of safety and efficacy would be required not only for the drug as a whole, but also for each of the components. In other words, each component must be shown to contribute individually to the claimed overall effects of the product. This contribution, however, need not relate to efficacy—a component may also be added if it is shown to increase the safety of the other component or components. Of key importance under the combination drug policy is the principle that prior efficacy (or safety) results on individual active components cannot be extrapolated to a proposed combination drug—rather, that combination drug must undergo its own clinical investigations to demonstrate safety, efficacy and the contribution of the active components.[190] Like many such principles in the drug approval setting, however, this one is not necessarily absolute, and FDA may exhibit more (or less) flexibility in individual cases.

In addition to proof of effectiveness, a drug may not be approved unless there are "adequate tests by all methods reasonably applicable to show whether or not such drug is safe for use under the conditions prescribed, recommended, or suggested in the proposed labeling thereof."[191] In applying this statutory standard, FDA recognizes that there is no such thing as an absolutely safe drug; in addition to the benefits it provides, every drug will present some risks. Therefore, FDA's assessment of safety necessarily contemplates consideration of efficacy. In the agency's words, "FDA weighs the product's demonstrated effectiveness against its risks to determine whether the benefits outweigh the risks."[192] This risk/benefit analysis takes account of information such as the seriousness of the disease, the presence and adequacy of existing remedies and adverse reaction and any other safety data.[193] FDASIA further requires FDA to implement a structured risk/benefit assessment framework that will facilitate the review of drug risk and benefit considerations. A draft five-year plan describing FDA's proposal to implement and develop such a framework was released in 2013.[194]

---

[187]   Combination *Drug* Products are not to be confused with "Combination Products" which, as discussed in Chapter 17 *infra*, involve a combination of two or more different types of products; e.g., drug/device, or biologic/device products.

[188]   The agency's regulations state that:

> (a) Two or more drugs may be combined in a single dosage form when each component makes a contribution to the claimed effects and the dosage of each component (amount, frequency, duration) is such that the combination is safe and effective for a significant patient population requiring such concurrent therapy as defined in the labeling for the drug. Special cases of this general rule are where a component is added:

> (1) To enhance the safety or effectiveness of the principal active component; and

> (2) To minimize the potential for abuse of the principal active component.

> 21 C.F.R. § 300.50.

[189]   *See* Combination Drugs for Human Use: Proposed Statement Amplifying Policy on Drugs in Fixed Combinations, 36 Fed. Reg. 3126 (1971).

[190]   *See, e.g.,* U.S. v. Articles of Drug...Promise Toothpaste, 826 F.2d 564 (7th Cir. 1987).

[191]   FDCA § 505(d)(1), 21 U.S.C. § 355(d)(1).

[192]   60 Fed. Reg. 39,180 (1995).

[193]   *Id.*

[194]   FDCA § 505(d), 21 U.S.C. § 355(d) (as amended by FDASIA § 905).

Under the Pediatric Research Equity Act (PREA)[195] (made permanent by FDASIA in 2012), an NDA or BLA must include assessments of the safety and efficacy of the product in all relevant pediatric subpopulations (as defined by FDA in consultation with the sponsor) as well as data to support dosing and administration for each pediatric subpopulation for which the product is safe and effective.[196] The applicant must first, however, submit an initial pediatric study plan prior to submission of the assessment.[197] Upon meeting with or receiving comments on the initial pediatric study plan from FDA, the applicant must document its agreement with the plan, which may be amended at any time.[198] FDA then must confirm its agreement with the plan and provide its recommendation in response to requests for deferral, partial waiver or waiver as described below.[199] The content of and process for submitting initial and amended pediatric study plans is described in a draft guidance released by FDA in July 2013.[200]

Assessment requirements may be deferred for various reasons, including an FDA finding that the product is ready for adult approval before pediatric studies are complete.[201] They may also be waived partially or entirely on a variety of grounds, including that 1) the necessary studies are impossible or highly impractical; 2) there is evidence strongly suggesting that the product would be ineffective or unsafe in children; 3) the product does not represent a meaningful benefit over existing therapies for children and is not likely to be used in a substantial number of children; or 4) (for a partial waiver applicable to a specific age group) reasonable efforts to produce a pediatric formulation necessary for that age group have failed.[202] FDA also has authority under PREA to require pediatric assessments for marketed products if the agency finds that 1) the product is used in a substantial number of children for the labeled indications and adequate pediatric labeling could confer a benefit on pediatric patients; 2) there is reason to believe the product would represent a meaningful therapeutic benefit over existing therapies for pediatric patients for one or more claimed indications; or 3) the absence of adequate pediatric labeling could pose a risk to pediatric patients.[203]

PREA was amended by FDASIA to permit the extension of deferrals by FDA on its own initiative or in response to an applicant's request for a new deadline.[204] The request for a new deadline must be submitted to FDA 90 days prior to the expiration of the existing deadline.[205] FDA is also required to issue noncompliance letters to any applicant that fails to submit or defer a required assessment, or if the applicant does not submit a request for approval of a pediatric formulation.[206]

---

[195]   Pub. L. No. 108-155, 177 Stat. 1936 (2003).

[196]   FDCA § 505B(a)(2), 21 U.S.C. § 355c(a)(2).

[197]   FDCA § 505B(e)(2)(B) (as amended by FDASIA § 506(a)).

[198]   FDCA § 505B(e)(3) (as amended by FDASIA§ 506(a)).

[199]   Id.

[200]   FDA, Draft Guidance, Pediatric Study Plans: Content of and Process for Submitting Initial Pediatric Study Plans and Amended Pediatric Study Plans (July 2013), available at http://www.fda.gov/downloads/Drugs/GuidanceComplianceRegulatoryInformation/Guidances/UCM360507.pdf.

[201]   FDCA § 505B(a)(3)(A), 21 U.S.C. § 355c(a)(3)(A).

[202]   FDCA § 505B(a)(4), 21 U.S.C. § 355c(a)(4).

[203]   FDCA § 505B(b), 21 U.S.C. § 355c(b).

[204]   FDCA § 505B(e)(3)(B) (as amended by FDASIA § 505(a)).

[205]   Id.

[206]   FDCA § 505B(d) (as amended by FDASIA § 505(c)).

In addition to evidence of safety and effectiveness, there must also be adequate manufacturing controls in place before FDA will approve a drug.[207] In particular, the methods used in, and the controls and facilities used for, manufacturing, processing, packing, and holding the drug substance and finished product must comply with FDA's cGMPs, and must be adequate to maintain the drug's purity, quality, strength, identity, and bioavailability.[208] A pre-approval inspection of the applicant's facilities will typically be conducted to verify compliance with these requirements.[209]

An additional prerequisite to approval is that the drug's labeling meets applicable statutory and regulatory requirements. The labeling cannot be false or misleading in any particular,[210] and must comply with general requirements concerning both the content and form of the information that must accompany a drug, such as indications, clinical data, warnings, precautions, side effects, and dosage and administration information.[211]

Comparative Effectiveness Research

In 2009 Congress passed the American Recovery and Reinvestment Act (ARRA) in support of comparative effectiveness research (CER).[212] Congress appropriated $1.1 billion to the Agency for Healthcare Research and Quality (AHRQ) for the development and use of clinical registries and clinical data networks that can be used to generate or obtain health outcomes data.[213] AHRQ transferred a portion of these funds to FDA to develop policies, standards, infrastructure, and tools for standardizing clinical study data to enable CER analysis across multiple studies.[214]

It is not FDA policy to require that new drug products or devices submitted for approval be more effective than other approved therapies for the same disease or condition; effectiveness is shown based on clinical data that does not necessarily involve a comparison to another known effective treatment or product.[215] However, in certain circumstances, FDA will consider comparative efficacy; namely when less effectiveness could present a public health danger.[216] Two specific circumstances where a new therapy must be as effective as already approved alternatives are when: 1) the disease to be treated is life-threatening or capable of causing irreversible morbidity (e.g., stroke or heart attack); or 2) the disease to be treated is a contagious illness that poses serious consequences to the health of others (e.g., sexually transmitted diseases).[217] New products developed for particular subpopulations that do not respond to or are unable to tolerate an existing approved therapy require only proof of

---

[207] FDCA § 505(d)(3), 21 U.S.C. § 355(d)(3). Manufacturing requirements are discussed more fully in Chapter 9 *supra*.

[208] 21 C.F.R. § 314.125(b)(1).

[209] *Id.* § 314.125(b)(12).

[210] FDCA § 505(d)(7), 21 U.S.C. § 355(d)(7); 21 C.F.R. § 314.125(b)(6).

[211] 21 C.F.R. § 314.125(b)(8). *See* 21 C.F.R. pt. 201 for a detailed description of labeling requirements.

[212] Pub. L. No. 111-5, 123 Stat. 115 (2009).

[213] *Id.* tit. VIII.

[214] *Id.*

[215] Statement Regarding the Demonstrations of Effectiveness of Human Drug Products and Devices, Notice, 60 Fed. Reg. 39,180, 39,181 (1995).

[216] *Id.*

[217] *Id.*

effectiveness in the targeted population and do not need to be as effective as alternative therapies in the broader population.[218]

Advisory Committee Review

Although the primary review of an NDA is, of course, carried out by the appropriate division within CDER, FDA refers many applications to outside advisory committees for their comments and recommendations. These advisory committees, which are composed primarily of prominent research and clinical specialists, review certain critical studies regarding drug products under consideration, as well as proposed labeling.[219] Advisory committees respond to specific questions posed by the agency regarding safety and efficacy, and evaluate whether additional studies are needed to support approval.[220] In addition to advisory committees, FDA also has discretion to consult outside expert reviewers from the scientific community for their views.[221] Under FDASIA, for example, FDA is required to maintain a list of experts who can provide consultation related to the review of drugs and biological products for rare diseases or that are genetically targeted.[222] Advisory committee and outside review recommendations, however, are not binding on the agency.

FDA has typically been more likely to use advisory committee review if the new drug being studied is particularly novel, presents significant new clinical issues, or if review of the drug involves evaluation of complex scientific data. The FDAAA requires FDA to refer any BLA or any NDA for a new chemical entity to an advisory committee for review prior to approval or to summarize in the action letter why it did not do so.[223] In an effort to ensure that advisory committees reflect the most current expert advice, conflict-of-interest rules were amended under FDASIA to improve outside expert recruitment by FDA and to expand the number of experts who can qualify for nomination to serve on an advisory committee.[224]

FDA Action and Time Frames for NDA Review

The FDCA provides that within 180 days after the filing of an NDA "or such additional period as may be agreed" between FDA and the applicant, FDA must either approve the application or give the applicant notice of an opportunity for a hearing as to whether the application is approvable (essentially, a procedural step required before FDA may formally reject an NDA).[225] Because FDA rarely is in a position to reach a final decision on an NDA within 180 days after it is filed, the agency has created a procedural framework that allows it to engage in multiple rounds of review of an NDA that may stretch on much longer than 180 days without running afoul of the statutory deadline.

---

[218]   *Id.* (citing the approval of atovaquone, although less effective than the standard therapy in the broad population, for the patient group unable to tolerate a widely used therapy for an AIDS-related pneumonia).
[219]   *Id.*
[220]   *Id.*
[221]   *Id.*
[222]   FDCA § 569(a), 21 U.S.C. § 360bbb (added by FDASIA § 903(a)).
[223]   FDCA § 505(s), 21 U.S.C. § 355(s) (added by FDAAA § 918).
[224]   FDCA § 712, 21 U.S.C. § 379d–1 (amended by FDASIA § 1142).
[225]   FDCA § 505(c)(1), 21 U.S.C. § 355(c)(1).

First, as described above, FDA has by regulation established a 60-day period following actual receipt of the NDA during which the agency decides if the application is sufficiently complete to allow it to be "filed." Only after this determination is made does the statutory "filing clock" start to run.

While the filing step effectively extends the 180-day statutory deadline by 60 days, even this additional amount of time is usually insufficient for FDA to reach a final decision on an application. Accordingly, the primary mechanism by which FDA ensures itself the timing flexibility it needs to complete its review of an application without violating the statutory deadline is to rely on the "or such additional period as may be agreed" language of the statute to create a system in which the NDA applicant in effect agrees to allow the review of the application to continue until FDA is either ready to approve it or makes clear that the application is not approvable in its current form, in which case the applicant typically withdraws the application on its own. (Situations in which an applicant forces FDA to provide a formal hearing on approvability, as the statute contemplates, are quite rare.)

This mechanism in turn is premised on the concept of the review cycle, formerly referred to in FDA regulations as the "review clock." FDA regulations, as amended effective August 11, 2008,[226] state that within 180 days of the receipt of an NDA, FDA will review it and send the applicant either an approval letter or a "complete response" letter describing the deficiencies that must be satisfactorily addressed before the application can be approved.[227] This 180-day period is called the "initial review cycle." Significantly, however, the regulations also provide that the initial review cycle "may be adjusted by mutual agreement between FDA and the applicant or as the result of a major amendment" (amendments to the NDA are discussed below).[228]

A key vehicle for documenting applicants' agreement to extending the initial review cycle is FDA's performance goals under the Prescription Drug User Fee Act (PDUFA), which are negotiated between industry and FDA and formally presented to Congress. First enacted in 1992 with the intent of providing additional resources for FDA drug review and accelerating drug review times, PDUFA is re-authorized on a five-year cycle, with the most recent re-authorization taking place in 2012 as part of the FDASIA. PDUFA applies only to NDAs and BLAs, not to ANDAs;[229] generic drug applications are subject to user fees under the Generic Drug User Fee Amendments (GDUFA), which were enacted as part of FDASIA in 2012.[230]

Under PDUFA, FDA collects a substantial user fee for each NDA (and BLA) it receives, with certain minor exceptions. In exchange, FDA commits to the PDUFA performance goals, which provide for specific review times for NDAs and BLAs. Though not legally binding, these performance goals represent FDA's side of a three-way bargain under which industry agrees to pay the user fees and Congress authorizes FDA to collect the fees and use them

---

[226]   See 73 Fed. Reg. 39,588 (July 10, 2008).
[227]   21 C.F.R. §§ 314.100, 314.110.
[228]   Id. § 314.100(c).
[229]   PDUFA is due for re-authorization in 2017. FDASIA also amended the "generic exception" to state that a prescription product is not subject to a fee if it "is the same product as another product." FDCA § 736(a)(3) (B)(ii) (amended by FDASIA § 103(D)(ii)).
[230]   FDCA § 744B(b), 21 U.S.C. § 379f (added by FDASIA § 302).

for drug reviews and related tasks. As such, the performance goals are taken seriously by the agency.

In its PDUFA performance goals under the 2012 re-authorization, FDA committed to review and act on 90 percent of standard original NDA and BLA submissions within 10 months of the 60-day filing date, and 90 percent of priority original NDA and BLA submissions (i.e., submissions for drugs that represent significant advances over existing treatments) within six months of the 60-day filing date. Additional performance goals apply to non-NME NDAs, Class 1 and 2 Resubmissions, Original Efficacy Supplements, and Class 1 and 2 Resubmitted Efficacy Supplements.[231] Thus, by signing on to the PDUFA performance goals, industry has effectively agreed to an extension of the statutory review cycle for standard NDA and BLA applications from six months to 10 months.[232]

As noted above, at the conclusion of the initial review cycle, FDA will send the applicant either an approval letter or a complete response letter outlining the additional steps that need to be taken before the application can be approved. Upon receipt of a complete response letter, the applicant must resubmit the application, addressing the deficiencies noted in the letter; withdraw the application; or ask FDA to provide an opportunity for a hearing on the approvability of the application.[233] Under FDA regulations, the applicant that receives a complete response letter automatically agrees to an extension of the statutory review deadline until it takes any of these actions.[234] Failure to take any of the specified actions within one year after the issuance of a complete response letter will be considered a request by the applicant to withdraw the application, unless the applicant has requested an extension.[235] If FDA considers the applicant's failure to take action within one year to be a request to withdraw the application, the agency will give the applicant written notice and a 30-day period in which to explain why the application should not be withdrawn and to request an extension of time to resubmit it.[236]

Resubmissions of an application following receipt of a complete response letter fall into two categories. A "Class 1" resubmission is one that contains relatively minor information such as final printed labeling, draft labeling, certain safety or stability updates, postmarketing study commitments, assay validation data, final release testing on lots used to support approval, or minor re-analyses of previously submitted data.[237] Under FDA's regulations a Class 1 resubmission constitutes an agreement by the applicant to start a new two-month review cycle beginning on the date FDA receives the resubmission.[238] A "Class 2" resubmission is one that includes any item not specified as part of a Class 1 resubmission, including any item that would require presentation to an advisory committee.[239] A Class 2 resubmission

---

[231]   PDUFA Performance Goals, *supra* note 72, at 4.
[232]   Some have claimed to observe an emerging trend toward FDA increasingly failing to meet user fee action dates. Because each re-authorization of the user fee law may involve renegotiation of FDA performance goals, the 2012 goals may be modified upon the next expected re-authorization in 2017.
[233]   21 C.F.R. § 314.110(b).
[234]   *Id.* § 314.110(c).
[235]   *Id.*
[236]   *Id.*
[237]   21 C.F.R. § 314.3(b).
[238]   *Id.* § 314.110(b)(1)(i).
[239]   *Id.* § 314.3(b).

constitutes an agreement by the applicant to start a new six-month review cycle beginning on the date FDA receives the resubmission.[240]

Submission by the applicant of an amendment to a pending application can also affect the review timelines. If the applicant submits a "major amendment" within three months of the end of a review cycle, FDA's regulations state that this constitutes an agreement by the applicant to extend the review cycle by three months.[241] In its PDUFA performance goals under the 2012 reauthorization, however, FDA noted that a major amendment at any time during the review cycle may extend the goal date by three months.[242] A major amendment may include, for example, a new clinical safety report, reanalysis of a previously submitted study, or the submission of a REMS including elements to assure safe use that were not included in the original application or that were significantly amended.[243] Submission of an amendment that is not major at any time during a review cycle will not extend the cycle, although FDA also may defer review of such an amendment to the next cycle.[244]

Expedited Availability

As discussed above, the history of the FDA drug approval process has been marked by pendular swings between two competing public health goals: ensuring that drugs are as safe and effective as possible before being approved; and avoiding undue regulatory delay in the availability of important new drugs that have the potential to save, extend or improve patients' lives. As the regulatory and scientific burden of meeting FDA's drug approval criteria has increased over the decades, Congress and FDA have recognized the need for, and have established, a variety of mechanisms to speed the availability of especially important and promising drugs. Additionally, in its PDUFA V Commitment Letter, FDA expressed dedication to "advancing and facilitating the development of drugs and biologics for rare diseases."[245] A summary of the options for expedited availability, as discussed herein, is detailed in FDA's 2014 Guidance.[246]

Priority Review

Priority review was established pursuant to the original PDUFA in 1992, where FDA agreed to specific goals for improving the drug review time and created a tiered system for reviewing applications, including faster promised review times for qualifying applications.[247] The program allows for an expedited timeline for the review of the clinical data necessary for approval of an NDA, shortening the clock from 10 months to six months.[248] Generally, to qualify, the drug must treat a serious condition and offer a potentially significant improvement in safety or effectiveness over existing therapies.[249] Sponsors may request

---

[240] *Id.* § 314.110(b)(1)(ii).

[241] *Id.* § 314.60(b)(1).

[242] PDUFA Performance Goals, *supra* note 72, at 32.

[243] *Id.*

[244] 21 CFR § 314.60(b)(3).

[245] *See* PDUFA Performance Goals, *supra* note 72, at 23.

[246] *See* FDA, Guidance: Expedited Programs for Serious Conditions – Drugs and Biologics (May 2014), *available at* http://www.fda.gov/downloads/Drugs/GuidanceComplianceRegulatoryInformation/Guidances/UCM35 8301.pdf.

[247] *See* Pub. L. No. 102-571, 106 Stat. 4491 (1992).

[248] *See* Expedited Programs Guidance, *supra* note 246, at 8.

[249] *Id.* at 7.

priority review, and FDA determines if priority review is appropriate on a case-by-case basis at the time of filing.[250]

Under the FDAAA, a sponsor of a drug approved for the treatment of specified tropical diseases may be granted a "Priority Review Voucher" (PRV), which, among other things, automatically allows an NDA to receive priority review.[251] A recipient of a PRV may use the PRV for a different application, and further may transfer the voucher to another sponsor.[252] In 2012, FDASIA expanded upon priority review by establishing a PRV for "rare pediatric disease" products.[253] A "rare pediatric disease" is defined as a "disease [that] primarily affects individuals aged from birth to 18 years, including age groups often called neonates, infants, children, and adolescents."[254] The program seeks to encourage the development of rare pediatric disease treatments by providing expedited review for drugs containing active ingredients that have not been previously approved.[255] Applicants must notify FDA of their intent to use PRV no later than 90 days prior to application submission,[256] and within five years after approval must report on the estimated population suffering from the disease, the estimated U.S. demand for the product and the actual product distribution.[257]

Fast Track

In FDAMA, Congress added new section 506 to the FDCA[258] leading to the creation of the Fast Track program for drugs intended to treat serious or life-threatening diseases for which there is an unmet medical need. Fast Track is a holistic process whereby FDA takes a much more active and collaborative role throughout the drug development and testing process for designated drugs, in order to "facilitate development and expedite review of drugs to treat serious and life-threatening conditions so that an approved product can reach market expeditiously."[259]

To qualify for Fast Track designation, the drug must be intended for either a life-threatening or serious condition,[260] and must show the potential to address an unmet medical need for such condition.[261] It is not sufficient, however, that the drug be intended for use in patients who have a serious or life-threatening condition. Rather, the drug must be specifically intended to treat the serious condition itself or a serious aspect or sequelae of the condition.[262] Additionally, under the Generating Antibiotics Incentives Now Act (GAIN

---

[250]   *Id.* at 24.

[251]   FDCA § 524, 21 U.S.C. § 360n (added by FDAAA § 1102).

[252]   FDCA § 524(b)(2), 21 U.S.C. § 360n(b)(2); *see also* FDA, Guidance for Industry: Tropical Disease Priority Review Vouchers, at 5 (Oct. 2008), *available at* http://www.fda.gov/downloads/Drugs/Guidances/UCM080599.pdf.

[253]   FDCA § 529, 21 U.S.C. § 360ff (added by FDASIA § 908).

[254]   *Id.*

[255]   FDCA § 529(a)(4)(A)(ii), 21 U.S.C. § 360ff(a)(4)(A)(ii).

[256]   FDCA § 529(b)(4), 21 U.S.C. § 360ff(b)(4).

[257]   FDCA § 529(e)(2), 21 U.S.C. § 360ff(e)(2).

[258]   21 U.S.C. § 356.

[259]   FDA, Guidance for Industry: Fast Track Drug Development Programs—Designation, Development, and Application Review, at 3 (Jan. 2006) [hereinafter Fast Track Guidance].

[260]   *Id.* All life-threatening diseases are deemed to be "serious" for Fast Track purposes.

[261]   *Id.*

[262]   *Id.*

Act), implemented as part of FDASIA, a drug designated by FDA as a Qualified Infectious Disease Product (QIDP) is eligible for the Fast Track designation.[263]

FDA recommends that sponsors request Fast Track status no later than the date of the sponsor's pre-NDA or pre-BLA meeting with the agency.[264] If the drug is given Fast Track status, the sponsor will have the opportunity to participate in FDA-sponsor meetings that can result in an expedited review process.[265] In addition, FDA may review portions of a drug application prior to submission of the sponsor's complete application.[266] This rolling review process may occur only after FDA conducts a preliminary assessment of the sponsor's clinical data and determines that the drug may be effective.[267] FDA's acceptance of a sponsor's application sections does not, however, obligate the agency to commence its review or to meet its review performance goals prior to receipt of the sponsor's complete application.[268]

The benefits of Fast Track programs include earlier and more frequent meetings between FDA and the sponsor, including broad pre-IND consultation, EOP-1 meetings, EOP-2 meetings, pre-NDA/BLA meetings, and early labeling discussion meetings. As part of a Fast Track program FDA will also provide more frequent, more timely, and more proactive interactions (including meetings and correspondence) on development and clinical trial issues. In addition, Fast Track drug candidate sponsors may be allowed to submit portions of an NDA or BLA as soon as they are ready, without waiting for the full application to be completed and ready for filing. Finally, Fast Track drugs are ordinarily eligible for priority review and also may be eligible for accelerated approval if the sponsor chooses to pursue that approval pathway. Where Fast Track products are approved based on surrogate endpoints, such approval may be conditioned upon postapproval studies and pre-dissemination review by FDA of the company's promotional materials.[269]

Breakthrough Therapy

The breakthrough therapy designation was established under FDASIA to expedite the development and review of a drug, whether alone or in combination with one or more drugs, to treat a serious or life-threatening disease or condition and preliminary clinical evidence indicates that the drug may demonstrate substantial improvement over existing therapies on one or more clinically significant endpoints.[270] Preliminary clinical evidence may be early evidence of both a clinical benefit and an effect on a mechanistic biomarker (i.e., a biomarker with activity that is conducted through a theoretical mechanism of action for a disease).[271] A clinically significant endpoint for breakthrough therapy purposes will measure an effect on irreversible morbidity or mortality or on serious symptoms.[272]

[263] See FDCA § 505E, 21 U.S.C. § 351 (added by FDASIA § 801-04); 21 U.S.C. § 356(b)(1).
[264] Expedited Programs Guidance, *supra* note 246, at 8.
[265] Id. at 35.
[266] Id.
[267] Id.
[268] Id. at 36.
[269] FDCA § 506, 21 U.S.C. § 356(b).
[270] FDCA § 506, 21 U.S.C. § 356 (amended by FDASIA § 902).
[271] FDCA § 506(a)(1), 21 U.S.C. § 356(a)(1).
[272] Expedited Programs Guidance, *supra* note 246, at 12.

A request for breakthrough designation can be made with the submission of an IND or at any time following submission of an application as an amendment to an IND, but should occur no later than the end-of-Phase-2 meeting.[273] A drug that qualifies for designation as a breakthrough therapy will also qualify for Fast Track status. As development and review of a breakthrough therapy may occur over a short period of time when compared to other drug development programs, FDA will likely meet with sponsors on a regular basis to discuss clinical trial designs that will yield the information that is needed to facilitate an accelerated review and approval process.[274]

Accelerated Approval

Unlike priority review and Fast Track, which are intended to expedite the development and review of the clinical data necessary for approval of an NDA, the accelerated approval program is aimed at abbreviating the approval timeline itself by reducing (at least initially) the evidentiary burden needed for drug approval. This procedure, which was adopted in its final form in December 1992,[275] is available only for drugs or biologics that offer meaningful therapeutic benefit compared to existing treatment for serious or life-threatening illnesses. There are two different routes to accelerated approval. Under the first route, FDA may approve a treatment subject to special distribution or use restrictions that address outstanding safety issues.[276] The second route, which is much more significant, provides for approval based on evidence of the drug's effect "on a surrogate endpoint that reasonably suggests clinical benefit or . . . on a clinical endpoint other than survival or irreversible morbidity."[277] Such approval may be conditioned upon the completion of postmarketing clinical studies to "verify and describe the drug's clinical benefit and to resolve remaining uncertainty" about the relationship of the surrogate endpoint to clinical benefit.[278] Drugs and biologics approved under the accelerated procedure are also subject to pre-dissemination review for promotional labeling and advertising, and a streamlined procedure for withdrawal of approval if, among other reasons, a postmarketing clinical study fails to verify clinical benefit.[279]

Postapproval Requirements

The Postapproval Period

An applicant's responsibilities with respect to its NDA do not cease upon the application's approval. The postapproval stage brings with it its own set of obligations for the NDA holder. In particular, in the wake of FDAAA the drug sponsor must reckon with expanded FDA powers over such areas as safety-related labeling changes and the conduct of postmarketing studies.

---

[273]   *Id.* at 8.
[274]   *See id.* at 13.
[275]   21 C.F.R. § 314, subpt. H, as codified at 57 Fed. Reg. 58,942 (Dec. 11, 1992), and amended 64 Fed. Reg. 402 (Jan. 5, 1999).
[276]   21 C.F.R. § 314.520.
[277]   *Id.* § 314.510.
[278]   *Id.*
[279]   *Id.* §§ 314.550, 314.530.

Changes Affecting an Approved Application

In order to make changes affecting an approved drug that go beyond the conditions established in the NDA, an applicant must address the requirements of the supplemental NDA process. Changes affecting an approved drug are grouped into three categories, each of which carries different procedural requirements. For some changes, the sponsor must submit a supplement to its NDA, and FDA must approve that supplement, before the sponsor can implement the desired changes—the so-called "prior approval" supplement. A second group of changes also requires supplementing the NDA, but the sponsor can implement the changes before FDA takes action on the supplement, subject to the risk that the agency may ultimately not approve the supplement.[280] These supplements are commonly referred to as "changes being effected," or CBE, supplements. A third category of changes need only be listed in the annual report that the sponsor must file with respect to the drug covered by the NDA.

Under FDA's regulation on supplements, prior approval supplements are required for any change to the drug or its manufacturing processes, equipment, or facilities that has "a substantial potential to have an adverse effect" on the drug's identity, strength, quality, purity, or potency as these factors may relate to its safety or effectiveness.[281] On the manufacturing side, this may include changes in the drug's qualitative or quantitative formulation or approved specifications; changes that may affect the sterility assurance of the drug; and changes in the synthesis of the drug substance that may affect its impurity profile or its physical, chemical, or biological properties.[282] And almost all changes in labeling— including new indications, dosing regimens, populations, and the like—require a prior approval supplement, with limited exceptions that will be discussed below.[283]

"Changes being effected" supplements are utilized for changes with only a "moderate" potential for an adverse effect on the performance of the drug. These supplements fall into two subcategories. The first subcategory requires the sponsor to wait 30 days after submitting the supplement before starting distribution of the drug product incorporating the change in question—the so-called "CBE-30."[284] CBE-30s are to be used, for instance, for a change in the drug's container-closure system that does not affect its quality, or for "relaxation of an acceptance criterion or deletion of a test to comply with an official compendium that is consistent with FDA statutory and regulatory requirements."[285] When an applicant submits a CBE-30, it may not distribute the drug incorporating the change in question if within the 30-day period following submission FDA informs it that the change requires prior approval or that required information is missing from the supplement.[286] For the second subcategory of CBE changes, the applicant may begin distribution of the affected drug product immediately upon receipt by FDA of the supplement; these CBEs are often referred to as "CBE-0s." CBE-0s may be used for changes involving an addition to a specification or changes in methods or controls to provide increased assurance that the drug will have the

---

[280]   For this reason sponsors typically consult informally with FDA before making certain kinds of CBE changes "at risk," particularly safety-related labeling changes.

[281]   21 C.F.R. § 314.70(b).

[282]   *Id.* § 314.70(b)(2)(i-iv).

[283]   *Id.* § 314.70(b)(3), (c)(2).

[284]   *Id.* § 314.70(c)(1).

[285]   *Id.* § 314.70(c)(2).

[286]   *Id.* §314.70(c)(5).

characteristics it purports to possess,[287] or a change in labeling that adds or strengthens a contraindication, warning, precaution, or adverse reaction; adds or strengthens dosage and administration information to increase safe use of the product; or deletes false or misleading information.[288]

Finally, changes in conditions with only a minimal potential for an adverse effect on the drug's performance need only be described in the annual report submitted by the applicant.[289] Examples of such changes include editorial or minor changes in labeling, deletion or reduction of an ingredient that only affects the product's color, and changes in the drug's container size or shape without changes in the closure system (for nonsterile solid dosage forms).[290]

Postmarketing Safety-Related Label Changes

As noted above, the enactment of the FDAAA was preceded by several years of intense public focus on FDA's oversight of postmarketing drug safety. One of the key provisions included in the new law aimed at strengthening FDA's safety oversight powers was new authority to compel a sponsor to make safety-related changes in drug labeling after approval of the drug. Under this new authority, if FDA becomes aware of "new safety information" about a serious drug risk that the agency believes should be included in the drug's labeling, it must promptly notify the sponsor, who then has 30 days to either submit a labeling supplement reflecting the new safety information or explain why the sponsor does not believe a labeling change is warranted.[291] If the agency disagrees with the sponsor's conclusion, it must initiate discussions with the sponsor that may not take more than 30 days from the due date of the sponsor's response, unless extended by the agency. Within 15 days of the conclusion of these discussions, FDA may issue an order requiring the sponsor to make those labeling changes the agency deems appropriate to address the new safety information. Violations of any of these requirements by the sponsor will subject the sponsor to misbranding charges and potential civil money penalties.[292]

In July 2013, FDA issued a final guidance providing details of the agency's interpretation of various aspects of this authority, such as what type of information constitutes "new safety information" that may trigger a labeling change.[293] Information FDA expects to trigger safety-labeling changes includes boxed warnings, contraindications, warnings and precautions, drug interactions, and adverse reactions.[294]

---

[287]   *Id.* § 314.70(c)(6)(i).

[288]   *Id.* § 314.70(c)(6)(iii).

[289]   *Id.* § 314.70(d). The annual report is a document the applicant must submit each year within 60 days of the anniversary date of the NDA's approval date. *Id.* § 314.81(b)(2). This annual report contains various current data about the drug, including a summary of significant new information that might affect the safety, labeling, or effectiveness of the drug product; information about the quantity of the drug distributed; the currently used labeling that accompanies the drug; and changes in chemistry, manufacturing, and controls. *Id.*

[290]   *Id.* § 314.70(d).

[291]   21 U.S.C. § 355(o)(4).

[292]   *Id.*

[293]   FDA, Guidance for Industry: Safety Labeling Changes – Implementation of Section 505(o)(4) of the FD&C Act (July 2013), *available at* http://www.fda.gov/downloads/drugs/guidancecomplianceregulatoryinformation/guidances/ucm250783.pdf.

[294]   *Id.*

The process of a safety label change will be initiated upon an FDA notification letter detailing the FDA determination that new safety information should be included in labeling.[295] Upon receipt, an application holder must either 1) submit a supplement[296] with proposed labeling changes to reflect the new safety information; or 2) notify FDA through a rebuttal statement that it does not believe a labeling change is warranted.[297] FDA will either approve an application holder's response or initiate a discussion period[298] for further modifications.[299] Although FDA expresses that it will be a rarity, the agency retains the authority to order a change to product labeling[300] if it concludes that an application holder's proposed labeling changes are inadequate at the end of the discussion period.[301] Further, if the application holder fails to respond, FDA has authority to enforce the section 505(o)(4) requirements through 1) an unapproved new drug charge, 2) a misbranding charge, 3) civil monetary penalties, and/or 4) seizure of the product and injunction.[302]

Adverse Reaction Reporting

"Adverse drug experiences" are somewhat circularly defined under FDA's regulations as any adverse events associated with the use of a drug in humans.[303] An applicant holding an approved NDA or ANDA must promptly review reports of adverse drug experiences associated with its drug, regardless of the source from which such reports were obtained.[304] If a reaction is both serious (e.g., fatal, life-threatening, or permanently disabling) and unexpected (not listed in labeling, or differing from reactions listed in the labeling due to greater severity or specificity), it must be reported in an "alert report" within 15 calendar days of the applicant's receipt of the information.[305] Finally, all adverse reactions that are not serious and unexpected must be reported at quarterly intervals for three years after an application is approved, and annually thereafter.[306]

The FDAAA did not amend the adverse drug event reporting system *per se*. However, with the extensive new safety authorities provided to FDA under the FDAAA to respond to newly reported safety information—including the power to impose a REMS, to mandate safety-related labeling changes, and to require postmarketing studies—the potential consequences of adverse event information submitted to FDA under the existing system have obviously increased dramatically. FDASIA, however, added a requirement that drug discontinuances and interruptions with supply additionally be reported.[307]

---

[295] *See id.* at 6.

[296] FDA will communicate whether a prior approval supplement or changes-being-effected supplement should be submitted. *See id.* at 6-7.

[297] *Id.* at 9. *See also* FDCA § 505(o)(4)(B)(i)-(ii).

[298] *See* FDCA § 505(o)(4)(C).

[299] Labeling Changes Guidance, *supra* note 293, at 8.

[300] *See* FDCA § 505(o)(4)(E).

[301] *See* Labeling Changes Guidance, *supra* note 293, at 10. FDA has implemented its authority under section 505(o)(4) in a number of cases including Advair Diskus, Aranesp, Epogen and Procrit, Geodon, Propylthiouracil, Symbicort, Symbyax, Vasotec, and Zyprexa. *See* FDA, Safety Labeling Change Orders, *available at* http://www.fda.gov/Drugs/DrugSafety/PostmarketDrugSafetyInformationforPatientsandProviders/ucm189280.htm.

[302] *See* Labeling Changes Guidance, *supra* note 293, at 14-15.

[303] 21 C.F.R. § 314.80(a).

[304] *Id.* § 314.80(b).

[305] *Id.* § 314.80(c)(1)(i).

[306] *Id.* § 314.80(c)(2).

[307] FDCA § 506C(a), 21 U.S.C. § 356c (amended by FDASIA § 1001(a)).

Sentinel Program

In May 2008, FDA launched the Sentinel Initiative to develop and implement a proactive, national electronic system for monitoring the safety of FDA-approved drugs and other medical products.[308] This was in response to section 905 of the FDAAA, which mandates FDA to develop an enhanced ability to monitor the safety of drugs after these products reach the market.[309]

The Sentinel Initiative is a new approach to postmarket risk identification and adverse event surveillance that requires FDA to "develop methods to obtain access to disparate data sources," in order to implement a "post-market risk identification and analysis system" capable of linking and analyzing safety data from these aggregate sources.[310] The initiative directs FDA collaboration with public, academic, and private entities[311] in a long-term effort to augment the agency's existing and largely passive postmarket safety surveillance systems, including the CDER's Adverse Event Reporting System (AERS).[312] The envisioned active surveillance would enable FDA to actively request information from Sentinel System data partners when a safety question arises about a medical product.[313]

Withdrawal of NDA Approval

Although FDA rarely invokes its authority to withdraw NDAs under section 505(e) of the FDCA, there are several circumstances under which the agency can take such action.[314] As might be expected, the conditions for NDA withdrawal generally relate to serious problems with the drug or the application. For instance, FDA can withdraw an NDA if the drug is unsafe for use under the conditions of use for which the application was approved.[315] Similarly, FDA can use its withdrawal authority if new clinical evidence shows that the drug is not safe under approved conditions, or if the drug is not effective.[316] Additionally, FDA can seek withdrawal of an application if the drug's labeling is false or misleading, or if there are inadequate assurances that the drug's quality, strength and purity are as claimed.[317] The agency can also withdraw an NDA if the sponsor fails to file required patent information in a timely manner, or if the NDA contains false statements of material fact.[318]

---

[308]   See The Sentinel Initiative July 2010 Report, *available at* www.fda.gov/downloads/.../FDAsSentinelInitiative/UCM233360.pdf.

[309]   See id. ("FDAAA set goals that FDA's new safety monitoring system must be able to access data from 25 million people by July 2010 and 100 million people by July 2012"; FDA met the July 2010 goal and continues to work toward the goal for 2012).

[310]   FDCA § 505(k)(3).

[311]   FDCA § 505(k)(4).

[312]   See The Sentinel Initiative Report, *supra* note 308 (FDA's passive safety surveillance has involved gathering risk information from external sources in reporting suspected adverse reactions; whereas, the active surveillance instituted through the Sentinel program will enable FDA to initiate its own safety evaluations utilizing available electronic healthcare data to investigate the safety of drugs and other medical products.).

[313]   See id. ("Data partners will include organizations such as academic medical centers and healthcare systems with electronic health record systems, and health insurance companies with administrative claims data.").

[314]   FDCA § 505(e), 21 U.S.C. § 355(e); 21 C.F.R. § 314.150.

[315]   Id. § 505(e)(1), 21 U.S.C. § 355(e)(1); 21 C.F.R. § 314.150(a)(2)(i).

[316]   Id. § 505(e)(2)-(3), 21 U.S.C. § 355(e)(2)-(3); 21 C.F.R. § 314.150(a)(2)(ii)-(iii).

[317]   21 C.F.R. § 314.150(b)(2)-(3).

[318]   FDCA § 505(e)(4)-(5), 21 U.S.C. § 355(e)(4)-(5). A complete list of grounds for NDA withdrawal is set forth in 21 C.F.R. § 314.150.

If FDA seeks to withdraw an NDA, normally it must give the applicant notice and the opportunity for a hearing.[319] If the drug in question presents an "imminent hazard," however, the Secretary of DHHS can summarily suspend approval of the application and give the applicant the opportunity for an expedited hearing.[320] The Secretary cannot delegate the authority to summarily suspend NDAs in this fashion, but can and has delegated to FDA the authority to hold the expedited hearing.[321] Historically, FDA rarely invoked its authority to withdraw or summarily suspend approval of NDAs.

More recently, however, FDA has taken several high-profile actions to withdraw drug approvals, including a proposal to withdraw the breast cancer indication for Avastin, securing the voluntary withdrawal of the weight loss drug Meridia after a tie vote by an FDA Advisory Committee on whether the drug should be involuntarily withdrawn, a proposal to withdraw approval of the low blood pressure drug Midodrine due to a failure of the sponsor to conduct required postapproval studies, and the withdrawal of the approval of propoxyphene products based on FDAAA-mandated postmarket safety studies.

Postmarketing Studies

Although clinical studies are generally thought of as a prerequisite to approval, there are also clinical studies that take place after approval—the so-called postmarketing or "Phase 4" studies. Such studies can be designed for a variety of purposes, including to 1) obtain additional safety data; 2) obtain additional efficacy data; 3) detect new uses for or abuses of a drug; or 4) determine effectiveness for labeled indications under conditions of widespread usage.

There are at least two reasons FDA may be interested in Phase 4 studies. First, such studies allow FDA to grant approval of a new drug on the condition that the applicant complete studies that resolve remaining questions about the drug's safety and efficacy. Using Phase 4 studies to implement a conditional approval of this sort avoids delaying approval of drugs with apparent therapeutic importance. Phase 4 studies can also be used to facilitate FDA's postapproval monitoring of an approved drug when concerns about its safety or efficacy arise.

The FDAAA added to FDA's postmarketing study toolkit new authority to require a sponsor to complete a previously agreed postmarketing study or to impose a new requirement to conduct and complete a postmarketing study on a marketed drug either to 1) assess a known serious risk related to use of the drug; 2) assess signals of serious risk related to use of the drug; or 3) identify an unexpected serious risk when available data indicate the potential for such risk.[322] This new authority comes with several restrictions. For example, FDA cannot require a postmarketing study unless adverse event reporting and active surveillance would not be sufficient to fulfill the purpose of the study, and the agency cannot require a clinical trial unless a less burdensome kind of study (e.g., a patient registry or an epidemiological

---

[319] FDCA § 505(e), 21 U.S.C. § 355(e); 21 C.F.R. § 314.150(a).

[320] 21 U.S.C. § 355(e)(5).

[321] Id.; see also 21 C.F.R. § 314.150(a)(1).

[322] 21 U.S.C. § 355(o)(3). In April 2011, FDA issued a final guidance on the implementation of this authority. FDA, Guidance for Industry: Postmarketing Studies and Clinical Trials – Implementation of Section 505(o) (3) of the Federal Food, Drug, and Cosmetic Act (April 2011).

study) would be inadequate. Failure to comply with a postmarketing study requirement imposed under this new authority carries with it a potential misbranding charge and substantial civil monetary penalties.[323]

Looking Ahead

As we have seen, over the long term FDA's approach to new drug approvals has involved a constant effort to balance the inherent tension between earlier access to new treatments and rigorous evidentiary standards for product approvals. This balancing process has not always been smooth, as multiple stakeholders, from patient advocacy groups to product sponsors to healthcare payors, have sought to influence the direction of the process, often forcefully. In recent years, questions of value have also emerged as important considerations in this equation, as the healthcare system looks for its own balance between affordability and effective patient care. As a result, the challenges and complexities for drug sponsors continue to mount. The ultimate effects of this trend on industry's ability to deliver innovative treatments to patients remain to be seen.

---

[323]   *Id.*

CHAPTER 11

GENERIC DRUGS:
ANDAS, SECTION 505(b)(2) APPLICATIONS,
PATENTS, AND EXCLUSIVITIES

....

FREDERICK R. BALL AND CAROLYN A. ALENCI[*]

Submission of a new drug application (NDA) under section 505(b)(1) following lengthy preclinical and clinical investigations, as discussed in Chapter 10, is not the only pathway to market for drugs. Indeed, there currently are two abbreviated pathways for traditional chemical drugs to reach the market: one for generic drugs, for which an abbreviated new drug application (ANDA) can be filed, and one for drugs approved under section 505(b)(2), for which an NDA must be filed but for which approval can be based in part on the safety and effectiveness of an already-approved drug.[1]

The term "generic drug" generally applies to a drug that is the same as its counterpart brand product with respect to active ingredient(s), dosage form, strength, route of administration, and conditions of use.[2] FDA advises that generic drugs that contain the same active ingredients as the brand, and have the same labeling and are shown to be available to the treatment site at the same rate as the brand, may be therapeutically equivalent to the brand.[3] Section 505(b)(2) applications may be submitted for new chemical entities or for modified versions of previously approved drugs. Section 505(b)(2) drugs differ from section 505(b)

---

[*]   This is an updated version of a chapter originally written by William B. Schultz and Margaret M. Dotzel and updated by Lisa Barclay.

[1]   On March 23, 2010, President Obama signed into law the Affordable Care Act, which contained the Biologics Price Competition and Innovation Act of 2009, which amends the Public Health Service Act (PHSA) and other statutes to create an abbreviated approval pathway for biological products shown to be highly similar (biosimilar) to, or interchangeable with, an FDA-licensed reference biological product. Section 351(k) of the PHSA (42 U.S.C. § 262(k)), which was added by the new legislation, allows a company to submit an application for licensure of a biosimilar or interchangeable biological product. Biosimilars are discussed more fully in Chapter 15.

[2]   21 C.F.R. § 314.92(a)(1).

[3]   See FDA, Approved Drug Products with Therapeutic Equivalence Evaluations (34th ed. 2014) at vii (hereinafter the Orange Book). Virtually every state has adopted laws and/or regulations that govern the substitution of drug products. Id. at iv. Some take the approach of permitting substitution only for drugs on a specific list (the positive formulary approach). Id. Others require that substitution be permitted for all drugs except those prohibited by a particular list (the negative formulary approach). Id.

(1) drugs because they may be approved based in part on the safety and effectiveness of an approved drug.

These abbreviated pathways to drug approval are important because they permit manufacturers to gain approval without having to repeat expensive clinical trials that have already been conducted by their brand counterparts.[4] Because generic drug manufacturers are not required to repeat expensive clinical trials and because they generally market their products to drug suppliers and do not undertake significant advertising directed at physicians or consumers, generic drugs typically are sold at a fraction of the cost of brand products.[5] Thus, generic drugs save consumers, healthcare providers, and state and federal governments billions of dollars per year.[6]

The History of Generic Drugs and Abbreviated Drug Applications

Although the Drug Price Competition and Patent Term Restoration Act of 1984, popularly known as the "Hatch-Waxman Amendments" or "Hatch-Waxman," is credited with creating the approval pathway for generic drugs and is responsible for creating the modern-day generic drug industry, prior to 1984 FDA took important steps to facilitate the marketing of generic drugs.

The Earliest Generics

Prior to enactment of the Federal Food, Drug, and Cosmetic Act (FDCA) in 1938, there were few regulatory barriers to the market entry of drugs, including generic versions of brand products. After the 1938 act was enacted, however, a new drug could not be marketed unless its NDA demonstrating the drug's safety became effective[7] or the drug was generally recognized as safe (GRAS).[8] With respect to the latter pathway, FDA adopted an informal practice whereby upon request it would inform an interested party whether a particular drug was GRAS or a new drug subject to a premarket application.[9] Thus, a manufacturer could make its own determination that a particular drug was GRAS, or it could seek a letter

---

[4]   Mova Pharmaceuticals Corp. v. Shalala, 140 F.3d 1060, 1063 (D.C. Cir. 1998).

[5]   United States v. Generix Drug Corp., 460 U.S. 453, 455 n.1 (1983). Generic drugs are discounted as much as 70 to 80 percent. *See* CONG. BUDGET OFF., HOW INCREASED COMPETITION FROM GENERIC DRUGS HAS AFFECTED PRICES AND RETURNS IN THE PHARMACEUTICAL INDUSTRY (July 1998), *available at* http://www.cbo.gov/sites/default/files/cbofiles/ftpdocs/6xx/doc655/pharm.pdf [hereinafter the 1998 CBO Study]; *see generally*, David Reiffen & Michael R. Ward, *Generic Drug Industry Dynamics*, 87 REVIEW OF ECON. & STAT. 37 (2005).

[6]   *See, e.g.,* FEDERAL TRADE COMMISSION, GENERIC DRUG ENTRY PRIOR TO PATENT EXPIRATION: AN FTC STUDY (July 2002), at 9 (citing Congressional Budget Office studies to show, among other things, that in 1994, the availability of generic drugs saved consumers $8 billion to $10 billion) [hereinafter FTC Report].

[7]   The 1938 act provided that a new drug application (NDA) would automatically become effective within 60 days unless the agency affirmatively refused to approve the application. Pub. L. No. 75-717, 52 Stat. 1040 (codified at 21 U.S.C. § 301 *et seq.*) (1938). The requirement for affirmative approval by FDA was not added until the 1962 Drug Amendments, Pub. L. No. 87-781, 76 Stat. 780 (1962).

[8]   Pub. L. No. 75-717, 52 Stat. 1040 (codified at 21 U.S.C. § 301 *et seq.*).

[9]   *See* New Drug Status Opinions; Statement of Policy, 33 Fed. Reg. 7758 (Jan 23, 1968); *see also* Abbreviated New Drug Application Regulations; Proposed Rule, 54 Fed. Reg. 28,872 (July 10, 1989).

from FDA stating that fact. The practice of informing manufacturers about the status of their drugs was discontinued in 1968 and all "not new drug letters" were formally revoked by the agency at that time.[10] Between 1938 and 1962, FDA considered drugs that were identical, similar, or related to drugs with effective applications to be covered by those approvals and allowed those drugs to be marketed without independent approval.[11]

The DESI Review

In 1962, Congress passed the Kefauver-Harris Drug Amendment, which added as a condition for approval that a drug be effective. The 1962 amendments also required a retrospective evaluation of the efficacy of drugs that had been approved as safe between 1938 and 1962.[12] Under the Drug Efficacy Study Implementation (DESI) Review, which FDA established in 1968 to implement the 1962 amendments, the National Academy of Sciences appointed expert panels to review available data on all drugs first marketed between 1938 and 1962 to make recommendations as to their efficacy.[13] FDA had approved generic versions of pre-1962 drugs without requiring independent evidence of safety or effectiveness if their manufacturers demonstrated that they were duplicates of drugs that the agency had determined had sufficient evidence of effectiveness to warrant continued approval and the manufacturer provided product quality information.[14] To do so, the agency created a new form of NDA, known as the ANDA, for which approval was based on sameness of active ingredients and bioequivalence rather than on safety and efficacy data.[15]

The Paper NDA Policy

The DESI program and the abbreviated mechanism for approval of duplicates did not apply to drugs first marketed after 1962. Although FDA initially concluded that the FDCA did not provide authority for an abbreviated pathway for approval of these drugs, it did recognize that sound public policy would allow duplicates to enter the market without undertaking expensive and repetitive testing.[16] Thus, FDA sought an alternate way to expand the ANDA policy to post-1962 drugs. Initially, it adopted the "paper NDA" policy. This policy permitted competing versions of approved new drugs to demonstrate safety and effectiveness on the basis of publicly available reports of well-controlled studies demonstrating the drug's safety and efficacy.[17] Although the paper NDA policy survived a court challenge,[18] it did little to

---

[10]   *Id.*

[11]   *See* FDA, Guidance for FDA Staff and Industry: Marketed Unapproved Drugs—Compliance Policy Guidance (June 2006).

[12]   Pub. L. No. 87-781, 76 Stat. 780 (1962).

[13]   *See* 54 Fed. Reg. at 28,873.

[14]   *See* Abbreviated Applications; Proposed Rule, 34 Fed. Reg. 2673 (Feb 27, 1969); Abbreviated Applications; Final Rule, 35 Fed. Reg. 6574 (Apr. 24, 1970). *See also* 54 Fed. Reg. at 28,872-73.

[15]   *Id.* As discussed herein, many drugs came onto the market before 1962 without FDA approvals, most often because they were claimed to have been marketed prior to 1938 or to be identical, similar, or related to such a drug. These drugs were not subject to DESI. In response to concerns about these unapproved drugs, FDA developed a program known as the "Prescription Drug Wrap-Up," which was designed to address the legal status of these drugs. *See* FDA, Guidance for FDA Staff and Industry: Marketed Unapproved Drugs—Compliance Policy Guide (June 2006).

[16]   Response to Petition Seeking Withdrawal of the Policy Described in the Agency's "Paper" NDA Memorandum of July 31, 1978; Notice, 45 Fed. Reg. 82,052 (Dec. 12, 1980).

[17]   Publication of "Paper NDA" Memorandum; Notice, 46 Fed. Reg 27,396 (May 19, 1981).

[18]   Burroughs Wellcome Co. v. Schweiker, 649 F.2d 221 (4th Cir. 1981); *see* also Upjohn Mfg. Co. v. Schweiker, 681 F.2d 480 (6th Cir. 1982).

foster generic competition because adequate published studies were available for only a fraction of post-1962 drugs.[19] In 1982, FDA announced that it was reconsidering its initial assessment of the scope of its authority and was contemplating changing its regulations to create an abbreviated pathway for post-1962 drugs similar to the DESI process for pre-1962 drugs.[20] FDA's efforts were overtaken by passage of the Hatch-Waxman Amendments in 1984, which eliminated the need for a regulatory change.

The Hatch-Waxman Amendments

At the same time that the generic drug industry was urging FDA and Congress to create an abbreviated pathway for generic drug approval, the brand drug industry was arguing that its companies were losing the effective period of their patent protection because of the length and complexity of the drug approval process. To address the brand industry concerns, Senator Orrin Hatch introduced a bill that would have provided for patent extensions where a company had lost patent time while testing its product and awaiting approval of its NDA. At approximately the same time, Congressman Henry Waxman introduced legislation to simplify the requirements for approval of generic drugs, modeled after the ANDA process that applied to pre-1962 drugs. Ultimately these bills were combined, and the Hatch-Waxman Act created two new abbreviated statutory pathways—ANDAs submitted under section 505(j), which were modeled after the ANDAs FDA had been accepting for DESI drugs; and NDAs submitted under section 505(b)(2), which under the law could be based in part on the agency's safety and efficacy finding for a different drug. The new statute also created a process for granting patent extensions to new drugs and incentives (in the form of exclusivity) both for research and for challenging patents.

Specifically, Hatch-Waxman established a process under section 505(j) pursuant to which duplicates of previously approved brand drugs could be approved on the basis of chemistry, manufacturing, and bioequivalence data without evidence from literature or clinical data to establish effectiveness and safety.[21] Under these provisions, if an ANDA applicant establishes that its proposed drug product has the same active ingredient, strength, dosage form, route of administration, labeling, and conditions of use as the brand drug and that it is bioequivalent to that drug, the applicant may rely on the fact that FDA previously found the brand drug to be safe and effective.[22] The legislation also permitted generic drug applicants to petition for permission to submit ANDAs for products that differ from the brand drug in any of four specified ways—dosage form, route of administration, strength, or active ingredients—where such changes do not require review of clinical data.[23] Such petitions are called "suitability petitions," and under section 505(j) the applicant must show that the generic product is sufficiently similar to the approved product for which safety and effectiveness have already been established so that no additional evidence of safety and effectiveness need be submitted for review.[24]

---

[19]   See 54 Fed. Reg. at 28,873-75.

[20]   Abbreviated New Drug Applications for New Drugs Approved After October 10, 1962 for Human Use; Calendar of Federal Regs., 47 Fed. Reg. 1765, 1767 (Jan. 13, 1982).

[21]   Pub. L. No. 98-417, 98 Stat. 1585 (1984).

[22]   FDCA § 505(j), 21 U.S.C. § 355(j).

[23]   FDCA § 505(j)(2)(C), 21 U.S.C. § 355(j)(2)(C). A change in active ingredient is permitted only where one active ingredient is substituted for one of the active ingredients in a listed combination drug. 21 C.F.R. § 314.93(b). A change in active ingredient is therefore not permitted in a single active ingredient product.

[24]   FDCA § 505(j)(2)(C), 21 U.S.C. § 355(j)(2)(C).

One of the goals of the Hatch-Waxman Act was to get safe and effective generic substitutes on the market as quickly as possible after expiration of the underlying patent.[25] To achieve that objective, Congress created a statutory scheme pursuant to which FDA could tentatively approve an ANDA before the patent for the "pioneer" drug had expired with an effective date as of the patent's expiration date.[26] Hatch-Waxman also overturned the holding of the 1984 decision of the Federal Circuit in *Roche v. Bolar*, which had prohibited testing on a patented drug before the expiration of the patent.[27] In addition, the law included a reward to the generic companies that contested the validity or infringement of brand patents, namely a 180-day period of "generic exclusivity," during which the first generic to challenge the patent would be protected from competition by subsequently filed ANDAs challenging the same patent.

The second abbreviated pathway created by Hatch-Waxman was a new type of NDA, the 505(b)(2) application. Section 505(b)(2) permits an applicant to rely on investigations not conducted by or for the applicant and for which the applicant has not obtained a right of reference. Although, as discussed in greater detail below, it has been argued that this provision was intended only to codify FDA's "paper NDA" policy, since 1984 FDA has concluded, based on the provision's language, that Congress intended a much broader application, namely to permit companies to rely on the agency's previous findings of safety and effectiveness for a drug if that finding is useful in reducing the data required to establish safety and effectiveness of the applicant's product. Section 505(b)(2) basically covers drugs that are not duplicates of already-approved drugs but for which a full NDA would require testing that would be duplicative and unnecessary. The patent extension provisions and exclusivities awarded to innovator products that apply to ANDAs also apply to 505(b)(2) applications.[28]

The Post Hatch-Waxman Years

The Hatch-Waxman Amendments dramatically increased the entry of generic drugs into the market. Today, generic drugs comprise 69 percent of all prescriptions dispensed, up from 19 percent in 1984, when the law was passed.[29] At the same time, generic medicines account for only 16 percent of all dollars spent on prescription drugs.[30] Despite the success

---

[25] See H.R. REP. No. 98-857, Part II at 8-9 (Aug. 1, 1984), 1984 U.S.C.C.A.N. 2686, 2692-3; see also Mead Johnson Pharmaceutical Group v. Bowen, 838 F.2d 1332, 1333 (D.C. Cir. 1988) ("The purpose of [the Drug Price Competition and Patent Term Restoration Act] was to increase competition in the drug industry by facilitating the approval of generic copies of drugs.").

[26] See H.R. REP. No. 98-857, Part I at 27 (June 21, 1984) ("The Committee recognizes that some ANDA's will be submitted and ready for approval before the patent on the listed drug has expired.").

[27] Roche v. Bolar, 733 F.2d 858 (Fed. Cir. 1984), cert. denied, 469 U.S. 856 (1984). The House Judiciary Committee rejected an amendment to the act that would have limited generic drug manufacturers' ability to conduct bioequivalency tests before the pioneer drug's patent expired to the last year of exclusivity because the amendment would have resulted in delays after the expiration of the patent before the generic drug could go on the market, in contradiction of the policy objective of "getting safe and effective generic substitutes on the market as quickly as possible after the expiration of the patent." H.R. REP. No. 98-857, Part II at 8-9.

[28] See FDCA § 505(c)(3), 21 U.S.C. § 355(c)(3).

[29] See "Facts at a Glance," Generic Pharmaceutical Industry Ass'n., available at http://gpha.hfwebdev.com/about-gpha/about-generics/facts (last visited Sept. 17, 2014) [hereinafter GPhA Facts at a Glance]; see also the 1998 CBO Study, supra note 5 at ix; FTC Report, supra note 6 at i.

[30] GPhA Facts at a Glance, supra note 29.

of the law, FDA's generic program got off to a difficult start. In addition, some aspects of the law led to controversial practices and strategies, which resulted in additional legislation. The significant issues and statutory changes designed to address those issues will be discussed throughout this chapter.

The first controversy grew out of what is now referred to as "the generic drug scandal." Following the passage of Hatch-Waxman, an investigation by the Subcommittee on Oversight of the House Committee on Energy and Commerce revealed that a number of generic companies were paying unlawful gratuities to FDA reviewers with the hope of receiving expedited or favorable consideration of their ANDAs. Others were submitting fraudulent data. Congress responded by referring some of the individuals whom it investigated for criminal prosecution and enacting the Generic Drug Enforcement Act of 1992.[31] That act provides for debarment of firms or individuals convicted of fraud and other crimes in the course of the ANDA process, and it authorizes FDA to impose civil money penalties for ANDA fraud.[32]

Since 1984, the courts and FDA have addressed a number of Hatch-Waxman issues. In response to allegations that certain provisions of Hatch-Waxman were being misused, in 2003, Congress included amendments to Hatch-Waxman in the Medicare Prescription Drug Improvement and Modernization Act of 2003 (MMA).[33] These provisions were designed to close some legal loopholes that continued to delay generic drug approval. In 2007, as part of the Food and Drug Administration Amendments Act of 2007 (FDAAA), Congress added additional new requirements related to ANDAs and generic drug approvals.[34] The specifics of these laws and the issues they sought to address are discussed in further detail below.

The ANDA Approval Process

ANDA Applications

As stated above, a generic drug typically is the same as the brand drug product with respect to active ingredient, dosage form, strength, route of administration, and intended use.[35] A company seeking to market a generic version of a brand-name drug first must submit an ANDA to FDA that includes:

(a) information showing that the proposed conditions of use previously have been approved for a drug that FDA has approved for safety and efficacy (hereinafter referred to as the "reference listed drug" or "RLD");[36]

---

[31]   Pub. L. No. 102-292, 106 Stat. 149 (codified at 21 U.S.C. §§ 335a-335c).
[32]   *See* 21 U.S.C. § 335a-335c.
[33]   Pub. L. No. 108-173, 117 Stat. 2066 (2003).
[34]   Pub. L. No. 110-85, 121 Stat. 823 (2007).
[35]   21 C.F.R. § 314.92(a)(1).
[36]   FDCA § 505(j)(2)(A)(i), 21 U.S.C. § 355(j)(2)(A)(i).

(b) proof that the active ingredient(s) is (are) the same as the active ingredient(s) in the RLD;[37]

(c) information showing that the route of administration, dosage form, and strength are the same as those for the RLD;[38]

(d) information to show that the drug is bioequivalent to the RLD;[39]

(e) information to show that the proposed labeling of the generic is the same as the labeling for the RLD except for changes required because of differences approved pursuant to the suitability petition process, discussed below, or because of differences related to different manufacturers;[40]

(f) the basic technical information required in an NDA (e.g., chemistry, manufacturing data);[41] and

(g) a certification that describes the applicant's belief regarding the status of each patent that claims the RLD.[42]

Reference Listed Drug—Orange Book Listing/Delisting

A reference listed drug is a drug identified by FDA in its list of approved drugs (the Orange Book) as a drug product upon which an ANDA applicant can rely in seeking approval.[43] A listing in the Orange Book means that the drug has been approved and not withdrawn from the market based upon safety or efficacy concerns.[44] Although FDA rarely withdraws an approval for a drug, manufacturers occasionally remove a drug voluntarily. In such cases, FDA must determine whether the drug was withdrawn for reasons of safety or effectiveness before approving any ANDA that references such drug or before permitting the continued marketing of any ANDA that has already been approved.[45] A firm that seeks to use a reference drug that is not designated as an RLD may submit a citizen petition to FDA seeking to have the agency designate its preferred listed drug as an RLD.[46] An interested person may also petition FDA to make such a determination.[47]

Suitability Petition

As noted above, although a generic drug generally must be the same as the brand drug product with respect to active ingredient, dosage form, strength, route of administration, and intended use,[48] Hatch-Waxman permits a generic applicant to petition FDA for permission to file an ANDA for a drug that has a different active ingredient, route of administration, dosage

---

[37] FDCA § 505(j)(2)(A)(ii), 21 U.S.C. § 355(j)(2)(A)(ii). The statute permits the use of a different active ingredient in a multiple-active-ingredient drug product provided the difference has been approved in a "suitability petition," which is discussed in further detail below.

[38] FDCA § 505(j)(2)(A)(iii), 21 U.S.C. § 355(j)(2)(A)(iii). The statute also permits differences here pursuant to an approved suitability petition.

[39] FDCA § 505(j)(2)(A)(iv), 21 U.S.C. § 355(j)(2)(A)(iv).

[40] FDCA § 505(j)(2)(A)(v), 21 U.S.C. § 355(j)(2)(A)(v).

[41] FDCA § 505(j)(2)(A)(vi), 21 U.S.C. § 355(j)(2)(A)(vi).

[42] FDCA § 505(j)(2)(A)(vii), (viii), 21 U.S.C. § 355(j)(2)(A)(vii), (viii).

[43] 21 C.F.R. §§ 314.3(b), 314.94(a)(3).

[44] 21 U.S.C. §§ 355(j)(7)(C); 21 C.F.R. § 314.3(b).

[45] 21 C.F.R. § 314.161.

[46] See id. §§ 10.25(a), 10.30, 314.94(a)(3).

[47] Id.

[48] 21 C.F.R. § 314.92(a)(1).

form or strength.[49] FDA is directed to approve such a petition (called a suitability petition) unless it finds that 1) investigations must be conducted to show safety and effectiveness; or 2) the drug with a different active ingredient cannot be evaluated for approval on the basis of information that is required in an ANDA.[50] An applicant may not submit an ANDA for a drug subject to a suitability petition until after FDA has granted the petition. Because of the time involved in FDA reviewing the petition and the significant backlog, many applicants forgo this route and instead submit a 505(b)(2) filing.

Bioequivalence

In order to rely on FDA's previous finding that the RLD is safe and effective, the ANDA applicant must show that its proposed product is bioequivalent to the RLD.[51] Bioequivalence is the foundation of generic drug approval. A generic will be found to be bioequivalent if:

- the rate and extent of the drug's absorption into the body (i.e., bioavailability) is not significantly different from the RLD when administered at the same molar dose of the therapeutic ingredient under similar experimental conditions in either a single dose or multiple doses;[52] or

- the extent of absorption of the drug into the body does not show a significant difference from the extent of absorption of the RLD when administered at the same molar dose of the therapeutic ingredient under similar experimental conditions in either a single dose or multiple doses and the difference from the RLD in the rate of absorption is intentional, is reflected in the proposed labeling, is not essential to the attainment of effective body drug concentrations on chronic use, and is considered medically insignificant for the drug.[53]

An ANDA submitted based on a suitability petition may be approved on the basis of a showing that the active ingredients of the new drug are of the same pharmacological or therapeutic class as those of the listed drug and that the new drug can be expected to have the same therapeutic effect.[54]

Same Labeling

Historically, as mentioned above, the Hatch-Waxman Amendments provided an avenue for generic drug manufacturers to submit more streamlined drug applications that no longer required expensive and lengthy clinical trials for generic drug products. Instead, the generic drug manufacturer had to prove that the drug was the same as the branded drug with regard to active ingredients, dosage form, strength, and route of administration, except for differences approved by FDA under a suitability petition.[55] This sameness requirement is the hallmark of the Hatch-Waxman Amendments.

---

49   FDCA § 505(j)(2)(C), 21 U.S.C.§ 355(j)(2)(C); 21 C.F.R.§ 314.93.
50   FDCA § 505(j)(2)(C), 21 U.S.C. § 355(j)(2)(C). Different active ingredients are allowed only for combination drugs in which at least one active ingredient is the same as the RLD and the second is approved in a similar drug.
51   FDCA § 505(j)(4)(F), 21 U.S.C. § 355(j)(4)(F); Pfizer Inc. v. Shalala, 182 F.3d 975, 977 (D.C. Cir. 1999).
52   FDCA § 505(j)(8)(B)(i), 21 U.S.C. § 355(j)(8)(B)(i).
53   FDCA § 505(j)(8)(B)(ii), 21 U.S.C. § 355(j)(8)(B)(ii).
54   FDCA § 505(j)(4)(F), 21 U.S.C. § 355(j)(4)(F).
55   21 U.S.C. § 355(j)(2)(A)(i)-(iv).

Likewise, the FDCA requires a generic drug's labeling to be the same as the RLD unless changes are required because of differences approved under a suitability petition or because the generic and the RLD are produced or distributed by different manufacturers.[56] FDA's regulations have interpreted the law to permit changes in a generic drug's labeling in a variety of circumstances, including for differences in expiration dates, formulations, bioavailability, or pharmacokinetics; because of labeling revisions made to comply with current FDA labeling guidelines; and because aspects of the RLD's labeling are protected by patent or by exclusivity (discussed below) and such differences do not render the generic drug less safe and effective than the RLD for all of the remaining, non-protected conditions of use.[57]

Brand companies have mounted several unsuccessful judicial challenges to FDA's regulations. For example, in one case, a brand company challenged the approval of an ANDA that included a label warning regarding an inactive ingredient (sulfite) found in the generic product but not in the brand.[58] The court rejected the challenge on the grounds that the changes were permitted based on differences in formulation and in order to comply with current FDA labeling guidelines and guidance on sulfite warnings.[59]

Equally unsuccessful court challenges were mounted against the part of the regulation that permits differences in labels that exclude protected information. For example, two companies argued that permitting a generic to be approved without the protected information undercuts their exclusivity or protection because a physician can prescribe the generic product for the protected indication. The courts rejected this argument.[60]

Brand manufacturers also have argued in administrative proceedings that the labeling change for which they were granted exclusivity or patent protection was so critical to the safe and effective use of the drug that no generic could be approved without it, and thus no generic could be approved until the three-year exclusivity or the patent had expired. FDA has generally rejected this argument and allowed the generics to carve out the protected information and market the drug without it.[61] In the one instance in which FDA determined

---

56   FDCA § 505(j)(2)(A)(v), 21 U.S.C. § 355(j)(2)(A)(v).

57   21 C.F.R. §§ 314.94(a)(8)(iv), 314.127(a)(7).

58   Zeneca v. Shalala, 213 F.3d 161 (4th Cir. 2000).

59   Id.

60   Bristol-Myers Squibb Co. v. Shalala, 91 F.3d 1493 (D.C. Cir. 1996) (holding that a generic drug manufacturer may omit labeling protected by the three-year exclusivity because the exclusivity would otherwise prevent the approved ANDA from entering the market at all during the three-year period and would expand the scope of the exclusivity beyond that intended by Congress); Sigma-Tau Pharmaceuticals, Inc. v. Schwetz, 288 F.3d 141, 148 n.3 (4th Cir. 2002) (agreeing with the D.C. Circuit's holding in *Bristol-Myers*).

61   *See, e.g.*, Letter from Steven K. Galson, Director, CDER, to Edward John Allere and Theodore Sullivan, Buchanan Ingersoll P.C., Docket No. 2005P-0383 (Dec. 1, 2006) (rejected Savient's argument that omission of protected geriatric use information was inconsistent with FDA's regulations and would render the generic less safe because the generic's label would lack important dosing and safety information for use in geriatric patients that comprise a significant portion of the patient population); Letter from Steven K. Galson, Acting Director, CDER, to David M. Fox, Esq., Hogan and Hartson, Docket No. 2003P-0321 (Apr. 6, 2004) (denied Citizen Petition asking FDA to refrain from approving generic ribavirin with labels that omit protected information regarding the use of ribavirin with PEG-Intron® arguing that generics with labeling for only the non-protected use (ribavirin used in combination with INTRON A®) would result in medication errors for patients prescribed generic ribavirin for use in combination with PEG-Intron® because appropriate dosage information would be missing); Letter from Janet Woodcock, Director, CDER, to Marcy MacDonald, Associate Director, Regulatory Affairs, Apotex Corp., Deborah A. Jaskot, Executive Director, Regulatory

that the protected information could not be omitted from the generic labeling and thus a generic could not be approved until the three-year period expired, FDA found that the protected labeling was critical prescribing information that all physicians should receive to appropriately determine treatment for all indications.[62]

The same labeling requirement has become an impediment in failure-to-warn claims brought by private citizens under state law against generic drug manufacturers. The United States Supreme Court in *PLIVA, Inc. v. Mensing*,[63] held that federal laws and regulations preempted state failure-to-warn claims because it would be impossible for generic manufacturers to fulfill their state-law duties to warn without violating the federal-law requirement that the labeling be the same as the approved brand drug.

For instance, FDA's regulations expressly require the same labeling and do not authorize divergent product warnings. FDA has specifically stated:

> Except for labeling differences under section 505(j)(2)(v) of the act, the ANDA product's labeling must be the same as the listed drug product's labeling because the listed drug product is the basis for ANDA approval. *Consistent labeling will assure physicians, health professionals, and consumers that a generic drug is as safe and effective as its brand-name counterpart.*[64]

Mensing established that FDA's interpretations of these types of regulations are "controlling unless plainly erroneous or inconsistent with the regulations or where there is another reason to doubt that these views reflect FDA's fair and considerate judgments."[65]

Until recently, FDA has stood its ground with respect to these "sameness" labeling requirements. However, just as it has permitted branded drug manufacturers to make certain changes to their labels prior to receiving FDA approval,[66] FDA has proposed new rules that would "allow[] generic drug makers to use the same process as brand drug manufacturers to update safety information in the product labeling."[67] In an effort to "speed the dissemination of new safety information about generic drugs," generic drug manufacturers would be

---

Affairs, Teva Pharmaceuticals, USA, and James F. Hurst, Esq., Winston and Strawn, Docket Nos. 2001P-0495, 2002P-0191, 2002P-0252 (June 11, 2002) (permitted generic applicants to omit from their labeling protected information regarding a 25-mg 16-day titration schedule; rejected brand argument that omission of the protected titration dosing information would decrease efficacy because slower titration increases tolerability); Letter from Janet Woodcock, Director, CDER, to Terry G. Mahn, Esq., Fish and Richardson, PC., Docket No. 2002P-0469 (May 21, 2003) (rejected argument that omission of pediatric information would prevent FDA from ensuring that generics are labeled for safe use in the pediatric population because section 11 of the Best Pharmaceuticals for Children Act would authorize it to include any necessary warnings or precautions in the labeling of the generic).

[62] *See* Letter from Steven K. Galson, Acting Director, CDER to Michael S. Labson and Elizabeth M. Walsh, Counsel for Wyeth Pharmaceuticals, Docket No. 2003P-0518 (Sept. 20, 2004).

[63] 79 U.S.L.W. 4606 (2011).

[64] Krelic v. Mutual Pharms. Co., Inc., C.A. No. GD-08-024513, 161 P.L.J. 329, 332 (emphasis added).

[65] *Id.* (*citing Mensing*, 131 S. Ct. at 2575).

[66] Wyeth v. Levine, 555 U.S. 555, 568 (2009).

[67] Supplemental Applications Proposing Labeling Changes for Approved Drugs and Biological Products, 78 Fed. Reg. 67,985 (Nov. 13, 2013), *available at* https://www.federalregister.gov/articles/2013/11/13/2013-26799/supplemental-applications-proposing-labeling-changes-for-approved-drugs-and-biological-products (last visited Dec. 29, 2014); *see also* FDA News Release, FDA takes action to speed safety information on generic

permitted to "independently update product labeling . . . with newly-acquired safety information before FDA's review of the change."[68] FDA's ultimate decision on these proposed labeling changes could affect both the branded and generic drug label, making sure that the branded and generic drug labeling information ultimately stay the "same" as each other.[69]

Fundamentally, it is unlikely FDA has legal authority to implement these changes. FDA takes the position that the FDCA and the Public Health Service Act provide it with the authority to regulate drug labeling.[70] For example, FDA points to FDCA section 502, which "allows it to consider a drug misbranded if it bears inadequate directions for use or insufficient warnings."[71] Similarly, FDA points to FDCA section 701, which allows it to "regulate CBE supplements and their use."[72] However, one commentator points out that "[t]he 'sameness' requirement that underlies preemption is in the statute, and is unique to generic drugs."[73] As such, FDA may be precluded by the statute from making such rules.[74] Ultimately, the promulgation of the proposed rule could upset the "delicate balance of rights and responsibilities of the brand and generic industry."[75] If nothing else, it would "change the entire regulatory and liability landscape for generic drug manufacturers."[76]

Patent Protection and Exclusivity

Today drug patents have a life of 20 years from the date of first filing of the patent application.[77] Because the U.S. Patent and Trademark Office (PTO) typically takes about one year to issue a patent, the new patent term generally lasts 19 years from the date of issuance. Nevertheless, because patents usually are obtained before a drug has been studied and approved for marketing, the effective patent term of the product is usually significantly less than the 19 or 20 years afforded under the law.

In 1984, when Congress passed Hatch-Waxman, it extended the patent life for drugs to compensate patent holders for time lost while developing their products and awaiting FDA approval. Under this law, approved drug products are eligible for a one-time patent extension of up to five years.[78] The extension period is calculated on the basis of length of time required to study and gain approval of the patented product. The total post-approval patent protection period may not exceed 14 years (e.g., if there are still 12 years left on the

---

drugs (Nov. 8, 2013), *available at* http://www.fda.gov/NewsEvents/Newsroom/PressAnnouncements/ucm374171.htm (last visited Dec. 29, 2014).

[68]   *Id.*

[69]   *Id.*

[70]   Alexander Gaffney, *Experts: FDA's Generic Drug Labeling Rule Likely Illegal,* Regulatory Affairs Professionals Society (Nov. 15, 2013), *available at* http://www.raps.org/regulatoryDetail.aspx?id=9655 (last visited Sept. 18, 2014).

[71]   *Id.*

[72]   *Id.*

[73]   *Id.*

[74]   *Id.*

[75]   *Id.*

[76]   Jennifer M. Thomas, *FDA Proposes a Rule That Would Undercut Generic Drug Preemption,* FDA Law Blog (Nov. 12, 2013), *available at* http://www.fdalawblog.net/fda_law_blog_hyman_phelps/2013/11/fda-proposes-a-rule-that-would-undercut-generic-preemption.html (last visited Sept. 18, 2014).

[77]   35 U.S.C. § 154. Prior to June 8, 1995, the effective date of the Uruguay Rounds Agreement, patents had 17 years of patent life from the date the patent was issued.

[78]   *Id.* § 156(d)(5)(E).

patent post-approval, the extension will be only two years; if there are 14 years left on the patent, no extension will be granted).[79]

Hatch-Waxman also made drug products approved under section 505 of the FDCA eligible for five years of new drug product exclusivity (also called NCE (new chemical entity) exclusivity), and/or three years of exclusivity for certain applications that include clinical data under the same provision of the FDCA.[80]

With regard to the NCE exclusivity, if there is no patent protection, the generic application may not be submitted until five years after the brand is approved, which means that the five-year exclusivity is effectively extended by the time it takes the generic to get approved. (This typically takes more than one year; the median approval time in 2007 was 18.9 months.) If the brand has a patent and the generic challenges the patent (on the grounds that it is not valid, not enforceable, or not infringed), the generic may submit an application four years after approval of the brand, but a timely patent suit by the brand will bar approval for an additional 30 months beyond what would have been the end of the five-year exclusivity period (unless the patent challenge is successful). Under the statute, if the brand files a timely patent suit, it gets a minimum of seven and one-half years of exclusivity.[81] The period will be shortened if before the expiration of the seven-and-one-half-year period, a district court rules that the patent is invalid or was not infringed. (Note: if the brand has a patent that is not challenged and the patent runs longer than the five years of NCE exclusivity, the exclusivity will expire before the patent and provide no additional market protection other than that afforded by a valid patent.)

The three-year period of exclusivity is available for a product that is not an NCE if clinical data is needed to obtain approval of the product.[82] To qualify for this type of exclusivity, a supplement to an application approved under section 505(b) must contain reports of new clinical investigations other than bioavailability studies.[83] This type of exclusivity is granted, for example, for changes to an approved drug product that affect its active ingredient(s), strength, dosage form, route of administration, or conditions of use if clinical investigations were essential to approval of the application or supplemental application containing those changes. In contrast to the five-year exclusivity, which prevents even the submission of an ANDA for four or five years, depending on the circumstances, the three-year exclusivity does not delay submission of an ANDA; it delays only the ANDA's approval. This means that an ANDA can be submitted during the period of exclusivity and be ready for final approval as soon as the period expires. Moreover, a generic may be able to avoid the exclusivity by relying on the original formulation of the RLD. For example, if the exclusivity is based

---

[79]   *Id.* § 156.The law defines drug product to mean the active ingredient of a new drug including any salt or ester of the active ingredient. *Id.* § 156(f). There has been litigation over the precise meaning of drug product. *See, e.g.,* Pfizer v. Dr. Reddy's Labs, Ltd., 359 F.3d 1361 (Fed. Cir. 2004); Glaxo v. Quigg, 894 F.2d 392 (Fed. Cir. 1990); Photocure ASA v. Kappos, 603 F.3d 1372 (Fed. Cir. 2010); Ortho-McNeil Pharm. v. Lupin, 603 F.3d 1377 (Fed. Cir. 2010).

[80]   FDCA §§ 505(c)(3)(E), (j)(5)(F), 21 U.S.C. §§ 355(c)(3)(E), (j)(5)(F); *see also* 21 C.F.R. § 314.108.

[81]   FDCA § 505(j)(5)(F), 21 U.S.C. § 355(j)(5)(F). Thus, if a generic applicant challenges a brand patent in an ANDA filed four years after approval and the brand files suit, the 30-month period becomes a 42-month period during which an ANDA may not be approved. The 42-month period begins to run on the date that is four years after the date of approval of the brand RLD.

[82]   FDCA § 505(j)(5)(F)(iv), 21 U.S.C. § 355(j)(5)(F)(iv).

[83]   *Id.*

on a formulation change, a generic can market the original formulation. Similarly, if the exclusivity is for a new use, the generic can market without the new use on its label. In some circumstances, however, the three-year exclusivity has the effect of blocking generics. For example, when the three-year exclusivity is granted in connection with a switch from prescription to over-the-counter (OTC) status, a generic cannot be approved until the expiration of the three years because the OTC status is protected by the three-year exclusivity.

Historically, FDA has interpreted the term NCE to be "a drug product that does not contain a previously approved active moiety."[84] According to FDA's Exclusivity Summary checklist for a fixed-combination product, if "'*any one* of the active moieties in the drug product' has been previously approved," the three-year exclusivity checklist applies and the drug product is not eligible for the five-year NCE exclusivity.[85] In other words, if "the combination contains one never-before-approved active moiety and one previously approved active moiety," it does not meet the criteria for five-year NCE exclusivity.[86] However, under FDA's "umbrella policy," if the drug product is eligible for five-year NCE exclusivity, then "drug products subsequently developed that contain the same active moiety would also benefit from the original product's 5-year NCE exclusivity until the exclusivity period for the original product expired."[87]

FDA recognizes that fixed-combination drug products "can simplify regimens to allow easier distribution and improved patient adherence," as well as provide "real clinical benefits, including potential increases in efficacy . . . reductions in adverse events and the development of resistance to antimicrobial treatments."[88] In order to incentivize the development of fixed-combination products, FDA has issued a Final Guidance for Industry that recognizes the term "drug" in these provisions to mean "drug substance" or "active ingredient."[89] Under this definition, the "5-year NCE exclusivity determination will be made for each drug substance in a drug product, not for the drug product as a whole."[90] Therefore, a drug product would be "eligible for a 5-year NCE exclusivity, provided that it contains a drug substance that meets the definition of *new chemical entity*, regardless of whether that drug substance is approved alone or in a fixed combination."[91] This change is applied prospectively and, therefore, does not apply to any products that have already been approved.[92]

[84]   See, e.g., Letter from Janet Woodcock, M.D., Director, CDER, to David M. Fox, Hogan Lovells US LLP, Theodore M. Sullivan and Edward J. Allera, Buchanan Ingersoll & Rooney PC, and Joy J. Liu, Ropes & Gray LLP, Docket Nos. 2013-P-0058, 2013-P-0119, 2013-P-0471 (Feb. 21, 2014) (denied Citizen's Petitions requesting FDA change its interpretation of the five-year NCE exclusivity provisions and regulations of implementation related to fixed-combination drug products); FDA Response to Citizens Petitions dated Feb. 21, 2014, at p. 6, available at http://www.duanemorris.com/site/static/Citizen_Petition_Denial_Response_from_FDA_CDER.pdf.
[85]   Id. at 7 (emphasis in original).
[86]   Id.
[87]   Id. at 8.
[88]   Id. at 15.
[89]   FDA, Guidance for Industry: New Chemical Entity Exclusivity Determinations for Certain Fixed-Combination Drug Products (Oct. 2014) available at http://www.fda.gov/downloads/Drugs/GuidanceComplianceRegulatoryInformation/Guidances/UCM386685.pdf.
[90]   Id. at 8.
[91]   Id. at 2.
[92]   Id. at 1.

Another type of exclusivity that is available is orphan drug exclusivity. The first sponsor to gain approval of a drug product that qualifies for orphan designation under section 526 of the FDCA will receive a seven-year period of marketing exclusivity under section 527 of the FDCA.[93] An orphan drug is a drug for a disease or condition that affects fewer than 200,000 persons.[94] This exclusivity applies only to the indication for which the drug has been designated and approved, permitting other applications for the same drug for a new use to be approved. The exclusivity applies broadly, however, to any application for the same drug, which is defined in the regulations generally to mean a drug that contains the same active moiety or the same principal molecular structural features for the same indication.[95] This means that orphan exclusivity will block even the submission of a full NDA for the same product for the protected indication. The one exception is when the sponsor of a drug that is otherwise the same as one that already has orphan-drug approval for the same rare disease or condition can show that its drug is clinically superior.[96]

In 1997, as part of the Food and Drug Administration Modernization Act of 1997 (FDAMA), Congress created a new type of exclusivity, pediatric exclusivity, which awards an additional six months of exclusivity for conducting pediatric studies.[97] In order to qualify for the exclusivity, FDA must request a pediatric study, the study must be conducted in accordance with the request, and FDA must accept the study. Even if the study does not result in a pediatric indication, if it was conducted in accordance with the request, exclusivity will be granted.[98] Pediatric exclusivity attaches to any exclusivity and patent protection listed in the Orange Book for any drug product containing the same active moiety as the drug studied and for which the party submitting the study holds the approved new drug application.[99] When a qualifying pediatric study is conducted prior to approval, pediatric exclusivity will attach to any exclusivity or patent protection listed in the Orange Book upon approval of that unapproved drug.[100]

Patent Listing and Certification

Because an ANDA may generally not be approved until all of the brand patents and relevant exclusivities have expired or have been successfully challenged, an ANDA applicant must include as part of its application a certification with respect to each patent that "claims" the RLD.[101]

Information as to which patents may be infringed if a generic is marketed is provided by the holder of the approval for the referenced listed drug, which, in its original NDA submission, must identify each patent that it believes "claims" the drug for which approval is sought.[102] Once an NDA is approved, FDA is required to "make available to the public" a list containing,

---

93   See 21 U.S.C. §§ 360bb, 360cc.
94   FDCA § 526, 21 U.S.C. § 360bb.
95   21 C.F.R. § 316.3(b)(13).
96   Id. See also 21 C.F.R. §§ 316.24, 316.25.
97   See generally FDCA § 505A, 21 U.S.C. § 355a.
98   Id.
99   FDCA §§ 505A(a), (c), 21 U.S.C. §§ 355a(a), (c).
100 Id.
101 FDCA § 505(j)(2)(A)(vii), 21 U.S.C. § 355(j)(2)(A)(vii).
102 FDCA §§ 505(b)(1), (c)(2), 21 U.S.C. §§ 355(b)(1), (c)(2). Process patents and patents that claim a method of use that is not in the NDA may not be submitted. 21 C.F.R. § 314.53(b).

among other things, patent information pertaining to approved drug products.[103] During the initial Hatch-Waxman rulemaking process, FDA identified the Orange Book, which was already in existence at the time Hatch-Waxman was enacted, as the publication that would be used to meet this statutory obligation.[104] The Orange Book thus provides publicly available, frequently updated information on the patents to which ANDA applicants must certify.[105] Patents listed in the Orange Book generally are referred to as "listed patents."

If an NDA holder is awarded a patent that it believes claims its product after the NDA has already been approved, the NDA holder must submit to FDA supplemental information on the newly issued patent. The holder of an approved NDA has 30 days after issuance of a patent by PTO to submit new patent information to FDA.[106]

The statute provides that "[u]pon the submission of [post-approval] patent information, the Secretary *shall* publish it."[107] With respect to post-approval patents submitted to FDA by an NDA holder, however, the agency will not publish the patent in the Orange Book until the agency determines that the patent submission is substantially complete and contains the information indicating that the patent is eligible for listing; i.e., that the patent "claims" the approved drug.[108] FDA bolstered these requirements in 2003, in response to concerns that NDA holders were submitting eleventh-hour patents to FDA that were ineligible for listing in an effort to delay improperly the onset of generic competition.[109] While FDA does not generally consider as part of its review of patent submissions the substantive patent law question of whether the patent in fact claims the approved drug, it does consider whether the

---

103 FDCA § 505(j)(7)(A), 21 U.S.C. § 355(j)(7)(A).

104 54 Fed. Reg. at 28,876 ("As a general rule, FDA intends to use the list [i.e., the Orange Book] and its supplemental updates as the primary means of announcing information regarding patent status [and] exclusivity . . . ."). *See also* Abbreviated New Drug Application Regulations; Patent and Exclusivity Provisions; Final Rule, 59 Fed. Reg. 50,338, 50,338 (Oct. 3, 1994) (noting that FDA publishes "patent information in its approved drug products list"—i.e., the Orange Book); 21 C.F.R. §§ 314.3, 314.53(e) (defining the Orange Book as "the list" and noting that FDA will publish in "the list" patent information that is required to be submitted to FDA by an NDA applicant or holder).

105 *See* Ranbaxy Labs., Ltd., v. Leavitt, 459 F. Supp. 2d 1, 9-10 (D.D.C. 2006), *aff'd*, 469 F.3d 120 (D.C. Cir. 2006) ("NDA patent information appears in the Orange Book because Congress included in [Hatch-Waxman] a provision requiring the publication of such information to facilitate the new ANDA process."); Merck & Co., Inc. v. Mediplan Health Consulting, Inc., 434 F. Supp. 2d 257, 264 (S.D.N.Y. 2006) (describing the Orange Book as "a catalogue that informs the public of [a] patent's existence"). Until 2005, the Orange Book was available both in "hard copy" and in an electronic format, the latter appearing on FDA's website. The "hard copy" Orange Book was traditionally updated on a monthly basis. 21 C.F.R. § 314.53(e). Before FDA began to update patent information daily via the Electronic Orange Book (EOB), patent information not yet published in the Orange Book was made available to the public by FDA's Freedom of Information staff. *Id.* Today the Orange Book is only available electronically at www.fda.gov/cder/ob, and patent information contained in the EOB is updated daily. FDA, Frequently Asked Questions about the Orange Book, *available at* http://www.fda.gov/Drugs/InformationOnDrugs/ucm114166.htm.

106 FDCA § 505(c)(2), 21 U.S.C. § 355(c)(2).

107 *Id.* (emphasis added).

108 21 C.F.R. § 314.53(c)(1); Applications for FDA Approval to Market a New Drug: Patent Submission and Listing Requirements and Application of 30-Month Stays on Approval of Abbreviated New Drug Applications Certifying That a Patent Claiming a Drug Is Invalid or Will Not Be Infringed; Final Rule, 68 Fed. Reg. 36,676, 36,687 (June 18, 2003).

109 *See generally* FTC Report, *supra* note 6 at iii-v (detailing concerns about post-approval patents).

NDA holder has provided the requisite "complete" documentation under FDA regulations in support of an Orange Book listing.[110]

An ANDA applicant that must certify to a patent claiming the RLD may submit to FDA one of four types of certifications with respect to that patent: a "paragraph I" certification asserting that patent information (for the relevant patent) has not been filed,[111] a "paragraph II" certification asserting that the relevant patent has expired,[112] a "paragraph III" certification stating that the relevant patent will expire on a date certain,[113] or a "paragraph IV" certification asserting that the patent is invalid, unenforceable or will not be infringed by the drug for which ANDA approval is sought.[114] With respect to any patent that has been listed in the Orange Book before the filing of the ANDA, the ANDA applicant's certification must appear in the original ANDA. With respect to patents added by the NDA holder after the submission of the ANDA, the ANDA holder must file a supplement to its application containing the appropriate certification, unless the patent was not listed in a timely manner.[115] Where the ANDA applicant has filed a paragraph III certification including the patent expiration date, the ANDA will not be approved until all of the paragraph III listed patents have expired. An ANDA applicant may convert its certification if it chooses to do so. For example, an applicant can convert from a paragraph III to paragraph IV certification or vice versa based on changes in circumstances or strategy.

If an ANDA applicant wishes to challenge the validity or enforceability of the patent or to assert that the patent will not be infringed by the product in the ANDA, the applicant must submit a paragraph IV certification to FDA. Although some applicants have served "preemptive" notice letters, FDA's position, with support from the courts, is that the applicant also must provide notice to the NDA holder and patent owner stating that the application has been submitted and explaining the factual and legal basis for the applicant's opinion that the patent is invalid, not infringed, or not enforceable, once the applicant received notice of "acceptance" of the ANDA filing from FDA.[116] Upon notification from the ANDA applicant that it has submitted to FDA a paragraph IV certification challenging the NDA holder's patent, the NDA holder may commence patent infringement litigation against the ANDA applicant—a process that the framers of Hatch-Waxman had intended would lead to the swift resolution of brand-generic patent disputes.[117] By commencing such litigation within 45 days of receiving the notice, the patent holder can trigger a 30-month stay of FDA

---

[110]   21 C.F.R. § 314.53(c)(1) ("We will not accept the patent information unless it is complete and submitted on the appropriate forms . . . .").

[111]   FDCA § 505(j)(2)(A)(vii)(I), 21 U.S.C. § 355(j)(2)(A)(vii)(I).

[112]   FDCA § 505(j)(2)(A)(vii)(II), 21 U.S.C. § 355(j)(2)(A)(vii)(II).

[113]   FDCA § 505(j)(2)(A)(vii)(III), 21 U.S.C. § 355(j)(2)(A)(vii)(III).

[114]   FDCA § 505(j)(2)(A)(vii)(IV), 21 U.S.C. § 355(j)(2)(A)(vii)(IV).

[115]   FDCA § 505(j)(2)(A)(vii), 21 U.S.C. § 355(j)(2)(A)(vii); 21 C.F.R. §§ 314.94(a)(12)(i), (vi). If the patent was not submitted to FDA within the statutory time frame (30 days from issuance), FDA regulations permit ANDA applicants to disregard the new patent listing and to avoid amending the ANDA with regard to the late-listed patent. 21 C.F.R. § 314.94(a)(12)(vi).

[116]   FDCA §§ 505(b)(2), (j)(2)(B), 21 U.S.C. §§ 355(b)(2), (j)(2)(B); *See* SB Pharmco Puerto Rico, Inc. v. Mutual Pharm. Co., 552 F. Supp. 2d 500 (E.D. Pa. 2008); Merck & Cie v. Watson Pharms., Inc., C.A. No. 12-161-RGA (D. Del. Sept. 25, 2012); and Otsuka Pharm. Co. v. Par Pharm., Inc., C.A. No. 13-1979 (RGA) (D. Del. Mar. 10, 2014). If FDA has already "accepted" the ANDA for filing, then the applicant must send the notice letter at the same time as the amended certification to FDA.

[117]   Apotex, Inc. v. Thompson, 347 F.3d 1335, 1338 (Fed. Cir. 2003) (paragraph IV process a "streamlined mechanism" created to "facilitate judicial resolution" of patent infringement claims). *See also In re* Barr Labs.,

approval of the ANDA.[118] As discussed below, under certain conditions, the 30-month stay of approval may be terminated, shortened, or even extended.[119]

Further, where an ANDA applicant believes that patent information in the Orange Book needs to be corrected or deleted, an applicant may assert a counterclaim under section 505(j)(5)(C)(ii)(I) of the FDCA.[120] Such a counterclaim is known as a "delisting" counterclaim. According to the United States Supreme Court, a delisting counterclaim may be employed "to force correction of a use code that inaccurately describes the brand's patent as covering a particular method of using the drug in question."[121]

Extension or Termination of the 30-Month Stay

The 30-month stay of approval that is triggered by the timely filing of a patent infringement suit can be terminated, and approval of an ANDA may be made effective as of:

- the date that the district court enters judgment reflecting its decision that the patent at issue is invalid or not infringed; or

- the date of a settlement order or consent decree signed and entered by the district court stating that the patent that is the subject of the certification is invalid or not infringed; or

- if the district court decides that the patent has been infringed and this decision is reversed on appeal, the date on which the court of appeals decides that the patent is invalid or not infringed or the date of a settlement order or consent decree that is signed and entered by the court of appeals stating that the patent is invalid or not infringed.[122]

The court may shorten or lengthen the 30-month period if either party fails to cooperate in expediting the litigation.[123] The 30-month stay will be extended if the court grants a preliminary injunction prior to the end of the 30-month stay prohibiting the ANDA

Inc., 930 F.2d 72, 76 (D.C. Cir. 1991) (purpose of Hatch-Waxman was "to get generic drugs into the hands of patients at reasonable prices—fast").

[118]   FDCA §§ 505(c)(3)(C), (j)(5)(B), 21 U.S.C. §§ 355(c)(3)(C), (j)(5)(B).

[119]   Id.

[120]   21 U.S.C. § 355(j)(5)(C)(ii)(I).

[121]   Caraco Pharm. Labs., Ltd. v. Novo Nordisk A/S, 80 U.S.L.W. 4324, 4327 (2012).

[122]   FDCA §§ 505(c)(3)(C), (j)(5)(B)(iii), 21 U.S.C. §§ 355(c)(3)(C), (j)(5)(B)(iii); FDA's Draft Guidance for Industry on Listed Drugs, 30-Month Stays, and Approval of Abbreviated New Drug Applications and 505(b)(2) Applications Under Hatch-Waxman, as Amended by the Medicare Prescription Drug Improvements and Modernization Act of 2003—Questions and Answers [hereinafter FDA Draft MMA Guidance]. In its initial regulations implementing Hatch-Waxman, FDA interpreted "court" to mean "the court that enters final judgment from which no appeal can be or has been taken," which is a final decision by a federal circuit court of appeals. Abbreviated New Drug Application Regulations: Patent and Exclusivity Provisions; Final Rule, 59 Fed. Reg. 50,338, 50,352-50,354 (Oct. 3, 1994). This interpretation was challenged and the court ruled that the 30-month stay expires upon a district court decision finding a patent invalid, unenforceable, or not infringed. TorPharm, Inc. v. Shalala, No. 97-1925, 1997 U.S. Dist. LEXIS 21983 (D.D.C. Sept. 15, 1997), appeal withdrawn and remanded, 1998 U.S. App. LEXIS 4681 (D.C. Cir. Feb. 5, 1998); vacated No. 97-1925 (D.C.C. Apr. 9, 1998). FDA subsequently issued a guidance adopting the TorPharm court's decision and defined "court" to mean the first court to render a decision finding the patent at issue invalid, unenforceable, or not infringed. See FDA, Guidance for Industry on Court Decisions, ANDA Approvals, and 180-Day Exclusivity Under the Hatch-Waxman Amendments to the Federal Food, Drug and Cosmetic Act (March 2000). When Congress amended the law as part of MMA, it specifically described the circumstances under which the 30-month stay would terminate. MMA, Title XI, section 1101(a)(2).

[123]   FDCA §§ 505(c)(3)(C), (j)(5)(B)(iii), 21 U.S.C. §§ 355(c)(3)(C), (j)(5)(B)(iii).

applicant from marketing the drug until the court decides the issues of patent validity and infringement.[124]

If the district court hearing the infringement suit decides that the patent at issue is infringed and this decision is not appealed or is affirmed on appeal, the ANDA will not be approved prior to the patent's expiration and any extension or exclusivity that remains.[125]

Multiple 30-Month Stays

As discussed above, Hatch-Waxman provided for a 30-month stay of FDA approval of an ANDA if a brand company files suit for patent infringement within 45 days of receiving notice of the ANDA's paragraph IV certification. Pursuant to FDA's initial interpretation of the act, multiple 30-month stays were possible. For example, an ANDA application that already had been subject to one 30-month stay based on a paragraph IV certification to a patent listed before the ANDA was filed could be subject to additional 30-month stays if the applicant filed a subsequent paragraph IV certification to a patent listed after the application's submission and that subsequent certification triggered another timely filed patent infringement suit.[126] A 2002 FTC report found that after 1998 there was a substantial increase in the number of patents being submitted to FDA after an ANDA had been filed and that these later-listed patents were resulting in multiple 30-month stays and additional delays to generic approval.[127] Even more disturbing was the finding that most of these late-listed patents ultimately were found to be invalid or not infringed. FTC concluded that some brand companies were filing questionable patents and delaying generic approval.[128]

In June 2003, FDA issued regulations that permitted only one 30-month stay per ANDA.[129] Several months later, Congress passed the MMA, which amended Hatch-Waxman to preclude most multiple 30-month stays for applications with paragraph IV certifications to patents submitted to FDA after August 13, 2003 (the effective date).[130] Specifically, MMA precludes 30-month stays for patents submitted to FDA after the date an ANDA is submitted.[131] There is still the possibility of multiple 30-month stays with regard to patents that were submitted before the ANDA, if the ANDA applicant amends one of its patent certifications. For example, if an ANDA applicant converts a paragraph III certification to a patent that was submitted to FDA before the ANDA was filed, then a second 30-month stay

---

[124]   *Id.*

[125]   *Id.*, FDA Draft MMA Guidance, *supra* note 122.

[126]   *See* Applications for FDA Approval to Market a New Drug: Patent Listing Requirements and Application of 30-Month Stays on Approval of Abbreviated New Drug Applications Certifying That a Patent Claiming the Drug Is Invalid or Will Not Be Infringed; Proposed Rule, 67 Fed. Reg. 65,448, 65,454-55 (Oct. 24, 2002); FDA Draft MMA Guidance, *supra* note 122.

[127]   FTC Report, *supra* note 6 at iii-iv, 36 and 45.

[128]   *Id.*

[129]   68 Fed. Reg. 36,676.

[130]   MMA, tit. XI, §§ 1101(a)(2)(A)(ii)(I), 1101(b).

[131]   *Id. See also* FDA Draft MMA Guidance, *supra* note 122. Following passage of MMA, FDA revoked its regulatory provision regarding 30-month stays on the basis that it was superseded by the MMA provision. Application of 30-Month Stays on Approval of Abbreviated New Drug Applications and Certain New Drug Applications Containing a Certification Certifying That a Patent Claiming the Drug is Invalid or Will Not Be Infringed; Technical Amendment, 69 Fed. Reg. 11,309 (Mar. 10, 2004).

is possible. Thus, after the MMA, the possibility of multiple 30-month stays is largely within the control of the applicant.[132]

180-Day Generic Drug Exclusivity

As an incentive for generic companies to initiate challenges, through paragraph IV certifications, to suspect brand company patents, Hatch-Waxman awards 180 days of market exclusivity to the generic applicant that is the first to submit a substantially complete ANDA containing a paragraph IV certification with respect to a patent that the NDA holder asserts claims the referenced brand drug. During this period no other ANDA with a paragraph IV certification for the same drug can be approved. Hatch-Waxman exclusivity is an extremely valuable incentive for generic companies to bring paragraph IV challenges to brand company patents. The success rate of generic company paragraph IV challenges has been quite high,[133] and numerous generic companies have earned significant profits as a result of exclusivity awards arising out of these challenges.[134] Because of the considerable value of Hatch-Waxman exclusivity, ANDA applicants aggressively vie for the position of "first-filer" of paragraph IV certifications in cases in which such certifications are deemed appropriate.

For example, until FDA issued a guidance clarifying that any ANDA applicant that submitted a paragraph IV certification on the first day that such certifications are appropriate would be entitled to a share of exclusivity, representatives of ANDA applicants lined up outside FDA for days or even weeks in advance in an effort to be the first paragraph IV filer with respect to a particular patent.[135] In 2003, FDA put an end to this practice by declaring that two or more same-day paragraph IV certifications to the same patent will share exclusivity.[136]

Another example of ANDA applicants aggressively vying for the position of first-filer relates to a practice that has been adopted when the Patent and Trademark Office grants a patent application that arguably covers a drug for which FDA has approved an NDA but for which no patents are listed in the Orange Book and the exclusivity period has expired. If the

---

132 *See* FDA Draft MMA Guidance, *supra* note 122.

133 *See* FTC Report, *supra* note 6 at 16 (noting that paragraph IV challenges leading to actual patent litigation have resulted in victory for the generic company in 73 percent of cases). Of course, the generic company also effectively prevails when no lawsuit is filed.

134 Mylan Pharms., Inc., 454 F.3d at 273 ("The 180-day exclusivity period . . . is a significant boon to the recipient.").

135 *See* FDA, Guidance for Industry: 180-Day Exclusivity When Multiple ANDAs Are Submitted on the Same Day (July 2003) *available at* http://www.fda.gov/downloads/Drugs/GuidanceComplianceRegulatoryInformation/Guidances/ucm072851.pdf.

136 *Id.* FDA also has addressed the situation in which different ANDA applicants were first to submit patent challenges as to *different* listed patents such that each applicant ends up blocking the other applicant[s] with its exclusivity creating an "exclusivity standoff" in which no application can be approved. Under these circumstances, FDA has adopted the shared exclusivity approach. Pursuant to this approach, when different applicants have submitted first paragraph IV ANDAs for different listed patents, resulting in mutually blocking exclusivities, each is eligible to share a single 180-day period of exclusivity. The eligible first paragraph IV ANDAs cannot block each other. The 180 days will begin to run for all eligible ANDAs sharing in the exclusivity when it begins to run for any one of the eligible ANDAs. *See, e.g.,* Letter from Gary Buehler, Director, FDA Office of Generic Drugs to Marcy Macdonald, U.S. Agent for Torpharm (July 30, 2003) (Re: Shared Exclusivity for Paroxetine Hydrochloride Tablets, ANDA 75-356); Letter from Gary Buehler, Director, FDA Office of Generic Drugs to Diane Servello, Andrx Pharmaceuticals, Inc. (Nov. 16, 2001) (Re: Shared Exclusivity for Omeprazole, ANDA 75-347).

NDA holder then asks FDA to list the newly issued patent, the ANDA applicant who is the first to certify against that patent receives the 180-day exclusivity. These types of patents are commonly known as "pop-up" patents. Although the ANDA holder can determine that a patent has been issued by the PTO, it cannot know when the NDA holder will actually submit the patent to FDA. FDA ultimately lists the patent in the Orange Book but this presumably happens some time after it has been submitted. In an effort to ensure that they are first filers, generic companies have adopted the practice of submitting to FDA daily paragraph IV certifications to a relevant patent once the patent has been issued by the PTO, stopping these daily submissions only after the patent is actually listed by FDA in the Orange Book. This approach is based on the generic companies' assumption that one of its paragraph IV certifications, though it does not know which one, will reach FDA on the first day that the certifications will be deemed effective by FDA and will therefore give rise to partial or full generic exclusivity.

Once a first filer has been identified by FDA, subsequent ANDA applicants cannot be approved until the 180-day period has expired.[137] A big question that both FDA and the courts have struggled with over the years is when the 180-day period actually begins; i.e., what triggers the start of the 180-day period. The answer to the question is of critical importance to those other ANDA applicants waiting to get on the market. The sooner the 180-day period begins, the sooner they can get on the market. As discussed below, the answer to the question has changed several times, and Congress sought to clarify the issue in the MMA.

Prior to the MMA, the FDCA provided that the 180-day exclusivity period was triggered by the earlier of the first commercial marketing of the generic drug for which the first ANDA was submitted or the first court decision holding the patent that was the subject of the paragraph IV certification invalid or not infringed.[138] Although FDA had interpreted "court decision" to mean the final decision from which no appeal can be or has been taken,[139] the D.C. district court overruled that interpretation and held that the "court decision" that could begin the running of the 180-day period may be the decision of the district court that the patent at issue is unenforceable or will not be infringed, even if the decision is appealed.[140] The rationale for FDA's initial interpretation was that the generic exclusivity would be significantly devalued if the generic manufacturer had to market at the risk of being subject to treble damages if the appeals court ruled in favor of the patent holder, and that Congress could not have intended this result.[141] Nevertheless, FDA adopted the D.C. district court's position.[142] The practical effect of that interpretation was that many generics chose not to market at risk and lost the benefit of the 180-day exclusivity, which ran during the pendency of an appeal.[143]

---

[137]   FDCA § 505(j)(5)(B)(iv), 21 U.S.C. § 355(j)(5)(B)(iv).

[138]   *See* Mylan Pharmaceuticals, Inc. v. Shalala, 81 F. Supp. 2d 30, 33 (D.D.C. 2000).

[139]   59 Fed. Reg. at 50,354-55.

[140]   Mylan Pharmaceuticals, Inc., 81 F. Supp. 2d 30.

[141]   59 Fed. Reg. at 50,354-55.

[142]   FDA, Guidance for Industry: Court Decisions, ANDA Approvals, and 180-Day Exclusivity Under the Hatch-Waxman Amendments to the Federal Food, Drug, and Cosmetic Act (Mar. 2000) *available at* http://www.fda.gov/downloads/Drugs/GuidanceComplianceRegulatoryInformation/Guidances/ucm072868.pdf.

[143]   In cases where there was no court decision and the first applicant did not begin commercial marketing, there could be prolonged or indefinite delays in the beginning of the running of the 180-day period and thus delays in the approval of any other ANDAs with an end result of no generic competition. The FTC

The MMA revised the precise conditions under which FDA can approve subsequent ANDAs. For paragraph IV ANDAs filed after the date of enactment of MMA (December 8, 2003), a court decision will no longer trigger the period of 180-day exclusivity. Instead, as discussed below, a court decision can be a forfeiture event. For ANDAs with paragraph IV certifications filed before December 8, 2003, a court decision can still trigger exclusivity. If the exclusivity was not already triggered before December 8, 2003, the triggering court decision is one from which no appeal has been or can be taken, other than a petition to the Supreme Court for a writ of certiorari.[144]

Although post-MMA court decisions no longer trigger the running of the 180-day exclusivity period, the law added provisions to ensure that first filers cannot block subsequent ANDA approvals by delaying the commercial marketing of their product.[145] Specifically, MMA sought to address the potential for blocking generic competition by adding provisions pursuant to which the first to file can forfeit its right to 180 days of exclusivity. The MMA added six possible forfeiture events.[146] With the exception of the fifth forfeiture event (regarding agreements that violate the antitrust laws), these forfeiture events apply only to ANDAs filed after the effective date of the MMA (December 8, 2003) certifying to patents for which no paragraph IV certification had been made in any ANDA before December 8, 2003. The collusive agreement forfeiture provision applies to ANDAs filed after December 8, 2003, regardless of when the first paragraph IV certification was made for the RLD.

Under the first forfeiture event, a first applicant will forfeit its 180 days if it fails to market its product by the later of (aa) 75 days after approval of the first ANDA or 30 months after the submission of the first ANDA, whichever is earlier, or (bb) the date that is 75 days after at least one of the following occurs: a court enters a final decision that the patent is invalid or not infringed, a court signs a settlement order or consent decree entering final judgment that includes a finding that the patent is invalid or not infringed, or the patent information for the listed drug is withdrawn by the NDA holder.[147] In a decision regarding Teva's eligibility for 180-day exclusivity in connection with its ANDA for granisetron hydrochloride, FDA determined that a failure-to-market forfeiture event could not occur if none of the events in the second subpart (bb) has occurred.[148] In a subsequent decision, FDA determined that the first filer, Cobalt Pharmaceuticals, did forfeit its 180-day exclusivity by failing to market by the later of (aa) September 22, 2007 (which was 30 months after it submitted its ANDA) or (bb) April 16, 2007 (which was the date that the NDA holder requested that the patent information be withdrawn from the Orange Book).[149]

---

report found instances of brand companies and first generic applicants entering agreements pursuant to which the generic agreed not to go to market. *See* FTC Report, *supra* note 6 at vii. As discussed below, MMA added provisions aimed at addressing this problem. *See* MMA, tit. XI, § 1102(b)(3).

[144] *See* MMA, tit. XI, § 1102(b)(3) (defining, for this purpose, "decision of a court" as used in section 505(j)(5) (B)(iv) of the act).

[145] As stated above, under the pre-MMA exclusivity provision, in a situation where there was not a court decision and the first applicant did not begin commercial marketing, there could be prolonged or indefinite delays in the beginning of the running of the 180-day period and thus delays in the approval of any other ANDAs during which there would be no generic competition.

[146] FDCA § 505(j)(5)(D), 21 U.S.C. § 355(j)(5)(D).

[147] FDCA § 505(j)(5)(D)(i)(I), 21 U.S.C. § 355(j)(5)(D)(i)(I).

[148] *See* Letter from Gary Buehler, Director, FDA Office of Generic Drugs to Marc A. Goshko, Teva North America, Docket No. 2007N-0389 (Jan. 17, 2008).

[149] *See* Letter from Gary Buehler, Director, FDA Office of Generic Drugs to William A. Rakoczy, Esq., Docket No. 2007N-0445 (May 8, 2008). Following that decision FDA approved Roxane's ANDAs for acarbose.

The second potential forfeiture event is the first applicant's withdrawal of its ANDA.[150] FDA can consider the ANDA withdrawn if it determines that the application does not meet the requirements for approval.[151] If the first applicant changes its paragraph IV certification (by withdrawing or amending its certification for all patents with respect to which it submitted a certification qualifying it for the 180 days), it will forfeit the 180-day exclusivity.[152] Under the fourth forfeiture event, a first applicant forfeits its 180 days of exclusivity if it fails to obtain tentative approval within 30 months of filing its application, unless the failure is caused by a change in or a review of the requirements for approval of the application imposed after the date on which the application was filed.[153]

A first applicant will forfeit its 180-day exclusivity if it enters into an agreement with the brand company that is found to violate antitrust law.[154] FDA recently was asked to find that Cobalt Pharmaceuticals was not entitled to 180-day exclusivity because it had entered into a settlement with the brand company, King Pharmaceuticals. FDA denied the request on the grounds that there was no final, unappealable order finding that the terms of the agreement violate antitrust law, as required by the law.[155] Finally, the 180-day exclusivity period will be lost if the qualifying patents expire.[156]

Because the 180-day exclusivity is so valuable and there are so many different and complicated factors at play when it comes to determining whether it has been forfeited, FDA has been interpreting the application of these forfeiture events on a case-by-case basis and has been establishing dockets for the purpose of soliciting comment from all interested parties as potential forfeiture issues arise.[157]

FDA has had the opportunity to address some of the issues raised by these new provisions, but it has yet to see or address all possible scenarios. For example, FDA has addressed the question of whether a forfeiture event occurs if an applicant fails to market its product due to the fact that it was blocked from approval by an unexpired patent or period of exclusivity. In that instance, FDA found that the first ANDA applicant, Hi-Tech, had forfeited its 180-day exclusivity for a generic form of COSOPT® opthalmic solution because the statute's "failure to market" forfeiture provision does not contain any qualifying language that would stay or toll the forfeiture provision due to circumstances outside of the applicant's control. Of

---

Cobalt unsuccessfully sought to stop the marketing of Roxane's products, but the D.C. district court declined to issue a temporary restraining order on the grounds that FDA's decision was likely to be upheld. Cobalt Laboratories v. FDA, No. 08CV798 (D.D.C.). Subsequently, Cobalt voluntarily dismissed the case.

[150] FDCA § 505(j)(5)(D)(i)(II), 21 U.S.C. § 355(j)(5)(D)(i)(II).

[151] *Id.*

[152] FDCA § 505(j)(5)(D)(i)(III), 21 U.S.C. § 355(j)(5)(D)(i)(III).

[153] FDCA § 505(j)(5)(D)(i)(IV), 21 U.S.C. § 355(j)(5)(D)(i)(IV).

[154] FDCA § 505(j)(5)(D)(i)(V), 21 U.S.C. § 355(j)(5)(D)(i)(V).

[155] *See* Letter from Gary Buehler, Director, FDA Office of Generic Drugs to Carmen M. Shepard and Kate C. Beardsley, Buc and Beardsley, Docket No. 2007N-0382 (Jan. 29, 2008). FDA also rejected the argument that a subsequent ANDA applicant should be permitted to change its paragraph IV certification after a final court decision finding the patent invalid and thus avoid being blocked by Cobalt's 180-day exclusivity. FDA requires unexpired patents to remain in the Orange Book until the end of the patent term or the end of the 180-day exclusivity, whichever occurs first so that the protection offered by the 180-day exclusivity cannot be undermined by changes from paragraph IV certifications. 21 C.F.R. § 314.94(a)(12)(viii). *See also* 59 Fed. Reg. 50,338, 50,348 (Oct. 3, 1994).

[156] 21 U.S.C. § 355(j)(5)(D)(i)(VI).

[157] *See, e.g.,* Docket Nos. 2007N-0382, 2007N-0389, 2007N-0417.

course, the interpretation and impact of these forfeiture provisions will continue to evolve over time.

Authorized Generics

The term "authorized generic" is generally used to describe an instance when an NDA holder, in the face of pending generic competition, markets a generic version of its own product.[158] Prior FDA approval is not needed for the NDA holder to market an authorized generic because the product has already been approved under the NDA. Moreover, because generic drug 180-day exclusivity only blocks approval of ANDAs for which paragraph IV certifications have been submitted, the courts have held that it does not block an authorized generic (which is really another version of the drug approved in the NDA) from entering the market.[159]

The marketing of authorized generics has been controversial. Although the brand industry argues that the additional competition lowers generic drug prices, generic manufacturers argue that in some cases the decreased profits caused by the marketing of authorized generics will deter generic manufacturers from challenging patents.[160] The generic companies also argue that the marketing of authorized generics is inconsistent with congressional intent because it devalues the exclusivity Congress gave to generic companies willing to challenge questionable patents.[161]

In 2006 and 2007, following requests from several Senators and Congressman Waxman, the Federal Trade Commission (FTC) announced that it would conduct a study on the short- and long-term competitive effects of authorized generics.[162] FDAAA includes a provision that requires FDA to compile and update quarterly a database of authorized generics and to provide that information to FTC and the Centers for Medicare and Medicaid Services.[163] The provision is intended to assist FTC's study on the impact of authorized generics.

Declaratory Judgment Actions

The MMA added a provision to the ANDA statutory provisions expressly authorizing declaratory judgment actions.[164] This new subparagraph, entitled "Civil Action to Obtain Patent Certainty," provides that an ANDA applicant may bring a civil action for a declaratory judgment that the patent at issue is invalid or will not be infringed by the ANDA applicant if the patentee or NDA holder does not bring an infringement action within 45 days after receiving notice of a paragraph IV certification.[165] The MMA also amended the companion patent statute to provide that in a civil action to obtain patent certainty, federal courts

---

[158] *See* Mylan Pharmaceuticals, Inc. v. FDA, 454 F.3d 270 (4th Cir. 2006); Teva Pharm. Indus. v. FDA, 410 F.3d 51 (D.C. Cir. 2005).

[159] *See* Mylan Pharmaceuticals, Inc., 454 F.3d at 276; Teva Pharm. Indus., 410 F.3d at 55.

[160] *See* Federal Trade Commission Information Collection Notice, 72 Fed. Reg. 25,304, 25,305 (May 4, 2007) and Federal Trade Commission Information Collection Notice, 71 Fed. Reg. 16,779, 16,780 (Apr. 4, 2006).

[161] 72 Fed. Reg. at 25,305; 71 Fed. Reg. at 16,780.

[162] *See* 72 Fed. Reg. at 25,305 (referring to Letters from Senators Grassley, Leahy, and Rockefeller and Representative Henry Waxman to Chairman Deborah Platt Majoras); 71 Fed. Reg. 16,779.

[163] FDAAA, tit. IX, § 920; 21 U.S.C. § 355(t).

[164] MMA, tit. XI, § 1101.

[165] FDCA § 505(j)(5)(C), 21 U.S.C. § 355(j)(5)(C).

"shall, to the extent consistent with the Constitution, have subject matter jurisdiction for a declaratory judgment action."[166] According to the legislative history of the MMA, Congress added this provision to level the playing field. Hatch-Waxman provided that patent owners and NDA holders may bring patent infringement suits against an ANDA applicant immediately upon receiving notice that the applicant is challenging the patent. The MMA provision simply clarifies that the generic applicant may also seek prompt resolution of these patent issues by bringing a declaratory judgment action if not sued within 45 days.[167]

Since enactment of the MMA, generic companies have filed lawsuits that test the limits of the new declaratory judgment provision. The Supreme Court addressed the issue in *MedImmune, Inc. v. Genentech, Inc.*, where the Court rejected the federal circuit's longstanding "reasonable apprehension of suit" test, holding that "Article III jurisdiction may be met where the patentee takes a position that puts the declaratory judgment plaintiff in the position of either pursuing arguably illegal behavior or abandoning that which claims a right to do."[168] The dispute must be "definite and concrete, touching the legal relations of parties having adverse legal interests" and "be real and substantial."[169]

The federal circuit subsequently opined that the *MedImmune* decision had changed the landscape, in a decision that requires a declaratory judgment plaintiff to satisfy only Article III of the Constitution by showing under all of the circumstances an actual or imminent injury caused by the defendant that can be redressed by judicial relief and that is of sufficient immediacy and reality to warrant the issuance of a declaratory judgment.[170] The Federal Circuit cited the MMA legislative history in which Congress states: "[W]e fully expect that in almost all situations where a generic applicant has challenged a patent by filing a paragraph IV certification and not been sued for patent infringement, a claim by the generic applicant seeking declaratory judgment will give rise to a justiciable case or controversy under the Constitution. The only circumstance in which a case or controversy might not exist is in the rare instance when a patent owner or brand company has given the generic a covenant not to sue or otherwise formally acknowledged that the generic applicant drug does not infringe."[171] Additional cases that have been decided since *MedImmune* and *Teva* illustrate that the determination is fact-specific and the courts will determine jurisdiction on a case-by-case basis.[172]

---

[166]   35 U.S.C. § 271(e)(5).

[167]   149 CONG. REC. S15,885 (Nov. 25, 2003) (remarks of Senator Kennedy, ranking member of the Senate Committee on Health, Education, Labor, and Pensions).

[168]   MedImmune, Inc. v. Genentech, Inc., 549 U.S. 118 (2007).

[169]   Id.

[170]   Teva Pharmaceuticals USA, Inc. v. Novartis Pharmaceuticals Corp. 482 F.3d 1330 (Fed. Cir. 2007).

[171]   Id. at 1343.

[172]   See, e.g., Pfizer Inc. v. Ranbaxy Laboratories Ltd., 525 F. Supp. 2d 680 (D. Del. 2007); Janssen Pharmaceutica, N.V. v. Apotex, Inc., No. 06-1020, 2007 U.S. Dist. LEXIS 75967 (D.N.J. Oct. 11, 2007); Rite Aid Corp. v. Purdue Pharma, L.P., No. 06-15304, 2007 U.S. Dist. LEXIS 61583 (S.D.N.Y. Aug. 21, 2007).

Antitrust Issues Raised By Settlements between Brand and Generic Companies

A relatively recent trend in the generics arena has been patent litigation settlements between a brand company and a generic company. In the late 1990s, FTC challenged several such agreements as being anticompetitive, and their use diminished.[173]

In 2003, the MMA included a provision that requires pharmaceutical companies to file certain agreements with FTC and the Department of Justice.[174] On June 17, 2013, the United States Supreme Court weighed in with its opinion in *FTC v. Actavis, Inc.*[175] In *Actavis, Inc.*, the FTC filed an antitrust complaint against a brand-name manufacturer of AndroGel, alleging that the manufacturer's reverse payment settlement agreements with certain generic drug manufacturers were unlawful agreements not to compete in violation of the Federal Trade Commission Act.[176] The Eleventh Circuit dismissed the FTC's complaint, and the United States Supreme Court reversed, finding that, while reverse payment settlement agreements are not per se lawful, in some instances they may violate antitrust laws.[177] Specifically, the Court held that:

> [A] reverse payment, where large and unjustified, can bring with it the risk of significant anticompetitive effects; one who makes such a payment may be unable to explain and to justify it; such a firm or individual may well possess market power derived from the patent; a court, by examining the size of the payment, may well be able to assess its likely anticompetitive effects along with its potential justifications without litigating the validity of the patent; and parties may well find ways to settle patent disputes without the use of reverse payments.[178]

Citizen Petitions Challenging ANDA Approvals

FDA regulations provide that any person (including a corporation) may file a "Citizen Petition" with the agency seeking FDA action or inaction on any issue before FDA.[179] The origin of Citizen Petitions is rooted in genuine concerns for the health and safety of the

---

[173] *See* Prepared Statement of the Federal Trade Commission Before the Subcommittee on Commerce, Trade, and Consumer Protection, Committee on Energy and Commerce, United States House of Representatives on Protecting Consumer Access to Generic Drugs: The Benefits of a Legislative Solution to Anticompetitive Patent Settlements in the Pharmaceutical Industry (May 2, 2007) [hereinafter FTC May 2007 House Testimony], *available at* http://www.ftc.gov/sites/default/files/documents/public_statements/ prepared-statement-federal-trade-commission-protecting-consumer-access-generic-drugs-benefits/ p85991020protecting_consume_20access_testimony.pdf; Prepared Statement of the Federal Trade Commission Before the Committee on The Judiciary of the United States Senate on Anticompetitive Patent Settlements in the Pharmaceutical Industry: The Benefits of a Legislative Solution (Jan. 17, 2007) [hereinafter FTC January 2007 Senate Testimony], *available at* http://www.ftc.gov//speeches/ leibowitz/070117anticompetitivepatentsettlements_senate.pdf.

[174] MMA, tit. XI, § 1112.

[175] 133 S. Ct. 2223 (2013).

[176] FTC v. Watson Pharms., Inc., 677 F.3d 1298, 1304-05 (11th Cir. 2012), rev'd 81 U.S.L.W. 4455 (2013).

[177] *Id.* at 2227.

[178] *Id.* at 2237.

[179] 21 C.F.R. §§ 10.25, 10.30.

American people. Citizen Petitions, which may be filed by a citizen or corporation, are a means of requesting administrative action by FDA.

Both FDA and FTC have found, however, that brand companies sometimes use the Citizen Petition process to delay generic drug approvals and thereby prolong the life-cycle of brand-manufacturer's drugs.[180] Some commentators argue that the process is "susceptible to systemic abuse . . . It is no coincidence that brand companies often file these petitions at the eleventh hour before generic entry and that the vast majority of citizen petitions are denied."[181] As a result of these tactics of delay, American purchasers have lost billions of dollars of cost savings from generic drugs.[182] With such extraordinary profits on the line, Citizen Petitions have become part of an arsenal used to protect drug manufacturers' profit and exclusivity in the marketplace.

In FDAAA, in an attempt to curb the baseless claims of some Citizen Petitions, Congress added a provision that is intended to counter the tactic of delaying generic approval by filing last-minute Citizen Petitions. The amendment to the FDCA prohibits FDA from delaying the approval of a generic drug while it is preparing a response to a Citizen Petition, unless there is a fairly rigorous certification that the petition raises a public health issue.[183] It is not clear, however, that this provision will solve the Citizen Petition problem. Today, FDA has authority to approve a generic drug while a related Citizen Petition is pending, but often, in anticipation of litigation, at the direction of the agency's Chief Counsel's office, the agency delays approval while it is preparing a response. It is difficult to show why a generic approval is being delayed and therefore it will be difficult to monitor the implementation of this well-intentioned provision. Moreover, some brand companies have begun to file challenges to ANDA approval in their NDA file. Because information in the NDA file is confidential, ANDA applicants have no opportunity to respond to the brand arguments unless FDA itself raises the issue.

Further congressional legislation increased FDA's responsibility and burden. For instance, the enactment of the Food and Drug Administration Safety and Innovation Act (FDASIA) section 1135 shortened FDA's timeframe for responding to petitions from 180 days to 150 days.

In 2013, about 32 Citizen Petitions with 505(q) certifications were submitted to FDA for consideration. Out of the 32 petitions 17 were denied, six were denied in part/granted in part, five received interim responses, three were withdrawn, and one remains pending.

---

[180]   FTC Report, *supra* note 6 at 65-68; *See* Citizen Petition Needs Reforming, FDA Chief Counsel Says, Drug Industry Daily, Sept. 21, 2005 (noting comments of FDA Chief Counsel Sheldon Bradshaw at the Annual Meeting of the Generic Pharmaceutical Manufacturers Association (Sept. 19, 2005) that he has "seen firsthand that many [citizen] petitions seem totally without merit" and that "[s]ometimes, stakeholders try to use the [citizen petition] mechanism to unnecessarily delay approval of a competitor's products").

[181]   Jon Leibowitz, Fed. Trade Comm'n, text based on speech given to Generic Pharmaceutical Annual Policy Conference, entitled "How Settlements Make Strange Bedfellows: Or How the Federal Trade Commission has Managed to Unite the Entire Pharmaceutical Industry" (Sept. 29, 2006), *available at* http://www.ftc.gov/public-statements/2006/09/how-settlements-make-strange-bedfellows-or-how-federal-trade-commission.

[182]   *See The Generic Drug Maze: Speeding Access to Affordable Life-Saving Drugs: Hearing Before the Special Committee on Aging*, 109th Cong. (2006) (statement of Gordon H. Smith, Sen. of the United States).

[183]   FDCA § 505(q), 21 U.S.C. § 355(q).

FDAAA

Although FDAAA included a number of provisions that affect ANDAs, as discussed earlier in this chapter, the principal focus of the legislation was on brand products. Thus, for example, the user fee provisions extended by the law apply only to new drug and biologic applications, and not to abbreviated new drug applications.[184] The most significant provisions of FDAAA (other than the extension of user fees) establish a program to regulate and evaluate the safety of new drugs after they have been approved. The legislation provided FDA with new enforcement authorities, including the authority to order label changes and some additional authority with respect to drug advertising and provided substantial funding for the agency. There is also authority to require applicants to conduct postmarket and other studies of drug safety after a drug has been approved.[185]

Generic drugs are exempt from most of the new drug safety obligations except the obligation to conform to new labeling and the obligation to comply with restricted distribution plans (where FDA for example restricts the sale of drugs to particular specialties or requires drug registries).[186] With regard to the restricted distribution requirements, the law requires the generic and brand to use a single shared system unless the burden of doing so outweighs the benefit or some aspect of the plan is subject to patent or trade secret protection and the generic has been unable to obtain a license to use the protected aspect of the plan.[187]

Generic Drug User Fees

The Generic Drug User Fee Amendments of 2012 (GDUFA) were signed into law on July 9, 2012, in an effort "to speed access to safe and effective generic drugs to the public and reduce costs to industry."[188] A failure to pay a required fee may result in a refusal to receive an ANDA, any supplement to an ANDA, or in a drug being deemed misbranded.[189] Some of the required fees include a backlog fee, Drug Master File (DMF) fee, ANDA fee, Active Pharmaceutical Ingredient (API) fee, Prior Approval Supplement (PAS) fees, and facilities fees.[190]

Under GDUFA, facilities are determined based on a self-identification process, which is required for 1) facilities that manufacture, or intend to manufacture, human generic drug APIs and/or final dosage forms (FDFs); 2) sites that package the FDF; 3) sites that are identified in a generic drug submission that subdivide the contents of the primary container/closure system; 4) bioequivalence/bioavailability sites that conduct clinical, bioanalytical, and/or in

---

[184]   Applications under section 505(b)(2) are also subject to user fees.

[185]   FDCA §§ 505(o), (p), 505-1, 21 U.S.C. §§ 355(o), (p), 355-1.

[186]   FDCA § 505-1(i), 21 U.S.C. § 355-1(i).

[187]   Id.

[188]   Generic Drug User Fee Amendments of 2012, Pub. L. No. 112-144, tit. III (July 9, 2012), available at http://www.fda.gov/ForIndustry/UserFees/GenericDrugUserFees/default.htm.

[189]   See generally FDA, Draft Guidance for Industry: Generic Drug User Fee Amendments of 2012: Questions and Answers (Sept. 2013), available at http://www.fda.gov/downloads/Drugs/GuidanceComplianceRegulatoryInformation/Guidances/UCM316671.pdf.

[190]   See http://www.fda.gov/ForIndustry/UserFees/GenericDrugUserFees/default.htm.

vitro testing; and 5) sites that perform testing of one or more attributes/characteristics of the FDF or API.[191]

FDA has also issued guidance regarding PASs under GDUFA. These PASs and amendments to PASs for ANDAs are submitted under section 505(j) of the FDCA.[192] FDA may refuse to receive a PAS for:

- failure to pay the application fee within 20 calendar days of submission;

- reference to a drug master file (DMF) that is not on the public available for reference list;

- reference to a facility on the facility arrears list;

- the applicant is the owner or is affiliated with the owner of a facility on the facility arrears list; or

- the applicant is on or affiliated with an entity on the backlog arrears list.[193]

FDA has also issued guidance regarding amendments and easily correctable deficiencies under GDUFA.[194] Such amendments fall into the following categories: solicited, unsolicited, and administrative. A solicited amendment is a submission made in response "to a complete response letter (CR) issued by FDA."[195] An unsolicited or "gratuitous" amendment is one that is submitted "on the applicant's own initiative and not in response to FDA's CR letter."[196] By

---

191   Generic Drug User Fee Amendments of 2012, Pub. L. No. 112-144, tit. III, pt. 7 (July 9, 2012); *see also* FDA, Draft Guidance for Industry: Self-Identification of Generic Drug Facilities, Sites, and Organizations (Aug. 2012), at 3-4, *available at* http://www.fda.gov/downloads/Drugs/GuidanceComplianceRegulatoryInformation/Guidances/UCM316672.pdf.

192   21 U.S.C. 355(j); FDA, Draft Guidance for Industry: ANDA Submissions—Prior Approval Supplements Under GDUFA (July 2014), at 1, *available at* http://www.fda.gov/downloads/Drugs/GuidanceComplianceRegulatoryInformation/Guidances/UCM404441.pdf.

193   *Id.* at 6-7.

194   FDA, Draft Guidance for Industry: ANDA Submissions—Amendments and Easily Correctable Deficiencies Under GDUFA (July 2014), at 1, *available at* http://www.fda.gov/downloads/Drugs/GuidanceComplianceRegulatoryInformation/Guidances/UCM404440.pdf.

195   *Id.* at 4. These amendments are classified as either Tier 1 or Tier 3 and either as a major amendment, a minor amendment, or an easily correctable deficiency (ECD). *Id.* A major amendment "contain[s] a substantial amount of new data or new information not previously submitted to or reviewed by FDA, requiring . . . a substantial expenditure of FDA resources." *Id.* The first solicited major amendment is classified as Tier 1; any subsequent major amendment is classified as Tier 3. *Id.* A minor amendment, on the other hand, "requires . . . fewer FDA resources than are necessary to review a major amendment but more than are necessary to review the information submitted in response to an ECD." *Id.* For instance, a minor amendment may address missing information but not require any new studies to be performed. *Id.* The first through fifth solicited minor amendments are classified as Tier 1; any subsequent minor amendment is classified as Tier 3. *Id.* Finally, ECDs "require[]. . . a modest expenditure of FDA resources." *Id.* They can be responded to quickly because the applicant should already have the necessary information. ECDs generally relate to requests for clarification, requests for postapproval commitments, or final resolution of technical issues. *Id.*

196   *Id.* at 5. These amendments are classified as either delaying or nondelaying. *Id.* All delaying amendments are Tier 1 and all nondelaying amendments are Tier 2. *Id.* at 5-6. A delaying amendment "address[es] actions by a third party that would cause delay or impede application review or approval timing and that were not a factor at the time of submission." *Id.* at 5. A nondelaying amendment "contain[s] information that is not requested by FDA and is not the result of changes to the RLD or USP monograph, changes to the RLD labeling, a REMS and REMS modification, or generic approval requirements reflected in citizen petition responses issued by FDA." *Id.* at 6.

contrast, an administrative amendment is "routine in nature and do[es] not require scientific review."[197]

Section 505(b)(2) Applications

A section 505(b)(2) application is an NDA for which one or more of the investigations relied upon by the applicant for approval come from studies not conducted by or for the applicant and for which the applicant has not obtained a right of reference or use from the person by or for whom the investigations were conducted.[198] A section 505(b)(2) application is similar to a full NDA in that it must satisfy the same requirements for safety and effectiveness. It is similar to an ANDA because it may rely on FDA's finding that the drug it references is safe and effective to support its own safety and effectiveness. A section 505(b)(2) NDA, however, can be for a drug that has substantial differences from the listed drug it references. The application must support those differences with appropriate safety and effectiveness information. The basic idea is that FDA will rely on its approval of the brand reference product to the extent it is scientifically relevant. This approach saves both agency and industry resources and prevents unnecessary delay. The section 505(b)(2) process fills a gap between the full NDA and the ANDA.

A section 505(b)(2) applicant may rely on published literature or on the agency's previous finding of safety and effectiveness for an approved drug. A section 505(b)(2) NDA may be submitted for a new chemical entity (NCE) when some part of the data necessary for approval is derived from studies not conducted by or for the applicant and to which the applicant has not obtained a right of reference. A section 505(b)(2) NDA may also be submitted for changes to a previously approved drug product that would not be permitted under section 505(j) because approval would require the review of clinical data. An application submitted pursuant to section 505(b)(2) is appropriate even when new clinical data are not required for approval and the application also could have been submitted in an ANDA based on a suitability petition.[199] This use of section 505(b)(2) for changes to previously approved drugs encourages innovation without requiring duplicate work. Like section 505(j), it reflects the principle that it is wasteful and unnecessary to carry out studies to demonstrate what is already known about a drug.[200]

Some examples of changes to approved drugs that would be submitted as section 505(b)(2) applications include formulation changes, a new dosing regimen, a change in the active ingredient (for example a different salt, ester, or racemate), a new molecular entity, a combination product for which the active ingredients were approved individually, a new

---

[197] *Id.* at 6. These types of amendments include "[r]equests for final approval with no scientific changes to the ANDA, patent amendments, and general correspondence submitted by applicants." *Id.*

[198] FDCA § 505(b)(2), 21 U.S.C. § 355(b)(2). If the applicant obtains a right of reference to the raw data underlying the relevant studies, it may be submitted as a full NDA under section 505(b)(1) of the FDCA.

[199] *See* 57 Fed. Reg. 17,950 (Apr. 28, 1992). Applications submitted pursuant to section 505(b)(2) are subject to user fees. 21 U.S.C. §§ 379g, 379h. This also means that such applications will be reviewed in accordance with FDA's user fee goals.

[200] *See* FDA, Draft Guidance for Industry: Applications Covered by Section 505(b)(2) (Oct. 1999).

indication, and a switch from prescription to OTC.[201] A section 505(b)(2) application would also be appropriate for drug products with active ingredients derived from animal or botanic sources or recombinant technology where clinical investigations are necessary to show that the active ingredient is the same as an active ingredient in a listed drug. Applications for drug products with rates and/or extents of absorption that are different from the listed drug (but are not less than the listed drug) also could be appropriately submitted as a section 505(b)(2) application.[202]

Changes in dosage form, strength, or route of administration and substitution of an active ingredient in a combination product might have to be submitted in a section 505(b)(2) application if they require studies beyond those permitted in an ANDA. As noted above, if they require only review of bioavailability or bioequivalence studies of data from limited confirmatory testing, they can be submitted either in a section 505(b)(2) application or a ANDA based on an approved suitability petition.[203]

An application that is a duplicate of an RLD and eligible for approval under section 505(j) cannot be submitted as a section 505(b)(2) application. Likewise, if the product's only difference from the RLD is the extent to which its active ingredient is absorbed or otherwise made available to the site of action is less than the RLD or if the product's only difference from the RLD is that the rate at which its active ingredient is absorbed or otherwise made available to the site of action is unintentionally less than that of the RLD, a section 505(b)(2) application is not appropriate.[204]

After FDA issued its 1999 guidance on section 505(b)(2) applications, several brand-name companies filed citizen petitions challenging the agency's interpretation of section 505(b)(2) that permits a section 505(b)(2) applicant to rely on the agency's finding of safety and effectiveness for another approved product.[205] Specifically, they argued that section 505(b)(2) permitted sponsors to rely only on studies in published literature. FDA has rejected these challenges and has taken the position, based on the language of the statute, that section 505(b)(2) is intended to encourage innovation in drug development without requiring duplicative studies to demonstrate what is already known about a drug while protecting the patent and exclusivity rights for the approved drug.[206]

As with ANDAs, the filing or approval of a section 505(b)(2) application may be delayed due to patent or exclusivity protections covering an approved product. Section 505(b)(2) applications must include the patent certifications described in the statute and must provide notice of such certifications to the NDA holder and patent owner.[207] A section 505(b)(2) NDA is eligible for all exclusivities that may be awarded to a full NDA, including the five-

---

[201] *See id.*

[202] *Id.*

[203] *Id.*

[204] *Id.*

[205] *See* Docket Nos. 2001P-0323; 2002P-0447 and 2003P-0408.

[206] *See* Letter from Janet Woodcock, Director FDA Center for Drugs to Katherine M. Sanzo and Lawrence S. Ganslaw, Morgan, Lewis & Bockius, LLP, Jeffrey B. Chasnow, Pfizer, Inc., Stephen E. Lawton and Gillian R. Woollett, Biotechnology Industry Organization, and William R. Rakoczy, Lord, Bissell & Brook LLP, Docket Nos. 2001P-0323, 2002P-0447 and 2003P-0408 (Oct. 14, 2003).

[207] FDCA §§ 505(b)(2), (b)(3), 21 U.S.C. §§ 355(b)(2), (b)(3).

year exclusivity for an NCE; the three-year exclusivity based on new clinical investigations, other than bioavailability or bioequivalence studies, essential to approval of the application and conducted or sponsored by the applicant; orphan drug exclusivity; and pediatric exclusivity.[208] A section 505(b)(2) NDA can neither be awarded 180-day exclusivity nor have its approval delayed by such exclusivity.[209]

Antibiotics

Until 1997, antibiotics were not approved under section 505 of the FDCA and thus were not subject to the Hatch-Waxman provisions. In 1997, FDAMA repealed section 507 of the FDCA, under which antibiotics had been approved for marketing.[210] Antibiotics, including generic antibiotics, subsequently were approved under section 505, in NDAs and ANDAs. Because generic antibiotics previously had not been subject to the Hatch-Waxman exclusivity and patent certification provisions, FDAMA excluded from those provisions antibiotics for which the active moiety of the RLD was approved prior to enactment of FDAMA.[211] Thus, under FDAMA, "old antibiotics" approved in NDAs were not entitled to Hatch-Waxman exclusivity, and thus, old antibiotics approved in ANDAs were not blocked by such exclusivity.[212] Applications for antibiotics filed after 1997 are subject to the Hatch-Waxman exclusivity and patent certification provisions.

Then, on October 8, 2008, Congress passed the Qualifying Individual Program Supplemental Funding Act of 2008 (the QI Act) and amended the FDCA to add new section 505(v) to extend Hatch-Waxman benefits to antibiotics approved prior to enactment of FDAMA in 1997.

Enantiomer Exclusivity

Enantiomers are stereoisomers of a chiral compound that are mirror images of each other. Enantiomers can be either left-handed or right-handed. A racemic mixture is one that has equal amounts of left- and right-handed enantiomers. In implementing Hatch-Waxman, FDA did not consider single enantiomers of approved racemates to be active ingredients eligible for Hatch-Waxman five-year new chemical entity exclusivity.[213] In 2007, FDAAA amended the FDCA to provide that NDA applicants for a non-racemic drug containing as an active ingredient a single enantiomer that is contained in a racemic drug approved in

---

208   FDCA §§ 505(c)(3)(E), (j)(5)(F), 21 U.S.C. §§ 355(c)(3)(E), (j)(5)(F); FDCA § 527, 21 U.S.C. § 360cc; FDCA § 505A, 21 U.S.C. § 355a.

209   FDCA § 505(c)(3)(E), (j)(5)(B), 21 U.S.C. § 355(c)(3)(E), (j)(5)(B).

210   Pub. L. No. 105-115, § 125; 111 Stat. at 2326-27.

211   Pub. L. No. 105-115, § 125(d); 111 Stat. at 2326-27.

212   See FDA, Guidance for Industry and Reviewers: Repeal of Section 507 of the Federal Food Drug and Cosmetic Act (May 1998), available at http://www.fda.gov/downloads/Drugs/GuidanceComplianceRegulatoryInformation/Guidances/ucm080566.pdf.

213   See 54 Fed. Reg. 28,872, 28,898 (July 10, 1989). FDA requested comment on whether granting a five-year period of exclusivity to single enantiomers of approved racemates was advisable, but never initiated a rule-making to do so. See 62 Fed. Reg. 2167 (Jan. 15, 1997).

another application under section 505(b) can elect to have the single enantiomer an active ingredient that is different than the ingredient contained in the approved racemic drug if the following conditions are met:

- the single enantiomer has not previously been approved except in the approved racemic drug;

- the application includes full reports of new clinical investigations (other than bioavailability studies) necessary for approval and conducted or sponsored by the applicant; and

- the enantiomer is not for a condition of use in a therapeutic category in which the approved racemic drug has been approved or for which any other enantiomer of the racemic drug has been approved.[214]

If the enantiomer is not considered to be the same active ingredient, then it would be eligible for five years of exclusivity. If the enantiomer NDA applicant elects to receive this exclusivity, however, the enantiomer drug cannot be approved for any condition of use in the therapeutic category in which the racemic drug is approved until 10 years after the enantiomer has been approved.[215] The provision applies only to applicants submitted after enactment of FDAAA and it expires in 2012.[216]

Reorganization of the Office of Generic Drugs

On December 10, 2013 FDA announced that FDA's Center for Drug Evaluation and Research (CDER) approved plans to reorganize the Office of Generic Drugs (OGD) into a "super office."[217] OGD now reports directly to the director of CDER and will be structured into four separate sub-offices: the Office of Research and Standards, the Office of Bioequivalence, the Office of Regulatory Operations, and the Office of Generic Drug Policy.[218] The restructuring was announced as a measure designed to "lead to greater efficiency and more consistency across review components" and "to expedite the availability of safe, effective, and high-quality generic drugs to patients."[219] In large part, the restructuring was motivated by FDA's desire to meet the challenges posed by the passage of GDUFA.[220]

The Office of Generic Drug Policy includes the Division of Legal and Regulatory Support, which is expected to focus its efforts on handling and resolving Hatch-Waxman disputes.[221]

---

[214] FDCA § 505(u), 21 U.S.C. § 355(u), added by FDAAA § 1113.

[215] *Id.*

[216] *Id.*

[217] U.S. Food & Drug Admin., Office of Generic Drugs Reorganization: *Development and Approval Process (Drugs)* (last updated July 21, 2014), *available at* http://www.fda.gov/drugs/developmentapprovalprocess/howdrugsaredevelopedandapproved/approvalapplications/abbreviatednewdrugapplicationandagenerics/ucm378126.htm.

[218] *Id.*

[219] *Id.*

[220] Bob Pollock, *OGD Elevation to Super Office in CDER* (Sept. 10, 2012), *available at* http://www.lachmanconsultants.com/ogd-evelvation-to-super-office-in-cder.asp.

[221] Kurt R. Karst, *Office of Generic Drugs "Super Office" Becomes a Reality: New "Office of Generic Drug Policy" Will Handle Hatch-Waxman Issues*, FDA Law Blog (Dec. 25, 2013), *available at* http://www.fdalawblog.net/

Prior to the reorganization, certain issues, such as 180-day exclusivity, were handled in a less focused manner and this division should "bring greater clarity (and speed?) to FDA's decisions and decision-making process," not unlike the CDER Exclusivity Board does for five- and three-year exclusivity disputes.[222] It has been further predicted that the restructuring should lead to a wave of new hiring in the OGD, which has proven to be accurate.[223]

In fact, improving the ANDA process appeared to be part of a larger strategy to meet GDUFA metrics in the future.[224] FDA provided further guidance on the content and format of ANDAs, including a closer look at "enhanced refuse-to-receive standards, the establishment of a public docket . . . to receive input and suggestions on ways to improve ANDA quality and on how to best communicate those suggestions to the generic drug industry."[225] The guidance was intended to be an accessible document containing much of OGD's advice for submissions, with links to other OGD documents. Again, this move was logical considering that high-quality ANDAs should be easier to review, thus making it easier for the OGD to meet its GDUFA performance goals.[226]

OGD's Acting Director also announced that starting on February 1, 2014, "OGD's CC officers will conduct a complete inventory of all the original ANDAs in our queue, and provide each applicant with an update regarding the status of its ANDAs."[227] This effort would extend to ANDAs submitted prior to GDUFA; it also covers ANDAs submitted in Fiscal Years 2013 and 2014, despite the lack of FDA performance goals regarding review and action on those ANDAs.[228] FDA Law Blog reported on a form-version of the correspondence that the OGD expects to send out in connection with this initiative.[229]

---

fda_law_blog_hyman_phelps/2013/12/office-of-generic-drugs-super-office-becomes-a-relity-new-office-of-generic-drug-policy-will-handle.html.

[222]   *Id.*

[223]   *Id.*

[224]   Kurt R. Karst, *Improving the Yield on ANDA Submissions: FDA Wants to Hear Industry's Concerns and Provide Guidance on How to Build a Better ANDA*, FDA Law Blog (Jan. 22, 2014), *available at* http://www.fdalawblog. net/fda_law_blog_hyman_phelps/2014/01/improving-the-yield-on-anda-submissions-fda-wants-to-hear-industrys-concerns-and-provide-gudance-on-.html.

[225]   Kurt R. Karst, *Gentlemen, We Can Rebuild the ANDA – Better, Stronger, Faster: FDA Issues Guidance on Quality ANDA Submissions*, FDA Law Blog (June 12, 2014), *available at* http://www.fdalawblog.net/fda_law_blog_ hyman_phelps/2014/06/gentlemen-we-can-rebuild-the-anda-better-stronger-faster-fda-issues-guidance-on-quality-anda-submiss.html.

[226]   *Id.*

[227]   Kurt R. Karst, *FDA's Office of Generic Drugs Says "We Hear You, and We're Willing to Bite the Bullet" in a Massive Effort to Address Post-GDUFA Stakeholder Transparency Concerns*, FDA Law Blog (Jan. 31, 2014), *available at* http://www.fdalawblog.net/fda_law_blog_hyman_phelps/2014/01/fdas-office-of-generic-drugs-says-we-hear-you-and-were-willing-to-bite-the-bullet-in-a-massive-effor.html.

[228]   *Id.*

[229]   *See* Kurt R. Karst, *The Rollout: FDA's Mission Critical ANDA Undertaking*, FDA Law Blog (Feb. 12, 2014), *available at* http://www.fdalawblog.net/fda_law_ blog_hyman_phelps/2014/02/the-rollout-fdas-mission-critical-anda-und ertaking.html.

CHAPTER 12

PRESCRIPTION DRUG PROMOTION AND MARKETING

KATHLEEN M. SANZO AND STEPHEN PAUL MAHINKA

Introduction

Few areas of food and drug law and regulation have undergone such far-reaching and substantial change in recent years as prescription drug promotion and marketing. Once characterized by limited methods of promotion, predominantly to a restricted target audience of physician-prescribers directly by detail force representatives, prescription drug promotion has expanded vastly in scale and scope. Consequently, the degree and sources of enforcement activity have increased.

Prescription drug promotion and marketing has expanded far beyond physician-prescribers to other audiences who influence the selection of therapeutic drugs, including managed care entities, consumers, and government and private reimbursement officials. Promotion and marketing sources now include direct-to-consumer (DTC) advertising, social media, and Internet information sites, direct mail, and medical science liaisons (MSLs).

With these significant changes in the scale and scope of prescription drug promotion and marketing, there has been, unsurprisingly, a substantial increase in the degree of enforcement activity and the number of entities focused on this area. In addition to the traditional enforcers, such as the Food and Drug Administration (FDA) and the Federal Trade Commission (FTC), now the Office of Inspector General of the Department of Health and Human Services (OIG DHHS), the Department of Justice (DOJ) and its U.S. Attorneys, State Attorneys General, and private entities also commonly investigate and challenge drug promotion and marketing.

The ongoing concern among payors and consumers regarding the cost of prescription branded and generic drugs and biologics is expected to generate sustained focus on promotion and marketing. Further, the rise in interest regarding development of cost-effectiveness, comparative effectiveness, clinical effectiveness, and health outcomes measurement as potential mechanisms of cost control, and the mandate for development of comparative effectiveness data from the healthcare reform law (the Patient Protection and Affordable Care Act of 2009[1]) also can be expected to significantly affect prescription drug promotion and marketing in the future.

Sources of Regulation

Federal Food, Drug, and Cosmetic Act (FDCA)

Since its inception, the Federal Food, Drug, and Cosmetic Act (FDCA) has provided regulatory authority over all prescription labeling, including promotional labeling. Authority over prescription drug advertising was added beginning with the Kefauver-Harris Amendment in 1962, in which Congress granted to FDA the statutory authority to enforce a "proof of efficacy" requirement for new drug approvals.[2] The Kefauver-Harris Amendment also created section 502(n) of the FDCA,[3] which provided FDA with broad statutory authority to regulate the advertising of prescription drugs. Prior to this legislation, the authority to regulate prescription drug advertising was placed solely with FTC.[4]

The primary requirements for drug labeling are well known (e.g., prohibition against false and misleading labeling; requirement for adequate directions for use), and are discussed more fully in Chapter 9 *supra*. Under section 502(n), all prescription drug advertisements must include the established (official)[5] name of the drug, name and amount of ingredients,[6] and a brief summary of side effects, contraindications, and effectiveness.[7] FDA promulgated regulations and guidelines on prescription drug advertising, intended for healthcare providers and consumers,[8] as well as regulations for prescription drug labeling that govern promotional labeling.[9] The advertising regulations establish many requirements, discussed *infra*, including, but not limited to: 1) prohibitions against the dissemination of claims of safety and efficacy for investigational drugs; 2) standards relating to the disclosure of risk

---

[1]   Patient Protection and Affordable Care Act (PPACA), Pub. L. No. 111-148, 124 Stat. 119 (2010) as amended by the Health Care and Education Reconciliation Act of 2010, Pub. L. No. 111-152 (2010).

[2]   Drug Amendments of 1962, Pub. L. No. 87-781, 76 Stat. 780 (1962).

[3]   21 U.S.C. § 352(n).

[4]   FDCA § 502(n), 21 U.S.C. § 352(n) (stating that "no advertisement of a prescription drug . . . shall . . . be subject to the provisions of sections 12 through 17 of the Federal Trade Commission Act"). This has been confirmed by repeated statements made by FTC staff. *See, e.g.,* Comments Submitted by FTC Staff on FDA-proposed Assessment of Physician and Patient Attitudes Toward Direct-to-Consumer (DTC) Promotion Drugs, at n. 9 (Sept. 24, 2001), *available at* http://www.ftc.gov/be/v010008.shtm.

[5]   21 U.S.C. § 352(n); 21 C.F.R. § 202.1(b)(1) (2008). The issue of whether a differentiating name will be mandated for biosimilars is under consideration by FDA. *See, e.g.,* Generic Pharmaceutical Assn, Naming of Biosimilars, http://www.gphaonline.org/gpha-media/gpha-resources/1naming-biosimilars.

[6]   *Id.* § 352(n); 21 C.F.R. § 202.1(c).

[7]   *Id.* § 352(n); 21 C.F.R. § 202(e)(1).

[8]   *Id.* § 202; *see also* http://www.fda.gov/Drugs/GuidanceComplianceRegulatoryInformation/Guidances/ucm064956.htm.

[9]   *Id.* § 201; *see also* 21 C.F.R. § 202.1(l)(2) (providing a description of what types of materials constitute drug labeling).

information pertaining to the drug; 3) price advertising; and 4) dissemination of claims inconsistent with FDA-approved labeling.

Products that are supported by advertisements and promotional labeling that are false or misleading in any particular are misbranded under 21 U.S.C. §§ 352(a) and (n) and FDA's implementing regulations, and are prohibited from entry into commerce under 21 U.S.C. §§ 331(a) and (k). Courts have upheld this standard, considering it neither unconstitutionally vague nor indefinite.[10] Consequently, FDA has authority—exercised through DOJ—to seek seizures, criminal fines, and imprisonment, and injunctions for activities such as false advertising, which result in distribution of a misbranded product.[11] However, as a practical matter, the overwhelming majority of FDA enforcement actions for noncompliant advertising and promotional labeling are through use of pre-enforcement untitled letters or Warning Letters issued by FDA's Office of Prescription Drug Promotion (OPDP) (formerly the Division of Drug Marketing, Advertising, and Communications (DDMAC)).[12] Warning Letters allege a violation of law, demand a cessation of the alleged violative practices, and in the vast majority of cases demand that the drug marketer issue corrective communications to the same audience (e.g., physicians). These corrective communications may be in the form of "Dear Healthcare Professional" letters[13] and/or in the form of corrective labeling[14] or advertising correlating to the format of the violative promotion.[15]

---

[10] See e.g., United States v. Dr. Salsbury's Rakos, 53 F. Supp. 746 (D.C. Minn. 1944); United States v. Marmola Prescription Tablets, 48 F. Supp. 878 (W.D. Wisc. 1943), aff'd, 142 F.2d 107 (7th Cir. 1944), cert. denied, 323 U.S. 731 (1945).

[11] See 21 U.S.C. §§ 332–334, discussed infra in Chapter 21.

[12] See FDA, REGULATORY PROCEDURES MANUAL, ch. 4. (Mar. 2010), available at http://www.fda.gov/ICECI/ComplianceManuals/RegulatoryProceduresManual/default.htm.

[13] See 21 C.F.R. § 200.5; see also FDA Center for Drug Evaluation and Research, MANUAL OF POLICIES AND PROCEDURES 6020.10, NDAs: Dear Health Care Professional Letters (July 2003), available at http://www.fda.gov/downloads/AboutFDA/CentersOffices/CDER/ManualofPoliciesProcedures/ucm082012.pdf; FDA, Guidance for Industry and FDA Staff: Dear Health Care Provider Letters: Improving Communication of Important Safety Information (Jan. 2014), available at http://www.fda.gov/downloads/Drugs/GuidanceComplianceRegulatoryInformation/Guidances/UCM233769.pdf (Dear Health Care Provider Letters are "intended to alert physicians and other health care providers about important new or updated information regarding a human drug or biologic").

[14] According to the Washington Legal Foundation's DDMAC Watch Program, more than 96 percent of all Warning Letters issued by DDMAC during the time period from January 2005 through June 2006 requested corrective communications. WASHINGTON LEGAL FOUNDATION, DDMAC WATCH: THE YEAR IN REVIEW, (Aug. 7, 2006), available at http://www.wlf.org/upload/0806DDMACWatch_%20Year%20in%20Review%20Report. pdf. Additionally, 64 percent of Warning Letters issued by DDMAC during the time period from July 2006 through May 2007 requested corrective communications. WASHINGTON LEGAL FOUNDATION, DDMAC WATCH: THE YEAR IN REVIEW (Jan. 30, 2008), available at http://www.wlf.org/upload/DDMACWatch%202007%20 Annual%20Report.pdf.

[15] See e.g., Warning Letter from Karen R. Rulli, Ph.D., Acting Group Leader, Division of Drug Marketing, Advertising, and Communications, FDA, to Lisa Drucker, PharmD, MBA, Director, Regulatory Affairs – Oncology, Novartis Pharmaceuticals Corp (July 29, 2010), available at http://www.fda. gov/downloads/Drugs/GuidanceComplianceRegulatoryInformation/EnforcementActivitiesbyFDA/WarningLettersandNoticeofViolationLetterstoPharmaceuticalCompanies/UCM221325.pdf; Warning Letter from Robert Dean, Division Director, Division of Consumer Drug Protection, Office of Prescription Drug Promotion, FDA, to Ian C. Reed, Chairman and Chief Executive Officer, Pfizer Inc. (May 24, 2012), available at http://www.fda.gov/downloads/Drugs/GuidanceComplianceRegulatoryInformation/EnforcementActivitiesbyFDA/WarningLettersandNoticeofViolationLetterstoPharmaceuticalCompanies/UCM306109.pdf (requesting complete corrective messages for overstatement of efficacy in a TV commercial for EpiPen® and EpiPen® Jr. (epinephrine) Auto-Injectors (EpiPen)); Warning Letter from Michael Sauers, Acting Division Director, Office of Prescription Drug Promotion, FDA, to Ron Cohen, President and Chief Executive Officer, Acorda Therapeutics, Inc. (July 25, 2013), available at http://www.

Anti-Kickback Statute and Civil Monetary Penalty Provision under the Social Security Act

The Anti-Kickback Statute, section 1128B(b) of the Social Security Act (SSA), makes it a criminal offense for anyone who knowingly and willfully solicits or receives any remuneration (including any kickback, bribe, or rebate) to induce referrals or services reimbursable by any federal healthcare program.[16] Violation of the statute constitutes a felony punishable by a fine (maximum $25,000 per violation) and imprisonment (up to five years) or both. Under section 1128A(a)(7), the OIG DHHS may also impose civil monetary penalties and exclude such party from the federal healthcare programs.

A pharmaceutical manufacturer may violate the Anti-Kickback Statute if it provides remuneration including any kickback or bribe, directly or indirectly, in cash or in-kind to physicians or other healthcare personnel with the intent to influence a referral, such as prescription of a drug that is paid for in full or in part by a federal or state government payor.[17]

The OIG, assisted by DOJ and its U.S. Attorneys, indirectly regulates under the False Claims Act[18] drug advertising and promotion through its investigation of and enforcement against promotion of unapproved (off-label) uses which allegedly result in the submission by physicians of false claims for reimbursement to federal or state healthcare programs. There have been a large number of settlements of these cases,[19] but very few cases have actually been litigated. The U.S. Court of Appeals for the First Circuit, however, has held that off-label marketing practices, while illegal, "are not a sufficient basis for an FCA [False Claims Act] action" if they do not involve claims for government reimbursement.[20]

In 2012, the U.S. Court of Appeals for the Second Circuit concluded that the First Amendment's free speech guarantee encompassed off-label promotion regarding prescription drugs. In *United States v. Caronia*,[21] the Second Circuit vacated the criminal conviction of a pharmaceutical sales representative who allegedly promoted the drug Xyrem for "off-

---

fda.gov/downloads/Drugs/GuidanceComplianceRegulatoryInformation/EnforcementActivitiesbyFDA/WarningLettersandNoticeofViolationLetterstoPharmaceuticalCompanies/UCM363213.pdf (requesting complete corrective messages in the same format due to omission of risk information in a print ad for AMPYRA® (dalfampridine) Extended Release Tablets).

[16]   SSA § 1128B(b), 42 U.S.C. § 1320a-7b(b); *see also* SSA § 1128A(a)(5), 42 U.S.C. § 1320a-7a(a)(5) (providing civil monetary penalty for inducements to beneficiaries).

[17]   *See* 42 U.S.C. § 1320a-7b(b). For further discussion of off-label promotion as a basis for a violation of the Anti-Kickback Statute and the False Claims Act, *see* Chapter 24.

[18]   *See* 31 U.S.C. § 3729; *see also* OIG, Allegations of Waste, Fraud and Abuse in Pharmaceutical Pricing: Financial Impacts on Federal Health Programs and the Federal Taxpayer (Testimony of Lewis Morris, Chief Counsel to the Inspector General, OIG, before the H. Oversight & Government Reform Comm.) (Feb. 9, 2007), *available at* http://www.oig.hhs.gov/testimony/docs/2007/020907tmy.pdf.

[19]   *See* OIG database of settlements of criminal enforcement actions at http://www.oig.hhs.gov/fraud/enforcement/criminal/.

[20]   United States ex rel. Rost v. Pfizer Inc., 507 F.3d 720, 732 (1st Cir. 2007). The case was remanded, United States ex rel. Rost v. Pfizer Inc., 253 F.R.D. 11 (D. Mass. 2008), and summary judgment subsequently was granted. United States ex rel. Rost v. Pfizer Inc., 736 F. Supp. 2d 367 (D. Mass. 2010). *See also* United States ex rel. Simpson v. Bayer Corp., 2:05-CV-03895-JLL-JAD (D. N.J.) (Apr. 11, 2014) (failure to comply with FDCA misbranding provisions is not a condition of payment under federal healthcare programs).

[21]   703 F.3d 149 (2d Cir. 2012).

label use." The court held that FDA's construction of the misbranding statute in support of DOJ's off-label promotion argument "provide[d] only ineffective or remote support for the government's purpose."[22] *Caronia* has been cited extensively since its publication to support the right of companies to discuss off-label uses in commercial/promotional context.[23]

Federal Trade Commission Act

The Federal Trade Commission has stated that the FTC and FDA have "overlapping authority over a number of products, including prescription drugs."[24] It is FTC's view that, although section 502(n) of the FDCA limits a portion of FTC's authority over prescription drug advertising, it "does not address FTC jurisdiction over statements other than those that fall into three categories: (1) drug name, (2) formula, and (3) summary of effectiveness and consequences of use."[25] Additionally, FTC has commented that section 502(n) does not affect "the FTC's basic jurisdiction over advertising, including prescription drug advertising," under section 5 of the FTC Act.[26] For example, the FTC staff "agrees with the FDA's suggestion that the Commission [FTC] has jurisdiction over help-seeking communications related to prescription drugs."[27]

For example, FTC takes the position that it can bring an enforcement action where "an online pharmacy makes false or misleading claims about the products or services it provides," because such marketing of prescription drugs online is deceptive in violation of section 5 of the FTC Act.[28] FTC also has attempted to prevent physicians from advertising unapproved uses of FDA-approved new drugs; however, a federal court held that advertising a treatment program (e.g., weight loss clinic) that uses an unapproved new drug (human chorionic

---

[22] 703 F.3d at 167 (quoting Central Hudson Gas & Elec. Corp. v. Public Serv. Comm'n, 447 U.S. 557, 564 (1980)).

[23] *See e.g.*, Bee v Novartis Pharms. Corp. 2014 U.S. Dist. LEXIS 64309 (E.D. N.Y. May 9, 2014, at 44-46; Wilcox v. Forest Pharms., Inc. (In re: Celexa & Lexapro Mktg. and Sales Practices Litig.), 2014 U.S. Dist. LEXIS 109667 (D. Mass. Aug. 8, 2014).

[24] *See, e.g.*, FTC, The Internet Sale of Prescription Drugs From Domestic Websites (Statement of Howard Beales, Director of the Bureau of Consumer Protection, FTC Before the Comm. on Government Reform, U.S. House of Rep.) (Mar. 27, 2003), *available at* http://www.ftc.gov/os/2003/03/030327 internetprescriptions.pdf (citing the Working Agreement Between FTC and FDA, 3 Trade Reg. Rep. (CCH) ¶ 9,859.01 (1971)). FTC's asserted authority to regulate prescription drug advertising has not been the subject of judicial review.

[25] Comments of the Staff of the Bureaus of Economics and Consumer Protection of FTC, In the Matter of Pharmaceutical Marketing and Information Exchange in Managed Care Environments, Public Hearings, Docket No. 95N-0228, at n. 5 (Jan. 16, 1996), *available at* http://www.ftc.gov/be/v960002.shtm.

[26] *Id.*

[27] Comments of the Staffs of the Bureaus of Consumer Protection and Economics, and the Office of Policy Planning of FTC, In the Matter of Request for Comments on Agency Draft Guidance Documents Regarding Consumer-Directed Promotions, Docket No. 2004D-0042, at 3 (May 10, 2004); *available at* http://www.ftc. gov/sites/default/files/documents/advocacy_documents/ftc-staff-comment-food-and-drug-administration-concerning-consumer-directed-promotion/040512dtcdrugscomment.pdf.

[28] *Id.* For example, FTC and FDA jointly reviewed Internet sites for the promotion and sale of the antibiotic Cipro to treat anthrax exposure to determine if the Cipro being sold was counterfeit. *See* FTC, The Internet Sale of Prescription Drugs from Domestic Websites, Before the Comm. on Gov't Reform of the U.S. House of Rep (Mar. 27, 2003), *available at* http://www.ftc.gov/os/2003/03/030327internetprescriptions. pdf. FTC and FDA on September 23, 2014, sent a joint Warning Letter to Natural Solutions Foundation concerning websites with an embedded YouTube video for silver solutions described to combat Ebola, which FDA asserted made the products drugs, *available at* http://www.fda.gov/ICECI/EnforcementActions/ WarningLetters/2014/ ucm416051.htm.

gonadotropin in this case) does not violate the FTC Act.[29] In 2013, FTC published updated guidelines advising businesses how federal advertising law applies to advertising and sales on the Internet, which encompasses healthcare products subject to FTC's enforcement jurisdiction.[30]

Despite the asserted overlapping jurisdiction, FTC and FDA have signed a memorandum of understanding (MOU) agreeing that FDA has primary jurisdiction over the regulation of advertisements for prescription drugs.[31] Note that a drug that is switched from prescription to OTC status for certain strengths or indications would be subject to FTC standards for advertising of the OTC product, whereas any advertising for prescription dosages of the product that continue to be marketed would remain regulated by FDA.

In 2009, FTC revised its Guides Concerning the Use of Endorsements and Testimonials in Advertising,[32] which consistent with the FTC's view of its jurisdiction noted above, would apply to prescription drug advertising. The Guides prohibit deceptive and unfair practices in the use of endorsements and testimonials in advertising, including by experts such as physicians as well as celebrities[33] and consumers/patients. The 2009 revisions extended the applicability of the Guides to social media, such as blogs and social network sites, in addition to traditional advertising contexts such as television and print advertisements.

Lanham Act

Pursuant to 15 U.S.C. § 1125(a), competitors can bring an action against a company that makes unsupported claims that lead to competitive harm. For many years, however, courts have held that it is not appropriate to allow a competitor to seek redress for alleged false advertising of a prescription drug through the Lanham Act, concluding that actions for false and misleading labeling and advertising are in the first instance within the sole jurisdiction of FDA, and the FDCA does not provide a private right of action.[34] At least one court has

---

29   FTC v. Simeon Mgmt. Corp., 391 F. Supp. 697 (N.D. Cal. 1975), *aff'd*, 532 F.2d 708 (9th Cir. 1976).

30   *See* FTC, FTC.COM DISCLOSURES, HOW TO MAKE EFFECTIVE DISCLOSURES IN DIGITAL ADVERTISING (March 2013), *available at* http://www.ftc.gov/sites/default/files/attachments/press-releases/ftc-staff-revises-online-advertising-disclosure-guidelines/130312dotcomdisclosures.pdf.

31   Memorandum of Understanding between FTC and FDA Concerning Exchange of Information, FDA MOU No. 225-71-8003 (May 14, 1971), *available at* http://www.fda.gov/AboutFDA/PartnershipsCollaborations/MemorandaofUnderstandingMOUs/DomesticMOUs/ucm115791.htm.

32   16 C.F.R. pt. 255.

33   *See, e.g.,* Direct-to-Consumer Advertising: Marketing, Education, or Deception?: Hearing Before the Subcomm. on Oversight and Investigations of the H. Comm. on Energy and Commerce, 110th Cong. (2008) (statement of Rep. Bart Stupak) (discussing Pfizer's DTC ads for Lipitor that featured Mr. Robert Jarvik, a celebrity and healthcare professional who invented the artificial heart, as a paid spokesperson for Lipitor. Mr. Jarvik admitted that he did not begin taking Lipitor until a few months after he began filming the commercials. Pfizer voluntarily stopped the ad after the subcommittee began its investigation).

34   *See, e.g.,* Schering-Plough Healthcare Prod. Inc. v. Schwarz Pharma, Inc., 547 F. Supp. 2d 939 (E.D. Wis. 2008), *aff'd*, 586 F.3d 500 (7th Cir. 2009) (the court concluded that ruling on the merits of Schering's Lanham Act claim would require the court to usurp FDA's responsibility for interpreting and enforcing its regulations.) *See also* Sandoz Pharms. Corp. v. Richardson-Vicks, Inc., 902 F.2d 222 (3d Cir. 1990) (as to claims for OTC drugs, the court found that neither of the agencies' constituent statutes creates an express or implied private right of action, and what the FDCA and the FTC Act do not create directly, the Lanham Act does not create indirectly, at least not in cases requiring original interpretation of these acts or their accompanying regulations) (citations omitted). *Cf.* Buckman v. Plaintiff's Legal Committee, 531 U.S. 341 (2001) (the Court discussed whether actions resting on violations of the Medical Devices Amendments of 1976 were improper assertions of a private right of action under the FDCA).

allowed a Lanham Act claim to proceed against a prescription drug advertisement when FDA independently had not approved it.[35]

In 2014, another court held that complying with FDA regulations does not preempt a Lanham Act claim, unless the claim would require the court to question FDA's scientific conclusions.[36] In *GlaxoSmithKline LLC v. Teva Pharmaceuticals*,[37] GlaxoSmithKline (GSK) alleged that Teva falsely advertised a generic antidepressant as equivalent to GSK's brand-name Wellbutrin, thereby damaging GSK's product's reputation. GSK argued that Teva improperly relied on the United States Supreme Court decision in *POM Wonderful LLC v. Coca Cola Co.*, and that *POM Wonderful* rejected efforts to narrow liability under the Lanham Act and the FDCA.[38] In that case, the Supreme Court held that competitors may bring Lanham Act claims challenging food and beverage labels regulated under the FDCA, and neither the Lanham Act nor the FDCA preempt such challenges.[39] On Motion for Reconsideration, the trial court found that GSK's claim is not preempted by FDA's determination that the two products are not bioequivalent. These decisions reflect an increasing willingness by federal courts to look beyond FDA determinations as the basis for false advertising claims and illustrate the tension between the Lanham Act and FDCA preemption.

Subsequently, in a case involved drug labeling, the United States District Court for the Central District of California, in 2014, relied on *POM Wonderful*[40] in concluding that "Congress did not intend the FDCA to preclude Lanham Act suits."[41] The District Court interpreted the *Pom Wonderful* decision to also apply to alleged misleading drug labeling that violates the Lanham Act.[42]

States

Many of the states have statutes similar to the FDCA that prevent false and misleading labeling.[43] In addition, some states have unfair competition and consumer deception laws; e.g., California's Unfair Competition Law (codified at California Business and Professions Code § 17200 *et seq.*), that allow for actions by the state attorney general and/or consumers against false and misleading advertising.[44] However, this section of the California statute has been held to be preempted by federal law, at least in areas such as credit reporting agencies,[45] interstate sales of wholesale electricity,[46] and homeowner's loans.[47]

---

[35] Solvay Pharms., Inc. v. Ethex Corp. & KV Pharm. Co., Food, Drug, Cosm. L. Rep. (CCH) ¶ 38,872 (D. Minn. 2006).
[36] GlaxoSmithKline LLC v. Teva Pharm. USA Inc., No. 2:13-cv-00726 (E.D. Pa. June 24, 2014).
[37] No. 2:13-cv-00726 (E.D. Pa. June 24, 2014).
[38] *See* POM Wonderful LLC v. Coca-Cola Co., 134 S. Ct. 2228, 2241 (2014).
[39] *Id.* at 2242.
[40] *See* POM Wonderful LLC v. Coca-Cola Co., 134 S. Ct. 2228, 2241 (2014).
[41] Par Sterile Products LLC v. Hospira Inc., 2014 U.S. Dist. Lexis 142797.
[42] *Id.*
[43] *See, e.g.*, CAL. HEALTH & SAFETY CODE §§ 111360, 111365, 111860-111895 (Lexis 2014).
[44] *See, e.g.*, California's Unfair Competition Law, codified at CALIFORNIA BUSINESS AND PROFESSIONS CODE § 17200, *et seq.*, prohibits "unfair competition," which includes "any . . . unfair, deceptive, untrue or misleading advertising." CAL. BUS. & PROF. §§ 17200-17210 (Lexis 2014).
[45] Howard v. Blue Ridge Bank, 371 F. Supp. 2d 1139 (N.D. Cal. 2005).
[46] In re Enron Corp., 328 B.R. 75 (2005).
[47] Silvas v. E*Trade Mortg. Corp., 421 F. Supp. 2d 1315 (S.D. Cal. 2006).

While the courts have not addressed whether the FDCA prescription drug advertising provisions preempt California's Unfair Competition Law, some courts have ruled that claims under similar state laws are preempted by federal law. In August 2007, for example, the Third Circuit Court of Appeals held that the plaintiffs' state fraud claims under Delaware law were preempted by the FDCA and FDA regulations because both the federal statute and regulations "provide specific requirements for prescription drug advertising," and this "high level of specificity . . . is irreconcilable with general state laws that purport to govern all types of advertising."[48] However, in *Wyeth v. Levine*, the Supreme Court held that there was "powerful evidence that Congress did not intend FDA oversight to be the exclusive means of ensuring drug safety and effectiveness."[49] The Court therefore held that FDA approval did not preempt product liability litigation challenges brought under state laws. Likewise, state courts are now much more likely to find an absence of preemption based on compliance with FDA regulations.

In addition, several states have adopted marketing and transparency codes, regulating various types of prescription drug marketing and promotional activities, including interactions with healthcare professionals and reporting of payments and other benefits provided to physicians.[50]

National Advertising Division (NAD)

Companies have also turned to the National Advertising Division (NAD) of the Council of Better Business Bureaus to challenge allegedly false advertising of prescription drugs.[51] For example, GSK's advertisement for Flonase Nasal Spray was challenged in 2005 by Schering-Plough Corporation, maker of Nasonex Nasal Spray.[52] More recently, in 2014, Merck brought a challenge based on Chattem's OTC Nasacort Allergy 24 HR allergy relief product advertisements.[53] Merck claimed there was insufficient scientific evidence including a lack of a head-to-head clinical trial between Claritin and Nasacort to provide a reasonable basis for Nasacort's comparative superiority claims. NAD reviewed the evidence and determined there was a reasonable basis for each of the Nasacort claims and, moreover, stated that conducting head-to-head trials was not the sole way to provide support for comparative

---

[48] Penn. Employees Benefit Trust Fund v. Zeneca, Inc., 499 F.3d 239, 251-252 (3rd Cir. 2007), vacated and remanded, 555 U.S. 555 (U.S. 2009), in light of Wyeth v. Levine, and dismissed without prejudice on remand, 710 F. Supp. 2d 458 (D. Del. 2010)

[49] Wyeth v. Levine, 555 U.S. 555 (2009).

[50] *See, e.g.,* Vermont's Prescription Drug Cost Containment Reporting Requirements, 18 Vt. Stat. Ann. § 4632 (2014); Massachusetts' Pharmaceutical and Medical Device Manufacturer Conduct Requirements, Mass. Gen. Laws ch. 111N § 4 (2014).

[51] *See, e.g.,* Code of Advertising, Nat'l Adver. Div., Better Bus. Bureau, *available at* http://www.bbb.org/council/for-businesses/code-of-advertising/ ("Advertisements which . . . shall not be used."). Challenges to advertising for OTC drugs are more common, for example, the manufacturer of Claritin's challenge before the NAD to certain claims made by the maker of another allergy medication, Allegra (*See* CHATTEM, Inc., Allegra, NAD/CARU Case Reports, #5360 (Aug. 2011)).

[52] The challenged advertisement for Flonase Nasal Spray was in the form of a "dosing card," distributed by GlaxoSmithKline (GSK) to sales representatives for use in sales calls with physicians. NAD/CARU Case Reports, #4,312 (Apr. 2005). Upon inquiry by NAD, GSK stated that the advertising in question was permanently discontinued prior to the challenge. *Id.* Also in 2005, Merck & Co., Inc.'s Vytorin broadcast commercial was challenged by Kraft Foods Global, Inc. Upon inquiry by NAD, Merck stated that the advertising piece had been discontinued "for reasons unrelated to the present challenge." NAD/CARU Case Reports, #4330 (Apr. 2005).

[53] Chattem, Inc., Nasacort Allergy 24HR, NAD/CARU Case Reports, #5740 (July 2014).

performance clams, especially when there is strong scientific consensus about the product efficacy[54] claims.

NAD reviews "only national advertisements," which involve "product performance claims, superiority claims against competitive products and all kinds of scientific and technical claims."[55] The NAD process is self-funded (through participants' review fees), voluntary, and not binding on the parties. When an advertiser elects not to participate in a NAD review, however, NAD "prepares a review of the facts with relevant exhibits and forwards them to the appropriate federal or state law enforcement agency."[56] NAD may also refer the file to the appropriate government agency, ordinarily FTC, if the advertiser fails to respond to an NAD inquiry, fails to respond to NAD's decision that the advertising was not substantiated, or fails to comply with NAD's decision.[57] However, occasionally NAD and federal agencies disagree. For example, in 2014, Pfizer Consumer Healthcare, maker of ThermaCare® over-the-counter heat wraps challenged through NAD broadcast, print, and Internet health-related superiority and pricing claims made by Hisamitsu America, Inc., maker of Salonpas® Brand Pain Relief Products.[58] Hisamitsu declined to participate in the NAD review of its claims, stating that the challenged claims were submitted as part of its NDA for use on the OTC drug product label and approved by FDA. NAD disagreed, stating that FDA approval of a claim does not preclude review by NAD to determine whether competing superiority claims are truthful and accurate. NAD referred the case to FTC. FTC declined to recommend enforcement action, finding that the net impression created by Hisamitsu's statements, graphics, and other depictions in the advertising was not misleading.[59]

Trade and Other Associations
PhRMA Codes

In response to criticism about the scope and frequency of direct-to-consumer advertising of prescription drugs, the Pharmaceutical Research and Manufacturers of America (PhRMA), the trade association representing innovator pharmaceutical companies, developed in 2005 the PhRMA Guiding Principles on DTC Advertisements About Prescription Medicines to

---

[54] The NAD decision is another example of third-party entities looking beyond FDA standards to review advertising claims, as here, the FDA standard to support a comparative superiority claim would have required a head-to-head clinical trial.

[55] NAD, How NAD Works, *available at* http://www.nadreview.org/HowNADWorks.aspx ("About NAD")

[56] NAD, Advertising Industry's Process of Voluntary Self-Regulation (Policies and Procedures by the National Advertising Review Board), § 2.1.F(iii), *available at* http://www.narcpartners.org/reports/2010_Procedures.pdf.

[57] NAD, Advertising Industry's Process of Voluntary Self-Regulation (Policies and Procedures by the National Advertising Review Board), at §§ 2.9.B, 2.10.B, 4.1.B. For further discussion of the NAD process, *see* the Advertising Industry's Process of Voluntary Self-Regulation (Policies and Procedures by the National Advertising Review Board) (revised March 8, 2010), *available at* http://www.narcpartners.org/reports/2010_Procedures.pdf.

[58] Hisamitsu America, Inc./Salonpas® Brand Pain Relief Products, NAD/CARU Case Reports, #5669 (Jan. 2014).

[59] *See* Letter from Mary K. Engle, Associate Director, Division of Advertising Practices, Federal Trade Commission, to Andrea C. Levine, Senior Vice President, Nat'l Advertising Division (May 13, 2014), *available at* http://www.ftc.gov/system/files/documents/public_statements/310491/140513salonpasresolutionltr.pdf.

"ensure that direct-to-consumer advertising in the future is even more informational and educational to patients and consumers."[60]

PhRMA also adopted a voluntary marketing code in 2002, its Code on Interactions with Healthcare Professionals (PhRMA Code).[61] The PhRMA Code provides standards for hiring physicians as consultants to promote drugs or render other services and providing financial grants for drug education and other purposes.[62] This Code was revised in July 2008, to further restrict promotion in the form of gifts and other payments to physicians.[63] The 2002 PhRMA Code was a precursor to the model compliance code for pharmaceutical manufacturers issued by the OIG in 2003, which is relied on by the pharmaceutical industry as a regulatory framework for marketing and promoting drugs.[64] According to OIG, compliance with the PhRMA Code, "[a]lthough it will not protect a manufacturer as a matter of law under the anti-kickback statute; it will substantially reduce the risk of fraud and abuse and help demonstrate a good faith effort to comply with the applicable federal healthcare program requirements."[65]

American Medical Association (AMA) Policy

AMA has also established principles for advertising and promotion in connection with AMA publications and websites as well as general guidelines for quality of medical information content on websites.[66] The guidelines set standards for disclosure of site ownership, funding and sponsorship, and privacy. For example, the guidelines prohibit the placement of advertisements for a product adjacent to an AMA editorial on the same topic.

Accreditation Council for Continuing Medical Education (ACCME)

The ACCME has established standards for financial support for continuing medical education (CME) to ensure that it is not unduly influenced by pharmaceutical industry supporters, and thus becomes drug "promotion" rather than education.[67] Despite these standards, there has been congressional scrutiny of the ACCME guidelines based on concern that the standards are not sufficiently well enforced to prevent undue commercial influence over content.[68] As a result, in June 2010, the ACCME released additional guidance

---

60   PhRMA Guiding Principles: Direct to Consumer Advertisements About Prescription Medicines (2009), *available at* http://www.phrma.org/sites/default/files/631/phrmaguidingprinciplesdec08final.pdf.

61   PhRMA Code on Interactions with Healthcare Professionals (2002), *available at* http://www.phrma.org/principles-guidelines/code-on-interactions-with-health-care-professionals..

62   *Id.* at p. 7-10.

63   *See* PhRMA Code on Interactions with Healthcare Professionals (July 2008; effective Jan. 2009), *available at* http://www.phrma.org/sites/default/files/108/phrma_marketing_code_2008.pdf (updating voluntary code on interactions with healthcare professionals with respect to marketed products and pre-launch activities).

64   OIG, Compliance Program Guidance for Pharmaceutical Manufacturers, 68 Fed. Reg. 23,731 (May 3, 2003).

65   *Id.* at 23,737.

66   *See* The AMA Principles Governing Advertising in Publications of the American Medical Association, *available at* http://jamanetwork.com/data/pdfs/ads/adPrinciples.pdf.

67   *See* The Standards for Commercial Support: Standards to Ensure Independence in CME Activities (2004), *available at* http://www.accme.org/printpdf/requirements/accreditation-requirements-cme-providers/standards-for-commercial-support. Additionally,

68   Letter from Senator Herb Kohl, Chairman of the Special Committee on Aging, United States Senate, to Dr. M. Kopelow, CEO, ACCME (June 20, 2008) (requesting documentation on ACCME accreditation process

about the role of ACCME-defined commercial interest employees in accredited CME, which outlines the ACCME standards for ensuring independence for CME about discovery and research. The guidance includes examples of important factors for accredited providers and the ACCME to consider in determining an appropriate role for an employee of an ACCME-defined commercial interest in planning or presenting accredited CME.[69]

Broadcasters

Broadcast and cable networks also have standards and guidelines on drug advertising in general, and on prescription drug advertisements in particular. For example, ESPN's Advertising Standards & Guidelines state that "[p]rescription drug advertisements must comply with FDA Guidelines," including the elements of 'Major Statement' and 'Adequate Provision.'"[70] The networks also have processes by which competitors can challenge advertisements under the broadcasters' standards.

Congressional Oversight

On occasion, Congress also may become involved concerning particular drug promotional activities. For example, in 2008, the U.S. House of Representatives Committee on Energy and Commerce sent a letter to Pfizer's CEO, expressing concerns that consumers may misinterpret its Lipitor DTC advertisements that utilize Dr. Robert Jarvik.[71] In particular, the committee was concerned that consumers "may misinterpret the health claims" of Lipitor, and that consumers also may misinterpret Dr. Jarvik's qualifications, as he "may not be a practicing physician with a valid license in any State."[72] The letter asked Pfizer to provide records relating to the advertising campaign for Lipitor and records relating to Dr. Jarvik's association with Pfizer, among others.[73] In a response letter to the committee, Pfizer announced that it was "voluntarily withdrawing Lipitor advertising and promotion featuring Dr. Jarvik."[74]

---

and criteria for scientific validity of materials used in CME).

[69] "Can accredited CME include the oral (e.g., presentations) or written reporting (e.g., abstracts) of 'scientific research' conducted by ACCME-defined commercial interests that is reported by employees of those commercial interests?" (last revised Nov. 2011), *available at* http://accme.org/ask-accme/can-provider-allow-oral-or-written-reporting-scientific-research-employee-commercial.

[70] ESPN, ESPN Advertising Standards & Guidelines (All Media) (2014), at 10, *available at* http://commops.espn.com/new_folder0/ESPN_AdStandardsGuidelines_1.pdf.

[71] Letter from Reps. Bart Stupak and John D. Dingell of the U.S. House of Rep., Comm. on Energy and Commerce, to Jeffrey B. Kindler, CEO, Pfizer (Jan. 7, 2008), *available at* http://democrats.energycommerce.house.gov/images/stories/Documents/PDF/Letters/110-ltr.010708.Pfizer.Jarvik.pdf.

[72] *Id.*

[73] *Id.*

[74] Letter from Anthony J. Principi, Senior Vice President, Pfizer, to Reps. Bart Stupak and John D. Dingell of the U.S. House of Rep., Comm. on Energy and Commerce (Feb. 25, 2008), *available at* http://democrats.energycommerce.house.gov/images/stories/Documents/PDF/Letters/110-ltr.022508.resptoour010708.Pfizer.pdf.

Promotion and Marketing of Prescription Drugs

What Is Regulated—Advertising Versus Labeling

Under the FDCA, FDA regulates the sale, manufacture, and distribution of drugs. This statutory grant of authority includes oversight over promotional materials for and marketing of all prescription drugs, including labels, labeling, advertising, and promotional activities such as trade show demonstrations, oral presentations by sales representatives and others, video and audio conferences, meetings, and press releases.[75] The FDCA defines "labeling" as "all labels and other written, printed, or graphic matter (1) upon any article or any of its containers or wrappers, or (2) accompanying such article."[76] The Supreme Court held that the phrase "accompanying such article" in the "labeling" definition applies to any materials that supplement or explain the drug, "in the manner that a committee report of the Congress accompanies a bill. No physical attachment one to the other is necessary. It is the textual relationship that is significant . . . ."[77] Thus, FDA has historically treated most written, printed, or graphic materials disseminated by or on behalf of a drug company as labeling rather than advertising, regardless of their physical proximity to the product. FDA regulations define "labeling" as a wide variety of written, printed, or graphic matter that bears a textual relationship with a drug or device, such as written materials handed out or otherwise distributed by the company or its representatives, such as brochures, detail pieces, file cards, coupons, calendars, and price lists.[78] Such materials may include electronic labeling such as software programs, CD-ROMs, and arguably PDA and podcasts.[79]

The Supreme Court's decisions in *Warner-Lambert v. Kent*[80] and *Wyeth v. Levine*,[81] concerning the product liability ramifications of changes and omissions in a product's FDA-approved label and the inapplicability of federal preemption of challenges under state laws, also affect pharmaceutical manufacturers' decisions regarding label and labeling revisions and updates.

Neither the FDCA nor FDA's regulations expressly address how to categorize a company's materials displayed on the Internet.[82] As a practical matter, FDA now regulates labeling and advertising in the same manner. FDA recently issued a draft guidance on Internet/social media platforms which indicates that companies should include both benefit and risk information within advertising and promotional labeling of their FDA-regulated medical products on electronic/digital platforms that are associated with character space

---

[75]   FDCA § 502(n), 21 U.S.C. § 352(n).

[76]   FDCA § 201(m), 21 U.S.C. § 321(m).

[77]   Kordel v. United States, 335 U.S. 345 (1948); *see also* United States v. Articles of Drug ... 5906 Boxes, 745 F.2d 105 (1st Cir. 1984), *cert. denied*, 470 U.S. 1004 (1985) (noting index cards provided to doctors are labeling because the cards explained the drug).

[78]   21 C.F.R. § 202.1(l)(2).

[79]   *Id.*

[80]   Warner-Lambert v. Kent, 552 U.S. 440 (2008).

[81]   Wyeth v. Levine, 555 U.S. 555 (2009).

[82]   FDA indicated its intent to evaluate which standards should apply to Internet sites in its notice of public meeting and request for comments on how to regulate Internet materials. *See* 61 Fed. Reg. 48,707 (Sept. 16, 1996). Prior FDA guidances, e.g., FDA Draft Guidance, Presenting Risk Information in Prescription Drug and Medical Device Promotion (May 2009), appear to equate promotional labeling and advertising. *Id* n. 9.

limitations.[83] In a second guidance document on social media use, FDA asserted it intends to regulate, as pharmaceutical company content, communications that are:

- generated by an employee or agent who is acting on behalf of the firm to promote the firm's product[84] owned, controlled, created, influenced or operated by, or on behalf of, the firm or affirmatively adopted by or endorsed by or on behalf of the firm;

- under certain circumstances, generated by a third party that is promoted by the firm to third-party sites; and

- generated by an employee or agent who is acting on behalf of the firm to promote the firm's product.

Similarly, FDA has issued untitled and Warning Letters concerning Internet sites[85] and search engines[86] that apply the same principles ordinarily applied to labeling and advertising.

---

[83] FDA Draft Guidance for Industry, Internet/Social Media Platforms with Character Space Limitations–Presenting Risk and Benefit Information for Prescription Drugs and Medical Devices (June 2014), *available at* http://www.fda.gov/downloads/Drugs/GuidanceComplianceRegulatoryInformation/Guidances/UCM401087.pdf.

[84] *Id.* The FDA Draft Guidance has been criticized by pharmaceutical companies and trade organizations, with the majority of objections citing that FDA proposes to review materials that fall outside of the FDCA's definition of labeling and FDA's regulatory description of advertising. *See Big Pharma Tears Into FDA's Social Media Guidance*, Law360 (Apr. 16, 2014), http://www.law360.com/articles/528723/big-pharma-tears-into-fda-s-social-media-guidance. Comments on the proposed guidance can be found at: http://www.regulations.gov/#!docketBrowser;rpp=25;po=0;dct=PS;D=FDA-2013-N-1430;refD=FDA-2013-N-1430-0001.

[85] *See* Untitled Letter from Oluwaseun Asante and Samuel M. Skariah, Office of Prescription Drug Program, FDA, to Naumann Chaudry, Director, Regulatory Affairs Advertising and Promotion, Gilead Sciences, Inc. (June 27, 2014), *available at* http://www.fda.gov/downloads/Drugs/GuidanceComplianceRegulatoryInformation/EnforcementActivitiesbyFDA/WarningLettersandNoticeofViolationLetterstoPharmaceuticalCompanies/UCM404063.pdf (warning Gilead Sciences that its sponsored link for the drug Viread on the Internet search engine, Google.com, is labeling that is intended for a new use for which it lacks approval, and renders Viread misbranded); Untitled Letter from Ankur Kalola and Adora Nadu, Office of Prescription Drug Promotion, FDA, to Steve A. Kates, Vice President, Citius Pharmaceuticals (June 9, 2014), *available at* http://www.fda.gov/downloads/Drugs/GuidanceComplianceRegulatoryInformation/EnforcementActivitiesbyFDA/WarningLettersandNoticeofViolationLetterstoPharmaceuticalCompanies/UCM400708.pdf (stating that the website homepage for its drug Suprenza is false or misleading because it omits risk information, includes unsubstantiated efficacy claims, and omits material facts). FDA's first direct effort to regulate all Internet references as labeling occurred on March 26, 2009, when FDA issued untitled letters to 14 pharmaceutical companies regarding their use of sponsored links on Internet search engines. FDA used its traditional standard for promotional materials to review the Internet-based advertising in these letters. The agency stated that a sponsored link violates the FDCA's misbranding provisions when the link contains inadequate or misleading information related to a drug product's risks or indications. Subsequently, in a 2010 Warning Letter to Novartis, FDA stated that, although a website produced a pop-up window disclaimer stating that the user was moving to an external website independently operated and not managed by Novartis, FDA asserted that there were several indicators that the manufacturer nonetheless was responsible for the content of the website. (*See* Warning Letter from Thomas Abrams, Director, Division of Drug Marketing, Advertising, and Communications, FDA to Ludwig Hantson, CEO, Novartis Pharmaceuticals Corporation (Apr. 21, 2010), *available at* http://www.fda.gov/Drugs/GuidanceComplianceRegulatoryInformation/EnforcementActivitiesbyFDA/WarningLettersandNoticeofViolationLetterstoPharmaceuticalCompanies/ucm259229.htm).

[86] *See* FDA Warning Letter from Alonza E. Crus, Director, Los Angeles District, FDA, to Clifford Woods, Vibrant Life Vitamins (April 7, 2013), *available at* http://www.fda.gov/iceci/enforcementactions/warningletters/2013/ucm364664.htm (websites, including a Facebook page and use of metatags, promoted its products for conditions that caused them to be considered unapproved new drugs under FDCA).

Materials that drug companies distribute will also be attributed to the company as labeling, even if not authored by the company.[87] For example, scientific articles written by academicians, if distributed by the company, are deemed to be statements of the company.[88]

FDA also considers oral statements to be labeling, and to be able to expand the labeling of a drug beyond its approved indications,[89] and thereby potentially misbrand it. A number of courts have held such oral statements may render a product misbranded for failure to bear adequate directions for use.[90]

Under the law and in practice, there are generally two types of labeling—the FDA-approved label or labeling that is on or physically accompanying the product, and "promotional" labeling. The label for a prescription drug that is principally intended for healthcare professionals, and sometimes labeling for patients, is submitted in the application for approval (a new drug application or abbreviated new drug application) or licensure (a biologics license application) and reviewed and approved by FDA *prior* to product approval.[91] FDA also may require or strongly recommend to an applicant that it include with the drug a Medication Guide (MedGuide),[92] which is labeling that must be dispensed to patients and that is reviewed by FDA prior to product approval.[93] Prescription drug manufacturers can also provide patient package inserts, which must also be reviewed by FDA prior to

[87]   *See* Warning Letter from Roberta Szydlo, Regulatory Review Officer, Division of Professional Drug Promotion, Office of Prescription Drug Promotion, FDA, to Ashlie Adams, Manager, Regulatory Affairs, Cornerstone Therapeutics (Oct. 31, 2012), *available at* http://www.fda.gov/downloads/Drugs/GuidanceComplianceRegulatoryInformation/EnforcementActivitiesbyFDA/WarningLettersandNoticeofViolationLetterstoPharmaceuticalCompanies/UCM327250.pdf (marketing firm sent a pitch letter promoting a Cornerstone press release regarding prescription drug Curosurf).

[88]   *See* Warning Letter from Thomas Abrams, Director, Division of Drug Marketing, Advertising, and Communications, FDA, to James Manuso, Chairman, SuperGen, Inc. (Aug. 18, 2005), *available at* http://www.fda.gov/downloads/Drugs/GuidanceComplianceRegulatoryInformation/EnforcementActivitiesbyFDA/WarningLettersandNoticeofViolationLetterstoPharmaceuticalCompanies/ucm054801.pdf.

[89]   *See* Warning Letter from Robert Dean, Division Director, Office of Prescription Drug Promotion, FDA, to Marc Beer, Chief Executive Officer, Aegerion Pharmaceuticals, Inc. (Nov. 8, 2013), *available at* http://www.fda.gov/downloads/Drugs/GuidanceComplianceRegulatoryInformation/EnforcementActivitiesbyFDA/WarningLettersandNoticeofViolationLetterstoPharmaceuticalCompanies/UCM374338.pdf (regarding statements CEO Marc Beer made about prescription drug Juxtapid during broadcast interviews on CNBC's television show "Fast Money." FDA stated the Mr. Beer's statements provided evidence that Juxtapid is intended for new uses for which it lacked approval, rendering it misbranded; Untitled Letter from Mathilda Fienkeng, Regulatory Review Officer, Division of Drug Marketing, Advertising, and Communications, FDA, to John Driscoll, Senior Manager, Regulatory Affairs, Forest Laboratories, Inc. (Apr. 28, 2011) (oral statements by sales representatives regarding the drug Savella, complaints regarding which were submitted through the DDMAC Bad Ad Program); Warning Letter from Lynn Panholdzer, Pharm.D and Debi Tran, Pharm.D, USPHS, Regulatory Review Officers, Division of Drug Marketing, Advertising, and Communications, FDA, to Andrea Czeizinger, J.D., Program Director, Drug Regulatory Affairs, Hoffman-LaRoche Inc. (July 15, 2005) concerning Fuzeon for Injection (oral statements by sales representatives made at scientific conference misbrand drug by recommending a use beyond the approved labeling) (citing 21 C.F.R. §201.5(a) and 201.128).

[90]   *See, e.g.,* United States v. Hohensee, 243 F.2d 367, 370 (3d Cir. 1957); *see also* V.E. Irons, Inc. v. United States, 244 F.2d 34 (1st Cir. 1957), cert. denied, 354 U.S. 923 (1957).

[91]   21 C.F.R. § 314.81(b)(3)(i); *see also id.* § 601.12(f)(4).

[92]   *Id.* § 208.20.

[93]   *Id.* § 208.24. Medication Guides can also be required as part of a Risk Evaluation and Mitigation Strategy. *See* FDA Guidance, Medication Guides — Distribution Requirement and Inclusion in Risk Evaluation and Mitigation Strategies (REMS) (Nov. 2011).

NDA approval and which in most cases do not have to be dispensed to patients.[94] All other labeling is considered by FDA to be promotional labeling, and is not subject to approval by FDA *prior* to dissemination. All promotional labeling must be consistent, however, with the FDA-approved labeling, and must be submitted to FDA at the time of distribution.[95] Promotional labeling must be accompanied by a copy of the full product labeling.

FDA also regulates advertising, which is not defined by statute or regulation, but includes such items as "advertisements in published journals, magazines, other periodicals, and newspapers, and advertisements broadcast through media such as radio, television, and telephone communication systems."[96] In one instance, FDA extended this categorization to broadcast over the Internet through YouTube.[97] Unlike labeling, advertisements need only include a brief summary relating to the side effects, warnings, precautions, and contraindications of the product, but not full product labeling.[98] The "brief summary," however, is often lengthy and may contain most of the information found in the package insert.

There are multiple types of promotional labeling and advertising subject to FDA oversight: 1) product claims, in which safety, efficacy, or other characteristics of the product are discussed, and 2) reminder labeling and advertising, which contain only a reference to drug name, ingredients, dosage, form, quantity, price, and the manufacturer. Reminder labeling and advertisements are not required to provide any risk or other information.[99] Help-seeking labeling and advertisements that are intended to give consumers general information about a disease and direct them to a healthcare provider, for further information are regulated by the Federal Trade Commission unless they include any written, graphic, or audio references which directly or indirectly imply a specific product.[100] The help-seeking advertisement would then be considered to be product promotion and subject to FDA's jurisdiction.

In May 2010, FDA instituted a program encouraging health professionals to submit reports of potentially untrue or misleading drug promotion to the agency (the "Bad Ad" program). During its first year of operation, DDMAC (now called the Office of Prescription Drug Promotion, or OPDP) reported that reports of potentially violative promotions to the agency tripled over the total received during the prior year.[101] Of the 328 complaints received by

---

[94] *See, e.g., id.* § 310.501.

[95] *Id.* § 314.81(b)(3)(i).

[96] *Id.* § 202.1(l)(1).

[97] *See* Warning Letter from Thomas Abrams, Director, Division of Drug Marketing, Advertising, and Communication, FDA, to Angus Russell, Chief Executive Officer, Shire Development, Inc. (Sept. 25, 2008), *available at* http://www.fda.gov/downloads/Drugs/GuidanceComplianceRegulatoryInformation/EnforcementActivitiesbyFDA/WarningLettersandNoticeofViolationLetterstoPharmaceuticalCompanies/ucm053995.pdf.

[98] 21 U.S.C. § 352(n).

[99] 21 C.F.R. §§ 201.100(f), 202.1(e)(2)(i).

[100] For example, a disease awareness advertisement bearing the distinctive color combination of a branded drug could be construed to violate the guideline, and convert the advertisement to a product-specific safety and efficacy claim. *See* FDA, Guidance for Industry: Help-Seeking and Other Disease Awareness Communications by or on Behalf of Drug and Device Firms (Jan. 23, 2004) at 5, *available at* http://www.fda.gov/downloads/Drugs/GuidanceComplianceRegulatoryInformation/Guidances/ucm070068.pdf.

[101] *See,* FDA's Truthful Prescription Drug Advertising and Promotion (Bad Ad Program), *available at* http://www.fda.gov/Drugs/GuidanceComplianceRegulatoryInformation/Surveillance/DrugMarketingAdvertisingandCommunications/ucm209384.htm#Report.

FDA during the first year of the program, 188 came from healthcare providers; more than a third of the reports (125) related to potentially misleading promotional activities.[102] FDA issued several Warning Letters that derived from the Bad Ad program in 2011, including to Forest Laboratories,[103] Warner Chilcott,[104] Shire,[105] and Pfizer.[106] In 2012, FDA issued Warning Letters to Merck & Co.[107] and Pfizer.[108] The OIG also has referenced FDA's Bad Ad program on its website, encouraging submission of potentially misleading programs.[109]

FDA Review and Clearance Procedures for Labeling and Advertising

Except in "extraordinary circumstances," the FDCA does not authorize FDA to require pre-clearance of promotional materials prior to dissemination.[110] FDA regulations, however, provide for the voluntary submission of promotional materials in advance of dissemination. FDA's OPDP will provide advisory comments on draft promotional materials (submitted before their distribution),[111] and it cannot act against an advertiser who follows these

---

[102]   See FDA, Bad Ad Program 2010-2011 Year End Report, available at http://www.fda.gov/drugs/guidancecomplianceregulatoryinformation/surveillance/drugmarketingadvertisingandcommunications/ucm258719.htm. See also FDA Bad Ad Program 2011-2012 Year End Report, available at http://www.fda.gov/Drugs/GuidanceComplianceRegulatoryInformation/Surveillance/DrugMarketingAdvertisingandCommunications/ucm258719.htm.

[103]   See Untitled Letter from Mathilda Fienkeng, Pharm.D., Regulatory Review Officer, Division of Drug Marketing, Advertising, and Communications, FDA, to John Driscoll, Senior Manager, Regulatory Affairs, Forest Laboratories, Inc. (Apr. 28, 2011) concerning Savella (oral statements by sales representatives that were submitted via the DDMAC Bad Ad Program), available at http://www.fda.gov/downloads/Drugs/GuidanceComplianceRegulatoryInformation/EnforcementActivitiesbyFDA/WarningLettersandNoticeofViolationLetterstoPharmaceuticalCompanies/UCM253625.pdf.

[104]   See Untitled Letter from Michelle L. Safarik, MSPAS, PA-C, Regulatory Review Officer, Division of Drug Marketing, Advertising, and Communications, FDA, to Brian Deutsch, Associate, Regulatory Affairs, Warner Chilcott, LLC (May, 5, 2011) concerning Atelvia (YouTube video by a member of Warner Chilcott's sales team, submitted via the DDMAC Bad Ad Program), available at http://www.fda.gov/downloads/Drugs/GuidanceComplianceRegulatoryInformation/EnforcementActivitiesbyFDA/WarningLettersandNoticeofViolationLetterstoPharmaceuticalCompanies/UCM254562.pdf.

[105]   See Warning Letter from Thomas Abrams, Director, Division of Drug Marketing, Advertising, and Communications, FDA, to Angus Russell, CEO, Shire Pharmaceuticals Inc. (May 6, 2011), available at http://www.fda.gov/Drugs/GuidanceComplianceRegulatoryInformation/EnforcementActivitiesbyFDA/WarningLettersandNoticeofViolationLetterstoPharmaceuticalCompanies/ucm259167.htm.

[106]   See Untitled Letter from Zarna Patel, Pharm.D., Regulatory Review Office, Division of Drug Marketing, Advertising, and Communications, FDA, to Robert Clark, Vice President, US Regulatory Affairs, Pfizer Inc. (Aug. 31, 2011), available at http://www.fda.gov/downloads/Drugs/GuidanceComplianceRegulatoryInformation/EnforcementActivitiesbyFDA/WarningLettersandNoticeofViolationLetterstoPharmaceuticalCompanies/UCM270607.pdf.

[107]   See Untitled Letter from Jessica N. Cleck Derenick, PhD, Regulatory Review Office, Division of Professional Promotion, Office of Prescription Drug Promotion, FDA, to Rachel Henderson, Pharm.D., Senior Manager, Office of Promotion and Advertising Review, Merck & Co., Inc. (Feb. 2, 2012), available at http://www.fda.gov/downloads/Drugs/GuidanceComplianceRegulatoryInformation/EnforcementActivitiesbyFDA/WarningLettersandNoticeofViolationLetterstoPharmaceuticalCompanies/UCM295164.pdf.

[108]   See Warning Letter from Robert Dean, Division Director, Division of Consumer Drug Promotion, Office of Prescription Drug Promotion, FDA, to Ian C. Reed, Chairman and Chief Executive Officer, Pfizer Inc. (May 24, 2012), available at http://www.fda.gov/downloads/Drugs/GuidanceComplianceRegulatoryInformation/EnforcementActivitiesbyFDA/WarningLettersandNoticeofViolationLetterstoPharmaceuticalCompanies/UCM306109.pdf.

[109]   See OIG, A Roadmap for New Physicians at http://oig.hhs.gov/compliance/physician-education/index.asp.

[110]   FDCA § 502(n), 21 U.S.C. § 352(n).

[111]   21 C.F.R. § 202.1(j)(4).

recommendations unless it first issues a "change of opinion letter."[112] The advertiser who receives such a letter "will be given a reasonable time for correction" before any regulatory action can be taken.[113]

FDA regulations also specify some of the "extraordinary circumstances" under which FDA may require preclearance of promotional materials. For instance, preclearance may be required if the sponsor of the drug or FDA has received material suggesting that the drug may cause fatalities or serious injury, and that the information has not been widely publicized in the medical literature.[114] FDA regulations also permit the agency to require preclearance of promotional materials for products approved under the Fast Track approval process,[115] as well as under FDA's accelerated approval process, called "subpart H."[116] These processes are described more fully in Chapter 10 *supra*. In circumstances of repeat violations of the regulations by a company as part of a voluntary corrective action, FDA may impose a preclearance requirement for promotional materials for a defined time period, usually ranging from six months to two years.[117]

Standards of Review—Principles of Advertising and Promotion of Product Claims

Not False or Misleading

As noted above, the FDCA provides that a drug is misbranded if its labeling is false or misleading in any particular manner. The FDCA further provides that a determination of whether a drug's labeling or advertising is misleading shall take into account "not only representations made or suggested," but also "the extent to which the labeling or advertising fails to reveal facts material in light of such representation."[118] Accordingly, both affirmative statements and material omissions can be false or misleading and will cause a drug to be misbranded. The determination of whether materials are false or misleading depends on the specific statements made and the overall impression created by the statements, such as size of print, placement of statements, colors and other graphics, music and videos.[119]

---

[112] *Id.*

[113] *Id.*

[114] 21 C.F.R. § 202.1(j)(1)(i). Note that this requirement may be appealed pursuant to 21 C.F.R. § 202.1(j)(5).

[115] *See* FDCA § 506(b), 21 U.S.C. § 356(b).

[116] *See* 21 C.F.R. § 314.550.

[117] *See* Warning Letter from Dr. Cheryl Graham, Acting Director, Division of Drug Marketing, Advertising, and Communications, FDA, to Joseph E. Smith, President, Parke Davis Group, Division of Warner-Lambert Co. (June 4, 1992) (FDA required as part of corrective action preclearance of all promotional materials for six months).

[118] FDCA § 201(n), 21 U.S.C. § 321(n).

[119] *See* FDA, Guidance for Industry: Presenting Risk Information In Prescription Drug and Medical Device Promotion (Draft Guidance) (May 2009), *available at* http://www.fda.gov/downloads/Drugs/GuidanceComplianceRegulatoryInformation/Guidances/UCM155480.pdf.

All product claims must be supported by substantial evidence,[120] or, in the case of advertisements, substantial clinical experience.[121] This will vary by claim, but is ordinarily expected to include two or more adequate and well-controlled studies.[122]

Fair Balance

FDA regulations require that each advertisement have fair balance "between information relating to side effects and contraindications and information relating to effectiveness of the drug."[123] This requirement derives from the statutory requirement that the advertisement contain a "true statement." The requirement of "fair balance" is applied to promotional labeling based on the statutory requirement that labeling not be false or misleading in any particular.

FDA looks at both content and format to determine whether an advertisement or a promotional labeling contains fair balance. The regulations for advertisements provide that the claims will be viewed in context with the "typography, layout, contrast, headlines, paragraphing, white space, and any other techniques apt to achieve emphasis."[124] The sum of this information must have "a prominence and readability reasonably comparable with the presentation of information relating to effectiveness of the drug."[125] Often, the lack of fair balance results from inadequate risk information, and over-emphasizing the positive benefits of the product. There are many examples of Warning Letters in which FDA asserts a lack of fair balance.[126]

Providing Risk Information in Advertisements: The Brief Summary

As noted above, advertisements must contain a "true statement of information in brief summary relating to side effects, contraindications and effectiveness,"[127] commonly referred to as the brief summary requirement. Typically, companies include the four risk information sections of FDA-approved labeling to fulfill this requirement. Although FDA

---

[120]   21 C.F.R. § 314.126(b).

[121]   21 C.F.R. § 202.1(e)(4)(ii)(b) and (c).

[122]   FDAMA section 115 codified prior FDA policy by changing the definition of "substantial evidence" to clarify that it does not always require two adequate and well-controlled studies. 21 U.S.C. § 355(d) (FDCA § 505(d)). FDA subsequently issued Guidance for Industry on Providing Clinical Evidence of Effectiveness for Human Drugs and Biological Products, 63 Fed. Reg. 27,093 (May 15, 1998), to assist companies in determining when one study is adequate support.

[123]   21 C.F.R. § 202.1(e)(5)(ii).

[124]   Id. § 202.1(e)(7)(viii).

[125]   Id.

[126]   See e.g., Warning Letter from Thomas Abrams, Director, Division of Drug Marketing, Advertising, and Communications, FDA, to Kos Pharmaceuticals, Inc. (July 13, 2001) (finding DTC advertisement for Niaspan lacking in fair balance because it failed to include bolded warnings concerning toxicity), available at http://www.fda.gov/downloads/Drugs/GuidanceComplianceRegulatoryInformation/ EnforcementActivitiesbyFDA/WarningLettersandNoticeofViolationLetterstoPharmaceuticalCompanies/ UCM166441.pdf; Untitled Letter from Ankur Kalola and Adora Nadu, Office of Prescription Drug Promotion, FDA, to Steve A. Kates, Vice President, Citius Pharmaceuticals (June 9, 2014) (omitting material facts and risk information indicates a lack of fair balance), available at http://www.fda. gov/downloads/Drugs/GuidanceComplianceRegulatoryInformation/EnforcementActivitiesbyFDA/ WarningLettersandNoticeofViolationLetterstoPharmaceuticalCompanies/UCM400708.pdf.

[127]   21 C.F.R. § 202.1(e).

accepts this approach to fulfill the brief summary requirement for advertising directed to both professionals and to consumers, the agency informally takes the position that such language, which is drafted for healthcare practitioners, is not optimal to inform consumers of the relevant risks. Accordingly, FDA has issued a draft guidance recommending that, for consumer-directed advertising, companies alter the wording of the language in the brief summary to be more consumer-friendly, while taking care not to minimize risk information.[128]

Types of Presentations That Are False or Misleading or Lacking in Fair Balance

FDA regulations provide specific guidance on circumstances that will or may identify an advertisement as false or lacking in fair balance or otherwise misleading. These include:

- claims that a drug is better, more effective, more useful in a broader range of indications or patients, safer, or has fewer or less serious side effects;

- unsupported comparative claims;

- favorable claims that are not supported by recent science or studies;

- selective use of scientific data or expert statements, or misrepresentation of the size or scope of a study;

- use of animal or in vitro data

- relying on data relating to dosage forms different from the advertised product;

- use of pooled data from dissimilar studies;

- erroneous use of statistical findings to claim clinical equivalence or deny the existence of a real clinical difference when they are not clinically significant.[129]

Specific Types of Product Advertising and Promotion

Pre-approval Promotion

In general, claims of safety and effectiveness for investigational drug products are prohibited, to prevent the promotion and commercialization of the drug prior to approval.[130] However, FDA regulations reserve an exception to this prohibition for the "full exchange of scientific information concerning the drug, including dissemination of scientific findings in scientific or lay media."[131] In addition, FDA does allow certain statements about drug products immediately before launch. Pursuant to now-withdrawn guidelines on pre-approval advertising, FDA previously required a manufacturer to choose between two formats—the

---

[128]   FDA, Draft Guidance for Industry: Brief Summary: Disclosing Risk Information in Consumer-Directed Print Advertisements, Center for Drug Evaluation and Research, FDA (Jan. 2004), *available at* http://www. fda.gov/downloads/Drugs/GuidanceComplianceRegulatoryInformation/Guidances/ucm069984.pdf.

[129]   21 C.F.R. § 202.1(e)(6).

[130]   *Id.* § 312.7(a).

[131]   *Id.*

"coming-soon" advertisement, noting only the name of the drug, the company name and an indication that the drug was "coming soon," or an institutional advertisement, stating that a company was conducting research in a particular therapeutic area; e.g., "Pharm-X is researching new treatments for AIDS." Once either format was selected during the pre-launch period, a company could not vary from it. Although FDA has withdrawn this guidance, OPDP (formerly DDMAC) still informally implements some parts of this approach. That is, OPDP considers unacceptable an advertisement for an investigational product which mentions both the drug name and the proposed indication in the same advertisement, to prevent doctors and consumers from receiving information about the drug that later turns out to be false and misleading compared to the approved labeling.[132] FDA's current policy, however, is that it will no longer require manufacturers to exclusively use only one of the formats; rather, each advertisement must adhere to the general principles, and not combine product name and indication. FDA continues to discourage use of pre-approval promotion for drugs that are likely to have a black box warning.

Press Releases

Competing requirements as to disclosure about drug products for publicly traded companies are presented by the investor disclosure requirements pursuant to the Securities and Exchange Act of 1934. In 1986, Upjohn Co. issued a press release detailing positive results of new studies evaluating the safety and effectiveness of minoxidil, an investigational drug for hair loss. In response, FDA issued a Warning Letter, asserting that these disclosure statements constituted promotion of an investigational drug and, therefore, resulted in the product being misbranded under section 502(a) of the FDCA.[133] Although Upjohn contended that the press release was directed to investors, not healthcare providers or consumers, FDA responded that the information was more detailed than that required under Securities and Exchange Commission (SEC) full disclosure requirements, and that the intended audience was irrelevant to what constitutes labeling under the FDCA.

---

[132]   See e.g., Untitled Letter from Thomas Abrams, Director, Office of Prescription Drug Promotion, FDA, to Dr. Burzynski, Burzynski Research Institute (Oct. 2012) concerning pre-approved promotion statements in press releases on company website, success stories on website concerning research subjects, and embedded videos of interviews with Dr. Burzynski, available at http://www.fda.gov/downloads/Drugs/GuidanceComplianceRegulatoryInformation/EnforcementActivitiesbyFDA/WarningLettersandNoticeofViolationLetterstoPharmaceuticalCompanies/UCM326631.pdf; Warning Letter from Thomas Abrams, Director, Division of Drug Marketing, Advertising, and Communications, FDA, to Geert Kersten, CEO, CEL-SCI Corporation (Aug. 2011) (concerning pre-approval promotion on company website relating to research subject success with investigational drug), available at http://www.fda.gov/downloads/Drugs/GuidanceComplianceRegulatoryInformation/EnforcementActivitiesbyFDA/WarningLettersandNoticeofViolationLetterstoPharmaceuticalCompanies/UCM268686.pdf; Untitled Letter from Nisha Patel, Division of Drug Marketing, Advertising, and Communications, FDA, to Robert Niecestro, AOI Pharmaceuticals/Keyx Biopharmaceuticals (Jun. 2011)(pre-approval promotion of investigational drug on firm website), available at http://www.fda.gov/downloads/Drugs/GuidanceComplianceRegulatoryInformation/EnforcementActivitiesbyFDA/WarningLettersandNoticeofViolationLetterstoPharmaceuticalCompanies/UCM263176.pdf; Warning Letter from Shefali Doshi, Regulatory Review Officer, Division of Drug Marketing, Advertising, and Communications, FDA, to Dr. Leslie Baumann, Baumann Cosmetic and Research Institute (Jan. 11, 2010) concerning pre-approval promotion of abobotulinumtoxinA for injection, available at http://www.fda.gov/downloads/Drugs/GuidanceComplianceRegulatoryInformation/EnforcementActivitiesbyFDA/WarningLettersandNoticeofViolationLetterstoPharmaceuticalCompanies/UCM198400.pdf.

[133]   See Warning Letter from William Purvis, Assistant Director, Division of Drug Advertising, FDA, to E.L. Schuman, Director of Regulatory Affairs, The Upjohn Company (May 15, 1986).

However, as a result of the increasing demands of the biotechnology industry, for which there is a greater need for disclosure of events related to drug development, such as the completion of clinical trials or trial results which are material for investors, disclosures have become more necessary and frequent. FDA reviews press releases and has issued Warning Letters for press releases that FDA concluded were misleading.[134] In addition, the Department of Justice has asserted criminal violations for issuance of a misleading press release regarding clinical trial results.[135]

In 2004, SEC and FDA set up an interagency system to increase communication and improve regulating this intersection of the SEC full disclosure requirement and the FDA prohibition against pre-approval promotion of drugs.[136] SEC subsequently suspended trading in securities of two FDA-regulated companies based on statements made in press releases and registration statements concerning studies on the product and evidence of efficacy.[137] Although no guidance is currently available from these regulatory agencies to assist companies in complying with the requirements of both agencies, companies take into account various factors in disseminating investor communications concerning investigational drugs. In general, such communications should 1) be identified as an investor communication; 2) not imply or state that the investigational drug is safe or effective; 3) not be disclosed only in the case of positive results or disclose results out of context; 4) take a *de minimis* approach to the information disclosed (i.e., disclose only the level of information required by SEC); 5) be precise in describing the status of the investigational drug in the drug approval process; and 6) not minimize independent reports of safety or efficacy concerns.[138] In addition to press

---

[134] *See* Untitled Letter from Roberta Szydlo, Regulatory Review Officer, Division of Professional Drug Promotion, FDA, to Ashlie Adams, Manager, Regulatory Affairs, Cornerstone Therapeutics, Inc. (Oct. 31, 2012), *available at* http://www.fda.gov/downloads/Drugs/GuidanceComplianceRegulatoryInformation/EnforcementActivitiesbyFDA/WarningLettersandNoticeofViolationLetterstoPharmaceuticalCompanies/UCM327250.pdf (concerning a press release Cornerstone issued concerning the omission of risk information and usage of unsupported comparative superiority claims of Curosurf). Untitled Letter from Thomas Abrams, Director, Division of Drug Marketing, Advertising, and Communications, FDA, to Stanislaw R. Burzynski, MD, PhD, Burzynski Research Institute, Inc. (Oct. 18, 2012) (concerning website which included posted press releases and embedded videos promoting investigational new drugs, Antineoplastons A10 and AS2-1 Injections, as safe and effective for which they were being investigated); Warning Letter from Thomas Abrams, Director, Division of Drug Marketing, Advertising, and Communications, FDA, to Brian A. Markinson, Chairman, President and CEO, King Pharmaceuticals, Inc. (Oct. 8, 2009) (concerning a video press release King issued concerning Ebmeda), *available at* http://www.fda.gov/downloads/Drugs/GuidanceComplianceRegulatoryInformation/EnforcementActivitiesbyFDA/WarningLettersandNoticeofViolationLetterstoPharmaceuticalCompanies/UCM187636.pdf.

[135] United States v. Harkonen, 2010 U.S. Dist. LEXIS 75528 (N.D. Cal. 2010) (court decision denying Harkonen's post-trial motion for an acquittal or new trial). The case arose out of InterMune, Inc.'s press release regarding clinical trial results of its drug Actimmune. *See* Untitled Letter from Lynn Panholzer, Regulatory Review Officer, Division of Drug Marketing, Advertising, and Communications, FDA, to Susan Vermeir, Vice President, Regulatory Affairs, InterMune, Inc. (Mar. 28, 2006), *available at* http://www.fda.gov/downloads/Drugs/GuidanceComplianceRegulatoryInformation/EnforcementActivitiesbyFDA/WarningLettersandNoticeofViolationLetterstoPharmaceuticalCompanies/ucm054382.pdf (concerning a journal advertisement regarding Intergen).

[136] *See FDA and SEC to Work to Enhance Public's Protection from False and Misleading Statements*, FDA NEWS (Feb. 5, 2004), *available at* http://www.fda.gov/NewsEvents/Newsroom/PressAnnouncements/2004/ucm108239.htm.

[137] *See, e.g.*, 69 Fed. Reg. 19,583 (Apr. 13, 2004) (Notice of order of suspension of trading).

[138] Jeffrey Reidler, SEC Corporate Finance Division Assistant Director, address to Food and Drug Law Institute Annual Meeting (Apr. 15, 2004).

releases concerning investigational drugs, FDA also reviews press releases on approved products to ensure that they are not false or misleading.[139]

Reminder Advertisements

Reminder advertisements are exempt from the requirement to include a brief summary of side effects, contraindications, and effectiveness.[140] To qualify as a reminder advertisement, the piece must contain the proprietary name of the drug product and the established names of all active ingredients, and may include 1) information relating to the dosage form; 2) quantity of the package contents; 3) price; 4) name and address of the manufacturer, packer, or distributor; and 5) other written, printed, or graphic matter that contains no representation or suggestion relating to the advertised drug product.[141] Thus, for example, a pen or note pad serving as a template could have the drug's name but not a small red heart to signal treatment for cardiovascular disease. Accordingly, reminder advertisements are prohibited from making any express or implied claims regarding the safety or effectiveness of the drug product.

Reminder advertisements are not allowed for drug products that carry boxed warnings (commonly referred to as "black boxes"), which are used by FDA to signal major risks associated with use of the drug.[142] Generic drug marketers may use reminder advertisements, but no reference may be made to bioequivalence or "AB" ratings. Reminder ads and labeling are frequently included on pens, pads, magnets, table covers, scrubs, gowns, calendars, mugs, post-its, and other similar products.[143]

Direct-to-Consumer (DTC) Advertisements

At the time of the Kefauver-Harris Amendment in 1962, and the promulgation of prescription drug advertising regulations, the practice of advertising prescription drugs direct to consumers ("DTC advertising") was uncommon. Consistent with the trend in the United States toward greater patient responsibility for participation in healthcare decisions, the use of DTC advertising has greatly expanded, especially in social media platforms. The balance that FDA intends to maintain in connection with its regulation of DTC advertising is to provide consumers with adequate efficacy and safety risk information in an understandable format and language. As discussed below, FDA regulations draw a distinction between DTC print and broadcast advertisements.[144] In response to this increasing communication

---

[139]   *See* Warning Letter from Thomas Abrams, Director, Division of Drug Marketing, Advertising, and Communications, FDA, to Dr. Raymond Gilmartin, President and CEO, Merck & Co. (Sept. 17, 2001) (concerning a press release Merck issued concerning the cardiovascular safety profile of Vioxx, and statements that the profile was "favorable," after multiple reports of large numbers of adverse cardiac events), *available at* http://www.fda.gov/downloads/Drugs/GuidanceComplianceRegulatoryInformation/EnforcementActivitiesbyFDA/WarningLettersandNoticeofViolationLetterstoPharmaceuticalCompanies/UCM166383.pdf.

[140]   21 C.F.R § 202.1(e)(2)(i).

[141]   *Id.*

[142]   *Id.*

[143]   Industry ethical codes (such as the PhRMA code) and state laws have had an impact on the types of items used and distributed by pharmaceutical and medical device companies for promotional and advertising purposes.

[144]   *See generally id.* § 202.1.

directly with consumers PhRMA, the pharmaceutical industry's trade association, also issued principles on DTC advertising.[145]

The primary difference between the regulation of print and broadcast advertisements is the nature, extent, and formatting of risk information that must be present in the advertisement.

Direct-to-Consumer Print Advertisements

In addition to complying with the standards identified *supra,* print advertisements must in all instances contain a brief summary, consistent with all of the requirements discussed *infra.* Most pharmaceutical companies use the majority of the full package insert for the brief summary notwithstanding current FDA guidelines on DTC print advertising that strongly recommend consumer-friendly language and organization.[146] Use of an abbreviated label as a brief summary as proposed by FDA in DTC advertisements could subject a pharmaceutical company to product liability challenges, based on incomplete warnings, and could reduce the potential ability to rely on preemption of state law defenses based on FDA review and approval of specific aspects of a more complete label.[147]

FDA has published guidance concerning how companies can comply with the adequate provision requirement. The guidance states that inclusion of the following components would satisfy this requirement: 1) disclosure in the advertisement of a toll-free number whereby consumers may call to either have full labeling mailed to them in four to six business days in a timely manner, or have the entire labeling read to them by phone as a prerecorded message; 2) reference in the advertisement to disclosure of the risk information by a mechanism to reach individuals with limited access to sophisticated technology such as the Internet (e.g., dissemination through brochures in publicly accessible sites such as libraries or reference in the broadcast advertisement to a print advertisement in a general interest magazine; 3) a website address in the advertisement that provides access to the full package labeling; and 4) disclosure in the advertisement that healthcare providers can provide further information to consumers.[148]

In 2011, FDA announced findings from three studies it had conducted, that, in the agency's view, confirmed that the manner in which information is conveyed and displayed in printed OTC drug advertising affects consumer understanding of prescription drugs. The studies examined ways to improve consumer understanding of how consumers use the "brief summary" section of printed prescription drug advertisements.[149]

---

[145]   PhRMA, Guiding Principles on Direct to Consumer Advertising about Prescription Medicines (2014), *available at* www.pharma.org/sites/default/files/pdf/phrmaguidingprinciplesdec08final.pdf.

[146]   FDA, Draft Guidance for Industry: Brief Summary: Disclosing Risk Information in Consumer-Directed Print Advertisements, at 4-6 (Jan. 2004), *available at* http://www.fda.gov/downloads/Drugs/GuidanceComplianceRegulatoryInformation/Guidances/ucm069984.pdf.

[147]   *But see* Wyeth v. Levine, 555 U.S. 555 (2009) (holding FDA approval of a brand name prescription drug label did not preempt state common law claims for injuries allegedly caused by the drug).

[148]   FDA, Draft Guidance for Industry: Brief Summary: Disclosing Risk Information in Consumer-Directed Print Advertisements (Jan. 2004).

[149]   *See* FDA, FDA examines ways to improve consumer understanding of prescription drug ads (June 20, 2011), *available at* http://www.fda.gov/NewsEvents/Newsroom/PressAnnouncements/2011/ucm259919.htm.

Direct-to-Consumer Broadcast Advertisements[150]

Broadcast advertisements include advertisements broadcast through such media as television, radio, or telephone.[151] Such advertisements "shall include information relating to the major side effects and contraindications of the advertised drugs in the audio or audio and visual parts of the presentation . . . ."[152] FDA provides no explicit guidance on compliance with this requirement, which is commonly referred to as the major statement. Accordingly, companies wishing to run broadcast advertisements must make the determination of which side effects, contraindications, and warnings should be included in the advertisement to fulfill the major statement requirement.

On March 29, 2010, FDA published a proposed guidance document entitled "Direct-to-Consumer Prescription Drug Advertisements: Presentation of the Major Statement in Television and Radio Advertisements in a Clear, Conspicuous, and Neutral Manner." The proposed guidance set out four requirements: that information be understandable for consumers, the audio information must be easy to follow and understandable, the text be easily readable, and the major statement is free from distractions.[153] FDA routinely issues enforcement letters concerning DTC[154] broadcast advertising.

Due to the prohibitive cost of including a print type of brief summary in DTC broadcast advertisements, FDA has provided broadcast advertisers an alternative mechanism for disclosing the full risks associated with use of the drug product. FDA regulations provide that a broadcast advertisement must contain the brief summary, "unless adequate provision is made for dissemination of the approved or permitted package labeling in connection with the broadcast presentation . . . ." This provision is commonly called the "adequate provision" requirement.[155]

In 2007 Congress granted FDA authority to require submission of any TV advertising before dissemination.[156] In 2012, FDA published a proposed guidance document for comment entitled "Direct-to-Consumer Television Advertisements: FDAAA DTC Television Ad Pre-Dissemination Review Program." The document stated the agency's intention to require

---

[150]   The Food and Drug Administration Amendments Act of 2007 (FDAAA) § 104, Pub. L. No. 110-85, 121 Stat. 823 (amending 21 U.S.C. §§ 301 et seq., created section 736A of the FDCA, 21 U.S.C. § 379h-1, which authorized a fee program for the advisory review of direct-to-consumer (DTC) prescription drug television advertisements, established a review fee for FY 2008 for each proposed television advertisement voluntarily submitted, but then later announced that it would not implement the user fee program.

[151]   See 21 C.F.R. § 202.1(e)(1).

[152]   Id.

[153]   On January 24, 2011, Thomas Abrams, Director of DDMAC, announced that DDMAC is considering modifying the proposed rule to include a fifth standard of requiring "the major statement to be presented in both audio and visual formats simultaneously." See Abrams: DDMAC Plans New Guidance on TV Ads, Changes to Brief Summary and the Major Statement. FDA ADVERTISING & PROMOTION MANUAL, 3-4 (March 2011).

[154]   See Warning Letter from Robert Dean, Division Director, Division of Consumer Drug Promotion, Office of Prescription Drug Promotion, FDA, to Ian Read, Chairman and CEO, Pfizer Inc. (May 24, 2012) (over statement of efficacy for TV and involving the EpiPen), available at http://www.fda.gov/downloads/Drugs/GuidanceComplianceRegulatoryInformation/EnforcementActivitiesbyFDA/WarningLettersandNoticeofViolationLetterstoPharmaceuticalCompanies/UCM306109.pdf.

[155]   See 21 C.F.R. § 202.1(e)(1).

[156]   Food and Drug Administration Amendments Act of 2007 (FDAAA), Pub. L. No. 110-85, § 901(d)(2) (codified at 21 U.S.C. 353B).

companies to submit six categories of high-risk advertisements for review before airing them. The categories covered advertisements for drugs with higher-than-usual risks, and contexts in which advertisements are more likely to misstate the product's risks.[157]

While the use of DTC advertising has continued to be carefully reviewed, a Congressional Budget Office analysis concluded that a moratorium on DTC advertising of prescription drugs would not affect prices in many cases.[158] The CBO report concluded that: "Although a moratorium would allow more time for safety concerns about a new drug to be revealed, it would entail health risks of its own, because some individuals who would benefit from a new drug might be unaware of its availability in the absence of consumer advertising."[159]

Direct-to-Consumer Internet Promotion

Generally, DTC Internet prescription drug promotion issues arise regarding the presentation and sequence of material facts and risk information. FDA has issued Warnings Letters for making efficacy claims while failing to state contraindications and adverse reactions associated with the drug's use on the same webpage. FDA noted that merely supplying a link to "full Prescribing Information" was not enough to "mitigate the misleading omission of risk information."[160] FDA holds traditional Web-based promotion to the same standard as print advertising.

FDA has also stated that links to external websites where the drug company controls or pays for the external website, makes the drug company responsible for the content related to their products.

Direct-to-Consumer Social Media Advertisements

As mentioned above, FDA issued its draft guidance for industry, "Internet/Social Media Platforms with Character Space Limitations — Presenting Risk and Benefit Information for Prescription Drugs and Medical Devices" on June 17, 2014.[161] The guidance followed FDA's November 2009[162] public hearing on the promotion of FDA-regulated medical

---

[157] FDA, Guidance for Industry: Direct-to-Consumer Television Advertisements — FDAAA DTC Television Ad Pre-Dissemination Review Program (March 2012).

[158] *Congressional Budget Office, Potential Effects of a Ban on Direct-to-Consumer Advertising of New Prescription Drugs* (May 2011).

[159] *Id.* at 1.

[160] *See* Warning Letter from Ankur Kalola, Regulatory Review Officer, Office of Prescription Drug Promotion, FDA, to Steven A. Kates, Ph.D., Vice President, Citius Pharmaceuticals, LLC (June 6, 2014), *available at* http://www.fda.gov/downloads/Drugs/GuidanceComplianceRegulatoryInformation/EnforcementActivitiesbyFDA/WarningLettersandNoticeofViolationLetterstoPharmaceuticalCompanies/UCM400708.pdf (Warning Letter for Suprenza (phentermine hydrochloride) Internet promotion). Warning Letter to Larry Doroney, Executive Vice President, Teva Pharmaceuticals USA, from Thomas Abrams, Office of Prescription Drug Promotion (March 2012) asserting superiority over statement of efficacy, present unsubstantiated claims, broaden the indication of Gopaxone, au ma drug, about risk information and materials facts in "Team Copakone" webpage featuring case study of USA Triathlon National Champion, and others); Untitled Letter from Sheetal Patel, Office of Prescription Drug Promotion, FDA, to Stephanie Dours, Director, Regulatory Affairs, Valeant Pharmaceuticals North America, LLC (July 2012) (concerning webpage for Zovirax Cream for over statement of efficacy, unsubstantiated superiority claims).

[161] *See* note 83 *supra.*

[162] Public Hearing on Promotion of FDA-Regulated Medical Products Using the Internet and Social Media Tools (Nov. 2009), *available at* http://www.fda.gov/AboutFDA/CentersOffices/OfficeofMedicalProductsandTobacco/

products using the Internet and social media tools, preparatory to issuance of proposed guidance,[163] which received comments from a variety of participants as to how the agency should regulate social media promotion.[164] Before FDA issued its guidance document, as its Warning Letters concerning social media promotion illustrate, the agency assessed social media and Internet promotion under its traditional print and broadcast advertisements regulations and guidances.[165] This approach resulted in ongoing criticism by the drug and social media industries that the FDA policy was not workable in the new media.[166] FDA's draft guidance attempted to address these criticisms, by reflecting the limited characters space of social media such as Twitter, and sponsored links. Under the guidance, advertisements on platforms with character space limitations must include the product's proprietary name, generic name, approved indications, any required information on the product's label, adequate risk information, and a hyperlink to a destination populated exclusively with more detailed risk information.[167]

FDA's principal direction in the guidance is that risk information comparable in content and prominence to the benefit information must be provided. FDA set out examples demonstrating how to draft social media promotions that will comply with the guidance and meet the structure and character limits of Twitter and Google's Sitelinks. FDA acknowledges that it may not be possible to provide all the required information for drugs "with complex indications or extensive serious risks" on character-space-limited platforms, and recommends that "[if] an accurate and balanced presentation of both risks and benefits of a specific product is not possible within the constraints of the platform, then the firm should reconsider using that platform."[168]

Correction of Misinformation on Internet/Social Media Platforms

FDA released a draft guidance on June 17, 2014, entitled "Internet/Social Media Platforms: Correcting Independent Third-Party Misinformation about Prescription Drugs and Medical

---

CDER/ucm184250.htm.

[163]   *See* http://www.fda.gov/AboutFDA/CentersOffices/OfficeofMedicalProductsandTobacco/CDER/ucm184250.htm.

[164]   For example, many participants provided FDA with ideas on the types of promotion that should be permitted on Internet search engines such as Google and Yahoo as well as social media tools such as Facebook, YouTube, Twitter, and Flickr.

[165]   *See* Untitled Letter from Kendra Y. Jones, Regulatory Review Officer, and Adora Ndu, Acting Team Leader, Office of Prescription Drug Promotion, FDA, to Clarence E. Jones, IBSA U.S. Agent, Institut Biochimique SA (Feb. 24, 2014), *available at* http://www.fda.gov/downloads/Drugs/GuidanceComplianceRegulatoryInformation/EnforcementActivitiesbyFDA/WarningLettersandNoticeofViolationLetterstoPharmaceuticalCompanies/UCM388800.pdf (FDA letter to Institut Biochimique SA in February 2014 for creating a Facebook page for TIROSINT (levothyroxine sodium) and omitting material labeling information regarding risk information associated with its use); *see also* Warning Letter from LaTonya M. Mitchell, District Director, Denver District Office, FDA, to Bryce L. Johnson, Owner, Zarbee's, Inc. (June 27, 2014), *available at* http://www.fda.gov/ICECI/EnforcementActions/WarningLetters/2014/ucm403255.htm (FDA claiming that Zarbee's "Liking" of customer testimonials that made unapproved therapeutic claims on Zarbee's products established company endorsement of the customers' comments which amounted to a misbranded drug claim).

[166]   *See, e.g.,* Facebook's reversal of its policy exempting pharmaceutical companies from open "walls," and thus allowing consumer comments on drugs to be viewed, resulted in several companies deciding to remove their Facebook pages on specific products. *See* WASH. POST, Aug. 17, 2011, at A-3.

[167]   *See* note 83 *supra*.

[168]   *Id.* at 5.

Devices."[169] Because allowing firms to correct misinformation might benefit public health, FDA announced that it does not intend to object if the corrections do not comply with the regulatory requirements for promotion, provided the corrections are made "in a truthful and non-misleading manner and as described in this draft guidance."[170] Moreover, the misinformation cannot be initiated by or on behalf of the pharmaceutical company. Corrective information must be presented in a way that connects it to and is narrowly related to the misinformation, and discloses the author's affiliation with the product. The correction must be supported by sufficient evidence, limited in scope to responding to the misinformation, and cannot have a promotional tone.[171] The guidance explains that firms are neither required to monitor for third-party misinformation, nor to correct third-party misinformation they find, however, firms that choose to correct misinformation must correct all the misinformation within a clearly defined portion of the forum at that time, including misinformation that overstates the efficacy of the product.[172]

The broad scope of potential enforcement authority with respect to DTC advertising through the Internet and social media is illustrated by the agreement in August 2011 by Google, Inc. with DOJ to forfeit $500 million for allowing Canadian online pharmacies to place online advertisements targeting U.S. consumers.[173] The government had challenged the behavior as leading to the unlawful importation of controlled and non-controlled prescription drugs into the United States in violation of the FDCA and the Controlled Substances Act. In addition to the monetary forfeiture, the company agreed to compliance and reporting obligations to ensure no recurrence of the challenged conduct.

PhRMA Guidelines for DTC Advertisements

As discussed above, PhRMA published its Guiding Principles, Direct to Consumer Advertisements About Prescription Medicines, in 2005 (PhRMA DTC Guidelines), and updated them in 2014.[174] Most member companies have agreed to follow these guidelines. Many of the principles set forth in the guidelines echo the requirements of FDA regulations, and there is an explicit requirement that member companies should comply with applicable FDA regulations. The PhRMA principles also place restrictions on the participating members that exceed the scope of FDA regulatory requirements.

Most significantly, the principles state that DTC advertisements that mention a specific product by name should also state the FDA-approved indication and the major risks associated with use of the drug. The PhRMA DTC Guidelines focus on education and encourage the use of help-seeking advertisements and disease awareness communications, as well as product-specific advertisements.

---

[169]   FDA, Internet/Social Media Platforms: Correcting Independent Third-Party Misinformation about Prescription Drugs and Medical Devices (June 2014), *available at* http://www.fda.gov/downloads/Drugs/GuidanceComplianceRegulatoryInformation/Guidances/UCM401079.pdf.

[170]   *Id.* at 3.

[171]   *Id.* at 5.

[172]   *Id.* at 7.

[173]   *See* DOJ, Google Forfeits $500 Million Generated by Online Ads & Prescription Drug Sales by Canadian Online Pharmacies (Aug. 24, 2011), *available at* http://www.justice.gov/opa/pr/2011/August/11-dag-1078.html.

[174]   *See* note 145 *supra*.

Other significant principles in the PhRMA DTC Guidelines include 1) the education of healthcare providers prior to launching a DTC drug advertising campaign; 2) predistribution review of all DTC advertisements by FDA, which is voluntary under FDA regulations; 3) targeting advertisements toward age-appropriate audiences (e.g., erectile dysfunction advertisements should be run during predominantly adult-viewed time slots and programming); 4) providing information on other treatment options, and 5) where feasible, including information regarding help for uninsured and underinsured.

Help-Seeking and Disease Awareness Advertisements

Two additional types of advertisements are permitted because they do not link specific products and particular indications. These communications are not considered product promotion. Disease awareness communications are directed at either consumers or healthcare practitioners, and discuss a particular disease or health condition;[175] however, these communications are prohibited from mentioning any specific drug, or making any representation or suggestion concerning a particular drug.[176] Help-seeking communications are a subset of disease awareness communications directed at consumers, and typically encourage the consumer to consult a healthcare practitioner concerning the disease or health condition identified in the ad.

Help-seeking and disease awareness communications are not regulated by FDA regulations. Through draft guidance, FDA has asserted that these communications are not regulated under the FDCA, because they are not intended to promote specific drugs, and are thus not labeling and product advertisements.[177] The help-seeking content of the advertisement, however, is not the sole determinant of whether the communication is promotional in nature; the "physical and temporal proximity" to the other communications is also considered. For example, a help-seeking advertisement and a reminder television advertisement may be considered by FDA to be nonpromotional when viewed independently; however, if both ads were presented during the same commercial segment or with the same color scheme, graphics, or similar musical presentation, they may collectively be viewed by FDA as promotional.[178] Similarly, if there is only one drug in a therapeutic class for which a help-seeking advertisement appears, FDA will look closely at whether the advertisement is likely to be perceived by consumers as directed to the one therapeutic option available.[179]

---

[175] FDA, Guidance for Industry: "Help-Seeking" and Other Disease Awareness Communications by or on Behalf of Drug and Device Firms (Draft Guidance) (Jan. 23, 2004), *available at* http://www.fda.gov/downloads/Drugs/GuidanceComplianceRegulatoryInformation/Guidances/ucm070068.pdf.

[176] *See* Warning Letter from Thomas Abrams, Director, Division of Drug Marketing, Advertising, and Communications, FDA, to Ludwig Hantson, CEO, Novartis Pharmaceuticals Corporation (Apr. 21, 2010), *available at* http://www.fda.gov/Drugs/GuidanceComplianceRegulatoryInformation/EnforcementActivitiesbyFDA/WarningLettersandNoticeofViolationLetterstoPharmaceuticalCompanies/ucm259229.htm.

[177] *See* note 175 *supra*.

[178] *See* Warning Letter from Thomas Abrams, Director, Division of Drug Marketing, Advertising, and Communications, FDA, to Dr. Garnier, CEO, GlaxoSmithKline (June 2006) (inclusion of website address www.zoviracontmentx.com on help seeking deck card rendered it drug promotion).

[179] *Id.* at 4.

Price Advertising

Subject to certain limitations, FDA regulates advertisement and labeling of the price of drugs similarly to reminder advertisements. To comply with these regulations, the sole purpose of the advertisement must be to advertise price, and may not contain any "representation or suggestion concerning the drug product's safety, effectiveness or indications for use."[180] Further, the advertisement must contain both the proprietary and established name of the drug product, as well as the dosage strength and form for each active ingredient present in the drug product.[181] Lastly, the price advertisement must state the charge for a specific quantity of the drug product, and must include all charges associated with the drug product (e.g., professional fees, handling fees, and mailing fees).[182]

In addition to these requirements, FDA regulations specify that price advertisements may contain other written, printed, or graphic material, such as identification of professional or convenience services provided by the pharmacy. These additions to the advertisement also must not be false or misleading, or contain representations or suggestions concerning safety and effectiveness.[183]

Healthcare Outcomes Effectiveness Research / Pharmacoeconomics Claims

Pharmacoeconomics, or healthcare outcomes effectiveness research (HOER), claims[184] are often made to third-party payors and formulary committees to communicate economic benefits claimed for the product.[185] Such claims made to formulary committees or managed care or similar entities are not false or misleading if the information "directly relates to an indication approved under section 505 or under section 351(a) of the Public Health Service Act for such drug and is based on competent and reliable scientific evidence."[186] HOER and cost-effectiveness claims to other healthcare providers (e.g., physicians) are regulated under general labeling and advertising provisions. FDA has continued to state that the agency is developing guidance to address the use of such claims in promotional labeling.[187] In 2011, the agency published a notice of opportunity for public comment regarding a proposed

---

[180] 21 C.F.R. § 200.200(a)(1).

[181] FDA, Guidance for Industry: Product Name, Placement, Size, and Prominence in Advertising and Promotional Labeling (Draft Guidance) (Jan. 20, 1999) at 1, *available at* http://www.fda.gov/downloads/Drugs/GuidanceComplianceRegulatoryInformation/Guidances/ucm070076.pdf.

[182] *See* 21 C.F.R. §§ 200.200(a)(2), (4); *see also infra* regarding state price reporting requirements.

[183] *Id.* § 200.200(a)(3).

[184] Healthcare economic information is defined as "any analysis that identifies, measures, or compares the economic consequences, including the costs of the represented health outcomes, of the use of a drug to the use of another drug, to another healthcare intervention, or to no intervention." FDCA § 502(a), 21 U.S.C. § 352(a).

[185] PhRMA renews calls for the FDA to issue Sec. 114 guidance that addresses manufacturer/payer communications. Sue Sutter, *CDER Policy Council Urged to Address Manufacturer/Payer Communications*, F-D-C REP. ("The Pink Sheet"), Sept. 2, 2013 at 21.

[186] *Id.* As noted in Chapter 24 *infra*, the standard employed under the Federal Trade Commission Act for claim substantiation is "competent and reliable scientific evidence."

[187] Warning Letter from Ele Iborra-Pratt, Regulatory Review Officer, Division of Drug Marketing, Advertising, and Communications, FDA, to Michele M. Hardy, Director, Advertising and Labeling Policy, Glaxo Wellcome Inc. (Mar. 13, 2000); Warning Letter from Janet Norden, Regulatory Review Officer, Division of Drug Marketing, Advertising, and Communications, FDA, to Richard A. Schupack, Director, Legal Affairs-Regulatory, Elon Pharmaceuticals (Feb. 15, 2000).

study of comparative advertising of prescription drugs, in view of the increasing interest in developing and presenting comparative research.[188] In 2014, the agency published another notice of opportunity for public comment regarding a proposed study to examine whether contextual information about efficacy and safety enables physicians and consumers to distinguish between drugs in comparative price advertisements.[189] In the absence of guidelines, FDA has issued Warning Letters concerning allegedly unsubstantiated claims in connection with product cost savings, reduced hospital stays, and other economic benefits.[190]

The increasing concern regarding the cost of drugs and biologics can be expected to result in significantly enhanced interest in and use of HOER, comparative effectiveness, and other cost-effectiveness claims. Numerous studies and legislative proposals have called for the establishment of agencies to encourage and/or undertake cost or comparative effectiveness research.[191] The Medicare Improvements for Patients and Providers Act of 2008[192] mandated that two studies be conducted by the Institute of Medicine, one identifying standards for conducting reviews of clinical effectiveness research and the other to assess best methods for development of clinical practice guidelines.[193] The American Recovery and Reinvestment Act of 2009 (the economic stimulus legislation) allocated $1.1 billion for comparative effectiveness research.[194] The healthcare reform law, the Patient Protection and Affordable Care Act (PPACA), mandated the development of comparative effectiveness research, including through establishment of the Patient-Centered Outcomes Research Institute (PCORI), whose purpose is to conduct and disseminate comparative effectiveness research findings.[195]

Comparative Claims

Claims comparing the safety and effectiveness of a drug product to other agents must support these claims with "substantial evidence derived from adequate and well-controlled studies."[196] FDA subjects comparative claims to the same evidentiary standards as required under the statute for approval of a drug as being effective. Accordingly, to provide "substantial evidence" to support the claims, sponsors should conduct at least two "adequate and well-controlled" studies[197] and, moreover, these must be head-to-head clinical trials comparing

---

[188]   See 76 Fed. Reg. 38,663 (July 1, 2011).

[189]   See 79 Fed. Reg. 26,255 (May 7, 2014).

[190]   See Warning Letter from John Markow, Division of Drug Marketing, Advertising, and Communications, FDA, to Audrey Hackman, Manager, World Wide Regulatory Affairs, Rhone Poulenc Rorer Pharms. Inc. (Apr. 8, 1999) (brochure describing a "shortened mean hospital stay" by use of Lovenox deemed false and misleading because not adequately substantiated).

[191]   See e.g., Report of the Medicare Payment Advisory Commission (June 2007); Report of the Congressional Research Service (Oct. 15, 2007) on the potential for comparative effectiveness research to reduce costs and improve treatment.

[192]   Medicare Improvements for Patients and Providers Act of 2008 (MIPPA), Pub. L. No. 110-275 (July 15, 2008).

[193]   MIPPA § 304.

[194]   American Recovery and Reinvestment Act, Pub. L. No. 111-5, 123 Stat. 115 (Feb. 19, 2009).

[195]   See note 1 supra at § 6301.

[196]   21 C.F.R. § 201.57(c)(2)(iii). See Stephen Paul Mahinka, Imperative: Comparative Effectiveness Research, LMG Life Sciences, Aug. 13, 2013, at 18.

[197]   DDMAC, FDA, Current Issues and Procedures (Apr. 1994) (withdrawn 1997); available at Wayne Pines, FDA Advertising and Promotion Manual (Wayne Pines ed., 2008).

the agents.[198] The observed difference between the agents should be statistically significant and indicative of some clinically meaningful benefit (i.e., not merely theoretical).[199]

Because comparative promotional claims must be consistent with the FDA-approved labeling, the products being compared must be approved for the same indication.[200] Furthermore, the "dosage regimens compared must be an appropriate basis for comparison, consistent with the dosage recommendations in the approved labeling, and in the same part of the dose range."[201] Consistent with this policy, FDA has issued Warning Letters to companies that make claims for the "once-a-day" administration of their drug product in the context of discussion of other products approved for the same indication, but for multiple daily doses.[202] These implied superiority claims—in the absence of substantial evidence—are likely to lead to FDA enforcement action. As with HOER/cost-effectiveness claims, the increasing focus on the cost of drugs and biologics can be expected to result in increasing use of comparative effectiveness claims.

In October 2010, DDMAC announced that it was considering developing new guidance on comparative claims,[203] responding to the likely increase in comparative claims based on HOER/comparative effectiveness research.

---

[198]   *See* Untitled Letter from Ankur S. Kalola, Regulatory Review Officer, Office of Prescription Drug Promotion, FDA, to Arthur M. Deboeck, Vice President and General Manager, Galephar Pharmaceutical Research Inc. [U.S. Agent for Cipher Pharmaceuticals Inc.] (Sept. 11, 2014) (superiority claims unsubstantiated in the absence of "well controlled head-to-head clinical trials comparing" Lipofen to other fenofibrate products); Warning Letter from Thomas Abrams, Director, Division of Drug Marketing, Advertising, and Communications, FDA, to Mr. Michael D. Becker, CEO, Cytogen Corp. (July 18, 2005); Warning Letter from Thomas Abrams, Director, Division of Drug Marketing, Advertising, and Communications, FDA, to Joseph Dieroni, Pres./CEO, Sankyo Pharma Inc. (Jan. 12, 2007) (superiority claims not substantiated because they were supported only by open-label, uncontrolled studies, were meta-analysis, were titration-to-effect comparisons, or did not compare the drugs administered at their maximum approved dosages). *See* Untitled Letter from Carole Broadnax, Regulatory Review Officer, Division of Drug Marketing, Advertising, and Communications, FDA, to Stacey Tosadori, Director, Regulatory Affairs, Amgen, Inc. (May 13, 2010) concerning comparative claims made regarding Vectibix; Warning Letter from Robert Dean, Director, Division of Consumer Drug Promotion, FDA, to Bruce C. Cozadd, Chairman, CEO, Jazz Pharmaceuticals (Sept. 18, 2012).

[199]   *See* Warning Letter from Ann M. Reb, Regulatory Review Officer, Division of Drug Marketing, Advertising, and Communications, FDA, to Jeffrey T. Whitmer, Director, Regulatory Affairs and Promotional Compliance, Bristol-Myers Squibb Co. (May 4, 1998). *See* Untitled Letter from Kathleen Klemm, Regulatory Review Officer, Division of Drug Marketing, Advertising, and Communications, FDA, to Harris Rotman, Director, Global Regulatory Affairs, Shire Development, Inc. (Apr. 27, 2010) concerning comparative claims made regarding Lialda.

[200]   *See* Warning Letter from Janet Norden, Regulatory Review Officer, Division of Drug Marketing, Advertising, and Communications, FDA, to Priya Janbhekor, Director of Regulatory Affairs, Boxter Pharm. Prod. Inc. (Oct 1, 1999).

[201]   DDMAC, FDA, Current Issues and Procedures (Apr. 1994) (withdrawn 1997); *available at* WAYNE PINES, FDA ADVERTISING and PROMOTION MANUAL (Wayne Pines ed., 2008).

[202]   *See e.g.,* Warning Letter from Jo Ann Spearmon, Regulatory Review Officer, Division of Drug Marketing, Advertising, and Communications, FDA, to Carol A. Sever, Associate Director, Bayer Pharmaceutical Division (Apr. 2, 1999); Warning Letter from Thomas Abrams, Director, Division of Drug Marketing, Advertising, and Communications, FDA, to R. Gilmartin, President and CEO, Merck & Co. (Sept. 17, 2001).

[203]   Ben Moscovitch, *FDA Drug Ad Review Shop Eyes Comparative Claims Guide in Move Seen As CER Preparation* (Oct. 25, 2010), *available at* http://InsideHealthPolicy.com.

Dissemination of HOER also may lead to competitor challenges. In the first case in this area, *ONY, Inc. v. Cornerstone Therapeutics, Inc.*,[204] a competing manufacturer challenged, under the Lanham Act and state unfair competition laws, a comparative study sponsored and disseminated by the defendants, Chiesi Farmaceutici and its U.S. subsidiary Cornerstone that was published in a peer-reviewed scientific journal. The Second Circuit affirmed the trial court's dismissal of the action on the basis that statements about contested scientific hypotheses are more closely akin to matters of opinion for purposes of the First Amendment and laws relating to defamation, and are so understood by the relevant scientific communities.[205] Such competitor litigation is likely to continue in view of the increasing demand for HOER, comparative, and cost effectiveness studies by both government and private payors in response to drug and biologics pricing.

Off-Label Promotion

A guiding principle of FDA advertising and promotion regulation is that FDA regulates the marketing of drug products, not the practice of medicine. Consistent with this approach, FDA does not attempt to interfere with physicians prescribing drugs for diseases and conditions that are not part of FDA-approved labeling (so called "off-label" use). In contrast, FDA does regulate and attempt to limit pharmaceutical company promotion of prescription drugs for off-label indications. This distinction is grounded not only in the language of the statute but also in FDA's belief that the promotion of off-label indications decreases the incentive for companies to seek premarket approval for safety and effectiveness for these indications, which potentially increases public health risk.

The issue of off-label promotion has been the subject of significant controversy. FDA regulations allow for the dissemination of information regarding the safety and effectiveness of investigational products and unapproved indications for approved products to promote the "scientific exchange" of information. Beginning in the early 1990s, FDA sought to define permissible pharmaceutical company-sponsored educational conferences that involved discussion of off-label indications for approved products by the conference speakers. The agency also restricted distribution of textbooks and articles discussing off-label use. For roughly a decade between the early 1990s and 2000s, the Washington Legal Foundation (WLF) tried to persuade FDA through filing citizens petitions and later in court that FDA's three guidance documents restricting 1) the distribution of reprints of independent, peer-reviewed articles; 2) industry-funded dissemination of independent textbooks; and 3) industry support of continuing medical education were unconstitutional, in that they violated the First Amendment.[206]

During this same time, section 401 of the Food and Drug Administration Modernization Act of 1997 (FDAMA) was enacted, which contained provisions allowing, under limited circumstances, the dissemination of "written information concerning the safety, effectiveness, or benefit of a use not described in the approved labeling of a drug."[207] The

---

[204]   720 F.3d 490 (2d Cir. 2013) (the authors were counsel for the manufacturer defendants in this action).

[205]   *Id.* at 494.

[206]   *See* Wash. Legal Found. v. Henney, 202 F.3d 331 (D.C. Cir. 2000); Wash. Legal Found. v. Friedman, 13 F. Supp. 2d 51 (D.D.C. 1998); Wash. Legal Found. v. Henney, 56 F. Supp. 2d 81 (D.D.C. 1999); Citizen Petition by the Wash. Legal Found. (Oct. 22, 1993), FDA Docket No. 92N-0434/CP1.

[207]   FDCA § 551(a), 21 U.S.C. § 360aaa(a).

legislation limited dissemination of off-label material to reprints of peer-reviewed journal articles and also required manufacturers making such claims to submit a supplemental new drug application for approval of the off-label use within a defined time frame.[208]

In July 1998, the U.S. District Court for the District of Columbia held that all three of FDA's guidance documents violated the First Amendment.[209] The court acknowledged a constitutional right to distribute certain materials, but stated that FDA could lawfully place certain restrictions on the dissemination of qualifying off-label information, including that: 1) journal articles and textbooks include a conspicuous notification that they discuss uses not approved by FDA; 2) all articles, textbooks, and CME be published or produced by independent entities; 3) journal articles should be peer-reviewed and sponsors who provide financial support for dissemination of articles or textbooks that discuss off-label uses may be required to disclose their financial interest; 4) FDA may continue to enforce rules that prohibit dissemination of material that is false and misleading. However, the U.S. Circuit Court of Appeals for the District of Columbia later in 2000 vacated the District Court's decision and instead agreed with FDA that there were no constitutional issues regarding FDA's restrictions on the dissemination of off-label information.[210]

FDA reiterated its position that FDAMA and the CME guidance[211] represent safe harbors that manufacturers may use to allow them to disseminate off-label materials without risk. FDA also reasserted its position, however, that when FDAMA is not followed, the agency remains free on a case-by-case basis to use "any and all evidence of the manufacturer's intent regarding the use of the product, including evidence of distribution of reprints or sponsorship of CME,"[212] to undertake enforcement action. FDA further stated that such restrictions on manufacturers are "the linchpin of the FDCA," and designed to ensure that products on the market are deemed by FDA to be safe and effective for "each and every use for which they are intended." FDA noted that, to hold otherwise, would "quash the incentive" to obtain new clearances or approvals.[213] Notwithstanding the notice, FDA has not cited any company for falling outside the safe harbor in connection with the dissemination of peer-reviewed articles and textbooks. FDA issued draft guidance in 2008 to manufacturers to describe the safe harbor for distribution of scientific reprints, including those that address off-label uses.[214] The Government Accountability Office (GAO) has strongly criticized FDA's ability to track drug company promotional activity in order to monitor off-label promotion and identify potential violations.[215]

On September 30, 2006, section 401 of FDAMA expired due to a statutory sunset provision. The Food and Drug Administration Amendments Act of 2007 did not renew these provisions, nor introduce an altered statutory provision.

---

[208]　FDCA § 551(b), 21 U.S.C. § 360aaa(b).

[209]　Wash. Legal Found. v. Friedman, 13 F. Supp. 2d 51 (D.D.C. 1998).

[210]　Wash. Legal Found. v. Henney, 202 F.3d 331 (D.C. Cir. 2000).

[211]　*Id.* at 10.

[212]　*Id.* at 2.

[213]　*Id.* at 3.

[214]　Draft Guidance for Industry on Good Reprint Practices for the Distribution of Medical Journal Articles and Medical or Scientific Reference Publications on Unapproved Devices, 73 Fed. Reg. 9342 (Feb. 20, 2008), *available at* http://www.fda.gov/RegulatoryInformation/Guidances/ucm125126.htm.

[215]　GAO Report, PRESCRIPTION DRUGS: FDA'S OVERSIGHT OF THE PROMOTION OF DRUGS FOR OFF-LABEL USES (July 2008).

FDA has continued to undertake enforcement actions regarding off-label promotion. During 2010, the agency issued a Warning Letter relating to the off-label promotion of Novartis' drug Gleevec through two websites.[216] FDA stated that, although the website produced a pop-up window disclaimer stating that the user was moving to an external website independently operated and not managed by Novartis, FDA asserted that there were several indicators that the manufacturer was responsible for the content of the website.

Several states have challenged pharmaceutical manufacturers' promotional activities following the issuance by FDA of Warning Letters concerning off-label promotion under state consumer protection statutes, including South Carolina, which won a $317 million judgment,[217] and Louisiana, which won a $257 million judgment.[218]

The continuing lack of clarity over the scope and application of FDA's regulations to off-label promotion, and the scope of civil and criminal penalties potentially applicable to allegedly unlawful promotion, led several pharmaceutical manufacturers to file a Citizen Petition on July 5, 2011, requesting the agency to clarify its regulations and policies with respect to when manufacturers legally may disseminate information on unapproved new uses for products.[219]

The scope of FDA's enforcement concerning off-label promotion also may be significantly affected by the Supreme Court's decision in *Sorrell v. IMS Health, Inc.,*[220] which declared a Vermont law designed to prevent pharmaceutical information data mining unconstitutional. The Court rejected Vermont's justifications for the law's burdens on speech, including medical privacy, reduced healthcare costs, and improved public health, finding that prohibiting pharmacies from selling prescriber-identifying information to other parties constituted viewpoint discrimination, as it restricted speech by restricting information distribution.[221] The Court explained that, while "Vermont may be displeased that detailers who use prescriber-identifying information are effective in promoting brand-name drugs," this does not mean that a state may enact a law that would "burden the speech of others in order to tilt public debate in a preferred direction."[222] The *Sorrell* decision thus is significant because it may provide a basis for successfully challenging agency restrictions on off-label or other forms of promotion that may unduly or differentially restrict the dissemination of truthful, non-misleading information.[223]

---

[216]   *See* Warning Letter from Thomas Abrams, Director, Division of Drug Marketing, Advertising, and Communications, FDA, to Ludwig Hantson, CEO, Novartis Pharmaceuticals Corporation (Apr. 21, 2010), *available at* http://www.fda.gov/Drugs/GuidanceComplianceRegulatoryInformation/Enforcement ActivitiesbyFDA/WarningLettersandNoticeofViolationLetterstoPharmaceuticalCompanies/ucm259229. htm.

[217]   State of South Carolina, ex rel. Alan Wilson v. Ortho-McNeil-Janssen Pharmaceuticals, Inc. et al., No. 07-CP-42-1438, S.C. Cir., Spartanburg Co. (June 2011).

[218]   James Caldwell ex rel. State of Louisiana v. Janssen Pharmaceutica, Inc. et al., No. 04-C-3967, La. Dist., St. Landry Parish (October 2010).

[219]   Citizen Petition submitted by Allergan, Inc. et al. to FDA, July 5, 2011.

[220]   Sorrell v. IMS Health, 131 S. Ct. 2653 (2011).

[221]   *Id.* at 2671.

[222]   *Id.*

[223]   Subsequent to the *Sorrell* decision, a pharmaceutical manufacturer brought an action seeking an injunction against FDA enforcement of its off-label promotion regulations as violative of the First Amendment. *See* Par Pharmaceutical Inc. v. United States, Civil Action 11-cv-01820-RWR (D.D.C.) (filed Oct.14, 2011).

In 2012, the Second Circuit Court of Appeals issued an opinion in *United States v. Caronia*.[224] Citing *Sorrell v. IMS Health, Inc.*, the court overturned a criminal conviction of a pharmaceutical sales representative who promoted the drug Xyrem for "off-label use." Though the government argued that it only used Caronia's statements as evidence of an intent to promote an off-label use, the court found that the government had prosecuted Caronia for truthful speech concerning legal activity, and held that the state interests involved failed to justify the limit on speech. The court held that FDA's construction of the misbranding statute in support of its off-label promotion argument "provide[d] only ineffective or remote support for the government's purpose."[225]

FDA chose not to seek certiorari in *Caronia*, and therefore the full implications of the case remain unclear. In response to Citizen Petitions[226] for clarification, FDA announced a revised draft guidance entitled "Distributing Scientific and Medical Publications on Unapproved New Uses – Recommended Practices" on March 3, 2014. The document proposed guidelines that manufacturers could follow to ensure that their distribution of information about off-label uses for drugs will not be used as evidence of an intent to promote off-label use.[227]

Thereafter, however, a DOJ official commented that the government will continue to bring enforcement actions against off-label promotion, even when the speech is not false or misleading.[228] To avoid a result similar to *Caronia*, where the enforcement action was based almost exclusively on speech, the official stated that the cases would likely focus on a theory of unlawful conduct that evinced an intent to promote off-label use.[229] It thus remains unclear what conduct or speech the government would consider a basis for an enforcement action based on an intent to promote off-label use.

United States v. Harkonen[230] illustrates a type of conduct and speech the government considers sufficient to support an enforcement action based on an intent to promote off-label or unapproved use. A jury found W. Scott Harkonen guilty of wire fraud for falsely portraying the results of a clinical trial.[231] The Ninth Circuit affirmed the defendant's conviction for wire fraud for issuing a fraudulent press release that promoted off-label uses for the drug Actimmune, rejecting his First Amendment freedom of speech defense.

---

[224]   703 F.3d 149 (2d Cir. 2012).

[225]   703 F.3d at 167 (quoting Central Hudson Gas & Elec. Corp. v. Public Serv. Comm'n, 447 U.S. 557, 564 (1980).

[226]   Citizen Petitions from Allergan, Inc., Eli Lilly, Johnson & Johnson, Novartis Pharmaceuticals Corporation, Novo Nordisk, Inc., Pfizer, Inc., and Sanofi-Aventis US LLC (Ropes & Gray), FDA-2011-P-0512 (July 2011), *available at* http://www.regulations.gov/#!documentDetail;D=FDA-2011-P-0512-0001; Citizen Petition from Medical Information Working Group, Ropes and Gray LLP, FDA-2013-P-1079 (Sept. 3, 2013), *available at* http://www.regulations.gov/#!documentDetail;D=FDA-2013-P-1079-0001.

[227]   FDA, Guidance for Industry: Distributing Scientific and Medical Publications on Unapproved New Uses –Recommended Practices, 79 Fed. Reg. 11,793, 11,796 (Mar. 3, 2014).

[228]   Dep't of Justice, Assistant Attorney General Stuart F. Delery Delivers the Keynote Address at the CBI Pharmaceutical Compliance Congress (Jan. 29, 2014), http://www.justice.gov/iso/opa/civil/speeches/2014/civ-speech-140129.html.

[229]   *Id.*

[230]   United States v. Harkonen, 510 Fed. App'x 633 (9th Cir. 2012), cert. denied, 134 S. Ct. 824 (2013).

[231]   United States v. Harkonen, No. C-08-00614 MHP, 2010 U.S. Dist. LEXIS 75528, at *1 (N.D. Cal. July 27, 2010).

Recently, DOJ filed a case against Millennium Pharmaceuticals and Schering-Plough Corp. for promoting Integrilin for unapproved new uses.[232] Millennium Pharmaceuticals and Schering-Plough Corp. allege that they are being prosecuted based on speech. In its amicus brief, the PhRMA characterizes DOJ's interpretation of an intent to promote unapproved new uses as having "no rational stopping point."[233] The DOJ contends that PhRMA's position would give a constitutional right to defraud the government under the guise of free speech.[234]

Scientific Exchange

CME/Educational and Scientific Events

In contrast to promotion and advertising by pharmaceutical companies, FDA encourages and promotes scientific exchange among scientists. Scientific exchange can occur at continuing medical education (CME) conferences, through distribution of peer-reviewed journal articles, or through communications from company medical science liaisons to doctors.[235] As discussed above, FDA issued a guidance document that describes factors it will consider in determining whether activities supported by pharmaceutical companies are independent CME or promotional events. Notwithstanding the asserted First Amendment legal basis for CME, Congress has raised concerns with FDA about the genuine independence of CME from its industry supporters.[236]

Scientific exchange about a drug often occurs at large professional meetings of health specialists. FDA officials frequently attend these meetings to ensure that the materials being distributed and presentations made comply with the standards for independence and educational value.[237] In the 1990s, FDA issued Warning Letters to companies concerning

---

[232] Second Amended Complaint at 1, United States v. Millennium Pharmaceuticals Inc., No. 2:09-cv-03010 (E.D. Cal. Apr. 15, 2014).

[233] Brief for Pharmaceutical Research & Manufacturers of America as Amicus Curiae Supporting Defendants filed in United States ex rel. Solis v. Millennium Pharmaceuticals, No. 2:09-cv-3010-MCE-JFM (E.D. Cal. Oct. 16, 2014).

[234] United States' Statement of Interest In Opposition to Amicus Curiae Brief Submitted by Pharmaceutical Research & Manufacturers of America, 2:09-CV-3010 MCE JFM (E.D. Cal. Aug. 28, 2014).

[235] FDA, Guidance for Industry-Supported Scientific and Educational Activities, 62 Fed. Reg. 64,074, 64,093 (Dec. 3, 1997).

[236] See Letter from Senator Henry Waxman, Chairman of the Committee on Oversight and Government Reform; House of Representatives to Andrew C. Von Eschenbach, M.D., Commissioner, FDA (Nov. 30, 2007). Promotion of investigational drugs is prohibited. See 21 C.F.R. § 312.7; Warning Letter from Thomas Abrams, Director, Office of Prescription Drug Promotion, FDA, to Stanislaw R. Burzynski, MD, PhD, Burzynski Research Institute, Inc. (Oct. 18, 2012).

[237] See Untitled Letter from Twyla Thompson, Regulatory Review Officer, Division of Professional Promotion, Office of Prescription Drug Promotion, FDA, to Susan Rinne, Vice President, Regulatory Affairs, NeurogesX, Inc. (Dec. 13, 2011), available at http://www.fda.gov/downloads/Drugs/GuidanceComplianceRegulatoryInformation/EnforcementActivitiesbyFDA/WarningLettersandNoticeofViolationLetterstoPharmaceuticalCompanies/UCM283644.pdf (warning exhibit booth at scientific meeting is false or misleading regarding claims for Qutenza because exhibit failed to present risk information in conjunction with efficacy claims); Untitled Letter from Nisha Patel, Regulatory Review Officer, Division of Professional Promotion, Office of Prescription Drug Promotion, FDA, to Lynda Tetarenko, Director, Regulatory Affairs, Celgene Corporation (Dec. 23, 2011), available at http://www.fda.gov/downloads/Drugs/GuidanceComplianceRegulatoryInformation/EnforcementActivitiesbyFDA/WarningLettersandNoticeofViolationLetterstoPharmaceuticalCompanies/UCM289192.pdf (warning that white paper obtained from promotional exhibit booth at scientific meeting

promotional activities at such meetings, including the use of physicians' presentations, scientific abstracts, and non-peer-reviewed articles.[238] In recent years there have been fewer such letters.

Responses to Unsolicited Requests for Information

Consistent with FDA's support of legitimate scientific exchange, FDA has not objected to pharmaceutical companies responding to unsolicited requests for information about their products, including questions or requests[239] for information on unapproved uses.[240] In order to ensure that such responses are not used for promotional purposes, which might trigger regulation under the labeling provisions of the statute, FDA recommends that such inquiries be handled by the medical affairs department of the company (not sales or marketing), that the information not be prepackaged for distribution, that it only be distributed in connection with approved products, and that a detailed log of all unsolicited requests be maintained by the company.[241]

Use of Medical Personnel to Communicate with Physicians

Increasingly, pharmaceutical companies have employed physicians and others with scientific backgrounds who report to the medical affairs division of the company to meet with healthcare providers and purchasers to discuss scientific issues, new studies, and findings concerning the company's drug products, and to respond to specific questions from the physicians. These individuals are often called medical science liaisons (MSLs). As with CME, while these interactions provide benefits to healthcare providers, some scientific exchanges can raise promotion concerns and result in enforcement action.[242] Notwithstanding industry's attempt to distinguish MSLs from traditional pharmaceutical sales representatives, FDA has taken the position that the nature of the individual's position in the company is irrelevant; rather, FDA will examine both the content and context of the interaction to determine if it is scientific exchange or promotional.[243]

---

regarding Abraxane for Injectable Suspension made unsubstantiated effectiveness and superiority claims, and omitted important risk information).

[238] *See e.g.,* Warning Letter from Minnie Baylor-Henry, Director, Division of Drug Marketing, Advertising, and Communications, FDA, to Richard J. Kogan, CEO, Schering Corp. (July 31, 1997).

[239] FDA, Draft Guidance for Industry: Responding to Unsolicited Requests for Off-Label Information (Dec. 2011), *available at* http://www.fda.gov/downloads/Drugs/GuidanceComplianceRegulatoryInformation/Guidances/UCM285145.pdf.

[240] *See* 59 Fed. Reg. 59,820, 59,823 (Nov. 18, 1994).

[241] DDMAC, FDA, Current Issues and Procedures, (Apr. 1994) (withdrawn 1997); *available at* WAYNE PINES, FDA ADVERTISING AND PROMOTION MANUAL A-107 (Wayne Pines ed., 2008).

[242] The improper use of MSLs to promote off-label uses was an activity alleged by the U.S. Attorney as a basis for its investigation concerning the sale of Neurontin by Pfizer. *See* Press Release, Dep't of Justice, Warner-Lambert to pay $430 Million to Resolve/Criminal & Civil Health Care Liability Relating to Off-Label Promotion (May 13, 2004), *available at* http://www.justice.gov/opa/pr/2004/May/04_civ_322.htm. *See* USA press release and complaint on Neurontin.

[243] FDA, Draft Policy Statement on Industry-Supported Scientific and Educational Activities, 57 Fed. Reg. 56,412 (Nov. 27, 1992).

State Regulation of Promotion and Marketing

The states have been increasingly active since the mid-1990s in regulation of marketing and promotion, especially as it relates to off-label promotion, often investigating in tandem with the Department of Justice.[244] Based on the concern that pharmaceutical company promotion was increasing healthcare costs, several states imposed requirements for disclosure of pharmaceutical company gifts and other contributions of value to physicians.[245] Some states exempt from disclosure the value of samples given to patients, legitimate CME support, payments for clinical and other research and, in some states, consulting payments.[246] None of the states with reporting requirements so far has taken enforcement action against noncompliant companies. Such state statutes may decline in use with the enactment of transparency provisions in PPACA (which are often referred to as the Physician Payment Sunshine Act) requiring disclosure by pharmaceutical, medical device, biologics, and other medical product suppliers whose products are paid for by public healthcare programs such as Medicare and Medicaid. These provisions of PPACA regulate payments and other transfers of value to physicians and teaching hospitals.[247]

Conclusion

Reacting to the expansion in scope and methods of prescription drug promotion and marketing, the number of enforcement entities focused on this area and their level of activity have grown dramatically. The resulting greater complexity of compliance and difficulty of formulating prescription drug marketing and promotion strategies are permanent features of the new marketing and communications environment.

---

[244] *See* Press Release, U.S. Dep't of Justice, AstraZeneca Pharmaceuticals Pleads Guilty to Health Care Crimes (June 20, 2003) (company paid $355 million to settle criminal and civil liabilities related to drug pricing and marketing practices); Press Release, U.S. Dep't of Justice, TAP Pharmaceutical Products Inc. and Seven Others Charged with Health Care Crimes (Oct. 3, 2001).

[245] District of Columbia Access Rx Act of 2004 and D.C. Code § 48-833 *et. seq.*, MAINE REV. STAT. tit. 22, § 2698-A (report of all expenses related to advertising, marketing, and direct promotion of prescription drugs through radio, television, magazines, newspapers, direct mail, and telephone, all CME programs, and gifts of more than $25); MINN. STAT. § 151.461 (prohibiting any gift of more than $50) and MINN. STAT. § 151.47 (reporting of payments). VT. STAT. ANN., tit. 18, § 4631(a), 4632 (reporting of all gifts, fee payments, or other value to physicians, hospitals, pharmacy nursing homes, etc. in connection with promotion or marketing). W. VA. CODE R. § 16-29-H-8 and W. VA. CODE CSR § 210-1 *et. seq.* (requiring reports of advertising costs for prescription drugs). Massachusetts also requires disclosure and regulates pharmaceutical and medical device manufacturer conduct under Massachusetts General Law (M.G.L.) Chapter 111N and 105 CMR 970.000 (*et seq.*). In addition, Conn. Public Act No. 10-117, §§ 93-94 requires pharmaceutical and medical device companies to adopt a comprehensive compliance program; CAL. HEALTH & SAFETY CODE § 119400 and § 119402 requires that a "pharmaceutical company" make an annual declaration relating to the company's compliance program; and NEV. REV. § 639.570 requires wholesalers and manufacturers to adopt a code of conduct and to annually report specific information relating to the code of conduct and compliance program.

[246] *See e.g.,* ME. REV. STAT. ANN. tit. 22, § 2698-A (2008); CAL. HEALTH & SAFETY CODE § 119402 (West 2008). Vermont requires the disclosure of samples (*see* http://ago.vermont.gov/divisions/for-lawyers-and-businesses/pharmaceutical-manufacturer-payment-disclosure.php).

[247] *See* note 1 *supra* § 6002.

Prescription drug promotion and marketing compliance will likely become increasingly complex in the future, with the use of new technologies for promotion, expanding consumer demand for content, and the expansion of marketing and communications based on HOER, cost-effectiveness, and comparative effectiveness claims, in response to growing interest in the development of cost control mechanisms for prescription drug expenditures.

CHAPTER 13
OVER-THE-COUNTER DRUGS

STACY L. EHRLICH AND DANIEL R. DWYER

Introduction and Summary

The term "over-the-counter (OTC) drugs" refers to the category of drugs that are sold legally without a healthcare provider's prescription. These are also called "nonprescription" drugs.

Historically, OTC drugs have been regulated differently than prescription drugs. Although the law has evolved so as to require increasingly rigorous evidence to support the safety and effectiveness of OTC drugs, there still remain significant differences between these two categories of products. To a large extent, this reflects the fact that OTC drugs typically present fewer safety risks than prescription drugs when used as recommended.

To understand the rather unusual regulatory structure that applies to OTC drugs, it is helpful to survey some of the main historical events that have impacted the regulation of these products. Here is a brief timeline:

1938: The Federal Food, Drug, and Cosmetic Act (FDCA)[1] was enacted, prohibiting the adulteration or misbranding of drugs and requiring the submission of a new drug application (NDA) to establish the safety of "new drugs." "New drugs" were defined as drugs not "generally recognized as safe" (GRAS).[2] Many OTC drugs that were on the market before 1938—and many that came onto the market later—were marketed without NDAs on the theory that they were not "new drugs" because they were GRAS. (Some were also marketed without NDAs on the theory that they were subject to the "grandfather" provisions of the law.[3])

---

[1]   Pub. L. No. 75-717, 52 Stat. 1040 (1938), as amended (codified at 21 U.S.C. §§ 301 *et seq.*).

[2]   FDCA § 201(p), 21 U.S.C. § 321(p). The definition of "new drug" is discussed more fully in Chapter 10.

[3]   *See* Chapter 10.

1951: Congress passed the Durham-Humphrey Amendment[4] to the FDCA to clarify the distinction between prescription and OTC drugs. The new law set forth three types of drugs that must be limited to prescription use: 1) certain habit-forming drugs; 2) drugs not safe for use except under the supervision of a licensed practitioner because of a) toxicity or other potential for harmful effects, b) method of use, or c) the collateral measures necessary for use; and 3) drugs limited to prescription use under an approved NDA.[5]

1962: Congress passed the Drug Amendments of 1962, which mandated an evaluation of a new drug's "effectiveness" in addition to "safety." That is, the law required FDA to affirmatively approve "new drugs" as both safe and effective. As a result, FDA evaluated the efficacy of all drug products marketed under NDAs between 1938 and 1962.[6] Most of these were prescription drugs, but there were also approximately 400 OTC drugs covered by NDAs. FDA's review of these OTC drugs was delayed for some years. When FDA's review finally began, the agency learned that thousands of OTC products were on the market without NDAs. FDA had to acknowledge that while an individualized, case-by-case product review was possible for the limited number of prescription products approved under NDAs, it was not feasible to conduct such a review for the many thousands of OTC products that had never received an assessment under the agency's NDA process.

1972: FDA began its "OTC Review," in which it evaluated the safety and effectiveness of OTC drug products by considering categories of active ingredients at specific dosage levels together with their labeled instructions for use, warnings, and other relevant information. Once safety and effectiveness had been evaluated through procedures involving notice-and-comment rulemaking, FDA would publish monographs for each OTC drug category in the form of final regulations. Under FDA's OTC regulations, a product may be marketed without approval of an NDA if it has active ingredients and labeling that conform to a final monograph, and its inactive ingredients are all "safe and suitable." Under the FDCA, an NDA is not required because a product marketed in conformity with an OTC monograph is "generally recognized as safe and effective" (GRASE) and therefore not a "new drug."

The OTC Review is the regulatory structure under which most OTC drugs are currently marketed. A much smaller number of OTC drugs are marketed under approved NDAs. These consist of both:

- drugs that were "switched" from prescription to OTC status via an NDA supplement, and
- drugs that were first approved as OTC drugs.

Importantly, whereas OTC monographs apply only to active ingredients and key labeling elements, an NDA reflects approval of a specific drug product, consisting of all active ingredients, inactive ingredients, and labeling.

Finally, another smaller category of OTC drugs consists of those previously prescription-only products subject to NDAs that were switched to OTC status under the authority of section 503(b)(3) of the FDCA and published in 21 C.F.R. § 310.201.

---

[4]   Pub. L. No. 82-215, 65 Stat. 648 (1951), as amended, FDCA § 503, 21 U.S.C § 353.

[5]   FDCA §§ 503(b)(1)(A)-(C), 21 U.S.C §§ 353(b)(1)(A)-(C).

[6]   *See* Chapter 11 (discussing DESI Review).

In the last 20 years, there have been a number of significant regulatory developments affecting OTC drugs:

- FDA has published a number of final monographs under its OTC Review covering various categories of OTC drugs.

- FDA has published standardized labeling requirements for important information on OTC drug labels. This information includes, for example, the products' uses, warnings, directions, and active and inactive ingredients. The information is required to be formatted in a box and displayed on the label under the heading "Drug Facts."

- FDA has developed a regulatory procedure for permitting new ingredients to be included in the OTC Review if those ingredients are GRASE and have been marketed for a material time and to a material extent, even if those ingredients were not marketed in the United States prior to 1972 (when the OTC Review began) and so were not previously considered eligible for the OTC Review. This provides a mechanism for certain ingredients marketed OTC in foreign countries to be considered for inclusion in the OTC Review.

- A number of prescription drugs have been "switched" to OTC status under NDAs, and several products have been approved for OTC use under NDAs, without ever having been marketed as prescription drugs.

The "OTC switch"—a change in a drug's status from prescription to OTC use—is likely to continue to be an important mechanism for introducing new drugs onto the OTC market. This route to market becomes more feasible with the enhanced desire and ability of patients to self-diagnose and treat their conditions, and with the rising cost of prescription drug insurance coverage. In 2014, FDA began a process of soliciting public comment on how to improve the current OTC monograph process.[7] If this process is successful, it may result in improvements that would enhance opportunities for OTC switches.

Because NDA approval for OTC use typically requires new clinical studies, an OTC switch can provide a manufacturer with three years of "exclusivity" for its OTC product. "Exclusivity" refers to a period of time during which generic versions of the drug may not be approved if the generic application relies on safety and effectiveness data upon which FDA relied in approving the original product. Such exclusivity can provide an incentive for manufacturers to develop OTC versions of prescription drugs after the exclusivity and patent periods for the prescription products have expired. OTC switches have raised interesting regulatory questions, however, such as: can FDA mandate a switch when FDA believes the drug is adequately safe for OTC use but the NDA holder is resistant?

One of the more interesting recent developments in this area is a practice that has emerged of limiting certain classes of OTC drugs to "behind-the-counter" sale. These products are available without a prescription, but a consumer can obtain them only by expressly asking a pharmacist for them (rather than just selecting them off the shelf). This phenomenon has arisen in different contexts, for example: 1) negotiated conditions for approving the switch of a controversial contraceptive drug from prescription to OTC status (e.g., "Plan B"); 2) attempts to control abuse or misuse of an OTC drug that can have other uses or is subject to abuse (e.g., pseudoephedrine under state law); and 3) attempts by retailers to limit pilferage

---

[7]   79 Fed. Reg. 10,168 (Feb. 24, 2014).

of relatively expensive OTC drugs (e.g., nicotine replacement therapy products). In the near future, the number of behind-the-counter sale switches may also increase.

To help put these recent developments into perspective, the following sections provide a general overview of the regulation of OTC drugs in the United States.

OTC Review Overview

As previously stated, FDA's OTC Review began in 1972. At that time, FDA published proposed regulations outlining the scope and procedures for this review.[8] FDA proposed to focus only on active ingredients for each therapeutic category of OTC drugs. It was anticipated that this review would be limited to approximately 200 active ingredients used in existing products. With regard to inactive ingredients, FDA contemplated imposing only general limitations: that the inactive ingredients selected by the manufacturer would be suitable and safe in the amounts administered, and would not interfere with the product's effectiveness or with tests used to determine the product's quality.[9] For each therapeutic category, an advisory panel would be convened to help review the data. Then, through notice-and-comment rulemaking, FDA would review each panel's conclusions and promulgate a regulation that would be a "monograph" of requirements applicable to each therapeutic category of OTC drugs.

In establishing OTC monographs of general applicability, FDA required sound scientific justification to show "general recognition" of the safety and effectiveness of the active ingredients. According to FDA, proof of effectiveness meant published data from controlled clinical investigations, "unless this requirement is waived on the basis of a showing that it is not reasonably applicable to the drug . . . ."[10] The preamble to FDA's proposed regulations establishing the OTC Review specified that "[e]xceptions [to the otherwise stringent standards of evidence] are permitted where they can be justified."[11] For example, the panel could consider unpublished data "if in its expert opinion there is a sound scientific basis for such a decision which is sufficiently widespread to establish general recognition."[12] In general, evidence supporting general recognition of safety and effectiveness could consist of "[o]bjective or subjective clinical studies; bioavailability of ingredients; documented clinical experience or uncontrolled clinical studies; market research studies; animal studies; general medical and scientific literature, published and unpublished; any use by the professional and the consumer; and common medical knowledge."[13] Thus, at the outset, the OTC Review evidentiary standards for GRAS status were, as a practical matter, less stringent than those applicable to prescription drugs and OTC drugs evaluated as "new drugs." Over the years, however, FDA has applied stricter data requirements to drugs under the OTC Review so

---

[8]   37 Fed. Reg. 85 (Jan. 5, 1972).
[9]   21 C.F.R. § 330.1(e).
[10]   37 Fed. Reg. 9464, 9469 (May 11, 1972).
[11]   Id. at 9469.
[12]   Id.
[13]   Id.

that, as a practical matter, they have evolved to become closer to those employed in the new drug approval process.[14]

Under the OTC Review as it has evolved, a finished OTC drug product is excluded from "new drug" status if the active ingredient or combination of active ingredients is deemed GRASE in a final OTC monograph (published as a final regulation), and if the labeling of the product conforms to the specifications in that monograph and to the general labeling rules for OTC drugs.[15] Drugs covered by the OTC Review need not comply with proposed monographs (or "tentative final monographs"), or even with final monographs, until the regulations become final and effective; they may continue to be marketed prior to an effective final monograph unless they are adulterated or misbranded (i.e., unless they present a health hazard or are likely to defraud consumers).[16] As a practical matter, however, manufacturers often seek to comply with proposed monographs to ensure that their products are deemed covered by the OTC Review (because, in general, an OTC drug that is marketed outside of the OTC Review must be the subject of an approved NDA). Also, manufacturers often seek to comply with proposed monographs to ensure that their products are not considered adulterated or misbranded.

Under sections 503(b)(4)(A) and (B) of the FDCA, a drug product is misbranded if it is subject to prescription limitations and is not labeled with the prescription legend (e.g., "Rx Only"), or if it is not subject to prescription limitations and is labeled with the prescription legend. Historically, these requirements were interpreted by FDA to mean that the same active ingredient could not be both prescription and OTC. This resulted in certain uses for OTC drugs (such as aspirin for preventing secondary heart attack) being subject to "Professional Use Only" labeling requirements.[17] In the recent past, however, FDA has interpreted the law to permit the marketing of the same active ingredient in both a prescription product and an OTC product if there is some meaningful difference between the two that makes use of the prescription product safe only under the supervision of a licensed practitioner (e.g., a different indication, strength, route of administration, or dosage form). Examples of such drugs include: meclizine (prescription for vertigo/OTC for nausea with motion sickness); clotrimazol (prescription for candidiasis/OTC for athlete's foot, ring worm, jock itch); loperamide (prescription for chronic diarrhea/OTC for acute diarrhea); nicotine products (prescription for administration through inhalers and nasal sprays/OTC in gums, lozenges, and patches); ibuprofen (prescription at 400 mg and above for arthritis/OTC at 400 mg and below for aches and pains); and H2 blockers (prescription at 300 mg and above for ulcers/OTC at 200 mg for heartburn). In 2014, FDA took action to withdraw abbreviated new drug application (ANDA) approvals for the prescription laxative Polyethylene Glycol 3350 on the basis that an OTC version had been approved and that the FDCA does not permit both Rx and OTC versions of the same drug product to be marketed at the same time.[18]

---

[14] For the legal basis for this approach, *see, e.g.,* Weinberger v. Hynson, Westcott & Dunning, 412 U.S. 609, 629-30 (1973) (holding that a drug cannot be "generally recognized" as safe and effective without the adequate and well-controlled studies that would be required for its approval).

[15] 21 C.F.R. § 330.1.

[16] 37 Fed. Reg. at 9472; *see also* 21 C.F.R. § 310.6; FDA, Guidance for FDA Staff and Industry Marketed Unapproved Drugs — Compliance Policy Guide Sec. 440.100 (2006); FDA, CPG Sec. 450.200 Drugs - General Provisions and Administrative Procedures for Recognition as Safe and Effective (1980).

[17] 21 C.F.R. § 201.5(a).

[18] *See, e.g.,* FDA letter to Paddock Laboratories, Inc. re: ANDA 77-893 (May 22, 2014).

Until 2006, the agency had not authorized the marketing of the same active ingredient for the same indication as a prescription product for one population and as an OTC product for a different population.[19] In 2006, however, the agency approved the switch of "Plan B" from prescription to OTC status for women aged 18 and older. Plan B is an emergency contraceptive drug (or "morning-after pill"). FDA initially required that it remain available as a prescription-only product for women age 17 and under. On March 23, 2009, a federal court issued an order directing FDA to permit the Plan B drug sponsor to make Plan B available to women 17 and older (rather than 18 and older) without a prescription.[20] On July 10, 2009, FDA approved an application for such use.

The OTC Review Procedures

FDA's OTC Review involves a complex four-step process for the development of final monographs for more than 25 broad therapeutic classes of OTC drugs (e.g., antacids, cough and cold preparations, sunscreens, skin protectants, and others).[21] Each step is designed to provide ample opportunity for public participation and comment.

In the first phase of the monograph development process, an expert panel reviews the available data relating to marketed OTC drug products within a particular therapeutic class and provides FDA with its recommendations regarding the safety, effectiveness and labeling for particular active ingredients within that class. Beginning in 1972, FDA convened 17 panels of qualified experts to review data. During the next 10 years, the panels reviewed data, conducted hearings, and heard testimony concerning more than 700 active ingredients and over 1,400 active ingredient uses (as some active ingredients have more than one use).

In the second phase of the OTC Review, FDA publishes each panel recommendation in the *Federal Register*, along with a "proposed monograph," as an advance notice of proposed rulemaking (ANPR). The ANPR sets out the conditions, including indications, under which the panel believes OTC drug products in particular therapeutic classes could be deemed GRASE and not misbranded.

The determination that an OTC product is GRASE and not misbranded would remove the product's new drug status and exempt it from the corresponding requirement for NDA approval.[22] In practice, the ANPR often provides FDA commentary on the panel's views, particularly when the agency disagrees with a specific panel recommendation.[23]

In the third phase of the monograph development process, the agency publishes a tentative final monograph (TFM) in the *Federal Register*, which has the regulatory status of a proposed rule. The TFM announces FDA's preliminary position regarding the safety and effectiveness

---

[19]   70 Fed. Reg. 52,050 (Sept. 1, 2005).

[20]   Tummino v. Torti, 603 F. Supp. 2d 519 (E.D.N.Y. 2009).

[21]   21 C.F.R. pt. 330.

[22]   As noted above, a "new drug" is one that, *inter alia*, is not generally recognized as safe and effective.

[23]   Some monographs have been re-opened to include additional ingredients or claims. *See, e.g.*, 55 Fed. Reg. 38,560 (Sept. 19, 1990) (plaque and gingivitis claims).

of particular active ingredients within a therapeutic class as well as acceptable labeling for indications, warnings, and directions for use. In addition, the preamble to the TFM contains a detailed discussion of and response to each comment submitted by interested parties in response to the ANPR. (As of the date of this publication, there is at least a TFM for each class of drugs covered by the OTC Review.)

In the fourth and final phase, FDA publishes a final monograph that is intended to have the status of a regulation with the force and effect of law. Before issuing a final monograph, the agency must evaluate and address all comments received in response to the TFM, as well as all requests for a public hearing. The agency usually addresses these issues in the preamble to its final rule. Once finalized, a monograph conclusively establishes the conditions under which a drug product within a particular therapeutic class will be considered GRASE and not misbranded. The final monograph is codified in FDA regulations and typically provides an effective date one year after publication in the *Federal Register.*

In the process leading up to the final monograph, active ingredients are categorized into three groups: Category I, covering drugs that are GRASE;[24] Category II, including all ingredients, labeling claims, and other conditions that would result in a drug being not GRASE;[25] and Category III, including all ingredients, labeling claims and other conditions for which available data are insufficient to justify classification in either of the other groups.[26]

As originally promulgated by FDA, the regulations authorized the marketing of any Category III drug after publication of the final monograph provided the manufacturer conducted additional testing.[27] The United States District Court for the District of Columbia, however, struck down this provision, holding that it directly contravened the FDCA by sanctioning for an indefinite period the marketing of drugs that were unable to satisfy the GRASE requirements.[28] In response to this decision, FDA amended its regulations to their present form, eliminating the post-final monograph marketing authorization for Category III drugs,[29] but adding a 12-month period following publication of the TFM in which the administrative record is kept open for receipt of new information regarding the safety and effectiveness of drugs tentatively placed in Category III.[30] This 12-month open record period was then challenged but upheld by the D.C. Circuit.[31]

Following the effective date of a final monograph, all drug products subject to the monograph that fail to conform to its requirements (i.e., "non-monograph" products) are subject to misbranding charges and/or to charges of being an unapproved new drug, in the absence of an approved NDA. FDA has issued final monographs that apply, either partially or completely, to many of the originally identified OTC therapeutic classes. In addition, the agency has issued numerous final regulations determining that certain types of OTC

---

[24]   21 C.F.R. § 330.10(a)(5)(i).

[25]   *Id.* § 330.10(a)(5)(ii).

[26]   *Id.* § 330.10(a)(5)(iii).

[27]   *Id.* § 330.10(a)(13) (1981).

[28]   Cutler v. Kennedy, 475 F. Supp. 838, 855 (D.D.C. 1979).

[29]   Cutler v. Hayes, 549 F. Supp. 1341, 1345 (D.D.C. 1982).

[30]   21 C.F.R. § 330.10(a)(7)(iii) (1986).

[31]   Cutler v. Hayes, 818 F.2d 879, 899 (D.C. Cir. 1987).

drug products are not GRASE and are new drugs.[32] There remain, however, a number of monographs that have not yet reached a final stage.

The OTC Review has proved a much more burdensome and protracted process than anyone expected at its outset in 1972. It was expected that the review would be completed within two to four years, but after more than 40 years, it is still years from completion. Many administrative records have been re-opened to accept new data and comments as new information about ingredients comes to light, further slowing the review process.[33] Despite the procedural delays and the lack of final effective monographs for some therapeutic classes, however, few would dispute that the review has been a useful and successful regulatory effort. Though ingredients in most available OTC products were first discovered and marketed long before the proliferation of today's potent prescription drugs, industry has collected and generated a vast quantity of data under the OTC Review in an attempt to meet FDA's standards of evidence. In addition, products have been, and are being, reformulated to meet proposed monograph conditions even before the applicable monograph becomes final and effective. In cases in which manufacturers have disagreed about the need for further evidence or reformulation of products, they have often individually or through coalitions sought to resolve the residual issues by supplementing the scientific evidence or seeking a mutually acceptable resolution with FDA.[34]

In 2012, FDA announced that it is considering a new "paradigm" under which it would switch prescription drugs to OTC status and approve drugs that would otherwise require a prescription for OTC use under "conditions of safe use." These conditions of safe use would be specific to the drug product and might involve restrictions on sale in certain pre-defined healthcare settings, such as a pharmacy, or restrictions based on the use of specific technology (such as diagnostic or monitoring tests). FDA held a public hearing to discuss this paradigm and, at this writing, it is still under consideration.[35]

As described above, the label and labeling of the products marketed under the OTC Review must conform to the applicable monograph and comply with other relevant regulations, such as those requiring warnings.[36] Under what was termed an "exclusivity" policy, FDA initially took the position that the "indications" section of OTC drug labeling must use the exact terminology set forth in the monograph. In 1986, the agency adopted the "flexibility policy," which permitted other truthful and nonmisleading statements to describe the indications established for the product.[37] The manufacturer now has the option of placing the exact monograph indication(s) in the "Uses" section of the Drug Facts box (described below), or using similar wording. Aspects of the label or labeling other than the indications must still follow the monograph precisely where specific language is specified by quotation

---

[32]   E.g., 21 C.F.R. § 310.528 (classifying products marketed as aphrodisiacs as "new drugs"). Most of the regulations found in 21 C.F.R. pt. 310, subpart E similarly designate specific product categories as "new drugs."

[33]   See, e.g., 59 Fed. Reg. 18,507 (Apr. 19, 1994) (proposing a monograph for OTC internal analgesics).

[34]   See, e.g., submissions by industry representatives on OTC antimicrobial drug products (the "Healthcare Continuum Model").

[35]   77 Fed. Reg. 12,059 (Feb. 28, 2012).

[36]   See, e.g., 21 C.F.R. §§ 330.1(g) (general warnings for OTC products), 330.2 (pregnancy-nursing warning).

[37]   Id. § 330.1(c)(2); 51 Fed. Reg. 16,266 (May 1, 1986).

marks.[38] The OTC monograph regulations also require that OTC drugs be manufactured in compliance with current good manufacturing practice (cGMP) as established by regulation.[39]

Once a monograph becomes final, new ingredients or indications may be added through the administrative rulemaking process by petitioning for an amendment to the monograph. The OTC Review procedures are so time-consuming, however, that this is generally not a very attractive option. New drug clearance is likely to be a quicker route to market, in addition to providing opportunities for exclusivity not available under the OTC Review.[40] This is particularly so in situations where a company can take advantage of the so-called "NDA deviation" provisions set forth in 21 C.F.R. § 314.11. Under this procedure, the applicant submits a section 505(b)(2) NDA relying on the safety and effectiveness findings of the monograph, thereby requiring the applicant to submit safety and effectiveness data relating only to the deviation.[41]

In 2002, FDA implemented a procedure whereby a manufacturer may seek to add an active ingredient to an OTC monograph that would not otherwise qualify for inclusion because it was not marketed in the United States before 1972 (when the OTC Review began). Ingredients marketed in the United States after 1972, or ingredients marketed in foreign countries (either as OTC drugs, or as dietary supplements or cosmetics if such products would be subject to regulation as OTC drugs under U.S. law) may potentially be included under the OTC Review if FDA accepts a "Time and Extent Application" (TEA) for the ingredients. The TEA must establish that the ingredient was marketed for OTC use for at least five years in the same country and in a sufficient quantity.[42] Although these rules have been in place for more than 10 years and FDA is currently reviewing the eligibility of several ingredients under them, as of this writing no ingredients have successfully negotiated the TEA procedures.

OTC Switches

A prescription drug may be switched to OTC status when FDA finds that prescription requirements are not necessary for protection of the public health and that the drug is safe and effective for OTC use as directed in the proposed product labeling.[43] FDA published one of the first switch regulations in September 1957.[44]

There are three different ways that an OTC switch may occur:

    (1) FDA may perform the switch by regulation, pursuant to section 503(b)(3) of the FDCA and 21 C.F.R. §§ 310.200 and 310.201 (FDA's so-called switch regulations);

---

[38]   21 C.F.R. § 330.1(c)(2).

[39]   21 C.F.R. § 330.1(a).

[40]   See Chapters 10 (full NDA) and 11 (section 505(b)(2) NDA and exclusivity).

[41]   21 C.F.R. § 330.11.

[42]   21 C.F.R. § 330.14; see also FDA, Guidance for Industry: Time and Extent Applications for Nonprescription Drug Products (Sept. 2011).

[43]   21 C.F.R. § 310.200(b).

[44]   22 Fed. Reg. 7315 (Sept. 13, 1957) (carbetapentacitrate preparations).

(2) FDA may approve a supplemental NDA or ANDA[45] that permits OTC marketing (with any necessary changes to the labeling and/or product); or

(3) FDA may include under its OTC Review, in appropriate monographs, new active ingredients or strengths that were previously available only by prescription or new indications that FDA previously determined required a healthcare provider's recommendation or supervision.

The switch regulation procedure has not been used very frequently; however, it was the vehicle for several switches that predated the OTC Review program, including acetaminophen, the active ingredient in Tylenol®. The switch regulations were also used as a vehicle by which a product could escape "new drug" status in that products previously subject to NDA approval were able to be marketed OTC pursuant to a switch regulation without such NDA or ANDA approval. Thus, for example, branded and generic acetaminophen were able to be marketed OTC without NDA approval following the switch.

In the past, the OTC Review program was effectively used to switch certain active ingredients from prescription to OTC status or to increase the permitted OTC strength of an active ingredient. The development of the OTC monograph for external analgesics provides examples of both.[46] In recent years, however, switches have usually been accomplished by an NDA holder submitting a supplement to its NDA requesting OTC approval.[47] Except in the case of complete switches in which the same product that was marketed as a prescription drug is marketed OTC (i.e., same strength, dose, dosage form, and indication), the switch generally requires the support of one or more clinical studies to demonstrate that OTC use is safe and effective. Approval often also requires label comprehension studies to determine how best to design a label that consumers will understand, as well as actual-use studies to show that consumers not only understand but also follow the directions for use.

For purposes of switching, the most important criterion is that the product must be safe for use without the ongoing supervision of a physician. This criterion has been considered by the courts in cases in which FDA has challenged a manufacturer's failure to market a drug under prescription limitations. A relevant court decision on this issue is *United States v. An Article of Drug . . . Decholin*,[48] wherein the court emphasized that the test was a practical one based on the benefits of the product as well as specific concerns about potential harm to users. The court also suggested that the adequacy of labeling to guide lay use was an important factor in determining whether OTC status was appropriate for a particular drug. FDA has commonly used label warnings to enhance the safety of OTC drugs.

---

[45]   An ANDA approval for prescription use can be switched to OTC use only if the reference drug for the ANDA is also approved for the OTC use. *See* Chapter 11 (discussing ANDAs and reference drugs).

[46]   *See* 44 Fed. Reg. 69,768, 69,813 (Dec. 4, 1979) (announcing the Advisory Panel's conclusion that hydrocortisone is safe and effective for use as an OTC antipruritic and noting that hydrocortisone was first marketed as a prescription drug in 1952); 48 Fed. Reg. 5852, 5868 (Feb. 8, 1983) (adopting the Advisory Panel's recommendation and including hydrocortisone as an approved active ingredient in the tentative final monograph); 55 Fed. Reg. 6932 (Feb. 27, 1990) (amending the tentative final monograph by increasing the maximum allowable concentration of hydrocortisone from 0.5 percent to 1 percent); 56 Fed. Reg. 43,025 (Aug. 30, 1991) (announcing an enforcement policy allowing the marketing of OTC external analgesic drug products containing hydrocortisone at concentrations between 0.5 percent and 1 percent).

[47]   *See e.g.*, switches for protein pump inhibitor (PPI) acid reducer products: NDA 22-327 for Prevacid®24HR (approved May 18, 2009); NDA 22-281 for Zegerid OTC™ (approved December 1, 2009).

[48]   264 F. Supp. 273 (D. Mich. 1967).

As noted above, in general—and particularly since the advent of user fees—it is likely to be more expeditious to file a section 505(b)(2) NDA to switch a prescription drug to OTC status than to submit a petition to amend an existing OTC monograph. In practice, rulemaking actions under the OTC Review have typically taken several years (or more) to accomplish, whereas the agency's current Prescription Drug User Fee Act (PDUFA) goal for approval of an NDA (or supplements requiring clinical data) is 10 months. For generic versions of products that are switched pursuant to an NDA or NDA supplement, ANDAs or ANDA supplements can be approved upon expiration of any applicable periods of exclusivity. The ability to file a supplemental ANDA ensures that generic versions can also be marketed OTC.

Data to Support an OTC Switch

In order to obtain approval of a prescription product for OTC use or to change the indication or patient population of an NDA-approved OTC product, an applicant must demonstrate that the intended population of consumers is able to self-treat and self-manage the condition covered by the proposed OTC indication.[49] These elements are generally assessed through label comprehension studies and actual use studies, both of which evaluate the ability of consumers to understand the information provided in the product labeling.[50]

Label Comprehension. Label comprehension studies are designed to determine if the label clearly communicates the uses, directions, and warnings to a diverse population and enables the consumer to make appropriate judgments about self-selection and conditions of use.[51] Label comprehension study data may not, however, be adequate to predict how consumers will actually use a drug product. Data on this issue may be obtained through an actual use study, discussed below. Label comprehension studies are generally conducted in advance of any actual use studies.

Actual Use. As the name implies, actual use studies are intended to evaluate actual use of the drug in the population for which it is intended. Thus, unlike subjects in a label comprehension study, subjects in an actual use study will self-administer the product. Actual use studies are intended to test parameters such as: 1) the adequacy of labeling for the OTC population; 2) compliance issues, including off-label usage; 3) overdose or abuse potential; and 4) specific safety issues related to use in the OTC population without the intervention of a healthcare professional.

Exclusivity Issues for OTC Switches

There can be significant economic rewards associated with newly switched products for the OTC marketplace. If an NDA supplement contains reports of new clinical investigations

---

[49]   In deciding whether or not a drug should be available without a prescription, FDA also considers whether the condition being treated can be self-diagnosed and recognized without the help of a healthcare practitioner. The inability to self-diagnose a medical condition, however, does not automatically prevent a product approved to treat that condition from switching to OTC status.

[50]   *See* FDA, Manual of Policies and Procedures 6532.1: Over-the-Counter (OTC) Labeling and Use Studies (1996).

[51]   *See* FDA, Guidance for Industry: Label Comprehension Studies for Nonprescription Drug Products (2010).

(other than bioavailability studies) essential to approval and conducted or sponsored by the applicant, that supplement is entitled to three years of nonpatent exclusivity.[52]

Over the years, there has been litigation over what studies qualify as "essential" for purposes of granting exclusivity as part of OTC switches.[53] When an OTC product is to be marketed at a lower strength than the prescription version, studies must be conducted to demonstrate efficacy, and those studies qualify for exclusivity.[54] If the product being switched is identical in dose and strength to the original prescription product, however, the agency will focus on the marketing history of the product, the safety profile, and OTC label comprehension studies. Although actual use studies, if necessary for approval, should qualify the switched product for exclusivity, there are occasions in which OTC switches are accomplished without the need for clinical studies.[55] In such instances, three-year exclusivity would not be available.

Importantly, however, the issue is not whether switch candidates are identical to prescription products, but whether the particular studies conducted by the applicant meet the statutory criteria for exclusivity. For example, Femstat, an antifungal switched with a dosage identical to that of the prescription version, received three-year exclusivity based on a clinical trial establishing that it was at least as effective as other OTC products on the market. Where the OTC switch requires a clinical study under conditions of OTC use in order to establish either safety or efficacy in an OTC setting, or FDA demands additional safety or effectiveness information (thereby effectively requiring a new clinical study to support the application), there is a strong argument that the statutory requirement that the clinical study be "essential" to approval has been met. Even in this situation, the agency must agree with the drug manufacturer on what data are "essential" before exclusivity will be granted.[56]

Finished Formulation Testing

Under the OTC Review, most monographs do not require finished formulation testing. Some do, however, and FDA has included in those monographs a standard in vitro or in vivo test. Examples are the in vitro acid neutralizing capacity test for antacids,[57] the in vitro USP dissolution tests for enteric-coated and delayed-release aspirin preparations,[58] and the in vivo and in vitro effectiveness tests for sunscreens.[59]

When there is no adequate standardized test or a clinical study is required, FDA may deny monograph status and require an NDA. For example, in 1995, FDA concluded that

---

52   FDCA § 505(j)(4)(D)(iii), 21 U.S.C. § 355(j)(4)(D)(iii).

53   *See, e.g.,* Upjohn Co. v. Kessler, 938 F. Supp. 439 (W.D. Mich. 1996).

54   There has been relatively little controversy regarding three-year exclusivity for switches of lower-strength versions of prescription drug products. Examples include ibuprofen 200 mg (Advil®), naproxen 100 mg (Aleve®), and cimetidine 100 (Tagamet HB®). In each of these cases, there was no question that new clinical studies were required to demonstrate that the products were effective at lower than previously approved doses.

55   OTC clotrimazole is an example.

56   *See, e.g.,* Upjohn Co., *supra* note 53.

57   *See* 21 C.F.R § 331.21.

58   *See* 53 Fed. Reg. 46,204 (Nov. 16, 1988) (proposing amendments to be codified at 21 C.F.R. § 343.90).

59   *See* 21 C.F.R. § 201.327(i) (sun protection factor (SPF) Test) and (21 C.F.R. § 201.327(j) (Broad Spectrum Test).

clinical trials were needed to assess the efficacy of each finished formulation of OTC vaginal contraceptives and proposed that manufacturers obtain approved NDAs for such products rather than permitting approval under the OTC Review.[60] Industry proposed such clinical trials, and FDA has allowed the continued marketing of these OTC products pending the completion and analysis of these trials.[61] In general, the trend has been to include in the monograph any testing requirements for drugs subject to the OTC Review, rather than requiring such drugs to be covered by NDAs.

Trade Names

FDA reviews proposed proprietary names for OTC drugs that will be marketed under an NDA or ANDA as part of the approval process. With respect to OTC products marketed under a monograph, FDA recommends that manufacturers review proprietary names for safety.[62]

Many OTC drugs are marketed as part of a line or family of products that may or may not contain one of the active ingredients present in the first marketed product. These products, sometimes referred to as umbrella brands or line extensions, often share the same root proprietary name with a suffix or other modifier to distinguish individual products. Because this practice creates inherent similarity among the names, FDA has expressed concern that these products may be subject to name confusion and medical error.

For example, in 2010 there were two examples of safety issues raised by umbrella branding. First, there were numerous adverse event reports for Benadryl Extra Strength Itch Stopping Gel based on mistaken ingestion by consumers, who apparently confused the product with Benadryl oral liquid products. As a result, Johnson & Johnson added the statement, "For Skin Use Only," to the label, but was not required to change the name of the product. In the other case, Novartis changed the name and packaging of Maalox Total Relief to avoid potentially serious side effects if the stomachache/diarrhea product was confused with antacid products marketed under the same brand name (but containing different active ingredients).

In the NDA/ANDA context, FDA evaluates OTC proprietary names that include brand-name extensions on a case-by-case basis to consider whether: 1) the products share at least one common active ingredient; 2) the products are differentiated by labeling; and 3) the modifiers used are appropriate and effectively differentiate the product among members of the same product line.

When a drug product is switched from prescription to OTC status, the proposed proprietary name for the OTC product might or might not be the same as the original (prescription) proprietary name. Continued use of the original proprietary name might be appropriate when there is a full switch (i.e., all indications, dosing, and strengths previously limited to prescription use will now all be available OTC). However, when the product switch is only partial (i.e., prescription-only status still applies to some indications, dosages, or strengths),

[60]   60 Fed. Reg. 6892 (Feb. 3, 1995).

[61]   *See* 68 Fed. Reg. 2254 (Jan. 16, 2003); 72 Fed. Reg. 71,769, 71,772 (Dec. 19, 2007).

[62]   FDA, Draft Guidance for Industry: Best Practices in Developing Proprietary Names for Drugs (2014).

it might be appropriate to market the OTC product under a different or modified proprietary name. Alternatively, the sponsor can propose a completely new proprietary name for the OTC product, whether the switch was full or partial. FDA evaluates these proposals on a case-by-case basis.

Labels and Labeling

OTC drug labels are subject to both FDA's general regulations and the specific monographs that cover different categories of OTC drugs. The general regulations provide for basic label elements (such as the statement of identity, net quantity of contents, and "Keep Out of Reach of Children" warning) and specify the standard format for the "Drug Facts" box, which must appear on virtually all OTC drugs. The contents of the Drug Facts box are derived from both the general regulations and the monographs, and include required information such as indications, warnings, and directions for use.

As discussed above, most of the required label information must appear exactly as stated in the OTC monographs. In response to industry demands for more flexibility in label wording, however, in 1986 FDA modified its so-called "exclusivity" policy to permit labels to bear either the exact words of the indication specified in FDA monographs or a variation on that wording that is truthful and not misleading.[63] FDA regulations only cover the required label elements;[64] the parts of an OTC drug label that are not governed by the regulations may generally contain any truthful and nonmisleading information.[65]

Section 412 of the Food and Drug Administration Modernization Act of 1997 (FDAMA) amended the FDCA to require, for the first time, that the outer retail package bear the name of each inactive ingredient listed in alphabetical order.[66] FDA may, if appropriate, require by regulation that the inactive ingredients also appear on the immediate container, although in general this information needs to appear only in the Drug Facts box, which must appear on the outer retail package.

In addition, certain contact information is required on the label of OTC drugs, depending on whether they are marketed pursuant to an approved NDA or ANDA or under the OTC Review. The Food and Drug Administration Amendments Act of 2007 (FDAAA)[67] mandated the promulgation of regulations requiring that the label of an OTC product that is marketed pursuant to an approved NDA or ANDA, and that does not include a toll-free number that consumers may call to report complaints to the manufacturer or distributor, must include

---

[63]   *See* 21 C.F.R. § 330.1(c)(2).

[64]   21 C.F.R. § 201.66.

[65]   Claims concerning nontherapeutic characteristics of drugs (e.g., "tastes great" or "4 out of 5 doctors recommend") are generally not addressed by the OTC monographs. Labeling claims of this type, however, would be subject to the misbranding provisions of the Act. FDCA § 502; 21 U.S.C. § 352.

[66]   FDCA § 502(e)(1)(A)(iii), 21 U.S.C. § 352(e)(1)(A)(iii). There is an exception to listing inactive ingredients in alphabetical order for OTC drugs that are also cosmetics.

[67]   FDAAA contains another provision applicable to OTC drugs marketed under an approved NDA or ANDA: a requirement mandating participation in a Clinical Trial Registry, which includes the posting of clinical trial results. 42 U.S.C. § 282(j).

in the Drug Facts box a statement that side effect information may be reported to FDA by calling 1-800-FDA-1088.[68]

Under the Dietary Supplement and Nonprescription Drug Consumer Protection Act of 2006 (DSNDCPA), the label of OTC drugs marketed without NDA or ANDA approval (i.e., marketed under an OTC monograph) must include "a domestic address or domestic phone number through which the responsible person . . . may receive a report of a serious adverse event."[69] FDA has interpreted this provision to require either 1) a full U.S. mailing address that includes the street address or a P.O. Box number and the city, state, and zip code or 2) a telephone number.[70] FDA also recommends, but does not require, that the label bear a statement informing consumers that the domestic address or phone number is for reporting serious adverse events associated with use of the product.[71]

FDA also has jurisdiction over OTC drug labeling, which, in addition to the product label, includes all "other written, printed or graphic matter . . . accompanying such article."[72] FDA and the courts have broadly interpreted this definition,[73] and the agency now routinely takes enforcement action on the basis of claims made on websites, Facebook, Twitter, YouTube and other forms of social media. This is particularly the case where the product label references a website address or where the product is available for sale via the website or social media site.

Advertising

The FDCA does not give FDA authority to regulate the advertising of OTC drugs. Instead, this statutory responsibility falls to the Federal Trade Commission (FTC).[74] FDA regulations, however, require that OTC drug advertising be limited only to the conditions for use specified in labeling.[75] This regulation is based on the statutory requirement that labeling bear "adequate directions for use."[76] FDA relies on this authority to object to advertising of OTC drugs for off-label uses. The agency takes the position that an OTC drug is misbranded if its advertising suggests uses for which the product is not labeled. If, however, the product was labeled with adequate directions for the advertised, non-monograph use, it would be

---

68 FDAAA § 501(f); 21 C.F.R. § 201.66(c)(5)(vii).
69 FDCA § 502(x), 21 U.S.C. § 352(x).
70 FDA, Guidance for Industry: Labeling of Nonprescription Human Drug Products Marketed Without an Approved Application as Required by the Dietary Supplement and Nonprescription Drug Consumer Protection Act: Questions and Answers (2009).
71 Id.
72 FDCA § 201(m), 21 U.S.C. § 321(m).
73 See, e.g., Kordel v. United States, 335 U.S. 345 (1948) (term phrase "accompanying such article" includes literature shipped separately and at different times from the drugs with which they were associated); SmithKline Beecham Consumer Healthcare, L.P. v. Watson Pharms., Inc., 211 F.3d 21, 26 (dictum) (copyrighted user's guide and audiotape for nicotine gum constitute "labeling"); FDA Response to Washington Legal Foundation Citizen Petition (Docket No. 01P-0187) (Nov. 1, 2001) (denying request that FDA determine that websites do not constitute "labeling").
74 Federal Trade Commission Act §§ 5, 12, 15(a), 15 U.S.C §§ 45, 52, 55(a).
75 21 C.F.R. § 330.1(d).
76 FDCA § 502(f)(1), 21 U.S.C § 352(f)(1).

an unapproved new drug. This legal dilemma is known as FDA's "squeeze play."[77] FDA has also used its new drug approval authority in the context of the ibuprofen "switch" to require assurances that advertising for an OTC drug will not undercut the required warnings in labeling.[78]

FDA and FTC have executed a Memorandum of Understanding that provides for cooperation in exercising their respective responsibilities with respect to OTC drugs.[79] Prior to its announcement of the "exclusivity" policy requiring that OTC drug labeling of indications for use conform to the exact wording of the applicable monograph (which, as noted above, was subsequently abandoned by the agency), FDA sought an FTC rulemaking that would similarly limit OTC drug advertising claims to the exact wording of the monographs. In 1981, FTC concluded that OTC drug advertising should not always be limited to labeling language approved by FDA.[80]

As a practical matter, FTC will, when evaluating the claims made for an OTC drug, require such claims to be supported by competent and reliable scientific evidence—and claims authorized in an FDA monograph are by definition supported by such evidence.[81] Moreover, FDA and FTC work closely together in reviewing OTC drug promotion and have in recent years issued joint Warning Letters claiming that certain claims violate both the FDCA and the Federal Trade Commission Act.

Inspection Authority

Section 412 of FDAMA changed FDA's inspection authority over OTC drug establishments to be similar to its authority over prescription drug establishments.[82] Previously, FDA's authority to inspect establishments in which OTC drugs are handled was limited to pertinent equipment, finished and unfinished materials, containers, and labeling, while its authority to inspect prescription drug establishments extended to everything in the plant (with certain limited exceptions) bearing on the products' compliance with the law.

Preemption

Section 412 of FDAMA created section 751 of the FDCA,[83] which preempts state and local laws that impose different or additional requirements on the marketing of OTC drugs. A

---

[77]   *See, e.g.*, United States v. An Article of Drug . . . B-Complex Cholinos Capsules, 362 F.2d 923, 925-926 (3d Cir. 1966).

[78]   *See* McNeil, Inc. v. Heckler, No. 84-1617 (D.D.C. June 5, 1985).

[79]   FDA-FTC Memorandum of Understanding, 36 Fed. Reg. 18,539 (Sept. 16, 1971).

[80]   46 Fed. Reg. 24,584 (May 1, 1981) (terminating the rulemaking proceeding to designate as a violation of the FTC Act using in advertising wording other than that required by the final monograph established for that therapeutic category).

[81]   *See* Chapter 12 (discussing FTC regulation of OTC drug advertising).

[82]   21 U.S.C. § 374(a)(1).

[83]   21 U.S.C. § 379r.

state or political subdivision can request an exemption from FDA if its unique requirement "protects an important public interest that would not otherwise be protected," would not cause the drug to be in violation of any federal law, and "would not unduly burden interstate commerce."

Registration Under the Public Health Security and Bioterrorism Preparedness and Response Act of 2002

By amending section 510(i) of the FDCA,[84] this legislation requires foreign drug manufacturing establishments to register on or before December 31 of each year by electronic means the name and place of business of the establishment, the name of the U.S. agent for the establishment, the name of each importer into the United States known to the establishment, "the name of each importer of such drug . . . in the United States that is known to the establishment," and "the name of each person, who imports or offers for import such drug . . . to the United States for purposes of importation." Under section 801(o) of the FDCA,[85] if the importer does not submit a statement that identifies the section 510(i) registration of each establishment that is required to be registered, FDA may refuse admission of the drug.

Adverse Event Reports

The FDCA requires the submission to FDA of reports of serious adverse reactions associated with the use of all OTC drugs used in the United States within 15 business days of notification. The report to FDA may be accompanied by a statement denying that the report constitutes an admission that the product involved caused or contributed to the serious adverse event.[86]

New information relating to adverse events associated with OTC drugs has led to FDA regulatory action in a number of cases. For example, based on potential liver injury and stomach bleeding associated with OTC internal analgesic, antipyretic, and antirheumatic drug products, FDA issued a final rule, codified at 21 C.F.R. § 201.326, requiring additional warnings for such products.[87] Similarly, based on serious side effects associated with the customary dose of OTC sodium phosphates solution for bowel cleansing prior to colonoscopy, FDA proposed that sodium phosphate salts are not GRAS for this use and that

---

84   21 U.S.C. § 360(i).

85   21 U.S.C. § 381(o).

86   *See* FDA, Guidance for Industry: Postmarketing Adverse Event Reporting for Nonprescription Human Drug Products Marketed Without an Approved Application (2009).

87   74 Fed. Reg. 19,385 (Apr. 29, 2009); *see also* FDA, Guidance for Industry: Organ-Specific Warnings: Internal Analgesic, Antipyretic, and Antirheumatic Drug Products for Over-the-Counter Human Use — Small Entity Compliance Guide (2010).

the professional labeling proposed for sodium phosphate salts in the 1985 TFM for OTC laxative drug products should be withdrawn.[88]

In addition, adverse event reports (highlighted, in some cases, by citizen petitions) have led FDA to issue public health advisories. For example, based on a wide variety of rare, serious adverse events associated with pediatric cough and cold products and reported to the agency, in 2008, FDA issued a Public Health Advisory for parents and caregivers, recommending that OTC cough and cold products not be administered to infants and children under two years of age.[89] Likewise, in 2011, FDA issued two Drug Safety Communications regarding topical benzocaine products.[90] Most recently, in June 2014, FDA issued a Drug Safety Communication warning the public that certain OTC topical acne products can cause rare but serious and potentially life-threatening allergic reactions or severe irritation.[91]

Homeopathic Drugs

A growing class of OTC drugs that generally falls outside the OTC Review is the class of homeopathic drugs. The practice of homeopathy is based on the belief that disease symptoms can be cured by small doses of substances that produce similar symptoms in healthy people. The FDCA recognizes as drug products substances listed in the Homeopathic Pharmacopeia of the United States (HPUS).[92] The FDCA also specifies that homeopathic drugs generally must meet the standards for strength, quality, and purity set forth in the HPUS.[93]

Since 1988, FDA has provided guidance on the regulation of OTC, as well as prescription, homeopathic drugs, and delineated those conditions under which homeopathic drugs may ordinarily be marketed in the United States.[94] FDA takes the position that the new drug definition and the requirement for new drug approval apply to homeopathic drugs, but it exercises its discretion not to enforce these provisions and certain related labeling

---

[88]   76 Fed. Reg. 7743 (Feb. 11, 2011).

[89]   *See* FDA Public Health Advisory: FDA Recommends that Over-the-Counter (OTC) Cough and Cold Products not be used for Infants and Children under 2 Years of Age, *available at* http://www.fda.gov/drugs/drugsafety/postmarketdrugsafetyinformationforpatientsandproviders/drugsafetyinformationforheathcareprofessionals/publichealthadvisories/ucm051137.htm.

[90]   *See* FDA Drug Safety Communication: FDA continues to receive reports of a rare, but serious and potentially fatal adverse effect with the use of benzocaine sprays for medical procedures (Apr. 7, 2011), *available at* http://www.fda.gov/Drugs/DrugSafety/ucm250040.htm; FDA Drug Safety Communication: Reports of a rare, but serious and potentially fatal adverse effect with the use of over-the-counter (OTC) benzocaine gels and liquids applied to the gums or mouth (Apr. 7, 2011), *available at* http://www.fda.gov/Drugs/DrugSafety/ucm250024.htm.

[91]   *See* FDA Drug Safety Communication: FDA warns of rare but serious hypersensitivity reactions with certain over-the-counter topical acne products (June 25, 2014), *available at* http://www.fda.gov/Drugs/DrugSafety/ucm400923.htm.

[92]   FDCA § 201(g)(1), 21 U.S.C. § 321(g)(1). The fact that the act passed by Congress in 1938 contains a section recognizing homeopathic drugs was largely due to the efforts of Senator Royal Copeland, one of the foremost homeopathic physicians of his day. *See* Pub. L. No. 75-717, 52 Stat. 1,040, 1,041 (1938).

[93]   FDCA § 501(b), 21 U.S.C. § 351(b).

[94]   FDA, Conditions Under Which Homeopathic Drugs May Be Marketed, Compliance Policy Guide § 400.400 (1995) [hereinafter Homeopathic Compliance Policy Guide].

requirements against homeopathic drugs recognized in the HPUS and meeting other conditions set forth in its compliance policy guide.[95]

Allopathic Versus Homeopathic Drugs

There is a peculiar dichotomy in the regulation of allopathic (i.e., conventional) versus homeopathic drugs. In contrast to allopathic drugs, homeopathic products have generally not been demonstrated to be safe and effective based on adequate and well-controlled clinical studies. When FDA focused on ensuring the safety of all new drugs following the Elixir of Sulfanilamide tragedy in 1938, the agency ignored the category of homeopathic drugs. Similarly, after the passage of the 1962 Kefauver-Harris Amendment in the wake of the thalidomide tragedy, FDA did not address the effectiveness of homeopathic products.[96] Indeed, because the 1962 Drug Amendments required efficacy review only of drugs approved between 1938 and 1962, and homeopathic drugs had not been approved during this time period (because they were thought to pose no safety concerns), homeopathic products were not reviewed during the DESI Review process. Homeopathic drugs were likewise excluded from the OTC Review: "Because of the uniqueness of homeopathic medicine, the Commissioner has decided to exclude homeopathic drugs from this OTC drug review and to review them as a separate category at a later time after the present OTC drug review is complete."[97]

Thus, homeopathic drugs have not been required to be proven effective against disease by the scientific standards that FDA applies to other drugs, such as randomized, controlled double-blind trials. The result is that, whereas allopathic drugs may not be marketed without rigorous and expensive scientific support, homeopathic drugs may be marketed with no such support.

Definition of Homeopathic Drug

FDA's Center for Drug Evaluation and Research has issued a compliance policy guide (CPG) that provides a definition of "homeopathic drug."[98] First, the drug must contain active ingredients listed in the HPUS. Second, the potencies of homeopathic drugs must be specified in terms of dilution (i.e., 1X (1/10 dilution), 2X (1/100 dilution), etc.). Third, homeopathic drug products must contain diluents commonly used in homeopathic pharmaceutics, such as water and alcohol. With regard to alcohol, under FDA's final rule establishing maximum alcohol concentration limits for orally ingested OTC drugs,[99] FDA declared that orally ingested homeopathic drugs are exempt from the FDA alcohol content limits. As an interim measure, however, FDA required such products to be relabeled to disclose their alcohol content and, in certain circumstances, to advise consumers to consult a physician before administering the product to children below certain ages.

Drug products containing homeopathic ingredients in combination with non-homeopathic ingredients, or drug products formulated as homeopathic products but labeled for non-

---

95   *Id.*

96   *FDA Talk Paper No. T-88-68* (Sept. 15, 1988).

97   37 Fed. Reg. 9464 (May 11, 1972).

98   *See* Homeopathic Compliance Policy Guide, *supra* note 94.

99   59 Fed. Reg. 51,030 (Oct. 6, 1994).

homeopathic use, are not considered homeopathic drugs.[100] FDA regularly issues Warning Letters to companies based on determinations that ostensibly homeopathic drugs fail to meet these standards.[101]

Prescription Versus OTC Status

The statutory criteria specified in section 503(b) of the FDCA for the determination of prescription status apply to homeopathic drug products.[102] However, if the HPUS declares a homeopathic drug to be a prescription drug based on strength (e.g., 20X), FDA will regard the drug as a prescription drug without regard to the criteria of section 503(b) of the FDCA. In practice, FDA has only permitted homeopathic products intended solely for "self-limiting disease conditions amenable to self-diagnosis (of symptoms) and treatment" to be marketed OTC. A homeopathic drug product that does not meet this standard must be marketed as a prescription drug bearing the prescription legend, "Caution: Federal law prohibits dispensing without prescription" or "Rx Only."[103]

In 1992, FDA took its first enforcement action against a homeopathic drug based on prescription drug status, issuing a Warning Letter based on its Health Fraud Bulletin Number 17, "Prescription Homeopathic Products Marketed Over-the-Counter."[104] The action is noteworthy because the agency stated that the diseases or conditions for which a homeopathic product is indicated determine the product's prescription or OTC status, rather than the homeopathic compendium's standard, which is based solely on strength. FDA's primary enforcement concern with respect to homeopathic drug products continues to be the OTC marketing of homeopathic products for indications that should require a prescription.

Labeling

Homeopathic drug product labeling must comply with the labeling provisions of sections 502 and 503 of the FDCA[105] and 21 C.F.R. Part 201. Regardless of container size, each product, at a minimum, must bear a label containing the statement of identity, potency, and the name and place of business of the manufacturer, packer, or distributor.[106] With regard to potency, labeling must bear a statement of quantity and amount of ingredients in the product expressed in homeopathic terms.[107] Each drug product offered for retail sale must also bear adequate directions for use[108] and an established name.[109] All labeling must be in

---

[100]   *See* Homeopathic Compliance Policy Guide *supra* note 94.

[101]   *See, e.g.,* Warning Letters to Dakota Laboratories, LLC (Mar. 17, 2011); Libido Edge Labs, LLC (June 10, 2010); Zone of Natural Remedies (May 21, 2010); Washington Homeopathic Products, Inc. (Aug. 25, 2009).

[102]   21 U.S.C. § 353(b).

[103]   FDCA § 503(f)(4), (b)(2), 21 U.S.C. § 353(f)(4), (b)(2).

[104]   Warning Letter to King Bio Pharmaceuticals, Inc. (Oct. 8, 1992); *see also* Warning Letters to Healthy World Distributing (May 19, 2004), Similasan (May 5, 2003), Dolisos (Mar. 23, 1995), L.b.L.–Bot. Bio. Hom. Corp. (Apr. 29, 1994).

[105]   21 U.S.C. §§ 352, 353.

[106]   21 C.F.R. § 201.1.

[107]   FDCA § 502(b), 21 U.S.C § 352(b); 21 C.F.R. § 201.10.

[108]   21 C.F.R. § 201.5.

[109]   FDCA § 502(e)(1), (3), 21 U.S.C. § 352(e)(1), (3); 21 C.F.R. § 201.10.

English, although it is permissible to include in the labeling both English and Latin names of the homeopathic ingredients.[110]

The labels of OTC homeopathic drug products must additionally comply with the principal display panel and the declaration of net quantity of contents provisions,[111] and contain a statement of identity,[112] which must include the established name of the drug, if any; a minimum of one indication for use; and adequate warnings.[113] Homeopathic drug products are, however, exempt from expiration dating requirements under 21 C.F.R. § 211.137.

Although FDA has not expressly exempted homeopathic drugs from the Drug Facts labeling requirements, it nevertheless stated, "[A]s emphasized in the proposed rule, the agency's stated policy is that [homeopathic] products ordinarily will not be recommended for regulatory action if the product is a homeopathic drug as described in Compliance Policy Guide 7132.15 . . . and the product follows the labeling and all other recommendations outlined in that guidance document. By its terms, the policy of generally not recommending homeopathic products for regulatory action will extend to this rule."[114]

Other Requirements

All firms that manufacture, prepare, propagate, compound, or otherwise process homeopathic drugs must register as drug establishments,[115] and all homeopathic drug products must be listed with FDA.[116] Homeopathic drug products must also be packaged in accordance with the FDCA[117] and be manufactured in conformance with good manufacturing practices.[118] Due to the unique nature of these drug products, however, some good manufacturing practices requirements are currently not applicable: homeopathic drugs are exempt from expiration dating requirements[119] and the requirement for laboratory determinations of the identity and strength of each active ingredient prior to release for distribution.[120] Also, homeopathic drug products in solid oral dosage form are required to bear a code imprint that identifies the manufacturer and their homeopathic nature, but the imprint need not identify the specific product.[121]

---

[110]   FDCA § 502(c), 21 U.S.C § 352(c); 21 C.F.R. § 201.15(c)(1).
[111]   21 C.F.R. § 201.62.
[112]   *Id.* § 201.61.
[113]   *See, e.g., id.* § 201.63.
[114]   64 Fed. Reg. 13,254, 13,258 (Mar. 17, 1999).
[115]   FDCA § 510, 21 U.S.C. § 360; 21 C.F.R. § 207.
[116]   21 C.F.R. § 207.
[117]   FDCA § 502(g), 21 U.S.C § 351(g).
[118]   FDCA § 501(a)(2)(B), 21 U.S.C § 351(a)(2)(B); 21 C.F.R. § 211.
[119]   21 C.F.R. § 211.137.
[120]   *Id.* § 211.165. In the *Federal Register* of April 1, 1983, the agency proposed to amend 21 C.F.R. § 211.165 to exempt homeopathic drug products from this testing requirement. 48 Fed. Reg. 14,003 (Apr. 1, 1983). According to the CPG, the testing requirement will not be enforced for homeopathic drugs, pending issuance of a final rule on the exemption.
[121]   21 C.F.R § 206.10; *see* 58 Fed. Reg. 47,948 (Sept. 13, 1993).

Recent Developments

In recent years, the popularity of complementary and alternative medicine has increased.[122] Homeopathy, which had once served the needs of a relatively small niche of licensed practitioners, is experiencing something of a renaissance. Nearly 22 centuries have passed since Hippocrates described his "like cures like" theory of homeopathy, and there is life in it yet. It remains to be seen whether, and how, FDA will respond to the increasing prominence of homeopathic medicines in the marketplace.

Conclusion

While OTC drugs are subject to a different regulatory scheme than prescription drugs, they are nevertheless actively and in many respects strictly regulated by FDA and FTC. Indeed, with the adoption of new statutory provisions in the past decade or so, the regulatory differences between OTC drugs and prescription drugs are being narrowed. As more products are switched from prescription to OTC status, FDA may become even more active in this area to ensure that consumers are using OTC products in a safe and effective manner.

---

[122] *See, e.g.,* FDA, Draft Guidance for Industry: Complementary and Alternative Medicine Products and Their Regulation by the Food and Drug Administration (2006).

CHAPTER 14
HUMAN BIOLOGICS

....

EDWARD L. KORWEK AND MICHAEL N. DRUCKMAN

Introduction

Biologics are revolutionizing medicine, healthcare, and life itself. We can now glimpse the day when we will be able to re-grow organs utilizing stem cells, tailor a biologic to an individual's genome, and correct—even improve—an individual's genes.[1] Pharmaceutical companies, grasping the direction that innovation is going, are moving increasingly into the biologics arena.[2] Naturally, the healthcare industry and the public want this revolution to benefit everyone. To help accomplish that goal, Congress crafted the Biologics Price Competition and Innovation Act of 2009 (BPCIA), which was signed into law by President Obama on March 23, 2010 as part of the Patient Protection and Affordable Care Act.[3] The BPCIA is intended to help bring cheaper biologics to the marketplace in the same way that the generics drug legislation adopted in 1984 gave birth to the engine that has brought forth many affordable other drugs.[4]

---

[1] See CHALLENGES FOR THE 21ST CENTURY IN SCIENCE AND THE REGULATION OF BIOLOGICAL PRODUCTS, *available at* http://www.fda.gov/AboutFDA/WhatWeDo/History/ProductRegulation/100YearsofBiologicsRegulation/ucm070022.htm#FromaRichHistorytoaChallengingFuture ("Gene therapy . . . is a means by which you can actually alter the genetic makeup of a cell. Instead of giving a person interferon—which is a protein used to treat certain cancers and other diseases—why not give the person the gene and then his own body will actually start to make the protein, and might never have to replace it again? That's one of the very intriguing theories of gene therapy.").

[2] *See, e.g.,* Walter Armstrong, *Into the Woods*, PHARM. EXEC. (Jan. 2008) at 47 (discussing implications of "Big Pharma launch[ing] more and more biologics").

[3] Pub. L. No. 11-148, tit. VII (Improving Access to Innovative Medical Therapies), Subtitle A (Biologics Price Competition and Innovation), § 7001, *et seq.*

[4] Throughout this chapter, nonbiological drugs will be referred to simply as "drugs" and nonbiological medical devices approved or cleared under the Federal Food, Drug, and Cosmetic Act will be referred to as "medical devices," or simply "devices," following the conventions that FDA most commonly uses. For biological drugs and biological medical devices licensed under the Public Health Service Act, the terms "biological products" or "biologics" will be used for discussions that apply to all such products, and the terms "biological drugs" and "biological devices" will be used when necessary to distinguish between them. For further discussion, *see* text at notes 124-125, *infra*.

With biologics' growing presence and the explosion of innovation can come new challenges. Whether implementation of the BPCIA ultimately will have favorable economic and other effects similar to that for generic drugs remains to be seen.[5] As with some drugs, but often for different reasons, it sometimes can be very difficult to predict exactly how biological products, such as those with complex structures, will act in the body[6] or to foresee the possible long-term effects that might lie dormant or otherwise not become apparent for decades because of the presence of latent viruses.[7] In addition, the anthrax attacks in 2001 not only have placed a new premium on the importance of our ability to develop, distribute and dispense rapidly new vaccines and other biologics but also have heightened concerns about bioterrorism.[8] Challenges and change, however, are not new to the United States Food and Drug Administration (FDA). Over the years, it has responded to challenges involving biologics, as well as other products, by retaining a flexible biological legal framework that can adapt readily to change.

This chapter discusses the existing legal framework governing biologics. The discussion is organized into four sections: 1) background; 2) the fundamental requirements for licensure; 3) the ambiguous and complex nature of biologics; and 4) postapproval regulation.

In the background portion, we explain, preliminarily, what biologics are and briefly describe the history of their regulation in this country. In the second section, we describe the process for licensing a biologic and the legal framework governing that process, including FDA's statutory authority, regulations, and guidance documents. We also describe some of the differences and similarities among the approval processes for biologics, drugs and medical devices. Finally, we discuss the important interplay between the Public Health Service Act (PHSA), which primarily governs biologics licensure, and the Federal Food, Drug, and Cosmetic Act (FDCA).

In the next part the ambiguous and complex nature of biologics is addressed, including how biologics law has accommodated this ever-changing category of products. We discuss the many types of biologics and the varied processes often used to manufacture them. The presentation includes the impact of modern biotechnology methods on developing new types of biologics, such as many recombinant DNA-derived drugs, monoclonal antibodies for diagnostic and therapeutic use, and cell and gene therapy products.

---

[5] *See, e.g.,* Edward L. Korwek, *Towards Understanding the "Generic" Debate About Biologics,* 7 J. Biolaw & Bus. 3, 6 (2004). For a discussion of the BPCIA and its implications, *see* Chapter 15.

[6] *See, e.g.,* Philip Noguchi, M.D., *Risks and Benefits of Gene Therapy,* 348 N. Eng. J. Med. 193-94 (Jan. 16, 2003) ("The manipulations needed to create genetic therapy add enormous complexity to considerations of safety and preclinical toxicity testing, and for every intended consequence of a complex biologic product, there are unintended consequences.").

[7] *See* FDA FY 2004 Justification and Estimates of Appropriations Committees, at 10 (Xenotransplantation) ("Potential cross species infection with persistent viruses, such as retroviruses, is of particular public health concern because they may be latent and lead to disease years after infection. Moreover, new or emerging infectious agents may not be readily identifiable with current techniques.").

[8] Notice, Office of the Assistant Secretary for Preparedness and Response; DHHS Public Health Emergency Medical Countermeasures Enterprise Strategy for Chemical, Biological, Radiological and Nuclear Threats, 72 Fed. Reg. 13,109 (Mar. 20, 2007) ("Advances in biotechnology support the development of new medical treatments, but also make those same tools more widely available to adversaries who might use them to modify biological organisms with the intention to inflict harm.").

Finally, in the fourth section FDA's statutory and regulatory authority over biologics after licensure is discussed. A few of the differences and similarities in regulation of biologics, drugs and medical devices are described. We also discuss how FDA's creative regulatory and enforcement approaches for biologics have paved the way for strategies that FDA uses with all products, primarily in the enforcement area involving consent decrees.

Background

Defining a Biologic

What is a biologic? Historically the answer to that question was relatively straightforward because most biologics were either vaccines or blood products.[9] In the past few decades, however, new biologics have blurred the line between biologics and drugs or devices. FDA's Center for Biologics Evaluation and Research (CBER), which regulates many biologics, sometimes characterizes them generally as "made from living organisms," including those "derived from human, plant, animal, or microorganism sources."[10] While their origin is certainly important in describing them, and such characterizations are often helpful, biologics are not fully defined by their origin.[11] Section 351(i) of the PHSA states that "the term 'biological product' means a virus, therapeutic serum, toxin, antitoxin, vaccine, blood, blood component or derivative, allergenic product, protein (except any chemically synthesized polypeptide), or analogous product, or arsphenamine or derivative of arsphenamine (or any other trivalent organic arsenic compound), applicable to the prevention, treatment or cure of a disease or condition of human beings."[12]

Although that definition can in most respects appear fairly clear and unambiguous on its face, many subtle and difficult issues have arisen over whether particular products fall within its terms. Those issues are reviewed in the third section below on the ambiguous and complex nature of biologics.[13] Undeniably, however, biologics' unique regulatory history has helped influence whether a specific product is a biologic or not.

History of Biologics Regulation in the United States

Early prophylactic or therapeutic biological products, such as the first laboratory-created vaccine, began to emerge on the market in the late 19th century—an exciting time for biological research.[14] Even through the early 1900s, however, this burgeoning industry

---

9   Kevin L. Ropp, *Just What Is a Biologic, Anyway?* FDA Consumer, Apr. 1993.

10   CBER, What Is CBER's Mission? (Apr. 15, 2008).

11   Korwek, *supra* note 5, at 3. For example, although antibiotics and hormones such as insulin and human growth hormone (hGH) are traditionally obtained from living organisms, they are not biologics. *Id.*

12   42 U.S.C. § 262(i) (2010).

13   For more extensive information on defining biologics, *see* Edward L. Korwek, *What Are Biologics? A Comparative Legislative, Regulatory, and Scientific Analysis*, 62 Food & Drug L.J. 257 (2007).

14   In 1879, Louis Pasteur created the first laboratory vaccine to protect chicken from chicken cholera. Subsequently, American bacteriologists Theobald Smith and Edmund Salmon introduced the concept of heat-cultured vaccines, which they used to inoculate swine against hog cholera. In addition to research on vaccines, researchers Emil von Behring and Shibasaburo Kitasato in Robert Koch's laboratory discovered that animals injected with toxins could produce antitoxins to cure and provide future immunity to other

had no regulation, standardization or quality control.[15] This all changed in 1901 when a young St. Louis girl died of tetanus, which she contracted from a contaminated diphtheria "antitoxin" derived from a horse named Jim.[16] In response to this and other similar episodes, Congress enacted the Biologics Control Act in 1902 to "ensure the safety, purity, and potency of vaccines, serums, toxins, antitoxins, and similar products."[17] The language from that original legislation continues to underpin federal biologics regulation even as the statutes and entities regulating biologics have changed.[18]

The Biologics Control Act imposed requirements that the federal government grant premarket approval for every biologic, as well as for its production process and facility.[19] In fact, manufacturers were required to submit two separate license applications: a product license application (PLA) and an establishment license application (ELA). The separate ELA requirement reflected the longstanding view that, for biologics, tight control over production processes and facilities was essential to assure the product's identity and consistency from batch to batch.[20]

The regulation of biologics under the Biologics Control Act was initially the responsibility of the U.S. Public Health and Marine Hospital Service of the Department of the Treasury, but was later passed to the Federal Hygienic Laboratory, which became the National Institutes of Health (NIH) in 1930. Within NIH a Division of Biologics Control (DBC) was created in 1937, which was later renamed the Laboratory of Biologics Control (LBC).[21] The Biologics Control Act was re-enacted in 1944 as part of the recodification of the PHSA, which consolidated and substantially revised all existing legislation relating to the Public Health Service.[22] Although the PHSA has been amended a number of times since 1944, the framework that it created for regulating biologics pretty much still remains in force today.[23]

In 1955, several cases of polio resulted from a vaccine containing undetected live viruses, which led to the creation of the Division of Biologics Standards (DBS) within NIH to provide for greater vaccine oversight.[24] The fix was temporary due to widespread claims that DBS failed to apply the requirements for proof of effectiveness,[25] that it suppressed or ignored

animals. Suzanne White Junod, *Biologics Centennial: 100 Years of Biologics Regulation*, Update (Nov./Dec. 2002) at 41.

[15] Ramanas A. Kondratas, *Biologics Act of 1902*, in The Early Years of Federal Food and Drug Control (J.H. Young ed., 1982).

[16] Junod, *supra* note 14, at 41.

[17] 32 Stat. 728 (1902).

[18] Peter Barton Hutt, Richard Merrill & Lewis A. Grossman, Food and Drug Law 1124 (4th ed., 2014) (citing Jonathan Liebenau, Medical Science and Medical Industry: The Formation of the American Pharmaceutical Industry (1987)).

[19] John P. Griffin & John O'Grady, The Textbook of Pharmaceutical Medicine 568 (2006).

[20] Hutt, Merrill & Grossman, *supra* note 18, at 1131.

[21] *Id.* at 879.

[22] 58 Stat. 682, 702 (1944).

[23] Among other things, section 351 of the PHSA provides statutory authority for FDA regulations on biologic products throughout Parts 600-680 of Title 21 of the *Code of Federal Regulations* (C.F.R.). *See also* Douglas J. Pisano & David Mantus, FDA Regulatory Affairs: A Guide for Prescription Drugs, Medical Devices, and Biologics 130 (2003).

[24] F.C. Robbins, *Polio—Historical*, in Vaccines 98-114 (S.A. Plotkin, E.A. Mortimer eds., 1988).

[25] A 1972 General Accounting Office report concluded that ineffective biologics were licensed under the Biologics Act because of the failure to apply the requirements for proof of effectiveness. Lauren B. Leveton, HIV and the Blood Supply: An Analysis of Crisis Decisionmaking 44 (1995).

scientific findings that would adversely affect the vaccine market due to a "passionate commitment to vaccine therapy,"[26] and that the division's combination of research and regulatory functions created an inherent conflict of interests.[27] As a result of these and other criticisms, the Secretary of Health, Education, and Welfare delegated concurrent authority to FDA and NIH to apply the drug provisions of the FDCA to biological products.[28] Finally, on July 1, 1972, DBS was transferred to FDA and elevated to become the Bureau of Biologics.[29]

Upon accepting responsibility for regulating biologics, the Commissioner of Food and Drugs issued a public notice making it clear that while the PHSA would continue to apply to biologics, the FDCA also applied.[30] In that notice, the Commissioner announced procedures through which FDA would review all biologics licensed before July 1, 1972, to ensure that they are safe, effective and not misbranded, under modern FDA requirements. In doing so, the Commissioner acknowledged "unique problems involved in applying the requirement of 'substantial evidence of effectiveness' to biological products" under the FDCA.[31] For example, he stated that adequate and well-controlled studies, normally required for all drug approvals, were not always feasible for biologics and that where, in those situations, "acceptable alternative scientific methods of demonstrating effectiveness" are available, the latter would be sufficient.[32] To address such problems and to initiate the review generally, independent advisory panels were charged with developing the standards and methodology for effectiveness for particular product classes.[33]

The Commissioner also declared that the review process "represents the first amalgamation of the licensing procedure established under section 351 of the [PHSA] and the new drug and misbranding provisions established under the [FDCA]."[34] That process was part of a larger plan to harmonize biologics law and regulation with drug law and regulation:

> This notice constitutes only the first step in bringing together the provisions of section 351 of the Public Health Service Act and the requirements of the Federal Food, Drug, and Cosmetic Act. New procedural and substantive regulations governing the licensing of biological products, which will incorporate all applicable provisions of the Federal Food, Drug, and Cosmetic Act, are in preparation and will be proposed for comment when they are available.[35]

---

26   Nicholas Wade, *Division of Biologics Standards: Scientific Management Questioned*, 175 SCIENCE 966 (1972).

27   HUTT, MERRILL & GROSSMAN, *supra* note 18, at 1125 (quoting a public statement made in 1972 by Dr. Anthony Morris, a DBS scientist).

28   37 Fed. Reg. 4,004 (Feb. 25, 1972).

29   37 Fed. Reg. 12,865 (June 29, 1972); *see* 37 Fed. Reg. 26,679 (Aug. 18, 1972); Korwek, *supra* note 13, at 260-61.

30   37 Fed. Reg. at 26,679

31   *Id.*

32   *Id.*

33   *Id.*

34   *Id.*

35   37 Fed. Reg. at 26,680.

The view was that after a period of transition, biologics would become fully subject to the FDCA and regulated like most drugs.[36]

Despite this ambitious vision, the organizational scheme did not yield so easily. Although the Bureau of Biologics was merged with the Bureau of Drugs in 1982,[37] the groups were again separated in 1988, and the biologics unit was given its present name, the Center for Biologics Evaluation and Research.[38] Eventually Congress took additional steps, through the Food and Drug Administration Modernization Act of 1997 (FDAMA),[39] to attempt to harmonize biologic and drug regulation. Among other changes, ELAs and PLAs were consolidated into a single biologics license application (BLA).[40] Congress also instructed the Secretary of Health and Human Services to minimize differences in the review and approval processes for biologics and drugs,[41] although it did leave in place the separate licensing process for biologics.[42]

That licensing process for biologics remains intact, even for products that are no longer handled by CBER. Specifically, on June 30, 2003, FDA transferred some therapeutic biologics, which CBER had been regulating, to the Center for Drug Evaluation and Research (CDER).[43] FDA continues to treat those transferred products as biologics.[44] Consequently, the PHSA's licensing requirements still apply to the transferred products, as well as to most products that fall within the PHSA's definition of biological products.[45]

Biologics License Application Requirement, Standards, and Process

Statutory Authority

The biologics license requirement, which appears in section 351(a)(1) of the PHSA, states: "No person shall introduce or deliver for introduction into interstate commerce any biological product unless . . . a biologics license is in effect for the biological product . . . ." In contrast

---

[36]   Id. at 26,679 ("As the provisions of the Federal Food, Drug, and Cosmetic Act are gradually applied to licensed biological products and new biological products . . . existing exemptions will be modified or revoked for a biological product or category of products, on a transitional basis.").

[37]   47 Fed. Reg. 26,913 (June 22, 1982).

[38]   52 Fed. Reg. 3275 (Feb. 3, 1987); 53 Fed. Reg. 8978 (Mar. 18, 1988).

[39]   Pub. L. No. 105-115, 111 Stat. 2296 (1997).

[40]   64 Fed. Reg. 56,441, 56,442 (Oct. 20, 1999).

[41]   FDAMA, § 123(f).

[42]   Id. ("The Secretary of Health and Human Services shall take measures to minimize differences in the review and approval of products required to have approved biologics license applications under section 351 of the Public Health Service Act (42 USC 262) and products required to have approved new drug applications under section 505(b)(1) of the Federal Food, Drug, and Cosmetic Act (21 USC 355(b)(1).").

[43]   68 Fed. Reg. 38,067, 38,067-68 (June 26, 2003).

[44]   See FDA, About FDA, Transfer of Therapeutic Products to the Center for Drug Evaluation and Research (updated Feb. 22, 2010), available at http://www.fda.gov/AboutFDA/CentersOffices/OfficeofMedicalProductsandTobacco/CBER/ucm133463.htm.

[45]   See PHSA § 351(j) ("The Federal Food, Drug, and Cosmetic Act applies to a biological product subject to regulation under this section, except that a product for which a license has been approved under subsection (a) of this section shall not be required to have an approved application under section 505 of such Act.").

to the FDCA's lengthy approval provisions of section 505, section 351 is a model of brevity. Its simplicity lies in its having delegated broad rulemaking authority to the Secretary of the Department of Health and Human Services,[46] allowing that individual the flexibility to incorporate detailed requirements and standards as science evolves. The same result is essentially achieved in a more complicated statutory fashion by section 505 of the FDCA.

Section 351(a)(2)(C) lists the fundamental biologics license standards quite succinctly:

> The Secretary shall approve a biologics license application—
>
> (i)   on the basis of a demonstration that—
>> (I) the biological product that is the subject of the application is safe, pure, and potent; and
>> (II) the facility in which the biological product is manufactured, processed, packed, or held meets standards designed to assure that the biological product continues to be safe, pure, and potent; and
>
> (ii) if the applicant (or other appropriate person) consents to the inspection of the facility that is the subject of the application, in accordance with [the provision allowing manufacturing facility inspections].

With a few exceptions,[47] section 351 delegates all other licensing details to the Secretary of Health and Human Services, stating that the "Secretary shall establish, by regulation, requirements for the approval, suspension, and revocation of biologics licenses."[48] That delegation has allowed for a great deal of regulatory flexibility and largely is responsible for the PHSA biologics provisions remaining relatively unchanged since their original precursors embodied in the Biologics Control Act of 1902.

Regulatory Authority

FDA (to which the Secretary of Health and Human Services has delegated rulemaking authority under section 351)[49] has followed section 351's model for succinctness when establishing the requirements for approval, suspension, and revocation of biologics licenses. The regulation on biologics license application standards, 21 C.F.R. § 601.2(a), starts simply by stating that "[t]o obtain a biologics license under section 351 of the [PHSA] for any biological product, the manufacturer shall submit an application to the Director, Center for Biologics Evaluation and Research or the Director, Center for Drug Evaluation and Research . . . on forms prescribed for such purposes, and shall submit data derived from

[46] The Secretary, in turn, has delegated to FDA's Commissioner "[f]unctions vested in the Secretary under sections 351 and 352 of pt. F, subpt. 1 of the PHSA (42 U.S.C. 262 and 263, as amended (Biological Products)), insofar as they relate to the functions assigned to the Food and Drug Administration." *Delegations of Authority to the Commissioner Food and Drugs*, in FDA Staff Manual Guides (SMG), § 1410.10(1)(A)(4), *available at* http://www.fda.gov/AboutFDA/ReportsManualsForms/StaffManualGuides/ucm080711.htm.

[47] Specifically: 1) section 351(a)(1)(B) requires each package of a biologic to be plainly marked with the product's proper name and expiration date and with the manufacturer's name, address and license number; 2) section 351(a)(2)(B) requires applicants to include pediatric assessments in their BLAs; and 3) section 351(j) states that biological products are licensed under the PHSA rather than approved under the Food, Drug, and Cosmetic Act (FDCA).

[48] 42 U.S.C. § 262(a)

[49] *See* SMG 1410.10(1)(A)(4), *supra* note 46.

nonclinical laboratory and clinical studies which demonstrate that the manufactured product meets prescribed requirements of safety, purity, and potency . . . ." It requires applications to include a "full description of manufacturing methods," "data establishing stability of the product through the dating period" and "summaries of results of tests performed on the lot(s) represented by the submitted sample(s) . . . ." Finally, it requires the applicant to provide product, container and labeling samples, several certifications,[50] the address of all manufacturing locations, and a signature.

Incorporating Requirements, Recommendations, and Standards by Reference

At first glance, the provision appears fairly uninformative. It merely repeats the PHSA's "safe, pure, and potent" standard, and provides only slightly more details about what manufacturers must include in their BLAs. Yet, a closer examination reveals a world of information and requirements packed into that limited verbiage, largely through the incorporation by reference of other regulations, standards and recommendations, both directly and indirectly, as has been done in other areas of drug regulation.

Incorporating Requirements Through the Form Prescribed for Submitting an Application

The first sentence of section 601.2(a), which states that the manufacturer shall submit an application "on forms prescribed for such purposes," allows FDA to prescribe a great deal more of its expectations for BLA content than appears. Form FDA 356h, entitled "Application to Market a New Drug, Biologic, or an Antibiotic Drug for Human Use,"[51] presents itself as a general cover sheet for applicants to inform FDA what the applicant has included in the package when submitting any of several types of applications. The form, however, includes a checklist of items that FDA expects applicants to include for particular applications, and indicates which items are relevant to which applications by including the regulatory citation following the item. As the instructions to Form FDA 356h explain, "[t]he CFR references are provided for most items in order to indicate what type of information should be submitted in each section." The form cites section 601.2 as requiring the following items and sections for BLAs: chemistry, manufacturing and controls (CMC) information; methods validation package; nonclinical pharmacology and toxicology; human pharmacokinetics and bioavailability; clinical data; safety update report; statistical information; case report tabulations; and case report forms.

By including on Form FDA 356h that comprehensive checklist of items applicable to BLAs, FDA has fleshed out its expectations in greater detail than appears in section 601.2; none of the items is specifically named in section 601.2, except for clinical data. Nevertheless, FDA interprets the regulation as requiring them. For example, CMC information is considered to

---

50   Those certifications include statements about the nonclinical laboratory studies' compliance with FDA's Good Laboratory Practice regulations and about the clinical trials' compliance with FDA's human subject protection regulations; financial disclosure statements for clinical investigators; and an environmental assessment or claim for a categorical exclusion.

51   An electronic version of Form FDA 356h is *available at* http://www.fda.gov/downloads/AboutFDA/ReportsManualsForms/Forms/ucm082348.pdf (last viewed September 2014).

be part of the "full description of manufacturing methods" that section 601.2(a) requires.[52] Similarly, the agency views the methods validation package as part of the full description of manufacturing methods.[53]

Incorporating Recommendations and Interpretations Through Preambles

Interpreting section 601.2 broadly is consistent with the preambles that FDA issued when it promulgated this regulation and amended it. For example, when amending the section in 1999, the agency stated: "A review of SOP's, physical plant information, and information on contracts have always been part of an assessment of a product's safety, purity, and potency. FDA has authority to require sponsors to submit such information in license applications under section 351 of the PHSA and 21 CFR part 601."[54] Although preambles do not have the force and effect of law,[55] they can inform the public how FDA interprets the regulations that it promulgates and serve as a valuable source of information for biologics manufacturers.

Incorporating Recommendations Through Guidance

In addition, manufacturers can look to guidance documents issued by FDA (referred to hereinafter as guidances) to add flesh to the bones of FDA's regulations. Like preambles, guidances do not have the force and effect of law. As FDA's Good Guidance Practice regulation states, "guidance documents do not establish legally enforceable rights or responsibilities. They do not legally bind the public or FDA."[56] Consequently, manufacturers "may choose to use an approach other than the one set forth in a guidance document," as long as the alternative approach complies with the relevant statutes and regulations."[57] Guidances do, however, "represent the agency's current thinking." FDA employees may depart from guidance documents "only with appropriate justification and supervisory concurrence."[58] As might be expected, manufacturers rely on guidances to a great extent, and FDA uses

---

[52] As FDA has stated in guidance, "All manufacturing methods and validations of the process should be described in the CMC section of the Biologics License Application." FDA, Guidance for Industry: For the Submission of Chemistry, Manufacturing and Controls and Establishment Description Information for Human Plasma-Derived Biological Products, Animal Plasma or Serum-Derived Products (Feb. 1999).

[53] See, e.g., 69 Fed. Reg. 18,728, 18,733 (Apr. 8, 2004) ("intermediates, raw materials, reagents, container closure systems, in process materials and other products and biologics are considered *part of the manufacturing method* . . . [and] while the extent of a specification (e.g. number or type of tests, strictness of acceptance criteria) for these materials may vary . . . FDA *has required specifications* for these materials to be *included in applications* as *part of the description of the manufacturing method* and will continue to do so.") (emphases added).

[54] 64 Fed. Reg. 56,441, 56,444 (Oct. 20, 1999).

[55] See 21 C.F.R. § 10.85(d)(1) (preambles to proposed and final rules constitute advisory opinions). Although an advisory opinion represents the formal position of FDA on a matter and usually obligates the agency to follow it until it is amended or revoked, id. § 10.85(e), in certain situations the Commissioner may take action contrary to an advisory opinion before it has been amended or revoked. Id. § 10.85(f). Moreover, an advisory opinion may be amended or revoked at any time after It has been Issued. Id. § 10.85(g). See also Proposed Rule, Administrative Practices and Procedures; Advisory Opinions and Guidelines, 57 Fed. Reg. 47,314 (Oct. 15, 1992) (proposal to amend section 10.85 to reflect the general legal principle that federal agencies cannot be estopped from enforcing the law).

[56] 21 C.F.R. § 10.115(d)(1).

[57] Id. at (d)(2).

[58] Id.

them extensively to communicate to manufacturers what they expect in a biologics license application, as it does in other product areas.[59]

Communicating Standards Through Approval Packages

Finally, manufacturers can also understand more fully what FDA expects in a biologics license application by reviewing the approval packages that it publishes after licensing a biologic. Regulations provide that after a license is issued, a set of eight categories of data and other information from the biological product file are immediately available for public disclosure unless extraordinary circumstances are shown.[60] With the passage of the Food and Drug Administration Amendments Act of 2007, the agency must now post on its Internet website a summary of its review within 48 hours after the date that FDA approved the BLA, except where redaction is required.[61] FDA must then publish the Action Package for Approval, as it is called, on its Internet website within 30 days after the licensure date.[62] Ordinarily, the agency is not bound by precedent regarding the type or extent of data it requires because almost any two biological products can differ in some respects.[63] Nevertheless, the Action Packages for Approval, including the approved labeling, can provide valuable insights and information to competitors and others about the data and information that will constitute a sufficient showing that the biological product is safe, pure and potent.

As illustrated by the foregoing, licensing requirements are built upon a pyramid of laws, regulations, guidances, and action packages, each of which is increasingly specific and detailed in the requirements and expectations it imposes on manufacturers. In adopting the specific requirements for the licensing of biologics, the agency also often looks to some of the other provisions and recommendations applicable to drugs, and devices.

Examples Where Section 601.2 Incorporates Requirements and Recommendations Applicable to Drugs or Devices

Clinical Study Data

A tiered, standards-incorporating approach has been applied to many licensing requirements. For example, section 601.2(a) requires that manufacturers "submit data derived from . . . clinical studies . . . ." Even though the PHSA expressly authorizes FDA

---

[59]   Unless otherwise indicated, all guidances cited herein are available on FDA's website, www.fda.gov, and will be cited only by title and date. FDA has provided guidances, for example, on what it expects in the CMC section for different product classes. *See, e.g.,* Guidance for Industry, For the Submission of Chemistry, Manufacturing and Controls Information for a Therapeutic Recombinant DNA-Derived Product or a Monoclonal Antibody Product for In Vivo Use (Oct. 31, 1996); Guidance for the Submission of Chemistry, Manufacturing and Controls Information and Establishment Description for Autologous Somatic Cell Therapy Products (Jan. 10, 1997); Guidance for Industry for the Submission of Chemistry, Manufacturing, and Controls Information for Synthetic Peptide Substances (Nov. 1994); and Guidance for Industry: For the Submission of Chemistry, Manufacturing and Controls and Establishment Description Information for Human Blood and Blood Components Intended for Transfusion or for Further Manufacture and for the Completion of Form FDA 356h Application to Market a New Drug, Biologic, or an Antibiotic for Human Use (May 1999).

[60]   21 C.F.R. § 601.51(e).

[61]   21 U.S.C. § 355(l)(2)(B) and (C)(iv).

[62]   *Id.* § 355(l)(2)(A) and (C).

[63]   *But see* Bracco Diagnostics, Inc. v. Shalala, 963 F. Supp. 20 (D.D.C. 1997) ("disparate treatment of functionally indistinguishable products is the essence of the meaning of arbitrary and capricious").

to prescribe clinical study requirements for biologics—as a condition for allowing those investigational biologics to be exempt from the requirement that they be licensed before being introduced into interstate commerce[64]—FDA did not promulgate separate regulations spelling out the requirements for biologics clinical trials. Instead, it applied to biologics the FDCA statutory and regulatory requirements for investigational drugs, or where the biologic is a device, applied the requirements for investigational devices. Specifically, 21 C.F.R. § 601.21 states:

> A biological product undergoing development, but not yet ready for a biologics license, may be shipped or otherwise delivered from one State or possession into another State or possession provided such shipment or delivery is not for introduction or delivery for introduction into interstate commerce, except as provided in sections 505(i) [governing investigational drugs] and 520(g) [governing investigational devices] of the Federal Food, Drug, and Cosmetic Act, as amended, and the regulations thereunder (21 C.F.R. Parts 312 and 812).

Consequently, all the procedures and requirements for an investigational new drug (IND) exemption or an investigational device exemption (IDE) apply to a biologic, depending on whether the biologic is also a drug or a device. Similarly, as mentioned above, section 601.2(a) simply incorporates by reference the human subject protection requirements of 21 C.F.R. Parts 50 and 56.[65] Nevertheless, as will be addressed further in the section on the ambiguous and complex nature of biologics,[66] some biologics carry characteristics that demand higher or different levels of protection for patients in whom they are being investigated. In those cases, although the applicable regulations are no different from those for drugs or devices, FDA has recommended different human subject protection measures, such as long-term patient monitoring and even life-time patient surveillance, through guidance.[67]

"Prescribed Requirements" of Safety, Purity and Potency

Another example of FDA's tiered, standards-incorporation approach is how it communicates what data are sufficient to demonstrate that the manufactured product meets "prescribed requirements" of safety, purity and potency. Like "prescribed forms" and "clinical studies," the phrase "prescribed requirements" is packed with meaning. Section 601.2(d) states that an approval of a biologics license application shall constitute a determination "that the establishment(s) and the product meet applicable requirements to ensure the continued

---

[64] 21 U.S.C. § 262(a)(3).

[65] 21 C.F.R. § 601.2(a) (requiring BLAs to include "statements regarding each clinical investigation involving human subjects contained in the application, that it either was conducted in compliance with the requirements for institutional review set forth in part 56 of this chapter; or was not subject to such requirements in accordance with § 56.104 or § 56.105, and was conducted in compliance with requirements for informed consent set forth in part 50 of this chapter.").

[66] *See infra,* section entitled "The Ambiguous and Complex Nature of Biologics."

[67] *See, e.g.,* PHS Guideline on Infectious Disease Issues in Xenotransplantation (Jan. 19, 2001) at 36, *available at* http://www.fetal-cells.com/PHS.pdf; Gene Therapy Patient Tracking System (June 27, 2002) at 12, *available at* http://www.fda.gov/downloads/biologicsbloodvaccines/cellulargenetherapyproducts/ucm150110.pdf; Guidance for Industry: Source Animal, Product, Preclinical, and Clinical Issues Concerning the Use of Xenotransplantation Products in Humans at VIII(G) (Apr. 2003), at 45; Guidance for Industry: Gene Therapy Clinical Trials—Observing Subjects for Delayed Adverse Events (2006), at 14-19.

safety, purity, and potency of such products." As discussed above,[68] the establishment's manufacturing processes are integral to ensuring a biologic's continued safety, purity and potency, and under 601.2(d), the manufacturer must demonstrate in the BLA that those processes will satisfy "applicable requirements."

Section 601.2(d) states that "[a]pplicable requirements for the maintenance of establishments for the manufacture of a product subject to this section shall include but not be limited to the good manufacturing practices requirements set forth in parts 210, 211, 600, 606, and 820 of this chapter." Similarly, section 601.4 requires CBER or CDER to make a determination that the establishments and the product meet applicable requirements established "in this chapter" before issuing a biologics license. The chapter—Chapter I of Title 21 of the C.F.R.—covers all regulations in Title 21, Parts 1-1299.[69] Thus, a BLA must contain everything that CBER or CDER determines satisfies all the regulations in Title 21 that apply.

The regulations that apply are varied and encompassing. The current good manufacturing practice (cGMP) requirements for drugs in Title 21 Parts 210 and 211 apply, if the biologic is also a drug.[70] Those regulations cover virtually all aspects of drug manufacturing: organization and personnel,[71] buildings and facilities,[72] equipment,[73] control of components and drug product containers and closures,[74] production and process controls,[75] packaging and labeling control,[76] holding and distribution,[77] laboratory controls,[78] records and reports,[79] and returned and salvaged drug products.[80] Not surprisingly, many of those drug provisions overlap with some of the biologics regulations,[81] although some contain requirements unique to biologics.[82] Where regulations from the drugs subchapter and the biologics subchapter both apply, the biologic manufacturer must satisfy both, except

---

[68] *See supra* notes 20 and 53 and accompanying text.

[69] Chapter II of Title 21, Parts 1300–1399, contains the DEA regulations, and Chapter III, Parts 1400–1499, contains the Office of National Drug Control Policy's regulations.

[70] 21 C.F.R. § 601.2(d). Where the biologic is a device, the Quality System Regulation, 21 C.F.R. Part 820, applies. *Id.* § 601.4.

[71] *Id.* pt. 211, subpt. B.

[72] *Id.* subpt. C.

[73] *Id.* subpt. D.

[74] *Id.* subpt. E.

[75] *Id.* subpt. F.

[76] *Id.* subpt. G.

[77] *Id.* subpt. H.

[78] *Id.* subpt. I.

[79] *Id.* subpt. J.

[80] *Id.* subpt. K.

[81] *Cf., e.g.,* 21 C.F.R. § 211.25, "Personnel qualifications" ("Each person engaged in the manufacture, processing, packing, or holding of a drug product shall have the education, training, and experience, or any combination thereof, to enable that person to perform the assigned functions") *with* section 600.10, "Personnel" ("Personnel shall have capabilities commensurate with their assigned functions, a thorough understanding of the manufacturing operations which they perform, the necessary training and experience relating to individual products, and adequate information concerning the application of the pertinent provisions of this subchapter to their respective functions.").

[82] *See, e.g., id.* § 600.11(e)(3)(ii) (requiring firms that manufacture using spore-forming microorganisms in multi-product manufacturing areas to conduct environmental monitoring specific to the spore-forming microorganism in adjacent areas during manufacturing to ensure that the spores are contained).

where the regulations explicitly state otherwise.[83] Where a conflict arises, "the regulation specifically applicable to the drug product in question shall supersede the more general."[84]

Other regulations in Chapter I that apply to biologics, and which the applicant must therefore show in its BLA are satisfied if applicable, include those in Part 606 establishing cGMP standards specific to blood and blood components, in Part 610 setting forth the General Biological Products Standards, and in Parts 640 through 680, setting forth additional standards for blood and blood products, for diagnostic substances for diagnostic tests (such as blood grouping reagents), and for miscellaneous products (allergenics). Some of those regulations are precise and exacting.[85] Recently, however, FDA has tended to promulgate regulations that articulate the appropriate standard more generally, leaving room for it to exercise regulatory discretion in determining whether the manufacturer has satisfied the standard, sometimes by providing more specific recommendations in guidance format to inform manufacturers about the details that are needed to satisfy the standard.

For example, the regulation on testing blood and blood components for communicable diseases does not specify the particular screening test that a manufacturer must use. Instead, it sets forth the following general standard:

> To test for evidence of infection due to communicable disease agents designated in paragraph (a) of this section, you must use screening tests that the Food and Drug Administration (FDA) has approved for such use, in accordance with the manufacturer's instructions. You must perform one or more such tests *as necessary* to reduce *adequately and appropriately* the risk of transmission of communicable disease.[86]

When promulgating that provision, FDA later explained:

> We are allowing for future advancements in testing methodologies by not specifying the test marker(s) for each disease agent.[87]

It added:

> Because we are not specifying the test or tests to be used in this regulation, we are listing in the following table the test or tests we currently believe reduce adequately and appropriately the risk for transmission

---

83   *Id.* § 211.1(b) (providing that cGMP regulations throughout the chapter that apply to drugs, including those in Parts 600 through 680 that apply to biological drugs, supplement and do not supersede the regulations in Part 211, "unless the regulations explicitly apply otherwise"); *see, e.g., id.* § 610.67 ("Biological products must comply with the bar code requirements at section 201.25 of this chapter. However, the bar code requirements do not apply to devices regulated by the Center for Biologics Evaluation and Research or to blood and blood components intended for transfusion. For blood and blood components intended for transfusion, the requirements at § 606.121(c)(13) of this chapter apply instead.").

84   *Id.* § 211.1(b).

85   *See, e.g.,* 21 C.F.R. § 610.21 (establishing minimum potency levels for particular products, such as 500 units per milliliter for diphtheria antitoxin).

86   *Id.* § 610.40(b) (emphasis added).

87   66 Fed. Reg. 31,146, 31,147 (June 11, 2001).

> of communicable disease agents . . . . As technology advances, we intend to regularly issue guidance describing those tests that we believe would adequately and appropriately reduce the risk of transmission of communicable disease agents.[88]

One such guidance states that FDA now expects hepatitis B screening tests to be sensitive enough to detect as little as 0.5 nanograms of hepatitis surface antigen per milliliter of blood product tested.[89] Like all guidances, this one provides that manufacturers may use an alternative approach as long as it satisfies the applicable statutes and regulations.[90] Nevertheless, the agency ties its recommendation to the regulatory standard, stating that it "believes that tests that are incapable of identifying [Hepatitis B surface antigen] at these limits are not adequate to reduce the risk of communicable disease transmission."[91] Consequently, sponsors would be hard-pressed to demonstrate that they satisfy the regulatory standard if they use tests that are less sensitive than the level specified in the guidance. Moreover, they know that their biologics license application will not be approved unless they list in their CMC section hepatitis B surface antigen tests that meet FDA's recommendation for adequate sensitivity.

FDA's Approach of Promulgating General, Standard-Setting Regulations and Imposing Specific Requirements in Licenses

The approach of promulgating general regulations responds to several forces that militate against the inclusion of particular numbers or other details in biologics regulations. One factor is the time that it now takes to promulgate new regulations.[92] For example, the 2001 final rule discussed above pertaining to testing blood for communicable diseases culminated from a process that was first initiated in 1994.[93] FDA cannot keep up with technology advancements in regulations and is better able to do so through guidances.

A second factor is the drive to harmonize biologic and drug approval requirements. The agency generally does not have product-specific regulations for products approved under NDAs.[94] Instead, the drug regulations describe the information that sponsors must submit in their applications in general terms and set forth general criteria for acceptable studies needed to support approval.[95] Given Congress' mandate in FDAMA to harmonize the

---

[88]   *Id.* at 31,149.

[89]   Guidance for Industry: Adequate and Appropriate Donor Screening Tests for Hepatitis B; Hepatitis B Surface Antigen (HGsAg) Assays Used to Test Donors of Whole Blood and Blood Components, Including Source Plasma and Source Leukocytes (Nov. 2007), at 3.

[90]   *Id.* at 1.

[91]   *Id.* at 3.

[92]   *See* Erica Seiguer & John J. Smith, *Perception and Process at the Food and Drug Administration: Obligations and Trade-Offs in Rules and Guidances*, 60 Food & Drug L.J. 17 (2005) ("A commonly held perception inside and outside the . . . FDA is that rulemaking is both time-consuming and resource-intensive, and this perception is believed to impact decision-making processes.").

[93]   *See* 64 Fed. Reg. 45,340 (Aug. 19, 1999) (preamble to proposed rule describing FDA's review of blood product and establishment regulations, which FDA initiated in 1994).

[94]   *See* 21 U.S.C. § 355; 21 C.F.R. pt. 314; Ann H. Wion, *Potential Implications of the Supreme Court's Decision in Berkovitz v. United States*, 44 Food Drug Cosm. L.J. 145, 153 (1989).

[95]   *Id.*

approval criteria for drugs and biologics as much as possible, moving to more general standards in biologics regulations is an expected outcome.

A third factor is a Supreme Court case, *Berkovitz v. United States*,[96] which involved allegations that FDA's predecessor, the Division of Biologics Standards (DBS), deviated from specific requirements in its regulations when licensing Orimune®, an oral polio vaccine. In *Berkovitz*, the plaintiffs sued the United States under the Federal Tort Claims Act (FTCA) alleging that DBS, among other things, issued a product license for the vaccine without first receiving data mandated by FDA regulations showing how the product matched up against regulatory safety standards.[97] The government moved to dismiss the case on the ground that DBS' licensing decisions fell within the discretionary function exception to the FTCA,[98] which shields the government from liability when performing functions that require judgment. The District Court denied the motion, but the Court of Appeals reversed.[99]

Initially, the Court of Appeals rejected the government's argument that the discretionary function exception bars all claims arising out of the regulatory activities of federal agencies.[100] It held, however, that federal law and regulations imposed no responsibilities on DBS in licensing the polio vaccine that were not wholly discretionary actions.[101] The Supreme Court disagreed, stating:

> The DBS has no discretion to issue a license without first receiving the required test data; to do so would violate a specific statutory and regulatory directive. Accordingly, to the extent the petitioners' licensing claim is based on a decision of the DBS to issue a license without having received the required test data, the discretionary function exception imposes no bar.[102]

Consequently, *Berkovitz* is another factor weighing against FDA including specific details in regulations and favoring more general standards.[103]

The agency has in fact amended some of its regulations to remove specific requirements, such as the 2001 change to section 610.40 discussed above.[104] Nevertheless, it still can

---

[96] 486 U.S. 531 (1988).

[97] *Id.* at 543. One of those regulatory safety standards, for example, was the neurovirulence test. That test involved injecting monkeys with the vaccine and examining the vaccine's capacity to produce pathologic effects—its neurovirulence—on the monkeys' central nervous system. The results were then compared with the neurovirulence of a reference polio vaccine, which DBS had previously selected. The test was satisfied if the vaccine's neurovirulence "did not exceed" the reference's neurovirulence. *Id.* at 543 n. 9.

[98] *Id.* at 533.

[99] *Id.* at 534.

[100] *Id.*

[101] *Id.*

[102] *Id.* at 542-43.

[103] *See* Ann H. Wion, *supra* note 94, at 152 ("A reasonable implication may be that agency officials wishing to minimize the government's exposure to tort liability should not establish detailed regulatory criteria in regulations.").

[104] *Compare* 21 C.F.R. § 610.40(a) (1999) ("Each donation of blood, plasma, or serum to be used in preparing a biological product shall be tested for the presence of hepatitis B surface antigen by a method of sufficient sensitivity to detect all sera labeled A, (A), B, (B), and C in the Reference Hepatitis B Surface Antigen Panel distributed by [CBER] . . . .") *with id.* § 610.40(b) (2002) (requiring manufacturers to perform one or

ensure that biologics satisfy particular requirements. Under section 601.5(b)(1)(iv), it has authority to revoke a biologics license if the establishment, any location with the establishment or the product fails to conform to the applicable standards "established in the license" designed to ensure the continued safety, purity and potency of the manufactured product. Consequently, the authority exists to enforce such requirements set forth in the biologics license application, even if they are not specifically mandated in regulations.

Given that the agency has the ultimate decision about whether to license a biologic, it has a great deal of leverage over what manufacturers must include in their BLAs. Through guidances and pre-BLA meetings,[105] FDA can and does communicate particular requirements.[106] Of course, a requirement cannot be imposed that is contrary to law, but where the regulations state standards in general terms, the agency has a fair degree of discretion in what it can require as a prerequisite to granting a license.

In addition, relying on specific requirements in licenses rather than in regulations provides additional flexibility. For example, manufacturers can submit supplemental biologics license applications, known as "supplements," seeking permission to change the standards and requirements set forth in a biologics license.[107] Except where those standards are mandated by statute or regulation, discretion exists over whether to approve that change. FDA is able to approve supplements much more rapidly than it is able to change regulations, which can require, among other things, notice-and-comment rulemaking, an analysis of the rule's likely impacts,[108] an assessment of the rule's likely environmental impact and effect on the states under Executive Order 13,132, and sometimes clearance by the Office of Management and Budget under the Paperwork Reduction Act of 1995.[109]

Not all specific measurements, numbers, and exacting requirements have been eliminated from the biologics regulations. For example, 21 C.F.R. § 610.11, on general safety tests for extraneous toxic contaminants, sets forth the specific weight and species of test animals to be used, the duration of the test, and the volume of liquid to be injected. Likewise, 21 C.F.R. § 610.30, on mycoplasma testing, specifies the temperature range for samples, the volume of samples to be mixed, the maximum duration of incubation, and the maximum strength of magnification at which the incubated samples shall be viewed. Similarly, 21 C.F.R. § 610.53 provides a table of dating periods prescribing the temperature and duration of storage for

---

more FDA-approved tests for listed communicable diseases, including hepatitis B, "as necessary to reduce adequately and appropriately the risk of transmission of communicable disease").

[105]   "CDER and CBER participate in many meetings each year with sponsors of investigations and applicants for marketing who seek guidance relating to the development of new [Prescription Drug User Fee Act (PDUFA)] products or the review of marketing applications for PDUFA products." Guidance for Industry: Formal Meetings with Sponsors and Applicants for PDUFA Products (Feb. 2000), at 1.

[106]   *See* Guidance for Industry: IND Meetings for Human Drugs and Biologics (May 2001), at 3 (stating that the purpose of end-of-phase 2 meetings is to "ensure that meaningful data will be generated during phase 3 studies to support a planned marketing application" and that the purpose of pre-NDA or pre-BLA meetings is to discuss filing and format issues); PDUFA III Reauthorization Performance Goals and Procedures (Enclosure to June 4, 2002 transmittal letter from Secretary Thompson to Congress (section VIII.b) (stating that one of the purposes of a pre-NDA/BLA meeting is "to provide industry with feedback" on proposed risk management plans so that such feedback "can be included in the NDA/BLA submission.").

[107]   21 C.F.R. § 601.12.

[108]   The assessment of impacts requires a review under Executive Order 12,866 as well as the Regulatory Flexibility and Unfunded Mandates Act of 1995.

[109]   44 U.S.C. § 3501-3520.

specific biologic products. Some areas are more easily amendable to standardization through the promulgation of regulations.

Where the agency has retained specific numbers and other details in regulations it has, in some instances, adopted strategies that provide additional flexibility, such as by promulgating regulations giving itself discretion to waive the requirements. For example, under 21 C.F.R. § 640.120, the Director of CBER may approve an exception or alternative to any requirement in Subchapter F of Chapter I of Title 21 of the C.F.R. regarding blood, blood components, or blood products.[110] Likewise, under 21 C.F.R. § 610.9, the Center Directors for CBER and CDER have authority to approve a modification of "any particular test method or manufacturing process," required by 21 C.F.R. Parts 610-680, or the conditions under which it is conducted. In addition, under an interim final rule on labeling of products intended for the U.S. Strategic National Stockpile (SNS), FDA Center Directors may exempt investigational, approved, or licensed products from labeling requirements when they find that these requirements adversely affect product safety, effectiveness, or availability.[111] Furthermore, 21 C.F.R. § 610.11 was amended in 2003 to permit manufacturers of biological products to apply for an exemption from the General Safety Test (GST) requirement, provided appropriate production controls and quality assurance safeguards exist.[112]

Those waiver provisions, however, are the exception. As discussed above, flexibility in establishing biologics licensing standards exists primarily because they contain standards that are worded in general terms, and because those regulations incorporate and rely on other regulations, and provide room for FDA to convey its current thinking and recommendations on how to interpret them through guidance documents, which can evolve in step with technological changes more easily than can the regulations themselves. In that way, the relatively terse articulation of licensing requirements set forth in section 601.2 does not leave BLA sponsors guessing at how they must be satisfied. Sponsors may turn to other regulations and FDA guidances to understand what is expected in their BLAs to satisfy the general requirements in section 601.2, such as a full description of manufacturing methods,[113] data establishing the stability of the product through the dating period,[114] and specimens of the labels to be used for the product.[115] This regulatory approach for biologics licensing, which incorporates and relies on sources of authority and direction outside the particular regulatory provision on licensing requirements, is not surprising given the parallel approach reflected in the PHSA, as well as in other facets of FDA law. Indeed, the PHSA borrows and relies on the provisions of the FDCA to provide some of the fundamental, core aspects of biologics regulation.

---

[110]   21 C.F.R. § 640.120. Of course, the Director may not waive any statutory requirements.

[111]   Exceptions or Alternatives to Labeling Requirements for Products Held by the Strategic National Stockpile, 21 C.F.R. pts. 201, 312, 314, 601, 610, 801, 807, 809, 812, and 814.

[112]   68 Fed. Reg. 10,158 (Mar. 4, 2003).

[113]   *See supra* text at note 50.

[114]   *See, e.g.,* 21 C.F.R. subpt. F (dating period limitations).

[115]   *See, e.g., id.* subpt. G (labeling standards); *id.* § 314.57.

Overlap Between PHSA Section 351 and the FDCA

Although many provisions of the FDCA, primarily those enacted in the last 15 years, specifically refer to biologics,[116] the usual triggers for application of the FDCA to biological products have been the definitions in the FDCA of a "drug" or a "device." Since these quoted terms are defined, in relevant part, primarily in relation to their intended use, such as in the diagnosis and prevention of disease or other conditions,[117] the jurisdictional boundaries of the FDCA are broad enough to cover biologics. This is in part because biological products are similarly defined in FDA regulations to be applicable to the "prevention, treatment, or cure of diseases or injuries of man . . . ."[118]

The definitional interplay between the FDCA and the biologics law seems not to have been recognized until the passage in 1938 of the FDCA.[119] For roughly 30 years no overlap therefore existed, and the legislative history of the 1938 act seems to indicate that biologics were not to be subject to it.[120] Upon recodification of the biologics law in 1944, however, the interplay seems to have become recognized and intended.[121] More recently, with the passage of FDAMA in 1997, subpart (j) was added to make clear that a biological product is also subject to the FDCA, except section 505, if it is licensed.[122]

---

[116]   See, e.g., 21 U.S.C. § 379g, pertaining to user fees, which refers to a "human drug application" as including "licensure of a biological product." Other more recently adopted provisions also refer indirectly to biologics in the context of specific mention of section 351 of the PHSA, 42 U.S.C. § 262. See, e.g., 21 U.S.C. § 355(o)(2) (B) (postmarket surveillance and other requirements); 42 U.S.C. § 282(j)(1)(A)(iii) (clinical trial database requirements); and 21 U.S.C. § 355(p) (risk evaluation and mitigation requirements). Interestingly, sections 355(o) and (p) are also incorporated by reference in section 351 of the PHSA. See 42 U.S.C. § 262(a)(2) (D) and (j). Portions of this section and the next sections are derived from previous articles, particularly, Edward L. Korwek, *Human Biological Drug Regulation: Past, Present, and Beyond the Year 2000,* 50 Food & Drug L.J. 123 (1995) and Korwek, *supra* note 13.

[117]   Section 201(g) of the FDCA defines a "drug" to include articles intended for use in the diagnosis, cure, mitigation, treatment, or prevention of disease in man or other animals, or articles (other than food) intended to affect the structure or any function of the body of man or other animals. Section 201(h) defines a device to include an:

> instrument, apparatus, implement, machine, contrivance, contrabands, implant, in vitro reagent, or other similar related article including any component, part, or accessory, which is . . . intended for use in the diagnosis of disease or other conditions, or in the cure, mitigation, treatment or prevention of disease, in man or other animals or … intended to affect the structure or any function of the body of man or other animals, and which does not achieve its primary intended purposes through chemical reaction within or on the body of man or other animals, and which is not dependent upon being metabolized for the achievement of any of its primary intended purposes.

[118]   21 C.F.R. § 600.3(h). *But see* 42 U.S.C. § 262(i), which refers to biologics somewhat differently as "applicable to the prevention, treatment, or cure of a disease or condition of human beings." This statutory language is a result of the passage in 1997 of FDAMA, which changed "injuries" to "conditions." Pub. L. No. 105-115, § 123(d), 111 Stat. 2295, 2324 (1997). The regulatory language has yet to be conformed with the statutory change, which seems broader. *See* Korwek, *supra* note 13, at 266.

[119]   William R. Pendergast, *Biologic Drug Regulation,* in 75th Anniversary Commemorative Volume of Food and Drug Law 293, 298-99 (FDLI 1984).

[120]   *Id.* For other discussion of the overlap, *see* David M. Dudzinski, *Reflections on Historical, Scientific, and Legal Issues Relevant to Designing Approval Pathways for Generic Versions of Recombinant Protein-Based Therapeutic and Monoclonal Antibodies,* 60 Food & Drug L. J. 143, 152-154 (2005).

[121]   *See* Hutt, Merrill & Grossman, *supra* note 18, at 1124-25. *But see* Pendergast, *supra* note 119 at 300, 303 (maintaining that the 1944 recodification did not clarify the status of biologics under the FDCA).

[122]   Pub. L. No. 105-115, § 123(g), 111 Stat. 2295, 2324 (1997). *See also* 21 C.F.R. §§ 310.4(a) and 314.1(b) (NDA requirements do not apply to licensed biologics).

Besides the definitional interplay, the overlap of the two statutes can also be traced to similar provisions in both laws, appearing in section 351(g) of the PHSA and section 902(b) of the FDCA. These sections state that nothing in either statute shall be construed in any way as "affecting, modifying, or repealing or superseding" the provisions of the FDCA or section 351 of the PHSA. The legislative history of the enactment of section 351(g) in 1944 arguably indicates that dual jurisdiction under both laws was legally appropriate, although debate has existed on this topic.[123] The enactment in 1997 of subsection (j) relating to coverage of biologics by the FDCA, a topic mentioned previously, has codified and clarified such dual jurisdiction.

Despite the clear overlap of the FDCA and section 351 of the PHSA, various products often have been referred to, even in scholarly texts, as "drugs, devices, or biologics," as if these classifications were mutually exclusive. Because human biological products are, by definition, simultaneously at least either drugs or devices,[124] the more appropriate regulatory characterization of such products is as biological drugs or biological devices. All other drugs and devices are nonbiological drugs or nonbiological devices.[125] Put another way, the important regulatory determination has often been whether a product that is a drug or device is also a biologic, a principle which is true yet today, even after the merger of several aspects of biological drug regulation with that of drug regulation, largely as a result of FDAMA and the advent of products developed through the use of modern biotechnology methods.

Provisions of the FDCA Applied to Biologics

More than 100 different provisions of the FDCA are applicable to human biologics, particularly with the enactment in 2007 of the Food and Drug Administration Amendments Act (FDAAA) and in 2012 of the Food and Drug Administration Safety and Innovation Act (FDASIA). The significant regulatory ramifications of this observation become apparent upon a summary review of a few of the key provisions. Enforcement powers of the FDCA, such as seizure and injunction under sections 304 and 302, respectively, are also applied to biologics,[126] as section 351 of the PHSA has neither. As discussed above, because section 351 also does not contain substantive provisions regarding clinical testing, section 505(i) of the FDCA governing investigational drugs and the implementing regulations also apply to

---

[123] Some debate has occurred about the application to biological drugs of various provisions of the FDCA as part of FDA administrative proceedings. *See, e.g.,* Biological Products: Procedures for Review of Safety, Effectiveness and Labeling, 38 Fed. Reg. 4319, 4319 (Feb. 13, 1973) (comment 3) (standards of safety and efficacy set forth in new drug provisions of section 505 of the FDCA applicable to biological products challenged as illegal). *See also* Registration of Blood Banks and Other Firms Collecting, Manufacturing, Preparing, or Processing, 38 Fed. Reg. 2965, 2965 (Jan. 31, 1973) (comment 2) (regulation requiring registration of blood banks was questioned as to whether it was the intent of Congress to classify blood as a drug).

[124] *See, e.g.,* 21 C.F.R. §§ 310.4(a), 809.3(a).

[125] Even though using such terminology consistently might improve clarity, FDA generally has not adopted such a convention. *See supra* note 4.

[126] *See, e.g.,* United States v. Miami Serpentarium Laboratories, Inc., Food Drug Cosm. L. Rep. (CCH) ¶ 38,164 (S.D. Fla. 1982)). The penalty provisions of section 303 of the FDCA are also usually applied, given the relatively limited monetary and other penalties of section 351.

biologics.[127] Investigational use principles pertaining to clinical studies of unapproved drugs seem to be one of the earliest aspects of the FDCA applied to biological drugs.[128]

Although section 351 of the PHSA requires that biological products be safe and potent, as well as pure, traditionally both the safety and efficacy requirements of the FDCA have been applied to biological drugs,[129] as alluded to previously. They are therefore sometimes said to be required to be "safe, pure, potent, and effective,"[130] criteria which reflect the literal requirements of both section 351 of the PHSA and section 505 of the FDCA.[131] The mention of efficacy in addition to potency seems to be because efficacy (which is not defined in section 351) has been viewed, at times, to be different from potency.[132] The two concepts are integrally related, however, since drugs must usually be potent to be effective. FDA's definition of potency currently recognizes this interrelationship, as it includes effectiveness.[133] Indeed, the 1902 biologics law (and the current statute) has been viewed by some to include as

---

127   *See* 21 C.F.R. § 312.2 (stating that the requirement for an investigational new drug application for clinical investigations applies to products subject to section 505 of the FDCA or to products subject to the licensing provisions of the PHSA). *See also id.* § 312.3(b) (defining the term "investigational new drug" to mean a "new drug, or biological drug that is used in a clinical investigation").

128   *See* Procedural and Interpretative Regulations; Recodification of Part, 21 Fed. Reg. 5576, 5577 (July 25, 1956).

129   *See generally* 21 C.F.R. § 601.25. *See also* 37 Fed. Reg. 16,679 (1972) (proposal to review safety, efficacy and labeling of biological products); 38 Fed. Reg. 4319 (1973) (final regulation).

130   *See, e.g.,* Donohue, *Blood and Blood Products: A Five Year Challenge,* 36 Food Drug Cosm. L.J. 27, 27 (1981) (speaking of safety, potency and effectiveness requirements); 45 Fed. Reg. 73,922, 73,922 (1980) (stating that for a biological product to be licensed it must be "tested to ensure that it is safe, pure, potent, and effective"); CBER, Frequently Asked Questions, *available at* http://www.fda.gov/cber/faq.htm ("CBER conducts laboratory research related to the regulatory standards on the safety, purity, potency, and effectiveness of biological products.").

131   Section 351(a)(2)(C) of the PHSA states that a product license may be approved upon demonstration that the product is "safe, pure, and potent." Section 505(d)(5) of the FDCA states that FDA can disapprove a new drug application if, *inter alia,* there is a lack of substantial evidence that the drug is effective.

132   An advisory panel charged with reviewing data and information concerning the safety, effectiveness and labeling of bacterial vaccines and bacterial antigens with no U.S. standard of potency stated:

> [P]otency may be distinct from an ability to prevent, ameliorate, or modify in a beneficial way a disease state (effectiveness). For example, a given antigen may induce specific antibodies after a specified interval of time . . . . Whether such antibodies prevent or alter the course of disease is a separate problem. To illustrate, agglutinating antibody induced by the antigen may be found not to correlate with the prevention or modification of a given disease state . . . . Thus evidence that a substance is potent as an immunogen would be insufficient to support effectiveness, unless a previously established correlation existed.

Bacterial Vaccines and Bacterial Antigens With No U.S. Standard of Potency; Implementation of Efficacy Review; Proposal, 42 Fed. Reg. 58,266, 58,273 (Nov. 8, 1977). *See also* William R. Pendergast, *Biologic Drugs, in* Food and Drug Law, ed. by Richard M. Cooper (Food and Drug Law Institute Series, 1991), at 311 (saying that the efficacy provisions of the FDCA were "more precise" than the potency standard of the PHSA).

133   Potency is defined as

> [T]he specific ability or capacity of the product, as indicated by appropriate laboratory tests or by adequately controlled clinical data obtained through the administration of the product in the manner intended, to effect a given result.

21 C.F.R. § 600.3(s). Interestingly, comparable veterinary biologics regulations promulgated by the Animal and Plant Health Inspection Service describe potency as the relative strength of a biologic and define efficacy as similar to potency for human biologics, stating efficacy is the "specific ability or capacity . . . to effect . . . [a] result . . . ." 9 C.F.R. §§ 101.5(f) and (g).

part of the potency requirement at least some measure of "effectiveness,"[134] long before that requirement was adopted as part of the Drug Amendments of 1962 for other human drugs.[135]

The establishment registration and product listing requirements of section 510 of the FDCA also have been applied to biological products,[136] as well as the drug advertising provisions of section 502(n).[137] FDA approval of commercial exports of unapproved drugs (including biologics that are "partially processed"[138]) is explicitly governed by section 802 of the FDCA, adopted as part of the Drug Export Amendments Act of 1986 (DEAA).[139] The Prescription Drug Marketing Act of 1987,[140] along with the Prescription Drug Amendments of 1992,[141] amended the FDCA to prohibit prescription drug re-importation and the sale of

---

[134] See, e.g., Pendergast, supra note 119, at 297, stating in the context of legislative changes to the biologics law in 1944 that

> Congress recognized that not only should a drug be safe and "pure," but it should also be potent, i.e., effective. In recognizing these concepts, Congressional regulation of biologics under the Virus Act was far more advanced than regulation of other human drugs. Demonstration of efficacy, . . . had been administratively required since 1902 and was legislatively imposed in 1944.

See also E. Timm, 75 Years of Compliance with Biological Product Regulations, 33 Food Drug Cosm. L. J. 225, 226 (1978) (stating that "such concern [for effectiveness] was built into the original 1902 Act for biologicals in its labeling dating requirements," referring to the fact that the 1902 Act required a label bearing an expiration date related to effectiveness. Id. at 225). See also Pittman, The Regulation of Biologic Products at NIH, 1902-1972, in National Institute of Allergy and Infectious Diseases, Intramural Contributions, 1887-1987, ed. H.R. Greenwald, V.A. Harden, pp. 61-70, U.S. Department of Health and Human Services, Public Health Service, National Institutes of Health, National Institute of Allergy and Infectious Diseases (Oct. 1987) (stating with respect to typhoid vaccine that since an evaluation of potency had been complicated, the use of a certain test finally confirmed the importance of a particular ingredient and therefore "that the relative potency of the vaccines reflected efficacy." [footnote omitted] As a strict technical matter, however, a product could be potent by a particular laboratory test, but not necessarily effective clinically unless the potency assay has been correlated in a positive way with efficacy.

[135] Pub. L. No. 87-781, 76 Stat. 780 (1962) (codified at 21 U.S.C. §§ 321, 331-332, 348, 351-353, 355, 357-360, 372, 374, 376, 381).

[136] See generally 21 C.F.R. pt. 207 and id. pt. 607 (establishment registration and product listing for manufacturers of human blood and blood products). FDA's initiative to require registration of blood banks and other entities collecting, manufacturing, preparing or processing blood and blood products was controversial for a variety of reasons, including whether FDA had the requisite legal authority, as well as whether registration was to be considered a prelude to product licensing. See, e.g., Registration of Blood Banks and Other Firms Collecting, Manufacturing, Preparing, or Processing, 38 Fed. Reg. 2965, 2965-66 (Jan. 31, 1973).

[137] Until relatively recently, promotional labeling and advertising was handled by various components of CBER, not by a separate group as is the case with drugs regulated by CDER. Much like for drugs, a separate entity has now been established within CBER to handle this area. It is called the Advertising and Promotional Labeling Branch (APLB), which is within the Office of Compliance and Biologics Quality. See Manual of Standard Operating Procedures, SOPP 8412 (Version # 2, Mar. 20, 2008), available at http://www.fda.gov/BiologicsBloodVaccines/GuidanceComplianceRegulatoryInformation/ProceduresSOPPs/ucm073510.htm, at 4.2.A.4 ("The Office of Compliance and Biologics Quality (OCBQ)/Advertising and Promotional Labeling Branch (APLB) reviews the content of labeling from a labeling comprehension and promotional perspective to ensure that it is not false or misleading.").

[138] Section 351(h) of the PHSA provides that a partially processed biologic not intended for sale in the United States which is intended for further manufacture outside the United States, does not require a license if the product either 1) satisfies U.S. cGMP requirements, or 2) meets international manufacturing standards as certified by an international standards organization recognized by the Secretary and meets the requirements in section 801(e)(1) of the FDCA.

[139] Pub. L. No. 99-660, 100 Stat. 3743 (1986) (codified at 21 U.S.C. §§ 301 note, 333 note, 382; 42 U.S.C. §§ 241, 262).

[140] Pub. L. No. 100-293, 102 Stat. 95 (1987) (codified at 21 U.S.C. §§ 301 note, 331(t), 333(v), 353(c)-(e), 381).

[141] Pub. L. No. 102-353, 106 Stat. 941 (1992) (codified at 21 U.S.C. §§ 301 note, 333, 353, 353 note, 381).

prescription drug samples, to restrict sales of prescription drugs purchased by hospitals and other healthcare entities, and to provide for state licensing of wholesale prescription drug distributors.[142] These provisions also apply to biologics that are prescription drugs, except blood and blood components intended for transfusion.[143]

Some other relevant provisions applicable to biologics include 1) those added to the FDCA as part of the Orphan Drug Act of 1983 (ODA);[144] 2) section 503(g), governing combination product regulation, which was adopted as part of the Safe Medical Devices Act of 1990 (SMDA);[145] and (3) section 361 of the PHSA,[146] which relates to the prevention of the transmission of communicable diseases. Other significant provisions applied to biologics include those adopted as part of FDAAA pertaining to pediatric testing requirements,[147] postmarketing studies and safety labeling, and risk evaluation and mitigation strategies (REMS);[148] those adopted as part of FDASIA[149] pertaining to biosimilar user fees[150] and breakthrough therapy designations;[151] and those adopted under the Drug Supply Chain Security Act for tracing and securing prescription drugs throughout the supply chain. [152]

Additional requirements that have been applied to biologics are based on a combination of statutory authorities. cGMP regulations governing drugs and biologics,[153] in particular blood and blood components in intrastate commerce,[154] have been promulgated under a variety of

---

142   *See generally* 21 C.F.R. pts. 203 and 205 (provisions regarding wholesale distribution of prescriptive drugs and guidelines for state licensing of wholesale prescription drug distributors).

143   *See, e.g., id.* §§ 203.1 and 205.3(f)(8).

144   Pub. L. No. 97-414, 96 Stat. 2049 (1983), as amended at 21 U.S.C. §§ 360aa, *et seq.*

145   Pub. L. No. 101-629, § 16, 104 Stat. 4511, 4526 (1990) (codified at 21 USC § 353(g)).

146   58 Stat. 682, 703 (codified at 42 U.S.C. § 264) (authorizing the Department of Health and Human Services to make and enforce regulations to prevent the spread of communicable diseases). *See also* 21 C.F.R. pts. 1240 (implementing regulations), 1270 (human tissue intended for transplantation), and 1271 (human cells, tissues and cellular and tissue-based products).

147   *See* 21 U.S.C. § 355c. The pediatric testing requirements of FDAAA illustrate that the legislative economy and uniformity achieved by applying a single set of statutory provisions to both drugs and biologics can sometimes lead to regulatory inefficiencies and duplicative requirements. FDAAA amended the Pediatric Research Equity Act (PREA) provisions of the FDCA to require that a Pediatric Review Committee review all sponsor requests for deferrals of and waivers from the obligation to submit a pediatric assessment. *See* 21 U.S.C. § 355c(f)(4). Congress mandated that review as a check on what it perceived to be overuse of PREA's deferral and waiver provisions. The requirement that waivers and deferrals of pediatric assessments—and waivers of the requirement to present to the Pediatric Review Committee—always be presented to the Pediatric Review Committee is ill-suited to childhood vaccines. These biological products are specifically developed for use in the pediatric population. Consequently, their pivotal trials uniformly include pediatric data and sponsors, and their labeling necessarily covers pediatric dosing and use instructions. In addition, the Advisory Committee on Immunization Practices, established under section 222 of the PHSA, 42 U.S.C. § 217a, reviews childhood vaccines and makes recommendations about the appropriate dose and frequency, precautions, and contraindications for these products. Imposing an additional Pediatric Review Committee assessment requirement creates duplicative regulatory reviews on an already-overburdened regulatory process. *See* Marion F. Gruber, *US FDA Review and Regulation of Preventive Vaccines for Infectious Disease Indications: Impact of the FDA Amendments Act 2007,* 10 Expert Rev. Vaccines 1011, 1015-1016 (2011).

148   *See id.* § 355-1.

149   Pub. L. No. 112-144, 126 Stat. 993 (2012).

150   *See* 21 U.S.C. §§ 379j–51, 379j-52.

151   *See* 21 U.S.C. § 356(a).

152   Pub. L. No. 113-54, 127 Stat. 599 (2013) (codified at 21 U.S.C. §§ 353(e), 581-585).

153   *See* 21 C.F.R. § 210.2 (stating that the cGMP regulations in Part 211 and the biologics regulations are considered usually to supplement, not to supersede each other).

154   *Id.* Part 606.

provisions. Section 501(a)(2)(B) of the FDCA, pertaining, in relevant part, to the adulteration of drugs not manufactured in accordance with cGMP requirements, section 361 of the PHSA pertaining to the prevention of transmissible diseases such as hepatitis,[155] and section 351(a)(2) of the PHSA governing the conditions for licensure of establishments and products, all have been used to assure that blood products (including blood) are prepared by proper manufacturing procedures and in compliance with relevant manufacturing regulations.[156] Adverse event reporting requirements applicable to biologics[157] also historically are based on a variety of provisions, such as the misbranding sections 502(a) and 502(f)(2) of the FDCA and section 351(b) of the PHSA, governing, respectively, misleading labeling of and inadequate warnings for drugs and false labeling of biologics.[158]

The Ambiguous and Complex Nature of Biologics

The subject of what biologics are and are not has been addressed frequently,[159] sometimes inaccurately or confusingly. This in part is because they traditionally have been an amorphous, ill-defined group of drugs or devices. Unless a product is called a "vaccine" or "blood," or is derived from blood,[160] such as plasma or platelets, whether it is a biologic is often difficult to decide. Less obvious biologics are allergenic products.[161] The situation is confused further by the fact that some products that *seem* like they would be biologics are regulated as drugs (e.g., insulin)[162] or devices (e.g., porcine heart valves transplanted into humans), and some products that seem like they would be drugs or devices are regulated as biologics (e.g., certain in vitro diagnostic devices). Other more recent complicating factors are that certain therapeutic biologics have been transferred to CDER even though they are

---

[155] *See* Biological Products, Current Good Manufacturing Practice for Blood and Blood Components, 39 Fed. Reg. 18,614, 18,614 (1974).

[156] FDA's efforts to impose cGMP requirements on intrastate blood banks, as well as interstate blood banking operations, were controversial. *See id.* at 18,614-15.

[157] *See* 21 C.F.R. subpt. D. For a history of adverse experience reporting requirements pertaining to biologics, *see* Adverse Experience Reporting Requirements for Licensed Biological Products; Final Rule, 59 Fed. Reg. 54,034, 54,034 (1994). *See also infra,* section entitled "Adverse Experience Reporting and Recordkeeping."

[158] *See, e.g.,* Adverse Experience Reporting Requirements for Licensed Biological Products; Proposed Rule, 55 Fed. Reg. 11,611, 11,613 (Mar. 29, 1990) (proposed rule on adverse experience reporting for licensed biological products).

[159] For a comprehensive article on the subject, *see* Korwek, *supra* note 13.

[160] The regulation of blood as a biologic has not always been straightforward or obvious. Three different courts addressed the issue of its status, ultimately resulting in the PHSA being amended in 1970 to explicitly cover blood products. For a discussion of the history of regulation of blood products as a biologic, *see* Korwek, *supra* note 13, at 270-73.

[161] *See* 42 U.S.C. § 262(i) (definition of biologic specifically mentions "allergenic product."). *See also* Allergenic Substances: Policy on Licensure of Oral Products Intended to Determine Allergies, Products Intended as Adjuncts to Allergy Skin Tests, and Materials Intended for Patch Tests of Humans, 51 Fed. Reg. 33,664 (Sept. 22,1986) (products used as oral challenges to determine whether persons are allergic to certain chemicals in food, products used adjunctively as positive controls, and allergenic skin tests and chemical reagents used in patch-testing kits are considered biological products subject to licensure).

[162] *See* APPROVED DRUG PRODUCTS WITH THERAPEUTIC EQUIVALENCE EVALUATIONS (known as the Orange Book)(34th ed. 2014), *available at* http://www.fda.gov/downloads/Drugs/DevelopmentApprovalProcess/UCM071436. pdf; *see also, e.g.,* 21 C.F.R. § 310.4(b) (radiolabeled biologics are regulated as drug-biologic combination products through the NDA process).

still regulated as biologics under section 351 of the PHSA, as mentioned previously, and the BPCIA has added to the biologic definition proteins, except chemically synthesized polypeptides.

The recent biosimilars legislation and the preceding[163] and ongoing debate about the issues it raises have often not helped to clarify what biologics are. Regulatory commentary sometimes has suggested or indicated inaccurately that insulin and human growth hormone are "biological proteins."[164] No simple, quick, all-encompassing definition exists. Biologics are often distinguished today in terms of their sources, chemical properties, immunogenicity,[165] macromolecular size or structure, or how they function. They have been characterized as complex macromolecules, as proteins, or as derived from living organisms or natural sources, as difficult to identify compared to so-called small molecule drugs, or as generally working through some immune mechanism or process.[166]

Section 351 itself is not particularly useful in understanding the nature of biologics. It does not define the term, other than usually by reference to particular types of products. Specifically mentioned in most relevant part are a "virus, therapeutic serum, toxin, anti-toxin, vaccine, blood, blood component or derivative, allergenic product, or protein (except any chemically synthesized polypeptide), or analogous product, or arsphenemine" or its derivatives. Many of these terms themselves are difficult to understand or define, even from a scientific standpoint. The scope of products that are subject to section 351 becomes almost impossible to comprehend because of the use of the language "analogous product." Depending upon the limits or expansiveness of one's imagination, almost nothing or anything can be viewed as "analogous" to another product, as a legal or scientific matter.

Therefore, time and again, FDA has construed the potentially boundless term "analogous product" to encompass a wide variety of products and procedures that do not squarely fall within the other categories of the definition.[167] This enables the agency to use existing statutory authority to accommodate rapid advances in molecular biology, genomics, immunology and transplant biology that lead to novel therapeutic approaches. For instance, xenotransplantation—the use of living, nonhuman animal cells, tissues or organs for

---

[163] One of the major issues in human biological product regulation today is the topic of "generic" or follow-on versions. *See* Chapter 15 *infra*. *See also* Korwek, *supra* note 5; Dudzinski, *supra* note 120; Donald E. Segal, et al., *Regulatory Pathway for "Biosimilar" Products Debated*, 22 WASHINGTON LEGAL FOUNDATION, LEGAL BACKGROUNDER, No. 6 (2007); and Tam Q. Dinh, *Potential Pathways for Abbreviated Approval of Generic Biologics under Existing Law and Proposed Reforms to the Law*, 62 FOOD & DRUG L.J. 77 (2007).

[164] For a discussion of hormones, *see infra* notes 176-177 and accompanying text.

[165] M. Wadhwa & R. Thorpe, *Unwanted Immunogenicity: Implications for Follow-On Biologicals*, 41 DRUG INFO. J. 1 (2007); Thomas Morrow, *Defining the Difference: What Makes Biologics Unique*, BIOTECHNOLOGY HEALTHCARE 25 (Sept. 2004).

[166] *See, e.g.,* FDA, Drugs, Frequently Asked Questions About Therapeutic Biological Products (updated Dec. 24, 2009), *available at* http://www.fda.gov/Drugs/DevelopmentApprovalProcess/HowDrugsareDevelopedandApproved/ApprovalApplications/TherapeuticBiologicApplications/ucm113522.htm; USDA, Animal Health, Common Questions about Veterinary Biologics (updated July 22, 2010), *available at* http://www.aphis.usda.gov/animal health/vet_biologics/vb_pel_faqs.shtml. *See also* Annabel Hecht, *Making Sure Biologicals Are Safe*, FDA CONSUMER (July-August 1977) at 21 ("[v]accines are . . . called 'biologics' because they are made from or with the aid of living organisms that are produced in man or animals").

[167] *See, e.g.,* 66 Fed. Reg. 4688 (Jan. 18, 2001) (proposed rule to require FDA submission and public disclosure of certain data and information related to gene therapy and xenotransplantation).

human therapeutic purposes—and gene therapy—the use of genetic material to correct defective genes or otherwise alter the biological properties of living cells responsible for disease development—represent two areas of treatment intervention that FDA has classified as biologics.[168] Yet, these products do not themselves necessarily qualify as a "virus, therapeutic serum, toxin, anti-toxin, vaccine, blood, blood component or derivative, [or] allergenic product," although they and other products may now be covered by the "protein" language of the definition, in accordance with the new provisions added by the BPCIA, if the products are not chemically synthesized polypeptides.

FDA further utilizes the delegation of authority under section 351(a) to issue regulations, guidance documents, or policy statements to describe whether and how its current statutory and regulatory authority applies to innovative technological advances. For instance, as gene therapy experimentation emerged in the late 1980s, FDA issued a policy statement clarifying its statutory authority to regulate such products, and it also drafted a guideline that "makes clear" that it "has regulatory oversight for xenotransplantation clinical trials conducted in the U.S."[169] Indeed, when in September 1999, Jesse Gelsinger, an 18-year-old who suffered from a rare genetic liver disorder, unexpectedly died while undergoing gene therapy treatment at the University of Pennsylvania,[170] the agency began to take a closer look at new initiatives to protect clinical trial participants.[171]

FDA's regulations provide little help in identifying the types of products subject to section 351.[172] They often focus on the source of the product, such a therapeutic serum, which is the product obtained from blood by removing the clotting components and the blood cells.[173] One of the more significant aspects of the regulations pertains to the definition for a biological product that is "analogous to a toxin or anti-toxin." Such a product is a biologic if it is applicable to the prevention, treatment, or cure of disease or injuries of man through a "specific immune process," irrespective of its source.[174] Again, what precisely constitutes a "specific immune process," is difficult to ascertain and complicated.[175]

---

[168]   See, e.g., 66 Fed. Reg. 4688, 4690 (2001).

[169]   FDA, Statement of Policy for Regulating Biotechnology Products, 51 Fed. Reg. 23,309, 23,311 (1986) (stating that nucleic acids or viruses used for gene therapy are biological drugs); FDA, Vaccines, Blood, & Biologics, PHS Guideline on Infectious Disease Issues in Xenotransplantation (Jan. 19, 2001) (updated June 18, 2009) *available at* http://www.fda.gov/BiologicsBloodVaccines/GuidanceComplianceRegulatoryInformation/Guidances/Xenotransplantation/ucm074727.htm.

[170]   *See* Larry Thompson, *Human Gene Therapy: Harsh Lessons, High Hopes,* FDA CONSUMER (Sept./Oct. 2000), at 1.

[171]   *See, e.g.,* Gene Therapy Patient Tracking System (June 27, 2002), *available at* http://www.fda.gov/downloads/biologicsbloodvaccines/cellulargenetherapyproducts/ucm150110.pdf; Guidance for Industry: Source Animal, Product, Preclinical, and Clinical Issues Concerning the Use of Xenotransplantation Products in Humans at VIII(G) (April 2003), *available at* http://www.fda.gov/biologicsbloodvaccines/guidancecomplianceregulatoryinformation/guidances/xenotransplantation/ucm074354.htm; Guidance for Industry: Gene Therapy Clinical Trials—Observing Subjects for Delayed Adverse Events (2006).

[172]   *See* 21 CFR § 600.3(h).

[173]   *Id.* § 600.3(h)(2).

[174]   *Id.* § 600.3(h)(5)(iii).

[175]   *See, e.g.,* Korwek, *supra* note 13, at 270 and *infra* notes 203-209 and accompanying text regarding combination products.

Despite the lack of definitional clarity in the biologics law and regulations, they do specify that one type of product is not a biologic: hormones.[176] For example, human growth hormone and human insulin, a few of the first "genetically engineered" products that have been commercialized, were approved as drugs through the NDA process. FDA also does not classify antibiotics as biologics, although they can be derived from living organisms, largely because they were once regulated, like insulin, under specific sections of the FDCA.[177]

The modern biotechnology commercial revolution that began in the early 1980s has pushed the limits of FDA's biologics definitions and other regulations, particularly in the area of combination products.[178] Examples of approved recombinant and monoclonal products are now commonplace. Such products include alpha, beta, and gamma interferons; thrombolytics, such as alteplase; blood clotting factors, such as Factors VIII and IX; and a variety of monoclonal antibodies such as infliximab, abcixemab, and basiliximab.[179] An example in the vaccine area is quadrivalent human papillomavirus recombinant vaccine for females for the prevention of cervical cancer.[180] Other sometimes less obvious biologics include cell and gene therapies,[181] cord blood,[182] human cloning methods,[183] transgenic plant or animal sources of certain drugs, xenotransplants, and certain human and cellular tissue products[184] (discussed below).[185] The diversity of marketed products produced by modern biotechnology methods led in part to the promulgation in 1991 of a number of Intercenter Agreements describing product characteristics or product types and their status as biologics, drugs, devices, or combination products.[186]

---

[176] See 21 C.F.R. § 600.3(h)(5)(ii). For further detailed discussion of this category, see Korwek, supra note 13 at 274.

[177] See Korwek, supra note 13, at 270.

[178] See, e.g., FDA, Combination Products Containing Live Cellular Components, Notice of Public Hearing, 67 Fed. Reg. 24,722 (May 15, 2002).

[179] For an excellent chart of many such products, see Dudzinski, supra note 120, Appendix A.

[180] Approval Letter for Human Papillomavirus Quadrivalent (Types 6, 11, 16, 18) Vaccine, Recombinant (June 8, 2006), available at http://www.fda.gov/BiologicsBloodVaccines/Vaccines/ApprovedProducts/ucm111283.htm.

[181] As early as 1986, the Food and Drug Administration stated that nucleic acids or viruses used for gene therapy are biological drugs. See supra note 169.

[182] See, e.g., Request for Proposed Standards for Unrelated Allogeneic Peripheral and Placental/Umbilical Cord Blood Hematopoietic Stem/progenitor Cell Products; Request for Comments, 63 Fed. Reg. 2985 (Jan. 20, 1998). See also 21 C.F.R. pt. 1271.

[183] See FDA's Role in the Use of Cloning Technology as a Cause for Public Health Concern: Hearing Before the S. Comm. on Oversight and Investigations, 107th Cong. 78, 79 (Mar. 28, 2001) (statement of Kathryn C. Zoon, Director, CBER), available at http://www.fda.gov/NewsEvents/Testimony/ucm115228.htm.

[184] See, e.g., PHS Guideline on Infectious Disease Issues In Xenotransplantation (Jan. 19, 2001), available at http://www.fda.gov/downloads/BiologicsBloodVaccines/GuidanceComplianceRegulatoryInformation/Guidances/Xenotransplantation/UCM092858.pdf; Guidance for Human Somatic Cell Therapy and Gene Therapy (March 1998), available at http://www.fda.gov/downloads/BiologicsBloodVaccines/GuidanceComplianceRegulatoryInformation/Guidances/CellularandGeneTherapy/ucm081670.pdf.

[185] See generally Korwek, supra note 13 (discussing the sometimes complex and arcane reasons for classifying various products as biologics).

[186] See generally Assignment of Agency Component for Review of Premarket Applications; Guidance Documents Entitled Intercenter Agreements for Biologic, Device and Drug Products; Availability, 56 Fed. Reg. 58,760 (Nov. 21, 1991) (announcing the availability of the Intercenter Agreements). The agreements are now dated and have been superseded in some respects. See FDA, Jurisdictional Update: Intercenter Agreements, at http://www.fda.gov/oc/combination/intercenterupdate.html.

Within these categories, one of the more confusing product areas relates to "human tissue" and "Human Cells, Tissues and Cellular and Tissue-based Products" (HCT/Ps).[187] The former includes tissues derived from the human body that were recovered before May 25, 2005 (the effective date of the comprehensive HCT/P rule), and that were 1) intended for transplantation to another human for the diagnosis, cure, mitigation, treatment or prevention of any condition or disease; 2) recovered, processed, stored or distributed by methods that do not change tissue function or characteristics; and 3) not regulated as a human drug, biological product or medical device.[188] In 2004, exercising its authority under section 361 of the PHSA to prevent the transmission of communicable disease, FDA established a comprehensive system for regulating HCT/Ps.[189]

The new rule defined HCT/Ps more broadly than "human tissue," including all articles containing or consisting of human cells or tissues that are intended for implantation, transplantation, infusion, or transfer into a human recipient, except for certain enumerated categories, such as vascularized human organs.[190] FDA determined that applying the new rule retrospectively would be overly burdensome and impractical, and consequently retained the prior, narrower definition for tissues recovered before the rule's effective date.[191] The new rule specifies that HCT/Ps are regulated solely under section 361 of the PHSA and the new regulations if they are 1) minimally manipulated; 2) not promoted or labeled for any use other than a homologous use;[192] 3) not combined with or modified by the addition of any article except for water, crystalloids or sterilizing, preserving, or storage agents that do not raise new clinical safety concerns; *and* 4) either a) do not have a systemic effect and are not dependent on the metabolic activity of living cells for their primary function, or b) have a systemic effect or depend on such metabolic activity, but are for autologous use,[193] allogeneic[194] use in first- or second-degree blood relatives, or reproductive use.[195] With this approach, cells or tissues derived from the body that comply with these characteristics are regulated by CBER solely as human tissues, and require no premarket approval or licensure submission.[196] Tissues or cells not meeting these criteria, and meeting the definition of a biological product or a drug, must, respectively, be licensed by CBER or CDER under section 351 of the PHSA or approved by CDER under section 505 of the FDCA prior to marketing.[197] Lastly, tissue or cells not qualifying as "section 361" HCT/Ps, and that achieve their intended

---

[187] *See* 21 C.F.R. § 1270.3(b) (tissue) and 21 C.F.R. § 1271.10(a) (HCT/Ps).

[188] 21 C.F.R. § 1270.3(j).

[189] Current Good Tissue Practice for Human Cell, Tissue, and Cellular and Tissue-Based Product Establishments; Inspection and Enforcement, 69 Fed. Reg. 68,612 (Nov. 24, 2004).

[190] 21 C.F.R. § 1271.3(d).

[191] 69 Fed. Reg. at 68,650. FDA indicated that it intends to revoke 21 C.F.R. Part 1270 in the future when it is confident that no human tissue regulated under that part is still available for use. *Id.*

[192] Homologous use means the repair, reconstruction, replacement, or supplementation of a recipient's cells or tissues with cellular products that perform the same basic function in the recipient as in the donor. *Id.* § 1271.3(c).

[193] Autologous use means the implantation, transplantation, infusion or transfer of cellular products back into the individual from whom the cells were recovered. 21 C.F.R. § 1271.3(a).

[194] Allogeneic use is not defined by FDA but generally means the implantation, transplantation, infusion, or transfer of cellular products into a person other than the original donor.

[195] 21 C.F.R. § 1271.10(a)(4).

[196] Current Good Tissue Practice for Human Cell, Tissue, and Cellular and Tissue-Based Product Establishments; Inspection and Enforcement; Final Rule, 69 Fed. Reg. at 68,613.

[197] *Id.*

effect in the human body as medical devices, are regulated by the Center for Devices and Radiological Health (CDRH) as medical devices pursuant to the FDCA.[198]

Human stem cells are an example of products that may be regulated either strictly as "section 361" HCT/Ps[199] or as HCT/Ps that are also drugs, devices, and/or biological products, depending on their intended use.[200] Two general categories of stem cells are embryonic stem cells (which are derived from embryos) and adult stem cells (which are obtained from blood, tissues or organs), but as knowledge about stem cells evolves many other categories are being identified. Unlike other cells in the human body, stem cells are not fully specialized as one particular organ or tissue type, but can be bioengineered or otherwise changed into different specialized cell types (e.g., heart cells, muscle cells).

One type of adult stem cells are peripheral blood stem cells (PBSCs). When minimally manipulated and used autologously (on the donor) at the point of care for direct re-administration, they meet the regulatory definition of HCT/Ps, which expressly includes "hematopoietic stem/progenitor cells derived from peripheral blood."[201] If they are more than minimally manipulated, or fail to meet the other criteria for "361 HCT/Ps," however, they become subject to regulation as a biological product, including requirements for investigation under the investigational new drug regulations (21 C.F.R. Part 312) and biologics license requirements.[202]

Apart from such "single entity" products, the assignment of combination product regulation can be difficult as applied to biologics, in part because section 503(g)(1) of the FDCA states that the Center that shall have primary jurisdiction depends upon the primary mode of action of the combination product. If the primary mode of action is that of a biologic, then CBER has primary jurisdiction, under section 503(g)(1)(C).[203] If the primary mode of action is that of a drug "(other than a biological product)," then CDER has primary jurisdiction under section 503(g)(1)(A), and so on. Interestingly, there is no parallel parenthetical language for devices in section 503(g)(1)(B), as there is for drugs, that excludes biologics.[204] This difference probably represents more of a technical drafting problem than a significant legal issue. The primary mode of action for a combination of a biologic and drug will determine whether it is assigned to CBER or CDER. If the primary mode of action involves a biologic assigned to CDER, then CDER has biologic jurisdiction. Otherwise, CBER is the appropriate review division.[205]

The "mode of action" test for determining primary jurisdiction can be problematic for at least a couple of reasons. First, it can be difficult as a scientific matter to ascertain the precise mode of action of a particular product, or which of several possible modes of action

---

[198]   *Id.*

[199]   21 C.F.R. § 1271.3(d).

[200]   *Id.* § 1271.20.

[201]   21 C.F.R. § 1271.3(d); *see also* Draft Guidance for Industry: Cell Selection Devices for Point of Care Production of Minimally Manipulated Autologous Peripheral Blood Stem Cells (PBSCs) (July 2007), at 2.

[202]   *See id.*

[203]   See 21 C.F.R. § 3.4(a)(3).

[204]   *See id.* § 503(g)(1)(B).

[205]   *See* FDA, Jurisdictional Update: Drug-Biologic Combination Products, *available at* http://www.fda.gov/oc/combination/biologic.html.

of any given product is "primary," as FDA clearly recognizes.[206] Second, neither the FDCA nor section 351 of the PHSA, or implementing regulations of the FDCA, define drugs or biologics strictly in terms of their mode of action. Sections 351(a) of the PHSA and section 201(g)(1) of the FDCA are both silent about how a biologic or a drug can or must function. Except for devices,[207] therefore, no statutory standards exist indicating the modes of action of biologics or drugs. Only FDA's regulations make a reference to biological products that act through a "specific immune mechanism," as mentioned previously. Even in this case, however, the description is one of the many possible characteristics of a biologic. This regulatory standard is therefore not dispositive of biologic status, either for a combination product or any other product.

The regulations on this point simply say that a combination product has a biological primary mode of action if it acts by the same means as the named products listed in section 351(i),[208] which contain an often interesting and confusing mix of very different products, sometimes with complicated means of therapeutic action. An example of a combination drug-biologic product that has been designated as having a biological primary mode of action is pegylated interferon and ribavirin to treat chronic hepatitis C. Combination biologic-device products with a biological primary mode of action are much more common.[209]

In addition to combination products, CBER regulates certain medical devices used to collect, process, or administer blood products and other biologics.[210] Some of those devices are biological devices licensed under the PHSA; others are medical devices approved or cleared under the medical device authorities, but which CBER regulates because they are intimately related to processing or administering blood products or other biologics and because regulating them, even though they are devices, requires in-depth familiarity with the biologics on which they are used.

Licensed biological devices regulated by CBER under section 351 of the PHSA include in vitro tests that are required for donor screening and related blood banking practices.[211] Also separately licensed as biological devices are certain specific reagents, such as the antibody to hepatitis B surface antigen and the Human Immunodeficiency Virus Type 1, that are components of those required in vitro tests.[212] As discussed above, combination biologic-devices whose primary mode of action is that of a biologic are licensed as well. Those include medical devices that are 1) packaged with licensed biologics and serve as their delivery system (such as an allergen patch and "tine" tests), 2) filled with licensed biologics during the manufacturing process and serve as the final container and delivery system (such as syringes filled with RhoD immunoglobulin), and 3) combined or impregnated with a licensed biologic during the manufacturing process.[213]

---

[206] *See* Definition of Primary Mode of Action of a Combination Product; Proposed Rule and Notice, 69 Fed. Reg. 25,527, 25,529 (May 7, 2004).

[207] *See supra* note 117.

[208] *See* 21 C.F.R. § 3.2(k)(1).

[209] *See* FDA, Jurisdictional Determinations, at http://www.fda.gov/oc/combination/ determinations.html.

[210] Intercenter Agreement Between the Center for Biologics Evaluation and Research and the Center for Devices and Radiological Health (1991), *available at* http://www.fda.gov/oc/combination/intercenter.html.

[211] *Id.* at 4 (Part VI).

[212] *Id.* at 5 (Part VI.B.1).

[213] *Id.* at 5 (Part VI.B.2).

In contrast, medical devices that are marketed separately from licensed biologics but that constitute systems dedicated for use with human subjects in collecting, processing, or administering biologics, are regulated by CBER under the medical device authorities.[214] Apheresis machines are one example. Similarly, medical devices, other than reagents, that blood banks use to prepare blood products or for quality assurance, are also regulated by CBER under the medical device authorities.[215] Examples include computer software programs for blood establishment data management, clinical laboratory devices with separate blood bank claims, and microwave ovens used to thaw blood products.[216] In addition, certain in vitro reagents, such as lectins, protectins, bovine albumin, and potentiating media, that are not required for blood donor screening or related blood banking practices but that are intended for use in processing licensed biologics, are regulated by CBER under the medical device authorities. [217]

CDRH, on the other hand, has the lead in regulating medical devices in this arena that are used directly in patients for therapeutic purposes. For example, where automated cell separators or blood processing equipment are applied to a particular patient with a specific disease to produce a direct clinical benefit through the removal of toxins or excess deleterious elements, CDRH regulates those products under the medical device authorities.[218] Similarly, where medical devices include filters, columns, or other matrices (such as magnetic beads) that are coupled with biological substances (such as monoclonal antibodies) to process blood or blood components, CDRH will regulate them under the medical device authorities if the devices are used for therapeutic purposes.[219] Roughly 300 monoclonal antibody in vitro diagnostic tests have been cleared by the device notification process. Finally, CDRH has the lead in regulating in vitro tests or reagents that detect certain infectious agents in blood, such as cytomegalovirus, when the tests are used only for diagnostic purposes or for both diagnostic and blood donor screening purposes, while CBER has the lead where they are intended only for blood and plasma donor screening.[220] The one exception is that all in vitro tests and other devices used specifically to diagnose HIV are regulated by CBER under the medical device authorities, due to CBER's extensive experience with HIV/AIDS.[221] HIV diagnostic kits fall into that category, whether they are used for blood donor screening or individual diagnoses.[222] Other devices that fall into that category include collection devices, specimen containers, test kit components, and devices used to inactivate the HIV virus.[223]

The distinction between which products are licensed by CBER through the BLA process and which are approved or cleared by CBER or CDRH as medical devices through the premarket approval (PMA) or 510(k) pathway can be important. The average review time and the cost of the preclinical and clinical studies necessary to support the safety and efficacy of each product can sometimes differ. CDRH clinical study requirements for PMA submissions historically have relied on one "pivotal" clinical study, which is typically a

---

[214]   *Id.* at 4 (Part VI.A.1).
[215]   *Id.* at 5 (Part VI.A.3).
[216]   *Id.*
[217]   *Id.* at 4 (Part VI.A.2.a).
[218]   *Id.* at 6 (Part VI.C.3).
[219]   *Id.* at 6 (Part VI.C.4.a).
[220]   *Id.* at 5-6 (Part VI.C.1).
[221]   *Id.* at 4 (Part VI).
[222]   *Id.*
[223]   *Id.*

multi-Center, randomized controlled study involving a large enough study population to provide statistically significant evidence of the device's safety and efficacy. CBER clinical study requirements for BLA submissions, on the other hand, have often required two larger "phase III" clinical studies involving a large number of subjects.

Postmarketing Biologics Regulation

FDA also has regulations mandating certain postapproval requirements, activities, and tools to verify that biologics continue to be safe, pure, and potent. Some of those tools are the same as for drugs, some are the same but have subtle differences unique to biologics, and some are completely unique to biologics.

Lot Release

One postapproval tool that is now completely unique to biologics is lot release, although this feature has not always been unique to biologics.[224] CBER's Center Director (or CDER's Center Director, for therapeutic biologics regulated by CDER) may at any time notify a manufacturer that it may not distribute a biological product lot until the Center Director grants permission.[225] The main limitation on the Center Director's discretion is that a lot release notice may be issued only when necessary for the safety, purity, or potency of the product. The Center Director may also require a manufacturer to submit samples of any lot of any licensed biologic, together with the protocols showing results of applicable tests.[226] Historically, FDA required lot release for most biologics because it was necessary to ensure lot-to-lot consistency for the complex mixtures produced by living organisms in most biologics, and also to ensure that contaminants were not introduced during production.[227] Over time, however, technology enabled the industrial scale production of biological products that were more easily characterized. In addition, improved analytical techniques were developed for characterizing starting materials and final products, and efficient methods of purification were developed to reduce process-related impurities to minimum levels. Based on those technological improvements, and years of product-specific inspections and testing in CBER laboratories, a guidance was issued establishing the circumstances in which manufacturers could submit amendments to their applications that would allow them to substitute alternatives to lot release requirements.[228] Little by little, even the presumption that all biologics would require lot release began to shift.[229] FDA now has a flexible policy, which imposes lot release only on certain products. That policy shift acknowledges the continued existence of lot-to-lot inconsistency in certain complex

---

[224] See Korwek, *supra* note 116 at 133, n. 89.

[225] 21 C.F.R. § 610.2(a).

[226] *Id.* § 610.2(a).

[227] Guidance on Alternatives to Lot Release for Licensed Biological Products, 58 Fed. Reg. 38,771, 38,772-73 (July 20, 1993).

[228] *Id.*

[229] See 58 Fed. Reg. 38,771, 38,772-38,773 (July 20, 1993); 60 Fed. Reg. 63,048, 63,048-49 (Dec. 8, 1995); 62 Fed. Reg. 29,353, 29,354 (May 30, 1997); 62 Fed. Reg. 49,244, 49,245 (Sept. 19, 1997); 65 Fed. Reg. 15,341, 15,342 (Mar. 22, 2000); 65 Fed. Reg. 41,678, 41,678 (July 6, 2000); 67 Fed. Reg. 79,127, 79,128 (Dec. 27, 2002); 68 Fed. Reg. 27,820, 27,821 (May 21, 2003); 71 Fed. Reg. 3856, 3857 (Jan. 24, 2006).

biologics, but also recognizes advancements in discerning which products should be subject to lot release.

License Revocation and Suspension

A postapproval biologics provision that is similar to a corresponding provision in drug regulation but that differs in important ways is CBER's license revocation and suspension authority. FDA has authority to revoke a biologics license on six grounds[230]: 1) inability to gain access to the establishment to inspect; 2) discontinuation of manufacturing such that FDA cannot conduct a meaningful inspection; 3) failure by the manufacturer to report a manufacturing change; 4) failure to conform to the applicable standards established in the license and in FDA regulations designed to ensure the continued safety, purity, and potency of the products; 5) change in the establishment or manufacturing methods that requires a new showing of compliance; and 6) a determination that the product is not safe and effective for all its intended uses, or is misbranded with respect to any such use. FDA must provide the license holder with a notice, known as a Notice of Intent to Revoke (NOIR), which sets forth the grounds for the proposed revocation and offer an opportunity for a hearing.[231]

Except in cases involving willfulness, or where FDA has already suspended the license without a hearing on the ground of danger to health, the agency must first provide a reasonable period for the licensed manufacturer to demonstrate or achieve compliance with the requirements of the regulations before instituting proceedings to revoke the license.[232] After providing the manufacturer with that opportunity, and finding that the manufacturer has not demonstrated or achieved compliance, and has not waived the opportunity for hearing, FDA must issue a notice of an opportunity for a hearing (NOOH) on the matter.[233]

Where "reasonable grounds" exist to believe that any of the six reasons for license revocation exists and that as a result a danger to health exists, FDA may immediately notify the manufacturer that its license is suspended.[234] In that event, the manufacturer may be required to notify all selling agents and distributors to whom the biologic has been delivered about the suspension, and to provide CBER or CDER with records documenting the deliveries and notice of suspension.[235] Upon suspension, FDA can either proceed to revoke the license, or hold the revocation in abeyance pending resolution of the issue, if the licensed manufacturer agrees.[236]

Although license revocation under section 601.5 applies only to biologics, the FDCA does contain a provision authorizing the Secretary of DHHS to withdraw approval of a new drug application (NDA) or abbreviated new drug application (ANDA).[237] It provides that the Secretary shall withdraw approval of an NDA or an ANDA if certain findings can be made, based on scientific evidence, that undermine the conclusion that the product is safe

---

[230]　21 C.F.R. § 601.5.

[231]　Id. § 601.5(b)(1).

[232]　Id. §§ 601.5 (b)(2); 601.6 (a).

[233]　Id. §§ 12.21(b) and 601.5(b)(2).

[234]　21 C.F.R. § 601.6(a).

[235]　Id.

[236]　Id. § 601.6(b).

[237]　21 U.S.C. § 355(e).

and effective.[238] The statute also requires that the approval be withdrawn if mandatory patent information was not timely filed, and if the application contains any untrue statement of material fact.[239] In addition to these mandatory provisions, withdrawal of marketing approval can occur if 1) the applicant failed to satisfy certain requirements related to recordkeeping; 2) new information indicates that the manufacturing methods, facilities and controls are inadequate to ensure the drug's continued identity, strength, quality, and purity, and the manufacturer did not make them adequate in a reasonable time; or 3) new information indicates that the drug's labeling is false and misleading and was not corrected in a reasonable time.[240] Finally, another regulation[241] incorporates the same basic withdrawal provisions of section 355(e), and then adds grounds for withdrawal.[242]

Similar to biologics license revocations, an applicant must be provided with due notice and an opportunity for a hearing before initiating withdrawal proceedings.[243] Also, like revocations, a withdrawal order must state the grounds for the action.[244] Finally, section 355(e) also resembles the biologics revocation provisions in that it contains a suspension provision. Specifically, section 355(e) states that where an "imminent hazard to the public health" exists, the Secretary may suspend the approval immediately. In that event, the applicant must be given prompt notice and an opportunity for an expedited hearing.

In sum, many similarities exist between the drug withdrawal and suspension provisions, on one hand, and the biologics regulations on license revocation and suspension, on the other. For example, they both require: notice and an opportunity for a hearing;[245] that manufacturers be provided a reasonable opportunity to correct manufacturing process deficiencies before the initiation of formal revocation or withdrawal proceedings;[246] and that FDA can proceed based on evidence calling into question the product's safety, or the manufacturing processes' ability to ensure the product's continued identity, strength, quality, and purity.[247] They both also allow action based on an applicant's failure to allow FDA to inspect records or failure to maintain required records.[248]

---

[238] *Id.* § 355(e).
[239] *Id.*
[240] *Id.*
[241] 21 C.F.R. § 314.150. *See also id.* at § 314.151, which adds provisions for withdrawing approval of an ANDA when FDA withdraws approval of the application which the ANDA referenced.
[242] The additional grounds for withdrawal are if FDA finds 1) that the applicant failed to update its drug listing as section 510(j)(2) of the FDCA requires; 2) that the applicant has failed to submit bioavailability or bioequivalence data required under 21 C.F.R. pt. 320; 3) that the applicant withheld information about the drug that it possessed and should have submitted in the application; 4) that essential nonclinical laboratory studies violated good laboratory practices without justification; 5) that any clinical investigation described in the application violated the human subject protection rules; 6) that the applicant or a CRO refused to submit to a bioresearch monitoring inspection; and 7) that an ANDA's labeling is no longer consistent with that of its reference drug and no exception is applicable. *See* 21 C.F.R. § 314.150(b)(4)-(10).
[243] 21 C.F.R. § 314.150(a).
[244] 21 U.S.C. § 355(e).
[245] *See* 21 C.F.R. pt. 12.
[246] 21 C.F.R. § 601.5(b)(2) for biologics and *id.* § 314.150(b)(2) for drugs.
[247] *Id.* §§ 601.5(b)(1)(vi), (b)(1)(iv) for biologics, and *id.* §§ 314.150(a)(2)(i), (a)(2)(ii), (b)(2) for drugs.
[248] *Id.* §§ 601.5(b)(1)(iv) (biologics), 314.150(b)(1) (drugs). The drug provision expressly provides for records inspections, whereas the biologics provision refers to standards established in the license, which may require records inspection, and standards established in this chapter designed to ensure the product's continued safety, purity and potency, which includes recordkeeping requirements Part 211, subpt. J.

Nevertheless, agency personnel generally regard license revocation to be much more readily available, easier to achieve, and more useful as an enforcement tool than drug approval withdrawal, for several reasons. First, several drug withdrawal provisions are more restrictive than the corresponding biologics revocation provisions. For example, a NOIR can be issued if the manufacturer fails to satisfy any requirement in the license or in any regulation designed to ensure the continued safety, purity, and potency of the product, without proving that the violation had any effect on the product.[249] In contrast, the drug regulations require a finding that the manufacturing controls, in fact, are inadequate to assure the drug's continued strength, identity, quality, and purity, and also require that the finding is based on at least some new information that the Secretary received since approving the drug.[250] Second, for drug approval suspension, the Secretary may not delegate its authority. In contrast, FDA's Commissioner has direct authority to suspend a biologics license and has further delegated that authority to the CBER and CDER Center Directors.[251] Moreover, the Center Directors may suspend a license any time they have "reasonable grounds" to believe that any ground for revocation poses a "danger to health,"[252] whereas the Secretary may suspend a drug approval only after finding that there is an "imminent hazard" to the public health resulting from one of the five mandatory reasons for withdrawal.[253]

Finally, the license revocation and suspension provisions can be tailored more easily than can the NDA withdrawal provisions. Drug approval withdrawal is an all-or-nothing remedy. If one particular location where the drug is being manufactured is out of compliance, withdrawing the NDA prohibits the company from distributing the drug completely, even where the drug is made at other, completely compliant locations. In contrast, license revocation can be more narrowly circumscribed. Before Congress merged PLAs and ELAs into consolidated BLAs,[254] FDA could revoke the ELA for just one location found to be out of compliance, or just one product within a multiproduct manufacturing facility. After Congress created the unified BLA, the revocation regulation was adjusted to retain its ability to focus the remedy. Specifically, at the same time as a license suspension or revocation, FDA may issue a new biologics license that excludes the location or locations that fail to comply with the regulations.[255]

This may be done without a request or submission from the manufacturer. Consequently, an applicant's license to market a biologic manufactured at a particular facility may be revoked, while allowing the applicant to continue to market that same biologic to the extent it is manufactured in other, compliant facilities. Conversely, in the case of multiple products included under a single biologics license application, FDA may re-issue the BLA, excluding any noncompliant products, at the same time that it suspends or revokes a biologics license for the noncompliant products. It may do so without any request or application from the applicant. In that way, license revocation is not the all-or-nothing remedy that drug approval withdrawal is.

---

[249]   *Id.* § 601.5(b)(1)(iv).
[250]   *Id.* § 314.150.
[251]   FDA STAFF MANUAL GUIDES, § 1410.203 (2003).
[252]   21 C.F.R. § 601.6.
[253]   21 U.S.C. § 355(e).
[254]   Pub. L. No. 105-115, § 123(d), 111 Stat. 2295, 2324 (1997).
[255]   21 C.F.R. § 601.9.

Recall Orders

Some other fairly focused postapproval enforcement tools exist that are unique to biologics. For example, the PHSA itself contains a provision authorizing the issuance of an order to recall.[256] Specifically, the provision states that "[u]pon determination that a batch, lot, or other quantity of a product licensed under this section presents an imminent or substantial hazard for public health, the Secretary shall issue an order immediately ordering the recall of such batch, lot, or the quantity of such product."[257] That provision allows FDA to pursue a focused remedy, by limiting regulatory action to just those batches, lots, or quantities of product that are determined to be problematic. In addition, Congress provided FDA with substantial power to enforce such a mandatory recall. Specifically, it provides civil money penalties of up to $100,000 per day for violating such a mandatory recall order.[258] This specific grant of recall authority illustrates Congress' view that lot-to-lot variability in biologics manufacturing requires narrowly focused enforcement tools.

Interestingly, the agency has never issued a mandatory recall order, to the best of our knowledge. Several factors probably can account for that. First, the success of the voluntary recall provisions has made it largely unnecessary to invoke any mandatory recall authority.[259] Second, like for the "imminent hazard to the public health" language in the drug approval suspension provision, FDA has interpreted the "imminent or substantial hazard for public health" language in the mandatory recall provision as very significant, and not to be imposed lightly. Finally, section 351(d) requires that a mandatory recall order be issued in accordance with the Administrative Procedure Act including the requirement that FDA afford the company notice and an opportunity for a hearing. Such hearings have tended to be avoided because they are highly labor intensive. For that reason, the agency greatly favors voluntary recalls, and maximizes its leverage to convince biologics manufacturers to conduct a voluntary recall whenever necessary.

Civil Money Penalties

To the best of our knowledge, FDA has also never used the narrowly focused civil money penalty authorities for biologics. The provision mentioned above authorizing civil money penalties for violating a mandatory biologic recall order has never been triggered, given that FDA has never issued such an order. The PHSA also authorizes civil money penalties against any vaccine manufacturer who intentionally destroys, alters, falsifies or conceals any record or report that the PHSA requires for vaccines that state laws make mandatory, or for vaccines covered by the National Vaccine Injury Compensation Act.[260] To the best of our knowledge, FDA has never sought civil money penalties under that provision of the PHSA. One reason, perhaps, is that imposing such penalties requires resource-intensive civil money penalty hearings, following specified procedures.[261]

---

[256]   42 U.S.C. § 262(d)(1).
[257]   *Id.*
[258]   42 U.S.C. § 262(d)(2).
[259]   *See* FRED H. DEGNAN, FDA'S CREATIVE APPLICATION OF THE LAW: NOT MERELY A COLLECTION OF WORDS (FDLI, 2d ed. 2006).
[260]   PHSA § 2128, 42 U.S.C. § 300aa-28.
[261]   21 C.F.R. § 17.1(g).

Court-Ordered Injunctions and Consent Decrees

Other notable enforcement options have involved violations of current good manufacturing practices by blood establishments. The AIDS crisis in the 1980s and 1990s brought intense focus on the blood industry and revealed widespread violative practices. FDA therefore adopted an aggressive policy of seeking court-ordered injunctions or consent decrees against the majority of major U.S. blood establishments. Although bringing those cases required significant resources initially, the flexibility that a court-ordered injunction or consent decree could provide achieved the leverage that FDA believed to be necessary to bring the blood industry into compliance. The FDCA provides U.S. district courts with jurisdiction to restrain most prohibited acts set forth in the FDCA.[262] It does not limit the remedies that district courts may use to restrain those violations, and FDA and the Department of Justice have convinced courts to use that flexibility to craft narrowly tailored remedies to bring blood establishments into compliance. A court-ordered consent decree with the American Red Cross issued in 1993 and amended in 2006 illustrates this point. The decree gave FDA the authority to levy civil money penalties for failure to comply with the terms of the decree.[263]

This flexible approach has also been utilized for other biologics. When FDA discovered extensive cGMP violations in the manufacture of certain medically necessary products,[264] it sought the remedy of disgorgement because it could not seek an injunction to shut down the manufacture of medically necessary products. The theory was that although it could not afford to have a stoppage in making the products, the agency could seek a court order forcing the disgorgement of all profits that the manufacturer derives from those noncompliant products.[265] The goal was to encourage the investment of the money necessary to bring the manufacturing facilities into full compliance, without depriving the public of important products in the interim period.[266]

Postapproval Manufacturing Changes Supplements

FDA does not limit its postapproval surveillance of biologics to simply ensuring that they meet the existing specifications and requirements of the BLA and existing regulations. As new information arises that has the potential to impact product specifications, manufacturers are obligated to investigate and implement scientifically sound changes as appropriate. Consequently, it is the manufacturer's responsibility under the cGMP regulations not only to establish appropriate specifications for their biologics, but also to continually improve their processes based on information accumulated from batch manufacturing, monitoring, and testing. For that reason, biologics regulations provide a process for manufacturers to

---

[262] 21 U.S.C. § 302.

[263] Amended Consent Decree of Permanent Injunction, United States v. American National Red Cross (D.D.C. Jan. 30, 2006), *available at* http://www.fda.gov/ora/frequent/letters/ARC_Amended_ Decree_1.html, at 54-55.

[264] Consent Decree of Condemnation and Permanent Injunction, United States v. Various Articles of Drug (Wyeth-Ayerst Laboratories), 3:00-CV-359 (E.D. Tenn. Oct. 3, 2000).

[265] *Id.* at ¶ 16.

[266] This disgorgement remedy has been controversial and subject to much debate. *See* W. Vodra & A. Levine, *Use of Disgorgement by FDA Under Recent Court Decisions*, PHARM. L. & INDUS. REPORT, Apr. 21, 2006.

"supplement" their BLAs (or NDAs) with information on manufacturing changes that they implement over time based on new information and experience.[267]

The regulatory provisions identify the criteria for determining whether such a change needs to be submitted as a supplement for pre-approval by FDA, as a changes being effected supplement (CBE), as changes being effected in 30 days supplement (CBE-30), or as an annual report. Some important differences exist between drugs and biologics. For example, the biologics regulations acknowledge that manufacturers may need to demonstrate through clinical studies (other than bioavailability or bioequivalence studies) that certain changes in the product, production process, quality controls, equipment, facilities, responsible personnel, or labeling do not adversely affect safety or effectiveness, whereas in vitro or in vivo bioequivalence studies may suffice for drugs.[268] Interestingly, FDA has treated applications for annual influenza vaccines as manufacturing supplements that do not require clinical data and allow for quick approval, even though the strain of the virus material in the vaccine often changes annually.[269]

Manufacturers planning postapproval chemistry, manufacturing, and control (CMC) changes could consider submitting a comparability protocol in a supplement.[270] Congress expanded the concept of comparability protocols to drugs as well as biologics in the federal Food and Drug Administration Modernization Act of 1997.[271] Such protocols represent agency- and manufacturer-negotiated agreements concerning the types of studies required to demonstrate that a specific CMC change does not have an adverse effect on the identity, strength, quality, purity, and potency as these factors relate to the safety and effectiveness of the product.

Establishment Inspections

Although the responsibility for monitoring the need to make changes to biologics based on new experience and information remains with the manufacturer, FDA has several other postapproval tools for ensuring not only that manufacturers meet all existing specifications, but also that they adjust those specifications as new information and experience dictates. One fundamental tool is not unique to biologics: establishment inspections. As discussed above, the Secretary may not approve a biologics license application unless "the applicant (or other appropriate person) consents to the inspection of the facility that is the subject of the application," in accordance with subsection (c) of section 351.

Subsection (c), in turn, provides that "[a]ny officer, agent, or employee of the Department of Health and Human Services, authorized by the Secretary for the purpose, may during all reasonable hours enter and inspect any establishment for the propagation or manufacture and preparation of any biological product."[272] Although that language might appear to provide

---

[267] See 21 C.F.R. §§ 601.12 and 314.70.

[268] Compare 21 C.F.R. § 601.12(b)(2)(ii) with 21 C.F.R. § 314.70(b)(2)(ii).

[269] Presentation by Karen Midthun, Director of FDA Office of Vaccines Research and Review, *Workshop on the Development of a Clinical Trial Plan for Pandemic Influenza Vaccines: Regulatory Considerations* (Sept. 22-23, 2003) (*available at* http://www3.niaid.nih.gov/about/organization/ dmid/PDF/midthun.pdf).

[270] See 21 C.F.R. § 601.12(e); 21 C.F.R. § 314.70(e).

[271] See FDAMA, § 116.

[272] 42 U.S.C. § 262 (c).

a blank check for the inspection of any records, spaces, or objects within a facility that is in any way involved in manufacturing a biologic, FDA's inspection authority for biologics also is subject to the limitations under the FDCA.[273] FDA investigators must restrict their inspection to records and things related to determining whether products within the facility are adulterated or misbranded, or otherwise in violation of the law.

Although the legal scope of inspections for biologics is, therefore, the same as that for drugs, the expertise necessary to conduct those inspections can vary for biologics. Consequently, FDA uses an approach called "Team Biologics," where inspection teams are assembled that include scientists with a range of expertise necessary to conduct a biologics inspection. The team usually consists of at least one product specialist from CBER (or from CDER, if the product is a therapeutic biologic), one field inspector from the Office of Regulatory Affairs, and sometimes a microbiologist, chemist, toxicologist or other scientists with specialized expertise. This approach recognizes that in general biologics can be highly complex and that to conduct a meaningful review of the manufacturing records requires a certain level of background and experience.[274]

Postapproval Reporting Requirements

Another postapproval tool for ensuring that biologics continue to be safe, pure and potent pertains to reporting requirements.

Biological Product Deviation Reports (BPDRs)

BPDRs are required where a distributed biologic involves either 1) a deviation from current good manufacturing practice, applicable regulations, applicable standards, or established specifications that may affect the safety, purity, or potency of the product; or 2) an unexpected or unforeseeable event that may affect the safety, purity, or potency of the product.[275] License holders who had control over the products when the deviation occurred have this reporting obligation. If the deviation occurred while the contract manufacturer was performing processing steps for the license holder, the license holder still has the duty to report the deviation.[276] This provision gives FDA access to information about manufacturing steps and other processes that take place on the way to distribution that may affect a biologic's safety, purity, or potency. This means that BLA license holders are required to develop systems to ensure that contract manufacturers, distributors, and other such vendors report product deviations received by the company or its agents to the BLA holder in a timely manner. Notably, drug manufacturers do not have a comparable product deviation reporting requirement. They are, however, required to submit field alert reports

---

[273]   21 U.S.C. § 374.

[274]   FDA, Investigations Operations Manual, § 5.7.2 (2011).

[275]   21 C.F.R. § 600.14 (b) (1)

[276]   Certain manufacturers who have deviation reporting obligations under other regulatory provisions are exempted from the requirements of this section. Specifically, those who manufacture only in vitro diagnostic products not subject to licensing must report under Part 803 of the device regulations, rather than under section 600.14. Those who manufacture blood and blood components must report deviations instead under section 606.171. Blood and blood components are deemed to be in the control of the licensed manufacturer, unlicensed registered blood establishment or transfusion service even if one of those entities has contracted or otherwise arranged with another entity to manufacture, hold, or distribute the product while under its control. Id. § 606.171(a). Licensed manufacturers are required to develop, maintain, and follow procedures with such entities to receive reports of deviations, complaints, and adverse experience. See id.

informing the agency of any bacterial contamination; any significant chemical, physical, or other change or deterioration in the distributed product; and any failure of one of the batches of the drug product to meet specifications.[277]

Adverse Experience Reporting and Recordkeeping

Another postapproval reporting requirement is adverse experience reporting, which is not very different from that for drugs. Licensed biologics manufacturers must promptly review all adverse experience information pertaining to their products that they receive from any source, and must report adverse events at different intervals depending on their seriousness and relationship to the biologic.[278] For serious and unexpected adverse experiences, licensed manufacturers must report them no later than 15 calendar days after first learning about them.[279] For adverse experiences not included in 15-day alert reports, licensed manufacturers must report them to FDA at quarterly intervals for three years after receiving a license, and then annually.[280] Manufacturers are required to review all reports of possible adverse event information relating to their products received by the company or its agents from any source, both domestic and foreign, including information from spontaneous reports from commercial use of the products, postmarketing clinical investigations, postmarketing epidemiological/surveillance studies, reports in scientific literature, and unpublished reports in company files or received from other sources.[281] Importantly, companies must report adverse experiences described by these sources, including any adverse event temporally associated with the use of the product in humans regardless whether it was product-related.[282] This includes adverse events resulting from an overdose, abuse of the product, and withdrawal of the product and failure of the product to have its expected pharmacologic action.[283]

In addition to the reporting requirements, licensed companies are required to retain records on adverse experiences, including raw data and any correspondence relating to the adverse experiences, for 10 years.[284] As discussed above, failing to establish and maintain records and to make the required reports is grounds for FDA to revoke a biologics license. The 10-year record maintenance requirement reflects the understanding that adverse effects from biologics and drugs are not always readily apparent[285] and sometimes difficult to connect with the treatment.[286]

---

[277] 21 C.F.R. § 314.81(b)(1).

[278] Id. § 600.80.

[279] Id. § 600.80 (c)(1).

[280] Id. § 600.80 (c)(2).

[281] Id. § 600.80(b).

[282] 21 C.F.R. § 600.80(a).

[283] Id.

[284] Id. § 600.80 (i)

[285] For example, a pig virus that can be passed to humans by certain therapeutic agents and tissues and is associated with "mad cow disease" and Creutzfeld-Jakob Disease (CJD) can lie dormant for decades after exposure.

[286] For example, patients with multiple sclerosis taking interferons have reported depression and suicidal ideation, both of which could be attributable to the progression of the disease itself or the therapeutic agent. FDA added a class warning to the labeling of these products in 2003.

Vaccine Adverse Event Reporting and Recordkeeping Provisions

For biologics that are vaccines, additional sources of postapproval requirements exist. First, Congress mandated additional recordkeeping and adverse event reporting for vaccines covered by the National Vaccine Injury Compensation Program.[287] The program provides compensation to individuals who develop certain recognized adverse reactions to vaccines, without their having to prove causality.[288] Those recognized vaccine adverse experiences are set forth in a table, the Vaccine Injury Table, in the PHSA.[289] The Secretary has authority to amend the Vaccine Injury Table by regulation,[290] and has done so.[291]

For vaccines listed on the Vaccine Injury Table, each healthcare provider who administers such vaccines must record in the recipient's permanent medical record certain important information: 1) vaccination date; 2) manufacturer name and lot number; 3) healthcare provider name and address; and 4) other identifying information on the vaccine.[292] Each healthcare provider and vaccine manufacturer must also report the occurrence of any event listed on the Vaccine Injury Table and the occurrence of the any adverse reaction to a vaccine that is listed in the contraindication section of the manufacturer's package insert.[293] Finally, each manufacturer of a vaccine listed on the Vaccine Injury Table, or of a vaccine that is mandated by the law or regulations of any state, must maintain records on the manufacturing history of each of the vaccines, including significant problems encountered in the production, testing or handling.[294] Manufacturers must also report within 24 hours the result of any safety test that indicates a potential imminent or substantial public health hazard, and to prepare, maintain, and upon request submit vaccine distribution records for those vaccine lots, batches, or quantities.[295]

To receive and accommodate the information required under the above provisions, the Vaccine Adverse Event Reporting System (VAERS) exists, which FDA and the Centers for Disease Control and Prevention (CDC) co-manage. The system satisfies the need to receive and collect the information that vaccine manufacturers and healthcare providers must report under the PHSA, but also is set up to receive other voluntary reports, such as reports from patients who have experienced health problems after receiving a vaccine.

---

[287] PHSA, tit. XXI, Subtitle 2.

[288] *Id.* § 2111(c)(1), 42 U.S.C. § 300aa-11(c)(1).

[289] *Id.* § 2114.

[290] *Id.* § 2114(c).

[291] *See, e.g.,* National Vaccine Injury Compensation Program: Addition of Trivalent Influenza Vaccines in the Injury Table, 70 Fed. Reg. 19,092, 19,029 (Apr. 12, 2005).

[292] PHSA § 2125(a), 42 U.S.C. § 300aa-25(a).

[293] *Id.* § 2125(b), 42 U.S.C. § 300aa-25(b).

[294] *Id.* § 2128(a)(1), 42 U.S.C. § 300aa-28(a)(1).

[295] *Id.* § 2128(a)(2)-(4), 42 U.S.C. § 300aa-28(a) (2)-(4). As mentioned previously, Congress provided a substantial penalty for any vaccine manufacturer who intentionally destroys, alters, falsifies, or conceals any record or report required by that section. PHSA § 2128(b), 42 U.S.C. § 300aa-28(b).

Conclusion

Since Congress first regulated biologics through the Biologics Control Act of 1902 the field has changed dramatically. Yet, some of the language from that first act of legislation, as well as the basic framework for licensing and regulating biologics, still remains intact, even though Congress has made various changes over the years. The biologics field will certainly continue to advance significantly as the biological sciences march forward. For now, however, FDA seems ready to regulate such changes by relying on the basic legal framework governing biologics, which has afforded it sufficient flexibility under most circumstances.

CHAPTER 15
BIOSIMILARS

....

ERIKA LIETZAN, EMILY ALEXANDER, AND LAURA SIM

In March 2010, Congress amended the Public Health Service Act (PHSA) and other statutes to create an approval pathway for biosimilars—biological products that are "highly similar" to reference biological products "notwithstanding minor differences in clinically inactive components" and that have no "clinically meaningful differences" from those reference products in terms of safety, purity, or potency.[1] This landmark legislation—the Biologics Price Competition and Innovation Act of 2009 (BPCIA)—represented the culmination of nearly 10 years of active stakeholder debate as well as four years of discussion of draft bills.[2]

FDA faces many scientific, legal, and policy decisions as it interprets and implements the new law. As of this writing, the agency had issued only a handful of draft guidance documents;[3] it had not finalized any guidance or issued proposed regulations. The agency had, however, approved one biosimilar under the new pathway and several applications were under review. In addition to any forthcoming guidance or regulations, FDA's continued review and approval of biosimilar applications will shed light on a number of key issues.

This chapter begins with a brief background on biosimilars, focusing on the U.S. legislative history, the current status at FDA, and the global landscape. It then discusses U.S. regulatory

---

[1] Patient Protection and Affordable Care Act, Pub. L. No. 111-148, tit. VII, subtit. A, 124 Stat. 119, 804 (2010); see PHSA § 351(i)(2); 42 U.S.C. § 262(i)(2) (defining "biosimilar").

[2] For a detailed legislative history, see Krista Hessler Carver, Jeffrey Elikan & Erika Lietzan, An Unofficial Legislative History of the Biologics Price Competition and Innovation Act of 2009, 65 FOOD & DRUG L.J. 671 (2010).

[3] FDA, Draft Guidance for Industry: Biosimilars: Questions and Answers Regarding Implementation of the Biologics Price Competition and Innovation Act of 2009 (February 2012) [hereinafter Q&A Guidance]; FDA, Draft Guidance for Industry: Quality Considerations in Demonstrating Biosimilarity to a Reference Protein Product (February 2012) [hereinafter Quality Guidance]: FDA, Draft Guidance for Industry: Scientific Considerations in Demonstrating Biosimilarity to a Reference Product (February 2012) [hereinafter Scientific Considerations Guidance]; FDA, Draft Guidance for Industry, Formal Meetings Between the FDA and Biosimilar Product Sponsors or Applicants (March 2013) [hereinafter Formal Meetings Guidance]; FDA, Draft Guidance for Industry: Clinical Pharmacology Data to Support a Demonstration of Biosimilarity to a Reference Product (May 2014) [hereinafter Clinical Pharmacology Guidance]; FDA, Draft Guidance for Industry: Reference Product Exclusivity for Biological Products Filed Under Section 351(a) of the PHSA (August 2014) [hereinafter Exclusivity Guidance].

requirements issue by issue, drawing from the statute, the draft guidance documents and, where necessary, public statements from the agency. It also identifies open issues as of this writing, as well as key stakeholder views. A discussion of patent litigation provisions, drawing from the statute, stakeholder comments, and pending or recent litigation, follows. Again, open issues and stakeholder views are identified. The chapter ends with a brief conclusion.

Background

Enactment of the BPCIA

A "biological product" is a "virus, therapeutic serum, toxin, antitoxin, vaccine, blood, blood component or derivative, allergenic product, protein (except any chemically synthesized peptide), or analogous product, . . . applicable to the prevention, treatment, or cure of a disease or condition of human beings."[4] Generally speaking, biologics are manufactured through biologic synthesis; they are manufactured in or extracted from living systems. A biological product may not be introduced into interstate commerce without a biologics license application (BLA) approved under the PHSA.[5] Most biological products also fall within the definition of "drug" in the Federal Food, Drug, and Cosmetic Act (FDCA), but the PHSA exempts biological products with approved licenses from the otherwise applicable new drug application (NDA) requirement.[6]

The overlap between "biological products" and "drugs" is at least partly responsible for the fact that several protein products have been marketed under NDAs when they could in theory have been regulated as biologics with approved BLAs.[7] These include bovine-derived and porcine-derived insulins, human growth hormone derived from human cadavers, and conjugated estrogens derived from the urine of pregnant mares. All were all regulated under NDAs, despite the fact that these products shared a key characteristic with many biologics: a manufacturing process that involved extraction from animals.[8] FDA also approved the first biotechnology product—a recombinant human insulin product—under an NDA in 1982, just as it had approved the product's naturally derived insulin predecessors.[9]

Because a number of protein products hold approved NDAs, a handful of follow-on protein products have been approved under the Hatch-Waxman provisions of the FDCA. The approval of Omnitrope (somatropin [rDNA origin]) in May 2006, in particular, helped

---

4   PHSA § 351(i), 42 U.S.C. § 262(i). As part of the BPCIA, Congress amended this definition to include proteins, except for "chemically synthesized polypeptides."

5   PHSA § 351(a)(1), 42 U.S.C. § 262(a)(1).

6   *See* PHSA § 351(j), 42 U.S.C. § 262(j) ("The Federal Food, Drug, and Cosmetic Act, including the requirements under sections 505(o), 505(p), and 505-1 of such Act, applies to a biological product subject to regulation under this section, except that a product for which a license has been approved under subsection (a) shall not be required to have an approved application under section 505 of such Act.").

7   These products are proteins, however, and likely satisfy the new definition of "biological product." The BPCIA contains special transition provisions to address biosimilar versions of these products. The transition provisions are discussed later in this chapter.

8   JUDITH A. JOHNSON, CONG. RESEARCH SERV., FDA REGULATION OF FOLLOW-ON BIOLOGICS 6-7 (2009).

9   *Id.* at 1; HHS NEWS, P82-50 (Oct. 29, 1982).

to push the U.S. legislative process on biosimilars into motion. The 505(b)(2) application for this human growth hormone product relied on approval of the innovative reference product Genotropin (somatropin [rDNA origin]). According to the agency, the 505(b)(2) applicant had established that "Omnitrope is sufficiently similar to Genotropin to warrant reliance on FDA's finding of safety and effectiveness for Genotropin to support the approval of Omnitrope."[10] Chemistry, manufacturing, and controls (CMC) data showed that the active ingredient in Omnitrope was "highly similar, physiochemically" to Genotropin's active ingredient.[11] The applicant had also conducted three pivotal clinical trials that demonstrated the "clinical comparability" of the products.[12] Omnitrope is widely regarded as the first U.S. "biosimilar" product because it was the first recombinant follow-on version of a recombinant innovative product.

Just a few months after FDA approved Omnitrope, Representative Waxman introduced the first bill proposing a comprehensive biosimilar approval pathway.[13] In the summer of 2007, Senators Kennedy, Hatch, Enzi, and Clinton developed a legislative proposal, working with both the generic industry and the innovative industry, in the hopes of crafting a compromise that would have widespread support.[14] These efforts resulted in language that would eventually form the backbone for the BPCIA.[15] In 2008, the House took up discussion of biosimilars, with many bills echoing the Senate language in broad brush strokes.[16]

Early consensus emerged with respect to key aspects of the regulatory pathway for biosimilars including, for example, that clinical data would often or perhaps always be needed; that applications would vary in size and nature, perhaps by product class; that interchangeability designations would require additional thought in part because of immunogenicity risks; and that a public process for providing FDA with input on application requirements and other implementation issues was generally desirable. At the same time, stakeholders disagreed about some of the details, including whether FDA should have complete discretion with respect to application contents; whether and what sort of structural differences between a biosimilar and a reference product should be permitted; whether and how the legislation should address nonproprietary names, labeling, and packaging for biosimilars; and whether the legislation should address interchangeability.

The major hurdles, however, were the length of the exclusivity period for reference products and a concern of the generic industry that reference product sponsors would "evergreen" their products by developing second-generation versions of those products that would be entitled to their own 12-year exclusivity periods. Indeed, through 2009, negotiations in both the House and Senate primarily focused on the length and scope of the data exclusivity period. Once compromise was reached, the biosimilar legislation was included in the

---

10   Letter from Stephen K. Galson, M.D., M.P.H. Director, CDER, to Kathleen Sanzo, Stephan Lawton, & Stephen Juelsfaard, FDA Docket Nos. 2004P-0231, 2003P-0176 & 2004P-0171, at 8 (May 30, 2006).

11   *Id.* at 9 (footnote omitted).

12   *Id.* at 10.

13   H.R. 6257, 109th Cong. (2006).

14   *Generic Biologics May See Life After PDUFA; Senate Mark-Up Possible in May*, F-D-C REP. ("The Pink Sheet"), Apr. 23, 2007, at 6.

15   S. 1695, 110th Cong. (2007).

16   *Bush Proposes Biosimilars in Budget; CBO Working to Score Savings*, FDA WEEK, Feb. 8, 2008; *Biogenerics Bill From Reps. Eshoo and Barton "Expects" Limits on Substitution*, F-D-C REP. ("The Pink Sheet"), Feb. 25, 2008, at 3.

consolidated healthcare reform package, which President Obama signed into law on March 23, 2010.

The Global Landscape

The U.S. legislative process took place, and the current FDA implementation process is taking place, within a larger global context that includes a relatively well-developed European biosimilar pathway. European authorities developed their framework for approval of biosimilars in 2003, fleshed it out in a series of highly detailed guidance documents beginning in 2004, and began to approve biosimilars in 2006—the year the U.S. legislative process began in earnest. The developing European framework put pressure on Congress to develop a similar pathway in a timely fashion and offered a scientifically vetted and workable model. European authorities have since steadily approved biosimilars in a variety of product classes, often proposed by applicants who ultimately intend to propose the same products in the United States and for global markets.[17] Although FDA may request different or additional information from these applicants, it is hard to escape the conclusion that so long as European approval generally precedes approval in the United States, the thinking of the European Medicines Agency (EMA) on biosimilar application requirements will be influential.

The process began in Europe with an amendment to Annex I of Directive 2001/83/EC to provide for a new marketing authorization procedure for "similar biological medicinal products."[18] This new provision recognized that the typical generic approval pathway generally would not be appropriate for biologics and that additional "toxicological and other non-clinical and appropriate clinical data" would be needed. The precise nature of the additional data was to be described in guidelines. The amendment to the Annex took effect in October 2003 and was later confirmed by an amendment to the directive itself.[19]

The EMA implemented the legislative amendments through a series of general guidelines on preclinical, clinical, and quality issues,[20] as well as a series of guidelines specific to individual product classes.[21] The general guidelines, and the early class-specific guidelines,

---

[17]   In 2006, the European Commission (EC) approved two biosimilars containing somatropin, the human growth hormone: Omnitrope and Valtropin. More than a dozen biosimilars are now approved in the European Union (EU), including biosimilar erythropoietin, filgrastim, insulin glargine, and infliximab products. Other applications, however, have been subject to negative opinions from the European authorities or withdrawn by the sponsor.

[18]   Directive 2001/83/EC of the European Parliament and of the Council, as amended 2003 O.J. (L159) 46, Annex I, Part II, Section 4.

[19]   Directive 2001/83/EC of the European Parliament and of the Council, as amended 2004 O.J. (L136) 34.

[20]   *See* EMA, Guideline on Similar Biological Medicinal Products (CHMP/437/04) (October 2005); EMA, Guideline on Similar Biological Medicinal Products Containing Biotechnology-Derived Proteins as Active Substance: Quality Issues (EMEA/CHMP/BWP/49348/2005) (February 2006); EMA, Guideline on Similar Biological Medicinal Products Containing Biotechnology-Derived Proteins as Active Substance: Non-Clinical and Clinical Issues (EMEA/CHMP/BMWP/42832/2005) (February 2006). The EMA has revised, or begun revising, all of these. *E.g.*, EMA, Guideline on Similar Biological Medicinal Products Containing Biotechnology-Derived Proteins as Active Substance: Quality Issues (EMA/CHMP/BWP/247713/2012) (May 2014).

[21]   *See, e.g.*, EMA, Guidance on Similar Medicinal Products Containing Recombinant Human Soluble Insulin (EMEA/CHMP/BMWP/32775/2005) (February 2006). The EMA continues to issue new product class guidelines, even as it revises some of the older ones. *E.g.*, EMA, Guideline on Non-Clinical and Clinical Development of Similar Biological Medicinal Products Containing Recombinant Human Follicle-Stimulating

issued in the early stages of the U.S. legislative process. As a general rule, they require physical, chemical, and biological characterization of each biosimilar, in comparison with the reference product. The guidelines also require comparative nonclinical studies assessing pharmacodynamics, pharmacokinetics, toxicity, and any special safety concerns, as well as comparative clinical trials that begin with pharmacokinetics and pharmacodynamics studies, followed by safety and efficacy trials (using, if appropriate, validated surrogate endpoints in lieu of clinical endpoints). The biosimilarity of each therapeutic indication must ordinarily be separately justified, but the European Union (EU) does allow extrapolation of data submitted for one indication to support approval of other indications, if scientifically justified. The guidelines also require immunogenicity testing both before and after approval.

Similar frameworks for the approval of biosimilars were developed in Canada and Japan, for example, in the years that followed,[22] and in 2009 the World Health Organization (WHO) issued a similar draft guideline for national regulatory authorities to consider.[23] Lawmakers and regulators around the globe have continued to develop pathways for the approval of biosimilars—many fashioned implicitly, or explicitly, on the European, WHO, and U.S. models.[24] Many biosimilar applicants continue to seek approval first in Europe, but some have started in other parts of the world.

Some differences have begun to emerge in countries' scientific judgments on particular issues, such as extrapolation. In 2013, for example, the European Commission approved a biosimilar infliximab that had been studied clinically in two diseases (rheumatoid arthritis and ankylosing spondylitis). The European Commission approved the biosimilar for all the indications of its reference product, including for the treatment of inflammatory bowel disorders (Crohn's disease and ulcerative colitis).[25] In contrast, when Health Canada approved this biosimilar in January 2014 on the basis of a similar data package as the one submitted in Europe, it did not approve it for the inflammatory bowel disorders.[26] Health Canada determined that it could not recommend extrapolation to Crohn's disease and ulcerative colitis "due to differences between [the biosimilar] and the reference product, that could have an impact on the clinical safety and efficacy of these products in these indications."[27]

Hormone (r-hFSH) (EMEA/BMWP/671292/2010) (February 2013); EMA, Guideline on Non-Clinical and Clinical Development of Similar Biological Medicinal Products Containing Recombinant Erythropoietins (EMEA/CHMP/BMWP/301638/2008) (April 2010) (superseding earlier erythropoietin guideline).

[22] *See* Health Products and Food Branch, Health Canada, Guidance for Sponsors: Information and Submission Requirements for Subsequent Entry Biologics (SEBs) (Mar. 5, 2010); Japan Ministry of Health, Labor and Welfare, Guideline for the Quality, Safety and Efficacy Assurance of Follow-on Biologics (PFSB/ELD Notification No. 0304007) (March 2009).

[23] Expert Comm. on Biological Standardization, WHO, Guidelines on Evaluation of Similar Biotherapeutic Products (SBPs) (2009).

[24] Ministry of Food and Drug Safety, Republic of Korea, Guidelines on the Evaluation of Biosimilar Products (2009).

[25] *See* EMA, Remsima (infliximab): EPAR (European Public Assessment Report) Summary for the Public, EMA/407240/2013 (September 2013).

[26] *See* Health Canada, Remsima Summary Basis for Decision (Jan. 4, 2014).

[27] *Id.* ("[S]ince differences in ADCC [Antibody-Dependent Cell-Mediated Cytotoxicity] have been observed between the [biosimilar and the reference product] and because ADCC may be an active mechanism of action for infliximab in the setting of IBD, but not in the setting of rheumatic disease (the studied populations), extrapolation from the settings of rheumatoid arthritis and ankylosing spondylitis to IBD cannot be recommended due to the absence of clinical studies in IBD.").

FDA Regulation of Biosimilars

Approval Standard

FDA must approve an application submitted under the biosimilar pathway, section 351(k) of the PHSA, if the agency determines that the information in the application is sufficient to show that the product is biosimilar to or interchangeable with the reference product and if the applicant (or other appropriate person) consents to a manufacturing inspection.[28] A product is biosimilar if it is "highly similar" to a reference product "notwithstanding minor differences in clinically inactive components" and it has no "clinically meaningful differences" from the reference product "in terms of the safety, purity, and potency."[29] The agency has not offered definitions of "highly similar" or "clinically meaningful differences," instead explaining that it will use a "totality-of-the-evidence" approach to determining whether an applicant meets the 351(a) standard.[30]

FDA confirmed in draft guidance that a biosimilarity exercise is different from, and may require more extensive and comprehensive data than, a comparability exercise. Comparability is the process by which a manufacturer of a biological product ensures the continuing quality, safety and efficacy of the product after a manufacturing change.[31] The goal of the exercise is to determine that the quality attributes of the pre-change and post-change product "are highly similar and that the existing knowledge is sufficiently predictive to ensure that any differences in quality attributes have no adverse impact upon safety or efficacy of the drug product."[32] During debate on legislation to establish a biosimilar pathway, several stakeholders had argued that the same process, standard, and data requirements should be used for both exercises, but others adamantly opposed efforts to analogize the exercises. In 2007, a key FDA official had explained that the exercises are not the same, stating that "it should be clear that demonstrating the similarity of a follow-on protein product to a reference product will typically be more complex, and thus require more new data, than assessing the similarity of products before and after manufacturing changes made by the approved product's sponsor."[33] The position taken in the February 2012 draft guidance is generally consistent with this comment.[34] Some stakeholders have raised the concern that biologic sponsors might ask FDA to approve applications filed under section 351(a) that nevertheless invite the agency to rely, directly or indirectly, on

---

[28]   PHSA § 351(k)(3), 42 U.S.C. § 262(k)(3).

[29]   PHSA § 351(i)(2), 42 U.S.C. § 262(i)(2).

[30]   *E.g.*, Scientific Considerations Guidance, *supra*, at 8 (emphasis omitted). It *did* note that clinically meaningful differences "could include a difference in the expected range of safety, purity, and potency" but added that "slight differences in rates of occurrence of adverse events . . . ordinarily would not be considered clinically meaningful differences." *Id.*

[31]   FDA, Guidance for Industry: Q5E Comparability of Biotechnological/Biological Products Subject to Changes in Their Manufacturing Process 3 (June 2005).

[32]   *Id.*

[33]   *See Assessing the Impact of a Safe and Equitable Biosimilar Policy in the United States: Hearing Before the Subcomm. on Health of the House Comm. on Energy and Commerce*, 110th Cong. 31 (2007) (statement of Janet Woodcock, M.D., Deputy Commissioner, Chief Medical Officer, FDA).

[34]   Nevertheless, some stakeholders have continued to encourage FDA to treat a biosimilarity demonstration between two products as it would a comparability demonstration involving a single product before and after a manufacturing change. Some have argued, for example, that the comparability approach is appropriate given that FDA may know more about a biosimilar upon approval (in light of postmarket experience with the reference product) than it typically knows about an innovative product upon approval.

the data in a previously approved application, or on a finding of safety, purity, and potency relating to a previously approved biological product (so-called "skinny BLAs"). If filed under section 351(a), such an application would not be subject to the exclusivity period that delays biosimilar approvals, nor would it be subject to the patent litigation provisions of section 351(l). Some stakeholders have suggested that Congress intended these applications to be submitted under section 351(k) and have asked the agency to categorize incoming applications using certain presumptions—such as a presumption that any application containing comparative analytical data, asserting similarity to a previously approved product, or proposing a product that has been approved as a biosimilar elsewhere in the world, should be submitted under section 351(k). The agency did not address this issue in its 2012 or 2014 draft guidance documents. The lawfulness of these "skinny BLAs" could be settled in the courts, particularly if—as some have suggested—there is a constitutional dimension to allowing applications that are effectively "biosimilar applications" to be filed without regard to exclusivity and premarket patent litigation.[35]

The Biosimilar Application

Contents

Every biosimilar application must include information demonstrating that the product is biosimilar to a reference product based on data from: 1) analytical studies that demonstrate that the two products are highly similar "notwithstanding minor differences in clinically inactive components"; 2) animal studies, including toxicology studies; and 3) one or more clinical studies, including an assessment of immunogenicity.[36] FDA has the authority to waive any of these data requirements, although the applicant must still demonstrate biosimilarity.[37]

FDA's draft guidance documents recommend a "stepwise" approach to demonstrating biosimilarity—a concept that has broad support among stakeholders. This approach "can include" comparative testing regarding structure, function, animal toxicity, human pharmacokinetics and pharmacodynamics, clinical immunogenicity, and clinical safety and effectiveness. At each step, the applicant should identify residual uncertainties about the biosimilarity of the product and design the next step to address them. A "selective and targeted approach to animal and/or clinical testing" might be appropriate in any particular case if, among other things: 1) comparative characterization shows minimal differences between the products; 2) a "*fingerprint*-like" analysis algorithm is available; 3) existing clinical knowledge elucidates the relevance of structural differences; and/or 4) a clinically relevant pharmacodynamics marker is available.[38] Some have cautioned that not

---

[35] In 2012, FDA approved an application filed under section 351(a) for Granix (tbo-filgrastim), a filgrastim product sponsored by Teva and marketed by Teva in Europe under a biosimilar marketing authorization application. Teva's U.S. application contained the results of additional research not presented to the European regulators, however, and the agency expressly declined to consider published literature relating to a product other than Teva's product. In any case, it appears that the application was not meaningfully smaller in size than Amgen's 351(a) application for Neupogen (filgrastim). Amgen's non-U.S. Neupogen was the active comparator in Teva's clinical trials. Teva filed this application prior to the enactment of the BPCIA. Whether FDA would (or could) permit this use of section 351(a) now, after enactment of the BPCIA, is unclear.

[36] PHSA § 351(k)(2)(A)(i)(I), 42 U.S.C. § 262(k)(2)(A)(i)(I).

[37] PHSA § 351(k)(2)(A)(ii), 42 U.S.C. § 262(k)(2)(A)(ii).

[38] *E.g.*, Scientific Considerations Guidance, *supra*, at 7.

all data warrant equal weight and some steps may need to take place in parallel rather than sequentially. And while some stakeholders support the concept of fingerprint-like analyses as a means to reduce residual uncertainty about potential differences, many commenters on FDA's 2012 draft guidances asked the agency to provide additional information about the type of analysis it envisions when it uses this term.

Analytical Testing. Analytical studies provide the foundation for an assessment of a proposed biosimilar and the extent of its similarity to its reference product.[39] Indeed, if the reference product and proposed biosimilar cannot be "adequately characterized," the proposed biosimilar may not be appropriate for an application using the section 351(k) pathway.[40] FDA has therefore explained that "[e]xtensive, robust comparative physicochemical and functional studies" should be performed to assess analytical similarity.[41] A "meaningful assessment" of similarity will turn on "the capabilities of available state-of-the-art analytical assays to assess, for example," higher order structure and post-translational modifications, degree of heterogeneity, impurity profiles, and degradation profiles.[42] Physicochemical and functional characterization studies should establish quality attributes that define product identity, quantity, purity, potency, and consistency.[43] Impurities should be identified, characterized as appropriate, quantified, and compared to those of the reference product to the extent feasible and relevant.[44] Identification and determination of the relative levels of protein variants should be included in the comparative analytical characterization studies.[45] Acceptance criteria should be based on the totality of the analytical data and not simply on the range of product attributes of the reference product.

The analytical standard seems to mean at least that the primary amino acid sequence should be identical,[46] although FDA has noted that minor modifications in primary amino acid sequence, such as N or C terminal truncations that do not have an effect on safety, purity, or potency, may be justified by the applicant.[47] Apart from this comment about the amino acid sequence, FDA has generally eschewed specifics about its expectations for the analytical characterization—leaving itself and sponsors with considerable flexibility to tailor the balance of the application according to the results of the preliminary work. Indeed, according to FDA, the comparative analytical characterization will lead to one of four findings: 1) not similar, in which case further development through the 351(k) pathway is not recommended; 2) similar, in which case further information is needed to determine if the product is highly similar; 3) highly similar, in which case the product meets the statutory standard for analytical similarity (i.e., "high confidence in the analytical similarity" and "it would be appropriate for the sponsor to conduct targeted and selected animal and/or clinical studies to resolve residual uncertainty"); and 4) "highly similar with fingerprint-like similarity," in which case it would be "appropriate for the sponsor to use a *more* targeted and selective approach."[48] FDA has therefore signaled that even when the comparative

---

[39]   Scientific Considerations Guidance, *supra*, at 7, 9; Q&A Guidance, *supra*, at 4; Quality Guidance, *supra*, at 4.
[40]   Quality Guidance, *supra*, at 4.
[41]   *Id.* at 6.
[42]   *Id.*
[43]   *Id.*
[44]   *Id.*
[45]   *Id.* at 7.
[46]   Scientific Considerations Guidance, *supra*, at 9.
[47]   *Id.*
[48]   Clinical Pharmacology Guidance, *supra*, at 6 (emphasis added).

analytical work shows that the products are only "similar"—i.e., not satisfying the statutory standard—additional "analytical data or other studies" may be sufficient to establish that they are "highly similar."[49] It offered the example of using comparative pharmacokinetic and pharmacodynamic studies to "resolve" differences in glycosylation patterns.[50]

Drift. Over time, biologic companies often make changes to their manufacturing processes, such as minor changes to the purification process. The cumulative effect of these minor changes may result in a meaningful "drift" in analytical characteristics over time. For instance, a biosimilar biological product could drift over the course of research and development—*after* the preliminary comparative analytical assessment that forms the basis for design of the preclinical and clinical program. Further, the reference product could similarly drift during the development of a biosimilar. In addition, once a biosimilar has been approved, it—and/or the reference product—may drift. FDA's draft guidance documents offer general comments relevant to premarket drift of the biosimilar product. For instance, on the question of premarket drift of the biosimilar itself, the agency comments that "[l]ots used for the [structural] analysis should support the biosimilarity of both the clinical material used in confirmatory clinical trials and the to-be-marketed [biosimilar]."[51] It further observes that "[i]dentification of the specific lots of the reference product used in the biosimilar studies together with expiration dates and timeframes of actual use" would be valuable,[52] but otherwise offers very little comment on drift of the reference product during the biosimilar research program. And the agency has said nothing to date on the implications of drift (in both products) after biosimilar approval. Thus, how subtle changes in the two separate products over time might affect regulatory findings of biosimilarity and interchangeability remains unclear. Several stakeholders have taken the position that upon approval, biosimilars (at least those not designated interchangeable) should stand on their own; in other words, biosimilars need not remain biosimilar to their reference products over time.

Nonclinical Testing. A draft guidance suggests FDA will probably not require animal data in all cases. For instance, animal toxicity data will be "considered useful" when structural and functional testing reveals safety questions that must be addressed before clinical testing.[53] In some cases, a single-dose comparative study in animals using pharmacokinetics and pharmacodynamics measures "may contribute to the totality of evidence" that "supports" a demonstration of biosimilarity.[54] Although animal immunogenicity studies generally do not predict human immune response, measurement of anti-protein antibody response in animals may sometimes provide relevant safety information.[55]

Many commenters on FDA's 2012 draft guidances supported FDA's flexible approach toward animal testing. They expressed the view that it is often difficult to identify a relevant species and animal testing will rarely provide valuable information. In contrast, others viewed at least some animal testing as necessary for patient safety. They argued that some nonclinical

---

[49]   *Id*, at 5.
[50]   *Id*.
[51]   Scientific Considerations Guidance, *supra*, at 9.
[52]   Quality Guidance, *supra*, at 7-8.
[53]   Scientific Considerations Guidance, *supra*, at 11.
[54]   *Id*. at 12.
[55]   *Id*.

toxicity and immunogenicity testing is essential before evaluating any new biologic in humans.

Clinical Pharmacology. Clinical pharmacology studies are normally a "critical" part of the biosimilarity showing.[56] FDA guidance explains that data from these studies describe the similarity in drug exposure between the two products.[57] "Exposure" in the context of this guidance refers broadly to pharmacokinetics variables.[58] These studies may also include pharmacodynamics endpoints (either pharmacological/therapeutic response or toxicological/safety response) and pharmacometric analyses.[59] According to FDA, when determining which pharmacodynamics markers to use, a sponsor should consider: 1) the time of onset of the marker relative to dosing; 2) the dynamic range of the marker over the exposure range to the biological product; 3) the sensitivity of the marker to differences between the products; 4) the relevance of the marker to the mechanism of action of the drug; and 5) the relationship between changes in the marker and clinical outcomes.[60] If these are "addressed" with the submission of "convincing" pharmacokinetics and pharmacodynamics results, "the extent of the clinical development program can be refined in both the design and extent" of additional testing needed.[61]

Clinical Safety and Efficacy Testing. Comparative safety and efficacy testing "will be necessary . . . if there are residual uncertainties" about biosimilarity following completion of, for example, analytical, nonclinical, clinical pharmacology, and clinical immunogenicity testing.[62] To determine the type and extent of required safety and efficacy testing, FDA will consider a variety of factors, including: 1) product complexity; 2) the extent to which analytical, functional, and nonclinical differences predict differences in clinical outcome; 3) the extent to which the mechanism of action and disease pathology are understood; 4) the extent to which human pharmacokinetics and pharmacodynamics results will predict clinical outcomes; 5) clinical experience with the reference product and therapeutic class; and 6) clinical experience with the proposed biosimilar.[63] Stakeholders commenting on FDA's 2012 draft guidances were roughly divided on the issue of whether it is ever scientifically justified for a biosimilar applicant to entirely omit clinical efficacy and safety testing.

FDA generally recommends that biosimilar sponsors use equivalence designs in their clinical trials evaluating efficacy and safety.[64] Non-inferiority designs may be appropriate

---

56   Clinical Pharmacology Guidance, *supra*, at 2.
57   *Id.*
58   *Id.* at 3.
59   *Id.*
60   *Id.* at 4.
61   *Id.*
62   Scientific Considerations Guidance, *supra*, at 16. *See also* Clinical Pharmacology Guidance, *supra*, at 11 ("[I]f clinical pharmacology similarity between products is demonstrated, in some instances this may complete the clinical evaluation, and in others it may support a more targeted clinical development program.").
63   Scientific Considerations Guidance, *supra*, at 16.
64   Scientific Considerations Guidance, *supra*, at 17. ("A study employing a two-sided test in which the null hypothesis is that either (1) the proposed product is inferior to the reference product or (2) the proposed product is superior to the reference product based on a pre-specified equivalence margin is the most straightforward study design for accomplishing this objective. The margins should be scientifically justified and adequate to enable the detection of clinically meaningful differences in effectiveness and safety between the proposed product and the reference product.").

"in some cases," for instance where higher-than-recommended doses of the products do not present safety concerns or where the study examines safety or immunogenicity.[65] FDA recommends a crossover design for products with half-lives shorter than five days and parallel designs for products with longer half-lives.[66] A biosimilar sponsor may use different endpoints than the reference product sponsor used where "scientifically justified," for instance where pharmacodynamics measures are more sensitive than clinical endpoints.[67] Biosimilar sponsors should, however, generally use study populations similar to those used in the reference product trials.[68] In any case, the endpoints and study populations should be clinically relevant and sensitive in detecting clinically meaningful differences.[69]

Immunogenicity. FDA generally will require at least one comparative human immunogenicity study.[70] The immunogenicity assessment might take place before licensure or through a combination of premarket and postmarket studies.[71] Immunogenicity studies should use a comparative, parallel, one-sided design.[72] Thus, the applicant need only show that its product does not result in increased immunogenicity compared to the reference product (unless decreased immunogenicity would raise efficacy concerns).[73] Observed differences in immune response may warrant further testing, even in the absence of observed clinical sequelae.[74] Commenters on FDA's 2012 draft guidances expressed broad agreement that clinical assessment of a biosimilar's immunogenicity profile is important. Views differed, however, as to how immunogenicity should be evaluated, the appropriate length of the assessment, and the extent to which the assessment should take place premarket or postmarket.

Extrapolation. As noted above, extrapolation refers to when data concerning one indication may support a biosimilar's approval for other indications (not studied clinically). Extrapolation is a critical component, some have argued, to making the biosimilar pathway a truly abbreviated pathway and to achieving development cost savings.

FDA will permit extrapolation of indications with scientific justification. The agency expects this justification to address, among other things: 1) the mechanism of action in each condition of use for which licensure is sought; 2) the pharmacokinetics and biodistribution of the product in the different patient populations; 3) any differences in expected toxicities in each condition of use and patient population (including whether expected toxicities are related to the pharmacological activity of the product or to off-target activities); and 4) any "other factor that may affect the safety or effectiveness of the product in each condition of use and patient population for which licensure is sought."[75] The sponsor should select, for

---

[65]   *Id.*
[66]   *Id.* at 18.
[67]   *Id.*
[68]   *Id.*
[69]   *Id.*
[70]   *Id.* at 14.
[71]   *Id. Cf.* Clinical Pharmacology Guidance, *supra,* at 8 ("Safety and immunogenicity data from the clinical pharmacology studies should be collected and evaluated . . . . [D]ata derived from these studies may need to be supplemented by additional evaluations either preapproval or postapproval.").
[72]   Scientific Considerations Guidance, *supra,* at 14-15.
[73]   *Id.*
[74]   *Id.*
[75]   *Id.* at 19-20.

study, the condition of use that is "the most sensitive" for detecting clinically meaningful differences in safety (including immunogenicity) and effectiveness.[76] And caution is generally warranted given the different co-morbidities and concomitant medications of different patient populations.[77] Stakeholders have expressed general support for FDA's enumerated extrapolation criteria. The true test, however, will be how FDA applies these criteria in practice.

Pediatric Assessments. A biosimilar biological product that has not been deemed interchangeable with its reference product is considered to have a new "active ingredient" for purposes of section 505B of the FDCA.[78] This provision requires every new drug and biologics license application for a new active ingredient to include the results of pediatric assessments on the safety and efficacy of the product for the claimed indications in all relevant pediatric subpopulations. Unless a biosimilar applicant proposes an interchangeability designation when it submits its application for approval, therefore, the application will need to contain pediatric assessments. Under section 505B, FDA may grant waivers or deferrals of the pediatric assessment requirement if the drug is ready for approval for use in adults before pediatric studies are complete.[79] Several commenters on FDA's 2012 draft guidances urged FDA to generally grant waivers, on the theory that biosimilars will have no clinically meaningful differences from their reference products—including with regard to use in pediatric populations.

Other Requirements. Every biosimilar application must also contain information demonstrating that the proposed biosimilar and the reference product use the same mechanism or mechanisms of action, if known, as well as information showing that the conditions of use in the labeling of the proposed biosimilar have previously been approved for the reference product.[80] Also, the route of administration, the dosage form, and the strength of the biosimilar must be the same as those of the reference product.[81] FDA has clarified in draft guidance that the applicant may obtain licensure for fewer than all of the reference product routes of administration, presentations, and conditions of use.[82] That said, if the applicant seeks licensure for a particular indication of the reference product that corresponds to a particular presentation of the reference product, the applicant *may* need to seek licensure for that particular presentation.[83] In addition, the application must contain manufacturing and processing data and publicly available information regarding FDA's determination that the reference product is safe, pure and potent.

These mandatory (i.e., non-waivable) elements of a biosimilar application have generated little controversy. They relate to other issues, however, for which the statute does not offer direction. For example, some stakeholders have asked FDA to clarify whether a biosimilar sponsor may submit a full data package to support approval of its product for a new condition of use (indication, route of administration, dosage form, etc.) for which the reference product

---

[76] *Id.* at 20.

[77] *Id.*

[78] FDCA § 505B(m), 21 U.S.C. § 355c(m).

[79] FDCA § 505B(a)(3), 21 U.S.C. § 355c(a)(3).

[80] PHSA § 351(k)(2)(A)(i)(II) & (III), 42 U.S.C. § 262(k)(2)(A)(i)(II) & (III).

[81] PHSA § 351(k)(2)(A)(i)(IV), 42 U.S.C. § 262(k)(2)(A)(i)(IV).

[82] Q&A Guidance, *supra*, at 6-7.

[83] *Id.* at 6.

is not approved, and if so, whether that approval would have consequences for the reference product. Similarly, stakeholders have asked whether and under what circumstances a biosimilar may receive approval of a new condition of use for which the reference product is approved after licensure of the biosimilar. FDA may choose to address questions like these only as the need arises and, even then, may proceed on a case-by-case basis.

Differences. In its draft guidances, FDA addressed some of the ways in which a biosimilar product may differ from its reference product. In every case, of course, the statutory standard must be met. But as noted above, the agency has signaled that in some cases it is open even to *structural* differences in the active ingredient, detectable analytically, within the parameters of a "highly similar" finding.[84] The statute is silent with respect to product-level issues like formulation, delivery device, container closure, and primary packaging, and the agency has indicated that some differences may be acceptable.[85] Any differences are likely to affect the extent of testing required.

A number of stakeholders commenting on FDA's 2012 draft guidances encouraged FDA to exercise caution when considering whether to permit a biosimilar applicant to introduce *intentional* differences between the products, such as a different formulation or delivery device. Each difference could create the potential for other differences that may go undetected. Others, however, strongly supported permitting applicants to introduce these kinds of intentional differences. They recognized that doing so will help biosimilar manufacturers develop products that may be less likely to infringe certain innovator patents and differentiate their biosimilars in the marketplace.

Biosimilar Product Development Program Meetings

FDA has created a biosimilar product development (BPD) program that involves frequent early meetings between the agency and sponsor.[86] The BPD program comprises five meeting types specific to biosimilar development programs. It begins with an initial advisory meeting, limited to a general discussion regarding whether licensure under section 351(k) might be feasible and to general advice on the expected content of the development program. The sponsor should submit in advance, among other things, manufacturing process information and sufficient comparative characterization data for the agency to determine whether the biosimilar pathway will be appropriate. Assuming the agency agrees that a biosimilar program is suitable, it might then offer advice on the proposed analytical methodology and assay development, as well as more general advice on nonclinical and clinical studies.

Meeting types 1 through 4 are available thereafter, depending on the needs of the sponsor. Type 1 meetings are those necessary for an otherwise stalled biosimilar development program to proceed; one might be warranted, for instance, to discuss a clinical hold or important safety issue that has emerged.[87] Dispute resolution meetings are also Type

---

[84] Scientific Considerations Guidance, *supra*, at 8.

[85] *Id.* at 14. *See also* Q&A Guidance, *supra*, at 4-6.

[86] Formal Meetings Guidance, *supra*. *See also* Leah Christl, FDA, *Biosimilar Use Fee Act of 2012 (BsUFA): Requirements and Implementation* (undated) (slide presentation), http://www.fda.gov/downloads/ForIndustry/UserFees/BiosimilarUserFeeActBsUFA/UCM321015.pdf.

[87] Formal Meetings Guidance, *supra*, at 3.

1.[88] Type 2 meetings for ongoing programs are those to discuss a specific issue (such as proposed study design or endpoints) or questions as to which FDA can provide targeted advice.[89] Type 3 meetings involve in-depth review of data and advice regarding an ongoing program—for example, review of completed study reports.[90] Type 4 meetings address the format and content of product applications.[91] BPD meetings will not be scheduled if the sponsor is delinquent with respect to applicable user fees, discussed in the next subsection. FDA meeting minutes, which are the "official record of the meeting," will be issued to the sponsor within 30 days of any BPD meeting.[92]

User Fees

The BPCIA contained transitional user fee provisions, which were never used (because no applications were submitted), and which have been superseded by the Biosimilar User Fee Act of 2012 (BsUFA).[93] This statute authorizes FDA to assess and collect fees for biosimilar biological products from October 2012 through September 2017, placing biosimilar user fees on the same reauthorization schedule as other drug program user fees. FDA will collect application fees, establishment fees, and product fees from biosimilar sponsors. The fee rates are identical to those applicable to other drug sponsors under the Prescription Drug Use Fee Act (PDUFA) provisions of the statute. For instance, in FY 2014, the fee for a marketing application requiring clinical data is $2,169,100.[94]

BsUFA also authorized collection of a new type of fee: the biosimilar biological product development (BPD) fee, for biosimilar products in the development phase. A biosimilar sponsor must pay an initial BPD fee within five calendar days after FDA grants a BPD meeting for the product in question or upon submission of an investigational new drug application (IND), whichever happens first.[95] The fee constitutes 10 percent of the PDUFA fee for an application requiring clinical data.[96] An additional 10 percent is due the first business day on or after October 1 of each subsequent year or "the first business day after the enactment of an appropriations Act providing for the collection and obligation of fees for such year under [the user fee provision]."[97] A fee is also required to reactivate participation in the BPD program, if the sponsor formally discontinues participation.[98] When the sponsor submits its eventual biosimilar marketing application, the user fee for that application is reduced by the cumulative amount of previously paid BPD fees for the product.[99]

---

[88]   *Id.*

[89]   *Id.*

[90]   *Id.* at 4.

[91]   *Id.*

[92]   *Id.* at 14.

[93]   Food and Drug Administration Safety and Innovation Act, Pub. L. No. 112-144, tit. IV, 126 Stat. 993, 1026 (2012), FDCA §§ 744G and 744H, 21 U.S.C. §§ 379j-51 and 379j-52.

[94]   *See* FDA, BsUFA Fee Schedule and Payment Instructions, http://www.fda.gov/ForIndustry/UserFees/BiosimilarUserFeeActBsUFA/ucm320765.htm (last visited Aug. 26, 2014).

[95]   FDCA § 744H(a)(1)(A)(i), 21 U.S.C. § 379j-52(a)(1)(A)(i).

[96]   FDCA § 744H(b)(1)(A), 21 U.S.C. § 379j-52(b)(1)(A).

[97]   FDCA § 744H(a)(4)(B), 21 U.S.C. § 379j-52(a)(4)(B).

[98]   FDCA § 744H(a)(1)(D), 21 U.S.C. § 379j-52(a)(1)(D).

[99]   FDCA § 744H(a)(2)(A)(i), 21 U.S.C. § 379j-52(a)(2)(A)(i).

As part of BsUFA, the agency committed to certain performance goals in a side letter to the legislation; these can be found on the agency's website.[100] Many of the goals are similar to PDUFA performance goals (with different timelines), but others reflect the novel BPD program that FDA has created. Further, the goals change over the first five years of the program: for instance, FDA commits to reviewing 85 percent of original biosimilar applications within 10 months of receipt in fiscal year 2016 and to reviewing 90 percent in fiscal year 2017.[101]

Reference Products and Foreign Innovative Products

Section 351(i) of the PHSA defines a reference product as "the single biological product licensed under subsection (a) against which" a biosimilar is evaluated.[102] The PHSA also states that a biosimilar can be evaluated against only one reference product.[103] Together, these provisions mean that a biosimilar must be evaluated against a single U.S.-licensed product.

There has been significant discussion, however, of the extent to which a biosimilar applicant may rely on data comparing a proposed biosimilar to a foreign (as opposed to FDA-approved) innovative product. Section 351(k) provides that a biosimilar application may include "any additional information in support of the application."[104] Some stakeholders have contended that this provision permits FDA to consider data from studies comparing the proposed biosimilar to a foreign innovative product. The issue is particularly important to biosimilar companies that are pursuing global development programs.

In its 2012 draft guidances, FDA acknowledged that in some circumstances, the use of data from a foreign innovative product may be permissible. At a minimum, "analytical studies and at least one human PK [(pharmacokinetics)] and/or PD [(pharmacodynamics)] study" would need to be conducted with the U.S.-licensed reference product. FDA has taken the position that a biosimilar sponsor is, however, permitted "to use data derived from animal or clinical studies comparing a proposed product with a non-U.S.-licensed product to address, in part, the requirements under section 351," provided that the sponsor establishes "an acceptable bridge" to the U.S.-licensed reference product.[105] In the Clinical Pharmacology Guidance, FDA clarified that "the type of bridging data needed will always include data from analytical studies . . . that directly compares all three products (i.e., ([sic] the proposed biosimilar

100   FDA, Biosimilar Biological Product Authorization Performance Goals and Procedures Fiscal Years 2013 through 2017 (undated), http://www.fda.gov/downloads/Drugs/DevelopmentApprovalProcess/HowDrugsareDevelopedandApproved/ApprovalApplications/TherapeuticBiologicApplications/Biosimilars/UCM281991.pdf.

101   Id. at 3. Type 1 BPD meetings will be scheduled to occur within 30 calendar days of FDA receipt of a written meeting request and meeting package; Type 2 within 75 calendar days; Type 3 within 120 calendar days; and Type 4 within 60 calendar days. Id. at 11.

102   PHSA § 351(i)(4), 42 U.S.C. § 262(i)(4).

103   PHSA § 351(k)(5)(A), 42 U.S.C. § 262(k)(5)(A).

104   PHSA § 351(k)(2)(A)(iii), 42 U.S.C. § 262(k)(2)(A)(iii).

105   Scientific Considerations Guidance, supra, at 6; Q&A Guidance, supra, at 7. Issues that a sponsor may need to address include: whether the foreign innovative product and U.S.-licensed reference product are manufactured in the same facility (during the same time period), whether the facility in question was licensed and inspected by a regulatory authority that has scientific and regulatory standards similar to those of FDA, and whether the product itself was licensed by a regulatory authority that has similar scientific and regulatory standards. Q&A Guidance, supra, at 7-8.

product, the U.S.-licensed reference product, and the non-U.S.-licensed product) and is likely to also include PK [pharmacokinetics] and, if appropriate, PD [pharmacodynamics] study data for all three products."[106]

Reliance on foreign innovative product data was one of the most commonly addressed topics in stakeholder comments on FDA's 2012 draft guidances. Some stakeholders praised FDA for what appeared to be the agency's willingness to accept foreign innovative product data, and thus, minimize "redundant" testing involving the U.S.-licensed reference product. Some thought that FDA should relax its proposed criteria for determining when reliance on these data was appropriate. Others, however, expressed concern that reliance on foreign innovator product data would unnecessarily introduce additional uncertainty about a proposed product's biosimilarity to a U.S.-licensed reference product (the product with which patients might be switched in practice) and would be contrary to the statute. Some stakeholders urged FDA to place additional limitations on when an applicant may rely on these data, such as by permitting reliance only if the U.S. and foreign innovative products are manufactured in the same facilities (information that, however, generally will not be publicly available) and have the same formulations, delivery devices, and containers. Some argued that comparative data involving a foreign innovative product cannot ever substitute for immunogenicity testing involving the U.S.-licensed reference product.

FDA still needs to flesh out under what circumstances it will permit applicants to rely on data from a foreign innovative product, as well as how comparable the U.S.-licensed reference product and the foreign innovative product must be for FDA to accept these data. The EMA recently updated its guidelines to potentially allow for greater use of data from foreign innovative products in certain circumstances.[107] Many other countries' guidelines still require the use of a single, domestically approved reference product,[108] but FDA's and the EMA's willingness to consider comparative data involving foreign innovative products data suggest that the use of data from a foreign innovative product may be more common in other jurisdictions in the future.

---

[106]   Clinical Pharmacology Guidance, *supra*, at 10.

[107]   *Compare* EMA, Guideline on Similar Biological Medicinal Products (CHMP/437/04) § 2.2 (October 2005) ("The chosen reference medicinal product must be a medicinal product authorised in the Community, on the basis of a complete dossier . . . . The chosen reference medicinal product, defined on the basis of its marketing authorisation in the Community, should be used throughout the comparability program for quality, safety and efficacy studies during the development of a similar biological medicinal product in order to allow the generation of coherent data and conclusions. Data generated from comparability studies with medicinal products authorised outside the Community may only provide supportive information."), *with* EMA, Draft Guideline on Similar Biological Medicinal Products (CHMP/437/04 Rev 1) § 3.2 (May 22, 2013) ("A single reference medicinal product, defined on the basis of its marketing authorisation in the EEA, should be used as the comparator throughout the comparability programme for quality, safety and efficacy studies during the development of a biosimilar in order to allow the generation of coherent data and conclusions. However, with the aim of facilitating the global development of biosimilars and to avoid unnecessary repetition of clinical trials, it may be possible for an Applicant to compare the biosimilar in certain clinical studies and in vivo non-clinical studies (where needed) with a non-EEA authorised comparator (i.e. a non-EEA authorised version of the reference medicinal product) which will need to be authorised by a regulatory authority with similar scientific and regulatory standards as EMA (i.e. ICH countries).").

[108]   *See, e.g.*, Japanese Follow-on Biologics Guideline, *supra*, § 3 (stating that "originator biodrugs should be drugs approved domestically and be the same product throughout the development period of the follow-on biologic (the entire quality, non-clinical and clinical development period)").

Reference Product Exclusivity

Section 351(k)(7) provides that a biosimilar may not be approved until 12 years after the date that the reference product was first licensed under section 351(a).[109] A biosimilar application may be filed four years after the reference product's first licensure.[110] The statute clarifies that this "first licensure" date does not include two types of approvals. First, it does not include approval of a supplement to the BLA for the reference product.[111] Second, it does not include approval of a subsequent application

> filed by the same sponsor or manufacturer of the biological product that is the reference product (or a licensor, predecessor in interest, or other related entity) for
>
> (I) a change (not including a modification to the structure of the biological product) that results in a new indication, route of administration, dosing schedule, dosage form, delivery system, delivery device, or strength; or
>
> (II) a modification to the structure of the biological product that does not result in a change in safety, purity, or potency.[112]

It is likely that products to which the first licensure exception applies (i.e., the innovative products that are the subject of those subsequent applications) will benefit from whatever amount of the 12-year exclusivity period protecting the first licensed product remains upon approval of the subsequent application. In the Hatch-Waxman context, FDA applies an "umbrella" exclusivity policy pursuant to which a company's subsequent applications for products containing its previously approved new chemical entity (NCE) (i.e., products not eligible for separate NCE exclusivity) are nonetheless protected by any remaining portion of the exclusivity term granted to the original NCE.[113] FDA has not yet addressed the issue publicly, despite requests by numerous stakeholders that it do so.

FDA has explained in draft guidance how it intends to interpret "licensor, predecessor in interest, or other related entity." Specifically, a licensor is "any entity that has granted the sponsor a license to market the biological product."[114] A "predecessor in interest" is any entity: 1) that the sponsor has "taken over, merged with, or purchased"; 2) "that has granted the sponsor exclusive rights to market the biological product" under the BLA; or 3) that

---

[109] PHSA § 351(k)(7)(A), 42 U.S.C. § 262(k)(7)(A).

[110] PHSA § 351(k)(7)(B), 42 U.S.C. § 262(k)(7)(B).

[111] PHSA § 351(k)(7)(C)(i), 42 U.S.C. § 262(k)(7)(C)(i).

[112] PHSA § 351(k)(7)(C)(ii), 42 U.S.C. § 262(k)(7)(C)(ii).

[113] *See* 54 Fed. Reg. 28,872, 28,897 (July 10, 1989) (preamble to 21 C.F.R. § 314.108) (noting that "when exclusivity attaches to an active moiety or to an innovative change in an already approved drug, the submission or effective date of approval of ANDA's and 505(b)(2) applications for a drug with that active moiety or innovative change will be delayed until the innovator's exclusivity has expired, whether or not FDA has approved subsequent versions of the drugs entitled to exclusivity, and regardless of the specific listed drug product to which the ANDA or 505(b)(2) application refers" and that the alternative approach "would seriously undermine [the value of exclusivity], reducing the incentives for research and innovation in the pharmaceutical industry").

[114] Exclusivity Guidance, *supra*, at 5.

had exclusive rights to the data underlying the BLA.[115] And two entities are related if: 1) either "owns, controls, or has the power to own or control" the other, whether directly or indirectly, or 2) they are under "common ownership or control."[116] FDA "may" find two parties are related, also, if they are engaged in certain "commercial collaborations relating to the development of the" product in question. The agency did not explain this, except by adding that it would consider ownership and control of the investigational new drug application (IND) and BLA, as well as the "level of collaboration" between the companies during the "development program as a whole."[117]

The agency's proposed approach to "licensor" and "predecessor in interest" implicitly takes an important position with respect to the drafting of the first licensure provision, but it is also internally inconsistent. The statute provides that the four-year and 12-year rules do not apply to a "*subsequent* application *filed by* the same sponsor or manufacturer of the biological product that is the reference product (or *a licensor* [or] *predecessor in interest*)." By its plain language, this seems to preclude a new term for a second product only if the *second company* is the licensor or predecessor in interest *of the first company*. In its explanation of this provision, FDA seems to have followed the plain language of the statute.[118] But the more likely scenario, of course, is that the second applicant in time is a licensee or successor in interest of the first applicant. Elsewhere in the draft guidance document, however, the agency seems to take the opposite approach—instructing (second) applicants to identify the previously licensed products for which a licensor or predecessor in interest was the (first) license holder.[119]

On the question of the type of structural change needed to earn a separate period of exclusivity, many have argued that the structural modification needs to be significant or result in a clinically superior product. Others have pointed out that the statute refers only to "a modification to the structure of the biological product" and does not permit evaluations of significance or superiority. The draft guidance makes no mention of a superiority or significance test, confirming that FDA will look only to "modification" in structure, and a resulting "change" in safety, purity, or potency.[120] The agency suggests structural differences might include: differences in amino acid sequence, glycosylation patterns, tertiary structure, post-translational events, and infidelity of translation or transcription.[121] It also indicated it would look to whether the modified product affects the same molecular target. FDA will apparently *not* presume structural differences, even in the case of deliberate genetic modification to the cell line.[122]

The applicant must demonstrate both structural modification and, separately, a change in safety, purity, or potency. FDA has asked for "measurable effects" that will "typically" be demonstrated in preclinical or clinical studies, and a clear description of "how" the modification "resulted" in the change in question. Changes in safety, purity, or potency

---

[115]   *Id.*
[116]   *Id.*
[117]   *Id.*
[118]   *Id.* at 4-5.
[119]   *Id.* at 8.
[120]   *Id.* at 5.
[121]   *Id.* at 5-6.
[122]   *Id.* at 6.

"may" include a meaningful benefit to public health, such as a "therapeutic advantage or other substantial benefit" compared to the previously licensed product. FDA *will* presume a change in safety, purity, or potency if the sponsor has demonstrated that the second product affects a different molecular target than did the first product.[123]

FDA's August 2014 draft guidance recommends that sponsors provide the following information when submitting a section 351(a) application or in correspondence to (or an amendment to) an already approved application: 1) a list of all previously licensed biological products that are "structurally related" to the product at issue, including products that "share some of the principal molecular structural features"; 2) a list of those for which the sponsor, or "one of its affiliates, including any licensors, predecessors in interest, or related entities, are the current or previous license holder"; 3) a description of the structural differences between the proposed product and the previously licensed products just identified; and 4) "[e]vidence of the change in safety, purity, and/or potency" between the two.[124] FDA explicitly warned that it may *not* make exclusivity decisions when it first approves biological products, particularly in complex cases or where it needs additional information.[125] The agency has now listed licensed biological products on its website in the *Purple Book*, and it plans to include reference product exclusivity.[126] As of this writing, however, it had posted first licensure dates and exclusivity expiry dates for few BLAs.

Biological products continue to be eligible for orphan drug exclusivity.[127] An uncodified section of the BPCIA provides that if a reference product has been designated as an orphan product, a biosimilar product labeled with the orphan indication cannot be licensed until after both the seven-year orphan drug exclusivity and the reference product exclusivity periods expire.[128] FDA noted in its draft guidance that it maintains a searchable database of orphan designations and approved orphan products on its website.[129]

The BPCIA amended the PHSA to provide that innovative biologics are also eligible for six months of pediatric exclusivity if FDA requests in writing that the sponsor conduct pediatric studies and the studies are completed in accordance with the request.[130] Pediatric exclusivity extends the four-year bar on submission of biosimilar applications, the 12-year bar on effective approval of biosimilar applicants, and seven-year orphan exclusivity.

Pharmacovigilance and Risk Management

All approved drugs are subject to postmarket pharmacovigilance requirements,[131] and since 2007 FDA has had statutory authority under the FDCA to require postmarket studies and

---

[123] *Id.*

[124] *Id.* at 8 (footnote omitted).

[125] *Id.* at 7.

[126] *See* FDA, PURPLE BOOK: LISTS OF LICENSED BIOLOGICAL PRODUCTS WITH REFERENCE PRODUCT EXCLUSIVITY AND BIOSIMILARITY OR INTERCHANGEABILITY EVALUATIONS, http://www.fda.gov/Drugs/DevelopmentApprovalProcess/HowDrugsareDevelopedandApproved/ApprovalApplications/TherapeuticBiologicApplications/Biosimilars/ucm411418.htm.

[127] FDCA § 526, 21 U.S.C. § 360bb.

[128] Pub. L. No. 111-148, § 7002(h).

[129] Q&A Guidance, *supra*, at 15.

[130] PHSA § 351(m), 42 U.S.C. § 262(m).

[131] *See* 21 C.F.R. § 600.80.

trials as well as risk evaluation and mitigation strategies (REMS).[132] The BPCIA included a provision explicitly stating that FDA's authority to impose a REMS on an innovative biologic applies with equal force to biosimilars.[133] This provision was likely unnecessary given that biosimilars meet the definition of a drug (like innovative biologics) and would therefore be subject to FDA's pharmacovigilance, postmarket studies and trials, and REMS requirements even in the absence of this provision.

Since passage of the BPCIA, some stakeholders have argued that the postmarket requirements, including any required surveillance, for a biosimilar should be at least as stringent as those for the reference product—and that in some cases the postmarket requirements may need to be more extensive. Others, citing concerns about additional burdens on pharmacies and distributors, have contended that the REMS and other postmarket requirements for biosimilars should be the same as those for reference products, or even less extensive (in light of postmarket experience with the reference product).

FDA has said little to date on the topic of pharmacovigilance and risk management for biosimilars. In guidance FDA briefly acknowledged the importance of postmarket safety monitoring for all biologics, including biosimilars.[134] The agency also stated that any "[p]ostmarket safety monitoring should take into consideration any particular safety or effectiveness concerns associated with the use of the reference product and its class, as well as the proposed product in its development and clinical use (if marketed outside the United States)."[135] The agency emphasized the need for postmarket safety monitoring to be able to accurately track any adverse events.[136] Finally, the agency suggested that in some cases, it will exercise its authority to require postmarket studies, including, for example, to assess rare, but potentially serious, safety risks (e.g., immunogenicity).[137]

FDA seems to view postmarket safety monitoring, as well as postmarket studies and trials, as critical to ensuring that the biosimilar development pathway is, in fact, abbreviated. For example, the Clinical Pharmacology Guidance states that, in some cases, clinical pharmacokinetics and pharmacodynamics data (without safety and efficacy clinical data) may provide sufficient clinical information to determine whether there are clinically meaningful differences between a biosimilar and a reference product. In such a case, "a full evaluation of safety and immunogenicity would still be necessary, either before or *after approval*."[138]

Many stakeholders have expressed concern that existing pharmacovigilance processes and practices, such as adverse event reporting and some registries, are often not capable of adequately distinguishing between products to ensure detection of safety signals and

---

[132] FDCA §§ 505(o) (postmarket clinical studies and trials, postmarket safety-related labeling changes), 505-1 (REMS), 21 U.S.C. §§ 355(o), 355-1.

[133] PHSA § 351(k)(5)(C), 42 U.S.C. § 262(k)(5)(C).

[134] Scientific Considerations Guidance, *supra*, at 20.

[135] *Id.*

[136] *Id.* ("Postmarketing safety monitoring for a proposed product should also have adequate mechanisms in place to differentiate between the adverse events associated with the proposed product and those associated with the reference product.").

[137] *Id.*

[138] Clinical Pharmacology Guidance, *supra*, at 12 (emphasis added).

accurate identification of the particular product involved. Some have also expressed concern that existing pharmacovigilance mechanisms are not capable of capturing certain safety events, such as an immunogenic event that might manifest itself in a reduction in efficacy, but that would require a more thorough assessment to properly identify.

Naming

Since the passage of the BPCIA in 2010, the issue of what names are appropriate for biosimilars has dominated much of the debate surrounding biosimilars in the United States. The key question is whether biosimilars should have nonproprietary names (also known as proper, established, or generic names) that are in some way distinguishable from those of their reference products. In recent years, however, the debate has expanded to include the question of whether *all* biologics, innovator and biosimilar alike, should have distinguishable nonproprietary names. At the time of this writing, an FDA policy on the naming conventions for biosimilars was expected within the year.[139]

Under the FDCA, a drug (which includes a biological product that falls within the drug definition) is misbranded unless its label includes its "established name."[140] The PHSA separately requires packages containing a biological product to be marked with the product's "proper name,"[141] but FDA treats the "proper name" for a biologic as synonymous with "established name" for a drug or ingredient.[142] The FDCA states that the established name of a drug is one of three names, in descending order of authority: 1) the applicable official name designated pursuant to section 508 of the FDCA; 2) the official title of the drug or ingredient in an official compendium (e.g., the United States Pharmacopoeia); or 3) the "common or usual name" of the drug.[143]

Section 508 of the FDCA lays out a process for FDA to designate official names for drugs pursuant to notice and comment rulemaking. FDA engaged in this process for decades, usually selecting the name adopted by the United States Adopted Names (USAN) Council.[144] In the early 1980s, FDA decided to stop routinely publishing official names and to publish

[139] FDA gave Sandoz's Zarxio, the first biosimilar approved under section 351(k), the "placeholder" nonproprietary name "filgrastim-sndz." FDA News Release, FDA approves first biosimilar product Zarxio (March 6, 2015), http://www.fda.gov/NewsEvents/Newsroom/PressAnnouncements/ucm436648.htm?source=govdelivery&utm_medium=email&utm_source=govdelivery. FDA stated that "[t]he provision of a placeholder nonproprietary name for this product should not be viewed as reflective of the agency's decision on a comprehensive naming policy for biosimilar and other biological products. While the FDA has not yet issued draft guidance on how current and future biological products marketed in the United States should be named, the agency intends to do so in the near future." Id.

[140] FDCA § 502(e), 21 U.S.C. § 352(e).

[141] PHSA § 351(a)(1)(B)(i), 42 U.S.C. § 262(a)(1)(B)(i).

[142] FDA draft guidance on drug and biologic promotional labeling states that "established name" encompasses both the "proper name" of a biological product and the "established name" of a drug product. See FDA, Draft Guidance for Industry: Product Name Placement, Size, and Prominence in Advertising and Promotional Labeling (November 2013), at 2 n.4. FDA Form 356h (Application to Market a New or Abbreviated New Drug or Biologic for Human Use (June 2014)) also asks for the product's "Established Name (e.g., *proper name, USP/USAN name).*"

[143] FDCA § 502(e); 21 U.S.C. § 352(e).

[144] 47 Fed. Reg. 31,008 (July 16, 1982). FDA's participation in the USAN Council dates to 1967, when sponsors of the Council and the agency signed an agreement pursuant to which one voting FDA member would be appointed to the Council and FDA would accept as the "official or established" name any drug name the USAN Council adopted. See Competitive Problems in the Drug Industry, Part 2: Hearings before the Subcomm. on

only official names generated by the agency after rulemaking under section 508(c) of the FDCA. The effect was that, unless the agency takes "positive action by publishing an official name under section 508 of the act, a drug name adopted by the USAN Council will be the drug's 'established name.'"[145]

Some of the biosimilar bills under consideration between 2006 and 2009 would have required distinguishable nonproprietary names (or distinctive labeling and packaging) for biosimilars. The final bill, however, did not include any provisions relating to biosimilar naming (or labeling or packaging). These products, of course, are drugs, and so the scheme discussed in the previous paragraphs apply. Accordingly, the open question is not which entity has authority over naming for biosimilars—it is clear that FDA has the final say—but what approach FDA will take.

Although generic drugs share a nonproprietary name with the reference drug, there are two key aspects of biosimilars, and biologics more generally, that have driven the debate about whether a different approach is needed for biosimilars. First, biosimilars will be similar to, but not the same as, their reference products. They will likely have somewhat different clinical profiles either at the time of approval or after approval (due to drift of the biosimilar, the reference product, or both), and differences in immunogenicity may not be fully understood until after years of postmarket monitoring or study. Biosimilars also may have other differences. For example, FDA may determine that a biosimilar cannot be approved for some indications of the reference product without additional data. Some biosimilars thus may not share all of their reference products' indications. Biosimilars and reference products also may have significant differences with regard to delivery devices that could affect their adverse event profiles or patient compliance. Second, all biologics may be sensitive to even small changes in the manufacturing process, and it is not always possible to fully predict the clinical effect of a manufacturing change. These two facts make accurate pharmacovigilance for biologics especially critical.

Prescribing and/or reporting adverse events by brand name is not required in the United States. Indeed, FDA lacks explicit statutory authority to require that a product have a brand name. Some stakeholders have suggested that shared nonproprietary names could result in healthcare provider or patient confusion and medications errors. Some have also expressed concern that if biosimilars and reference products share nonproprietary names, if a biologic is prescribed by nonproprietary name or an adverse event is reported by nonproprietary name then it will be challenging to determine which product a patient actually received and/or whether the responsible product was accurately identified in the adverse event report. Data from the generic drug context has contributed to this concern. There is often widespread misattribution of adverse events associated with generic drugs to the reference drugs.[146] Many stakeholders therefore view distinguishable names as critical to ensuring that adverse events and postmarket safety signals are identified and attributed to the correct product. FDA officials appeared to agree with this reasoning in a 2011 article:

Monopoly of the S. Select Comm. on Small Business, 90th Cong. 752-53 (1967). FDA reserved the right to select the official name in instances where the USAN Council could not reach a unanimous agreement. *Id.*

[145]   47 Fed. Reg. at 31,009.

[146]   Erika F. Lietzan, Laura E. Sim, & Emily A. Alexander, *Biosimilar naming: How do adverse event reporting data support the need for distinct nonproprietary names for biosimilars?*, 3 FDLI's Food and Drug Policy Forum 1-20 (2013).

History suggests that pharmaceutical companies will make manufacturing-related changes to biologics periodically throughout their lifecycles, and even small changes could affect safety or efficacy. Tracking adverse events associated with the use of reference and biosimilar products will be difficult if the specific product or manufacturer cannot be readily identified . . . .[147]

FDA also agreed with this reasoning when it assigned distinguishable nonproprietary names to three innovative products approved via section 351(a) of the PHSA that were related to previously approved innovator products: tbo-filgrastim, ziv-aflibercept, and ado-trastuzumab emtansine. For example, as discussed above, Teva's tbo-filgrastim is a follow-on version of the innovator product Neupogen (filgrastim), but was approved via section 351(a). The agency cited the need to facilitate pharmacovigilance when assigning it a name distinguishable from that of filgrastim:

> FDA . . . has concluded that unique nonproprietary names will facilitate postmarketing safety monitoring by providing a clear means of determining which "filgrastim" product is dispensed to patients. Due to the fact that health care providers may use nonproprietary names instead of proprietary names when prescribing and ordering products, and pharmacovigilance systems often do not require inclusion of proprietary names, the use of distinct proprietary names is insufficient to address these concerns.[148]

The most common suggestion for creating distinguishable names is to add a distinguishing prefix or suffix to the nonproprietary name of the reference product. Stakeholders argue that the common core portion of the name would signify that the products are in fact related, while the distinguishing prefix or suffix would facilitate more accurate prescribing, dispensing, and adverse event reporting.[149] This approach is consistent with the nonproprietary name FDA gave the first biosimilar approved under section 351(k), Sandoz's Zarxio, upon approval: filgrastim-sndz.

---

[147] Steven Kozlowski et al., *Developing the Nation's Biosimilar Program*, 365 NEW ENG. J. MED. 385, 387-88 (2011).

[148] Biological Product Naming Working Group, FDA, Memorandum re: BLA 125294 - [xxx]-filgrastim, at 2 (Aug. 2, 2012), http://www.accessdata.fda.gov/drugsatfda_docs/nda/2012/125294Orig1s000NameR. pdf. Similarly, when FDA approved Zaltrap (ziv-aflibercept), a product that shares some similarities with another innovative biologic, Eylea (aflibercept), FDA required a distinguishing prefix in order to reduce potential confusion. Melanie Pierce, FDA, Memorandum re: BLA 125418/0; Advice/ Information request-teleconference (July 17, 2012), http://www.accessdata.fda.gov/drugsatfda_docs/ nda/2012/125418Orig1s000Admincorres.pdf ("FDA concluded that a different nonproprietary name would minimize the possibility of medication errors and reduce confusion among healthcare practitioners who may consider use of the same nonproprietary name to mean the biological products are indistinguishable."). FDA also assigned a distinguishing prefix when it approved Kadcyla (ado-trastuzumab emtansine) in order to prevent medication errors. Robert L. Justice, M.D., M.S., FDA, Summary Review for Regulatory Action, BLA 125427 Kadcyla (ado-trastuzumab emtansine), at 22 (Feb. 21, 2013), http://www.accessdata.fda.gov/ drugsatfda_docs/nda/2013/125427Orig1s000Sumr.pdf.

[149] FDA seemed open to this option in its *Federal Register* notice announcing the 2010 public meeting and posing a series of questions. The agency asked "[i]f each product were given a unique nonproprietary name, should a distinguishing prefix or suffix be added to the nonproprietary name for a related biological product that has not been demonstrated to be biosimilar, a biosimilar product, or an interchangeable product to facilitate pharmacovigilance?" 75 Fed. Reg. 61,497, 61,499 (Oct. 5, 2010).

Other stakeholders—primarily some biosimilars manufacturers, pharmacies, and related trade organizations—have argued that biosimilars should have the *same* nonproprietary names as their reference products. They suggest that other mechanisms, such as brand name, national drug code (NDC), lot number, and manufacturer name, can adequately ensure the traceability of adverse events. Many of these stakeholders have contended that, even though some related innovative biologics share the same nonproprietary name (such as human growth hormone products), this convention has not resulted in any safety issues or confusion. They also point to Europe, where all but one biosimilar has the same nonproprietary name as the reference product, to suggest that effective pharmacovigilance can be obtained in the absence of distinguishable nonproprietary names. All biosimilars are required to carry a distinguishable trade or brand name in Europe.[150]

Outside of Europe, a number of regulatory and public health authorities seem to have embraced the need for distinctive naming. For example, the Japanese biosimilar guidance provides that "the nonproprietary names and brand names of follow-on biologics should be readily distinguishable from the nomenclature of originator biodrugs and other follow-on biologics."[151] More specifically, "Follow-on 1" (or 2, 3, etc.) must be added as a suffix to the nonproprietary name of the originator biodrug. And "BS" should be added to the product's brand name.[152] This applies to all but the simplest of biologics.

The World Health Organization (WHO) separately assigns international nonproprietary names (INNs) to pharmaceutical substances and active ingredients. Historically, the WHO had taken the position that there was no need for biosimilars and reference products to have distinguishable nonproprietary names, though the WHO's guidelines do provide that biosimilars should have unique brand names.[153] In addition, a Greek letter suffix was used as part of the INN to indicate differences in glycosylation profiles.

However, beginning in April 2013, the WHO began to discuss the possibility of assigning distinguishable INNs to biosimilars. The reasoning focused not only on the need to facilitate pharmacovigilance, but also on the need to prevent unintended substitution of the biosimilar and the reference product or of one biosimilar for another.[154] No policies have been finalized, but the current discussion has focused on the use of a "biological qualifier" (BQ) that would be assigned to each biologic (biosimilars and innovative biologics alike).[155] In July 2014, the WHO released a proposal under which 1) a biologic sponsor could voluntarily apply for a BQ from the WHO; 2) the BQ would be a four-letter code assigned at random based on where the biologic drug substance was manufactured; 3) the BQ could be used retrospectively

150   For example, some biosimilars are distinguished by manufacturer name (e.g., Tevagrastim (filgrastim), which is manufactured by Teva and is a biosimilar of Neupogen). Some of the EPO products are distinguishable by brand name only (e.g., Binocrit (epoetin alfa), which is a biosimilar of Eprex (epoetin alfa)).

151   Japan Ministry of Health, Labor and Welfare, Memorandum to Directors, Health Bureaus, Prefectural Government re: Handling of nonproprietary and brand names of follow-on biologics (PFSB/ELD No. 0304011, at 1 (Mar. 4, 2009).

152   *Id.*

153   Expert Comm. on Biological Standardization, WHO, Guidelines on Evaluation of Similar Biotherapeutic Products (SBPs) § 12 (2009).

154   WHO, 56th Consultation on International Nonproprietary Names for Pharmaceutical Substances, Geneva, 15-17 April 2013, Executive Summary (2013).

155   WHO, 57th Consultation on International Nonproprietary Names for Pharmaceutical Substances, Geneva, 22-24 October 2013, Executive Summary (2013).

(i.e., with already approved biologics); and 4) the BQ would not formally be considered part of the INN. Individual regulatory authorities could require use of the BQ in addition to the INN in labeling, prescribing, adverse event reporting, or otherwise.[156] Depending on whether and how the BQ proposal is finalized, and the extent to which it is supported by national authorities, it has the potential to lead to a more widespread global movement encouraging the distinguishable identification of biologics.

Labeling

Many stakeholders have recognized that the debate surrounding biosimilar naming is related to the question of the content of the labeling (in particular, the Prescribing Information) of biosimilars. By law, generic drugs must have labeling identical to that of their reference drugs (with a few exceptions).[157] As mentioned in the preceding section, however, the BPCIA does not contain any provisions related to labeling. FDA's Draft Scientific Considerations Guidance touches briefly on the topic, stating that:

> Labeling of a proposed product should include all the information necessary for a health professional to make prescribing decisions, including a clear statement advising that
>
> - This product is approved as biosimilar to a reference product for stated indication(s) and route of administration(s).
>
> - This product (has or has not) been determined to be interchangeable with the reference product.[158]

The labeling for one biosimilar that FDA had approved at the time of this writing, however, does not contain either statement. In its 2015 guidance agenda, the agency committed to publishing additional guidance on biosimilar labeling.[159]

Naming and labeling are related issues. For example, many stakeholders have argued that the labeling for a biosimilar should distinguish between data generated from testing of the reference product and data generated from testing of the biosimilar. This may be more challenging, however, if the products share a nonproprietary name. In addition, the nonproprietary name of a product and its labeling are key to communicating to physicians and other stakeholders about a product.

Labeling is likely to garner increased interest in the years ahead, given its potential to affect the advertising and promotion of a biosimilar, as well as other issues such as products liability for biosimilars and possibly reference products sponsors.

---

[156] WHO, Biological Qualifier: An INN Proposal (July 2014).

[157] *See, e.g.,* FDCA § 505(j)(2)(A)(v), 21 U.S.C. § 355(j)(2)(A)(v).

[158] Scientific Considerations Guidance, *supra,* at 21.

[159] FDA, Guidance Agenda: New & Revised Draft Guidances CDER is Planning to Publish During Calendar Year 2015 (February 2015).

Interchangeability and Substitution

The vast majority of generic drugs approved in the United States are eligible for automatic substitution at the pharmacy. This results from two separate processes: a determination of therapeutic equivalence by FDA and individual state laws that regulate the process of substitution.

In the late 1960s and early 1970s, FDA developed by regulation an abbreviated new drug application (ANDA) process for copies of certain reference drugs.[160] "[I]n response to requests from State health agencies for assistance in administering their drug product selection laws,"[161] FDA created the *Orange Book*, which was first published in 1980.[162] The *Orange Book* explains that drugs are "therapeutically equivalent" if they are, among other things, pharmaceutical equivalents (i.e., contain the same active ingredient(s), are of the same dosage form and route of administration, and are identical in strength or concentration) and bioequivalent (i.e., they present no known or potential bioequivalence problem or are shown to meet an appropriate bioequivalence standard).[163]

According to FDA, "if one ['[']therapeutically equivalent drug product' is substituted for another under State law, with due professional regard for the individual patient, there is no substantial reason to believe that the patient will receive a drug product that is different in terms of the therapeutic effect intended."[164] FDA's statement recognizes that the practice of pharmacy (including the circumstances in which a pharmacist can substitute an alternative product) has historically been regulated at the state level.

As justification for creating the *Orange Book*, FDA cited several general provisions of the PHSA and the FDCA—which remain the law today—for the authority to issue therapeutic equivalence ratings.[165] Congress codified the concept of bioequivalence when it created a

---

[160]   34 Fed. Reg. 2673 (Feb. 27, 1969); 35 Fed. Reg. 6574 (Apr. 24, 1970). Specifically, FDA decided to permit "abbreviated new drug applications," or ANDAs, that contained no safety or effectiveness data. 45 Fed. Reg. 82,052 (Dec. 12, 1980); 21 C.F.R. § 314.1(f) (1980).

[161]   45 Fed. Reg. 72,582, 72,583 (Oct. 31, 1980) ("[T]he List is intended to assist the States in establishing a formulary that would list therapeutically equivalent drug products . . . .").

[162]   *Id.* at 72,582.

[163]   FDA, Approved Prescription Drug Products with Therapeutic Equivalence Evaluations I-4 (Orange Book) (1st ed. 1980); 44 Fed. Reg. 2932, 2937 (Jan. 12, 1979).

[164]   44 Fed. Reg. at 2937; *see also* 45 Fed. Reg. at 72,852 ("Those products on the List that are evaluated as therapeutically equivalent can be expected, in the judgment of FDA, to have equivalent therapeutic effect and equivalent potential for adverse effects when administered to the patient under the conditions specified in the labeling.").

[165]   It cited section 310 of the PHSA, which directs the Secretary to issue "information related to public health, in the form of publications or otherwise, for the use of the public" and to publish "other pertinent health information for the use of persons and institutions concerned with health services." It cited section 311(a) of the PHSA, which directs the Secretary to "advise the several States on matters relating to the preservation and improvement of the public health." It cited section 705(b) of the FDCA, which authorizes the Secretary to disseminate information regarding drugs "in situations involving, in the opinion of the Secretary, imminent danger to health, or gross deception to the consumer." And it cited section 306 of the FDCA, which stated at the time that "[n]othing in this chapter shall be construed as requiring the [FDA] to report for prosecution, or for the institution of libel or injunction proceedings, minor violations of this chapter whenever he believes that the public interest will be adequately served by a suitable written notice or warning." *See generally* 45 Fed. Reg. at 72,584-589.

statutory ANDA pathway by enacting the Hatch-Waxman Act in 1984.[166] The law directed FDA to publish a list of reference drugs.[167] But it did not mention therapeutic equivalence ratings, interchangeability, or substitution.

Congress took a different approach with the BPCIA, creating effectively two separate approval standards: biosimilarity and interchangeability. FDA must find a product that meets the biosimilarity standard to be "interchangeable" with its reference product if the applicant establishes that the product "can be expected to produce the same clinical result as the reference product in any given patient."[168] For products that are administered more than once (i.e., most biologics), there is an additional requirement: "the risk in terms of safety or diminished efficacy of alternating or switching between" the biosimilar and the reference product must not be "greater than the risk of using the reference product" alone.[169] According to the definitions set forth in the BPCIA, a determination of "interchangeability" means that the biosimilar "may be substituted for the reference product without the intervention of the health care provider who prescribed the reference product."[170]

In its 2015 guidance agenda, FDA committed to releasing a guidance document on interchangeability. As of this writing, the agency has said little on interchangeability. But in the Q&A Guidance the agency stated that "[a]t this time, it would be difficult as a scientific matter for a prospective biosimilar applicant to establish interchangeability in an original 351(k) application given the statutory standard for interchangeability and the sequential nature of that assessment."[171] It is therefore generally expected that in the near term, obtaining an interchangeability designation will require a two-step process through which a sponsor initially seeks approval as a biosimilar and then, after the product has been on the market for some time, subsequently seeks an interchangeability designation.

As mentioned above, FDA has published the *Purple Book* on its website.[172] FDA has indicated that the *Purple Book* will identify whether biologics are biosimilar or interchangeable, as well as their reference products.

At the federal level, the open questions related to interchangeability largely fall into three buckets. First, FDA will need to determine what type of data are needed to obtain an initial interchangeability designation. Several stakeholders have asked FDA to require switching studies and postmarket experience with a biosimilar to support an interchangeability designation. FDA has yet to provide public guidance on whether a switching study will be required and the appropriate design of such (e.g., the minimum number of switches that would need to be included in the trial and how long patients should be maintained

---

[166] FDCA § 505(j)(2)(A)(iv), 21 U.S.C. § 355(j)(2)(A)(iv) (requiring an ANDA to include information showing that the proposed generic is bioequivalent to the reference listed drug).

[167] FDCA § 505(j)(7), 21 U.S.C. § 355(j)(7).

[168] PHSA § 351(k)(4), 42 U.S.C. § 262(k)(4).

[169] *Id.*

[170] PHSA § 351(i)(3), 42 U.S.C. § 262(i)(3).

[171] Q&A Guidance, *supra*, at 11.

[172] FDA, Purple Book: Lists of Licensed Biological Products with Reference Product Exclusivity and BiosimilarityorInterchangeabilityEvaluations, http://www.fda.gov/Drugs/DevelopmentApprovalProcess/ HowDrugsareDevelopedandApproved/ApprovalApplications/TherapeuticBiologicApplications/ Biosimilars/ucm411418.htm.

on the biologic before a switch occurs). A few stakeholders have argued, in contrast, that an applicant's demonstration that its product meets the biosimilarity standard should be sufficient to obtain an (automatic) interchangeability determination.[173]

Second, FDA will need to determine whether certain types of differences between a biosimilar and its reference product may preclude an interchangeability designation. For example, some stakeholders have taken the position that if the two products have meaningful differences in delivery device or container closures, or if the biosimilar is not approved for all the conditions of use or routes of administration of the reference product, the biosimilar cannot meet the interchangeability standard.

Third, FDA will need to address how an interchangeability designation will work in the long-term and with an increasingly complex biologic marketplace. In some ways, these questions may be more challenging for the agency to address. For example, when FDA deems a generic drug therapeutically equivalent to the reference drug, it is also therapeutically equivalent with other generics citing the same reference drug.[174] Substitution of one generic for another, and substitution of any generic for the reference drug, is therefore commonplace. For biologics, however, two or more biosimilars that share the same reference product may not be interchangeable with each other or with the reference product (and scientific issues aside, it is not clear whether FDA has the authority to designate a biosimilar as interchangeable to another biosimilar as a legal matter). FDA will therefore need to determine what, if any, safeguards (such as requiring cautionary language in labeling) it will put in place to prevent inadvertent substitution of products not deemed interchangeable with one another.

As another example, FDA will need to assess whether and how an interchangeability designation must be maintained over time. Health Canada has recently stated that it will not issue interchangeability designations for biosimilars (as it does bioequivalence ratings for generic drugs) because of the potential that a biosimilar and reference product could "drift" apart as a result of independent manufacturing changes over time and the sensitivity of biologic products to these changes.[175] FDA has yet to address this issue publicly.

The debate is not limited to the federal level. As noted, states maintain authority over pharmacy practice (and therefore establish the rules on automatic substitution of biologics). State substitution laws that existed before passage of the BPCIA did not contemplate the substitution of biologics. They often permitted or required substitution of products listed

---

[173] The first company to file a biosimilar application in the United States, Sandoz, noted publicly that "FDA desires a two-step process—first approval of biosimilarity followed by a subsequent submission for interchangeability." *See* Sandoz Briefing Information for the January 7, 2015 Meeting of the Oncologic Drugs Advisory Committee, 12 (Jan. 2015), http://www.fda.gov/AdvisoryCommittees/ CommitteesMeetingMaterials/Drugs/OncologicDrugsAdvisoryCommittee/ucm428779.htm. Sandoz's product, Zarxio, did not receive an interchangeability designation upon initial approval in March 2015.

[174] In addition, in some cases applicants may submit studies demonstrating that their generic drugs are therapeutically equivalent to other innovative products (in addition to the reference products).

[175] Bradley J. Scott, Agnes V. Klein, & Jiang Wang, *Biosimilar Monoclonal Antibodies: A Canadian Regulatory Perspective on the Assessment of Clinically Relevant Differences and Indication Extrapolation*, J. CLIN. PHARMACOL. (2014) (Epub ahead of print) ("[D]ata used in the demonstration of 'similarity' are only valid at the time of market authorization due to possible significant postmarket changes and 'manufacturing drift'").

in the *Orange Book*,[176] therapeutically equivalent drugs approved under the FDCA,[177] or products with the same "active ingredient."[178] More than half a dozen states have now amended their laws to permit the automatic substitution of biosimilars that have been designated by FDA as interchangeable.[179] The debate at the state level has primarily focused on whether any substitution should be communicated to the prescribing physician. Proponents of this requirement argue that it would help to facilitate accurate adverse event reporting by increasing physician awareness of which product a patient received, but others suggest that it may deter automatic substitution of biosimilars. Given that many biologics are administered in hospitals or clinics rather than in the retail pharmacy setting, the extent to which state automatic substitution rules and practices will affect market uptake of biosimilars remains to be seen.

Separately, the first biosimilar product that is deemed interchangeable for any condition of use of the reference product is eligible for a period of exclusivity during which FDA cannot designate another biosimilar with the same reference product as interchangeable for any condition of use.[180] Although eligibility for this statutory incentive is not connected to patent challenges (as is the case with 180-day exclusivity for ANDA applicants under Hatch-Waxman), expiry of the exclusivity period may depend on the timing of patent litigation. Specifically, exclusivity for the first biosimilar designated as interchangeable with a particular reference product ends on the earlier of: 1) one year after first commercial marketing of the first interchangeable biosimilar; 2) 18 months after either a final court decision on all patents in suit or the dismissal of a patent action with or without prejudice (if a patent infringement case was brought against the applicant for the first interchangeable biosimilar biological product under the new law's provisions for "immediate" patent litigation); 3) 42 months after licensure of the first interchangeable biosimilar biological product (if a patent action was commenced against the applicant under these provisions and the litigation is still ongoing); or 4) 18 months after licensure of the first interchangeable biosimilar biological product (if the applicant was not sued under these provisions).[181]

Regulations and Guidance Documents

Although earlier biosimilar bills explicitly required FDA to issue regulations, guidance, or both,[182] the enacted legislation requires neither. FDA is thus free to regulate directly under the statute. Nevertheless, section 351(a) of the PHSA—which predates the BPCIA—requires FDA to issue regulations governing the approval, suspension, and revocation of biologics licenses. This includes licenses under section 351(k), and many expect the agency to amend

---

[176] *See, e.g.*, D.C. CODE § 48-803.02 ("When a pharmacist receives a prescription for a brand name drug, the pharmacist may dispense a generically equivalent drug product that is listed in the Orange Book . . . .").

[177] *See, e.g.*, CONN. GEN. STAT. § 20-619 ("'Therapeutically equivalent' means drug products that are approved under the provisions of the federal Food, Drug and Cosmetics Act for interstate distribution and that will provide essentially the same efficacy and toxicity when administered to an individual in the same dosage regimen . . . .").

[178] *See, e.g.*, NEV. REV. STAT. § 639.2583 (requiring a pharmacist to substitute a drug that, among other things, has the same "active ingredient or ingredients" as the prescribed drug).

[179] *See, e.g.*, DEL. CODE § 2549A; FLA. STAT. § 465.0252; IND. CODE § 16-42-25-4.

[180] PHSA § 351(k)(6), 42 U.S.C. § 262(k)(6).

[181] *Id.* "Final court decision" means a final decision of a court from which no appeal (other than a petition for a writ of certiorari to the United States Supreme Court) has been or can be taken. *Id.*

[182] *See, e.g.*, S. 726, 111th Cong. (2009).

part 601 of its regulations in due course. Various regulations, including the regulation governing release of confidential commercial information in BLAs,[183] will need to be updated to reflect the existence of an abbreviated pathway.

Thus far, however, FDA has issued only draft guidance documents. FDA must allow for public comment prior to finalizing any guidance document.[184] The statute provides that the issuance or non-issuance of guidance must not preclude agency action on a biosimilar application.[185] In other words, FDA cannot use the lack of biosimilar guidance as a reason to delay or withhold approval of a biosimilar.

If FDA issues product class-specific guidance documents, as the EMA has done, the guidance must include a description of the criteria that the agency will use to determine whether a proposed biosimilar is highly similar to or interchangeable with a reference product in that class.[186] Many have argued that a public process for the development of class guidance would provide a key opportunity for the scientific and medical communities, manufacturers, and others to provide input into the standards for biosimilars. Others have argued, however, that it would be of little value for FDA to engage in a potentially time- and resource-intensive process to effectively repeat the work that the EMA has done. And some have pointed out that the science in this area is rapidly changing, such that any final guidance documents would quickly become obsolete. Indeed, as noted earlier, the EMA is already revising several class-specific guidelines issued in the mid-2000s. At this stage, it appears unlikely FDA will issue class-specific guidance. Assuming the agency does not engage in a class guidance process, stakeholders will need to consider whether and how questions relevant to a product class can be effectively raised and addressed.

Section 351(k)(8) states that FDA may indicate in guidance that existing science and experience do not allow approval of a biosimilar for a specific product or product class.[187] It adds, however, that FDA may not make such a statement with respect to a recombinant protein.[188] Several stakeholders have urged FDA to exclude vaccines and blood products from the scope of the biosimilar pathway (whether by guidance or other means), which would be consistent with biosimilar guidance from the WHO and many other jurisdictions.[189] Others have taken the position that FDA should not expend resources determining which products can serve as reference products. They have reasoned that if the data in an

---

[183]   21 C.F.R. § 601.51.

[184]   PHSA § 351(k)(8)(B), 42 U.S.C. § 262(k)(8)(B). This provision states that section 701(h) of the FDCA applies to guidance on biosimilars, and it eliminates the narrow exception to prior comment available in that section. *See* FDCA § 701(h), 21 U.S.C. § 371(h) (requiring the agency to permit public participation prior to implementation of guidance documents that set forth initial interpretations of statutes or regulations, non-minor changes in prior interpretations or policies, complex scientific issues, and highly controversial issues, unless this prior participation would be infeasible or inappropriate).

[185]   PHSA § 351(k)(8)(C), 42 U.S.C. § 262(k)(8)(C).

[186]   PHSA § 351(k)(8)(D), 42 U.S.C. § 262(k)(8)(D).

[187]   PHSA § 351(k)(8)(E)(i), 42 U.S.C. § 262(k)(8)(E)(i).

[188]   *Id.*

[189]   *See, e.g.,* Expert Comm. on Biological Standardization, WHO, Guidelines on Evaluation of Similar Biotherapeutic Products (SBPs) (2009), at 4 ("This guideline applies to well-established and well-characterized biotherapeutic products such as recombinant DNA-derived therapeutic proteins. Vaccines, plasma derived products, and their recombinant analogues are excluded from the scope of this document."); Japanese Follow-on Biologics Guideline, *supra,* § 2 (stating that "conventional vaccines" are excluded from the scope of the biosimilar guidance).

application establish biosimilarity or interchangeability, FDA must approve the application, and if the data do not, FDA must reject the application—regardless of the product class and the existence or non-existence of relevant guidance. To date, FDA has not addressed this provision in guidance, nor has it issued such a pronouncement with respect to any class of biological product.

Definition of a Biological Product

Prior to 2010, the PHSA defined a "biological product" as "a virus, therapeutic serum, toxin, antitoxin, vaccine, blood, blood component or derivative, allergenic product, or analogous product, ... applicable to the prevention, treatment, or cure of a disease or condition of human beings."[190] The BPCIA added "a protein (except any chemically synthesized polypeptide)" after "allergenic product." After soliciting comments in the fourth quarter of 2010, FDA offered definitions of "protein" and "chemically synthesized polypeptide" in its 2012 draft guidance documents. FDA's interpretation of these terms will determine whether certain products are regulated under the PHSA or the FDCA and, accordingly, the available regulatory pathways, exclusivities, and premarket litigation scheme.

FDA explained that a protein is "any alpha amino acid polymer with a specific defined sequence that is greater than 40 amino acids in size."[191] Larger compounds "will be scrutinized to determine whether they are related to a natural peptide of shorter length and, if so, whether the additional amino acids raise any concerns about the risk/benefit profile of the product."[192] The significance of this comment is unclear, but FDA may intend to treat compounds more than 40 amino acids in length as peptides, rather than proteins, if they relate to a shorter strand and the additional amino acids have no discernible clinical impact. The agency relied on scientific literature for the position that "protein" does not include "peptides," and it relied on certain scientific literature (while admitting a lack of agreement therein) for the threshold of 40 amino acids.[193]

FDA also stated that a "chemically synthesized polypeptide" is "any amino acid polymer" that is both 1) "made entirely by chemical synthesis" and 2) fewer than 100 amino acids in length. These molecules will be regulated under NDAs rather than BLAs, because they fall outside the definition of "biological product." The agency noted that a chemically synthesized polypeptide with more than 99 amino acids would be scrutinized, as well, to determine whether it relates to a shorter natural peptide and whether the additional amino acids raise any concerns about risk or benefit. Finally, it noted that there might be "additional considerations" for combination device-biologic products.[194] The agency again cited scientific literature in support of its approach, this time noting competing views and selecting the narrower definition specifically in order to avoid making the "exception" refer to a "larger category of molecules."[195]

---

[190]   PHSA § 351(i), 42 U.S.C. § 262(i).
[191]   Q&A Guidance, *supra*, at 13.
[192]   *Id.*
[193]   *Id.*
[194]   *Id.* at 13-14.
[195]   *Id.* at 14.

While some stakeholders have expressed support for FDA's interpretation of the meaning of "protein" and "chemically synthesized polypeptide," many have urged the agency to not base its definitions primarily on the number of amino acids. Many have asked the agency to consider the complexity of a molecule's higher order structure or another more nuanced approach. Others, however, have argued that reliance on the size of the amino acid sequence will be more easily administrable and will promote predictability.

A number of products and product classes will likely fall under the new definition (i.e., products that are proteins, but not chemically synthesized polypeptides). These will likely include recombinant human growth hormone, recombinant human insulin and insulin analogues, and conjugated estrogens. The PHSA also now covers products that are "analogous to" proteins, but it is unclear what products fall into this category. A longstanding FDA regulation explains what is analogous to the other covered product categories (a virus, therapeutic serum and toxin, for instance),[196] and presumably the agency will eventually amend this regulation to explain what is analogous to a protein.

Transition Provisions

As already noted, FDA approved a number of protein products under the FDCA, some naturally derived and some manufactured through biotechnology. Most or all of these products likely satisfy the new definition of "biological product." As amended, the PHSA states a general requirement that all applications for biological products must now be submitted under the PHSA.[197] Congress included transition provisions for the earlier-approved biological products. Specifically, all approved NDAs for biological products will be deemed "licenses" under the PHSA 10 years after enactment, i.e., on March 23, 2020.[198] During the 10-year period, however, the sponsor may submit an NDA if another product in that class was approved under the FDCA before enactment of the BPCIA, i.e., March 23, 2010.[199]

The agency has explained in draft guidance how it intends to interpret the term "product class" for purposes of this provision. Specifically, a proposed biological product is in the same product class as a protein with an NDA if "both products are homologous to the same gene-coded sequence"—with "allowance for additional novel flanking sequences (including sequences from other genes)."[200] Further, products with "discrete changes in gene-coded sequence" or "discrete changes in post-translational modifications" may be in the same product class as an earlier approved protein product, *even if* the result is a change in pharmacokinetics. If the FDCA-approved protein product is naturally derived and lacks an identified sequence linked to any specific gene, the subsequent protein product is in the same class "if both products share a primary biological activity." Whether or not the protein product is naturally derived, if the difference between the two products "alters a biological target or effect," then they are not in the same product class for purposes of the transition provisions.[201]

---

[196]   21 C.F.R. § 600.3.

[197]   Pub. L. No. 111-148 § 7002(e)(1).

[198]   *Id.* § 7002(e)(4).

[199]   *Id.* § 7002(e)(2).

[200]   Q&A Guidance, *supra*, at 14.

[201]   *Id.* at 14-15.

A follow-on version of an FDA-approved product must be submitted under one of the two follow-on pathways in the FDCA, i.e., the pathway in section 505(b)(2) or, if the active ingredients can be shown identical and if clinical data are not needed, the generic pathway in section 505(j). Congress addressed one special follow-on scenario that might arise during the transition period. Specifically, an application may not be submitted under the FDCA if there is "another biological product" approved under section 351(a) of the PHSA that "could be a reference product" for the application in question.[202] This provision raises a number of issues. FDA must determine what needs to be true, for the finding that a PHSA product "could" be the reference product. The agency will also need to determine how early (or late) the agency may inform a biosimilar applicant that it must use a PHSA reference product, and whether the agency may or should do so if use of a PHSA reference product will require the applicant to restart its development program and/or invest additional time and money. The agency has not offered any views on this provision, to date.

There will be additional issues when FDA transitions products to the PHSA in 2020, such as whether litigation commenced under the Hatch-Waxman scheme will remain subject to the Hatch-Waxman scheme after the innovative application has been reclassified as a BLA. Another question is whether, once an NDA has been reclassified as a BLA, subsequent biosimilar applications would be subject to the PHSA litigation scheme. If both propositions are true, some innovators could be engaged in both types of litigation at the same time with respect to the same product.

Premarket Patent Litigation

Section 351(l) of the PHSA lays out a detailed process for identification and litigation of patents potentially implicated by the marketing of a biosimilar. The process differs significantly from the patent challenge process set forth under the Hatch-Waxman Act. Among other differences, section 351(l)'s patent litigation provisions have no effect on FDA's ability to approve a biosimilar (i.e., the agency can approve a biosimilar even if there is still relevant patent protection or pending patent litigation).

There are four stages to the patent litigation process: 1) the biosimilar applicant provides information about its product to the reference product sponsor; 2) the parties identify a master list of relevant patents; 3) the parties identify a subset of patents for the first phase of litigation; and 4) in the final six months before market entry, the parties may litigate the remaining patents. Each stage is discussed in turn below.

Exchange of Information

Within 20 days after FDA notifies a biosimilar applicant that its application has been accepted for review, the applicant must provide a copy of its application and information about the manufacturing process to the reference product sponsor.[203] The PHSA includes a set of default rules to govern the confidentiality of this information, but the parties may agree to a different set of rules.[204]

---

[202]   Pub. L. No. 111-148 § 7002(e)(3).

[203]   PHSA § 351(l)(2), 42 U.S.C. § 262(l)(2).

[204]   PHSA § 351(l)(1)(A), 42 U.S.C. § 262(l)(1)(A).

If the biosimilar applicant fails to provide a copy of its application and manufacturing information to the reference product sponsor within this timeframe, the reference product sponsor may bring a declaratory judgment action with respect to a patent that claims the biological product or a use of that product.[205] Submission of the application itself constitutes an act of infringement as to any patent that could have been identified by the reference product sponsor in its initial list of relevant patents (discussed in the next section).[206] This creates federal court jurisdiction to hear the controversy between the parties. The biosimilar applicant is not permitted, however, to bring a declaratory judgment action in this situation.[207]

Several stakeholders have asked FDA to require biosimilar applicants to certify to the agency that they have provided or will provide copies of their applications and manufacturing information to reference product sponsors. Others, however, have taken the position that the statute gives FDA no role, and FDA should play no role, in implementing or enforcing section 351(l)'s patent litigation provisions.

Identification of Relevant Patents

Within 60 days of receiving the biosimilar application, the reference product sponsor must provide the biosimilar applicant with a list of patents for which it believes it (or a third-party patent owner that has granted an exclusive license to it) could reasonably assert a claim of infringement.[208] It must also indicate which of those patents it would be prepared to license. The owner of a patent that should have been, but was not, included on the reference product sponsor's list may not bring suit on that patent with respect to the biosimilar product either before or after product approval.[209] The reference product sponsor's initial list of relevant patents thus appears to bind not only the reference product sponsor (where it is the patent owner) but also a third party that had licensed the patent to the reference product sponsor.

Within another 60 days, the biosimilar applicant must respond to the reference product sponsor's list. In this response it may, if it wishes, provide its own list of patents as to which it believes the reference product sponsor (or a third-party patent owner that has granted an exclusive license to the reference product sponsor) could reasonably assert a claim of infringement.[210] Whether or not it adds patents to the list, the applicant must provide the reference product sponsor with a detailed statement as to each patent (listed by the reference product sponsor or itself) to the effect that either: 1) it will not market its product prior to patent expiry; or 2) on a claim-by-claim basis, why the patent is invalid, unenforceable, or not infringed.[211] The biosimilar applicant must also respond to any offer to license.[212] If the biosimilar applicant fails to provide a detailed statement in response to the reference product sponsor's list, the latter may immediately bring a declaratory judgment action on

[205]   PHSA § 351(l)(9)(C), 42 U.S.C. § 262(l)(9)(C).
[206]   35 U.S.C. § 271(e)(2)(C)(ii).
[207]   PHSA § 351(l)(9)(C), 42 U.S.C. § 262(l)(9)(C).
[208]   PHSA § 351(l)(3)(A), 42 U.S.C. § 262(l)(3)(A).
[209]   35 U.S.C. § 271(e)(6)(C).
[210]   PHSA § 351(l)(3)(B), 42 U.S.C. § 262(l)(3)(B).
[211]   Id.
[212]   PHSA § 351(l)(3)(B)(iii), 42 U.S.C. § 262(l)(3)(B)(iii).

any patent on its own initial or supplemental list (in the case of newly issued or licensed patents, as discussed below).[213]

Within 60 days of receiving the applicant's detailed statement, the reference product sponsor must provide a response. The response must consist of a detailed, claim-by-claim statement as to why each patent will be infringed and responding to the biosimilar applicant's statements about validity and enforceability (as appropriate).[214]

If a relevant patent issues or is licensed to the reference product sponsor after it provides its initial patent list, then it must supplement the list within 30 days and the biosimilar applicant must provide its detailed statement explaining why the patent is not infringed or is invalid or unenforceable within 30 days of receiving the supplemental list.[215] These supplemental patents will not be part of the first phase of patent litigation. The owner of a patent that should have been, but was not, included on the supplemental list may not bring suit on that patent with respect to the biosimilar product.[216] And if the biosimilar applicant fails to provide a detailed statement in response to the supplemental list, the reference product sponsor may immediately bring a declaratory judgment action on any patent on that list.[217]

First Phase of Litigation

The parties next identify a subset of patents for immediate litigation. Specifically, for 15 days after the reference product sponsor provides its response, the biosimilar applicant and the reference product sponsor must negotiate a list of patents that should be litigated immediately.[218] If they agree, the reference product sponsor has 30 days to bring suit on the listed patents.[219] In theory, the parties could agree to litigate every relevant patent in the first phase.

If the parties cannot agree, the biosimilar applicant must specify the number of patents it intends to list in a subsequently exchanged list of patents.[220] No more than five days later, the parties must exchange lists of patents that they want litigated immediately.[221] The reference product sponsor may not list more patents than the number provided by the biosimilar applicant, except that the statute permits the reference product sponsor to always list at least one patent.[222] The reference product sponsor must then bring suit on the listed patent(s) within 30 days.[223] If the biosimilar applicant fails to state a number of patents that it will list for immediate litigation, the reference product sponsor may immediately bring a declaratory judgment action on any patent on its own initial or supplemental list.[224]

---

213 PHSA § 351(l)(9)(B), 42 U.S.C. § 262(l)(9)(B).
214 PHSA § 351(l)(3)(C), 42 U.S.C. § 262(l)(3)(C).
215 PHSA § 351(l)(7), 42 U.S.C. § 262(l)(7).
216 35 U.S.C. § 271(e)(6)(C).
217 PHSA § 351(l)(9)(B), 42 U.S.C. § 262(l)(9)(B).
218 PHSA §§ 351(l)(4)(A), (B), 42 U.S.C. §§ 262(l)(4)(A), (B).
219 PHSA § 351(l)(6)(A), 42 U.S.C. § 262(l)(6)(A).
220 PHSA § 351(l)(5)(A), 42 U.S.C. § 262(l)(5)(A).
221 PHSA § 351(l)(5)(B), 42 U.S.C. § 262(l)(5)(B).
222 PHSA § 351(l)(5)(B)(ii), 42 U.S.C. § 262(l)(5)(B)(ii).
223 PHSA § 351(l)(6)(B), 42 U.S.C. § 262(l)(6)(B).
224 PHSA § 351(l)(9)(B), 42 U.S.C. § 262(l)(9)(B).

The statute provides that an applicant's submission of an application for a biosimilar product is an act of infringement with respect to any patent on the patent lists provided by the reference product sponsor or biosimilar applicant or on any supplement to those lists.[225] This is an artificial act of infringement that creates federal court jurisdiction to hear the first phase of litigation.

Once the complaint is served, the biosimilar applicant has 30 days to provide FDA with notice and a copy of the complaint.[226] FDA must publish notice in the *Federal Register*.[227] If the biosimilar applicant fails to provide notice of the litigation and a copy of the complaint to FDA, the reference product sponsor may immediately bring a declaratory judgment action on any patent on its own initial or supplemental list.[228]

If the reference product sponsor does not initiate patent litigation within 30 days of the finalization of the list, or if a timely lawsuit is initiated but the suit is dismissed without prejudice or is not prosecuted in good faith,[229] only a reasonable royalty (thus, no injunction) is available in a subsequent lawsuit following a finding that the biological product that is the subject of a suit infringes the patents in question. This, too, appears to apply to both the reference product sponsor and a third-party patent owner. Also, if the reference product sponsor does not file a patent infringement suit within 30 days after agreeing upon the patents subject to immediate litigation or exchanging patent lists, the reference product sponsor must either return all confidential information it received or destroy it.[230]

As noted earlier in this chapter, a biosimilar application may be submitted any time after the date that is four years following first licensure of the reference product. Although the statute provides for two phases of litigation, it directs entry of an injunction only if there is a final court decision of infringement[231] in the first phase of litigation and before expiry of the 12-year data exclusivity term. If a biosimilar application is submitted immediately after the four-year submission bar has ended, the parties should have more than seven years to resolve the first phase of litigation, and it should be possible to reach a final court decision on the patents included in that first phase. If, however, a biosimilar application is not submitted until later in the data exclusivity term—for example, if it is submitted 10 years after first licensure—there may not be sufficient time for a final court decision in the first-phase litigation before expiry of the 12-year term. In this case, the statutory injunction provision does not apply. It should still be possible to obtain the remedy of a permanent injunction from the court, but this will presumably be governed by the traditional four-part test for injunctions.

---

[225]   35 U.S.C. § 271(e)(2)(C)(i).

[226]   PHSA § 351(l)(6)(C), 42 U.S.C. § 262(l)(6)(C).

[227]   PHSA § 351(l)(6)(C)(ii), 42 U.S.C. § 262(l)(6)(C)(ii).

[228]   PHSA § 351(l)(9)(B), 42 U.S.C. § 262(l)(9)(B).

[229]   35 U.S.C. §§ 271(e)(6)(A), (B).

[230]   PHSA § 351(1)(1)(F), 42 U.S.C. § 262(l)(1)(F).

[231]   "Final court decision" means one from which appeal (other than a petition to the United States Supreme Court for a writ of certiorari) has not been taken or could not be taken. PHSA § 351(k)(6), 42 U.S.C. § 262(k) (6).

Second Phase of Litigation

The biosimilar applicant must provide notice to the reference product sponsor no later than 180 days before commercial marketing of its biosimilar product.[232] It could in theory provide this notice considerably longer (even years) before it intends to market the product. This notice simply makes it possible for the second phase of litigation to begin. If the biosimilar applicant fails to provide timely notice, the reference product sponsor may immediately bring a declaratory judgment action on any patent on its own initial or supplemental list.[233]

Prior to the 180-day notice, and assuming the applicant provided the reference product sponsor with confidential access to its application and other information, neither the reference product sponsor nor the biosimilar applicant may bring an action for a declaratory judgment with respect to any patent that was on the initial lists but was not part of the first litigation phase.[234] Once the 180-day notice has been received, either party may seek a declaratory judgment. In addition, after the 180-day notice has been received and before the date of commercial marketing of the biosimilar, the reference product sponsor may seek a preliminary injunction on any patent identified in the initial lists that was not included in the first litigation phase,[235] as well as on any patent identified in a supplement to the list.[236] It may bring a suit at any time, including after market entry.

Pending Patent Litigation

As of early March 2015 when this chapter was finalized, no biosimilar and reference product sponsor had engaged in patent litigation resulting from the exchange process outlined above. Two significant cases, however, have tested the willingness of courts to hear patent disputes related to biosimilars outside of this designated process.

In 2013, Sandoz sued Amgen and Hoffman La-Roche in a declaratory judgment action seeking a declaration of non-infringement, unenforceability and invalidity for two patents covering Enbrel (etanercept).[237] At the time, Sandoz had not yet filed an application for its etanercept biosimilar. To date, no application has been publicly announced. The court dismissed the case, ruling that Sandoz could not have provided notice of commercial marketing because its biosimilar had not yet been approved. The statute provides that a biosimilar must provide notice "not later than 180 days before the date of the first commercial marketing of the biological *product licensed under subsection (k).*"[238] Because Sandoz's product had not yet been licensed, the court reasoned that Sandoz could not have provided notice of commercial marketing. In addition, the court found that even after an applicant provides a "notice of commercial marketing," it cannot bring a declaratory judgment action until it has complied with its obligations under section 351(l)(2)(A) of the PHSA (i.e., providing a copy of the application and manufacturing information to trigger the patent exchange process).[239] The district court's opinion has the effect of adding a six-month period between a biosimilar's

---

[232] PHSA § 351(l)(8)(A), 42 U.S.C. § 262(l)(8)(A).

[233] PHSA § 351(l)(9)(B), 42 U.S.C. § 262(l)(9)(B).

[234] PHSA § 351(l)(9)(A), 42 U.S.C. § 262(l)(9)(A).

[235] PHSA § 351(l)(8)(B), 42 U.S.C. § 262(l)(8)(B).

[236] PHSA § 351(l)(7), 42 U.S.C. § 262(l)(7).

[237] Sandoz v. Amgen, No. 3:13-cv-02904-MMC, 2013 U.S. Dist. LEXIS 161233 (N.D. Cal. 2013) (Compl.).

[238] PHSA § 351(l)(8)(A), 42 U.S.C. § 262(l)(8)(A) (emphasis added).

[239] *Sandoz,* 2013 U.S. Dist. LEXIS 161233 at *6.

approval by FDA and the date on which it can first be commercially marketed. The United States Court of Appeals for the Federal Circuit affirmed the dismissal, reasoning that Sandoz did not allege an injury of sufficient immediacy and reality to create jurisdiction.[240] The court of appeals did not address the district court's interpretation of the BPCIA.

In a separate case between these parties, Amgen sued Sandoz in October 2014, alleging that by failing to provide Amgen with a copy of Sandoz's application for a biosimilar version of Neupogen (filgrastim) (as required by the BPCIA once the application was accepted for filing by FDA), Sandoz had engaged in unfair competition under California state law, had wrongfully converted Amgen's property under California state law, committed a statutory act of patent infringement, and had infringed an Amgen patent covering Neupogen.[241] In July 2014, Sandoz had announced that its application for its filgrastim biosimilar had been accepted by FDA.[242] According to Sandoz, this application is the first biosimilar application filed in the United States. As discussed above, under section 351(l)(2), no later than 20 days after FDA notifies a biosimilar applicant that its application has been accepted for filing, the applicant "shall provide to the reference product sponsor a copy of the application . . . and such other information" relating to the manufacturing process for the product. Sandoz elected to withhold its application and manufacturing information from Amgen. The case is pending as of early March 2015.

Conclusion

FDA faces a monumental task in implementing the BPCIA—a task that may be even more complicated than implementing its generic drug authority given the unique scientific issues raised by biosimilars. Some issues will be decided in the near term. At the time of this writing, FDA had approved the first section 351(a) application, and several biosimilar applications were pending before the agency. The agency's initial approach with regard to naming and labeling was thus starting to be clarified.

It will take many years for the scientific, policy, and legal nuances to be resolved. And if experience with the Hatch-Waxman premarket litigation scheme for generic drugs is any indication, it could take decades to resolve interpretive questions related to section

---

240   Sandoz Inc. v. Amgen Inc., 2014 U.S. App. LEXIS 22903. Similarly, Celltrion and Hospira filed declaratory judgment actions concerning patents for Remicade (infliximab) against Janssen Biotech, as well as the Kennedy Trust for Rheumatology Research, which holds third-party patents for Remicade. Celltrion Healthcare Co. v. Janssen Biotech, Inc., No. 1:14-cv-11613 (D. Mass. Mar. 31, 2014) (Compl.); Celltrion Healthcare Co. v. Kennedy Trust for Rheumatology Research, No. 1:14-cv-02256-UA (S.D.N.Y. Mar. 31, 2014) (Compl.); Hospira Inc. v. Janssen Biotech, Inc., et al., No. 1:14-cv-7049-PAC (S.D.N.Y. Aug. 29, 2014) (Compl.). At the time of Celltrion and Hospira's filings, neither party had submitted to FDA an application for a biosimilar infliximab. By December 2014, all of the cases were either dismissed based on jurisdictional reasons or voluntarily withdrawn. Celltrion Healthcare Co. v. Janssen Biotech, Inc., 1:14-cv-11613 (D. Mass. Oct. 23, 2014) (Notice of Voluntary Dismissal Without Prejudice by Celltrion Healthcare Co.); Celltrion Healthcare Co. v. Kennedy Trust for Rheumatology Research, No. 1:14-cv-02256-PAC (S.D.N.Y. Dec. 1, 2014) (Opinion & Order); Hospira Inc. v. Janssen Biotech, Inc., et al., No. 1:14-cv-7049-PAC (S.D.N.Y. Dec. 1, 2014) (Opinion & Order).

241   Amgen Inc. v. Sandoz Inc., No. 3:14-cv-04741-EDL (N.D. Cal Oct. 24, 2014) (Compl.).

242   *FDA Accepts First Application in US for Biosimilar*, Specialty Pharmacy Times (July 24, 2014), http://www.specialtypharmacytimes.com/news/FDA-Accepts-First-Application-in-US-for-Biosimilar.

351(l)'s patent dispute resolution provisions. In addition, FDA may need to revisit some policies or adopt new policies as the complexity of the biologics marketplace increases over time. Biosimilars are often discussed in the context of a single reference product and a single biosimilar. But over time, there will likely be multiple biosimilars with the same reference product. Some of these biosimilars may be interchangeable, while others may not. Similarly, some of these biosimilars may be approved for all of the indications for the reference product, while others may have failed to obtain full extrapolation. FDA will not be the only stakeholder affected by this complexity; biologic sponsors, patients, physicians, pharmacists and payers will all need to be aware of and adapt to this marketplace reality over time.

CHAPTER 16
MEDICAL DEVICES

JONATHAN S. KAHAN, EDWARD C. WILSON, JR.,
AND MICHAEL S. HEYL[*]

Introduction

The Food and Drug Administration's (FDA) regulation of medical devices is extremely complex. As new technologies emerge, the challenges of determining how products will be regulated, and navigating the premarket clearance and approval process, are complicated and often daunting. Once products are cleared or approved to market, companies face rigorous regulatory requirements to keep them there. Until 1976, Congress had never enacted specific legislation governing the regulation of medical devices. Prior to that date, public protection from defective devices depended on FDA's enforcement of the limited provisions in the Federal Food, Drug, and Cosmetic Act of 1938 (FDCA) and on judicial interpretations that extended FDA's regulatory authority over drugs to devices. This combination of sources for the agency's authority proved cumbersome. By the mid-1970s, it had become clear that, due to significant and rapid scientific advances, and because some unsafe, ineffective, and even fraudulent devices were occasionally marketed, an increase in federal regulation was needed. Since that time, Congress has enacted several pieces of legislation in an attempt to create a workable system to ensure the safety and effectiveness of medical devices.

Congress' first and most comprehensive legislative effort was the Medical Device Amendments, enacted on May 28, 1976,[1] which vastly expanded FDA's statutory authority by creating a comprehensive regulatory scheme for devices. Implementation of the 1976 amendments, however, proved more challenging and time consuming than anticipated. The 1976 law also contained what Congress perceived as significant regulatory gaps. Thus, in 1990, Congress further revised and expanded FDA's regulatory authority over devices in

---

[*] The authors appreciate the assistance of Jodi K. Scott, Dennis C. Gucciardo, Danielle Woodlee, Lina Kontos, Michael Kasser, and Chan Lee in updating this chapter.

[1] Medical Device Amendments of 1976, Pub. L. No. 94-295, 90 Stat. 539 (1976) (codified at 15 U.S.C. § 55 (1994) and 21 U.S.C. *passim* (1994)).

the Safe Medical Devices Act of 1990 (SMDA).[2] Among other things, the SMDA provided FDA with new enforcement authority, enabling the agency to seek civil penalties, order device recalls, and temporarily suspend premarket approval (PMA) applications. It also codified FDA's interpretation of section 510(k) of the FDCA regarding device clearances and imposed time limits on FDA's implementation of certain key provisions of the 1976 legislation, including decisions whether to downclassify or require PMAs for a number of Class III devices (defined below). Two years later, in the 1992 Medical Device Amendments, Congress "fine tuned" several provisions of the FDCA, specifically with respect to the medical device reporting, tracking, postmarket surveillance and repair, replacement, and refund provisions of the statute.[3]

By enacting the federal Food and Drug Administration Modernization Act of 1997 (FDAMA), Congress sought to strike a balance between the need to ensure that products are safe and effective and the need to facilitate the timely availability of new products. Many of FDAMA's provisions were intended to provide clarity regarding the product review process, including provisions intended to streamline FDA's procedures and make the agency more accountable for its actions. FDAMA touched nearly every aspect of medical device regulation, including investigational device exemptions (IDEs), PMA, and 510(k) requirements; recognition of device standards; addition of third-party review of 510(k)s; narrowing of device tracking and postmarket surveillance requirements; and adding requirements for the dissemination of information about off-label uses of devices.[4]

In 2002, Congress passed the Medical Device User Fee and Modernization Act (MDUFMA) to help expedite the marketing of safe and effective devices.[5] The most important MDUFMA reform authorized FDA to require user fees for the review of certain medical device submissions, such as PMAs and 510(k)s. To help ensure that the submissions subject to user fees were reviewed by FDA in a timely manner, MDUFMA tied some of the Center for Devices and Radiological Health's (CDRH) budget to a performance goal requirement for the review of those submissions. Another provision of MDUFMA created FDA's Office of Combination Products (OCP). Congress envisioned OCP's role both to help facilitate the review of combination products, such as drug-device combinations, by the proper FDA Center, and ensure that all combination product reviews proceeded quickly and fairly.

It took five years for Congress to enact additional legislation to affect the regulation of medical devices in the United States with the Food and Drug Administration Amendments Act of 2007 (FDAAA). This legislation was passed amid rising concerns over FDA oversight, chiefly related to a number of high-profile safety concerns for approved drugs and the release of a Government Accountability Office (GAO) report on postmarket surveillance. Most significantly, FDAAA renewed the user fee program, but with a modified structure. Under FDAAA, the user fee rates for PMAs were reduced. New fees were added, however, for 30-day notices for manufacturing changes to products subject to PMAs; requests for

---

[2]   Safe Medical Devices Act of 1990, Pub. L. No. 101-629, 104 Stat. 4511 (1990) (codified at 21 U.S.C. § 301 *passim* and 42 U.S.C. §§ 263b-n (1994)).

[3]   Medical Device Amendments of 1992, Pub. L. No. 102-300, 106 Stat. 238 (1992) (codified at 21 U.S.C. §§ 301 *passim* and 42 U.S.C. § 26).

[4]   Food and Drug Administration Modernization Act of 1997, Pub. L. No. 105-115, 111 Stat. 2296 (1997) (codified at 21 U.S.C. §§ 301 *et. seq. passim* and 42 U.S.C. *passim*).

[5]   Medical Device User Fee and Modernization Act of 2002, Pub. L. No. 107-250, 116 Stat. 1588 (2002).

classification under section 513(g) of the FDCA; annual fees for PMA annual reports; and fees tied to establishment registration. Another significant change under FDAAA was the adoption of exclusively electronic registration and listing. In addition, FDAAA increased the transparency of the regulatory process by expanding the clinical trial registry database previously reserved to drug trials to include medical device trials. Finally, FDAAA expanded the laws regarding pediatric regulations both to strengthen the agency's ability to regulate postmarket surveillance of pediatric uses and provide incentives to encourage device companies to seek pediatric approvals and clearances.

Just a few years after FDAAA was enacted, in response to concerns raised by both industry and consumers and to increasing congressional pressure, in September 2009, CDRH commissioned both internal and external evaluations of the 510(k) process to assess how well the 510(k) program was meeting its two public health goals of facilitating innovation and assuring that medical devices are safe and effective.[6] On January 19, 2011, CDRH released its 510(k) and Science Report Recommendations, which announced a plan for implementing 25 initiatives to improve the 510(k) program in 2011.

As of this printing, FDA has taken action on a number of the proposed initiatives. For example, FDA has established a "direct de-novo" process, created a new pre-submission process and, though ultimately withdrawn, issued a draft guidance governing device modifications. Others have been identified as priorities for implementation in 2014. Several other initiatives were referred to the Institute of Medicine (IOM) for consideration and comment. On July 29, 2011, the IOM released its report evaluating the 510(k) process.[7] Rather than continuing to modify the 510(k) process, the IOM concluded that FDA's limited resources would be better directed toward "developing an integrated premarket and postmarket regulatory framework that provides a reasonable assurance of safety and effectiveness throughout the device life cycle."[8] Essentially, the primary conclusion of the report is that FDA should completely dismantle the existing 510(k) program for Class II devices and replace that paradigm with a new system explicitly based on safety and effectiveness. The IOM report outlines its criteria for this recommended framework. Specifically, the IOM report indicates that any such new process should 1) be based on sound science; 2) be clear, predictable, straightforward, and fair; 3) be self-sustaining and self-improving; 4) facilitate innovation that improves public health by making medical devices available in a timely manner and ensuring their safety and effectiveness throughout their life cycle; 5) apply relevant and appropriate regulatory authorities and standards throughout the life cycle of devices to ensure safety and effectiveness; and 6) be risk-based.[9]

On July 9, 2012, President Obama signed into law the Food and Drug Administration Safety and Innovation Act of 2012 (FDASIA). The law implements nearly three dozen provisions relevant to the medical device industry, in addition to reauthorizing the Medical Device User

---

[6] Center for Devices and Radiological Health, U.S. Food and Drug Administration, 510(k) and Science Report Recommendations: Summary and Overview of Comments and Next Steps (Jan. 19, 2011), *available at* www.fda.gov/downloads/AboutFDA/CentersOffices/CDRH/CDRHReports/UCM239449.pdf.

[7] Institute of Medicine, National Academy of Sciences, Medical Devices and the Public's Health: The FDA 510(k) Clearance Process at 35 Years (July 29, 2011), *available at* http://www.iom.edu/Reports/2011/Medical-Devices-and-the-Publics-Health-The-FDA-510k-Clearance-Process-at-35-Years.aspx.

[8] *Id.*

[9] *Id.*

Fee Act (MDUFA III). Reauthorization of MDUFA links higher device user fees with concrete and escalating goals for improving premarket review times, and implements significant changes to how FDA's performance will be tracked and measured. FDASIA made a number of significant changes to the regulation of medical devices. The following is a summary of some of the more salient changes:

- **IDE enhancements:** FDASIA explicitly prohibited the agency from disapproving an IDE application when a clinical trial, in FDA's view, might not fully support a device clearance or approval. Specifically, FDASIA prohibits FDA from rejecting an IDE solely because the investigation would not support device approval, a de novo finding, or substantial equivalence, or any data requirement associated with those decisions.

- **De novo downclassification:** Companies may now submit a de novo petition directly to FDA, without first submitting a 510(k) notification and then receiving a Not Substantially Equivalent (NSE) determination. Because of FDASIA, sponsors can now directly file de novo petitions with the agency and expect a response within 120 days.

- **Unique device identifier improvements:** FDASIA created a new program for FDA to more systematically track information regarding device recalls, streamline recall audits, and develop more detailed criteria for evaluating recall corrective action plans. FDASIA also put pressure on the agency to finalize the newly proposed Unique Device Identifier (UDI), which it ultimately did on September 24, 2013.

- **Allows reclassification by administrative order:** Attempting to encourage FDA to finally complete the task of reclassifying all pre-amendment devices, FDASIA now allows the agency to reclassify a device by administrative order, rather than by regulation. As appropriate, stakeholders will still have input in the reclassification process, as FDA will need to publish any proposed reclassification order in the *Federal Register*, complete with a discussion of valid supporting scientific evidence, as well as hold an advisory panel meeting and consider public comments.

- **Key changes to custom device program:** FDASIA codified both FDA's and the court's interpretation of the custom device exemption, imposed a new "five-unit" limit on custom device production, and imposed annual reporting requirements for custom devices.

Other changes implemented by the law include allowing all submitters of humanitarian device exemptions to make a profit for devices intended for the pediatric patient population, withdrawing a controversial guidance document regarding when a 510(k) needs to be submitted for a device modification, increased willingness by the agency to accept clinical data from abroad, and modifications to the appeals process. Since its passing, the agency has published many guidance documents describing how the provisions in the law are being implemented. The agency's progress toward meeting the law's provisions can be tracked online.[10]

This chapter provides highlights of various premarket requirements that apply to products before they can be marketed in the United States, as well as various postmarket requirements that are triggered when a product is marketed in this country.

---

[10]   FDASIA-TRACK, U.S. Food and Drug Administration at http://www.fda.gov/aboutfda/transparency/track/ucm328907.htm.

The Regulation of Medical Devices under the FDCA—Premarket Regulations

Is It a Device?

The FDCA defines the term "device" as "an instrument, apparatus, implement, machine, contrivance, implant, in vitro reagent, or other similar or related article, including any component, part, or accessory, which is: 1) recognized in the official National Formulary, or the United States Pharmacopoeia, or any supplement to them; 2) intended for use in the diagnosis of disease or other conditions, or in the cure, mitigation, treatment, or prevention of disease, in man or other animals; or 3) intended to affect the structure or any function of the body of man or other animals, and which does not achieve its primary intended purposes through chemical action within or on the body of man or other animals and which is not dependent upon being metabolized for the achievement of its primary intended purposes."[11]

The drafters of the 1976 amendments recognized it was important to decide whether particular products are "drugs" or "devices," and determined that if a product's primary mode of action was mechanical, it should be treated as a device. Thus, if a health-related product achieves its primary purpose by means not involving chemical reactions or metabolism, it is a device.[12] If the primary intended use of the product is achieved through chemical action or by being metabolized by the body, the product is usually a drug. According to FDA, however, the fact that a product is not metabolized and does not achieve its principal purpose by chemical action does not automatically make it a device.

This policy decision is exemplified by a letter FDA wrote to the manufacturer of a product called Quick-Prep,[13] in response to its request for an FDA opinion whether a saline solution was a drug or a device. FDA ruled that it was a drug although it did not accomplish any of its primary purposes either by being metabolized or by chemical action on or within the body. This position is curious in light of the definition of "device." Similarly, products such as laxatives that work by mechanical action still may be considered drugs because they are "drug-like" substances. FDA's countenance of this position increases the uncertainty about whether some products are drugs or devices.

In addition, the SMDA introduced the concept of combination products and allowed FDA to begin to clarify product jurisdiction issues.[14] Shortly thereafter, in 1991, the Center for Biologics Evaluation and Research (CBER), the Center for Drug Evaluation and Research (CDER), and CDRH entered into three Intercenter Agreements (ICAs): a CBER–CDER

---

[11] FDCA § 201(h), 21 U.S.C. § 321(h). The definition was modified slightly by the Safe Medical Devices Act of 1990.

[12] FDCA § 201(g), (h), 21 U.S.C. § 321(g), (h).

[13] Letter from William Randolph, Acting Associate Comm'r for Regulatory Affairs, FDA, to Lester J. Lifton, M.D.

[14] A general definition is given in 21 C.F.R. § 3.2(e) that describes combination products as:

  1. Two or more regulated components that are physically, chemically, or otherwise combined, or mixed and produced as a single entity;

  2. Two or more separate products that are packaged together in a single package or as a unit;

Intercenter Agreement, a CBER–CDRH Intercenter Agreement and a CDER–CDRH Intercenter Agreement.

The ICAs help to explain how various categories of combination products were classified and assigned at the time the agreements were written. In 1991, the agreements were the major jurisdictional statements issued by the agency. While the ICAs continue to provide useful guidance related to product jurisdiction, their usefulness is becoming limited as new products are developed, as new uses are developed for existing products, and as additional laws, regulations, and guidance are promulgated. FDA has continued to classify and assign many new products not specifically covered by the ICAs. For these and other reasons, the ICAs have become incomplete statements.

In general, the drug or device determination often rests on whether the primary mode of action of these products is performed by the "drug or by the device" segment of the combination. Additionally, the greater the concern about the risks presented by a "drug-type" substance, the more likely it is that the agency will consider the combination a drug under the primary jurisdiction of CDER. FDA's policies in this area are based upon the fact that drugs usually are regulated more stringently than devices.

FDA's product jurisdiction regulations[15] provide manufacturers with a mechanism for obtaining an official agency determination as to how a product will be primarily regulated. In general, manufacturers can prepare a request for designation (RFD) for submission to the OCP.[16] Under the regulations, RFDs are appropriate whenever the product jurisdiction is not covered by an ICA or when the product jurisdiction is in dispute. It is not uncommon for CDER and CDRH to have differing views over which Center has primary jurisdiction over a product.

On November 23, 2005, a rule defining the methods for classifying products based on their primary mode of action became effective.[17] The new rule redefined the primary mode of action[18] and provided a two-tiered assignment algorithm for classification of products.[19] In June 2011, FDA issued new draft guidance regarding device classification issues as well as a guidance document with respect to preparing an RFD.[20] While those rules, coupled with the RFD requirements and FDA's recent guidance, added clarity to the regulatory regime, issues still arise regarding how particularly novel or complex products will be regulated.

---

3. Two or more separate products that are packaged separately, intended for use only with an approved individual specified product, where both are required to achieve the intended use, indication, or effect, and the labeling of the approved product would need to be changed.

[15]   21 C.F.R. pt. 3. See Chapter 17 *infra*.

[16]   OCP was created in 2002 as a result of the Medical Device User Fee and Modernization Act. Its main duties include assigning combination product reviews to a Center and coordinating timely premarket reviews involving more than one Center. It also must ensure the consistency and appropriateness of combination product postmarket regulation.

[17]   70 Fed. Reg. 49,848 (2005).

[18]   21 C.F.R. § 3.2.

[19]   *Id.* § 3.4.

[20]   Office of Combination Products, Food and Drug Administration, Classification of Products as Drugs and Devices and Additional Product Classification Issues (June 2011); Interpretation of the Term "Chemical Action" in the Definition of Device Under Section 201(h) of the Federal Food, Drug, and Cosmetic Act (June 2011); How to Write a Request for Designation (RFD) (April 2011).

For example, in September 2012, French manufacturer Prevor sued and won summary judgment[21] against the FDA's decision to regulate its combination product as a drug in the United States District Court for the District of Columbia (referred to as *Prevor I*). FDA claimed that Prevor's Diphoterine Skin Wash (DSW), a chemical wash applied through an aerosol canister that mitigates burns in industrial workplaces, should be regulated as a drug because the liquid contained within the spray canister achieves its primary intended purpose, "at least in part," through chemical action (FDA found that the wash liquid had two purposes: 1) wash chemical off the skin and 2) neutralize the chemical that is on the skin). The court found FDA acted arbitrarily and capriciously because it failed to address or explain what makes the chemical effect within DSW the primary intended purpose of the product and, thus, subject to regulation as a drug. Specifically, the court found lacking from the administrative record FDA's qualitative analysis or scientific information that it relied on when determining that the product's primary intended purpose is the chemical effect. The court rejected FDA's argument that if a chemical reaction of a product is "at least in part" an element of the mode of action of the combination product, it can thus be regulated as a drug. The court remanded the decision back to FDA to determine whether there were solid scientific reasons for FDA's classification.

On May 25, 2013, FDA again classified the Prevor combination product as being subjected to the drug regulations by finding that the product's drug solution is the primary mode of action because the solution is expected to make the greatest contribution to the overall intended therapeutic effect of DSW. FDA claimed that a combination product is not subject to device regulation if the chemical action "meaningfully contributes" to its primary intended purpose. This time around, FDA reviewed publications and Prevor material to support its decision making. In addition, the agency found that DSW had only a single primary purpose (as opposed to the two purposes the agency had previously identified) of preventing and minimizing accidental chemical burn injuries. Accordingly, the agency did not have to select a primary purpose among a number of purposes, the product's primary intended purpose.

Again, Prevor sought for relief from the United States District Court for the District of Columbia (referred to as *Prevor II*) claiming that its product should not be subjected to the drug regulations. On September 9, 2014, the court upheld Prevor's motion for summary judgment.[22] The court accepted FDA's conclusion concerning DSW's purpose but rejected FDA's interpretation of the FDCA. Specifically, the court disagreed with the agency's statutory interpretation in that FDA only needs to determine that the product's chemical reaction "meaningfully contributes" to its primary purpose in order to subject the combination product to the drug regulations. The court found that "meaningfully contributes" does not equate to the statutory requirement that a combination product must "achieve its primary intended purposes through chemical action within or on the body of man" to be regulated as a drug.[23] The court did not rule that FDA was required to quantify the exact contribution of a product component in achieving its ultimate goal. The Court did find, however, that the FDCA required more than simply finding that the product would not work as claimed

---

21   Prevor v. U.S. Food and Drug Admin., 895 F. Supp. 2d 90 (D.D.C. Sept. 25, 2012).

22   Prevor v. U.S. Food and Drug Admin., No. 13-1177 (D.D.C. Sept. 14, 2014).

23   21 U.S.C. § 321(h).

without chemical action. Again, the court remanded the case to FDA to determine a standard that complies with the FDCA and to classify DSW accordingly.

Classification/Reclassification/Downclassification

The regulatory pathway to bring a new product to market depends on the class in which the device is regulated. Device classification proceedings had begun even before the passage of the 1976 Medical Device Amendments. To date, FDA has established classifications for approximately 1,700 different generic types of devices.[24] Each of these generic types of devices is assigned to one of three regulatory classes based on the level of control necessary to assure the safety and effectiveness of the device. The three classes and the requirements that apply to them are:

- **Class I.** Class I devices are those devices that pose the least risk and are subject to FDA's general controls. General controls include: adulteration and misbranding provisions; registration and listing; premarket notification (510(k)) (for a limited number of Class I devices); notification and repair; replacement or refund; records and reports; banned devices, and Good Manufacturing Practices (unless exempt).

- **Class II.** Class II devices are those devices for which general controls are not sufficient to ensure safety and effectiveness. Class II devices must meet general controls (including premarket notification requirements unless exempt) as well as special controls, if applicable. Special controls include: performance standards; postmarket surveillance; patient registries; guidelines recommendations; and "other appropriate actions."

- **Class III.** Class III devices are those devices for which general and special controls alone are not sufficient to establish safety and efficacy and devices that: i) are used in supporting or sustaining human life or ii) are for a use which is of substantial importance in preventing impairment of human health or iii) present a potential unreasonable risk of illness or injury.

One option for seeking guidance from FDA is to file a request for classification under section 513(g) of the FDCA. As experience and knowledge about a device increase, the original classification can be adjusted through the process of reclassification. Changes in classification are based on FDA's receipt of new information about a device. FDA may, on its own, or in response to an outside petition, change a device's classification by regulation. A manufacturer who wishes to have a device reclassified to a lower class must convince FDA that the less stringent class requirements will be sufficient to provide reasonable assurance of safety and effectiveness.

FDA notifies petitioners of determinations made on petitions for reclassification by a reclassification letter. If a determination is made to reclassify a device, FDA may publish a proposed rule to reclassify in the *Federal Register,* which includes the scientific justification for reclassification and that affords a period for comment. Subsequently, a final rule is published in the *Federal Register* that changes the reclassification.[25] However, with the enactment of

---

[24]   Center for Devices and Radiological Health, U.S. Food and Drug Administration, Device Advice, at http://www.fda.gov/MedicalDevices/DeviceRegulationandGuidance/default.html (last updated May 3, 2011) [hereinafter "Device Advice"].

[25]   Note: As a result of FDA's reclassification efforts in the 1990s, most Class I devices are now exempt from the agency's 510(k) requirements.

FDASIA in 2012, FDA can now reclassify a device by administrative order, rather than by regulation. As appropriate, stakeholders will still have input in the reclassification process, as FDA will need to publish any proposed reclassification order in the *Federal Register*, complete with a discussion of valid supporting scientific evidence, as well as hold an advisory panel meeting and consider public comments.

The Section 510(k) Process

Section 510(k) of the FDCA, coupled with its implementing regulations in 21 C.F.R. Part 807, requires the filing of a premarket notification (510(k)) by a manufacturer prior to: 1) initial marketing of a device; 2) making a change or modification to a cleared device that "could significantly affect the safety or effectiveness" of the device; or 3) making a major change or modification to the intended use of a cleared device.[26] FDA uses the 510(k) provision of the FDCA to permit access to the market for new devices that are claimed to be similar to a legally marketed Class I device, Class II device or Class III device for which premarket approval is not required (i.e., predicate device(s)).

Under this premarket pathway, manufacturers are required to submit a 510(k) notification to FDA at least 90 days prior to the applicant's intended introduction into the market of a device that requires premarket clearance. A device that requires 510(k) clearance, however, may not be marketed until the applicant receives an "order" from FDA, which states that the new device is substantially equivalent to a legally marketed predicate device. FDA's regulations require manufacturers to include in the notification the classification status of the device and information such as proposed labeling and information (including nonclinical and, in some instances, clinical data) that demonstrates that the new device is substantially equivalent to a legally marketed predicate device.

In order for a new device to be found "substantially equivalent" to one or more legally marketed predicate devices, the new device must have: 1) the same intended use as a predicate; *and* 2) either a) the same technological characteristics as the predicate device or b) different technological characteristics, but the different characteristics must not raise new questions of safety and effectiveness as compared to the predicate devices and must demonstrate substantial equivalence. The agency strongly prefers that substantial equivalence decisions be based on a single predicate device whenever possible. However, a device that is the subject of a 510(k) notification may have multiple predicate devices, as certain technological features of the device may be substantially equivalent to certain predicate devices, while other features may be substantially equivalent to other predicates.[27] In such a case, a "primary predicate" should be identified with indications for use and technological characteristics most similar to the device under review. FDA no longer accepts "split predicates," that is, one predicate for intended use and another predicate for technological characteristics. With regard to the intended use of the device, FDA is directed

---

26   *See* FDCA § 510(k), 21 U.S.C. § 360(k). *See also* 21 C.F.R. § 807.81.

27   FDCA § 513(i)(l)(a), 21 U.S.C. § 360c(i)(l)(a). Note: FDA has developed a decision tree that facilitates making the substantial equivalence determination. See Office of Device Evaluation, Guidance The 510(k) Program: Evaluating Substantial Equivalence in Premarket Notifications [510(k)] (July 28, 2014). FDCA § 513(i)(1)(E)(i), 21 U.S.C. § 360c(i)(1)(E)(i).

to limit its determination as to whether the product is substantially equivalent based on the device's proposed labeling included in the 510(k) filing. [28]

On July 28, 2014, FDA finalized its guidance, "The 510(k) Program: Evaluating Substantial Equivalence in Premarket Notifications [510(k)]"[29] (a draft version was released on December 27, 2011). Among other items, this guidance included a definitive statement that "split predicate" arguments are inconsistent with the 510(k) review standard. It also affirmed the agency's novel concept of a "reference device," which was first articulated in the 2011 draft version, and clarifies that FDA will rely on such "reference devices" only in assessing the acceptability of the scientific methods proposed in a 510(k) notice for determining whether a new device with different technological characteristics that do not raise different questions of safety or effectiveness is as safe and effective as the predicate. It should be noted that since implementation of the concepts and standards contained through release of the draft guidance in 2011, the not substantially equivalent (NSE) rate has risen from a historically low rate of 2 percent to more than 10 percent in the current environment. Questions have been raised as to whether these new concepts and standards are precluding the 510(k) pathway for a fair number of devices that would otherwise not have raised any questions under prior guidance and practice.

Because FDA allows manufacturers to vary their methods of presentation in order to properly put forward their arguments for substantial equivalence, there is no single way to put together a 510(k) notification. However, certain basic elements are found in all 510(k) applications. The information required in a 510(k) premarket notification, outlined below, is specified in several sections of the *Code of Federal Regulations*.[30] The contents of a premarket notification are as follows:

- **Device Name.** The device name, including both the trade or proprietary name and the classification name, must be included in a 510(k) premarket notification.

- **Identification.** The applicant's name and street address must be included in a 510(k) premarket notification.

- **Registration Number.** If applicable, the FDA establishment registration number of the owner or operator submitting the premarket notification should be included.

- **Classification.** The applicant should include the class of the device, (i.e., Class I, II, or III). If known, include the appropriate classification panel.

- **Description.** The 510(k) notification should include a physical description of the new device, together with an explanation of its intended use, principles of operation, power source, composition, and other information necessary to understand the device.

- **Substantial Equivalence Comparison.** Applicants should attempt to make a comparison of the new device to its predicate as easy as possible for the FDA reviewer. The 510(k) notification should, therefore, include a discussion of the similarities and differences between the device and its predicate device(s), and should make use of comparative tables whenever possible.

---

[28]   *Id.*

[29]   *Available at* http://www.fda.gov/downloads/MedicalDevices/.../UCM284443.pdf (last visited Nov. 20, 2014).

[30]   21 C.F.R. §§ 807.87, 807.90, 807.92, 807.93.

- **Software.** Applications for computerized devices must follow the appropriate CDRH guidance.[31]

- **Standards.** The applicant should identify any mandatory or voluntary standards met by the device.

- **Performance.** Performance data are often needed to help demonstrate that the proposed device is as safe and effective as the predicate device.

- **Biocompatibility.** Submissions for devices that directly contact the body must include a description of the characteristics of their materials. This description should compare the device to its predicates in sufficient detail to determine biocompatibility, as well as the kind of tests needed to determine biocompatibility. Any material differences between the new device and the claimed predicate device must be stated explicitly, but it is just as important to state whether the materials comprising the two devices are identical. Manufacturers need to provide biocompatibility test data for any materials found in the new device that are not present in other cleared or approved devices that have the same nature and duration of contact as the device under review.

- **Sterility.** Submissions for devices that are labeled sterile must cite their sterilization method, sterility assurance level, and the method used to validate the sterilization cycle.

- **Labeling.** Although applicants may submit drafts of their device labeling, the submission should be representative of the final version.

- **Class III Certification and Summary.** All 510(k) submissions for Class III devices must have a special added certification statement by which the applicant must certify in its 510(k) premarket notification that it has searched for all available information relative to that device's safety and effectiveness, and the 510(k) notification must include citations to any adverse safety and effectiveness data.

- **510(k) Summary or Statement.** A premarket notification must include either a summary of the 510(k) safety and effectiveness information upon which the substantial equivalence determination is based or a statement that this information will be made available by the 510(k) applicant to any person within 30 days of a written request.

- **Truthful and Accuracy Statement.** All 510(k) applicants must include a statement certifying that all information in the application is truthful and accurate and that no material fact has been omitted.

510(k) submitters also must pay certain fees to the agency. MDUFMA authorized FDA to charge a user fee for premarket submissions, including 510(k)s. In 2012, the Medical Device User Fee Amendments (MDUFA III) reauthorized user fees through Fiscal Year (FY) 2017. The intent of the user fees is to, among other things, help defray the cost of the review of a significant number of 510(k)s and to help the agency meet certain performance goals for making substantial equivalence determinations.

In addition to the premarket contents described above, the Office of Device Evaluation (ODE) has issued many device-specific guidance documents that contain requirements

---

[31] Office of Device Evaluation, Center for Devices and Radiological Health, Food and Drug Administration, Guidance for Industry and FDA Staff: Guidance for the Content of Premarket Submissions for Software Contained in Medical Devices (May 11, 2005).

for data and information to be submitted with the 510(k).[32] The data and information may include engineering testing data, information regarding applicable national and international standards, and/or human clinical data. These documents are posted on FDA's website, which should be consulted frequently as documents are added and removed from the site as necessary.

Premarket notification submissions that include clinical information in order to demonstrate substantial equivalence are often referred to as "hybrid 510(k)s."[33] When a 510(k) includes clinical data, FDA requires study sponsors to either disclose certain financial interests of the clinical investigators or certify that the clinical investigators do not hold any disclosable financial interests. Moreover, under FDAAA, any 510(k) that contains clinical data must be accompanied by a certification that the applicant has complied with the clinical trial registration requirements.

Initially, the agency required proof of substantial equivalence to a device that was marketed prior to May 28, 1976, the date of enactment of the 1976 Medical Device Amendments. However, section 513(i) of the FDCA (which was enacted with the passage of the Safe Medical Devices Act of 1990) makes it clear that a postamendments Class I or Class II device may be found substantially equivalent to any "legally marketed" Class I or Class II device or Class III device for which FDA has not yet called for PMAs.[34] The predicate device, therefore, need not be a pre-amendments device (a device on the market prior to May 28, 1976), but it cannot be a device that was removed from the market by FDA or determined to be misbranded or adulterated by judicial order.

FDA responds to a 510(k) notification in one of three ways. FDA can 1) decide that a device is substantially equivalent to a legally marketed device that does not require premarket approval; 2) decide that a device is not substantially equivalent; or 3) notify the applicant that additional information is required in order to determine whether the device is, in fact, substantially equivalent to one or more predicate devices. In FDA's view, a finding that a device is NSE to the predicate device means that it is a new Class III device, which requires FDA approval of a PMA before being marketed.

In the past, when CDRH reviewed a 510(k) for a device for which there was no legally marketed predicate device, but that would have otherwise been appropriately placed in Class I or Class II, the agency was required to find the product to be not substantially equivalent, leaving the reclassification or premarket approval processes as the only viable paths to market. As a result of FDAMA, however, section 513(f)(2) was added to the FDCA.[35]

---

[32]   ODE is the office within FDA that is responsible for the program areas through which medical devices are evaluated or cleared for clinical trials and marketing.

[33]   If information concerning similarity to a predicate device must be obtained through a clinical trial, the trial is subject to the requirement of the IDE regulation, 21 C.F.R. § 812.

[34]   Note: Section 206 of FDAMA exempts almost all Class I devices from FDA's premarket notification requirements; however, this exemption does not apply to devices that are of substantial importance in preventing the impairment of human health or that present a potentially unreasonable risk of injury or illness. FDAMA also requires FDA to publish each type of Class II device that the agency determines does not require 510(k) clearance in the *Federal Register.*

[35]   Congress included this section to limit unnecessary expenditure of CDRH and manufacturer resources that could occur if low-risk devices were subject to premarket approval (PMA) under section 515. The section was not intended to significantly increase the number of not substantially equivalent (NSE) determinations

Under what has become known as the "de novo" downclassification process, if a device manufacturer receives written notification from FDA that its device is not substantially equivalent to a legally marketed predicate and, therefore, is designated as a Class III device, the manufacturer may submit a "de novo" request arguing that the device should be placed in Class I or II based on its level of risk.[36] The manufacturer must file such a request with the agency within 30 days of receiving the Class III notification.[37] FDA then has 60 days to respond with a written order classifying the device.[38] Under FDASIA, FDA is authorized to accept "direct de novo" petitions, meaning the company does not need to file a 510(k) and have the device be found NSE first. If FDA reclassifies the device as either Class I or Class II, then it may be marketed and may serve as a predicate for future substantial equivalence determinations.[39] However, if the agency determines that the device should remain a Class III device, PMA approval will be required.[40]

Although FDA's response to applications under section 510(k) establishes, for all practical purposes, whether a particular device can be marketed without a PMA, FDA does not "approve" a premarket notification in the same way that it approves a PMA. FDA's response to section 510(k) notifications, known as a "clearance," states that its determination extends only to whether a device is substantially equivalent to a predicate device and not whether it is safe and effective for its intended use(s).

One of the most difficult decisions for 510(k) holders is when to submit a new premarket notification for changes that the 510(k) holder intends to make to one of its legally marketed devices. FDA's regulations require that a new 510(k) notification be cleared by FDA before the 510(k) holder makes a change or modification to the device that "could significantly affect the safety or effectiveness of the device, e.g., a significant change or modification in design, material, chemical composition, energy source, or manufacturing process"; or makes a major change or modification in the intended use of the device.[41] Typically, 510(k) sponsors place emphasis on the word "significantly" and try to argue that the proposed modification could not *significantly* affect the device's safety or effectiveness, whereas FDA typically places emphasis on the word "could," in other words, the *possibility* that the change could significantly affect the safety or effectiveness of the cleared device.

Although the 510(k) holder is responsible for making the initial determination as to whether a change or modification could significantly affect safety or effectiveness, FDA may second-guess the company's decisions. If FDA disagrees with the company's decision not to file a new 510(k) notification for a device modification or change, the agency may make the company file a 510(k) notification retrospectively and discontinue marketing the device while the 510(k) is pending. The agency may also take enforcement action against the company. As a practical matter, however, if the company has made a good-faith effort to document the reasons that it did not submit a new 510(k) for the device change, if the

---

or to otherwise alter the 510(k) provisions of the act or CDRH's approach to the 510(k) classification process.

[36] FDCA § 513(f), 21 U.S.C. § 360c(f).
[37] *Id.*
[38] *Id.*
[39] *Id.*
[40] *Id.*
[41] 21 C.F.R. § 807.81(a)(3)(i).

reasons are defensible and appear genuine, and there are no demonstrated safety problems with the modified device, FDA may (but is certainly not bound to) use its enforcement discretion and allow the company to continue marketing the device while the new 510(k) notification is pending.

To assist industry in making 510(k) determinations for device modifications, FDA issued a policy in 1997 regarding the criteria that should be used in deciding whether a device modification or change requires a new 510(k) submission.[42] In July 2011, the agency issued an updated draft version of this guidance for public comment purposes.[43] Due to significant opposition to the guidance by parties that believed it would significantly expand the situations in which 510(k)s are required for changes, in FDASIA, Congress ordered FDA to withdraw the document. The agency is in the process of re-issuing the guidance, which is expected to mirror the 1997 guidance more closely. In the interim, the 1997 guidance is still in effect.

Though not binding on either industry or FDA, this guidance document provides a framework for making decisions about whether device changes require premarket clearance. When making such decisions, 510(k) holders should carefully consider the reason why the changes are being made and the cumulative effect of the changes. For example, changes made to address field complaints are more likely to trigger the 510(k) filing requirement than those made to enhance a product that is performing well. FDA requires the 510(k) holder to compare the modified device to the last cleared version of the device (not the last marketed version of the device) in assessing whether the modifications trigger the criteria for submitting a new 510(k) notice. In addition, the standard for whether a new 510(k) notice is required to be submitted applies to changes that could significantly affect *either* in a positive *or* negative way the safety or effectiveness of the cleared device. It also is important to note that the criteria for when a new 510(k) notice is required for a modified device is *not* whether the device is actually substantially equivalent to one or more predicate devices. That is a determination made by FDA once the criteria for needing to submit a new 510(k) notice have been triggered.

On March 20, 1998, FDA published a guidance document entitled, "A New 510(k) Paradigm—Alternate Approaches to Demonstrating Substantial Equivalence in Premarket Notifications."[44] Under this scheme, manufacturers of devices subject to the 510(k) requirements have the option of submitting 1) a traditional 510(k) notification (described above), 2) a Special 510(k): Device Modification, or 3) an Abbreviated 510(k) in order to market the device. Under the Special 510(k): Device Modification option, a manufacturer that intends to modify its own legally marketed cleared device may conduct the necessary verification and validation activities to demonstrate that the design outputs of the modified device meet the design input requirements. The manufacturer also has the option of using a third party to assess conformance with design controls. In this case, the Special 510(k) application includes both a conformance statement from the third party, as well as a

42   Office of Device Evaluation, 510(k) Memorandum: Deciding When to Submit a 510(k) for a Change to an Existing Device (Jan. 10, 1997).

43   Office of Device Evaluation, Guidance for Industry and FDA Staff - 510(k) Device Modifications: Deciding When to Submit a 510(k) for a Change to an Existing Device (July 27, 2011).

44   Office of Device Evaluation, The New 510(k) Paradigm—Alternate Approaches to Demonstrating Substantial Equivalence in Premarket Notifications—Final Guidance (Mar. 20, 1998).

declaration of conformity signed by the manufacturer. Special 510(k)s are usually processed by ODE within 30 days of receipt. Modifications that affect the intended use or alter the basic fundamental scientific technology of the device are not eligible for this alternate type of submission, but may be eligible for the proposed new Abbreviated 510(k) route as described below.

Under the Abbreviated 510(k) option, device manufacturers are permitted to submit Abbreviated 510(k)s for devices subject to the 510(k) requirements when a special controls guidance document (SCGD) exists or when FDA has recognized an individual special control such as a relevant standard. Abbreviated 510(k)s include summary information that describes how special controls have been used to address the risks associated with the device type and a declaration of conformity with any relevant recognized standards, if applicable. In an Abbreviated 510(k), a manufacturer also has the option of using a third party to assess conformance with the recognized standard.

Premarket Approval Applications

In 1986, FDA promulgated a regulation that outlines the expected content of an original PMA and any supplements to that submission. It also sets forth the criteria to be used by FDA for evaluating a PMA. PMAs are required for the following types of devices:

- Pre-amendments devices: devices on the market at the time of the 1976 amendments that were subsequently classified or reclassified into Class III (and devices that were found to be substantially equivalent to these pre-amendments devices before being classified into Class III);
- Transitional devices: devices on the market at the time of the 1976 amendments that were then considered "new drugs," and devices substantially equivalent to these devices; and
- All devices developed after the 1976 amendments that are not substantially equivalent to a legally marketed predicate device.

FDA may require PMAs for products in the first category of medical devices—i.e., those pre-amendments devices placed in Class III after review by one of FDA's outside advisory panels—only after the agency publishes a regulation that establishes a timetable for their submission. Under section 515(i) of the FDCA, by December 1, 1995 (or December 1, 1996, after FDA requested a one-year extension), FDA was required to downclassify any pre-amendments Class III device for which FDA had not published a final regulation requiring the submission of a PMA.

FDA has been slow to call for PMA applications for pre-amendments Class III devices and, consequently, missed the December 1, 1995, and December 1, 1996, deadlines for most pre-amendments Class III devices and subsequent deadlines that were established.

FDA has not yet called for PMAs for all the 25 remaining pre-amendments devices or down-classified these device classes. The device classification regulations for these devices state that a PMA has not yet been requested and that a 510(k) is required prior to marketing the device. If and when FDA does publish a final regulation requiring a PMA for a device that falls into this category, the PMA must be submitted within 90 days of the date of promulgation of that final regulation, or 30 months after the publication of the final classification of the device, whichever is later.

In addition to devices categorized as Class III, certain other devices may require a PMA prior to marketing. In particular, new high-risk devices (a device that supports or sustains human life, is of substantial importance in preventing impairment of human health, or presents a potential, unreasonable risk of illness or injury) that have been found to be not substantially equivalent to a 510(k) device must have an approved PMA prior to marketing. Companies also may use the product development protocol (PDP) process (discussed below) though this mechanism is rarely used.

A PMA differs significantly from a 510(k) premarket notification in the amount of information (particularly clinical data) that must be submitted to FDA. In contrast to 510(k) notices, which must demonstrate that the new device is "substantially equivalent" to a predicate device, a PMA must be supported by valid scientific evidence to demonstrate the "safety and effectiveness" of the device for its intended use(s). As explained more fully below, PMAs typically include the results of extensive clinical trials, bench tests, laboratory studies, animal studies, and references to any standards relevant to a device's safety or effectiveness. The PMA also must contain a complete description of the device and its components; a detailed description of the methods, facilities, and controls used to manufacture the device; the proposed labeling and advertising literature; and any training materials. In addition, all published and unpublished literature concerning the prior use of the product must be included, as well as a bibliography of all published reports that were not submitted and were known to the applicant concerning the device's safety and effectiveness. The review time for a PMA is significantly longer than for 510(k) notifications. The following table summarizes the major distinctions between 510(k) notices and PMAs.

	510(k) Premarket Notification	Premarket Approval (PMA)
Devices Subject to Requirement	Some Class I, most Class II, and Class III pre-amendments devices for which PMAs have not been called	All Class III postamendments devices and Class III pre-amendments devices for which PMAs have been called
Clinical Data Requirements	Many are not supported by clinical data; Hybrid 510(k) notifications include clinical data	Clinical studies usually required to support submission
Evidence of Safety and Efficacy Required	Information and data to support the "substantial equivalence" of the device to a legally marketed predicate device	Clinical data and/or scientific evidence supporting "safety and efficacy" claims

	510(k) Premarket Notification	Premarket Approval (PMA)
Marketing Rights	No exclusivity	Like a Product License
Average FDA Review Time*	74 days	208 days
Regulations on Device Changes	Must file new 510(k) if the change "could significantly affect" the safety or efficacy of the device or constitutes a major change to the intended use of the device	Must file a new PMA, some form of PMA supplement, or annual report depending on the nature and effect of the change on the safety and effectiveness of the device
Advisory Panel Review	No Advisory Panel Review for almost all 510(k) devices	Advisory Panel Review for some but not all PMAs. Generally, no Advisory Panel Review for PMA supplements

*As of Fiscal Year 2010; taken from Improvements in Device Review: Results of CDRH's Plan of Action for Premarket Review of Devices, U.S. Food and Drug Administration, November 2012.

In evaluating the safety and effectiveness of a device, FDA is permitted to consider only valid scientific evidence. Companies may use data obtained with earlier versions of the device in order to support the safety and efficacy of the new device, if the changes between device versions are not significant and do not invalidate the relevance of the data.[45] Nonetheless, in most cases, as described above, FDA requires studies on Class III medical devices that are designed like new drug trials (e.g., prospective, randomized controls).

The format and information required in a PMA are outlined in 21 C.F.R. 814.20 as follows:

- The name and address of the applicant.
- A table of contents that specifies the volume and page number for each item referred to in the table.
- A summary in sufficient detail that shall contain the following information:
  - Indications for use.
  - Device description.
  - Alternative practices and procedures for diagnosing, treating, preventing, curing, or mitigating the disease or condition for which the device is intended.
    - A brief description of the foreign and U.S. marketing history

---

[45] FDCA § 520(g), 21 U.S.C. § 360j(g).

- Summary of studies. An abstract of any study information or report described in the PMA including nonclinical laboratory studies and clinical investigations involving human subjects.
  - Conclusions drawn from the studies.
- A complete description of:
  - The device, including pictorial representations;
  - Each of the functional components or ingredients of the device if the device consists of more than one physical component or ingredient;
  - The properties of the device relevant to the diagnosis, treatment, prevention, cure, or mitigation of a disease or condition;
  - The principles of operation of the device; and
  - The methods used in, and the facilities and controls used for, the manufacture, processing, packing, storage, and, where appropriate, installation of the device, in sufficient detail so that a person generally familiar with current good manufacturing practice can make a knowledgeable judgment about the quality control used in the manufacture of the device.
- Reference to any performance standard under section 514 of the Act or the Radiation Control for Health and Safety Act of 1968 (42 U.S.C. 263b *et seq.*) in effect or proposed at the time of the submission and to any voluntary standard that is relevant to any aspect of the safety or effectiveness of the device and that is known to or that should reasonably be known to the applicant. The applicant shall—
  - Provide adequate information to demonstrate how the device meets, or justify any deviation from, any performance standard established under section 514 of the Act or under the Radiation Control for Health and Safety Act, and
  - Explain any deviation from a voluntary standard.
- Technical sections which shall contain data and information in sufficient detail to permit FDA to determine whether to approve or deny approval of the application. Companies should consult device-specific guidance documents to determine the level of evidence that FDA expects for the specific type of device.
  - Results of the nonclinical laboratory studies with the device including microbiological, toxicological, immunological, biocompatibility, stress, wear, shelf life, and other laboratory or animal tests as appropriate.
  - Results of the clinical investigations involving human subjects with the device including clinical protocols, number of investigators and subjects per investigator, subject selection and exclusion criteria, study population, study period, safety and effectiveness data, adverse reactions and complications, patient discontinuation, patient complaints, device failures and replacements, tabulations of data from all individual subject report forms and copies of such forms for each subject who died during a clinical investigation or who did not complete the investigation, results of statistical analyses of the clinical investigations, device failures and replacements, contraindications and precautions for use of the device, and any other appropriate information from the clinical investigations. Any investigation conducted under

an IDE shall be identified as such. Information on clinical investigations involving human subjects shall include the following:

- A statement with respect to each study that it either was conducted in compliance with the institutional review board regulations in 21 C.F.R. Part 56, or was not subject to the regulations under 21 C.F.R. §§ 56.104 or 56.105, and that it was conducted in compliance with the informed consent regulations in 21 C.F.R. Part 50; or if the study was not conducted in compliance with those regulations, a brief statement of the reason for the noncompliance.

- A statement that each study was conducted in compliance with 21 C.F.R. Part 812 or 21 C.F.R. Part 813 concerning sponsors of clinical investigations and clinical investigators, or if the study was not conducted in compliance with those regulations, a brief statement of the reason for the noncompliance.

- For a PMA supported solely by data from one investigation, a justification showing that data and other information from a single investigator are sufficient to demonstrate the safety and effectiveness of the device and to ensure reproducibility of test results.

- The following:

  - A bibliography of all published reports not submitted under this section, whether adverse or supportive, known to or that should reasonably be known to the applicant and that concern the safety or effectiveness of the device.

  - An identification, discussion, and analysis of any other data, information, or report relevant to an evaluation of the safety and effectiveness of the device known to or that should reasonably be known to the applicant from any source, foreign or domestic, including information derived from investigations other than those proposed in the application and from commercial marketing experience.

  - Copies of such published reports or unpublished information in the possession of or reasonably obtainable by the applicant if an FDA advisory committee or FDA requests.

- One or more samples of the device and its components, if requested by FDA. If it is impractical to submit a requested sample of the device, the applicant shall name the location at which FDA may examine and test one or more devices.

- Copies of all proposed labeling for the device. Such labeling may include, e.g., instructions for installation and any information, literature, or advertising that constitutes labeling under section 201(m) of the act.

- An environmental assessment. If the applicant believes that the action qualifies for exclusion, the PMA shall provide information that establishes to FDA's satisfaction that the action requested is included within the excluded category and meets the criteria for the applicable exclusion.

- A financial certification or disclosure statement or both as required by 21 C.F.R. Part 54.

- Such other information as FDA may request. If necessary, FDA will obtain the concurrence of the appropriate FDA advisory committee before requesting additional information.

When clinical data are included in the PMA (which is almost always), FDA requires the applicants to either disclose certain financial interests of the clinical investigators or certify that the clinical investigators do not hold any disclosable financial interests. Under FDAAA, PMAs that contain clinical data must also be accompanied by a certification that the applicant has complied with the clinical trial registration requirements.

Prior to submitting a PMA application, a company may request a meeting with the agency to discuss the type of scientific evidence that will be needed to obtain marketing approval. This process can be done informally through the pre-submission meeting process, or through a Determination Meeting or Agreement Meeting. To obtain informal feedback, often at an early stage of development of the company's testing plan, companies have the opportunity to meet with the agency to discuss potential data requirements under the pre-submission meeting process discussed in the Investigational Devices section below. As PMAs often require extensive scientific and clinical data, discussing the necessary elements to establish the safety and efficacy of a device at an early stage is often productive and potentially cost-saving for the company. A Determination Meeting is intended to provide the company with FDA's formal determination of the type of scientific evidence that will be required to support the marketing application. FDA will provide the company with its written determination 30 days after the meeting, and this determination is binding upon the agency with certain exceptions. Additionally, Agreement Meetings are available to sponsors planning to investigate the safety or effectiveness of any Class III product to discuss and reach an agreement on the key parameters of an investigational plan. The meeting is to be granted within 30 days of the request, and the resulting agreement is to be written. The agreement is binding on the agency with certain exceptions.

Once the PMA has been submitted, FDA is required to meet with the company upon written request no later than 100 days after a "filable" PMA was submitted to discuss the status of the review. A filable PMA is defined under 21 C.F.R. § 814.42 as a submission for which "FDA has made a threshold determination that the application is sufficiently complete to permit a substantive review." Within 180 days of submission of a "filable" PMA, FDA must issue a letter to the company regarding the approvability of the submission. While it is theoretically possible to have an application approved at the first submission, because of the high-risk nature of these devices and the large volume of information contained in these submissions, it is virtually certain that FDA will pose additional questions for the company to address. In practice, FDA typically asks multiple rounds of questions on the various sections of the PMA. While the main body of the PMA submission is reviewed by ODE, the Office of Compliance (OC) reviews the manufacturing section.

A pending PMA can be amended either by the company's initiation or in response to a request from FDA. If significant new data is submitted in the amendment, the review period for the submission may be extended up to 180 days.

During the review process, FDA has the option to refer the PMA to an advisory panel for review and recommendation regarding approval of the submission. These advisory panel meetings are open to the public and are not binding on the agency. Prior to approval of the device, FDA's OC will typically inspect the manufacturing facilities to confirm that the device is manufactured in accordance with the information provided in the PMA, and that the company's quality system conforms with 21 C.F.R. Part 820, Quality System Regulation.

If FDA's evaluations of both the PMA and the manufacturing facilities are favorable, FDA may issue either an approval letter (an order authorizing the marketing of the device in the United States) or an "approvable" letter, which contains a number of conditions that must be met in order to secure final PMA approval. When and if the manufacturer satisfies those conditions, FDA will issue an approval letter authorizing commercial marketing of the device for specific indications. If FDA's evaluation of the PMA or the manufacturing facilities is not favorable, FDA will deny approval of the application (a final order rejecting the submission) or a "non-approvable" letter, which identifies the major deficiencies with the PMA. In such instances, the company can attempt to amend the PMA submission to meet FDA's requirements in order to obtain approval of the PMA.

Upon approval of the PMA, or as a condition of approval, FDA has the authority to impose postapproval requirements on the device sponsor or manufacturer. Often, these postapproval requirements take the form of labeling restrictions or requirements, continuing evaluations of the safety and efficacy of the device in clinical use, record maintenance and device tracking, and submission of annual reports.

As an alternative to the standard voluminous submission of an original PMA, in 1998, FDA proposed a modular PMA process through a series of guidance documents to permit companies to submit discrete sections of the standard PMA submission for review by the agency as the sections are ready. This was later codified in MDUFMA, and subsequent guidance documents have been issued to clarify the procedure. The modular PMA permits FDA and the company to review sections of the standard submission one at a time, and because each module has a 90-day review clock, the review of the final module may be completed more quickly.

PMA Supplements

Once a PMA has been approved, in order to make a change to the device that affects its safety or effectiveness, FDA must approve the change through a PMA supplement. Supplements to a PMA often require the submission of the same type of information required for an initial PMA, except that the supplement generally is limited to the information needed to support the safety and effectiveness of the proposed modification, or to clarify the safety and effectiveness of the existing device (i.e., new adverse event information, higher than predicted failure rates, etc.). The regulations identify several types of changes that require the submission of a PMA supplement if the change affects safety or effectiveness. These include: 1) new indications for use of the device; 2) labeling changes; 3) the use of a different facility or establishment to manufacture, process, or package the device; 4) changes in manufacturing facilities, methods, or quality control procedures; 5) changes in sterilization procedures; 6) changes in packaging; 7) changes in the performance or design specifications, circuits, components, ingredients, principle of operation, or physical layout of the device; and 8) extension of the expiration date of the device based on data obtained under a new or revised stability or sterility testing protocol that has not been approved by FDA. Many of these changes, such as a change in the manufacturing site, are presumed to affect safety and efficacy and require a PMA supplement.

There are several types of supplements that may be used to obtain FDA approval for a modification to a PMA device. These include: a new PMA; a Panel Track Supplement; a traditional PMA supplement; a 30-Day Notice; a 30-Day Supplement; a Special PMA Supplement for Changes Being Effected; or a PMA Manufacturing Site Change Supplement. FDA has disseminated a guidance document to assist manufacturers in determining which type of PMA supplement is required for various types of device modifications.[46] The suggested outcomes in the guidance document are driven by the level and nature of the nonclinical and clinical data that are necessary to support the proposed modifications and approved device. The suggested outcomes are not binding on either the agency or industry.[47]

Submission of a New PMA

FDA's PMA Supplement Guidance states that in general, a new original PMA application (rather than a PMA supplement) is appropriate when the modifications result in a new device. FDA considers a new device to be one where a modification results in a device design so different from the original that the preclinical and clinical data submitted in the original device are no longer applicable in demonstrating reasonable assurance of the safety and effectiveness of the modified device.

Panel-Track PMA Supplements

A "Panel-Track Supplement" is defined as:

> a supplement to an approved premarket application or premarket report under section 515 that requests a significant change in design or performance of the device, or a new indication for use of the device, and for which substantial clinical data are necessary to provide a reasonable assurance of safety and effectiveness.[48]

In FDA's PMA Supplement Guidance, the agency notes that Panel-Track Supplements are most appropriate for changes in the indication for use, or significant design changes that require the applicant to conduct new preclinical tests and clinical studies to demonstrate that there is reasonable assurance of safety and effectiveness of the modified device. Thus, FDA believes that a Panel-Track Supplement should be submitted for a change in indication for use of the device because:

- new clinical data are necessary to provide reasonable assurance of safety and effectiveness for the change in indication for use, and

- indication changes generally either do not require or require very limited new preclinical test data (i.e., all or most of the preclinical data previously submitted and reviewed in the original PMA are still applicable for the change in indication).[49]

---

[46]   Office of Device Evaluation, Center for Devices and Radiological Health, Food and Drug Administration, Draft Guidance for Industry and FDA Staff—Modifications to Devices Subject to Premarket Approval (PMA)—The PMA Supplement Decision-Making Process (Dec. 11, 2008) [hereinafter PMA Supplement Guidance].

[47]   21 C.F.R. § 814.39.

[48]   FDCA § 737(4)(B), 21 U.S.C. § 379i(4)(B).

[49]   PMA Supplement Guidance, *supra* note 46.

Traditional, or "180-Day" PMA Supplements

The FDCA requires "a supplement to an approved premarket application or premarket report under section 515 that is not a Panel-Track Supplement and requests a significant change in components, materials, design, specification, software, color additives, and labeling."[50] FDA requires the submission of a 180-Day Supplement for certain changes to the approved device that affect the safety or effectiveness of the device. FDA's PMA Supplement Guidance states:

> . . . in general, in order for a change to be submitted as a 180-Day Supplement, the clinical data provided in support of the original device approval should still be applicable in supporting the approval of the modified device. In most cases, for such modifications, only new pre-clinical testing is needed to demonstrate reasonable assurance of safety and effectiveness of the modified device. In some instances, however, additional limited confirmatory clinical data may be necessary to provide a bridge between the clinical data set for the original device and the expected clinical performance of the modified device. Confirmatory clinical data typically involve a limited number of patients, shorter study duration, and/or a subset of endpoints as compared to the clinical data set for a traditional PMA. In these situations, FDA believes that a 180-Day Supplement, rather than a Panel-Track Supplement, is appropriate because of the limited nature of the supplementary clinical data.

The applicant should submit a 180-Day Supplement for certain significant changes, including the following changes:

- the principle of operation;
- the control mechanism;
- the device design or performance;
- the labeling; or
- new testing requirements or acceptance criteria.[51]

30-Day Notices

Traditional PMA supplements are not required if the change is a modification in a manufacturing procedure or method of manufacturing, and certain conditions are met. Certain changes in a manufacturing procedure or method may be made within 30 days after providing written notice to FDA (called a "30-Day Notice").[52] That notice must describe the manufacturing change in detail and summarize the data and information supporting the change. Although the change may be made 30 days after providing written notice to FDA, during that 30-day period FDA may notify the manufacturer that the agency has

---

50   FDCA § 737(4)(C), 21 U.S.C. § 379i(4)(C).

51   *See* PMA Supplement Guidance, *supra* note 46.

52   Office of Compliance, Center for Devices and Radiological Health, Food and Drug Administration. Guidance for Industry and FDA Staff - 30-Day Notices, 135-Day Premarket Approval (PMA) Supplements and 75-Day Humanitarian Device Exemption (HDE) Supplements for Manufacturing Method or Process Changes (Apr. 13, 2011).

determined that a 135-Day Supplement will be required rather than a 30-day notice. The 135-Day Supplement must contain the information that FDA determines is missing from the 30-Day Notice in order to approve the change. If a 135-Day Supplement is required, FDAMA provides that FDA has 135 days to review the supplement, but the time FDA spent reviewing the 30-day notice is subtracted from the 135 days.[53]

30-Day Supplements

FDA may allow certain changes to a PMA-approved device to be reported in a 30-Day Supplement. FDA will notify applicants of this alternative through an advisory opinion to the affected industry or in correspondence with the applicant. If FDA requires that the change be reported in a 30-day PMA supplement, the change may be made 30 days after FDA files the 30-Day Supplement, unless FDA informs the PMA holder that additional information is required, the supplement is not approvable or the supplement is denied. The 30-day PMA supplement must follow the instructions in the correspondence or advisory opinion. This mechanism is rarely used.[54]

Real-Time Review Supplements

Real-Time Review Supplements are supplements to an approved PMA that propose minor changes to the device and that would involve review by only one scientific discipline, as opposed to multiple disciplines. Specifically, pursuant to FDA's 2006 guidance document, "Real-Time Premarket Approval Application (PMA) Supplements," the minor modification at issue would be appropriate for real-time review when: 1) the change is of a type expected for that device type; 2) the change has been validated according to scientific principles, accepted test methods for that type of device or via an FDA-recognized standard or guidance document; and 3) the change is adequately supported by preclinical or animal testing, without the need for clinical data. Unlike other PMA supplements, applicants must request approval from the agency to submit this type of supplement for a particular modification. Once agreed to, the applicant submits the supplement for review of the modification and supporting information in real-time, in an interactive forum.

Special PMA Supplement—Changes Being Effected

A "Special PMA Supplement—Changes Being Effected" is a type of PMA supplement that allows the sponsor to implement certain changes upon FDA's receipt of the changes being effected.[55] This type of supplement is limited to the labeling, quality control and manufacturing process changes specified under FDA's regulations. It allows for the addition of, but not the replacement of, previously approved quality control specifications and test methods. This procedure is not applicable to changes in device design, composition, specifications, circuitry, software or energy source. From a practical perspective, as with other submissions such as the 30-Day Notice and 30-Day PMA Supplements, it is advisable not to implement changes under this provision until FDA agrees that the changes are indeed candidates for this type of submission. Otherwise, if the changes are implemented before FDA agrees that this type of submission is appropriate, FDA can (as it has in some

---

[53]   21 C.F.R. § 814.39(f).

[54]   See id. § 814.39(e).

[55]   21 C.F.R. § 814.39(d).

cases) require the company to revert to the pre-modified device until a PMA supplement is approved and even recall devices that were modified inappropriately.

PMA Supplement—Manufacturing Site Change

PMA supplements that involve a change of a manufacturing facility are generally considered to be 180-day supplements. However, FDA is generally sensitive to the business issues concerning facility moves and may be willing to work with the sponsor to try to complete the agency's review sooner than the 180 days allowed. Site change supplements typically require an FDA pre-approval inspection of the new facility. However, if the new facility has been the subject of a successful FDA quality systems inspection within the last two years, FDA may determine that a pre-approval inspection is not required. CDRH intends to issue a guidance document for manufacturing site change supplements that provides criteria for such supplements and when an inspection would likely occur.[56] As of this printing, this guidance has not yet been issued.

PMA Annual Reports

FDA requires that the PMA holder report a change for which a PMA supplement is not required in a periodic (annual) report that is due each year on the anniversary date of the PMA approval. These changes may be made before they are reported to FDA because, by definition, they are changes that the manufacturer has determined do not affect the safety or effectiveness of the approved device. FDA's PMA Supplement Guidance also allows manufacturers to make certain very minor changes to their approved devices by simply documenting the change information in the firm's files. As a practical matter, most companies include in their annual reports at least general information about all changes that have been made to the device during the reporting period that have not been the subject of an approved supplement, in order to put FDA on notice of the changes. FDA can disagree that changes reported in an annual report do not affect safety or efficacy and require the retrospective submission of PMA supplements and take enforcement action against the company.

Annual reports must also contain a bibliography and a summary of any unpublished reports of data from any clinical investigations or nonclinical laboratory studies involving the device or related devices and any reports in the scientific literature concerning the device. The annual report should summarize information pertaining to the original PMA, as well as any subsequent PMA supplements, and should include all postapproval reports for PMA supplements. The annual report should also describe any adverse device effects.[57]

Product Development Protocol

As an alternative to the full PMA process, certain Class III devices may be approved through a product development protocol (PDP).[58] The PDP mates clinical evaluation of a device

---

[56]   PMA Supplement Guidance, *supra* note 46.

[57]   Center for Devices and Radiological Health/Center for Biologics Evaluation and Research, Annual Reports for Approved Premarket Approval Applications (PMA) (Oct. 26, 2006).

[58]   FDCA § 515(f), 21 U.S.C. § 360e(f).

with the necessary information for marketing approval into one regulatory mechanism. In practice, the PDP is generally only a useful tool for devices with well-established technology.

The distinguishing feature of a PDP is FDA's early involvement and close relationship with the sponsor, allowing the sponsor and FDA to agree at the design stage on the testing required to demonstrate the new device's safety and effectiveness. The PDP essentially creates a contract between the sponsor and FDA, which includes the required testing and reporting milestones agreed on by FDA and the sponsor. FDA has a 120-day time frame to review a PDP. Once FDA determines that the requirements of the PDP are met, a device subject to a completed PDP is considered to have an approved PMA.[59]

Although the PDP offers a theoretically shorter time frame for review, the requirements to prove device safety and effectiveness are as stringent under a PDP as for a PMA. Therefore, the PDP process offers little advantage if the device already has undergone considerable design investigation and evaluation. The PDP has rarely been proven feasible for a manufacturer and is overly demanding of FDA's resources.

Investigational Devices

Devices used on human subjects to conduct investigations of the device's safety and effectiveness are considered "investigational devices" under section 520(g) of the FDCA. These devices have not been approved for commercial distribution by FDA for their investigational use. An investigational device exemption (IDE) allows an unapproved device to be shipped in interstate commerce for purposes of conducting clinical research that can be submitted in support of a 510(k) or PMA submission to establish substantial equivalence or a reasonable assurance of safety and effectiveness, as applicable. Without this exemption, shipment of an unapproved device in interstate commerce would violate the FDCA.

The IDE regulations[60] apply to most clinical investigations involving new devices or new uses for existing devices. For the following clinical investigations of medical devices, however, manufacturers need not comply with the IDE requirements[61]:

- legally marketed devices that are being investigated i) in the case of pre-amendments devices, in accordance with the indications in the labeling in effect at that time; or ii) in the case of postamendments devices, in accordance with the labeling included in the cleared 510(k) notice.

- investigations of diagnostic devices under certain conditions;

- consumer preference testing;

- investigations of devices intended solely for veterinary use; and

- custom devices meeting the definition of 21 CFR § 812.3(b).

---

59   21 C.F.R. § 814.19.

60   21 C.F.R. pt. 812.

61   45 Fed. Reg. 3732, 3751 (1980)); 21 C.F.R. § 812.2(c).

The IDE regulations describe two types of studies of devices that are categorized as significant risk (SR) and nonsignificant risk (NSR) studies. A significant risk device is an investigational device that:

(1) Is intended as an implant and presents a potential for serious risk to the health, safety, or welfare of a subject;

(2) Is purported or represented to be for use in supporting or sustaining human life and presents a potential for serious risk to the health, safety, or welfare of a subject;

(3) Is for a use of substantial importance in diagnosing, curing, mitigating, or treating disease, or otherwise preventing impairment of human health and presents a potential for serious risk to the health, safety, or welfare of a subject; or

(4) Otherwise presents a potential for serious risk to the health, safety or welfare of a subject.[62]

Conversely, a nonsignificant risk device study is one that does not pose a significant risk to patients.

An assessment of whether an investigation of a device for a particular intended use is nonsignificant risk is made initially by the sponsor. If the sponsor believes a study poses only nonsignificant risk, the sponsor may begin the study without obtaining FDA approval (nonsignificant risk studies are "deemed" to have IDE approval by FDA[63]), provided that each reviewing Institutional Review Board (IRB) approves the study. While the sponsor makes the initial determination regarding whether a device is NSR or SR and thus whether an IDE is necessary, FDA is the final arbiter of whether an IDE is required. Examples of devices and studies that do/do not require an IDE are provided in FDA's 2006 guidance "Significant Risk and Nonsignificant Risk Medical Device Studies."

For studies of NSR devices, the sponsor provides the IRB with the study proposal, an explanation of why the study is a nonsignificant risk, and other supporting information; e.g., any reports of prior investigations. The sponsor or investigator must also advise the IRB whether the study subjects must undergo a procedure as part of the investigational study (e.g., a surgical procedure), so the IRB can evaluate the potential harm that could be caused by the procedure in addition to the potential harm that could be caused by the device.

Studies of significant risk devices must meet all of the regulatory requirements set forth in 21 C.F.R. Part 812, including the requirement that the sponsor obtain FDA approval of an IDE application, and approval of the investigational plan and informed consent form from each participating IRB before commencing the study. IRB approval and informed consent from each subject must be obtained, regardless of whether it is a significant or nonsignificant risk study.

Per 21 C.F.R. § 812.20, a sponsor of a proposed human clinical investigation that is not exempt per 21 C.F.R. § 812.2(c), and that meets the definition of a significant risk study, must submit an IDE application with the following information:

---

[62]   21 C.F.R. § 812.3(m).
[63]   21 C.F.R. § 812.2(b)

- Name and address of sponsor;
- Report of prior investigations, including biocompatibility, in vitro and in vivo testing, as well as published and unpublished adverse information;
- Investigational plan, including a description of the intended use of the device, objectives and duration of the study, analysis of risk, justification, patient population, monitoring procedures, and the clinical study protocol;
- Device description and description of manufacturing;
- Example of investigator agreement;
- Certification that all investigators who will participate in the study have signed the investigator agreement;
- Names, addresses, and chairpersons of IRBs;
- Participating institutions;
- Statement of noncommercialization;
- Claim of categorical exclusion from environmental assessment;
- Labeling; and
- Informed consent materials.

If an IDE does not contain all of these elements, it will likely be returned to the sponsor for revision before FDA begins a substantive review.

Per the IDE regulations, sponsors of IDE investigations and the investigators participating in the IDE investigation have various responsibilities depending on whether the study is a significant or nonsignificant risk study. Participating investigators are responsible for ensuring that the study is conducted according to the investigational plan and applicable FDA regulations; obtaining informed consent from study subjects; supervising the use of the device; and returning unused investigational devices to the sponsor or disposing of them as the sponsor directs. Sponsors are responsible for selecting qualified investigators and providing them with the information they need to conduct the study properly; obtaining IRB review and approval as necessary; ensuring proper monitoring of the study; investigating any unanticipated adverse events that occur during the study and taking appropriate action; and informing FDA and IRBs about significant new information.[64]

In addition to the above responsibilities, both sponsors and investigators are subject to recordkeeping and reporting responsibilities which, again, vary depending on whether the study is a significant or nonsignificant risk study. Specifically, investigators must keep records of correspondence with the sponsor, FDA, IRB, other investigators, and monitors; receipt and disposition of investigational devices; study subjects' case history and exposure to the device; documentation of informed consent; and the protocol as well as any protocol deviations.[65] Sponsors are responsible for maintaining records of correspondence with investigators, FDA, IRB, other sponsors, and monitors; shipment and disposition

---

[64]   21 C.F.R. § 812.40.
[65]   *Id.* § 812.140(a). Note that there are abbreviated requirements for NSR studies. See 21 C.F.R. § 812.2(b).

of investigational devices; signed investigator statements; the name and address of each investigator; and the name and address of each IRB that has reviewed the study.[66]

With regard to reporting responsibilities, participating investigators must report unanticipated adverse effects reports and submit progress reports and final reports to the study sponsor and the applicable IRB.[67] Sponsors' reporting requirements include evaluating the reports of unanticipated adverse effects from the investigator and reporting the results to FDA, all reviewing IRBs, and participating investigators; submitting to FDA a current investigator list; submitting progress reports to all IRBs and, for significant risk devices, to FDA; notifying FDA of the termination of a study within 30 days (for significant risk devices), and submitting final reports to FDA, all reviewing IRBs, and participating investigators. For nonsignificant risk devices, a final report must be submitted to all reviewing IRBs within six months after study termination.[68]

During the course of the investigation, study sponsors may make certain modifications to investigational devices and study protocols without submitting an IDE supplement to FDA for approval or to notify the agency of the change. The regulations set forth several specific changes that do not require IDE supplements: 1) developmental changes in the device (including manufacturing changes) that do not constitute a significant change in design or basic principles of operation and that are made in response to information gathered during the course of investigation; and 2) changes or modifications to clinical protocols that do not affect: a) the validity of data or information resulting from the completion of an approved protocol, or the relationship of likely patient risk to benefit relied upon to approve a protocol; b) the scientific soundness of an investigational plan submitted in the IDE; or c) the rights, safety, or welfare of the human subjects involved in the investigation.

The IDE regulations state that these types of changes can be made if the sponsor of the study determines that the change or modification meets the specified criteria and the sponsor submits a notice of the change or modification not later than five days after making the change or modification. The intent of this provision is to place the burden on the study sponsor to determine whether proposed changes necessitate the filing of an IDE supplement. Of course, FDA has the option to disagree with the sponsor's determination and can later require an IDE supplement at its discretion.

Since publication of the IDE regulations in 1980, the regulations have remained largely unchanged. However, FDAMA established what is now known as the "pre-IDE meeting," to allow sponsors who intend to conduct clinical studies in the United States the opportunity to meet with FDA prior to submitting an IDE application to discuss their investigational plan.[69] Such a meeting can be obtained by submitting a written request setting forth a description of the device, the proposed conditions of use, a proposed investigational plan, and the expected performance of the device, if available.[70] The ability to meet with and have

---

66   21 C.F.R. § 812.140(b). Note that there are abbreviated requirements for NSR studies. *See* 21 C.F.R. § 812.2(b).

67   21 C.F.R. § 812.150(a). Note that there are abbreviated requirements for NSR studies. *See* 21 C.F.R. § 812.2(b).

68   21 C.F.R. § 812.150(b).

69   FDCA § 520(g), 21 U.S.C. § 360j(g).

70   *Id.*

an open dialogue with the agency was so useful that this program has been expanded and generalized to include all submission types, prompting a change in program name from pre-IDE to pre-submission. The pre-submission process can be used to discuss a variety of topics including clinical trial design, significant/non-significant risk determination, testing requirements for new devices, response strategies to agency requests for additional information, and likely regulatory pathway. The agency has recently published guidance related to this program titled "Requests for Feedback on Medical Device Submissions: The Pre-Submission Program and Meetings with Food and Drug Administration Staff." This document describes several pre-submission types including informational meetings, study risk determinations, formal early collaboration meetings, and submission issue meetings. In general, the agency aims to schedule a pre-submission meeting within 75 days, but no longer than 90 days, of receipt of the complete pre-submission and will provide written feedback prior to the meeting. Although the company may receive valuable feedback from the agency during these meetings, the discussions and decisions are not binding on FDA.

FDAAA also established registration requirements with the ClinicalTrials.gov database for "applicable clinical trials." An applicable device clinical trial is defined as:

> (1) "a prospective clinical study of health outcomes comparing an intervention with a device subject to [510(k), PMA and Humanitarian Device Exemptions premarket requirements] against a control in human subjects (other than a small clinical trial to determine the feasibility of a device, or a clinical trial to test prototype devices where the primary outcome measure relates to feasibility and not to health outcomes);" and

> (2) "a pediatric postmarket surveillance [requirement]."

Thus, per FDAAA, it may be the case that a study being conducted under an IDE must be registered with the ClinicalTrials.gov database.

Humanitarian Device Exemption Regulation

On June 26, 1996, FDA published regulations prescribing the procedures for submitting humanitarian device exemption (HDE) applications for humanitarian use devices (HUD).[71] The regulations implemented section 520(m) of the FDCA, which was intended to create an incentive for the development of devices for use in the treatment or diagnosis of diseases or conditions affecting a small number of individuals. The regulations require a manufacturer to show only that a device is safe and has a probable benefit to patients, but not a demonstration of effectiveness.

Section 520(m) authorizes FDA to exempt a HUD from the effectiveness requirements of sections 514 (performance standards) and 515 (premarket approval) of the FDCA provided that 1) the device is to be used to treat or diagnose a disease or condition that affects fewer than 4,000 individuals in the United States; 2) the device would not be available to a person with such a disease or condition unless the exemption is granted; 3) no comparable device (other than a device that has been granted such an exemption) is available to treat or diagnose

---

71   61 Fed. Reg. 33,232 (1996).

the disease or condition; and 4) the device will not expose patients to an unreasonable or significant risk of illness or injury, and the probable benefit to health from using the device outweighs the risk of injury or illness from its use, taking into account the probable risks and benefits of currently available devices or alternative forms of treatment. Exempting a HUD from the effectiveness requirements relieves manufacturers of a major disincentive to bringing devices for rare conditions to market—the great expense of conducting controlled clinical studies.

In accordance with the regulations, there are two distinct steps necessary to obtain approval to obtain an HDE for a device. First, the sponsor must submit a request to FDA's Office of Orphan Products Development (OOPD) seeking a HUD designation for the device. This designation is based on a determination that the disease or condition that the device is intended to treat or diagnose affects or is manifested in fewer than 4,000 individuals in the United States per year. The request for HUD designation should provide the following: 1) based upon current medical and scientific knowledge, the precisely defined proposed indication(s) for use; 2) a brief description of the device, including illustrations and a discussion of its principle of operation; and 3) documentation, with authoritative references appended, of the target population demonstrating that the rare disease or condition affects or is manifested in fewer than 4,000 people in the United States per year.

Second, if OOPD determines that the device is eligible for a HUD designation, an HDE application must be submitted to FDA's Office of Device Evaluation. The HDE application is similar in both form and content to a PMA application, however, the HDE application is not required to contain the results of scientifically valid clinical investigations demonstrating that the device is effective for its intended purpose. Additionally, there are no user fees associated with a HDE application.

The HDE application must include a summary of the indications for use of the device, a description of the disease or condition the device is intended to treat, significant physical and performance characteristics of the device, an explanation of why the probable benefit to health from use of the device outweighs the risk of injury or illness from its use, taking into account the probable risks and benefits of currently available devices or alternative forms of treatment, and any clinical and nonclinical data that are relevant to evaluating the safety and probable benefit of the device. The application must also contain sufficient information for FDA to determine that the device does not pose an unreasonable risk of illness or injury to patients and that the probable benefit outweighs the risk of injury or illness from its use, taking into account the probable risks and benefits of currently available devices or alternative forms of treatment.[72] The applicant is also required to include information regarding any clinical experience or investigations with the device, where available, and information that will enable FDA to determine that the device would not otherwise be available unless an HDE were granted and that no comparable device (other than another HUD with an approved HDE or a device with an approved IDE) is available to treat or diagnose the disease or condition. Certification on clinicaltrials.gov is required for any clinical studies. Regardless of the degree of information provided to the agency for review, the labeling for the device must state that FDA has not evaluated its effectiveness. All applications must include information on any pediatric subpopulations that suffer from the

---

[72]   FDCA § 520(m)(2)(C); 21 C.F.R. 814.104(b)(3).

disease or condition that the device is intended to treat, diagnose, or cure; and the number of affected pediatric patients, if such information is readily available, in order to comply with the Pediatric Medical Device Safety and Improvement Act of 2007 and 21 C.F.R. 814.100(c).

The application must also provide the amount to be charged for the device and, if the amount is more than $250, a report by an independent certified public accountant or an attestation by a responsible individual of the organization verifying that the amount charged does not exceed the costs of the device's research, development, fabrication, and distribution. Exceptions to these cost restrictions, allowing companies to change for HUD devices above cost, is permitted only for devices intended for pediatric populations and those populations where the development of the device for such patients is impossible, highly impracticable, or unsafe. FDASIA expanded the pediatric exemption to include all medical devices that qualify for a HUD exemption.

Custom Devices

The FDCA prohibits the introduction of any adulterated device into interstate commerce with few exceptions. One such exception, the custom device exemption, exempts custom medical devices from performance standards, premarket clearance and approval, and IDE requirements. Although this longstanding exemption has been clearly defined in FDA law and regulation for decades,[73] until recently, device manufacturers were left to interpret the definition on the basis of Warning Letters and court opinions. Without firm FDA guidance, interpretations of the definition historically varied and frequently have been a source of confusion for medical device manufacturers. Adding to the confusion is the skepticism with which FDA viewed devices that were purported to be within the custom device exemption; both in terms of whether they met the four corners of the definition and volume of devices purported to be customs.

Seeking to bring clarity to the custom device exemption, upon its enactment in 2012, FDASIA redefined custom devices essentially codifying FDA's and the courts' historical interpretation. Under FDASIA, the following are considered to generally meet the definition of a "custom device":

• Device is created or modified in order to comply with the order of an individual physician or dentist;

• Device is not generally available in the United States in finished form through labeling or advertising by the manufacturer, importer, or distributor for commercial distribution;

• Device is designed to treat a unique pathology or physiological condition that no other device is domestically available to treat;

---

[73]   Prior to the enactment of FDASIA in 2012, FDCA § 520(b) defined a custom device as "[a device] intended for use by an individual patient named in [an] order by such physician, dentist (or other specially qualified person so designated) and is to be made in a specific form for such patient, or . . . intended to meet the special needs of such physician or dentist (or other specially qualified person so designated) in the course of [his] professional practice . . . ."

- Device is intended to meet the special needs of such physician or dentist in the course of the professional practice of such physician or dentist; or is intended for use by an individual patient named in such order of such physician or dentist; or

- Device is assembled from components or manufactured and finished on a case-by-case basis to accommodate the unique needs of a patient.

FDASIA further explained that:

- A custom device does not lose its designation despite that it may have common, standardized design characteristics, chemical and material compositions, and manufacturing processes as commercially distributed devices;

- The custom device must be for the purpose of treating a sufficiently rare condition such that conducting clinical investigation on such a device would be impracticable; and

- A custom device cannot be replicated more than five times in a manufacturing year.

While exempt from premarket requirements, custom devices must comply with other general control requirements including, among others, the Quality System Regulation (QSR) and restrictions on sale, adulteration, and misbranding. In addition, FDASIA has imposed an annual reporting requirement for manufacturers of custom devices.[74] The agency's preferred format and required content for custom device annual reports is set forth in FDA's September 24, 2014, guidance document, "Custom Device Exemption."[75] FDA has indicated that it will not enforce the reporting requirement until the end of 2014, but that the first report should contain information on custom devices manufactured from the date of enactment of FDASIA (July 9, 2012) through the date of the first report.

Traditionally, FDA interpreted the term "custom device" very strictly to mean essentially a "one of a kind device" that is unique and crafted specifically for an individual patient or physician but did not impose a clear numerical limit although many in industry believed would allow approximately 10 devices. The statutory definition of custom devices set forth in FDASIA appears to broaden the scope of the custom device exemption and clarifies that companies may produce no more than five units of a custom device type in a given year, assuming that the replication otherwise complies with the statutory definition. FDA 2014 guidance provides details regarding the agency's interpretation of the new statutory definition of a custom device, as well as the agency's interpretation of FDASIA's annual "five-unit" limit on the production of custom devices.[76]

Although FDASIA has slightly broadened the definition of a custom device, such a device is distinguishable from a *"customized"* device, which is a device or system of components that is more widely disseminated but can be varied in size, shape, or material on order of a physician to meet the needs of individual patients. FDA's regulations, which have not changed with the enactment of FDASIA, effectively exclude *customized* devices from the regulatory definition a

---

[74]   *See* FDCA § 520(b)(2)(C), 21 U.S.C. § 360j(b)(2)(C).

[75]   Center for Devices and Radiological Health, Custom Device Exemption (Sept. 2014).

[76]   *Id.*

custom device[77] and, therefore, customized devices are generally subject to FDA's premarket approval or 510(k) clearance requirements. A number of regulatory enforcement actions have been taken against companies that have misapplied this regulation and have marketed devices as "custom" that would, in fact, require premarket clearance or approval.

Performance Standards, Special Controls, and Voluntary Consensus Standards

Under the 1976 amendments, section 514 of the FDCA[78] authorized FDA to establish performance standards for Class II devices[79] and set forth a complex process for the development of these standards. In addition, section 514 specified some of the features of devices that may be subjected to standards and mentioned other organizations, including other federal agencies, that may be eligible to develop standards. Nevertheless, although a final procedural regulation for the development of standards was published on February 1, 1980,[80] not one section 514 performance standard was developed.

Recognizing that performance standards under section 514, as originally enacted, were difficult to prepare, FDA officials devoted considerable attention to other ways of addressing device problems, such as requesting voluntary action by manufacturers to resolve device problems; publicizing particular device problems; publishing educational and technical information for the users of devices; encouraging agency participation in developing voluntary standards; developing guidelines for product testing and product labeling; and preparing and sending letters to companies notifying them of their violative conduct and requesting corrective action. Some of these alternatives, however, posed questions of procedural fairness, as well as questions about the rights and obligations of manufacturers and users.

Congress recognized that the procedures for establishing performance standards in the 1976 amendments were unworkable. As a result, as discussed above, the SMDA attempted to decrease the procedural complexity of promulgating performance standards, permitting

---

[77]   According to FDA regulation, a custom device is defined as one that—

(1) Necessarily deviates from devices generally available or from an applicable performance standard or premarket approval requirement in order to comply with the order of an individual physician or dentist;

(2) Is not generally available to, or generally used by, other physicians or dentists;

(3) Is not generally available in finished form for purchase or for dispensing upon prescription;

(4) Is not offered for commercial distribution through labeling or advertising; and

(5) Is intended for use by an individual patient named in the order of a physician or dentist, and is to be made in a specific form for that patient, or is intended to meet the special needs of the physician or dentist in the course of professional practice.

21 C.F.R. § 812.3(b).

Notably, the regulatory definition for a custom device, set forth above, has not been updated since the enactment of FDASIA.

[78]   FDCA § 514, 21 U.S.C. § 360d.

[79]   Section 514 should be read as granting discretionary authority, since section 514(a)(1) does say "may." However, section 513(a)(1)(B) defines Class II as consisting of those devices for which a performance standard is "necessary . . . to provide reasonable assurance of its safety and effectiveness." Another view is that FDA is required to promulgate performance standards for all Class II products. See Address by Allen Greenberg, FDA Medical Device Forum 3-A (Jan. 26, 1982).

[80]   45 Fed. Reg. 7474 (1980).

FDA to issue standards via the ordinary notice-and-comment rulemaking process.[81] The SMDA also permitted FDA to use other types of "special controls," such as postmarket surveillance, device-specific guidance documents (e.g., in vitro fertilization/assisted reproductive device guidance, medical image management devices), and other mechanisms, as an alternative to formal performance standards.[82] Device manufacturers commonly rely on these special controls in the development, manufacture, and control of all classes of medical devices.

In addition to device-specific guidance documents and special controls, CDRH also allows manufacturers to rely on FDA-recognized voluntary consensus standards developed by external organizations. FDAMA amended section 514 of the FDCA[83] to authorize the agency specifically to recognize all or part of national and international standards by publication of notices of their recognition in the *Federal Register*. Recognized consensus standards could then be cited in guidance documents or individual policy statements, or established as special controls to address specific risks associated with different types of devices or device characteristics. FDA's recognition of voluntary consensus standards, combined with modified review procedures, have, since 1997, streamlined the review of 510(k) notices with the development of the Abbreviated 510(k) paradigm, and aided manufacturers and sponsors of PMA submissions to rely on the recognized standards through declarations of conformity, rather than through the development of nonstandardized test methods. Manufacturers choosing to develop alternate methods, or who elect to deviate from such FDA-recognized consensus standards, may do so provided that the manufacturer explains to the agency in the relevant premarket submission why the company's approach in lieu of conformance with a consensus standard is sufficient to ensure the safety and effectiveness of the device.

To alert manufacturers to these approaches and to educate stakeholders about the process of relying on voluntary consensus standards, FDA has published a number of relevant guidance documents. As outlined in these documents, manufacturers required to submit a premarket application (i.e., 510(k) notice, IDE, PMA, HDE, or PDP) must provide information as required by the statute and regulations for CDRH to make an appropriate decision regarding the clearance or approval of the submission. In accordance with the SOP Guidance, CDRH may use information demonstrating a manufacturer's conformance with recognized consensus standards to satisfy the agency's premarket review requirements.

The agency, by acceptance of manufacturer declarations of conformity to the recognized consensus standards, has simplified the premarket submission process by allowing manufacturers to provide the declaration and, in many cases, eliminate the need for FDA review of the actual test data for those aspects of the device addressed by the standards. FDA notes in the guidance, however, that "if a recognized standard describes a test method, but does not specify a performance limit or pass/fail criteria, the manufacturer should submit the test results."[84]

---

[81]   FDCA § 514(b)(1)(A), 21 U.S.C. § 360d(b)(1)(A).

[82]   FDCA § 513(a)(1)(B), 21 U.S.C. § 360c(a)(1)(B).

[83]   FDCA § 514(c), 21 U.S.C. § 360d(c).

[84]   Office of Science and Engineering Laboratories, Center for Devices and Radiological Health, Guidance for Industry and FDA Staff—Recognition and Use of Consensus Standards, 4 n.1 (Sept. 17, 2007).

Restricted Devices

The 1938 Federal Food, Drug, and Cosmetic Act included a provision characterizing drugs and devices as misbranded if their labeling failed to give adequate directions for use.[85] The FDCA also permitted FDA to exempt drugs and devices from that provision. FDA interpreted the exemption provision as a grant of authority to limit the distribution of certain drugs (and later medical devices) to sale only on the prescription of a physician, and agency regulations to this effect were upheld by the courts.[86] It was FDA's position that "adequate directions for use" meant adequate directions for lay use. Therefore, drugs and devices that could safely and effectively be used only under the supervision of a physician could not, as a matter of law, bear adequate directions for lay use. FDA, by regulation, exempted such drugs and devices if they were labeled to be dispensed only by prescriptions.[87]

The 1976 amendments expanded FDA's authority to restrict the distribution, and use of certain devices by enabling FDA to characterize them as "restricted devices." Accordingly, the agency may impose stringent limitations on the sale, distribution or use of devices when it believes that these limitations are needed and will provide reasonable assurance of safety and effectiveness.[88] Devices characterized as restricted under section 520(e) are automatically subject to additional FDA regulatory authority. For example, FDA has jurisdiction over advertising for restricted devices, although advertising for nonrestricted devices is regulated under less stringent rules by the Federal Trade Commission.[89] Finally, the manufacturers of restricted devices must give FDA inspectors access to virtually all of their manufacturing and distribution records.[90]

Laboratory Developed Tests

On July 31, 2014, FDA announced plans to formally regulate laboratory developed tests (LDTs). The announcement came in the form of letters to Congress attaching the preliminary drafts of two guidance documents describing the agency's proposed risk-based framework for regulatory oversight of LDTs. The first draft guidance, "Framework for Regulatory Oversight of Laboratory Developed Tests (LDTs),"[91] addresses the proposed regulatory framework, while the second, "FDA Notification and Medical Device Reporting for Laboratory Developed Tests (LDTs),"[92] describes the methods that industry may be able to use to address the requirements the agency is proposing (both drafts were issued publicly on October 3, 2014). In providing the draft documents, FDA commented that it was taking this step in part because it does not feel that the Clinical Laboratory Improvement Amendments (CLIA), which also contain regulatory requirements applicable to laboratories, are sufficient to "ensure that LDTs are properly designed, consistently manufactured, and

---

[85] FDCA § 502(f)(1), 21 U.S.C. § 352(f)(1).

[86] *See* United States v. Sullivan, 332 U.S. 689 (1948); United States v. El-O-Pathic Pharmacy, 192 F.2d 62 (9th Cir. 1951).

[87] FDCA § 503, 21 U.S.C. § 353.

[88] FDCA § 520(e), 21 U.S.C. § 360j(e). The authority to restrict use of a device to certain categories of practitioners, however, is limited.

[89] *See* FDCA § 502(r), 21 U.S.C. § 352(r).

[90] FDCA § 704, 21 U.S.C. § 374.

[91] *Available at* http://www.fda.gov/downloads/MedicalDevices/DeviceRegulationandGuidance/GuidanceDocuments/UCM416685.pdf (last visited Nov. 20, 2014).

[92] *Available at* http://www.fda.gov/downloads/MedicalDevices/DeviceRegulationandGuidance/GuidanceDocuments/UCM416684.pdf (last visited Nov. 20, 2014).

are safe and effective for patients." While this position has been very controversial, FDA asserted that external review of test validity, as well as clinical assessment of validity, by regulators is important to ensuring good test design. FDA further cited the complexity and widespread use of LDTs as an important factor in FDA's decision to change the existing regulatory policy. FDA stated that its proposed regulatory framework recognizes that, as with in vitro diagnostic devices (IVDs), LDTs also have different risks depending on their use and thus "a risk-based approach to regulatory oversight is appropriate and necessary to protect patient safety." Under this regulatory framework, LDTs would be classified consistent with the approach taken for existing medical devices, placing the tests into class I (i.e., low risk devices), class II (i.e., moderate risk devices) or class III (i.e., high risk and not substantially equivalent devices). Using this approach, the level of regulatory oversight and the time frame for compliance with applicable requirements would be based, ultimately, on the test's classification. If and when the guidance documents are finalized, FDA plans to initiate enforcement using a phased approach.

The Regulation of Medical Devices under the FDCA—Postmarket Regulations

Good Manufacturing Practices

As a result of the 1976 amendments, the FDCA states that FDA may prescribe Good Manufacturing Practice (GMP) requirements to ensure that medical devices are safe and effective for their intended uses. Specifically, the FDCA requires the promulgation of "regulations requiring that the methods used in, and the facilities and controls used for, the manufacture, pre-production design validation (including a process to assess the performance of a device but not including an evaluation of the safety or effectiveness of a device), packing, storage, and installation of a device conform to current good manufacturing practice, as prescribed in such regulations, to assure that the device will be safe and effective and otherwise in compliance with this Act."[93]

The agency had begun drafting a device GMP regulation—probably the single most important device regulation applicable to devices of all classes—before the amendments were enacted. The original GMP regulation became final on July 21, 1978,[94] and effective as of December 18, 1978. A GMP Advisory Committee, mandated by the amendments,[95] devoted a substantial portion of its deliberations to successive versions of the GMP regulation. The regulation specified general requirements covering virtually all aspects of manufacturing. It was intended to ensure that regulated devices are consistently made according to written specifications. Failure to comply with the GMPs specified in the regulation renders a device violative of the FDCA.

---

93   FDCA § 520(f)(1)(A), 21 U.S.C. § 360j(f)(1)(A).
94   43 Fed. Reg. 31,508 (1978), 21 C.F.R. § 20.
95   2 Med. Devices Rep. (CCH) ¶ 15,090 (D. Md. June 19, 1987).

Nearly 20 years after the original GMPs were promulgated, on October 7, 1996, FDA published its final QSR rule[96] to revise the GMP regulations for the purposes of 1) replacing quality assurance program requirements with quality system requirements that include design, purchasing, and servicing controls; 2) clarifying recordkeeping requirements for device failure and complaint investigations; 3) clarifying requirements for qualifying, verifying, and validating processes and specification changes; and 4) clarifying requirements for evaluating quality data and correcting quality problems.[97] In addition, the QSR was intended to better harmonize FDA's GMP requirements for devices with the specifications for quality systems contained in ISO 9001 and other applicable international standards. The effective date of the QSR was June 1, 1997.

The QSR requires that domestic and foreign manufacturers have a quality system in place for the design, manufacture, packaging, labeling, storage, installation, and servicing of finished medical devices intended for commercial distribution in the United States. Specifically, the QSR requires medical device manufacturers to implement and comply with procedures covering the following activities:

- Management Responsibility;[98]
- Quality Audits;[99]
- Personnel (and Training);[100]
- Design Controls;[101]
- Document Controls;[102]
- Purchasing Controls;[103]
- Device Identification and Traceability;[104]
- Production and Process Controls;[105]
- Inspection, Measuring, and Test Equipment;[106]
- Process Validation;[107]
- Receiving, In-Process, and Finished Device Acceptance;[108]
- Nonconforming Product;[109]
- Corrective and Preventive Action (CAPA);[110]

---

[96]   61 Fed. Reg. 52,601 (1996).
[97]   *Id.*
[98]   21 C.F.R. § 820.20.
[99]   *Id.* § 820.22.
[100]   *Id.* § 820.25.
[101]   *Id.* § 820.30.
[102]   *Id.* § 820.40.
[103]   *Id.* § 820.50.
[104]   *Id.* §§ 820.60, 820.65.
[105]   *Id.* § 820.70.
[106]   *Id.* § 820.72.
[107]   *Id.* § 820.75.
[108]   *Id.* § 820.80.
[109]   *Id.* § 820.90.
[110]   *Id.* § 820.100.

- Device Labeling and Packaging;[111]
- Device Handling, Storage, Distribution, and Installation;[112]
- Device Recordkeeping;[113]
- Complaint Handling;[114]
- Servicing;[115] and
- Statistical Techniques.[116]

Though comprehensive with respect to the scope of the activities covered, the QSR also provides flexibility to medical device manufacturers as to what provisions may apply to a particular medical device or company. For example, the regulation states that "[i]f a manufacturer engages in only some operations subject to the requirements in this part, and not in others, that manufacturer need only comply with those requirements applicable to the operations in which it is engaged."[117] In addition, although the subject of extensive debate, manufacturers of device components and third-party servicers are not covered by the QSR.

In addition to the regulations, FDA has published several guidance documents that provide FDA's interpretations and recommendations regarding compliance with the general nature of the QSR's requirements. For example, Design Control Guidance for Medical Device Manufacturers is intended to "ensure that good quality assurance practices are used for the design of medical devices and that they are consistent with quality system requirements worldwide . . . ."[118] Another guidance provides the agency's expectations as to what issues are to be included in quality system procedures that are submitted as part of a PMA application.[119] Although the scope of that guidance pertains to procedures submitted as part of a PMA application, FDA's recommendations are applicable to QSR procedures irrespective of the type of devices manufactured. Lastly, FDA's Guide to Inspections of Quality Systems identifies the particular issues that the agency reviews during a typical quality system inspection.[120]

There have been few judicial decisions involving FDA's GMP and QSR regulations. A notable exception is *United States v. Utah Medical Products, Inc.*[121] At issue in that case was whether Utah Medical had properly validated its extrusion and injection molding processes; whether Utah Medical had properly validated the software programs used as part of its production or quality system; and whether Utah Medical properly processed certain of its complaints.

---

[111]   *Id.* §§ 820.120, 820.130.
[112]   *Id.* §§ 820.140, 820.150, 820.160, 820.170.
[113]   *Id.* §§ 820.180, 820.181, 820.184, 820.186.
[114]   *Id.* § 820.198.
[115]   *Id.* § 820.200.
[116]   *Id.* § 820.250.
[117]   *Id.* § 820.1(a).
[118]   Center for Devices and Radiological Health, Design Control Guidance for Medical Device Manufacturers (Mar. 11, 1997).
[119]   Center for Devices and Radiological Health, Quality System Information for Certain Premarket Application Reviews; Guidance for Industry and FDA Staff (Aug. 3, 1999).
[120]   *See* Center for Devices and Radiological Health, Guide to Inspections of Quality System, Quality Systems Inspection Technique (Aug. 1999).
[121]   404 F. Supp. 2d 1315 (D. Utah 2005).

After a series of inspections, FDA alleged that Utah Medical failed to comply with the QSR and as a result, was seeking to enjoin production at Utah Medical's facility until the company complied with FDA's interpretation of the QSR. Utah Medical argued that it had a comprehensive quality system in place that was compliant with the QSR. In an order denying FDA's request, the court relied upon the inherent flexibility of the QSR and Utah Medical's efforts to comply with FDA's regulations. Specifically, the court stated:

> Product safety is not an issue in this case. Processes and procedures are. "Validation" is the key word, and has often been noted, "many roads lead to Rome." The fact that the road chosen by Utah Medical may be different in degree than that thought to be appropriate by a regulator, does not mean that it is wrong, or in violation of the regulations.[122]

The judge also described the QSR as having the virtue of generality and the vice of imprecision. In this regard, the judge stated:

> This endemic problem is perhaps augmented by decision makers who themselves rely too much on inspectors' reports without taking a fresh look themselves at ongoing changes made by Utah Medical in response to questions raised.[123]

As a result, because Utah Medical had addressed FDA's concerns, the court denied FDA's request for injunction. Specifically, the court noted: "Without a doubt, the United States captured Utah Medical's attention in the past, and whatever modest deviations from regulations may have occurred in times past no longer exist at the present. It makes no sense for the court to order Utah Medical to do something they are already doing."[124] The impact of this case is often debated but one likely result is that FDA will ensure that it has current inspectional information about the company's state of QSR compliance before seeking an injunctive action.

Registration, Listing, and Inspection

Under 21 C.F.R. Part 807, device manufacturers, repackagers, relabelers, specification developers, and distributors of medical devices or ready-to-use components in commercial distribution must register their establishment and submit device listing information.[125] Specifically, owner/operators of device establishments are required to register their establishments with FDA within 30 days of engaging in an activity that requires registration, including the production of a medical device. In addition, manufacturers of medical devices intended for commercial distribution in the U.S. are required to list each device marketed in the U.S. within 30 days of U.S. commercial distribution. As a result of FDAAA in 2007, all establishment registration and device listing information is required to be submitted to FDA electronically using FDA's Unified Registration and Listing System (FURLS), unless

---

[122]   *Id.* at 1324.

[123]   *Id.* at 1323.

[124]   *Id.*

[125]   21 C.F.R. § 807.20.

a waiver has been granted by FDA.[126] FDA requires an amendment to an establishment registration and device listing when there are changes to individual ownership, corporate or partnership structure, or location of a registered establishment.[127] Such amendments are due at the time of annual registration, or within 30 days of such changes.[128] With respect to changes to device listing, modifications are to be updated during the registration period.[129] FDA also has published regulations requiring that foreign manufacturers (including contract manufacturers) who export devices into the United States designate a person as their U.S. agent.[130]

FDAAA also expanded FDA's user fee authority to include an annual fee for each medical device establishment that is required to register with the agency.[131] The annual fee for FY 2015 for all medical device establishments is $3,646 and is projected to be $3,872 for FY 2016 and FY 2017. To collect these annual fees in a timely manner, the timing of annual registration was modified to occur between October and December of each year.[132]

FDA uses the establishment registration and device listing information to maintain a database of companies that are subject to FDA inspection as well as the types of products manufactured or distributed by each firm. FDA uses this information to schedule inspections and to target mass mailings to segments of the medical device industry, or to the industry as a whole.

FDA conducts periodic inspections of registered facilities. The frequency of inspection is based on a number of factors including the level of risk of the devices manufactured by the firm; the date of the company's last inspection; whether major QSR violations were observed during previous inspections; whether the firm is viewed as a recidivist/repeat offender; whether the firm conducted a recall recently; and whether FDA has received consumer or competitor trade complaints. The manufacturing facilities of devices that are the subject of pending premarket approval applications (and, in some cases, PMA supplements) are typically inspected before FDA approves the submission. Based on the results of the inspection, FDA can take a number of actions, including enforcement actions. Typically, FDA will issue a Form FDA 483 List of Inspectional Observations that identifies deficiencies observed during the inspection. In addition, FDA can initiate a wide variety of enforcement actions including, but not limited to, the issuance of a Warning Letter, implementation of an import alert, initiation of a product seizure action, or injunction. FDA's enforcement authority and options are discussed in Chapter 21 *infra*.

Medical Device Reporting Requirements

FDA requires manufacturers, importers, and user facilities to report certain adverse events involving marketed devices in order to ensure that the agency is promptly informed of all

---

[126] FDCA § 510(p), 21 U.S.C. § 360(p).
[127] 21 C.F.R. § 807.26.
[128] *Id.*
[129] *See id.* § 807.30(b).
[130] 60 Fed. Reg. 63,606 (1995) (codified at 21 C.F.R. § 807.40).
[131] FDCA § 738(a), 21 U.S.C. § 379j(a).
[132] FDCA § 510(b), 21 U.S.C. § 360(b).

serious problems or potentially serious problems associated with marketed devices. The Medical Device Reporting (MDR) requirements are found in 21 C.F.R. Part 803.

Specifically, manufacturers must submit an MDR to FDA within 30 days after receiving or otherwise becoming aware of information, from any source, that reasonably suggests that a device marketed by the manufacturer 1) may have caused or contributed to a death or serious injury; or 2) has malfunctioned and such device or a similar device marketed by the manufacturer would be likely to cause or contribute to a death or serious injury, if the malfunction were to recur.[133] In addition, manufacturers must submit a five-day report to FDA within five working days after 1) becoming aware from any source, including trend analysis, that remedial action is necessary to prevent an unreasonable risk of substantial harm to the public health; or 2) becoming aware of an MDR reportable event for which FDA has made a written request for the submission of a five-day report.[134] Manufacturers also are required to submit supplemental reports.[135]

A user facility is required to report to FDA and the manufacturer, if known, within 10 working days whenever it receives or becomes aware of information, from any source, that reasonably suggests that a device has or may have caused or contributed to the death of a patient of the facility.[136] If there is a serious injury rather than a death, the user facility must report the incident within 10 working days to the manufacturer only.

Following the enactment of FDAMA, FDA updated the MDR regulations to, among other things, revoke the distributor reporting requirements.[137] Thus, distributors of medical devices who do not also qualify as manufacturers are no longer required to submit MDRs. Distributors are required, however, to maintain certain records of adverse events.[138] FDA further modified the MDR regulations in February 2005 to make each section of the regulation "easy to understand by using clear and simple language rather than jargon, by keeping sentences short, and by using active voice rather than passive voice whenever possible."[139] Despite the implementation of the plain language now used in the regulation, there were no substantive modifications promulgated by the agency.

In July 2013, FDA issued a draft guidance document entitled "Draft Guidance for Industry and Food and Drug Administration Staff – Medical Device Reporting for Manufacturers."[140] As stated in the draft guidance, the purpose of the document is to provide FDA's current interpretation of the MDR regulation. The document is written in a question-and-answer format and re-emphasizes FDA's interpretation of how the regulation applies to certain device failures. The draft guidance also changed a number of longstanding FDA interpretations

---

[133]   21 C.F.R. § 803.50(a).
[134]   *Id.* § 803.53.
[135]   *Id.* § 803.56.
[136]   *Id.* § 803.30.
[137]   65 Fed. Reg. 4112 (2000). Under this notice, FDA formally revoked 21 C.F.R. Part 804, which contained the distributor reporting requirements.
[138]   *See* 21 C.F.R. § 809.18.
[139]   70 Fed. Reg. 9558 (2005).
[140]   U.S. Food and Drug Admin., Medical Device Reporting for Manufacturers: Draft Guidance (July 9, 2013), *available at* http://www.fda.gov/downloads/MedicalDevices/DeviceRegulationandGuidance/GuidanceDocuments/UCM359566.pdf.

and policies. For example, the draft guidance defines the term "similar" with respect to malfunction reporting. As noted above, manufacturers are required to submit MDRs for malfunctions for events when that device or a similar device marketed by the manufacturer would be reasonably likely to cause or contribute to a death or serious injury if the malfunction were to recur. In the draft guidance, FDA defines "similar devices" as devices with the same basic design and performance characteristics, intended use and function, and device classification and product code. Other factors include brand name and whether the device was cleared under the same 510(k) or PMA.[141]

Exportation of Medical Devices

The FDCA does not govern the exportation of approved medical devices. Accordingly, cleared and approved devices may be exported to anywhere in the world without prior FDA approval or notification provided that they are exported for those uses that FDA has cleared or approved. For a device to be legally marketed in the United States, the following requirements must be met:

- The manufacturing facility must be registered with FDA;
- The device must be listed with FDA;
- The device must have a cleared 510(k) or approved PMA unless exempted by regulation or if the device was on the market prior to May 28, 1976;
- The device must meet the labeling requirements of 21 C.F.R. Part 801 and 21 C.F.R. 809, if applicable; and
- The device must be manufactured in accordance with the QSR.

Sections 801 and 802 of the FDCA govern the export of devices that are uncleared or unapproved by FDA. Under section 801(e)(1), a device that may be cleared for marketing under section 510(k) of the FDCA (e.g., a "510(k)able" device) may be exported without prior FDA approval provided the device 1) accords to the specifications of the manufacturer; 2) is not in conflict with the laws of the country to which it is intended for export; 3) is labeled on the outside of the shipping package that it is intended for export; and 4) is not sold or offered for sale in domestic commerce. Prior to the enactment of the FDA Export Reform and Enhancement Act on April 26, 1996,[142] devices that were not "510(k)able" were required to meet the above requirements as well as obtain FDA approval of their exportation, pursuant to section 801(e)(2).

The FDA Export Reform and Enhancement Act, which expedited the export of many Class III devices, permits the export of a Class III device that complies with the laws of the receiving country and has marketing authorization in any country identified in section 802(b)(1)(A) of the FDCA. The countries listed in that section, known as "Tier I countries," are Australia, Canada, Israel, Japan, New Zealand, Switzerland, South Africa, a member of the European Union (United Kingdom, Spain, Ireland, Denmark, Greece, Belgium,

---

[141]   Id.
[142]   FDCA §§ 304, 802, 21 U.S.C. §§ 334, 382; 42 U.S.C. § 262.

Portugal, Germany, France, Italy, Luxembourg, Netherlands, Sweden, Finland, and Austria) or the European Economic Area (includes the European Union countries and Norway, Iceland, and Liechtenstein). As of May 2004, the European Union also includes Cyprus, the Czech Republic, Estonia, Hungary, Latvia, Lithuania, Malta, Poland, Slovakia, and Slovenia. Exportation under section 802(b) requires the subject device to:

- meet the requirements of section 801(e)(1);

- substantially meet the QSR or an international quality standard recognized by FDA (currently, none are recognized);

- not be adulterated other than by the lack of marketing approval;

- not be the subject of a notice by Department of Health and Human Services that re-importation would pose an imminent hazard, nor pose an imminent hazard to the receiving country; and

- not be mislabeled other than by possessing the language, units of measure, or any other labeling authorized by the recipient country. In addition, the labeling must comply with the requirements and conditions of use in the listed country which gave marketing authorization, and must be promoted in accordance with its labeling.

Although FDA approval for exportation is not required if all of the above requirements are met, once companies first begin to export a device under section 802(b) of the FDCA, they must provide written notification of such export to FDA. The notification must identify:

- The product's trade name;

- The type of device;

- The product's model number; and

- The country that is to receive the exported article if the export is to a Tier II country.

The notification may, but is not required to, identify the Tier I countries to which the product is intended to be exported or may state that the export is intended for a listed Tier I country without identifying the listed country.

Under section 802(c) of the FDCA, a device may be exported to a Tier I country for investigational use without FDA approval so long as it is, among other things, exported in accordance with the laws of the receiving country. Specifically, in order to qualify for export under section 802(c), devices must:

- meet the requirements of section 801(e)(1) of the FDCA (discussed above);

- be manufactured, processed, packaged, and held in substantial compliance with the QSR, or an international standards organization recognized by FDA has certified that it meets international standards;[143]

- not be adulterated as: 1) it does not consist in whole or in part of any filthy, putrid, or decomposed substance; 2) it has not been prepared, packed, or held under unsanitary conditions, whereby it may have been contaminated with filth, or whereby it may have

---

[143]   FDA has not yet recognized any such international standards.

been rendered injurious to health; 3) its container is not composed, in whole or in part, of any poisonous or deleterious substance which may render the contents injurious to health; and 4) its strength does not differ from, or its purity or quality fall below, that which it purports or is represented to possess;

- not be the subject of a notice of export prohibition issued by FDA or the U.S. Department of Agriculture because the probability of re-importation of the exported device would present an imminent hazard to the public health;

- not present "an imminent hazard to the public health of the country" to which it would be exported;

- be labeled in accordance with the requirements and conditions for use in the country in which it received valid market authorization *and* the country to which it would be exported; and

- be labeled in the language and units of measurement of the country to which it would be exported or in the language designated by that country.

If a company intends to export a device that is not "510(k)able," is not approved in any of the Tier I countries, and is intended to be exported to a nonlisted country, the requirements of section 801(e)(2) must be met. Section 801(e)(2) is the most restrictive of the FDCA's medical device export provisions. Under this provision, prior FDA approval must be obtained to export an unapproved device. In order to obtain this approval, a manufacturer must initially meet the four conditions required in section 801(e)(1). In addition, the manufacturer also must provide adequate information, including a detailed device description, to FDA for the agency to determine that 1) exportation of the device is not contrary to the public health and safety and 2) the device is approved for use in the country to which it is intended for export. After a section 801(e)(2) submission is received, FDA reviews the above information to determine whether the export should be approved. This review typically can be completed within 20 to 30 days if no safety issues arise.

In 2007, FDA issued guidance regarding exports under the Export Reform Act of 1996.[144] Among other things, that guidance identifies the agency's current thinking with respect to what companies need to do to comply with the FDCA's export provisions.

Manufacturers that export medical devices are often asked by foreign governments to provide a certificate that states that the device is legally marketed in the United States. Section 801(e)(4) of the FDCA authorizes FDA to certify in writing that a device being exported is cleared, approved, or exempt from premarket clearance or approval, or that it meets the requirements of the applicable export provisions of the FDCA (i.e., sections 801(e)(1), 801(e)(2) or 802).

The most commonly issued certification is the Certificate to Foreign Governments (CFG). CFGs are issued for legally marketed devices that are in compliance with the FDCA. All such requests must be submitted on form FDA-3613, Supplementary Information Certificate to Foreign Government Requests. This form is available on FDA's website. The form also may be submitted electronically via the CDRH Export Certification and Tracking System (CECATS).

---

[144]   Office of International Programs, Food and Drug Administration. Guidance for Industry: Exports Under the FDA Export Reform and Enhancement Act of 1996 (July 23, 2007).

CECATS is the agency's voluntary electronic system that allows manufacturers and initial importers to request export documents online as an alternative to paper submissions.[145]

FDA also requires an initial fee and a fee for additional certificate(s) issued for the same product(s) in the same letter of request.

FDA's Recall Regulations—Reports of Corrections and Removals

FDA defines a recall as the *removal* or *correction* of a marketed product that the agency considers to be in violation of the laws it administers and against which the agency would initiate legal action, e.g., seizure.[146] A correction is defined as a means of repair, modification, adjustment, relabeling, destruction, or inspection (including patient monitoring) of a product without its physical removal to some other location.[147] A removal is defined as the physical removal of a device from its point of use to some other location for repair, modification, adjustment, relabeling, destruction, or inspection.[148] Although corrections and removals are typically initiated voluntarily by device manufacturers, FDA has the legal authority to order device manufacturers to cease distribution of devices regulated by the agency and notify health professionals and user facilities to cease using such devices, where it makes a finding that there is "a reasonable probability that a device intended for human use would cause serious, adverse health consequences or death."[149]

Voluntary Recalls

FDA's regulations address the processes by which medical device manufacturers should determine whether to conduct a recall, as well as how such recalls should be implemented.[150] FDA's regulations also require, among other things, that certain types of corrections and removals be reported to FDA.[151] In general, FDA entrusts companies to use reasonable judgment in determining whether potential safety or compliance issues rise to the level of recalling product from the field. When faced with a recall decision, FDA expects every medical device manufacturer to make a judgment as to whether it is appropriate to continue to ship (and not recall) devices that may be experiencing a problem. This determination should be made based on a variety of data developed and/or acquired through the company's quality system. For example, because the safety profile of such a product is not always clear, the agency expects manufacturers to prepare a Health Hazard Analysis or to otherwise review available quality and safety data and information to make decisions with respect to whether the continued marketing and use of the device is appropriate.[152] Based on this

---

[145]   See   http://www.fda.gov/MedicalDevices/DeviceRegulationandGuidance/ImportingandExportingDevices/ExportingMedicalDevices/ucm346619.htm.

[146]   21 C.F.R. § 7.3(g) (emphasis added).

[147]   *Id.* § 7.3(h).

[148]   *Id.* § 806.2(i).

[149]   *See* 21 C.F.R. pt. 810.

[150]   *See generally,* 21 C.F.R. pt. 7.

[151]   *See generally,* 21 C.F.R. pt. 806.

[152]   *See, e.g.,* 21 C.F.R. § 7.41(a).

information, recalls are classified into a numerical designation (I, II, or III) to indicate the relative degree of health hazard presented by the product being recalled.[153] Specifically, recalls are to be classified into one of three classes.

- Class I—a situation in which there is a reasonable probability that the use of, or exposure to, a violative product will cause serious adverse health consequences or death.

- Class II—a situation in which use of, or exposure to, a violative product may cause temporary or medically reversible adverse health consequences or where the probability of serious adverse health consequences is remote.

- Class III—a situation in which use of, or exposure to, a violative product is not likely to cause adverse health consequences.[154]

Although a company that is initiating a voluntary recall can propose the recall classification, FDA ultimately determines the recall classification.[155]

In addition to the recall decision-making and implementation processes addressed above, FDA's medical device corrections and removals reporting regulations, found in 21 C.F.R. Part 806, require manufacturers to submit a written report to FDA of any nonexempt product removal or correction initiated either 1) to reduce a risk to health posed by the device or 2) to remedy a violation of the FDCA caused by the device which may present a risk to health, unless that information has previously been reported to FDA under the MDR regulation. Thus, FDA requires that a report be filed for all Class I and Class II recalls. In practice, however, certain FDA districts expect to be notified of Class III recalls as well. Reports of corrections and removals must be submitted to FDA within 10 working days of the initiation of the removal or correction and must include the following:

- Registration number, date the report is made, sequence number (001, 002, etc.);

- Name, address, phone number, and contact person of the firm responsible for conducting the correction or removal;

- Brand name and common name of the device and intended use;

- FDA marketing status, i.e., 510(k), PMA, pre-amendment status, and device listing number;

- Model/catalog number, lot/serial number;

- Manufacturer's contact information (name, address, phone number, contact person) if different from above;

- Description of event(s) and the corrective and removal actions that have been and are expected to be taken;

- Any illness or injuries that have occurred with the use of the device. If applicable, include any MDR numbers;

---

[153] *Id.* § 7.3(m).
[154] Center for Devices and Radiological Health, U.S. Food and Drug Administration, Device Registration and Listing, at http://www.fda.gov/MedicalDevices/DeviceRegulationandGuidance/HowtoMarketYourDevice/RegistrationandListing/default.htm (last updated June 30, 2009).
[155] 21 C.F.R. § 7.41(b).

- The number of devices subject to the Correction or Removal;

- Date of manufacture or distribution; expiration date or expected life;

- Name, address and telephone number of all consignees (domestic and foreign) and the dates and number of devices distributed to each consignee;

- A copy of all communications regarding the correction or removal; and

- A statement as to why any required information is not available and a date when it will be submitted.[156]

FDA does not require notification of the following actions:

- Market withdrawals: a correction or removal of a distributed device that involves a minor violation of the act that would not be subject to legal action by FDA or that involves no violation of the act, e.g., normal stock rotation practices.[157]

- Routine servicing: any regularly scheduled maintenance of a device, including the replacement of parts at the end of their normal life expectancy, e.g., calibration, replacement of batteries, and responses to normal wear and tear. Repairs of an unexpected nature, replacement of parts earlier than their normal life expectancy, or identical repairs or replacements of multiple units of a device are not routine servicing.[158]

- Stock recoveries: the correction or removal of a device that has not been marketed or that has not left the direct control of the manufacturer, i.e., the device is located on the premises owned, or under the control of, the manufacturer, and no portion of the lot, model, code, or other relevant unit involved in the corrective or removal action has been released for sale or use.[159]

FDA requires certain recordkeeping requirements for corrections or removals that are not required to be reported to FDA.[160] In addition, actions taken by device manufacturers to improve the performance or quality of a device but that do not reduce a risk to health posed by the device or remedy a violation of the act caused by the device are not required to be reported as recalls. FDA clarified this position in an October 15, 2014 guidance clarifying the difference between medical device recalls and device enhancements.[161] This document, entitled "Distinguishing Medical Device Recalls from Medical Device Enhancements: Guidance for Industry and Food and Drug Administration Staff," replaced a controversial draft guidance issued by the agency in February 2013. The guidance seeks to clarify when a change to a device constitutes a medical device recall, to distinguish those instances from device enhancements that do not meet the definition of a medical device recall, and to identify the associated regulatory reporting requirements for each type of activity. The guidance defines a device enhancement as a change to improve a device's performance or quality that is not meant to resolve a violation of the FDCA or FDA regulations. Enhancements may also be changes designed to better meet the user's needs, to make the device easier to manufacture,

---

[156]   *Id.* § 806.10.
[157]   *Id.* § 806.2(h).
[158]   *Id.* § 806.2(k).
[159]   21 C.F.R. § 806.2(l).
[160]   *See generally, id.* § 806.20.
[161]   Distinguishing Medical Device Recalls from Medical Device Enhancements: Guidance for Industry and Food and Drug Administration Staff (Oct. 15, 2014), *available at* http://www.fda.gov/downloads/MedicalDevices/DeviceRegulationandGuidance/GuidanceDocuments/UCM418469.pdf.

or to improve a non-violative device's safety or performance. Per the guidance, a device enhancement does not require the submission of a report under Part 806 as such a change is not considered to be a recall. The guidance uses a question-and-answer format and also provides a number of examples to put FDA's position into context. However, the examples in the guidance appear to focus on changes to devices that have already been distributed to the field. One issue that is not specifically addressed in the guidance is whether a change to production units and/or units in inventory, without correcting or removing product in the field, is considered to be a recall and thus requires the submission of a report under 21 C.F.R. Part 806. It would appear that the same logic set forth in the guidance would apply to that situation, in that if a change that is made exclusively on a going forward basis meets the definition of a product enhancement, and product in the field is non-violative, the change would not require the submission of a report under 21 C.F.R. Part 806, but again, that scenario is not spelled out in the guidance

FDA Mandated Recalls

In accordance with 21 C.F.R. Part 810, if, after providing a manufacturer with an opportunity to consult with the agency, FDA finds that there is a reasonable probability that a device intended for human use would cause serious, adverse health consequences or death, the agency may issue a cease distribution and notification order requiring the company named in the order to immediately:

- cease distribution of the device;
- notify health professionals and device user facilities of the order; and
- instruct health professionals and device user facilities to cease use of the device.[162]

FDA's regulations provide companies the opportunity for a regulatory hearing to challenge the order[163] as well as the opportunity to submit a written request to the agency to seek that the order be modified, vacated, or amended.[164]

Federal Preemption

The 1976 amendments included a provision that preempted certain state regulations of medical devices. Section 521 of the amendments stated, in pertinent part, that:

> (a) Except as provided in subsection (b), no State or political subdivision of a State may establish or continue in effect with respect to a device intended for human use any requirement—
>> (1) which is *different from, or in addition to, any requirement applicable under this Act* to the device, and
>> (2) which relates to the safety or effectiveness of the device or to any other

---

[162] *Id.* § 810.10(a).
[163] *Id.* § 810.11.
[164] *Id.* § 810.12.

matter included in a requirement applicable to the device under this Act.[165]

The precise scope of this preemption provision remained ambiguous for nearly 20 years following its enactment. Federal circuits were divided on the meaning of the terms "requirement" and "different from, or in addition to."[166] Thus, some circuits interpreted the provision to mean that clearance of a premarket notification for a device preempted some or all state common-law claims,[167] while other circuits construed the provision to preserve all state common-law claims.[168]

To resolve this split among the federal circuit courts, the U.S. Supreme Court granted certiorari in 1995 in *Medtronic v. Lohr*.[169] In *Lohr*, Lora Lohr, who had received a pacemaker manufactured by Medtronic, and her spouse brought a state common-law negligence and strict liability action against Medtronic for damages allegedly resulting from the device's failure. The Lohrs claimed that Medtronic was negligent due to defective device design and failure to provide adequate instructions. The plaintiffs also presented a strict liability claim, alleging that the device was, at the time of sale, in a defective condition and unreasonably dangerous to foreseeable users. Medtronic counterargued that all of the plaintiffs' state law claims were preempted by the provision in section 521, quoted above.

The issue presented before the Supreme Court was the precise scope of the preemption provision. Because Medtronic's pacemaker had been cleared by FDA through the 510(k) process and was subject to continuing regulatory monitoring of its manufacture and labeling, Medtronic argued that the availability of state law remedies imposed a requirement "different from or in addition to" federal requirements, thus triggering the preemption provision.

The Court rejected Medtronic's argument, concluding that the 510(k) process does not preempt state law claims. Justice Stevens, writing for the majority, stated that:

> The company's defense exaggerates the importance of the § 510(k) process . . . . As the court below noted, "the 510(k) process is focused on equivalence, not safety." . . . As a result, "substantial equivalence determinations provide little protection to the public . . . ."[170]

While *Lohr* appears to resolve the issue of the scope of the preemption provision for state law claims regarding products cleared through the 510(k) process, the opinion expressly leaves open the question of whether PMA approval would preempt state law claims.

---

[165]   21 U.S.C. § 360k(a) (emphasis added).

[166]   *See, e.g.,* English v. Mentor Corp., 67 F.3d 477 (3d Cir. 1995) (510(k) clearance preempts state regulation); Feldt v. Mentor Corp., 61 F.3d 431 (5th Cir. 1995) (510(k) clearance does not preempt state regulation); Kennedy v. Collagen Corp., 67 F.3d 1453 (9th Cir. 1995) (state common law claims are not preempted by section 521 of Medical Device Amendments).

[167]   *See, e.g.,* English v. Mentor Corp., 67 F.3d 477 (3d Cir. 1995).

[168]   *See, e.g.,* Kennedy v. Collagen Corp., 67 F.3d 1453 (9th Cir. 1995).

[169]   116 S. Ct. 2240 (1996).

[170]   *Id.* at 2254.

Following the Supreme Court's decision in *Lohr*, a majority of the circuit courts of appeal concluded that state law claims regarding products approved by FDA through the exceptionally rigorous PMA process, by which federal regulators ensured that the device met federal requirements, are preempted.[171] Then, on February 20, 2008, the U.S. Supreme Court decided the case of *Riegel v. Medtronic, Inc.*[172]

Charles Riegel and his wife brought suit against Medtronic after Medtronic's Evergreen Balloon Catheter, a Class III, PMA-approved device, ruptured in Charles Riegel's coronary artery during heart surgery. The Riegels alleged that the device was manufactured, labeled and designed in a manner that violated New York common law. At issue was whether PMA approval preempts state common-law challenges to the safety and effectiveness of a medical device.

The Court found in favor of Medtronic, concluding that the MDA's preemption clause bars common-law claims that challenge the safety and effectiveness of a medical device marketed in a form that received premarket approval from FDA.[173] The Court's decision was based on its findings that through the PMA approval process, the federal government has established "specific requirements applicable to a particular device," within the meaning of the MDA's preemption provision and that the Riegels' claims were based on state requirements, which were "different from and in addition to" those requirements imposed by FDA.[174]

In distinguishing the PMA approval process in question in *Riegel* from the 510(k) clearance process in question in *Lohr*, the Court stated, "While § 510(k) is 'focused on *equivalence*, not safety,' premarket approval is focused on safety, not equivalence."[175] The Court's decision in *Riegel* decisively restricts the right of device users to sue medical device firms for faulty products that have been approved through the PMA process, to the extent that the device complies with the FDA-approved specifications.

A number of cases that have applied the Supreme Court rulings provide additional insight into the scope of the MDA's preemption clause. For example, in *Cornett v. Johnson & Johnson*,[176] the plaintiff alleged that the design of an approved medical device was less safe than possible alternatives. The court held that the state products liability statute, under which the claim was brought, provided a different standard from the federal requirements for adequacy of the device's design, and thus, was preempted.

Even more recently, in *Walker v. Medtronic, Inc.*,[177] an approved programmable pump for delivering medication to patients requiring a chronic infusion of drugs delivered an excess

---

[171]   *See* Riegel v. Medtronic, Inc., 451 F.3d 104, 106 (2d Cir. 2006); Horn v. Thoratec Corp., 376 F.3d 163, 169 (3d Cir. 2004); Martin v. Medtronic, Inc., 254 F.3d 573, 585 (5th Cir. 2001); Brooks v. Howmedica, Inc., 273 F.3d 785 (8th Cir. 2001); Kemp v. Medtronic, Inc., 231 F.3d 216, 230 (6th Cir. 2001); Mitchell v. Collagen Corp., 126 F.3d 902, 913 (7th Cir. 1997); Papike v. Tambrands, Inc., 107 Fed 737, 742 (9th Cir. 1997); *but see* Goodwin v. Medtronic, Inc., 167 F.3d 1367, 1377 (11th Cir. 1999) (holding § 360(a) does not preempt common-law claims involving PMA approved devices).

[172]   Riegel v. Medtronic, Inc. 555 U.S. 312 (2008).

[173]   *Id.*

[174]   *Id.*

[175]   *Id.*

[176]   Cornett v. Johnson & Johnson, 414 N.J. Super. 365, 998 A.2d 543 (App. Div. 2010).

[177]   Walker v. Medtronic, Inc., 670 F.3d 569 (4th Cir. 2012).

of medication resulting in the death of a patient. The pump's approved operating manual specified that medication would accurately flow from the pump within 15 percent of the programmed rate and warned of various factors that could compromise the pump's accuracy. The plaintiff sued in state court for negligence, strict liability, and breach of warranty arguing that the flow accuracy specification constituted a performance standard under the MDA from which the device deviated. Accordingly, the plaintiff alleged that the state law claims paralleled those that could be brought under the MDA. The court held that the flow accuracy specification in the device labeling was intended to inform the medical community of the results that the device was likely to achieve under optimal circumstances. This aspect of the device labeling did not constitute a performance standard required to be met by FDA. Because the plaintiff's claims sought to impose requirements more restrictive than those imposed by the MDA, the court concluded that the claims were preempted by the MDA.

Courts have also rejected attempts to break down medical devices into their component parts for purposes of avoiding preemption. In the course of the last several years, the courts have held that preemption applies to all components of a PMA-approved device, even if the component at issue had previously been marketed through the 510(k) clearance process. For example, in *Bass v. Stryker Corp.*,[178] the Fifth Circuit Court of Appeals affirmed the district court's preemption finding in a case involving the acetabular shell of the Trident artificial hip system, holding that the district court was correct not to break the device into component parts.

Further, plaintiffs seeking ways to avoid dismissal on preemption grounds have included parallel claims in their complaints alleging, for example, off-label promotion by the device manufacturer.[179]

There also appears to be a split in views among the circuit courts as to whether a plaintiff's claims, which are premised on the defendant's alleged failure to report postapproval information to FDA, are preempted.[180]

The theory of preemption continues to develop as plaintiffs seek to avoid dismissal based on the pleadings, including a series of cases in which preemption was considered and, in many cases, applied to devices used under an approved IDE.[181]

---

[178]   Bass v. Stryker Corp., 669 F.3d 501 (5th Cir. 2012).

[179]   See Caplinger v. Medtronic, Case No. 5:12-cv-630 (W.D. Okla. Feb. 6, 2013) (in which allegations of off-label promotion would not prevent dismissal on preemption grounds).

[180]   *Compare* Stengel v. Medtronic, Inc., 704 F.3d 1224 (9th Cir. 2013) (finding preemption) *with* In re Medtronic, Inc., Sprint Fidelis Leads Products Liability Litigation, 623 F.3d 1200 (8th Cir. 2010) (rejecting preemption).

[181]   *Compare for example* Martin v. Telectronics Pacing Systems, Inc., 105 F.3d 1090 (6th Cir. 1997); Gile v. Optical Radiation Corp., 22 F.3d 540 (3d Cir. 1994); Chambers v. Osteonics Corp., 109 F.3d 1243 (7th Cir. 1997); Slater v. Optical Radiation Corp., 961 F.2d 1330 (7th Cir. 1992); Becker v. Optical Radiation Corp., 66 F.3d 18 (2d Cir. 1995); Burgos v. Satiety, Inc., 2010 WL 4907764 (E.D.N.Y. Nov. 30, 2010); Blinn v. Smith & Nephew Richards, Inc., 55 F. Supp. 2d 1353 (N.D. Fla. 1999), (finding preemption) *with* Caccia v. Biomet, Inc., et al., 2013 WL 4502211 (N.D. Ind. Aug. 21, 2013) (rejecting preemption).

Conclusion

FDA's regulations on devices are quite extensive and often complex. This chapter summarizes both FDA's premarket and postmarket regulatory requirements. However, it is certainly not an exhaustive account of what is necessary to comply with all of the agency's requirements as well as FDA's expectations.

CHAPTER 17
COMBINATION PRODUCTS
AND JURISDICTIONAL ISSUES

....

JEFFREY K. SHAPIRO

A combination product employs a combination of drug, device, and/or biologic modalities that act together to achieve a therapeutic effect. The Food and Drug Administration (FDA) is organized in different Centers equipped to regulate each of these modalities separately. The relevant Centers are the Center for Drug Evaluation and Research (CDER) (drugs); the Center for Devices and Radiological Health (CDRH) (devices); and the Center for Biologics Evaluation and Research (CBER) (biologics). Because of this modality-based organization, the task of regulating combination products has long caused difficulties for FDA. The creation of the Office of Combination Products (OCP) in 2002 was intended to improve the agency's management of combination products. Still, as will be discussed, there continue to be regulatory obstacles to technological innovation in combination products.[1]

History

Early on, FDA decided how to regulate combination products on an *ad hoc* basis. For example, prophylaxis pastes containing fluoride were regulated as drugs, although prophylaxis pastes without fluoride were considered medical devices.[2] Bone cement, however, is treated as a device, regardless of whether it is combined with an antibiotic drug.[3]

---

[1]   FDA's Office of Combination Products also reviews and provides jurisdictional designations for single entity products that do not involve combinations (as defined by the agency), based on which of the single entity's products achieves the product's primary intended effect. Where relevant, this distinction between the primary mode of action (for combination products) and the characteristics of a single entity that achieves a product's primary intended effect, is noted.

[2]   Letter from William F. Randolph, Dep. Assoc. Comm'r for Regulatory Affairs, FDA, to Robert A. Abodeely, Dir., Regulatory Affairs and Quality Assurance, Johnson & Johnson Dental Prods. Co. (Sept. 18, 1981).

[3]   Letter from William F. Randolph, Dep. Assoc. Comm'r for Regulatory Affairs, to Timothy M. Wendt, Vice President, Div. Counsel, Zimmer (Jan. 17, 1983) (re: bone cement containing an antibiotic); 21 C.F.R. § 888.3027 (1996) (re: bone cement itself).

Sometimes consistency was elusive even when there was no combination, and just a single entity product. For example, in vitro diagnostics for detecting antibodies to HIV are regulated as biologics when they are used for screening the blood supply, but as medical devices when used for diagnostic or other screening purposes.[4] Over the years, when FDA decided quickly and unequivocally on the regulatory status of a product, whether it was deemed a single entity product or was in combination with another product, there was relatively little objection to the agency's decisions about how to regulate combination products and products whose status was uncertain. When FDA required two separate approvals, one for the device and one for the drug element of the product, as it did with the drug ursodiol for use with lithotripters, the agency created difficulty and delay in getting the products licensed so they could be used together.[5]

In the Safe Medical Devices Act of 1990 (SMDA),[6] Congress took these issues in hand and amended the Federal Food, Drug, and Cosmetic Act (FDCA)[7] to make it easier for FDA to regulate combination products in a rational fashion. The new provisions altered the substantive provisions of the FDCA only in minor respects.[8] The main thrust of the new law was managerial, directing FDA to make decisions about which Center would have "primary jurisdiction" over a combination product, based on the agency's decision about the "primary mode of action" of the product.[9] The SMDA provisions also explicitly stated that nothing in the new amendment prevented FDA from using any of its resources necessary to ensure adequate review of the safety, effectiveness, or substantial equivalence of an article.[10]

The SMDA also ordered FDA to issue regulations implementing market clearance procedures in accordance with the new section 503(g) within one year.[11] FDA did so, and published its new regulations on November 21, 1991.[12]

---

[4]   FDA, Intercenter Agreement Between the Center for Biologics Evaluation and Research and the Center for Devices and Radiological Health at 5 (Oct. 25, 1991) [hereinafter CDER-CDRH ICA]; FDA, Talk Paper, *Update on AIDS Test Kits* (Oct. 26, 1987).

[5]   M-D-D-I Rep. ("The Gray Sheet"), Jan. 8, 1996, at 9-10; M-D-D-I Rep. ("The Gray Sheet"), Sept. 24, 1990, at 4-5.

[6]   Safe Medical Devices Act, Pub. L. No. 101-629, 104 Stat. 4511 (1990).

[7]   Federal Food, Drug, and Cosmetic Act, Pub. L. No. 75-717, 52 Stat. 1040 (1938) (codified at 21 U.S.C. § 301 *et seq.*).

[8]   Specifically, Congress deleted from the definition of "drug" the phrase "but does not include devices or their components," thus allowing FDA to approve a combination product as a drug. S. REP. No. 513, 101st Cong., 2d Sess. 30 (1990). Congress also changed the definition of "device." Pre-SMDA, a product could not be a device if it "achieve[d] any of its principal purposes through chemical action" . . ., etc. The SMDA deleted "any of" and substituted "primary" for "principal." *Id.*

[9]   FDCA § 503(g)(1), 21 U.S.C. § 353(g)(1). Because FDA considered the new statute to govern administration and management rather than substance, it decided that its procedures for issuing implementing regulations were exempt from notice and comment under the Administrative Procedure Act. Assignment of Agency Component for Review of Premarket Notifications, Preamble to Final Rule, 56 Fed. Reg. 58,754, 58,755 (Nov. 21, 1991).

[10]   FDCA § 503(g)(2), 21 U.S.C. § 353(g)(2). Presumably FDA already had this authority, for nothing in the FDCA or the Public Health Service Act otherwise requires or prevents the Commissioner of Food and Drugs' delegation of authority (as delegated to him or her by the Secretary of the Department of Health and Human Services (DHHS)) to any of the agency's employees.

[11]   FDCA § 503(g)(3), 21 U.S.C. § 353(g)(3).

[12]   Assignment of Agency Component for Review of Premarket Applications, Final Rule, 56 Fed. Reg. 58,754 (Nov. 21, 1991) [hereinafter, "Final Rule"].

As will be discussed, the regulations implemented the new statutory provisions governing combination products, and also provided a means of resolving questions about which Center will have primary jurisdiction for any drug, device, or biological product, whether a combination product or not, where such jurisdiction is unclear or in dispute.[13]

Although neither the statute nor the regulations explain what "primary jurisdiction" means, it seems clear that FDA intends it to mean that the Center that has primary jurisdiction will review the combination product and ordinarily give it just one approval; that is, a new drug application (NDA), premarket approval (PMA), or biologic license application (BLA) as appropriate. Section 3.4(b) makes it clear, however, that FDA's designation of one agency component as having primary jurisdiction does not preclude, in appropriate cases, the requirement for separate applications; e.g., a 510(k) and a BLA. When separate applications are required, both can be reviewed by the lead Center, but "exceptional" cases may involve a second application to be reviewed by a different Center.[14] To facilitate this, the agency published new delegations giving officials in each of the three Centers the authority to clear devices and to approve devices, drugs, biologics, or any combination of two or more of them.[15]

Contemporaneous with publication of the new regulations, FDA made public three new Intercenter Agreements (ICAs) between CDRH and CBER, CDRH and CDER, and CDER and CBER. They describe the allocations of responsibility for numerous categories of specific products, both combination and noncombination. According to the regulations, these Intercenter Agreements are not binding; they are intended to "provide useful guidance to the public,"[16] and, as a practical matter, to FDA staff as well.[17]

For about 15 years after the ICAs and the regulations implementing section 503(g), FDA's management of combination products remained fairly stagnant. It also was subject to serious criticism. FDA was charged with inconsistency, unpredictability, and lack of transparency in the product assignment process; excessive delays and lack of coordination in the review process when two or more Centers had review responsibilities for a combination product; a lack of clarity about the postmarket regulatory controls applicable to combination products; and a lack of clarity regarding when applications to more than one Center would be needed.

Some of these concerns were highlighted when FDA was sued in *Bracco Diagnostics v. Shalala*.[18] This case examined FDA's regulatory treatment of injectable ultrasound contrast agents for use with diagnostic ultrasound equipment in the diagnosis of cardiac dysfunction. Some of these contrast agents had been assigned to CDER and subject to the drug legal authorities; a similar product was assigned to CDRH under the device legal authorities. The court found that FDA probably had discretion under section 503(g) to regulate the products as either devices or drugs. But the court held: "What the FDA is not free to do, however, is to treat them dissimilarly and to permit two sets of similar products to run down two

---

13   *Id.* at 58,756.
14   Preamble to Final Rule, 56 Fed. Reg. at 58,755.
15   21 C.F.R. § 5.33; Final Rule, 56 Fed. Reg. at 58,758.
16   21 C.F.R. § 3.5(a)(2).
17   The Intercenter Agreements can be viewed from the combination products page on FDA's website, *available at* www.fda.gov/oc/combination.
18   Bracco Diagnostics, Inc. v. Shalala, 963 F. Supp. 20 (D.D.C. 1997).

separate tracks, one more treacherous than the other, for no apparent reason."[19] Thus, FDA was held to have acted arbitrarily and capriciously. The case also highlighted FDA's inability to produce a written administrative record that would rationally explain its decision making as to the classification of these various contrast agents.

In 2002, Congress mandated the establishment of FDA's OCP.[20] OCP, which sits within the Office of the Commissioner, has management and congressional reporting obligations designed to ensure efficient reviews and transparent standards for all combination products (except veterinary combination products regulated by the Center for Veterinary Medicine or veterinary biologics regulated by the U.S. Department of Agriculture). OCP has authority to determine which FDA Center has jurisdiction over the combination product, but also has the authority to rule whether single entity products should be regulated as drugs, devices, or biologics based on the characteristic of the single entity which achieves the product's primary intended effect.

With this history in mind, we turn now to a systematic analysis of combination product regulation.

Definition of a Combination Product

A *combination product* is one that combines a drug, a device, and/or a biological product.[21] Neither the FDCA nor the Public Health Service Act (PHSA) defines combination products. Still, Congress has recognized combination products as distinct from stand-alone drugs, devices, and biologics.[22] Thus, FDA has established a definition by regulation, which defines four types of combination products:

(1) A product comprised of two or more regulated components, i.e., drug/device, biologic/device, or drug/biologic, that are physically, chemically, or otherwise combined or mixed and produced as a single entity;

(2) Two or more separate products packaged together in a single package or as a unit and comprised of drug and device products, device and biological products, or biological and drug products;

(3) A drug, device, or biological product packaged separately that according to its investigational plan or proposed labeling is intended for use only with an approved individually specified drug, device, or biological product where both are required to achieve the intended use, indication, or effect and where upon approval of the proposed product

---

19   *Id.* at 28.

20   This requirement was part of the Medical Device User Fee and Modernization Act of 2002, Pub. L. No. 107-250, 116 Stat. 1588 (2002).

21   The statutory definitions of drugs, devices, and biological products are provided in Chapters 9, 16, and 14, respectively.

22   *E.g.*, 21 U.S.C. § 360bbb-2(a) (stating that a product may be classified as a drug, device, biological product, *or* combination product). This provision was added by the SMDA.

the labeling of the approved product would need to be changed, e.g., to reflect a change in intended use, dosage form, strength, route of administration, or significant change in dose; *or*

(4) Any investigational drug, device, or biological product packaged separately that according to its proposed labeling is for use only with another individually specified investigational drug, device, or biological product where both are required to achieve the intended use, indication, or effect.[23]

The Choice of Lead Center

If a product falls within the regulatory definition of a combination product, FDA is required under the FDCA to refer it to a *single* Center with primary regulatory jurisdiction over the product.[24] The SMDA amended the FDCA to require FDA to determine the *primary mode of action* (PMOA) of the product and on that basis choose a lead Center with primary jurisdiction.[25] For example, if a combination product has a drug primary mode of action, then CDER would be designated to take the lead in regulating it. Even so, the FDCA specifically authorizes FDA to apply resources as necessary from the other Centers to ensure an appropriate premarket review.[26] Thus, if a drug-device combination product is under CDER's primary jurisdiction, it is likely that CDRH will be consulted on the device-related aspects of the product.

To improve the coordination between Centers, OCP issued a *Manual of Standard Operating Procedures and Policies* (SOPP) addressed to the Intercenter Consultative/Collaborative Review Process.[27] As stated in the SOPP, its purpose was "to describe appropriate handling of the intercenter reviews of combination products, devices, drugs, and biologics throughout the review process. The objectives are to improve intercenter communication on combination products as well as the timeliness and consistency of intercenter consultative and collaborative reviews."[28] In the SOPP, the OCP distinguished between *collaboration* and *consultation* activities among the Centers:

- *Collaboration:* "A review activity in which reviewers in two or more Centers have primary review responsibilities, generally for a defined portion of a submission. Regulatory and scientific decisions will be made by the management of each Center for that portion of the review assigned to it, including the decision to approve or disapprove the product."[29]

- *Consult:* "A review activity in which a reviewer in one Center requests advice from a reviewer in *another* Center on a specific question or issue raised in the review of a

---

[23]   21 C.F.R. § 3.2(e)(1)-(4).

[24]   FDCA § 503(g)(1), 21 U.S.C § 353(g)(1).

[25]   *Id.*

[26]   FDCA § 503(g)(2), 21 U.S.C. § 353(g)(2).

[27]   FDA, MANUAL OF STANDARD OPERATING PROCEDURES AND POLICIES (June 18, 2004), *available at* http://www.fda.gov/downloads/RegulatoryInformation/Guidances/UCM126016.pdf.

[28]   *Id.* at 3.

[29]   *Id.* at 1.

submission. The consultative review will be used to assist the requesting reviewer in making appropriate regulatory/scientific decisions."[30]

Most reviews are consultations rather than collaborations, but both types are available to FDA as tools in the management of combination products.

In 2005, FDA issued a regulation defining the PMOA and setting forth an algorithm for the agency to use in making this determination.[31] The regulation defines "mode of action" as "the means by which a product achieves an intended therapeutic effect or action."[32] The regulation observes that a combination product is one having some combination of biologic, drug, and device modes of action.[33] The *primary* mode of action is:

> the single mode of action of a combination product that provides the most important therapeutic action of the combination product. The most important therapeutic action is the mode of action expected to make the greatest contribution to the overall intended therapeutic effects of the combination product.[34]

The regulation recognizes that "[i]n some situations, it is not possible to determine, with reasonable certainty, which one mode of action will provide a greater contribution than any other mode of action to the overall therapeutic effects of the combination product."[35] FDA had previously provided as an example a hypothetical contact lens combined with a drug to treat glaucoma. The product has both a device action (to correct vision) and a drug action (to treat glaucoma). Both of these actions are independent, and neither appears to be subordinate.[36]

In these types of cases, the regulation provides that:

> the agency will assign the combination product to the agency component that regulates other combination products that present similar questions of safety and effectiveness with regard to the combination product as a whole. When there are no other combination products that present similar questions of safety and effectiveness with regard to the combination product as a whole, the agency will assign the combination product to the agency component with the most expertise related to the most significant safety and effectiveness questions presented by the combination product.[37]

Thus, in the hypothetical contact lens example above, FDA stated that it might apply the foregoing algorithm as follows: .

---

[30]   *Id.* at 2 (emphasis added).

[31]   Definition of Primary Mode of Action of a Combination Product, Final Rule, 70 Fed. Reg. 49,848 (Aug. 25, 2005).

[32]   21 C.F.R. § 3.2(k).

[33]   *Id.*

[34]   21 C.F.R. § 3.2(m).

[35]   *Id.* § 3.4(b).

[36]   Definition of Primary Mode of Action of a Combination Product, Preamble to Proposed Rule, 69 Fed. Reg. 25,527, 25,530 (May 7, 2004).

[37]   21 C.F.R. § 3.4(b).

CDRH regulates devices intended to correct vision. CDER regulates drugs intended to treat glaucoma. In this hypothetical example, no combination product intended to treat these different conditions simultaneously has yet been submitted to the agency for review. Though both CDER and CDRH regulate products that raise similar safety and effectiveness questions with regard to the constituent parts of the product, neither agency component regulates combination products that present similar safety and effectiveness questions with regard to the product as a whole.

. . . .

In this hypothetical example, the most significant safety and effectiveness questions are related to the characterization, manufacturing, and clinical performance of the drug component, while the safety and effectiveness questions raised by the vision-correcting contact lens are considered routine. Based on the application of this criterion, this product would be assigned to CDER because CDER has the most expertise related to these issues.[38]

FDA's decision making as to the choice of lead Center is also reflected in the ICAs. The ICAs were negotiated primarily by the offices of compliance in CDER, CDRH, and CBER. They allocated responsibility for several categories of combination products. For example, the ICA between CDER and CDRH provides that CDER will take the lead in regulating prefilled drug delivery devices (although CDRH will likely be consulted as to review of the device component).[39] The ICAs also set forth general principles that would apply to *ad hoc* decisions on new products that might arise. The ICAs, for example, allow FDA to empanel intercenter jurisdictional committees on *ad hoc* bases to resolve jurisdictional questions informally.

Although the ICAs were adopted in 1991, they are still valid written guidance and should be consulted when considering the potential jurisdictional status of a combination product. The preamble to the 2005 regulation establishing a definition of PMOA makes it clear that this definition does not supersede the ICAs or FDA's prior PMOA decisions. Rather, the preamble states that the regulatory definition of PMOA is "consistent with agency practice regarding the assignment of combination products. This rulemaking will codify criteria the agency has generally used since 1990."[40] Many of those criteria are set forth in the ICAs.

Nonetheless, the OCP has shown an increasing penchant for charting its own course despite precedent such as the ICAs. This tendency has created confusion, and certainly makes the ICAs less valuable as a guide to OCP's likely decision making. In draft guidance on product classification, the OCP summarizes the status of the ICAs in a manner that makes apparent their increasingly tenuous status:

In 2006, the [a]gency reviewed these agreements and preliminarily determined that they continued to provide helpful, nonbinding guidance.

---

[38] Definition of Primary Mode of Action of a Combination Product , 69 Fed. Reg. at 25,530.

[39] CDER-CDRH ICA at VII(A)(1)(b).

[40] Definition of Primary Mode of Action of a Combination Product, 70 Fed. Reg. at 49,849.

See U.S.C. § 353(g)(4)(F). The [a]gency proposed to continue them in effect, with the understanding that they should not be independently relied upon as the [a]gency's most current, complete jurisdictional statements (71 FR 56,988, Sept. 28, 2006). However, in light of current scientific understanding, we are currently reviewing the agreements to determine whether it would be appropriate to modify them or replace them with new agreements. In the interim, we note that these agreements should be considered in light of statutory definitions and current scientific understanding. Products that might appear to fall within a category addressed in one of these agreements can only be classified consistent with other products in that category if such a classification is legally permissible in light of the specific characteristics of that particular product. In addition, to the extent that those agreements appear to support classification determinations that are inconsistent with this guidance, this guidance supersedes those agreements with respect to such classifications.[41]

In some cases, even after designating a lead Center, FDA may require concurrent review of a second marketing application by a second Center. Thus, the regulations provide: "The designation of one agency component as having primary jurisdiction for the premarket review and regulation of a product does not preclude . . . in appropriate cases, the requirement by the FDA of separate [marketing] applications."[42] In the preamble to this regulation, FDA explained:

[W]here the agency finds it necessary, the agency reserves the option to require separate applications to be approved by separate agency components. FDA recognizes that requiring the approval of a second agency component would represent the exception rather than the rule and, in those instances, the reviews will be coordinated to the greatest extent possible.[43]

The Choice of Legal Authorities

The FDCA is silent about whether the choice of Center requires application of that Center's legal authorities. For example, if CDER is assigned the lead role for regulating a combination product, is FDA restricted to requiring an NDA approval and postmarket drug authorities? The legal authorities for each Center are quite different, so this question is not academic.

---

41   FDA, Draft Guidance for Industry, Classification of Products as Drugs and Devices & Additional Product Classification Issues at 6 (June 2011).
42   21 C.F.R. § 3.4(c).
43   Assignment of Agency Component for Review of Premarket Notifications, Preamble to Final Rule, 56 Fed. Reg. at 58,755.

FDA takes the position that it has "discretion to decide which statutory authorities it [will] use in regulating a particular combination product."[44] Thus, the ICAs expressly contemplate the possibility that one Center will have primary jurisdiction but apply legal authorities belonging to another Center. For example, pursuant to the CDER-CDRH ICA, a prefilled drug delivery system may be regulated by "CDER using drug authorities and device authorities, as necessary."[45]

There has always been great uncertainty about how postmarket regulation applies to combination products in areas such as manufacturing, user fees, adverse event reporting, and labeling and advertising. In recent years, OCP has begun issuing guidance and rules in major areas of postmarket regulation. For example, the OCP in 2013 issued a final rule on the application of GMPs to combination products.[46]

In 2009, OCP issued a proposed rule that would provide a framework for adverse event reporting for combination products.[47] Obviously, until the rulemaking is complete, there will continue to be uncertainty.[48]

The extent of FDA's discretion in regulating combination products has not been definitively addressed in court decisions. In *FDA v. Brown & Williamson Tobacco Corp.*,[49] the Supreme Court acknowledged FDA's position that it could use "drug authorities, device authorities, or both, depending on how the public health goals of the act can be best accomplished" to regulate a drug-device combination product.[50] The Court, however, decided the case on other grounds without ruling on the validity of this position.[51]

Request for Designation

When the identity of the Center with primary jurisdiction is unclear or in dispute, or a sponsor believes its combination product is not covered by the ICAs, a sponsor can request a designation from FDA's product jurisdiction officer.[52] Similarly, when the classification of

---

[44]   Regulations Restricting the Sale and Distribution of Cigarettes and Smokeless Tobacco to Protect Children and Adolescents, Final Rule, 61 Fed. Reg. 44,396, 44,000 (Aug. 28, 1996).

[45]   CDER-CDRH ICA at VII(A)(1)(b).

[46]   Current Good Manufacturing Practice Requirements for Combination Products, Final Rule, 78 Fed. Reg. 4.307 (Jan. 22, 2013) (codified at 21 C.F.R. pt. 4, subpt. A).

[47]   Postmarketing Safety Reporting for Combination Products, Proposed Rule, 74 Fed. Reg. 50,744 (Oct. 1, 2009).

[48]   A logical rule of thumb for now would be to report under the same authorities that apply to the premarket review of the product. Thus, if a combination product receives a PMA approval from CDRH, it would be logical to report adverse events pursuant to the Medical Device Reporting regulation (21 C.F.R. pt. 803), which applies to devices. If a product is marketed based upon two concurrent marketing approvals (e.g., 510(k), NDA), the decision is more difficult. One approach might be to make a determination, if possible, as to whether the drug or device component is implicated in an adverse event and report under the appropriate authorities. Another approach might be to simply report under both drug and device authorities, even at the risk of duplication.

[49]   FDA v. Brown & Williamson Tobacco Corp., 529 U.S. 120 (2000).

[50]   *FDA v. Brown & Williamson*, 529 U.S. at 129 (internal quotation marks omitted).

[51]   *Id.* at 133.

[52]   21 C.F.R. § 3.5(b), 3.7(a).

a single entity product is in question, sponsors should submit a request for designation to OCP. A sponsor "should" file a request for designation (RFD) with the product jurisdiction officer before submitting its application for marketing approval or an investigational notice.[53] If the jurisdictional issue becomes evident after the review process has already begun, FDA may ask the sponsor to file an RFD, or the sponsor may decide to do so.[54] If the sponsor prefers that a particular Center have primary jurisdiction, a discussion with the product jurisdiction officer associated with that Center may provide valuable information about previous classification decisions and other considerations that should be addressed when formulating an argument as to why that Center should have primary jurisdiction.

The RFD may not exceed 15 pages, and its elements are dictated by section 3.7 of FDA's regulations:

1)   The identity of the sponsor, including company name and address, establishment registration number, company contact person, and telephone number (3.7(c)(1)).

2)   A description of the product, including:

a)   Classification, name of the product, and all component products, if applicable (3.7(c)(2)(i));

b)   Common, generic, or usual name of the product and all component products (3.7(c)(2)(ii));

c)   Proprietary name of the product (3.7(c)(2)(iii));

d)   Identification of any component of the product that already has received premarket approval, is marketed as not being subject to premarket approval, or has received an investigational exemption, the identity of the sponsors, and the status of any discussions or agreements between the sponsors regarding the use of this product as a component of a new combination product (3.7(c)(2)(iv));

e)   Chemical, physical, or biological composition (3.7(c)(2)(v));

f)   Status and brief reports of the results of developmental work, including animal testing (3.7(c)(2)(vi));

g)   Description of the manufacturing processes, including the sources of all components (3.7(c)(2)(vii));

h)   Proposed use or indications (3.7 (c)(2)(viii));

---

[53]   *Id.* § 3.7(b).

[54]   One disincentive for making designation requests after an application has been submitted is that filing or review by the product jurisdiction officer stays the review clock during the pendency of the review. 21 C.F.R. § 3.10.

i)   Description of all known modes of action, the sponsor's identification of the single mode of action that provides the most important therapeutic action of the product, and the basis for that determination (3.7(c)(2)(ix));

j)   Schedule and duration of use (3.7(c)(2)(x));

k)   Dose and route of administration of drug or biologic (3.7(c)(2)(xi));

l)   Description of related products, including the regulatory status of those related products (3.7(c)(2)(xii)); and

m) Any other relevant information (3.7(c)(2)(xiii)).

3)   The sponsor's recommendation as to which agency component should have primary jurisdiction . . . .[55]

OCP has posted a guidance for drafting RFDs on its web page.[56] In drafting the RFD, the most important aspects are the product description and intended use, the modes of action, the discussion of the PMOA (including a summary of any developmental work or testing that helps describe the modes of action and/or PMOA), and the argument supporting the jurisdictional recommendation.

The RFD should be sent by email to the OCP (combination@fda.gov). Within five days of receipt, OCP will review the submission for administrative completeness and determine whether the RFD contains the information FDA needs to make its jurisdictional determination. The OCP will then either send the sponsor an acknowledgment letter confirming the filing date of an RFD, or notify the sponsor that the RFD was not filed, and identify the information needed to make the RFD complete. For filed RFDs, the acknowledgment letter will also identify the date by which FDA will respond to the RFD.

In recent years, the OCP has increased markedly the number of times it refuses to file an RFD. Typically, the issues are minor, but the OCP nonetheless requires that the entire RFD be refiled. The obvious purpose of this approach is to start the 60-day decision clock all over again. In one case, however, the OCP refused to file an RFD twice, demanding detailed scientific data that was virtually impossible to provide. The applicant finally gave up.

If FDA does not issue a designation letter within 60 days of the filing of the RFD, as required by 21 C.F.R. 3.8(b), the sponsor's recommendation of the agency component with primary jurisdiction will become the designated agency component. The letter of designation will be emailed back to the sponsor (with hard copy to follow). Typically, the letter will offer the sponsor 15 days to request reconsideration if the sponsor disagrees with the outcome. The OCP takes the position that the time begins to run from the receipt of the email, not the hard copy (just as the time for decision begins to run when the RFD is first submitted by email). A request for reconsideration must be based upon the facts as presented in the

---

[55]   Section 563 of the FDCA establishes a parallel procedure for requesting a classification decision for either a single entity product or a combination product. It offers slightly more protection against change of the decision after the fact. It is prudent to state in an RFD request that it is submitted both under section 563 and 21 C.F.R. Part 3.

[56]   FDA, Guidance for Industry, How to Write a Request for Designation (RFD) (April 2011).

original RFD and may not introduce new evidence. FDA does not have a required timeline for responding to such requests, but the OCP has been generally prompt in providing a ruling. The chances for success on a request for reconsideration are generally low.

In recent years, the OCP's decisions have become increasingly aggressive in pushing products into CDER and CBER. These decisions have been especially questionable when the OCP is asked to decide whether an article is a single entity device or a drug.

The OCP typically begins its analysis with the statutory definition of a drug as any article that prevents, treats, or diagnoses disease.[57] Thus, every single entity article that comes before the OCP is presumptively a drug. An applicant seeking to convince the OCP otherwise must establish that the article falls within the statutory definition of a device, in that it does not achieve its "primary intended purposes through chemical action within or on the body of man . . . and which is not dependent upon being metabolized for the achievement of its primary intended purposes."[58]

In June 2011, the OCP issued draft guidance to define the OCP's understanding of "chemical action":

> Through either chemical reaction or intermolecular forces or both, the product: [1] Mediates a bodily response at the cellular or molecular level, or [2] [c]ombines with or modifies an entity so as to alter that entity's interaction with the body of man or other animals.[59]

A companion draft guidance issued describes the OCP's approach to applying the statutory definitions of drug and device, as follows:

> A product may be classified as a device if it "does not achieve its primary intended purposes through chemical action within or on the body of man or other animals . . .", provided the product also meets the rest of the device definition under section 201(h). Interpretation of this phrase is often at issue in classification determinations. ***
>
> First, [under the statute] a product that exhibits chemical action within or on the body of man may meet the device definition provided that the product "does not achieve its primary intended purposes through" such chemical action. Thus, if a product's chemical action contributes to an effect other than a primary intended purpose of the product, the product could fall within the scope of section 201(h). *In contrast, a product that depends, even in part, on chemical action within or on the body of man to achieve any one of its primary intended purposes, would not be a device. In addition, if a product has multiple therapeutic effects, each of these would be a "primary intended purpose" of the product, and the product would not meet the device*

---

[57]   FDCA § 201(g), 21 U.S.C. § 321(g).

[58]   FDCA § 201(h), 21 U.S.C. § 321(h).

[59]   FDA, Draft Guidance, Interpretation of the Term "Chemical Action" in the Definition of Device under Section 201(h) of the Federal Food, Drug, and Cosmetic Act at 3 (June 2011).

definition if it achieves any one of these primary intended purposes through chemical action within or on the body of man. Second, under this phrase, a product that "achieves its primary intended purposes through chemical action" still meets the device definition provided that the chemical action does not occur "within or on the body of man or other animals."[60]

This approach has been challenged in litigation brought against FDA by a French company, PREVOR, which makes Diphoterine® Skin Wash (DSW), a liquid substance inside a canister. DSW is intended to help prevent and minimize chemical burn injuries that occur due to accidental exposure to chemicals and is intended to be used in the industrial setting as a "first response" method. DSW is sprayed onto the skin to physically and mechanically remove or wash away the offensive chemical from the skin. A secondary purpose is to neutralize the acids and bases that are washed off the skin. On the basis of the latter, the OCP ruled that this product is a drug-device combination product with a "drug" primary mode of action.

PREVOR filed suit in the U.S. District Court for the District of Columbia challenging FDA's determination. The complaint alleges that uncontradicted data show that more than 90 percent of the overall intended purpose of the product comes from a physical washing effect, and that less than 10 percent of the intended purpose comes from a chemical neutralization effect. Yet, the OCP ruled that the product is a drug. The District Court rejected the OCP's ruling, finding that the italicized language in the draft guidance impermissibly altered the statutory definition of a device.[61] First, it treated "any" purpose of a product as a primary purpose. Second, it treated achievement "even in part" of "any" purpose through chemical action as achievement of a primary intended purpose through chemical action. In both cases, FDA's requirement for excluding the product from the definition of a device potentially was unduly expansive and did not comport with the statutory definition. The court allowed that there might be a scientific justification for this approach, but FDA had provided none. Accordingly, the case was remanded to FDA to narrow its definition of primary purpose and explain its conclusion that the chemical effect of DSW achieves a primary, as opposed to secondary, intended purpose.[62]

On remand, FDA once again ruled that DSW is a drug, in part based upon a newly created standard, in which a product cannot be a device if a chemical effect "meaningfully contributes" to the achievement of its primary purpose. The Court found that the "meaningfully contributes" threshold was lower than the statutory requirement that a device be excluded from the definition of a device if it "achieves" a primary purpose via chemical effect. Once again, the court remanded the matter to FDA for further proceedings in light of the opinion.[63]

---

60   FDA, Draft Guidance, Classification of Products as Drugs and Devices & Additional Product Classification Issues at 4-5 (June 2011) (emphasis added).

61   FDCA § 201(h), 21 U.S.C. § 321(h).

62   Prevor v. FDA, 895 F. Supp. 2d 90 (D.D.C. 2012) [hereinafter, *Prevor I*]. The court did not reach the question as to whether FDA's draft guidance (or reliance upon a draft guidance) complied with the Administrative Procedure Act. *Id.* at 94.

63   Prevor v. FDA, No. 13-1177, 2014 WL 4459174, *7 (D.D.C. 2014) [hereinafter, *Prevor II*]. As of this writing, FDA's third decision in this matter had not yet been issued.

In many instances, the OCP's involvement begins with a sponsor seeking 510(k) clearance of a product based upon substantial equivalence to predicate devices that have already received 510(k) clearance. During the review process, CDRH may spontaneously raise a concern that perhaps this product is a drug, or contains a drug component, and will request that the sponsor submit an RFD to the OCP.

The OCP may then rule that the product is a drug, despite the sponsor's protest that the product is actually substantially equivalent to numerous devices cleared via the 510(k) process. The OCP's stock response is that they are bound by their own prior decisions regarding product designation, but not by prior CDRH decisions to regulate a product as a device.

This refusal to take into account FDA's prior administrative practice means that the OCP is sending products to CDER that are very similar to other products already regulated by CDRH. That is precisely the type of conduct that was ruled arbitrary and capricious in *Bracco Diagnostics v. Shalala*.[64] In one unpublished matter, the OCP indicated that it would rectify an admitted inconsistency in designating a product as a drug by an unspecified future administrative action aimed at similar products already regulated as devices. This promise of a level playing field in the hereafter is not sufficient. Sponsors are entitled to a level playing field in the here and now.

After the OCP has classified a product as a drug, or as having a drug PMOA, the sponsor's only choice is to submit the product to CDER or appeal to the Associate Commissioner for Special Medical Programs in the Office of the Commissioner. Unfortunately, the chances of success on appeal are not high, and the process is slow. It can take months to obtain an appeal meeting, and as long as 18 months afterward to obtain a decision.

The Cross-Labeling Conundrum

FDA's regulation of labeling is central to its mission to ensure product safety and effectiveness. Typically, FDA looks to the intended use and claims in product labeling in order to determine the type of supporting safety and effectiveness data that the agency will require to clear or approve the product for marketing.[65] When two therapeutic products are developed together, for use together as a system, the task of drafting appropriate labeling (supported by appropriate data) may be relatively straightforward, once the lead Center with primary jurisdiction over the system has been chosen. But where one product is developed for use in combination with a prior approved product, the task of bringing the labeling of the two products into mutual conformity may not be so straightforward.

One area where this problem arises often is when innovative drug delivery or medical imaging devices are intended for use with drugs and contrast agents that are already on the

---

64   *Bracco Diagnostics*, 963 F. Supp. 20.

65   E.g., New Drug and Antibiotic Regulations, Final Rule, 50 Fed. Reg. 7452, 7470 (Feb. 22, 1985) ("Drug labeling serves as the standard under which the FDA determines whether a product is safe and effective.").

market with an existing approval. This situation corresponds to the third prong of FDA's four-prong definition of combination products quoted above. This is the third prong again:

> A drug, device, or biological product packaged separately that according to its investigational plan or proposed labeling is intended *for use only with an approved individually specified drug, device, or biological product* where both are required to achieve the intended use, indication, or effect *and where upon approval of the proposed product the labeling of the approved product would need to be changed,* e.g., to reflect a change in intended use, dosage form, strength, route of administration, or significant change in dose.[66]

If FDA believes that approval of a proposed drug delivery or medical imaging device would require a conforming change in the labeling of a previously approved drug or contrast agent, then it may be necessary for the manufacturer of the latter to cooperate in obtaining a labeling change from FDA, including potentially providing a right of reference to the safety and effectiveness data already on file with FDA. Unfortunately, such manufacturers often do not have an incentive to cooperate as the impact on sales may not be large, and there may be generic versions of the drug sold by other manufacturers who could reap the lion's share of any sales increase associated with a labeling change. Such manufacturers may even have disincentives to cooperate based upon the regulatory cost involved in changing the labeling and/or products liability risks potentially associated with the new intended use.

There are some possible workarounds for this regulatory impasse, none of which is entirely satisfactory. Most frequently, FDA will permit a drug delivery or medical imaging device to be labeled with broad indications that do not name any specific drug. For example, FDA might allow the device to be labeled for infusion of "physician specified agents" or "local anesthetics" without being any more specific. Labeled this way, the device is not deemed a combination product under FDA's regulatory definition. This approach can only be used if the device and drug/contrast agent are sold separately. It also creates vexing issues concerning what the respective device and drug manufacturers should be permitted to say about the new use in labeling and advertising without being deemed either to have created a combination product through labeling or advertising, or to have gone beyond the scope of FDA's clearance or approval.

Another possibility is for FDA to allow the device company to put sufficient information about the administration of the drug or contrast agent with the device that the drug labeling does not need to be changed. The most prominent example to date of this approach was FDA's approval of drug-eluting stents. In that case, the device mode of action was clearly primary, and CDRH was the lead Center with CDER consulting. It is not clear that this approach can be applied if the drug mode of action is primary, or if neither the drug nor device mode of action is subordinate to the other. It is also not feasible to apply this approach in cases where FDA needs to be able to review the underlying drug approval data and the manufacturer does not grant a right of reference. Finally, FDA believes that allowing this type of umbrella device labeling may raise some safety concerns. One is the possibility of end user confusion since the drug information in the device labeling will differ from the

---

[66]   21 C.F.R. 3.2(e)(3) (emphasis added).

approved drug labeling. Another is that a drug company could make formulation changes adversely impacting use of the drug with the device, but the device manufacturer would not necessarily know about it, since by hypothesis there is no cooperation between the two firms. These concerns need to be addressed in any sponsor's proposal to FDA for umbrella device labeling.

A step in the right direction is FDA's issuance of a guidance focused on the development of new contrast indications for imaging devices for use with already approved imaging drug (contrast agent) or biological products. The guidance opens the door to the umbrella device labeling approach. It permits a new indication for an imaging drug to be added to device labeling even if the indication is not in the drug labeling.[67]

A third possible workaround arises under section 505(b)(2) of the FDCA. This provision allows a device company potentially to obtain NDA approval for the drug without the usual clinical studies. This approach is rarely used, and would only benefit a device company that is in a position to manufacture the drug under its own NDA approval or with a contract manufacturer.

FDA has been considering these issues for a number of years, but has been slow to provide definitive resolutions. Thus, the development of improved drug delivery and medical device imaging has been impeded in the United States, while many useful innovations are implemented quite readily outside the United States. Congress could help by amending the FDCA to improve FDA's ability to address the cross-labeling issue in a meaningful way. At any rate, reform is urgently needed, because the status quo is hindering the development of innovative products that could contribute to improved patient care.

---

[67]   FDA, Guidance for Industry, New Contrast Imaging Indication Considerations for Devices and Approved Drug and Biological Products (Dec. 2009).

CHAPTER 18
TOBACCO PRODUCTS

JOSEPH A. PAGE

Introduction

In 2009, four and a half decades after the publication of a U.S. Surgeon General's Report recognizing a causal link between cigarette smoking and cancer,[1] Congress enacted the Family Smoking Prevention and Tobacco Control Act (hereafter referred to as the Tobacco Control Act, or the TCA),[2] which for the first time subjected the manufacture, labeling, marketing, and distribution of tobacco products to pervasive federal regulation. The new law gave the Food and Drug Administration (FDA) authority to carry out its directives, most of which have become part of the Federal Food, Drug, and Cosmetic Act (FDCA).[3]

Historical Background

The effort to bring the number-one cause of preventable deaths in the United States[4] under legal control has been of epic dimensions.[5] In its initial phase, the struggle took the form of tort suits by smokers against cigarette manufacturers,[6] and regulatory initiatives by both the

---

[1] U.S. DEPARTMENT OF HEALTH, EDUCATION, AND WELFARE, SMOKING AND HEALTH: REPORT OF THE ADVISORY COMMITTEE TO THE SURGEON GENERAL OF THE PUBLIC HEALTH SERVICE, P.H.S. Doc. No. 1103 (1964).

[2] Pub. L. No. 111-31, 123 Stat. 1776 (2009) [hereinafter cited as TCA].

[3] Pub. L. No. 75-717, 52 Stat. 1040 (1938), as amended 21 U.S.C. §§ 301 et seq. (2014). Other statutes amended by the Tobacco Control Act include the Cigarette Labeling and Advertising Act (see TCA §§ 201-03, 206); the Comprehensive Smokeless Tobacco Health Education Act (see id. § 204-05); and the Federal Meat Inspection Act (see id., § 103(o)).

[4] See David A. Kessler et al., The Food and Drug Administration's Regulation of Tobacco Products, 335 NEW ENG. J. MED. 988, 990, col. 1 (Sept. 26, 1996).

[5] For an exhaustive account that takes the story to the 1990s, see RICHARD KLUGER, ASHES TO ASHES: AMERICA'S HUNDRED-YEAR CIGARETTE WAR, THE PUBLIC HEALTH, AND THE UNABASHED TRIUMPH OF PHILIP MORRIS (1996).

[6] See Robert L. Rabin, Institutional and Historical Perspectives on Tobacco Tort Liability, in SMOKING POLICY: LAW, POLITICS, AND CULTURE 118-25 (Robert L. Rabin & Stephen Sugarman eds., 1993).

Federal Trade Commission (FTC) and the Federal Communications Commission, the former to impose mandatory warning labels on cigarette packages,[7] the latter to require radio and television stations to provide free time for anti-smoking commercials.[8] Congress intervened with a series of federal statutes forcing cigarette companies to put cautionary statements on the packages of cigarettes and other tobacco products, and restricting advertisements for them.[9]

From the very beginning, FDA took the position that so long as cigarette manufacturers made no disease-prevention claims, their products escaped the legal definition of "drug."[10] But in 1996, as a result of the discovery of evidence demonstrating that tobacco-industry officials had not only long been fully aware of the addictive properties of nicotine, but had also manipulated nicotine levels in order to keep cigarette smokers smoking, the agency ruled that cigarettes were medical devices designed and intended to deliver a drug—nicotine—into the human body, and put a number of restrictions on the marketing of these products to minors.[11] The United States Supreme Court, in *Food and Drug Administration v. Brown & Williamson Tobacco Corporation*,[12] invalidated the rules on the ground that Congress had never meant to include cigarettes within the meaning of the statutory terms "drug" and "medical device," unless their manufacturers made disease-prevention claims for them. However, pressure on Congress to take action had become irresistible, and in 2009 it finally enacted legislation that authorized FDA to regulate tobacco products.

A Preliminary Look at the Tobacco Control Act

What Congress Might Have Done

Once Congress decided to act, it might simply have banned all tobacco products, on the basis of a legislative finding that they are inherently, massively, addictively, and unjustifiably dangerous to the public health.[13] However, this would have triggered serious enforcement problems, given the intense level of dependence nicotine had generated in a substantial

---

7   For a perceptive look at FTC's efforts to regulate cigarettes, *see* A. LEE FRITSCHLER, SMOKING AND POLITICS: POLICYMAKING AND THE FEDERAL BUREAUCRACY (1969).

8   *See* Television Station WGBS-TV, Applicability of the Fairness Doctrine to Cigarette Advertising, 9 F.C.C.2d 921 (1967), *aff'd sub nom.* Banzhaf v. F.C.C., 405 F.2d 1082 (D.C. Cir. 1968), *cert. denied sub nom.* Tobacco Institute, Inc. v. F.C.C., 396 U.S. 842 (1969).

9   *See, e.g.,* the Federal Cigarette Labeling and Advertising Act, Pub. L. No. 89-92, 79 Stat. 282 (1965); the Public Health Cigarette Smoking Act, Pub. L. No. 91-222, 84 Stat. 87 (1969); the Little Cigar Act, Pub. L. No. 89-92, 79 Stat. 282 (1973); the Comprehensive Smoking Education Act, Pub. L. No. 98-474, 98 Stat. 2200 (1984).

10   *See* Action on Smoking and Health v. Harris, 655 F.2d 236 (D.C. Cir. 1980), upholding FDA's denial of a petition from a consumer group asking the agency to assume jurisdiction over cigarettes on the ground that they were by definition "drugs." *See generally* FRED H. DEGNAN, FDA'S CREATIVE APPLICATION OF THE LAW 152-54 (2000).

11   *See* Food and Drug Administration, Regulations Restricting the Sale and Distribution of Cigarettes and Smokeless Tobacco to Protect Children and Adolescents, 61 Fed. Reg. 44,396 (Aug. 28, 1996).

12   529 U.S. 120 (2000).

13   One approach would have been to require legislatively that tobacco products be included within the term "other substance" in section 102(6) of the Controlled Substances Act (CSA), Pub. L. No. 91-513, 84 Stat.

number of smokers. A gradual ban plus comprehensive medical care for those addicted to tobacco might have been a sensible alternative. But instead, Congress opted to impose requirements and restrictions on the manufacture and marketing of tobacco products.

In so doing, Congress had as one alternative the passage of a simple amendment incorporating cigarettes within the definition of "medical devices." This would have validated FDA's 1996 regulations. But such an approach would have left open up the possibility that the agency would eventually rule that under any plausible interpretation of the language of the FDCA it had no recourse but to conclude cigarettes were so unavoidably hazardous that they should not be permitted to remain on the market.[14] (Of course, Congress could simply have prohibited the agency from imposing such a ban.) In addition, treating cigarettes as medical devices would not have had any effect on other tobacco products. Another alternative would have been to create a fresh regulatory framework and a new federal agency to administer and enforce it. This would have imposed increased costs and set the regulation of tobacco products adrift on uncharted waters, which may not have had much appeal for either Congress or the industry.

What Congress Did

The statute eventually signed into law by President Barack Obama adopted a more cautious, eclectic approach. It brought all tobacco products within the purview of the FDCA, and gave FDA administrative responsibility over them, on the ground that the agency was the most logical choice within the existing federal regulatory universe. This meant that the same enforcement mechanisms the government might use against manufacturers of food, drugs, cosmetics, medical devices, and dietary supplements would for the most part be available in proceedings against the makers of tobacco products.

The TCA, which bristles with detail, creates a new Chapter IX within the FDCA. It constructs a regulatory regime governing tobacco products with elements that are in part novel, and in part borrowed from pre-existing statutory language applicable to other products, and it incorporates elements of the 1996 FDA rules as well.

What FDA Has Done

A half decade has passed since the Tobacco Control Act became law. During that time, FDA created and staffed a Center for Tobacco Products and began to implement various provisions of the act.[15] The industry launched judicial challenges to several of these initiatives, a signal that the agency could expect vigorous resistance to regulation that the manufacturers of tobacco products deemed excessively burdensome or beyond legal bounds set by the act or

---

1236 (1970), and place them in Schedule I, which would have the effect of a total ban. See CSA § 202(b)(1), 21 U.S.C. § 812(b)(1).

[14] FDA Commissioner Charles C. Edwards had taken this position in 1972. See *Public Health Cigarette Amendments of 1971: Hearings Before the Consumer Subcomm. of the Senate Comm. on Commerce,* 92d Cong., 2d Sess. 239 (1972).

[15] For the agency's description of its initial four years of existence, see Report to Congress, Progress and Effectiveness of the Implementation of the Family Smoking Protection and Tobacco Control Act, U.S. Dep't of Health and Human Services, Food and Drug Administration, May 23, 2013, http://www.fda.gov/downloads/tobaccoproducts/guidancecomplianceregulatoryinformation/ucm371271.pdf.

by the Constitution. This chapter will describe the statutory scheme created by Congress, the initial efforts by FDA to exercise its legal authority, and the litigation that resulted.

The Preamble of the Tobacco Control Act

The TCA comprises the first of two totally unrelated divisions of Public Law No. 111-31. (The second reforms the existing system of retirement benefits for federal employees.) The initial six sections of the act amount to a preamble, and include factual findings, a statement of purposes, and limitations on scope and effect, as well as a severability provision[16] and modifications of deadlines that other sections of the statute impose on FDA.[17]

The TCA does not incorporate its preamble into the text of the FDCA.[18] Language in a preamble cannot be used to contradict directive parts of a statute that are expressed clearly, but may be of help in construing ambiguities.[19]

Findings

The findings listed in section 2 are lengthy and detailed. Several themes emerge. Subsections (1) to (29) spell out the scope and dimensions of the health problem caused by tobacco products, as well as a somewhat understated yet unmistakable indictment of the behavior of the industry for the responsibility it bears, especially in purposefully addicting minors to nicotine. Subsections (30) to (32) give reasons why the restrictions the act places on the advertising and promotion of tobacco products do not violate the free-speech guarantee of the First Amendment to the Constitution. Subsections (33) to (35) insert miscellaneous facts, such as the chronic nature of tobacco dependence, the need to achieve smoking cessation because it is the only safe alternative to smoking, and the link between the illicit trade of tobacco products and organized crime as well as terrorist activity. Subsections (36) to (43) stress the importance of risk reduction as a regulatory goal. Subsections (44) and (45) indicate why Congress decided to give FDA the task of administering the Tobacco Control Act.[20] Subsection 46 explains why manufacturers should not be allowed to include

---

16   Section 5 keeps the rest of the Tobacco Control Act intact in the event that a court should invalidate any of its individual provisions. Congress clearly had in mind here the constitutional challenges portions of the statute would inevitably invite, and the possibility that courts might uphold some of them.

17   Section 6 introduces an element of flexibility by easing deadlines the Tobacco Control Act imposes on FDA's obligations to take mandated steps. Given the historic difficulty the agency has experienced in fulfilling statutory duties that did not carry time limits with them (see, e.g., The FDA Food Additive Review Process: Backlog and Failure to Observe Statutory Deadline, H.R. REP. No. 104-436, 104th Cong., 1st Sess. (1995)), Congress saw fit to include deadlines on a number of action directives to which FDA would be subjected, although how these time limits might be enforced remains problematic.

18   Other statutes that amend the Federal Food, Drug, and Cosmetic Act and contain findings of fact that do not appear in the FDCA include the Dietary Supplement Health and Education Act, Pub. L. No. 103-417, 108 Stat. 4325, § 2 (1994); the Prescription Drug User Fee Act, Pub. L. No. 102-571, 106 Stat. 4491, § 102 (1992); and the Food and Drug Administration Act, Pub. L. No. 100-607, 102 Stat. 3120, § 502 (1988).

19   See WILLIAM N. ESKRIDGE, JR., PHILIP P. FRICKEY & ELIZABETH GARRETT, LEGISLATION AND STATUTORY INTERPRETATION 280 (2d ed. 2006), citing 2A SUTHERLAND, STATUTES AND STATUTORY CONSTRUCTION § 47.04, at 146.

20   The statute actually gives regulatory responsibility to the Secretary of Health and Human Services, but since the latter department delegates to FDA the task of administering the FDCA, this chapter will treat

in labeling or labeling any statement to the effect that FDA regulates the product. The last three subsections (47, 48, and 49) return to the backdrop of industry blameworthiness, and cite findings of fact made in an exhaustive 2006 opinion by a United States District Court Judge, concluding that tobacco companies continued to target young people as potential smokers and adjust nicotine levels in order to keep them addicted.[21]

Purposes

The act's purposes, set out in section 3, are more succinct and focused. However, they betray traces of internal inconsistency, with subsection (9) calling for the promotion of the cessation of smoking, and subsection (7) directing FDA to continue to allow adults to purchase tobacco products. Subsection (6) speaks to a need to inform consumers about the ill effects that flow from the use of tobacco products, a goal that would not seem to have any impact on persons already so helplessly addicted to nicotine that they are in no position to make free choices. Accurate information would be useful only to non-addicted adults willing and able to stop using tobacco products, or non-users capable of making a choice about whether or not to begin using a tobacco product. Perhaps what Congress had in mind was the preservation of a libertarian value, the right of competent adults to decide to engage or continue to engage in risky conduct that endangers no one but themselves. However, neither the stated findings nor the goals make this point, nor do they refer to what some have deemed massive market manipulation on the part of the tobacco industry,[22] suggesting that the decision to smoke often does not derive from the exercise of individual freedom.

Scope and Effect

Section 4, dealing with the act's scope and effect, places certain broad limits on the reach of the TCA. Subsection (a)(1) is somewhat enigmatic, stating that the act is not to be "construed to . . . establish a precedent with regard to any other industry, situation, circumstance, or legal action." Statutes, of course, cannot take on the force of precedent that binds the legislative branch, since lawmakers, subject only to constitutional constraints, are free to borrow from or ignore existing statutes when they enact new laws. Hence, this language would seem to be directed at the courts. Yet it does not clearly indicate what kind of statutory interpretations are meant to fall under the "no-precedent" rule it purports to establish.[23]

FDA as the entity wielding authority under the Tobacco Control Act.

[21] United States of America v. Philip Morris, USA, Inc., 449 F. Supp. 2d 1 (D.D.C. 2006).

[22] *See* Jon D. Hanson & Douglas A. Kysar, *Taking Behavioralism Seriously: Some Evidence of Market Manipulation*, 112 HARV. L. REV. 1420, 1467-1553 (1999) (behavior of tobacco industry as case study of demand manipulation).

[23] It might be useful to contrast this language in the TCA with sections 520(n)(1) and (2) of the FDCA. Subsection (n)(1) provides that "All contact lenses shall be deemed to be medical devices," while (n)(2) states that (n)(1) "shall not be construed as bearing on or being relevant to the question whether any product other than contact lenses is a device . . ." Here Congress appears to be saying that contact lenses are a special case, in its view worthy to be regulated as medical devices even if they do not fit comfortably within the contours of the statutory definition of a "device," and that the unique treatment afforded them is not to influence courts, one way or the other, if they are called on to decide whether to interpret the term "medical device" to apply to any other product. Thus, section 320(n)(2) makes very clear under what circumstances section 320(n)(1) will not carry precedential weight. Moreover, it is a special statutory provision that has placed contact lenses within the device definition.

Section 4 also declares that nothing in the act affects any authority currently exercised by the Secretary of Agriculture over raw tobacco. This prevents FDA from imposing any health-related restrictions over tobacco until it leaves the control of the farmers who grew it, or on the domain of the Internal Revenue Service with respect to excise taxes levied on tobacco products.

Broad Limitations on FDA Authority

The TCA particularizes the scope of FDA's new regulatory authority, by both detailing the powers delegated to the agency and by placing express limitations on them. On a broad level, Congress subjected FDA to two important restrictions. First, the Tobacco Control Act defines terms in ways that limit the scope of the TCA. Second, the act excludes from FDA's reach certain entities engaged in tobacco-related activity.

Definitions

"Tobacco Product." Section 201(rr) of the FDCA spells out the meaning of the key phrase "tobacco product." The term encompasses "any product made or derived from tobacco that is intended for human consumption, including any component, part, or accessory of a tobacco product (except for raw materials other than tobacco used in manufacturing a component, part, or accessory of a tobacco product)." However, the mere fact that an item falls within the statutory definition does not mean that it is subject to regulation under the Act. Section 901(b) provides that Chapter IX applies to cigarettes, cigarette tobacco, roll-your-own tobacco, and smokeless tobacco. Thus, these tobacco products are automatically subject to regulation under Chapter IX. With respect to all other tobacco products, the section states that, in order to regulate them, FDA must first promulgate a regulation that "deems [the product] to be subject to this chapter."

To make sense of this cryptic language, one must imagine a tobacco product that does not meet one of the definitions of the four products mentioned by name in section 901(b). For example, suppose that a dissolvable nicotine lozenge does not consist of cut, ground, powdered, or leaf tobacco, and hence does not meet the definition of "smokeless tobacco,"[24] but it is still a product that is "made or derived from tobacco," and hence is a "tobacco product." Section 901(b) is a barrier that blocks FDA from regulating these kinds of lozenges under Chapter IX until the agency first goes through the administrative process of promulgating a rule that deems them to be suitable for regulation under the TCA. The statutory implication here is that some tobacco products may be unsuitable for regulation.

An item that would otherwise fall within the definition of "tobacco product" is excluded from that category if it also falls within the definition of "drug" or "medical device,"[25] a proviso that eliminates the possibility of dual classification. In addition, once an item is

---

[24]   FDCA § 900(18), 21 U.S.C. § 387(18).
[25]   FDCA §§ 201(rr)(2), (3), 21 U.S.C. §§ 321(rr)(2), (3).

by definition a "tobacco product," it cannot legally be sold in combination with any other product regulated under the FDCA.[26]

Electronic Cigarettes. FDA tried to circumvent the need for a "deeming" regulation when it took the position that electronic cigarettes, which vaporize a liquid nicotine mixture in such a way as to enable users to inhale it, should be considered a drug-device combination and therefore would not fall within the definition of "tobacco products."[27] FDA reasoned that the electronic cigarettes fell outside the holding in *Brown & Williamson*[28] because they were not traditional tobacco products like cigarettes and smokeless tobacco, and the manufacturers not only intended them to affect the structure or function of the body, but also meant them to be useful in the prevention, mitigation, or treatment of a smoker's symptoms associated with nicotine withdrawal.

Two distributors successfully enjoined FDA from barring the importation of electronic cigarettes, when a United States District Court judge ruled that these products were not drug-device combinations, but instead fell within the definition of "tobacco products."[29] On appeal, a three-judge panel of the United States Court of Appeals also rejected FDA's position.[30]

FDA's "Deeming" Regulation. The electronic-cigarette industry then increased its production and intensified its marketing of what are now commonly referred to as e-cigarettes, and thereby aroused substantial concern over the safety and public-health implications associated with them.[31] However, FDA decided to take a broad approach. Instead of addressing only the e-cigarette problem, the agency proposed a general regulation deeming that all other tobacco products (except accessories to them) in addition to those listed in section 901(b) merited regulation under the TCA.[32] This would encompass items such as cigars, pipe tobacco, and gels, in addition to e-cigarettes.

---

[26] FDCA § 201(rr)(4), 21 U.S.C. § 321(rr)(4). The agency has published a draft guidance giving examples of what it would consider prohibited combinations. See FDA, Draft Guidance: The Scope of the Prohibition Against Marketing a Tobacco Product in Combination with Another Article or Product Regulated under the Federal Food, Drug, and Cosmetic Act (Sept. 30, 2009), http://www.fda.gov/TobaccoProducts/GuidanceComplianceRegulatoryInformation/ucm184283.htm (for example, a mouthwash added to the ingredients of a cigarette, where the cigarette is identified as containing mouthwash).

[27] The definition of a "tobacco product" excludes "an article that is a drug under subsection (g)(1), a device under subsection (h), or a combination product described in section 503(g)." FDCA § 201(rr)(2), 21 U.S.C. § 321(rr)(2).

[28] 529 U.S. 120 (2000). If electronic cigarettes fell within the holding in *Brown & Williamson,* they would not be subject to regulation as drugs or devices.

[29] Smoking Everywhere, Inc. v. U.S. Food and Drug Administration, 680 F. Supp. 2d 62 (D.D.C. 2010). For a discussion of the relevant legal issues, *see* Azim Chowdhury, *The Evolution of the Electronic Cigarette,* UPDATE, May/June 2011, at 30.

[30] Sottera, Inc. v. Food and Drug Administration, 627 F.3d 891 (D.C. Cir. 2010).

[31] *See, e.g.,* Megan McArdle, *E-Cigarettes: A $1.5 Billion Industry Braces for FDA Regulation,* http://www.businessweek.com/articles/2014-02-06/e-cigarettes-fda-regulation-looms-for-1-dot-5-billion-industry. Proponents of e-cigarettes claimed they would reduce the incidence of cigarette smoking, while opponents argued that they would attract new smokers.

[32] Food and Drug Administration, Deeming Tobacco Products to be Subject to the Federal Food, Drug, and Cosmetic Act, 79 Fed. Reg. 23,142 (Apr. 25, 2014). The agency also proposed, as an alternative, to exempt "premium cigars" from the rule.

The proposed rule would immediately and automatically expose manufacturers to sections of the statute prohibiting the sale of adulterated or misbranded tobacco products, requiring registration and submission of lists of ingredients and potentially harmful constituents, restricting the use of modified-use descriptors, making the distribution of free samples illegal and, most problematically, imposing premarket-review obligations. The last of these restrictions would raise serious problems as to how FDA should treat new tobacco products, such as e-cigarettes, which are already on the market. The document also carried with it a further proposal to impose minimum-age and identification requirements and health warnings, and would eliminate the use of vending machines from the marketing process.

"Additive." The definition of "additive" in section 900(1) is identical to the first part of the statutory definition of "food additive,"[33] and includes a similar specific parenthetical inclusion of materials "intended for use in producing, manufacturing, packing, processing, preparing, treating, packaging, transporting, or holding." It does not replicate the food-additive exclusion for substances generally recognized as safe, but it does exclude "tobacco or a pesticide chemical residue in or on raw tobacco or a pesticide chemical." Falling within the definition of tobacco "additive," however, does not carry with it the same consequences as classification as a "food additive." In the latter instance, the additive could not be marketed without premarket approval by FDA.[34] There is no similar requirement for tobacco "additives."[35]

"Smokeless Tobacco." Section 900(18) defines "smokeless tobacco" as "any tobacco product that consists of cut, ground, powdered, or leaf tobacco, and that is intended to be placed in the oral or nasal cavity." Products that fall squarely within this definitional category include snuff and chewing tobacco.

FDA has issued a statement asserting its authority to regulate dissolvable tobacco products as "smokeless tobacco."[36] These items would include nicotine lozenges meant to be placed in the mouth, where they gradually dissolve, allowing the ingestion of nicotine. To meet the definition, they would also need to consist of "cut, ground, powdered, or leaf tobacco,"[37] which seems to be the case with most of these items,[38] since they are made from compressed

---

[33]   FDCA § 201(s), 21 U.S.C. § 321(s).

[34]   For a discussion of FDA's authority to regulate food additives, *see* Chapter 2 *supra.*

[35]   To illustrate, assume that Chemical X is detected in both food-packaging material and cigarette paper, its presence cannot be eliminated, and it is not generally recognized as safe. A company wishing to use it in food-packaging material could not do so without prior approval by FDA. Moreover, since it could be considered a "component" of food, it would be by definition "food" under section 201(f), and might be subject to seizure under section 304. See Natick Paperboard Corp. v. Weinberger, 525 F.2d 1103 (1st Cir. 1975). A company wishing to use it in cigarette paper would not need to secure premarket approval. Moreover, the definition of "tobacco products" in section 201(rr)(1) excludes "raw materials other than tobacco used in . . . [an] accessory of a tobacco product." Hence, Chemical X would not be deemed a "tobacco product," and would not be subject to seizure under section 304(a)(2)(E). If FDA wanted to take regulatory action against cigarettes using paper that contained Chemical X, it would have to bring an enforcement action that would require the government to prove that the cigarettes were adulterated under section 902(1). For criticism of this disparity of treatment, see James T. O'Reilly, *FDA Regulation of Tobacco: Blessing or Curse for FDA Professionals?,* 64 Food & Drug L.J. 459, 464 (2009).

[36]   *See* http://www.fda.gov/TobaccoProducts/NewsEvents/ucm248801.htm.

[37]   FDCA § 900(18), 21 U.S.C. § 387(18).

[38]   The hypothetical lozenge discussed *supra* at note 24 and accompanying text was not derived from cut, ground, powdered, or leaf tobacco.

tobacco.[39] The broad requirement that they be "intended to be placed in the oral cavity" would logically encompass pellets designed to dissolve in the mouth.

Exclusion for Raw Tobacco

The TCA explicitly exempts raw tobacco and those who produce it. The definition of "tobacco product" in section 201(rr)(1) embraces "any product made or derived from tobacco," which would not logically include the raw tobacco itself. Section 901(c)(2)(A), moreover, removes from the scope of Chapter IX "tobacco leaf that is not in the possession of a manufacturer of tobacco products," as well as "the producers of tobacco leaf, including tobacco growers, tobacco warehouses, and tobacco grower cooperatives . . . ." Reflecting an awareness of FDA's occasional forays into imaginative statutory construction, Congress added section 901(c)(2)(C), which declares that no exercise of interpretation should permit the agency "to promulgate regulations on any matter that involves the production of tobacco leaf or a producer thereof, other than activities by a manufacturer affecting production."

Prohibited Acts

Adulteration

The Tobacco Control Act sets out eight distinct ways in which FDA might deem a tobacco product to have been adulterated. Three of them relate to actual or potential contamination caused by a direct exposure to a harmful substance or condition. Four relate to what might be termed indirect adulteration caused by the failure to conform to regulatory requirements designed to protect against actual or potential contamination. One has very little, if anything, to do with adulteration in the dictionary sense of the term.

Actual or Potential Contamination. Section 902(1) of the FDCA provides that a tobacco product is adulterated if "it consists in whole or in part of any filthy, putrid, or decomposed substance, or is otherwise contaminated by any added poisonous or added deleterious substance that may render the product injurious to health." The first clause is copied verbatim from section 501(a)(1), dealing with adulterated drugs and devices. The second is less straightforward, taken from the "may-render-injurious" standard for added substances in food.[40] Neither the courts nor FDA have elaborated on the meaning of this language,[41] mainly because of the multitude of special provisions Congress has inserted into the FDCA to regulate specific kinds of added substances.[42] The adverb "otherwise" suggests that the harmful effect from an added substance must result from a causative factor other than filth, putrescence, or decomposition. This section seems to deal with health risks that are marginal, certainly when compared to the inherent dangers posed by tobacco products, so that FDA is not likely to assign a high priority to its enforcement.

---

[39]   See Gregory N. Connolly et al., *Unintentional Child Poisonings Through Ingestion of Conventional and Novel Tobacco Products*, 125 Pediatrics 896, 898, col. 1 (May 2010).

[40]   FDCA § 402(a)(1), 21 U.S.C. § 342(a)(1).

[41]   The leading case is still *U.S. v. Lexington Mill & Elevator Co.*, 232 U.S. 399 (1914).

[42]   See, e.g., FDCA § 409, 21 U.S.C. § 348, dealing with food additives.

Subsections (2) and (3), dealing with insanitary conditions and packaging composed of poisonous or deleterious substances, copy verbatim the standards for the adulteration of drugs and medical devices.[43]

Indirect Adulteration. The Tobacco Control Act authorizes FDA to set tobacco product standards,[44] review certain tobacco products before they can be marketed,[45] promulgate rules that specify good manufacturing practices,[46] and regulate modified-risk tobacco products.[47] These provisions aim in part to prevent from entering the stream of commerce tobacco products that might carry with them risks even greater than the hazards inherent in them. Section 902 classifies as adulterated any tobacco products that have been marketed although they do not comply with regulations designed to protect consumers from these additional risks, without regard to whether the products in question were actually harmful, or had been exposed to actual insanitary conditions, or had come into contact with any actually or potentially harmful substance.

Technical Adulteration. Section 902(4) deals with tobacco products whose manufacturer has violated provisions of section 919, requiring the payment of user fees. The link between user fees and the factual adulterating of a product is highly tenuous, perhaps based on the supposition that a manufacturer's refusal to pay the fees might in some way hinder FDA in its efforts to prevent the marketing of tobacco products that subject consumers to the risk of adulteration. Yet Congress in its wisdom may deem anything to be by definition "adulterated" for the purpose of enforcing the statute.

Misbranding

Section 903 takes a multi-pronged approach to misbranding, which, like adulteration, is a prohibited act.[48] First, it contains a general prohibition against false or misleading labeling[49] or advertising of a tobacco product. Second, the section specifically lists certain information that must appear on the labels[50] of tobacco products, and provides that a label not bearing this information will be deemed misbranded.[51] Third, with respect to advertising as well as labeling, the section categorizes as misbranding failures to conform to certain statutory requirements specifying information that must be conveyed to potential consumers and customers.[52]

In addition to the substantive requirements that certain information must appear on labels and labeling, section 903 speaks to the method by which this information is to be conveyed.

---

[43]   FDCA §§ 501(a)(2)(A) and (3), 21 U.S.C. §§ 351(a)(2)(A) and (3).

[44]   See FDCA § 907, 21 U.S.C. § 387g.

[45]   See FDCA § 910, 21 U.S.C. § 387j.

[46]   See FDCA § 906(e), 21 U.S.C. § 387f(e).

[47]   See FDCA § 911, 21 U.S.C. § 387k.

[48]   See FDCA § 301(a), 21 U.S.C. § 331(a).

[49]   The FDCA defines "labeling" as "all labels and other written, printed or graphic matter (1) upon any article or any of its containers or wrappers, or (2) accompanying such article." FDCA § 201(m), 21 U.S.C. § 321(m).

[50]   The statute defines "label" as a "display of written, printed, or graphic matter upon the immediate container of any article." See FDCA§ 201(k), 21 U.S.C. § 321(k). The prototypical label for a tobacco product would be the informational display on a cigarette package.

[51]   FDCA § 903(a)(2), 21 U.S.C. § 387c(a)(2).

[52]   E.g., FDCA § 903(a)(9), 21 U.S.C. § 387c(a)(9) (labeling required under tobacco product standards).

Subsection (a)(3) provides that mandated information must be prominent and conspicuous, and must be comprehensible to the ordinary consumer under ordinary conditions of purchase and use; if not, the product may be deemed misbranded.

General Prohibition Against False or Misleading Statements. Section 903(a)(1) begins with a general proposition, found elsewhere in the FDCA,[53] to the effect that the labeling of a tobacco product is misbranded if it is "false or misleading in any particular."[54] Section 903(a)(8) applies this rule to advertising as well.

The supplementary language in section 201(n), to the effect that the failure to reveal material facts may be relevant in determining whether labeling or advertising is false or misleading in any particular, is also applicable to tobacco products. Hence, the prohibition against misbranding covers not only untrue affirmations but also omissions that create misimpressions.

As a general proposition, FDA may use its informal rulemaking authority to declare as misleading the failure to disclose information not specifically required by other sections of Chapter IX. The extensive jurisprudence that section 201(n) has generated in cases involving other product categories[55] may be relevant in cases involving tobacco products. However, the TCA contains so many particularized disclosure requirements that FDA is unlikely to make frequent or significant use of section 903(a)(1).

Specific Requirements Contained in Section 903. Section 903(a)(2) requires that the labels of tobacco products in package form bear certain factual information, such as the name and place of business of the manufacturer. Section 903(a)(8) imposes a similar mandate for advertisements.

Specific Requirements Contained in Other Sections. Section 903 puts teeth into provisions found in other sections of the Tobacco Control Act and requiring that specific information designated either by those provisions or by FDA regulations appear on the labeling or advertisements of tobacco products. These include section 920(a) (origin labeling for tobacco products other than cigarettes), section 905 (registration information), and section 907 (labeling required by a tobacco product standard).

In addition, section 903 designates as misbranding the failure to comply with certain statutory or regulatory requirements imposed elsewhere in Chapter IX and having nothing to do with the transmission of information to consumers. These mandates encompass restrictions on the sale and distribution of tobacco products,[56] the failure to comply with requirements to furnish health information to FDA,[57] the failure to comply with FDA orders

---

[53] See, e.g., FDCA § 403(a)(1), 21 U.S.C. § 343(a)(1) (misbranding of food); FDCA § 502(a), 21 U.S.C. § 352(a) (misbranding of drugs and devices); FDCA § 602(a), 21 U.S.C. § 362(a) (misbranding of cosmetics).
[54] See FDCA § 903(a)(1), 21 U.S.C. § 387c(a)(1); FDCA § 903(a)(7)(A), 21 U.S.C. § 387c(a)(7)(A).
[55] For example, section 201(n) helped to provide legal authority for FDA regulations requiring patient package inserts. See Pharmaceutical Manufacturers Ass'n v. FDA, 484 F. Supp. 1179 (D. Del. 1980), aff'd per curiam, 634 F.2d 106 (3d Cir. 1980).
[56] FDCA § 903(a)(7)(B), 21 U.S.C. § 387c(a)(7)(B), referencing FDCA § 906(d)(1), 21 U.S.C. § 387f(d)(1).
[57] FDCA § 903(a)(10)(A), 21 U.S.C. § 387c(a)(10)(A), referencing FDCA § 904, 21 U.S.C. § 387d.

that notices of risks be given or recalls undertaken,[58] and the failure to keep required records and reports and provide them to FDA when requested.[59]

Violation of Regulations Requiring Directions for Use or Warnings. Section 903(a)(5) provides that a tobacco product is misbranded if it fails to comply with FDA regulations that require its labeling to carry adequate directions for use, or adequate warnings against use by children. Some of the language here seems to have been borrowed from section 502(f), which deals with the misbranding of drugs and devices, except that the latter does not include as a prerequisite the issuance of regulations. This subsection does not cross-reference any other provision that grants to FDA specific authority to issue such regulations. One possible source of such authority would be section 907(a)(4)(C), which permits FDA to include in tobacco product standards requirements for labeling that will assure the appropriate use of the product.

Other Prohibited Acts

In addition to applying the concepts of adulteration and misbranding to the manufacture and marketing of tobacco products, the TCA adds a number of particularized items to the long list of prohibited acts in section 301 of the FDCA. These include: failure to comply with recordkeeping and reporting requirements mandated by sections 909 and 920;[60] failure to furnish health information, as required by section 904; and failure to comply with substantive obligations as they relate to labeling (section 903(b)), tobacco product standards (section 907), notification (section 908), modified-risk tobacco products (section 911), and advertising (section 913). Other miscellaneous prohibitions relate to the shipping of a detained product,[61] the sale of tobacco products in violation of a no-sale order,[62] the counterfeiting of tobacco products,[63] their charitable distribution,[64] and the failure on the part of a manufacturer or distributor to report knowledge of the illegal trade of tobacco products.[65]

Finally, section 301(tt) contains an explicit prohibition against any representation in the labeling or advertising of tobacco products to the effect that FDA approves or endorses them, or considers them safe, or that tobacco products are safe and less harmful because they are regulated by FDA. To the extent that such representations are false or misleading, they would also constitute misbranding. This provision has subsequently been held unconstitutional.[66]

---

[58]   FDCA § 903(a)(10)(A), 21 U.S.C. § 387c(a)(10)(A), referencing FDCA § 908, 21 U.S.C. § 387h.

[59]   FDCA § 903(a)(10)(B), 21 U.S.C. § 387c(a)(10)(B), referencing FDCA § 909, 21 U.S.C. § 387i.

[60]   In addition, the inclusion of any false or misleading information in a report required by law constitutes a prohibited act. FDCA § 301(q)(2), 21 U.S.C. § 331(q)(2).

[61]   FDAC § 301(r), 21 U.S.C. § 331(r). This subsection also prohibits removing or altering any symbol identifying a tobacco product as detained.

[62]   FDCA § 301(oo), 21 U.S.C. § 331(oo).

[63]   FDCA § 301(qq), 21 U.S.C.§ 331(qq).

[64]   FDCA § 301(rr), 21 U.S.C. § 331(rr).

[65]   FDCA § 301(ss), 21 U.S.C. § 331(ss).

[66]   See Discount Tobacco City Lottery Inc. v. United States, 674 F.3d 509 (6th Cir. 2012), discussed *infra* at note 224 and accompanying text.

Enforcement

The enforcement options that the government can invoke in response to the commission of prohibited acts relating to tobacco products fall into three categories: 1) they may be identical to mechanisms generally applicable to food, drugs, medical devices, and cosmetics, 2) they may be identical to mechanisms applicable only to certain products regulated under the FDCA; and 3) they may be *sui generis.*

Common Mechanisms. The rules that govern criminal penalties[67] and injunctions[68] in enforcement actions dealing with food, drugs, cosmetics, and medical devices apply also to tobacco products. This means that the case law and rules interpreting the imposition of these mechanisms in proceedings involving these products will also govern cases affecting tobacco products. Moreover, tobacco establishments registered with FDA are subject to mandatory biennial inspections governed by section 704, which also authorizes inspections of food, drug, medical device, and cosmetics establishments.[69] Finally, the provision of the act giving FDA authority to generate publicity also applies to tobacco products.[70]

Selective Mechanisms. Also applicable to tobacco products are the substantive and procedural rules governing actions to seize medical devices, and administrative proceedings to detain them.[71] Moreover, section 303(f)(5), containing procedural rules for the imposition of civil penalties, applies to all products, including tobacco products, implicated in statutory violations for which the government might impose civil penalties.[72]

Unique Mechanisms. The TCA creates a special section authorizing the assessment of civil penalties for statutory violations in cases involving tobacco products, and taking effect on the issuance of FDA guidelines.[73] This provision specifies the amounts of penalties that may be awarded, and the mitigating effect of a defendant's efforts to correct a violation.

The Tobacco Control Act also permits the government to impose a no-tobacco-sale order on retail outlets found to have committed repeated violations of regulations promulgated under section 906(d), dealing with restrictions on the sale and distribution of tobacco products.[74]

---

[67] FDCA § 303(a), 21 U.S.C. § 333(a).

[68] FDCA § 302, 21 U.S.C. § 332.

[69] FDCA § 905(g), 21 U.S.C. § 374(g).

[70] FDCA § 705, 21 U.S.C. § 375.

[71] FDCA § 304(a)(2)(E), 21 U.S.C. § 334(a)(2)(E) (seizure; counterfeit drugs included in same subsection); FDCA § 304(g), 21 U.S.C. § 334(g) (administrative detention).

[72] For a summary of the statutory violations that might justify the imposition of civil penalties, *see* PETER BARTON HUTT, RICHARD A. MERRILL & LEWIS A. GROSSMAN, FOOD AND DRUG LAW: CASES AND MATERIALS 262-63 (4th ed., 2014).

[73] FDCA § 303(f)(9), 21 U.S.C. § 333(f)(9). On FDA's current thinking about civil penalties as applied to retailers, *see* Food and Drug Administration, Draft Guidance for FDA and Tobacco Retailers: Civil Money Penalties and No-Tobacco-Sale Orders for Tobacco Retailers (March 2011), http://www.fda.gov/downloads/TobaccoProducts/GuidanceComplianceRegulatoryInformation/UCM252955.pdf.

[74] FDCA § 303(f)(8), 21 U.S.C. § 333(f)(8). The procedural rules in subsections (f)(5) and (f)(6) also apply to no-tobacco-sale orders, which bar individual retailers from selling tobacco products.

Reporting Requirements

The TCA requires all manufacturers of tobacco products to report certain information to FDA. These mandates can help the agency fulfill a principal goal of the act, "to impose appropriate regulatory controls on the tobacco industry,"[75] a task that will require access to data that only the industry can provide. The statute itself particularizes some of these reporting requirements. In other instances, it authorizes FDA to promulgate rules mandating the submission of additional information.

Section 905 calls for the annual registration of entities engaged in the manufacture of tobacco products. Section 904 obliges the submission of health-related information to FDA. Section 909 authorizes FDA to issue regulations requiring the maintenance of records and the submission of reports deemed necessary for assuring that tobacco products are not adulterated or misbranded, and for otherwise protecting the public health. Section 915 directs FDA to finalize rules requiring tests and the disclosure of test results when the agency deems this necessary to safeguard the public.

The act also places limitations on reporting requirements, in order to protect the tobacco industry from data requests that are either quantitatively or qualitatively unreasonable. Moreover, some reporting obligations apply only to certain tobacco products, such as those intended to modify risks.

Registration

Section 905, dealing with annual registration, applies to existing domestic manufacturers, new domestic manufacturers, and foreign manufacturers, whose tobacco products will be imported into the United States. Domestic manufacturers must report their names, places of business, and all other tobacco-related establishments they operate.[76] Foreign establishments will be subject to registration requirements established by FDA regulations.[77]

These mandates closely track the language of section 510, which sets out the requirements for the registration of producers of drugs and devices. Thus, subsection 905(b) copies section 510(b) by requiring the registration of all establishments engaged in "manufacture, preparation, compounding or processing;" section 905(a) includes repackagers; and subsection (b) requires that in the case of partnerships the "name" include each partner, and in the case of corporations, the "name" include each corporate officer, director, and the state of incorporation, language taken directly from sections 510(a) and (b).

The information that must accompany registration includes not only names and places of business, but also "a copy of all consumer information and other labeling," and a sample

---

[75]   TCA, Pub. L. No. 111-31, § 3(8), 123 Stat. 1776, 1782 (2009).

[76]   Section 905(c), dealing with new owners and operators engaged in the manufacture or preparation of any tobacco product or products in any establishment they own or operate, requires the reporting of the "name, place of business and such establishment." This subsection is poorly drafted, since a new business might begin operations with more than one establishment. Hence, it should refer to any "establishment or establishments," so as to require that FDA be notified immediately about the existence of multiple establishments.

[77]   FDCA § 905(h), 21 U.S.C. § 387e(h).

of advertisements for the product.[78] The act does not define the somewhat vague term "consumer information." Its linkage to the phrase "other labeling" suggests strongly that it incorporates information that has the same characteristics as labeling. Hence, it would seem to embrace any material that a tobacco company communicates to consumers even if it does not fall within the sweep of the terms "labeling" and "advertising."

Health-Related Information

Section 904(a) obligates tobacco companies to submit to FDA a list of all ingredients in their products, and a description of the content, delivery, and form of nicotine contained therein; a list of all product constituents determined by FDA to be hazardous;[79] and all documents concerning the health, toxicological, behavioral, or physiologic effects of their tobacco products.

Section 904(b) expands even further the duty to report health-related information. It gives FDA authority to promulgate regulations requiring the submission of all documents incorporating research done, supported by or in the possession of tobacco companies and relating to the health, toxicological, behavioral, or physiological effects of tobacco products, or relating to the existence of technology that might reduce health risks associated with tobacco products; and all documents relating to marketing research and its effectiveness.

Records and Reports

Section 909(a) gives FDA broad authority to issue regulations requiring the maintenance of records and the making of reports deemed necessary to protect the public health. The only example provided here specifies "information that reasonably suggests that ... marketed tobacco products may have caused or contributed to a serious unexpected adverse experience associated with the use of the product or any significant increase in the frequency of a serious, expected adverse product experience."[80]

The Tobacco Control Act does not explain the meaning of the term "serious adverse experience," a curious omission, since the expression "serious adverse drug experience" is defined in Chapter V of the FDCA.[81] Since the ordinary use of tobacco products can cause death or certain kinds of serious bodily harm, the reference to "unexpected" adverse experience must refer to other types of serious bodily harm, or an increase in the rate of death or serious bodily harm usually caused by these products.

---

[78] FDCA § 905(i)(1)(B), 21 U.S.C.§ 387e(i)(1)(B). FDA, for good cause, may also obtain copies of all advertisements promoting a particular tobacco product. *Id.*

[79] Section 904(e) obliges FDA to compile and maintain a list of harmful and potentially harmful constituents. For the agency's views on what constitutes such a constituent, *see* FDA, Guidance for Industry and FDA Staff: "Harmful and Potentially Harmful Constituents" in Tobacco Products as Used in Section 904(e) of the Federal Food, Drug, and Cosmetic Act (June 2010), http://www.fda.gov/downloads/TobaccoProducts/GuidanceComplianceRegulatoryInformation/UCM214600.pdf.

[80] FDCA § 909(a)(1), 21 U.S.C. § 387i(a)(1). Subsection (2) allows FDA to designate additional "significant adverse tobacco product experiences" that would have to be reported.

[81] FDCA § 505-1(b)(4), 21 U.S.C. § 355-1. For the statutory definition of an analogous term, *see* FDCA § 760(a)(3), 21 U.S.C. § 379aa(a)(3) (defining "serious adverse event" in context of reporting requirement imposed on manufacturers of nonprescription drugs).

Subsection 909(a) requires FDA to provide reasons for the reporting rules it is imposing.[82] It also contains some specific limitations on FDA's authority to promulgate regulations dealing with records and reports. For example, they must not be "unduly burdensome," and FDA must balance the cost of complying with them against the health benefits they are expected to produce.[83] Curiously, this is the only Tobacco Control Act provision that directs FDA to take into account financial burdens that a regulation might impose on tobacco companies.

A further reporting requirement is contained in section 909(b), which calls on FDA to issue regulations mandating that the agency be notified whenever a tobacco producer takes corrective action on its own to remove a tobacco product from the market in order to reduce a health risk, or because the product violates some provision of Chapter IX.

Test Data

Section 915(b) directs FDA to finalize regulations that will require the tobacco industry to test product ingredients and additives by brand and sub-brand, and to report the results; and to make public disclosures of the results of tests on tar, nicotine, and other constituents as determined by the agency. Section 915(c) permits FDA to conduct or to require tests on constituents, including constituents of smoke, and to require the public disclosure of results.

Tobacco Product Standards

Although section 907 bears the title "Tobacco Product Standards," it in fact conflates the concepts of standards and bans by authorizing (or barring) the prohibition of certain types of tobacco products while at the same time legalizing the regulatory imposition of requirements relating to their composition, design, labeling, or marketing.[84] Thus, the section gives FDA authority to set the latter type of standard, and at the same time creates self-executing rules prohibiting the inclusion of certain flavors as the characterizing ingredients in cigarettes, and certain pesticide residues in tobacco. Violations of these rules and standards would amount to prohibited acts.[85]

Special Rules

Flavors. Consistent with a major purpose of the Tobacco Control Act—the protection of minors from the perils of cigarette smoke—section 907(a)(1)(A) bars the inclusion of flavors, herbs, and spices as constituents or additives amounting to ingredients that characterize

---

[82] FDCA § 909(a)(4), 21 U.S.C. § 387i(a)(4).

[83] FDCA § 909(a)(3), 21 U.S.C. § 387i(a)(3).

[84] This is by no means the first time that an agency has conflated standards and bans. For example, the Consumer Product Safety Commission has used its authority to ban products under the Hazardous Substances Act (HSA) to set standards that prohibited the sale of products that did not incorporate certain design characteristics. See Consumer Product Safety Commission, Bicycles: Banning of Hazardous Bicycles; Establishment of Safety Requirements, 39 Fed. Reg. 26,100 (July 16, 1974). The fact that the procedures for banning under the HSA were much less onerous than the procedures for setting standards under the Consumer Product Safety Act explains this choice of methodology.

[85] FDCA § 301(q)(1)(C), 21 U.S.C. § 331(q)(1)(C).

cigarettes. They may be artificial or natural, and might include strawberry, grape, orange, clove, cinnamon, pineapple, vanilla, coconut, licorice, cocoa, cherry, or coffee—all flavors that might be appealing to young people.[86] FDA may use this version of its standard-setting authority to set rules for artificial or natural flavors, herbs, or spices not enumerated in section 907(a)(1)(A).[87] Tobacco flavor receives a permanent exemption from this ban.

A flavor given special treatment is menthol, because of its special appeal to African-American smokers, more than three-quarters of whom use cigarettes spiced with it, and because of increased risks of harm associated with menthol cigarettes.[88] Section 907(a)(1)(A) permits FDA to ban these products, but only after first obtaining a report and recommendation from its Tobacco Products Scientific Advisory Committee,[89] and then promulgating a regulation under section 907(a)(3).[90]

The special rules in section 907(a)(1)(A) apply only to cigarettes and their component parts. Thus, a manufacturer might be able to circumvent the ban by converting its flavored cigarettes into flavored cigars. FDA would then have to go through the process for setting a tobacco product standard that would extend the flavor ban beyond cigarettes.[91]

---

[86]   The House Report mentioned the names of flavored-cigarette brands that target young people. See H.R. REP. No. 111-58, Pt. 1, 111th Cong., 1st Sess. 37 (2009). It pointed out that addicted adult smokers did not ordinarily smoke these types of cigarettes, and hence removing them from the market would not cause the sorts of problems that result from suddenly depriving addicts of their source of addiction. Id. at 38.

[87]   To do so, FDA would have to use the mechanism of a tobacco product standard, which would also instance the melding of the notions of standards and bans in Chapter IX.

[88]   See C. Stephen Redhead & Vanessa K. Burrows, FDA Tobacco Regulation: The Family Smoking Prevention and Tobacco Control Act of 2009, Congressional Research Service Report, No. 7-5700, 11-12 (May 28, 2009).

[89]   See § 907(e), 21 U.S.C. § 387g(e).

[90]   For the judicial nullification of the first report submitted by the Committee recommending that FDA ban menthol cigarettes, see infra notes 204-05 and accompanying text. The special treatment given to menthol flavoring led to a complaint by Indonesia to the World Trade Organization (WTO) panel, to the effect that by statutorily banning clove-flavored cigarettes (to the economic detriment of Indonesian exporters) while allowing domestically produced menthol-flavored cigarettes to remain on the market amounted to disparate treatment that violated international trade laws. The panel's decision, in favor of Indonesia, was upheld by the Appellate Body of the WTO. The Appellate Body found that the disparate treatment did not derive from a bona fide regulatory distinction. The dispute is still pending. For an account of it, see Tania Voon, World Trade Organization—Agreement on Technical Barriers to Trade—national treatment—discrimination— public health objectives, 106 AMERICAN J. OF INT'L LAW 824 (2012).

[91]   FDA is attempting to elude this requirement in response to an effort by a flavored-cigarette importer to avoid the ban by using tobacco leaf instead of paper as wrapping and rechristening its clove-flavored cigarettes as cigars. See Letter from Hon. Henry A. Waxman, Letter to FDA Commissioner Margaret Hamburg (Mar. 28, 2011), http://democrats.energycommerce.house.gov/sites/default/files/documents/Hamburg.FDA_. Kretek.2010.3.28.pdf. The agency takes the position that it can regulate flavored cigars as cigarettes if they meet the statutory definition of "cigarettes." See FDA, Guidance for Industry and FDA Staff: General Questions and Answers on the Ban of Cigarettes that Contain Certain Characterizing Flavors (Edition 2), (Dec. 23, 2009), http://www.fda.gov/downloads/TobaccoProducts/ProtectingKidsfromTobacco/FlavoredTobacco/ ucm195420.pdf, at 2-3. The definition of a "cigarette" in section 900(3) of the FDCA includes a requirement that the product include tobacco as a functional ingredient, and because of its appearance and packaging is likely to be purchased by a consumer as a cigarette. However, the definition also includes the definition in section 3(1) of the FCLAA, which excludes products wrapped in any tobacco-containing substance (i.e., cigars). Moreover, cigars have been consistently viewed as not falling within the definition of "cigarette" in the FCLAA. See, e.g., Lorillard Tobacco Co. v. Reilly, 533 U.S. 525, 537 (2001) (statement by Justice O'Connor that "[t]he FCLAA's preemption provision does not cover . . . cigars").

Pesticides. Section 907(a)(1)(B) creates another special rule banning the use of both domestic and foreign tobacco bearing pesticide residues at levels higher than the tolerance levels set by federal law for domestic tobacco. The purpose of this provision, as stated in the House Report, is to "create a level playing field between domestic tobacco growers and foreign tobacco growers."[92]

Promulgation of Standards for Tobacco Products

In addition to creating the special, self-executing rules in subsection (a)(1), section 907 gives FDA the power to develop tobacco product standards. The act spells out with considerable detail the types of standards that might be adopted; the factors FDA must take into account in promulgating a standard; and the procedure the agency must use.

Types of Standards. Although the act nowhere defines the term "tobacco product standard," section 907(a)(4) gives a number of examples of standards that might be appropriate for the safeguarding of the public health. They all relate to the composition, design, testing, and marketing of tobacco products, and hence cover broad ground. Thus, standards may set levels of nicotine yields,[93] or lessen or eliminate the presence of other constituents.[94] They also may affect the construction, components, ingredients, additives, constituents, and properties of a tobacco product.[95] Finally, standards may impose requirements for testing,[96] sale, and distribution,[97] and labeling necessary to assure the proper use of the product.[98]

Section 907(d)(3) places an important limitation on FDA's authority to set standards. It prohibits FDA from issuing a regulation that bans cigarettes, smokeless tobacco products, cigars, pipe tobacco, and roll-your-own tobacco products, or that reduces nicotine yields to zero.[99] The reason given is the importance of such a regulation, most likely in the sense that it implicates the sort of decision that should be left to the legislative and executive branches, given the public-health, cultural and law-enforcement ramifications that a total prohibition might provoke.

Considerations. In order to justify the setting of a tobacco product standard, FDA must make a finding that it would be "appropriate for the protection of the public health."[100] Section 907(a)(3)(B)(i) requires FDA to take into account scientific evidence establishing the risks and benefits of the standard to both consumers and affected third parties; any increase or decrease in the odds that current consumers will stop using the tobacco product

---

92   H.R. Rep. No. 111-58, Pt. 1, 111th Cong., 1st Sess. 40 (2009).

93   FDCA § 907(a)(4)(A)(i), 21 U.S.C. § 387g(a)(4)(A)(i).

94   FDCA § 907(a)(4)(A)(ii), 21 U.S.C. § 387g(a)(4)(A)(ii).

95   FDCA § 907(a)(4)(B)(i), 21 U.S.C. § 387g(a)(4)(B)(i).

96   FDCA § 907(a)(4)(B)(ii)-(iv), 21 U.S.C. § 387g(a)(4)(B)(ii)-(iv).

97   FDCA § 907(a)(4)(B)(v), 21 U.S.C. § 387g(a)(4)(B)(v). FDA's authority here is explicitly limited by the restrictions section 906(d) places on regulatory constraints dealing with the sale and distribution of tobacco products.

98   FDCA § 907(a)(4)(C), 21 U.S.C. § 387g(a)(4)(C).

99   An explicit ban would not seem to qualify as a "standard." However, it is conceivable that the agency could craft a standard that could not be met under existing technology, and hence would amount to a ban. This subsection does leave open the possibility that FDA might reduce nicotine to non-addictive levels.

100   FDCA § 907(a)(3)(A), 21 U.S.C. § 387g(a)(3)(A).

involved; and any increase or decrease in the danger that non-consumers will begin to use it.[101]

Noticeably absent here is any express mandate that FDA take into account the extent of any economic burden with which a standard might saddle the tobacco industry.[102] Moreover, an executive order issued by the Office of Management and Budget directs federal agencies to consider the costs and the benefits of all possible regulatory options, and to choose regulatory options that maximize societal benefits.[103] Since the act forbids FDA from banning cigarettes and other tobacco products,[104] FDA may be precluded from promulgating a standard that would impose such heavy costs that it would amount to a *de facto* ban.

In addition to determining the appropriateness of a proposed standard in terms of public health, FDA must also consider whether compliance with the standard is technologically achievable,[105] and whether the standard might have any countervailing (or negative) effects on the health of young users, adult users, and non-users.[106]

Standard-Setting Procedure. Section 907(c) sets out the procedures FDA must follow when proposing to set, amend, or revoke a tobacco product standard. They generally track the informal processes the agency normally utilizes in promulgating regulations under section 701(a), except that here the statute specifies certain requirements, such as the providing of a justification to support the necessary finding that the standard will appropriately protect the public health,[107] an invitation to interested parties that they submit a competing proposal for a standard,[108] and consultation with the Secretary of Agriculture.[109]

Section 907(d) provides for the promulgation of a final rule, along with the findings that subsection (c) directs FDA to make. It also requires the consideration of a number of factors relevant to the establishment of an effective date for the regulation. These include the technical feasibility of complying, the existence of patents that might make compliance impossible, and alterations in the methods of producing home-grown tobacco.

---

[101] Subsection (ii) adds the provision that if FDA proposes to reduce or eliminate an additive, constituent, or component on the ground that it is or may be harmful, any party contesting this finding may supply FDA with evidence that the standard will not lessen or eliminate the risk of injury or illness. The rulemaking process normally gives interested parties this opportunity, so this subsection may serve no more than an expressive function.

[102] Other consumer protection statutes explicitly require the consideration of the costs of compliance with standards. *See, e.g.,* Consumer Product Safety Act § 9(c)(1), 15 U.S.C. § 2058(c)(1).

[103] Office of Management and Budget, Regulatory Planning and Review, Exec. Order 12,866 (Sept. 30, 1993), 58 Fed. Reg. 51,735 (Oct. 4, 1993), *as amended,* Exec. Order 13,258, 67 Fed. Reg. 9385 (Feb. 28, 2002).

[104] FDCA § 907(d)(3)(A), 21 U.S.C. § 387g(d)(3)(A).

[105] FDCA § 907(b)(1), 21 U.S.C. § 387g(b)(1).

[106] FDCA § 907(b)(2), 21 U.S.C. § 387g(b)(2).

[107] FDCA § 907(c)(2)(A), 21 U.S.C. § 387g(c)(2)(A). A proposed rule that would revoke an existing tobacco product standard must provide justification to support a finding that the standard will no longer appropriately protect the public health. FDCA § 907(c)(3), 21 U.S.C. § 387g(c)(3).

[108] FDCA § 907(c)(2)(B), 21 U.S.C. § 387g(c)(2)(B).

[109] FDCA § 907(c)(2)(D), 21 U.S.C. § 387g(c)(2)(D). Section 907(c)(2)(C) also specifically invites comments on how the structure of the standard might be modified so as to prevent it from favoring imported tobacco over domestic tobacco.

Appellate Review. Section 912(a) provides for judicial review of the establishment, amendment, or revocation of a tobacco product standard by a United States Court of Appeals, in accordance with section 706(2)(a) of the Administrative Procedure Act, which directs the setting aside of agency actions if they are "arbitrary, capricious, an abuse of discretion, or otherwise not in accordance with the law." In this respect, tobacco product standards differ from medical device performance standards, motor vehicle safety standards, and consumer product safety standards, all of which must be justified by substantial evidence in the record as a whole.[110]

On the other hand, as has been demonstrated, the act spells out in great detail the numerous findings FDA must make in support of standards the agency promulgates. To comply with these requirements will not only strain FDA resources, but it may also heighten judicial scrutiny. Given the reduction in the deference courts have traditionally paid to FDA expertise,[111] there exists a very real possibility that the standard setting might turn out to be so exacting and so burdensome that FDA will rarely engage in it.

Will History Repeat Itself? In this regard, it is useful to recall that in the past, federal agencies have faced such enormous difficulties in setting product-safety standards that they have all but abandoned the process. Take, for example, the performances of the National Highway Traffic Safety Administration in promulgating motor vehicle safety standards under the National Traffic and Motor Vehicle Safety Act;[112] the Consumer Product Safety Commission setting consumer product safety standards under the Consumer Product Safety Act;[113] and FDA itself in finalizing performance standards for medical devices under the FDCA.[114] In each instance, procedural as well as substantive obstacles in enabling statutes made the standard-setting process so time- and resource-consuming, and the development of a sufficient factual predicate so difficult, that the agencies opted to concentrate on other regulatory mechanisms, such as recalls.

Substantive Labeling Requirements

The Tobacco Control Act uses the misbranding provisions to require manufacturers to place a considerable amount of factual information on the labeling of tobacco. Normally, labeling conveys directions for the safe use of a product, as well as hazard-related communications that enable both actual and potential consumers to make informed choices about whether or not to expose themselves to risks arising from the use of a product. What makes tobacco-product regulation unique is that the most widely marketed items, such as cigarettes and smokeless tobacco, are inherently dangerous, and there is no way to consume them in a safe

---

[110]   See FDCA § 517(c), 21 U.S.C. § 360g(c) (medical devices); Consumer Product Safety Act § 11(c), 15 U.S.C. § 2060(c).

[111]   *See* James T. O'Reilly, *Losing Deference in the FDA's Second Century: Judicial Review, Politics, and a Diminished Legacy of Expertise*, 93 CORNELL L. REV. 939 (2008).

[112]   *See* Jerry L. Mashaw & David L. Harfst, *Regulation and the Legal Culture: The Case of Motor Vehicle Safety*, 4 YALE J. ON REG. 257 (1987).

[113]   *See* Teresa M. Schwartz, *The Consumer Product Safety Commission: A Flawed Product of the Consumer Decade*, 51 GEO. WASH. L. REV. 32 (1982).

[114]   *See* Robert B. Leflar, *Public Accountability and Medical Device Regulation*, 2 HARV. J.L. & TECH. 1 (1989).

way. Moreover, the deadly risks to which they expose consumers, when compared to the benefits they provide, would seem to suggest only one rational choice—non-consumption.

This section will first touch on some general labeling requirements applicable to all tobacco products. Then it will consider how the law mandates the disclosure of information on labeling for the purpose of discouraging non-smokers, especially those who have not reached adulthood, from becoming consumers of cigarettes. It will also cover labeling obligations applicable to tobacco products other than cigarettes. Finally, it will survey briefly labeling requirements that are less directly related to consumer protection.

General Labeling Requirements

Section 903(a)(1) provides that a tobacco product will be deemed misbranded "if its labeling is false or misleading in any particular." In addition, section 903(b) provides that FDA may issue a regulation mandating prior approval of statements appearing on the label of a tobacco product to make certain that the statements do not violate either the general prohibition against misbranding or any other provision of the act. The failure to comply with a directive issued under the section would amount to a prohibited act under section 301(q)(1)(A).

Cigarette Labeling

In drafting the TCA, Congress might have repealed prior statutes mandating the placement of specific cautionary statements on the labeling of cigarettes and smokeless tobacco—laws that were enacted at a time when FDA had no jurisdiction over tobacco products—and given FDA exclusive authority to administer and enforce a new warnings regime. This would have the advantage of simplification and consolidation. In the alternative, it could have maintained the existing structure, and merely revised and expanded the existing statutory requirements. Congress chose the latter, and passed amendments to the Federal Cigarette Labeling and Advertising Act (FCLAA) and the Comprehensive Smokeless Tobacco Health Education Act (CSTHEA), as well as to the FDCA. The result, in the case of cigarettes, has produced a complex system of labeling regulation.

The TCA amends the FCLAA to provide more explicit warnings about the risks related to smoking. It authorizes FDA to promulgate regulations providing for graphic warnings on packages, and to make substantive revisions of these new cautionary statements. Also, it requires FDA to use notice-and-comment rulemaking to determine whether to mandate the label disclosure of the tar and nicotine yields of cigarettes. Finally, it directs FDA to re-promulgate a substantial portion of its invalidated 1996 regulations,[115] except for two subsections dealing with cigarette and smokeless-tobacco packages.[116]

Amending FCLAA. The FCLAA mandated a warning statement on cigarette packages, and included specifications on the appearance and placement of the required cautionary

---

[115]   One of the regulations requires that labeling and advertising of cigarettes and smokeless tobacco use only a black text on a white background. TCA § 102(a)(2), 21 U.S.C. § 387a-1(a)(2) (directing FDA to adopt 21 C.F.R. § 897.32(a)).

[116]   TCA § 102(a)(2)(B), 21 U.S.C. § 387a-1(a)(2)(B). The regulations contained established names, such as "Cigarettes" and "Dry Snuff," that would have to be used on packages, which would also have to bear the statement: "Nicotine Delivery Device for Persons 18 or Older."

language.[117] Failure to comply would amount to a federal crime.[118] The law contained a four-year "sunset" provision.[119] It delegated no administrative authority to any agency, but it did direct FTC and the Secretary of Health, Education, and Welfare to submit to Congress reports on various issues relating to smoking and health.[120] Four years later, Congress amended the act to make the warnings more forceful.[121] In 1984, as part of the Comprehensive Smoking Education Act, amendments to the FCLAA further strengthened the cautionary message on cigarette packages.[122]

Section 201(a) of the TCA amends the FCLAA once again, and calls for the placement of one of nine health-warning statements that describe in even starker terms the dangers of smoking.[123] It specifies where on the package the warning must appear, the size of the type, and the color of the print and background (white on black, or black on white). It also exempts manufacturers and distributors who are not marketing their products in the United States, and retailers, if they meet certain requirements.

However, at this point the Tobacco Control Act differs from its predecessors, in that it vests in FDA the authority to revise the statutorily required warnings, and even to add to them. This may represent a congressional deferral to agency expertise, and also a recognition that warnings may become ineffective or dated, especially in the light of advances in scientific knowledge, and agencies may be better able to adjust to these changes in a timely fashion.

FDA-Mandated Warnings. Section 201(d) authorizes FDA to promulgate regulations requiring graphic displays to accompany the warning statements on cigarette packages, and to illustrate the adverse health effects caused by cigarettes,[124] and to use informal rulemaking to promulgate regulations changing both the way warnings are conveyed and their textual substance, if the agency could find that "such a change would promote greater public understanding of the risks associated with the use of tobacco products."[125]

On June 22, 2011, FDA promulgated regulations that required color images to accompany each of the statutorily mandated warnings.[126] Although the statutory authority enabling FDA to do this was subsequently upheld, FDA's initial effort to implement these provisions has been set aside as unconstitutional.[127]

---

[117]   The Federal Cigarette Labeling and Advertising Act, § 4, Pub. L. No. 89-92, 79 Stat. 282 (1965). The act blocked an FTC administrative proceeding that would have promulgated a trade regulation rule requiring a stronger cigarette-package warning. Federal Trade Commission, Trade Regulation Rule: Unfair or Deceptive Advertising and Labeling of Cigarettes in Relation to the Health Hazards of Smoking, 29 Fed. Reg. 8324 (June 22, 1964).

[118]   FCLAA, § 6.

[119]   Id. § 10.

[120]   Id. §§ 5(d)(1), (2).

[121]   The Public Health Cigarette Smoking Act, Pub. L. No. 91-222, 84 Stat. 87 (1969).

[122]   The Comprehensive Smoking Education Act, Pub. L. No. 98-474, 98 Stat. 2200 (1984).

[123]   The warnings include: "Cigarettes are addictive," "Cigarettes cause cancer," and "Smoking can kill you."

[124]   FDA proposed such regulations 17 months after the TCA became law. See Food and Drug Administration, Required Warnings for Cigarette Packages and Advertisements, 75 Fed. Reg. 69,523 (Nov. 12, 2010).

[125]   TCA § 202(d).

[126]   Food and Drug Administration, Required Warnings for Cigarette Packages and Advertisements, 76 Fed. Reg. 36,628 (June 22, 2011).

[127]   For a discussion of the judicial decisions involved, see infra notes 224-37 and accompanying text.

Tar and Nicotine Levels. Section 206 of the TCA amends the FCLAA to give FDA authority to determine, via informal rulemaking, whether cigarette packages should also include tar and nicotine levels. Since FTC had already established regulations for the reporting of tar and nicotine yields in cigarettes,[128] the section also directs the two regulatory entities to work out any discrepancies by way of a memorandum of understanding.

Labeling of Other Tobacco Products

Smokeless Tobacco. Section 204 of the TCA amends the Comprehensive Smokeless Tobacco Health Education Act of 1986 in a way that parallels the changes it makes to the FCLAA. It sets out four different mandatory warnings, which must appear individually and on a rotating basis on the packages of smokeless tobacco products; specifies the size and form of the type; and gives FDA authority to promulgate rules that adjust the format and type sizes.[129] Section 205 amends the CSTHEA to enable FDA to use rulemaking to revise the warning statements on the label, conditioned on a finding that "such a change would promote greater public understanding of the risks associated with the use" of such products.

Other Specific Types of Tobacco Products. In addition to smokeless tobacco, several other particular categories of tobacco products are subject to special labeling requirements. These include tobacco products for which standards have been set,[130] new tobacco products,[131] and modified-risk tobacco products.[132]

Miscellaneous Labeling Requirements

Section 903(a)(2) requires the labels of tobacco products sold in package form to bear the name and place of business of the manufacturer, packer, or distributor, an accurate statement of the quantity of contents, and, in a bow to economic protectionism, the percentage of both domestic- and foreign-origin tobacco in the product.[133] The label must also carry the established name of the product in prominent type, as required by FDA regulations.[134]

Regulation of Advertising

Efforts to regulate the advertising of tobacco products on a nationwide basis began in 1964, when the FTC proposed a trade regulation rule that would have required health warnings on cigarette advertising as well as on packages.[135] The 1965 Federal Cigarette Labeling and Advertising Act temporarily barred the FTC from mandating health warnings

---

[128]   *See, e.g.,* Federal Trade Commission, Cigarettes: Testing for Tar and Nicotine Content, 32 Fed. Reg. 11,178 (Aug. 1, 1967).

[129]   As in the case of cigarettes, it also exempts manufacturers and distributors of products to be exported, and retailers who comply with certain requirements.

[130]   *See* FDCA § 907(a)(4)(C), 15 U.S.C. § 387g(a)(4)(C).

[131]   *See* FDCA § 910(b)(1)(F), 15 U.S.C. § 387j(b)(1)(F).

[132]   *See* FDCA § 911(d)(4), 15 U.S.C. § 387k(d)(4).

[133]   For a criticism of the latter requirement, *see* James T. O'Reilly, *supra* note 35, at 466.

[134]   FDCA § 903(a)(4), 21 U.S.C. § 387c(a)(4).

[135]   Federal Trade Commission, Trade Regulation Rule for the Prevention of Unfair or Deceptive Advertising and Marketing of Cigarettes in Relation to the Health Hazards of Smoking, 29 Fed. Reg. 8324, 8354 (1964).

in cigarette advertisements.[136] The 1969 Public Health Cigarette Smoking Act then extended the moratorium, and at the same time banned cigarette advertising from radio and television.[137] In 1972, the moratorium having expired, the FTC required the major cigarette companies to include health warnings in cigarette advertisements.[138] Twelve years later, the Comprehensive Smoking Education Act replaced the FTC-imposed rule with a requirement of rotational warnings for advertisements.[139]

A decade later, FDA took up the cudgels, and in 1996 promulgated regulations that would have placed sweeping limitations on the advertising and promotion of cigarettes and smokeless tobacco products to minors. The rules restricted to a black-on-white, text-only format advertisements that might reach the eyes of children, and placed limits on outdoor advertising, the distribution of promotional items (which might include tote bags and T-shirts), and the use of tobacco product brand names in the sponsoring of athletic, musical, or other performance events that might appeal to young audiences.[140] The United States Supreme Court then invalidated the regulations, on the ground that FDA had no authority to impose them.[141]

Illustrating the truth of the old saw that "the postman always rings twice," Congress included in the TCA a provision that directed FDA to revive its 1996 advertising regulations as part of an even more extensive effort to curb the promotion of tobacco products. Whereas FDA's original initiative confined itself to print advertisements aimed directly or indirectly at minors, the Tobacco Control Act recognized the harm that can also result from advertising aimed at consumers and potential customers who have reached the age of majority.[142] Thus, the reach of some of the advertising controls the act authorizes may affect the promotion of tobacco products to adults. Here the regulatory objective would be to make certain that adults capable of making a choice about whether to begin or continue smoking have a full and non-manipulated understanding of the extent and gravity of the health hazards involved.

The act nowhere defines "advertising," and often uses the broader term "promotion" to refer to efforts to expand a product's pool of consumers.[143] Thus, advertisements might be viewed as one form of promotion, through the use of various forms of communication to convey information or to cultivate a positive emotional response toward a product or a brand name.

---

[136]   Federal Cigarette Labeling and Advertising Act, § 10, Pub. L. No. 89-92, 79 Stat. 284 (1965).

[137]   Public Health Cigarette Smoking Act, § 6, Pub. L. No. 91-222, 84 Stat. 89 (1970).

[138]   *See* Lorillard et al., 80 F.T.C. 455, 460-65 (1972).

[139]   Comprehensive Smoking Education Act, § 4, Pub. L. No. 98-474, 98 Stat. 2201 (1984).

[140]   Food and Drug Administration, Regulations Restricting the Sale and Distribution of Cigarettes and Smokeless Tobacco to Protect Children and Adolescents, 61 Fed. Reg. 44,396, 44,617-618 (Aug. 28, 1996).

[141]   *See* Food and Drug Administration v. Brown & Williamson Tobacco Co., 529 U.S. 120 (2000).

[142]   Thus, section 2(16) cites promotional expenditures of more than $13 billion to "retain current users, increase current consumption, and generate favorable long-term attitudes toward smoking and tobacco use," as well as to entice new users. Section 2(27) alludes to international experience demonstrating that stringent advertising restrictions "have a greater impact on *overall tobacco use and* young people's use than weaker or less comprehensive ones." (Emphasis added.)

[143]   FDA uses the term "promotional labeling" for promotional forms of drug labeling that do not require premarket approval by the agency. The drug-advertising regulations give examples. On "promotional labeling," *see supra* Chapter 12.

Promotion would include not only advertisements but also non-media initiatives such as the distribution of free samples.

First of all, the TCA makes applicable to cigarette and smokeless-cigarette advertisements the warnings requirements applicable to the labels of those products. Secondly, it directs FDA to promulgate a final rule that incorporates regulations the agency had issued in 1996, with some limitations. In addition, it more broadly authorizes FDA to develop regulatory restrictions on the advertisement of any tobacco product, upon a finding that "such regulation would be appropriate for the protection of the public health."[144] With respect to advertisements and other descriptive printed material issued by the manufacturer, packer, or distributor, section 903(a)(8) mandates the inclusion of certain specific information. Finally, section 903(a)(7)(A) provides that a tobacco product is misbranded if its advertising is false or misleading in any particular.

Warnings

Section 201 of the TCA amends the Federal Cigarette Labeling and Advertising Act to require that advertisements of cigarettes bear the same cautionary statements as mandated for labeling. It makes allowances for different types of advertising[145] and foreign language publications.[146] The act authorizes FDA to use informal rulemaking to make adjustments in these requirements.[147] Advertisers must rotate warnings quarterly for each brand of cigarettes they advertise, in accordance with a plan submitted to and approved by FDA.[148] Section 204 amends the CSTHEA to require smokeless tobacco advertisements to bear the same warning statements as those required for labels, with similar adjustments. It also bans radio and television advertisements for those kinds of products.[149] These provisions coordinate the regulation of labels and advertisements, as well as the label and advertising requirements imposed on cigarettes and smokeless tobacco.

Implementation of FDA Regulations

Section 102 of the TCA directs FDA to publish as a final rule, and with certain designated exceptions[150] and changes, section 897 of its 1995 regulations, which place restrictions on the sale, distribution, and use of cigarettes and smokeless tobacco. It also specifies the procedure that the agency must use in promulgating the rule. Finally, it provides that the preambles to the proposed and final 1996 rule, and supporting documents on the jurisdictional justification for the rule, should not be considered FDA advisory opinions,

---

[144] FDCA § 906(d)(1), 21 U.S.C. § 387f(d)(1).

[145] *See* Federal Cigarette Labeling and Advertising Act, § 4(b)(2), 15 U.S.C. § 1333(b)(2) (authorizing FDA to revise type sizes as the agency deems appropriate).

[146] FCLAA § 4(b)(2)(A), (B), 15 U.S.C. § 1333(b)(2)(A), (B).

[147] FCLAA § 4 (b)(4), 15 U.S.C. § 1333(b)(4).

[148] FCLAA § 4(c)(2), 15 U.S.C. § 1333(4)(c)(2).

[149] CSTHEA, § 3(c), 15 U.S.C. § 4402(c).

[150] As with labeling, section 102(a)(2)(B) eliminates the requirement in 21 C.F.R. § 897.32(c) that certain established names would have to be used in advertising, which would also have to carry the identifier: "Nicotine Delivery Device for Persons 18 or Older."

except as they relate to tobacco products. In the spring of 2010 FDA published regulations that implemented section 102.[151]

Advertising and Promotional Media. Section 1140.30 of the implementing regulations lists media where advertising of cigarettes, and smokeless tobacco may be disseminated: newspapers, magazines, and other publications; billboards, posters, and placards; non-point-of-sale promotional material; point-of-sale promotional material; and audio or visual formats delivered at point of sale. To disseminate this type of advertising in media not specifically listed requires prior notice to FDA.[152] These restrictions also apply to labeling.

Limitations on Form and Content. Section 1140.32 provides that advertising (as well as labeling) must use only black text on a white background. Exempted from this restriction are ads in facilities where machines and self-service displays are permitted, and in publications whose readership is primarily adult. Audio formats may have only words, with no music or sound effects. Video formats may have only static black text on a white background.

Indirect Promotion. Section 1140.34(a) prohibits the promotion of cigarettes or smokeless tobacco by marketing other products or services that carry the brand name, logo, symbol, motto, or any other indicia of product recognition of a particular brand of cigarette or smokeless tobacco. Section 1140.34(b) forbids the offering of any other item in exchange for the purchase of cigarettes or smokeless tobacco. This eliminates both point-of-sales and non-point-of-sales rewards programs. Section 1140.34(c) prohibits tobacco companies from sponsoring "any athletic, musical, artistic, or other social or cultural event," or any team or entry bearing any indication of product identification with any brand of cigarettes or smokeless tobacco.[153]

Outdoor Advertising. Section 897.30(b) of the 1995 regulations provided that outdoor advertising of cigarettes and smokeless tobacco could not be situated within 1,000 feet of a public playground or playground area in a public park. Section 102 of the statute directs FDA to modify this rule in accordance with governing First Amendment case law. The FDA regulation implementing the 1995 rules opted for further consideration of constitutional objections that have been directed at restrictions on outdoor advertising.[154]

Procedural Requirements. Section 102 of the TCA allowed FDA to implement its 1995 regulations by publishing a final rule, without having to repeat the notice-and-comment

---

[151] Food and Drug Administration, Regulations Restricting the Sale and Distribution of Cigarettes and Smokeless Tobacco to Protect Children and Adolescents, 75 Fed. Reg. 13,225 (Mar. 19, 2010).

[152] Notification must also include the extent to which the advertising might be seen by persons below the age of 18.

[153] An exception is made for sponsorship of such events, teams, or entries in the name of a corporation manufacturing a tobacco product where the corporate name and corporation were registered and in use in the U.S. before January 1, 1995, and the corporate name does not contain anything that might identify any brand of cigarettes or smokeless tobacco.

[154] *See* Food and Drug Administration, Advance Notice of Proposed Rulemaking: Request for Comment on Implementation of the Family Smoking Prevention and Tobacco Control Act, 75 Fed. Reg. 13,241 (Mar. 19, 2010). In this regard, section 102(a)(2)(E) of the statute specifically directs FDA to consider the holding of the United States Supreme Court in *Lorillard Tobacco Co. v. Reilly*, 533 U.S. 525 (2001).

process that preceded the formulation of the prior regulations.[155] Moreover, it also relieved FDA from having to comply with the detailed congressional review provisions of Title 5, section 801 of the U.S. Code.[156]

Preambles to the 1996 Regulations. Preambles to proposed and final FDA regulations are ordinarily treated as advisory opinions issued by the agency.[157] However, section 102(b) provides that the preambles to the proposed and final 1996 regulations, as well as the accompanying documents arguing that nicotine is a drug and cigarettes are drug-delivery devices, do not constitute advisory opinions, except as they relate to tobacco products, and cannot be cited by the Secretary of Health and Human Services or FDA as binding precedent.[158]

General Authority to Regulate Advertising

Section 906(d)(1) of the FDCA gives FDA broad authority to promulgate rules putting restrictions on the advertising and promotion of tobacco products upon a finding that "such regulation would be appropriate for the protection of the public health." The act requires that any limitations be consistent with the First Amendment, a proposition that would not seem to require iteration. FDA would have to consider "the risks and benefits to the population as a whole," the likelihood or improbability that existing consumers would stop using the products, and the likelihood or improbability that non-consumers would begin using the products.

Inclusion of Specific Information

Section 903(a)(8) provides that a tobacco product is misbranded if advertisements (as well as other descriptive printed matter issued by the manufacturer, packer, or distributor) do not include the product's established name,[159] a brief indication of its intended uses, and warnings, precautions, side effects, and contraindications relevant to the product.

---

[155] This prevented interested parties from having further input. FDA justified this expedited procedure by pointing to the more than 700,000 comments it received in the process of publishing the 1996 regulations. See Food and Drug Administration, *supra* note 151, at 13,226.

[156] TCA § 102(a)(7).

[157] 21 C.F.R. § 10.85(d)(1).

[158] It is difficult to imagine a scenario in which these documents might serve as a precedent binding on FDA with respect to the regulation of non-tobacco products. Hence, this provision might be expressive only, stressing once again the uniqueness of tobacco regulation.

[159] The Tobacco Control Act nowhere defines the term "established name." The FDCA elsewhere defines "established name" as the term applies to drugs and devices. See § 522(e)(3), (4), 21 U.S.C. § 352(e)(3), (4). The only portion of these definitions that would plausibly apply to tobacco products incorporates the "common or usual name" of the drug or device as its "established name." *See id.* Section 508 specifically grants FDA the legal authority to designate the established name of a drug or device through informal rulemaking. FDA has implied such authority to designate common or usual names for foods via informal rulemaking. See American Frozen Food Institute v. Mathews, 413 F. Supp. 548 (D.D.C. 1976), *aff'd* sub nom. American Frozen Food Institute v. Califano, 555 F.2d 1059 (D.C. Cir. 1977), upholding FDA's authority to do so.

Distribution Controls

One reason for FDA's original choice to regulate cigarettes as medical devices was the availability of existing statutory provisions that empower the agency to restrict distribution of devices,[160] authority FDA would not have enjoyed if it had classified cigarettes as "drugs."[161] Moreover, the 1996 rules were meant to protect minors, which would have been very difficult to do without restricting how these products might get into the hands of underage consumers.

The TCA shares this goal, and hence places limitations on the distributors[162] and retailers[163] who form the links between manufacturers and consumers. The act does so in four ways. First, as in the case of advertising, it directs FDA to promulgate the distribution requirements and restrictions that the 1996 regulations would have imposed. Second, it puts limitations on the distribution of free samples. Third, it authorizes FDA to promulgate additional restrictions on the sale and distribution of tobacco products. Finally, it requires FDA to develop new regulations governing non-face-to-face contacts between retailers and consumers.

Implementation of the 1996 Regulations

Sections 102(a)(1) and (2) of the statute oblige FDA to re-promulgate its 1996 regulations dealing with the distribution of cigarettes and smokeless tobacco. The agency fulfilled this requirement in regulations published in 2010,[164] and issued a draft guidance a year later.[165] Both deal with matters such as age limits, non-face-to-face sales and retailer responsibilities.

Age Limits. FDA regulations now prohibit retailers from selling cigarettes or smokeless tobacco to anyone younger than 18 years of age, and mandate that retailers require photographic identification for purchasers under the age of 26. Section 916(a)(1) of the FDCA reserves to the states and their political subdivisions the authority to enact more stringent age requirements for tobacco-product purchases.

---

[160]   *See* FDCA § 520(e)(1), 21 U.S.C. § 360j(e)(1).

[161]   For a judicial rejection of an attempt by FDA to exercise distribution controls over drugs by implication, *see* American Pharmaceutical Ass'n v. Weinberger, 377 F. Supp. 824 (D.D.C. 1974), *aff'd*, 530 F.2d 1054 (D.C. Cir. 1976) (per curiam).

[162]   The statute defines a "distributor" as "any person who furthers the distribution of a tobacco product, whether domestic or imported, at any point from the original point of manufacture to the person who sells or distributes the product to individuals for personal consumption." FDCA § 900(7), 21 U.S.C. § 387(7). Common carriers are specifically exempted. *Id.*

[163]   The statute defines a retailer as "any person, government, or entity who sells tobacco products to individuals for personal consumption, or who operates a facility where self-service displays of tobacco products are permitted." FDCA § 900(14), 21 U.S.C. § 387(14).

[164]   Food and Drug Administration, *supra* note 154.

[165]   FDA, Draft Guidance for Industry: Compliance with Regulations Restricting the Sale and Distribution of Cigarettes and Smokeless Tobacco to Protect Children and Adolescents [Revisions to Draft Guidance] (March 2011), www.fda.gov/downloads/TobaccoProducts/GuidanceComplianceRegulatoryInformation/UCM248241.pdf. This guidance spells out FDA's thinking as to the meaning and application of its re-published regulations. It contains a number of specific examples, along with the agency's view as to the line between what is legally permitted and what amounts to a violation of the act.

Non-Face-to-Face Sales. Section 897.16(c) of the 1996 regulations, republished as 21 C.F.R. § 1140.16(c), permits sales of cigarettes and smokeless tobacco only in face-to-face exchanges between retailers and customers. One exception to this ban is the use of vending machines and self-service displays, if the responsible retailer can ensure that persons under 18 years of age will not have access to them. Another is the use of mail-order sales, although the regulations prohibit the mail-order redemption of coupons and the sending of free samples through the mail.

Free Samples

Section 897.16(d) of the 1996 rules contained a flat ban on the distribution of free samples of cigarettes and smokeless tobacco. Section 101(a)(1)(G) of the TCA directs FDA to amend the ban by subjecting other tobacco products to the prohibition, and by creating an exception for smokeless tobacco in a "qualified adult-only facility," defined at some length in such a way as to try to make sure that minors would not have access to the samples.[166] Samples may not be distributed to any sports team or entertainment group, and "at any football, basketball, baseball, soccer or hockey event or any other sporting or entertainment event determined by [FDA]."[167]

General Restrictions on Sales and Distribution

Section 906(d)(1) of the FDCA gives FDA broad authority to promulgate regulations restricting the sale and distribution of tobacco products, if the agency can justify a finding that they are "appropriate for the protection of the public health." As in the case of regulations restricting the advertising and promotion of tobacco products, a determination of appropriateness must derive from consideration of the increased or decreased odds that current consumers would cease their consumption of the products,[168] and the increased or decreased odds that non-consumers might begin to consume them.[169] The one limitation that the act bars FDA from imposing is sale by prescription only.[170]

New Tobacco Products

When Congress imposed new rules on the manufacturers of new drugs and certain medical devices, by requiring premarket approval for efficacy in the case of the former and premarket clearance for both safety and efficacy for certain devices, it also made these obligations apply retroactively.[171] This served to provide consumers with the benefit of demonstrated efficacy with respect to both older and newer drugs.

---

[166] The number and size of the samples allowed to be taken out of the facility are also severely restricted. It will obviously be extremely difficult, as a practical matter, to enforce these limitations. Section 897.16(d)(4) of the regulation requires FDA to implement a program to ensure compliance with the rules on free samples, and to report back to Congress with 18 months of the enactment of the TCA.

[167] 21 C.F.R. § 897.16(d)(3).

[168] FDCA § 906(d)(1)(A), 21 U.S.C. § 387f(d)(1)(A).

[169] FDCA § 906(d)(1)(B), 21 U.S.C. § 387f(d)(1)(B).

[170] *Id.* § 906(d)(1), 21 U.S.C. § 387f(d)(1).

[171] *See* Peter Barton Hutt, Richard A. Merrill & Lewis A. Grossman, *supra* note 72, at 580-81, 987-89.

Another reason for this was to allow manufacturers of new drugs and risk-generating devices introduced into the marketplace after the effective date of the new rules to compete on a level playing field with marketers of new drugs and potentially hazardous devices already in the stream of commerce. However, the same concern clearly does not animate provisions in the TCA dealing with new tobacco products, which must surmount restrictions that do not apply to tobacco products marketed before February 15, 2007. This may reflect a recognition on the part of Congress that except in the case of modified-risk tobacco products, there are no persuasive policy reasons to encourage the development of new products with serious inherent risks and questionable benefits by putting them on an equal footing with competitors, or it may reflect a political trade-off to help secure the enactment of the bill.

The Tobacco Control Act defines what constitutes a "new tobacco product," and directs FDA to grant or deny premarket approval to tobacco products deemed "new" in accordance with specified standards and procedures.

Definition of a "New Tobacco Product"

Section 910(a)(1) defines a "new tobacco product" as a tobacco product either not commercially available in the United States before February 15, 2007, or a tobacco product marketed before that date and subject to modification after that date. Examples of modification include any change in overall design, the change of a component, part or constituent, a change in the content, delivery, or form of nicotine, or any other additive or ingredient. How FDA will interpret the term "modification" will be of critical import because of the onerous regulatory obligations that the law imposes on "new tobacco products."[172]

Exemptions from Requirement of Premarket Approval

There are two ways by which a manufacturer can avoid having to secure premarket approval of a "new tobacco product." First, it can make a showing that the product is substantially equivalent to a tobacco product marketed before February 15, 2007. This approach is modeled after the system of premarket notification in the medical device section of the act.[173] Second, the manufacturer can demonstrate that the product falls within a special exemption.

Substantial Equivalence. Under section 905(j), a manufacturer wishing to market a new tobacco product deemed substantially similar to a tobacco product in commercial distribution before February 15, 2007,[174] must submit to FDA a report explaining the basis for that

---

[172]   An FDA guidance document states that the agency does not presently intend to enforce the "new tobacco product" rules in cases of blending changes required to deal with natural variations in tobacco in order to maintain a consistent product. See Food and Drug Administration, Guidance for Industry and FDA Staff, Section 905(j) Reports: Demonstrating Substantial Equivalence for Tobacco Products 4 (Jan. 5, 2011), http://www.fda.gov/TobaccoProducts/GuidanceComplianceRegulatoryInformation/ucm238876.htm. This suggests a very broad reading of "modification." The question remains open whether changes in a product made necessary by the act will also constitute "modification." A strong argument based on the element of legal compulsion can be made that it does not.

[173]   See FDCA § 510(k), 21 U.S.C. § 360(k).

[174]   The act permits "piggy-backing," in the sense that substantial similarity to a product marketed after February 15, 2007, and subsequently found to be substantially similar to a product marketed before that date will also satisfy the requirement. FDCA § 905(j)(1)(A)(i), 21 U.S.C. § 387e(j)(1)(A)(i). For FDA's views

determination.[175] Section 910(a)(3)(A) defines the latter term as requiring the possession of the same characteristics as the predicate tobacco product, that is, the product to which the new tobacco product is substantially similar. Subsection (B) defines "characteristics" as "materials, ingredients, design, composition, heating source, or other features of a tobacco product." If the product characteristics are different, substantial equivalence may still be found if the new tobacco product does not raise questions of public health that are different from those raised by the predicate product.[176] Section 910(a)(3)(C) bars a finding of substantial equivalence if FDA had removed the predicate tobacco product from the market, or if a court decision had found it to be adulterated or misbranded.

Special Exemption. Section 905(j)(3) authorizes FDA to exempt from the premarket approval requirements a tobacco product modified by the adding or deleting of a tobacco additive, or the changing of the amount of an existing additive, on findings that the modification was minor, filing a report under this section would not be necessary to establish that allowing the product onto the market would be appropriate for safeguarding the public health, and an exemption would otherwise be appropriate. The minor-modification exemption has the potential to become a major gateway, if FDA defines the term broadly.

Premarket Approval

If a manufacturer of a new tobacco product cannot establish the requisite substantial equivalence and cannot qualify for an exemption, the only remaining recourse is to apply to FDA for premarket approval. Given the difficulty and cost of compliance with the new rules, it seems likely that they will see infrequent use.

What an Application Must Include. Section 910(b)(1) mandates the submission of an application containing full reports of information showing the health risks linked to the product and an indication that these risks are less than those attributable to other tobacco products;[177] a full description of the components, ingredients, additives, and properties of the new tobacco product and a description of how it operates; a full account of how it is manufactured, processed, and, if relevant, packed and installed; a reference to any applicable tobacco product standard and information to demonstrate that either the new product conforms to it or why any deviation from the standard is justifiable; product samples and any other information FDA might request.

---

on one aspect of substantial equivalence, *see* FDA, Draft Guidance for Industry and Staff: Establishing that a Tobacco Product was Commercially Marketed in the United States as of February 15, 2007 (Apr. 22, 2011), http://www.fda.gov/downloads/TobaccoProducts/ResourcesforYou/For Industry/ucm252235.pdf.

[175] For FDA's current thinking, *see* FDA, Guidance for Industry and FDA Staff: Section 905(j) Reports: Demonstrating Substantial Equivalence for Tobacco Products (Jan. 5, 2011), http://www.fda.gov/downloads/TobaccoProducts/GuidanceComplianceRegulatoryInformation/ucm239021.pdf. For a criticism of aspects of the Guidance Document, *see* William McGrath & Nick Peterson, *A Look at FDA's New Substantial Equivalence Requirements for Tobacco Products*, UPDATE, May/June 2011, at 25.

[176] FDCA § 910(a)(3)(A)(ii), 21 U.S.C. § 387j(a)(3)(A)(ii). Public health concerns might relate both to the type and the gravity of the inherent risks in the product. Both would be relevant to a finding of similarity.

[177] Unlike the requirements of proof of substantial similarity, this provision of the act does not specify to what other tobacco products a new tobacco product should be compared. This opens up the possibility that FDA might prioritize public health protection and use as a predicate the least risky type of tobacco product currently on the market.

Standards for Denial. Under section 910(b)(2), FDA must deny the application if there is no proof that letting the product on the market would be appropriate for the protection of the public health; if the methods used to manufacture, process, or pack the product do not conform to the Good Manufacturing Practice requirements of section 906(e); if the proposed labeling is false or misleading in any particular; or if the new product does not meet an applicable product standard.

Meaning of "Appropriate for the Protection of the Public Health." The critical part of the standard for the approval for new tobacco products is the meaning of the phrase "appropriate for the protection of the public health." This is the same test FDA must meet in order to justify regulations placing restrictions on the advertising, promotion, and distribution of tobacco products under section 906(d)(1), and when promulgating tobacco product standards under section 907(a)(3). The agency must consider whether existing users of tobacco products will stop using those products, and whether non-consumers will begin to use them.

Procedures for Withdrawal. Section 910(d) sets out procedures for the withdrawal or temporary suspension of new tobacco products previously approved by FDA. The agency must first submit the issue to the Tobacco Products Scientific Advisory Committee, and then provide an opportunity for an informal hearing.[178] On the basis of the facts before it, including the recommendation of the Advisory Committee and any additional information and argumentation that surfaced at the hearing, FDA will then make its determination.

Standards for Withdrawal. FDA may then withdraw its approval order if the agency can conclude that keeping the product on the market would no longer be appropriate to protect the public health; the application contained an untrue statement of a material fact; the applicant's conduct fell below standards set out elsewhere in the act;[179] or that certain new information[180] has surfaced, justifying the withdrawal.

Temporary Suspension. Section 910(d)(3) enables FDA, after giving an opportunity for an informal hearing, to suspend on a temporary basis a premarket approval order, if the continued marketing of the product "would cause serious adverse health consequences or death, that is greater than ordinarily caused by tobacco products on the market."

Modified-Risk Tobacco Products

Amid the lengthy list of findings of fact in the TCA are eight that express serious congressional concern about the marketing of tobacco products for which manufacturers make assertions that they reduce risks or exposures to risks inherent in similar products, and about the harm this can cause to the public health if the claims made for them do not come to fruition

---

[178]   Since these procedures will be "informal," they presumably will not be in the nature of trial-type adversarial hearings before an administrative law judge.

[179]   The specific provisions cited are FDCA § 909, 21 U.S.C. 387i, requiring the maintenance and making of reports; FDCA § 704, 21 U.S.C. § 374, requiring access to, copying, or verification of records; and *id.* § 905, 21 U.S.C. § 387e, requiring annual registration.

[180]   The new information must involve good manufacturing practices, as specified in *id.* § 906(e), 21 U.S.C. § 387f(e); the labeling of the product; or the product's conformity to an applicable tobacco product standard.

or consumers misunderstand them.[181] To deal with this problem, the act includes a set of comprehensive, richly detailed directives that create a demanding approach to premarket approval for what are termed "modified-risk tobacco products."[182]

Thus, modified-risk tobacco products join new tobacco products in triggering a requirement of premarket approval.[183] There are some similarities in the applicable rules, but the regime for modified-risk products is much more comprehensive.

Premarket Approval

Premarket Approval. The act first defines "modified-risk tobacco products," to which the requirement of premarket approval will apply. It then sets out the procedures that applicants and FDA must follow and the substantive standards the agency must apply in passing judgment on the application. Finally, it establishes a special exception applicable to certain modified-risk products.

Definition. A "modified risk tobacco product" is one which a manufacturer markets with a claim that it is less risky than other similar products, or causes less exposure to a substance of substances (presumably that are harmful or potentially harmful).[184] The representation may be made through a label, labeling, advertising, or, after the enactment of the TCA, any other action directed by the manufacturer to consumers.[185] Thus, the definition covers new tobacco products as well as tobacco products already on the market. Moreover, the definition would apply if the label, labeling, or advertising uses the descriptive terms "light," "mild," "low," or a similar adjective.[186]

Application Process. Section 911(d) mandates submissions of applications that contain a description of the product and the proposed labeling and advertising; the conditions for its use; its formulation; sample labels and labeling; all health-related documents (favorable or unfavorable, and including scientific data) relating to the capacity of the product to reduce risk or exposure and relating to human health; data concerning how consumers actually use the product; and any other information FDA may require. The agency must make this information available to the public, subject to protections normally afforded trade secrets and otherwise confidential commercial information, and solicit comments about this material

---

[181] TCA, Pub. L. No. 111-31, §§ 36-43, 123 Stat. 1776, 1779-80 (2009).

[182] For a discussion of an unsuccessful constitutional challenge to the premarket approval requirement, *see infra* note 226 and accompanying text.

[183] A third class of tobacco products, which meet the definition of "drug" under the FDCA, are subject to the standards and procedures applicable to the premarket approval of new drugs. FDCA §§ 201(rr)(2)-(3), 21 U.S.C. §§ 321(rr)(2)-(3).

[184] FDCA § 911 (b), 21 U.S.C. § 387k(b). Section 911(b)(2)(C) exempts smokeless tobacco products from the statutory definition of modified-risk tobacco products even though their label, labeling, or advertising uses the terms "smokeless tobacco," "smokeless tobacco product," "not consumed by smoking," "does not produce smoke," "smokefree," "smoke-free," "without smoke," "no smoke," or "not smoke." The act does not specify what would qualify as a predicate product. Logic would seem to suggest that it should be similar in type to the product for which the claim is being made.

[185] FDCA § 911(b)(2)(A)(iii), 21 U.S.C. § 387k(b)(2)(A)(iii).

[186] FDCA § 911 (b)(2)(A)(ii), 21 U.S.C. § 387k(b)(2)(A)(ii).

and about the label, labeling, and advertising samples included in the application. FDA must also submit the application to the Tobacco Products Scientific Advisory Committee for review and recommendation.

Standard for Approval. The test FDA must use to determine whether or not to approve an application to market a modified-risk tobacco product is whether it will "significantly reduce harm and the risk of tobacco-related disease to individual tobacco users,"[187] and will "benefit the health of the population as a whole taking into account both users of tobacco products and persons who do not currently use tobacco products."[188] The burden of proof here falls on the applicant.[189]

Special Rules for Certain Products. Section 911(g)(2) creates an exception for applicants unable to meet the requirements for modified-risk tobacco products. To qualify, four conditions must be met. FDA must determine: 1) that an approval order would promote the public health; 2) that what makes the label, labeling, and advertising qualify the product for modified-risk treatment arises from explicit or implicit representations that the product or its smoke does not contain, or contains a reduced level of, a substance or presents a reduced exposure to a substance in tobacco smoke;[190] 3) that the only available evidence to show this would have to derive from long-term epidemiological studies; and 4) that the only other scientific evidence available indicates that "a measurable and substantial reduction in morbidity or mortality among individual users is reasonably likely in subsequent studies."[191]

Conditions of Marketing for Special Cases. Section 911(g)(2)(C) provides that approval under these special rules will last only for a five-year term, subject to renewal; and the applicant must conduct postmarket surveillance and studies, and submit results of them to FDA annually.

Additional Conditions for Marketing All Modified-Risk Products. Section 911(h) spells out additional preconditions for the marketing of modified-risk tobacco products. They include proof that the advertising, and labeling of the product will enable the public to understand the information conveyed about modified risk and the relative importance of this information in relation both to overall health and the tobacco-related diseases and conditions. In addition, FDA may exercise regulatory oversight over comparative claims

---

[187]   FDCA § 911(g)(1)(A), 21 U.S.C. § 387k(g)(1)(A).

[188]   FDCA § 911(g)(1)(B), 21 U.S.C. § 387k(g)(1)(B).

[189]   *See* FDCA § 911(g)(1), 21 U.S.C. § 387k(g)(1).

[190]   Presumably this substance must be in some way harmful.

[191]   This section also requires FDA to make a number of other findings, which include a determination that the applicant has established that the size of the overall reductions in the substance or substances cited in the application is substantial, the substance is harmful, and the product actually exposes users to the specified reduced level; the product as actually used by consumers will not subject them to more than minimal higher levels of other harmful substances when compared to other similar types of tobacco product on the market, and the reasonably expectable overall impact of the use of the product would be a substantial, measurable reduction in overall morbidity and mortality; testing of actual consumer perception of the label and promotion of the product would not create the misleading impression that the product is or has been shown to be less harmful, or is or has been shown to present less of a risk of disease than one or more commercially available tobacco products; and approval is expected to benefit the overall health of Americans, taking into account both users and current non-users of tobacco products.

and quantitative comparisons, and require additional label disclosures and labeling about conditions of use.

Postmarket Obligations. Under section 911(i), FDA must require postmarket surveillance and studies, and annual submissions of results.[192] The required focus here is on consumer perception, behavior, and health, for the purpose of enabling FDA to review the soundness of its premarket approval.

Withdrawal of Authorization. If FDA determines that it has grounds to withdraw its approval of an application to make modified-risk claims, section 911(j) provides that it must first give the applicant the opportunity for an informal hearing.[193] The agency must then decide whether to take the product off the market. The grounds for withdrawal are: new information indicating that FDA can no longer make the findings it had to make under section 911(g); the subsequent discovery of the absence of material information, or the inclusion of any untrue statement of a material fact, in the application; a finding that a representation that the product reduces risk or exposure is no longer valid; or the applicant's failure to conduct required postmarket surveillance or submit results of it or of any other required studies.

Drugs Intended to Treat Tobacco Dependence

Section 918 directs FDA to consider classifying new drug products for smoking cessation, including nicotine-replacement products, as fast-track research and approval products within the scope of section 506. It also mandates that FDA give thought to authorizing the prolonged use of nicotine-replacement products such as patches, gums, and lozenges, for the treatment of tobacco dependence, and of evidence for additional indications for nicotine-replacement products, such as for relief of craving, and relapse avoidance. Finally, it calls on FDA to prepare and submit to Congress a report on how best to regulate, promote, and spur the development of innovative products and treatment to achieve total abstinence from tobacco use, reductions in tobacco consumption, and reductions in the harm caused by continued tobacco use.

Postmarketing Controls

The Tobacco Control Act creates two types of postmarketing controls that FDA might exercise over all tobacco products. Section 908 permits the agency to notify the public of a risk discovered after a tobacco product has entered the stream of commerce, or to order a recall of the product. Section 909 requires manufacturers and importers to notify FDA about adverse reactions that they have discovered after the products linked to them

---

[192]   Applicants must submit in advance surveillance protocols, which FDA must approve.

[193]   This is similar to an analogous requirement providing an opportunity for a hearing on the withdrawal of the approval of a new tobacco product, discussed *supra* at note 178 and accompanying text.

entered the marketplace. In addition, section 911 imposes extra postmarketing mandates on manufacturers of modified-risk tobacco products.

Notice Requirements

Section 908(a) mirrors language in section 518(a) dealing with medical devices.[194] It enables FDA to order the issuance of warnings relating to product-related risks that have come to light after the initial marketing of the product. FDA must make two factual findings: the product must "present an unreasonable risk of substantial harm to the public";[195] and notification must be both "necessary" and "the most practicable means" for eliminating that risk.[196] Once it has made these determinations, FDA may require that notification be given "in an appropriate form by the persons and means best suited under the circumstances involved, to all persons who should properly receive such notification in order to eliminate such risk."[197] One method of notification—public-service announcements—is specifically mentioned as an option.

Recalls

As in the case of notification, the TCA borrows liberally from the medical device section of the FDCA to give FDA authority to mandate recalls of tobacco products.[198] The agency must first make a finding of a reasonable probability that "serious adverse health consequences or death" would result from "a manufacturing or other defect not ordinarily contained in tobacco products on the market."[199] An order based on this finding must target an "appropriate person (including the manufacturers, importers, distributors, or retailers of the tobacco product)," and must call for an immediate cessation of distribution. The act then gives any person subject to the order an opportunity for an informal hearing within 10 days of the issuance of the directive. At issue in the hearing would be whether the actions required by the order are appropriate, and whether the order should be amended to include a recall.

If FDA opts to go ahead with a recall, the agency must develop a time table and require progress reports. Recalls may not reach down to the level of individual purchasers, and must include notification to persons put at risk by the use of the product. If these individuals cannot be found, FDA is authorized to contact them through the use of its authority to generate publicity, as spelled out in section 705(b), which contains a further limitation, to the effect that the product put consumers in "imminent danger to health."

---

[194] The two sections are nearly identical. Section 518(a), however, takes into account a role for health professionals, and recognizes that there may be instances in which notification might create additional risks for persons in whom medical devices have been implanted.

[195] FDCA § 908(a)(1), 21 U.S.C. § 387h(a)(1).

[196] FDCA § 908(a)(2), 21 U.S.C. § 387h(a)(2).

[197] *Id.*

[198] *See* FDCA § 518(e), 21 U.S.C. § 360h(e).

[199] FDCA § 908(c)(1), 21 U.S.C. § 387h(c)(1).

Miscellaneous Provisions

Tobacco Products Scientific Advisory Committee

Section 917 directs FDA to set up a 12-member Tobacco Products Scientific Advisory Committee (TPSAC). The responsibilities of the committee are to furnish FDA with advice, recommendations, and information, as specifically provided for in the act, on the effects of reducing nicotine levels in tobacco products, on the possibility of finding a nicotine level that will not produce tobacco dependence, and on any other issues as requested by FDA.[200] The provisions of the act that call for input from the committee include sections 906(e) (1)(B)(i) (good manufacturing practice requirements), 907(d)(1) and (5) (tobacco product standards), 907(e)(1) (menthol cigarettes), 910(b)(2) (new tobacco products), and 911(f) (modified-risk tobacco products).

Committee members must have appropriate technical expertise and "appropriately diversified professional backgrounds."[201] However, the diversity requirement does not extend to interest-group representation, at least with respect to voting. The Act designates the appointment of one individual to represent the general public as a voting member, and three representatives of various industry groups as non-voting members only.[202] The voters are subject to a conflict-of-interest provision that bars individuals who have received money or support from the tobacco industry for the 18-month span before, and during, their committee membership.[203]

Alleged conflicts of interest on the TPSAC have already sparked litigation. *Lorillard, Inc. v. United States Food and Drug Administration*[204] involved a challenge to the appointment of three voting members and to a report it sent to FDA recommending the banning of menthol cigarettes. Relying on applicable provisions of the Federal Advisory Committee Act,[205] the court ruled that service as witnesses for plaintiffs in personal-injury suits against the tobacco industry and consultancies for companies seeking expert advice on nicotine-replacement therapies and other smoking-cessation products amounted to an impermissible conflict that disqualified them from committee membership and irrevocably tainted the menthol report, which will need to be re-done.

User Fees

Section 919 establishes a schedule of user fees to be assessed against the manufacturers and importers of tobacco products. A unique aspect of the system of users fees established by the TCA is the requirement that they be the sole source of federal funds available for the regulation of tobacco products.[206] According to subsection (b)(3), fees are to be calculated according to the type of product being made or imported, and the percentage of market share, based on the total volume of domestic sales of the class of product during the fiscal

---

[200] FDCA § 917(c), 21 U.S.C. § 387q(c).
[201] FDCA § 917(b)(1)(A), 21 U.S.C. § 387q(b)(1)(A).
[202] *Id.*
[203] FDCA § 917(b)(1)(C), 21 U.S.C. § 387q(b)(1)(C).
[204] No. 11-440 (D.D.C. July 21, 2014).
[205] Pub. L. No. 92-463, 86 Stat. 770, 5 U.S.C §§ 1-16 (1972).
[206] FDCA § 919(c)(2)(B)(i), 21 U.S.C. § 387s(c)(2)(B)(i).

year.[207] Failure to pay user fees will cause a manufacturer's or importer's products to be considered adulterated under section 902(4).

Prevention of Illicit Trade

Although the TCA explicitly bars FDA from banning cigarettes and other specific tobacco products,[208] and from mandating that nicotine yields of a tobacco product be reduced to zero,[209] the act does prohibit the sale of many kinds of flavored cigarettes.[210] It also imposes on manufacturers a number of costly obligations, which could in turn force them to discontinue the marketing of certain tobacco products or to increase prices. In the latter instance, some consumers may not be able to afford these items. Both unavailability and unaffordability could give rise to illegal commerce.

To deal with this possibility, the TCA includes several provisions aimed at discouraging the illegal trade of tobacco products. They include requirements of origin labeling,[211] record-keeping to monitor the commercial movement of tobacco products,[212] and access to certain records when FDA has reason to believe that the product is part of illegal trade or is counterfeit.[213]

Preemption

The preemption provision in section 5 of the Federal Cigarette Labeling and Advertising Act declares that "(a) No statement relating to smoking and health, other than the statement required by . . . this Act, shall be required on any cigarette package." According to subsection (b), "No requirement or prohibition based on smoking and health shall be imposed under State law with respect to the advertising or promotion of any cigarettes the packages of which are labeled in conformity with the provisions of this Act."[214] The United States Supreme Court has held that when Congress expressly preempts certain state action, the courts may not invoke the doctrine of implied preemption to bar additional state activity.[215] It also held

---

[207]   The calculation is to be made under terms spelled out in the American Jobs Creation Act §§ 625(e)-(h), Pub. L. No. 108-357, 118 Stat. 1418 (2004).

[208]   FDCA § 907(d)(3)(A), 21 U.S.C. § 387g(d)(3)(A). Also exempted from banning are all smokeless tobacco products, all cigars except little cigars, all pipe tobacco, and all roll-your-own tobacco products.

[209]   FDCA § 907(d)(3)(B), 21 U.S.C. § 387g(d)(3)(B).

[210]   FDCA § 907(a)(1)(A), 21 U.S.C. § 387g(a)(1)(A). This section also specifies different effective dates for different types of tobacco products.

[211]   FDCA § 902(a), 21 U.S.C. §387t (a).

[212]   FDCA § 920(b), 21 U.S.C. §387t(b).

[213]   FDCA § 920(c), 21 U.S.C. §387t(c).

[214]   The Comprehensive Smokeless Tobacco Health Education Act has a similar preemption clause that excludes outdoor building advertisements. CSTHEA §§ 7(a)-(b), 15 U.S.C. §§ 4406(a)-(b).

[215]   Cipollone v. Liggett Group, Inc., 505 U.S. 504 (1992). Federal preemption derives from the Constitution's Supremacy Clause, which provides that the laws of the United States "shall be the supreme Law of the Land." U.S. Const., Art. VI, Cl. 2. It may arise from express language in a federal statute or by implication. See Lorillard Tobacco Co. v. Reilly, 533 U.S. 525, 541 (2001).

that subsection (b) of the FCLAA preempted only state action directly linked to advertising and promotion, and not to obligations other than those imposed by the FCLAA.[216]

When the tobacco industry challenged the Attorney General of Massachusetts when he promulgated regulations restricting outdoor cigarette advertising on billboards and certain practices dealing with the distribution and sales of cigarettes, the Supreme Court had another occasion to interpret the preemption provision of the FCLAA. In *Lorillard Tobacco Co. v. Reilly*,[217] the Court in a 5-4 decision interpreted the words "with respect to" broadly, and refused to distinguish, as defendants had urged, between the location of advertisements and their contents, and to limit preemption to state efforts to regulate only the former.

With the enactment of the Tobacco Control Act, the preemption panorama underwent a change. The act addressed the issue in three ways. First, it amended the preemption provisions in both the FCLAA and the CSTHEA, so that they no longer stand in the way of the new federal requirements and restrictions imposed on the labeling and advertising of cigarettes and smokeless tobacco by statute and FDA regulations. Second, it further amended the FCLAA and CSTHEA to allow states or localities to regulate the time, place, and manner of cigarette advertising. Third, it created a limited preemption scheme applicable to the regulation of tobacco products generally.

A Green Light for TCA Regulation of Labeling and Advertising

Sections 202 and 205 of the TCA coordinate the FCLAA and CSTHEA with the new regime of tobacco product regulation. They amend the preemption provisions in both statutes to accommodate both the new cigarette and smokeless-tobacco labeling and advertising requirements imposed by the Tobacco Control Act itself and the new authority that the latter statute gave to FDA for the imposition of further directives on the manufacturers of these products.[218]

"Time-Place-Manner" Barrier Removed

Section 203 of the Tobacco Control Act enables states and localities to pass laws and promulgate regulations putting bans or limitations on the "time, place, and manner, but not content, of the advertising or promotion of any cigarette." This provision removes the obstacle that *Lorillard Tobacco* had created, so that the preemption doctrine would no longer proscribe the type of billboard regulation imposed by the regulations of the Massachusetts Attorney General.[219]

---

[216] *Cipollone*'s main focus was on the preemption of state product-liability decisions that held a defendant liable for failing to take greater precautionary measures than those mandated by federal law or regulation. It held that the preemption clause of the FCLAA as first enacted did not preempt judicial impositions of tort liability for failure to include additional warnings on cigarette packages, but the amendments to the clause made by the Public Health Cigarette Smoking Act of 1969 did preempt certain kinds of tort liability.

[217] 533 U.S. 525, 541 (2001).

[218] Technically, what these amendments brought about did not fall within the ambit of federal preemption, which bans only state laws and regulations that conflict with federal directives or fall within certain defined areas of federal regulation.

[219] For a list of state advertisement regulations that the Tobacco Control Act might now permit, *see* Tobacco Control Legal Consortium, Federal Regulation of Tobacco: Impact on State and Local Authority, 6 (July 2009).

New Preemption Rules

In a somewhat awkward way, section 916 of the FDCA spells out a new set of preemption rules for all tobacco products. They erect a preemption barrier for certain kinds of regulation by entities other than FDA, and for products other than cigarettes and smokeless tobacco. The section first details the kinds of regulatory activity that will not be preempted. It then enumerates exceptions. It then specifies exceptions to the exceptions. Finally, it places product liability lawsuits outside the reach of federal preemption.

What Others Can Do. Section 916(a)(1) applies not only to states and their subdivisions, but also to federal agencies and Indian tribes. These entities many adopt and enforce laws, administrative rules, or other measures that are in addition to or more stringent than requirements imposed under the Tobacco Control Act. More specifically, they can take action "relating to or prohibiting the sale, distribution, exposure to, access to, advertising and promotion of, or use of tobacco products by individuals of any age, information reporting to the State, or measures relating to fire safety standards for tobacco products." Moreover, no part of the act may "limit or otherwise affect any State, tribal or local taxation of tobacco products."

What Others Cannot Do. After bestowing authority on other government entities to impose additional or stricter rules on sales, distribution, advertisements, and promotion, as well as reporting and fire safety, section 916(a)(2)(A) then imposes a broad preemption rule applicable to "tobacco product standards, premarket review, adulteration, misbranding, labeling, registration, good manufacturing standards, or modified risk products."

What Others Can Do (Revisited). In a disconcerting reversal of direction, section 916(a)(2)(B) then posits that the prohibitions in subsection (A) will not govern "requirements relating to the sale, distribution, possession, information reporting to the State, exposure to, access to, the advertising and promotion of, or use of, tobacco products by individuals of any age, or relating to fire safety standards for tobacco products." What this seems to suggest, for example, is that a state might regulate the advertising and promotion of a modified-risk product.

Products Liability. Section 916(b) makes clear that tobacco regulation under the act will not preempt "any action or the liability of any person under the product liability law of any State." This leaves the door open for state tort claims that a tobacco company should in the exercise of due care have included additional or more dramatic cautionary statements on the labeling or in the advertising of a tobacco product, and the failure to do so renders the company liable for money damages.[220] However, if in so doing a manufacturer would have committed an act prohibited by law, the courts should not imply preemption.

---

[220]   Section 916(b) would not affect the preemption provision of the FCLAA relating to cigarette labeling, since the former applies only to the preemption provisions in the TCA.

Constitutional Challenges

In 1999, the Attorney General of the Commonwealth of Massachusetts promulgated regulations limiting the advertising and sale of cigarettes, smokeless tobacco, and cigars. In response to an industry challenge, the United States Supreme Court held that the Federal Cigarette Labeling and Advertising Act preempted state regulation of cigarette advertising; and the First Amendment invalidated restrictions the regulations would have imposed on the outdoor and point-of-sale advertising of smokeless tobacco and cigars.[221] To support the latter holding, the Court applied the commercial speech doctrine it had adopted in *Central Hudson Gas & Elec. Corp. v. Public Service Commission of New York*,[222] which applies to government attempts to regulate speech that is neither false nor misleading. Under *Central Hudson*, the government must demonstrate that it has a substantial interest in the restriction, that the restriction directly advances that interest, and that it is not more extensive than would be necessary to promote that interest. A majority of the Court found that the restrictions Massachusetts sought to impose constituted an undue infringement on the right of defendants to communicate with adult smokers, because as a practical matter they would ban all such advertising.[223]

A decade later, the TCA explicitly gave the government broad power over the marketing of cigarettes and other tobacco products. Hence, it came as no surprise that soon after the Act became law, tobacco companies launched a constitutional assault on the statutory provisions of the act creating this authority and subsequent attempts by FDA to implement them provoked a similar reaction. In *Discount Tobacco City Lottery Inc. v. United States*,[224] the Sixth Circuit upheld most of the marketing provisions targeted, including the grant of authority to FDA to devise graphic warnings and mandate that cigarette companies place them on all packages. At the same time, in *R.J. Reynolds Tobacco Company v. Food and Drug Administration*,[225] the District of Columbia Circuit set aside regulations requiring cigarette packs to bear highly graphic images depicting examples of the harms cigarettes can inflict on smokers. The reasoning that underpinned these decisions to a certain extent conflicted, thus setting up a situation that might eventually necessitate resolution by the United States Supreme Court.

The discussion that follows will first consider the Sixth Circuit's treatment of constitutional issues not implicating graphic images. It will then examine the Court's upholding of Congress' authority to mandate graphic warnings. The latter holding will then be contrasted with the D.C. Circuit's decision in *R.J. Reynolds*.

---

[221] Lorillard Tobacco Co. v. Reilly, 533 U.S. 525 (2001).

[222] 447 U.S. 557 (1980).

[223] The regulation prohibited smokeless tobacco and cigar advertising within a 1,000-foot radius of a school or playground. See 533 U.S. at 556. This tracked a similar rule, applicable to cigarettes and smokeless tobacco, and included in FDA's 1996 Regulations. See FDA, *supra* note 11, at 21 C.F.R. § 897.30(b). The Court held that Massachusetts had not demonstrated that the ban was not more extensive than necessary to prevent underage tobacco use.

[224] 674 F.3d 509 (6th Cir. 2012).

[225] 696 F.3d 1205 (D.C. Cir. 2012). For commentary on the decision, *see* Note, 126 HARV. L. REV. 818 (2013).

Discount Tobacco

Regulation of Modified-Risk Claims. The TCA authorizes the premarket review of risk-reduction claims made in the labeling and advertising of tobacco products.[226] Plaintiffs in *Discount Tobacco* asserted that this restriction would preclude them from participating in public debate about tobacco-harm reduction, and hence would infringe on their right to free speech. The Sixth Circuit upheld the constitutionality of these provisions. The Court, however, ruled that the statute precludes only commercial speech conveyed by the labeling and advertising of specific products, a limitation justified by the industry's long history of using misleading claims to market reduced-risk cigarettes; the prohibition would not interfere with non-commercial speech in public-health discourse.[227]

Brand-Name Event Sponsorship and Merchandise. The Sixth Circuit also upheld the regulatory ban on the use of brand names to sponsor events to which children might be exposed, or to distribute items such as caps and T-shirts bearing a brand name or corporate logo, on the ground that it was not more extensive than necessary to reduce youth exposure to brand names or possession of branded merchandise.[228]

Color and Graphics. Plaintiffs challenged the requirement that labeling and advertising use only black text on a white background, with no graphics, as well as the narrowness of the exceptions to it. The Court rejected the government's argument that all uses of colors and graphics are likely to attract minors to use tobacco products, and agreed with plaintiffs' contention that they communicate to adults important commercial information about their products. Because of the absence of a reasonable fit between the government's goal of protecting young people and a total prohibition on color and graphics, the court invalidated the broad prohibition, but left open the government's authority to ban particular uses of colors and graphics.[229]

Safety Claims Based on FDA Approval. The suit also zeroed in on that part of section 301(tt)(4) that lists as a prohibited act the making of any statement to consumers through the media implying that a tobacco product is safe or less harmful because of FDA regulation or its compliance with FDA regulations. The court indicated that applied literally, the ban might apply to anyone (whether connected to the tobacco industry or not) making such an assertion through the media, and hence would transcend commercial speech; therefore, a rule of strict scrutiny would apply in order to determine its validity; since the government offered no justification, section 301(tt)(4) is unconstitutional on its face.[230]

Warnings and Graphic Images on Cigarette Packages. Plaintiffs also challenged the additional and updated cigarette-package warnings (including graphic images) mandated by section 201 of the Tobacco Control Act, and the new mandates as to their size and location, on the ground that consumers already understand the risks of smoking, and hence the regulation is unduly burdensome. However, by a 2-1 vote, the court opted to apply a rule

---

[226]   See FDCA § 911, U.S.C. § 387k, discussed *supra* at notes 181-92 and accompanying text.

[227]   *See Discount Tobacco*, 674 F.3d at 531-37.

[228]   *See id.* at 537-44.

[229]   *See id.* at 544-48. The imposition of plain-packaging requirements for cigarettes has become a global issue. *See* Public Health and Plain Packaging of Cigarettes: Legal Issues (Tania Voon et al. eds., 2012).

[230]   674 F.3d at 548-51.

fashioned by the United States Supreme Court in *Zauderer v. Office of Disciplinary Counsel*,[231] which refused to overturn a state regulation that forced certain disclosures by attorneys advertising contingent-fee services. Under this compelled-speech test, a regulation would be constitutional if it had a rational basis, in the sense that the regulation was reasonably related to the state's interest in protecting consumers against deception. The Sixth Circuit pointed to evidence "that current warnings ineffectively convey the risks of tobacco use and that most people do not understand the full risks,"[232] and ruled that FDA's authority to require graphic images was not in itself unconstitutional, since it was reasonably related to the act's goal of preventing consumer deception; thus, the regulations might directly advance a substantial government interest in a sufficiently tailored way.[233]

R.J. Reynolds

The holding of the D.C. Circuit in *R.J. Reynolds* likewise upheld FDA's authority to require cigarette manufacturers to place graphic warnings on their packages and print advertisements, but in a 2-1 decision it invalidated the hard-hitting images that the agency had mandated by regulation.[234] The Court explicitly rejected the so-called "rational-basis" test that the Sixth Circuit had derived from *Zauderer*, on the ground that the latter would apply only if marketing without graphic images would create a real danger of misleading consumers, and the government had failed to establish this; in addition, the graphics did not amount to information, but rather sought only to promote emotional responses.[235] Hence, the majority applied the test the Supreme Court had fashioned for commercial speech in *Central Hudson*, a case not involving compelled speech but rather suppressed speech. Under *Central Hudson*, the government must show that its claimed interest is substantial, its regulation directly promotes that interest, and the regulatory action is no more extensive than necessary to advance the stated goal. The graphic images FDA sought to mandate, according to the court, failed the third prong of the test. In response to the D.C. Circuit's opinion in *R.J. Reynolds*, the government decided not to seek a rehearing *en banc*. In March 2013, FDA withdrew the

---

[231] 471 U.S. 626 (1985).

[232] 674 F.3d at 564.

[233] *Id.* at 551-69.

[234] *See* Required Warnings for Cigarette Packages and Advertisements, 76 Fed. Reg. 36,628, 36,629 (June 22, 2011). The pictorial elements included, *inter alia*, an addicted smoker exhaling cigarette smoke through a hole in his throat apparently caused by a tracheotomy, and a corpse whose chest bore the marks of major surgery.

[235] For a critical analysis of the court's treatment of emotion, *see* Rebecca Tushnet, *More Than a Feeling: Emotion and the First Amendment*, 127 HARV. L. REV. 2392, 2404-15 (2014).

The majority and the dissent disagreed, *inter alia*, about how the court should take into account the many years of deceptive marketing engaged in by the industry. The dissent argued that weight be given to a context defined by decades of misleading conduct that suppressed public awareness and appreciation of the harms caused by smoking. The majority took a narrower position and insisted that prior deception was relevant only if the compelled speech was specifically intended to counter it. For the Sixth Circuit's reference to past misconduct by the tobacco industry to support a finding that FDA's restrictions on speech concerning modified-risk tobacco products was constitutional, *see supra* note 227 and accompanying text. The majority opinion also referred to "decades-long deception" by the industry to justify its holding that the statutory authorization of graphic warnings did not violate the Constitution. *See Discount Tobacco*, 674 F.3d at 569. Thus, the courts seem to be struggling to work out a consistent approach to the deceptive practice that long characterized the marketing of tobacco products.

regulation and announced its intention to return to the drawing board and re-design the graphic warnings.[236]

However, the D.C. Circuit subsequently considered the applicability of *Zauderer* in the context of a U.S. Department of Agriculture regulation mandating the country-of-origin labeling of certain meat products. In an *en banc* decision, the majority ruled that the *Zauderer* test applies to government-required disclosures aimed at other interests in addition to preventing deception in commercial speech.[237] In so doing, the court specifically overruled language in *R.J. Reynolds* indicating otherwise.[238] This may create uncertainty that will require eventual resolution by the Supreme Court.

---

[236]   Food and Drug Administration, Report to Congress, Progress and Effectiveness of the Implementation of the Family Smoking Prevention and Tobacco Control Act, May 23, 2013, *id.* p. 32.

[237]   American Meat Institute v. United States Dep't of Agriculture, 760 F.3d 18 (D.C. Cir. 2014).

[238]   *Id.* at 23.

CHAPTER 19
FDA REGULATION
OF HEALTHCARE PROFESSIONALS

....

DAVID G. ADAMS

Introduction

One of the most persistent controversies facing the Food and Drug Administration (FDA) over the years has been the agency's application of the provisions of the Federal Food, Drug, and Cosmetic Act (FDCA) to healthcare professionals such as medical practitioners[1] and pharmacists. While it is clear from the legislative history of the FDCA that Congress did not intend the statute as a general mandate for federal regulation of these professions, certain provisions of the law do clearly affect, and in many instances restrict, the practices of healthcare professionals. The statute provides express authority over clinical research by physicians involving investigational new drugs or investigational devices[2] and over labeling and dispensing of prescription drugs by pharmacists.[3] Acknowledging Congress' admonitions in the legislative history, however, FDA has traditionally asserted that it does not regulate the practice of medicine or pharmacy, and has generally sought to avoid regulatory actions that would directly restrict or interfere with professional service to patients.

Nevertheless, the agency has identified circumstances in which it will seek to regulate the conduct of physicians, pharmacists, and other healthcare professionals in the same manner that it regulates manufacturers and distributors of medical products. In the case of medical practitioners, the agency has sought to regulate promotion and sale of unapproved medical products, as well as promotion of approved products for "off-label use."[4] In the case of

---

[1]   The term "medical practitioners" as used herein is intended to include physicians, chiropractors, nurses, nurse practitioners, and others who use human drugs or devices in the practice of the healing arts. Although the focus of this chapter is on human healthcare, corollary provisions and policies related to veterinary medicine are noted.

[2]   *See* Chapters 10 (drugs) and 16 (medical devices).

[3]   *See* Chapter 9.

[4]   The term "off-label use" generally refers to the use of a drug or device in a manner that is outside of the product's labeling that has been approved or authorized by FDA. *See* Washington Legal Foundation v.

pharmacists, the agency has sought to regulate not only promotion of approved products but also promotion, preparation, and dispensing of drugs that are compounded by pharmacists, and Congress has amended the statute to provide express authority over compounding.[5] Although FDA's policies affecting the practices of medicine and pharmacy are similar in certain respects, they have developed separately in numerous judicial enforcement actions and agency pronouncements. The discussion below addresses regulation of healthcare professionals with regard to drugs (including therapeutic biologics) and devices for human use. Regulation of veterinary products is addressed in Chapter 7.

Medical Practitioners

The "Practice of Medicine Exception"

Both the agency and the courts have recognized the many significant statements in the legislative history of the FDCA that the legislation was not intended to regulate the "practice of medicine," or, as it was later described, the "healing art."[6] Senator Royal Copeland, who introduced the legislation that was to become the FDCA, is commonly quoted in this regard:

> [T]he bill is not intended as a medical practices act and will not interfere with the practice of the healing art by chiropractors and others in the States where they are licensed by law to engage in such practice. It is not intended to permit the sale in interstate commerce or otherwise in Federal jurisdiction of adulterated or misbranded drugs or devices under the guise of the practice of a healing art. It is likewise not intended to permit the false advertising of drugs and devices under such guise.[7]

The references in the legislative history to the practice of medicine and of the healing art, however, do not define those phrases, and neither phrase is found in the FDCA, itself.[8] Thus, while agreeing that FDA does not regulate the practice of medicine, the courts have

---

Kessler, 880 F. Supp. 26, 28 n. 1 (D.D.C. 1995). *See* also letter to Hon. Joseph Barton, Chairman, Subcomm. on Oversight and Investigation, Comm. on Commerce, U.S. House of Rep., from Diane E. Thompson, Assoc. Comm'r for Legislative Aff., FDA (Apr. 14, 1995).

[5]   *See* Compounding, *infra.*

[6]   References to the practice of the "healing art" were intended to clarify that Congress' concerns extended to chiropractors as well as medical doctors. See S. REP. No. 493, 73d Cong., 2d Sess. (1934), reprinted in C. DUNN, FEDERAL FOOD, DRUG AND COSMETIC ACT 111 (1938).

[7]   S. REP. No. 361, 74th Cong., 1st Sess. (1935), *reprinted in* DUNN, *supra* note 5. Senator Copeland made this remark while explaining the significance of a qualification provided in the bill's definition of "drug." The definition stated at the outset that "[t]he term 'drug,' for the purposes of this Act and *not to regulate the practice of medicine,* includes . . . ." S. 2800, 73d Cong, 2d Sess., § 2 (1934), *reprinted in* DUNN, *supra* note 6, at 72 (emphasis added). In the next draft of the bill, the phrase was changed slightly to "not to regulate the *legalized practice* of *the healing art.*" *Id.* at 93 (emphasis added). The qualification was dropped from the drug definition prior to passage because it was deemed unnecessary and possibly confusing. *See id.* at 403 (Senate debate); H.R. REP. No. 2755, 74th Cong., 2d Sess. (1935), *reprinted in* DUNN at 554; *see also id.* at 578 (House debate).

[8]   FDA has, in response to a congressional inquiry, defined the practice of medicine as "the examination, diagnosis, and treatment of individual patients based on judgments made by licensed health care professions . . . regulated by State Boards of Medicine, which license physicians." Letter to Hon. Joseph Barton, *supra* note 4.

not fashioned a general exemption to shield physicians from the adulteration, misbranding, and new drug provision of the FDCA.[9] Nor have the courts found constitutional limitations on FDA's authority to regulate physicians.[10] Thus, the regulatory regimes for drugs and devices have been applied to medical practitioners, and, unavoidably, to the practice of medicine, itself.[11]

Regulation of Off-Label Use of Approved or Authorized Products

Drugs

Off-label use of drugs (prescribing drugs for uses that are not approved and set forth in drug labeling) is common and well accepted in the practice of medicine,[12] and FDA has long held that it is not subject to regulation under the FDCA.[13] The agency's 1972 proposed rulemaking on off-label use remains the most significant statement of agency policy on this issue.[14]

The agency sought in the proposed rule to address the "widespread use of certain prescription drugs for conditions not named in the official labeling."[15] The agency proposed to address the issue not by regulating off-label use itself, but, rather, by imposing labeling and other requirements on manufacturers and distributors of drugs that are commonly used off-label.[16] In declining to regulate actual off-label use, the agency acknowledged that

---

[9]   Although one court has stated that the legislative history "expressed a specific intent to prohibit FDA from regulating physicians' practice of medicine," it did so at the prodding of FDA where a plaintiff requested that FDA intervene in a case involving capital punishment by lethal injection of approved drugs. Chaney v. Heckler, 718 F.2d 1174 (D.C. Cir. 1984), rev'd, 470 U.S. 821 (1985).

[10]   Although the Supreme Court stated in Linder v. United States, 268 U.S. 5, 18 (1925), that direct control of medical practice was beyond the reach of the federal government, lower courts have refused to limit FDA's authority in response to arguments that the practice of medicine must be left to the states. See United States v. Regenerative Services, LLC, 741 F.3d 1314, 1319-20 (D.C. Cir. 2014); United States v. Evers, 643 F.2d 1043, 1048-49 (5th Cir. 1981); Simeon Management Corp. v. FTC, 579 F.2d 1137, 1144 (9th Cir. 1978). The Supreme Court has generally held that doctors have no special constitutional rights related to medical practice other than those deriving from patient's rights. See Whalen v. Rose, 429 U.S. 589, 605 (1977) (confidentiality of medical records); Griswold v. Connecticut, 381 U.S. 479, 481 (1965) (right to contraceptives). Attempts to limit FDA's authority based on assertions of patients' constitutional rights have not fared well. See, e.g., United States v. Burzynski Cancer Research Inst., 819 F.2d 1301, 1313-14 (5th Cir. 1987) (cancer patients have no constitutional privacy right to obtain medical treatment when the treatment consists of an unapproved new drug) (citing United States v. Rutherford, 442 U.S. 544 (1979)).

[11]   For a discussion of the historical background of the FDCA and FDA policy development related to the practice of medicine, see Peter Barton Hutt, Regulation of the Practice of Medicine Under the Pure Food and Drug Laws, 33 FOOD & DRUG OFFICIALS OF THE U.S. Q. BULL. 3 (1969).

[12]   Buckman v. Plaintiffs' Legal Comm., 531 U.S. 341, 350-51 (2000). A study conducted in 2006 found that more than 20 percent of prescriptions written for 160 of the 500 most commonly used prescription drugs were written for off-label use. D.C. Radley et al., Off-Label Prescribing Among Office-Based Physicians, 166 ARCH. INTERN. MED. 1021 (2006).

[13]   See William L. Christopher, Off-Label Drug Prescription: Filling the Regulatory Vacuum, 48 FOOD & DRUG L.J. 247, 247 n. 6 (1993). The agency has followed a different policy with regard to animal drugs. See Chapter 7.

[14]   Legal Status of Approved Labeling for Prescription Drugs; Prescribing for Uses Unapproved by the Food and Drug Administration, 37 Fed. Reg. 16,503 (Aug. 15, 1972).

[15]   Id. at 16,503.

[16]   The proposed rule authorized the following actions when "an unapproved use of a new drug may endanger patients or create a public health hazard, or provide a benefit to patients or to the public health": 1) requiring the manufacturer to revise the package insert to add the new use and related contraindications, warnings,

package inserts often do not contain the most current information about new uses of drugs, and that such new uses may sometimes be appropriate in the practice of medicine.[17] The agency stated unambiguously that such off-label uses would not violate the FDCA or its implementing regulations.[18]

While acknowledging the repeated statements in the legislative history that Congress did not intend the FDCA to interfere with or regulate medical practice, the agency concluded that "Congress clearly required the Food and Drug Administration to control the *availability* of drugs for prescribing by physicians.[19] The agency added:

> As the law now stands, therefore, the Food and Drug Administration is charged with the responsibility for judging the safety and effectiveness of drugs and the truthfulness of their labeling. The physician is then responsible for making the final judgment as to which, if any, of the available drugs his patient will receive in light of the information contained in their labeling and other adequate scientific data available to him.[20]

Although the proposed rule was never adopted, due in part to the strong opposition from medical professionals,[21] the discussion of off-label use has remained an important statement of agency policy.[22]

---

and similar information; 2) restricting refills; 3) requiring the manufacturer to substantiate the unapproved use; 4) restricting distribution, prescribing, dispensing, and administration (e.g., to physicians with specified qualifications); and 5) withdrawing approval of the product. *Id.* at 16,504-05.

[17]   *Id.*

[18]   *Id.*

[19]   *Id.* at 16,503-04 (emphasis added).

[20]   *Id.* at 16,504.

[21]   *See* DEP'T OF HEALTH, EDUCATION & WELFARE, REVIEW PANEL ON NEW DRUG REGULATION, INTERIM REPORT—PRESCRIBING DRUGS FOR UNAPPROVED USES 7-10 (1977).

[22]   See *Use of Approved Drugs for Unlabeled Indications,* 12 FDA DRUG BULL. 5 (1982):

> Once a product has been approved for marketing, a physician may prescribe it for uses or in treatment regimens or patient populations that are not included in approved labeling . . . "[U]napproved" or, more precisely, "unlabeled" uses may be appropriate and rational in certain circumstances, and may, in fact reflect approaches to drug therapy that have been extensively reported in medical literature . . . . Valid new uses for drugs already on the market are often first discovered through serendipitous observations and therapeutic innovations, subsequently confirmed by well-planned and executed clinical investigations.

Although in 1991, the agency considered whether to withdraw the 1972 proposed rule, the agency ultimately declined to withdraw the proposed rule. FDA noted, however, that it did not intend to proceed to a final rule at that time because it planned to assemble an "Unlabeled Use Task Force to examine the promotion and use of prescription drugs for indications not included on their approved labeling." Withdrawal of Certain Pre-1986 Proposed Rules; Final Action, 56 Fed. Reg. 67,440, 67,442 (Dec. 30, 1991). In 1994 the agency confirmed the policy expressed in a notice requesting comments on the agency's policy in promotion of unapproved uses of approved drugs and devices. Citizen Petition Regarding the Food and Drug Administration's Policy on Promo-tion of Unapproved Uses of Approved Drugs and Devices; Request for Comments, 59 Fed. Reg. 59,820 (Nov. 18, 1994). See also Stuart L. Nightingale, *Unlabeled Uses of Approved Drugs,* 26 DRUG INFO. J. 141, 145 (1992); Proposed New Drug, Antibiotic, and Biologic Drug Regulations, 48 Fed. Reg. 26,720, 26,733 (June 9, 1983).

The policy is currently reflected in FDA's investigational new drug (IND) regulations, which govern investigational use of unapproved new drugs and unlicensed biological products.[23] These regulations provide that no IND is required where a physician is prescribing an approved or licensed product for an unapproved (off-label) use in the practice of medicine.[24] In applying this policy, the agency has drawn a critical distinction between off-label use in the practice of medicine and commercialization of an off-label use. The seminal case in this regard is *United States v. Evers*,[25] where FDA challenged a physician's promotion and advertising of chelating drugs for a use that was not within the approved labeling.[26] Although the agency acknowledged that Dr. Evers could prescribe the drugs for an off-label use, it argued that Dr. Evers' commercial activities had misbranded the product under section 502(f)(1) of the FDCA[27] by creating a new intended use for which there were no "adequate directions" in the labeling.[28] The court of appeals rejected the agency's position, however, because Dr. Evers had distributed the drugs only to his own patients.[29] The court found that Dr. Evers had 1) no duty under the FDCA to provide adequate directions to other physicians since he had not distributed the drugs to other physicians; 2) no duty to provide adequate directions to his patients because the drug was a prescription drug;[30] and 3) for obvious reasons, no duty to provide adequate directions to himself.[31]

---

[23]   21 C.F.R. pt. 312.

[24]   FDA generally distinguishes clinical research from practice of medicine involving approved drugs. See 21 C.F.R. § 312.2(b). See also David A. Kessler, *The Regulation of Investigational Drugs*, 320 N. ENG. J. MED. 281 (1989).

[25]   643 F.2d 1043 (5th Cir. 1981).

[26]   *Id.* at 1045-46. Dr. Evers was using a chelating drug in the treatment of atherosclerosis, a use for which the drug was contraindicated. *Id.* at 1044-45. The agency had previously obtained relief against Dr. Evers in a case brought in Louisiana, where he was not licensed. United States v. An Article of Drug . . . Diso-Tate, No. 75-1790 (E.D. La. Sept. 28, 1976). Dr. Evers subsequently moved to Alabama, where he was licensed, and resumed administering and promoting the drug. United States v. Evers, 453 F. Supp. 1141, 1142-43 (M.D. Ala. 1979), *aff'd*, 643 F.2d 1043, 1052-53 (5th Cir. 1981).

[27]   21 U.S.C. § 352(f)(1).

[28]   643 F.2d at 1048-49 ("[T]he government agrees with Dr. Evers that the provisions of the Act and the regulations of FDA that are now in force do not prevent him from prescribing for uses not approved by FDA drugs which had been approved by FDA for some other purposes. The object of the government's case against Dr. Evers is not, therefore, his *prescription* of Calcium EDTA for use in the treatment of circulatory disorders. Instead, the government seeks to challenge Dr. Evers' *promotion* and *advertising* of chelating drugs for that use.") (emphasis added).

[29]   Although Dr. Evers promoted the drug to other physicians, the court noted that such promotion did not constitute a violation of the FDCA because he did not sell or distribute the product to other physicians. *Id.* at 1053 n.16. The court emphasized in this regard that "the Act was intended to regulate the distribution of drugs in interstate commerce, not to restrain physicians from public advocacy of medical opinions not shared by FDA." *Id.*

[30]   Although section 502 requires adequate directions for use by laymen, 21 C.F.R. § 201.100 provides an exemption from this requirement for prescription drugs.

[31]   United States v. Evers, 643 F.2d at 1044. The view of the *Evers* court may not be shared by other courts. In an earlier case involving a seizure of drugs held by physicians for their medical practice, the court appeared to reach a different result:

> It may be that physicians are not understood as holding for sale the drugs which they administer or prescribe in connection with their treatment of patients. But the potentiality of harm to the public from misbranded drugs is not less because the intervening agency of distribution may be a physician rather than a layman . . . . If forfeiture works any interference with claimants' practice of medicine it is a mere incident of their violation of the law in making representations concerning their drugs which the jury found were unwarranted, false or misleading.

Although Dr. Evers argued the broader proposition that FDA had no jurisdiction over the practice of medicine, the court declined to reach the issue and appeared to accept the distinction drawn by FDA in the preamble to the 1972 proposed regulation: "Of course, while the Act was not intended to regulate the *practice of medicine,* it was obviously intended to control the *availability of drugs* for prescribing by physicians."[32]

Devices

In the case of medical devices, FDA and the courts have provided less flexibility for physicians than in the case of human drugs. The courts have shown a willingness to require adequate directions for use even for devices held by physicians for their own use,[33] and have enjoined physicians from using misbranded or adulterated devices and permitted seizures of devices in physicians' offices.[34] Although the agency's regulatory approach to drugs and devices has, for the most part, appeared the same with regard to promotion, distribution, and off-label use,[35] the agency had for many years reserved the right to regulate off-label use of devices.[36] In 1997, however, Congress amended the FDCA to require that the statute not

---

United States v. 10 Cartons . . . Article of Drug Labeled in Part "Hoxey," 152 F. Supp. 360, 364 (W.D. Pa. 1957). *See also* United States v. Articles of Animal Drug Containing Diethylstilbestrol, 528 F. Supp. 202, 205 (D. Neb. 1981), in which the court held that, although prescription drugs are exempt from the requirement of adequate directions for use when dispensed in patients, FDCA § 503(b)(2), 21 U.S.C. § 353(b)(2), there is no such exemption while the drugs are held for sale prior to being dispensed. The court also noted that "an article of drug or device is 'held for sale' if it is used for any purpose other than personal consumption." *Id.*

[32]   United States v. Evers, 643 F.2d at 1048 (emphasis added).

[33]   *See, e.g.,* United States v. Device Labeled "Cameron Spitler, Etc.," 261 F. Supp. 243, 246 (D. Neb. 1966). The court quoted United States v. Ellis Research Lab., 300 F.2d 550 (7th Cir.) (1962), in support of its position:

> Licensed practitioners are not exempt from the terms of the Act, and we see no reason why a device used solely by licensed practitioners should, for that reason alone, be exempt from that portion of the Act requiring the labeling to bear adequate directions for use.

[34]   *See, e.g.,* United States v. Diapulse Corp. of America, 514 F.2d 1097, 1098 (2d Cir.) (1975):

> The contention that the injunction [prohibiting interstate shipment of a misbranded device] was improperly extended to cover devices held by practitioners [was] also without merit. Such devices, used in the treatment of patients, may properly be considered "held for sale" within the meaning of the Food, Drug and Cosmetic Act, 21 U.S.C. § 331(k).

[35]   In an informal notice dated February 1989, the agency noted:

> Good medical practice and the best interests of the patient require that physicians use legally available drugs, biologics and devices according to their best knowledge and judgment. . . . Use of a marketed product in this manner when the intent is the "practice of medicine" does not require the submission of an Investigational New Drug Application (IND), Investigational Device Exemption (IDE) or review by an Institutional Review Board (IRB).

FDA, "Off-Label" and Investigational Use of Marketed Drugs, Biologics, and Medical Devices – Information Sheet, *available at* http://www.fda.gov/RegulatoryInformation/Guidances/ucm126486.htm.

[36]   The agency stated in response to a 1995 congressional inquiry that "[t]he Medical Device Amendments . . . give FDA authority to regulate the unapproved use of the medical devices," Letter to Hon. Joseph Barton, *supra* note 4 (citing 21 U.S.C. §§ 360, 360c, 360f, 360h, 360i, 360j, 360k (FDCA §§ 510, 513, 516, 518, 519, 520, 521)). Agency personnel had suggested informally that the use of a device outside of authorization in the context of a device classification or finding of substantial equivalence would render the device a Class III device under FDCA § 513(f), 21 U.S.C. § 360c(f) (requiring an approved premarket approval application (PMA)), and that the use of a Class III device outside the labeling approved in a PMA would render it unapproved, and, thus, adulterated under section 351(f) (FDCA § 501(f)). Although the agency has apparent authority to regulate physician use of restricted devices under 21 U.S.C. § 360j(e) (FDCA § 520(e)), ("sale, distribution or *use*" outside of labeled restrictions) (emphasis added), there are few devices that qualify as restricted devices.

"be construed to limit or interfere with the authority of a healthcare practitioner to prescribe or administer any legally marketed device to a patient for any condition or disease within a legitimate healthcare practitioner-patient relationship."[37] In the same section, Congress expressly preserved the agency's authority to enforce restrictions on the sale, distribution and labeling of devices and the agency's "prohibition on the promotion of unapproved uses of legally marketed devices."[38]

Regulation of Use and Distribution of Unapproved or Unauthorized Products

Drugs

Although FDA generally does not attempt to intervene directly in the prescribing and administration of human drugs in the practice of medicine, the agency has in some cases sought to regulate the preparation and distribution of unapproved or otherwise unlawful drugs by physicians. Shortly after its loss in the *Evers* case, FDA successfully challenged the activities of another physician, Dr. Stanislaw R. Burzynski, under a different legal theory.[39] Unlike Dr. Evers, Dr. Burzynski was distributing an unapproved and controversial cancer treatment that he, himself, manufactured. In Dr. Burzynski's case, the agency obtained injunctive relief under the new drug provisions of the FDCA, which prohibit introduction of unapproved new drugs into interstate commerce.[40] The agency's relief did not extend to intrastate sales by Dr. Burzynski in Texas because the FDCA does not prohibit holding unapproved new drugs for sale after shipment in interstate commerce.[41]

Devices

The agency's approach to drugs formulated by physicians cannot be applied to devices that are customized to meet the needs of individual patients. If a physician procures or develops a new device for a single patient, it may be protected as a custom device.[42] A device that is produced in multiples and is not in a specific form for an individual patient, however, may subject the physician to liability under the FDCA.[43] A policy based on such distinctions poses obvious difficulties for physicians seeking to provide the best care for their patients.

---

[37] Pub. L. No. 105-115, § 214, 111 Stat. 2296, 2348 (1997), FDCA § 906, 21 U.S.C. § 396.

[38] *Id.*

[39] *See* United States v. Burzynski Cancer Research Inst., No. H-83-2069 (S.D. Tex. May 24, 1983); United States v. Burzynski Cancer Research Inst., 819 F.2d 1301, 1304 (5th Cir. 1987).

[40] FDCA § 201(d)(3), 21 U.S.C. § 321(d)(3).

[41] *See Burzynski Cancer Research Inst.,* 819 F.2d at 1305. *See also* Trustees of the Northwest Laundry & Dry Cleaners Health & Welfare Fund v. Burzynski, 27 F.3d 153, 155 & n.3 (5th Cir. 1994). Unlike the adulteration and misbranding provisions of the FDCA, FDA's jurisdiction over unapproved new drugs is limited to introduction into interstate commerce. See FDCA § 301(d), 21 U.S.C. § 331(d). The adulteration or misbranding of the drugs in Texas would have resulted in a violation of FDCA § 301(k), 21 U.S.C. § 331(k) (held for sale after shipment in interstate commerce) if any of the drug's components came from out of state. The court in *Trustees of the Northwest Laundry* also noted that state laws may preclude intrastate marketing of an unapproved new drug. 27 F.3d at 155 & n.4.

[42] FDCA § 520(b), 21 U.S.C. § 360j(b).

[43] In *United States v. Fulton,* Food Drug Cosm. Law Rep. (CCH) ¶ 15,164 (C.D. Cal. July 29, 1992), a physician was enjoined from using unapproved liquid silicone in his medical practice. The physician was charged with violating 21 U.S.C. § 331(q) by "using a device which lacks pre-market approval, without an investigational device exemption, as required by 21 U.S.C § 360j(g)." *Id.* The court held that the liquid silicone did not meet the requirements of the custom device exemption, 21 U.S.C. § 360j(b)(2)(A)(i), (ii). *Id.*

Restrictions on Availability to Medical Practitioners

Drugs

As discussed above, FDA and the courts have generally agreed that the FDCA is designed to restrict the availability of unapproved and otherwise unlawful drugs to physicians. Such drugs are considered experimental under the agency's regulations, and manufacturers cannot provide such drugs to physicians in the absence of an IND authorizing the physicians' use of the product.[44] As discussed below, however, drugs compounded by a physician, or by a pharmacist pursuant to a physician's prescription, are generally not subject to this requirement.

In 2007, Congress amended the FDCA to permit FDA to impose restrictions on availability of approved drugs where necessary to "assure safe use of the drug, because of its inherent toxicity or potential harmfulness."[45] Under this provision the agency may require special training, experience, or certification for healthcare professionals who prescribe or dispense the drug, restrictions on settings in which the drug may be dispensed, and patient testing, monitoring, and enrollment in a registry.[46]

Prior to this amendment, in the one notable case in which the agency attempted to impose controls on the availability of an *approved* drug, the agency was successfully challenged. In *American Pharmaceutical Association v. Weinberger,*[47] a federal district court held that FDA had no authority to limit the distribution of methadone to certain hospitals for certain specific uses. Despite this holding, in 1992 FDA promulgated a regulation that would authorize restrictions on distribution of drugs approved under special criteria, known as an accelerated approval process.[48] In response to comments that such restrictions would interfere with the practice of medicine, the agency asserted "broad authority . . . to issue regulations to help assure the safety and effectiveness of new drugs,"[49] and argued that, "rather than interfering

---

[44]   21 C.F.R. § 312.3(a). The statute authorizes INDs for emergency use, compassionate use and treatment use. FDCA § 561, 21 U.S.C. § 360bbb. These provisions, enacted in 2003, largely codified the approach already taken by the agency in its IND regulations. The agency's treatment IND regulations, for example, make possible the distribution of promising experimental drugs for patients with serious or immediately life-threatening diseases where there is no satisfactory alternative therapy, the drug is already the subject of a controlled trial under an IND, and the sponsor of the trial is actively pursuing agency approval. *Id.* § 312.34. The regulations also authorize emergency uses of investigational drugs where time does not allow the submission of an IND. *Id.* § 312.36.

[45]   Pub. L. No. 110-85, § 901(b), 121 Stat. 823, 926 (2007). This may be required in the approval of an NDA as part of a risk evaluation and mitigation strategy or "REMS," FDCA § 505-1(a), 21 U.S.C. § 355-1(a). *See* Chapter 10 for a further discussion of REMS.

[46]   *Id.* § 505-1(f), 21 U.S.C. § 355-1(f).

[47]   377 F. Supp. 824 (D.D.C. 1974), *aff'd sub nom.* APhA v. Mathews, 530 F.2d 1054 (D.C. Cir. 1976).

[48]   New Drug, Antibiotic, and Biologic Drug Product Regulations; Accelerated Approval, 57 Fed. Reg. 58,942, 58,951 (Dec. 11, 1992). See 21 C.F.R. §§ 314.520, 601.42. Included in this rule are certain postmarketing regulations, under which FDA may "(1) Restrict distribution to certain facilities or physicians with special training or experience, or (2) condition distribution on the performance of specified medical procedures." 57 Fed. Reg. at 58,943. See Chapter 10 for a further discussion of accelerated approval.

[49]   *Id.* at 58,951.

with physician or pharmacy practice, the regulations permit, in exceptional cases, approval of drugs with restrictions so that the drugs may be available for prescribing or dispensing."[50]

Devices

FDA's statutory authority over medical devices provides express authority to place restrictions on the availability of products for medical practitioners. The agency can establish through regulation or administrative order restrictions on the sale, distribution, or use of devices. Specifically, FDA may promulgate regulations specifying that a device must be sold, distributed, or used only upon the authorization of a practitioner licensed to administer or use the device.[51] The agency may confine the use of a device to persons with specific training or experience or to certain facilities where the restriction is required for the safe and effective use of the device.[52] The agency may also require that the label of a restricted device bear statements reflecting the restrictions that have been imposed.[53] The agency has, to date, used this authority very sparingly.

Pharmacists

Statutory Exemptions for Pharmacy Practice

As in the case of practice of medicine, there is no general exemption in the FDCA for the practice of pharmacy.[54] Thus, FDA has regulated the preparation, holding, promotion, and dispensing of prescription drugs by pharmacists under the misbranding, adulteration, and new drug provisions of the act.[55] The act, does, however, contain certain specific, limited exemptions for pharmacy practice.

Adequate Directions for Use

The primary exemption applies generally to any person authorized to dispense prescription drugs. It exempts drugs dispensed by pharmacists from most statutory labeling requirements, including the requirement of adequate directions for use.[56]

---

[50]   *Id.* at 58,952.

[51]   FDCA § 520(e)(1), 21 U.S.C. § 360j(e)(1). A person may not be excluded from using a device because he or she is not eligible for certification or has not been certified by the American Board of Medical Specialties. *Id.*

[52]   *Id.*

[53]   FDCA § 520(e)(2), 21 U.S.C. § 360j(e)(2).

[54]   See Professionals and Patients for Customized Care v. Shalala, 56 F.3d 592, 593 n.3 (5th Cir. 1995); United States v. Algon Chem. Inc., 879 F.2d 1154, 1162-63 (3d Cir. 1989).

[55]   *See, e.g.,* United States v. Sullivan, 332 U.S. 689, 692 (1948) (pharmacist failing to provide warnings and adequate directions for use for drug dispensed without a prescription). United States v. Jamieson-McKames Pharms, Inc., 651 F.2d 532, 536-38, 544-45 (8th Cir. 1981) (inspecting retail pharmacy without a warrant; affirming conviction for counterfeiting, misbranding, and adulterating drugs).

[56]   FDCA § 503(b)(2), 21 U.S.C. § 353(b)(2). This exemption is not limited to pharmacies, but applies to any person authorized to dispense prescription drugs. Under the exemption, dispensed drugs are required to comply only with the labeling requirements of FDCA § 502(a), (i)(2)-(3), 21 U.S.C. § 352(a), (i)(2)-(3), and with the packaging requirements of § 352(g), (h), (p). The labeling for dispensed drugs is required to contain only minimal information, including the specific directions for used contained in the prescription. *Id.* § 503(b)(2), 21 U.S.C. § 353(b)(2).

Registration and Listing

Another provision exempts certain pharmacies from the registration and drug listing provisions of the act.[57] The exemption is limited to pharmacies that dispense drugs "upon prescriptions of practitioners licensed to administer such drugs to patients under the care of such practitioners in the course of their professional practice, and which do not manufacture, prepare, propagate, compound, or process drugs or devices for sale other than in the regular course of their business of dispensing or selling drugs or devices at retail."[58] The agency interprets this provision to apply only to pharmacies engaged in the "traditional practice of pharmacy," and has received support for this interpretation from the courts. In *Cedars North Towers Pharmacy, Inc. v. United States*,[59] a Florida district court found a number of practical considerations to be relevant to determining whether a pharmacy is engaged in the "normal" practice of pharmacy within the meaning of the registration provisions in section 510(g)(1),[60] including, among other things, the geographic area of distribution and the use of advertising and promotion.[61]

Inspection

The statute also provides an exemption from certain FDA inspection requirements, again restricting the exception to pharmacies that dispense drugs "upon prescriptions of practitioners licensed to administer such drugs or devices to patients under the care of such practitioners in the course of their professional practice, and which do not . . . manufacture, prepare, propagate, compound, or process drugs or devices for sale other than in the regular course of their business of dispensing or selling drugs or devices at retail."[62] In *Wedgewood Village Pharmacy, Inc. v. United States*, the U.S. Court of Appeals for the Third Circuit agreed with FDA that the exemption from records inspection in section 704(a)(2)(A)[63] does not apply to pharmacies engaged in "large scale" compounding, viewed by FDA as "inconsistent with [the pharmacy's] status as a retail pharmacy."[64] In *Medical Center Pharmacy v. Gonzales*, however, a district court in Texas held that pharmacies compliant with local laws, dispensing per prescriptions, and compounding in the normal course of their business are exempt from records inspection.[65]

---

[57]   FDCA § 510(g)(1), 21 U.S.C. § 360(g)(1).

[58]   *Id.*

[59]   Food Drug Cosm. Law Rep., (CCH) ¶ 38,200 (S.D. Fla. Aug. 20, 1978) (Civ. No. 77-4695), reprinted in Federal Food, Drug, and Cosmetic Act: Judicial Record 1978-1980, at 668-71 (1980).

[60]   21 U.S.C. § 360(g)(1).

[61]   Food Drug Cosm. Law Rep., *supra* note 59 at ¶ 38,828.

[62]   FDCA § 704(a)(2)(A), 21 U.S.C. § 374(a)(2)(A).

[63]   21 U.S.C. 374(A)(2)(a).

[64]   421 F.3d 263, 273 (3d Cir. 2005).

[65]   451 F. Supp. 2d 854, 866 (W.D. Tex. 2006), *rev'd on other grounds, sub nom.* Med. Ctr. Pharmacy v. Mukasey, 536 F.3d 383 (5th Cir. 2008). On remand the district court held that FDA had authority to conduct limited inspections of records to determine whether pharmacies are engaged in unlawful compounding, but the court of appeals reversed that decision on procedural grounds. Med. Ctr. Pharmacy v. Holder, 634 F.3d 830 (5th Cir. 2011).

Mandatory Dissemination of Patient Information and Restrictions on Distribution under a REMS

As discussed in Chapter 10, FDA may require pharmacists to disseminate patient information and impose restrictions on dispensing approved drugs under risk evaluation and mitigation strategies (REMS), including training, experience, or certification requirements for pharmacists who dispense such drugs and restrictions on the settings in which the drugs are dispensed.[66]

Compounding

Compounding has a complex regulatory history under the FDCA, and is currently regulated under sections 503A[67] and 503B,[68] which were added to the Act in 1997 and 2013, respectively. Although the term "compounding" is not defined in the FDCA, the Supreme Court has broadly described "drug compounding" as "a process by which a pharmacist or doctor combines, mixes, or alters ingredients to create a medication tailored to the needs of an individual patient."[69] As noted below, certain specific types of product preparation are deemed to be "compounding" under section 503B but not under section 503A.[70]

Regulation of Compounding Prior to Enactment of Sections 503A and 503B

Prior to the enactment of section 503A in 1997,[71] the FDCA provided no express exemption for compounding, and consequently exposed pharmacists and physicians to potential regulation under most of the same standards that apply to manufacturers, including the requirement that new drugs be approved. Until the 1980s, however, FDA left regulation of compounding almost exclusively to the states. The agency turned its attention to compounding when it began to see examples of large-scale pharmacy compounding and promotion of compounded drugs, which the agency considered to be more similar to commercial drug manufacturing and marketing than to "traditional practice of pharmacy." These concerns led to the issuance of a compliance policy guide on pharmacy compounding in 1992 (1992 CPG)[72] listing factors the agency would consider in determining whether to

---

[66]   FDCA § 505-1, 21 U.S.C. § 355-1.

[67]   21 U.S.C. § 353a.

[68]   21 U.S.C. § 353b.

[69]   Thompson v. W. States Med. Ctr., 535 U.S. 357, 360-61 (2002).

[70]   *See infra* notes 77 and 106.

[71]   Pub. L. No. 105-115, § 127(a), 111 Stat. 2328 (1997).

[72]   FDA, Manufacture, Distribution, and Promotion of Adulterated, Misbranded or Unapproved New Drugs for Human Use by State-Licensed Pharmacies, Compliance Policy Guide 7132.16 (1992). The 1992 CPG followed earlier, less expansive policy statements on compounding. A 1980 compliance policy guide provided that *hospital* pharmacies that compound and/or repackage drugs are not required to register under FDCA § 510, 21 U.S.C. § 360, unless they sell to other hospitals or drugstores. FDA, Hospital Pharmacies— Status as Drug Manufacturers, Compliance Policy Guide § 406.100 [originally published as § 7132.06] (1980). It also provided that such pharmacies may compound drugs in limited quantities prior to the receipt of prescription as long as the pharmacy can document a historical demand for the quantities it compounds. *Id.* Another policy statement issued as a draft guideline in 1984 provided parameters in which the agency would not seek to regulate compounding of radiopharmaceuticals. FDA, Nuclear Pharmacy Guideline: Criteria for Determining When to Register as a Drug Establishment (May 1984).

regulate a pharmacy as it would a manufacturer.[73] Shortly after publication of the 1992 CPG, an organization of pharmacists and pharmacies sued FDA to overturn the policy. Although the lawsuit was unsuccessful,[74] continuing controversy over the 1992 CPG resulted in the 1997 enactment of section 503A.

Section 503A

Section 503A operates to exempt compounding[75] of human drugs from the statutory requirements of new drug approval, good manufacturing practice and adequate directions for use based on a set of set of standards and requirements.[76] The compounded drug must be dispensed based on an unsolicited prescription for an identified patient indicating that the drug is medically necessary.[77] Section 503A reinforces the concept of medical necessity by prohibiting compounding "regularly or in inordinate amounts (as defined by the Secretary) any drug products that are essentially copies of a commercially available drug product."[78] This language does not include a compounded product with "a change, made for an identified individual patient, which produces for that patient a significant difference, as determined by the prescribing practitioner, between the compounded drug and the comparable commercially available drug product."[79]

Section 503A also provides quality standards and further limitations on compounding. These include standards for active ingredients[80] and inactive ingredients,[81] and prohibitions

---

[73]   1992 CPG at 4-5. These factors, providing the contours of the agency's concept of "traditional practice of pharmacy" largely coincided with the agency's interpretations of the statutory exemptions from registration requirements and inspection authority for pharmacies that fill prescriptions "in the course of their professional practice . . . ." See *supra* notes 58 and 62. Most of the agency's criteria reflected concerns similar to those expressed in the *Cedars* and *Sene X* decisions over the physician-patient-pharmacist relationship and the similarity of the pharmacy operation to commercial manufacture and distribution, and most were embraced by Congress in section 503A.

[74]   See *Professionals and Patients for Customized Care, supra* note 54.

[75]   The term "compounding" as used in section 503A does not include "mixing, reconstituting, or other such acts that are performed in accordance with directions contained in approved labeling provided by the product's manufacturer and other manufacturer directions consistent with that labeling." FDCA § 503A(e), 21 U.S.C. § 353a(e).

[76]   FDCA § 503A(a) (exempting compounded drugs from sections 505, 501(a)(2)(B), and 502(f)(1)), 21 U.S.C. § 353a(a).

[77]   FDCA § 503A(a), 21 U.S.C. § 353a(a). The drug may be compounded "in limited quantities before the receipt of a valid prescription order for such individual patient based on a history of the licensed pharmacist or licensed physician receiving valid prescription orders for the compounding of the drug product, which orders have been generated solely within an established [physician/patient/pharmacist] relationship . . . ." FDCA § 503A(a)(2), 21 U.S.C. § 351(a)(2).

[78]   FDCA § 503A(b)(1)(D), 21 U.S.C. § 353a(b)(1)(D).

[79]   FDCA § 503A(b)(2), 21 U.S.C. § 353a(b)(2).

[80]   Bulk drug substances (active ingredients) in compounded drugs must 1) comply with compendial standards (USP or National Formulary), be components of approved drugs, or appear on a list in a regulation promulgated by FDA; 2) be manufactured in facilities registered under FDCA § 510; and 3) be accompanied by valid certificates of analysis for the bulk active substance. FDCA § 503A(b)(1)(A), 21 U.S.C. § 353a(b)(1)(A). Because FDA has not yet promulgated a bulk drug substances list, drugs must be compounded with drug substances that are approved or are the subject of USP or National Formulary monograph. See FDA, Guidance: Pharmacy Compounding of Human Drug Products Under Section 503A of the Federal Food, Drug, and Cosmetic Act, 5 (2014), *available at* http://www.fda.gov/downloads/drugs/guidancecomplianceregulatoryinformation/guidances/ucm377052.pdf.

[81]   Inactive ingredients must comply with compendia standards or with the USP chapter on pharmacy compounding. FDCA § 503A(b)(1)(B), 21 U.S.C. § 353a(b)(1)(B).

against compounding drugs that have been listed by FDA as drugs removed from the market on the basis of safety or efficacy[82] or determined by regulation to be demonstrably difficult to compound.[83] There are also limitations on interstate sales.[84] As originally enacted, section 503A contained a prohibition against advertising and promotion of compounded drugs. That provision was later found unconstitutional[85] and was removed by Congress in 2013 in the Drug Quality and Security Act.[86]

Section 503B

In addition to amending section 503A, the Drug Quality and Security Act added a new section 503B to provide an alternative regulatory scheme for "outsourcing facilities" that operate under the supervision of a pharmacist and compound sterile drugs.[87] If these facilities voluntarily register with FDA and comply with section 503B, they are exempt from the new drug approval, adequate directions for use, and drug supply chain provisions of the FDCA.[88] They are not, however, exempt from the statutory requirement of current Good Manufacturing Practice (cGMP) in section 501(a)(2)(B). Although FDA has indicated that these facilities will not have to meet all of the cGMP requirements that are applicable to drug manufacturers, FDA has taken the position that such facilities must meet "standards necessary to protect patients from the risks of contaminated or otherwise substandard compounded drug products," and has published interim guidance on such standards in anticipation of proposing regulations.[89]

---

[82]   FDCA § 503A(b)(1)(C), 21 U.S.C. § 353a(b)(1)(C). FDA's list of products removed from the market on the basis of safety or efficacy is established by regulation. See 21 C.F.R. § 216.24.

[83]   FDCA § 503A(b)(3)(A), 21 U.S.C. § 353a(b)(3)(A). FDA has not yet promulgated a list of products that are demonstrably difficult to compound.

[84]   The compounding entity may not distribute more than 5 percent of prescription orders in interstate commerce unless the pharmacist or entity is licensed in a state that has entered into a memorandum of understanding with FDA "which addresses the distribution of inordinate amounts of compounded drug products interstate and provides for appropriate investigation by a State agency of complaints relating to compounded drug products distributed outside such State." FDCA § 503A(b)(3)(B), 21 U.S.C. § 353a(b)(3)(B).

[85]   See W. States Med. Ctr., supra note 69, at 360. Prior to Congress' 2013 amendment to section 503A, there had been a split in the circuits regarding the constitutionality of the entire section. Although the Supreme Court did not address whether the unconstitutional ban on promotion was severable from the remainder of the section, the U.S. Court of Appeals for the Ninth Circuit had ruled in the underlying case that the ban was not severable. W. States Med. Ctr. v. United States, 238 F.3d 1090 (9th Cir. 2001), aff'd, 535 U.S. 357 (2002). On the basis of this ruling, FDA deemed section 503A to be invalid, and returned to its practice of regulating pharmacy compounding under a compliance policy guide that enumerated factors distinguishing "traditional practice of pharmacy" from compounding activities resembling commercial manufacture. FDA, Guidance for FDA Staff and Industry, Compliance Policy Guides Manual: § 460.200: Pharmacy Compounding, 2 (2002). In 2008, however, the U.S. Court of Appeals for the Fifth Circuit held in Medical Center Pharmacy v. Mukasey that the provision in section 503A banning promotion is severable, and that the other provisions in section 503A remain applicable. 536 F.3d 383 (5th Cir. 2008), rev'g Med. Ctr. Pharmacy v. Gonzales, 451 F. Supp. 2d 854 (W.D. Tex. 2006). Although the government did not appeal the Medical Center Pharmacy decision, FDA announced shortly after the decision that the agency would follow the court's ruling and apply section 503A only within the Fifth Circuit. See FDA, Compliance & Regulatory Information: Pharmacy Compounding, Medical Center Pharmacy v. Mukasey (May 6, 2009). Outside the Fifth Circuit, the agency continued to regulate pharmacy compounding under its Compliance Policy Guide.

[86]   Pub. L. No. 113-54, § 106(a), 127 Stat. 587, 598 (2013).

[87]   FDCA § 503B(d)(4), 21 U.S.C. § 353b(d)(4). The outsourcing facility need not, itself, be a pharmacy licensed under state law. FDCA § 503B(4)(d)(iii)(B), 21 U.S.C. § 353b(4)(d)(iii)(B).

[88]   FDCA § 503B(a) (exempting affected drugs from FDCA §§ 505, 502(f)(1), and 582), 21 U.S.C. § 353b(a).

[89]   FDA, Guidance for Industry: Current Good Manufacturing Practice—Interim Guidance for Human Drug Compounding Outsourcing Facilities Under Section 503B of the FD&C Act (2014), available at http://www.

Certain restrictions under section 503B are similar to those in section 503A. These include standards for active ingredients[90] and inactive ingredients[91] and requirements that the compounded drug not be on FDA's list of drugs removed from drug from the market on the basis of safety or efficacy[92] and not be determined by regulation to be a drug that is demonstrably difficult to compound.[93] There is also a requirement that the compounded drug not be "essentially a copy of one or more approved drugs."[94] The definition of "essentially a copy of an approved drug" in section 503B, however, differs from the definition of "essentially a copy of a commercially available drug product" in section 503A. Under section 503B, the compounded drug is considered "essentially a copy of an approved drug" if it contains an active ingredient that is a component of an approved drug or an unapproved non-prescription drug unless the compounded drug is modified to "produce[] for an individual patient a clinical difference, as determined by the prescribing practitioner, between the compounded drug and the comparable approved drug"[95] or if the compounded drug is "identical or nearly identical" to an approved drug or unapproved non-prescription drug (unless the approved drug appears on FDA's drug shortage list under section 506E).[96]

Because outsourcing facilities are permitted to engage in large-scale production of sterile drugs outside of traditional practice of pharmacy, many provisions in section 503B are significantly more onerous than those in section 503A. Outsourcing facilities under section 503B must register with FDA,[97] pay user fees,[98] report on products that they compound,[99] and report on adverse events.[100] FDA is provided with express authority to conduct inspections under a "risk-based schedule" with enumerated risk factors,[101] and to inspect records.[102]

---

fda.gov/downloads/drugs/guidancecomplianceregulatoryinformation/guidances/ucm403496.pdf.

[90] If an outsourcing facility compounds from bulk drug substances rather than from commercially available products, the drug substance used in the compounding must appear on an FDA list of drug substances for which there is a clinical need or on FDA's drug shortage list under section 506E. FDCA § 503B(a)(2)(A), 21 U.S.C. § 353b(a)(2)(A). The drug substance must also comply with any applicable USP, NF or other compendial monograph. FDCA § 503B(a)(2)(B), 21 U.S.C. § 353b(a)(2)(B).

[91] FDCA § 503B(a)(3), 21 U.S.C. § 353b(a)(3).

[92] FDCA § 503B(a)(4), 21 U.S.C. § 353b(a)(4). FDA has indicated that its list of products removed from the market on the basis of safety or efficacy in 21 C.F.R. § 216.24 will govern requirements in both sections 503A and 503B. Additions and Modifications to the List of Drug Products That Have Been Withdrawn or Removed From the Market for Reasons of Safety or Effectiveness, 79 Fed. Reg. 37,687, 37,688 (July 2, 2014).

[93] FDCA § 503B(a)(6), 21 U.S.C. § 353b(a)(6). As mentioned above in the context of section 503A, FDA has not promulgated this list.

[94] FDCA § 503B(a)(5), 21 U.S.C. § 353b(a)(5).

[95] FDCA § 503B(d)(2)(B), 21 U.S.C. § 353b(d)(2)(B).

[96] FDCA § 503B(d)(2)(A), 21 U.S.C. § 353b(d)(2)(A).

[97] FDCA § 503B(b)(1)(A), 21 U.S.C. § 353b(b)(1)(A). See also FDA, Registration of Human Drug Compounding Outsourcing Facilities Under Section 503B of the FD&C Act: Guidance for Industry (2014). FDA must maintain a list of the registered outsourcing facilities on the agency's website. FDCA § 503B(b)(1)(B)(ii), 21 U.S.C. § 353b(b)(1)(B)(ii).

[98] FDCA § 503B(a)(9), 21 U.S.C. § 353b(a)(9). Outsourcing facilities must pay an annual establishment fee and a re-inspection fee. FDCA § 744K, 21 U.S.C. § 379j-62. See also FDA, Fees for Human Drug Compounding Outsourcing Facilities Under Sections 503B and 744K of the FD&C Act: Guidance for Industry (2014).

[99] FDCA § 503B(b)(2), 21 U.S.C. § 353b(b)(2). See also FDA, Electronic Drug Product Reporting for Human Drug Compounding Outsourcing Facilities Under Section 503B of the Federal Food, Drug, and Cosmetic Act: Guidance for Industry: Revised Draft Guidance (2014).

[100] FDCA § 503B(b)(5), 21 U.S.C. § 353b(b)(5).

[101] FDCA §§ 503B(4)(B), 21 U.S.C. § 353b(b)(4)(B). Inspection determinations will be based on the known safety risks of outsourcing facilities based on compliance history, record, and nature of recalls linked to the facility, the inherent risk of the drugs compounded at the facility, and other factors. FDCA § 503B(b)(4)(C), 21 U.S.C. § 353b(b)(4)(C).

[102] FDCA § 503B(b)(4)(A)(ii), 21 U.S.C. § 353b(b)(4)(A)(ii).

Outsourcing facilities must also demonstrate that they will use controls comparable to the controls applicable under any applicable REMS.[103] Section 503B also contains special labeling requirements for drugs compounded by outsourcing facilities.[104]

Outsourcing facilities are also relieved from some of the requirements in section 503A. They may compound without a prescription[105] and reconstitute and make other modifications to approved products that are specified in labeling.[106] There is also no limitation on interstate sales under section 503B but the drugs must not be sold or transferred by an entity other than the outsourcing facility.[107]

Misbranding and Enforcement

In addition to the new standards and requirements in sections 503A and 503B, the Drug Quality and Security Act added a misbranding provision and prohibited acts related to compounding. A compounded drug is deemed misbranded if its advertising or promotion is false or misleading in any particular.[108] The Act further prohibits the resale of a compounded drug that is labeled "not for resale" under section 503B, the intentional falsification of a prescription for a drug subject to section 503A or 503B, and the failure by an outsourcing facility to report drugs or adverse events by an outsourcing facility under section 503B.[109]

In an unusual additional provision, Congress enlists state boards of pharmacy in enforcing the requirements of sections 503A and 503B by requiring FDA to receive submissions from them with regard to actions they have taken against compounding pharmacies (including Warning Letters, sanctions, or suspension or revocation of a state license) or concerns they have that a compounding pharmacy may be acting contrary to one or more FDA requirements.[110] FDA is required to notify a state pharmacy board if it finds that a compounding pharmacy is violating federal regulations.[111]

---

[103] FDCA § 503B(a)(7), 21 U.S.C. § 353b(a)(7). See discussion of REMS requirements in Chapter 10.

[104] The product label must state "This is a compounded drug" or must contain a "reasonable comparable alternative statement (as specified by the Secretary)" that may be specified by FDA. FDCA § 503B(a)(10)(A)(i), 21 U.S.C. § 353b(a)(10)(A)(i). It must also contain the name of the outsourcing facility, the lot or batch number of the drug, dosage form and strength, and other key information. FDCA § 503B(a)(10)(A), 21 U.S.C. § 353b(a)(10)(A).

[105] FDCA § 503B(d)(4)(A)(iii)(C), 21 U.S.C. § 353b(d)(4)(A)(iii)(C).

[106] For purposes of section 503B, the term "compounding" includes "the combining, admixing, mixing, diluting, pooling, reconstituting, or otherwise altering of a drug or bulk drug substance to create a drug." FDCA § 503B(d)(1), 21 U.S.C. § 353b(d)(1). As noted above, "compounding" under section 503A expressly excludes from its scope for purposes of that section "mixing, reconstituting, or other such acts that are performed in accordance with directions contained in approved labeling provided by the product's manufacturer and other manufacturer directions consistent with that labeling." See supra note 77.

[107] FDCA § 503B(a)(8), 21 U.S.C. § 353b(a)(8).

[108] FDCA § 502(bb), 21 U.S.C. § 352(bb).

[109] FDCA § 301(ccc), 21 U.S.C. § 331(ccc).

[110] Pub. L. No. 113-54, supra note 86, § 105, 127 Stat. at 597.

[111] Id. § 105(d).

Conclusion

Although Congress and FDA have been willing to exercise greater regulatory control over pharmacists than over medical practitioners, regulation of both professions remains largely in the hands of the states. The greater degree of regulation of pharmacists results mainly from activities such as large-scale compounding that resemble pharmaceutical manufacturing and distribution. As the lines between pharmacy, drug manufacturing and distribution, and healthcare delivery become less distinct in today's healthcare marketplace, FDA's policies and precedents suggest the potential for an even more intrusive regulatory presence for healthcare professionals. This tendency may be countered, however, by the need for greater flexibility and efficiency in the healthcare marketplace and by the continued evolution of the marketplace model for which the FDCA was originally designed.

CHAPTER 20

FDA ADMINISTRATIVE PROCEDURES

....

ANN H. WION

Introduction

The Food and Drug Administration (FDA) acts primarily as a regulatory agency, overseeing the marketing in interstate commerce of a broad range of foods, drugs, medical devices, cosmetics, and electronic products.[1] The principal statute administered by FDA is the Federal Food, Drug, and Cosmetic Act (FDCA),[2] which establishes the agency within the Department of Health and Human Services (DHHS) and sets forth its mission to promote and protect the public health.[3] The agency's decisions interpreting statutory provisions are generally embodied in "orders" and "rules," as defined by the Administrative Procedure Act (APA).[4] For example, FDA reviews various types of premarket applications and issues decisions (orders) granting or denying approval.[5] In some cases, the agency's decisions are embodied in final rules issued in response to petitions described by statute.[6] FDA also

---

[1] For a very useful brief overview of FDA's statutory authorities and activities, *see* Chapter 1.

[2] Pub. L. No. 75-717, 52 Stat. 1040 (1938), as amended 21 U.S.C. §§ 321-399 (2012).

[3] FDCA § 1003, 21 U.S.C. § 393.

[4] "Rule" is defined in the APA in essence as "the whole or a part of an agency statement of general or particular applicability and future effect designed to implement, interpret, or prescribe law or policy or describing the organization, procedure, or practice requirements of an agency . . . ." 5 U.S.C. § 551(4) (2012). "Order" is defined in the APA as "the whole or a part of a final disposition, whether affirmative, negative, injunctive, or declaratory in form, of an agency in a matter other than rule making but including licensing." 5 U.S.C. § 551(6).

[5] For example, FDA reviews and approves new drug applications under section 505 of the FDCA and medical device premarket approval applications under section 515. 21 U.S.C. §§ 355, 360e. The agency reviews and approves biologics license applications under section 351 of the Public Health Service Act (PHSA). 42 U.S.C. § 262 (2012).

[6] For example, under section 409 of the FDCA, the agency reviews and makes decisions on petitions proposing the issuance of regulations prescribing conditions under which food additives may be safely used. 21 U.S.C. § 348. Under section 403 of the FDCA, in response to petitions, the agency promulgates regulations authorizing so-called "nutrient content claims" or "health claims" to be made in food labeling. 21 U.S.C. § 343.

establishes by regulation various pre- and postmarketing requirements for products within its jurisdiction.[7]

It follows, then, that the more formal processes through which FDA administers the law are primarily adjudications and rulemakings.[8] The agency's interpretations of the law are also often reflected in guidance documents or in responses to petitions that are not part of a marketing-authorization process. Like other federal agencies, FDA also uses many informal communication tools—such as press or other media communications, speeches, and responses to letters—to inform and educate the regulated industry and the public.[9]

Of course, as a regulatory agency, FDA's interpretations of the law are reflected in its enforcement actions and policies. For example, FDA exercises its authority and conveys its views through communications during inspections, Warning Letters and other regulatory correspondence, initiation and prosecution of administrative actions and civil and criminal judicial actions, and import-detention actions.[10]

The FDCA specifies many of the procedures FDA is to follow in implementing the statute's substantive requirements.[11] As an agency within the executive branch, FDA is also subject to constitutional constraints, general statutes that govern its activities, judicial opinions, and executive orders issued by the President.[12]

This chapter focuses on particular administrative procedures governing FDA's policy formulation and decision making.[13] FDA has been a government leader in procedural innovation for many decades. Since the mid-1970s, when the agency first promulgated its administrative practice and procedures regulations, FDA has both charted and reflected

---

[7]   For example, FDA's regulations prescribe conditions for studying certain unapproved drugs, biological products, and devices prior to submission of marketing applications. 21 C.F.R. pts. 312, 812 (2014). Similarly, the agency prescribes in regulations postmarketing adverse experience reporting requirements for certain drugs, biological products, and devices. 21 C.F.R. §§ 314.80, 600.80, 803.1-.58 (2014).

[8]   The APA defines "adjudication" as "agency process for the formulation of an order" and "rule making" as "agency process for formulating, amending, or repealing a rule." 5 U.S.C. §§ 551(7), 551(5).

[9]   Many of the agency's current informal communications may be accessed through FDA's website at http://www.fda.gov.

[10]   For valuable discussions and informative excerpts related to FDA's enforcement activities, *see* PETER BARTON HUTT, RICHARD A. MERRILL & LEWIS A. GROSSMAN, FOOD AND DRUG LAW: CASES AND MATERIALS 1196-1370 (3d ed. 2007) and Chapter 21, *infra*.

[11]   For a useful discussion of many of these procedures, *see* Joel E. Hoffman, *Administrative Procedures of the Food and Drug Administration*, in I FUNDAMENTALS OF LAW AND REGULATION 13-53 (Robert P. Brady et al. eds., 1997).

[12]   For a brief description of some of the general statutes and executive orders to which FDA is subject, *see* Cooper, *supra* note 1. Constitutional limitations on potential FDA activities are reflected in the Supreme Court's decision in *Thompson v. W. States Med. Ctr.*, 535 U.S. 357 (2002) (holding certain advertising restrictions related to compounded human drugs in the Food and Drug Administration Modernization Act of 1997 to be unconstitutional under the First Amendment). *See* Margaret Gilhooley, *Drug Regulation and the Constitution After* Western States, 37 U. RICH. L. REV. 901 (2003).

[13]   This chapter does not address certain topics in administrative law and practice that apply to FDA and other agencies, such as standing to challenge FDA decisions in court, ripeness of challenges to FDA decisions, the laws governing information disclosure (e.g., the Freedom of Information Act), when notice-and-comment rulemaking is required, and many others. For more information on such topics, *see, e.g.*, RICHARD J. PIERCE, JR., ADMINISTRATIVE LAW TREATISE (4th ed. 2002), JACOB A. STEIN ET AL., ADMINISTRATIVE LAW (2006), OFFICE OF INFORMATION AND PRIVACY, U.S. DEPARTMENT OF JUSTICE, FREEDOM OF INFORMATION ACT GUIDE (2007) (also *available at* http://www.gov/o4foia/04_7.html).

the course of modern administrative law.[14] Describing in detail the agency's procedures for every type of FDA action would require a prohibitively extensive discussion. Consequently, this chapter concentrates on procedures in four main areas: regulations, hearings, guidance documents, and petitions. Each of these areas illustrates FDA's effective approaches to reasoned decision making through structured participation by interested persons.

Regulations

FDA's Historical Approach to Regulations

From as early as 1906, in the Pure Food and Drugs Act, FDA's predecessor agency was authorized to make rules and regulations to enforce the law.[15] The 1906 act, however, prescribed neither standards for the regulations nor procedures for their promulgation.[16] Chapter VII of the FDCA, as originally enacted, contained three separate general rulemaking provisions: section 701(a), authority for the Secretary[17] to promulgate regulations "for the efficient enforcement of this Act"; section 701(b), authority for the Secretary and the Secretary of the Treasury jointly to prescribe regulations "for the efficient enforcement of . . . section 801" of the act, regarding imports and exports; and section 701(e), regarding regulations issued under specific authorities elsewhere in the act.[18]

With enactment of the APA[19] in 1946 and subsequent case law, it became clear that section 701(a) and (b) rulemakings are subject to the procedural requirements for informal

---

[14] For a general description of some of FDA's pioneering efforts, *see* HUTT, *supra* note 10, at 1522-1614, and Hoffman, *supra* note 11.

[15] The Secretary of Agriculture was responsible for enforcing the 1906 statute. *See* Pub. L. No. 59-384, 34 Stat. 768 (1906). The Secretaries of Agriculture, Commerce and Labor, and Treasury had joint rulemaking authority. *Id.* § 3.

[16] *See* Pub. L. No. 59-384, 34 Stat. 768, § 3. The rules were required only to be "uniform." *Id.*

[17] Functions vested in the Secretary of the Department of Health and Human Services under the FDCA have been delegated to the Commissioner of Food and Drugs. FOOD & DRUG ADMIN., STAFF MANUAL GUIDES 1410.10.1.A.1. (2014), http://www.fda.gov/aboutfda/reportsmanualsforms/staffmanualguides/default.htm. The Secretary has reserved authority to approve certain FDA regulations. *Id.* at 1410.10.2. The Office of the Secretary designates the specific FDA regulations that are to be reviewed by DHHS officials before publication.

[18] Pub. L. No. 75-717, 52 Stat. 1040 (1938) (codified as amended at 21 U.S.C. §§ 301-399). *See* 21 U.S.C. § 371(a), (b), (e) (2012). Under current section 701(b), the regulations "shall be promulgated in such manner and shall take effect at such time, after due notice, as the Secretary of Health and Human Services shall determine." 21 U.S.C. § 371(b).

[19] Pub. L. No. 404, §§ 1-12, 60 Stat. 237 (1946), repealed by Pub. L. No. 89-554, 80 Stat. 381 (1966). The APA, as amended, was subsequently codified at 5 U.S.C. §§ 551-559, 701-706, 1305, 3105, 3344, 5372, 7521 (2012).

rulemaking set out in 5 U.S.C. § 553.[20] Similarly, section 701(e) rulemakings are subject to the requirements of 5 U.S.C. §§ 556 and 557 for formal evidentiary hearings.[21]

FDA Regulations on Rulemaking

As part of extensive rulemakings on administrative practices and procedures begun in 1975, FDA developed regulations governing its procedures for promulgating regulations for the efficient enforcement of the law.[22] These regulations, now codified at 21 C.F.R. § 10.40,[23] govern the agency's informal rulemaking and, to the extent applicable, formal rulemaking.[24]

FDA's rulemaking regulation specifically provides for the agency to propose regulations not only on its own initiative but also in response to petitions from interested persons.[25] The general format for proposed rules is prescribed in 21 C.F.R. § 10.40(b)(1). Under this regulation, the agency ordinarily will provide at least 60 days for comment on a proposed rule, although the comment period may be as short as 10 days for good cause.[26] In common practice, FDA usually provides longer than 60 days for the public to comment, especially when the proposal is lengthy or complex.[27] Interested persons may also request extensions of the comment period;[28] extensions of 30 days or longer are published in the *Federal Register.*[29]

---

[20]   *See* 40 Fed. Reg. 40,682, 40,688 (Sept. 3, 1975). Although for some period of time there was uncertainty about FDA's authority to promulgate substantive rules, a series of cases, beginning with the Supreme Court's decision in *Abbott Laboratories v. Gardner,* 387 U.S. 136 (1967), confirmed the agency's rulemaking authority. *See, e.g.,* Nat'l Ass'n of Pharmaceutical Mfrs. v. FDA, 637 F.2d 877 (2d Cir. 1981); Nat'l Nutritional Foods Ass'n v. Weinberger, 512 F.2d 688 (2d Cir. 1975). *See also* Richard A. Merrill, *FDA and the Effects of Substantive Rules,* 35 Food Drug Cosm. L.J. 270 (1980).

[21]   *See id. See also* United States v. Florida East Coast Ry. Co., 410 U.S. 224 (1973). The 1938 act included specific procedures for promulgating rules establishing standards of identity, quality, and fill of food containers (Pub. L. No. 75-717, § 401, 52 Stat. at 1046); tolerances for poisonous and deleterious substances in food (*id.* § 406(a), 52 Stat. at 1049)); lists of coal-tar colors for use in food, drugs, and cosmetics (*id.* § 406(b), 52 Stat. at 1049; § 504, 52 Stat. at 1052; § 604, 52 Stat. at 1055); and standards of strength, quality, and purity for drugs (*id.* § 501(b), 52 Stat. at 1049).

[22]   *See* 40 Fed. Reg. 40,682 (proposed rule); 42 Fed. Reg. 4680 (Jan. 25, 1977) (final rule). The agency had issued final rules in May 1975 without following notice-and-comment procedures, on the basis of two theories: 1) under the APA, regulations governing agency practice and procedure may be published without notice and public procedure and 2) the regulations met the APA's "impracticable, unnecessary, or contrary to the public interest" standard for issuance without notice and public procedure. *See* 40 Fed. Reg. 22,950 (May 27, 1975). In *American College of Neuropsychopharmacology v. Weinberg,* C.A. No. 75-1187 (D.D.C. 1975), however, the court held that the notice-and-comment requirements of the APA did apply to these FDA regulations. The agency then issued the proposed rule for comment in September 1975 and issued the final rule in January 1977.

[23]   21 C.F.R. § 10.40 (2014).

[24]   *See* 21 C.F.R. § 10.40(a)(1).

[25]   21 C.F.R. § 10.40(a)(2). *See* discussion of the citizen petition process at pp. 715-20, *infra.*

[26]   21 C.F.R. § 10.40(b)(2).

[27]   Executive Order No. 12889, "Implementation of the North American Free Trade Agreement," requires a 75-day comment period for, with certain exceptions, "any proposed Federal technical regulation or any Federal sanitary or phytosanitary measure of general application." Exec. Order No. 12889, § 4, 58 Fed. Reg. 69,681 (Dec. 30, 1993). Certain FDA proposed regulations would fall within the scope of this executive order.

[28]   21 C.F.R. § 10.40(b)(3) (detailing permissible grounds for extension of comment period).

[29]   21 C.F.R. § 10.40(b)(3)(ii).

Docket Submission Requirements

At the same time it promulgated the regulation governing rulemakings, FDA issued a regulation governing submissions of documents, such as comments on proposed rules, to the agency's Division of Dockets Management.[30]

The docket submission regulations, now codified at 21 C.F.R. § 10.20, require that submissions be signed by the submitter or by an attorney or other authorized representative.[31] These regulations make clear that a submission to an FDA docket is a representation that the statements in the submission are true and accurate, and an acknowledgment that such statements are subject to the False Reports to the Government Act (18 U.S.C. § 1001).[32] Information referred to or relied on generally must be included in full, not incorporated by reference.[33] Materials in a foreign language must be accompanied by an English translation verified to be complete and accurate.[34] Irrelevant information, personal privacy information, and any defamatory, scurrilous, or intemperate matter are not to be included in a submission.[35]

If the Division of Dockets Management is aware that a submission, on its face, does not meet an applicable requirement, it will not file the submission, but will return it to the submitter to correct the deficiencies.[36] Filing means only that the Division has not identified a technical deficiency.[37]

With the advent of electronic communication through the Internet, FDA permits submission of rulemaking comments electronically, through the federal electronic rulemaking portal.[38] Submissions by facsimile, mail, courier, and hand delivery (including paper, disk, or CD-ROM submissions) also continue to be accepted.

Comments submitted to FDA are available for public examination. All comments received may be posted to the dockets website without change, including any personal information provided.[39]

---

[30] 40 Fed. Reg. at 40,719 (proposed rule); 42 Fed. Reg. at 4,698 (final rule) (now codified at 21 C.F.R. § 10.20 (2014)).

[31] 21 C.F.R. § 10.20(b).

[32] 21 C.F.R. § 10.20(i). The statements are "to the best of the knowledge, information, and belief" of the submitter to be true and accurate. *Id.*

[33] 21 C.F.R. § 10.20(c). An article or other cited source may be incorporated by reference if it is a reported federal court case, a federal law or regulation, an FDA document that is routinely publicly available, or a readily available recognized medical or scientific textbook. 21 C.F.R. § 10.20(c)(1).

[34] 21 C.R.R. § 10.20(c)(2). A brief statement of the translator's qualifications is also required. *Id.*

[35] 21 C.F.R. § 10.20(c)(3), (4), (5).

[36] 21 C.F.R. § 10.20(c)(6).

[37] 21 C.F.R. § 10.20(d).

[38] Under section 206(c) of the E-Government Act of 2002, agencies are, to the extent practicable, to accept comments in informal rulemakings by electronic means. Pub. L. No. 107-347, 116 Stat. 2910 (2002). A centralized portal for submission of electronic comments to many federal agencies' rulemakings has been established at Federal eRulemaking Portal: http://www.regulations.gov.

[39] *See* http://www.regulations.gov.

Promulgation Without Notice and Comment

Consistent with the APA, 5 U.S.C. § 553(b), FDA may publish a final rule without first providing for public comment when the agency, for good cause, finds that procedure "impracticable, unnecessary, or contrary to the public interest."[40] In those cases, the final rule would provide an opportunity for subsequent comment.[41]

In 1997, FDA published its policy and procedures for issuing "direct final rules."[42] Consistently with a recommendation of the Administrative Conference of the United States,[43] the agency announced its approach to streamlining the regulations-promulgation process for rules it believes will be noncontroversial.[44] When the agency does not anticipate receiving any significant adverse comment, it will publish a final rule and, in the same issue of the *Federal Register*, a companion proposed rule.[45] Ordinarily, FDA will allow at least 75 days for comment on the direct final rule. If the agency receives no significant adverse comment, the direct final rule goes into effect 60 days after the end of the comment period. If the agency receives a significant adverse comment, it will withdraw the direct final rule and, in developing the final rule under the usual APA notice-and-comment procedure, will consider the comment as a comment on the proposed rule.

Final Regulations

In considering the provisions of any final rule, the agency may avail itself of additional procedures, such as public meetings, hearings, and revised proposed rules.[46]

Title 21 C.F.R. § 10.40 also specifies the format for final rules. The preamble to the codified regulation summarizes each type of comment and the agency's conclusions as to each, with a "thorough and comprehensible explanation of the reasons for the Commissioner's decision on each issue."[47] Many FDA regulations contain lengthy preambles with extensive discussions of the submitted comments and the agency's responses.[48] The preambles also contain any

---

[40]   21 C.F.R. § 10.40(e)(1).

[41]   *Id.* FDA generally styles such regulations as "interim final rules."

[42]   *See* 62 Fed. Reg. 62,466 (Nov. 21, 1997).

[43]   *See* ACUS Recommendation 95-4, Procedures for Noncontroversial and Expedited Rulemaking, 60 Fed. Reg. 43,108 (Aug. 18, 1995), referred to by FDA at 62 Fed. Reg. 62,466 (Nov. 21, 1997).

[44]   *See* Guidance for FDA and Industry: Direct Final Rule Procedures, at 62 Fed. Reg. 62,466.

[45]   *Id.* "Significant adverse comment" is defined as one "where the comment explains why the rule would be inappropriate, including challenges to the rule's underlying premise or approach, or would be ineffective or unacceptable without a change." *Id.* at 62,469. Comments that are frivolous, insubstantial, or outside the scope of the rule are not considered "adverse." *Id. See* 63 Fed. Reg. 19,185, 19,196 (Apr. 17, 1998) for an example of a direct final rule and companion proposed rule issued by FDA.

[46]   21 C.F.R. § 10.40(f).

[47]   21 C.F.R. § 10.40(c)(3). Prior to issuance of the final rule that established section 10.40(c)(3), FDA's rulemaking classifying certain vitamins as prescription drugs had been examined by the Second Circuit in relation to "the agency's obligation to publish a statement of reasons that will be sufficiently detailed to permit judicial review" and an admonition to "provide a thorough and comprehensible statement of the reasons for its decision." Nat'l Nutritional Foods Ass'n v. Weinberger, 512 F.2d 688, 701 (2d Cir. 1975).

[48]   *See, e.g.,* FDA's final rule on current good manufacturing practice for dietary supplements, with more than 200 pages of text as printed in the *Federal Register*. 72 Fed. Reg. 34,752 (June 25, 2007).

applicable analyses under the Regulatory Flexibility Act,[49] the Paperwork Reduction Act,[50] the National Environmental Policy Act,[51] and the Unfunded Mandates Reform Act.[52]

Record for Judicial Review

An FDA regulation specifies the documents that constitute the administrative record of a rulemaking.[53] The validity of the regulation when reviewed in a court action is then to be determined solely on the basis of the administrative record specified.[54] In judicial review of FDA's informal rulemaking under 701(a), the arbitrary and capricious standard applies.[55]

Formal Rulemaking

As originally enacted in 1938, section 701(e) of the FDCA required the agency to hold a formal evidentiary hearing on each proposal to issue, modify, or repeal a regulation under certain provisions of the statute.[56] For a proposed rule under this section, the agency was required to hold a formal hearing and make a record containing substantial evidence to support its proposal even if there had been no objection to the proposal. In response to criticisms of such situations, Congress revised the law, first in 1954 in relation to food standards,[57] and two years later for all section 701(e) proceedings.[58]

After subsequent amendments over the years,[59] current section 701(e) specifically refers to the issuance, amendment, or repeal of any regulation under:

- section 403(j) (labeling of foods for special dietary uses),

- section 404(a) (food emergency permit controls),

- section 406 (tolerances for poisonous and deleterious substances in food),

---

[49] 5 U.S.C. §§ 601-621 (2012).

[50] 44 U.S.C. §§ 3501-3520 (2012).

[51] 42 U.S.C. §§ 4321-4322 (2012). *See* 21 C.F.R. pt. 25 (2014) for FDA's regulations on consideration of environmental impacts.

[52] 2 U.S.C. §§ 1501-1571 (2012).

[53] 21 C.F.R. § 10.40(g). The record includes, for example, the proposed rule, comments received, the final rule, all information identified or filed as part of the administrative record, and transcripts or minutes of meetings related to the notice. *Id.* In a case involving the agency's regulation banning sulfite agents on fresh potatoes, the court concluded that FDA's failure to follow its own regulations on making the entire record available for public inspection was arbitrary and capricious. Hanover Potato Prods., Inc. v. Sullivan, No. 1:CV-90-0746 (M.D. Pa. Aug. 3, 1990), *aff'd*, No. 90-5738, 1991 WL 35857 (3d Cir. Mar. 20, 1991). *See also* Hanover Potato Prods., Inc. v. Shalala, 989 F.2d 123 (3d Cir. 1993).

[54] *See* 21 C.F.R. § 10.45(f) (2014). *See also, e.g.,* Citizens to Preserve Overton Park v. Volpe, 401 U.S. 402, 415 (1971).

[55] *See* 5 U.S.C. § 706. *See Overton Park,* 401 U.S. at 416; United States v. Nova Scotia Food Prods. Corp., 568 F.2d 240, 249 (2d Cir. 1977).

[56] Pub. L. No. 75-717, § 701(e), 52 Stat. at 1050.

[57] Pub. L. No. 83-336, 68 Stat. 54 (1954). For further discussion of this amendment, known as the Hale Amendment [of 1954], *see* Hoffman, *supra* note 11 at 26.

[58] Pub. L. No. 84-905, 70 Stat. 919 (1956). *See* Hoffman, *supra* note 11 at 26 for a discussion of the Hale Amendment of 1956.

[59] Section 701(e) was subsequently amended in 1960 (Pub. L. No. 86-618, 74 Stat. 397 (1960)), 1990 (Pub. L. No. 101-535, 104 Stat. 2353 (1990)), 1993 (Pub. L. No. 103-80, 107 Stat. 778 (1993)), and 1994 (Pub. L. No. 103-396, 108 Stat. 4153 (1994)). *See* note to 21 U.S.C. § 371. Although section 701(e) continues to refer to section 502(d), that section was eliminated by Pub. L. No. 105-115, § 126(6), 111 Stat. 2296, 2327 (1997).

- section 501(b) (tests for strength, quality or purity of drugs),

- section 502(h) (packaging and labeling of drugs liable to deterioration), or

- any action for amendment or repeal of a definition and standard of identity under section 401 for any dairy product.[60]

The procedure specified in section 701(e) calls for publication of a proposal,[61] followed by an opportunity for all interested persons to present their views.[62] Then FDA is to issue a public order with a 30-day period for any person who would be adversely affected to file objections, "specifying with particularity the provisions of the order deemed objectionable, stating the grounds therefor, and requesting a public hearing upon such objections."[63] The filing of objections stays the provisions to which objections have been made. After the request for a hearing, the agency is to hold "such a public hearing for the purpose of receiving evidence relevant and material to the issues raised by such objections."[64]

After the hearing, an order is issued on the basis of substantial evidence of record at the hearing.[65] The order is to take effect no sooner than 90 days after publication, during which time an adversely affected person may petition the U.S. court of appeals for the circuit within which the person resides or has a principal place of business.[66]

FDA's administrative procedure regulations list these additional provisions of the act (not specifically listed in section 701(e)) as affording an opportunity for a formal evidentiary hearing in rulemaking matters:

- section 409(c), (d) and (h) (food additive regulations); and

- section 721(b) and (c) (regulations for color additive listing and certification).[67]

---

[60]   21 U.S.C. § 371(e)(1). Codified references are to 21 U.S.C. §§ 343(j), 344(a), 346, 351(b), 352(h), and 341.

[61]   The proposal may be made on the agency's initiative or by "petition of any interested person, showing reasonable grounds therefor." 21 U.S.C. § 371(e)(1).

[62]   The opportunity to present views is "orally or in writing," 21 U.S.C. § 371(e)(1); typically, the agency affords the opportunity for written comments at this stage.

[63]   21 U.S.C. § 371(e)(2).

[64]   21 U.S.C. § 371(e)(3).

[65]   Id.

[66]   21 U.S.C. § 371(e)(3), (f)(1).

[67]   21 C.F.R. § 10.50(c)(5) & (13) (2014). Section 409 of the FDCA does not refer to section 701(e), but describes similar procedures. 21 U.S.C. § 348. One difference is that section 409(f) states that the order is to be based on a "fair evaluation of the entire record at such hearing," 21 U.S.C. § 348(f), whereas the order under 701(e) is to be based "on substantial evidence of record at such hearing," 21 U.S.C. § 371(e)(3). This textual difference has not made any practical difference in the agency's approach to these rulemaking hearings. Section 721(d) specifically refers to section 701(e). 21 U.S.C. § 379e(d). See Simpson v. Young, 854 F.2d 1429 (D.C. Cir. 1988). FDA's regulations also list, as subject to formal rulemaking procedures, regulations under section 4(a) of the Fair Packaging and Labeling Act, 15 U.S.C. 1453(a) (2012) (food, drug, device, and cosmetic labeling) and section 5(c) of the Fair Packaging and Labeling Act, 15 U.S.C. 1454(c) (2012) (additional economic regulations relating to food, drugs, devices, and cosmetics). 21 C.F.R. 10.50(c)(14), (15) (2014); see 15 U.S.C. 1453(a), 1454(c) and 1455(a) (2012). The agency's regulations also continue to list section 502(n) (prescription drug advertising regulations) and section 512(n)(5) (regulations for animal antibiotic drugs and certification requirements). 21 C.F.R. 10.50(c)(9), (12) (2014). Section 502(n), however, was modified by Pub. L. No. 110-85, § 901(d)(3), 121 Stat. 823, 940 (2007), to delete the previous reference in section 502(n) to 701(e) rulemaking; and section 512(n)(5) was repealed by Pub. L. No. 100-670, § 101(b), 102 Stat. 3971 (1988).

Hearing Denials

Although section 701(e) does not expressly provide for the denial of hearing requests, FDA has taken the position that hearing requests under this section may, in certain circumstances, be denied.[68] In the context of regulations for the listing of coal-tar colors for use in food, FDA had denied a hearing request on the basis that the requesters' grounds were insufficient to warrant a hearing. Because the requesters sought a regulation the agency had no authority to promulgate, FDA determined that there would be no purpose in holding a hearing. In upholding the agency's decision, the Eighth Circuit relied in part on the language in section 701(e) that provides that the purpose of the hearing is to receive evidence "relevant and material to the issues raised by such objections."[69] The court stated that

> the objections, in order to be effective and necessitate the hearing requested, must be legally adequate so that, if true, the order complained of could not prevail. The objections must raise "issues." The issues must be material to the question involved; that is, the legality of the order attacked. They may not be frivolous or inconsequential . . . . Congress did not intend the governmental agencies created by it to perform useless or unfruitful tasks.[70]

When FDA promulgated its administrative procedure regulations governing formal rulemaking, the agency expressly relied on this and other judicial precedent to permit denials of hearing requests.[71] The current regulations at 21 C.F.R. Part 12, which govern hearings in formal rulemaking proceedings, authorize hearing denials unless the requester has submitted material showing that:

- there is a genuine and substantial issue of fact, not only an issue of policy or law;

- the factual issue can be resolved by available and specifically identified reliable evidence;

- the data and information would be adequate to justify resolution of the factual issue in the way sought by the requester;

- resolution of the factual issue in the way sought is adequate to justify the action requested;

- the requested action is not inconsistent with a statutory provision or a regulation particularizing statutory standards; and

- the requirements in other applicable regulations are met.[72]

---

[68] See, e.g., 41 Fed. Reg. 51,706, at 51,708-10 (Nov. 23, 1976). Although the question whether the language of section 701(e) requires development of a formal record pursuant to the APA, 5 U.S.C. 556 and 557, has never been directly adjudicated, FDA decided to follow the Supreme Court's dictum on this matter in United States v. Florida East Coast Railway Co., 410 U.S. 224, 237-238 (1973), where the Court used section 701(e) as an example of a statutory provision that requires a hearing "on the record" and, therefore, a formal evidentiary hearing under the APA. See 40 Fed. Reg. at 40,691.

[69] Dyestuffs & Chems., Inc. v. Flemming, 271 F.2d 281, 286 (8th Cir. 1959). But see Certified Color Indus. Comm. v. Flemming, 283 F.2d 622 (2d Cir. 1960) (hearing request impermissibly denied because objections raised issue of fact).

[70] Id. at 286.

[71] See 40 Fed. Reg. at 40,700 (proposed rule); 41 Fed. Reg. 51,708, 51,708-10 (Nov. 23, 1976) (final rule).

[72] 21 C.F.R. §§ 12.24(b), 12.28 (2014). Subsequent litigation has upheld particular aspects of these regulations. See Pineapple Growers Ass'n v. FDA, 673 F.2d 1083, 1085-1086 (9th Cir. 1982) (hearing must be held only "where 'material' issues of fact are raised 'that should not be dispelled at the outset without a hearing, . . .

Rulemaking Plans

Since 1978, federal agencies have been directed by executive orders to publish an agenda of significant regulations under development.[73] The Regulatory Flexibility Act, enacted in 1980, requires agencies to publish semiannual regulatory flexibility agendas identifying upcoming rules likely to have a "significant economic impact on a substantial number of small entities."[74] This law also mandates periodic review of agencies' existing rules that have such an impact.[75] As part of the government-wide publication effectuating the directives in both statute and executive order, FDA announces in the Unified Regulatory Agenda its list of regulations under development, as well as its list of existing regulations undergoing periodic review.[76] Also included in this publication is a Regulatory Plan identifying the most important significant proposed and final regulations the agency expects to issue in the fiscal year.[77]

OMB's Role

The Office of Management and Budget (OMB) reviews certain FDA regulations before publication. Under a series of executive orders, federal agencies have been directed to send certain proposed and final regulations to OMB for review before publication.[78]

---

objections [are] 'made in good faith' and are neither frivolous or inconsequential'"). *See also* Pactra Indus., Inc. v. CPSC, 555 F.2d 677 (9th Cir. 1977) (review of rulemaking conducted under section 701(e) pursuant to 15 U.S.C. § 1262).

[73]   Executive Order 12,044, issued by President Carter in 1978, required an agency, at a minimum, to describe "the regulations being considered by the agency, the need for and the legal basis for the action being taken, and the status of regulations previously listed on the agenda." Exec. Order 12,044, § 2, 43 Fed. Reg. 12,661 (Mar. 24, 1978). Executive Order 12,291, issued by President Reagan in 1981, revoked Executive Order 12,044, but directed agencies to publish, in October and April of each year, an agenda of proposed regulations they had issued or expected to issue. Exec. Order 12,291, § 5, 46 Fed. Reg. 13,193, 13,195 (Feb. 19, 1981). Executive Order 12,498, issued in 1985, added a regulatory program designed to provide an overview of agencies' regulatory policies, goals, and objectives for the program year. Exec. Order 12,498, 50 Fed. Reg. 1,036 (Jan. 4, 1985). Executive Order 12,866, issued by President Clinton in 1993, revoked Executive Order 12,291 and Executive Order 12,498, but retained the requirement that agencies prepare an agenda of all regulations under development or review. Exec. Order 12,866, § 4, 58 Fed. Reg. 51,735, 51,738 (Oct. 4, 1993). As part of the Unified Regulatory Agenda, agencies were also directed to prepare a Regulatory Plan of the most important significant proposed and final rules expected to be issued in the fiscal year. *Id.* Executive Order 12,866, amended by Executive Order 13,422, issued by President Bush in 2007, continued to require federal agencies to develop the agenda of regulations and plan for significant rules for the upcoming fiscal year. Exec. Order 12,866, as amended by Exec. Order 13,422, 72 Fed. Reg. 2763 (Jan. 23, 2007). Executive Order 13,497, issued by President Obama in 2009, revoked Executive Order 13,422, thereby returning Executive Order 12,866 to the text as issued in 1993. Executive Order 13,497, 74 Fed. Reg. 6113 (Feb. 4, 2009). Executive Order 13,563, issued by President Obama in 2011, reaffirmed and supplemented Exec. Order 12,866, which continues to require development of the agenda of regulations and plan for significant rules. Exec. Order 13,563, 76 Fed. Reg. 3821 (Jan. 21, 2011).

[74]   Pub. L. No. 96-354, § 3(a), 94 Stat. 1164, 1166 (1980) (codified at 5 U.S.C. § 602).

[75]   *Id.* § 3(a), 94 Stat. at 1169 (codified at 5 U.S.C. § 610). These periodic reviews are often referred to as "610 reviews." Executive Order 13,563 also directed each agency to develop a plan under which the agency would "periodically review its existing significant regulations to determine whether any such regulations should be modified, streamlined, expanded, or repealed so as to make the agency's regulatory program more effective or less burdensome in achieving the regulatory objectives." Exec. Order 13,563 § 6(b), 76 Fed. Reg. 3821, 3822 (Jan. 21, 2011).

[76]   *See, e.g.,* 71 Fed. Reg. 73,197, 73,197-200 (Dec. 11, 2006).

[77]   *See, e.g.,* 71 Fed. Reg. 73,211, 73,211-39 (Dec. 11, 2006).

[78]   Executive Order 12,291, issued in 1981, required agencies to transmit "major rules" to OMB at least 60 days before publication, and most other proposed and final rules at least 10 days before publication. Exec. Order

Under Executive Order 12,866,[79] FDA sends OMB's Office of Information and Regulatory Affairs (OIRA) a list of proposed and final rules, and indicates which would meet the definition of "significant regulatory action" under the executive order.[80] For proposed and final rules identified as "significant" by OIRA, FDA sends the draft document to OIRA for review within 90 days.[81] Either in the document, itself, or accompanying the document, the agency is to provide an assessment of the potential costs and benefits of the regulation.[82] The document is not published until the process for OMB review specified in Executive Order 12,866 is complete.[83] As part of its review process, OIRA may share the draft document with other federal agencies whose programs or policies may be affected by it.[84]

OIRA maintains a public log of regulations it is currently reviewing.[85] Some information about OIRA's communications with persons outside the executive branch and about documents exchanged between OIRA and the agency is also made public.[86]

12,291, § 3(c), 46 Fed. Reg. 13,193, 13,194 (Feb. 19, 1981). Formal rulemaking, governed by 5 U.S.C. §§ 556 and 557, was excluded from the scope of Executive Order 12,291. *Id.* § 1(a)(1), 46 Fed. Reg. at 13,193. Executive Order 12,866 established a more elaborate centralized review of agency regulations by the Office of Information and Regulatory Affairs within OMB. Exec. Order 12,866, § 6, 58 Fed. Reg. at 51,740. Minor revisions to Executive Order 12,866 were made by Executive Order 13,258 in 2002. Exec. Order 13,258, 67 Fed. Reg. 9385 (Feb. 28, 2002). More significant changes to Executive Order 12,866, especially relating to guidance documents, were made by Executive Order 13,422 in 2007. Exec. Order 13,422, 72 Fed. Reg. 2763 (Jan. 23, 2007). Executive Order 13,497 revoked Executive Order 13,258 and Executive Order 13,422, thereby returning Executive Order 12,866 to the text as issued in 1993. Exec. Order 12,499, 74 Fed. Reg. 6113 (Feb. 4, 2009).

[79] Executive Order 13,563 reaffirmed the "principles, structures, and definitions governing contemporary regulatory review that were established in Executive Order 12,866 of September 30, 1993." Exec. Order 13,563, § 1(b), 76 Fed. Reg. 3821 (Jan. 21, 2011).

[80] Exec. Order 12,866, § 6. "Regulatory action" is an action that promulgates or is expected to lead to "promulgation of a final regulation, including notices of inquiry, advance notices of proposed rulemaking, and notices of proposed rulemaking." Exec. Order 12,866, § 3. Regulations issued under the formal rulemaking provisions of 5 U.S.C. §§ 556 and 557 are excluded from the scope of the executive order. *Id.* "Significant regulatory action" is defined as likely to result in a regulation that may:

- have an annual effect on the economy of $100 million or more or adversely affect in a material way the economy, a sector of the economy, productivity, competition, jobs, the environment, public health or safety or governments or communities;

- create a serious inconsistency or interfere with another agency's planned action;

- alter the budgetary impact of entitlements, grants, user fees or loan programs or the recipients of these; or

- raise novel legal or policy issues.

Id.

[81] Exec. Order 12,866, § 6. The review period may be extended by OMB or FDA. *Id.*

[82] *Id.*

[83] OIRA may waive review, review the document, and return it to the agency for further consideration or complete its review without request for further consideration. Exec. Order 12,866, § 8. If the 90-day period expires without OIRA having notified the agency that it is returning the document for further consideration, the agency may proceed to publish the document. *Id.* To the extent permitted by law, if OIRA and the agency cannot resolve disagreements, the matter is resolved by the President, with the assistance of the Chief of Staff. Exec. Order 12,866, § 7.

[84] *Id.*

[85] *See* Exec. Order 12,866, § 6.

[86] *Id.*

Congressional Review

Under the Small Business Regulatory Enforcement Fairness Act of 1996, before a federal agency's rule can take effect the agency must submit a copy of the rule, along with other information, to Congress.[87] With certain exceptions, no "major rule" may take effect sooner than 60 days after its submission to Congress.[88] During this period, Congress may pass a joint resolution of disapproval, which blocks the rule from taking effect.[89] The President may veto such a resolution, subject to congressional override of the veto.[90] As of mid-2014, no FDA regulations had been delayed or prevented from taking effect under this provision of law.

Hearings

As part of its promulgation of administrative procedures in the mid-1970s, FDA developed extensive hearing procedures covering a range of formal and informal adjudications.[91] As additional statutory authorities, such as authority to impose civil monetary penalties, became available to FDA, the agency revised its procedural regulations accordingly.[92]

Formal Evidentiary Public Hearings (Part 12)

In addition to the statutory provisions for formal rulemakings discussed above, FDA has identified the other statutory provisions under which it will offer adversely affected persons an opportunity for a formal evidentiary hearing.[93] These are primarily situations in which the agency proposes to deny or revoke the approval to market a medical product,[94] including under:

---

[87] Pub. L. No. 104-121, § 251, 110 Stat. 868 (1996) (codified at 5 U.S.C. § 801). The Comptroller General also receives this information. 5 U.S.C. § 801(a)(1).

[88] 5 U.S.C. § 801(a)(2). The exceptions include determinations made by the President by executive order relating to imminent health or safety threats or other emergencies, criminal law enforcement, national security, or international trade agreements. 5 U.S.C. § 801(c). "Major rules" are those determined by OIRA to be likely to result in:

- an annual effect on the economy of $100 million or more;

- a major increase in costs or prices for consumers, industries, government agencies, or geographic regions; or

- significant adverse effects on competition, employment, investment, productivity, innovation or on the ability of U.S.-based enterprises to compete with foreign-based enterprises in domestic and export markets.

5 U.S.C. § 804(2).

[89] 5 U.S.C. §§ 801, 802.

[90] *Id.*

[91] *See* 40 Fed. Reg. at 40,682 (proposed rule); 41 Fed. Reg. 48,258 (Nov. 2, 1976) (final rule); 41 Fed. Reg. 52,148 (Nov. 26, 1976) (same); 41 Fed. Reg. 51,706 (Nov. 23, 1976) (same); 41 Fed. Reg. 26,636 (June 28, 1976) (same). As discussed *supra*, certain hearing procedures also apply in some rulemaking contexts.

[92] *See* 60 Fed. Reg. 38,626 (July 27, 1995) (establishing 21 C.F.R. pt. 17 on civil-money-penalties hearings).

[93] *See* 21 C.F.R. § 10.50(c)(16)-(20) (2014).

[94] Although the agency did not concede that the law required an opportunity for a formal hearing under 5 U.S.C. §§ 556 and 557 in the case of all listed provisions, FDA concluded that it would be appropriate to offer this opportunity. *See* 40 Fed. Reg. at 40,691.

- section 505(d) and (e) on new drug applications;

- section 512(d), (e), and (m)(3) and (4) on new animal drug applications;

- section 515(g) on device premarket approval applications and product development protocols;

- section 351(a) of the Public Health Service Act on biologics licenses for biological products; and

- section 306 on debarment, debarment period and considerations, termination of debarment under section 306(d)(3), suspension and termination of suspension.[95]

As a discretionary matter, the Commissioner may order a formal evidentiary hearing on any matter when "it would be in the public interest to do so."[96] Conversely, a person who has a right to a formal hearing may waive that right and choose a hearing before a Public Board of Inquiry, a public advisory committee or the Commissioner.[97]

Prior to promulgation of the general procedural regulations, FDA had also established the principle of threshold requirements for granting hearing requests in administrative adjudications. Particularly in the new drug context, the agency had established standards in regulations for meeting the statutory evidentiary burden for product approval. If a hearing request did not provide evidence that the new drug application on its face met the standards in FDA's regulations, the agency denied the request. The Supreme Court upheld the agency's hearing-denial principles in *Weinberger v. Hynson, Westcott & Dunning, Inc.*,[98] a case related to FDA's program to implement the effectiveness requirements added to the FDCA in 1962.[99] Given the vast scope of the undertaking, which was to review approximately 4,000 marketed drugs to determine whether they met the new effectiveness standard,[100] the court noted that, "[i]f FDA were required automatically to hold a hearing for each product whose efficacy was questioned . . ., even though many hearings would be an exercise in futility, we have no doubt that it could not fulfill its statutory mandate . . . ."[101] In these circumstances, the Court found FDA's hearing regulations "unexceptionable on any statutory or constitutional ground."[102] The principle that a hearing requester must present "material" evidence to justify

---

[95] 21 C.F.R. § 10.50(c)(16)-(20); *see* 21 C.F.R. § 12.21(a) (2014). Statutory references, as codified, are 21 U.S.C. §§ 355(d), (e), 360b(d), (e), (m)(3), (4), 360e(g)(1), 42 U.S.C. § 262(a); and 21 U.S.C. §§ 355a, 355a(d)(3). The debarment provisions preclude from participation in certain activities individuals or corporations who have been convicted of felonies or engaged in other specified activities related to drug development or approval, food importation, or third-party inspection of devices. *See* 21 U.S.C. § 355a.

[96] 21 C.F.R. §§ 10.50(b), 12.1(b) (2014).

[97] 21 C.F.R. § 12.32 (2014).

[98] 412 U.S. 609 (1973).

[99] *See* Pub. L. No. 87-781, §§ 102(a), 104(a) and 102(c), 76 Stat. 780, 781, 784 (1962) (codified at 21 U.S.C. §§ 321(p), 355(a) and (d)). Sponsors of drugs approved before 1962 were given two years to submit effectiveness data, after which FDA could proceed to withdraw approvals of NDAs for lack of effectiveness, as appropriate. *See* Pub. L. No. 87-781, § 107(c)(3)(B), 76 Stat. at 788-89.

[100] As of 1973, in a review conducted for FDA by expert panels convened by the National Academy of Sciences-National Research Council, only 434 of these 4,000 drugs had been found effective for all of their claimed uses. 412 U.S. at 623. FDA has continued to take final actions related to the Drug Efficacy Study Implementation (DESI) Review over the years, with final action on about a dozen drugs pending in late 2014.

[101] *Id.*

[102] 412 U.S. at 622. Although the Supreme Court upheld the validity of FDA's summary-denial procedures, it disagreed with FDA on whether Hynson's submission was sufficient to warrant a hearing. *Id.* at 623. Subsequent judicial decisions acknowledged the validity of the agency's hearing-denial procedures, but did

a hearing has subsequently been upheld even in the absence of standards particularized in regulations.[103] The agency's regulations governing formal evidentiary hearing procedures, now codified at 21 C.F.R. Part 12, reflect the developed case law on denial of hearing requests in adjudicatory, as well as formal rulemaking, contexts.[104]

When requests for formal hearings are granted, the agency observes separation of functions and prohibits *ex parte* communications.[105] This approach, consistent with the APA restrictions in 5 U.S.C. § 557(d), also incorporates the sanction that making *ex parte* communications may, "consistent with the interests of justice and the policy of the underlying statute," result in an adverse decision to the person knowingly making such a communication.[106]

Perhaps in part because of the agency's position on denials of hearings, FDA has held few formal evidentiary hearings. The opportunity continues, however, to be available and, if appropriate, such trial-type hearings before an administrative law judge are occasionally still held.[107] For example, in 2005 the Commissioner withdrew approval of a new animal drug application for enrofloxacin (an antibiotic within the fluoroquinolone class of drugs) in poultry after a Part 12 hearing.[108]

Hearing Before a Public Board of Inquiry (Part 13)

In the mid-1970s, when FDA developed its hearing regulations, FDA and other federal agencies had been much criticized for long delays in administrative action because of trial-type procedures.[109] In offering an alternative approach at 21 C.F.R. Part 13, FDA opined that, in situations involving complex scientific and medical issues, a "searching scientific

---

not always agree with FDA's application of them to the facts before it. *See, e.g.,* Am. Cyanamid Co. v. FDA, 606 F.2d 1307 (D.C. Cir. 1979); SmithKline Corp. v. FDA, 587 F.2d 1107 (D.C. Cir. 1978); Edison Pharm. Co. v. FDA, 513 F.2d 1063 (D.C. Cir. 1975).

[103]   *See* John D. Copanos & Sons, Inc. v. FDA, 854 F.2d 510 (D.C. Cir. 1988); Cmty. Nutrition Inst. v. Novitch, 773 F.2d 1356 (D.C. Cir. 1985).

[104]   *See* 21 C.F.R. §§ 12.24, 12.28 (2014) and discussion at pp. 694-96, *supra.*

[105]   *See* 21 C.F.R. § 10.55 (2014).

[106]   21 C.F.R. § 10.55(f); 5 U.S.C. § 557(d)(1)(D). Title 21 C.F.R. §§ 314.200(f) (2014) (concerning new drug applications), 514.200 (2008) (concerning new animal drug applications), and 601.7(a) (2014) (concerning biologics license applications) specify that separation of functions commences upon receipt of a hearing request, and applies as specifically detailed in each of those sections. Otherwise, separation of functions applies, as detailed in section 10.55(b)(2), upon publication of the notice announcing a formal hearing.

[107]   For many years, one administrative law judge, Judge Daniel J. Davidson, who is now retired, presided over FDA's formal evidentiary hearings.

[108]   *See* 70 Fed. Reg. 44,048-49, 44,105 (Aug. 1, 2005) and www.fda.gov/oc/antimicrobial/baytril.pdf. The Commissioner agreed with the determination in the administrative law judge's initial decision, but with different reasoning on several points.

[109]   *See* 40 Fed. Reg. at 40,698. In the context of withdrawing approval of a new animal drug application, the D.C. Circuit noted that the hearing "need not borrow the characteristics of conventional courtroom controversy, burdened with the impediments of the kind of arcane questions with which lawyers often bedevil expert witnesses," but rather "can perhaps best be provided by an on-the-record conference-hearing procedure, modeled on conference discussions between lawyers and experts." Cooper Labs., Inc. v. Comm'r, 501 F.2d 772, 792-793 (D.C. Cir. 1974). The agency's hearing under section 701(e) on the standard of identity for peanut butter, which extended over 10 years, especially prompted recommendations for reform. *See, e.g.,* Robert W. Hamilton, *Rulemaking on a Record*, 26 FOOD DRUG COSM. L.J. 627 (1971); William W. Goodrich, *A Reply to Professor Hamilton's Comments and Recommendations for Procedural Reform*, 26 FOOD DRUG COSM. L.J. 639 (1971).

inquiry conducted by independent experts may well be more appropriate than a formal evidentiary public hearing."[110]

This alternative hearing procedure is available to a person entitled to a formal evidentiary hearing who waives that right and requests review by a Public Board of Inquiry (Board), if the Commissioner accepts the request.[111] The three-member Board is appointed by the Commissioner from among nominees submitted by the director of the FDA Center involved in the matter, other parties to the proceeding, and any person whose petition is granted and is the subject of the hearing.[112] Board members must have relevant medical, technical, scientific, or other expertise and must comply with the conflict-of-interest rules applicable to special government employees.[113]

Board proceedings are to be "conducted as a scientific inquiry rather than a legal trial."[114] Participants may make oral presentations to the Board, whose members may ask questions. Other participants may comment orally and with written rebuttal information.[115] The Board then issues a decision with findings, references, and a detailed statement of reasoning.[116]

As of mid-2014, Boards under Part 13 had been convened only twice: to review FDA's proposed approval of a food additive petition for aspartame[117] and FDA's refusal to approve the injectable contraceptive Depo-Provera.[118] In both cases, the Board ultimately upheld the agency's original position. In practice, the Public Board of Inquiry does not offer as streamlined and less costly an approach to administrative adjudication as anticipated.[119]

Hearing before a Public Advisory Committee (Part 14)

Although FDA has used a Public Board of Inquiry very rarely, the agency frequently uses its advisory committees. The agency's creation and use of advisory committees must be consistent with the Federal Advisory Committee Act (FACA),[120] which sets forth general requirements.[121] In the mid-1970s, FDA promulgated regulations establishing for its advisory committees procedures that reflect FACA requirements as well as agency policies as to such committees.[122]

---

[110] 40 Fed. Reg. at 40,699.

[111] 21 C.F.R. § 13.1(c) (2014).

[112] 21 C.F.R. § 13.10 (2014).

[113] 21 C.F.R. § 13.10(a). A Board functions as an "administrative law tribunal," and is not subject to the requirements of the Federal Advisory Committee Act. 21 C.F.R. § 13.10(e).

[114] 21 C.F.R. § 13.30(a) (2014).

[115] 21 C.F.R. § 13.30(c), (d), (e) (2014).

[116] 21 C.F.R. § 13.30(j) (2014).

[117] See Aspartame, 46 Fed. Reg. 38,285 (July 24, 1981).

[118] See Depo-Provera [1984-1985 Transfer Binder] Food Drug Cosm. L. Rep. (CCH) ¶ 38, 291 (FDA Public Bd. of Inquiry Oct. 17, 1984).

[119] See Sidney A. Shapiro, Scientific Issues and the Function of Hearing Procedures: An Evaluation of FDA's Public Board of Inquiry, 1986 Duke L.J. 288 (1986) (report for Administrative Conference of the United States).

[120] Pub. L. No. 92-463, 86 Stat. 776 (codified as amended at 5 U.S.C. app. 2).

[121] For example, FACA requires that an advisory committee have membership that is "fairly balanced in terms of the points of view represented and the function to be performed" by the committee (§ 5(b)(2)); have meetings open to the public, with limited exceptions (§ 10(a), (d)); make its records, transcripts, minutes etc., available to the public under the Freedom of Information Act (§ 10(b)); and have only an advisory role (§ 2(b)(6)). 5 U.S.C. app. 2.

[122] See 40 Fed. Reg. 40,682; 41 Fed. Reg. 52,148 (Nov. 26, 1976).

Currently codified at 21 C.F.R. Part 14, these regulations govern all aspects of FDA's advisory committees, from establishment through termination. The agency determined that its advisory committees would provide advice both on policy matters and on specific technical or scientific issues, which might relate to pending regulatory decisions.[123] In 1990, the Commissioner received direct authority to establish "technical and scientific review groups," or advisory committees, and to appoint and pay advisory committee members.[124] In 1997 Congress directed the agency to establish panels of experts (or use previously established panels) to provide "expert scientific advice and recommendations" on clinical investigations and approvals of drugs and biological products.[125] One of the oldest of FDA's standing advisory committees is the Technical Electronic Product Radiation Safety Standards Committee (TEPRSSC), established by statute in 1968, to advise on performance standards for electronic products to control the emission of radiation.[126] FDA currently has approximately 30 standing committees, most of which are managed by the agency's centers.[127]

In general, the agency has considerable discretion about whether and when to hold meetings of particular advisory committees, and which issues to present to the committees for recommendations.[128] Congress, however, has expressly provided for the use of advisory committees in certain situations. For example, the FDCA authorizes advisory committee recommendations in relation to device performance standards, review of device premarket approval applications and product development protocols, and device good manufacturing practice regulations.[129] In 1997, Congress provided that, in certain circumstances, drug, device, or biological product manufacturers could request review of scientific disputes by an advisory committee.[130] In the context of drug labeling changes related to pediatric use, referral to an advisory committee is directed by statute when the drug sponsor does not agree to make the change.[131] FDA is required to consult with the TEPRSSC before prescribing a performance standard for an electronic product.[132] In the Food and Drug Administration Amendments Act of 2007 (FDAAA), Congress required FDA to seek recommendations on priority drug safety questions at least biannually from the Drug Safety and Risk Management Advisory Committee, and from other committees as appropriate.[133] Under the Family

---

[123]   See 21 C.F.R. § 14.1(b)(2) (2014).

[124]   21 U.S.C. § 394 (2012). See also 21 U.S.C. § 393(e), which gives similar authority to "the Secretary through the Commissioner of Food and Drugs."

[125]   Pub. L. No. 105-115, § 120, 111 Stat. 2296, 2318 (1997) (codified at 21 U.S.C. § 355(n)). This provision also authorizes delegation of the appointment and oversight authority of section 904 (21 U.S.C. § 394) to Center Directors within FDA. 21 U.S.C. § 355(n)(2).

[126]   See Pub. L. No. 90-602, § 2(3), 82 Stat. 1177 (1968) (formerly codified at 42 U.S.C. § 263f(f)(1)(A), now codified at 21 U.S.C. § 360kk(f)(1)(A)). See also 21 C.F.R. § 14.100(d)(3) (2014); 21 C.F.R. § 14.120-.130 (2014). For a very long time, the oldest standing advisory committee was the Board of Tea Experts, originally established in 1897, to advise on standards of purity, quality, and fitness for consumption of imported tea. See former 21 U.S.C. § 42, repealed by Pub. L. No. 104-128 in 1996.

[127]   See FDA's website at http://www.fda.gov/oc/advisory/default.htm for the list of current committees and committee member vacancies, under "FDA Advisory Committee Vacancies." Each committee's purpose is reflected in its charter. See 21 C.F.R. § 14.40(c) (2014).

[128]   See 21 C.F.R. § 14.1(a)(1), (3) (2014).

[129]   See 21 U.S.C. §§ 360d(b)(5), 360e(b)(3), 360e(f)(2), 360j(f)(1).

[130]   Pub. L. No. 105-115, § 404, 111 Stat. 2296, 2368 (1997) (codified at 21 U.S.C. § 360bbb-1). See 21 C.F.R. § 10.75(b) (2014) for FDA's implementing regulations.

[131]   See 21 U.S.C. § 355a(i)(2).

[132]   21 U.S.C. § 360kk(f)(1)(A).

[133]   Pub. L. No. 110-85, § 905(a), 121 Stat. 823, 946 (2007) (codified at 21 U.S.C. § 355(k)(4)(C)).

Smoking Prevention and Tobacco Control Act (Tobacco Control Act), FDA was required to establish the Tobacco Products Scientific Advisory Committee.[134] Applications filed with FDA for "modified risk tobacco products" must be referred to this advisory committee for recommendations to the agency.[135]

Members of one of FDA's technical advisory committees are required to have expertise in the subject matter with which the committee is concerned and "diverse professional education, training, and experience" to reflect a "balanced" composition.[136] Section 505(n) of the FDCA, added in 1997, specifies the expertise to be represented on panels making recommendations about clinical investigations or approvals of drugs or biologics.[137] FDA also includes nonvoting members on its advisory committees to represent consumer interests and industry interests.[138]

Voting members of FDA's advisory committees are subject to the conflict-of-interests laws and regulations.[139] In 1997, Congress enacted additional requirements for members of panels under section 505(n) with conflicts of interests.[140] Then, in 2007, Congress revised these provisions and extended them to the members of all advisory committees providing advice or recommendations regarding FDA activities.[141] In 2012 Congress again revised these provisions, so that current section 712 of the FDCA directs FDA to undertake certain recruitment activities related to advisory committee membership and to disclose certain financial interests of advisory committee members in advance of advisory committee meetings.[142] The previously enacted special conflict-of-interest provisions for FDA advisory committee members were eliminated. When FDA grants conflict-of-interest waivers under 18 U.S.C. § 208(b)(1) or (b)(3), the agency ordinarily is required to post on its website at

---

[134]   21 U.S.C. § 377q.

[135]   21 U.S.C. § 387k(f). Upon request by the applicant, or on FDA's initiative, an application concerning a "new tobacco product" may also be referred to the Tobacco Products Scientific Advisory Committee for recommendation. 21 U.S.C. § 387j(b)(2).

[136]   21 C.F.R. § 14.80(b)(1)(i) (2014). This regulation also reflects the FACA requirement of balanced membership. See FACA § 5(b)(2), 5 U.S.C. app. 2.

[137]   Pub. L. No. 105-115, § 120, 111 Stat. 2296, 2319 (1997) (codified at 21 U.S.C. § 355(n)).

[138]   See 21 C.F.R. §§ 14.84-14.86 (2014). Section 505(n) of the FDCA also specifies that the drug and biologic panels include "a representative of consumer interests, and a representative of interests of the drug manufacturing industry not directly affected by the matter to be brought before the panel." 21 U.S.C. § 355(n)(3)(C) (2012).

[139]   See 18 U.S.C. § 208(a) (2012); 21 C.F.R. §§ 14.80(b)(1)(ii), 14.127(d) (2014).

[140]   Under the 1997 provision, each member was required to disclose publicly all conflicts of interest the member may have with respect to the work to be undertaken by the panel. 21 U.S.C. § 355(n)(4). In addition, no member could vote on any matter where the member or an individual in the member's immediate family could gain financially from the advice given. Id. FDA could grant a waiver upon public disclosure of the conflict if the waiver were "necessary to afford the panel essential expertise," as long as the member's own scientific work was not involved. Id.

[141]   See Pub. L. No. 110-85, tit. VII, 121 Stat. 823, 900-04 (2007). Under the 2007 provisions, with limited exceptions, a member could not participate with respect to a particular matter considered at an advisory committee meeting if the member or an individual in the member's immediate family had a financial interest that could be affected by the committee's advice. FDA could grant waivers to permit members with such conflicts to participate as either nonvoting or voting members if "necessary to afford the advisory committee essential expertise." Congress, however, limited the number of conflict-of-interest waivers to increasingly smaller percentages over a five-year period.

[142]   21 U.S.C. §§ 379d-1(b)-(c).

least 15 days before an advisory committee meeting the "type, nature, and magnitude of the financial interests" to which the waivers apply and the reasons for granting the waivers.[143]

Most FDA advisory committee meetings consist largely of open public hearings and open committee discussions.[144] Portions of the meetings may be closed to the public only if the agency determines that one of the reasons set forth in 5 U.S.C. § 552b(c) applies.[145] The reasons for closing meetings that are most commonly applicable to FDA advisory committees include discussions of trade secret or confidential commercial information and matters involving personal privacy.[146]

In addition to requiring that meetings be generally open to the public, FACA requires that materials provided for or by advisory committees be publicly available, subject to the exemptions under the Freedom of Information Act (FOIA).[147] Because review of materials provided to advisory committees to determine whether any information may be withheld from disclosure can be complex and time consuming, FDA has issued guidance to industry on developing and organizing materials to be provided to committee members.[148] Given all the steps that need to be accomplished before an advisory committee's briefing materials are posted on FDA's website, the materials need to be prepared and reviewed well in advance of a meeting.[149]

Members of the public may make oral presentations at an FDA advisory committee meeting, and may also submit written materials to the committee.[150] The agency has also provided guidance to members of the public on how to participate in advisory committee meetings.[151] Individuals attending an FDA advisory committee meeting may record it.[152] The agency also makes transcripts of the open portions of its advisory committee meetings available to the public.[153]

---

[143]   21 U.S.C. § 379d-1(c). The reasons must also include "as appropriate, the public health interest in having the expertise of the member with respect to the particular matter before the advisory committee." 21 U.S.C. § 379d-1(c)(1)(B). The transcript of each advisory committee meeting must also include these required disclosures. 21 U.S.C. § 379d-1(d). For FDA's views on the disclosure issues related to conflict-of-interest waivers, see FDA, Guidance for the Public, FDA Advisory Committee Members, and FDA Staff: Public Availability of Advisory Committee Members' Financial Interest Information and Waivers (March 2014). FDA's guidance documents related to advisory committees may be found on FDA's website at http://www. fda.gov/AdvisoryCommittees/default.htm.

[144]   See 21 C.F.R. § 14.25 (2014).

[145]   See FACA § 10, 5 U.S.C. app. 2; 21 C.F.R. § 14.27(b) (2014).

[146]   See id. Other possible reasons for closing meetings include matters involving law enforcement investigatory files; accusing persons of crimes; censuring persons; national defense or foreign policy; and certain agency information the premature disclosure of which would significantly impede implementation of the proposed action. Id.

[147]   FACA § 10(b), 5 U.S.C. app. 2.

[148]   See FDA, Guidance for Industry: Advisory Committee Meetings—Preparation and Public Availability of Information Given to Advisory Committee Members (Aug. 2008).

[149]   Id. The goal in the draft guidance is to have the sponsor's and FDA's publicly available briefing materials posted at least two full business days before discussion of the topic at an advisory committee meeting. Id.

[150]   See 21 C.F.R. §§ 14.30, 14.35 (2014).

[151]   See FDA, Guidance for the Public, FDA Advisory Committee Members, and FDA Staff: The Open Public Hearing at FDA Advisory Committee Meetings (May 15, 2013).

[152]   See 21 C.F.R. § 14.61 (2014).

[153]   See id.

Public Hearing before the Commissioner (Part 15)

In addition to adjudicatory hearings and advisory committee meetings, FDA also holds legislative-type hearings. The procedures for such hearings, which are conducted by the Commissioner or a designee, are set forth at 21 C.F.R. Part 15.[154]

When FDA first promulgated the procedures for these hearings, the agency had already had experience with such hearings in the context of its Over-the-Counter Drug Review (OTC Drug Review).[155] Although not required by statute to do so, in the context of this three-stage OTC drug-rulemaking procedure, FDA had provided opportunities for interested persons to object to the agency's proposals and to request an oral hearing before the Commissioner.[156] After enactment of the Medical Device Amendments of 1976,[157] the agency revised the scope of Part 15 to include hearings requested under certain provisions of the FDCA relating to custom devices, device-good-manufacturing-practice regulations, and proposed exemptions from preemption of state and local device requirements.[158]

The most frequent use of the Part 15 procedures has not been under these specific statutory or regulatory provisions, but, rather, as a matter of the agency's discretion to inform its decision making in other areas. Most commonly, the agency has arranged under these hearing procedures for panels of employees to listen to presentations by individuals and organizations on complex or controversial regulatory matters.[159] Panel members may ask questions of those presenting at a hearing, in order to further elucidate the issues.[160]

---

[154]   See 21 C.F.R. § 15.30 (2014) for a description of the conduct of such hearings. Modified Part 15 procedures, which include participation by an advisory committee constituted under Part 14 govern withdrawals of approvals under FDA's "accelerated approval" and "animal efficacy" regulations for new drugs and biological products. See 21 C.F.R. §§ 314.530, 314.620, 601.43 and 601.92 (2014).

[155]   See 40 Fed. Reg. at 40,711 (proposed rule); 41 Fed. Reg. 48,258 (Nov. 2, 1976) (final rule).

[156]   See 21 C.F.R. § 330.10(a)(7) (2014) (hearing opportunity after publication of the agency's proposal, called a "tentative final monograph"). For notices of hearing in this context, see also 38 Fed. Reg. 12,769 (May 15, 1973); 39 Fed. Reg. 1359 (Jan. 8, 1974). Although most Part 15 hearings are conducted by senior FDA officials other than the Commissioner, under 21 C.F.R. § 330.10(a)(8) (2014) such hearings in the OTC review may not be delegated. Hearings were held in the early days of the OTC review; since then, however, hearing requests in this context have generally been denied. See 21 C.F.R. 330.10(a)(8) (requiring "reasonable grounds" in support of a hearing request).

[157]   Pub. L. No. 94-295, 90 Stat. 539 (1976).

[158]   See 43 Fed. Reg. 51,971 (Nov. 7, 1978) (proposed rule); 44 Fed. Reg. 22,366 (Apr. 13, 1979) (final rule). Title 21 C.F.R. § 15.1(b) (2014) lists sections 520(b) and (f)(1)(B) and 521(b) of the FDCA as providing for public hearings on these matters. See 21 U.S.C. §§ 360j(b), 360j(f)(1)(B) and 360k(b). As discussed at p. 602, supra, persons who have a right to a formal evidentiary hearing under Part 12 may waive that right and request a hearing under Part 15. 21 C.F.R. § 15.1(c) (2014).

[159]   See, e.g., notices of Part 15 hearings on combination-product labeling, 70 Fed. Reg. 15,633 (Mar. 28, 2005); reporting of adverse events to institutional review boards, 70 Fed. Reg. 6,693 (Feb. 8, 2005); electronic submission of regulatory information, 71 Fed. Reg. 67,356 (Nov. 21, 2006); and the safety of fresh produce, 72 Fed. Reg. 8750 (Feb. 27, 2007).

[160]   See 21 C.F.R. § 15.21(e) (2014). The presiding officer often will receive questions from those attending the hearing, and will ask the presenters or panel members to respond. See 21 C.F.R. § 15.30(e).

Part 15 hearings are recorded, and transcripts are subsequently made available to the public.[161] Usually, the record of such a hearing remains open for at least 15 days after the hearing for additional written submissions.[162]

Informal Public and Private Meetings

In addition to the various types of hearings described in FDA's regulations, the agency also provides many opportunities for informal public and private meetings. Public meetings on developing scientific issues often take the form of "workshops," where experts and others may exchange information and views.[163] FDA also holds educational meetings for industry and for members of the public on regulatory requirements or other public health matters.[164] At the agency's discretion, it also may convene public meetings on pending matters, with broad opportunities for public participation.[165]

Members of the public may also request private meetings with FDA. Although those requesting such meetings are not entitled to meet with agency officials, the agency is to "make reasonable efforts to accommodate" such requests.[166] When the agency determines that documenting such meetings is useful, employees will prepare meeting memoranda.[167] For certain high-level agency officials, there is a public calendar showing, as feasible, significant events of the previous week, including significant meetings with persons outside the executive branch.[168]

Regulatory Hearings (Part 16)

FDA promulgated the procedures at 21 C.F.R. Part 16 to govern all informal fact-finding hearings held by FDA to determine "whether any, or what type of, regulatory action should be taken with respect to a particular matter involving a specified person."[169] This type of hearing could concern specific fact situations involving particular companies.[170] Such hearings would not involve policy issues usually considered in legislative-type hearings or other general matters, such as are considered in developing regulations.[171]

---

[161]   *See* 21 C.F.R. § 15.30(b); 21 C.F.R. pt. 20 (2014). Such hearings may also be videotaped under FDA's policy on electronic media coverage of public proceedings. *See* 21 C.F.R. §§ 10.205-10.206 (2014).

[162]   *See* 21 C.F.R. § 15.25 (2014).

[163]   *See, e.g.,* public workshops on adolescent over-the-counter drug products, 72 Fed. Reg. 62,481 (Nov. 5, 2007); correlates of protection related to anthrax vaccine, 72 Fed. Reg. 33,508 (June 18, 2007); licensure of apheresis blood products, 72 Fed. Reg. 33,509 (June 18, 2007); in vitro analysis of cell/scaffold medical products, 72 Fed. Reg. 58,102 (Oct. 12, 2007); and immune correlates of protection against influenza A viruses, 72 Fed. Reg. 60,681 (Oct. 25, 2007).

[164]   *See, e.g.,* educational workshops on current good manufacturing practices, 72 Fed. Reg. 53,778 (Sept. 20, 2007); clinical trial requirements, 72 Fed. Reg. 14,583 (Mar. 28, 2007); and women's-health-information-sharing network, 72 Fed. Reg. 14,822 (Mar. 29, 2007).

[165]   *See* 21 C.F.R. § 10.65(b) (2014).

[166]   *See* 21 C.F.R. § 10.65(c) (2014). Although the person requesting the meeting may ask for a specific FDA employee to attend, the agency determines which employees will attend when a meeting is granted. *Id.*

[167]   *See* 21 C.F.R. § 10.65(e) (2014).

[168]   *See* 21 C.F.R. § 10.100 (2014). The officials include the Commissioner, Deputy Commissioners, Senior Associate Commissioners, Associate Commissioner for Regulatory Affairs, Center Directors, and Chief Counsel. *Id.*

[169]   40 Fed. Reg. at 40,712.

[170]   *Id.*

[171]   *Id.*

These procedures were crafted specifically to meet or exceed the constitutional procedural due process standards.[172] Shortly after FDA proposed these Part 16 procedures, Congress enacted specific provisions of the Medical Device Amendments of 1976 creating opportunities for an "informal hearing" before an order or regulation is issued.[173] In that legislation, section 201 of the FDCA was also amended to add a definition of "informal hearing" that, in essence, specified certain procedures to be followed:

- the presiding officer is to be an agency employee who has not participated in the action that is the subject of the hearing, and is not directly responsible to an employee who has participated in that action;[174]

---

[172] *Id.* At the time Part 16 was first issued in the mid-1970s, the procedural due process standard had been relatively recently articulated in Goldberg v. Kelly, 397 U.S. 254 (1970). Although there have been subsequent refinements in Supreme Court due process opinions (*see, e.g.,* Mathews v. Eldridge, 424 U.S. 319 (1976); *See generally* Richard J. Pierce, Jr., Administrative Law Treatise, ch. 9 (4th ed. 2002)), the agency has continued to consider its Part 16 regulations as satisfying any due process requirements applicable to this type of hearing. For example, in 1997, the agency amended its medical-device-clinical-investigator-disqualification regulations, and continued to specify Part 16 procedures for the hearing opportunity. *See* 62 Fed. Reg. 12,096 (Mar. 14, 1997).

[173] *See* Pub. L. 94-295, §§ 2, 7(a), 90 Stat. 539, 582, 555, 557, 558, 560, 562, 568, 570, 571 (1976). These sections providing for informal hearings related to medical devices were added to the FDCA:

- section 304(g), on administrative detention;
- section 515(e)(1), on withdrawal of a premarket approval application (PMA);
- section 515(f)(6), on proposed orders to revoke a product development protocol (PDP) or declare the protocol not complete;
- section 515(f)(7), on revocation of a notice of completion of a PDP;
- section 516, on proposed banned devices;
- section 518(b), on determination that a device is subject to an order for repair, replacement or refund or that a correction plan is inadequate;
- section 520(f)(2)(D), on exemptions or variances from requirements for current good manufacturing practices; and
- section 520(g)(4) and (g)(5), on disapproval and withdrawal of approval of an investigational device exemption.

See 21 C.F.R. § 16.1 (2014); 21 U.S.C. §§ 334(g), 360e(e)(1), (f)(6), (f)(7), 360f, 360h(b), 360j(f)(2), (g)(4), (g)(5). In the Safe Medical Devices Act of 1990, additional sections providing for informal hearings were enacted:

- section 515(e)(3), on temporary suspension of PMA approval; and
- section 518(e), on orders to cease distribution, recall a device, or give notification of a risk.

See Pub. L. No. 101-629, §§ 8, 9, 104 Stat. 4511, 4520-21 (1990) (codified at 21 U.S.C. § 360e(e)(3), 360h(e)). Subsequently, section 303 of the Public Health Security and Bioterrorism Preparedness and Response Act of 2002 added to the FDCA subsection 304(h), which authorizes administrative detention of food, and provides an opportunity for an informal hearing after the food has been detained. *See* Pub. L. No. 107-188, § 303, 116 Stat. 594, 663 (2002); 21 U.S.C. § 334(h) (2012); *see also* 21 C.F.R. § 16.1(b)(1).

[174] The Part 16 regulations permit designation of a presiding officer subordinate to the Commissioner even if the Commissioner has participated in the matter. 21 C.F.R. § 16.42(b) (2014). The agency has stated, however, that it intends to arrange matters subject to the provisions listed in section 16.1(b) so that it will not be necessary to appoint a presiding officer subordinate to the Commissioner when the Commissioner has had any participation in the action. For example, initiation of the action may be made without the Commissioner's review. *See* 41 Fed. Reg. 48,259 (Nov. 2, 1976). The Commissioner has delegated authority to a number of agency officials to preside at regulatory hearings (e.g., the agency Ombudsman, Center Directors, Regional and District Directors) and, in 2002, revised the regulations to permit an administrative law judge to preside. *See* 21 C.F.R. § 16.42 (2014); 67 Fed. Reg. 53,305 (Aug. 15, 2002).

- each party has the right to be advised and accompanied by an attorney;

- each party is given reasonable notice of the matters to be considered, including a comprehensive statement of the basis for the action and a general summary of information to be presented at the hearing;

- at the hearing, the parties have the right to hear a full and complete statement of the action and supporting reasons, to ask questions, and to present relevant oral or written information;

- the presiding officer is to prepare a written report, accompanied by the written material presented at the hearing, and participants may review and correct or supplement the report; and

- a party has the right to have the hearing transcribed at its expense, and any transcription is to be included in the presiding officer's report.[175]

Each of these statutory "informal hearing" procedures is reflected in the Part 16 regulations.[176]

In addition to providing an opportunity for a hearing under the Part 16 procedures when the FDCA specifies an opportunity for an "informal hearing," the agency provides such an opportunity in relation to 25 regulations governing a variety of actions on FDA-regulated products.[177] In general, at the agency's discretion, on its own initiative, or at the suggestion of any person, the agency may offer such an opportunity before taking any regulatory action.[178] Certain actions, including several related to law enforcement as well as refusals to allow products to be imported, are specifically outside the scope of Part 16.[179] Those matters are governed by separate procedures, described, in many cases, in FDA's *Regulatory Procedures Manual*.[180]

---

[175] Pub. L. No. 94-295, § 3, 90 Stat. 539, 575 (1976), adding paragraph 201(y). Subsequently, paragraph 201(y) was redesignated as paragraph 201(x). *See* Pub. L. No. 103-80, § 3(b), 107 Stat. 775, 779 (1993); current 21 U.S.C. § 321(x).

[176] *See, e.g.,* 21 C.F.R. §§ 16.62, 16.26(f)-(g), 16.60(b), (d), (e) (2014).

[177] *See* 21 C.F.R. § 16.1(b)(2) (2014).

[178] *See* 21 C.F.R. § 16.1(a) (2014).

[179] *See* 21 C.F.R. § 16.5 (2014). For example, section 305 of the FDCA provides for "notice and an opportunity to present . . . views" before a person is reported to a U.S. Attorney for a criminal proceeding. 21 U.S.C. § 335. Providing this opportunity, however, is not a prerequisite to prosecution, United States v. Dotterweich, 320 U.S. 277, 278-79 (1943); and Part 16 does not apply to such an informal presentation of views. *See* 21 C.F.R. § 16.5(a)(1); *see also* 40 Fed. Reg. at 40,712; FDA REGULATORY PROCEDURES MANUAL, Chap. 5-2 (2006). Procedures for presentations of views under section 305 (commonly called "305 hearings") are set forth in 21 C.F.R. §§ 7.84-7.87 (2014). Similarly, Part 16 explicitly does not apply to hearings on refusal of admission of foods, drugs, devices, or cosmetics under section 801(a) of the FDCA, 21 U.S.C. § 381(a), which hearings are conducted in accordance with the procedures prescribed by 21 C.F.R. § 1.94 (2014), or to refusal of admission of electronic products under section 538 of the FDCA, 21 U.S.C. § 360ooo, which hearings are conducted in accordance with the procedures prescribed by 21 C.F.R. § 1005.20 (2014). Factory inspections, voluntary recalls, and regulatory letters also fall outside the scope of these procedures. 21 C.F.R. § 16.5(a)(3). Hearings on orders for relabeling, diversion, or destruction of shell eggs have special procedures under 21 C.F.R. § 101.17(h) and 115.50(e)(2014), promulgated pursuant to section 361 of the Public Health Service Act, 42 U.S.C. § 264 (2012). *See* 21 C.F.R. § 16.5(a)(4).

[180] *See* http://www.fda.gov/iceci/compliancemanuals/regulatoryproceduresmanual/default.htm for the current version of the *Regulatory Procedures Manual*.

Historically, the most frequent use of the Part 16 hearing procedures has been for disqualifications of clinical investigators under 21 C.F.R. § 312.70.[181] On occasion, there have also been expeditious Part 16 hearings on medical device detentions.

Although FDA's Part 16 hearing regulations did not originally provide for denials of hearing requests or for summary decisions on issues in a hearing, FDA revised the regulations in 1988 to allow such actions.[182] Currently, a Part 16 hearing request may be denied if the Commissioner decides that "no genuine and substantial issue of fact" has been raised by the material submitted in support of the request.[183] After a hearing has commenced, the presiding officer may also make a summary decision on any issue under this same standard.[184] A summary decision by the presiding officer may be reviewed by the Commissioner on the Commissioner's own initiative, or at the request of a party to the hearing.[185] Although these options for denial and summary decision have been available since 1988, FDA has very seldom used them in the Part 16 context.

The presiding officer has considerable discretion in conducting a Part 16 hearing, which is to be "fair, expeditious, and impartial."[186] The rules of evidence do not apply to these informal hearings, and objections to the admissibility of evidence are not entertained.[187] The parties are allowed to conduct "reasonable cross-examination" of those making statements at the hearing.[188] Part 16 hearings are open to the public, with limited exceptions.[189]

Although separation-of-functions requirements do not apply to Part 16 hearings,[190] FDA's Office of the Chief Counsel historically has followed an informal separation-of-functions approach to these hearings. *Ex parte* communications are to be avoided; but, if they occur, they are to be made part of the record of the proceeding.[191] After the hearing, the presiding officer prepares a report with recommendations, upon which the parties may then comment.[192] The Commissioner then makes the final decision on the matter.[193] For hearings conducted under specific statutory authority for informal hearings or specific regulations identifying Part 16 procedures, the Commissioner's written decision is to be based solely on the administrative record.[194]

---

[181]   21 C.F.R. § 312.70 (2014). *See* http://www.fda.gov/ICECI/EnforcementActions/ucm321308.htm for the list of disqualified clinical investigators, including those disqualified through the hearing process.

[182]   21 C.F.R. § 16.26 (2014); *see* 51 Fed. Reg. 43,217 (Dec. 1, 1986) (proposed rule); 53 Fed. Reg. 4,613 (Feb. 17, 1988) (final rule).

[183]   21 C.F.R. § 16.26(a).

[184]   21 C.F.R. § 16.26(b).

[185]   21 C.F.R. § 16.26(c).

[186]   21 C.F.R. § 16.60(g), (h) (2014).

[187]   21 C.F.R. § 16.60(c) (2014).

[188]   21 C.F.R. § 16.60(b) (2014).

[189]   *See* 21 C.F.R. § 16.60(a) (2014) (permitting closing of all or part of a hearing to protect personal privacy, trade secret or confidential commercial information, or investigatory records).

[190]   *See* 21 C.F.R. § 16.44(a) (2014).

[191]   *See* 21 C.F.R. § 16.44(b) (2014).

[192]   21 C.F.R. § 16.60(e) (2014).

[193]   21 C.F.R. § 16.95 (2014).

[194]   21 C.F.R. § 16.95(b). The administrative record is defined in 21 C.F.R. § 16.80 (2014). For discretionary Part 16 hearings, the Commissioner may consider other relevant information and views as well. 21 C.F.R. § 16.95(a). After final agency action that has been the subject of a Part 16 hearing, any party may petition for reconsideration under 21 C.F.R. § 10.33 (2014) or for a stay under 21 C.F.R. § 10.35 (2014). 21 C.F.R. § 16.119 (2014); *see* p. 720, *infra*.

Civil Money Penalty Hearings (Part 17)

Beginning in 1986, a series of legislative changes authorized administrative imposition of civil money penalties by FDA.[195] Under the National Childhood Vaccine Injury Act of 1986 (NCVIA), which added section 351(d)(2) to the Public Health Service Act (PHSA), FDA may impose civil money penalties for violations of biological-product-recall orders.[196] This legislation also authorized such penalties for vaccine manufacturers that intentionally violate certain recordkeeping and reporting requirements.[197] The Prescription Drug Marketing Act of 1988 (PDMA) amended the FDCA to provide for civil money penalties in connection with convictions for violation of certain laws prohibiting the sale, purchase, or trade of drug samples.[198] Neither the NCVIA nor the PDMA expressly stated whether the civil money penalties were to be imposed judicially or administratively. FDA has interpreted both laws as implicitly authorizing the agency either to impose these penalties administratively or to seek judicial imposition of them.[199]

Express statutory authority for FDA to impose substantial civil money penalties administratively came in the Safe Medical Devices Act of 1990 (SMDA).[200] Adding section 303(f) to the FDCA, the SMDA authorized civil money penalties for most violations of the act concerning devices.[201] For certain violations, there must have been a "significant and knowing departure" from the requirements or a "risk to the public health."[202] Exceptions to liability for civil money penalties also apply for certain minor violations and for certain violations of an adulteration provision.[203] Although the SMDA was not explicit on this point, FDA interpreted the law as authorizing the agency to request the Department of Justice (DOJ) to seek a civil penalty in court in lieu of initiating an administrative proceeding.[204]

---

[195]   Violations of certain requirements of the Radiation Control for Health and Safety Act of 1968 (RCHSA) also subject persons to civil money penalties. *See* FDCA § 539(b)(1), 21 U.S.C. § 360pp(b) (2012) (previously codified at 42 U.S.C. § 263k(b)). Under the RCHSA, district courts have jurisdiction to impose such penalties. 21 U.S.C. § 360pp(a). In 2004, FDA amended its regulations to include section 539(b)(1), 21 U.S.C. § 360pp(b)(1), within the scope of its civil money penalty procedural regulations in 21 C.F.R. Part 17. *See* 69 Fed. Reg. 43,299 (July 20, 2004) (adding 21 C.F.R. § 17.1(d)).

[196]   Pub. L. No. 99-660, § 315, 100 Stat. 3751, 3783 (1986) (codified at 42 U.S.C. § 262(d)(2)).

[197]   Pub. L. No. 99-660, § 311(a), 100 Stat. at 3777, which added section 2128 to the PHSA (codified at 42 U.S.C. § 300aa-28). *See* redelegation of authority to FDA, 53 Fed. Reg. 36,127 (Sept. 16, 1988).

[198]   Pub. L. No. 100-293, § 7(b), 102 Stat. 95, 99 (1988), which added section 303(b)(2)-(5) to the FDCA (codified at 21 U.S.C. § 333(b)(2)-(5)). The manufacturer or distributor may also be subject to civil money penalties for failing to report these convictions to DHHS. 21 U.S.C. § 333(b)(3).

[199]   *See* 58 Fed. Reg. 30,680-81 (May 26, 1993); 60 Fed. Reg. 38,613 (July 27, 1995). As of mid-2014 this interpretation had not been subject to judicial challenge.

[200]   Pub. L. No. 101-629, § 17, 104 Stat. 4511, 4526 (1990).

[201]   21 U.S.C. § 333(f)(1).

[202]   These limitations apply to violations of section 519(a), 21 U.S.C. § 360i(a), with respect to recordkeeping and reporting, and to violations of section 520(f), 21 U.S.C. § 360j(f), with respect to current good manufacturing practices. 21 U.S.C. § 333(f)(1)(B). *See* TMJ Implants, Inc. v. DHHS, 584 F.3d 1290, 1302 (10th Cir. 2009) for a discussion of "knowing departure" in the context of FDA's assessment of civil money penalties for failure to submit medical device reports under 21 U.S.C. § 360i(a).

[203]   Minor violations of section 519(e), 21 U.S.C. § 360i(e), with respect to tracking requirements, or minor violations of section 519(f) (only with respect to reports of corrections), 21 U.S.C. § 360i(f), are not subject to civil money penalties if the defendant demonstrates substantial compliance with these requirements. 21 U.S.C. § 333(f)(1)(B). Violations of section 501(a)(2)(A), 21 U.S.C. § 351(a)(2)(A), concerning adulteration through insanitary conditions also are not subject to civil money penalties if the violations involve one or more devices that are not defective. 21 U.S.C. § 333(f)(1)(B).

[204]   *See* 58 Fed. Reg. 30,681 (May 26, 1993).

Subsequently, the Generic Drug Enforcement Act of 1992 (GDEA) expressly authorized FDA either to assess a civil money penalty administratively or, in lieu of an administrative proceeding, to request DOJ to institute a court action to recover a civil money penalty.[205] The GDEA authorizes civil money penalties for certain actions related to abbreviated new drug applications (ANDAs), such as bribing DHHS employees or knowingly obstructing a DHHS investigation into a drug subject to an ANDA.[206] Civil money penalties are also authorized for persons debarred under section 306 of the FDCA[207] or for employers who use the services of such debarred persons.[208] The Mammography Quality Standards Act of 1992 (MQSA) also included express authority for administrative assessment of civil money penalties for violations of certain new requirements for mammography facilities.[209]

In 1996 Congress added civil money penalty authority for violations of certain requirements of the Food Quality Protection Act (FQPA) related to pesticide chemical residues on food.[210] Unlike the other statutory provisions authorizing civil money penalties, this provision, section 303(f)(2) of the FDCA, precludes the use of the criminal, seizure, or injunction authorities when civil money penalties have been assessed.[211]

Although these statutory authorizations vary in their descriptions of hearing opportunities, certain of the provisions specify imposition of civil money penalties "by an order made on the record after opportunity for a hearing provided in accordance with [5 U.S.C. § 554]."[212] In 1993, FDA proposed procedural regulations to be applied "whenever a person has a right to an opportunity for a hearing on the administrative imposition of civil money penalties by FDA."[213] While consideration of those new specific procedures was pending, however, the agency temporarily amended its regulations to apply its procedures in 21 C.F.R. Part 12 for formal evidentiary hearings to proceedings for civil money penalties.[214] These Part 12 procedures had been promulgated to conform to the APA requirements in 5 U.S.C. 554 for

---

[205] Pub. L. No. 102-282, § 3, 106 Stat. 149, 159 (1992), which added section 307(b) to the FDCA (codified at 21 U.S.C. § 335b).

[206] *See* 21 U.S.C. § 335b(a). These provisions were enacted in the wake of a bribery scandal involving generic drug companies and FDA employees. *See* Bae v. Shalala, 44 F.3d 489 (7th Cir.1995) (concerning former president of a generic drug company debarred under the GDEA).

[207] The GDEA also added section 306 of the FDCA, codified at 21 U.S.C. § 335a.

[208] 21 U.S.C. § 335b(a)(6), (7) (2012).

[209] Pub. L. No. 102-539, § 2, 106 Stat. 3547 (1992) (codified at 42 U.S.C. § 263b). Penalties may be assessed for failure to obtain a required certificate or to substantially comply with mammography standards, and for violation of regulations by an owner, operator, or employee. 42 U.S.C. § 263b(h)(3) (2012). Subsequent amendments in 1998 by Pub. L. No. 105-248, 112 Stat. 1864 (1998), added civil money penalties for failure to notify patients of a risk when required by FDA to do so. 42 U.S.C. § 263b(h)(3)(C).

[210] Pub. L. No. 104-170, § 407, 110 Stat. 1489, 1535 (1996), added section 303(f)(2) to the FDCA, 21 U.S.C. § 333(f)(2).

[211] 21 U.S.C. § 333(f)(2)(B). FDA had made clear its view that use of the other civil money penalty authorities did not preclude use of other judicial and administrative remedies, if appropriate. *See* 60 Fed. Reg. 38,613.

[212] 21 U.S.C. § 333(f)(3) (civil money penalty provisions relating to devices and adulterated food). The GDEA requires assessment "by an order made on the record after an opportunity for an agency hearing on disputed issues of material fact and the amount of the penalty." 21 U.S.C. § 335b(b). The MQSA requires procedures to provide for "notice" to the facility owner or operator and "reasonable opportunity . . . to respond to the proposed sanctions and appropriate procedures for appealing determinations relating to the imposition of sanctions." 42 U.S.C. § 263b(h)(4). The other statutory provisions authorizing FDA to impose civil money penalties are silent as to the administrative procedures to be followed.

[213] 58 Fed. Reg. 30,682 (May 26, 1993).

[214] 58 Fed. Reg. 49,190 (Sept. 22, 1993).

adjudications "required by statute to be determined on the record after opportunity for an agency hearing."[215]

Although the existing Part 12 procedures satisfied any statutory or constitutional requirements for civil money penalty hearing procedures, the agency decided to develop regulations specifically tailored to such proceedings.[216] FDA believed that a "complaint-and-answer" procedure would be more appropriate than the published "notice-of-hearing" procedure under Part 12.[217] This new approach, embodied in 21 C.F.R. Part 17, was intended to be a faster, more efficient approach to joining and resolving civil money penalty issues.[218] For example, the rules in Part 17 governing production of documents are more similar to the rules governing discovery requests in court than they are to the Part 12 process for disclosure of information being relied upon.[219] Unlike a judge in a court proceeding, however, a presiding officer in a Part 17 hearing may order a deposition only upon a showing that the information sought could not be obtained in another way, and that there is substantial reason to believe that, without the deposition, the evidence might not be preserved.[220]

Certain of the statutes authorizing civil money penalties also authorize FDA to issue subpoenas related to these proceedings.[221] As a result, the Part 17 hearing regulations, unlike any other FDA administrative procedure regulations, describe the process for the presiding officer to issue subpoenas "when authorized by law."[222]

FDA decided that appeals from decisions of the presiding officers in civil money penalty proceedings would be made not to the Commissioner, as in other FDA proceedings, but, instead, to the DHHS Department Appeals Board.[223] Consequently, FDA also decided not to observe separation of functions in its Part 17 proceedings.[224] *Ex parte* contacts are, however, restricted under the civil money penalty procedures.[225]

---

[215] *See* discussion of Part 12 regulations at pp. 694-96, *supra*.

[216] *See* 58 Fed. Reg. at 30,682; 60 Fed. Reg. 38,612 (July 27, 1995). The agency's goal was to "establish an efficient, predictable system that processes cases in a fair and responsible manner, while affording defendants adequate procedural safeguards." *Id.* at 38,612. The regulations were modeled in part on existing civil money penalty processes, especially those of the Environmental Protection Agency and the Inspector General of DHHS. *Id.*

[217] 58 Fed. Reg. at 30,682.

[218] *Id.*

[219] *See id.*

[220] 21 C.F.R. § 17.23(e) (2014); *see* 60 Fed. Reg. at 38,619. Discoverable information under the Part 12 procedures is, however, broader than under the Part 17 procedures. *See* 58 Fed. Reg. at 30,682.

[221] The SMDA and FQPA provide that, "[i]n the course of any investigation, [FDA] may issue subpoenas requiring the attendance and testimony of witnesses and the production of evidence that relates to the matter under investigation." 21 U.S.C. § 333(f)(3)(A). FDA has interpreted this language to allow the agency to issue subpoenas related to a civil-money-penalty proceeding at any time, including during the adjudication of the penalty. *See* 60 Fed. Reg. at 38,619. Similarly, the GDEA provides that, "[i]n the course of any investigation or hearing . . ., [FDA] may . . . issue subpoenas requiring the attendance and testimony of witnesses and the production of evidence that relates to the matter under investigation." 21 U.S.C. § 335b(b)(1)(A) (2012).

[222] 21 C.F.R. § 17.27 (2014).

[223] 21 C.F.R. § 17.47 (2014). *See* 60 Fed. Reg. 38,634 (July 27, 1995).

[224] *See* 60 Fed. Reg. at 38,616.

[225] *Id.*; 21 C.F.R. § 17.20 (2014).

Final decisions on civil money penalty matters after appeal are subject to judicial review under the various authorizing statutes.[226] All amounts assessed are to be deposited in the Treasury of the United States.[227]

The various civil money penalty statutory provisions specify the maximum dollar amounts; however, the Federal Civil Penalties Inflation Adjustment Act of 1990 requires agencies to issue regulations to adjust for inflation each such penalty within its jurisdiction.[228] Therefore, FDA includes in its Part 17 regulations a periodically updated chart showing the adjusted maximum penalty amounts for civil money penalties assessed by the agency.[229]

Historically, FDA had not imposed civil money penalties frequently; it had used this authority primarily in relation to violations of requirements for medical devices and mammography facilities.[230] In the FDAAA, Congress provided FDA additional civil money penalty authorities related to dissemination of false or misleading direct-to-consumer drug advertisements[231] and violations of requirements for postmarket studies and clinical trials on prescription drugs, drug-safety labeling changes, and drugs with required risk evaluation and mitigation strategies.[232] The Tobacco Control Act added civil money penalty authority for violations of the FDCA that relate to tobacco products.[233] FDA has initiated civil money penalty actions under this Tobacco Control Act authority in numbers far exceeding such actions relating to non-tobacco products.[234] Most recently, the FDA Food Safety Modernization Act gave FDA authority to assess civil money penalties against persons who do not comply with recall orders involving food.[235]

---

[226] 21 C.F.R. § 17.51 (2014). Civil money penalties imposed by FDA have been held to be nondischargeable in bankruptcy. In re Christensen, No. 10-35387 (Bankr. D. Colo. May 3, 2011).

[227] 21 C.F.R. § 17.54 (2014).

[228] 28 U.S.C. § 2461 (2012).

[229] 21 C.F.R. § 17.2 (2014). *See* 79 Fed. Reg. 6090 (Feb. 3, 2014)

[230] *See, e.g.,* Office of Enforcement, Office of Regulatory Affairs, Food and Drug Administration, The Enforcement Story 21 (2003); Office of Enforcement, Office of Regulatory Affairs, Food and Drug Administration, The Enforcement Story 39 (2004). *See also* Korangy v. FDA, 498 F.3d 272 (4th Cir. 2007) (upholding imposition of FDA order imposing civil money penalties against owner of mammography facility).

[231] Pub. L. No. 110-85, § 901(d)(4), 121 Stat. 823, 940 (2007), adding to the FDCA § 303(g), 21 U.S.C. § 333(g).

[232] *Id.* § 902, 121 Stat. at 943, adding to the FDCA § 303(f)(4), 21 U.S.C. § 333(f)(4). FDAAA also authorized civil money penalties for certain violations relating to submission of certifications and/or clinical trial information to the clinical trial data bank required under section 402(j) of the Public Health Service Act (42 U.S.C. § 282(j)). *Id.* section 801(b), 121 Stat. at 920, adding to the FDCA section 303(f)(3), 21 U.S.C. § 333(f)(3).

[233] Pub. L. No. 111-31, § 103(c), 123 Stat. 1776, 1835(2009), amending section 303(f) of the FDCA, 21 U.S.C. § 333(f). *See* Guidance for FDA and Tobacco Retailers: Civil Money Penalties and No-Tobacco-Sale Orders For Tobacco Retailers (March 2011), *available at* http://www.fda.gov.

[234] From October 1, 2009 through March 31, 2014 FDA had assessed 1,347 civil money penalties under the Tobacco Control Act authority. *See* U.S. Gov't Accountability Office, GAO-14-561, Tobacco Product Regulation at 31 (June 2014).

[235] Pub. L. No. 111-353, § 206(c), 124 Stat. 3885, 3943 (2011), amending section 303(f)(2) of the FDCA, 21 U.S.C. § 333(f)(2)).

Guidance Documents

FDA's Historical Approach to Guidance

For many decades, FDA used various informal procedures and various types of documents to communicate to the public its positions on technical and policy matters. When the agency formalized its administrative procedures in regulations adopted in the 1970s, it included specific procedures addressing "guidelines," "recommendations," and "interpretive rules."[236] "Guidelines" were described as stating "procedures or standards of general applicability" that were not legal requirements but were acceptable to FDA for subject matter falling within the laws the agency administered.[237] Guidelines adopted by the agency were included in a public file, and were announced to the public through a *Federal Register* notice of availability that offered interested persons an opportunity to submit written comments.[238] FDA's regulations obligated the agency to follow a guideline until it was amended or revoked, and provided that a guideline could be used in a court or administrative proceeding to illustrate acceptable standards, but not as establishing a legal requirement.[239]

"Recommendations" were described as about matters authorized by the laws FDA administered, but not involving direct regulatory action.[240] At the agency's discretion, recommendations could be handled using the same procedures as for guidelines, but with a different public file.[241]

Although not required by the APA to do so, the agency decided as a matter of policy to follow notice-and-comment procedures for issuing interpretive rules and rules of agency practice and procedure.[242] General statements of policy published as informational notices in the *Federal Register* and matters involving agency organization were excluded from this voluntarily assumed requirement of notice and comment.[243] As case law interpreting the concept of "rule" under the APA developed,[244] however, FDA determined that it was no longer feasible for the agency to follow informal rulemaking procedures for all agency pronouncements that a court might find to be interpretive rules or rules of agency practice and procedure.[245] Consequently, in 1991, the agency amended its regulations to provide that procedures for notice-and-comment rulemaking would apply only to the extent required by

---

[236]   42 Fed. Reg. at 4703, 4709.
[237]   Guidelines were further described as relating to "performance characteristics, pre-clinical and clinical test procedures, manufacturing practices, product standards, scientific protocols, compliance criteria, ingredient specifications, labeling, or other technical or policy criteria." *Id.* at 4709.
[238]   42 Fed. Reg. at 4709, 4710.
[239]   *Id.*
[240]   *Id.* at 4710. Examples included model state and local ordinances or personnel practices for reducing radiation exposure. *Id.*
[241]   *Id.*
[242]   40 Fed. Reg. at 40,689, 40,724 (proposed rule); 42 Fed. Reg. at 4703 (final rule). This decision was consistent with then current recommendations of the Administrative Conference of the United States and with agency practice in the previous few years. *See* 40 Fed. Reg. at 40,689.
[243]   42 Fed. Reg. at 4703.
[244]   *See, e.g.,* Community Nutrition Inst. v. Young, 818 F.2d 943 (D.C.Cir. 1987).
[245]   58 Fed. Reg. 31,080 (July 31, 1990) (proposed rule to revise 21 C.F.R. § 10.40(d)); 56 Fed. Reg. 13,757 (Apr. 4, 1991) (final rule).

the APA, and that FDA could follow such procedures voluntarily, as a matter of discretion, when not so required.[246]

Good Guidance Practices

In the mid-1990s, evolving case law and a citizen petition served as catalysts for FDA to revamp significantly its approach to providing guidance to the public. In May 1995, the Indiana Medical Device Manufacturers Council, Inc., and the law firm representing it petitioned FDA to develop written procedures to control the development of guidance documents. The petitioners also asked FDA to undo the change to its procedural regulations made in 1991 and restore the self-imposed requirement to use rulemaking to issue interpretive rules and rules of agency practice and procedure.[247] These petitioners expressed a number of concerns about the agency's guidance-document process, including their beliefs that FDA was treating such documents as creating legal obligations without using APA-required notice-and-comment rulemaking; that needed guidance was not being developed; and that the document-issuance process was confusing (because of different titles, forms of guidance, and lack of clarity about current versions). Acting on the petition, FDA decided to embark on a process to improve its development and use of guidance documents, but denied the request to amend its procedural regulations to restore the pre-1991 version.[248]

Following a request for public comment on its suggestions for improved guidance procedures[249] and a public meeting on the issues, FDA published its new "Good Guidance Practices" (GGPs) in February 1997.[250] GGPs were designed to ensure uniformity in development, issuance, and use of guidance documents.[251] The announced goals of GGPs were to help ensure that the agency's guidance documents were developed with adequate public participation, were readily available to the public, and were not applied as binding requirements.[252]

1997 Statutory Amendment

Within months of FDA's publication of the GGPs, Congress expressed approval of these agency policies by amending the FDCA to incorporate the basic principles of GGPs, and

---

[246] *Id., See* 21 C.F.R. § 10.40(d) (2014). Similarly, in 1992, FDA proposed to revise its regulation on "advisory opinions," which included guidelines issued under section 10.90(b), to remove the provision that such an opinion obligates the agency to follow it until it is amended or revoked, and precludes the agency from recommending legal action taken in conformity with the opinion. 57 Fed. Reg. 47,314 (Oct. 15, 1992) (proposing to revise 21 C.F.R. § 10.85). The agency pointed out that certain language in section 10.85 was both inconsistent with the principle that federal agencies may not be estopped from enforcing the law and potentially in conflict with case law on procedures through which an agency can bind itself. *Id.* at 47,315. Although the agency did not publish a final rule to revise section 10.85, on this point its subsequent regulations on guidance documents, *see* 21 C.F.R. 10.115 (2014), have largely superseded the provisions of section 10.85 as a practical matter.

[247] Petition to FDA from Baker & Daniels on behalf of the Indiana Medical Device Manufacturers Council, Inc. (IMDMC) and Baker & Daniels, representing IMDMC and companies selling food, drugs, and medical devices, FDA Dkt. No. 95P-0110 (May 2, 1995) [hereinafter IMDMC petition].

[248] Letter from William B. Schultz, Deputy Comm'r for Policy, FDA, to Bradley Merrill Thompson, Baker & Daniels, FDA Dkt. No. 95P-0110 (Oct. 30, 1995).

[249] 61 Fed. Reg. 9181 (Mar. 7, 1996).

[250] 62 Fed. Reg. 8961 (Feb. 27, 1997).

[251] *Id.* at 8967.

[252] *Id.*

to require the agency to evaluate the effectiveness of GGPs.[253] Section 701(h) of the FDCA (21 U.S.C. § 371(h)) captures the essential elements of the GGPs previously issued by FDA concerning public participation, public availability, legal effect, nomenclature, uniform procedures, employee training and monitoring, and appeals.

First, the statute directs the agency to develop guidance documents with public participation.[254] For guidances setting forth initial interpretations of a statute or regulation, more than minor changes in interpretation or policy, complex scientific issues or highly controversial issues, the agency is to ensure public participation prior to implementation unless "not feasible or appropriate."[255] In those cases, the agency is to provide for public comment after implementation.[256] If a guidance sets forth only existing practices or minor changes in policy, the agency may implement it and provide for public comment at that time. Second, the law clearly delineates the nonbinding effect of FDA guidance documents.[257] Although the documents are not to bind either the agency or others, they do present the agency's views; and FDA employees are not to deviate from guidances without appropriate justification and supervisory concurrence.[258] FDA is to train its employees on how to develop and use guidances and to monitor the process for development and issuance of guidances.[259] The agency also has to have an appeals process to address complaints about the agency's development or use of guidances.[260]

The statute requires that the guidance documents, themselves, be available to the public both in written form and, as feasible, electronically, as well as that an updated list of guidances be maintained electronically and published periodically in the *Federal Register*.[261] The agency is to use uniform nomenclature and uniform internal approval procedures for guidances, and is to ensure that the documents and revisions are properly dated.[262] Periodically, all guidance documents are to be reviewed and, where appropriate, revised.[263]

GGP Regulations

Finally, the statute requires FDA to promulgate a regulation specifying the policies and procedures for the development, issuance, and use of guidance documents.[264] Consistently

---

[253]   Food and Drug Administration Modernization Act of 1997, Pub. L. No. 105-115, § 405, 111 Stat. 2296, 2368 (1997), adding to the FDCA § 701(h), 21 U.S.C. § 371(h). *See* S. Rep. No. 105-43, at 26 (1997) (describing Senate committee views of problems with FDA's increasing reliance on policy statements, and committee's intent that policies governing guidance documents be in regulations).

[254]   FDCA § 701(h)(1)(A), 21 U.S.C. § 371(h)(1)(A).

[255]   FDCA § 701(h)(1)(C), 21 U.S.C. § 371(h)(1)(C).

[256]   *Id.*

[257]   FDCA § 701(h)(1)(A), 21 U.S.C. § 371(h)(1)(A). The statute provides that the documents, themselves, shall indicate their nonbinding nature. FDCA § 701(h)(2), 21 U.S.C. § 371(h)(2). Several FDA-related cases concern the distinction between substantive rules and statements of policy or interpretive rules, *see, e.g.*, Syncor Int'l Corp. v. Shalala, 127 F.3d 90 (D.C. Cir. 1997); Professionals & Patients for Customized Care v. Shalala, 56 F.3d 592 (5th Cir. 1995); Community Nutrition Inst. v. Young, 818 F.2d 943 (D.C. Cir. 1987); Bellarno Int'l Ltd. v. FDA, 678 F. Supp. 410 (E.D.N.Y. 1988).

[258]   FDCA § 701(h)(1)(A), (B), 21 U.S.C. § 371(h)(1)(A), (B).

[259]   FDCA § 701(h)(1)(B), 21 U.S.C. § 371(h)(1)(B).

[260]   FDCA § 701(h)(4), 21 U.S.C. § 371(h)(4).

[261]   FDCA § 701(h)(1)(A), (3), 21 U.S.C. § 371(h)(1)(A), (3).

[262]   FDCA § 701(h)(2), 21 U.S.C. § 371(h)(2).

[263]   *Id.*

[264]   FDCA § 701(h)(5), 21 U.S.C. § 371(h)(5).

with this congressional mandate, FDA evaluated GGPs and, in 2000, promulgated a regulation on good guidance practices.[265] This regulation, codified at 21 C.F.R. § 10.115, fleshed out the statutory requirements on the basis of the agency's experience with the new GGPs since 1997.

The regulation defines "guidance documents" as "documents prepared for FDA staff, applicants/sponsors, and the public that describe the agency's interpretation of or policy on a regulatory issue."[266] Specified examples of guidance documents include documents relating in various ways to regulated products, submissions, and inspection and enforcement policies.[267] Examples of documents that are not guidance documents are those relating to internal FDA procedures, general informational documents provided to consumers or health professionals, speeches, various media materials, Warning Letters, memoranda of understanding and other communications directed to individual persons or firms.[268]

One concern raised by the IMDMC petition and by commenters on GGPs was the perception that FDA had too often announced new interpretations or regulatory positions through speeches.[269] The regulation makes clear that FDA may not use means of communication excluded from the definition of "guidance documents"—e.g., speeches—to "communicate new or different regulatory expectations to a broad public audience for the first time."[270]

FDA termed the guidances for which the statute requires an opportunity for public participation prior to implementation "Level 1 guidance documents," and termed all others "Level 2 guidance documents."[271] For most Level 1 documents, FDA publishes in the *Federal Register* a notice of availability announcing that a draft is available both on the Internet and in hard copy, and that FDA seeks public comment.[272] When the agency determines that prior public participation is "not feasible or appropriate," the notice of availability explains that the Level 1 guidance is being implemented immediately, and invites comments at that time.[273] If the agency receives comments, it reviews them and revises the document when it determines revision is appropriate.[274] Unlike the process for notice-and-comment rulemaking, however, FDA's GGP process does not obligate the agency to address each comment specifically.[275]

---

[265]   65 Fed. Reg. 7321 (Feb. 14, 2000) (proposed rule); 65 Fed. Reg. 56,468 (Sept. 19, 2000) (final rule).

[266]   21 C.F.R. § 10.115(b)(1) (2014). The statute does not define "guidance document." The definition in the regulation is a modification of the definition FDA included in its 1997 GGP policy statement. *See* 62 Fed. Reg. 8961, at 8967 (Feb. 27, 1997).

[267]   21 C.F.R. § 10.115(b)(2) (2014).

[268]   21 C.F.R. § 10.115(b)(3) (2014).

[269]   *See* IMDMC petition at 1, 5, 6.

[270]   21 C.F.R. § 10.115(e) (2014).

[271]   21 C.F.R. § 10.115(c) (2014).

[272]   21 C.F.R. § 10.115(g)(1) (2014).

[273]   21 C.F.R. § 10.115(g)(2), (3) (2014). FDA stated in the preamble to the final rule that, as with the 1997 GGP policy, the agency intended to implement Level 1 documents immediately if 1) there are public health reasons; 2) there is a statutory requirement, executive order or court order requiring immediate implementation; or 3) the guidance presents a less burdensome policy consistent with public health. 65 Fed. Reg. 7321, 7324 (Feb. 14, 2000). That statement is not included in the codified regulation.

[274]   21 C.F.R. § 10.115(g)(3)(ii).

[275]   *See* 65 Fed. Reg. at 7324; 65 Fed. Reg. 56,468, 56,470 (Sept. 19, 2000) (stating that the agency may continue the practice of discussing very significant comments or those causing the agency to revise a guidance in the notice of availability for the final guidance document or in the final guidance document, itself).

Level 2 documents are simply posted on the Internet, made available in hard copy and implemented immediately, with an invitation for public comment.[276]

Opportunities for public influence on FDA's guidance documents begin before documents are drafted. The regulation invites the public to suggest topics for new guidances, including drafts of such documents, and to suggest revisions or withdrawals.[277] FDA publishes annual lists of possible topics for future guidance-document development during the coming year—again with opportunities for public comment on the lists.[278] The agency also often seeks early comment from outside individuals or groups, such as through public meetings and workshops on guidance topics.[279] Moreover, the opportunity to comment on FDA's guidance documents does not end when a particular comment period closes: anyone may comment on a guidance document at any time.[280]

The GGP regulation also makes explicit that guidance documents do not establish legally enforceable rights or responsibilities—i.e., they do not bind the public or FDA.[281] The agency has developed as a standard element a statement of nonbinding effect, which appears prominently in all its recent guidance documents.[282] Mandatory language is also prohibited in FDA's guidance documents unless used to describe a statutory or regulatory requirement.[283]

---

[276]   21 C.F.R. § 10.115(g)(4) (2014). No notice of availability in the *Federal Register* is published for Level 2 documents; however, the comprehensive list to be published annually in the *Federal Register* identifies documents, including Level 2 documents, added to or deleted from the list since the previous publication of the list. 21 C.F.R. § 10.115(n)(2) (2014). Moreover, a current list of all guidance documents is maintained on the Internet, and is updated within 30 days of issuance of a new document. 21 C.F.R. § 10.115(n)(1) (2014).

[277]   21 C.F.R. § 10.115(f) (2014).

[278]   21 C.F.R. § 10.115(f)(5).

[279]   21 C.F.R. § 10.115(g)(1) (2014).

[280]   21 C.F.R. § 10.115(g)(5) (2014). However, to ensure that the agency will consider a comment on a draft guidance before it begins work on the final version of the guidance, comments are to be submitted by the specified comment date. *See, e.g.,* "Dates" section, Draft Guidance for Industry on Diabetes Mellitus: Developing Drugs and Therapeutic Biologics for Treatment and Prevention; Availability, 73 Fed. Reg. 11,420 (Mar. 3, 2008).

[281]   21 C.F.R. § 10.115(d)(1) (2014).

[282]   21 C.F.R. § 10.115(i)(iv) (2014). The statement that appears bolded in a box on the first page of text in FDA's guidance documents is, with minor variations, as follows: "This guidance represents the Food and Drug Administration's (FDA's) current thinking on this topic. It does not create or confer any rights for or on any person and does not operate to bind FDA or the public. You can use an alternative approach if the approach satisfies the requirements of the applicable statutes and regulations. If you want to discuss an alternative approach, contact the FDA staff responsible for implementing this guidance. If you cannot identify the appropriate FDA staff, call the appropriate number listed on the title page of this guidance." *See, e.g.,* Guidance for Industry, Considerations for Plasmid DNA Vaccines for Infectious Disease Indications, at 1 (Nov. 2007), *available at* http://www.fda.gov/cber/guidelines.htm. Other standard elements required by the GGP regulation deal with nomenclature (use of term "guidance"), date of issuance, activity addressed, issuing Center, and status of document (*e.g.,* draft, replacement, or revision of previous document). 21 C.F.R. § 10.115(i) (2014).

[283]   21 C.F.R. § 10.115(i)(2). An additional boilerplate paragraph that usually appears in the "Introduction" section of FDA guidance documents states: "FDA's guidance documents, including this guidance, do not establish legally enforceable responsibilities. Instead, guidances describe the agency's current thinking on a topic and should be viewed only as recommendations, unless specific regulatory or statutory requirements are cited. The use of the word *should* in Agency guidances means that something is suggested or recommended, but not required."

The statutory provision that FDA employees shall not depart from guidance documents except with appropriate justification and supervisory concurrence is also reflected in the regulation, along with the mandates for training of and monitoring by FDA employees.[284] Those who believe the agency or an employee is not complying with the GGP regulation are directed to appeal to the employee's supervisor and, if no satisfactory resolution is achieved, to appeal up the supervisory chain or to the appropriate FDA ombudsman.[285]

Petitions

Background of Citizen Petition Regulations

Prior to FDA's promulgation of its procedural regulations in the 1970s, the agency had no form or other procedural requirements relating to petitions. As a result, there was uncertainty and confusion both among those wishing to petition FDA and among agency employees trying to handle many different forms of requests.[286]

The First Amendment to the Constitution recognizes the "right of the people to petition the Government for a redress of grievances."[287] Under the APA, every agency must give interested persons the "right to petition for the issuance, amendment, or repeal of a rule."[288] Whatever the scope of these two legal entitlements, FDA decided to provide an extremely broad scope for its citizen-petition regulation. In essence, in 1975 FDA proposed to permit petitions relating to all forms of agency administrative activity, including refusals to act, and including factual, policy, and legal issues.[289] The only activity the agency expressly proposed to exclude from the petition process was enforcement-related activity.[290]

Scope

FDA's final regulations on citizen petitions, first published in 1977, have retained their broad scope, and have remained in effect with few subsequent changes. Currently codified at 21 C.F.R. Part 10, these regulations permit any "interested person"[291] to petition the Commissioner to:

---

284   21 C.F.R. § 10.115(d)(3), (l) (2014).

285   21 C.F.R. § 10.115(o) (2014). In 2007, 10 years after FDA established its original GGP policy, President Bush issued Executive Order 13,422, which modified Executive Order 12,866 to include provisions on guidance documents. Exec. Order 13,422 (Jan. 18, 2007), 72 Fed. Reg. 2763 (Jan. 23, 2007). Under the revised executive order, agencies were directed to adhere to certain principles when issuing guidance documents. In addition, for "significant guidance documents," agencies were required to notify OIRA in advance of issuance and, if requested by OIRA, to provide the draft guidance along with a brief explanation of the need for the document and how the need would be met. Exec. Order 12,866, § 9 (as in 2007). In 2009, President Obama revoked Executive Order 13,422, thereby removing the provisions relating to guidance documents. Exec. Order 13,497, 74 Fed. Reg. 6113 (Feb. 4, 2009).

286   See 40 Fed. Reg. 40,682 at 40,686; 42 Fed. Reg. 4680 at 4684.

287   U.S. Const. amend. I.

288   5 U.S.C. § 553(e) (2012).

289   See 40 Fed. Reg. at 40,686.

290   Id.

291   Although these petitions are referred to as "citizen petitions," a petitioner need not be a U.S. citizen. 21 C.F.R. § 10.30(a) (2014). See 43 Fed. Reg. 51,967, 51,975 (Nov. 7, 1978) (proposing amendment to clarify that citizen petitions may be submitted by any person who seeks to persuade FDA to take (or refrain from

- issue, amend or revoke a regulation;

- issue, amend or revoke an order; or

- take or refrain from taking any other form of administrative action.[292]

Referrals to the DOJ to initiate judicial enforcement action and related correspondence are specifically excluded from the scope of the citizen-petition regulations.[293] This exclusion applies to compliance activities that may ultimately lead to court action, such as inspections, sample collections, Warning Letters and similar matters.[294] Such enforcement actions and related activities are within the exclusive discretion of the agency.[295] Nevertheless, through correspondence or otherwise (except by a citizen petition), anyone may bring to the agency's attention, for exercise of its enforcement discretion, apparent violations of any of the laws FDA administers, or of any of the agency's regulations.

Form

Unless the form of the petition is specified in another regulation,[296] the form of a citizen petition must follow the specifications of 21 C.F.R. § 10.30(b).[297] These specifications contain not only format requirements, but also, more importantly, content requirements for petitions submitted to FDA. In essence, petitions must include statements of:

- the statutory authority under which the petitioner requests action by FDA;

- the action being requested;[298]

- the factual and legal grounds the petitioner relies on;

- the environmental impact if the request were granted;[299]

- the economic impact if the request were granted (only if the agency asks for this information after reviewing the petition); and

---

taking) action, including an individual who may not be a citizen of the United States); 44 Fed. Reg. 22,325 (April 13, 1979) (making this proposal final).

[292] 21 C.F.R. § 10.25(a) (2014). "Administrative action" is defined in 21 C.F.R. § 10.3(a) (2014) as including "every act, including the refusal or failure to act, involved in the administration of any law by the Commissioner, except that it does not include the referral of apparent violations to U.S. attorneys for the institution of civil or criminal proceedings or an act in preparation of a referral."

[293] 21 C.F.R. § 10.30(k) (2014). *See also* definition of "administrative action" in 21 C.F.R. 10.3(a), *supra* note 292.

[294] *See* 40 Fed. Reg. 40,682 at 40,683.

[295] *See id.*; 42 Fed. Reg. at 4684. *See also* Heckler v. Chaney, 470 U.S. 821 (1985).

[296] For example, the form for a color additive petition is set forth in 21 C.F.R. § 71.1 (2014), for a food additive petition in 21 C.F.R. § 171.1 (2014), for a new drug application in 21 C.F.R. § 314.50 (2014). *See* 21 C.F.R. § 10.25(a)(1).

[297] 21 C.F.R. § 10.30(b) (2014).

[298] For requests related to regulations or orders, the petitioner is to include the exact wording of the regulation or order being requested. 21 C.F.R. § 10.30(b).

[299] The environmental impact information requested is limited to a claim for categorical exclusion under FDA's environmental impact regulations, 21 C.F.R. §§ 25.30-25.34 (2014), or an environmental assessment under 21 C.F.R. § 25.40 (2014). 21 C.F.R. § 10.30(b). A full environmental impact statement is not required. *See* 42 Fed. Reg. at 4686.

- certification that the petition includes all information and views being relied on and "representative data and information known to the petitioner which are unfavorable to the petition."[300]

Petitions also must be signed and must include the petitioner's name, mailing address, and telephone number.[301]

Routine correspondence that does not purport to meet these requirements is not a "petition" within the scope of 21 C.F.R. 10.30.[302] Consequently, informal correspondence to FDA may include requests or suggestions for action by FDA; but, unlike action on a citizen petition, the agency's action on informal correspondence—favorable or unfavorable—does not constitute final agency action subject to judicial review.[303]

Petitions must be submitted to FDA's Division of Dockets Management (DDM), and must comply with the requirements of 21 C.F.R. § 10.20,[304] which also apply to submissions of many other types of documents to DDM.[305] Petitions that appear to meet the formal requirements of 21 C.F.R. § 10.30(b) as well as the docket-submission requirements of section 10.20 will be filed and assigned a docket number.[306]

Public Comments and Agency Review

Once filed, petitions and supporting materials are available for the public to review and to comment on.[307] During the course of its review, FDA may choose to solicit further comment through a notice in the *Federal Register*, public meetings or hearings, or other processes.[308]

The regulations require FDA to respond to a citizen petition within 180 days of receipt of the petition[309] by:

---

[300]   21 C.F.R. § 10.30(b). The most contentious issues at the time the rule was promulgated were the requirements to include unfavorable information and to so certify. *See* 42 Fed. Reg. at 4685-86. Commenters argued, *inter alia*, that the requirement might violate the constitutional protections against self-incrimination, might conflict with an attorney's professional obligations, and might have a "chilling" effect on petitions. *Id.* The agency had stated that requiring submission of unfavorable information was necessary to provide a more balanced and reasonable presentation and to prevent FDA and the public from being misled. 40 Fed. Reg. at 40,686. In rejecting the commenters' position, FDA stated that a decision favorable to a petition that reflects a review of information both supportive of and adverse to the petition is likely to be credible and, ultimately, more supportable. 42 Fed. Reg. at 4685. The agency also concluded that the certification, although perhaps technically redundant with the requirements of the False Reports to the Government Act, 18 U.S.C. 1001 (1976), would remind petitioners to verify the accuracy of their submissions. *Id.*

[301]   21 C.F.R. § 10.30(b).
[302]   21 C.F.R. § 10.30(k).
[303]   *Id. See also* 21 C.F.R. § 10.85(k) (2014). The agency's goal was not to impede the normal flow of informal correspondence with FDA, but to reserve the citizen-petition process for particular matters calling for more formal procedures. *See* 40 Fed. Reg. at 40,686. *See* discussion of judicial review of citizen petitions, *infra* pp. 719-21.
[304]   21 C.F.R. § 10.20 (2014).
[305]   21 C.F.R. § 10.30(b). *See* discussion of 21 C.F.R. § 10.20 at p. 687, *supra*.
[306]   21 C.F.R. § 10.30(c) (2014).
[307]   21 C.F.R. §§ 10.20(j)(1), 10.30(c), (d) (2014).
[308]   21 C.F.R. § 10.30(h) (2014).
[309]   Petitions filed under FDCA § 505(j)(2)(C), 21 U.S.C. § 355(j)(2)(C) (commonly known as "suitability petitions"), have the statutory 90-day deadline for response. 21 C.F.R. § 10.30(e)(4) (2014).

- approving the petition (and concurrently taking implementing action[310]);
- denying the petition; or
- providing a tentative response indicating why the agency has not yet decided.[311]

Resource constraints have consistently made it difficult for the agency to respond rapidly to citizen petitions.[312] The agency explicitly stated that its responses to petitions would reflect agency resources, priorities, and statutory deadlines.[313]

Before the agency rules on a petition, the petitioner may supplement, amend, or withdraw the petition without prejudice to resubmission.[314] When a decision is made, the agency may grant or deny the petition, in whole or in part, and may grant other relief or take other action as warranted by the petition.[315]

Record of the Agency's Decision

The administrative record for FDA's decision on a citizen petition consists of:

- the petition, including information it relies on, as filed;
- all comments on the petition received by FDA;
- records of any other procedures the agency chose to use during its reviews, such as meetings, hearings, and *Federal Register* notices requesting comments (these records may be transcripts, meeting minutes, or other documents); and
- the agency's decision on the petition, including all information identified or filed in the petition docket.[316]

---

[310] For example, publication of a *Federal Register* notice could occur simultaneously with a petition approval. 21 C.F.R. § 10.30(e)(2)(i) (2014).

[311] 21 C.F.R. § 10.30(e)(2) (2014). The regulation includes as examples of reasons for a tentative response other agency priorities or a need for additional information. 21 C.F.R. § 10.30(e)(2)(iii). An FDA tentative response to a citizen petition citing delay due to "complex issues requiring extensive review and analysis by agency officials" survived a judicial challenge based on alleged APA and due process violations. Biovail Corp. v. FDA, 448 F. Supp. 2d 154 (D.D.C. 2006).

[312] "Perhaps the greatest problem facing the Food and Drug Administration today is the scarcity of resources to deal with petitions and other similar requests . . . . A determination with respect to the priority to be assigned to any particular petition or other matter must of necessity be within the discretion of the Commissioner, who is charged with the responsibility for implementing all provisions of the laws subject to his jurisdiction." 40 Fed. Reg. 40,682 at 40,721 (proposing responses "as promptly as is feasible," but anticipating delays in responding to petitions with a relatively low priority). Responding to comments, the agency in the final rule established the 180-day deadline for responses to petitions, and concluded that overdue responses should be considered priorities. 42 Fed. Reg. 4680 at 4685.

[313] 21 C.F.R. § 10.30(e)(1) (2014).

[314] 21 C.F.R. § 10.30(g) (2014). If the petition has been referred to a hearing under Parts 12, 13, 14, or 15, the petition may be supplemented, amended, or withdrawn only with the agency's approval. *Id.*

[315] 21 C.F.R. § 10.30(e)(3) (2014). The petitioner must be notified of the decision in writing. *Id.*

[316] 21 C.F.R. § 10.30(i) (2014).

Petitions for Reconsideration

Any interested person (including, of course, the petitioner) may ask the agency to reconsider a decision on a citizen petition.[317] Even a person who was not a party to the proceeding before FDA issued the decision as to which reconsideration is sought may file such a petition. The petition for reconsideration must be submitted within 30 days of the date of the decision, unless the agency, for good cause, permits late filing.[318] No new information or views may be included in the petition for reconsideration, which must show that relevant information or views already in the record were not previously considered at all or were not adequately considered.[319]

The agency may grant the petition for reconsideration if it is "in the public interest and in the interest of justice" to do so.[320] The agency will grant the request to reconsider if the petition shows *all* of the following:

- relevant information or views in the record of the original petition were not previously or not adequately considered;
- the petitioner's position is not frivolous and is being pursued in good faith;
- sound public policy grounds support reconsideration; and
- reconsideration is not outweighed by public health or other public interests.[321]

If the agency decides to reconsider, it puts that written determination into the docket, and proceeds to review and rule on the merits of the matter.[322] At this point, the agency could avail itself of the same ancillary procedures (meetings, hearings, etc.) it could use in reviewing an original petition.[323] The ultimate decision could be to reaffirm, modify, or overrule the original decision, in whole or in part, and could be to "grant such other relief or take such other action as is warranted."[324]

Petitions for Stay of Action

Any interested person may also ask the agency to stay the effective date of any administrative action for a specific or indefinite period of time.[325] As with a petition for reconsideration, a petition for stay must be filed within 30 days of the decision involved, unless the agency for good cause permits later filing.[326]

---

[317] 21 C.F.R. § 10.33 (2014). The agency may also initiate the reconsideration of a matter. 21 C.F.R. § 10.33(a), (h).

[318] 21 C.F.R. § 10.33(b) (2014). *See* 43 Fed. Reg. 51,967 (Nov. 7, 1978) (proposed rule to permit filing later than 30 days after decision); 44 Fed. Reg. 22,327 (Apr. 13, 1979) (final rule).

[319] 21 C.F.R. §10.33(e). A petitioner for reconsideration who wants to rely on new information or views may submit a new petition to modify the decision under 21 C.F.R. § 10.25(a). *Id.*

[320] 21 C.F.R. § 10.33(d).

[321] *Id.*

[322] 21 C.F.R. § 10.33(f), (i).

[323] 21 C.F.R. § 10.33(j).

[324] 21 C.F.R. § 10.33(i). The record of the decision on the merits of a petition for reconsideration is also very similar to that for the original petition. *See* 21 C.F.R. § 10.33(k); 21 C.F.R. § 10.30(i).

[325] 21 C.F.R. § 10.35(b). The agency, itself, may at any time stay or extend the effective date of a pending or decided matter. 21 C.F.R. § 10.35(a).

[326] 21 C.F.R. § 10.35(b).

The filing of a petition for stay, or any other kind of petition, will not lead to a stay or delay of the decision in question unless:

- the agency determines that a stay or delay is in the public interest and stays the action;
- a statute requires the stay; or
- a court orders the stay.[327]

Similar to the grounds for granting petitions for reconsideration, the agency may grant a petition for stay if it is "in the public interest and in the interest of justice."[328] The agency will grant a request for stay if *all* of the following apply:

- the petitioner will otherwise suffer irreparable injury;
- the petitioner's case is not frivolous and is being pursued in good faith;
- the petitioner has demonstrated sound public policy grounds for the stay;
- the delay from the stay is not outweighed by public health or other public interests.[329]

As with a citizen petition, the agency may grant or deny a petition for stay, in whole or in part; and may take other action warranted by the petition.[330] A petition for a stay is also subject to the docket submission requirements in 21 C.F.R. § 10.20.[331] Interested persons may comment on such petitions as well.[332]

Judicial Review of Final Action on a Petition

As a general rule, FDA's final decision on a citizen petition, a petition for reconsideration or a petition for stay of action is final agency action reviewable in court.[333] The agency takes the position that, when a court reviews FDA's decision, the validity of the agency's decision is to be determined solely on the basis of the administrative record (with no further record development in court).[334]

If a person complains in court about an FDA action or failure to act without first filing a citizen petition with FDA (or having participated in some other proceeding before the agency, e.g., an application for approval of a product), the agency may ask the court to dismiss the action or to refer the matter to the agency for an initial determination.[335]

---

[327]   21 C.F.R. § 10.35(d).

[328]   21 C.F.R. § 10.35(e).

[329]   *Id.*

[330]   *Id.*

[331]   21 C.F.R. § 10.35(c). *See* discussion of docket submission requirements, *supra* p. 687.

[332]   21 C.F.R. § 10.35(c).

[333]   21 C.F.R. § 10.45(d) (2014). If applicable law expressly requires that the petitioner take further action before judicial review is available, then FDA would not consider the matter ripe for judicial review. 21 C.F.R. § 10.45(d)(1)(i).

[334]   21 C.F.R. § 10.45(f) (2014). *See* Bradley v. Weinberger, 483 F.2d 410 (1st Cir. 1973). *See* 21 C.F.R. 10.30(i) (citizen petitions); 21 C.F.R. 10.33(k) (petitions for reconsideration); and 21 C.F.R. 10.35(h) (petitions for stay) for the description of the administrative record for each type of petition.

[335]   21 C.F.R. § 10.45(b) (2014). The agency's request may be based on grounds of failure to exhaust administrative remedies, lack of final agency action, and/or lack of an actual controversy. *Id. See, e.g.,* Public Citizen Health Research Group v. Comm'r, 740 F.2d 21 (D.C. Cir. 1984); Ass'n of Am. Physicians & Surgeons v. FDA, C.A. No. 07-0668 (D.D.C. Mar. 4, 2008).

1999 Proposed Changes to Citizen-Petition Regulations

Despite numerous efforts to improve its procedures for handling citizen petitions, FDA historically has had a large backlog of pending petitions.[336] Various criticisms of the agency's lack of timeliness in responding to citizen petitions led in 1999 to a proposed rule that would have amended the citizen-petition regulations.[337]

The proposal would have narrowed the scope of actions that could be requested by a citizen petition. Although a person could still petition FDA to issue, amend or revoke a regulation, a proposed or modified regulation would have to pertain to a subject appropriately addressed by a regulation.[338] For example, a petition seeking a regulation prohibiting the approval of a particular product would no longer be accepted.[339]

The proposed rule also would have precluded petitions to amend a pending order or for the issuance of a future order.[340] This change was intended primarily to eliminate wasted agency effort focused on speculation about future orders.[341] Another proposed change would have eliminated the broad category, "any form of administrative action."[342] Instead, the scope for actions other than regulations and orders that could be requested by petition would be limited to such actions "as specifically provided by regulation."[343]

At the time of the proposal, questions had been raised about whether the citizen-petition process was being used for improper purposes, such as to delay competition.[344] In response to such concerns, the agency also proposed to revise the certification statement for petitions to include a statement that the petition was "not submitted for any improper purpose, such as to harass or to cause unnecessary delay."[345]

Other proposed changes included specifically authorizing actions other than preparing a formal response to a petition. For example, if a petition involved issues that could be considered in another administrative proceeding or involved requests that could be addressed through correspondence, the agency could refer the petition for other action, rather than provide a formal response to the petition.[346]

---

[336] See 68 Fed. Reg. 16,461 (Apr. 4, 2003) ("[FDA] receive[s] nearly 290 citizen petitions annually, and in most years, the number of incoming citizen petitions exceeded the number of responses [issued]. . . . In the past, the response was approximately 100 responses per year. This resulted in a steadily growing backlog of citizen petitions.").

[337] 64 Fed. Reg. 66,822 (Nov. 30, 1999). For example, a 1998 report from the Office of Inspector General in the DHHS urged FDA to reduce its petition backlog by implementing some of the changes then being discussed within the agency. See 64 Fed. Reg. 66,823 (Nov. 30, 1999).

[338] 64 Fed. Reg. at 66,823.

[339] Id.

[340] Id.

[341] Id.

[342] 64 Fed. Reg. at 66,824.

[343] Id. At the time, there were more than 20 such FDA regulations expressly providing for interested persons to submit citizen petitions. Id.

[344] See 64 Fed. Reg. at 66,822. Such concerns had been raised by the Federal Trade Commission, especially in the context of approvals of generic drugs. Id.

[345] Id. at 66,824.

[346] Id. at 66,825.

Other parts of the proposal were designed to make the process more efficient. For example, if the agency asked for clarification because the petition was vague or contained conflicting requests, and the petitioner did not answer, the agency could consider the petition withdrawn.[347] FDA could also combine petitions on the same or similar subjects, and give one response.[348]

Most of the comments on the proposal, including those from industry and public interest groups, opposed it.[349] They emphasized the importance of citizen petitions to public participation in agency action, and expressed concern about unduly restricting the use of these petitions.[350] In 2003, FDA noted its internal progress in responding to citizen petitions, concluded that changing the regulations was not warranted and withdrew the proposed rule.[351]

2007 Amendment to FDCA on Certain Citizen Petitions

Although FDA withdrew its proposed changes to the citizen-petition regulations, concerns about the timeliness of agency responses and about potential abuses of the citizen-petition process to delay competition did not abate. Congress responded to certain of these concerns by enacting section 914 of the FDAAA, which amended section 505 of the FDCA.[352] A few revisions to this provision were subsequently enacted in the Food and Drug Administration Safety and Innovation Act (FDASIA) in 2012.[353]

Under revised section 505(q), FDA may not delay approval of a pending application submitted under section 505(b)(2) or section 505(j) of the FDCA[354] or section 351(k) of the Public Health Service Act[355] due to a request to take action relating to the application, unless:

- the request is a petition submitted pursuant to 21 C.F.R. § 10.30 (citizen petition) or § 10.35 (petition for stay); and

- FDA determines that a delay is necessary to protect the public health.[356]

FDA may not consider such a petition[357] unless it contains a signed certification similar to that in 21 C.F.R. § 10.30, with additional certifications about when the information became

---

[347] *Id.*

[348] *Id.*

[349] 68 Fed. Reg. 16,461 (Apr. 4, 2003).

[350] *Id.*

[351] *Id.*

[352] *See* Pub. L. No. 110-85, § 914, 121 Stat. 823, 953 (2007), amending 21 U.S.C. § 355.

[353] *See* Pub. L. No. 122-144, § 1135, 126 Stat. 993, 1123 (2012), amending 21 U.S.C. § 355(q).

[354] Applications under FDCA § 505(b)(2), 21 U.S.C. § 355(b)(2) are commonly called "505(b)(2) applications"; applications under FDCA § 505(j), 21 U.S.C. § 355(j) (2012) are commonly called "generic drug applications," "abbreviated new drug applications," or "ANDAs."

[355] Applications under § 351 of the PHSA are commonly called "biosimilar product applications."

[356] 21 U.S.C. § 355(q)(1)(A). *See* FDA Guidance for Industry: Citizen Petitions and Petitions for Stay of Action Subject to Section 505(q) of the Federal Food, Drug, and Cosmetic Act (June 2011) for a discussion of how FDA determines whether a petition would delay approval of an ANDA or section 505(b)(2) application, as well as other guidance on 505(q) petitions. *Available at* http://www.fda.gov/Drugs/ GuidanceComplianceRegulatoryInformation/Guidances/default.htm.

[357] Section 505(q), 21 U.S.C. § 355(q), does not apply to petitions relating solely to the timing of approval under section 505(j)(5)(B)(iv) or to petitions by sponsors about their own applications. 21 U.S.C. § 355(q)(4). From fiscal year 2008 through fiscal year 2012, FDA received a total of 116 petitions subject to section 505(q). *See*

known to the party on whose behalf the petition is being filed, and about who is paying for the filing of the petition.[358] Moreover, if there is any supplemental information, or if comments are submitted on a petition, a similar signed verification must be included.[359] This verification concerning additional information or comments includes the specific statement: "I have not intentionally delayed submission of this document or its contents."[360]

FDA may deny a petition if it determines that

- either the petition or a supplement to the petition was submitted with the primary purpose of delaying the approval of an application; and
- the petition does not on its face raise valid scientific or regulatory issues.[361]

If FDA has determined that delay of approval of a pending application because of a petition is necessary to protect the public health, the agency must so notify the applicant within 30 days of the determination.[362] If applicable, the notification would include any clarification or additional data that the applicant should submit to the petition docket to make possible FDA's prompt review of the petition.[363]

To address the lack of timely action by FDA on many such petitions, Congress mandated "final agency action" no later than 150 days after the petition is submitted.[364] No extensions are permitted for any reason.[365] FDA is considered to have taken final agency action on such a petition related to section 505(b)(2) or 505(j) if it makes a final decision, as described in

---

Food and Drug Administration, Fifth Annual Report on Delays in Approvals of Applications Related to Citizen Petitions and Petitions for Stay of Action for Fiscal Year 2012, Report to Congress, at 4 (2012).

[358] 21 U.S.C. § 355(q)(1)(H) requires this certification: " 'I certify that, to my best knowledge and belief: (a) this petition includes all information and views upon which the petition relies; (b) this petition includes representative data and/or information known to the petitioner which are unfavorable to the petition; and (c) I have taken reasonable steps to ensure that any representative data and/or information which are unfavorable to the petition were disclosed to me. I further certify that the information upon which I have based the action requested herein first became known to the party on whose behalf this petition is submitted on or about the following date: _____. If I received or expect to receive payments, including cash and other forms of consideration, to file this information or its contents, I received or expect to receive those payments from the following persons or organizations: _____. I verify under penalty of perjury that the foregoing is true and correct as of the date of the submission of this petition.', with the date on which such information first became known to such party and the names of such persons or organizations inserted in the first and second blank space, respectively."

[359] 21 U.S.C. § 355(q)(1)(I) requires this "verification": "I certify that, to my best knowledge and belief: (a) I have not intentionally delayed submission of this document or its contents; and (b) the information upon which I have based the action requested herein first became known to me on or about _____. If I received or expect to receive payments, including cash and other forms of consideration, to file this information or its contents, I received or expect to receive those payments from the following persons or organizations: _____. I verify under penalty of perjury that the foregoing is true and correct as of the date of the submission of this petition.', with the date on which such information first became known to the party and the names of such persons or organizations inserted in the first and second blank space, respectively."

[360] Id.

[361] 21 U.S.C. § 355(q)(1)(E).

[362] 21 U.S.C. § 355(q)(1)(B). The notification may be through either a document or a meeting with the applicant. Id.

[363] Id.

[364] 21 U.S.C. § 355(q)(1)(F).

[365] Id. Not even consent of the petitioner can extend the period. Id.

21 C.F.R. § 10.45(d), within 150 days or if the 150-day period expires without FDA having made such a final decision.[366]

Congress also required exhaustion of administrative remedies by providing that courts must dismiss civil actions filed against FDA on any issues raised in such petitions related to section 505(b)(2) or 505(j) before "final agency action" on the petition.[367]

The law puts additional pressure on timely agency review of and responses to petitions under section 505(q) related to section 505(b)(2) or 505(j) by limiting the administrative record of an application approval about which a petition was submitted.[368] For purposes of judicial review of such approvals, the record on any issue raised by a petition essentially includes the petition (and supplements and comments); FDA's response, if issued; and other information considered by the agency by the date of final agency action on the petition.[369]

Conclusion

For many decades, FDA has been a governmental leader in developing and codifying sound, clearly delineated administrative procedures. The FDCA specifies many procedural requirements to effectuate the statutory controls governing the various types of FDA-regulated products. FDA has further refined and articulated the processes governing its implementation of the law. These processes, which are generally set forth in regulations, afford interested persons clear and structured opportunities to contribute to the agency's decision making.

The agency's procedures for developing requirements through rulemaking provide opportunities for all interested persons to submit relevant information and views. FDA's extensive review, analysis and response to comments on its proposed rules help to ensure that the final rules reflect reasoned decision making.

FDA's hearing procedures also offer a broad range of opportunities for interested persons to inform agency employees, to challenge the agency's proposed actions and to defend their own past behavior as regulated individuals or entities. These procedures range from very informal meetings to highly structured adjudications, where detailed scientific and factual information can be carefully scrutinized.

The agency has also developed effective procedures for developing guidance to industry, to agency employees and to the public on regulatory issues. Developed with input from affected and interested persons, FDA's guidance documents often facilitate compliance with complex statutory or regulatory requirements.

---

[366] 21 U.S.C. § 355(q)(2)(A).
[367] 21 U.S.C. § 355(q)(2)(B). Such dismissals are without prejudice. *Id.*
[368] 21 U.S.C. § 355(q)(2)(C).
[369] *Id.*

Finally, FDA's petition procedures provide clear opportunities for interested persons to ask the agency to take appropriate action. This structured process not only assures people a pathway to obtaining an agency decision but also results in an articulated response that, in most cases, can be reviewed in court.

All of these administrative procedures provide structure to FDA and to others to help resolve even the most complex issues of science, law, and policy. Through these procedures, FDA's mission to promote and protect the public health is advanced in fair, orderly, and transparent ways.

CHAPTER 21
FDA ENFORCEMENT POWERS

....

SCOTT BASS AND WILLIAM MCCONAGHA[*]

Introduction

The Food and Drug Administration (FDA) is a relatively small federal agency with a huge job. It employs about 13,000 people and receives annual appropriations of approximately $2.6 billion, but it is responsible for regulating nearly 20 percent of the U.S. economy.[1] For every consumer dollar spent in the United States, nearly 25 cents is spent on items that fall under the agency's jurisdiction.[2] The products that FDA regulates now account for more than $1 trillion in annual sales each year.[3]

Given the size of this portfolio, FDA has been forced to become increasingly strategic in the development and execution of its enforcement policy. Over the last 20 years, the agency has institutionalized a risk-based approach to enforcement, focusing its limited resources on actions that address a public health threat, vindicate an important regulatory principle, or have an important deterrent value. With the latter goal in mind, FDA announced in 2010 that it would increase the number of misdemeanor criminal prosecutions initiated for violations of the Federal Food, Drug, and Cosmetic Act (FDCA) and would hold a corporation's executives, not just the corporation itself, personally liable for crimes under the Responsible Corporate Officer Doctrine. The verdict is out as to whether the agency has made good on this threat.

Several Centers of FDA are involved in the development of enforcement policy. FDA's Office of Enforcement, which was once the lead office on these issues, manages FDA's debarment

[*] The authors thank Ryan Kaat and Kathy Lee for their invaluable help in preparing the update to this chapter.

[1] FOOD AND DRUG ADMINISTRATION, DEPARTMENT OF HEALTH AND HUMAN SERVICES, FISCAL YEAR 2015 JUSTIFICATION OF ESTIMATES FOR APPROPRIATIONS COMMITTEES 21, 163 (2014).

[2] SUBCOMMITTEE ON SCIENCE AND TECHNOLOGY, FDA SCIENCE AND MISSION AT RISK: REPORT OF THE SUBCOMMITTEE ON SCIENCE AND TECHNOLOGY 1 (2007).

[3] Legislation, U.S. FOOD AND DRUG ADMINISTRATION, http://www.fda.gov/RegulatoryInformation/Legislation/default.htm (last updated July 9, 2012).

program, partners with the product Centers, and helps set priorities for field inspections. Each of FDA's product Centers has an Office of Enforcement, and each of these Offices has assumed a greater role in setting FDA enforcement policy in the last 15 years. Their growth in influence corresponded with a period of decentralized management of enforcement policy, but that trend appears to be changing. The Office of Commissioner is now assuming an even more prominent role in the process with the advent of the new Global Directorate, which is tasked with helping FDA manage the increasingly global nature of FDA-regulated supply chains.

These recent changes in the development of enforcement policy coincide with Congress' increased interest in preventive regulation. In several recent health crises, especially those related to foodborne illnesses and contaminated compounded pharmaceuticals, FDA was thrust into a reactive role, often initiating enforcement action well after the public health incident. Congress responded in 2011 and 2012 by strengthening FDA's current Good Manufacturing Practice (cGMP) authority and enacting the FDA Food Safety Modernization Act, which modernizes the regulation of the domestic food supply by requiring manufacturers to take steps to prevent foodborne outbreaks in the first place.

Over the past 30 years, Congress has also provided FDA with more administrative enforcement tools. These tools—which include civil monetary penalties,[4] debarment,[5] enhanced documentary requirements for imports,[6] administrative detention,[7] suspension of food registration,[8] and mandatory recalls[9] for most products—have enabled FDA to address and deter unlawful conduct with greater speed and more precision. They have also enabled the agency to tailor remedies to the specific nature of the misconduct at issue.

FDA is also leveraging its relationships with other regulatory agencies now more than ever. FDA continues to rely on state agencies to inspect domestic manufacturing plants and pursue misconduct under applicable state laws. FDA is also enhancing its partnerships with many foreign regulators to help facilitate the exchange of inspection information, increase oversight of global supply chains, and interdict violative products before they reach the U.S.

Over the past generation, FDA's responsibilities have grown substantially, the products the agency regulates have become decidedly more complex, and the supply chains for those products have become increasingly global. Congress has responded with new enforcement authorities, and user fees for medical products can now be used in certain circumstances to oversee supply chains, not just review product applications.[10] The result is an FDA that has more enforcement tools than ever but faces complicated questions about how best to use them. The current strategy is risk-based enforcement, prevention, and deterrence. Barring a major change in appropriations or political leadership, there is little reason to think these priorities will change meaningfully in the foreseeable future.

---

[4]   See FDCA §§ 303, 307, 21 U.S.C. §§ 333, 335b.
[5]   See FDCA § 306, 21 U.S.C. § 335a.
[6]   See FDCA § 801(r), 21 U.S.C. § 381(r).
[7]   See FDCA § 304(g), 21 U.S.C. § 335a(g).
[8]   See FDCA § 415(b), 21 U.S.C. § 350d(b).
[9]   See FDCA §§ 423, 518, 908(c), 21 U.S.C. §§ 350l, 360h, 387h(c).
[10]   See FDCA § 744A(11), 21 U.S.C. § 379j-41(11).

The Historical Development
of FDA's Enforcement Authority

Laws relating to the adulteration of drugs were enacted in a large number of states and territories in the late 19th century.[11] The proliferation of fraudulent patent medicines led to federal legislation proscribing poor-quality imported drugs.[12] Import interception was an early tool of both food enforcement and drug enforcement.

The Pure Food and Drugs Act of 1906,[13] the first wide-scale federal effort at drug regulation, granted to FDA's precursor agency the power to seize drugs and foods.[14] There were, however, a number of enforcement limitations under that statute. A product was "misbranded," for example, only if its label contained false statements about its ingredients. False claims about a product's effects were not proscribed.[15] In 1912, the Sherley Amendment[16] added fraudulent therapeutic claims to the misbranding provisions, but the amendment did not close a number of other gaping enforcement loopholes in the 1906 act.

In 1938, Congress enacted the Federal Food, Drug, and Cosmetic Act, the law under which FDA currently operates. This new law closed many of the loopholes in the 1906 act by increasing federal oversight and strengthening federal penalties.[17] The FDCA expanded FDA's jurisdiction to cover medical devices and cosmetics; it provided explicit authority for establishment inspections; and it imposed criminal penalties for a host of additional acts, including the distribution or sale of adulterated or misbranded drug products.[18]

The principal enforcement mechanisms provided by the 1938 act are *in rem* seizure, injunction, and criminal prosecution.[19] Together, seizure and injunction proceedings enable FDA to keep unsafe products from entering the stream of commerce; criminal prosecution is used to punish and deter serious violations of the FDCA (*see* sections on seizures, injunctions, and criminal proceedings, *infra*). All are judicial remedies that must be pursued through legal actions filed in federal district court.

The enforcement regime in the FDCA was (and is) grounded in three critical concepts: pre-approval, adulteration, and misbranding. The term "pre-approval" refers to the multiple provisions in the FDCA that require certain products, such as new drugs and food additives, to be pre-approved by FDA before they can be offered for sale in the United States.[20] The term "adulteration" refers to the physical integrity and quality of FDA-regulated products. Products that are contaminated with filth, sub- or super-potent, outside their approved

---

[11]   Wallace F. Janssen, *America's First Food and Drug Laws*, 30 Food Drug Cosm. L.J. 665 (1975).

[12]   The Import Drugs Act of 1848, 30 Cong. Ch. 70, 9 Stat. 237 (1848).

[13]   Pub. L. No. 59-384, 34 Stat. 768 (1906).

[14]   By 1907, FDA already had collected more than 13,000 samples for possible seizure recommendations. Food & Drug Law Inst., Federal Food, Drug, and Cosmetic Law Administrative Reports 1907-1949 (1951), *cited in* Eugene M. Pfeifer, *Enforcement, in* Seventy-Fifth Anniversary Commemorative Volume of Food and Drug Law 72, 78 (FDLI 1983).

[15]   United States v. Johnson, 221 U.S. 488 (1911).

[16]   Pub. L. No. 62-301, 37 Stat. 416 (1912).

[17]   Pub. L. No. 75-717, 52 Stat. 1040 (1938) (codified as amended at 21 U.S.C. §§ 301-399).

[18]   FDCA §§ 301, 303, 501, 502, 505, 21 U.S.C. §§ 331, 333, 351, 352, 355.

[19]   *See* FDCA §§ 302, 303, 304, 21 U.S.C. §§ 332, 333, 334.

[20]   *See* FDCA §§ 409, 505, 21 U.S.C. §§ 348, 355.

specifications or otherwise unfit for consumption are deemed adulterated under the law.[21] The term "misbranding" refers to the claims made for a product, including claims made on packaging, in labeling, or through advertisements. Product packaging that includes misleading claims, fails to disclose material information, or (as to drugs and medical devices) lacks adequate directions for use is deemed misbranded under the law.[22]

In the early years following passage of the 1938 act, FDA litigation consisted almost entirely of seizures and criminal prosecutions.[23] Injunctions were not widely used, in part because of the administrative burdens attendant to their approval within FDA.[24] As the modern era of enforcement evolved, FDA began to rely more heavily on administrative pronouncements, rather than solely on enforcement litigation and judicial precedents, to achieve wide-ranging compliance.[25]

Over time, FDA increasingly turned to Warning Letters (*see* section on warning notices, *infra*) as a means of communicating its enforcement intentions. Voluntary compliance was thereby encouraged without litigation. Recalls represented an additional FDA effort to secure compliance without having to resort to product seizures (*see* section on "voluntary" recalls, *infra*).[26]

In the 1970s, FDA sought and obtained legislation to clarify and expand its authority over all aspects of the marketing of medical devices.[27] When enforcement of the new requirements lagged, Congress responded with the Safe Medical Devices Act of 1990 to strengthen FDA's hand.[28] For the first time, Congress authorized FDA and the courts to require recalls with respect to an entire class of products,[29] an enforcement power previously available only on a "voluntary" basis (except for infant formulas[30]). In addition, provisions authorizing temporary suspensions of product approvals and civil penalties were enacted.[31]

The use of draconian penalties in the FDCA to offset enforcement budget limitations was ushered in by passage of the Prescription Drug Marketing Act of 1987 (PDMA).[32] The PDMA significantly enhanced FDA's enforcement authority to respond to growing concerns about

---

[21]   *See* FDCA §§ 301, 402, 501, 601, 902, 21 U.S.C. §§ 331, 342, 351, 361, 387b.

[22]   *See* FDCA §§ 301, 402, 502, 602, 903, 21 U.S.C. §§ 331, 343, 352, 362, 387c.

[23]   *See* Federal Food, Drug, and Cosmetic Law Administrative Reports 1907-1949, *supra* note 14, at 84.

[24]   *See id.*

[25]   *Id.* at 86.

[26]   Both enforcement tools were made the subject of *Federal Register* announcements. *See* Enforcement Policy for Certain Compliance Correspondence, 43 Fed. Reg. 27,498 (June 23, 1978) (Warning Letters); Recalls (Including Product Corrections)—Guidelines on Policy, Procedures, and Industry Responsibilities, 43 Fed. Reg. 26,202 (June 16, 1978) (recalls).

[27]   Those efforts culminated in the Medical Device Amendments of 1976, Pub. L. No. 94-295, 90 Stat. 539 (1976) (codified in scattered sections of 21 U.S.C.). FDA's enforcement powers also extend to biologics. 42 U.S.C. § 262(j).

[28]   Pub. L. No. 101-629, 104 Stat. 4511 (1990) (codified in scattered sections of 21 U.S.C.).

[29]   *Id.* § 8, 104 Stat. at 4520 (codified at 21 U.S.C. § 360h(e)).

[30]   FDCA § 412(e)(1), 21 U.S.C. § 350a(e)(1). Mandatory recall authority for all food products was added in the Food Safety Modernization Act of 2011, Pub L. No. 111-353, 124 Stat. 3885 (2011), *available at* http://www.gpo.gov/fdsys/pkg/PLAW-111publ353/pdf/PLAW-111publ353.pdf.

[31]   Pub. L. No. 101-629, § 9, 104 Stat. 4521 (1990) (codified at 21 U.S.C. §§ 360(e), 351(f)) (temporary suspension of approval); *id.* § 17, 104 Stat. 4526-28 (1990) (codified at 21 U.S.C. § 333(f)) (civil penalties).

[32]   Pub. L. No. 100-293, 102 Stat. 95 (1988) (codified at 21 U.S.C. §§ 331, 333, 353, 381).

the introduction of counterfeit and "grey market" products into the domestic drug supply. It included an "American goods returned" provision that made it more difficult to send drugs that had been exported out of the U.S. back into the country, for fear that unlawful foreign products could be co-mingled with the returned goods. The law also targeted unscrupulous practices in the secondary pharmaceutical sales market and the diversion of pharmaceutical samples by pharmaceutical company sales representatives (known originally as "detail men").[33] Large civil penalties, increased criminal penalties and whistleblower provisions were added to the FDCA.[34] Until the PDMA, felony criminal violations of the FDCA were punishable by a period of incarceration up to three years, but the PDMA increased this period to 10 years for certain knowing violations. Shortly thereafter, the Safe Medical Devices Act of 1990 authorized civil penalties of up to $1 million for violations relating to devices.[35]

Similarly, pervasive fraud uncovered in the manufacture and approval of generic pharmaceutical products led to passage of the Generic Drug Enforcement Act of 1992.[36] Lifetime debarment of individuals convicted of fraud in the approval process,[37] suspension of approvals,[38] mandatory and temporary debarment of corporations,[39] temporary denial of approval of applications,[40] civil penalties[41] and withdrawal of approvals[42] are among the enforcement tools now available to FDA with respect to generic drugs.

In September 2007, Congress passed the Food and Drug Administration Amendments Act of 2007 (FDAAA).[43] In addition to enhancing FDA's authority over products approved for marketing and supervision of clinical trials, the law significantly broadened FDA's civil monetary penalty authority by applying it to a range of conduct not previously liable to incur civil penalties.[44]

On June 22, 2009, Congress authorized FDA to regulate tobacco products under the Family Smoking Prevention and Tobacco Control Act (FSPTCA).[45] FDA's Center for Tobacco Products has stated that it will utilize a number of tools, such as Warning Letters, civil

---

33 STAFF OF THE SUBCOMM. ON OVERSIGHT AND INVESTIGATIONS OF THE H. COMM. ON ENERGY AND COMMERCE, PRESCRIPTION DRUG DIVERSION AND THE AMERICAN CONSUMER: WHAT YOU THINK YOU SEE MAY NOT BE WHAT YOU GET (Comm. Print 99-R 1985).

34 Pub. L. No. 100-293, § 7(b), 102 Stat. at 99 (codified at 21 U.S.C. § 333(a), (b)).

35 Pub. L. No. 101-629, § 17(a), 104 Stat. at 4526 (codified at 21 U.S.C. § 333(f)(1)(A)); *see also* 21 C.F.R. § 17.2 (2010) (setting the maximum civil penalties available under the FDCA and Public Health Service Act after adjustment for inflation pursuant to the Federal Civil Penalties Inflation Adjustment Act of 1990, Pub. L. No. 101-410, 104 Stat. 890 (1990) (codified as amended at 28 U.S.C. § 2461 note)).

36 Pub. L. No. 102-282, 106 Stat. 149 (1992).

37 *Id.* § 2, 106 Stat. at 152 (codified at 21 U.S.C. § 335a(c)(2)(A)(ii)).

38 *Id.* § 2, 106 Stat. at 156-57 (codified at 21 U.S.C. § 335a(g)).

39 *Id.* § 2, 106 Stat. at 150 (codified at 21 U.S.C. § 335a(a)).

40 *Id.* § 2, 106 Stat. at 155-56 (codified at 21 U.S.C. § 335a(f)).

41 *Id.* § 3, 106 Stat. at 159-60 (codified at 21 U.S.C. § 335b).

42 *Id.* § 4, 106 Stat. at 160-61 (codified at 21 U.S.C. § 335c).

43 Pub. L. No. 110-85, 121 Stat. 823 (2007).

44 *Id.* § 801(b)(2), 121 Stat. at 920-21 (codified at 21 U.S.C. § 333(f)(3)) (violation of clinical trial registry certification requirements); *id.* § 901(d)(4), 121 Stat. at 940-42 (codified at 21 U.S.C. § 333(g)) (dissemination of false or misleading direct-to-consumer advertisements); *id.* § 902(b), 121 Stat. at 943 (codified at 21 U.S.C. § 333(f)(4)) (violation of requirements for postmarket study or for risk evaluation and mitigation strategy).

45 Pub. L. No. 111-31, 123 Stat. 1776 (2009).

money penalties, seizures, injunctions, and criminal prosecutions.[46] It also can issue a "no-tobacco-sale order," which prohibits the sale of tobacco products "indefinitely or for a specified period of time at a particular retail outlet."[47]

In January 2011, the Food Safety Modernization Act (FSMA) became law.[48] The act grants FDA mandatory recall authority when a food company fails to undertake an FDA-requested, voluntary recall, and permits FDA to suspend registration of a facility if it determines that the food it processes poses a reasonable probability of serious health consequences or death.[49] It also transforms the regulation of the food supply in the United States by requiring the vast majority of food processors who sell food in (or into) the country to develop, implement, and monitor a preventive controls systems to prevent outbreaks of foodborne illness.[50]

In 2012, Congress passed the Food and Drug Administration Safety and Innovation Act (FDASIA), which enhances FDA's enforcement authority over medical products.[51] With respect to medical devices, FDASIA enhances FDA's ability to place investigational devices on clinical hold, and clarifies FDA's authority to require postmarket studies under risk of penalty.[52] With respect to drugs, FDASIA requires manufacturers to submit records to FDA in advance of FDA inspections, enhances the penalties associated with delaying or denying an FDA inspection abroad, and authorizes FDA to exchange inspection information with trusted foreign governments to streamline its oversight and enforcement efforts.[53] The law authorizes the ex-parte administrative detention of drugs, requires the registration of commercial importers, and significantly increases the agency's authority to require certain information as a condition of entry for drugs or drug ingredients manufactured abroad.[54]

The law also amends the longstanding cGMP provision in section 501 of the FDCA to clarify that manufacturers must verify that their suppliers meet cGMP requirements as well.[55] FDASIA raises the criminal penalty for intentionally adulterating a drug product from a maximum sentence of three years to a maximum sentence of 20 years.[56] It also enhances the criminal penalty for counterfeiting drugs to a maximum sentence of 20 years in prison and a $4 million fine.[57] In addition, FDASIA directs the U.S. Sentencing Commission to review

---

[46]   FDA, Enforcement Action Plan for Promotion & Advertising Restrictions (Sept. 29, 2010), *available at* http://www.fda.gov/downloads/TobaccoProducts/GuidanceComplianceRegulatoryInformation/UCM227882.pdf.

[47]   FDCA § 303(f)(8), 21 U.S.C. 333(f)(8).

[48]   Pub. L. No. 111-353, 124 Stat. 3885 (2011)

[49]   FDCA §§ 423, 415, 21 U.S.C. §§ 350l, 350d.

[50]   FDCA § 418(b)-(i), 21 U.S.C. § 350g(b)-(i).

[51]   Pub. L. No. 112-144, 126 Stat. 993 (2012).

[52]   *Id.* § 606, 126 Stat. at 1054 (codified at 21 U.S.C. § 360j(g)(8)(A)) (clinical holds on investigational device exemptions); *id.* § 608, 126 Stat. at 1055-56 (codified at 21 U.S.C. § 360c(e)(1)).

[53]   *Id.* § 706, 126 Stat. at 1067-68 (codified at 21 U.S.C. § 374(a)(4)(A)) (records for inspection); *id.* § 707, 126 Stat. at 1068 (codified at 21 U.S.C. § 351(j)) (prohibition against delaying, denying, limiting, or refusing inspection); *id.* § 712, 126 Stat. at 1072 (codified at 21 U.S.C. § 384e) (recognition of foreign government inspections).

[54]   *Id.* § 709, 126 Stat. at 1069 (codified at 21 U.S.C. § 358a(g)) (administrative detention); *id.* § 714, 126 Stat. at 1073-74 (codified at 21 U.S.C. § 381(s)) (registration of commercial importers); *id.* § 713, 126 Stat. at 1072-73 (codified at 21 U.S.C. § 381(r)) (standards of admission for imported drugs).

[55]   *Id.* § 711, 126 Stat. at 1071 (adding language to FDCA § 501 clarifying that "the term 'current good manufacturing practice' includes the implementation of oversight and controls over the manufacture of drugs . . . .").

[56]   *Id.* § 716, 126 Stat. at 1075-76 (codified at 21 U.S.C. § 333(b)(7)).

[57]   *Id.* § 717, 126 Stat. at 1076 (codified at 18 U.S.C. § 2320(a)).

and amend its guidelines as appropriate to reflect this congressional intent with respect to penalizing counterfeiters.[58]

In 2013, Congress enacted the Drug Quality and Security Act (DQSA), which amends the FDCA to address both pharmacy compounding and oversight of domestic pharmaceutical supply chains.[59] With respect to compounding, the DQSA clarifies the status of extemporaneous pharmacy compounding under federal law, and creates a new legal entity, called an "outsourcing facility," that operates as a sort of hybrid between a pharmacy and a traditional manufacturer. The law includes several new prohibited act provisions that penalize the resale of a compounded drug labeled "not for resale," the intentional falsification of a prescription for a compounded drug, and the failure by an outsourcing facility to report adverse events as required in the new law.[60] It also deems a compounded drug misbranded if its advertising or promotion is false or misleading in any particular.[61] With respect to the drug supply chain, the DQSA supersedes portions of the PDMA by replacing the pedigree system enacted in 1987 with a new track and trace system that will evolve to universal electronic package level traceability over time. The supply chain provisions include a new prohibited act provision that penalizes failure to comply with the requirements in the new law.[62] It also deems misbranded any drug that fails to bear the new serialized product identifier required under the statute.[63]

Enforcement by Other Agencies

Enforcement of the FDCA is not limited to FDA.[64] Seizure, injunction, and misdemeanor or felony proceedings are instituted by the U.S. Attorney in the district in which a case is brought.[65] The Department of Justice (DOJ), through its Consumer Protection Branch, enforces civil and criminal matters related to the FDCA,[66] and the Office of Legal Counsel may also become involved in court cases and consent decrees related to FDCA matters.[67] In addition, the U.S. Department of Health and Human Services (DHHS) Inspector General has been given the responsibility for investigating felony violations of the FDCA,[68] except for

---

[58]   *Id.* § 717, 126 Stat. at 1076-77 (codified at 28 U.S.C. § 994 note).

[59]   Pub. L. No. 113–54, 127 Stat. 587 (2013).

[60]   *See* FDCA § 303(ccc), 21 U.S.C. § 333(ccc).

[61]   *See* FDCA § 502(bb), 21 U.S.C. § 352(bb).

[62]   *See* FDCA § 303(t), 21 U.S.C. § 333(t).

[63]   *See* FDCA § 502(cc), 21 U.S.C. § 352(cc).

[64]   The Department of Justice has recently brought several cases alleging violations of the False Claims Act, 37 U.S.C. § 3729 *et. seq.*, premised on underlying FDCA violations. *See, e.g.*, Complaint, United States ex rel. Thorpe v. GlaxoSmithKline plc, No. 11-10398-RWZ (D. Mass. Oct. 26, 2011). GlaxoSmithKline ultimately settled this complaint for $3 billion. Often, these cases are initially brought by whistleblowers. *See, e.g.*, United States ex rel. Fox Rx, Inc. v. Omnicare, Inc., No. 1:11-cv-962-WSD (N.D. Ga. May 23, 2014). There is, however, no private right of action under the FDCA. *See, e.g.*, Buckman Co. v. Plaintiffs' Legal Committee, 531 U.S. 341 (2001); Bailey v. Johnson, 48 F.3d 965, 968 (6th Cir. 1995).

[65]   28 U.S.C. § 547 (2011). Since 2000, U.S. Attorneys' Offices have increasingly combined allegations of violations of the FDCA with allegations of violations of the False Claims Act, 31 U.S.C. §§ 3729-3733.

[66]   Consumer Protection Branch, U.S. Dep't of Justice, http://www.justice.gov/civil/consumer-protection-branch-home (last visited Nov. 4, 2014).

[67]   Office of Legal Counsel, U.S. Dep't of Justice, http://www.justice.gov/olc (last visited Nov. 4, 2014).

[68]   Letter from Dr. Louis Sullivan, Sec'y of DHHS, to Richard Kusserow, Inspector Gen. of DHHS (July 24, 1989).

matters "that should remain a function of the Food and Drug Administration."[69] FDA also shares jurisdiction with the Federal Trade Commission (FTC) with respect to the advertising of over-the-counter (OTC) drugs, devices, cosmetics and, under section 707 of the FDCA, foods, including dietary supplements.[70] The Environmental Protection Agency (EPA) also administers section 408 of the FDCA regarding tolerances for pesticide residues, and the Drug Enforcement Administration has certain jurisdiction over drugs that are controlled substances.[71]

Violations of the FDCA can also be pursued under other federal statutes, including the False Claims Act (FCA).[72] The FCA prohibits knowingly filing or causing the filing of false or fraudulent claims with the United States government. It imposes treble damages and statutory penalties for each false claim.[73] It can be enforced by the DOJ or by private individuals, who are empowered to file lawsuits on behalf of the government through a process called a *qui tam* action.[74] In FY 2013, private citizens initiated a record 752 *qui tam* suits, and the United States recovered about $3.8 billion in damages.[75] A common theory in such cases is that the government is defrauded when it reimburses through Medicare or Medicaid for the cost of a drug that has been manufactured or sold in violation of the FDCA. The alleged violation of the FDCA typically relates to off-label promotion of a drug by a company in violation of sections 505 and/or 502(f)(1) of the FDCA, or the sale of a drug that fails to meet cGMP in violation of section 501(a)(2)(B) of the FDCA. For example, in 2013, Genzyme paid $22 million in an FCA case involving off-label promotion of Seprafilm; Johnson & Johnson paid $2.2 billion in an FCA case involving, among other things, the off-label promotion of Risperdal, Invega, and Natrecor; and Wyeth paid $491 million in an FCA case involving off-label promotion of Papamune.[76]

The DOJ can also prosecute violations of the FDCA under several sections of Title 18 of the *United States Code*, including sections 371, 1001, 1505, 1341, 1343, and 2320. In many instances, indictments returned against FDA-regulated companies will include charges under the FDCA as well as charges under applicable provisions of Title 18 such as mail or wire fraud or product tampering.[77]

A large share of food, drug, and device enforcement is also borne by state agencies. FDA has long worked cooperatively with such agencies. In the 1980s, as a deregulatory philosophy and

---

[69] *Id.* The Nuclear Regulatory Commission (NRC) has assumed joint regulatory responsibility over certain drugs, medical devices, and biological products as well. *See* Memorandum of Understanding Between FDA and the NRC (Dec. 4, 2002), *available at* http://pbadupws.nrc.gov/docs/ML0235/ML023520399.pdf.

[70] FDCA § 707, 21 U.S.C. § 378; Memorandum of Understanding Between Federal Trade Commission and the Food and Drug Administration, 36 Fed. Reg. 18,539 (Sept. 16, 1971).

[71] FDCA § 408, 21 U.S.C. § 346a.

[72] 31 U.S.C. §§ 3729-3733.

[73] *See* 31 U.S.C. § 3729(a).

[74] *See* 31 U.S.C. §§ 3730(b)-(e).

[75] U.S. DEP'T OF JUSTICE, FRAUD STATISTICS OVERVIEW, OCTOBER 1, 1987 - SEPTEMBER 30, 2013 (2013), *available at* http://www.justice.gov/civil/docs_forms/C-FRAUDS_FCA_Statistics.pdf.

[76] *Id. See also supra* note 64.

[77] *See, e.g.*, Indictment, United States v. Parnell, No. 1:13-CR-12-WLS, 2013 U.S. Dist. LEXIS 75700 (M.D. Ga. Feb. 15, 2013) (alleging that the executives of the Peanut Corporation of America introduced adulterated and misbranded products with the intent to defraud or mislead, in violation of 18 U.S.C. §§ 2, 371, 1341, 1343, 1349, 1505).

budgetary limitations contracted FDA enforcement efforts,[78] states increased enforcement of their own food and drug laws.[79] Recognition of this increased state activity was reflected in the Nutrition Labeling and Education Act of 1990, which provides specific authority for states to institute civil proceedings if FDA fails to act against a food misbranding violation after 30 days' notice.[80] The recent indictment of several owners of New England Compounding Center (NECC) illustrates the role states can and do play in enforcing their consumer protection laws.[81] The indictment charges the owners with violating the adulteration and misbranding provisions of the FDCA, as well as state law second degree murder statutes, in connection with an outbreak of meningitis traced back to contaminated products compounded at NECC.

Numerous memoranda of understanding (MOUs) between FDA and other governmental agencies, foreign and domestic, have delineated FDA's enforcement responsibilities in actual practice.[82] Many have also discussed the means for interagency cooperation and coordination when joint jurisdiction exists.[83]

---

[78] *See, e.g.,* Julie Kosterlitz, *Reagan Is Leaving His Mark on the Food and Drug Administration,* 17 Nat'l J. 1568 (1985).

[79] *See, e.g.,* Stephen Gardner, *Litigation as a Tool in Food Advertising: A Consumer Advocacy Viewpoint,* 39 Loy. L.A. L. Rev. 291, 300-01 (2006); Marian Burros, *Food Companies Agree to Modify Claims on Fat,* N.Y. Times, Oct. 30, 1991, at C1.

[80] Pub. L. No. 101-535, § 4, 104 Stat. 2353, 2362 (1990) (codified at 21 U.S.C. § 337(b)).

[81] Indictment, United States v. Cadden, Case No. 1:14-cr-10363-RGS (D. Mass, Dec. 16, 2014), *available at* http://www.justice.gov/sites/default/files/opa/press-releases/attachments/2014/12/17/necc-indictment. pdf. *See also* Press Release, DOJ, 14 Indicted in Connection with New England Compounding Center and Nationwide Fungal Meningitis Outbreak, Dec. 17, 2014, http://www.justice.gov/opa/pr/14-indicted-connection-new-england-compounding-center-and-nationwide-fungal-meningitis.

[82] *See, e.g.,* MOU between FDA and The National Service of Agro Alimentary Health, Safety and Quality and The Federal Commission for the Protection From Sanitary Risks of the United Mexican States (July 24, 2014) (establishes regulatory cooperation regarding the safety of fresh and minimally processed produce focusing on preventive practices and verification measures); MOU between FDA and General Administration of Quality Supervision, Inspection and Quarantine (AQSIQ) of the People's Republic of China (Dec. 7, 2011) (establishes regulatory cooperation regarding improving the safety of food exported from China); MOU between FDA and the Centers for Disease Control and Prevention (CDC), No. 225-06-8401 (June 14, 2006) (establishing a framework for coordination and information exchange between FDA and CDC); MOU between FDA and the Federal Aviation Administration, No. 225-99-6000 (Nov. 25, 1998) (delineates responsibilities for regulating laser projection into navigable airspace); MOU between FDA and the Animal and Plant Health Inspection Service of the U.S. Department of Agriculture, No. 225-82-7000 (May 7, 1982) (delineates responsibilities for regulating animal biological products as biologicals under the Virus-Serum-Toxin Act of 1913, ch. 145, Pub. L. No. 62-430, 37 Stat. 832 (1913) (codified at 21 U.S.C. §§ 151-58), or as drugs under the FDCA); MOU between FDA and the Environmental Protection Agency (EPA), No. 225-79-2001 (June 22, 1979) (discusses control of direct and indirect additives to and substances in drinking water); MOU between FDA and the Consumer Product Safety Commission, No. 225-76-2003 (July 26, 1976) (delineates areas of jurisdiction for administration of the Consumer Product Safety Act, 15 U.S.C. §§ 2051-2085, and the FDCA with respect to food, food containers, and food-related articles and equipment). FDA maintains a library of the MOUs it has entered into at http://www.fda.gov/AboutFDA/PartnershipsCollaborations/MemorandaofUnderstandingMOUs/DomesticMOUs.

[83] *See, e.g.,* MOU between FDA and the CDC, No. 225-08-8002 (Jan. 24, 2008) (establishes a procedure for communication between agencies regarding a clinical trial involving the use of an investigational product that contains a select agent or toxin); MOU between FDA and Customs and Border Protection, No. 225-04-4001 (Dec. 3, 2003) (allows FDA to commission Customs officers to assist with examinations and investigations at ports and other facilities and locations); MOU among FDA, DHHS, and EPA, No. 225-93-4005 (June 4, 1993) (clarifies jurisdiction in the regulation of certain liquid germicides); MOU between FDA and EPA, No. 225-73-8010 (Aug. 28, 1973) (coordinates activities pertaining to pesticides).

By granting FDA authority to issue administrative-detention orders for food, the Public Health Security and Bioterrorism Preparedness and Response Act of 2002 has further expanded FDA's enforcement powers.[84]

From 1991 to 1993, FDA and states entered into numerous MOUs providing for joint enforcement efforts.[85] FDA has essentially abandoned its reliance on these MOUs, however, and relies instead on "contracts" and/or "partnerships" with local enforcement agencies.[86] These cover inspection of food and medicated feed firms; investigation of fraud and deception involving foods, drugs, devices, and cosmetics; investigation and control of violative levels of drugs, pesticides, and toxic chemical residues in edible tissues derived from food animals; and other related regulatory activities.[87]

Jurisdictional and Other Definitions

Section 201 of the FDCA[88] contains the definitions utilized in the act. The most important for purposes of enforcement are those of "person,"[89] "interstate commerce,"[90] "drug,"[91] "new

---

[84]   Pub. L. No. 107-188, 116 Stat. 594 (2002).

[85]   *See, e.g.*, MOU with Wyoming Department of Agriculture Regarding the Inspection of Food, Drugs and Medical Device Firms, CPG 7157.45 (FDA-225-92-4001) (Mar. 20, 1992); MOU with Utah Department of Agriculture Regarding the Inspection of Food, Drugs, and Medical Device Firms, CPG 7157.46 (FDA-225-92-4006) (Apr. 16, 1992); MOU with State of Arkansas Attorney General and Arkansas Department of Health Regarding the Inspection of Foods, Drugs, Devices, and Cosmetics, CPG 7157.47 (FDA-225-92-4004) (Apr. 17, 1992); MOU with Alabama Department of Agriculture and Industries Regarding Regulation of Wholesale Food Storage Warehouses, Disasters, Recalls, and Exchange of Information, CPG 7157.26; MOU with California Department of Health Services Regarding Inspections, Investigations, Recalls and Emergencies, CPG 7157.20; MOU with Colorado Department of Health and Department of Law Regarding Inspections of Food, Drug, Cosmetic and Medical Device Firms, CPG 7157.48; MOU with Connecticut Department of Consumer Protection Regarding the Coordination of Joint Efforts in Monitoring Pesticide and Industrial Chemical Residues in Foods, CPG 7157.37; MOU with Delaware Board of Pharmacy Concerning Regulatory Activities Relating to the Inspection of Drug Manufacturers, Wholesalers and Distributors, CPG 7157.24; MOU with Florida Department of Agriculture and Consumer Services Delineates Activities Relating to the Regulation of Milk, Foods, Medicated Feeds, and Pesticides, CPG 7157.18; MOU with Georgia Department of Agriculture and USDA/FSIS Regarding Regulatory Investigations Involving Drug, Pesticide, and Toxic Chemical Residues in Animal Feeds and in Meat Tissues, CPG 7147.41; MOU with Illinois Attorney General Regarding Development and Implementation of Appropriate Sanctions Concerning Fraud and Deception Involving Foods, Drugs, Devices, and Cosmetics, CPG 7157.04; MOU with Kansas Department of Health and Environment Concerning Inspection, Investigation, and Analytical Findings Related to Food and Drug Firms, CPG 7157.21; CPG 7157.13 with Maryland Department of Health and Mental Hygiene Concerning the Inspection of Food Processing and Storage Industries; MOU with Michigan Department of Agriculture Regarding Inspections, Investigations, and Analytical Findings Related to Food Firms, CPG 7157.49; MOU with Minnesota Department of Agriculture Regarding the Inspection of Food and Medicated Feed Firms, CPG 7157.50; MOU with Virginia Department of Health Concerning the Inspection of the Crabmeat Industry, CPG 7157.15.

[86]   Telephone conversation with the FDA Office of the Executive Secretariat (Feb. 29, 2008).

[87]   *See supra* note 83.

[88]   21 U.S.C. § 321.

[89]   FDCA § 201(e), 21 U.S.C. § 321(e).

[90]   FDCA § 201(b), 21 U.S.C. § 321(b).

[91]   FDCA § 201(g)(1), 21 U.S.C. § 321(g)(1).

drug,"[92] "labeling,"[93] "new animal drug,"[94] "counterfeit drug,"[95] "device,"[96] "food,"[97] "food additive,"[98] "dietary supplement,"[99] "processed food,"[100] "knowingly or knew,"[101] "high managerial agent,"[102] "reportable food,"[103] and "tobacco product."[104]

The definition of "interstate commerce" is read in conjunction with section 301,[105] which prohibits, *inter alia*, "the introduction or delivery for introduction into interstate commerce" of violative articles,[106] their "receipt in interstate commerce,"[107] and their "delivery or proffered delivery" in interstate commerce.[108] In enforcement litigation, it generally has been necessary for FDA to prove the movement in interstate commerce as an element of its case. In 1997, Congress amended section 709 of the FDCA so that FDA no longer has the initial burden to demonstrate a nexus to interstate commerce.[109] For example, violative devices can be seized and condemned without evidence that they have moved in interstate commerce.[110] As a practical matter, however, FDA continues to document movement in interstate commerce for all judicial interventions, because, section 709 notwithstanding, the government ultimately bears the burden of proof in judicial enforcement actions.

Two frequently cited prohibited acts in section 301 proscribe the introduction of violative articles into interstate commerce. Section 301(a) prohibits the introduction into interstate commerce of any FDA-regulated article that is adulterated or misbranded.[111] Section 301(d) prohibits the introduction into interstate commerce of an unapproved new drug.[112] The government must prove that a product was introduced (or offered for introduction) into interstate commerce. So what could FDA do if a product that had been lawfully shipped in interstate commerce was adulterated or misbranded after its receipt and then sold in the same state in which the misbranding or adulteration occurred? Congress offered as a solution section 301(k), which makes it unlawful to commit an act that renders an article adulterated or misbranded after receipt of that article (or its components) in interstate commerce while the article is held for sale.[113]

---

92   FDCA § 201(p), 21 U.S.C. § 321(p).
93   FDCA § 201(m), 21 U.S.C. § 321(m).
94   FDCA § 201(v), 21 U.S.C. § 321(v).
95   FDCA § 201(g)(2), 21 U.S.C. § 321(g)(2).
96   FDCA § 201(h), 21 U.S.C. § 321(h).
97   FDCA § 201(f), 21 U.S.C. § 321(f).
98   FDCA § 201(s), 21 U.S.C. § 321(s).
99   FDCA § 201(ff), 21 U.S.C. § 321(ff).
100   FDCA § 201(gg), 21 U.S.C. § 321(gg).
101   FDCA § 201(bb), 21 U.S.C. § 321(bb).
102   FDCA § 201(cc), 21 U.S.C. § 321(cc).
103   FDCA § 417(a)(2), 21 U.S.C. 350f(a)(2).
104   FDCA § 201(rr), 21 U.S.C. § 321(rr).
105   21 U.S.C. § 331.
106   FDCA § 301(a), (d), 21 U.S.C. § 331(a), (d).
107   FDCA § 301(c), 21 U.S.C. § 331(c).
108   *Id.*
109   Pub. L. No. 105-115, § 419, 111 Stat. 2296, 2379 (1997) (codified at FDCA § 709, 21 U.S.C. § 379a); *see* PETER BARTON HUTT, RICHARD A. MERRILL & LEWIS A. GROSSMAN, FOOD AND DRUG LAW: CASES AND MATERIALS 272 (4th ed. 2014).
110   FDCA § 304(a)(2)(D), 21 U.S.C. § 334(a)(2)(D).
111   FDCA § 301(a), 21 U.S.C. § 331(c).
112   FDCA § 301(d), 21 U.S.C. § 331(d).
113   FDCA § 301(k), 21 U.S.C. § 331(k).

The interstate commerce requirement of the FDCA thus confers a more limited grant of jurisdictional authority than that provided to federal agencies in other statutes or permitted by the U.S. Constitution.[114] To this end, the limitation should not be confused with the authority of Congress to enact the FDCA or to establish FDA under the Commerce Clause of the Constitution. Rather, the limiting issue here is the degree to which Congress made interstate movement of FDA-regulated articles an explicit element of violations of the FDCA. In recent years, Congress has de-linked the two in some instances. For example, the PDMA added criminal penalties for certain knowing conduct unrelated to interstate shipment.[115] Still, the prominence of the element in most of the original prohibited acts has presented challenges to the government, and led to a body of case law in which FDA has established that all unapproved prescription drug products are necessarily misbranded under section 502(f)(1) of the FDCA.[116] This body of law enables the government to pursue what is known as a "backdoor" new drug charge in instances where the misbranding occurs after the shipment of a product or any of its components has been introduced (or delivered for introduction into) interstate commerce, thus enabling use of section 301(k) rather than section 301(d), which has an explicit interstate commerce element.[117]

Section 301(k) was amended in 1948 to clarify that that the term "held for sale" does not necessarily mean the product's first sale.[118] The fix was vindicated in *United States v. Sullivan*, which held that the phrase "held for sale after shipment in interstate commerce" includes the resale of a product six months after it was received in interstate commerce.[119] Other cases helped give meaning to the multiple elements in 301(k). In *United States v. Wiesenfeld Warehouse Co.*, the Supreme Court ruled that the word "holding" may be sufficient to impose liability on a defendant who is merely a bailee, not a seller, of the food in question.[120] The

---

[114]   *See* FDCA § 301, 21 U.S.C. § 331, which is limited to articles that have traveled into or will travel into interstate commerce. The constitutionality of federal statues that regulate entirely intra-state conducts is well settled, meaning Congress imposed the interstate commerce elements in the FDCA by choice. For example, the Supreme Court has held permissible, under the interstate commerce clause, the regulation of the marketing of home-grown, home-consumed wheat that never left the state in which it was grown. The Court reasoned that its sale, in the aggregate, could have a substantial effect on interstate commerce. *See* Wickard v. Filburn, 317 U.S. 111 (1942). Unlike the FDCA, the reach of the Controlled Substances Act, 21 U.S.C. § 801 *et seq.*, is not limited to articles that move across state lines, but instead extends to all controlled substances in any of the United States. *Cf.* Gonzales v. Raich, 545 U.S. 1 (2005).

[115]   *See* FDCA § 303(b)(1)(B), 21 U.S.C. § 333(b)(1)(B).

[116]   *See, e.g.*, United States v. Evers, 643 F.2d 1043, 1047 (5th Cir. 1981) (government alleging that certain products were misbranded on the "sole basis" of 502(f)(1)).

[117]   *See, e.g.*, United States v. Articles of Drug, 625 F.2d 665, 675 (5th Cir. 1980); United States v. Premo Pharm. Labs., Inc., 511 F. Supp. 958, 977 n.23 (D.N.J. 1981).

[118]   *See* Pub. L. No. 80-749, 62 Stat. 582 (1948) (codified as amended at 21 U.S.C. § 331(k)); *see also* United States v. Cassaro, Inc., 443 F.2d 153 (1st Cir. 1971).

[119]   United States v. Sullivan, 332 U.S. 689, 696 (1948). *See also* United States v. An Article of Food, 752 F.2d 11 (1st Cir. 1985) ("'shipment in interstate commerce' requirement is satisfied when adulterated articles held for in-state sale contain ingredients shipped in interstate commerce"); Farm-to-Consumer Legal Def. Fund v. Sebelius, 734 F. Supp. 2d 668, 688-89 (N.D. Iowa 2010) (plaintiffs had standing under FDCA even though actual purchases were intrastate, because plaintiffs traveled across state lines to make such purchases and returned the purchased products across state lines); United States v. Varela-Cruz, 66 F. Supp. 2d 274, 279 (D. P.R. 1999) (holding that "wholly intrastate manufacturers and sales of drugs are covered by [section 331(k) of the FDCA] as long as an ingredient used in the final product traveled in interstate commerce")).

[120]   United States v. Wiesenfeld Warehouse Co., 376 U.S. 86, 92 (1964); United States v. Articles of Animal Drug Containing Diethylstilbestrol, 528 F. Supp. 202, 205 (D. Neb. 1981) ("an article or drug is 'held for sale' if it is used for any purpose other than personal consumption").

Court reasoned that having title to the goods was not a prerequisite to imposing the FDCA's public protection mechanisms on those who handle violative products within the act's scope.[121] Similarly, courts have held that a complete transfer of title is not required for liability. For example, in *United States v. Diapulse Corp. of America*, "holding for sale" was held to include a physician's use of a device in the treatment of patients.[122] As with the other prohibited act provisions, however, no element in section 301(k) can be ignored. In *United States v. Geborde*, a conviction under section 301(k) for distributing a misbranded drug was reversed because the defendant did not "hold for sale," but rather gave away, a designer drug that killed a teenager.[123]

Once an article has entered the stream of interstate commerce, whether from a domestic origin or by passage through U.S. Customs and Border Protection (CBP),[124] the statutory prohibitions and remedies apply.[125] Moreover, as long as any constituent—no matter how small—of an article sold in the United States has arrived in interstate commerce, the courts will generally view that article as within the reach of the FDCA's definition of "interstate commerce" for purposes of the prohibited acts.[126] In a case where a blend of edible oils was manufactured completely in New York, sold in New York, and stored there as well, the Second Circuit held that the foreign origin of a small proportion of the blend of oils rendered the finished food product subject to the FDCA.[127] Similarly, where soft drink beverages were manufactured and consumed within the Commonwealth of Puerto Rico, the inclusion of potassium nitrate, a minor ingredient that had been shipped previously in interstate commerce, rendered the beverages subject to the act.[128] Finally, dietary supplements composed of ingredients shipped in interstate commerce have also been held subject to the act.[129]

The scienter definition in section 201(bb) was added to the FDCA by the Generic Drug Enforcement Act to establish that "knowledge" means, "with respect to information" (e.g., in a pre-approval application), both "actual knowledge" and "acts in deliberate ignorance or reckless disregard of the truth or falsity of the information."[130] Subsection (cc), added by the same act, assigns responsibility for violations to those individuals in a corporation, association, or partnership who "may fairly be assumed to represent the policy" of that

---

121   *Id.*

122   United States v. Diapulse Corp. of Am., 514 F.2d 1097, 1098 (2d Cir. 1975); *Articles*, 528 F. Supp. at 205.

123   United States v. Geborde, 278 F.3d 926 (9th Cir. 2002).

124   230 Boxes, More or Less, of Fish…v. United States, 168 F.2d 361 (6th Cir. 1948); *see also* United States v. First Phoenix Group, 64 F.3d 984 (5th Cir. 1995) (plain language of section 334 permits FDA to initiate a seizure and condemnation action when goods are seized at the port of entry, not just when released by Customs).

125   United States v. Food, 2,998 Cases, 64 F.3d 984 (5th Cir. 1995).

126   *See* Baker v. United States, 932 F.2d 813, 814 (9th Cir. 1991) ("[T]he 'shipment in interstate commerce' requirement is satisfied even when only an ingredient is transported interstate.") (citing 21 U.S.C. § 331(k)).

127   United States v. 40 Cases…"Pinocchio Brand…Oil," 289 F.2d 343 (2d Cir. 1961).

128   United States v. An Article of Food…CoCo Rico, 752 F.2d 11, 14 (1st Cir. 1985).

129   Hi-Tech Pharms., Inc. v. Crawford, 505 F. Supp. 2d 1341, 1358 (N.D. Ga. 2007).

130   Pub. L. No. 102-282, § 6, 106 Stat. 149, 162 (1992) (codified as amended at 21 U.S.C. § 321(bb)). *See also* Arthur Pew Constr. Co. v. Lipscomb, 965 F.2d 1559, 1576 (11th Cir. 1992) (under 18 U.S.C. § 1001, misrepresentation "must have been deliberate, knowing and willful, or at least with a reckless disregard of the truth"); United States v. Mitcheltree, 940 F.2d 1329 (10th Cir. 1991) ("knowledge of the essential nature of the alleged fraud is a component of the intent to defraud") (*quoting* United States v. Hiland, 909 F.2d 1114, 1128 (8th Cir. 1990)).

entity, including those with "management responsibility" for FDA submissions, quality control, or research and development.[131]

An Overview of Statutory Offenses

Chapter III of the FDCA enumerates the prohibited acts, specifies most of the enforcement powers that are available to FDA, and prescribes the penalties for violations.[132]

Both specific "acts" and "the causing thereof" are prohibited. The latter prohibition has been used to prosecute, for example, laboratories that have been involved in either the formulation or testing of products that were later found to be adulterated or misbranded.[133] The prohibition can also be used to prosecute those who purchase or order a violative article on the grounds that placing the order or making the purchase caused the violative article to be introduced into interstate commerce. Consider, for example, a person in the United States who purchases an unlawful drug product from abroad over the Internet. The FDCA reaches both the person abroad who introduced the unlawful product into interstate commerce and the person in the United States whose order "caused" it to be so introduced.

Two major types of violations specific to the FDCA relate to "adulteration" and "misbranding." These terms underlie the majority of enforcement actions instituted under the act. The types of adulterated foods are set forth in section 402(a) through (e), (h), and (i);[134] adulterated dietary supplements and ingredients, in sections 402(f) and (g);[135] adulterated cosmetics, in section 601;[136] adulterated drugs and devices, in section 501;[137] and adulterated tobacco products in section 902.[138] Most of the "adulteration" offenses incorporate the common meaning of the term; that is, they encompass, for example, filthy or putrid products, foods with added poisons, foods in which a valuable constituent has been omitted or substituted for, foods with concealed defects or unapproved color additives,[139] and drugs and devices that fail to meet compendial standards, and foods, drugs, devices, and tobacco products that

---

[131]   *Id.* (codified as amended at 21 U.S.C. § 321(cc)).

[132]   The limits on fines set forth in FDCA § 303, 21 U.S.C. § 333, are superseded by 18 U.S.C. § 3571. With respect to sentencing, U.S. Sentencing Guideline § 2N2.1 has been in effect since November 1, 1987, and covers violations of statutes and regulations dealing with any food, drug, biological product, device, cosmetic, agricultural, or consumer product. *See* U.S. SENTENCING GUIDELINES MANUAL § 2N2.1 (2010). Currently, the base offense level is 6, and a specific offense characteristic set forth in the guideline provides that, "[i]f the defendant was convicted under 21 U.S.C. § 331 after sustaining a prior conviction under 21 U.S.C. § 331, increase by 4 levels." *Id.* Downward departure may be warranted only if negligent conduct was involved, and an upward departure may be warranted if "[t]he offense created a substantial risk of bodily injury or death; or bodily injury, death, extreme psychological injury, property damage, or monetary loss resulted from the offense." *See id.* cmt. n. 1, 3. Furthermore, "if the offense involved fraud," the fraud guideline, 2B1.1 is to be used. *See id.* § 2N2.1(b)(1). The Supreme Court has held that the Sentencing Guidelines are not mandatory, though appellate courts may "presume" that sentences consistent with the guidelines are reasonable. *See* Rita v. United States, 551 U.S. 338 (2007); United States v. Booker, 543 U.S. 220 (2005).

[133]   *See, e.g.*, United States v. Indus. Testing Labs. Co., 456 F.2d 908 (10th Cir. 1972).

[134]   21 U.S.C. § 342(a)-(e), (h), (i).

[135]   *Id.* § 342(f), (g).

[136]   *Id.* § 361.

[137]   *Id.* § 351.

[138]   *Id.* § 387b.

[139]   FDCA § 402, 21 U.S.C. § 342. The current Good Manufacturing Practice (cGMP) regulations governing the manufacture of foods are implemented in 21 C.F.R. Part 110 (2014).

diverge from the rigorous requirements of good manufacturing practices.[140] An unapproved Class III medical device is also deemed to be adulterated.[141]

The concept of "misbranding" derives from historical notions of economic fraud, but has been extended to other types of misstatements and miscellaneous types of violation, such as drugs or devices that are not listed with FDA or are from a facility that has not been registered with FDA, as required.[142] Misbranded foods and dietary supplements are described in section 403 of the act;[143] misbranded drugs and devices, in section 502;[144] misbranded cosmetics, in section 602;[145] and misbranded tobacco products, in section 903.[146]

Over time, legislation has expanded FDA's regulation of adulterated and misbranded food. In response to findings that 25 percent of certain processed food products did not list a major allergen on their labels, and that major allergens result in more than 30,000 visits to emergency rooms and 150 deaths per year, Congress enacted the Food Allergen Labeling and Consumer Protection Act of 2004.[147] A food that contains an allergenic ingredient and has a label that fails to bear the common or usual name of such ingredient is misbranded.[148] Labels must also list trans fatty acids on a separate line immediately under the line for the declaration of saturated fatty acids.[149] In determining whether an article is misbranded, the statute specifically relies not only on words and visual representations, but also on a failure to reveal "facts material" to claims or representations actually made.[150]

FSMA also expanded FDA's regulation of adulterated and misbranded food by providing FDA with the authority to require a recall when a company is unwilling to undertake a voluntary recall, and by expanding the authority to inspect all records (excluding those of farms and restaurants) relating to adulterated food, or a related article of food if FDA

---

[140] FDCA § 501(b)-(e), 21 U.S.C. § 351(b)-(e); FDCA § 902, 21 U.S.C. § 387b. In April 2011, the cGMP regulations for dietary supplements (see 21 C.F.R. pt. 111) were upheld as constitutional, despite a challenge by industry groups that terms such as "adequate," "qualified" and "suitable" were impermissibly vague. See Alliance for Natural Health U.S. v. Sebelius, C.A. No. 09-1523 (BAH), — F. Supp. 2d —, 2011 WL 1296888 (D.D.C. Apr. 6, 2011); see also Nat'l Ass'n of Pharm. Mfrs. v. DHHS, 586 F. Supp. 740 (S.D.N.Y 1984) (rejecting a similar vagueness challenge to the drug cGMP regulations for containing terms such as "adequate" and "appropriate.").

[141] FDCA § 501(f)(1), 21 U.S.C. § 351(f)(1). In contrast, an unapproved new drug is not considered adulterated; the introduction of such a drug into interstate commerce violates a provision of the FDCA that is distinct from its adulteration provisions. See FDCA §§ 301(d), 505(a), 21 U.S.C. §§ 331(d), 355(a).

[142] FDCA § 510(j), 21 U.S.C. § 360(j); 21 C.F.R. § 807.20 (2011).

[143] 21 U.S.C. § 343.

[144] Id. § 352.

[145] Id. § 362.

[146] Id. § 387c.

[147] Food Allergen Labeling and Consumer Protection Act of 2004, Pub. L. No. 108-282, 118 Stat. 891 (2004).

[148] FDA COMPLIANCE POLICY GUIDES MANUAL, § 555.250 (2001) (revised 2005), available at http://www.fda.gov/ICECI/ComplianceManuals/CompliancePolicyGuidanceManual/ucm074552.htm.

[149] Food Labeling; Trans Fatty Acids in Nutrition Labeling; Consumer Research to Consider Nutrient Content and Health Claims and Possible Footnote or Disclosure Statements; Final Rule and Proposed Rule, 68 Fed. Reg. 41,433 (July 11, 2003).

[150] FDCA § 201(n), 21 U.S.C. § 321(n); see Stauber v. Shalala, 895 F. Supp. 1178 (W.D. Wis. 1995) ("Information disclosing differences in performance characteristics (e.g., physical properties, flavor characteristics, functional properties and shelf life) is a material fact under section 201(n) of the act because it bears on the consequence of the use of the article.").

believes that there is a reasonable probability that the food will cause serious adverse health consequences to humans or animals.[151]

In 2012, FDASIA amended the FDCA to enhance the statutory cGMP requirement for drugs and to deem adulterated any drug produced at a firm that delays, denies, limits or refuses an FDA inspection.[152] FDASIA also substantially increases the penalties associated with deliberately adulterating or counterfeiting drugs.[153]

Section 301 enumerates 53 statutory offenses. They prohibit the manufacture, sale, delivery, receipt, or holding for delivery or sale of adulterated or misbranded products.[154] They also bar the introduction, and the delivery for introduction, into interstate commerce of unapproved new drugs; unapproved Class III medical devices; and unapproved new animal drugs, food additives, and antibiotics and tobacco products not authorized for marketing.[155] FDAAA amended section 301 to prohibit the failure to submit the certification required by Public Health Service Act section 402(j)(5)(B) or knowingly submitting a false certification.[156] As amended, section 301 further prohibits the failure to submit required clinical trial information and the submission of false or misleading clinical trial information.[157] FDAAA also amended section 301 to prohibit the introduction, and delivery for introduction, into interstate commerce of any food to which a drug or a biological product has been added, unless certain requirements are met.[158]

Section 301 additionally encompasses offenses relating to counterfeit products,[159] furnishing a false guarantee to a customer that a product is not adulterated or misbranded,[160] misuse by FDA personnel of certain types of trade secret information submitted to the agency,[161] failure of manufacturers or importers to register with the agency[162] and, *inter alia*, the sale or importation of drugs in violation of PDMA.[163] PDMA proscribes the import of American goods returned, the sale or trade of drug samples, and the resale or distribution of prescription drugs by healthcare entities.[164] PDMA at one time criminalized the failure to supply a "paper trail" (known as a "pedigree") in connection with sales of prescription drugs by certain wholesalers, but those requirements were recently superseded and expanded under the Drug Supply Chain Security Act, which requires certain new pedigree information to be provided to trading partners beginning in 2015 and will require fully electronic pedigrees bearing unique serialized identifiers to be provided to trading partners in another decade.[165] The

---

[151]   *See supra* notes 48-50 and accompanying text.

[152]   *See* Pub. L. No. 112–144, §§ 716-717, 126 Stat. 993 (2012) (codified as amended at FDCA § 501(j), 21 U.S.C. § 351(j)).

[153]   *See* Pub. L. No. 112–144, § 707, 126 Stat. 993 (2012) (codified as amended at FDCA § 303(b)(7), 21 U.S.C. §§ 333(b)(7), 2320).

[154]   FDCA § 301(a)-(d), (g), (k), 21 U.S.C. § 331(a)-(d), (g), (k).

[155]   FDCA § 301(a), (d), (p), 21 U.S.C. § 331(a), (d), (p); FDCA § 409, 21 U.S.C. § 348.

[156]   FDAAA § 801(b)(1) (codified at 21 U.S.C. § 331(jj)(1)).

[157]   *Id.* § 801(b)(1) (codified at 21 U.S.C. § 331(jj)(2), (3)).

[158]   *Id.* § 912(a) (codified at 21 U.S.C. § 331(ll).

[159]   FDCA § 301(i), (pp), (qq), 21 U.S.C. § 331(i), (pp), (qq).

[160]   FDCA § 301(h), 21 U.S.C. § 331(h).

[161]   FDCA § 301(j), 21 U.S.C. § 331(j).

[162]   FDCA § 301(o), (p), 21 U.S.C. § 331(o), (p).

[163]   FDCA § 301(t), 21 U.S.C. § 331(t).

[164]   Pub. L. No. 100-293, §§ 4-8, 102 Stat. 95 (1988) (codified at 21 U.S.C. §§ 333(b), 353(c)-(e)).

[165]   *See* Pub. L. No. 113–54, tit. II, 127 Stat. 587 (2013).

Bioterrorism Act[166] encompasses offenses related to the detention of food;[167] the importation of food by a debarred person;[168] the failure to register a food facility;[169] the importation of a food article without satisfying the prior-notice requirements;[170] the failure to submit a registration statement for an imported drug or device;[171] and the making of a false statement about the re-importation of a device or drug component or a food additive, color additive, or dietary supplement.[172] Another key enforcement concept that has evolved in section 301 is compliance with cGMP. FDAAA required FDA to promulgate cGMP requirements for Positron Emission Tomography products, FSMA attempted to apply cGMP-like requirements across the food supply, and FDASIA enhanced the longstanding cGMP provision in section 501(a)(2)(B) of the FDCA[173] to require drug manufacturers to look beyond their own facilities and ensure that their suppliers comply with cGMP as well.[174]

The FDCA is unusual in that it authorizes both civil and criminal remedies for the same violations. A first-time criminal violation is a misdemeanor, except where there is intent to defraud or mislead.[175] Repeat offenses and those with the requisite criminal intent are felonies.[176] Civil penalties also may be imposed for certain violations relating to medical devices[177] and radiation-emitting products,[178] violation of PDMA,[179] submitting false or misleading clinical trial information,[180] disseminating false or misleading direct-to-consumer advertising,[181] and violating postmarketing requirements or an FDA strategy for risk evaluation and mitigation.[182] In addition, FDA is authorized by statute to debar persons convicted of certain crimes from future participation in the drug industry.[183]

The various enforcement means available to FDA, most of which are set forth in Chapter III of the FDCA, are the subject of the remaining sections of this chapter.[184] Briefly, section 302[185] provides for injunctions and for a jury trial in the case of an alleged violation of an injunction. Section 303[186] contains the FDCA civil and criminal penalty provisions and a delineation of PDMA, device, and direct-to-consumer advertising offenses that

---

[166] Public Health Security and Bioterrorism Preparedness and Response Act of 2002, Pub. L. No. 107-188, 116 Stat. 594 (2002).

[167] FDCA § 301(bb), 21 U.S.C. § 331(bb).

[168] FDCA § 301(cc), 21 U.S.C. § 331(cc).

[169] FDCA § 301(dd), 21 U.S.C. § 331(dd).

[170] FDCA § 301(ee), 21 U.S.C. § 331(ee).

[171] FDCA § 301(ff), 21 U.S.C. § 331(ff).

[172] FDCA § 301(w), 21 U.S.C. § 331(w).

[173] 21 U.S.C. § 351(a)(2)(B).

[174] See Pub. L. No. 112–144, § 711, 126 Stat. 993 (2012) (codified at FDCA § 501, 21 U.S.C. § 351).

[175] FDCA § 303(a)(1), 21 U.S.C. § 333(a)(1).

[176] FDCA § 303(a)(2), 21 U.S.C. § 333(a)(2).

[177] FDCA § 303(f), 21 U.S.C. § 333(f).

[178] FDCA § 539, 21 U.S.C. § 360pp; see also Radiation Control for Health and Safety Act of 1968, Pub. L. No. 90-602, 82 Stat. 1173 (1968) (codified as amended at 21 U.S.C. §§ 360hh-360ss) (enforced by FDA).

[179] FDCA § 303(b)(2)(B), (f)(1)(A), 21 U.S.C. § 333(b)(2)(B), (f)(1)(A).

[180] FDAAA § 801(b)(2) (codified at 21 U.S.C. § 333(f)(3)(A)).

[181] Id. § 901(d)(4) (codified at 21 U.S.C. § 333(g)(1)).

[182] Id. § 902(b) (codified at 21 U.S.C. § 333(f)).

[183] FDCA § 306, 21 U.S.C. § 335a.

[184] FDA can use additional enforcement strategies beyond those described here, such as by withdrawing or temporarily deferring its approval of a new drug or device in order to achieve compliance with the FDCA. See FDCA §§ 306(f), 308, 505(e), 515(e), 21 U.S.C. §§ 335a(f), 335c, 355(e), 360e(e).

[185] 21 U.S.C. § 332.

[186] Id. § 333.

are subject to civil penalties. Seizures of drugs, devices, foods, cosmetics, and tobacco products are authorized by section 304.[187] That section further provides for detention of medical devices,[188] and for multiple seizures of adulterated products and, in certain cases, misbranded products.[189]

FDA inspections of manufacturing and processing facilities, warehouses, common carriers, seafood packers, and other establishments are authorized expressly by sections 702-704 and 706 of the FDCA.[190] The agency's powers over imports and exports are delineated in sections 801 and 802,[191] which grant to FDA substantial sampling powers that are exercised in conjunction with the U.S. Customs and Border Protection. Section 705 provides a broad publicity power, which FDA has utilized very effectively.[192]

The Generic Drug Enforcement Act added the powers set forth in sections 306,[193] 307,[194] and 308[195] dealing with debarment,[196] temporary denial of approval and suspension, civil penalties, and withdrawal of approvals of abbreviated new drug applications for generic drugs.[197]

Other enforcement provisions of note are section 309,[198] which confirms FDA's prosecutorial discretion by providing that minor violations may be dealt with by written notice or warning rather than by prosecution, injunction, or seizure, and section 305,[199] providing for a regulated party to have an opportunity to discuss with FDA informally potential criminal charges before FDA finally decides whether to refer the charges to the DOJ.[200]

In FDASIA, Congress clarified that there is extraterritorial jurisdiction over any violation of the FDCA related to an article intended for import into the United States.[201] The amendment formalized a position that FDA had long asserted even in the absence of such language, but it does little to address the practical difficulties that FDA and the DOJ confront in trying to enforce domestic laws against foreign actors located in foreign countries.

---

[187] *Id.* § 334.

[188] *Id.* § 334(g).

[189] *Id.* § 334(a)(1).

[190] *Id.* §§ 372-74, 376. FDAAA § 1006 authorizes FDA to enhance its inspection regime for aquaculture and seafood. Pub. L. No. 110-85, § 1006, 121 Stat. at 969 (codified at 21 U.S.C. § 2105).

[191] 21 U.S.C. §§ 381, 382.

[192] *Id.* § 375; *see also infra* notes 327-343 and accompanying text.

[193] 21 U.S.C. § 335a.

[194] *Id.* § 335b.

[195] *Id.* § 335c.

[196] Bac v. Shalala, 44 F.3d 489, 496 (7th Cir. 1995) (holding that, in permitting permanent debarment of convicted individuals, the Generic Drug Enforcement Act, designed to "safeguard the integrity of the generic drug industry," does not violate the constitutional prohibition against *ex post facto* laws).

[197] Pub. L. No. 102-282, §§ 2-4, 106 Stat. at 150-161.

[198] 21 U.S.C. § 336. FDA also was granted new emergency powers by the Dietary Supplement Health and Education Act. *See* SCOTT BASS & ANTHONY L. YOUNG, DIETARY SUPPLEMENT HEALTH AND EDUCATION ACT: A LEGISLATIVE HISTORY AND ANALYSIS 44 (FDLI 1996).

[199] 21 U.S.C. § 335.

[200] *Id.; see also* 21 C.F.R. §§ 7.84-7.87 (2010).

[201] *See* Pub. L. No. 112–144, § 718, 126 Stat. 993 (2012) (codified at FDCA § 311, 21 U.S.C. § 338).

Finally, FDA derives its enforcement authority indirectly from delegations of authority from the Secretary of Health and Human Services to the Commissioner of Food and Drugs.[202] FDA exercises these enforcement powers pursuant to specific delegations.[203] The delegations empower FDA to enforce not only the FDCA, but certain other statutes as well.[204] The Commissioner of Food and Drugs, in turn, has redelegated to the Principal Deputy Commissioner and the Associate Commissioner for Regulatory Affairs authority to perform the enforcement functions of the Commissioner.[205] It is extremely rare for the Commissioner to become personally involved in an individual enforcement case, though he or she may help spearhead an enforcement initiative.

Civil and Administrative Enforcement of the FDCA

The primary enforcement powers available to FDA are:[206]

- establishment inspections;

- Warning Letters and other regulatory correspondence;

- recalls;

- publicity;

- administrative detention, product seizures, and related reconditionings or destructions;

- injunctions, including restitution, disgorgement of profits, and "liquidated damages";

---

[202] FDA STAFF MANUAL GUIDES, Vol. II, SMG-1410.10(1)(A) (2011), *available at* http://www.fda.gov/downloads/ AboutFDA/ReportsManualsForms/StaffManualGuides/UCM273771.pdf. *See* Removal of Delegations of Authority and Conforming changes to Regulations, 69 Fed. Reg. 17,285 (Apr. 2, 2004).

[203] *See* 21 C.F.R. § 1.4(a) (2014). *See also* STAFF MANUAL GUIDES *available at* http://www.fda.gov/AboutFDA/ ReportsManualsForms/StaffManualGuides/default.htm.

[204] FDA STAFF MANUAL GUIDES, Vol. II, SMG-1410.10(1)(A)(1) (2014).

[205] *Id.*; SMG-1410.21(1)(b) (2014).

[206] Sources of FDA enforcement information are:
  - the statute: 21 U.S.C. §§ 301 *et seq.*;
  - the regulations: primarily title 21 of the *Code of Federal Regulations*, as well as other titles that may be relevant to specific products, such as dairy and meat;
  - the *Federal Register* (containing proposed regulations, explanatory preambles to final rules, interpretative rules, policy announcements, and notices);
  - the FDA *Compliance Policy Guides Manual* (an internal but publicly available document utilized by FDA field offices in interpreting regulatory policies and in communicating various enforcement actions such as import alerts), *available at* http://www.fda.gov/ora/compliance_ref/cpg/default.htm;
  - the FDA *Regulatory Procedures Manual* (RPM) (an internal but publicly available FDA document that sets forth agency policy on various enforcement matters), *available at* http://www.fda.gov/ora/ compliance_ref/rpm/default.htm;
  - the FDA *Investigations Operations Manual* (an internal but publicly available FDA guide for field inspectors), *available at* http://www.fda.gov/ora/inspect_ref/iom/; and
  - the FDA *Compliance Program Guidance Manual* (a publicly available supplement to FDA's *Investigations Operations Manual* that provides details on certain inspection programs), *available at* http://www.fda. gov/ora/cpgm/default.htm.

- import inspections, detentions, and refusals, and re-export refusals;
- product approval or license withdrawals and suspensions and "alert/reference" lists;
- application integrity policy (deferral of review of applications);
- civil penalty proceedings;
- debarment;
- misdemeanor prosecutions;
- felony prosecutions;
- Government Wide Quality Assurance Program (GWQAP).

The First Interface: Inspections

Since FDA does not have general civil subpoena powers,[207] it must rely principally on inspections for the acquisition of documentary and other information about regulated parties' states of compliance. Under sections 703 and 704 of the FDCA, the agency is permitted access to, respectively, interstate shipment records held by a common carrier, and to most records held in a facility that manufactures, ships, or holds "food, drugs, devices, tobacco products or cosmetics" as long as they are manufactured, processed, packed, or held for introduction into interstate commerce (including vehicles used therefor).[208] Section 704 provides for much broader inspection powers in the case of plants that manufacture prescription drugs, nonprescription drugs for human use, restricted devices, tobacco products, and infant formulas.[209]

FDASIA authorized FDA to request from a firm the documents to which it is entitled under section 704 without physically appearing at the firm to present credentials and conduct an inspection.[210] FDASIA also deems adulterated any drug sold by a firm that delays, denies, limits, or refuses an FDA inspection.[211] This provision will enable FDA to achieve parity between its oversight of domestic product manufacturers and those who operate abroad. Until the amendment in FDASIA, it had been a prohibited act in section 301 to refuse an FDA inspection,[212] but the provision was of limited value as applied to regulated parties overseas since it is a practical impossibility to prosecute someone abroad for a violation of the FDCA. Now that the drugs sold by an uncooperative foreign establishment are

---

[207]   *See supra* n. 35. The Act did provide FDA with limited subpoena authority with respect to medical devices. In addition, the Patient Protection and Affordable Care Act (Pub. L. No. 111-148, 124 Stat. 119) (2010), includes a modification to 18 U.S.C. § 24, which defines the term "federal health care offense." The act expands the definition of that term to include violations of "section 301 of the Federal Food, Drug, and Cosmetic Act (21 U.S.C. 331)" that relate to a healthcare benefit program. This expanded definition would give the Attorney General the authority to serve a subpoena when investigating violations of section 301 that relate to a healthcare benefit program.

[208]   21 U.S.C. §§ 373, 374.

[209]   FSMA expanded both FDA's authority to detain products that may be in violation of the law, and FDA's inspection authority by mandating inspection frequency for food facilities based on risk, providing FDA with access to food-related records, and requiring testing by accredited laboratories for certain foods. Pub. L. No. 111-353, §§ 414(a), 421 & 422, 124 Stat. at 3887, 3923 & 3926. *See also* FDA, Background on the FDA Food Safety Modernization Act, *available at* http://www.fda.gov/downloads/Food/GuidanceRegulation/UCM263773.pdf.

[210]   *See supra* note 51.

[211]   *See supra* note 152.

[212]   FDCA § 301(f), 21 U.S.C. 331(f).

considered adulterated, FDA has grounds to refuse their admission into the United States. This change gives FDA important economic leverage it lacked prior to FDASIA, and helps to ensure that foreign firms that do not comply with section 704 will not have access to the domestic market.

Although a search warrant normally is required by the Fourth Amendment for inspections of premises, an exception to this protection has been carved out by the Supreme Court as to regulatory inspections of industries "long subject to close supervision and inspection." This exception was articulated in *Colonnade Catering Corp. v. United States* in 1970,[213] and re-articulated for "pervasively regulated business[es]" in *United States v. Biswell* in 1972.[214] *Colonnade* involved inspections by the then Bureau of Alcohol, Tobacco and Firearms (ATF) to regulate liquor; *Biswell* involved an ATF inspection of firearms.

In 1981, the Eighth Circuit put to rest the question whether the *Colonnade-Biswell* exception applies to inspections under the FDCA:

> We think the drug-manufacturing industry is properly within the *Colonnade-Biswell* exception to the warrant requirement. The drug-manufacturing industry has a long history of supervision and inspection.... That Act was an attempt by Congress "to exclude from interstate commerce impure and adulterated foods and drugs..." and to prevent the transport of such articles "from their place of manufacture."[215]

This reasoning almost certainly extends to the other types of products regulated by FDA.[216]

Conceptually, in the absence of a warrant, FDA can inspect an establishment only with the consent of those in charge of it. A refusal to permit an inspection by an FDA investigator[217] who presents proper identification and a valid Notice of Inspection (Form FDA 482), however, is a prohibited act under FDCA section 301(f).[218] A refusal constituting a violation of section 301(f) can be total or partial.[219] A partial refusal can include denying an

---

[213]   397 U.S. 72, 77 (1970).

[214]   406 U.S. 311, 316 (1972). *But cf.* Marshall v. Barlows, Inc., 436 U.S. 307 (1978) (emphasizing that the *Biswell-Colonnade* exception is a narrow one, and refusing to allow warrantless searches for workplace safety inspections under OSHA); Camara v. Mun. Court, 387 U.S. 523 (1967) (warrantless searches generally are unreasonable).

[215]   United States v. Jamieson-McKames Pharms., Inc., 651 F.2d 532, 537 (8th Cir. 1981) (quoting McDermott v. Wisconsin, 228 U.S. 115, 128 (1913)). The holding applies to intrusions "limited to the purposes specified in the statute," *id.* at 542. It has been held that the Fourth Amendment exclusionary rule does not apply to condemnation proceedings pursuant to FDCA § 304. United States v. An Article of Food...Lumpfish Roe, 477 F. Supp. 1185, 1991 (S.D.N.Y. 1979). *But see* United States v. Various Articles of Drug, No. C94-1120C (W.D. Wash. 1994) (holding that the Fourth Amendment's warrant requirement applies to seizures under FDCA § 304, in contrast to inspections under FDCA § 704).

[216]   Although arguments can be made that the device industry has been regulated for only the last 30 years, most devices were in fact regulated as drugs before 1976. This reasoning has not been applied to tobacco products, which were recently put under FDA's jurisdiction.

[217]   FDA calls the employees who conduct inspections "investigators." An inspection may be performed by more than one investigator.

[218]   21 U.S.C. § 331(f).

[219]   *Compare* United States v. Cruez, 144 F. Supp. 229 (E.D. Ill. 1956) (prosecution for refusal to permit inspection), *with* United States v. Stanack Sales Co., 387 F.2d 849 (3d Cir. 1968) (prosecution for refusal to

investigator access to certain records or to particular parts of a facility, or refusing to agree to certain sampling requests. Evidence obtained by FDA in a warrantless inspection where a company representative has refused access may be excluded under the Fourth Amendment in a criminal trial on the ground that the company did not "consent" to the inspection.[220]

When consent to an inspection is refused, FDA generally seeks an inspection warrant from a district court.[221] Once that step has been taken, further enforcement action usually follows. For example, where a laboratory accused FDA of harassment by excessive searches and requests for too many expensive samples, the district court upheld FDA's inspection authority and found the laboratory in civil contempt of the warrant that was issued following the refusal of inspection.[222] Seizures, an injunction action, or a criminal prosecution can result from a refusal of inspection.[223]

Sometimes, an inspection may be conducted as part of a criminal investigation. In the wake of the generic drug scandal, FDA created the Office of Criminal Investigations (OCI), which directs criminal investigations in coordination with other federal and local authorities.[224] OCI personnel may be involved in FDA inspections as part of an ongoing criminal investigation. OCI helps implement criminal investigations, policy and training, and participates in grand jury proceedings as requested by DOJ.[225]

Inspections normally are carried out in a fairly cooperative fashion. An investigator must first present credentials and a Notice of Inspection. On request, the investigator conducting the inspection will inform the company whether a directed or general inspection is involved, i.e., whether the investigator is there solely with respect to specific products or literature, or for a full premises inspection. It is incumbent on the inspected company to give the investigator access to all areas where foods, drugs, cosmetics, biologics, devices, tobacco products, or dietary supplements are held or are being manufactured (including labeling) and to all records subject to inspection under the FDCA.[226]

---

[220] allow review of drug distribution records).
        Jamieson-McKames Pharm., Inc., 651 F.2d at 540; cf. supra note 215.
[221] See FDA INVESTIGATIONS OPERATIONS MANUAL (IOM) ch. 5, § 5.2.6, "Inspection Warrant" (2014), available at http://www.fda.gov/downloads/ICECI/Inspections/IOM/UCM150576.pdf; FDA RPM ch. 6, § 6-3-2, "Inspection Warrants" (2011), available at http://www.fda.gov/ICECI/ComplianceManuals/RegulatoryProceduresManual/ucm176735.htm. The showing needed for the issuance of an inspection warrant is less than the probable cause needed for a criminal search warrant. See, e.g., In re Establishment Inspection of Medtronic, Inc., 500 F. Supp. 536 (D. Minn. 1980); cf. United States v. Roux Labs., Inc., 456 F. Supp. 973, 976-78 (M.D. Fla. 1978).
[222] Roux Labs., Inc., 456 F. Supp. at 975-78.
[223] The question has arisen as to whether Miranda warnings (see Miranda v. Arizona, 384 U.S. 436 (1966)) are required in FDA inspections where a criminal investigation is under way. In the Eighth Circuit's Jamieson-McKames decision, such warnings were held inapplicable because FDA inspectors have no authority to make arrests. 651 F.2d at 543. Since the defendant employees were not in custody, the court ruled that Miranda warnings were not required, and it upheld the admission of their statements into evidence.
[224] See Office of Criminal Investigations, Duties and Functions, U.S. Food and Drug Administration, http://www.fda.gov/AboutFDA/CentersOffices/OfficeofGlobalRegulatoryOperationsandPolicy/ORA/ucm136613.htm (last updated Aug. 13, 2014); IOM, supra note 221, ch. 8, § 8.9, "Office of Criminal Investigations (OCI)."
[225] IOM, supra note 221 (ORA Headquarters Directory).
[226] Id.

FDA maintains the *Investigations Operations Manual (IOM)*,[227] which contains descriptions of the procedures and the training materials utilized by field office personnel. Most inspection issues are dealt with in that volume. The manual is supplemented by the *Compliance Policy Guides Manual (CPG)*,[228] the *Compliance Program Guidance Manual*[229] and *the Regulatory Procedures Manual (RPM)*.[230]

A great deal has been written about the inspectional powers of FDA and the tactics to be used by regulated firms during inspections.[231] Accordingly, most large companies under the jurisdiction of FDA have developed inspection procedures (as have trade associations for their FDA-regulated members) and are well aware of FDA's powers.

Nonetheless, certain issues with respect to the scope of inspections occasionally are contested. Section 704 of the FDCA states that inspections must be conducted during "reasonable times," "within reasonable limits," and in a "reasonable manner."[232] These standards rarely are litigated, and, when they are, the determination of reasonableness usually favors the agency.[233] On a practical basis, however, the agency often compromises with a company if the matter is resolved without resort to inspectional warrants or litigation.

Another issue is the applicability of the immunity provision of section 703, which states that "evidence obtained under this section, or any evidence which is directly or indirectly derived from such evidence, shall not be used in a criminal prosecution of the person from whom obtained."[234] Although many defendants seek this criminal immunity, few obtain it. Section 703 has been interpreted quite strictly to cover only inspections of common carriers and a few limited categories of persons receiving regulated products, thereby eliminating the vast majority of inspections that are conducted pursuant to section 704.[235] In a food-warehouse criminal case in which the inspection issues were heavily litigated, the court fairly easily found that FDA did not invoke section 703 in order to obtain the documents relied upon by the prosecution.[236]

---

[227]   *Id.*

[228]   FDA Compliance Policy Guides Manual, *available at* http://www.fda.gov/ICECI/ComplianceManuals/CompliancePolicyGuidanceManual/default.htm.

[229]   FDA Compliance Program Guidance Manual, *available at* http://www.fda.gov/ICECI/ComplianceManuals/ComplianceProgramManual/default.htm.

[230]   RPM, *supra* note 221.

[231]   *See, e.g.,* Linda R. Horton, *Warrantless Inspections Under the Federal Food, Drug, and Cosmetic Act,* 42 Geo. Wash. L. Rev. 1089 (1974); Peter B. Hutt, *Factory Inspection Authority—The Statutory Viewpoint,* 22 Food Drug Cosm. L.J. 667 (1967).

[232]   FDCA § 704(a)(1), 21 U.S.C. § 374(a)(1).

[233]   *See, e.g.,* United States v. Gel Spice Co., 601 F. Supp. 1214 (E.D.N.Y. 1983); *Roux Labs., Inc.,* 456 F. Supp. at 973, 976.

[234]   21 U.S.C. § 373.

[235]   *See e.g.,* Gel Spice Company, *supra* n. 233.

[236]   *Id.* The court reasoned that section 703 provides immunity in a criminal prosecution only to one who has permitted FDA personnel to inspect records of interstate shipments after 1) FDA has requested the records, 2) the custodian has refused to provide them and 3) the investigator has again requested the records, specifically under the authority of section 703, and has presented a written statement as required by that section. If the custodian has shown the document voluntarily, then the immunity granted by section 703 would not apply. *Id.* at 1220.

Many investigators request permission to take photographs. Inspected companies have been reluctant to permit such photographs because of the possibility of distortion of conditions, particularly in a food-sanitation dispute. The statute is silent as to photographs, and no case law expressly addresses whether FDA has authority to take them. In *United States v. Gel Spice Company*, a motion to suppress photographs was denied on the grounds that the probative value of the photographs was not "outweighed by the danger of unfair prejudice," and that "FDA personnel followed all applicable procedural requirements."[237] The evidence was thus admitted under rule 403 of the Federal Rules of Evidence, without any discussion of whether FDA had the power to take such photographs without consent.

Until recently, the IOM informed investigators that they are not to request permission from management to take photographs.[238] The IOM cites two decisions in support of FDA's position on taking photographs: *Dow Chemical Company v. United States*[239] and *United States v. Acri Wholesale Grocery Company*.[240] In *Dow Chemical*, the taking of an aerial photograph by EPA pursuant to the Clean Air Act was upheld as a valid exercise of EPA's inspectional powers, and not a violation of Dow Chemical's privacy rights. The *Dow Chemical* decision does not directly address the issues concerning photographs under the FDCA, nor does it deal with the taking of photographs inside a plant not open or visible to the general public. Instead, the IOM relies on the Court's general statement that, "[w]hen Congress invests an agency with enforcement and investigatory authority, it is not necessary to identify explicitly each and every technique that may be used in the course of executing the statutory mission."[241] In *Acri*, the court upheld the admission into evidence of photographs taken by FDA investigators inside a warehouse. Whether FDA had the right to take the photographs was not decided in that case. No objection was raised at the time of inspection to the taking of photographs; the court accordingly found that there had been full consent by the company.

Following the enactment of FDASIA, however, FDA issued a draft guidance on delaying inspections authorized by section 704 of the FDCA. In the guidance, FDA asserts the right to take photographs during an inspection. That aspect of the guidance has not yet been challenged in court, although nothing in FDASIA explicitly authorizes the conduct..[242]

Section 704 permits FDA to take samples of food, drugs, devices, tobacco products, and cosmetics, and of the labeling thereof. Although manufacturing records and quality-control procedures are not specifically within the purview of section 704 for nonrestricted devices, FDA demands access to these documents, and normally obtains them. As to restricted devices, tobacco products, prescription drugs, and nonprescription drugs intended for

---

[237] *Id. See also* United States v. Agnew, 931 F.2d 1397, 1409-10 (10th Cir. 1991) (finding proper chain of custody established for admission of photographs).

[238] IOM, *supra* note 221, § 5.3.4.1.

[239] 476 U.S. 227 (1986).

[240] 409 F. Supp. 529, 533 (S.D. Iowa 1976).

[241] IOM, *supra* note 221, § 5.3.4.1 (quoting *Dow Chemical Co.*, 476 U.S. at 233).

[242] FDA, Draft Guidance for Industry: Circumstances that Constitute Delaying, Denying, Limiting, or Refusing a Drug Inspection (July 2013) *available at* http://www.fda.gov/downloads/RegulatoryInformation/Guidances/UCM360484.pdf.

human use, the statute broadly and explicitly permits inspection and copying of records bearing on whether such products are in violation of the statute.[243]

Under section 704, confidential pricing, sales data (other than shipment data), and personnel records (other than records as to qualifications of technical and professional personnel performing functions subject to the FDCA) are not to be part of the inspection of documents. In reality, however, much confidential information is contained in documents that are part of a statutorily authorized inspection, and that information can be reported in internal FDA inspectional reports. In such circumstances, companies often seek and obtain FDA's agreement to expunge the confidential information from records released under the Freedom of Information Act (FOIA).[244]

In the course of an inspection, FDA investigators frequently request that an individual at the inspected company sign an affidavit confirming particular results of the inspection. The affidavit usually lists the documents taken, and it records answers provided by company personnel to questions posed orally during the inspection. Company personnel are under no duty to sign or even review such affidavits.

As required by section 704(b), at the conclusion of an inspection, the investigator provides to the head of the inspected facility or to a designee, on Form FDA 483, a list of "observations" of violative conditions made during the inspection. An exit interview is provided when requested by the inspected company. FDA 483 observations do not constitute formal FDA notices of violations, but rather the opinion of the investigator as to possible violations.[245] It is expected that an inspected firm will respond to FDA in writing within 15 working days as to each observation reported on the form.[246] If a response is submitted within the 15-day time frame, FDA will "conduct a detailed review of the response before determining whether to issue a Warning Letter."[247] If the response is submitted after the 15-day time frame, FDA may evaluate the response only as part of the firm's response to a Warning Letter.[248] FDA 483 reports and company responses are available for public disclosure in redacted form.[249]

After returning to the district office, the investigator prepares a draft of an establishment inspection report (EIR), which is then put into final form by the supervisory investigator, and is sent to FDA headquarters. If particularly egregious conditions are found, an official action indicated (OAI) alert will be communicated to agency headquarters, in which case further enforcement action may be taken against the inspected company. The investigator may also classify an inspection as voluntary action indicated (VAI). In contrast to OAI, a VAI inspection indicates that certain practices or conditions were identified during the inspection

---

[243] 21 U.S.C. § 374(a).

[244] *See* Pub. L. No. 89-487, 80 Stat. 250 (1966) (codified as amended at 5 U.S.C. § 552). FDA generally is cooperative in deleting confidential information from publicly released documents, although the agency is less so when a company seeks overbroad protection of information. FDA's policy as to protection of trade secrets and confidential commercial or financial information is set forth in 21 C.F.R. § 20.61 (2014).

[245] *See generally* 21 C.F.R. § 10.85(k) (2014).

[246] Richard M. Cooper & John R. Fleder, *Responding to a Form 483 or Warning Letter: A Practical Guide*, 60 FOOD & DRUG L.J. 470 (2005); Review of Post-Inspection Responses, 74 Fed. Reg. 40,211, 40,211-12 (Aug. 11, 2009).

[247] *Id.*

[248] *Id.*

[249] 21 C.F.R. § 20.20 (2014).

that do not meet the threshold of regulatory significance to warrant an OAI classification. These reports may be provided upon request directly to the inspected company. They also are subject to disclosure under the FOIA, except during an ongoing investigation, when the exemption for investigatory files applies.[250]

Depending on the complexity of the subject matter and the interest of the FDA district office in obtaining evidence of suspected violations, an inspection can take anywhere from a matter of minutes to weeks or months. The FDCA requires inspection of drug manufacturing facilities at least once every two years;[251] food plants are to be inspected by FDA at varying intervals.[252] A representative example of how an inspection is conducted and the manner in which it may lead to enforcement action appears in *United States v. General Foods Corporation*.[253]

The FDCA grants FDA authority to inspect and copy records where FDA has a reasonable belief that food has been adulterated and presents a threat of adverse health consequences.[254] FDA has implemented multiple rules under this authority,[255] which was granted by the Bioterrorism Act of 2002.[256]

Warning Notices: Letters and Other Regulatory Correspondence

Following an inspection or the discovery by other means of an alleged violation, either FDA headquarters or the relevant district office may formally communicate to a company by letter the finding of an alleged violation. Such a communication constitutes an official enforcement mode known as a "Warning Letter."[257] Although the types of violations addressed in Warning Letters generally do not lead to immediate enforcement action in a court, FDA considers them significant enough to warrant application of agency enforcement resources.

Until May 1991, there were two officially designated types of letters, "notices of adverse findings" and "regulatory letters," both discussed in an FDA *Federal Register* announcement in 1978.[258] The notice of adverse findings, previously known as an "information letter,"

---

[250] *See* 5 U.S.C. § 552(b)(5); 21 C.F.R. § 20.64 (2014).

[251] FDCA § 510(h), 21 U.S.C. § 360(h). FDA lacks the resources, however, to meet this statutory requirement. *See* FDA, Risk-Based Method for Prioritizing cGMP Inspections of Pharmaceutical Manufacturing Sites—A Pilot Risk Ranking Model 3 (Sept. 2004), *available at* http://www.fda.gov/ohrms/dockets/ac/04/briefing/2004-4080b1_04_risk-based.pdf.

[252] *See generally* GAO, Federal Oversight of Food Safety: High-Risk Designation Can Bring Needed Attention to Fragmented System 4-5 (Feb. 8, 2007), *available at* http://www.gao.gov/new.items/d07449t.pdf.

[253] 446 F. Supp. 740 (N.D.N.Y.), *aff'd*, 591 F.2d 1332 (2d Cir. 1978). There, FDA was denied an injunction despite the presence of green, slimy material on green-bean processing machinery. *Id.* at 754.

[254] FDCA § 414, 21 U.S.C. § 350c.

[255] *See, e.g.*, Registration of Food Facilities Under the Public Health Security and Bioterrorism Preparedness and Response Act of 2002, 70 Fed. Reg. 57,505 (Oct. 3, 2005); Establishment and Maintenance of Records Under the Public Health Security and Bioterrorism Preparedness and Response Act of 2002, 69 Fed. Reg. 71,561 (Dec. 9, 2004); *see* 21 C.F.R. § 1, subpart J (2014).

[256] Public Health Security and Bioterrorism Preparedness and Response Act of 2002, Pub. L. No. 107-188, §§ 305-306, 116 Stat. 594, 667-70 (2002) (codified at 21 U.S.C. §§ 350c, 350d).

[257] Warning Letters have the legend "Warning Letter" near the top of the first page.

[258] Enforcement Policy for Certain Compliance Correspondence, 43 Fed. Reg. 27,498 (June 23, 1978).

requested voluntary action by a party, and a response to FDA within 30 days. When a notice of adverse findings was issued, it stated that, although FDA believed that violations existed, no decision had been made by the agency as to whether further enforcement action would be taken. A regulatory letter, however, was a threat to sue if corrective action was not taken.[259] A response was demanded within 10 days, and enforcement action very often did follow a refusal or failure to provide a response the agency considered adequate.[260]

In May 1991, FDA Commissioner David Kessler issued a memorandum announcing the revocation of the warning system based on notices of adverse findings and regulatory letters.[261] Explaining that "FDA cannot afford to be perceived as a 'paper tiger' that inspects a firm, writes a letter, waits, then writes another letter," Commissioner Kessler introduced the new Warning Letter system (along with a streamlined review procedure for injunctions and criminal fraud cases).[262]

FDA's guidelines characterize the Warning Letter as "the agency's principal means of notifying regulated industry of violations and achieving prompt voluntary correction."[263] Warning Letters are intended to be issued only for those violations of regulatory significance (i.e., violations that could lead to enforcement action if they are not promptly and adequately corrected).[264] The agency advises, however, that "responsible individuals should not assume that they would receive a Warning Letter, or other prior notice, before FDA initiates enforcement action."[265] Warning Letters request a response and notify the addressee that FDA may take further action, including criminal action, without further notice. In instances where FDA wants to convey formally its concern about apparent violations of law, but does not believe the violations are serious enough to demand a response or threaten further legal action, FDA can send an "untitled" letter, which provides legal notice to an addressee but is softer in tone (and symbolism) than a Warning Letter.[266]

FDA District Directors may issue Warning Letters without the concurrence of headquarters, except when a letter addresses an issue as to a specific subject matter enumerated in FDA's *RPM*.[267] In such a case, the letter will be issued directly by one of FDA's Centers or by the District Office after referral to the appropriate Center.

---

[259]   *Id.* at 27,499.

[260]   *See, e.g.,* United States v. Sandoz Pharm. Corp., 894 F.2d 825 (6th Cir. 1990) (affirming seizure instituted against Fiorinal with Codeine products after FDA deemed inadequate Sandoz's response to regulatory letter asserting that products were unapproved new drugs).

[261]   FDA Memorandum from Commissioner David Kessler to all FDA enforcement and field offices (May 23, 1991).

[262]   *Id.*

[263]   RPM, *supra* note 221, ch. 4, § 4-1-3, "Issuing Warning Letters-Factors to Consider."

[264]   *Id.* § 4-1-1, "Warning Letter Procedures." At the same time FDA began to issue Warning Letters, the agency also began to issue "notice of violation" letters. These were later re-designated as "Untitled Letters." The violations that lead to an Untitled Letter do not meet the threshold of regulatory significance for a Warning Letter. *Id.* § 4-2-1, "Policy."

[265]   *Id.*

[266]   RPM, *supra* note 221, ch. 4, § 4-1, "Warning Letters."

[267]   *See id.* § 4-1-4, "Center Concurrence and Letters Issued by Centers."

In 2000, FDA began issuing "cyber" letters to website operators that promoted products that could be considered unapproved new drugs, and thus potentially violated the FDCA.[268] These letters do not meet the definition of a Warning Letter in the RPM in that they do not call for a response, nor do they threaten that FDA could take action without further notice. Instead, these letters are intended to deter unlawful conduct and achieve voluntary compliance by advising actors that their conduct is unlawful and known to FDA. In most instances, however, cyber letters are addressed to URLs because the individuals behind the websites are unknown. As a result, there are strong arguments that the letters do not constitute legal notice to any particular website operator or sponsor. Nevertheless, FDA continues to use this tool to address the proliferation of unlawful products offered through the medium.

Between March 2002 and August 2009, all Warning Letters and so-called "untitled" letters were submitted to FDA's Office of the Chief Counsel (OCC) prior to issuance, for review for legal sufficiency and consistency with agency policy.[269] In 2009, FDA amended the OCC review procedures "on an interim basis," to apply only to certain categories of Warning and Untitled Letters, which are specified by the relevant FDA Center.[270] FDA finalized the new review procedures in December 2010.[271] Under the revised procedures, OCC reviews, among other categories specified in the RPM, any Warning or Untitled Letter "involving a novel, controversial, or sensitive legal issue."[272] When OCC review is required, OCC has 15 working days to review a proposed Warning or Untitled Letter after receiving a complete set of supporting materials.[273]

A firm must respond to a Warning Letter within 15 working days after receipt of the letter.[274] When drugs or devices are involved, the letters often state that FDA is advising federal agencies of the issuance of the letter, so that those agencies may consider the information in the letter when awarding contracts for the affected products.[275] A Warning Letter may further place a hold on pending product or export approvals by FDA.[276]

On September 1, 2009, FDA created a new "close-out" process for Warning Letters.[277] After a firm responds to a Warning Letter, the issuing District Office or Center will evaluate the firm's response.[278] If the response is inadequate, or no response is received, the District Office or Center will begin follow-up action to achieve the requested correction. If, however, the response "appears adequate" and the corrections have been verified by FDA, usually

---

[268]   Cyber Letters, U.S. Food and Drug Administration, http://www.fda.gov/cder/warn/cyber (last updated July 23, 2013); *see also*, Nicholas Freitag, *Federal Food and Drug Act Violations*, 41 AM. CRIM. L. REV. 647, 669 (2004); FDA Launches "Cyber" Letters Against Potentially Illegal, Foreign-Based Online Drug Sites, FDA Talk Paper (Feb. 2, 2000), http://web.archive.org/web/20080229052621/fda.gov/bbs/topics/ANSWERS/ANS01001.html.

[269]   RPM, *supra* note 221, ch. 4, § 4-1, "Warning Letters" at Exhibit 4-1.

[270]   *Id.*

[271]   *Id.*

[272]   *Id.*

[273]   *Id.*

[274]   *Id.* § 4-1-10, "Warning Letter Format."

[275]   *Id.*

[276]   *Id.*

[277]   *Id.* § 4-1-8, "Warning Letter Follow-Up."

[278]   *Id.*

through a follow-up inspection, the District Office or Center will issue a "Warning Letter close-out letter" verifying that commitments appears to have been fulfilled and that correction appears to have been achieved.[279]

FDA takes the position that a Warning Letter is not final agency action, and so is not subject to judicial review:

> A Warning Letter is informal and advisory. It communicates the agency's position on a matter, but it does not commit FDA to taking enforcement action. For these reasons, FDA does not consider Warning Letters to be final agency action on which it can be sued.[280]

The U.S. District Court for the District of Columbia reached the same conclusion as to the analogous regulatory letter. In *Estee Lauder, Inc. v. FDA*, a cosmetics company sought a declaration that anti-aging claims for face creams did not render the products unapproved new drugs.[281] FDA had sent more than 20 manufacturers regulatory letters taking the position that such claims did have that effect.[282] FDA nonetheless moved to dismiss on the ground that the action was not ripe for adjudication, and that the plaintiff had failed to exhaust available administrative remedies.[283] *Estee Lauder* argued that FDA *had* taken final action by sending the regulatory letters, and that the next step was merely the procedural nicety of an action for seizure or some other enforcement action.[284] The court accepted FDA's position that its regulatory letters were not final agency action because they were an equivocal, not final, enforcement threat.

Six years later, however, the same court refined its position by concluding that Warning Letters can be considered evidence of a final agency policy, at least when evaluated with additional actions by FDA establishing such a policy.[285] In *Washington Legal Foundation v. Kessler*, a public interest organization brought a First Amendment challenge to FDA's policy prohibiting physician members of the organization from receiving from manufacturers information regarding "off-label" uses of the manufacturers' drugs and medical devices. FDA had issued Warning Letters and policy pronouncements threatening further enforcement against the distribution of scholarly articles and speeches by regulated firms. Despite FDA's assertion, in a motion to dismiss, that no final agency position had been adopted, the court held that the question of finality of conduct turned not on FDA's view of whether a final policy existed, but rather on the effect of the agency's conduct on the industry.[286] The case was held ripe for review.[287]

---

[279] *Id.*

[280] *Id.* § 4-1-1, "Warning Letter Procedures."

[281] 727 F. Supp. 1 (D.D.C. 1989). *See also* Dietary Supplemental Coal., Inc. v. Sullivan, 978 F.2d 560, 561 (9th Cir. 1992).

[282] 727 F. Supp. at 2-3.

[283] *Id.* at 2.

[284] *Id.* at 4-5.

[285] Washington Legal Found. v. Kessler, 880 F. Supp. 26 (D.D.C. 1995), *sub nom.* Washington Legal Found. v. Henney, 56 F. Supp. 2d 81 (D.D.C. 1999), *vacated in part on other grounds*, 202 F.3d 331 (D.C. Cir. 2000).

[286] *Id.* at 34.

[287] *Id.* at 36. *See also* Den-Mat Corp. v. United States, Dkt. No. 92-444, 1992 U.S. Dist. LEXIS 9,255 (D. Md. Apr. 24, 1992) (final agency action may be found where FDA has done more than simply threaten enforcement action in a Warning Letter and has taken additional "affirmative adverse action"). Den-Mat's

Although *Washington Legal Foundation* guides future judicial determinations, it probably has limited precedential value in most enforcement cases, in part because it involved a First Amendment challenge to FDA policy. Virtually every court that has considered the effect of a Warning Letter in the more typical enforcement context has agreed with FDA's and the *Estee Lauder* court's position that it does not, in and of itself, constitute final agency action.[288]

Nonetheless, judicial review of a position taken only in a Warning Letter can be obtained through exhaustion of FDA's citizen-petition process. When faced with a letter based on a questionable legal position, a regulated entity can seek final agency action by filing a citizen petition challenging the position.[289] If FDA still responds unfavorably or fails to respond within a reasonable amount of time, the petitioner can then seek judicial review under the Administrative Procedure Act[290] of FDA's action or inaction on the petition.[291]

Even without having the clear status of final agency action, a Warning Letter can create enough publicity that it will exert overwhelming pressure to comply with FDA's position. Thus, Warning Letters significantly expand FDA's effective enforcement powers, regardless of the ripeness of a later challenge in court.

Before FDA revised the RPM to allow for review of fewer Warning Letters by OCC, FDA's issuance of Warning Letters had been in significant decline due to changes in the agency's enforcement tactics. FDA had adopted a new approach that utilized more product recalls and press releases, so as to reserve Warning Letters for more serious deviations.[292] That trend has changed recently—at least in terms of real numbers—due in part to the commitment

---

subsequent motion to dismiss FDA's enforcement action was denied. Den-Mat Corp. v. United States, Dkt. No. 92-444, 1992 U.S. Dist. LEXIS 12,233 (D. Md. Aug. 17, 1992).

[288] *See* Holistic Candlers & Consumer Ass'n v. FDA, No. 10-582, 2011 U.S. Dist. LEXIS 27598 (D.D.C. Mar. 16, 2011) (holding that Warning Letters do not constitute final agency action); Regenerative Sciences, Inc. v. FDA, No. 09-cv-00411-WYD-BNB, 2010 U.S. Dist. LEXIS 29349 (D. Colo. Mar. 26, 2010) ("[T]he July 25, 2008, FDA Warning Letter is not a 'final agency action' as defined under the APA. Instead, it is a 'tentative or interlocutory action' which does not constitute a final agency action."); *Bracco Diagnostics, Inc. v. Amersham Health, Inc.,* 627 F.2d 384, 470 n.250 (D.N.J. 2009) ("None of the FDA letters introduced by Bracco at trial constitute [sic] final agency action ...."); Genendo Pharm. N.V. v. Thompson, 308 F. Supp. 2d 881, 885 (D. Ill. 2003) ("Statements of lower-level agency officials likewise do not rise to the level of final agency action—even when they are contained in Warning Letters or other official regulatory correspondence."); Summit Tech., Inc. v. High-Line Med. Instruments Co., 922 F. Supp. 299, 306 (C.D. Cal. 1996) ("regardless of any Warning Letter that the FDA may have sent to Defendants, it is clear that the FDA has not completed this investigation"); Professionals & Patients for Customized Care v. Shalala, 847 F. Supp. 1359, 1365 (S.D. Tex. 1994) ("[w]arning letters issued by the FDA are deemed to be informal communications that do not constitute final agency action" but "merely establish a dialogue between [sic] the FDA and do not necessarily lead to further sanctions") (citing Biotics Research Corp. v. Heckler, 710 F.2d 1375, 1378 (9th Cir. 1983)).

[289] 21 C.F.R. §§ 10.25(a), 10.30 (2014).

[290] 5 U.S.C. § 551 *et seq.*

[291] *See, e.g.,* Henley v. FDA, 873 F. Supp. 776 (E.D.N.Y. 1995) (reviewing denial of a citizen petition); Hill Dermaceuticals, Inc. v. FDA, 524 F. Supp. 2d 5 (D.D.C. 2007) (reviewing claim that FDA had unreasonably delayed in providing substantive response to a citizen petition); *cf.* Sandoz, Inc. v. Leavitt, 427 F. Supp. 2d 29 (D.D.C. 2006) (finding that FDA had unreasonably delayed in responding to a new drug application). Under section 505(q) of the FDCA, 21 U.S.C. § 355(q), moreover, for certain petitions related to pending applications submitted under sections 505(b)(2) or 505(j) of the FDCA, 21 U.S.C. §§ 355(b)(2), (j), FDA is required to "take final agency action" within 180 days. 21 U.S.C. § 355(q)(1)(F). If FDA fails to take action on the petition within 180 days, the agency "shall be considered to have taken final agency action" on the petition, and the petitioner would be able to seek judicial review. *Id.* § 355(q)(2)(A).

[292] Jared Favole, *FDA Warning Letters to Companies Decline Sharply,* Wall St. J., June 7, 2008, at A2.

by the Center for Tobacco Products to police tobacco retailers. On August 13, 2013, FDA announced that it had issued its 10,000th tobacco retailer Warning Letter.[293]

"Voluntary" Recalls

Until recently, except for infant formulas,[294] and medical devices since 1990,[295] FDA had no authority to require a recall of products. In 2009, FDA was given the authority to require tobacco product recalls,[296] and in 2011, FSMA provided FDA with mandatory recall authority for foods when a company fails to undertake an FDA-requested voluntary recall.[297] The recall is one of FDA's most effective enforcement tools. In short, FDA now has the authority to require recalls of medical devices, tobacco products, foods (including dietary supplements and infant formula), and biologics approved under § 351 of the Public Health Service Act. FDA cannot require recalls for drugs and cosmetics.

Not every product withdrawal or upgrade is technically a "recall." In FDA's terms, a "recall" is a withdrawal or correction of a product that is in violation of the FDCA or another statute administered by the agency, and the violation is serious enough to warrant enforcement action by the agency.[298] Thus, FDA views a recall as an alternative to a seizure, injunction, or other enforcement action by the agency to achieve a prospective effect. An implicit or explicit threat of such enforcement action, together with the risk that the agency will initiate adverse publicity, generally brings about any recall desired by the agency, and does so without time-consuming procedures.

From the perspective of a manufacturer or distributor, a "market withdrawal" is preferable to a "recall" because of the publicity accorded the latter. A market withdrawal does not trigger the listing in the *FDA Enforcement Reports*[299] and other publicity that a recall triggers.[300] FDA may, however, unilaterally classify a product correction or removal as a recall, rather than as a market withdrawal.

The use of recalls has increased significantly over time. The number of recalls of FDA-regulated products rose from 1,162 in 1991 to a high of 9,469 in 2012.[301] As FDA recognizes

---

293   *See* FDA Issues New Warning Letters, U.S. FOOD AND DRUG ADMINISTRATION, http://www.fda.gov/TobaccoProducts/NewsEvents/ucm364781.htm (last updated Aug. 27, 2014).

294   FDCA § 412(e)(1), 21 U.S.C. § 350a(e)(1).

295   Safe Medical Devices Act of 1990, Pub. L. No. 101-629, § 8, 104 Stat. at 4501 (codified at 21 U.S.C. § 360(h) (e)).

296   FSPTCA, Pub. L. No. 111-31, at § 101(b), 123 Stat. at 1805 (codified at 21 U.S.C. § 387h(c)).

297   Food Safety Modernization Act, Pub. L. No. 111-353, at § 206, 124 Stat. at 3939-42 (codified at 21 U.S.C. § 350l).

298   *See* 21 C.F.R. §§ 7.3(g), 7.40 (2010). FDA's Part 7 regulations do no not currently specify whether tobacco products are within the scope of the regulations, but the agency has proposed to amend the regulations specifically to include tobacco products. *See* Further Amendments to General Regulations of the Food and Drug Administration to Incorporate Tobacco Products, 76 Fed. Reg. 20,901 (Apr. 14, 2011).

299   FDA still issues the *FDA Enforcement Report* weekly, although it is now published electronically on FDA's website. *See* FDA Enforcement Reports, *available at* http://www.fda.gov/Safety/Recalls/EnforcementReports/default.htm (last visited Jan. 5, 2015).

300   21 C.F.R. § 7.50 (2014).

301   *Compare* Office of Enforcement, Office of Reg. Aff., FDA, The Enforcement Story: Fiscal Year 2001 (2003), *available at* http://www.fda.gov/ICECI/EnforcementActions/EnforcementStory/EnforcementStoryArchive/ucm090830.htm, *with* Office of Enforcement, Office of Reg. Aff., FDA, Enforcement Statistics Summary: Fiscal Year 2012 (2013), *available at* http://www.fda.gov/downloads/ICECI/EnforcementActions/UCM346964.pdf.

in the *RPM*, recalls "generally are more efficient and timely than formal administrative or civil actions, especially when the product has been widely distributed."[302]

Recall requests by FDA are still relatively rare.[303] FDA instead attempts to lead a company to initiate a recall voluntarily. Most commonly, FDA investigators or other employees aware of a violative situation warranting a recall point out the violations and possibly the potential effects on consumers, and leave it to the company involved to draw the obvious inference. By characterizing a withdrawal or correction of a product as a "recall," FDA takes a position on the compliance status of the product. Thus, although recalls technically are voluntary for many products under FDA's jurisdiction, in reality an FDA request for a "recall" informs the company involved that other enforcement action will be taken if a recall is not commenced. FDA often has sought recalls as part of the injunctive relief granted in successfully concluded lawsuits. Many courts have, however, declined to include such provisions in injunctions when they were requested by FDA because the FDCA generally did not authorize FDA or a court to order a recall.[304]

FDA expects to be notified of any recall, and to be actively involved in shaping it and confirming its effectiveness. This is true regardless of whether a firm initiates a recall on its own or in response to a request from FDA.[305] Once a recall situation has been identified, the agency will work with the recalling company to determine the classification of the recall, the types of notices and publicity that will be used to effectuate the recall, the depth (distribution level) to which the recall will go, and the means for conducting a check on the effectiveness of the recall.[306]

Much of the recall procedure is a matter of negotiation. Companies that voluntarily notify FDA are more likely to obtain a more favorable recall classification or a less onerous effectiveness check. Consequently, although there is no legal requirement to inform FDA of a defect-related market withdrawal (except as to medical devices and tobacco products),[307] it is considered good practice to notify the agency in any event. The agency considers it bad form for a regulated firm to conduct a "recall" without involving the agency, and can pressure a company to issue a second recall notification if FDA believes that the company's initial recall communication was inadequate.

In any recall situation, FDA takes an active role in classifying the recall, reviewing the notices utilized by the recalling company, inspecting the effectiveness-check response (often in the form of return postcards), and monitoring the publicity issued by the company. In addition,

---

[302] RPM, *supra* note 221, § 7-2, "Background."
[303] *Id.*
[304] *See, e.g.,* United States v. Superpharm Corp., 530 F. Supp. 408 (E.D.N.Y. 1981); United States v. X-Otag Plus Tablets, 441 F. Supp. 105 (D. Colo. 1977); United States v. C.E.B. Prods., Inc., 380 F. Supp. 664 (N.D. Ill. 1974). *But see, e.g.,* United States v. Barr Labs., Inc., 812 F. Supp. 458 (D.N.J. 1993) (concluding that the remedy of a recall, although not authorized expressly in the FDCA, is "consistent with the broad equitable relief powers district courts enjoy"); United States v. K-N Enters., Inc., 461 F. Supp. 988 (N.D. Ill. 1978) (same).
[305] 21 C.F.R. § 7.46 (2010). FDA expects firms to notify the agency of any firm-initiated recall; such notice is now mandated for medical devices by the Safe Medical Devices Act of 1990, Pub. L. No. 101-629, § 7, 104 Stat. at 4501 (codified at 21 U.S.C. § 360i(f)(1)).
[306] RPM, *supra* note 221, § 7-6-4, "Recall Strategy"; 21 C.F.R. §§ 7.41-7.45 (2014).
[307] 21 U.S.C. §§ 360i(g), 387i(b).

FDA, pursuant to regulation, promptly makes available in its weekly *FDA Enforcement Reports*[308] a listing of all recalls, and utilizes public media when the agency believes that a critical health hazard warrants such recourse.[309]

In detailed regulations governing the agency's recall policy,[310] FDA has divided product recalls into three classes.[311] The classification depends on a health hazard evaluation,[312] and it is the principal factor that determines FDA's views as to the appropriate notification strategy, publicity, depth, and effectiveness checks for a recall.

A Class I recall is the most serious. It occurs when there is a "reasonable probability that the use of, or exposure to, a violative product will cause serious adverse health consequences or death.[313] The depth of such a recall generally is to the consumer or user level, including intervening wholesalers and retailers.[314] Public warnings also are utilized in Class I recalls.[315]

A Class II recall is one in which the product may "cause temporary or medically reversible adverse health consequences or where the probability of serious adverse health consequences is remote."[316] A Class II recall may reach only to the retail level.[317]

A Class III recall is one in which the violative product "is not likely to cause adverse health consequences."[318] Class III recalls generally are conducted to the wholesale level.[319]

Effectiveness checks range from level A, constituting 100 percent of the total number of consignees to be contacted, to level E, which requires no effectiveness check.[320] FDA permits the use of personal visits, telephone calls, letters, or a combination of these methods, and ordinarily permits the recalling firm itself to do the effectiveness checks.[321]

As noted earlier, the Safe Medical Devices Act of 1990, by amending section 518 of the FDCA, granted FDA authority to order a recall where "there is a reasonable probability

---

[308] *See* FDA, Enforcement Report Index, http://www.fda.gov/Safety/Recalls/EnforcementReports/default.htm.

[309] 21 C.F.R. §§ 7.42(b)(2), 7.50 (2010). In addition to listing of the recall in the *FDA Enforcement Reports*, for recalls of human or pet food FDAAA § 1003 specifically requires FDA to "use existing networks of communication, including electronic forms of information dissemination, to enhance the quality and speed of communication with the public" and to post recall information on FDA's website as part of a searchable database that can be readily accessed and understood by the public. 21 U.S.C. § 2103. Section 206(a) of the Food Safety Modernization Act, moreover, requires FDA to "ensure that a press release is published" regarding a food recall, and to issue "alerts and public notices, as appropriate," to ensure that consumers and retailers are aware of the recall and understand the risks associated with the recalled product. 21 U.S.C. § 350l(g). If one is available, FDA is also required to publish on its website a picture of the recalled product. *Id.*

[310] 21 C.F.R. §§ 7.40-7.59 (2014).

[311] *Id.* § 7.3(m).

[312] *Id.* § 7.41.

[313] *Id.* § 7.3(m)(1).

[314] *See id.* § 7.42(b)(1).

[315] *See id.* § 7.42(b)(2).

[316] *Id.* § 7.3(m)(2).

[317] *See id.* § 7.42(b)(1).

[318] *Id.* § 7.3(m)(3).

[319] *See id.* § 7.42(b)(1).

[320] *Id.* § 7.42(b)(3)(i), (v).

[321] *Id.* § 7.42(b)(3).

that a device intended for human use would cause serious, adverse health consequences or death."[322] The order may be issued after an informal hearing. No recall order is issued until FDA first has notified the manufacturer, distributors, and retailers to cease distribution of the device, and has instructed the manufacturer to notify health professionals and device users to cease use of it. Once a recall order is issued, it does not apply to devices held by individuals or to devices in the possession of facilities where the risk of recalling a device presents a greater risk than not recalling it.[323] Although FDA has this authority, it rarely uses it; most device recalls are voluntary. The FSPTCA granted FDA similar authority and utilizes similar procedures for mandatory recalls of tobacco products.[324]

Finally, FSMA grants FDA authority to require a recall where "there is a reasonable probability that an article of food (other than infant formula) is adulterated . . . or misbranded . . . and the use of or exposure to such article will cause serious adverse health consequences or death to humans or animals," and the manufacturer refuses to initiate a recall voluntarily.[325] As under the device and tobacco provisions, FDA is required to provide the manufacturer with an informal hearing before issuing the recall order.[326]

The Power of Publicity

The publicity provisions in the recall regulations are only a small portion of FDA's powers under section 705 of the FDCA,[327] which affords FDA various publicity options. FDA not only issues public notices of health hazards associated with violative products during a recall; it also regularly issues press releases and *FDA Enforcement Reports*, holds press conferences, testifies at congressional hearings, and sends representatives to comment before the national media on current issues.

Section 705 provides that FDA shall cause "to be published from time to time reports summarizing all judgments, decrees, and court orders,"[328] and that the agency shall disseminate "information regarding food, drugs, devices, or cosmetics in situations involving, in the opinion of [FDA], imminent danger to health, or gross deception of the consumer."[329] FDA has issued press releases and televised warnings when products have been discovered to present a previously unknown risk of death or other serious harm. The ban on ephedra, an ingredient in dietary supplements, is exemplary. Following the publication of several studies suggesting that consumption of ephedra may be associated with serious adverse events, FDA, on December 30, 2003, issued a Consumer Alert to warn the public about the deleterious effects of consuming dietary supplements containing ephedra. According to the alert "[c]onsumers are urged to stop buying and using these products immediately."[330] At

---

322   See *supra* note 292.
323   FDCA § 518(e)(2)(B), 21 U.S.C. § 360h(e)(2)(B).
324   FDCA § 908(c), 21 U.S.C. § 387h(c).
325   FDCA § 423, 21 U.S.C. § 350l.
326   FDCA § 423(c), 21 U.S.C. § 350l(c).
327   FDCA § 705, 21 U.S.C. § 375.
328   FDCA § 705(a), 21 U.S.C. § 375(a).
329   FDCA § 705(b), 21 U.S.C. § 375(b).
330   Consumer Alert, FDA Plans Regulation Prohibiting Sale of Ephedra-Containing Dietary Supplements and Advises Consumers to Stop Using These Products (Dec. 30, 2003).

the same time that FDA issued this alert, it notified dietary supplement manufacturers of its intent to issue a final rule prohibiting the sale of ephedra.[331]

Similarly, when a large number of L-tryptophan-induced cases of *eosinophilia myalgia* surfaced, FDA was most effective not only in instigating recalls[332] but also in stopping sales of the product almost immediately through the use of widespread national publicity in print and on television.[333]

In the case of a batch of Chilean grapes that allegedly had been found to contain cyanide, FDA mounted a major consumer publicity campaign, and virtually stopped the importation of Chilean fruit for a period long enough for the agency to establish a meaningful sampling procedure.[334]

In 2009, FDA issued a public warning regarding serious adverse events associated with Hydroxycut, a weight loss supplement manufactured by Iovate Health Sciences.[335] The warning reported that FDA had received 23 reports of serious health problems associated with Hydroxycut.[336] In connection with FDA's public warning to consumers, Iovate agreed to recall all Hydroxycut products from the market.[337]

Even where public health is not an issue *per se*, FDA may use widespread publicity to signal a new enforcement posture in order to elicit voluntary industry compliance. A classic example was FDA's seizure of Procter and Gamble's product, Citrus Hill Orange Juice, on the ground that its use of the term "fresh" rendered the pasteurized juice misbranded.[338] As an unusually dramatic enforcement action taken against a major manufacturer, the seizure garnered substantial media attention, and prompted many to take note of FDA's willingness to enforce the FDCA aggressively.[339]

The means of publicity, as well as the publicity, itself, can sometimes be negotiated with FDA. If the agency determines that there is an imminent risk of a public health disaster, however, it may not consult with industry before issuing a public announcement. FDA also has participated in joint publicity efforts, such as that involving the manufacturer of Tylenol®.[340] Many large pharmaceutical manufacturers have prepared emergency publicity

---

[331]   *Id.* The final rule is at 21 C.F.R. § 119.1 (2014).

[332]   Malcolm Gladwell, *FDA Recalls Products Based on L-Tryptophan*, WASH. POST, Mar. 23, 1990, at A8.

[333]   *See, e.g., FDA Warns Against L-Tryptophan Use While It Investigates Illnesses*, L.A. TIMES, Nov. 12, 1989, at 4; *U.S. Officials Issue Warning to Users of Diet Supplement*, N.Y. TIMES, Nov. 14, 1989, at C16.

[334]   A later evaluation of the episode in the wake of industry complaints found that FDA had acted responsibly and promptly. GAO, GAO-HRD-90-164 Food Tampering: FDA's ACTIONS ON CHILEAN FRUIT BASED ON SOUND EVIDENCE (1990), *available at* http://www.gao.gov/assets/220/213116.pdf.

[335]   *See* FDA, FDA Warns Consumers to Stop Using Hydroxycut Products, FDA News Release (May 1, 2009), available ai http://www.fda.gov/NewsEvents/Newsroom/PressAnnouncements/ucm149575.htm.

[336]   *Id.*

[337]   *Id.*

[338]   George Gunset, *U.S. Raiders Put Squeeze on P&G in Juice-Labeling Dispute*, CHI. TRIB., Apr. 25, 1991, at 1; Warren Leary, *Citing Labels, U.S. Seizes Orange Juice*, N.Y. TIMES, Apr. 25, 1991, at A18.

[339]   *See, e.g.,* Stuart Elliott, *FDA Puts Squeeze on Food Label Claims*, USA TODAY, April 26, 1991, at 1A; Malcolm Gladwell, *FDA Aggressively Expanding Its Role*, S.F. CHRON., May 8, 1991, at B6.

[340]   Michael Waldholz, *Tainted Tylenol Found in 2 More Bottles in New York; Nationwide Alert Issued*, WALL ST. J., Feb. 14, 1986; *see also* Robert D. McFadden, *Poison Deaths Bring U.S. Warning on Tylenol Use*, N.Y. TIMES, Oct. 2, 1982, at 1.

procedures, to be implemented in conjunction with FDA in the event of a tampering-type incident.

FDA's power to conduct long-term publicity campaigns through press releases, seminars, and public announcements has been challenged as an "unlawful interference" with the business rights of regulated firms. In *Ajay Nutrition Foods, Inc. v. FDA*,[341] this challenge, premised on FDA's characterization of health food industry participants as "quacks" and "faddists," was dismissed.[342] The court adverted, *inter alia*, to FDA's duty under section 705 to disseminate information to the public.[343]

Enforcement Against the Product: Seizures
The Seizure Remedy in General

The civil remedy provided in section 304 of the FDCA[344] is a powerful one. The outcome of a successful seizure action is a judicial condemnation of the goods at issue and either the destruction of the goods at issue or a reconditioning procedure supervised by FDA pursuant to a court order.[345] A company that seeks to recondition its condemned goods must post a bond and subject itself to judicial and FDA discretion as to whether the company's reconditioning proposal is reasonable.[346] Section 304(d)(1) permits re-exportation of a seized article if it became adulterated or misbranded *before* it was imported, was imported in good faith by the claimant, and meets the general conditions of section 801(e) of the act for export.[347]

FDA may initiate a seizure proceeding under section 304 to have U.S. marshals or other employees of the U.S. government seize any adulterated or misbranded food, drug, device, cosmetic, or tobacco product that is in violation of section 404 (relating to emergency permit control),[348] and any new drug that lacks a required approval under section 505,[349] where the FDCA test for interstate commerce is satisfied.[350] Section 304(g) and (h) also permit FDA to detain medical devices, tobacco products, and foods in certain circumstances for 20 to 30 days (prior to a seizure pursuant to judicial process).[351] Section 304 does not provide for pre-seizure detention of drugs. Most states, however, provide for an embargo without resort to court action in the case of potentially adulterated products, including drugs, foods, dietary

---

[341] 378 F. Supp. 210 (D.N.J.), *aff'd*, 513 F.2d 625 (3d Cir. 1975).

[342] *Id.* at 218-19.

[343] *Id.* at 217-18.

[344] 21 U.S.C. § 334.

[345] FDCA § 304(d)(1), 21 U.S.C. § 334(d)(1).

[346] United States v...Article of Drug [Copanos], Food Drug Cosm. L. Rep. (CCH) ¶ 38,112 (W.D. Mo. 1989). FDA can require destruction of imported violative goods, even if they were never released by Customs. United States v. 2,988 Cases..., 64 F.3d 984, 988-89 (5th Cir. 1995).

[347] 21 U.S.C. § 334(d)(1). *See also* RPM, *supra* note 221, ch. 9, § 9-14 "Priority Enforcement Strategy for Problem Importers."

[348] 21 U.S.C. § 344.

[349] 21 U.S.C. § 355.

[350] Pursuant to amendments to supplemental rules effective December 1, 1991, any U.S. officer or employee authorized to enforce a warrant, not just a marshal, is permitted to execute the order of attachment that effectuates a seizure. Fed. R. Civ. P., Supp. R. for CERTAIN ADM. AND MARITIME CLAIMS C(3)(b)(ii).

[351] 21 U.S.C. § 334(g), (h).

supplements and cosmetics.[352] Thus, FDA often seeks the cooperation of state agencies in imposing an embargo while it pursues its judicial seizure remedy.

FDA's RPM sets forth in detail the procedural requirements for the issuance of an FDA referral to DOJ for a seizure action.[353] Seizures usually are instituted by means of a recommendation letter sent by an FDA District Office to the U.S. Attorney for the district where the articles are to be seized, after the recommendation has been reviewed by the FDA Center with responsibility for the product, the Division of Compliance Management and Operations, and the OCC at FDA headquarters.[354] Generally, seizures are not brought against out-of-compliance articles that "could have been easily corrected by the owner without litigation."[355]

A seizure action is filed against the goods that are claimed to be violative rather than against a company or individual. Thus, the title of a case will be of the form "*United States v. 200 Cases…-[Brand]*." Because the seizure action is filed against property, it is an *in rem* action, which is subject to the Federal Rules of Admiralty, found as the "Supplemental Rules for Certain Admiralty and Maritime Claims" appended to the *Federal Rules of Civil Procedure*.[356]

The procedure for the institution and prosecution of a seizure case differs slightly from that for other federal civil cases.[357] The government must file a Verified Complaint and seek an order from the court authorizing the process of attachment (i.e., an order for arrest of the *res*, or property).[358] Once a court issues the order, it is delivered to the clerk, who prepares a warrant for delivery to the U.S. marshal or other U.S. government employee. The marshal, in turn, executes the order by going to the location of the property to be seized, affixing a copy of the order to a conspicuous place on the property, and leaving a copy of the complaint with the person having possession of the property.[359] It is common for companies to be confronted with more than one U.S. marshal and an FDA district compliance officer, who arrive to execute the seizure warrant. Efforts to hide the goods subject to the seizure may be met with personal arrest by the U.S. marshal for obstruction of justice or contempt of court for disobedience of a lawful order.

Once a product has been seized, the government must provide to persons who reasonably appear to be potential claimants direct notice of the need to file in court a claim to the property.[360] Public notice is also generally required to alert other persons who might

---

[352]   *See, e.g.*, MS Code § 75-29-27 (2013) (providing for the embargo of adulterated or misbranded food).

[353]   RPM, *supra* note 221, ch. 6, § 6-1 "Seizure."

[354]   *Id.* §§ 6-1-7, "Methods of Recommending Seizure," 6-1-9, "Action on Seizure Recommendations."

[355]   *Id.* § 6-1-2, "General Guidelines for Seizures."

[356]   FED. R. CIV. P., SUPP. R. A.; FDCA § 304(b), 21 U.S.C. § 334(b). (The Admirality Rules provide a well-established jurisprudence of *in rem* actions originally relating to ships.)

[357]   The Federal Rules of Civil Procedure include supplemental rules for admiralty or maritime claims and asset forfeiture actions. On December 1, 2006, a new supplemental rule took effect (Rule G); it governs "forfeiture action[s] in rem arising from a federal statute." FED. R. CIV. P. SUPP. R. G. Since Rule G took effect, several seizure complaints brought by U.S. Attorneys' Offices have cited Rule G as governing seizure actions under FDCA § 304. *See, e.g.*, Verified Complaint, United States v. An Undetermined Quantity of Variously Labeled Cases, No. 3:07CV05388 (N.D. Cal. Oct. 22, 2007); Verified Complaint, United States v. Articles of Drug in the Possession of Charron Nutrition, No. 4:07CV365 (N.D. Fla. Aug. 23, 2007); Verified Complaint, United States v. Undetermined Quantities of Boxes of Articles, No. 2:07CV1769 (D.N.J. Apr. 16, 2007).

[358]   FED. R. CIV. P. SUPP. R. G(2), (3)(b).

[359]   *Id.* E(4).

[360]   *Id.* G(4).

have an interest in the property of the need to file a claim to it.[361] Normally, this notice is published in local newspapers "generally circulated in the district" or posted on an official Internet government forfeiture site for at least 30 consecutive days.[362] The costs of such notice are borne ultimately by an unsuccessful claimant.[363] Notice must also be provided "to any person who reasonably appears to be a potential claimant on the facts known to the government."[364] If no person claims the property, or if a seizure action is contested and lost by the claimant, then FDA is authorized, pursuant to instructions of the court, to destroy or sell the property at issue.[365]

Those wishing to challenge a seizure must file a claim to the seized property.[366] The claim must be filed within 30 to 60 days after publication of the notice, depending upon the notification method. An answer must be served within 21 days after the filing of the claim.[367] A failure to file a timely claim or answer can, and often does, lead to a default.[368]

Some parties have attempted to withdraw their claim after the case has proceeded past the joinder of issue, either to avoid imposition of costs or to prevent entry of an injunction if FDA amends its complaint to add an *in personam* claim for injunction. Case law supports FDA's position that the agency is entitled to a full adjudication once a claim has been filed, and that no withdrawal is permitted.[369]

Once an answer has been filed, the *Federal Rules of Civil Procedure* apply, and the seizure action is treated as if it were an injunction proceeding.[370] FDA usually seeks an injunction against the claimant in contested seizure cases. For this reason, some companies decide not to contest certain seizure actions. The judgment entered in an uncontested seizure action is against the seized *res*, and not against other units of the product or against the company that could have claimed it. A potential claimant can thus avoid a decision that would have *res judicata* effect in the same and other jurisdictions by choosing to default in one jurisdiction and await a possible seizure action in a more favorable forum.

Where a seizure is contested, even if FDA does not seek an injunction in the seizure case itself, the agency takes the position that a successfully litigated seizure action operates as

---

[361]   *Id.*

[362]   *Id.*

[363]   28 U.S.C. § 1921. In order to find a claimant, the government is required to publish a notice of the seizure in publications "reasonably calculated to notify potential claimants of the action." *Id.* Litigants may dispute whether the government has exceeded its mandate and incurred excessive costs by placing notices in expensive daily newspapers when a trade press listing, or even a telephone call, would have sufficed.

[364]   FED. R. CIV. P. SUPP. R. G(4)(b).

[365]   FDCA § 304(d)(1), 21 U.S.C. § 334(d)(1).

[366]   FED. R. CIV. P. SUPP. R. G(5). Generally, there is no release of the seized goods *pendente lite* under bond. United States v. 893 One-Gallon Cans…Labeled Brown's Inhalant, 45 F. Supp. 467 (D. Del. 1942).

[367]   FED. R. CIV. P. SUPP. R. G(5)(b).

[368]   *See, e.g.,* United States v. An Article of Drug…"Wilfley's Bio Water," Civ. No. 88-1482-FR, 1989 U.S. Dist. LEXIS 12833, at *4 (D. Or. Oct. 20, 1989).

[369]   *See, e.g.,* United States v. Articles of Drug…Penapar VK, 458 F. Supp. 687 (D. Md. 1978); United States v. 4 Cases of 12 Packages, More or Less, Etc., Notices of Judgment Under the Federal Food, Drug, and Cosmetic Act, FDA Papers No. 33 (Feb. 1968) *reprinted* in FEDERAL FOOD, DRUG, AND COSMETIC ACT JUDICIAL RECORD 1965-1968, at 45 (Vincent A. Kleinfeld & Alan H. Kaplan, eds.) (FDLI 1973).

[370]   United States v. Nysco Labs., Inc., 215 F. Supp. 87, 89 (E.D.N.Y. 1963), *aff'd*, 318 F.2d 817 (2d Cir. 1963); United States v. An Article… Sudden Change, 36 F.R.D. 695, 698-99 (E.D.N.Y. 1965).

res judicata in any subsequent proceeding for an injunction against the company that filed the claim.[371] The Fifth Circuit has held that the *res judicata* effect can run either way: it benefits the prevailing party in the seizure action, whether FDA or a claimant.[372] Because the proceeding is *in rem*, the destruction of the seized *res* renders any further proceedings (including appellate proceedings) moot.[373] Therefore, to obtain appellate review, a claimant that loses in the district court needs to obtain a stay of destruction of the *res*.

Seizure cases are often resolved by a strongly worded consent injunction, with FDA supervising any reconditioning of the products or their destruction.[374] The claimant pays the costs of FDA supervision, and generally posts a bond to ensure that the goods are kept intact until they have been reconditioned.[375]

As seen in the accompanying table, the number of seizure actions has dramatically decreased in recent years. This decline may be attributable to a combination of FDA initiating recalls in lieu of seizures, FDA's increased workload, the effective use of publicity, tightened and earmarked food enforcement, and budgetary limitations.[376]

Number of FDA Seizure Actions 1991-1993 and 2004-2013

Year	Seizures
1991	168
1992	183
1993	117
2004	10

---

[371] *See* United States v. All Articles of Drug...Labeled as Containing L-Tyrosine, 242 F. Supp. 2d 617, 620-21 (D. Minn. 2002) (describing arguments that the government is entitled to a judgment having *res judicata* effect once a claimant has voluntarily submitted to the court's *in personam* jurisdiction in a seizure action).

[372] United States v. An Article of Drug...[Neoterramycin], 725 F.2d 976, 984 (5th Cir. 1984). *But see* United States v. All Articles of Drug...Labeled as Containing L-Tyrosine, 242 F. Supp. 2d at 620-21 (permitting a claimant to withdraw from a seizure action after the government had moved for summary judgment on the ground that the contested articles were unapproved new drugs, despite the government's arguments that it was entitled to a judgment with *res judicata* effect).

[373] United States v. 3 Unlabeled 25-Pound Bags [of] Dried Mushrooms, 157 F.2d 722 (7th Cir. 1946).

[374] *See, e.g.*, Consent Order, United States v. Undetermined Quantities ... of Device, No. 07-CV-1769 (D.N.J. June 22, 2007); Consent Decree of Condemnation and Permanent Injunction, United States v. 7,140 Boxes ... of an Article of Device, No. 05-C-5852 (N.D. Ill. June 29, 2006); Consent Decree of Condemnation and Permanent Injunction, United States v. Undetermined Quantities of ... Drug, No. 5:05-CV-141 (E.D.N.C. May 5, 2005); Consent Decree of Condemnation and Permanent Injunction, United States v. Various Articles of Drug, No. 3:00-CV-00359 (E.D. Tenn. Oct. 4, 2000).

[375] FDCA § 304(d)(1), 21 U.S.C. § 334(d)(1). One court has permitted the government to reclaim even the costs of a state agency where the federal government requested the state's assistance in immediately stopping the sale of adulterated shrimp. United States v. 489 Cases [of] Shrimp, 154 F.3d 1261, 1261 (11th Cir. 1998).

[376] Science and Technology Subcommittee of the FDA Science Board, *FDA Science and Mission at Risk*, B-22 (Nov. 2007).

2005	20
2006	17
2007	6
2008	8
2009	6
2010	10
2011	15
2012	8
2013	6

Multiple and Mass Seizures

The FDCA permits FDA to initiate seizure actions simultaneously in multiple jurisdictions against different lots of the same product.[377] These "multiple seizures" are available to FDA as to products that the agency alleges are adulterated or lack a statutorily required approval.[378] Multiple seizures are also available against an allegedly misbranded product, but only if it: 1) has been the subject of a prior court judgment, 2) poses a danger to health, or 3) bears labeling that is "fraudulent, or would be in a material respect misleading to the injury or damage of the purchaser."[379]

If FDA files multiple seizures, section 304(b) of the act permits the claimant to choose, from among the jurisdictions in which the seizure actions have been filed, the jurisdiction where the proceedings will be consolidated.[380] No matter what convenience factors militate in favor of the government's retention of the case in another jurisdiction, venue is placed in a district chosen by the claimant that is within "reasonable proximity to claimant's principal place of business."[381]

The multiple-seizure remedy is a powerful tool for FDA, and is utilized when an effective nationwide cessation of sales is needed quickly and an adequate recall is not forthcoming. Because of the devastating impact of multiple seizures, a number of constitutional challenges were made to the statutory scheme. They culminated in the Supreme Court's decision in *Ewing v. Mytinger & Casselberry, Inc.*[382] Units of a dietary supplement were seized in a number of jurisdictions throughout the country due to misbranding caused by health claims for

---

[377]   FDCA § 304(a), 21 U.S.C. § 334(a).
[378]   *Id.*
[379]   *Id.*
[380]   FDCA § 304(b), 21 U.S.C. § 334(b).
[381]   FDCA § 304(a), 21 U.S.C. § 334(a).
[382]   339 U.S. 594 (1950).

the supplement. The Court held that the opportunity afforded a claimant to appear and have a full judicial hearing after the seizures satisfied the Due Process Clause of the Fifth Amendment.[383] As long as "there is at some stage an opportunity for a hearing and a judicial determination," a party's constitutional rights are protected.[384]

Another enforcement option that may have enormous consequences is a mass seizure, usually filed pursuant to the adulteration provisions of sections 402(a)(4) or 501(a)(2)(B) of the FDCA.[385] Those sections provide that food will be deemed to be adulterated if it has been prepared or held under "insanitary conditions," and that drugs will be deemed adulterated if the process for manufacturing them did not conform to cGMP. An entire warehouse may be shut down in such a case, on the ground that general unsanitary conditions or failures to conform to cGMP render every article in the facility potentially filthy or otherwise violative.

Procedural Limitations of the Seizure Remedy

Although seizures continue to be a very effective enforcement tool for FDA, the inherent problem with this procedure is that a company is free to sell its products in other jurisdictions even after a condemnation of the seized *res* occurs in the district where FDA brought the case. In addition, there have been instances where companies have obtained stays of enforcement of a judgment for condemnation pending appeal,[386] thus permitting the continued sale of an allegedly misbranded or adulterated product for years without penalty.

Another limitation of the seizure remedy is that the products condemned under a final judgment must be reasonably within the scope of the initial seizure order. In a case where the government seized approximately $680,000 worth of pharmaceuticals, the claimant sought release of two-thirds of the drugs (intermediates) on the ground that they were not intended for use in the manufacture of the finished drug products that were the subject of the seizure order.[387] The district court held that the intermediate drug products at issue were both perishable and capable of being utilized in other, lawfully marketed drugs. Accordingly, it released those products from the seizure order.[388] After FDA filed a follow-up injunction action, the Seventh Circuit enjoined the sale of the intermediate products.[389]

Civil Enforcement Against the Company: Injunctions

For FDA "[i]njunctions with temporary restraining orders have the highest priority ranking of all legal actions."[390] Injunctions are authorized by section 302 of the FDCA,[391] and are utilized to enjoin conduct where there is a likelihood that violations will continue or recur.[392] Unlike a private plaintiff in an injunction action, FDA need not prove that there will be

---

[383]   *Id.* at 599.
[384]   *Id.*
[385]   21 U.S.C. §§ 342(a)(4), 351(a)(2)(B).
[386]   *See, e.g.,* United States v. Sandoz Pharm. Corp., 894 F.2d 825, 826 (6th Cir. 1990); United States v. 225 Cartons ... "Fiorinal with Codeine," 687 F. Supp. 946 (D.N.J. 1988), *aff'd,* 871 F.2d 409 (3d Cir. 1989).
[387]   United States v. Undetermined Quantities of Drugs ... [Travenol Labs.], 675 F. Supp. 1113 (N.D. Ill. 1987).
[388]   *Id.* at 1117.
[389]   United States v. Baxter Healthcare Corp., 901 F.2d 1401 (7th Cir. 1990).
[390]   RPM, *supra* note 221, § 6-2-6.
[391]   21 U.S.C. § 332.
[392]   RPM, *supra* note 221, § 6-2-4.

"irreparable injury,"[393] but merely that there has been violative conduct by the defendant(s), and that, in the absence of an injunction, such conduct is likely to continue or recur.[394] Many FDA injunctions are consent decrees negotiated by FDA, DOJ, and the company and individuals involved (FDA almost always names individual corporate officers in injunctive actions), and then approved by the court where FDA's complaint and the consent decree are filed.

Injunctions under the FDCA may be entered against both corporations and individuals,[395] and they can range from a prohibition on the introduction of new products with specified ingredients[396] to the shutdown of a business until FDA is satisfied that it has been brought into compliance.[397]

The injunction remedy generally is utilized by FDA where: 1) "[t]here is a current and definite health hazard or a gross consumer deception, requiring immediate action," 2) "[t]here are significant amounts of violative products owned by the same person in many locations … and seizures are impractical or uneconomical," or 3) there have been chronic violations that have not been corrected voluntarily by the company.[398]

The only practical limitation on the scope of an injunction is that it must properly delimit the acts enjoined. Thus, for example, an injunction issued against the sale of "drug products identical or similar to those described in [the complaint]" was remanded for greater specificity so as not to preclude the defendant from properly marketing other products that might be subject to a shifting interpretation by FDA of the word "similar."[399]

In an injunction case involving violations of FDA's cGMP regulations, a company's operations typically will be shut down pending rehabilitation procedures ultimately reviewed by FDA.[400] The company is required to bring its manufacturing practices into compliance, to relabel improperly labeled products, to destroy adulterated or outdated ingredients or products, to revise standard operating procedures, to remedy unsanitary conditions, and to produce for introduction into interstate commerce only products that satisfy the terms

---

[393]   United States v. Diapulse Corp., 457 F.2d 25, 28 (2d Cir. 1972).

[394]   United States v. W.T. Grant Co., 345 U.S. 629, 633 (1953). Although courts recognize that, for a preliminary injunction under FDCA § 302(a), the government may have a lesser burden of showing harm, the government must provide some evidence of harm to consumers from the alleged violative products. See United States v. Nutri-Cology, Inc., No. C-91-1332-DLJ, 1991 WL 1092506, at *1 (N.D. Cal. July 19, 1991) (refusing the government's request for injunctive relief where it could not demonstrate any harm to consumers despite nine years of investigation, and where defendants had made extensive showings supporting the merits and reliability of their products).

[395]   United States v. Blue Ribbon Smoked Fish, Inc., 179 F. Supp. 2d 30, 41 (E.D.N.Y. 2001) (rejecting, in a case of alleged FDCA violations, the argument that it was unnecessary to enjoin corporate officers when FDA also sought an injunction against the corporation).

[396]   See, e.g., United States v. Articles of Drug…Midwest Pharms., Inc., 825 F.2d 1238, 1247-48 (8th Cir. 1987).

[397]   See, e.g., United States v. Utah Med. Prods., Inc., 404 F. Supp. 2d 1315 (D. Utah 2005); United States v. Lit Drug Co., 333 F. Supp. 990 (D.N.J. 1971). FDA has, on occasion, been denied requests for injunctive relief where a company has demonstrated adequate safeguards to prevent future violations. See, e.g., United States v. Flea-Tabs, Inc., Food Drug Cosm. L. Rep. (CCH) ¶ 38,123 (C.D. Cal. 1981); United States v. Sars of Louisiana, Inc., 324 F. Supp. 307 (E.D. La. 1971).

[398]   RPM, supra note 221, § 6-2-4.

[399]   Midwest Pharms., Inc., 825 F.2d at 1247.

[400]   See, e.g., Lit Drug Co., 333 F. Supp. at 990.

of the injunction.[401] Commonly, an injunction will require certification by an independent expert that the defendant is in compliance before FDA will conduct an inspection to confirm compliance.[402]

Since 1990, FDA has turned to draconian consent decrees to address many of the pharmaceutical manufacturing deficiencies that were uncovered in the wake of the generic drug criminal investigations. *Barr Laboratories*[403] is the most exhaustive judicial decision analyzing FDA's cGMP authority. Although the decision's underlying premise—that a judge is a qualified party to determine extra-statutory manufacturing standards—is questionable, FDA has utilized this decision in extracting strong decree language in subsequent enforcement actions.[404] On the basis of the strength of this favorable decision and the absence of any contrary judicial pronouncements, FDA has taken strong positions in negotiating subsequent decrees. Although many courts have been deferential to FDA in its efforts to enjoin alleged FDCA violations, at least one court has required FDA to demonstrate that the firm to be enjoined is currently violating the applicable cGMP regulations.[405]

Two of the more prominent decrees were entered against reputable pioneer drug and device companies. Six Warner-Lambert facilities were closed until compliance with cGMP was demonstrated; product certifications by outside consultants were required; and $25,000 was assessed in contempt penalties for noncompliance by the company and responsible individuals.[406] In the *Siemens* medical device decree, three plants were shut down until cGMP compliance was demonstrated; the company also had to certify the cGMP compliance of foreign manufacturers of components for its products.[407]

The government's authority to require disgorgement as part of a consent decree has raised significant controversy.[408] Over the last decade, cGMP consent decrees have included

---

[401] *See, e.g., id.* at 997-99. The RPM contains a number of model injunction provisions that provide not only for assay and supervision methodology, but also specify that all costs for the supervision will be borne by the defendant pursuant to preset schedules of charges. RPM, *supra* note 221, §§ 6-2-15 and 6-2-16.

[402] *See, e.g.,* Consent Order, United States v. Undetermined Quantities ... of Device, No. 07-CV-1769 (D.N.J. June 22, 2007); Consent Decree of Condemnation and Permanent Injunction, United States v. 7,140 Boxes ... of an Article of Device, No. 05-C-5852 (N.D. Ill. June 29, 2006).

[403] United States v. Barr Labs., Inc., 812 F. Supp. 458 (D.N.J. 1993).

[404] Since the beginning of the new millennium, consent decrees have involved a variety of very strict provisions. *See, e.g.,* Consent Decree of Condemnation and Permanent Injunction, United States v. Undetermined Quantities of ... Drug, No. 5:05-CV-141 (E.D.N.C. May 5, 2005) (assessing "liquidated damages" for each day GlaxoSmithKline is late in achieving a specified milestone for a corrective action); Consent Decree of Condemnation and Permanent Injunction, United States v. Schering-Plough Corp., No. 2:02-CV-02397 (JAP) (D.N.J. May 20, 2002) (requiring annual inspections by outside experts); Consent Decree of Condemnation and Permanent Injunction, United States v. Various Articles of Drug, No. 3:00-CV-00359 (E.D. Tenn. Oct. 4, 2000) (imposing specific reporting obligations on Wyeth-Ayerst Labs' management).

[405] United States v. Utah Med. Prods., Inc., 404 F. Supp. 2d 1315, 1324 (D. Utah 2005) (holding that "whatever modest deviations from *regulations* may have occurred in times past no longer exist at present ... [so that it] makes no sense for the court to order Utah Medical to do something they are already doing").

[406] United States v. Warner-Lambert Co., Civ. No. 93-3525 (D.N.J. 1993).

[407] United States v. Siemens Med. Sys., Inc., Civ. No. 940-912 (D.N.J. 1994).

[408] *Compare* Eric M. Blumberg, Universal Management, Abbott, Wyeth, Schering-Plough, *and ...: Restitution and Disgorgement Find Another Home at the Food and Drug Administration,* 58 FOOD & DRUG L.J. 169 (2003) (arguing that the courts must presume that they have authority to grant equitable relief unless expressly forbidden by statute), *with* Jeffrey N. Gibbs & John R. Fleder, *Can FDA Seek Restitution or Disgorgement?,* 58 Food & Drug L.J. 129 (2003) (arguing that fundamental canons of statutory construction strongly suggest that FDA lacks authority to seek disgorgement of profits or restitution in court actions), *and* William W.

provisions calling for disgorgement of profits.[409] Courts have largely upheld FDA's authority to seek such equitable remedies.[410] Despite these decisions, questions remain about whether routine use of these remedies represents sound public policy, and whether FDA has the authority to seek other forms of relief in consent decrees, such as "liquidated damages" for each day a company fails to meet a milestone for a required corrective action.[411]

Import/Export Powers

The Herculean task of protecting U.S. citizens from the importation of drugs, medical devices, biologics, foods, cosmetics, and tobacco products that are unapproved, adulterated, or misbranded is placed on FDA through the enforcement powers conferred in sections 801 and 802 of the FDCA.[412] Section 801 covers both imports and exports, and provides to FDA and to the U.S. Customs Service in the U.S. Department of the Treasury (superseded by CBP in the Department of Homeland Security) the power to sample, detain, refuse admission to, and ultimately destroy, products pending their importation into domestic commerce. Section 802 was enacted to regulate the export of unapproved products manufactured or held in U.S. commerce. Unapproved drugs, biologics, and devices must meet a number of stringent conditions for FDA to permit them to be exported.

Pursuant to an MOU with CBP, FDA district offices handle most of the procedural aspects of such imports.[413] FDA utilizes the Operational and Administrative System for Import Support (OASIS) to make admissibility determinations.[414] OASIS generates a "Notice of FDA Action," which provides specific information on the actions taken (e.g., sample collected, intended for sampling, detained, released, refused entry).[415]

Pursuant to the Bioterrorism Act of 2002, food importers must provide FDA with electronic prior notice that includes the identification of the article to be imported, the manufacturer or grower, the shipper, arrival information, and country of origin.[416] An article of food may be

---

Vodra & Arthur N. Levine, *Anchors Away: The Food and Drug Administration's Use of Disgorgement Abandons Legal Moorings*, 59 FOOD & DRUG L.J. 1 (2004) (arguing that FDA's use of disgorgement departs significantly from precedents defining the remedy).

[409]   United States v. Terumo Cardiovascular Systems Corp., Civil No. 11-11179 (E.D. Mich. Mar. 29, 2011) (providing for $35 million in disgorgement); United States v. Genzyme, 1:10-CV-10865 (D. Mass May 24, 2010) (providing for $175 million in disgorgement); United States v. Eli Lilly & Co., No. 1:05-CV-1884 (S.D. Ind. Feb. 10, 2006) (providing for $24 million in equitable disgorgement); United States v. Schering-Plough Corp., No. 2:02-CV-02397 (JAP) (D.N.J. May 20, 2002) (providing for $500 million in equitable disgorgement); United States v. Wyeth-Ayerst Labs., No. 3:00-CV-00359 (E.D. Tenn. Oct. 3, 2000) (providing for $30 million in equitable disgorgement).

[410]   *See* United States v. Rx Depot, Inc., 438 F.3d 1052, 1061 (10th Cir. 2006) (disgorgement), United States v. Lane Labs-USA Inc., 427 F.3d 219, 235 (3d Cir. 2005) (restitution); United States v. Universal Mgmt. Servs., Inc., 191 F.3d 750, 759 (6th Cir. 1999) (restitution).

[411]   *See* Richard M. Cooper, *The Need for Oversight of Agency Policies for Settling Enforcement Actions*, 59 ADMIN. L. REV. 835 (2007).

[412]   21 U.S.C. §§ 381, 382.

[413]   MOU 225-79-4003; Import Sampling; Memorandum of Understanding With the Customs Service, 44 Fed. Reg. 53,577 (Sept. 14, 1979).

[414]   RPM, *supra* note 221, § 9-1, "Import Procedures."

[415]   *Id.*

[416]   Pub L. No. 107-188, 116 Stat. 672 (2002); FDCA § 801(m), 21 U.S.C. § 381(m); 21 C.F.R. §§ 1.279, 1.281 (2010).

refused entry for lack of prior notice.[417] Pursuant to an MOU with CBP, FDA may commission CBP officers to assist with the implementation of the prior-notice requirements.[418]

If FDA finds that a product is in violation of the FDCA or any other law under its jurisdiction, it states "Detained" on the Notice of FDA Action in OASIS. This designation satisfies the requirement to provide notice to the owner or consignee of the right to a hearing on the detention.[419] The hearing is generally held within 10 days, or such other time as agreed by the agency. The "hearing" may take the form of telephone calls or letters of protest, which are then considered by FDA before further action is taken.

If a product has been refused entry, minor reconditioning may be accomplished under section 801 to bring it into compliance for importation. An example is labeling that has relatively insignificant omissions that can be remedied by the addition of a sticker with the requisite information. FDA, however, generally will not permit the relabeling of a product that, by virtue of its original label claims, is an unapproved new drug.[420] If FDA refuses entry to a product, it may be exported under the conditions set forth in sections 801(a) and 802.[421] FDA often issues Import Alerts to identify problematic commodities, shippers, and importers, and to identify products that have met the criteria for automatic detention.[422]

Even with its broad powers to sample, detain, and refuse entry, the import burden on FDA is overwhelming. In response to rising concerns about FDA's oversight over imports both from Congress[423] and within FDA,[424] the agency has established several overseas offices in the past five years. These include offices in China, India, Costa Rica, Chile, and Belgium, Mexico, the United Kingdom, and South Africa.[425] The recent establishment of the Global Directorate in the Office of the Commissioner also signals FDA's realization that enhanced oversight of global supply chains is an important way improve the quality of FDA-regulated articles offered for entry into the United States.

Congress also enhanced FDA's authority over, and attention to, imported food in FSMA. Under FSMA, FDA is required to inspect at least 600 foreign facilities in 2011, 1,200 in 2012, 2,400 in 2013, and 4,800 in 2014. The agency is required to inspect at least 9,600 facilities in 2015, and 19,200 in 2016. Authorities added by the FSMA include: importer accountability (i.e., importers have an explicit responsibility to verify that their foreign suppliers have adequate preventive controls in place to ensure that the food they produce is safe); third-party certification (i.e., the establishment of a certification program to facilitate the entry of imports); certification for high-risk foods (i.e., the authority to require that

417 FDCA § 801(m)(1), 21 U.S.C. § 381(m)(1).
418 MOU 225-04-4001.
419 RPM, *supra* note 221, § 9-7; 21 C.F.R. § 1.94.
420 *Id.* § 9-10.
421 21 U.S.C. §§ 381(a), 382.
422 RPM, *supra* note 221, § 9-13, "Import Information Directives."
423 *Foreign Drug Inspections Would Be Funded by Registration Fees in Draft Bill*, F-D-C REP. ("The Pink Sheet"), Apr. 21, 2008, and *FDA's Price Tag For Foreign Facility Inspections Tops $225 Million*, F-D-C REP. ("The Pink Sheet"), May 5, 2008.
424 Testimony by Andrew C. von Eschenbach, M.D., April 22, 2008, FDA Actions to Improve Safety of Medical Products with Foreign Components, *available at* http://www.hhs.gov/asl/testify/2008/04/t20080422a.html.
425 *See* FDA, FDA's International Posts: Improving the Safety of Imported Food and Medical Products (2010), http://www.fda.gov/ForConsumers/ConsumerUpdates/ucm185769.htm.

high-risk imported foods be accompanied by a credible third-party certification or other assurance of compliance); the establishment of a voluntary qualified-importer program; and the authority to deny entry into the U.S. of food from a foreign facility if FDA is denied access by the facility or by the country in which the facility is located.[426] As of the date of publication of this book, FDA is in the process of implementing these requirements through rulemaking.[427]

In addition, Title VII of FDASIA provided FDA with two new enforcement tools to help manage the importation of drugs into the U.S. Section 708 of FDASIA amended section 801 of the FDCA to allow FDA to destroy unlawful drugs offered for import into the U.S. that are valued at under $2,500.[428] Until this amendment, all unlawful drug products refused entry by FDA could be re-exported by the importer as a matter of right unless FDA went to the trouble to formally seize them. Under the amendment, such drugs cannot be exported from the U.S. and then shipped to another port of entry in the U.S. in the hope that they will slip through (a practice commonly called "port shopping").

Civil Monetary Penalties and Other Administrative Remedies

Beginning with the enactment of the PDMA,[429] Congress embarked on a new phase of FDA enforcement strategy. Since then, in addition to the basic enforcement tools discussed above, various amendments of the FDCA have contained provisions for civil penalties and other administrative sanctions that can have both retributive consequences and deterrence value.[430]

Persons who violate prohibitions in the PDMA against the sale or trade of drug samples face civil penalties of up to $50,000 for each of the first two violations, and up to $1,000,000 thereafter.[431] Companies that fail to issue drug-sample reports are subject to $100,000 in civil penalties.[432]

Under the Safe Medical Devices Act of 1990[433] civil penalties up to $15,000 for each violation, with a ceiling of $1,000,000 for all violations combined in one proceeding, are provided for in section 303(f)(1)(A) of the FDCA.[434]

---

[426]   *Id.*

[427]   Foreign Supplier Verification Programs for Importers of Food for Humans and Animals, 79 Fed. Reg. 58,573 (Sept. 29, 2014).

[428]   Pub. L. No. 112-144, § 708, 126 Stat. at 1068-69 (codified at 21 U.S.C. § 381(a)).

[429]   Pub. L. No. 100-293, § 7, 102 Stat. 95 (1988) (codified at 21 U.S.C. §§ 331(t), 333).

[430]   There are also civil monetary penalties for certain violations of the Public Health Service Act. *See* 42 U.S.C. § 262(d)(2) (authorizing civil monetary penalties for a violation of a biological product recall order); 42 U.S.C. § 300aa-28(b)(1) (authorizing civil monetary penalties for destroying, altering, falsifying, or concealing any vaccine record or report).

[431]   FDCA § 303(b)(2)(A)-(B), 21 U.S.C. § 333(b)(2)(A)-(B).

[432]   *Id.* § 303(b)(3), 21 U.S.C. § 333(b)(3).

[433]   Pub. L. No. 101-629, § 17, 104 Stat. at 4511 (codified at 21 U.S.C. § 333(f)(1)).

[434]   21 U.S.C. § 333(f)(1)(A). The Federal Civil Penalties Inflation Adjustment Act of 1990 (Inflation Adjustment Act) is codified at 28 U.S.C. 2461. The Inflation Adjustment Act was amended in 1996 by the Debt Collection Improvement Act, which added the requirement that agencies adjust their civil penalties by regulation (Pub. L. No. 104-134, § 31001, 110 Stat. 1321-373). Section 3 of the Inflation Adjustment Act defines a covered civil penalty as any "penalty, fine, or other sanction that…is for a specific monetary amount as provided by

The Generic Drug Enforcement Act[435] imposes civil penalties of up to $250,000 for individuals and $1,000,000 for corporations.

When it is determined that a civil monetary penalty is appropriate, the District Office submits a recommendation to the Center with principal jurisdiction over the matter.[436] The complaint served on the respondent must be signed by the OCC attorney for the Center.[437] After an answer has been filed, the Center must serve a notice of hearing on the respondent.[438] The hearing takes place before an administrative law judge.[439] Either party may appeal the decision of the administrative law judge to the DHHS Departmental Appeals Board (DAB).[440] The final decision of the DAB constitutes final agency action, from which a respondent may petition for judicial review.[441]

The FDAAA added new civil monetary penalties for drug violations.[442] A "responsible person" who violates section 505(o), 505(p), or 505-1 (postmarketing safety provisions added by the FDAAA) is subject to a civil penalty of up to $1 million for an initial violation[443] and up to $10 million for each subsequent violation.[444] Civil penalties may also be assessed for the failure to submit a certification of compliance with the required clinical trial information, the knowing submission of a false certification, failure to comply with the requirements to submit clinical trial information for drugs or devices, or the submission of false or misleading clinical trial information.[445]

The FDAAA also included civil penalty provisions strengthening FDA's enforcement powers relating to direct-to-consumer (DTC) prescription drug advertising that is false or misleading. In such a case, FDA may impose civil monetary penalties on the holder of an approved new drug application or biologics license application for a prescription drug.[446]

Federal law" or "has a maximum amount provided for by Federal law," and "is assessed or enforced by an agency pursuant to Federal law" and "is assessed or enforced pursuant to an administrative proceeding or a civil action in the Federal courts." FDA's OCC drafted a list of civil penalties that it considered covered by the Inflation Adjustment Act. Letter from Victor S. Rezendes, Managing Director Strategic Issues, United States General Accounting Office ("GAO"), to The Honorable Tommy Thompson, Secretary, Department of Health and Human Services ("DHHS") (Aug. 1, 2003), *available at* http://www.gao.gov/new.items/d02933r.pdf. The Safe Medical Devices Act of 1990 is included in this list.

[435] Pub. L. No. 102-282, § 307(a) 106 Stat. 149, 159 (1992) (codified at 21 U.S.C. § 335b(a)).

[436] RPM, *supra* note 221, § 5-8-3.

[437] 21 C.F.R. § 17.5(a) (2014).

[438] *Id.* § 17.13 (2014).

[439] *Id.* §§ 17.3(c), 17.9 (2014).

[440] *Id.* § 17.47. The Commissioner of Food and Drugs designated the Departmental Appeals Board to decide such appeals.

[441] *Id.* § 17.51 (2014).

[442] Pub. L. No. 110-85, § 902, 121 Stat. at 943 (2007).

[443] FDCA § 303(f)(4)(A)(i), 21 U.S.C. § 333(f)(4)(A)(i).

[444] FDCA § 303(f)(4)(B), 21 U.S.C. § 333(f)(4)(B).

[445] FDCA § 301(jj)(1), 21 U.S.C. § 331(jj)(1).

[446] FDCA § 303(g)(1), 21 U.S.C. § 333(g)(1). A civil monetary penalty for DTC advertising shall be assessed pursuant to an administrative process that requires written notice, an opportunity for a hearing, and "an order made on the record." 21 U.S.C. § 333(g)(2). In determining the amount of the civil penalty for a DTC advertisement, FDA is directed to consider a number of factors, including whether the advertisement was submitted to FDA for review under the DTC user-fee program established by the FDAAA. *Id.* § 333(g)(3). Because Congress did not appropriate required funds, however, the DTC user-fee program did not commence. User Fee Program for Advisory Review of Direct-to-Consumer Television Advertisements for Prescription Drug and Biological Products; Program Will Not Be Implemented, 73 Fed. Reg. 2924 (Jan.

Under the FSPTCA, FDA may impose civil penalties for violations of FDCA requirements that relate to tobacco products.[447] The penalties for violating FDCA requirements relating to tobacco products may not exceed $15,000 for each violation or $1,000,000 for all violations adjudicated in a single proceeding.[448]

In FSMA, Congress gave FDA authority to assess a civil money penalty for failure to comply with a mandatory recall order issued by FDA under section 423 of the FDCA.[449] It also authorized the government to assess a civil money penalty against persons who violate the whistleblower protections added in section 1012 of the FDCA.[450]

Additional Civil Powers

FDA has recourse to several additional enforcement means of a purely administrative nature. For example, the Secretary of Health and Human Services may immediately suspend the approval of a new drug application upon a finding of an imminent hazard to the public health.[451] FDA may withdraw a product approval because of a false statements in an application or for failure to file two or more annual reports.[452] FDA also has looked to the cGMP regulations as the grounds for withdrawal of approval of applications for new drug products.[453] FDA may revoke biologic product and establishment licenses for various types of noncompliance.[454] In the investigational phase of the drug or device approval procedure, FDA may disqualify investigators, Institutional Review Boards, laboratories, or sponsors, and may terminate investigational new drug exemptions (INDs) or investigational device exemptions (IDEs) for noncompliance.[455] FDA may issue an order to a sponsor to delay a proposed clinical investigation or to suspend an ongoing investigation.[456]

Another civil remedy provided by the Safe Medical Devices Act is the temporary suspension of approvals of applications.[457] A related regulatory remedy available to FDA where medical devices present substantial deception or an unreasonable risk of illness or injury is formal banning, a power conferred by section 516 of the FDCA.[458]

16, 2008). As a result, it is unclear how the agency will use its authority to assess monetary penalties for violative DTC advertisements. *See* F-D-C REP. ("The Pink Sheet"), Jan. 21, 2008; *see also* F-D-C REP. ("The Pink Sheet"), Apr. 19, 2010 (noting pressure for more DTC advertisement regulation during the fifth round of reauthorization of the Prescription Drug User Fee Act).

[447]   FDCA § 303(f)(9), 21 U.S.C. § 333(f)(9).
[448]   FDCA § 303(f)(9)(A), 21 U.S.C. § 333(f)(9)(A).
[449]   FDCA § 303(f)(2)(A), 21 U.S.C. § 333(f)(2)(A).
[450]   FDCA § 1012(b)(3)(C), 21 U.S.C. § 399d(b)(3)(C).
[451]   21 U.S.C. § 355(e).
[452]   21 C.F.R. § 314.150(a)(2)(v), (b)(1).
[453]   21 C.F.R. § 210 (2010). *See, e.g., Copanos*, Food Drug Cosm. L. Rep. (CCH) ¶ 38,112; *see also* F-D-C REP. ("The Pink Sheet"), Jan. 1, 1990 at 3-4.
[454]   21 C.F.R. § 601.5 (2014).
[455]   *Id.* § 312.44.
[456]   *Id.* § 312.42.
[457]   21 U.S.C. § 360e(e)(3).
[458]   21 U.S.C. § 360f.

Remedies specific to devices include notification when a device presents an unreasonable risk of substantial harm to the public health.[459] FDA may also order a manufacturer, importer, or distributor to repair, replace the device, or provide a refund.[460]

In addition, FDA has established an administrative procedure to address the issue of fraud in product applications. The policy is commonly known as the Application Integrity Policy (AIP), but is formally entitled, "Fraud, Untrue Statements of Material Facts, Bribery, and Illegal Gratuities; Final Policy."[461] Established in 1991, the AIP describes the agency's approach to the review of applications that may be affected by wrongful acts that raise significant questions regarding data reliability.[462] If FDA determines that there is a "pattern or practice" of wrongful conduct, it can invoke the AIP.[463] Under the policy, FDA can refuse to approve an application that contains unreliable data and may proceed to withdraw approval if the application in question has been approved.[464] Under FDA's fraud policy, the agency will withdraw approvals or refuse to approve new applications, and will seek recalls, where fraud, bribery or material false statements in connection with applications are discovered.[465] FDA's fraud policy also recommends corrective actions for an applicant to take.[466] If the evidence of fraud is widespread, FDA can apply the policy to all of a company's pending or future submissions.[467] Once a firm is subjected to the AIP, it can take years to be released from it.[468] In recent years, a number of high-profile companies, such as Ranbaxy, have been subject to the AIP.[469]

Congress also has enacted a number of other provisions intended to safeguard the public by enhancing the authority of FDA, state and whistleblowers. The Generic Drug Enforcement Act imposes sanctions of debarment of corporations from the pharmaceutical approval process,[470] debarment of individuals from the pharmaceutical industry,[471] withdrawal and suspension of product approvals,[472] and whistleblower awards of up to $250,000.[473] FDASIA strengthened protections for federal whistleblowers in the FDCA.[474] The Nutrition Labeling and Education Act of 1990 added civil enforcement by state authorities for violations of FDCA food misbranding provisions.[475] Permission for state enforcement is contingent on notice by the state to FDA of alleged violations, and on a waiting period of between 30 and

---

[459] FDCA § 518(a), 21 U.S.C. § 360h(a).

[460] FDCA § 518(b), 21 U.S.C. § 360h(b).

[461] *See* 56 Fed. Reg. 46,191 (Sept. 10, 1991). The Policy was initially issued by FDA as Compliance Policy Guide (CPG) 7150.09, § 120.100.

[462] FDA, Application Integrity Policy Procedures (Mar. 5, 1998), *available at* http://www.fda.gov/downloads/ ICECI/EnforcementActions/ApplicationIntegrityPolicy/UCM072631.pdf.

[463] *See* 56 Fed. Reg. 46,191, 46,194 (Sept. 10, 1991).

[464] *Id.* at 46,192.

[465] Fraud, Untrue Statements of Material Facts, Bribery, and Illegal Gratuities; Final Policy, 56 Fed. Reg. 46,191 (Sept. 10, 1991); CPG § 120.100 (7150.09).

[466] *Id.*

[467] *Id.* at 46,199.

[468] *See* Application Integrity Policy List, U.S. Food and Drug Administration, http://www.fda.gov/ICECI/ EnforcementActions/ApplicationIntegrityPolicy/ucm134453.htm (last updated Oct. 7, 2011).

[469] *Id.*

[470] Pub. L. No. 102-282, 106 Stat. 149 (1992) (codified at FDCA § 306(a)(1), 21 U.S.C. § 335a(a)(1)).

[471] FDCA § 306(c)(1)(B), 21 U.S.C. § 335a(c)(1)(B).

[472] FDCA § 306(g)(1), 21 U.S.C. § 335a(g)(1).

[473] FDCA § 307(e), 21 U.S.C. § 335b(e).

[474] *See, e.g.,* FDCA § 303(b)(5), 21 U.S.C. § 333(b)(5).

[475] Pub. L. No. 100-293, § 7, 102 Stat. 95 (1988); FDCA § 310(b), 21 U.S.C. § 337(b).

90 days dependent on FDA's institution of an investigation or enforcement action.[476] No state enforcement is permitted if FDA is "diligently prosecuting" a court action, or has settled a formal or informal enforcement action.[477]

The Dietary Supplement Health and Education Act confers emergency authority on DHHS to declare a dietary supplement adulterated, although this authority cannot be delegated to FDA.[478] This provision addresses concerns that the absence of pre-approval mechanisms left the U.S. public exposed.

FDA may also impose a no-tobacco-sale order against a person found to have committed repeated violations of the sale/distribution restrictions promulgated under section 906(d) of the FDCA at a particular retail outlet.[479]

When FDA Decides to Set an Example: Criminal Proceedings

FDA's Criminal Powers

Over the last 70 years, the number of cases FDA criminally prosecutes has dwindled.[480] The fear of criminal prosecution, however, has remained a serious deterrent to those involved in the industries regulated by FDA. All violations of the FDCA are subject to civil or criminal enforcement—or both—within FDA's and DOJ's discretion. The FDAAA has authorized expansion and enhancement of FDA's resources involved in FDCA criminal enforcement.[481]

FDA generally decides to recommend to DOJ a criminal prosecution in cases where there are: 1) gross violations that evidence management's disregard for unsafe conditions; 2) obvious and continuing violations where management has not exercised normal care; 3) life-threatening violations or those where injuries already have occurred; and 4) "deliberate attempts to circumvent the law," such as the submission of false data to the agency.[482]

FDA's OCI has primary responsibility for all criminal investigations conducted by FDA, and for determining when a matter should be recommended for prosecution. OCI was established in the early 1990s, largely in response to public criticism that FDA lacked the capability to enforce all of the laws under its jurisdiction and to identify and investigate

---

[476]   21 U.S.C. § 337(b)(2)(A)-(B).

[477]   Id. § 337(b)(2)(C).

[478]   Pub. L. No. 103-417, § 4, 108 Stat. 4325, 4496-97 (1994); FDCA § 402(f)(1)(C), 21 U.S.C. § 342(f)(1)(C).

[479]   FDCA § 303(f)(8), 21 U.S.C. § 333(f)(8).

[480]   Minority Staff of House Comm. on Government Reform, *Prescription for Harm: The Decline in FDA Enforcement Activity*, 109th Cong., 2d Sess. (2006); PETER B. HUTT, RICHARD A. MERRILL & LEWIS A. GROSSMAN, FOOD AND DRUG LAW: CASES AND MATERIALS 164-165 (4th ed. 2014) (observing that there were 626 criminal prosecutions in 1939 compared to 262 in 2012).

[481]   21 U.S.C. § 355e(c).

[482]   Sam D. Fine, *The Philosophy of Enforcement*, 31 FOOD DRUG COSM. L.J. 324 (1976). Mr. Fine's observations remain a basis of FDA's enforcement philosophy today.

criminal activity adequately.[483] Placed within FDA's existing Office of Regulatory Affairs (ORA), OCI was designed to be the FDA's "police force," and is staffed with fully trained criminal investigators. Thus, OCI directs all criminal investigation activities at FDA, and coordinates investigation activities with ORA's district offices and other federal, state, and local law enforcement agencies.[484] OCI often coordinates its enforcement efforts with DHHS and its Office of Inspector General.

The numerous prohibitions set forth in section 301 of the FDCA are subject to the criminal penalties set forth in section 303.[485] A first offense is a misdemeanor unless it was committed with "the intent to defraud or mislead," in which case it is a felony.[486]

Penalties of up to 10 years imprisonment and fines of not more than $250,000 are authorized by the PDMA,[487] and a five-year maximum sentence was added under section 303(e) for the intentional unlawful distribution of anabolic steroid products.[488] The maximum sentence increases to 10 years, however, if the offense involves an individual under 18 years old.[489] In FDASIA, Congress enhanced the penalty under the FDCA for intentional adulteration of a drug to 20 years of incarceration in certain instances.[490]

In federal criminal cases, prosecutors can use Title 18 of the *United States Code* to bring FDA-related charges against individual defendants. These charges could include, for example, conspiracy to defraud FDA or making false statements to FDA.[491] Title 18 statutory maximum penalties and federal sentencing guidelines would apply in the event of a conviction.

Once FDA has decided to seek criminal prosecution against a company and/or an individual, it asks DOJ to obtain an information or indictment, depending on whether a misdemeanor or felony charge is involved. DOJ's Office of Consumer Protection Branch then takes over the case as FDA's representative, though most cases are prosecuted primarily by an Assistant U.S. Attorney in the district in which the prosecution is brought. Thereafter, FDA no longer serves as the lead actor, and may have only minimal involvement. The role of FDA OCC varies widely from active involvement to bare notice until an indictment is obtained.

If serious criminal conduct has been widespread, as in the case of the generic drug scandal of the late 1980s and early 1990s, the government may seek to prosecute a large number of companies and individuals, rather than merely make an example by one prosecution.[492]

---

483 *See* Howard Schneider, *New Tools Help FDA Get Tougher in Tracking Threats to Product Safety*, L.A. TIMES, Jan. 2, 1994, at 21; *Edwards Committee Recommendations Have Led to Changes in the Status Quo*, M-D-D-I REP. ("The Gray Sheet"), June 15, 1992, at 4.

484 District management must communicate with its local OCI office before pursuing any criminal matter. RPM, *supra* note 221.

485 21 U.S.C. § 333.

486 *Id.* § 333(a)(2).

487 FDCA § 303(b)(1), 21 U.S.C. § 333(b)(1).

488 21 U.S.C. § 333(e).

489 21 U.S.C. § 331(e)(2).

490 See *supra* note 153.

491 *See, e.g.*, United States v. Mitcheltree, 940 F.2d 1329, 1332-33 (10th Cir. 1991) (holding that the government must offer evidence demonstrating the defendant's intent to defraud or mislead a government agency to convict for conspiracy to commit an FDCA violation under Title 18).

492 *See* F-D-C REP. ("The Pink Sheet"), Dec. 3, 1990, at 9.

FDA rarely obtains a criminal search warrant as part of its criminal investigations. This enforcement tool is utilized, however, where FDA believes that a company under investigation is being recalcitrant.

In the context of enforcement against off-label promotion, the principal source of referrals to DOJ is not FDA, but, rather, plaintiffs' lawyers representing *qui tam* whistleblowers who allege violations of the FCA.[493] These plaintiffs' lawyers refer the cases to U.S. Attorneys' Offices, who then work closely with *qui tam* plaintiffs to investigate their allegations of off-label promotion and to prosecute when considered appropriate.

The "Park" Doctrine: Strict Liability Criminal Misdemeanor

FDA names individual corporate officers or employees in all of its criminal referrals. The FDCA imposes on responsible corporate officials strict vicarious misdemeanor liability. The fact that a corporate officer has no direct involvement in or even knowledge of the actions or conditions that give rise to a criminal violation does not excuse that officer from criminal liability.

The seminal case of *United States v. Dotterweich* involved the prosecution of a chief executive officer of a company with 26 employees located in one facility.[494] J. H. Dotterweich was found guilty of distributing misbranded and adulterated drugs in interstate commerce.[495] He argued that his lack of direct involvement with the distribution at issue was a bar to an individual conviction. The Supreme Court strongly held otherwise:

> [U]nder § 301 a corporation may commit an offense and all persons who aid and abet its commission are equally guilty. Whether an accused shares responsibility in the business process resulting in unlawful distribution depends on the evidence . . . . Balancing relative hardships, Congress has preferred to place it upon those who have at least the opportunity of informing themselves of the existence of conditions imposed for the protection of consumers . . . rather than to throw the hazard on the innocent public who are wholly helpless.[496]

Dotterweich's holding was significantly extended in *United States v. Park*, which involved a chain of retail food stores with 36,000 employees, 874 retail outlets, and 16 warehouses.[497] John Park, the chief executive officer of the chain, whose office was in Pennsylvania, was charged by an information based on a rodent-infested warehouse in Baltimore, Maryland. There was no dispute that the chain had employees who were in charge of legal affairs and regulatory matters, and who oversaw the sanitary conditions at the company's facilities, and that all phases of the warehouse operation were assigned to "dependable subordinates."[498]

---

[493]   31 U.S.C. §§ 3729-3733.

[494]   320 U.S. 277 (1943).

[495]   *Id.* at 278. The jury hung as to the guilt of the corporation. *See also* United States v. Buffalo Pharmacal Co., 131 F.2d 500 (2d Cir. 1942), *rev'd*, 320 U.S. 277 (1943).

[496]   320 U.S. at 284-85.

[497]   421 U.S. 658 (1975).

[498]   *Id.* at 664.

Nonetheless, the Court found that the bylaws of the corporation prescribing the duties of the chief executive officer placed ultimate responsibility for all of the relevant functions on him. The Court, in a majority opinion by Chief Justice Burger, applied the *Dotterweich* doctrine and explained the FDCA's governing concept of misdemeanor responsibility:

> [T]he Act imposes not only a positive duty to seek out and remedy violations when they occur but also, and primarily, a duty to implement measures that will ensure that violations will not occur.[499]

> [I]t is equally clear that the Government establishes a prima facie case when it introduces evidence sufficient to warrant a finding by the trier of the facts that the defendant had, by reason of his position in the corporation, responsibility and authority either to prevent in the first instance, or promptly to correct, the violation complained of, and that he failed to do so.[500]

Although *Park* states the standard for criminal liability to be incorporated in a jury instruction or to be applied by a court in reviewing a verdict, the government uses a more demanding standard in deciding whom to charge.[501]

In *dictum*, the *Park* Court stated that an instruction on the defendant's lack of power or capacity to prevent a violation ("objective impossibility") should be given if the defendant presents sufficient evidence to put such a defense at issue.[502] This *dictum* derived from a 1964 Supreme Court decision that characterized the issue as factual, rather than legal, and ruled that it must first be raised defensively at trial.[503]

In subsequent cases, some defendants have asserted an "objective impossibility" defense based on that *dictum*. In *United States v. Y. Hata & Co., Ltd.*, the court declined to rule on whether the defense was available to corporations as distinct from individuals. Instead, it found that the absence of proof that the responsible officers were unable to install a sufficient protective mechanism to prevent continuing aviary infestation in a food warehouse rendered the defense inapplicable.[504] In *United States v. Starr,* the defense was rejected on the merits.[505] Starr, the defendant corporate officer, was held to a standard of reasonable foresight that the plowing of a nearby field would cause mice to flee to the adjacent food warehouse. In addition, the court ruled that the refusal of a janitor to comply with clean-up instructions was not only not "impossible" to prevent, but was, in the court's view, foreseeable.[506]

---

[499]   *Id.* at 672.

[500]   *Id.* at 672. *See also Gel Spice Co.*, Crim. No. 80 CR 650, *reprinted* in Federal Food, Drug, and Cosmetic Act Judicial Record 1983-1984, at 115. For a discussion of *Park* and *Dotterweich*, *see* Stephen C. Jones, *Individual Liability Under the Federal Food Drug, and Cosmetic Act: The Defenses Find a Defendant*, 39 Food Drug Cosm. L.J. 385 (1984); Daniel F. O'Keefe, *Criminal Liability; Park Update*, 32 Food Drug Cosm. L.J. 392 (1977); Richard A. Merrill, *The Park Case*, 30 Food Drug Cosm. L.J. 683 (1975).

[501]   Brief for the United States, United States v. Park, 421 U.S. 658 (1975).

[502]   421 U.S. at 676-78.

[503]   United States v. Wiesenfeld Warehouse Co., 376 U.S. at 91 (1964).

[504]   535 F.2d 508 (9th Cir. 1976).

[505]   535 F.2d 512 (9th Cir. 1976).

[506]   *Id.* at 515-16. Courts have extended the Park doctrine beyond the FDCA to violations of other "public welfare" laws. *See, e.g.*, United States v. Sexton Cove Estates, Inc. 526 F.2d 1293, 1300 n.19 (*dictum*) (violation

In *United States v. New England Grocers Supply*,[507] a magistrate's finding of strict liability under *Park* for three corporate officers was reversed and remanded. The court held that there had been no explicit finding that these officers were "not powerless to prevent" the violations.[508] On remand, the magistrate found the defendants not guilty.[509] The defendants having established the affirmative defense, the magistrate held that the government had then to present evidence to support a finding beyond a reasonable doubt that the defendants "could by the use of extraordinary care correct or prevent the violations."[510]

FDA has threatened to step up enforcement against individuals since 2009.[511] It is not clear that FDA made good on this threat, but there have certainly been a number of FDA-related criminal actions since 2009 in which charges have been filed against individuals. In 2009, Sally Qing Miller, Stephen S. Miller, and their company, Chemnutra, Inc., each pleaded guilty to one count of selling adulterated pet food and one count of selling misbranded food.[512] The defendants had shipped wheat gluten, contaminated with melamine, which was then used to manufacture pet food. The government charged the individuals and the company with the felony of conspiracy to commit wire fraud.[513] In 2009, a federal grand jury indicted four senior executives of Synthes, a medical device manufacturer that specializes in trauma products, for alleged violations of the FDCA in their role as "responsible corporate officers of Synthes."[514] The indictment alleged that the defendants marketed Norian XR, an orthopedic bone void filler, for spinal surgeries, an unapproved use that was specifically warned against in the labeling. Each defendant pleaded guilty to a strict liability offense of misdemeanor misbranding for shipping adulterated and misbranded Norian XR in interstate commerce.[515, 516]

---

of Rivers & Harbors Act).

[507]   488 F. Supp. 230 (D. Mass. 1980).

[508]   *Id.* at 234-36.

[509]   Federal Food, Drug, and Cosmetic Act Judicial Record 1978-80, at 233 (Vincent A. Kleinfeld & Alan H. Kaplan, eds., 1983).

[510]   *Id.* at 234. The *Park* standard also has been utilized in a civil context. *See* United States v. Hodges X-Ray, Inc., 759 F.2d 557 (6th Cir. 1985) (Radiation Control for Health and Safety Act violation). *See also* United States v. Able Lab., Inc., Civ. No. 91-4916 (filed D.N.J. May 2, 1992); United States v. Physio-Control Corp., Civ. No. C-92-1163CC (filed W.D. Wash. July 21, 1992).

[511]   Statements by FDA Commissioner Dr. Margaret A. Hamburg and Deputy Chief Counsel Eric Blumberg are indicative of this increased focus on enforcement against individuals. In a March 4, 2010 letter, Commissioner Hamburg stated that "[criteria have been developed] to increase the appropriate use of misdemeanor prosecutions, a valuable enforcement tool, to hold responsible corporate officials accountable." Letter from FDA Commissioner Margaret A. Hamburg, M.D., to Senator Charles E. Grassley (Mar. 4, 2010). At a Food and Drug Law Institute conference in April 2010, Mr. Blumberg stated: "Very soon, and I have no one particular in mind, some corporate executive is going to be first." He advised persons to "do what you can, do the right thing, before we find out about it." *See Corporate Responsibility Standards Coming; Don't Be First Case, FDA Warns*, F-D-C Rep. ("The Pink Sheet"), May 24, 2010.

[512]   Press Release, Department of Justice, U.S. Attorney's Office for the Western District of Missouri (June 16, 2009), *available at* http://www.usdoj.gov/usao/mow/news2009/miller.ple.htm.

[513]   Indictment, United States v. Sally Miller et al., No. 08-CR-00023 (W.D. Mo. Feb. 6, 2008).

[514]   Indictment, United States v. Norian Corp. et al., No. 02:09CR00403 (E.D. Pa. June 16, 2009).

[515]   Press Release, Department of Justice, U.S. Attorney's Office for the Eastern District of Pennsylvania (Oct. 4, 2010), *available at* http://www.justice.gov/usao/pae/News/Pr/2010/Oct/synthes,norian_release.pdf.

[516]   For additional examples of prosecution of individuals, *see* United States v. W. Scott Harkonen, No. 08-cr-164 (N.D. Cal. Sept. 29, 2009), affirmed Case No. 11-10209 (9th Cir. Mar 4, 2013) and United States v. Purdue Frederick Company et al., No. 07-cr-00029 (W.D. Va. July 23, 2007). In *Harkonen*, a company CEO was charged with felony misbranding in violation of FDCA §§ 301(k), 303(a)(2), and 502(f) and wire fraud in violation of 18 U.S.C. § 1343 for the creation and dissemination of a press release containing false and misleading information about the efficacy of InterMune's drug, Actimmune® (Interferon gamma-1b),

In January 2011, FDA published revised guidelines for the submission and review of prosecution recommendations.[517] Amended Chapter 6 of the RPM provides agency personnel greater discretion in recommending criminal prosecutions. In addition, FDA introduced criteria that it will consider when recommending *Park* prosecutions. Chapter 6 of the RPM provides: "[w]hen considering whether to recommend a misdemeanor prosecution against a corporate official, consider the individual's position in the company and relationship to the violation, and whether the official had the authority to correct or prevent the violation." It further provides that "[k]nowledge of and actual participation in the violation are not a prerequisite to a misdemeanor prosecution but are factors that may be relevant when deciding whether to recommend charging a misdemeanor violation." Other factors to be considered include, but are not limited to, whether the violation involves actual or potential public harm, whether the violation is obvious, whether the violation reflects a pattern of illegal behavior and/or failure to heed prior warnings, whether the violation is widespread, whether the violation is serious, the quality of the legal and factual support for the potential prosecution, and whether the potential prosecution is a prudent use of FDA's resources.

In 2011, the DHHS Office of Inspector General raised the stakes further by informing the CEO of Forest Laboratories that it intended to use against him in connection with the company's 2010 guilty plea to a misdemeanor off-label marketing offense its authority[518] to exclude individuals from federal health benefit programs.[519] The attempt to use a strict liability misdemeanor as grounds for exclusion generated widespread concern among FDA-regulated businesses, but DHHS OIG eventually reversed its position—announcing its intention not to bring an exclusion action against the CEO.[520]

The government has recently obtained two significant victories in enforcing the food safety provisions of the FDCA. In 2013, Peter and Jack DeCoster, owners of Quality Egg, LLC, pled guilty to shipping adulterated food into interstate commerce. The owners admitted to affixing labels with false expiration dates on their egg products.[521] And in 2014, a Georgia jury found Stewart Parnell, the former owner of the Peanut Corporation of America, guilty of conspiracy to introduce adulterated and misbranded foods into commerce with intent

---

as a treatment for idiopathic pulmonary fibrosis. He was convicted of wire fraud and found not guilty of felony misbranding. He was sentenced to three years' probation, with six months of home confinement. He was ordered to pay a $20,000 fine and to perform 200 hours of community service. *See* Criminal Post-Trial Minutes, United States v. W. Scott Harkonen, No. 08-cr-164 (N.D. Cal. Apr. 13, 2011) In *Purdue*, the company CEO, General Counsel, and Chief Scientific Officer each pleaded guilty to one count of strict liability misdemeanor misbranding of the painkiller OxyContin®. The CEO agreed to pay $19 million in fines; the General Counsel, $8 million and the Chief Scientific Officer, $7.5 million. The executives did not serve time in prison. Plea Agreement addressing claims against The Purdue Frederick Co. for claims in United States v. The Purdue Frederick Co., Inc., No. 1:07CR00029 (W.D. Va.); Civil Settlement Agreement addressing claims against The Purdue Frederick Co. for claims in United States v. The Purdue Frederick Co., Inc., Attachment D to Plea Agreement; *see also* United States v. The Purdue Frederick Co., 495 F. Supp. 2d 569 (W.D. Va. 2007) (approving plea agreement).

[517] RPM, *supra* note 221, § 6-5 "Prosecution."

[518] 42 U.S.C. § 1320a-7.

[519] *See* Alicia Mundy, *U.S. Efforts to Remove Drug CEO Jolts Firms*, WALL ST. J., Apr. 26, 2011, at A1.

[520] *See DHHS-OIG Drops Potential Action against Forest CEO Howard Solomon*, REUTERS, Aug. 5, 2011, *available at* http://www.reuters.com/article/2011/08/05/idUS265153+05-Aug-2011+BW20110805.

[521] *See* Press Release, Department of Justice, Quality Egg, Company Owner, and Top Executive Plead Guilty in Connection with Distribution of Adulterated Eggs (Jun. 4, 2014), *available at* http://www.fda.gov/ICECI/CriminalInvestigations/ucm400380.htm.

to defraud and mislead, in addition to various other charges.[522] The charges stemmed from a deadly *Salmonella* outbreak traced back to Mr. Parnell's peanut manufacturing facility.[523] Prosecutors had argued that Mr. Parnell had cut corners on food safety and covered up laboratory results that had tested positive for *Salmonella*. However, Mr. Parnell plans to challenge the guilty verdict.[524]

The Role of Guaranties

Sections 303(c)(2) and (3) of the FDCA provide a safe harbor from criminal liability under the general criminal penalty provisions of section 303(a)(1).[525] A guaranty received by a corporation, an employee of a corporation, or other individual should state that the articles delivered by the guarantor are not adulterated or misbranded within the meaning of the FDCA, and (as applicable) that they are not unapproved food additives, color additives, new drugs, or Class III devices subject to an approval requirement. A guaranty may be limited to a specific shipment or may be general and continuing.[526] A guaranty covering color additives under section 303(c)(3)[527] must be signed by the manufacturer of the colors, and, if from a foreign source, must be signed by both the foreign manufacturer and an agent of that manufacturer who resides in the United States.[528]

In its enforcement regulations covering guaranties,[529] FDA provides that "[t]he application of a guaranty . . . shall expire when," after the covered products are shipped or delivered by the guarantor, the products become adulterated or misbranded, or become products unauthorized under sections 404, 505, or 512 of the act.[530] The original guarantor's guaranty is not operative, therefore, if the product subsequently is adulterated, misbranded, or caused to become an otherwise violative product.

Under section 301(h) of the FDCA, furnishing a false guaranty is a prohibited act that can give rise to criminal liability.[531] Under that provision, however, a company that receives a guaranty and then, in good faith, provides a subsequent guaranty premised on the original guarantor's representations does not commit a prohibited act.[532]

The guaranty provisions are contained in the criminal-penalties section of the FDCA. The recipient of a guaranty is not protected against the imposition of civil remedies such as injunctions, seizures, or recalls. In the civil setting, fairness to the recipient is outweighed by the interest in protecting the public.

---

[522]   *See* Special Verdict, United States v. Parnell, 2014 WL 5106465 (M.D. Ga. Sept. 19, 2014).
[523]   *Id.*
[524]   *See* Moni Basu, *Unprecedented Verdict: Peanut Executive Guilty in Deadly Salmonella Outbreak*, CNN, Sept. 19, 2014, *available at* http://www.cnn.com/2014/09/19/us/peanut-butter-salmonella-trial/.
[525]   21 U.S.C. § 333(c)(2), (3).
[526]   21 C.F.R. § 7.13(a)-(b) (2014).
[527]   21 U.S.C. § 333(c)(3).
[528]   21 C.F.R. § 7.13(d) (2014).
[529]   *Id.* § 7.12-7.13.
[530]   *Id.* § 7.13(c).
[531]   21 U.S.C. § 331(h).
[532]   *Id. See, e.g.,* United States v. Crown Rubber Sundries Co., 67 F. Supp. 92 (N.D. Ohio 1946).

Section 305 "Hearing"

Section 305 of the FDCA provides that, "[b]efore any violation of this Act is reported by [FDA] to any U.S. attorney for institution of a criminal proceeding, the person against whom such proceeding is contemplated shall be given appropriate notice and an opportunity to present his views, orally or in writing, with regard to such contemplated proceeding."[533] Despite the statutory "shall," the Supreme Court held in *Dotterweich* that a hearing under section 305 is not mandatory.[534] Moreover a section 305 "hearing" will not be provided "if the Commissioner has reason to believe that [the opportunity for a hearing] may result in the alteration or destruction of evidence or in the prospective defendant's fleeing to avoid prosecution."[535] An opportunity for a section 305 hearing is normally provided when FDA contemplates a referral to DOJ for institution of a misdemeanor prosecution, but not when FDA contemplates a referral for institution of a grand jury investigation of a possible felony or felonies.[536]

The district consults with DCMO, which consults with OCC, to determine whether to issue a section 305 notice.[537] If no section 305 notice is to be issued, DCMO will notify the district. The district will prepare a Summary and Recommendation (S&R) and explain why the notice is not required. DCMO will then forward the relevant materials to OCC.[538]

The hearing is held pursuant to a formal notice (known as a "Section 305 Notice"). The event actually is a meeting, and is referred to as such, and its procedures are explained in the *RPM*.[539] FDA's regulation governing such meetings is titled: "Opportunity for presentation of views before report of criminal violation."[540] The meeting is informal, often held in a district office, and is designed to give a party an opportunity to convince FDA not to make a criminal referral to DOJ. FDA usually is involved alone when a section 305 notice initially is sent to a company or individual, but there are times following the entry of consent orders in civil cases when the U.S. Attorney's Office also is involved in the recommendation to consider instituting criminal proceedings.

There are many strategic considerations involved for a company or individual invited to a section 305 hearing because participation in the procedure is completely voluntary and can be accomplished either through a written or oral presentation, or both. Usually, potential specific charges and the evidence FDA has gathered are not disclosed to a respondent before or at the hearing. Generally, FDA listens to an oral presentation (or reads a written presentation) and may ask questions, but does not provide information. Anything said by or on behalf of a respondent at the hearing may be used against the respondent in a subsequent criminal proceeding. Consequently, a respondent needs to weigh the likelihood of persuading FDA not to make a criminal referral against the risks of participating in the

---

[533] 21 U.S.C. § 335. *See also* RPM, *supra* note 221, ch. 5, § 5-2-2 "Authority."
[534] 320 U.S. at 279. *See also* United States v. Prigmore, 243 F.3d 1, 23 (1st Cir. 2001).
[535] 21 C.F.R. § 7.84(a)(2) (2014).
[536] *See id.* § 7.84(a)(3).
[537] RPM, *supra* note 221 at ch. 6-5-7.
[538] *Id.*
[539] *Id.* ch. 5, § 5-2 "Section 305 Meeting."
[540] 21 C.F.R. § 7.84 (2014).

hearing and thereby possibly creating additional evidence for a potential prosecution and revealing potential defenses.

If a party takes the opportunity to make an oral presentation or answer questions, it is FDA's position that no *Miranda* warnings are necessary because section 305 meetings do not involve a person being "taken into custody or otherwise deprived of his freedom."[541] Where defendants failed to show that the government had already decided to prosecute them before section 305 hearings were held, the statements made at the hearings were not taken in violation of the defendants' constitutional rights; and, therefore, the evidence gathered at the hearings was not suppressed in a subsequent criminal proceeding.[542] At the section 305 hearing, a party claiming the protection of a guaranty under section 303(c) should provide FDA with a verified copy of the guaranty.

The section 305 proceeding may be transcribed at the expense of the respondent.[543] If there is no transcript, an FDA employee dictates a summary of the presentation, which thereafter is available to the respondent.[544] The respondent has a later opportunity to submit supplemental information before the summary is passed on to FDA headquarters.[545]

Following a section 305 hearing, the district will forward the 305 citation-request package and the S&R to the DCMO in the Office of Enforcement.[546] DCMO will perform a limited review to determine whether the proposed prosecution conforms to agency policy and enforcement strategies and objectives. Once DCMO concurs with the prosecution recommendation, it will forward all relevant materials to the OCC.[547] OCC will review the recommendation and, if it agrees with it, typically will prepare a referral letter and form of information or indictment and send them to the appropriate U.S. Attorney's Office and to the Consumer Protection Branch.[548]

Notwithstanding the foregoing, an FDA enforcement official contends that FDA no longer conducts section 305 hearings, principally because they are not required under *United States v. Dotterweich*.[549]

---

[541] RPM, *supra* note 221, ch. 5, § 5-2-5 "Conducting the 305 Meeting," subsec. "Miranda Warning."

[542] United States v. Gel Spice Co., 601 F. Supp. 1214, 1226-27 (E.D.N.Y 1983). *See also* United States v. Andreadis, 234 F. Supp. 341, 347-49 (E.D.N.Y. 1964).

[543] 21 C.F.R. § 7.85(e) (2014).

[544] *Id.* § 7.85(f).

[545] *Id.* § 7.85(g).

[546] RPM, *supra* note 221, § 6-5-6 "Criminal Prosecution after Section 305 Notice."

[547] *Id.*

[548] *Id.*

[549] Telephone conversation with FDA Office of Chief Counsel (2008).

FDA's Enforcement Strategies

Enforcement Discretion

Apart from the language of section 309 of the FDCA, which states that FDA will not be required to pursue minor violations when it believes "that the public interest will be adequately served by a suitable written notice or warning,"[550] there is no statutory provision dictating how FDA is to use its limited resources to remedy all the violations that are reported to, or discovered by, the agency.

In 1985, the Supreme Court addressed a major challenge to FDA's decision not to take action against a drug that was being used by states for execution by lethal injection, a use outside the drug's labeled indications. The Court in *Heckler v. Chaney* upheld, as an unreviewable exercise of enforcement discretion, FDA's decision not to pursue the unapproved use of this drug.[551]

Moreover, in *National Milk Producers Federation v. Harris*, the Eighth Circuit found no basis for a mandamus action against FDA for the agency's failure to take enforcement action against allegedly misbranded cheese substitutes. Enforcement proceedings, according to the court, were committed to FDA's discretion by law.[552] Similarly, in *International Center for Technology Assessment v. Thompson*, the court rejected plaintiff's claim that FDA had improperly refused to regulate a type of genetically engineered fish under the new animal drug provisions of the FDCA. The court noted that FDA had simply exercised its discretion not to take enforcement action against the fish.[553]

Pearson v. Shalala declared that the First Amendment limited FDA's authority to reject petitions for qualified health claims on foods.[554] Thereafter, FDA established a framework to permit qualified health claims under its "enforcement discretion." The agency issued guidance to explain how it would exercise that discretion as to health claims for conventional foods and dietary supplements.[555] In addition, FDA has attempted at various times to regulate the homeopathic and pharmacy compounding industries through the exercise of enforcement discretion.[556] The agency's authority to use enforcement discretion as a regulatory tool was clarified in two important cases in the 1970s, both of which offered insights on how FDA could promulgate a policy of inaction without contravening the FDCA.[557] A recent decision reminded FDA of the limits of this approach, however. In *Cook v. FDA*, the D.C. Circuit ruled that FDA could not ignore the word "shall" in the importation provisions of the FDCA.

---

[550] 21 U.S.C. § 336.

[551] 470 U.S. 821 (1985).

[552] 653 F.2d 339 (8th Cir. 1981). *See also* Pan Am. Pharms., Inc. v. Kessler, Food Drug Cosm. L. Rep. (CCH) ¶ 38,212 (W.D. Mich. 1991).

[553] 421 F. Supp. 2d 1, 7 (D.D.C. 2006).

[554] 164 F.3d 650 (D.C. Cir. 1999).

[555] FDA, Guidance for Industry: Qualified Health Claims in the Labeling of Conventional Foods and Dietary Supplements (2003), *available at* http://www.fda.gov/Food/GuidanceRegulation/GuidanceDocumentsRegulatoryInformation/LabelingNutrition/ucm053832.htm.

[556] *See* Pharmacy Compounding, CPG § 460.200 (withdrawn Dec. 4, 2013); Conditions Under Which Homeopathic Drugs May be Marketed, CPG § 400.400 (March 1995).

[557] *See* Hoffman-LaRoche v. Weinberger, 425 F. Supp. 890 (D.D.C. 1975); Cutler v. Kennedy, 475 F. Supp. 838 (D.D.C 1979).

The court explained that section 801(a) of the FDCA "imposes mandatory duties upon the agency" and that FDA's individual admission of foreign drug products in violation of that provision could not be justified as an exercise of enforcement discretion.[558]

Notwithstanding these decisions and the plain language of section 309, where FDA has initiated enforcement actions, several courts have required it to account for its decision to proceed against some parties but not others. In *United States v. Undetermined Quantities of an Article of Drug Labeled as "Exachol,"* FDA had seized, and subsequently sought an injunction against the marketing of, a dietary supplement that made claims for the prevention of cardiovascular disease.[559] The claims were similar to those made for cereal products and other low-fat or low-cholesterol foods. Because FDA had issued a proposed "health messages" regulation under which it had permitted the marketing of a bran cereal with colon-cancer claims and of vegetable oils with heart-disease claims,[560] the court denied a summary judgment motion by the government on the ground that an examination had to be made as to whether the claims at issue fell within the same proposed regulatory policy.

In *United States v. Diapulse Corp.*, the Second Circuit reviewed FDA decisions to take enforcement action against one medical device that failed to meet certain internal FDA scientific standards but not to proceed against a similar device that had the same compliance problems.[561] The court chastised FDA's failure to "apply its scientific conclusions even-handedly," and held that: "[d]eference to administrative discretion or expertise is not a license to a regulatory agency to treat like cases differently."[562] Similarly, FDA's failure to take enforcement action against one of two companies that received Warning Letters and failed to alter their allegedly illegal conduct led the D.C. District Court to require FDA to "treat similarly situated entities" in a "fair and even-handed manner."[563]

Despite these cases, however, it is very difficult to challenge any particular enforcement action by an executive agency on the ground that the action is selective or arbitrary and capricious. For example, in *United States v. Sage Pharmaceuticals*,[564] FDA initiated an enforcement action against Sage for the sale of unlawful drug products, notwithstanding the fact that other pharmaceutical companies were selling similar illegal drug products under the same trade name at the same time.[565] Sage argued on appeal "that the government's action against it violates the Administrative Procedure Act (APA) as it is arbitrary and capricious because

---

[558]   Cook v. FDA, 733 F.3d 1 (D.C. Cir. 2013). Cook involved the importation of foreign manufactured sodium thiopental into the United States for lethal injection of prisoners. Although importation of the drug was not lawful under the FDCA, FDA allowed its importation through an exercise of enforcement discretion.

[559]   716 F. Supp. 787 (S.D.N.Y. 1989).

[560]   Food Labeling; Public Health Messages on Food Labels and Labeling, 52 Fed. Reg. 28,843 (Aug. 4, 1987).

[561]   748 F.2d 56 (2d Cir. 1984).

[562]   *Id.* at 62.

[563]   Allergan, Inc. v. Shalala, Civ. No. 94-1223 (D.D.C. Nov. 10, 1994) (finding that, once FDA began industry-wide enforcement by means of a Drug Efficacy Study Implementation notice and Warning Letters, "it must do so in a fair and even-handed manner"); *cf.* Bracco Diagnostics, Inc. v. Shalala, 963 F. Supp. 20, 28 (D.D.C. 1997) (finding likelihood of success on claim that FDA acted arbitrarily and capriciously by regulating plaintiff's product as a drug and its competitor's product as a device where they were "identical in all material respects, and the FDA has not provided a legitimate reason for failing to regulate these similar products in the same way").

[564]   210 F.3d 475 (5th Cir. 2000).

[565]   *Id.* at 479.

the government has not taken similar action against its competitors."[566] The Fifth Circuit rejected this argument on the grounds that, under *Heckler v. Chaney*, the APA prohibits a review of the FDA's enforcement decisions, and that a claim that FDA's action was arbitrary and capricious was not a defense to an enforcement proceeding.[567]

In *Kisser v. Cisneros*, the Department of Housing and Urban Development (HUD) suspended multiple officers of a funding corporation, including Mr. Kisser, for improper handling of mortgage payments.[568] HUD then initiated a debarment action against Kisser, but not the other similarly situated officers, and eventually debarred Kisser. Kisser challenged HUD's decision, and the district court vacated the debarment, on the grounds that HUD's failure to explain why it had chosen to single out Kisser constituted arbitrary and capricious action.[569] The D.C. Circuit reversed and held that judicial authority to compare the completed case against Kisser with HUD's decision not to pursue enforcement against the other DRG employees was precluded by *Heckler v. Chaney*.[570]

In short, the reasoning of *Heckler* survives, with FDA often choosing to pursue enforcement against a principal target and varying strategies against other violators.[571]

How FDA Chooses to Employ Its Enforcement Powers

The number of FDA-initiated criminal prosecutions does not reflect the number of proposed criminal referrals, some of which are resolved through the section 305 hearing process, or the number of actual referrals, some of which are declined by DOJ. In addition, many pharmaceutical-related enforcement actions that are pursued by DOJ, U.S. Attorney's Offices, and DHHS OIG no longer originate with FDA. For example, DOJ has increasingly taken the lead in prosecuting enforcement actions involving fraud or promotion of drugs for unapproved uses and, in recent years, has developed prosecutions for FDCA violations without any involvement by FDA.[572] Criminal jurisdiction with respect to controlled drug substances also lies with the Drug Enforcement Administration (DEA) in DOJ, which actively monitors the distribution of such pharmaceuticals and their predicate substances, including FDA-approved controlled substances that might be diverted into unlawful channels. Additionally, FDA meets regularly with organizations such as the National Association of Attorneys General and the Association of Food and Drug Officials to discuss the institution of test cases or the development of new enforcement policies.

---

[566] *See id.* at 480 (citing Allergan, Inc. v. Shalala, 6 FDC Law Rep. (CCH) ¶ 38,375 (D.D.C. November 10, 1994) (action to compel FDA to treat similarly situated companies alike by continuing enforcement action against Allergan's competitor), vacated as moot (1995)).

[567] 210 F.3d at 480.

[568] 14 F.3d 615 (D.C. Cir. 1994).

[569] *Id.* at 618.

[570] *Id.* at 620.

[571] One example involved FDA's two seizure actions against a combination drug composed of pre-1983 "old drugs." The manufacturer of the seized drug lost both cases, appealed, obtained stays, and continued to sell millions of dollars worth of the product. United States v. Sandoz Pharm. Corp., 894 F.2d 825 (6th Cir. 1990); United States v. 225 Cartons ..."Fiorinal with Codeine," 687 F. Supp. 946 (D.N.J. 1988), *aff'd.* 871 F.2d 409 (3d Cir. 1989). Ostensibly, neither *Exachol* nor *Diapulse* would have assisted the manufacturer of a subsequently seized indistinguishable drug.

[572] *Rx Compliance Enforcement Is Moving Away from "FDA" Cases, Sheehan Says*, F-D-C REP. ("The Pink Sheet"), Sept. 10, 2007; *Clinical Trial Conduct May Be Subject to DOJ Enforcement*, F-D-C REP. ("The Pink Sheet"), Feb. 7, 2005, at 27.

FDA issues a large number of warning and other letters that lead firms to alter their practices and numerous FD483 exit interviews and exchanges of correspondence that frequently make further enforcement action unnecessary. Inspections have also played an effective and considered role in enforcement of manufacturing standards. For example, new pre-approval inspection procedures serve as a powerful enforcement tool, and FDA has used them effectively to defer approvals until cGMP compliance is achieved in the plant where a new drug or device is to be manufactured.

In addition to the powerful injunctive remedies outlined in the immediately preceding section of this chapter, FDA has utilized its enforcement power to negotiate civil penalties, such as the $30.5 million civil penalty as part of the *United States v. C.R. Bard, Inc.* litigation, $800 million civil penalty as part of the *United States ex rel. Robert Rudolf* litigation and $1.1 billion civil penalty as part of the *United States ex rel. Blair Collins v. Pfizer, Inc.* litigation.[573]

Since FDA has limited resources, it usually performs an informal risk-benefit analysis before initiating an enforcement action. Recently, FDA has chosen to pursue pharmacy compounders,[574] companies that manufacture contaminated drugs,[575] and pet-food manufacturers whose products contained melamine.[576] It has also taken action against companies marketing unapproved drug products,[577] often by issuing "cyber" letters to website operators.[578]

During the last decade, the U.S. Attorneys' Offices and DOJ have brought numerous off-label enforcement actions.[579] State attorneys general have also probed pharmaceutical companies'

---

[573]   United States v. C.R. Bard, Inc., 848 F. Supp. 287 (D. Mass. 1994); United States ex rel. Robert Rudolf, 2:03-cv-00943-LP (E.D. Pa. 2009); United States et al. ex rel. Blair Collins v. Pfizer, Inc., Civ. No. 04-11780-DPW (D. Mass.).

[574]   United States v. Main Street Family Pharmacy LLC, No. 1:14-cv-01326 (W.D. Tenn. Dec. 3, 2014). In Warning Letters to compounders, FDA has cited to such FDCA sections as 301(d), 502(f)(1), 502(o), 505(a), and 510(g).

[575]   United States v. McNeil-PPC, Inc. et al., No. 11-1745 (E.D. Pa. Mar. 10, 2011).

[576]   United States v. Xuzhou Anying Biologic Tech. Dev. Co., No. 08-27 (W.D. Mo); United States v. Miller, No. 08-23 (W.D. Mo).

[577]   Marketed New Drugs Without Approved NDAs and ANDAs, FDA Compliance Policy Guides Manual § 440.100 (revised Sept. 16, 2011); *FDA Crackdown on Unapproved Drugs Has Incentives for Voluntary Submissions*, F-D-C Rep. ("The Pink Sheet"), June 12, 2006, at 10-11. Recent targets have included marketers of unapproved prescription drug products containing hydrocodone, a narcotic used to treat pain and suppress coughs; guaifenesin, a substance commonly used to relieve cough and cold symptoms by stimulating removal of mucous from the lungs; and colchicine, a drug used to treat gout. *Unapproved Colchicine Drugs Face FDA Enforcement*, F-D-C Rep. ("The Pink Sheet"), Feb. 11, 2008; *Unapproved Hydrocodone Crackdown*, F-D-C Rep. ("The Pink Sheet"), Oct. 1, 2007; Malcolm Spicer, *Mucinex Sales Could Climb With FDA Action Against Unapproved Products*, F-D-C Rep. ("The Tan Sheet"), May 28, 2007.

[578]   Cyber Letters, U.S. Food and Drug Administration, http://www.fda.gov/cder/warn/cyber (last updated July 23, 2013); *see also*, Nicholas Freitag, *Federal Food and Drug Act Violations*, 41 Am. Crim. L. Rev. 647, 669 (2004); FDA Launches "Cyber" Letters Against Potentially Illegal, Foreign-Based Online Drug Sites, FDA Talk Paper (Feb. 2, 2000), http://web.archive.org/web/20080229052621/fda.gov/bbs/topics/ANSWERS/ANS01001.html.

[579]   *See* Press Release, DOJ, Johnson & Johnson to Pay More Than $2.2 Billion to Resolve Criminal and Civil Investigations (Nov. 4, 2013), http://www.justice.gov/opa/pr/johnson-johnson-pay-more-22-billion-resolve-criminal-and-civil-investigations; Brenda Sandburg, *Off-Label Promotion Probes May Focus on Companies' R&D Plans*, F-D-C Rep. ("The Pink Sheet"), Dec. 3, 2007. *See also* Complaint, United States ex rel. Thorpe v. GlaxoSmithKline, No. 11-10398-RWZ (D. Mass. Oct. 26, 2011); United States et al. ex rel. Blair Collins v. Pfizer, Inc., Civ. No. 04-11780-DPW (D. Mass.).

sales and marketing practices and brought numerous civil enforcement proceedings.[580] Government probes have resulted in an $875 million settlement and a plea of guilt for conspiracy to violate the Prescription Drug Marketing Act,[581] $20 million in penalties and victim compensation to resolve parallel criminal and civil investigations,[582] $700.6 million to resolve criminal charges and civil liabilities related to illegal marketing and selling of pharmaceuticals,[583] and $2.3 billion to resolve civil and criminal liability arising from the allegedly illegal promotion of pharmaceuticals.[584] Additionally, officers and company counsel have pled guilty to misdemeanor charges of misbranding.[585] Budgetary limitations have led to even greater cooperation among FDA and FTC, the U.S. Postal Service, the U.S. Department of Agriculture, DEA, and state agencies.

In an era when Congress has had to address an increasing reliance upon imported foods and medical product components, and has expressed skepticism about corporate integrity, it has conferred stronger enforcement powers on FDA. FDA continues to explore how best to use these new powers given its limited resources. The establishment of the Global Directorate inside the Office of the Commissioner and the proliferation of new FDA offices abroad evidence the agency's commitment to increase its scrutiny of the new global marketplace. The growth of OCI over the last decade[586] and the agency's propensity to prosecute high-profile violations of the FDCA also signal that the agency continues to believe there is important deterrent value in criminal enforcement of violations of the FDCA.[587]

---

[580] E.g., Maxi Drug N., Inc. v. Comm'r, N.H. HHS, 907 A.2d 974 (N.H. 2006); Jones v. Howell, 877 So. 2d 691 (Miss. 2002); 2006-033 Op. Att'y Gen (2005), 2005 Ala. AG LEXIS 202; 03-0437 Op. Att'y Gen (2003), 2003 La. AG LEXIS 521.

[581] Settlement addressing claims against TAP Pharmaceutical Products, Inc. for claims in United States v. TAP Pharm. Products Inc., Crim. No. 01-10354-011-WGY (D. Mass.); United States v. TAP Holdings Inc., Civ. No. 98-10547-GAO (D. Mass), and United States v. TAP Holdings Inc., Civ. No. 00-12618-GAO (originally filed in May 1996 in the E.D. Pa. and later transferred to the D. Mass.) (settled in 2001).

[582] Plea Agreement addressing claims against Orphan Medical, Inc. for claims in United States v. Orphan Med., Inc., Crim. No. 07-CR-531-ENV (E.D.N.Y.); Civil Settlement addressing claims against Orphan Medical, Inc. for claims in United States v. Orphan Med., Inc., Civ. No. 05-CR-0387 (E.D.N.Y.); Non-Prosecution Agreement Between Jazz Pharmaceuticals, Inc. and the U.S. Attorney's Office for the Eastern District of New York for claims in United States v. Orphan Med., Inc., Crim. No. 07-CR-531-ENV (E.D.N.Y.).

[583] Plea Agreement addressing claims against The Purdue Frederick Co. for claims in United States v. The Purdue Frederick Co., Inc., No. 1:07CR00029 (W.D. Va.); Civil Settlement Agreement addressing claims against The Purdue Frederick Co. for claims in United States v. The Purdue Frederick Co., Inc., Attachment D to Plea Agreement; see also United States v. The Purdue Frederick Co., 495 F. Supp. 2d 569 (W.D. Va. 2007) (approving plea agreement).

[584] Civil Settlement Agreement addressing claims against Pfizer Inc. for claims in United States et al. ex rel. Blair Collins v. Pfizer, Inc., 1:04-11780-DPW (D. Mass.); Plea Agreement addressing claims against Pharmacia & Upjohn Company, Inc. in United States v. Pharmacia & Upjohn Company, Inc., 1:09-cr-102580DPW (D. Mass.).

[585] Plea Agreement addressing claims against Michael Friedman for claims in United States v. Friedman, No. 1:07CR29 (W.D. Va.); Plea Agreement addressing claims against Paul Goldenheim in United States v. Goldenheim, No. 1:07CR29 (W.D. Va.); Plea Agreement addressing claims against Howard Udell in United States v. Udell, No. 1:07CR29 (W.D. Va.); Plea Agreement addressing claims against Peter Decoster, No. 3:14cr3024 (N.D. Iowa).

[586] See U.S. Gov't Accountability Office, GAO-10-221, Improved Monitoring and Development of Performance Measures Needed to Strengthen Oversight of Criminal and Misconduct Investigations (Jan. 2010) (observing that OCI staffing increased 40 percent from 1999 to 2008).

[587] See United States v. Parnell, No. 1:13-CR-12-WLS, 2013 U.S. Dist. LEXIS 75700 (M.D. Ga. Feb. 15, 2013); United States v. Quality Egg, LLC et al., No. 3:14-cr-03024 (N.D. Iowa June 3, 2014).

Still, the agency is facing a number of strategic questions about how to allocate its resources most effectively, given the growing universe of products it regulates and the complexities of modern supply chains. The enactment of FSMA in 2011, FDASIA in 2012, and DQSA in 2013 may lead to new priorities. On the one hand, Congress again enhanced FDA's enforcement authorities by substantially increasing the criminal penalties related to intentional adulteration of drugs and empowering FDA to suspend a food facility's registration through administrative means after an outbreak. On the other, however, the new laws call for preventive action across supply chains. FDASIA requires drug manufacturers to audit their suppliers, FSMA requires development and implementation of preventive controls for food processors, and Title II of DQSA sets forth significant track-and-trace requirements aimed at safeguarding the integrity of the domestic drug supply.

How FDA will modify its enforcement priorities, if at all, to align with this movement is not yet clear. FDA has expended enormous resources drafting the rules necessary to implement the new legislative requirements. It thus stands to reason that FDA will focus considerable energy on enforcing them. More enforcement of these requirements, however, will require more inspections (including more foreign inspections) and more document review. Such efforts are costly. Moreover, it can be very difficult to measure the effectiveness of actions taken to ensure compliance with preventive systems. Nevertheless, FDA seems poised to effectuate these new laws, so the numbers of Warning Letters directed at cGMP and preventive control lapses should increase in the next few years. The focus on criminal enforcement and high-profile civil cases should continue, as well, but FDA will have to balance those efforts with new enforcement initiatives aimed at preventing the adulteration and misbranding of FDA-regulated articles in the first place.

CHAPTER 22

MEDICAL COUNTERMEASURES: EMERGENCY PREPAREDNESS AND RESPONSE ROLES AND AUTHORITIES

BROOKE COURTNEY AND ELIZABETH SADOVE

Introduction

Since the 2001 anthrax attacks in the United States, which led to five deaths and sickened 17 individuals, the nation's approach to preparing for and responding to public health emergencies has evolved into a set of comprehensive, coordinated systems involving global, federal, state, tribal, territorial, local, and private sector partners.[1] As an agency of the U.S. Department of Health and Human Services (DHHS), the Food and Drug Administration (FDA), which has multifaceted roles in preparing for and responding to disasters and emerging threats, is a vital component of the nation's health security. FDA's responsibilities in preventing and mitigating the impacts of public health emergencies on the U.S. population, such as those involving chemical, biological, radiological, and nuclear (CBRN) threat agents, including emerging infectious disease threats (e.g., pandemic influenza), as well as natural disasters, range from efforts to secure the nation's food and drug supplies to helping to ensure the availability of safe and appropriate medical countermeasures (MCMs) to counter such threats.

Although achieving the nation's overarching MCM development and response goals involves a wide range of government (federal, state, and local), academic, and industry stakeholders,

---

[1] See, e.g., U.S. Dep't of Homeland Security (DHS), National Response Framework (2d ed. May 2013), available at https://s3-us-gov-west-1.amazonaws.com/dam-production/uploads/20130726-1914-25045-1246/final_national_response_framework_20130501.pdf. "The National Response Framework is a guide to how the Nation responds to all types of disasters and emergencies . . . [It] describes specific authorities and best practices for managing incidents that range from the serious but purely local to large-scale terrorist attacks or catastrophic natural disasters, . . . [and] describes the principles, roles and responsibilities, and coordinating structures for delivering the core capabilities required to respond to an incident and further describes how response efforts integrate with those of the other mission areas." Id. at i.

this chapter focuses on FDA's role in the development, approval,[2] emergency use, and postmarket oversight of MCMs. It defines "medical countermeasures" and "public health threats"; describes FDA's domestic and global MCM roles in public health emergency preparedness and response; and outlines the legal and regulatory authorities and mechanisms that FDA uses to facilitate MCM development, regulatory review, stockpiling, and emergency use.

Background

Definition of "Medical Countermeasures"

Medical countermeasures are the drugs, biologics (e.g., vaccines), and devices (e.g., in vitro diagnostics (IVDs) and respiratory protective devices (RPDs)) that are used to diagnose, prevent, or treat the human health effects of CBRN emergencies and emerging infectious disease threats.[3] Through diagnosing, preventing, or treating exposure or illness, MCMs are a critical component of securing the nation against naturally occurring, deliberate, and accidental threats. They are particularly important for emergencies involving biological threats, for which interdiction is unlikely or very difficult. Because of its regulatory oversight of medical products, FDA is involved in a range of activities in the life cycle of MCMs, including product development, stockpiling, dispensing to the populations that need to use them, monitoring of adverse events, and handling of stockpiled products that are held beyond their labeled expiration date but that may nevertheless be safe and effective. MCMs are developed by both government and industry sponsors, with government being the primary purchaser and stockpiler of such products.

MCMs and Public Health Threats

Emergencies such as the 2001 anthrax attacks, 2009 H1N1 influenza pandemic, 2011 Japan earthquake and tsunami (and resulting nuclear disaster), 2013 emergence of the novel H7N9 influenza virus and Middle East Respiratory Syndrome Coronavirus (MERS-CoV), and 2014 Ebola outbreak demonstrate the range of threats—both natural and deliberate—to public health that the nation faces and for which MCMs might be needed to mitigate the resulting health impacts. These events also reinforce the critical and often complex role that FDA plays in collaboration with multiple global, federal, tribal, state, territorial, local, private sector, and academic partners in public health and medical disaster preparedness and response and in national security. It is a role that is continually evolving with the occurrence of new

---

[2]   For purposes of this chapter, products that are "approved" include products that are "FDA-approved, licensed, or cleared" under sections 505, 510(k), or 515 of the Federal Food, Drug, and Cosmetic Act (FDCA) or under section 351 of the Public Health Service Act (PHSA).

[3]   Medical countermeasures include "qualified countermeasures" as defined in section 319F-1(a) of the PHSA (42 U.S.C. § 247d–6a(a)); "qualified pandemic or epidemic products" as defined in section 319F-3 of the PHSA (42 U.S.C. § 247d-6d)); and "security countermeasures" as defined in section 319F-2(c)(1)(B) of the PHSA (42 U.S.C. § 247d-6b). Food & Drug Admin. (FDA), FDA Medical Countermeasures Initiative (MCMi) Fiscal Year 2013 Program Update, 1 (2014), *available at* http://www.fda.gov/EmergencyPreparedness/Counterterrorism/MedicalCountermeasures/AboutMCMi/ucm390308.htm.

disasters, emergence of novel infectious diseases, advancements in regulatory science,[4] development of new MCMs, and establishment of new or enhanced legal and regulatory authorities and approaches.

A wide-area attack with aerosolized *Bacillus anthracis* (*B. anthracis*), the bacterium that causes anthrax, provides an example to demonstrate the variety of FDA-regulated MCMs and actions that might be needed for a response. At the outset of the emergency, FDA might need to authorize the emergency use of uncleared rapid diagnostic tests to determine antimicrobial susceptibility. FDA might also need to authorize the emergency use of vaccines or drugs, including unapproved, or unapproved uses of approved, drugs or vaccines, to prevent or treat anthrax disease among those exposed. In addition, FDA would need to monitor and assess the performance of MCMs used during the response as well as post-event. RPDs (e.g., N95 respirators) might also be used to protect response workers engaged in decontamination efforts during the recovery phase.

FDA's Role in MCM Emergency Preparedness and Response

Overview of FDA and Emergency Response

When a public health emergency strikes, or threatens to strike, domestically or abroad, FDA may have significant—and varied—response roles. During routine, non-emergency times, FDA's mission is broad. FDA is responsible for protecting the nation's public health by assuring the safety, efficacy, quality, and security of human and veterinary drugs, biological products, and medical devices and the safety of the nation's food supply, cosmetics, and products that emit radiation, and by regulating the manufacture, marketing, and distribution of tobacco products. During an emergency, FDA may also need to respond to unique incident-related circumstances while still continuing to fulfill its general mission. Depending on the local impact of the disaster and resulting emergency needs, some FDA-regulated products may be deployed and/or authorized for emergency use, while FDA-regulated industries may be adversely affected.

To provide structure and organization to FDA's response efforts, the agency's Office of Crisis Management (OCM) in the Office of the Commissioner (OC) facilitates the coordination of agency operations and resources, such as through implementing FDA's emergency operations plan, supporting DHHS response and recovery activities, assessing damage to

---

[4]   Regulatory science is "the science of developing new tools, standards, and approaches to assess the safety, efficacy, quality, and performance of all FDA-regulated products." FDA, Advancing Regulatory Science: Moving Regulatory Science into the 21st Century, *available at* http://www.fda.gov/scienceresearch/ specialtopics/regulatoryscience/default.htm (last visited Oct. 23, 2014). The goal of the Regulatory Science Program for MCMs is "to develop the tools, standards, and approaches to assess medical countermeasure safety, efficacy, quality, and performance and to help translate cutting-edge science and technology into innovative, safe, and effective medical countermeasures—including for at-risk populations." FDA, *supra* note 3, at 20.

FDA-regulated industries, and issuing safety alerts to the public.[5] In addition to OCM's role in overall coordination of FDA's emergency response activities, FDA's Centers and other offices (e.g., Office of the Chief Counsel (OCC) and Office of International Programs (OIP)) have critical and complementary roles in public health emergency preparedness and response efforts and, as needed, coordinate and collaborate on responses. The Center for Biologics Evaluation and Research (CBER), Center for Drug Evaluation and Research (CDER), and Center for Devices and Radiological Health (CDRH) have counterterrorism coordinators and teams who focus on emergencies and emerging threats. In addition, the Office of Counterterrorism and Emerging Threats (OCET) within OC facilitates intra- and interagency coordination, communications, and legal, regulatory, and policy activities specifically related to MCMs.

In carrying out its various response functions to address threats to public health, FDA actively engages with industry and with its global (e.g., World Health Organization (WHO)), federal (e.g., sister DHHS agencies and offices, Department of Defense (DOD), Department of Homeland Security (DHS), etc.), state, territorial, tribal, and local public health and medical response partners in support of emergency efforts. FDA's work in this area often falls under established federal coordinating structures. For example, as an agency of DHHS, which leads public health and medical responses to public health emergencies and incidents covered by the National Response Framework (NRF) in preparation for, during, and following disasters for which federal assets and assistance are needed, FDA interacts with other components of DHHS to help protect the population.[6]

Public Health Emergency Medical Countermeasures Enterprise

Within DHHS, FDA collaborates on MCM preparedness and response issues with the Office of the Assistant Secretary for Preparedness and Response (ASPR) of the DHHS Office of the Secretary. The ASPR serves as the Secretary's principal advisor on all matters related to federal public health and medical emergency preparedness and response.[7] This collaboration includes working with ASPR's Biomedical Advanced Research and Development Authority (BARDA), which provides an integrated and systematic approach to the advanced research on and the development and purchase of MCMs against public health threats.[8] FDA also partners with other DHHS agencies, such as the National Institutes of Health (NIH) on early product development and on conducting research during disasters[9] and the Centers for Disease Control and Prevention (CDC), which, among its many functions, manages the Strategic National Stockpile (SNS) and supports state and local public health agencies in their emergency response roles.[10] Further, FDA's response activities and authorities within

---

5   FDA, FDA Emergency Operations Plan (v. 2.0) (March 2014), *available at* http://www.fda.gov/downloads/emergencypreparedness/emergencypreparedness/ucm230973.pdf.

6   DHS, *supra* note 1; PHSA § 2801 (codified at 42 U.S.C. § 300hh).

7   PHSA § 2811 (codified at 42 U.S.C. § 300hh-10).

8   DHHS, Biomedical Advanced Research and Development Authority, *available at* https://www.medicalcountermeasures.gov/BARDA/BARDA.aspx (last visited Oct. 23, 2014).

9   N. Lurie, T. Manolio, A.P. Patterson, et al., *Research as a Part of Public Health Emergency Response*, 368 N. ENGL. J. MED. 1251-1255 (2013).

10   CDC, Strategic National Stockpile, *available at* http://www.cdc.gov/phpr/stockpile.htm (last visited Oct. 23, 2014). The SNS (formerly the National Pharmaceutical Stockpile) is the nation's repository of MCMs and includes large quantities of medical products (e.g., antibiotics, chemical antidotes, antitoxins, life-support

the context of the DHHS response paradigm extend to facilitating MCM-related efforts of state and local public health agencies, which have critical roles in emergency responses (e.g., stockpiling, distributing, and dispensing MCMs) in close coordination with ASPR and CDC.

Coordinated efforts to develop and stockpile MCMs began more than a decade ago, and the federal government's role in this area has expanded significantly over time, particularly following the 2001 anthrax attacks and, as described later in this chapter, the subsequent enactment of new federal authorities focused on MCMs.[11] These authorities set out to address significant challenges in MCM development,[12] which included a perceived lack of commercial viability since the products primarily are for purposes of emergency stockpiling and use, and the scientific complexity of developing and regulating them given that, for many of these products, it is unethical or infeasible to conduct human efficacy studies. These and other factors, such as liability protection, uncertainty of sustained government commitment, and unpredictable and continually evolving threats to public health historically deterred developers from engaging in research on and development of MCMs.[13,14]

To determine which MCMs are needed to counter various health threats to the U.S. population and to support and encourage the development, procurement, and stockpiling of them, ASPR leads the Public Health Emergency Medical Countermeasures Enterprise (Enterprise). FDA participates in the Enterprise, which is a coordinated, interagency effort to define and prioritize requirements for public health emergency MCMs; focus research, development, and procurement activities on the identified requirements; support MCM research and development; and establish deployment and use strategies for MCMs stockpiled in the SNS.[15] Other Enterprise partners include the CDC, NIH, DHS, DOD, Department of Veterans Affairs, and U.S. Department of Agriculture.

DHHS is also leading efforts to build and strengthen the nation's capacity to rapidly develop and produce MCMs in response to a sudden-onset CBRN emergency. In 2012, for example, DHHS announced the establishment of the Centers for Innovation in Advanced Development

---

medications, airway maintenance supplies, and medical/surgical items) to supplement and re-supply state and local health agencies in response to public health emergencies within the U.S. or its territories. *Id.*

[11] DHHS, The Public Health Emergency Medical Countermeasures Enterprise Review: Transforming the Enterprise to Meet Long-Range National Needs (August 2010), *available at* http://www.hhs.gov/nvpo/nvac/meetings/upcomingmeetings/korch_presentation.pdf.

[12] *Id.* at 5.

[13] For example, "[t]he review consistently found that most of the developers attracted to the MCM arena are small biotechnology companies that bring innovation to the . . . development of a new product, and in doing so, take on high risk. These companies are often challenged due to limited experience in taking a product through advanced development to licensure. They often lack the capability and/or experience in areas such as animal testing, assay development, product manufacturing, clinical trials, and navigating the regulatory process. For companies that do not have the existing *infrastructure* to undertake these activities, accessing such services is often too difficult or expensive to assume on their own. This problem is similar to medical product development in other sectors with small downstream markets, such as orphan drugs and drugs for neglected diseases." *See id.* at 8.

[14] *See* Institute of Medicine (IOM), *The Public Health Emergency Medical Countermeasures Enterprise: Innovative Strategies to Enhance Products from Discovery Through Approval: Workshop Summary* (2010). Washington, DC: The National Academies Press.

[15] DHHS, Public Health Emergency Medical Countermeasures Enterprise (PHEMCE) Management, *available at* https://www.medicalcountermeasures.gov/BARDA/PHEMCE/phemce.aspx (last visited Oct. 23, 2014).

and Manufacturing. These three new centers, which are supported by ASPR/BARDA, will aid in developing and manufacturing MCMs by bringing them to the market more quickly.[16]

FDA Medical Countermeasure Roles

The efforts and successes of the Enterprise and statutory mechanisms to facilitate MCM development have resulted in considerable advancements in the arsenal of MCMs that could be deployed to address the highest priority threats. The development and regulatory review of MCMs require specialized knowledge and scientific expertise. Because it is responsible for evaluating product safety and efficacy, FDA has the requisite understanding of the steps necessary for successful product development. Advancing MCM development and emergency preparedness is one of FDA's cross-cutting strategic priorities.[17,18]

FDA-wide MCM goals, and engagement in the Enterprise, include helping to accelerate MCM development toward approval and establishing clear regulatory pathways for review and approval of high-priority MCMs based on advanced scientific foundations. They also include advancing regulatory science to improve MCM development and evaluation (e.g., through supporting the continued modernization of scientific infrastructure that enhances and streamlines the development of tools and standards for assessing new medical product safety, efficacy, and quality); supporting new technologies for flexible, rapidly scalable development and manufacturing of vaccines and other MCMs; and modernizing the legal, regulatory, and policy framework for effective public health responses and emergency use of MCMs (e.g., through implementation of the Pandemic and All-Hazards Preparedness Reauthorization Act of 2013 (PAHPRA)), as discussed in this chapter.[19] FDA has also established a robust professional development program to educate staff in relevant offices about the unique challenges of MCMs, as well as the threats and diseases for which they are being developed.

Further, FDA and its federal partners work to build and strengthen the nation's capacity and capability to better understand how MCMs perform when used during emergencies. In some cases, MCMs used during responses may have very little historical clinical experience in humans. They may have been FDA-approved based on studies of efficacy in animals instead of humans, may be unapproved but authorized for use during the emergency, or may not previously have been used in certain populations. Effectively monitoring and assessing MCM performance (e.g., through enhanced adverse event tracking, reporting, analysis, and

---

[16]   DHHS, HHS Centers for Innovation in Advanced Development and Manufacturing, *available at* https://www.medicalcountermeasures.gov/hhscentersforinnovation.aspx (last visited Oct. 23, 2014).

[17]   In December 2009, to further address challenges and identify new and transformative approaches to facilitate and encourage MCM development, then-DHHS Secretary Sebelius called for a review of the entire Enterprise, with the goal of modernizing it through improved production processes, regulatory frameworks, and approaches to stockpiling and dispensing MCMs. The review identified FDA as a critical partner and spurred establishment of FDA's Medical Countermeasures Initiative (MCMi) in 2010 to enable innovative regulatory science and oversight and foster flexible manufacturing and advanced development, thereby expanding the product pipeline. The implementation of the MCMi has been led by FDA's Office of Counterterrorism and Emerging Threats (OCET), in close collaboration with the Center for Biologics Evaluation and Research (CBER), Center for Drug Evaluation and Research (CDER), Center for Devices and Radiological Health (CDRH), and Office of the Chief Counsel (OCC).

[18]   FDA, Strategic Priorities 2011-2015: Responding to the Public Health Challenges of the 21st Century (2011), *available at* http://www.fda.gov/downloads/AboutFDA/ReportsManualsForms/Reports/UCM252092.pdf.

[19]   FDA, *supra* note 3.

communication) in near-real time in an emergency are critical to helping to inform clinical decisions during the response and in future responses.

FDA Engagement in Global Health Security

In addition to its domestic MCM roles, FDA engages in international efforts to enhance global health security, including preparedness for and response to emergencies that would involve the use of MCMs.[20] FDA works closely with its DHHS sister agencies and offices, and with WHO and other partners, through several international initiatives to strengthen MCM preparedness, including the Global Health Security Agenda,[21] Beyond the Border,[22] and the Global Health Security Initiative (GHSI).[23] For example, GHSI is focused in part on sharing MCM stockpiles and expertise with other countries (which might lack their own supplies of needed MCMs and/or sufficient legal and regulatory structures to allow for the emergency use of certain medical products) during public health emergencies through helping to strengthen operational frameworks and regulatory capacity.

Federal MCM Statutes

Underlying FDA's efforts and authorities related to MCM development, approval, and emergency use is a comprehensive legal and regulatory framework. In addition to FDA's routine review and enforcement functions under the FDCA and the PHSA, the statutory basis of FDA's MCM and emergency response capacities lies in statutes that were enacted during the decade after the 2001 terrorist and anthrax attacks and are specifically focused on facilitating public health emergency preparedness and response efforts. In many cases, these statutes amended the FDCA and the PHSA.

Public Health Security and Bioterrorism Preparedness and Response Act (Bioterrorism Act) (2002)

Following the 2001 terrorist and anthrax events, the Bioterrorism Act was the first comprehensive legislative effort aimed at strengthening the nation's ability to prepare for and respond to public health emergencies at the federal, state, and local levels.[24,25] Among its many provisions, the Bioterrorism Act included FDA requirements related to the accelerated approval of priority MCMs[26] and the development of a final rule on animal models when

---

[20]   B. Courtney, K.C. Bond, C. Maher, *Regulatory Underpinnings of Global Health Security: FDA's Roles in Preventing, Detecting, and Responding to Global Health Threats*, BIOSECUR BIOTERROR, 12(5):239-246 (2014).

[21]   *See, e.g.*, CDC, The Global Health Security Agenda, *available at* http://www.cdc.gov/globalhealth/security/ghsagenda.htm (last visited Oct. 23, 2014).

[22]   DHS, Beyond the Border: A Shared Vision for Perimeter Security and Economic Competitiveness, *available at* http://www.dhs.gov/beyond-border-shared-vision-perimeter-security-and-economic-competitiveness (last visited Oct. 23, 2014).

[23]   Global Health Security Initiative, GHSI, *available at* http://www.ghsi.ca/english/index.asp (last visited Oct. 23, 2014).

[24]   Pub. L. No. 107-188, 116 Stat. at 594 (2002).

[25]   Prior to the Bioterrorism Act, the Public Health Improvement Act of 2000, Pub. L. No. 106-505, 114 Stat. 2314-2319, included several provisions related to public health emergencies and emerging threats to public health.

[26]   Pub. L. No. 107-188, § 122, 116 Stat. at 613 (codified at 21 U.S.C. § 356-1).

efficacy studies in humans are infeasible or cannot be conducted ethically.[27] The act also provided mechanisms for protecting the food and drug supplies, and established the SNS as "a stockpile or stockpiles of drugs, vaccines, and other biological products, medical devices, and other supplies in such numbers, types, and amounts as are determined by the Secretary [of DHHS] . . . to provide for the emergency health security of the United States . . . in the event of a bioterrorist attack or other public health emergency."[28]

Project BioShield Act (2004)

After the 2001 anthrax attacks, the federal government increasingly recognized the importance of having appropriate MCMs readily available to address CBRN threats, and the need to create incentives to address developers' concerns about entering an unpredictable market with limited prospects for financial gain.[29] The purpose of the Project BioShield Act[30] was to encourage the development of MCMs against CBRN threat agents by providing "additional and more flexible authorities and funding to financially support and expedite [their] development and procurement."[31] The BioShield Act, which also included provisions to streamline processes related to research on and development of qualified MCMs and procurement of security countermeasures,[32],[33] amended the FDCA to authorize the Commissioner of Food and Drugs to issue Emergency Use Authorizations (EUAs) for use of MCMs during emergencies under section 564.[34] This authority, which was amended in 2013 by PAHPRA, is described further below. The act also authorized the use of a special reserve fund for procuring countermeasures, even those that are not yet approved by FDA.[35] This authorization enabled DHHS to develop an essentially new federal market that reduced developers' risk by allowing for the purchase of MCMs for the SNS while the products were still being developed.[36]

---

[27]   *Id.* at § 123, 116 Stat. at 613.

[28]   Pub. L. No. 107-188, § 121, 116 Stat. 611-13 (codified as amended 42 U.S.C. § 247d-6b; originally codified at 42 U.S.C. § 300hh-12).

[29]   *See, e.g.,* Congressional Research Service (CRS), Project BioShield: Authorities, Appropriations, Acquisitions, and Issues for Congress (Mar. 3, 2011), *available at* http://assets.opencrs.com/rpts/R41033_20110303.pdf.

[30]   Pub. L. No. 108-276, 118 Stat. 835 (2004).

[31]   DHHS, Project BioShield Annual Report to Congress: January 2009-December 2009, at 4, *available at* https://www.medicalcountermeasures.gov/BARDA/documents/2009BioShieldReportFINAL.pdf (last visited Oct. 28, 2014).

[32]   *Id.*

[33]   A "qualified countermeasure" is "a drug (as that term is defined by section 201(g)(1) of the Federal Food, Drug, and Cosmetic Act (21 U.S.C. 321(g)(1))), biological product (as that term is defined by section 351(i) of this Act (42 U.S.C. 262(i))), or device (as that term is defined by section 201(h) of the Federal Food, Drug, and Cosmetic Act (21 U.S.C. 321(h))) that the Secretary determines to be a priority" to "treat, identify, or prevent harm from any biological, chemical, radiological, or nuclear agent that may cause a public health emergency affecting national security" or treat, identify, or prevent harm from a condition that may result in adverse health consequences or death and may be caused by administering a drug, biological product, or device." Pub. L. No. 108-276, § 2, 118 Stat. at 835-36 (codified at 42 U.S.C. § 247d-6a).

[34]   The Secretary of DHHS has delegated the authority to issue an EUA under section 564 of the FDCA to the FDA Commissioner, as permitted under section 1003 and existing delegations of authority. *Id.* at § 4, 118 Stat. at 853-59 (codified at 21 U.S.C. § 360bbb-3).

[35]   *Id.* at § 3, 118 Stat. at 843 (codified at 42 U.S.C. § 247d-6b).

[36]   *See, e.g.,* CRS, *supra* note 29.

Public Readiness and Emergency Preparedness (PREP) Act (2005)

To mitigate concerns about liability in the full range of MCM activities (i.e., from manufacturing and testing through dispensing to the public) and to encourage MCM development, the Department of Defense, Emergency Supplemental Appropriations to Address Hurricanes in the Gulf of Mexico, and Pandemic Influenza Act, 2006, added new authorities under the PHSA through the PREP Act.[37] The PREP Act authorizes the Secretary of DHHS to provide immunity from liability under federal and state law for covered persons (e.g., MCM manufacturers and state or local government program planners and qualified persons who dispense or administer "covered countermeasures").[38] It also established an injury compensation program.[39]

The PREP Act defined a "covered countermeasure" as a qualified pandemic or epidemic product;[40] a security countermeasure; or an unapproved drug, biological product, or device authorized for emergency use in accordance with section 564 of the FDCA.[41] This definition included products approved under the FDCA or the PHSA, authorized for investigational use under the FDCA, or authorized under an EUA under the FDCA. In 2013, however, PAHPRA added to the definition products that are authorized for emergency use in accordance with section 564A or 564B of the FDCA.[42]

To authorize PREP Act protections, the DHHS Secretary must first issue a PREP Act declaration after making "a determination that a disease or other health condition or other threat to health constitutes a public health emergency, or that there is a credible risk that the disease, condition, or threat may in the future constitute such an emergency."[43] Thus, the PREP Act's liability protections do not automatically apply as a whole to all MCMs. Rather, the immunity comes into effect only for those categories of disease and covered countermeasures for which PREP Act declarations have been issued and remain in effect; and the immunity applies only to those persons and entities specified in each declaration. Declarations also specify the effective time period, population of individuals receiving

---

[37] Pub. L. No. 109-148, 119 Stat. 2818 (2005) (codified at 42 U.S.C. § 247d-6d); P. Binzer, *The PREP Act: Liability Protection for Medical Countermeasure Development, Distribution, and Administration*, 6 BIOSECUR BIOTERROR 293-298 (2008).

[38] DHHS, PREP Act Q&As, *available at* http://www.phe.gov/Preparedness/legal/prepact/Pages/prepqa.aspx (last visited Oct. 23, 2014).

[39] *See* DHHS, Countermeasures Injury Compensation Program, *available at* http://www.hrsa.gov/cicp/ (last visited Oct. 23, 2014). The Countermeasures Injury Compensation Program is administered by the DHHS Health Resources and Services Administration. DHHS provides compensation as payor of last resort for medical expenses, lost employment income, and survivor death benefits to individuals for serious injury or death from use of covered countermeasures.

[40] The Pandemic and All-Hazards Preparedness Reauthorization Act of 2013 (PAHPRA) amended the definition of "qualified pandemic or epidemic product" to also include "a product or technology intended to enhance the use or effect of a drug, biological product, or device." Pub. L. No. 113-5, § 402, 127 Stat. 196.

[41] Pub. L. No. 109-148, § 2, 119 Stat. at 2827-28.

[42] Pub. L. No. 113-5, § 402, 127 Stat. 196. "In general, [covered countermeasures now include] products that are approved, cleared, or licensed by FDA; authorized for investigational use . . . by FDA; authorized under an EUA by FDA; or otherwise permitted to be held or used for emergency use in accordance with Federal law." DHHS, *supra* note 38.

[43] Pub. L. No. 109-148, § 2, 119 Stat. at 2819-20 (codified at 42 U.S.C. § 247d-6d).

the covered countermeasure, geographic limitations on covered countermeasure use, and limitations on the method of distribution.

Pandemic and All-Hazards Preparedness Act (PAHPA) (2006)

PAHPA, which was reauthorized in 2013, addressed a broad range of issues to further strengthen the nation's public health preparedness and response capacities, including those related to MCMs.[44] For example, the legislation established within FDA:

> a team of experts on manufacturing and regulatory activities (including compliance with current Good Manufacturing Practices [cGMPs]) to provide both off-site and on-site technical assistance to the manufacturers of qualified countermeasures (as defined in section 319F-1 of the Public Health Service Act), security countermeasures (as defined in section 319F-2 of such Act), or vaccines, at the request of such a manufacturer and at the discretion of the Secretary, if the Secretary determines that a shortage or potential shortage may occur in the United States in the supply of such vaccines or countermeasures and that the provision of such assistance would be beneficial in helping alleviate or avert such shortage.[45]

To foster advanced research on and development of MCMs, PAHPA created BARDA within DHHS for advanced research and development of MCMs. BARDA is also responsible for Project BioShield acquisitions.[46]

Pandemic and All-Hazards Preparedness Reauthorization Act (PAHPRA) (2013)

In 2013, Congress reauthorized PAHPA and further amended the PHSA and the FDCA to enhance DHHS public health emergency preparedness and response capabilities.[47] Among its many preparedness and response flexibilities, PAHPRA includes specific provisions to facilitate and foster the emergency use and development of MCMs. For example, as described in the section below, PAHPRA amended the EUA authority under section 564 of the FDCA and establishes FDCA sections 564A and 564B. For approved MCMs, section 564A created emergency use authorities (which can be used without the need to issue an EUA) related to emergency dispensing, expiration dating extensions, development and distribution of emergency use instructions (EUIs), and waivers of cGMP and Risk Evaluation and Mitigation Strategies (REMS) requirements. Under section 564B, federal, state, and local governments are permitted to pre-position MCMs in anticipation of approval, clearance, or issuance of an EUA to support rapid deployment during an actual CBRN emergency. PAHPRA also codifies and builds on FDA's ongoing, agency-wide MCM development efforts, including through provisions to increase FDA's interactions with government and industry MCM sponsors, enhance review processes, and advance regulatory science for MCM development.

---

[44]   Pub. L. No. 109-417, 120 Stat. 2831.

[45]   *Id.* at § 404, 120 Stat. at 2875 (codified at 21 U.S.C. § 360bbb-4).

[46]   *Id.* at § 401, 120 Stat. at 2867-72 (codified at 42 USC 247d-7e); *see also* DHHS, *supra* note 31.

[47]   Pub. L. No. 113-5, 127 Stat. 161 (2013).

FDCA Authorities for Facilitating MCM Availability

FDA's responsibilities include facilitating the availability of safe and effective MCMs for responding to CBRN emergencies through a range of mechanisms, including routine and expedited product review and approval. When proposed clinical studies are deemed unethical or infeasible under FDA's standard regulatory processes, an alternative pathway commonly referred to as the "Animal Rule" may be applicable.[48] In addition, FDA has tools to address some of the unique challenges associated with MCM use and stockpiling, including mechanisms to authorize the emergency use of unapproved products and unapproved uses of approved products, and to allow certain activities related to the emergency use of approved products that otherwise might violate provisions of the FDCA.

Development and Approval of MCMs

The desired end goal of the MCM Enterprise is to have a full arsenal of FDA-approved products for each high-priority threat agent. As with all medical products, MCMs are subject to FDA's rigorous review and approval regulations and policies, as discussed in detail in other chapters, including those for a marketing application (i.e., a new drug application (NDA),[49] a biologics license application (BLA),[50] and a premarket notification 510(k)[51] and premarket approval (PMA)[52] application for a device) and for the conduct of clinical investigations (i.e., investigational new drug application (IND),[53] investigational device exemption (IDE),[54] and humanitarian device exemption[55]).

FDA can also apply to MCMs its expedited programs for making "therapeutically important" drugs and biologics available earlier than they would otherwise be made available through its standard review processes.[56] For example, a sponsor of a product may request from FDA a fast track designation to facilitate development and expedite review of the product if it is intended for the treatment of a serious or life-threatening disease or condition and it demonstrates the potential to address an unmet medical need, or if it is a certain type of antibacterial or antifungal drug.[57] With a fast track designation, the drug sponsor is, among other things, eligible for more frequent meetings with FDA to discuss the development plan

---

[48] *See* 21 C.F.R. subpt. I (2014) (for drugs); 21 C.F.R. subpt. H (2014) (for biological products); FDA, New Drug and Biological Drug Products; Evidence Needed to Demonstrate Effectiveness of New Drugs When Human Efficacy Studies Are Not Ethical or Feasible, 67 Fed. Reg. 37,988 (May 31, 2002).

[49] 21 C.F.R. pt. 314 (2014).

[50] 21 C.F.R. pts. 600-680 (2014).

[51] 21 C.F.R. pt. 807 (2014).

[52] 21 C.F.R. pt. 814 (2014).

[53] 21 C.F.R. pt. 312 (2014).

[54] 21 C.F.R. pt. 812 (2014).

[55] 21 C.F.R. pt. 814, subpt. H (2014).

[56] FDA, Guidance for Industry: Expedited Programs for Serious Conditions—Drugs and Biologics (May 2014), *available at* http://www.fda.gov/downloads/drugs/guidancecomplianceregulatoryinformation/guidances/ucm358301.pdf; FDA, Fast Track, Breakthrough Therapy, Accelerated Approval and Priority Review: Expediting Availability of New Drugs for Patients with Serious Conditions, *available at* http://www.fda.gov/ForConsumers/ByAudience/ForPatientAdvocates/SpeedingAccesstoImportantNewTherapies/ucm128291.htm (last visited Oct.23, 2014).

[57] FDCA § 506(b), 21 U.S.C. § 356(b). Certain antibacterial and antifungal drugs may qualify for incentives under FDCA § 505f, 21 U.S.C. § 355f.

and design of proposed clinical trials, as well as a rolling review of completed sections of a marketing application for the product.

Another type of designation is for a "breakthrough therapy." Under section 506(a) of the FDCA, FDA may apply more timely advice and interactions, including rolling review of submissions, if FDA determines that the "preliminary clinical evidence indicates that the drug may demonstrate substantial improvement over existing therapies or on one or more clinically significant endpoints."[58] FDA may also use the accelerated approval process under section 506(c), which allows for approval of a drug for a serious or life-threatening disease or condition based on an effect on a surrogate endpoint or an intermediate clinical endpoint that is reasonably likely to predict a drug's clinical benefit.[59] FDA may also apply priority review, whereby FDA can reduce the time period for review and action on the marketing application from the standard 10 months to six months.[60] Priority review can apply to drugs and biologics that are used for serious conditions and that meet other specified criteria.[61]

Additionally, the FDCA directs FDA to meet with sponsors, if certain conditions are met, for the purpose of reaching an agreement on the design and size of clinical trials intended to form the primary basis of an efficacy claim in a marketing application.[62] Prescription Drug User Fee Act (PDUFA) performance goals for these agreements, called special protocol assessments (SPAs), provide that, "upon request, FDA will evaluate within 45 days certain protocols and issues relating to the protocols to assess whether they are adequate to meet scientific and regulatory requirements identified by the sponsor,"[63] thereby "significantly reducing regulatory uncertainty and business risks in drug development."[64] PAHPRA amended the FDCA to clarify that the animal efficacy studies conducted under the Animal Rule used to support marketing applications are included in the SPA provisions of the FDCA.[65]

MCMs may also qualify for FDA's orphan product designations and grants. The orphan designations and grant programs are designed to provide incentives, including tax credits for qualified clinical testing and waiver of prescription drug user fees, for sponsors to develop medical products for rare diseases.[66] Finally, MCMs are subject to FDA requirements related

---

[58]   FDCA § 506(a), 21 U.S.C. § 356(a).

[59]   FDCA § 506(c), 21 U.S.C. § 356(c); 21 C.F.R. pt. 314, subpt. H (for drugs); 21 C.F.R. pt. 601, subpt. E (for biologics) (2014).

[60]   For products that contain new chemical entities, the review periods are measured from the date at which FDA makes a decision on filing the application (60 days after its submission). FDA, PDUFA Reauthorization Performance Goals and Procedures Fiscal Years 2013 through 2017, at 4, *available at* http://www.fda.gov/downloads/forindustry/userfees/prescriptiondruguserfee/ucm270412.pdf. The priority review program was established under the Prescription Drug User Fee Act of 1992, Pub. L. No. 102-571, 106 Stat. 4491; FDA, *supra* note 56, at 7.

[61]   *Id.* FDA, *supra* note 56, at 7-8.

[62]   FDCA § 505(b)(5), 21 U.S.C. § 355(b)(5).

[63]   FDA, Guidance for Industry: Special Protocol Assessment 1-2 (May 2002), *available at* http://www.fda.gov/downloads/Drugs/GuidanceComplianceRegulatoryInformation/Guidances/ucm080571.pdf.

[64]   Press Release, FDA, FDA Seeks Public Input on Renewal Process for Prescription Drug User Fee Act (PDUFA) (Nov. 10, 2005), *available at* http://www.fda.gov/NewsEvents/Newsroom/PressAnnouncements/2005/ucm108516.htm.

[65]   PAHPRA, Pub. L. No. 113-5, § 301, 127 Stat. 179.

[66]   The Orphan Drug Act, Pub. L. No. 97-414, § 526, 96 Stat. 2050 (1983), authorizing FDA to designate drugs and biologics, is implemented in 21 C.F.R. pt. 316; the Safe Medical Devices Act, Pub. L. No. 101-

to obtaining safety and efficacy data for pediatric populations.[67] Because it is particularly challenging to develop MCMs for pediatric populations, PAHPRA includes provisions to ensure that pediatric experts are consulted, and the needs of pediatric populations are appropriately considered, in the development of MCMs, and to ensure that MCMs are duly considered when prioritizing funding for pediatric research.[68]

Animal Rule

As mentioned, for some threat agents (e.g., smallpox), clinical studies in humans to assess product efficacy for obtaining FDA approval are neither ethical nor feasible. To address this challenge, FDA published the Animal Rule in 2002[69] and issued revised draft guidance for industry in 2014.[70] The Animal Rule amended FDA's "new drug and biological product regulations to allow appropriate studies in animals in certain cases to provide substantial evidence of the effectiveness of new drug and biological products used to reduce or prevent the toxicity of chemical, biological, radiological, or nuclear substances."[71]

Under the Animal Rule, "FDA may grant marketing approval based on adequate and well-controlled animal studies when the results of those studies establish that the drug or biological product is reasonably likely to produce clinical benefit in humans."[72] Specifically, if the following criteria set forth under the rule are met, the effectiveness of the product in animals can reasonably be expected to be a reliable indicator of the product's effectiveness in human populations:

(1) There is a reasonably well-understood pathophysiological mechanism of the toxicity of the substance and its prevention or substantial reduction by the product;

629, § 14, 104 Stat. 4524-4525 (1990), authorized FDA to establish the Humanitarian Use Device (HUD) Program. For information on Orphan Product Programs, *see* FDA, Developing Products for Rare Diseases and Conditions, *available at* http://www.fda.gov/forindustry/developingproductsforrarediseasesconditions/ default.htm (last visited Oct. 23, 2014); FDA, Draft Guidance, Meetings with the Office of Orphan Products Development (April 2014), *available at* http://www.fda.gov/downloads/ForIndustry/ DevelopingProductsforRareDiseasesConditions/OOPDNewsArchive/UCM392593.pdf.

[67] For information on pediatric drug development authorities and programs, *see* FDA, Pediatric Product Development, *available at* http://www.fda.gov/drugs/developmentapprovalprocess/developmentresources/ ucm049867.htm (last visited Oct. 23, 2014); for information on the Pediatric Device Consortia Grants Program, *see* FDA, Pediatric Device Consortia Grants Program, *available at* http://www.fda.gov/ forindustry/developingproductsforrarediseasesconditions/pediatricdeviceconsortiagrantsprogram/ default.htm (last visited Oct. 23, 2014).

[68] PAHPRA, Pub. L. No. 113-5, § 307, 127 Stat. 191-192.

[69] FDA, *supra* note 48.

[70] FDA, Product Development under the Animal Rule, Revised Draft Guidance for Industry; Availability, 79 Fed. Reg. 31,950 (June 3, 2014), *available at* http://www.fda.gov/downloads/Drugs/ GuidanceComplianceRegulatoryInformation/Guidances/UCM399217.pdf. The revised draft guidance replaced a draft guidance issued in 2009 (74 Fed. Reg. 3610 (Jan. 21, 2009)), and expanded the scope of the guidance to address issues raised in numerous written comments, including from the IOM and the National Biodefense Science Board, and comments solicited from industry, academia, and government during a 2010 public meeting. FDA, Transcript: Public Meeting on the Draft Guidance for Industry Animal Models—Essential Elements to Address Efficacy under the Animal Rule (Dkt No. FDA-2009-D-0007) (Nov. 5, 2010), *available at* http://www.fda.gov/downloads/BiologicsBloodVaccines/ NewsEvents/WorkshopsMeetingsConferences/UCM245299.pdf.

[71] FDA, *supra* note 48, at 37,988-89.

[72] 21 C.F.R. §§ 314.600 (drugs), 601.90 (biological products) (2014); *see also* FDA, *supra* note 48.

(2) The effect is demonstrated in more than one animal species expected to react with a response predictive for humans, unless the effect is demonstrated in a single animal species that represents a sufficiently well-characterized animal model for predicting the response in humans;

(3) The animal study endpoint is clearly related to the desired benefit in humans, generally the enhancement of survival or prevention of major morbidity; and

(4) The data or information on the kinetics and pharmacodynamics of the product or other relevant data or information, in animals and humans, allows selection of an effective dose in humans.[73]

Although effectiveness is demonstrated through studies using animal models, clinical trials in humans are conducted to demonstrate safety and inform dosing.[74] To support product development under the Animal Rule, FDA established the Animal Model Qualification Program under FDA's Drug Development Tools (DDT) Qualification Programs. Sponsors can submit an animal model for qualification to support its use for multiple investigational products developed for the same targeted disease or condition.[75]

FDA has approved a number of MCMs under the Animal Rule, including: 1) pyridostigmine bromide for pretreatment against the nerve agent, Soman;[76] 2) hydroxocobalamin for exposure to cyanide;[77] 3) Levaquin (levofloxacin) to treat patients with plague and to reduce the risk of getting plague after exposure to *Yersinia pestis*, the bacterium that causes the disease;[78] 4) raxibacumab for treatment of patients with inhalational anthrax due to *Bacillus anthracis* in combination with appropriate antibacterial drugs (this was the first monoclonal antibody approved under the Animal Rule);[79] and 5) Botulism Antitoxin Heptavalent for treatment of adult and pediatric patients showing signs of botulism following exposure to

---

[73] 21 C.F.R. §§ 314.610(a)(1)-(4), 601.91(a)(1)-(4)) (2014).

[74] FDA, *supra* note 48, at 37,989; FDA, *Transcript: Public Meeting on the Draft Guidance for Industry Animal Models—Essential Elements to Address Efficacy under the Animal Rule (Dkt. No. FDA-2009-D-0007), supra* note 70, at 24-25; G.K. Gronvall, D. Trent, L. Borio, et al., *The FDA Animal Efficacy Rule and Biodefense*, 25 Nature Biotechnology 1084-1087 (2007).

[75] FDA, Guidance for Industry and Staff: Qualification Process for Drug Development Tools (Jan. 2014), *available at* http://www.fda.gov/downloads/Drugs/GuidanceComplianceRegulatoryInformation/Guidances/UCM230597.pdf; for additional information about FDA's DDT program, *see* FDA, Drug Development Tools (DDT) Qualification Programs, *available at* http://www.fda.gov/Drugs/DevelopmentApprovalProcess/DrugDevelopmentToolsQualificationProgram/default.htm (last visited Oct. 28, 2014).

[76] Press Release, FDA, FDA Approves Pyridostigmine Bromide as Pretreatment against Nerve Gas (Feb. 5, 2003), *available at* http://www.fda.gov/Drugs/EmergencyPreparedness/BioterrorismandDrugPreparedness/ucm130342.htm. "During the Gulf War, FDA had allowed distribution of pyridostigmine bromide under its Investigational New Drug provisions because pretreatment with this drug had the potential to help save lives if nerve agents were used." *Id.* Although pyridostigmine bromide was already an FDA-approved product at a different dose for treatment of myasthenia gravis, approval for its use as a pretreatment against nerve agent exposure required use of the Animal Rule. Gronvall *et al., supra* note 74.

[77] Press Release, FDA, FDA Approves Drug to Treat Cyanide Poisoning (Dec. 15, 2006), *available at* http://www.fda.gov/NewsEvents/Newsroom/PressAnnouncements/2006/ucm108807.htm.

[78] Press Release, FDA, FDA Approves New Antibacterial Treatment for Plague (Apr. 27, 2012), *available at* http://www.fda.gov/newsevents/newsroom/pressannouncements/ucm302220.htm.

[79] Press Release, FDA, FDA Approves Raxibacumab to Treat Inhalational Anthrax: First Monoclonal Antibody Approved Using the Animal Efficacy Rule (Dec. 14, 2012), *available at* http://www.fda.gov/NewsEvents/Newsroom/PressAnnouncements/ucm332341.htm.

botulinum neurotoxin (this was the first polyclonal antibody approved under the Animal Rule).[80]

Other FDCA Provisions to Facilitate MCM Development

PAHPRA codifies and builds on ongoing FDA-wide efforts to establish clear regulatory pathways for MCM products and to advance regulatory science for MCM development. Certain PAHPRA provisions amended the FDCA to ensure that MCMs benefit from focused FDA interactions with government and industry MCM sponsors. For example, PAHPRA amended FDA's SPA authorities to require FDA to meet with sponsors on the design and size of pivotal animal studies supporting claims of efficacy,[81] and amended the authorities to ensure that pediatric populations are duly considered when developing MCMs and that MCMs are considered when funding pediatric research.[82] In addition, PAHPRA includes provisions to ensure that FDA personnel are appropriately involved in interagency activities related to MCM advanced research and development, to ensure that those who are involved in review of applications for approval of MCMs have sufficient training and expertise in MCMs, and to finalize guidance on the development of animal models for purposes of establishing claims of efficacy. The enhanced authorities and resources devoted to MCM development and availability have resulted in significant advances in regulatory science and in MCM approvals that are contributing to helping the nation reach its MCM goals.[83]

Emergency Use of Approved and Unapproved MCMs

During CBRN and other emergencies, state and local public health agencies and their response partners (e.g., healthcare facilities and practitioners) typically have the primary responsibility for coordinating MCM storage, distribution, and dispensing or administration to the public.[84] However, such efforts occur in close coordination with DHHS partners, primarily ASPR, CDC, and FDA. Other government (e.g., DHS, DOD) and private sector entities also may be involved in MCM responses.

If FDA-approved MCMs are stockpiled by such response partners in accordance with cGMPs and are distributed and dispensed by them in a manner that is consistent with their product approval and FDA laws and regulations, then no additional FDA authorization for use during the emergency is required. However, any deviations from product approval and any uses of unapproved and investigational products require the use of special FDA mechanisms to ensure that such products are used in a safe and lawful manner. For example, a certain drug might be the most effective option during a particular emergency, but might not yet be approved by FDA for any indication. A drug, such as an antimicrobial, may be approved for one disease or condition, such as anthrax, yet in a response is intended to be put to a different use, such as for plague. Certain FDA-approved drugs may be intended to be used in response to the disaster for the approved disease or condition, yet in ways beyond their

---

80 Press Release, FDA, FDA Approves First Botulism Antitoxin for Use in Neutralizing All Seven Known Botulinum Nerve Toxin Serotypes: Product to Be Stored in Strategic National Stockpile for Emergency Preparedness and Responses (Mar. 22, 2013), *available at* http://www.fda.gov/newsevents/newsroom/pressannouncements/ucm345128.htm.

81 PAHPRA, *supra* note 65.

82 PAHPRA, *supra* note 68.

83 *See, e.g.,* FDA, *supra* note 3.

84 CDC, *supra* note 10.

approved labeling (e.g., in different dosing regimens or with modified, more user-friendly patient and practitioner product information). Additionally, a response agency may need to dispense an MCM without individual patient prescriptions or by responders who are not licensed healthcare professionals, or to use the MCM beyond its labeled expiration date to meet an emergency need.

For these reasons, FDA is authorized to use several alternative approaches, when appropriate, to facilitate the use of certain MCMs during emergency situations to protect the public health. These include mechanisms for expanded access to investigational drugs, the EUA authority, emergency use authorities for approved MCMs, and pre-positioning.

Expanded Access Mechanisms: IND and IDE

In some circumstances, the IND or IDE mechanism may be an appropriate approach for use of an unapproved, experimental product that could help to meet patient needs "when there is no comparable or satisfactory alternative therapy to diagnose, monitor, or treat the patient's disease or condition."[85] The FDCA and FDA regulations permit the shipment and use of investigational drugs or devices for serious or life-threatening diseases or conditions in certain emergency situations, as well as during circumstances not related to CBRN threat agents.[86] These regulations provide for expanded access under an IND for intermediate-sized patient populations (i.e., "smaller than those typical of a treatment IND or treatment protocol") and for a treatment use IND or treatment protocol under an IND for widespread access.[87] In addition, during an emergency, when it might not be possible for the sponsor to submit an IND in accordance with regulatory requirements, FDA may authorize the emergency use of an investigational drug for individual patient use under an emergency use IND.[88]

When the IND approach is used, certain requirements, such as informed consent, Institutional Review Board (IRB) supervision of investigations, and reporting to FDA, apply in most cases.[89] These measures help to ensure a layer of oversight until additional information is known about a product. An example of when an IND may be appropriate during an emergency is a situation involving a biological threat agent. In this scenario, if the only available vaccine for use against the agent lacks safety or efficacy data in a certain population (e.g., children under the age of 18 years), the IND's informed consent requirement

---

[85]   FDA, Expanded Access to Investigational Drugs for Treatment Use, 74 Fed. Reg. 40,900 (Aug. 13, 2009), *available at* http://edocket.access.gpo.gov/2009/pdf/E9-19005.pdf, 21 C.F.R. § 312 (2011).

[86]   *See, e.g.,* FDCA § 561 (21 U.S.C. § 360bbb; 21 C.F.R. §§ 312.300-320 (2014). The final rule "amends regulations on expanded access to investigational new drugs for treating patients . . . [and] clarifies existing regulations and adds new types of expanded access for treatment use. Under the final rule, expanded access to investigational drugs for treatment use will be available to individual patients, including in emergencies, intermediate-size patient populations, [and] larger populations under a treatment protocol or treatment investigational new drug application." FDA, Final Rules for Expanded Access to Investigational Drugs for Treatment Use and Charging for Investigational Drugs (2009), *available at* http://www.fda.gov/Drugs/DevelopmentApprovalProcess/HowDrugsareDevelopedandApproved/ApprovalApplications/InvestigationalNewDrugINDApplication/ucm172492.htm.

[87]   FDA, *supra* note 85, at 40,942; 21 C.F.R. §§ 312.315 (intermediate-size patient populations), 312.320 (treatment IND or treatment protocol) (2014).

[88]   21 C.F.R. § 312.310 (2014).

[89]   21 C.F.R. pts. 50, 56 (2014).

would, for example, help to ensure that those receiving the vaccine (or their guardians) are appropriately informed of its possible risks and benefits.

The IDE mechanism allows an investigational device to be used in a clinical study to collect safety and effectiveness data, and permits the device to be shipped lawfully for conducting investigations without complying with other requirements of the FDCA that apply to commercial distribution.[90] Clinical evaluation of devices that have not been cleared for marketing includes such requirements as IRB approval (and, if the study involves a significant risk device, FDA approval), informed consent, labeling for investigational use, and record keeping and reporting.

As with expanded access INDs, FDA may permit use of an investigational device prior to final action on the marketing application, such as under a treatment IDE.[91] Treatment IDE criteria include: the device is intended to treat or diagnose a serious or immediately life-threatening disease or condition; no comparable or satisfactory alternative device or other therapy is available; the device is under investigation in a controlled clinical trial for the same use under the approved IDE or such clinical trials have been completed; and the investigation's sponsor is actively pursuing marketing approval/clearance of the investigational device with due diligence.[92] As with expanded access IND requirements, IDEs have requirements for requests and submissions.[93]

Emergency Use Authorization (EUA)

During an emergency, novel or investigational products may be the only available MCMs to meet response needs. However, requirements for clinical investigations or expanded access, such as IRB approval or informed consent, can be difficult or impossible to meet given the exigent demands of the emergency, especially when very large populations are at risk. In addition, certain deviations from the conditions for product approval that may be needed to address the emergency may render a product misbranded under section 502 of the FDCA or adulterated under section 501 of the FDCA.

To address these types of concerns, FDA was delegated the authority to issue EUAs under section 564 of the FDCA, as amended by the Project BioShield Act[94] and PAHPRA.[95] Through EUAs, which are not considered to be a type of product approval, the FDA Commissioner may authorize the use of unapproved medical products, or authorize the unapproved use of approved medical products, during or in anticipation of CBRN emergencies (including

---

[90]   21 C.F.R. pt. 812; FDA, Device Advice: Investigational Device Exemption (IDE), *available at* http://www.fda.gov/MedicalDevices/DeviceRegulationandGuidance/HowtoMarketYourDevice/ InvestigationalDeviceExemptionIDE/default.htm (last visited Oct. 23, 2014).

[91]   21 C.F.R. § 812.36. For a description of other early/expanded access mechanisms for devices, *see* FDA, IDE Early/Expanded Access, *available at* http://www.fda.gov/MedicalDevices/DeviceRegulationandGuidance/ HowtoMarketYourDevice/InvestigationalDeviceExemptionIDE/ucm051345.htm (last visited Oct. 23, 2014).

[92]   FDA, *id.*

[93]   *Id.*

[94]   FDCA § 564, 21 U.S.C. § 360bbb-3, as amended.

[95]   FDA, Pandemic and All-Hazards Preparedness Reauthorization Act of 2013 (PAHPRA), *available at* http://www.fda.gov/EmergencyPreparedness/Counterterrorism/MedicalCountermeasures/MCMLega lRegulatoryandPolicyFramework/ucm359581.htm (last visited Oct. 23, 2014).

emerging infectious disease threats). In other words, if FDA grants a request for an EUA, it is finding that, if circumstances exist to justify EUA issuance and if the conditions set forth in the EUA are observed, an FDA-approved product may be used to diagnose, prevent, or treat an unapproved disease or condition, or a product that has not yet been approved by FDA for any disease or condition may be permitted to be used in response to the emergency despite lacking the quantum of data that would be necessary for approval. Because use under an EUA is not considered to be investigational, an EUA can help to streamline MCM response efforts because informed consent, IRB review, and reports to FDA typically mandated for investigational use are not required.

Before the FDA Commissioner may issue an EUA, the Secretary of DHHS must first declare that circumstances exist to justify the EUA on the basis of a determination by: 1) the Secretary of DHS that there is a domestic emergency (or a significant potential for such an emergency) involving a heightened risk of attack with a CBRN agent(s); 2) the Secretary of DOD that there is a military emergency (or a significant potential for such an emergency) involving a heightened risk to U.S. military forces of attack with a CBRN agent(s); 3) the Secretary of DHHS that there is a public health emergency (or a significant potential for a public health emergency) that affects, or has a significant potential to affect, national security or the health and security of U.S. citizens living abroad, and that involves a CBRN agent(s) or a disease or condition that may be attributable to such an agent(s); or 4) the identification by the Secretary of DHS of a material threat pursuant to section 319F-2 of the PHSA sufficient to affect national security or the health and security of U.S. citizens living abroad.[96] Depending on their content, it is possible for a DHHS EUA declaration and its supporting determination to be used for issuance of a single EUA for a specific product or of multiple EUAs for more than one product.

After the requisite determination and declaration have been made, the FDA Commissioner consults about the EUA, to the extent feasible given the emergency circumstances, with the ASPR and the Directors of NIH and CDC. The statutory criteria for EUA issuance that FDA must ensure are met include: 1) a serious or life-threatening illness or condition caused by a CBRN agent referred to in the DHHS EUA declaration; 2) a reasonable belief, based on the totality of the scientific evidence available (including data from adequate and well-controlled clinical trials, if available), that the product may be effective in diagnosing, treating, or preventing the illness or condition caused by the agent, or an illness or condition caused by an approved or authorized MCM for the agent; 3) the product's known and potential benefits, when used for the disease or condition, outweigh its known and potential risks and 4) no adequate, approved, available alternative to the product exists.[97] Factors that FDA considers for EUA issuance include, but are not limited to, the public health need, emergency circumstances, the product's regulatory status, available safety and efficacy data, product quality and shelf-life, and operational issues (e.g., who will dispense or administer the product, and when the product will be dispensed). An EUA is effective until the DHHS EUA declaration is terminated under section 564(b)(2) of the FDCA (i.e., due to the emergency circumstances no longer existing or due to a change in the product's approval status) or the EUA is revoked under section 564(g) of the FDCA.[98]

---

[96]   FDCA § 564(b), 21 U.S.C. § 360bbb-3(b).
[97]   FDCA § 564(c), 21 U.S.C. § 360bbb-3(c).
[98]   FDCA §§ 564(b)(2), 564(g), 21 U.S.C. §§ 360bbb-3(b)(2), 360bbb-3(g).

EUAs, which typically are requested by U.S. government agencies (e.g., CDC, DOD) and industry sponsors, also include various conditions of authorization. These conditions are based on whether the authorization is for an unapproved product or for an unapproved use of an approved product, and may also vary depending on the specific product and emergency circumstances. Examples include conditions related to which entities may distribute the product for emergency use, who may administer the product, and monitoring and reporting of adverse events. Notices of EUA declarations (and, if applicable, the determinations that support EUA declarations), issuance, termination, and revocation are published in the *Federal Register*.

Examples of EUAs

FDA has exercised its EUA authority in response to several actual or anticipated emergencies. For example, in 2008, FDA issued an EUA for pre-positioning emergency kits containing doxycycline hyclate tablets for post-exposure prophylaxis of inhalational anthrax.[99] The kits were made available to United States Postal Service employee volunteer participants and their household members under a special mass dispensing program. This EUA was subsequently amended to address programmatic changes.[100] During the H1N1 influenza pandemic in 2009-2010, FDA used the authority broadly to respond to the evolving event by providing increased access, through multiple EUAs, for antiviral drugs (including the first EUA for an unapproved product—the antiviral, peramivir), personal protective equipment, and diagnostic devices.[101] Because the declarations for the H1N1 EUAs terminated when the public health emergency determination for 2009 H1N1 influenza expired on June 23, 2010, and the H1N1 virus does not currently present the same public health threat as it once did, these EUAs are no longer in effect.[102] An EUA was not needed for the H1N1 vaccine because licensed vaccine was used during the response.

More recently, FDA issued multiple EUAs in 2013 and 2014 for IVDs for the emerging threats of the H7N9 influenza virus, MERS-CoV, and Ebola Zaire virus.[103] These EUAs, which were issued after PAHPRA's enactment, are focused on both preparedness and response for such public health threats. In some cases, these IVDs were also authorized for use outside of the U.S., such as for use by DOD to further enhance preparedness and protection of U.S. government personnel and U.S. citizens living abroad or by foreign laboratories.

---

[99]   FDA, Authorization of Emergency Use of Doxycycline Hyclate Tablet Emergency Kits for Eligible United States Postal Service Participants in the Cities Readiness Initiative and Their Household Members; Availability, 73 Fed. Reg. 62,507 (Oct. 21, 2008). This EUA has been amended several times, most recently on October 14, 2011.

[100] FDA, Amended Authorization of Emergency Use of Doxycycline Hyclate Tablet Emergency Kits for Eligible United States Postal Service Participants and Their Household Members; Availability, 76 Fed. Reg. 72,935 (Nov. 28, 2011).

[101] See, FDA, Emergency Use Authorization, *available at* http://www.fda.gov/EmergencyPreparedness/Counterterrorism/ucm182568.htm (last visited Oct. 23, 2014).

[102] DHHS, Termination of Declarations Justifying Emergency Use Authorizations of Certain In Vitro Diagnostic Devices, Antiviral Drugs, and Personal Respiratory Protection Devices, 75 Fed. Reg. 36,432 (June 25, 2010).

[103] See, e.g., FDA, Emergency Use Authorizations, *available at* http://www.fda.gov/MedicalDevices/Safety/EmergencySituations/ucm161496 (last visited Oct. 23, 2014).

Pre-EUA Activity

FDA also prepares for emergencies through engaging in pre-EUA activity, which involves a sponsor's submission of data and information about an MCM to the applicable FDA product Center for review prior to submission of a formal request for FDA to issue an EUA. Although pre-EUA activity can occur at any time prior to an emergency, an EUA may not be issued until the criteria for issuance are met and the DHHS EUA declaration that circumstances exist to justify an EUA has been issued (based on an appropriate determination, as described above).

Emergency Use Authorities for Approved MCMs

PAHPRA added several authorities related to the emergency use of approved, eligible MCMs. As defined in section 564A of the FDCA, "eligible products" include drugs, biologics, or devices that are approved, licensed, or cleared by FDA; intended for use to prevent, diagnose, or treat a disease or condition involving a CBRN agent or agents, or a serious or life-threatening disease or condition caused by a product used for such a purpose; and intended for use during circumstances in which a determination as described in subparagraph (A), (B), (C), or (D) of section 564(b)(1) has been made.[104] These emergency use authorities for eligible MCMs allow for certain response activities without FDA needing to issue an EUA and without rendering such products adulterated, misbranded, or unapproved under the FDCA.

Emergency Dispensing Orders (FDA)

Under section 564A(d), FDA may authorize emergency dispensing (including mass dispensing) of approved MCMs during a CBRN emergency without requiring an individual patient prescription for each recipient of the MCM.[105] This authority also allows such dispensing without all of the information otherwise required to be provided when a product is dispensed under section 503(b) or 520(e) of the FDCA.[106] However, emergency dispensing must occur in accordance with either: 1) an emergency dispensing order issued by FDA or 2) state law.[107] Emergency dispensing orders may be issued in advance of emergencies for preparedness purposes (but dispensing would not take place until the emergency circumstances occur) or during emergency responses. Also, in some cases as appropriate, FDA emergency dispensing orders may include waivers of cGMP requirements (as described below) and, to facilitate response coordination, may be issued in tandem with CDC's issuance of EUIs.

Emergency Use Instructions (CDC)

PAHPRA also establishes the authority, which was delegated by the Secretary of DHHS to CDC, to create and issue EUIs about an MCM's approved conditions of use.[108,109] EUIs are intended to be similar to the fact sheets for healthcare professionals and fact sheets

---

[104]   21 U.S.C. § 360bbb-3a(a)(1)-(2).

[105]   21 U.S.C. § 360bbb-3a(d).

[106]   *Id.* 21 U.S.C. §§ 353(b), 360j(e).

[107]   21 U.S.C. § 360bbb-3a(d)(2)(A)-(B).

[108]   FDCA § 564A(e), 21 U.S.C. § 360bbb-3a(e).

[109]   DHHS, Delegation of Authority of section 564(A)(e) of the Federal Food, Drug, and Cosmetic Act, Dec. 16, 2013.

for patients/recipients that are included in EUAs and are made available to response stakeholders (including government agencies responsible for dispensing MCMs). They provide streamlined, user-friendly information about use of the MCM in the emergency. EUIs, which may be informed by consultations with FDA, as well as other experts as needed, may be issued in advance of emergencies for preparedness purposes or during emergency responses.

Waivers of cGMP and REMS Requirements (FDA)

Under section 564A(c) of the FDCA, FDA may waive otherwise applicable cGMP requirements for approved MCMs.[110] This authority is intended to accommodate emergency response needs, such as the temporary shipment, holding, and storage of MCMs at local mass dispensing sites. In such situations, temporary deviations in storage or handling requirements might be unavoidable in order to meet public health response needs. Also to facilitate response needs, FDA may waive any REMS elements based on the same types of CBRN emergencies or threats that could trigger an EUA.[111]

Expiration Dating Extensions (FDA)

After MCMs are developed and procured, they are often stockpiled in appropriate locations (primarily by federal, state, and local government agencies) to ensure ready access in the event of a public health emergency. Because the shelf-life of a medical product is limited, MCM stockpiles can be costly to maintain. In 1986, this challenge led to development of the federal Shelf-Life Extension Program (SLEP), a fee-for-service program administered by DOD's Defense Medical Materiel Program Office (DMMPO).[112,113] Under SLEP, FDA conducts the testing and evaluation that determine whether adequate supporting data are available to extend the expiration date of specified lots of properly stored drug products owned by DOD and certain federal government agencies (e.g., CDC/SNS). The DMMPO identifies the medical products to be considered for extension of their labeled expiration dates. Current SLEP testing focuses on militarily significant or contingency-use products, drugs that have limited commercial use (e.g., nerve agent antidotes), and drugs that are purchased in very large quantities (e.g., certain antimicrobials). The program does not apply to biologics[114] or to non-federal stockpiles.

As amended by PAHPRA, the FDCA expressly authorizes FDA to extend the expiration date (i.e., "the date established through appropriate stability testing . . . to ensure that the product meets applicable standards of identity, strength, quality, and purity at the time of use") of approved MCMs stockpiled for use during a CBRN emergency.[115] Such extensions are limited to eligible products, must be intended to support the nation's public health or

---

110 21 U.S.C. § 360bbb-3a(c).

111 FDCA § 505-1, 21 U.S.C. § 355-1.

112 R.C. Lyon, J.S. Taylor, D.A. Porter, et al., *Stability Profiles of Drug Products Extended Beyond Labeled Expiration Dates*, 95 J PHARM SCI 1549-1560 (2006). The DOD Defense Medical Standardization Board (DMSB) is now referred to as the Defense Medical Materiel Program Office (DMMPO).

113 S.R. Kahn, R. Kona, P.J. Faustino, et al., *United States Food and Drug Administration and Department of Defense Shelf-Life Extension Program of Pharmaceutical Products: Progress and Promise*, 103 J PHARM SCI 1331-1336 (2014).

114 However, CBER has mechanisms to extend the dating period for biologics on the basis of manufacturer data, if necessary and appropriate.

115 FDCA § 564A(b), 21 U.S.C. § 360bbb-3a(b).

military preparedness and effectiveness, and must be supported by an appropriate scientific evaluation (conducted or accepted by FDA).[116] Also, each dating extension authorized by FDA must identify the product unit (e.g., lot, batch), duration of the extension, and any other requirements or conditions specified by FDA (e.g., related to storage, sampling, packaging, labeling, etc.).[117]

The section 564A(b) expiry dating extension authority may be applied to extensions that occur through SLEP or outside of SLEP. As an example of use of the authority outside of SLEP, in 2013 FDA addressed supply disruptions by allowing for specific lots of properly stored auto-injector product intended for CBRN use to be used for up to an additional year beyond the manufacturer's labeled expiry date.[118]

Pre-Positioning MCMs

Under section 564B of the FDCA, federal, state, and local government stakeholders (or persons acting on behalf of a government entity) may pre-position MCMs regardless of the product's regulatory status.[119] Government stakeholders may purchase, ship, or stockpile MCMs in anticipation of their being approved, licensed, cleared, or authorized for investigational use or use under an EUA, without violating the FDCA. However, such MCMs must be held in accordance with cGMPs, and may not be used in anticipation of or during an emergency until permitted 1) under FDA approval, licensure, or clearance, 2) under an IND or IDE, or 3) pursuant to an EUA.

International Responses—Export and Import

In addition to various product approvals and authorizations that help to facilitate the availability of needed MCMs in the U.S. to help counter health threats that may be emerging in the U.S. or throughout the world, FDA's roles and regulatory authorities may come into play during international responses involving the deployment and export of approved or investigational MCMs from the U.S. and the import of such products into the U.S.

Approved, licensed, or cleared MCMs may be exported from the U.S. in the same manner and under the same conditions that they can lawfully be shipped from one state to another in the U.S. However, federal laws administered by other departments, such as the Department of State or Department of Commerce, may apply to the export of approved MCMs. Certain FDA emergency use mechanisms, as described above, may also be used, when appropriate, to facilitate the export for preparedness or response purposes of approved MCMs intended for unapproved uses. For example, an EUA may allow the shipment of an approved product from the U.S. to other countries, provided the scope of the authorization and conditions on emergency use are met. Also, for approved, stockpiled products for which FDA has granted expiry dating extensions (even if they have not been relabeled with the new expiry date), FDA could use the expiration dating extension authority so that such products that are exported would be not rendered unapproved, adulterated, or misbranded under the FDCA.

---

[116]   21 U.S.C. § 360bbb-3a(b)(1).

[117]   21 U.S.C. § 360bbb-3a(b)(2).

[118]   FDA, Memorandum: DuoDote (atropine and pralidoxime chloride injection) Auto-Injector Expiry Dating (Sept. 5, 2013), *available at* http://www.fda.gov/downloads/Drugs/DrugSafety/UCM376385.pdf.

[119]   21 U.S.C. § 360bbb-3b.

FDA also has mechanisms to allow for the export of investigational new drugs and devices.[120] For example, under the "sudden and immediate national emergency provision," export of investigational therapies or vaccines may occur, provided that certain requirements are met (e.g., although FDA authorization is not required prior to export of such products, a determination by the Secretary of DHHS or a designee must be made prior to the export, and the exporting firm must submit a certification and related information to FDA when the product is first exported).[121] An EUA may also allow the shipment of an unapproved product from the United States (e.g., use of an uncleared IVD in other countries by foreign laboratories or U.S. laboratories located abroad), provided the criteria for issuance, scope of authorization, and conditions on emergency use are met.[122] For uncleared devices, export under the FDCA could occur under section 801(e)(1) and (2),[123] section 802(e),[124] or an EUA, depending on the situation. FDA has used its regulatory tools and flexibility to facilitate the emergency use of MCMs, such as uncleared IVDs, in other countries (e.g., by foreign laboratories or U.S. laboratories located in other countries) to help prepare for or respond to emerging threats (e.g., the 2014 Ebola outbreak in West Africa).

To date, the import of medical products from other countries has not been necessary for responses to emergencies occurring in the U.S. However, if such products were needed in future responses, FDA could allow import through several mechanisms, depending on the situation. FDA-regulated medical products being imported into the U.S. must meet the same FDCA requirements as domestic products.[125] If a medical product is not approved in the U.S., then import could occur under an emergency use mechanism described above (i.e., IND, IDE, expanded access mechanism), if appropriate. For example, 21 C.F.R. § 312.110(a) allows for the import of an investigational new drug if it is subject to an IND under certain conditions and 21 C.F.R. § 812.18 allows for the import of an investigational device under certain conditions.

Liability Protections and Injury Compensation

Liability is a significant concern among many MCM stakeholders, ranging from product sponsors to volunteers and health professionals directly administering MCMs during a public health emergency. As described in greater detail above, the PREP Act provides "liability immunity related to the manufacture, testing, development, distribution, administration, and use of medical countermeasures against chemical, biological, radiological and nuclear agents of terrorism, epidemics, and pandemics."[126] PREP Act declarations may provide coverage for products that are approved, authorized for investigational use, authorized for

---

[120] *See* 21 C.F.R. § 312.110 (drugs) and 21 C.F.R. §812.18 (devices) (2014). For exporting unapproved medical products, section 802 of the FDCA applies to unapproved new human drugs, biological products, and devices, and to approved human drugs, biological products, and devices being exported for unapproved uses.

[121] 21 C.F.R. § 312.110(b)(5)(ii). For a complete description of mechanisms for the export of unapproved drugs and vaccines for investigational use, *see* 21 C.F.R. § 312.110 and FDA, Guidance for Industry: Exports under the FDA Export Reform and Enhancement Act of 1996 (July 23, 2007), *available at* http://www.fda.gov/downloads/RegulatoryInformation/Guidances/ucm125898.pdf.

[122] *See, e.g.,* FDA, Authorization of Emergency Use of an In Vitro Diagnostic Device for Detection of Ebola Zaire Virus; Availability, 79 Fed. Reg. 55,804 (Sept. 17, 2014).

[123] 21 U.S.C. § 381(e)(1)-(2).

[124] 21 U.S.C. § 382(e).

[125] FDCA § 801.

[126] DHHS, *supra* note 38.

use under an EUA, or authorized for emergency use in accordance with section 564A or 564B of the FDCA (i.e., eligible approved MCMs that have received expiry dating extensions, received waivers of cGMP or REMS requirements, or for which emergency dispensing orders or emergency use instructions have been issued, as well as products held for emergency use in anticipation of approval, licensure, or clearance; authorization for investigational use; or authorization under an EUA).

Multiple PREP Act declarations have been issued. Examples include those for H1N1 influenza pandemic antivirals and vaccines[127] and for anthrax countermeasures.[128] Litigation related to the PREP Act has occurred, but courts have upheld PREP Act protections.[129] In addition, the PREP Act's Countermeasures Injury Compensation Program (which is separate from the National Vaccine Injury Compensation Program) provides a list of covered MCMs for which compensation for severe injuries or adverse health reactions resulting from MCMs used for declared public health emergencies may be available.[130]

Conclusion

Since the 2001 anthrax attacks, FDA has played an increasingly significant and essential role in efforts to safeguard public health in response to catastrophic emergencies and to strengthen the nation's MCM Enterprise. FDA's ongoing engagement with Enterprise partners has helped lead to important product approvals and has helped establish for MCM product innovators clear regulatory pathways that are based on a strong legal and regulatory framework and the most advanced science. Continued achievement of FDA's MCM goals will, ultimately, further help to accelerate MCM development toward approval and facilitate the safe and effective use and surveillance of such products during public health emergencies.

As new disasters occur, novel threats to public health emerge, science and technology advance, and international collaborations strengthen and develop, FDA's emergency preparedness and response functions related to ensuring the availability of safe and effective MCMs, as well as protecting and securing products from deliberate contamination, will

---

127   *See, e.g.,* DHHS, Pandemic Influenza Vaccines—Amendment, 77 Fed. Reg. 13,329 (Mar. 6, 2012); DHHS, Declaration Under the Public Readiness and Emergency Preparedness Act, 74 Fed. Reg. 50,968 (Oct. 2, 2009).

128   *See, e.g.,* DHHS, Declaration Under the Public Readiness and Emergency Preparedness Act, 73 Fed. Reg. 58,239 (Oct. 6, 2008).

129   DHHS, *supra* note 38. "On November 21, 2012, the Appellate Division of the New York Supreme Court in *Parker v. St. Lawrence County Public Health Department,* 102 A.D.3d 140 (2012) upheld PREP Act protections for a county that conducted a school based vaccination clinic in response to the H1N1 outbreak . . . In another case, *Kehler v. Hood,* [No. 4:11CV1416 FRB,] 2012 WL 1945952 (E.D. Mo. [May 30, 2012]), plaintiffs alleged that the physician and her employing hospital were negligent in failing to obtain the adult patient's informed consent and a consult from a specialist prior to the administration of the vaccination, which resulted in a severe case of transverse myelitis to the patient, and loss of consortium to the spouse. Defendants then brought third party product liability/failure to warn claims against the manufacturer. The parties did not dispute that the manufacturer was protected by the PREP Act, nor did they allege that it engaged in willful misconduct. As a result, the federal Eastern District Court of Missouri dismissed the claim against the manufacturer. Finding that it had no jurisdiction over plaintiffs' remaining claims, the federal court remanded the case to state court for further consideration of the plaintiffs' claims." *Id.*

130   *See* DHHS, *supra* note 39.

continue to strengthen, evolve, and further define FDA's critical role in protecting domestic public health, national security, and global health security in response to catastrophic emergencies.

CHAPTER 23

FOOD AND DRUG REGULATION IN THE EU

ELISABETHANN WRIGHT,
FABIEN ROY, AND CIARA FARRELL

Introduction

This chapter covers the legal foundation for international activities relating to food, pharmaceutical, medical device, and cosmetic regulation. The chapter provides a general overview of the international activities of the Food and Drug Administration (FDA), including harmonization, information sharing, arrangements with regulatory counterparts, and bilateral efforts with European Union (EU) authorities. The chapter also covers the principal activities at the international level—including relevant EU requirements—relating to medical devices, drugs (including biologics), food and veterinary medicine, and cosmetics.

European Union Directives, Regulations, and Other Acts

Since 2013, the EU has 28 members: Austria, Belgium, Bulgaria, Croatia, Cyprus, the Czech Republic, Denmark, Estonia, Finland, France, Germany, Greece, Hungary, Ireland, Italy, Latvia, Lithuania, Luxembourg, Malta, the Netherlands, Poland, Portugal, Romania, Slovakia, Slovenia, Spain, Sweden, and the United Kingdom (UK).

The EU institutions involved in lawmaking are the European Commission (which has the exclusive power to initiate the process), the European Parliament, and the European Council (top Member State officials). Any time these EU lawmaking institutions legislate via a "Directive," the 28 EU Member States must then implement that Directive into their national law by means of statutes, regulations, and other legally binding documents. Any

EU "Regulation," such as the EMA Regulation, takes effect throughout the EU upon the effective date stated in it, without need for any Member State action.

International Harmonization of Food Regulation

Codex Alimentarius

The paramount global organization for food regulation is the Codex Alimentarius Commission—an activity of two United Nations (UN) bodies, the Food and Agriculture Organization (FAO) and World Health Organization (WHO)—that was formed in 1963 to develop a food-standards program for the UN.[1] In addition to serving as the principal source of international standards for food, Codex has helped upgrade safe food production and processing all over the world, and provides a forum for regulators, scientists, and business and consumer representatives to exchange information and views.[2] The stated purposes of Codex are to facilitate world trade in foods and to promote consumer protection.[3] The FAO administers the Codex Secretariat. All member countries of the UN are invited to join the Commission, and approximately 183 countries have done so.[4] All members are eligible to send a delegate to participate in a plenary session of the Commission every year. The Commission decides upon the documents that will be included in a multi-volume code of authoritative guidance known as the Codex Alimentarius. Codex standards cover food commodity standards (similar to FDA standards of identity), food additives, food contaminants, and residues of veterinary drugs in food. Codex guidelines cover such topics as food labeling and inspection systems. Under the WTO Agreement on the Application of Sanitary and Phytosanitary Measures (SPS Agreement), countries with food-safety requirements that differ from Codex standards may have to justify them, in the event of any dispute with another country in the WTO. A Codex standard thus provides a safe harbor in WTO disputes.

The Codex Executive Committee is composed of the Chairman of the Commission (elected at each Commission meeting), the Vice-Chairs, and representatives from each of the principal regions (North America, Latin America, Europe, Africa, Asia, Near East, and the South Pacific). The Codex Alimentarius Commission is organized into a number of committees, and the substantive work of Codex is done in commodity and general subject committees. Several commodity committees have active operations, including those on fish products, milk products, and fruits and vegetables.

---

[1]   See www.codexalimentarius.net (last visited Dec. 8, 2014). For an overview of the Codex Alimentarius Commission, see Linda R. Horton, *Globalization and the Emerging Rule of Law on Regulatory Standards: Transatlantic Corporate Compliance and Governance of Food Safety* in GLOBAL GOVERNANCE OF FOOD AND AGRICULTURE INDUSTRIES: TRANSATLANTIC REGULATORY HARMONIZATION AND MULTILATERAL POLICY COOPERATION FOR FOOD SAFETY, at 202-34 (R. Carruth ed., 2006).

[2]   Donald L. Houston, *Codex Alimentarius Commission: 25 Years of Fair Trade and Consumer Protection*, 42 FOOD DRUG COSM. L.J. 163-64 (1987).

[3]   The discussion in this section draws from the FAO/WHO, CODEX ALIMENTARIUS COMMISSION, PROCEDURAL MANUAL *available at* ftp://ftp.fao.org/codex/Publications/ProcManuals/Manual_17e.pdf (last visited Dec. 8, 2014).

[4]   See http://www.who.int/topics/food_safety/en/ (last visited Dec. 8, 2014).

Codex's general subject committees include its Committees on General Principles (dealing with overall procedural issues), Food Hygiene, Import and Export Food Inspection and Certification Systems, Methods of Analysis and Sampling, Food Additives, Contaminants, Veterinary Drug Residues, Pesticide Residues, and Food Labeling. In developing food standards and guidelines, Codex Committees receive technical advice from the Joint Expert Committee on Food Additives (JECFA) and the Joint Meeting on Pesticides (JMP). These expert committees are organized by WHO and FAO.

The process by which Codex develops food standards is divided into eight steps[5]:

(1) The Commission decides that a standard is needed, and assigns its development to a committee or occasionally to another body, such as an *ad hoc* task force.

(2) The committee prepares a proposed draft standard.

(3) The proposed draft standard is circulated to Codex members and interested international organizations (e.g., international nongovernmental organizations, generally consumer or trade groups that have been recognized by Codex).

(4) The Commission sends the comments it has received to the committee drafting the standard, which reviews them and amends the standard as appropriate.

(5) The proposed draft standard goes to the Commission or Executive Committee, which decides whether to move it forward or send it back for further work.

(6) Once adopted as a draft standard, it is sent again to all members and international organizations for comment, as it was at step 3.

(7) As in step 4, all comments received are sent to the committee drafting it, for its consideration.

(8) The draft standard is sent to the Commission for adoption as a Codex standard.

The Codex standards process can take several years. It is possible for the Commission to omit steps 6 and 7, when it appears that the draft standard does not need further review. In such circumstances, a standard might be adopted more quickly. Decisions are generally made by consensus, although voting can take place in very controversial situations.

The U.S. government is required to publish information on its Codex activities each year in the *Federal Register*, as a result of a provision in the 1994 Uruguay Round Agreements Act[6] implementing the WTO SPS Agreement. Under this provision, the President must "designate an agency to be responsible for informing the public of the sanitary and phytosanitary standard-setting activities of each international standard-setting organization."[7] This annual *Federal Register* notice requirement applies not only to Codex activities[8] but also to U.S. participation in certain animal and plant health organizations.[9] Within the U.S.

---

5   Codex Procedural Manual (Uniform Procedures for the Elaboration of Standards and Related Texts). *See also* International Standard-Setting Activities, 73 Fed. Reg. 31,950 (June 5, 2008).

6   Pub. L. No. 103-465, 108 Stat. 4809 (Dec. 8 1994). *Id.* § 101(d)(3) (implementing SPS Agreement).

7   19 U.S.C. § 2578(a).

8   *See e.g.*, International Standard-Setting Activities, 73 Fed. Reg. 31,950 (June 5, 2008).

9   These include the International Office of Epizooties (OIE), the International Plant Protection Convention (in cooperation with the North American Plant Protection Organization), and any other international standard-setting organizations agreed to by North American Free Trade Agreement (NAFTA) countries or by WTO

government, a U.S. Codex Secretariat has for many years been a part of the U.S. Department of Agriculture (USDA). Consistent with the assignment of U.S. Codex leadership to the USDA, and the presence in USDA of the Animal and Plant Health Inspection Service (APHIS), which oversees U.S. animal-health[10] and plant-health (phytosanitary) matters, USDA was designated to be responsible for informing the public of activities of Codex and other international SPS standard-setting bodies.[11]

The U.S. government, and in particular the food safety agencies—FDA, USDA, and the Environmental Protection Agency (EPA)—always have considered Codex to be an important organization, and have been active participants. The WTO SPS Agreement gave added stature and importance to Codex Alimentarius standards, and its recognition of Codex standards led to intensified efforts to modernize Codex's approaches. Although FDA always invested significant resources in Codex, and certain of its standards (e.g., Hazard Analysis and Critical Control Points (HACCP)) were largely embraced by Codex, FDA has rarely completely accepted Codex standards. One reason is that Codex standards frequently contain elements that conflict with FDA food standards or are extraneous to FDA requirements. Statutes enacted in 1996 make it easier for the United States to adopt Codex standards for pesticides and veterinary drug residues in food.[12]

International Organization of Epizooties (OIE)

The OIE (World Organization for Animal Health) is an international organization, established by treaty,[13] that promotes animal health. Like Codex standards, OIE standards enjoy a recognized, safe-harbor status under the WTO SPS Agreement. USDA and FDA Center for Veterinary Medicine (CVM) officials participate in OIE activities.

The International Organization for Standardization (ISO)

ISO is the principal international standards organization of interest to the food industry and regulators. Private organizations and government agencies participate in ISO activities through the American National Standards Institute (ANSI). ANSI represents the United States in the ISO, and coordinates much of the standards-development activity in the United States. ISO has written hundreds of standards on food including ISO 22000, which seeks

---

members. The OIE is a treaty-based organization, headquartered in Paris, France, aimed at controlling animal diseases.

[10] Animal health measures include those taken to protect domestic herds against such diseases as foot-and-mouth disease, rinderpest, swine fever, Newcastle disease, rabies, anthrax, tuberculosis, brucellosis, and bovine spongiform encephalopathy (BSE).

[11] Proclamation No. 6780 of March 23, 1995, 60 Fed. Reg. 15,845 (Mar. 27, 1995).

[12] The Food Quality Protection Act of 1996, Pub. L. No. 104-170, amended section 408 of the FDCA to add a new subsection (b)(4) (21 U.S.C. § 346a(b)(4)) to facilitate adoption of Codex maximum residue levels in U.S. pesticide tolerances set by the Environmental Protection Agency (EPA) and enforced by FDA. The Animal Drug Availability Act, Pub. L. No. 104-250 (Oct. 9, 1996), amended the FDCA to add a new section 512(a)(6) to allow FDA to establish import tolerances for veterinary drugs used in other countries, if found safe by FDA, and allowed use of Codex standards for these tolerances.

[13] See www.oie.int, International Agreement for the Creation at Paris of an International Office for Epizooties, January 25, 1994, T.I.A.S. No. 8141. "Epizooties" is a French term for animal diseases.

to bring together in one document the concepts of good manufacturing practice (GMP), HACCP, and quality-systems management.

European Union Regulation of Food

Through bilateral "Europe agreements," several other countries at various stages of accession to the EU are aligning their regulatory requirements to those of the EU. Among these are Turkey and several countries that had been republics of Yugoslavia before its dissolution.

Some of the earliest European Community Directives had concerned food regulation, beginning with the European Council's first harmonizing law, a 1962 Directive on colors in food.[14] This action was followed by many recipe-type standards along the lines of those once favored by FDA.[15] Several landmark judgments by the European Court of Justice[16] stimulated new thinking about the powers granted to European Community institutions by EU members. According to these judicial opinions, EU Member States had only limited ability to restrict marketing of foods that meet Essential Requirements established at Community level.

Today's EU system for food regulation was shaped by a food safety crisis in the 1990s involving bovine spongiform encephalopathy (BSE) or "mad cow disease."[17] In early 1997 the EU re-organized food safety responsibilities within the European Commission under a Directorate General for Health and Consumer Protection (DG SanCo), and began an ambitious program of legislative reform, including[18]:

- Regulation 178/2002 on the General Principles of Food Law and the Establishment of the European Food Safety Authority (EFSA);[19]

- Regulation 882/2004 on Food and Feed Controls; and

- Regulation (EC) No 1829/2003 on genetically modified food and feed.

EFSA's main responsibilities are to provide independent scientific advice; to provide scientific support to the Commission on technical issues, such as food additive specifications; to provide literature reviews; to establish a centralized mechanism for collecting and analyzing information of relevance to food safety; to identify emerging risks; to participate in crisis

---

[14]   Council Directive 2645/62, 1962 O.J. 279.

[15]   Alain Gérard, *Food Law in the Common Market*, 27 FOOD DRUG COSM. L.J. 483 (1972); Alain Gérard, *EEC Directives on the Approximation of Member States' Legislation Relating to Foodstuffs*, 36 FOOD DRUG COSM. L.J. 543 (1981).

[16]   Rewe-Zentral AG v. Bundesmonopolverwaltung fur Branntwein, 1979 E.C.R. 649; 3 C.M.L.R. 494 (1979) (Cassis de Dijon); Case 178/84, Commission v. Germany, 1987-3 E.C.R.1227 (1987) (German beer case).

[17]   *See* Bovine Spongiform Encephalopathy *in* Linda R. Horton, *International Harmonization of Food and Veterinary Medicine Regulation*, 1 FUNDAMENTALS OF LAW & REGULATION, ch. 13 at 401 (FDLI 1997).

[18]   An in-depth discussion of EU food regulation is found in A. Konig, *Governance of Food Safety in the European Union*, *in* GLOBAL GOVERNANCE OF FOOD AND AGRICULTURE INDUSTRIES: TRANSATLANTIC REGULATORY HARMONIZATION AND MULTILATERAL POLICY COOPERATION FOR FOOD SAFETY at 133-62 (R. Carruth ed., 2006).

[19]   Regulation (EC) No 178/2002 of the European Parliament and of the Council of January 28, 2002 Laying Down the General Principles and Requirements of Food Law; Establishing the European Food Safety Authority and Laying Down Procedures in the Area of Food Safety, OJ L 031 of Febuary 1, 2002.

management in the event of a food safety crisis; and to communicate with the public concerning food risks. Headquartered in Parma, Italy, the EFSA's internal organization includes:

- a Management Board;
- an Executive Director and staff to serve as the legal representative of the Authority and to be responsible for day-to-day administration;
- an Advisory Forum to act as EFSA's consultative body, assist the Executive Director and advise on scientific matters, priorities and the work program, and to serve as a forum for exchange of views on risk assessment and food and feed safety issues; and
- a Scientific Committee and Scientific Panels, to undertake EFSA's risk assessments.

The basic principles of the EU General Food Law emphasize protection of health and protection of consumer interests, the concept of informed choice, the prohibition against misleading information, risk analysis (risk assessment and management as the basis for regulation), the precautionary principle, and transparency. The precautionary principle is an option open to EU risk managers when decisions have to be made to protect health, but scientific uncertainty exists.[20] It is applied when risk managers have identified a risk and find reasonable grounds for concern that the level of risk is unacceptable, but the supporting information and data may not be sufficiently complete to enable a comprehensive risk assessment. Decision makers may take provisional risk-management measures or other actions to protect health on the basis of the precautionary principle while seeking more complete scientific data. Any measures taken must comply with the principles of nondiscrimination and proportionality, and should be considered provisional until more comprehensive information concerning the risk has been gathered and analyzed.[21]

Those in the food business in the EU are required to comply with food-safety law, which includes the concept of traceability (i.e., the ability to trace and follow food, feed, and ingredients through all stages of production, processing, and distribution). Starting in 2005, all businesses in the EU food and feed sector have been required to maintain records of traceability. Importers are required to identify from whom a product was exported in the country of origin, and businesses need to be able at least to identify the immediate supplier of a product and the immediate subsequent recipient (one step back-one step forward), with the exception of retailers to final consumers.

In addition, the competent authorities of the EU Member States must implement adequate and effective controls. EU authorities have implemented a number of procedures to strengthen EU food regulation, including a Rapid Alert System for Food and Feed (to provide the control authorities with an effective tool for exchange of information on measures taken to ensure food safety), emergency procedures, crisis-management procedures, and a Regulatory Committee to assist the European Commission in the development of food-safety measures at all stages of the food chain. The European Commission must inform a non-EU country if it is known that a product subject to an alert notification has been exported to that country,

---

[20] Communication from the European Commission on the Precautionary Principle, COM (2000) 1-C5-014/2000.

[21] Under Art. 5.7 of the SPS Agreement, WTO members are allowed to take nondiscriminatory provisional measures for limited periods of time.

or when a product originating from that country has been the subject of a notification, so as to induce it to take corrective measures and thus avoid repetition of the problem.

The EU also has specific legislation on novel foods, food additives, food labeling, health and nutrition claims, food supplements such as vitamins and minerals marketed as pills, tablets, capsules, and in other forms, dietetic foods, foods for infants and young children, foods for special medical purposes, and foods for diabetics.

Many of these rules have been reviewed or amended in recent years. A general trend may be noted toward stricter EU-wide harmonization of the rules governing food as legislators often opt for legislation in the form of a Regulation rather than a Directive. A Regulation is an act that is directly applicable across the EU without the need to transpose it into the national legal systems of the EU Member States. The practical application of Directives in individual EU Member States is generally possible only following implementation of related national legislation by the States. Legislation at the EU level through use of Regulations also permits many aspects of risk management to be established at the EU level and leads to harmonized application at the national level in the EU Member States. Since the establishment of EFSA, a clear division may be made between risk-assessment task carried out by EFSA and the risk-management role conferred upon the European Commission. By means of Regulations, the Commission is able to propose EU-wide risk-management measures that will be applicable in a uniform way in all EU Member States.

An example of such an approach is found in the Package on Food Improvement Agents adopted in December 2008.[22] This package included Regulations governing food additives, food enzymes and flavorings, and food ingredients with flavoring properties. A fourth Regulation established a common authorization procedure for additives, enzymes, and flavorings.[23] The Regulations and related implementing measures establishing the permitted lists of substances falling within their application have repealed around 14 existing Directives applicable in this field.[24] The new Regulations are accompanied by a safety re-evaluation of all currently permitted food additives. This re-evaluation is currently being carried out by EFSA. The review has started with food colors. Review of other food additives will follow.[25]

---

[22]   *Inter alia* Regulation (EC) No 1331/2008 establishing a common authorization procedure provides for a centralized authorization procedure for food additives, food enzymes, and flavorings; Regulation (EC) No 1332/2008 on food enzymes creates harmonized rules for their scientific evaluation and authorization in the EU; Regulation (EC) No 1333/2008 on food additives consolidates all food additives legislation in one single legal instrument and will make legislation more user-friendly; and Regulation (EC) No 1334/2008 on flavoring and certain food ingredients with flavoring properties updates the previous legislation taking into account the latest scientific advice.

[23]   Regulation (EC) No 1331/2008 of the European Parliament and of the Council of December 16, 2008 establishing a common authorization procedure for food additives, food enzymes, and food flavorings; Regulation (EC) No 1332/2008 of the European Parliament and of the Council of December 16, 2008 on food enzymes; Regulation (EC) No 1333/2008 of the European Parliament and of the Council of December 16, 2008 on food additives; Regulation (EC) No 1334/2008 of the European Parliament and of the Council of December 16, 2008 on flavorings and certain food ingredients with flavoring properties for use in and on foods.

[24]   *Inter alia*, Directive 88/388/EEC on flavorings, Directive 89/107/EEC on food additives, Directive 94/35/EC on Sweeteners and Directive 94/36/EC on Colors.

[25]   Article 30 of Regulation EC 1333/2008 requires EFSA to re-evaluate by 2020 all food additives authorized for use in the EU prior to January 20, 2009 before they can be included on the EU list. All substances authorized under previous legislation (Directives 94/35/EC on sweeteners, 94/36/EC on colors, 95/2/EC on

EU harmonization of food law by substitution of Regulations for Directives is also demonstrated by the recently adopted EU Regulation on Food Information to Consumers.[26] The Regulation aims to merge, clarify, and simplify the rules governing labeling and nutrition labeling of foods, which are currently provided in two Directives.[27] The Regulation makes nutrition labeling mandatory, and requires the indication of energy value, fat, saturated fat, carbohydrates, sugars, proteins, and salt. Mandatory labeling information will have to be printed in a minimum font size, and origin labeling of fresh or frozen meat, not only beef, will become compulsory. Among key changes is a requirement to highlight allergenic ingredients in the list of ingredients. Industry must adapt to the new rules by December 13, 2014 but has an additional two years to comply with the Regulation's provisions on mandatory nutrition declaration.

The EU Nutrition and Health Claims Regulation[28] is a much-debated example of an EU food enactment focused on the objective of consumer protection and the concept of informed choice. The Regulation harmonizes the rules applicable to statements made on foods that refer to their nutritional properties or relationship with health.[29] The key requirements include use of only scientifically substantiated claims. This requirement complements the prohibition of the use of medicinal claims on foods that was established by EU food labeling rules.[30]

Medicinal claims are usually understood as those that "attribute to any foodstuff the property of preventing, treating or curing a human disease, or refer to such properties."[31]

The EU Nutrition and Health Claims Regulation establishes different categories of health claims. "General function claims" (known as Article 13 claims) were permitted, in principle, to be based on generally accepted scientific evidence. The Commission has established a positive list of such claims "in consultation" with EFSA. [32]

Another category of claims, those referring to reduction of a disease risk factor or to children's development and health (known as Article 14 claims), were required to be subject to a separate authorization procedure that would include a scientific assessment by EFSA based on an individual dossier.[33] However, due to the fact that the term "generally

food additives) are allowed until their review is complete. Regulation EU 257/2010 establishes a program for the re-evaluation of approved food additives, the details of which are in Annex II.

[26]   Regulation (EU) No 1169/2011 of the European Parliament and of the Council of 25 October 2011 on the provision of food information to consumers, amending Regulations (EC) No 1924/2006 and (EC) No 1925/2006 of the European Parliament and of the Council, and repealing Commission Directive 87/250/EEC, Council Directive 90/496/EEC, Commission Directive 1999/10/EC, Directive 2000/13/EC of the European Parliament and of the Council, Commission Directives 2002/67/EC and 2008/5/EC and Commission Regulation (EC) No 608/2004, OJ L 304, 22.11.2011, p. 18–63.

[27]   Directive 2000/13/EC on the labeling, presentation, and advertising of foodstuffs; Directive 90/496/EEC on nutrition labeling for foodstuffs.

[28]   Regulation (EC) No 1924/2006 on nutrition and health claims made on foods.

[29]   Nutrition claims that are permitted are listed in the Annex to the EU Nutrition and Health Claims Regulation. At the time of this writing, there was no equivalent list available for health claims.

[30]   Article 2(1)(b) of Directive 2000/13 on the labeling, presentation and advertising of foodstuffs.

[31]   Id.

[32]   See the EU Register of nutrition and health claims made on foods available at: http://ec.europa.eu/nuhclaims/ (last visited Dec. 8, 2014).

[33]   With a possibility to request protection of proprietary data on the basis of Article 13.5 of the Regulation.

accepted scientific evidence" proved to be insufficiently precise to permit determination of claims falling within Article 13, EFSA has used the thorough scientific-evaluation process provided for claims falling within Article 14 to determine the suitability of claims falling within Article 13. The large number of claims falling within Article 13 that were submitted by manufacturers to individual EU Member States and subsequently by the EU Member States[34] to the European Commission for evaluation by EFSA made the related review process very lengthy. It required more than four years after the Regulation entered into application in July 2007 before EFSA completed the evaluation process. Article 14 claims submitted by individual companies were being assessed in parallel. Only a fraction of the claims submitted on the basis of both Article 13 and Article 14 were approved by EFSA. These included the mainly noncontroversial and well-established health benefits of vitamins and minerals, and left a majority of the industry questioning the possibility of effectively marketing their products. The European Commission, assisted by EU Member States' experts, has established a list of permitted "general function" claims on the basis of EFSA opinions.[35]

Another challenge facing EU regulators in the future will be the regulation of innovations in food. The Council of the EU and the European Parliament have recently failed to reach a compromise concerning the ongoing review of the existing Novel Foods Regulation.[36] The institutions could not agree on suitable labeling of foods resulting from offspring of cloned animals. The European Commission has published a draft proposal for a Regulation on novel foods; it would revise the existing Regulation (EC) No 258/97 on novel foods and novel food ingredients.[37] However, genetically modified foods and foods from cloned animals are excluded from the proposal. The draft Regulation, if adopted in its current form, would streamline and simplify the authorization process and establish a Union list of authorized novel foods.

The regulation of the use of nanotechnology in food is also an issue of potential future controversy in EU food regulation. At present, a number of EU legislative provisions, such as the existing Biocides Directive[38] or the Regulation on Food Information to Consumers, contain only definitions of engineered nano-materials and requirements to label nano-ingredients. It appears that, provided related safety data are available, no comprehensive EU regulatory initiatives on nano-foods will be put forward.

A number of disputes have arisen between the United States and the EU on food-safety issues in recent years (e.g., EU restrictions on genetically modified food and EU objections to

---

[34]   The final list scrutinized by the Commission and submitted to EFSA contained more than 4,000 claims.

[35]   *Id.* footnote 147. In the process of evaluation of health claims the European Commission asked EFSA to exclude for the moment from the scope of assessment claims referring to botanical ingredients. This decision was due to the advocacy of food supplement producers that indicated, *inter alia*, inconsistencies of the assessment of botanicals under the EU Nutrition and Health Claims Regulation and under Traditional Herbal Medicines Directive (Directive 2004/24/EC of the European Parliament and of the Council of March 31, 2004 amending, as regards traditional herbal medicinal products, Directive 2001/83/EC on the Community code relating to medicinal products for human use); the Commission did not yet decide when the evaluation of botanicals will be re-opened.

[36]   Regulation (EC) No 258/97 concerning novel foods and novel food ingredients.

[37]   *Available at* http://ec.europa.eu/food/food/biotechnology/novelfood/initiatives_en.htm (last visited Dec. 8, 2014).

[38]   Directive 98/8/EC concerning the placing of biocidal products on the market.

antimicrobial treatments for poultry that are common in the United States). The best known is a U.S.-EU food trade dispute regarding a beef hormone matter. In 1998, a WTO appellate body ruled against the EU, in a case brought by Canada and the United States, following an EU ban on meat from cattle treated with hormones for growth-promotion purposes.[39] The WTO appellate body held that the EU had failed to produce a risk assessment justifying its refusal of such meat. The ruling against the EU was based in part on the fact that the Codex Alimentarius Commission had established standards for five of the six hormones in question. The EU was unable to produce a risk assessment or otherwise justify its continued ban of these hormones in the face of these international Codex standards, which had been adopted by the relevant food safety standards body under the SPS agreement. Therefore, the WTO permitted the United States and Canada to impose sanctions on EU exports. The sanctions consisted of increased tariffs on a list of European goods exported to North America, and total $116.8 million for the United States and C$11.3 million for Canada per year.

In 2003, the European Commission published documents citing new scientific information supporting its refusal to allow imports of beef from cattle treated with hormones, and requested that the United States and Canada lift the trade sanctions. The Commission asserted that the EU had now complied with the WTO ruling, by supplying a risk assessment to justify its departure from the Codex standards. The United States and Canada refused to lift the sanctions, and in 2008 the matter was again before a WTO dispute resolution panel and appellate body.[40] On March 31, 2008, the WTO panel ruled against the EU. The EU appealed. An appellate body issued a report dated October 16, 2008, that was a complex mixed ruling, which found against the EU in some respects and for it in others. All participants, of course, claimed victory.[41]

Pharmaceuticals

If each country—or even each of a few dozen countries—devised its own peculiar regulatory system for pharmaceuticals, with its own unique testing and production requirements, the costs of testing and developing pharmaceuticals would be astronomical; and these costs would be passed on to consumers and third-party players as increased healthcare costs.[42] Worse, the introduction of lifesaving products would be delayed. Moreover, regulatory costs would also be multiplied, as each country applied its own laws.

ICH

The fact that we do not today have a situation in which every country "reinvents" pharmaceutical regulation is a credit to the work done by the International Conference on

---

[39]   The WTO panel decision and the WTO appellate body decision may be found at www.wto.org.

[40]   *See* http://www.wto.org/english/tratop_e/dispu_e/cases_e/ds320_e.htm.

[41]   The United States and Canada will be able to maintain high tariffs on European products such as Roquefort cheese, truffles and Dijon mustard. B. Klapper, *WTO Said to Rule Against EU in Beef Hormone Dispute*, Int'l Herald Trib., Mar. 28, 2008.

[42]   Linda R. Horton, *Harmonization, Regulation and Trade: Where Do We Go From Here?*, 50 PDA J. Pharm. Sci. Tech. 61-5 (1996).

Harmonisation of Technical Requirements for Registration of Pharmaceuticals for Human Use (ICH).[43] ICH is an example of how FDA has joined with counterparts in other countries to write harmonized guidelines that protect the public and benefit industry by reducing duplicative testing. ICH developed a guideline whereby a single set of data, known as the Common Technical Document (CTD)—showing that a drug is effective, safe, and high quality—qualifies for marketing approval around the world. Even if agencies such as FDA insist on conducting independent reviews, at least the data requirements can be harmonized and regulatory reviews streamlined.

The purposes of ICH, which was launched in 1989, are to: 1) provide a forum for dialogue between regulatory agencies and the pharmaceutical industry on differences in the technical requirements for product marketing in countries such as Canada, Japan, the United States, and in the EU; 2) identify areas where modifications in technical requirements or greater mutual acceptance of research and development procedures could lead to more efficient use of human, animal, and material resources without compromising effectiveness, safety, or quality; and 3) make recommendations on practical ways to achieve greater harmonization in the interpretation and application of technical guidelines and requirements for registration.

ICH projects include the Medical Dictionary for Regulatory Activities (MedDRA), an international medical terminology designed to improve the electronic transmission worldwide of regulatory information and data on medical products during clinical and scientific reviews and marketing, including adverse event reporting and coding of clinical trial data. ICH has also produced dozens of guidance documents that create consistency in the requirements for new drug approval.

A factor in ICH's success is that, since its inception, ICH has included participants not only from the three government agencies but also from industry. Manufacturers can help identify inconsistencies in testing or submission requirements. Industry participates through the principal trade association for the research-oriented manufacturers in each of the regions, as discussed below. Representatives of the generic industry participate in quality-related discussions of interest to all companies. The ICH Secretariat is administered in conjunction with the International Federation of Pharmaceutical Manufacturers and Associations (IFPMA), discussed below. ICH operates under the direction of the ICH Steering Committee, which comprises representatives from FDA, the EU, the Ministry of Health, Labor and Welfare, Japan (MHLW), Pharmaceutical Research and Manufacturers of America (PhRMA), the European Federation of Pharmaceutical Industries and Associations (EFPIA), and the Japanese Pharmaceutical Manufacturers Association (JPMA). Official observer status has been given to WHO, the European Free Trade Association (EFTA), and the Health Products and Food Branch of Health Canada, which adopts ICH guidelines as Canadian guidelines. WHO publicizes ICH's harmonized guidelines to WHO members.

ICH has carried out its activities not only through large public meetings marking ICH progress, held at approximately two-year intervals, but also through guideline-drafting by representatives of the six ICH members (Ministry of Health, Labour and Welfare in Japan,

---

[43]   *See* www.ich.org (last visited Dec. 8, 2014).

JPMA, EU, EFPIA, FDA and PhRMA) with approximately 50 Expert Working Groups that meet as needed, sometimes several times in a year.

The work products of ICH consist of a series of consensus guidance documents. These guidance documents, after successive ICH steps of review and acceptance, including an opportunity for public review and comment in the respective jurisdictions, are forwarded to the regulatory agencies with the expectation that they will be formally adopted by the agencies. The ICH steps are:

- Step 1: Consensus sought—technical experts sign.
- Step 2: Steering Committee signs; public comment or consultation at the national level.
- Step 3: Comments reviewed—drafts revised by technical experts.
- Step 4: Final draft endorsed by regulatory agency members of steering committee, and draft prepared for adoption at the national level.
- Step 5: Final guideline adopted at the national level by the three regions.

A major focus of ICH activities has been the development of harmonized guidelines for the assessment of toxicity of pharmaceutical products. Areas of harmonization activity have included testing for carcinogenicity, genotoxicity, toxicokinetics and pharmacokinetics, and reproductive toxicity, as well as development of principles for the safety testing of biotechnology products.

ICH GCPs and Global Clinical Trials

The assessment of safety and efficacy of products during clinical studies depends on the quality of clinical trials and resulting data. ICH has produced harmonized guidelines on Good Clinical Practices (GCPs), an international ethical and scientific quality standard for designing, conducting, recording, and reporting trials that involve the participation of human subjects.[44] The resulting ICH guideline is widely followed around the world.

Many companies are sponsoring clinical studies in countries that have limited capacity for oversight of human research. Thus, international standards for both the conduct and oversight of clinical trials play an important role in filling this regulatory gap.[45] In recent years, the ICH GCP document has emerged as the leading standard, building on the

---

[44]   *See* International Conference on Harmonisation; Good Clinical Practice: Consolidated Guidelines, 62 Fed. Reg. 25,692 (May 9, 1997); ICH E6 Good Clinical Practice: Consolidated Guidance (April 1996).

[45]   *See* National Bioethics Advisory Commission, Ethical and Policy Issues in International Research: Clinical Trials in Developing Countries (Apr. 2001). Under 45 C.F.R. § 46.101 (2013), the normal policies of the U.S. Department of Health and Human Services (DHHS) for U.S. government-funded clinical research apply fully to DHHS-funded research conducted outside the United States, except where the relevant department or agency head determines that the procedures prescribed by the foreign institution afford protections that are at least equivalent to those provided in the DHHS policies, in which case that department or agency head may approve the substitution of the foreign procedures for the DHHS procedures. *Id.* § 46.101(h). *See* DHHS, Protection of Human Subjects, Proposed Criteria for Determinations of Equivalent Protection, 70 Fed. Reg. 15,322 (Mar. 25, 2005). Also, the U.S. Office of Human Research Protections has several international programs in this area, including registration of ethics committees in countries other than the United States. *See* http://www.hhs.gov/ohrp/assurances/index.html for the procedure and http://ohrp.cit.nih.gov/search/search.aspx?styp=bsc for a list of registered boards and committees.

Nuremberg Code,[46] a formal statement on medical ethics that led to present standards in the United States and elsewhere that protect human research subjects (whose central feature is the right of a subject to be told about the benefits, risks, and purpose of the research, i.e., "informed consent") and the declaration of Helsinki.[47] All of these documents are based on fundamental principles of ethical research involving human subjects.

These principles require that human subjects be used in research only if the research is based on scientific principles; all research utilizing human subjects should be preceded by adequate laboratory and animal experimentation; and a thorough review of the scientific literature should have been conducted to prevent unnecessary or ill-advised studies. In addition, clinical research should be conducted in accordance with a written protocol that has been reviewed by an independent committee, and should be conducted only by scientifically qualified persons under supervision of clinically competent medical personnel; most importantly, human subjects must give informed consent while not under duress.

Provided that GCP principles and local legal requirements are met, FDA accepts data from foreign studies, even if not conducted under an investigational new drug (IND) permit.[48] Sponsors of clinical trials in other countries should consider carefully whether their sites outside of the United States sites should be covered by an IND permit.[49]

International Organizations

FDA in general adopts ICH Guidelines as guidance documents.[50]

World Health Organization (WHO). WHO advises countries on the structure and functions of national drug regulatory authorities, including laws and regulations; enforcement powers; advisory bodies; independence of operation; licensing for products, manufacturers, and distributors; clinical trial regulation; and new drug assessments (small regulatory authorities are encouraged to accept approvals of leading regulatory authorities rather than conduct independent assessments).[51] A key responsibility of WHO in the pharmaceutical

---

[46]   The Nuremberg Code (1947) 313 BMJ 1448 (1996).

[47]   The declaration is issued by the World Medical Association, www.wma.org, an international non-governmental organization comprising national associations such as the American Medical Association. Until 2008, FDA cited the Declaration of Helsinki in its investigational new drug regulations. *See* 21 C.F.R. § 312.120; FDA, Final Rule, Human Subject Protection: Foreign Clinical Studies Not Conducted Under an Investigational New Drug Application, 82 Fed. Reg. 22,800 (Apr. 28, 2008). FDA had announced earlier that the version of the declaration to be followed was the 1989 version rather than later versions that were premised on the notion that placebo trials (often required by FDA) are unethical. FDA decided that, due to widespread adoption of the ethical standards in the ICH GCP standard, reference in its regulations to the Declaration of Helsinki is unnecessary.

[48]   21 C.F.R. §§ 312.120, 314.106 (2014). As discussed in the preceding footnote, this regulation was amended in 2008 to delete reference to the Declaration of Helsinki.

[49]   For a discussion of requirements for IND studies pertaining to need for signed Statements of Clinical Investigators (Form FDA 1572) and for FDA waivers where foreign ethics committees do not comply precisely with FDA requirements for institutional review committees, *see* FDA, Draft Information Sheet Guidance for Sponsors, Clinical Investigators, and Institutional Review Boards on Frequently Asked Questions—Statement of Clinical Investigator (Form FDA 1572); Availability, 73 Fed. Reg. 43,940 (July 29, 2008).

[50]   62 Fed. Reg. 8961 (Feb. 27, 1997).

[51]   WHO, *Guiding Principles for Small National Drug Regulatory Authorities*, 3 WHO DRUG INFORMATION 43 (1989); *in* WHO EXPERT COMMITTEE ON SPECIFICATIONS FOR PHARMACEUTICAL PRODUCTS, TECHNICAL REPORT SERIES, No.

area involves the establishment of international nonproprietary names (INNs).[52] INNs, also known as "generic names," facilitate the identification of active pharmaceutical ingredients.

International Conference of Drug Regulatory Authorities (ICDRA). In 1980, FDA convened a meeting to which the agency invited the heads of the drug regulatory authorities from all around the world. Attendees found the meeting worthwhile, and ICDRA was born. ICDRA comprises representatives from more than 100 countries, meets biennially, and is viewed by WHO as its principal network of regulatory agencies.

Organization for Economic Cooperation and Development (OECD). OECD is an international organization consisting of the most advanced economies in the world. It has been a leader in harmonization of good laboratory practices (GLPs) and chemical testing guidelines for pesticides and toxic chemicals. It issues decisions and recommendations. OECD has issued two decisions of particular interest to FDA. First, a 1981 Decision on Mutual Acceptance of Data sets forth conditions under which data generated in the testing of chemicals in an OECD member country shall be accepted in other OECD countries for the purposes of assessment and other uses relating to the protection of humans and the environment.[53] Second, a 1989 Council Decision-Recommendation places more stringent requirements on countries to assure compliance with GLP requirements, as well as mechanisms to strengthen information exchange among OECD countries.[54]

International Federation of Pharmaceutical Manufacturers and Associations (IFPMA). IFPMA is a nongovernmental organization, founded in 1968, which has had an official voice in WHO on behalf of the pharmaceutical industry since 1971.[55] PhRMA is the U.S. member of the IFPMA. The IFPMA maintains, and periodically updates, a Code of Pharmaceutical Marketing Practices.[56] EFPIA and the trade associations of individual countries throughout Europe and the rest of the world likewise have codes of practice on advertising and marketing of pharmaceuticals.

FDA International Activities: CDER

FDA's Center for Drug Evaluation and Research (CDER) has several unique international activities. CDER has developed a forum for international drug regulatory authorities, where its officials provide information about the U.S. drug regulatory processes as well as the underlying science, technology, regulations, and processes. The forum, which meets periodically and is open only to drug regulatory authorities, provides a more efficient way to share information about FDA's programs than is possible in piecemeal visits by foreign officials and workshops. Also, CDER has developed a Manual of Policies and Procedures (MAPPs) for international activities. (MAPPs are approved practices and procedures followed

790, Geneva (1990).

[52]   *Available at* http://www.who.int/medicines/services/inn/en/index.html.

[53]   Decision of the Council Concerning the Mutual Acceptance of Data in the Assessment of Chemicals, C (81) 30 (Final) (May 12, 1981), as amended.

[54]   Council Decision-Recommendation on Compliance with Principles of GLP, C (89) 87 (Final) (Oct. 2, 1989), as amended.

[55]   The IFPMA also has consultative status with the World Intellectual Property Organization, the United Nations Industrial Development Organization (UNIDO), the UN Conference on Trade and Development (UNCTAD), and the Council of Europe. It is on the UN Roster of Non-Government Organizations.

[56]   *See* www.ifpma.org (last visited Dec. 8, 2014).

by CDER staff to help standardize the new drug review process and other activities.) MAPP, § 4160.2, on "Prioritizing of Requests for Training and Visits by Foreign Regulatory Agencies and International Regulatory Organizations," describes how CDER prioritizes requests for visits and training by representatives from foreign regulatory agencies and international regulatory organizations.

CDER participates actively in the President's Emergency Plan for AIDS Relief (PEPFAR), which was announced in the 2003 State of the Union address. PEPFAR provides billions of U.S. dollars to fight the HIV/AIDS pandemic, with a special focus on 15 of the hardest hit countries. The President's plan is designed to prevent seven million new HIV infections, treat at least two million HIV-infected people, and care for 10 million HIV-affected individuals, AIDS orphans, and vulnerable children. It targets three specific areas: prevention of HIV transmission; treatment of AIDS and associated conditions; and care, including palliative care, for HIV infected-individuals, as well as orphans and vulnerable children.

As part of the PEPFAR program, FDA has granted tentative approvals to a number of anti-retroviral drugs that help keep the AIDS virus from reproducing. Some are fixed-dose combination products meant to simplify the administration of multidrug therapy. Under the agency's tentative approval approach, FDA makes a finding that the product in question meets all of FDA's manufacturing quality and clinical safety and efficacy standards.

Pharmaceutical Regulation in the EU

This section of the chapter answers eight questions[57]:

- Who regulates pharmaceuticals in the EU?
- What are the basic requirements?
- What authorization options are available?
- How does the EU regulate generics?
- What are the special laws on orphan medicines, medicines for children, and advanced therapies?
- How does the EU regulate biosimilars?
- How does the EU regulate Good Manufacturing Practices (GMPs)?
- How does EU competition law affect regulation of pharmaceuticals?

The discussion that follows focuses on distinctive aspects of EU regulation, and it should be borne in mind that ICH documents are always relevant in an EU context.

---

[57]   In the interest of brevity, and considering the constant evolution of EU pharmaceutical law, this section includes minimal footnotes. Readers are referred to the websites of the European Medicines agency, http://www.EMA.europa.eu, the European Commission http://ec.europa.eu/health/human-use/index_en.htm and the Rules governing the marketing of pharmaceuticals in the European Union (sometimes called notice to applicants) at http://ec.europa.eu/health/documents/eudralex/index_en.htm and the Heads of Medicines Agencies, http://www.hma.eu or may use Internet search engines to locate particular documents mentioned.

Who Regulates Pharmaceuticals?

EU regulation of "medicinal products"—as pharmaceuticals are called in the relevant EU legislation—is a rapidly changing work in progress. Without question, the European Medicines Agency (EMA) has emerged as the principal pharmaceutical advisory body in Europe. Since it began operations in 1995, this agency has become an international heavyweight. Within the EU, the EMA is viewed as having so masterfully carried out the tasks originally entrusted to it that its scope of responsibility has been steadily expanded.

The EMA's main responsibility is the protection and promotion of human and animal health, through the evaluation and supervision of medicines for human and veterinary use.[58] The specific responsibilities of the EMA include:

- the scientific evaluation of applications for European marketing authorizations for both human and veterinary medicines (centralized procedure);

- the monitoring of the safety of medicines through a pharmacovigilance network, and taking appropriate actions if adverse drug reaction reports suggest that the benefit-risk balance of a medicinal product has changed since its distribution was authorized;

- establishing safe limits for residues of veterinary medicinal products in food of animal origin;

- stimulating innovation and research in the pharmaceutical sector;

- forging close ties with partner organizations around the world, including the WHO and the regulatory authorities of non-European nations; and

- referral or arbitration procedures relating to medicines that are approved or under consideration by EU Member States in noncentralized authorization procedures.

EMA's Committee on Medicinal Products for Human Use (CHMP) prepares opinions on whether individual products should be authorized for marketing in the EU. However, the European Commission in Brussels makes the actual authorization decisions. The Commission generally endorses CHMP's opinion, and must give reasons if it chooses not to do so.

The European Commission is the principal administrative body in the EU, and is headed by a President. The Commission comprises Directorates-General corresponding to departments in the U.S. government. The department in the European Commission to which the EMA forwards CHMP opinions is the Pharmaceuticals Unit of the Directorate-General for Health and Consumer Policy (DG Sanco). The Pharmaceuticals Unit was moved to DG Sanco from the Directorate-General Enterprise and Industry (DG Enterprise) following the entry into force of the new Treaty on the Functioning of the European Union. Other parts of the European Commission that are important in the public health area are the Directorate-General for Research and the European Centre for Disease Prevention and Control (ECDC) which is overseen by DG Sanco.

---

[58]   See http://www.ema.europa.eu/ema/index.jsp?curl=pages/about_us/general/general_content_000091. jsp&murl=menus/about_us/about_us.jsp&mid=WC0b01ac0580028a42.

Patients' rights in cross-border healthcare is an emergent area in EU law that will affect both those who sell medical products in the EU and patients. Following several cases in which the European Court of Justice upheld the rights of EU citizens to seek (and be reimbursed for) healthcare in other EU countries, or even outside the EU, the European Commission and Member State officials intensified activities in this area. In July 2008, the European Commission published a Proposal for a Directive of the European Parliament and of the Council on the application of patients' rights in cross-border healthcare.[59] After prolonged negotiations involving the EU Institutions and the EU Member States, the Directive on Patients' Rights in Cross-Border Healthcare[60] was adopted on March 9, 2011. The Directive aims to facilitate access to safe and high-quality cross-border healthcare, and promotes cooperation on healthcare among EU Member States, in full respect of national competencies in organizing and delivering healthcare.

The EMA, since 1995, has become the principal gateway to the European Union marketplace for new pharmaceutical entities, as well as the exclusive route to market for biotechnological medicines and a growing list of other products. Located in London, the EMA is headed by an Executive Director, appointed by the agency's management board for a five-year term. The EMA management board is principally responsible for budgetary matters. It consists of two Members of the European Parliament, two senior officials of the European Commission, one representative from each EU Member State, one representative each from physicians' organizations, veterinarians' organizations and two representatives from patients' organizations. Representatives of certain EU accession candidates and the three other European countries that are members of the EEA—Iceland, Liechtenstein, and Norway—participate as observers in board proceedings and other EMA activities.

By the end of 2013, the EMA had a staff of 785 including 92 contract agents and 16 national experts. The EMA is able to operate with such a relatively small staff because it functions largely as a secretariat. The EU regulatory system's key distinguishing feature is that it essentially functions as a network. The EMA operates in partnership with the national competent authorities for human and veterinary products in the EU Member States. The authorities make scientific resources available in the form of a network of more than 3,600 European Union experts who assist the agency in performing its scientific tasks.[61]

Most product reviews and guideline-drafting activities are carried out by EU Member State experts serving on the CHMP and other scientific groups. In fact, a large share of the EMA's budget pays EU Member State drug regulatory agencies (so-called "competent authorities") for the scientific services of their experts in carrying out functions for the EMA. More than a third of the EMA's budget goes to Member State regulatory agencies for these services. The national authorities include the United Kingdom's Medicines and Health Products Regulatory Agency (MHRA), the French Health Products Safety Agency (AFSSAPS), the German Federal Institute for Drugs and Devices (BFARM) and Paul Ehrlich Institute (PEI), the Swedish Medical Products agency (MPA), and others. EU Member State

---

[59]   COM (2008) 414 final, 2008/0142 (COD), Brussels, July 2, 2008.

[60]   Directive 2011/24/EU of the European Parliament and of the Council of March 9, 2011 on the Application of Patients' Rights in Cross-Border Healthcare, OJ L 88, April 4, 2011, p. 45–65.

[61]   Information in this paragraph is from the overview of the European Medicines Agency's policy on conflicts of interests for scientific-committee members and experts 2013, EMA/546668/2013, at 1.

agencies have authority to approve certain products, and they also carry out a host of important regulatory responsibilities, including approval of clinical trials, inspections, and postapproval surveillance.

The principal contact point in Europe for scientific advice on the tests needed to satisfy EU requirements for authorization of a pharmaceutical is the EMA. However, many carefully designed product-development plans also involve contacts with EU Member State experts. In the European Union, there is no single, all-powerful focal point throughout the product-development process that is analogous to the relevant review division in CDER or the Center for Biologics Evaluation and Research (CBER).

What Are the Basic Requirements?

Whether a medicinal product enters the EU market through the centralized or decentralized routes discussed below, a complex array of requirements and guidelines at both the EU and EU Member State levels governs preclinical testing and GLPs, GCPs, GMPs, and related chemistry and manufacturing controls, inspections, labeling, advertising, and promotion, parallel trade, imports, exports, and compliance and enforcement. There has been a rapid expansion of law on these subjects at the EU level, with increased harmonization in many areas. Still, EU Member State requirements and guidelines remain essential parts of the EU regulatory picture, and there are considerable differences among Member States in implementation and enforcement.

EU regulation is similar in many respects to regulation in the United States. Its detailed requirements in many areas are similar to FDA requirements. Therefore, the discussion that follows focuses on novel EU aspects.

Three key laws govern the EU authorization procedure: the Clinical Trials Directive,[62] the Community Code on Medicinal Products[63] and the EMA Regulation.[64] No medicinal product can be placed on the market in the EU unless it has been authorized. This legal framework is in contrast to the U.S. system, in which a few categories of older drugs (most over-the-counter drugs covered by monographs and a shrinking number of prescription drugs) have been allowed to be marketed as "not new" drugs or "grandfathered" drugs.

EU pharmaceutical law contains "legal presence" requirements. Because a Marketing Authorization Holder (MAH) of an authorized medicinal product must be "established" in the EEA, the Marketing Authorization Application (MAA) requires a demonstration that the applicant has established such a presence. In addition, where a sponsor of a clinical trial is

---

[62]   Directive 2001/20 of the European Parliament and of the Council. By the second quarter of 2016, the Clinical Trials Directive will be replaced by Regulation (EU) No 536/2014 of the European Parliament and of the Council of April 16, 2014 on clinical trials on medicinal products for human use, and repealing Directive 2001/20/EC.

[63]   Directive 2001/83/EC of the European Parliament and of the Council of November 6, 2001 on the Community Code relating to medicinal products for human use, as amended.

[64]   Regulation (EC) no 726/2004 of the European Parliament and of the Council of March 31, 2004 laying down community procedures for the authorization and supervision of medicinal products for human and veterinary use and establishing a European Medicines Agency, as amended.

not established in the EEA, the sponsor must appoint a legal representative in the EEA for purposes of liability and communication with regulators.

Under the Clinical Trials Directive and the EU Member State implementing laws, all approval and supervision of clinical trials in the EU is carried out at the EU Member State level, and the Directive is a floor rather than a ceiling. EU Member States have layered a number of additional requirements on top of the EU-level basics, and legal research at EU Member State level is essential whenever there are clinical trial sites in an EU Member State. As a result, the Clinical Trials Directive has had only partial success in achieving harmonization of clinical trial regulation in the EU. In 2012, the European Commission published a proposal for a new Clinical Trials Regulation to replace the Clinical Trials Directive and overhaul the existing regulation of clinical trials in the EU. On April 16, 2014, the new Clinical Trials Regulation was adopted and is expected to enter into force during the second quarter of 2016.[65] Until the regulation enters into force, the Clinical Trials Directive will still be applicable to clinical trials conducted in the EU.

The Directive, through national implementing legislation, regulates the conduct of clinical trials, including multi-center trials, on human subjects involving medicinal products. It does not apply to non-interventional trials, also known as observational studies, although some EU Member States regulate such trials at the national level. The Directive applies without prejudice to national requirements for protection of clinical trial subjects, and obliges EU Member States to adopt, if they have not done so already, detailed rules to protect individuals unable to give consent.

Key features of the Directive are:

- common time limits and harmonized format for applying for opinions and approval from ethics committees and competent authorities;

- adoption of a single opinion by each EU Member State's lead ethics committee;

- standard procedure for all EU Member States on content of applications and on start and completion of clinical trials;

- creation of an EU-wide clinical trials database;

- formal notification procedure for adverse reactions, with reports to be collected in an EU database; and

- inspection procedures to ensure compliance with GCP and GMP in production of investigational medicines.

An area of focus in the EU has been first-in-human clinical trials. In 2007, the EMA issued guidelines on first-time-in-humans clinical trials.

EU authorities will accept data from clinical trials conducted outside the EU, provided that these trials met the ethical requirements of the Clinical Trials Directive as well as GCP.[66]

---

[65] Regulation (EU) No 536/2014 of the European Parliament and of the Council of April 16, 2014 on clinical trials on medicinal products for human use, and repealing Directive 2001/20/EC, OJ L 158, May 27, 2014, p. 1–76.

[66] Article 8.3(i)(b), Directive 2001/83/EC, the Community Code relating medicinal products for human use.

Clinical trials conducted for EU authorities often include an active comparator arm. FDA and the EU authorities, with counterparts from Japan, worked together to develop the ICH E10 guideline on Choice of Control Group and Related Issues in Clinical Trials. The EU agrees with FDA's view that placebo groups are justified in many drug trials, and neither FDA nor EMA has adopted the 2000 version of the Declaration of Helsinki, which expresses a negative view of placebo-controlled trials. (The European Commission and EMA follow the 1996 version of the Declaration.)

The Clinical Trials Directive applies only to pharmaceutical trials, not to trials or other clinical studies of medical devices, nor to other forms of biomedical research not involving products (e.g., experimental surgery). Such matters are dealt with by EU Member State laws. A few EU Member States (e.g., France), in implementing the Clinical Trials Directive, made corresponding changes in national legislation covering medical device trials.

Key Features of the New Clinical Trials Regulation

The new Clinical Trials Regulation will be directly binding in all EU Member States without the need for any national implementing legislation. The Clinical Trials Regulation is expected to enter into force six months following the achievement of full functionality of a new EU database and single online EU Portal (hereafter "EU Portal") created under the new Regulation. However, the Regulation states that, in any event, it will enter into force no later than the second quarter of 2016.

• Coordinated authorization procedure

The new Clinical Trials Regulation replaces the national approval procedures with a single EU-wide coordinated procedure initiated through an EU Portal managed by the EMA in cooperation with the European Commission and the EU Member States. Under the new coordinated procedure, the sponsor of a clinical trial will be required to submit a single application for approval of a clinical trial to a reporting EU Member State (RMS) through the EU Portal. The submission procedure will be the same irrespective of whether the clinical trial is to be conducted in a single EU Member State or in more than one EU Member State.

The application will be assessed in two parts: Part I involves the RMS's initial assessment of the scientific, therapeutic, and safety aspects of the proposed clinical trial. The conclusions of the RMS will be applicable in all concerned EU Member States. Part II of the assessment will involve an assessment of the application for approval by the individual EU Member States on the basis of their national requirements, including ethical requirements, concerning the conduct of clinical trials.

• Extending the clinical trial to another EU Member State

The Clinical Trials Regulation permits the extension of a clinical trial to a new EU Member State in a more efficient procedure than the current process of having to initiate a completely new authorization procedure for each Member State.

• Increased transparency

The new Clinical Trials Regulation also aims to increase the transparency of data generated from authorized clinical trials conducted within the EU. The EMA, in cooperation with the European Commission and the EU Member States, must establish and maintain a publicly accessible and searchable EU database of all approved clinical trial data relating to medicinal products. Confidentiality may be claimed for an exhaustive list of data, including personal data processed on the basis of Regulation (EC) No 45/2001, commercially confidential information, and actions to ensure effective supervision of the conduct of a clinical trial by an EU Member State.

• New reporting requirements

The Clinical Trials Regulation aims to streamline and simplify the rules on safety reporting for clinical trials. As an example, suspected unexpected serious adverse reactions (SUSARs) can be reported by the sponsor directly to EudraVigilance instead of being submitted to each EU Member State. EudraVigilance is an electronic data network and system for reporting and evaluating suspected premarketing and postmarketing adverse drug reactions in the European Economic Area.

• Data privacy issues

The sponsor of a clinical trial will be permitted to seek the consent of a human subject to use his or her data for purposes outside the scope of the trial Protocol. Such purposes must be exclusively scientific.

• Indemnity and Insurance

The Clinical Trials Regulation provides that insurance covering the investigator, the institution, or product liability insurance will be sufficient for low-intervention clinical trials. The Privacy Data Protection Directive[67] and EU Member State implementing laws have an effect on pharmaceutical and medical device companies engaged in clinical trials and other activities in the EU. For example, the informed consent forms provided to clinical trial subjects should unambiguously request permission for the personal data from their participation in the study to be transferred outside the EU for analysis and regulatory assessments. Anonymization of personal data is an option in some cases. It should be emphasized that each Member State has its own laws on the subject of data privacy protection, and there is wide variation in what they require.

What Authorization Options Are Available in the EU?

General Requirements

Marketing authorization (approval) of medicinal products is regulated by the Community Code on Medicinal Products and related EU Member State implementing legislation. Under these laws, the procedures for applying for marketing authorization, and the contents of applications, are essentially the same in all 28 EU Member States. The EMA Regulation governs the authorization of medicinal products under the "centralized authorization procedure." However, the provisions of the Community Code concerning the types of testing

---

[67] Directive 95/46/EC of the European Parliament and of the Council of October 24, 1995 on the protection of individuals with regard to the processing of personal data and on the free movement of such data.

needed, and the contents of applications to be submitted, apply even to the centralized marketing authorization procedure.

Under requirements that apply EU-wide and are spelled out in Annex I to the Community Code on Medicinal Products,[68] an applicant must demonstrate the quality, safety, and efficacy of any product for which authorization is sought in the EU. Annex I requires that the application follow the data content and format requirements in the ICH CTD. Any so-called full application must be accompanied by evidence that the necessary research and testing in animals and in human subjects has been conducted. The demonstration of efficacy, safety, and quality of the drug is achieved through submission of information on the chemistry, manufacturing, and pharmaceutical aspects of the product, as well as the nonclinical and clinical data. (However, there also are various alternatives to full applications, discussed below in the sections on generics and biosimilars.) The application must include all information relevant to the product's evaluation, whether is favorable or unfavorable. It must include, in particular, all relevant details about any incomplete or abandoned preclinical or clinical tests, whether or not related to a therapeutic indication for which marketing authorization is sought.

The European Commission and the EMA have developed additional guidelines that substantially clarify (and detail) the testing requirements and application procedure for authorization. Most important of these is the "notice to applicants" (NTA), a constantly updated, multivolume publication covering all aspects of applications for marketing authorization in the EU.[69] In addition, the EMA has issued many guidelines, which an applicant needs to consult. For example, applications to the EMA require an EU Risk Management Plan.[70]

A key document related to EU approvals is the Summary of Medicinal Product Characteristics (SMPC), which provides basic information on the approved indications and other aspects of approval. Also, the Community Code on medicinal products, as well as Commission and EMA guidelines, spell out in detail what is required for labeling. In the EU, package leaflets for patients are required in all cases (aided by the fact that pharmaceutical companies generally must sell their products in multi-unit packs of typical dosage supply).

Marketing authorizations granted by the European Commission or the EU Member States are valid for an initial five-year period. Following that period, market authorizations are unlimited in duration, unless postmarketing safety evaluation (pharmacovigilance) leads the Commission or the relevant national authorities to impose an additional five-year renewal requirement.

A marketing authorization holder that wishes to request approval of a change in the product or in its methods of production needs to file a "line extension" application or "variation" application. These applications are similar to a U.S. supplemental new drug application (or supplemental biologics license application). In 2008, the EU lawmaking bodies agreed to a

---

[68]   Commission Directive 2003/63 Amending Directive 2001/83/EC of the European Parliament and of the Council of November 6, 2001 on the Community Code Relating Medicinal Products for Human Use.

[69]   See http://ec.europa.eu/health/documents/eudralex/vol-2/index_en.htm (last visited Dec. 8, 2014).

[70]   See http://eudravigilance.ema.europa.eu/human/evRiskManagement.asp (last visited Dec. 8, 2014).

new legislative instrument on variations aimed at achieving greater harmonization in how such applications and approvals are handled for pharmaceutical marketing authorizations issued by national authorities.[71] Commission Regulation (EC) No 1234/2008 concerning the examination of variations to the terms of marketing authorizations for medicinal products for human use and veterinary medicinal products was adopted on of November 24, 2008.

Alternative Pathways

Under the EU system for authorizing medicinal products, there are both a "centralized authorization procedure" led by the EMA and an authorization procedure led by the EU Member State competent authorities in which the EMA plays a much smaller role. Legislation that became effective in late 2005 increased the proportion of products that must go through the centralized process and added to the existing mutual recognition process a new decentralized procedure.

The EMA/Commission Centralized Authorization Procedure

Where the centralized authorization procedure is used, an applicant submits one single marketing authorization application to the EMA. A single evaluation is carried out through the CHMP, which is made up of senior physicians and other experts from the EU Member State agencies. If the CHMP concludes that the efficacy, safety, and quality of the medicinal product are sufficiently proven, it adopts a positive opinion. The EMA then sends the opinion to the Commission, which, if it agrees with the CHMP's positive opinion, adopts a decision granting a market authorization valid for the whole of the EU. The European Parliament is entitled to a "droit de regard" of the Commission's decision to grant or refuse a marketing authorization. The European Parliament may object to the decision if it considers that the Commission has exceeded its powers granted by the EMA Regulation.

For some products, use of the centralized process is mandatory; for others, it is optional. The EMA Regulation identifies the following types of products as ones for which centralized authorization is mandatory: medicinal products developed by means of recombinant DNA technology; controlled expression of gene coding for biologically active proteins in prokaryotes and eukaryotes, including transformed mammalian cells, hybridoma and monoclonal antibody methods; and orphan medicinal products. In addition, medicinal products that are for human use and that contain a new active substance that was not authorized in the EU on the date of entry into force of the revised EMA Regulation (May 20, 2004) and are intended for treatment of specified diseases are subject to the mandatory centralized procedure. These diseases are acquired immunity deficiency syndrome, cancer, neurodegenerative disorder, diabetes, auto-immune diseases and other immune dysfunction, and viral diseases. In December 2008, tissue-engineered medicinal products became subject to the mandatory centralized approval process (joining the other categories of "advanced therapies," which are cell therapy and gene therapy).[72] One category of medicinal products as to which use of the centralized process is optional—and the option

---

[71] Earlier EU laws had covered variations of marketing authorizations under the mutual recognition and decentralized procedures (Commission Regulation 84/2003) and under the centralized procedure (Commission Regulation 1085/2003).

[72] Regulation (EC) 1394/2007 of the European Parliament and of the Council of November 13, 2007 on advanced therapy medicinal products.

is to be exercised by the applicant—is where a product contains a new active substance that had not been authorized in the EU on the date of entry into force of the EMA Regulation. This is a route the applicant can choose for cases where the new substance is non-biotech, even where its intended indication is something other than the diseases (AIDS, cancer etc.) whose treatments are subject to the mandatory centralized procedure, as discussed above.

A potentially very broad category eligible for the optional use of the centralized procedure is situations where an applicant demonstrates that a product constitutes a significant therapeutic, scientific or technical innovation or can demonstrate that the granting of authorization in accordance with the EMA Regulation is in the interest of patients at the Community level.

In its review of an application, the CHMP takes into account appropriate benefit/risk scenarios in the populations and conditions of use as documented in the submitted clinical data. No medicine is considered free of risks or possible side effects, but the overall assessment must satisfy the reviewers and the CHMP as a whole that the benefits of using the new product outweigh the known or predicted risks.

After an application for authorization is submitted, an EMA staff member is selected as Product Team Leader. However, the actual in-depth review of an application is carried out by a "rapporteur" and a "co-rapporteur," both appointed from among the members of the CHMP. A CHMP guideline governs appointment of these individuals. The CHMP is made up of one expert per EU Member State plus a few extra members (so-called "co-opted members") to round out the committee's expertise. The rules of procedure of the CHMP permit it to establish and consult with expert groups known as "working parties" composed of members selected from a European experts list maintained by the EMA. The CHMP consults its working parties on scientific issues relating to their particular fields of expertise, and delegates to them certain tasks associated with the scientific evaluation of marketing authorization applications or the drafting of scientific guidance documents. In addition, several scientific advisory groups advise on medicinal products for specific medical specialties.

When an application for authorization is ready for CHMP consideration at one of its 11 meetings per year, the matter is put on the agenda well in advance. The applicant and the rapporteur address the CHMP in writing and in oral sessions. CHMP members pose questions and seek additional information from both. There is almost always a list of questions for the applicant. Furthermore, a request for special commitments prior to authorization, such as addition of a warning or other information to labeling, may be made. Applicants may be asked to submit a written commitment to conduct a post-authorization clinical trial and to submit its results to the CHMP, via the EMA Product team Leader. After these consultations and information exchanges, the CHMP provides its opinion to the EMA and the Commission. The opinion concerns whether, in light of the product's efficacy, safety, and quality and its overall benefit-risk ratio for its intended use, the product should be granted a marketing authorization in the EU. The opinion is announced in the press release issued by the EMA at the end of each CHMP meeting. This generally is the first time the EMA discloses to the public that an application for marketing authorization is pending.

The decision to grant or refuse an authorization is made by the European Commission. The Commission is not bound by the opinion of the CHMP. However, it must provide a justification if it chooses not to follow the opinion. In practice, the Commission generally follows the opinions of the CHMP. The Commission submits its draft opinion for a vote to the Standing Committee representing the EU Member States. The vote is followed by a "droit de regard" by the European Parliament. The Commission should wait for the expiry of the period for "droit de regard" of the European Parliament before adopting the decision. Each authorization decision is published on the Commission website in a register and also in the official *Journal of the European Communities.*

The CHMP assessment report on a medicinal product and the reasons for the favorable CHMP scientific opinion are made available on the EMA website (http://www.ema.europa.eu), after consultation with the applicant on deletion of any information of a commercially confidential nature. This document is called the European Public Assessment Report (EPAR). The CHMP can perform a benefit/risk review at any time. In some cases and taking into account the pharmacovigilance reporting received, CHMP can revise its opinion on the basis of a reassessment of the benefit/risk profile of the product. Generally, this is in response to emerging information on safety issues with marketed products or a referral by a Member State. Such revisions will be reflected in updates to the EPAR and in product information. Just as the CHMP publishes its reasons for any withdrawals of applications from the review queue as well as for any negative opinions on submitted applications, the CHMP also publishes its reasons when it decides that an authorized product should be taken off the market. A product-removal decision can pertain to any product marketed in the EU, whether it originally reached the market via the centralized route or via one of the EU Member State authorization processes discussed below. Generally, a reference to the CHMP of a product approved by EU Member States originates from an EU Member State agency in response to serious adverse events.

Article 58 of the EMA Regulation permits the EMA to provide a scientific opinion, in co-operation with the WHO, for the evaluation of certain medicinal products for human use that are intended exclusively for markets outside the EU. Many developing countries with limited regulatory capacity rely on prior assessment of a medicinal product by a developed country as an indicator for marketing suitability. However, many products needed by developing countries have no marketing authorization in a developed country (e.g., where the disease that a medicine targets has no, or low, prevalence in developed countries and so development for developed countries' markets is not economically viable). The effort to facilitate access to these, often life-saving, medicines was partly responsible for the introduction of the scientific opinion procedure provided for in Article 58.

Because an application to the EMA for a scientific opinion under Article 58 must conform to the usual, extensive requirements for an application for a centralized authorization, an Article 58 scientific opinion is considered to have a status equal to that of the opinions provided for medicinal products intended to be marketed in the EU. Yet, any medicinal product that is the subject of this scientific opinion process is not, at the end of this procedure, granted an EU marketing authorization by the European Commission, which for most applicants would be more beneficial. The Article 58 scientific opinion procedure has been used for opinions on antiretroviral products that are exact duplicates of EU-authorized products except that they have a color different from that of the EU version. The changed color is part of a program to assist the company and EU authorities in combating diversion back into the EU of exports intended for donation or reduced-price sales into developing countries.

Member State Authorizations

A fundamental difference between the procedure for authorization of medicinal products in the United States and that used in the EU is that there are, as mentioned above, two types of authority with the power to authorize marketing of medicinal products: 1) the European Commission (following EMA review) and 2) drug regulatory authorities of the EU Member States.

Three different types of marketing authorization may be granted at the national level in the EU Member States. These are the decentralized procedure, whereby one or more national marketing authorizations are granted in a coordinated manner; the mutual recognition procedure, whereby an authorization already granted by one EU Member State is recognized by the authorities of other EU Member States; and the national authorization procedure, which applies only to an authorization within a single EU country. As explained earlier, the format-and-content requirements and the standards of review of applications for marketing authorization are the same whether the applicant uses one of the national procedure routes and/or is seeking authorization through the centralized EMA/Commission procedure.

How Does the EU Regulate Generics?

Striking the balance between innovator rights and generic opportunities has been one of the most contentious issues in EU medicines law. Amendments to the Community Code on medicinal products enacted in 2004 and effective in late 2005:

- added to the Code a definition of "generic medicinal product," that codified case law;
- included a related definition of "global marketing authorization" aimed at blocking innovators from seeking a restart of exclusivities through product changes;
- harmonized the EU regulatory data-protection period, described as "8+2+1" (referring to the number of years in which an innovator's reference product is shielded from generic competition);
- created the opportunity for a generic company to:
  - submit an abridged application to an EU Member State regulatory agency other than the one that authorized the reference product; or
  - use the centralized process for a generic copy of a centrally authorized product; or
  - use a Member State process for a generic copy of a centrally authorized product; or
  - use the centralized process for generics of products originally approved by a Member State;

- inaugurated a "Bolar" amendment to allow generic manufacturers to do testing during the reference product's patent life;[73] and

- defined "similar biological medicinal product" ("biosimilar") as well as a pathway for authorization through the EMA/Commission centralized process.

Definitions

Under the Community Code, a "generic medicinal product" is one that has the same qualitative and quantitative composition in active substances and the same pharmaceutical form as the reference medicinal product, and whose bioequivalence with the reference medicinal product has been demonstrated by appropriate bioavailability studies.[74] A "reference medicinal product" is one authorized under the procedures applicable to full applications. The legislation also uses the term "global marketing authorization"[75] as a legal construct seeking to reduce innovators' ability to claim that an innovation in its product warrants a new regulatory exclusivity period. The term is a companion to the new definition of "generic medical product."

Types of Applications for Marketing Authorizations

Several types of EU marketing authorization applications (MAAs) are available:

---

[73] "Conducting the necessary studies and trials with a view to the application of [provisions on abridged applications] and the consequential practical requirements shall not be regarded as contrary to patent rights or to supplementary protection certificates for medicinal products." Art. 10.6, Community Code. Prior to the enactment of this provision in 2004, testing a generic drug during the innovator product's patent life—to develop copies and test them for bioequivalence with the patented drug—was regarded by many EU countries (and the European Commission) as patent infringement. In a WTO case, *Canada – Patent Protection of Pharmaceutical Products*, the EU had challenged a provision of Canada's Patent Act that explicitly permitted both the manufacture and the stockpiling of drugs six months prior to the expiration of the patent. A WTO Panel held that the provision was permissible insofar as it permitted manufacture, but in violation of the WTO Agreement on Trade-Related Intellectual Property Rights (TRIPS) agreement insofar as it permitted stockpiling, during the patent life of the pioneer. The parties agreed that the stockpiling provision violated the exclusive rights provided for in TRIPS Article 28.1, and the question was whether the stockpiling provision qualified as an exception to a patent right under the three conditions set out in TRIPS Article 30: 1) the exception must be limited; 2) the exception must not unreasonably conflict with normal exploitation of the patent; and 3) the exception must not unreasonably prejudice the legitimate interests of the patent owner, taking into account the legitimate interests of third parties. The Panel found that the Canadian stockpiling provision went far beyond a "limited exception" permissible under TRIPS Article 30. The Panel observed that the Canadian stockpiling provision did not limit the quantity of production and constituted a "substantial curtailment of the exclusionary rights" granted to patent holders under the TRIPS Article 28.1. Panel Report, *Canada – Patent Protection of Pharmaceutical Products* (WT/DS114/R 2000). Canada subsequently changed its law to repeal the stockpiling provision.

[74] Article 10.2(b), Community Code. "The different salts, esters, ethers, isomers, mixtures of isomers, complexes or derivatives of an active substance shall be considered to be the same active substance, unless they differ significantly in properties with regard to safety and/or efficacy. In such cases, additional information providing proof of the safety and/or efficacy of the various salts, esters or derivatives of an authorized active substance must be supplied by the applicant. The various immediate-release oral pharmaceutical forms shall be considered to be one and the same pharmaceutical form. Bioavailability studies need not be required of the applicant if he can demonstrate that the generic medicinal product meets the relevant criteria as defined in the appropriate detailed guidelines." *Id.*

[75] "When a medicinal product has been granted an initial marketing authorization in accordance with the first sub-paragraph, any additional strengths, pharmaceutical forms, administration routes, presentations, as well as any variations and extensions shall also be granted an authorization in accordance with the first subparagraph or be included in the initial marketing authorization . . . ." Article 6(1) of Directive 2001/83/EC of the European Parliament and of the Council of 6 November 2001 on the Community Code relating to medicinal products for human use, OJ L 311, 28.11.2001, p. 67–128.

Full (or Complete) Application. A Full Application consists of the results of physicochemical, biological, or microbiological tests; pharmacological and toxicological tests; and clinical trials. The data requirements are described in great detail in EU legislation and guidelines issued by the European Commission and the EMA.

"Mixed Data" Applications. These are applications in which published scientific literature is presented together with original test and trial results. Such applications must be submitted and processed in accordance with the requirement for a complete, full, and independent marketing authorization dossier.

"Well-Established Medicinal Use" Application. In a "well-established medicinal use" application, it is possible to replace results of pharmacological and toxicological tests or clinical trials with detailed references to published scientific literature (information available in the public domain), if it can be demonstrated that the constituents of a medicinal product have a "well-established medicinal use," with recognized efficacy and an acceptable level of safety. Well-established medicinal use applications have been treated as a type of full and independent application. For example, there are old medicinal products that have long been marketed, but for which there is no original or reference product to which sameness or similarity could—in an abridged application—be claimed. Typically, these old medicinal products are well-established and have known indications, strengths, and pharmaceutical forms. Due to the years in which they have been marketed and used, there generally is public information available about their safety and efficacy.

Abridged Applications. These are applications in which, subject to certain conditions, the applicant is not required to provide the results of pharmacological and toxicological tests or clinical trials, because the applications refer to information contained in the dossier of a reference product's authorization. Among the types of abridged applications are:

Informed consent applications. The owner of certain privileged information gives or sells a right of reference to such data, which can be a right of reference to a full application, similar to the common use of master files covering substances contained in a medicine.

Generic applications. An application for a generic medicinal product that has the same qualitative and quantitative composition in active substances and the same pharmaceutical form as the reference medicinal product, and whose bioequivalence with the reference medicinal product has been demonstrated by appropriate bioavailability studies.

There is also a requirement that the reference product have been authorized within the Community for the time period set forth in the relevant legislation on regulatory data exclusivity, discussed below. The contents of an abridged application for a generic medicinal product include complete quality information, evaluation of bioequivalence studies or justification why studies were not performed, with the reference product, grounds for claiming biosimilarity, summary and evaluation of impurities, data showing bioavailability and bioequivalence, an update of relevant published literature, discussion and substantiation of every claim in the SMPC not known or inferred from the properties of the medicinal product and/or its therapeutic group; and, if applicable, additional data to demonstrate evidence of the equivalence of efficacy and safety properties of different salts, esters, or derivatives of an authorized active substance.

Hybrid abridged procedure. There are two possible hybrid abridged procedure scenarios:

- Where the active substance of the medicinal product for which marketing authorization through the hybrid abridged procedure is sought contains the same therapeutic moiety as the original authorized product [reference product] associated with a different salt/ ester-complex/derivative, evidence that there is no change in the pharmacokinetics of the moiety, pharmacodynamics, and/or in toxicity that could change the safety/efficacy profile shall be demonstrated [with the admonition that, should this not be the case, this version shall be considered a new active substance].

- Where a medicinal product is intended for a different therapeutic use or to be administered by different routes or in different doses or with a different posology, the results of appropriate toxicological and pharmacological tests and/or of clinical trials shall be provided.

It is not required that the reference product to which a generic application refers be authorized for marketing at the time of the generic product application. However, the marketing authorization of the reference medicinal product should not have been withdrawn for safety reasons.

In sum, to be approved in the EU, a generic medicinal product must go through one of several variants of an abridged product application process. Generic companies must generally prove bioequivalence to the innovator's reference product and in all cases meet other requirements, such as GMPs and labeling requirements. However, they do not need to conduct preclinical and clinical trials to prove product efficacy and safety, because the innovator's submitted and approved dossier for the reference product is treated as having demonstrated efficacy and safety. The generic company does not have a right to obtain a copy of the reference product's dossier, but is allowed to refer the regulatory reviewer to that dossier, as long as the reference product is no longer under regulatory data exclusivity. As a practical matter, the regulator may not even need to refer to the reference product's dossier, because the efficacy and safety of the active substance are treated as having been established by the innovator's efforts.

Regulatory Data Protection: "8+2+1" and "Global Marketing Authorization"

Data exclusivity laws prevent regulators from reviewing or processing a generic manufacturer's abridged marketing application that references an innovator's clinical efficacy and safety data, for a set period of time after the reference product's marketing authorization is granted. During this time period, a competitor may conduct its own original preclinical testing and clinical trials. However, a generic company that does not want to conduct trials of its own, but needs to prove that its product meets the legal standard, may be barred from referring the regulator to the innovator's data until the relevant data exclusivity period expires.

As in the United States, in the EU patent protection continues to be the primary mechanism to reward innovation and protect innovators' research and development (R&D) investments from early generic competition that would erode incentives. Regulatory data exclusivity is an additional incentive to innovation, consistent with the requirement in Article 39.3 of the TRIPS, which bars WTO members from unauthorized use of undisclosed pharmaceutical testing information.

Notably, however, there is no EU counterpart to a "Paragraph IV" process to try to resolve reference products' patent status prior to regulatory approvals of generic copies. The competent authorities granting marketing authorizations for medicinal products in the EU are not permitted to refuse to grant a marketing authorization for a medicinal product on the ground that the product may infringe one or more patents covering another medicinal product already on the market. This point was emphasized by the European Commission in the report of the Sector Inquiry conducted in the pharmaceutical sector. Where an EU drug regulatory authority grants an authorization to a generic medicine that the reference product's manufacturer believes is still patent-protected, the latter manufacturer must bring patent infringement litigation against the generic company in each EU Member State in which a patent is being allegedly infringed. Any patent infringement litigation proceeds on its own track, with no "linkage" to the regulatory agency approval processes. As discussed above, the EU legislation does not provide any legal ground for attacking the decision granting marketing authorization to a medicinal product that may infringe the patents covering another medicinal product placed on the market in the EU.

Under the EU law's "8+2+1" system, a generic company may submit its abridged application that references the innovator's data to the EMA or a Member State drug regulatory authority as early as the eighth anniversary of the innovator authorization. However, no matter when authorization of the generic is granted, its marketing is not allowed until the tenth anniversary of the reference product's authorization. An additional year of protection applies if the innovator sought and obtained approval for a new indication during the first eight years of its product's exclusivity. However, in order to benefit from the additional year, the innovator should demonstrate that this new therapeutic indication brings significant clinical benefit in comparison with existing therapies. The result would be a total of 11 years of exclusivity as to all indications. This harmonized "8+2+1" exclusivity period applies throughout the EU for all approvals (centralized and decentralized) for which applications were submitted after October 30, 2005, or, in the case of applications to EMA, after November 20, 2005. Also, there is a separate "+1" for a new use for a well-established product, or for an Rx-to-OTC switch.

The semi-harmonized "10/6" system that preceded enactment of the new legislation will continue to be significant for applications submitted prior to October 30, 2005, or to the EMA prior to November 20, 2005. Elements of the old 10/6 regulatory data exclusivity system were:

• centrally approved products had a full 10 years of market exclusivity, starting with authorization (Commission's publication of a decision granting the marketing authorization)

- nationally approved products had either 10 or 6 years (EU Member States' choice):

  - ten years: Belgium, France, Germany, Italy, Luxembourg, Netherlands, Sweden, UK

  - six years: Austria, Denmark, Finland, Greece, Ireland, Portugal, Spain, and all the "new EU Member States" (Bulgaria, Cyprus, Czech Republic, Estonia, Hungary, Latvia, Lithuania, Malta, Poland, Romania, Slovakia, and Slovenia).

What Special Laws Govern Orphan Medicines, Medicines for Children and Advanced Therapies?

Orphan Medicines

A medicinal product may be designated as an orphan product if:

> [i]t is intended for the diagnosis, prevention, or treatment of a life-threatening or chronically debilitating condition affecting not more than five in 10 thousand persons in the [EU] . . .,[76]

or

> [i]t is intended for the diagnosis, prevention, or treatment of a life-threatening, seriously debilitating, or serious and chronic condition in the [EU] that without incentives is unlikely that the marketing of the medicinal product in the [EU] would generate sufficient return to justify the necessary investment.[77]

In either case, the sponsor must demonstrate also that "no satisfactory method of diagnosis, prevention, or treatment of the condition has been authorized in the [EU] or, if such a method exists, the medicinal product will be of significant benefit to those affected by the condition."[78]

"Significant benefit" is "a clinically relevant advantage or a major contribution to patient care."[79] For example, a demonstration of significant benefit may be based on expected benefit to a particular subset of the disease population, the expectation of an improved safety profile, a more convenient formulation or route of administration of the product, if there are serious difficulties with the current formulation or route of administration, more favorable and clinically relevant pharmacokinetic properties, or insufficient quantity or limitation in availability of the authorized product.[80]

Any claim of significant benefit "must be justified by the applicant through the provision of evidence/data, which must be considered in the light of the particular characteristics of the

---

[76]   *See* Communication from the [European] Commission on Regulation (EC) No. 141/2000 on Orphan Medicinal Products, August 1, 2003 at 2 [2003 Communication].

[77]   European Parliament and of the Council 141/2000, Art. 3.1(a), 2000 O.J. (L 18) 1 (EC).

[78]   *Id.* at Art. 3.1(b).

[79]   Commission Regulation 847/2000, establishing the provisions for implementation of the criteria for designation of a medicinal product as an orphan medicinal product and definitions of the concepts "similar medicinal product" and "clinical superiority," 2000 O.J. (L 10) 1, Art. 3.2 (EC).

[80]   2003 Communication, at 4.

condition and the existing methods." Because there may be little or no clinical experience with the medicinal product in question, the justification for significant benefit is "likely to be made on assumptions of benefit."[81] For some sponsors, this may prove to be a substantial hurdle, because clinical trials may be necessary to show preliminary efficacy. In any case, in considering orphan designation requests, the EMA's Committee on Orphan Medicinal Products (COMP) will assess whether the applicant has supported the assumptions of significant benefit with sufficient data and other evidentiary support, in light of the characteristics of the condition and existing treatments.

A company whose product has been designated as an orphan drug can, upon approval, receive 10 years of market exclusivity. Multiple products in a class of "similar medicinal product[s]" with the "same therapeutic indication" may be designated as orphan products, but it is the first product that achieves marketing authorization in the EU that will be granted 10 years of marketing exclusivity. During this 10-year period, the EMA may not accept (nor may the European Commission approve) another application for marketing authorization for a "similar medicinal product" for the "same therapeutic indication."[82] Marketing exclusivity is intended to allow the innovator to recoup its investment in a product that, because it is for a rare disease or conditions, would not otherwise attract the necessary interest among investors and manufacturers. Orphan medicinal products are authorized through the centralized process only, following evaluation by the CHMP and input from the COMP.

Medicines for Children

The EU Pediatric Regulation[83] aims to increase the development of medicines for use in children, encourage research in this area, and improve available information. It imposes a system of far-reaching requirements on companies and also offers rewards. The Regulation sets up an expert pediatric committee in the EMA. According to a European Commission progress report on the Regulation, there has been an increase in the use of authorized medicinal products for children and new pharmaceutical forms of such products adapted for use in children.[84] A company applying for a marketing authorization for a new medicine or a line extension for existing patent-protected medicines authorized at the EU or national level must provide the results of studies performed in accordance with a Pediatric Investigation Plan (PIP) agreed to with the expert committee. This requirement was effective on July 26, 2008, for new medicines and January 26, 2009, for new indications, new pharmaceutical forms or new routes of administration. A sponsor may ask the committee for a waiver where the product is unlikely to benefit children, or a deferral where it is unsafe to test it on children or the tests would delay authorization for adults.

---

[81]   *Id.*

[82]   *Id.* Art. 8.1. *See also* Commission Regulation (EC) no. 847/2000, April 4, 2000, elaborating on "similar medicinal product" and "clinical superiority" and Communication from the European Commission C (2008) 4077 Final, September 19, 2008, a guideline on assessing similarity of medicinal products versus orphan medicinal products benefiting from marketing exclusivity and applying derogations from that market exclusivity.

[83]   Regulation (EC) No. 1901/2006 of the European Parliament and of the Council of December 12, 2006 on Medicinal Products for Paediatric Use. This chapter uses the U.S. "pediatric" spelling.

[84]   Progress Report on the Paediatric Regulation (EC) No 1901/2006, COM (2013) 443 Final.

Several possible rewards are available for companies complying with the PIP, where significant studies contained in an agreed PIP are completed after entry into force of the Regulation. For newer medicines, these include:

- six months' extension of the supplementary protection certificate (SPC)[85] or, for orphan medicines, two years' extension of market exclusivity, provided that, among other things, the product is authorized in all EU Member States (the reward is for conducting studies in the pediatric population and is therefore granted even when a pediatric indication is not authorized);

- optional access to the centralized EU-level procedure for marketing authorization applications that include one or more pediatric indications on the basis of studies conducted in accordance with the agreed PIP.

In addition, there is a new type of marketing authorization, a Pediatric Use Marketing Authorization (PUMA), which applies to off-patent products developed exclusively for use in the pediatric population in accordance with an agreed PIP.[86] There is optional access to the centralized EU level procedure for PUMA applications.

The SPC extension is not available where the applicant applies for, and obtains, a one-year extension of the period of marketing protection for the medicinal product concerned under the "8+2+1" system discussed earlier, where a new pediatric indication brings a significant clinical benefit in comparison with existing therapies.[87]

A marketing authorization holder may be required to provide a completed PIP for a product but may be ineligible for an incentive, e.g., because the SPC has expired before the PIP is completed or because the marketing authorization holder had already obtained an eleventh year of exclusivity based on a nonpediatric new indication.

Advanced Therapies

In recent years, the issuance of cell-derived products, tissue-engineered products, and gene therapies has led to the issuance of new regulations. Special regulatory consideration is often given to those products derived from human blood or tissues because the risk of disease transmission is well documented.[88] Beginning on December 30, 2008, authorizations

---

[85]   SPCs extend the period of patent protection. European drug patents run for 20 years from the time of filing. Created by a 1992 regulation, now replaced by Regulation (EC) No 469/2009 adopted in 2009, the SPC for a medicine provides up to five years of additional patent protection to compensate for part of the lost patent life between the time of patent filing and EU marketing authorization. This extended protection is provided for in Articles 13(1) and 13(2) of Regulation (EC) No 469/2009. An SPC may be granted once, at the expiry of patent protection.

[86]   The PUMA is intended to stimulate the development of off-patent products for use in the pediatric population. It is hoped that the PUMA will encourage the development of new pediatric formulations for these older products. Applications for PUMAs, which must contain the results from an agreed PIP, can refer to third-party data for the same active substance, are able to use the centralized procedure for authorization, and, if authorized, will benefit from 10 years' market exclusivity.

[87]   The one-year extension is provided by Article 14(11) of Regulation (EC) No 726/2004 or the fourth subparagraph of Article 10(1) of Directive 2001/83/EC.

[88]   By April 2006, EU Member States were required to enact laws on the EU Tissue Handling Directive 2004/23/EC of the European Parliament and of the Council of March 31, 2004 on setting standards of quality and safety for the donation, procurement, testing, processing, preservation, storage, and distribution of human

of tissue-engineered products falling within the definition of "advanced therapies" are governed by the EU legislation on the approval of medicinal products.[89] Three types of advanced therapy fall within the Advanced Therapies Regulation, and all are subject to the EMA/Commission centralized procedure. These are gene therapy, somatic cell therapy, and tissue-engineered products. Gene therapy and somatic cell therapy had already been classified as medicinal products.[90] So, the Regulation did not directly affect the current authorization procedure for these products to the same extent as tissue-engineered products. The most significant change under the new Regulation is the extension of the application of the medicinal product framework to tissue-engineered products, defined as products containing or consisting of engineered cells or tissues and presented as having properties for or used in or administered to human beings with a view to regenerating, repairing, or replacing a human tissue.

Cells or tissues are not considered to have been engineered if they have undergone certain treatments listed in Annex I to the Regulation: cutting, grinding, shaping, soaking in antibiotic or antimicrobial solutions, sterilization, irradiation, cell separation/concentration/purification, filtering, lyophilization, freezing, cryopreservation, or vitrification.

A tissue-engineered product may contain cells or tissues of human origin, animal origin, or both. The cells or tissues may be viable or nonviable. However, products that contain or consist exclusively of nonviable human or animal cells and/or tissues, which do not contain any viable cells or tissues, and which do not act principally by pharmacological, immunological, or metabolic action, do not fall within the definition of a tissue-engineered product, and thus are outside the scope of the Regulation.[91] However, if the product contains nonviable cells, but acts principally by pharmacological, immunological, or metabolic action (i.e., through a medicinal product mechanism of action), the product will be subject to the Regulation. Tissue-engineered products may also contain additional substances, such as cellular products, bio-molecules, biomaterials, chemical substances, scaffolds, or matrices.

Products that consist of both an advanced therapy and a medical device are specifically addressed in the Regulation and defined as a "combined advanced therapy medicinal product." The device element of such products must respect EU provisions governing medical devices including, where relevant, the results of the assessment by a notified body. However, irrespective of the role of the device element, for tissue-engineered products the medicinal product mechanism of action of the cells or tissues will be considered to be the principal mode of action of the combination product. As such, for purposes of authorization the product is classified as a medicinal product irrespective of the prior regulation of the device component under the Medical Devices Directive (MDD).[92] It must, therefore, be authorized through the EU's centralized authorization procedure for medicinal products.

tissues and cells, Official Journal L 102, April 7, 2004 P. 0048-0058. Earlier legislation affected similar activities involving blood.

89   Regulation (EC) 1394/2007 of the European Parliament and of the Council of November 13, 2007 on advanced therapy medicinal products.

90   *See, e.g.,* EMA CHMP Guideline on Human Cell-Based Medicinal Products, EMA /CHMP/410869/2006 (May 21, 2008).

91   These products also are outside the scope of the Medical Devices Directive 93/42/EEC of June 14, 1993, as amended and thus lack a harmonized pathway at EU level. *Id.* Art. 5(f).

92   Council Directive 93/42/EEC of June 14, 1993, as amended.

This procedure involves a single scientific evaluation by the EMA of the quality, safety, and efficacy of the product and authorization by the European Commission. Products prepared by doctors or hospitals for use within a common facility that fall within the definition of advanced therapies will also fall within the application and requirements of the Regulation. The only exception will be for custom-made products that are prepared on a nonroutine basis according to particular quality standards and used within the same Member State in a hospital in accordance with an individual prescription for an individual patient and under the exclusive professional responsibility of a medical practitioner.

The Regulation includes provisions permitting requests for a scientific recommendation by the EMA concerning borderline products and for advice concerning pharmacovigilance obligations. The Regulation also introduces specific requirements for traceability to the patient, the SMPC, and the packaging, labeling, and package leaflet. Specialized provisions for the authorization application, GCPs, and GMPs are also contemplated.

How Does the EU Regulate Biosimilars?

All medicinal products derived from biotechnology must be reviewed by the EMA, as discussed above. This requirement includes biotechnology-derived biosimilars. There are certain additional data requirements and testing requirements for biological medicinal products.

The definition of "similar biological medicinal product," popularly referred to as a "biosimilar," is as follows:

> Where a biological medicinal product which is similar to a reference biological product does not meet the conditions in the definition of generic medicinal products, owing to, in particular, differences relating to raw materials or differences in manufacturing processes of the biological medicinal product and the reference biological medicinal product, the results of appropriate pre-clinical tests or clinical trials relating to these conditions must be provided. The type and quantity of supplementary data to be provided must comply with the relevant criteria stated in the annex and the related detailed guidelines. The results of other tests and trials from the reference medicinal product's dossier shall not be provided.[93]

In the United States, the terms "follow-on biologics" or "follow-on proteins" are commonly used. The EU legislation provides for biosimilars a legal framework under which it is understood that these products will need less supporting data than had been required for the original reference product. A key question, answered in part by guidelines but also in discussions between follow-on applicants and regulators, concerns the data requirements for a biosimilar approval. As regulators are well aware, even experienced manufacturers have encountered serious immunogenicity problems as biologics production processes evolve. Therefore, the EMA has issued a series of guidelines to detail biosimilar requirements. Based on positive opinions from the CHMP, the European Commission has authorized 17

---

[93]   Article 10.4, Community Code Directive.

biosimilar medicinal products containing as active substances recombinant somatropin, epoetin alfa, epoetin zeta, and filgrastim.

How Does the EU Regulate GMPs?

All medicinal products for human use manufactured in or imported into the EU, including active pharmaceutical ingredients and medicinal products intended for use in clinical trials, are required to have been manufactured in accordance with GMPs. The Community Code on medicinal products outlines GMP requirements, and requires EU Member States to license manufacturing facilities in their territories and ensure that they follow GMPs.[94]

The manufacturer must ensure that manufacturing operations are carried out in accordance with GMPs and with the license and product authorizations. This requirement also applies to medicinal products for export. For medicinal products and investigational medicinal products imported from non-EU countries, the importer shall ensure that products have been manufactured in accordance with standards at least equivalent to EU GMP standards. For investigational medicinal products, the manufacturer shall ensure that all operations are carried out in accordance with sponsor information provided in the relevant clinical trial application as accepted by the relevant Member State drug regulatory agencies. Manufacturers shall regularly review production methods in the light of scientific progress and investigational product development. If a variation to the marketing authorization dossier, or an amendment to the clinical trial application is necessary, the application for modification shall be submitted to the relevant authorities.

The manufacturer shall establish and implement an effective pharmaceutical quality assurance system, involving active participation by management and personnel from different departments. At each production site, the manufacturer shall have a sufficient number of competent and appropriately qualified personnel available to achieve the pharmaceutical quality assurance objective.

Concerning quality control, the manufacturer shall establish and maintain a system placed under the authority of one individual—the Qualified Person (QP)—who has the requisite qualifications and is independent of production. The QP ensures that medicinal products (including investigational products) released into the EU have been produced under GMPs and meet other quality requirements. The QP must have, or have access to, one or more quality control laboratories, appropriately staffed and equipped to carry out necessary examination and testing of starting materials and packaging materials, as well as testing of intermediate and finished products. Contract laboratories may be used. However, under the Community Code Directive, there is the possibility that controls within a non-EU country where the medicinal product is manufactured can relieve the QP of certain responsibilities for recheck.

---

[94]   GMP requirements have been further elaborated in Commission Directive 2003/94/EC (Oct. 8, 2003) on GMPs for both finished dosage form products and active starting materials; the 2001 Clinical Trials Directive 2001/23 (and its successor, the Clinical Trials Regulation (EU) No 536/2014), the Notice to Applicants (NTA), as revised, and a Compilation of Community Procedures on Inspections and Exchange of Information.

Contract manufacturing is also covered, and any manufacturing operation that is carried out under contract shall be the subject of a written agreement that clearly defines each party's responsibilities and specifies that GMPs must be followed. The Community Code on medicinal products also specifies provisions on complaints, product recall and records and reports. Any complaint concerning a defect shall be recorded and investigated by the manufacturer. The manufacturer shall inform the competent authority of any defect that could result in a recall or unusual restriction on supply and, insofar as is possible, indicate the countries of destination. These requirements apply at both the clinical trial and post-authorization stages.

The Community Code on medicinal products requires EU Member States to license wholesalers and distributors of medicinal products and to require observance by them of Good Distribution Practices (GDPs). To this end, the European Commission has published a Guideline on GDPs, with provisions resembling GMPs but focused on responsibilities of the middlemen in the supply chain to maintain product quality. GDPs are particularly important in the EU due to internal parallel trade from countries where prices are lower to countries with higher prices, discussed below.

How Does EU Competition Law Affect Pharmaceutical Regulation?

Parallel trade results from the fact that most EU countries limit the prices of pharmaceuticals, and prices are higher in some countries than others. This price difference creates an opportunity for distributors to purchase original products in lower-price markets for resale in higher-price markets. The Directorate-General on Competition of the European Commission traditionally has viewed parallel trade as good for both consumers and healthcare payors and, in any case, permitted under EU competition law (Regulation 17/1962). The pharmaceutical industry believes that price controls and safety considerations should distinguish it from other economic sectors,[95] and questions whether parallel trade benefits anyone other than the distributors who engage in it.[96] In January 2013, Directive 2011/62/EC on the prevention of the entry into the legal supply chain of falsified medicinal products ("Falsified Medicines Directive") came into force.[97] During discussions on the proposed Falsified Medicines Directive to reduce the threat posed by counterfeit products, the part of the European Commission responsible for pharmaceuticals legislation, the Directorate-General on Enterprise and Industry, had shown willingness to consider the concerns of pharmaceutical manufacturers that repackaging activities carried on by parallel traders open the EU pharmaceutical distribution system to counterfeit and substandard products.[98] However, the final version of the Falsified Medicines Directive does not ban or restrict parallel trade of a medicinal product. Repackaging of medicinal products is also not prohibited.

---

[95]   See EFPIA, Parallel Trade; http://www.efpia.org/Content/default.asp?Pageid=536.

[96]   EurActiv, Parallel Trade in Medicines (Aug. 3, 2007) available at http://www.euractiv.com/en/health/parallel-trade-medicines/article-117528.

[97]   Directive 2011/62/EU of the European Parliament and of the Council of June 8, 2011 amending Directive 2001/83/EC on the Community code relating to medicinal products for human use, as regards the prevention of the entry into the legal supply chain of falsified medicinal products, OJ L 174, July 1, 2011, p. 74–87.

[98]   The European Commission announced its intent to propose such legislation in December 2008. See http://ec.europa.eu/health/files/pharmacos/pharmpack_12_2008/ip-08-1924_en.pdf (last visited Dec. 8, 2014).

Parallel traders contend that they are unfairly blamed for problems of counterfeiting. The matter appears likely to be debated in the EU for many years to come.[99]

The Commission's Directorate-General for Competition investigates competition issues in the pharmaceutical industry.[100] In the beginning of 2008, the Directorate-General for Competition launched an inquiry into competition in the pharmaceutical sector. The Final Report of the sector inquiry, published in July 2009, identified a number of strategies allegedly used by innovative pharmaceutical companies to prevent generic entry on the market and to distort competition. The alleged anticompetitive practices included, among others, excessive patenting strategies, vexatious patent litigation, settlement agreements with generic manufacturers, and intervention in regulatory approval procedures. The European Commission Directorate-General for Competition has continued to monitor patent settlements and in 2010 and 2011 launched two consecutive monitoring exercises. A number of pharmaceutical companies were invited by the European Commission to submit patent settlement agreements concluded with other companies. The Directorate-General for Competition published its fourth report on the monitoring of patent settlements in December 2013.[101]

Marketing Practices; Relationships with Healthcare Professionals

Most countries have both laws and industry codes governing advertising and marketing of pharmaceuticals as well as relationships between the drug industry and healthcare professionals. In addition, IFPMA has a Code of Marketing Practices that is periodically updated and available on its website.[102]

EU

Within the EU, the Community Code on medicinal products[103] establishes EU-level rules that are implemented in national laws concerning the marketing of pharmaceuticals. The Community Code legislation contains provisions to ensure that the content of advertisements to health professionals, or to the public about nonprescription medicines, is not false or misleading. Advertising of prescription products to the general public is forbidden. There are provisions controlling visits to healthcare professionals by sales representatives, requirements that any hospitality provided be subordinate to the substantive part of the meeting (whether promotional or medical/scientific in nature) and not lavish, limits on gifts (they must be modest in value and be medical-related), limiting samples, and requiring each company to have a scientific services unit to respond to medical queries. Under the Community Code, it is forbidden to advertise pharmaceuticals before they are authorized

---

[99]   See http://ec.europa.eu/comm/competition/sectors/pharmaceuticals/overview_en.html (last visited Dec. 8, 2014).

[100]   In January 2008, the European Commission's Directorate-General on Competition launched a sectoral inquiry into competition in the pharmaceuticals sector. The Preliminary Report was issued on November 28, 2008, and the Final Report was issued on July 8, 2009.

[101]   See http://ec.europa.eu/competition/sectors/pharmaceuticals/inquiry/patent_settlements_report4_en.pdf (last visited Dec. 8, 2014).

[102]   See www.ifpma.org (last visited Dec. 8, 2014).

[103]   Article 86-100 of Directive 2001/83 of the Council and of the Parliament, as amended.

or for indications other than those for which they are approved. Any communications about products or indications not authorized in the EU are permissible only if they are of any entirely medical and scientific nature and are subject to scrutiny by both regulators and industry code officials. In addition to implementing the Community Code and related EU legislation, such as the Advertising Directive,[104] EU Member States have laws relating to administration of healthcare delivery services, antibribery, and even tax laws that can come into play in regard to the financial aspects of companies' relationships with healthcare professionals.

In addition, industry codes of conduct, and associated enforcement by industry trade associations, are an integral part of the marketing practice compliance environment in the EU. EFPIA has adopted a Code on the Promotion of Prescription-only Medicines to, and Interactions with, Healthcare Professionals, dealing not only with the industry's advertising and promotional interactions with healthcare professionals but also with a range of medical and scientific interactions and fee-for-service relationships, such as consultancies.[105] At the national level, industry associations such as the Association of the British Pharmaceutical Industry (ABPI) have likewise adopted codes of practice.[106] Like the EFPIA code, the national codes have been expanded to encompass such topics as medical education and contractual relationships in which healthcare professionals serve as investigators, consultants, advisory board members, speakers, and writers. The law and industry code of the jurisdiction where the healthcare professional practices establishes the rules that apply to him or her. In recent years there has been a pronounced trend toward stricter rules, under the Community Code on medicinal products, national laws, the EFPIA Code and national-level codes. This is especially true in the area of hospitality, at both promotional events and nonpromotional medical/scientific events. There is also an increased trend towards transparency in the industry, following EFPIA's recent adoption of the Disclosure Code, which requires public disclosure of all direct and indirect payments made by industry to healthcare professionals and organizations.[107] Similar disclosure requirements are also beginning to be reflected in the national-level codes and legislation. Although the EFPIA Code has been instrumental in harmonizing the rules on a regional basis, it remains necessary in all cases to examine national legislation and codes to have an understanding of requirements pertaining to relationships between companies and healthcare professionals in a particular country. In France, for example, the government approves all sponsorships of physicians to attend medical congresses, and drug companies that have contracts with doctors must follow a procedure to disclose such sponsorships to the government.[108] Furthermore, the French

---

[104]   Directive 2006/114/EC of the European Parliament and of the Council of December 12, 2006 concerning misleading and comparative advertising (codified version).

[105]   Amended on June 24, 2013. *See* www.efpia.eu (last visited Dec. 8, 2014).

[106]   *See* www.abpi.org.uk (last visited Dec. 8, 2014).

[107]   *Id.*, footnote 96.

[108]   As a general rule and as provided in Article L.4113-6 of the Code de Santé Publique (French Public Health Code or FPHC), pharmaceutical companies that produce or market products in France, or that provide services reimbursed by the French social security scheme, are prohibited from granting free advantages or compensation, whether directly or indirectly, to healthcare professionals. Such professionals are likewise generally barred from receiving any advantage or compensation, directly or indirectly, from pharmaceutical companies. Two exceptions are provided, provided that a company goes through a procedure to obtain a prior opinion from a competent professional board. One relates to contracts concerning research or scientific evaluations between manufacturers and health professionals. The other relates to hospitality offered to health professionals during events of a scientific or promotional nature. Healthcare professionals

Sunshine Laws[109] go beyond the EFPIA Disclosure Code and require industry to disclose certain benefits and agreements between industry and healthcare professionals and organizations. In Germany, institutional approval of physicians' participation in contracts with companies is required by law.[110] In addition, many national medical societies regulate their members' relationships with industry, and even private-sector employers, such as hospitals, may have requirements for approval of outside activities by employees.

EU Member States vary as to whether there are continuing medical education (CME) requirements for physicians and, if so, whether there is a system for accreditation of CME to help ensure unbiased and independent content.[111] Such systems are rare. In most countries, pharmaceutical companies are major providers of CME and, where there is neither a CME accreditation system nor locally arranged independent medical educational programs organized by universities, hospitals, or medical societies, companies on their own sometimes devise policies and procedures so that their payments for medical education are not misconstrued as advertising and promotion—or even as corruption forbidden by national antibribery laws or the Foreign Corrupt Practices Act (FCPA). A key difference between the United States and other countries is that, outside the United States, it is still common for pharmaceutical companies to be permitted to pay the expenses of physicians to register for medical congresses and their reasonable travel expenses (although it is generally forbidden for companies to pay an honorarium to physicians who merely attend a conference without providing other services such as speaking). A few countries (e.g., Sweden and Switzerland) require a physician to bear part of the cost of attendance.

Another significant difference is that, in the EU, pharmaceutical trade associations can enforce their codes; in the United States, such enforcement would be seen as contrary to the antitrust law. Enforcement measures include adverse publicity ("shaming"), audits, corrective advertisements, fines, and suspensions of membership. One particularly active and transparent body is the Prescription Medicines Code of Practice Authority, established by the ABPI in 1993 to independently receive and adjudicate complaints alleging violations of the ABPI Code of Practice for the Pharmaceutical industry. The PMCPA website is an informative resource concerning the interpretation of various EU and UK laws and codes.[112]

---

covered by article L.4113-6 of FPHC are physicians registered with l'Ordre des Médecins, dental surgeons and nurses.

[109] Law no. 2011-2012 of December 29, 2011 on the reinforcement of the safety of medicinal and health products, Decree n°2013-414 of May 21, 2013 on the transparency of benefits granted by companies producing or marketing human products for sanitary and cosmetic purposes and Order of December 3, 2013 on the operating conditions of the centralised public website.

[110] In Germany, it is an offense under section 331(1) of the Criminal Code for an official to accept a benefit for the carrying out of an official duty. The primary official function of a physician employed by state-owned or municipal hospitals generally is the treatment of patients of the hospital, and the prescription of drugs is an official duty. German authorities treat this provision as applicable where a physician acts as a consultant or as an investigator in a clinical trial. The penal prosecution can be avoided only if the physician applies for, and receives, an authorization from the responsible body (e.g., the director of the hospital) that expressly authorizes the physician to receive the benefit or participate in the activity in question. Public employment law requires that outside employment be disclosed to, or even approved by, the public institution. *See*, *e.g.*, sections 65 and 66 of the Federal Civil Servants Code and Section Federal Civil Servants Spare-time Work Ordinance. Therefore, if civil servants or employees in state-owned and municipal hospitals want to perform a clinical trial and enter into agreements with the sponsor of the trial, they would need to apply for a prior approval.

[111] *See* www.game-cme.org (last visited Dec. 8, 2014).

[112] *See* www.pmcpa.org.uk (last visited Dec. 8, 2014).

Antibribery Laws

In recent years, the U.S. FCPA and other countries' antibribery laws have become part of the regulatory landscape in the international compliance arena. Broadly speaking, a violation of the antibribery provisions occurs when a person 1) gives, offers or promises something of value 2) directly or indirectly to a covered foreign official 3) with corrupt intent 4) to obtain or retain business.

The United Kingdom's Bribery Act came into force on July 1, 2011. In a number of respects, the UK Bribery Act is stricter and broader in its jurisdictional scope than the U.S. FCPA. The Bribery Act provides for very significant penalties, including substantial fines and personal exposure for individuals. Individuals may be sentenced to up to 10 years of imprisonment for violation of the act,[113] or up to 14 years for money laundering. Sanctions also include fines and/or debarment from serving as a company director. "Senior officers" of companies may be held personally liable even if not directly involved in any wrongdoing.[114]

The Bribery Act applies to any company incorporated in or carrying on business in the United Kingdom, irrespective of where in the world the offending conduct occurs. As to individuals, the Bribery Act applies to all conduct that takes place in the United Kingdom and, in the case of United Kingdom nationals, anywhere in the world.

The Bribery Act does not require a corrupt or dishonest state of mind for a practice to be considered a violation. The provision of an "advantage" coupled with an intention to induce or reward "improper performance" of the recipient's function constitutes the basic offense under the Act.[115]

The offenses under the Bribery Act include:

- offering, promising, or giving a bribe;

- requesting, accepting, or agreeing to receive a bribe;

- bribing a foreign official to obtain or retain business or a business advantage;

- consent to or connivance of a "senior officer" in the commission of one of the above offenses;

- failure by a commercial organization to prevent a third party paying a bribe on its behalf.[116]

Bribes are defined as any "financial or other advantage," which can capture corporate hospitality.[117] However, according to the Ministry of Justice, reasonable and proportionate hospitality that seeks to improve the image of a commercial organization, to present products and services, or establish cordial relations is recognized as an established and important part of doing business.[118]

---

[113]   See Section 11 of the Bribery Act 2010.
[114]   See Section 14 of the Bribery Act 2010.
[115]   See Sections 1, 2, and 4 of the Bribery Act 2010.
[116]   See Section 7 of the Bribery Act 2010.
[117]   See Sections 1 and 2 of the Bribery Act 2010.
[118]   Ministry of Justice Guidance on The Bribery Act 2010. See http://www.justice.gov.uk/downloads/legislation/bribery-act-2010-guidance.pdf (last visited Dec. 8, 2014).

The definition of public official in the EU may include physicians, pharmacists, laboratory technicians, and other healthcare professionals, as well as state or customs officials. Thus, the UK Bribery Act may apply to interactions of a company carrying on business in the United Kingdom with such individuals in the United Kingdom or in the EU.

Counterfeit Products

A worldwide problem, for developed and developing countries alike, is the trade in counterfeit drugs. According to the Pharmaceutical Security Institute, there were known 2,193 incidents of such pharmaceutical crime during 2013. This number represented an 8.7 percent increase over 2012.[119] In 2013, "1,156 counterfeiting incidents involved either customs seizures or police/health inspector raids."[120]

In 2006, WHO set up an International Medical Products Anti-Counterfeiting Taskforce (IMPACT), a voluntary grouping of governments, organizations, institutions, agencies, and associations, from developing and developed countries. IMPACT aims to share expertise, identify problems, seek solutions, coordinate activities, and fight the counterfeiting of medical products (drugs and medical devices).[121] Among other activities, WHO IMPACT has developed principles for model anticounterfeits legislation for adoption at the national level.[122]

Biologics

Most of the discussion above of pharmaceutical harmonization and EU law applies to biologics as well as to chemically derived pharmaceuticals. WHO has led standard-setting for biological product safety, efficacy, and quality for more than 60 years. It has been particularly active as to vaccines. In addition to WHO, other organizations active in standard-setting and harmonization for biologics include ICH and the Council of Europe, which administers the European Pharmacopeia. Many other international organizations, including the United Nations Children's Fund (UNICEF), the World Bank, and the U.S. Agency for International Development, promote vaccination by funding purchases of vaccines to prevent many childhood deaths.

---

[119]   See http://www.psi-inc.org/incidentTrends.cfm (last visited Dec. 8, 2014).
[120]   Id.
[121]   See http://www.who.int/impact/activities/lisbon_ppt/en/index.html (last visited Dec. 8, 2014).
[122]   257 WHO International Medical Products Anti-Counterfeiting Taskforce (IMPACT), Principles and Elements for National Legislation Against Counterfeit Medical Products (text Endorsed by IMPACT General Meeting, Lisbon, December 12, 2007), *available at* http://www.who.int/impact/en (last visited Dec. 8, 2014).

Medical Devices

Global Harmonization Task Force

Efforts to achieve harmonization of medical device regulation have made significant progress, particularly in the areas of medical device quality systems, adverse event reporting, product standards, and clinical evaluation. These efforts have been undertaken through an international cooperation initiative, known as the Global Harmonization Task Force (GHTF), led by officials from FDA, the European Commission, EU States, Japan, Canada, and Australia along with industry representatives.

Formed in 1992, GHTF consisted of a steering committee and study groups that concentrated on particular aspects of medical device regulation and met several times a year. In early 2011, the founding members of the GHTF decided to discontinue the task force.

Study Group 1. The Study Group developed a document known as the Summary Technical Document (STED), which aims to harmonize the format and content of manufacturer premarket submissions.

Study Group 2. The main objective of this group was to harmonize the criteria for reporting device-related incidents (i.e., death, serious injuries, and devices performing out of specifications) that should be reported to national authorities by manufacturers, as well as the format for such reports. The Study Group also established a mechanism for sharing information regarding devices and events. Success in this area is closely linked to progress concerning medical device nomenclature.

Study Group 3. The harmonization of a quality systems standard, as well as guidance documents on such subjects as quality control validation, was an early GHTF success. The group also commented on countries' quality system regulations and guidelines. The GHTF quality systems standard was the starting point for what is now the ISO 13485 quality systems standard for medical device manufacture. This globalization of the GHTF standard was achieved by an ISO committee, TC-210 on "Quality management and corresponding general aspects for medical devices," which works closely with Study Group 3 as well as experts in FDA, other regulators, and industry.

Study Group 4. This group prepared a GHTF guidance document on regulatory auditing of quality systems of medical device manufacturers. Its work contributed to the development of regulatory confidence in audits conducted by third-party conformity-assessment bodies.

Study Group 5. This group was developing harmonized approaches to clinical data and clinical evaluation.

In October 2011, representatives from the medical device regulatory authorities of Australia, Brazil, Canada, China, the European Union, Japan, and the United States, as well as WHO met in Ottawa to create the International Medical Device Regulatory Forum (IMDRF). The aim of the IMDRF is to accelerate international medical device regulatory harmonization based on the work already performed by the GHTF. The IMDRF, which will meet bi-annually, is composed of representatives from the medical device regulatory authorities of Australia, Brazil, Canada, China, the European Union, Japan, the Russian Federation, and the United States.

National Systems for Regulating Medical Devices

In the EU, medical device regulation is a more recent field than food and drug regulation; virtually all countries have, for some years, had a food and drug regulatory system. Medical device technology is generally newer. Only in the last few decades have many governments decided to regulate medical devices. The work of the GHTF, which has been replaced by the IMDRF, standards committees and WHO can be useful to policymakers around the world when they are developing national systems for regulating medical devices. In addition, a number of countries have been inspired by the example of FDA or the EU, whose system is discussed in detail below.

A number of elements might be included in a medical device regulatory system, depending upon a country's needs. Among these are:

- categories of control (classification);
- methods for identifying manufacturers and products (registration);
- adverse event reporting and investigation;
- product removal authority;
- Good Manufacturing Practices (GMPs), inspections, and compliance;
- standards; and
- evaluation, including clinical evaluation, and approval.

For medical devices produced in an individual country, it is important that that country have in place a regulation based on the ISO 13485 quality systems standard, and that it apply the regulation to domestically produced devices, imported devices, and devices intended for export.

Many countries appear to follow the lead of other countries' regulators, including FDA, in deciding what devices will be allowed on the market, rather than undertaking independent assessments. In many countries, an important factor in whether to admit a medical device to the domestic market is whether FDA has approved the product or cleared it under section 510(k) of the FDCA.[123] This is not surprising given the challenge and costliness of building a regulatory program that includes an independent review of products by experts. Countries are also increasingly looking to the CE mark, which evidences compliance with the EU medical devices legislation, or have sought to emulate the EU model, described below, as a basis for a regulatory system in which private sector assessment bodies might play a role in quality systems audits, product evaluations, or both. Several countries, e.g., Australia,

---

[123]   For example, Argentina, Australia, Canada, China, Israel, Mexico and Taiwan closely follow FDA decisions on products; and some of these countries streamline marketing requirements for FDA-approved imports.

Canada, and Japan, have crafted systems that adopt selected features of the FDA and/or the EU systems.

Medical Device Clinical Trials: International Aspects

Many clinical trials of medical devices are conducted outside the United States. Many such trials are not conducted under an FDA investigational device exemption (IDE).[124] In all cases, companies conducting clinical trials outside the United States and intending to submit the restuls to FDA in support of an application for approval or clearance need to comply with the regulatory requirements of the country where a trial is conducted, the ISO 14155 international standard on medical device clinical trials, requirements for export of investigational devices to countries where trials are taking place,[125] the criteria in an FDA regulation for acceptance of data from non-IDE foreign clinical trials,[126] regulations governing data protection, and any additional requirements imposed by local ethics committees or regulators. ISO 14155 resembles in many respects the ICH GCP standard.

European Union Regulation of Medical Devices
Three Main Directives

The three principal EU medical devices Directives that have been enacted are the Active Implantable Medical Devices Directive,[127] the Medical Devices Directive (MDD),[128] and the In Vitro Diagnostic Medical Devices Directive.[129] Under EU law, Directives are addressed to EU Member States. The Directives establish basic aims to be achieved, and leave to the national legislation of the EU Member States the determination of the legally binding ways in which these aims will be achieved. As a result, after adoption of a Directive, each EU Member State must enact legislation that implements the Directive. It is this national implementing legislation that directly applies to manufacturers.

The European Commission has also issued guidance documents, known as "MEDDEVs," on medical device vigilance, classification, auditing, and regulation of products at the borderline with other EU laws.[130]

Different interpretative documents, consensus statements, and borderline manuals are also published on the European Commission website to help manufacturers to place medical devices lawfully on the EU market.

Definition of "Medical Device." Article 1 of the MDD defines the term "medical device" as:

---

124 Investigational Device Exemptions, 21 C.F.R. pt. 812.

125 21 U.S.C. § 381(e), 21 U.S.C. § 382(c).

126 21 C.F.R. 814.15 (citing the Declaration of Helsinki, 1983 version).

127 Council Directive 90/385/EEC on the approximation of the laws of the Member States relating to active implantable devices, O.J. L 189 July 20, 1990 p. 17.

128 Council Directive 93/42/EEC concerning medical devices, O.J. L169 July 12, 1993 p. 1.

129 Directive 98/79/EC of the European Parliament and of the Council of October 27, 1998 on in vitro diagnostic medical devices, O.J. L 331 Dec. 12, 1998 p. 1.

130 See website of European Commission Directorate-General for Consumer Affairs, http://ec.europa.eu/health/medical-devices/documents/guidelines/index_en.htm (last visited Dec. 5, 2014).

any instrument, apparatus, appliance, software, material or other article, whether used alone or in combination, including the software intended by its manufacturer to be used specifically for diagnostic and/or therapeutic purposes and necessary for its proper application, intended by the manufacturer to be used for human beings for the purpose of:

a.   diagnosis, prevention, monitoring, treatment or alleviation of disease,

b.   diagnosis, monitoring, treatment, alleviation of or compensation for an injury or handicap,

c.   investigation, replacement or modification of the anatomy or of a physiological process,

d.   control of conception,

and which does not achieve its principal intended action in or on the human body by pharmacological, immunological or metabolic means, but which may be assisted in its function by such means.

According to Article 1(5)(c) of the MDD, in deciding whether a product falls within the MDD, particular attention should be paid to the principal mode of action of the product. Further clarification on this point is provided below.

Emergence of "New Approach" Regulation. The EU medical device regulatory system was established at a time when there was keen interest in a "new approach" that would replace the difficult and frustrating harmonization process that then applied to food and pharmaceuticals. Backed by judgments of the European Court of Justice holding that EU Member States have limited power to exceed the Essential Requirements specified in Directives, the European Commission began proposing new-approach Directives aimed at creating a single market and eliminating barriers and inconsistencies among EU Member States. The new approach was seen as a way to avoid both detailed regulations prescribing technical requirements and excessive use of government approvals, especially duplicative approvals, as a regulatory tool. Product categories handled under new-approach legislation include pressure vessels, toys, and personal protective equipment, as well as medical devices.

A new-approach Directive contains a legislative statement of Essential Requirements that are elaborated by technical standards. It is the responsibility of manufacturers to meet, and document how they meet, Essential Requirements. For some products, self-declaration of conformity is sufficient. For others, including medium- to high-risk medical devices, there must be a third-party assessment of a manufacturer's conformity, with the manufacturer given a degree of choice among methods for conformity assessment of the product and production system.[131] The endpoint is issuance of a certificate of conformity. A manufacturer applies a CE mark to the product to show conformity with Essential Requirements.[132]

---

[131]   Article 11 of MDD.
[132]   Article 17 of MDD.

An important element of EU new-approach Directives that distinguishes them from the law in other territories is the fact that there is no procedure in the EU according to which products falling within the scope of these Directives are classified, regulated, or approved by a competent authority either at the national level in one of the 28 EU Member States, or at the EU level prior to their use or marketing in the EU. The entire responsibility for placing the product on the market, therefore, lies with the manufacturer.

Notified Bodies. For medical devices in the EU, the third-party conformity assessment is carried out not by the EU Member States' competent authorities (the drug and device regulatory agencies) but, rather, by conformity-assessment bodies called "notified bodies." These are private organizations that have been demonstrated to possess the necessary technical competence to review specified types of medical devices. They are designated by the competent authorities of EU Member States. Each EU Member State must notify the European Commission of the notified bodies that it believes capable of reviewing the various categories of medical devices that fall within the application of the different Directives. The European Commission publishes periodic listings of these notified bodies in the *Official Journal of the European Union*. Manufacturers of medical devices select a notified body listed as having the technical qualifications for particular classes of product under the relevant Directive. Class I devices (with the exception of some aspects of Class I devices that are sterile and Class I devices with a measuring function) and most in vitro diagnostic devices enter the EU market on the basis of a manufacturer's self-assessment and a Declaration of Conformity by the manufacturer that the device complies with the Essential Requirements provided for in the relevant medical devices Directive. The intervention of a notified body is not required for these devices.

Finally, although a notified body may participate in the examination and approval of the technical data related to a product, the decision to affix the CE mark to the product lies entirely with the manufacturer of the product. Moreover, when a manufacturer affixes a CE mark to a product, the manufacturer is declaring that, for the purposes for which the device is CE marked, the product meets all of the requirements related to it that are set forth in the relevant EU medical devices Directive.

EEA "Presence" Requirement. Companies that do not have an establishment within the European Economic Area[133] (EEA) and that wish to affix a CE mark to the medical devices and to market them in the EEA must either establish an EU presence or select a local representative to serve as its "European Authorized Representative." Determination as to whether a non-EU company should establish a presence in the EEA will often depend on the size of the undertaking. For smaller companies, a European Authorized Representative may be the most cost-effective option.

A number of dispositions of the medical devices Directives deal with the role and responsibilities of the European Authorized Representative. However, concern has been expressed by stakeholders due to the lack of clarity of these provisions. In particular, manufacturers have expressed difficulties in understanding the responsibilities that can be delegated to the European Authorized Representatives and what information these

---

[133]   The EEA is made up of the 28 EU Member States plus three of the four EFTA States (Iceland, Liechtenstein, and Norway). Switzerland, although an EFTA State, is not an EEA State.

European Authorized Representatives should be able to provide to the competent authorities of the EU Member States. As a consequence of this concern, in January 2012 the European Commission published a Guideline for Authorized Representatives.[134] The intention of this Guideline is to clarify the requirements that may be imposed by the competent authorities of the EU Member States. The European Authorized Representative is not required to have medical qualifications. However, good administrative facilities, understanding of the requirements and functioning of the national measures implementing the MDD, and ability to communicate with national authorities are essential. European Authorized Representatives' agents serve as the manufacturer's point of contact with the competent authorities. They do not provide marketing services, but hold any files that need to be kept for possible inspection by the authorities. They also act as a go-between with European authorities. They forward to the manufacturer potential inquiries from the authorities, and they forward correspondence from the manufacturer back to the relevant authority. Importantly, the EU Directives require that 1) the labeling (the outer package of the device) bear the name and contact details of the European Authorized Representative, and 2) the name of the European Authorized Representative appear in the Declaration of Conformity. It is also advised, although not required, that the name of the European Authorized Representative be included in the Instruction For Use. It is important that the non-EU manufacturer and its European Authorized Representative have a written agreement detailing the Representative's obligations.

For a non-EU manufacturer, the laws of the EU Member State where the manufacturer's EU subsidiary is established or, in the absence of such a subsidiary, where the European Authorized Representative is located govern many aspects of the manufacturer's compliance responsibilities. In addition, the laws of the EU Member State where the manufacturer's selected notified body is located can be relevant to matters relating to the performance of that body. The laws of the EU Member State where a patient suffers a reportable adverse event govern the reporting of that event. Reporting obligations are also guided by European Commission guidelines on this subject.

Classification. The MDD groups medical devices into four product classes.[135] These classification rules are based on the potential risks associated with the technical design and manufacture of a medical device. The classification rules distinguish among non-invasive, invasive, and active medical devices. Some extra rules govern specific medical devices. Devices in Class I represent a low level of vulnerability. Those in Class IIa are considered to present a risk sufficient to require the compulsory intervention of a notified body at the production stage. Classes IIb and III are reserved for devices that present a high risk potential. It is the intended purpose of a medical device that determines the class of the device, and not the particular technical characteristics of the device, unless these have a direct bearing on its intended purpose. If a given device can be classified in several classes, on the basis of the performance specified for the device by the manufacturer, the strictest rules resulting from the highest applicable classification shall apply.[136]

---

[134]   European Commission Guideline for Authorised Representatives, MEDDEV 2.5/10 (January 2012).
[135]   Article 9 of MDD.
[136]   Directive 93/42/EEC as amended, Annex IX, Paragraph 2.

It is initially for the manufacturer to determine the classification of its product(s). Therefore, the manufacturer can select a notified body, if required, with the ability to carry out the appropriate conformity-assessment procedure. It will then be for that notified body to confirm whether the Technical File provided by the manufacturer supports the classification determined by embarking upon the process of conformity assessment. In the event that the manufacturer and its selected notified body cannot agree on the classification, either party can refer the matter for a decision to the competent authority that designated the notified body. In certain circumstances, the European Commission, acting in conjunction with a regulatory committee composed of experts from the EU Member States, may be approached for a decision.

Standards. To facilitate compliance with the Essential Requirements laid down in Annex I to the medical devices Directives, the Directives foresee recourse to harmonized European standards. Where the reference of these standards has been published in the *Official Journal of the European Union*, compliance with such standards will provide a presumption of conformity with Essential Requirements set forth in the Directives. Whereas the Essential Requirements are obligatory, the standards remain voluntary. For medical devices, the European Commission has adopted many harmonized standards,[137] including the EU version of ISO 13485, the international quality systems standard.

Conformity Assessment Procedures. The procedure to be followed in order to affix the CE mark to a medical device depends on the classification of the device. The procedure is substantially more complex for products falling within Class III than for those falling within Class IIa. Moreover, as indicated above, the intervention of a notified body in the conformity assessment procedure will be required for Class IIa, IIb, and III medical devices, as well as for Class I medical devices that are supplied sterile or with a measuring function. Independently of their classification, the general principle is that medical devices may be placed on the EU market only if any risks that may be associated with their use constitute acceptable risks when weighed against the benefits to the patient and are compatible with a high level of protection of health and safety.

In order to demonstrate the safety and performance of their medical devices, all manufacturers must demonstrate compliance with the relevant Essential Requirements set forth in Annex I of the MDD.[138] This Annex provides general and specific requirements such as requirements on chemical, physical, and biological properties, infection and microbial contamination, construction and environmental properties, devices with a measuring function, protection against radiation, requirements for medical devices connected or equipped with an energy source, and requirements regarding information supplied by the manufacturer (on the label and in the Instructions for Use).

As part of the conformity-assessment procedures, manufacturers of medical devices are required to prepare a Technical File containing information such as the product description and specifications, information about the manufacturing process, design and construction, a clinical evaluation, an Essential Requirements checklist, a risk analysis and related risk

---

[137]   http://ec.europa.eu/enterprise/policies/european-standards/harmonised-standards/medical-devices/index_en.htm last (last visited Dec. 5, 2014)

[138]   Article 3 of MDD.

management, information about the manufacturer's vigilance system, the product labeling and the declaration of conformity. This Technical File shall be held at the disposal of the competent authorities by all manufacturers. For Class IIa, IIb, and III, review and approval of the Technical File by the notified body is required prior to marketing of the device in the EU.

The different conformity-assessment procedures are described in Article 11 of the MDD. As explained above, distinctions shall be made among Class I, IIa, IIb, and III medical devices.

Class I

Article 11 of the MDD provides that, for Class I medical devices that are not custom-made or intended for clinical investigations, the manufacturer must follow the procedure referred to in Annex VII (EC Declaration of Conformity) to the Directive and draw up an EC Declaration of Conformity in order to affix the CE mark to the device before placing it on the market.

However, paragraph 5 of Annex VII provides that, for sterile products and products with a measuring function, the manufacturer must observe not only the provisions set forth in this Annex but also one of the procedures referred to in Annex II, IV, V, or VI that requires the intervention of a notified body (quality system). The application of these Annexes and the intervention by the notified body is, however, limited to the aspects of manufacture concerned with securing and maintaining sterile conditions, or the aspects of manufacture concerned with the conformity of the products with the metrological requirement for products with a measuring function.

Finally, registration of the medical device with the relevant competent authority of the EU Member State in which either the device manufacturer or, where the manufacturer has no presence in the EU, its European Authorized Representative is established is also required.

Class IIa

In the case of devices falling within Class IIa, other than devices that are custom-made or intended for clinical investigations, Article 11 of the MDD provides that the procedure to be followed is the procedure relating to the EC Declaration of Conformity set out in Annex VII (EC Declaration of Conformity), coupled with either:

(a) the procedure relating to the EC verification set out in Annex IV; or

(b) the procedure relating to the EC Declaration of Conformity set out in Annex V (production quality assurance); or

(c) the procedure relating to the EC Declaration of Conformity set out in Annex VI (product quality assurance).

Instead of applying these procedures, it is also possible to follow the procedure relating to the EC Declaration of Conformity set out in Annex II (full quality assurance); in this case, point 4 of Annex II is not applicable.

Class IIb

Article 11 of the MDD further provides that, for devices falling within Class IIb, other than devices that are custom-made or intended for clinical investigations, the procedure to be followed is either:

(a) the procedure relating to the EC Declaration of Conformity set out in Annex II (full quality assurance); in this case, point 4 of Annex II is not applicable; or

(b) the procedure relating to the EC type-examination set out in Annex III, coupled with:

  (i) the procedure relating to the EC verification set out in Annex IV; or

  (ii) the procedure relating to the EC Declaration of Conformity set out in Annex V (production quality assurance); or

  (iii) the procedure relating to the EC Declaration of Conformity set out in Annex VI (product quality assurance).

Class III

In the case of devices falling within Class III, other than devices that are custom-made or intended for clinical investigations, Article 11 of the MDD indicates that the procedure to be followed is either:

(a) the procedure relating to the EC declaration of conformity set out in Annex II (full quality assurance); or

(b) the procedure relating to the EC type-examination set out in Annex III, coupled with (i) the procedure relating to the EC verification set out in Annex IV; or (ii) the procedure relating to the EC Declaration of Conformity set out in Annex V (production quality assurance).

Manufacturer's Role in CE Marking. Medical devices that meet the Essential Requirements and have undergone the appropriate conformity-assessment procedures can be CE marked. However, as emphasized above, although a notified body may participate in the conformity-assessment procedure, the decision to affix the CE mark to the product lies entirely with the manufacturer of the product. There is no regulatory approval from a competent authority. Moreover, when a manufacturer affixes a CE mark to a product, the manufacturer is declaring that, for the purposes for which the device is CE marked, the product fulfills all of the requirements related to it that are set forth in the relevant EU medical devices Directive.

Member State Authorities' Role. Although not involved in the premarketing stage, EU Member State authorities have important responsibilities not only to approve and oversee notified bodies but also to regulate medical device clinical trials and oversee marketing.

Manufacturers that intend to begin clinical investigations on their devices must obtain a positive opinion from the competent Ethics Committee and notify the competent national authorities prior to commencement of the investigations. Either of these entities may oppose a study if, on the basis of the documents and data provided by the sponsor, they consider that the safety of the trial subjects is not ensured. In certain EU Member States, such as Germany, clinical investigations for medical devices are subject to a formal authorization similar to the authorization that must be delivered for clinical trials on medicinal products. Manufacturers intending to conduct clinical investigations on their medical devices should, therefore, understand the procedures, rules, and guidance governing clinical trials in the relevant EU Member State. From an EU perspective, the key regulatory documents governing clinical trials are the MDD, principally Article 15 and Annex VIII, and ISO 14155. The ISO 14155 standard applies to all clinical investigations for which a device's performance and safety are being studied, i.e., totally new devices or modifications to existing devices. EU national requirements for clinical trials also differ on such issues as insurance and translations. Manufacturers at present consult with external technical experts and notified bodies as much as or more than with national authorities for guidance on what clinical evidence or other information is needed to meet Essential Requirements.

The competent authorities of the EU Member States also oversee postmarket surveillance, including adverse event reporting.[139] They are also responsible for enforcement actions where needed, and participate in various EU committees and working groups.

Aware of the differing requirements applicable in the different EU Member States, the European Commission in December 2008 published a "Guide for Competent Authorities in Making an Assessment of Clinical Investigation; Notification."[140] This document provides a checklist of the main criteria and the documents to be assessed when reviewing an application for clinical investigation. In December 2010, the European Commission also published a guide for manufacturers and notified bodies on clinical investigation[141] as well as guidance on serious adverse-events reporting obligations.[142] In addition, the European Commission also released specific guidance on clinical evaluation for manufacturers and notified bodies.[143] The rules and principles provided in these MEDDEVs are commonly applied in the EU Member States and, therefore, constitute key tools for manufacturers.

Recent Legislation. The most recent technical revision to the medical device regulatory framework was through the Directive 2007/47/EC,[144] which was adopted in September 2007. This Directive makes no change to the Directive on In Vitro Diagnostic Medical Devices.

---

[139]   European Commission DG Consumer Affairs, Guidelines on a Medical Devices Vigilance System, MEDDEV 2.12-1 rev 8 (January 2013).

[140]   European Commission Guide for Competent Authorities in Making an Assessment of Clinical Investigation; Notification, MEDDEV 2.7/2 (December 2008).

[141]   European Commission Guidelines on Clinical Investigations: A Guide for Manufacturers and Notified Bodies, MEDDEV 2.7/4 (December 2010).

[142]   European Commission Guidelines on Clinical Investigations: Serious Adverse Event Reporting, MEDDEV 2.7/3 (December 2010).

[143]   European Commission Guideline on Clinical Evaluation: Guide for Manufacturers and Notified Bodies, MEDDEV 2.7/1 rev 3 (December 2009).

[144]   Directive 2007/47/EC of the European Parliament and of the Council of September 5, 2007 amending Council Directive 90/385/EEC on the Approximation of the Laws of the Member States Relating to Active Implantable Medical Devices, Council Directive 93/42/EEC Concerning Medical Devices and Directive 98/8/EC Concerning the Placing of Biocidal Products on the Market, OJ 2007 L247/21, Sept. 21, 2007.

On March 21, 2010, the modifications provided for in Directive 2007/47/EC entered into force in all EU Member States. The impact of this revision on certain types of medical devices currently on the EU market is important due to the number of modifications to the current EU regime governing active implantable medical devices and clinical data requirements.

The most important changes to the former regime concern clinical investigations and clinical evaluation. Since March 2010, manufacturers have been required to conduct clinical investigations when an initial clinical evaluation concludes that the available clinical data do not make possible a full evaluation of the clinical effectiveness and/or safety of the medical device. In addition it is made clear that clinical investigation is required for all implantable and Class III devices unless reliance on existing clinical data is duly justified. Directive 2007/47/EC also provides that technical documentation related to all medical devices must include a clinical evaluation document containing all the clinical data to support the declaration of conformity. This document must be actively updated, and must incorporate relevant postmarketing surveillance data.

Other important changes introduced by Directive 2007/47/EC include the refinement of definitions and classification provisions; the establishment of a central data bank for certain information on medical devices; the classification of software, whether stand-alone or incorporated into a medical device, as a medical device in its own right; and the introduction of specific requirements concerning the safety, labeling, and information with respect to certain high-risk medical devices, namely devices containing phthalates.

Regarding the classification of software as a medical device, on January 23, 2012 the European Commission published Guidelines on the Qualification and Classification of Stand Alone Software Used in Healthcare within the Regulatory Framework of Medical Devices.[145] The purpose of these Guidelines is to define the criteria permitting classification of stand-alone software as a medical device. Where stand-alone software qualifies as a medical device, the Guidelines list the criteria to be applied in determining whether this stand-alone software falls within the scope of the In Vitro Diagnostic Medical Devices Directive or the MDD.

Directive 2007/47/EC introduced provisions creating the potential for provision of Instructions for Use of medical devices in electronic format, rather than paper format. In light of these provisions, the European Commission can, where justified, "*adopt measures allowing instruction for use to be provided by other means.*" On the basis of this provision, the European Commission Regulation 207/2012/EU on electronic Instructions for Use of medical devices was published in the *Official Journal of the European Union* on March 10, 2012. The Regulation, which has applied since March 1, 2013, permits manufacturers of certain medical devices to provide electronic instructions for their use if these devices and accessories are intended exclusively for use by professional users. The Regulation imposes additional obligations, such as the requirement for manufacturers to conduct a risk assessment in order to demonstrate that the Instructions for Use provided in electronic form maintain or improve the level of safety in use of the medical device when compared to instructions for use provided in paper form.

---

[145] European Commission Guidelines on the Qualification and Classification of Stand Alone Software Used in Healthcare within the Regulatory Framework of Medical Devices, MEDDEV 2.1/6, (January 2012).

Recent Proposals. On September 26, 2012, the European Commission published two draft Regulations intended to replace the current MDD, the Active Implantable Medical Devices Directive and the In Vitro Diagnostic Medical Devices Directive:

- The Proposal for a Regulation of the European Parliament and of the Council on medical devices, and amending Directive 2001/83/EC, Regulation (EC) No. 178/2002 and Regulation (EC) No. 1223/2009 (to replace the Active Implantable Medical Devices Directive and the MDD).

- The Proposal for a Regulation of the European Parliament and of the Council on in vitro diagnostic medical devices (to replace the In Vitro Diagnostic Medical Devices Directive).

On October 22, 2013, during a plenary session, the European Parliament voted to approve the draft Regulations. At the time of this writing, the draft Regulations were being discussed by the Council of the European Union. If the proposed Regulations are adopted in their current form, they will lead to an overhaul of the regulation of medical devices in the EU. Many new provisions would be introduced by the draft Regulations, if adopted without changes by the Council. An outline of some of the most noteworthy revisions concerning the medical devices industry proposed in the draft Regulations is provided below.

Scope of the Regulations

Following proposed revisions of the draft Regulation on medical devices by the European Parliament, a new definition of "medical device" has been added to the draft. This definition would provide that medical devices can have direct and indirect medical purposes. The current definition of "medical device" provided in the Directives would be amended to provide that a product providing information concerning direct or indirect impact on health would be considered to constitute a medical device. In the draft Regulation on in vitro diagnostics, this amendment would include nutrigenetic tests and life-cycle tests.

New Procedure Concerning Certain High-risk Medical Devices

The draft Regulation on medical devices also introduced specific provisions governing "high-risk medical devices." Devices falling within this category would include:

(1) implantable Class III devices;

(2) Class IIb devices intended to administer and/or remove a medicinal product;

(3) devices manufactured utilizing non-viable tissues or cells of human or animal origin, or their derivatives; and

(4) Class D IVDs where no common technical standard exists.

These devices would be considered high-risk medical devices. For these medical devices, the proposed conformity-assessment procedure would include the intervention of special notified bodies, designated by the European Medicines Agency on the basis of their specific staff qualifications and training. These special notified bodies would be required to notify the European Commission of all applications for conformity assessment that they receive from manufacturers concerning high-risk medical devices.

When the European Commission received such a notification, it would immediately transmit the notification and the accompanying documents to a newly created Medical Device Coordination Group (MDCG). This Group could seek a clinical assessment from the relevant experts in a newly created Assessment Committee for Medical Devices (ACMD). On the basis of the ACMD assessment, the MDCG would provide an opinion concerning the clinical evaluation report and the postmarketing clinical follow-up plan related to the high-risk medical device. In its opinion, the MDCG would be entitled to recommend changes to these documents. In such circumstances, the notified body would be permitted to issue the relevant CE Certificate of Conformity to the manufacturer only if these proposed changes have been incorporated into the documents.

New Report Requirements

In addition to the procedure described above, manufacturers of high-risk medical devices and Class D IVDs would also be required to draw up a report concerning the safety and clinical performance of their devices, and prepare a summary of this report. The report summary would be made available to the public through the European data bank on medical devices (Eudamed). In light of the fact that it would be available to the public, this summary should be prepared in a manner that is easy for a layperson to understand and is available in the official languages of the countries within which the device is marketed.

Manufacturers of Class III medical devices would also be required to submit periodic safety-update reports to the competent authorities of the EU Member States. Such reports would be submitted either immediately upon request, or at least once a year during the first two years following the initial placing of the related device on the market in the EU. These periodic safety-update reports would be assessed by the MDCG. In the case of an unfavorable assessment, the MDCG would be entitled to contact the manufacturer's notified body concerning the potential suspension or withdrawal of the CE Certificate of Conformity.

Single-use Devices and Reprocessing of Devices

The draft Regulation on medical devices provides that medical devices would now be considered as suitable for reprocessing and as reusable devices by default. The only exception to this provision would be when they are placed on a list of single-use devices that are unsuitable for reprocessing.

The draft Regulation provides the European Commission with the power to establish the list of single-use devices unsuitable for reprocessing. This list would be established following a mandatory consultation with the Medical Device Advisory Committee (MDAC), an expert committee of stakeholders providing guidance to the European Commission and the MDCG. With the assistance of the IMDRF, which recently replaced the GHTF, and international standardization bodies, the European Commission would also define a clear set of high quality and safety standards for reprocessing single-use devices, including specific requirements for the manufacturers of reprocessed devices.

The draft Regulation also provides that any natural or legal person who wishes to reprocess a single-use device to make it suitable for further use must be considered the manufacturer of the reprocessed device and be held liable for its reprocessing activities. This provision would mean that this natural or legal person would be required to ensure the traceability of the reprocessed device and to assure compliance with the requirements of the draft Regulation, with the exception of obligations linked to the conformity-assessment procedure.

Unique Device Identification

The draft Regulation on medical devices would require manufacturers to fit devices with an implant card containing a Unique Device Identification (UDI) to make possible traceability and transparency of the devices. The UDI would identify the specific device, any warnings, precautions or measures to be taken by a patient or a healthcare professional in relation to the device, and include a description of potential related adverse events.

The proposed UDI would enable all economic operators to identify those to whom they have supplied a device and those from whom they have received the device. This identification would include any healthcare professional or institution to whom economic operators have supplied a device. The UDI would be placed on the label of the device.

Clinical Investigations

Irrespective of the outcome of any clinical investigation in relation to a medical device, the draft Regulation on medical devices provides that, within one year from the end of any clinical investigation or from its early termination, the sponsor would be required to submit a report of the results of the investigation to the EU Member States in which the study was conducted. This report would have to be accompanied by a summary presented in terms that are easily understandable to a layperson. Both the report and the summary would be made available to healthcare professionals and the public through Eudamed. The reports would include information concerning serious adverse events that occurred during the investigations.

It would be necessary for sponsors to provide to all EU Member States information concerning the reasons for early termination of a clinical investigation. The purpose is to permit the EU Member States to inform sponsors conducting similar clinical investigations throughout the EU of the results of that clinical investigation at the same time.

Designation and Monitoring of Notified Bodies

The draft Regulation on medical devices and the draft Regulation on in vitro diagnostic medical devices would impose stricter and more detailed criteria concerning the designation of notified bodies. The purpose is to improve the functionality of the notified bodies. In line with European Commission Implementing Regulation 920/2013/ EU of September 24, 2013 on the designation and the supervision of notified bodies, the draft Regulations provide that a joint assessment team composed of three experts chosen by the European Commission would be involved in the review of the documentation submitted by notified bodies in support of their application for designation by the EU Member States. At least one of these experts would be a representative of the European Commission, and at least one other would come from an EU Member State other than the one in which the applicant is established. The European Commission representative would lead the joint assessment team. The joint assessment team would submit its final opinion regarding the assessment report and the draft notification to the MDCG. The MDCG would then draft a final recommendation regarding the draft notification. The national competent authority of the EU Member State in which the applicant notified body is established would base its decision concerning the designation of the notified body on the recommendation made by the MDCG.

The draft Regulations also provides that, when a manufacturer approaches a notified body established in an EU Member State other than that in which the manufacturer is registered, the manufacturer would be required to inform the competent authority in its own EU Member State about the approach.

Person Responsible for Regulatory Compliance

Both the draft Regulation on medical devices and the draft Regulation on in vitro diagnostic medical devices would require all manufacturers to appoint a person responsible for regulatory compliance. This person would be required to have the "requisite expertise" in the field of medical devices, which would be demonstrated by appropriate qualifications or professional experience in medical device regulation.

European Data Bank on Medical Devices

Both draft Regulations provide for increased transparency by requiring more information to be shared in the Eudamed database. This information would include information concerning medical devices placed on or removed from the EU market, information concerning notified bodies' subsidiaries and subcontractors, CE Certificates of Conformity issued by the notified bodies, information concerning ongoing clinical investigations conducted with medical devices, vigilance data, market surveillance activities, Field Safety Correction Actions, Field Safety Notices, periodic safety update reports, Manufacturer's Incident Report, and Manufacturer's Trend Reports. The database will become accessible to the public.

New Essential Requirements

The draft Regulations would also introduce a number of new additions to the Essential Requirements. These would include provisions requiring that the Instructions for Use be easy for a layperson to understand and be reviewed by the representatives of relevant stakeholders, including patient and healthcare professionals' organization. In addition, the CE Mark would be accompanied by the term "Medical Device."

In light of the ongoing differences of opinion between the European Parliament and some members of the Council of the European Union it cannot be excluded that the current texts of the draft Regulations will be substantially amended before their final adoption, which is unlikely to take place before the end of 2015 or beginning of 2016 at earliest. Following adoption, entry into force of the Regulations would take place in 2017-2018 at the earliest.

Borderline and Combination Products

Unlike the United States, the EU does not have a special statutory provision to require timely regulatory decisions on borderline issues or combination products.[146] Nor is there an Office of Combination Products to address regulatory classification and assignment issues. Borderline issue resolution is affected by Article 2.2 of Directive 2001/83/EC,[147] which states that, "*in cases of doubt, where, taking into account all its characteristics, a product may fall within the definition of a 'medicinal product' and within the definition of a product covered by other Community legislation [such as the MDD] the provisions of this [Medicinal Products] directive shall apply.*" Thus, where a given product falls within the definition of more than one regulatory classification including that of a medicinal product, there is a presumption in favor of handling the product as a medicinal product, unless the product falls clearly under the definition of other categories (e.g. food, food supplement, medical device, biocide, or cosmetic).

The MDD describes the regulatory handling of several combination product categories. Article 1(3) of the MDD mandates that "a device that is intended to administer a medicinal product" shall be governed by the MDD. Any medicinal product that a device is intended to administer must be independently authorized and approved by prescribed medicinal-products procedures. If, however, "such a [drug-delivery] device is placed on the market in such a way that the device and the medicinal product form a single integral product which is intended exclusively for use in the given combination and which is not reusable," that single product shall be governed by the Community Code on Medicinal Products. EU medicinal product regulators must assess these combinations, but the device component must also meet the Essential Requirements provided in Annex I of the MDD.

Article 4.1 provides that " . . . *where a device incorporates, as an integral part, a substance which, if used separately, may be considered to be a medicinal product . . . and which is liable to act upon the body with action ancillary to that of the device, that device must be assessed and authorized in accordance with [the medical devices] directive.*" Provided that the action of the medicinal substance is ancillary to that of the device, as reflected in the product claim and as supported by the scientific data provided by the manufacturer, the product will still fall within the MDD. However, the presence of a medicinal product brings the device within Class III and substantially increases the requirements that must be fulfilled before the CE mark is available for a product. According to Annex I, Section 7.4 of the MDD, the notified body, having verified the usefulness of the substance as part of the medical device and taking account of the intended purpose of the device, shall seek a scientific opinion from one of the competent authorities designated by the EU Member States or the EMA on the quality and safety of the substance, including the clinical benefit/risk. Where the integral ancillary medicinal substance is derived from blood, the regulatory authority that must be consulted is the EMA.

---

[146]   David Fox & Jeffrey Shapiro, *Combination Products: How to Develop the Optimal Strategic Path for Approval* (FDA News 2005).

[147]   Directive 2001/83/EC of the European Parliament and of the Council of November 6, 2001 on the Community Code relating to medicinal products for human use, OJ L311 Nov. 28, 2001 p. 67.

The competent authority responsible for the assessment of the medicinal product shall take into account the manufacturing process and the data related to the usefulness of incorporation of the substance into the device as determined by the notified body. The quality, safety, and usefulness of the substance must be verified by analogy with the methods specified in Annex I to Directive 2001/83/EC. According to the European Commission guideline on drug-delivery devices and medical devices incorporating, as an integral part, an ancillary medicinal substance, which was updated in December 2009,[148] where well-known medicinal substances for established purposes are the subject of the consultation, all aspects of safety and usefulness may not be required and many of the headings will be addressed by reference to literature, including standard textbooks, experience, and other information generally available. However, all headings should be addressed, either with relevant data or justification for absence of data. The latter may be based on the manufacturer's risk assessment. For new active substances and for known substances used for a non-established purpose, comprehensive data are needed to address the requirements of Annex I to Directive 2001/83/EC. The evaluation of such an active substance would be performed in accordance with the principles of evaluation of new active substances.

Following the opinion from the competent authority, the notified body shall assess the product in accordance with the requirements of the MDD. According to Annex IX, Rule 13 of the MDD, all medical devices incorporating, as an integral part, a substance that, if used separately, can be considered to be a medicinal product, and that is liable to act on the human body with action ancillary to that of the devices, fall within Class III. The corresponding conformity assessment must, therefore, be carried out. The notified body shall finally ensure that its decision is communicated to the competent authority consulted on the ancillary substance.

Determination of a product's "principal mode of action" is crucial for classification. According to Article 1(5)(c) of the MDD, particular account shall be taken of the principal mode of action of the product when deciding whether a product falls within the MDD.[149] Medical devices typically function by physical means, whereas medicinal products generally function by pharmacological, immunological, or metabolic action. To determine a product's "principal mode of action," EU competent authorities consider a manufacturer's labeling and claims, as well as scientific data, regarding mechanisms of action.

In addition to the principal mode of action of the product, the intended purpose of the product is also considered by taking into account the manufacturer's labeling and claims.

The European Commission guideline on drug-delivery devices and medical devices incorporating, as an integral part, an ancillary medicinal substance explains that, as a general rule, a product is regulated as either a device or a medicinal product. In order to fall under the MDD, the guideline indicates that a product must fulfill the definition of "medical device" and must also not be excluded from the scope of the MDD. It is, therefore, necessary

---

[148]   European Commission Guideline on borderline products, drug-delivery products and medical devices incorporating, as integral part, an ancillary medicinal substance or an ancillary human blood derivative – MEDDEV 2.1/3 rev (Dec. 3, 2009).

[149]   This method of classification constitutes a change introduced by Directive 2007/47/EC. Previously, it was the intended purpose that was the main criterion for classification.

to examine both prerequisites. As mentioned above, a product will not as a rule be regulated under both Directives. However, for defined features, some cross-references are made within one regime to specific provisions of the other regime. The guideline provides a number of examples of products falling within the medical device definition. The examples include products intended to be used for medical purposes, not products intended as toiletries or cosmetics, e.g., toothbrushes, dental floss, or baby diapers.

Finally, manufacturers facing borderline classification issues should also refer to the *European Commission Manual on Borderline and Classification in the Community Regulatory Framework for Medical Devices*,[150] which provides guidance on borderline situations relating to in vitro diagnostic medical devices, active implantable medical devices, medicinal products, biocide products, and cosmetic products. This manual seeks to serve as a tool for the case-by-case application of EU legislation by the EU Member States. The manual's cover states that "only the European Court of Justice can give an authoritative interpretation of Community law," and that "*it is for the national competent authorities and the national courts to assess [product categorization decisions] on a case-by-case basis.*"

Cosmetics

Like other FDA-regulated industries, cosmetic manufacturers operate increasingly in a global market. It is, therefore, important for companies to understand the requirements of the countries in which they wish to sell products and to support harmonization of requirements wherever possible. Yet even the "cosmetic" definition is unharmonized. For example, in the United States, sunscreen products are considered over-the-counter (OTC) drugs, and suntan lotion products lacking ultraviolet filters and sunscreen active ingredients are simply cosmetics. In the EU, all such products are regulated as cosmetics.

Industry and regulators would generally agree that GMPs should be observed by manufacturers, but there may not be agreement on whether GMPs should be mandatory or simply recommended.

In the U.S. regulatory system for cosmetics, industry self-regulation plays a large role, along with some degree of regulatory oversight. The basis for the present U.S. system is the improbability of a major health risk arising from the use of a cosmetic product. In addition, in the United States, the success of a particular cosmetic product depends heavily on industry self-regulation, brand loyalty, product safety and reliability, and product marketing. A manufacturer strives to protect the reputation of its brands, and failure to substantiate product safety creates a risk of injuries that can result in lawsuits, adverse publicity, FDA actions, and loss of retailer and consumer goodwill. Consequently, the U.S. FDA regulatory system cannot be viewed in isolation, as the sole method of control over cosmetics, as the legal, political, and social climate that support product safety also must be considered. Due to the existence of product liability law, consumer demands, the power of the press, and the Internet to publicize product safety problems and other unique aspects of the U.S. system,

---

[150]   European Commission, Manual on Borderline and Classification in the Community Regulatory Framework for Medical Devices, Version 1.16 (July 2014).

he numerous deterrents to marketing unsafe cosmetics in the United States may not be as
ffective in other countries where more prescriptive regulatory requirements may be found.

Harmonization

Despite the lack of complete harmonization as to what constitutes a "cosmetic," divergences
n regulatory systems, and a lack of consensus about which controls should be mandated
by government and which left to industry initiative, FDA and its counterparts have found it
possible to identify areas in which harmonization is possible and desirable.

The principal forum for cosmetics harmonization is the International Cooperation on
Cosmetic Regulations (ICCR), which consists of representatives of FDA, the European
Commission, Health Canada, and the Japanese Ministry of Health, Labor and Welfare. Topics
that have been discussed in this forum include GMPs, ingredient labeling and adoption
of a harmonized system for names of cosmetic ingredients, nanotechnology, exchange of
nformation on market surveillance, harmonization as to composition of cosmetics, animal
testing and alternative methods, trace contaminants, and sunscreens.[151]

Regulation of Cosmetics in the European Union

Many countries have regulatory systems that aim to ensure that cosmetics are safe. A number
of these are similar to that of the United States; others are quite different. The EU system
is worthy of discussion both because of the importance of the EU as a market and because
of the global influence of this system. In the EU, cosmetic products fall within the scope of
Cosmetics Regulation.[152] The new Cosmetics Regulation simplified the previous Cosmetics
Directive 76/768/EEC in the form of a recast. A "recast" is a legislative technique which
enables codification of a legislative text and its amendments and to introduce substantive
improvements. Article 1 of the Cosmetics Regulation defines a "cosmetic" product as "any
substance or mixture intended to be placed in contact with the various external parts of
the human body (epidermis, hair system, nails, lips, and external genital organs) or with
the teeth and the mucous membranes of the oral cavity with a view exclusively or mainly
to cleaning them, perfuming them, changing their appearance, protecting them or keeping
them in good condition or correcting body odors." The definition of "cosmetic" is, therefore,
based on two cumulative elements. These are the target site of application "placing on
body/teeth/mucous membranes" and the intended main (cosmetic) function of the product
"cleaning, perfuming, changing appearance, protecting, keeping in good condition or
correcting body odors."

In the EU, a product may be either a cosmetic or a medicinal product (drug), depending
on its presentation (principally the claims made by the manufacturer) and its function, but
it may not be both. Certain products that have effects on the structure or function of the
human body, such as fluoride toothpastes, anti-dandruff shampoos, antiperspirants, and
sunscreens, are considered cosmetics in the EU but are regulated in the United States as

---

[151]   Meeting outcomes can be found on the European Commission website, Directorate-General for
Consumer Affairs, http://ec.europa.eu/consumers/sectors/cosmetics/cooperation-trade/international-
level/index_en.htm (last visited Dec. 5, 2014).

[152]   Regulation (EC) No 1223/2009 of the European Parliament and of the Council of November 30, 2009 on
cosmetic products, OJ L 342, Dec. 22, 2009, p. 59–209.

OTC drugs.[153] The regulatory systems, however, have similar features, in that the EU does specify permitted ingredients (as does FDA for color additives in cosmetics as well as for active ingredients in cosmetics regulated as OTC drugs) and prescribes conditions of use, including labeling requirements.

The principal objective of EU cosmetics regulation is to ensure that any cosmetic product placed on the market in the EU does not cause harm to human health when used under normal and expected conditions of use, taking into consideration the product's presentation, labeling, instructions for use, and any other indications or information provided by the manufacturer. The Cosmetics Regulation requires manufacturers to maintain an illustrative inventory of cosmetic ingredients, ingredient labeling, and product information files. In 1993, a proposal[154] for a future ban on animal testing of new cosmetic ingredients quickly proved to be extremely contentious, both within the EU[155] and with the EU's trading partners, including the United States. EU authorities on several occasions postponed the effective date of the proposed ban. However, the Commission confirmed in a Communication adopted on March 11, 2013 that from March 11, 2013, there is a ban on animal testing for finished cosmetic products and cosmetic ingredients.[156] It is also prohibited to market finished cosmetic products and ingredients included in cosmetic products that have been tested on animals.

Like the United States, the EU does not require registration of cosmetic products manufactured or imported for sale in the EU, and premarket approvals are not necessary to market a cosmetic. The Regulation does, however, require manufacturers to notify the European Commission, by means of a centralized online portal, of all cosmetic products on the EU market.[157]

Currently, manufacturers marketing cosmetics in the EU must comply with obligations relating to ingredient/substance lists contained in annexes to the Cosmetics Regulation. These lists are regularly updated by amendments to the Cosmetics Regulation. The annexes

---

153   Annex III of the Cosmetics Regulation. In the EU, only the European Court of Justice can decide the regulatory classification of a product. In the absence of an ECJ decision, the EU Member States' "national authorities, acting under the supervision of the courts, must decide on a case-by-case basis, taking account of all the characteristics of the product . . ." ECJ 211/03, C 209/03 to C 318.03 of June 9, 2005, HLH Warenvertriebs GmbH, Orthica BC v Germany, paragraph 51. The European Commission has fostered harmonization efforts in which Commission officials and EU Member State representatives reach a consensus as to the regulatory status of a product. Toward this end, the European Commission has published useful guidelines on the distinction between cosmetics and medicinal products: Guidance document on the demarcation between the Cosmetic Products Directive 76/768 and the Medicinal Products Directive 2001/83 as agreed between the Commission services and the competent authorities of the EU Member States (2007), *available at* http://ec.europa.eu/consumers/sectors/cosmetics/files/doc/ guidance_doc_cosm-medicinal_en.pdf; Manual on the scope of application of the Cosmetics Regulation (EC) No 1223/2009, version 1 (Nov. 2013). The Commission has likewise published guidance on the borderline between the Cosmetics Directive and the Biocides Directive 98/8/EC.
154   Council Directive 93/35, 1993 O.J. (L 151) 32.
155   *See, e.g.,* the Judgment of the European Court of Justice in France v. European Parliament and Council, Case C-244/03 (May 24, 2005). France sought annulment of a provision of Directive 2003/15/EC, an amendment to the 1976 Cosmetics Directive, with respect to the timetable for implementing an EU ban on the testing of cosmetic products on animals. The court declined to invalidate one provision of Directive 2003/15/EC, viewing the provision as nonseverable from other provisions.
156   *See* http://ec.europa.eu/consumers/consumers_safety/cosmetics/ban_on_animal_testing/index_en.htm.
157   *See* http://ec.europa.eu/consumers/consumers_safety/cosmetics/cosing/index_en.htm.

include one negative list (Annex II) of substances that must not form part of the composition of cosmetic products; one restricted list (Annex III) of substances the use of which is subject to certain restrictions and conditions; and several positive lists of substances such as coloring agents (Annex IV), preservatives (Annex V), and UV filters (Annex VI) subject to particular conditions. Once an ingredient is listed in any of the restricted or positive annexes, a manufacturer is able to use it freely in a cosmetic product as long as all conditions or restrictions are complied with. A new ingredient or substance, subject to prior approval, that does not appear on a positive list must be submitted to the European Commission or an EU Member State for approval prior to marketing. The EU also maintains and publishes an inventory of all ingredients used within the cosmetic industry, based on information supplied by the industry.[158] This inventory is not a list of authorized substances, but is, in effect, an informational listing of ingredient identities, functions, restrictions, conditions of use, and warnings. Although FDA does not maintain a similar list, an industry program initiated by the Cosmetics, Toiletries, and Fragrances Association, the industry trade association in the United States, maintains a widely used list of cosmetic ingredients used in the United States.[159]

The Cosmetics Regulation prohibits products that may cause harm to consumers. Warning statements are required for certain ingredients as prescribed by the annexes. Manufacturers are required to disclose serious undesirable effects to competent national authorities through the designated qualified person. Safety data are not required to be reviewed by the health authorities prior to marketing; as in the United States, it is the manufacturer's responsibility to substantiate a product's safety. Manufacturers are required to maintain a "dossier" or information packet, which must be available upon request of any EU Member State. The dossier must include the following:

- a description of the cosmetic product, which enables the product information file to be clearly attributed to the cosmetic product;

- method of manufacture, showing compliance with GMPs established by European Community law or by the relevant EU Member State, if applicable;

- an assessment of the safety for human health of the finished product;

- proof of the effect claimed for the finished product; and

- information on any animal testing performed by the manufacturer, its agents, or suppliers, relating to the development or safety evaluation of the product or its ingredients.

Certain information must appear on the container and packaging of a cosmetic. In particular, according to Article 19 of the Cosmetics Regulation, manufacturers are required to adhere to full ingredient labeling. The Cosmetics Regulation also requires a listing of colors based on Color Index Number. Cosmetic products imported from outside the EU must have a label that names the country of origin. Manufacturers and importers may also use a new symbol introduced in the Cosmetics Regulation that shows the product's date of minimum durability. This symbol allows cross-border distribution of cosmetic products without the

---

[158]   Commission Decision of May 8, 1996 establishing an inventory and a common nomenclature of ingredients employed in cosmetic products.

[159]   For further information, contact the Cosmetic Ingredient Review, 1101 17th Street, NW, Suite 412, Washington, DC 20036, ph 202.331.0651, fax 202.331.0088, andersena@cir-safety.org.

need to translate the declaration "best before" into all relevant languages. The use of this symbol is not mandatory, and the traditional "best before" declaration may still be used.

Article 8 of the Regulation requires manufacturers to comply with GMPs. Compliance will be presumed where the manufacture is in accordance with the relevant harmonized standards published, i.e., EN ISO 22716:2007.[160]

Conclusion

As people and goods move freely across borders, national regulatory agencies are turning to look at their challenges and opportunities in international terms. Also, companies increasingly are multinational in their operations. The globalization of public health and of the health-product industries presents a challenge to regulatory authorities such as FDA that have traditionally focused on domestic compliance.

Yet accompanying the international challenge is the opportunity to advance global public health through international cooperatives, including regulatory harmonization.

Given the current pressure around the world to control costs of food and healthcare, any steps that can be taken by regulators and regulated companies to apply common approaches that assure a high level of product safety will benefit everyone.

---

[160]   Official Journal C 123, Apr. 21, 2011 p. 3.

CHAPTER 24

FTC REGULATION OF ADVERTISING

....

ANNE V. MAHER AND LESLEY FAIR[*]

Introduction

The Federal Trade Commission (FTC) and the Food and Drug Administration (FDA) exercise concurrent jurisdiction over the labeling and advertising of foods, drugs, medical devices, cosmetics, and other health-related products. Pursuant to a longstanding liaison agreement between the two agencies, FTC exercises primary authority over the advertising of those products, while FDA exercises primary authority over their labeling.[1] The one exception to this general division of labor is prescription drugs, over which FDA exercises primary authority over both advertising and labeling.[2]

Although FTC has never endorsed one standard definition of the word "advertising," over the years the commission has successfully challenged deceptive representations conveyed to consumers in virtually every kind of marketing medium, including the Internet.[3] Unlike

---

[*] The opinions expressed herein are solely those of the authors, and do not reflect the opinions of the Federal Trade Commission or any of its bureaus, divisions, or offices. In addition, the citation of Federal Trade Commission settlements (called "consent orders") is for illustrative purposes only. A company's decision to settle FTC charges against it does not constitute an admission of a violation of law.

[1] FTC-FDA Liaison Agreement, 4 Trade Reg. Rep. (CCH) ¶ 9851 (1971), *available at* http://www.fda.gov/AboutFDA/PartnershipsCollaborations/MemorandaofUnderstandingMOUs/DomesticMOUs/ucm115791.htm. Although the Liaison Agreement gives primary authority over labeling to FDA, FTC has challenged deceptive claims made on product labels when the commission has also challenged claims in the product's advertising. *See, e.g.*, Nutramax Labs., Inc., 138 F.T.C. 380, 383 (2004) (consent order) (challenging as deceptive representations on the product label that Senior Moment enhanced memory); Panda Herbal Int'l, Inc., 132 F.T.C. 125 (2001) (consent order) (challenging as a deceptive representation on the label of a product containing St. John's wort, the statement "No known warnings or contraindications").

[2] FTC-FDA Liaison Agreement, 4 Trade Reg. Rep. (CCH) ¶ 9851(III)(b), *available at* http://www.fda.gov/AboutFDA/PartnershipsCollaborations/MemorandaofUnderstandingMOUs/DomesticMOUs/ucm115791.htm. Although the Liaison Agreement does not expressly address restricted medical devices, as a practical matter FTC cedes primary authority to FDA over the advertising of these products as well.

[3] In addition to advertising in broadcast and print media, FTC has challenged deceptive representations conveyed through packaging, labeling, direct mail promotions, telemarketing scripts, infomercials, radio

FDA's regulatory framework, FTC's caselaw and regulations draw no distinction among foods, drugs, medical devices, cosmetics, and other products. Regardless of the nature of the product, the agency applies one legal standard across the board: advertisers must possess and rely upon a reasonable basis for all objective claims—express and implied—that reasonable consumers take from their advertisements.[4]

This chapter provides an overview of FTC's structure, mission, and enforcement authority. It sets forth the legal standards, policy considerations, and application of FTC's authority to challenge unfair and deceptive practices, and provides examples from FTC case precedent. It also explains the relationship between the FTC and FDA, the FTC's enforcement framework, and its analytical approach and application of the advertising substantiation doctrine. Finally, the chapter discusses the wide range of remedies available to the commission to address unfair and deceptive advertising.

Overview of the Federal Trade Commission

How the FTC Is Organized

FTC's mission is to ensure that the nation's markets function vigorously and competitively. Established in 1914 by the Federal Trade Commission Act (FTC Act),[5] FTC is an independent agency, whose five Commissioners, no more than three of whom may be members of the same political party, are appointed by the President and confirmed by the Senate for staggered seven-year terms.[6] The Chairman is selected by the President and confirmed by the Senate, and all official acts of the commission require a majority vote of the Commissioners.

---

programs, shop-at-home television channels, billboard advertising, point-of-purchase displays, oral statements by sales personnel, pop-up advertisements, banner advertisements, email, and social media. *See, e.g.*, Wacoal Am., Inc., FTC Dkt. No. 4496 (Sept. 29, 2014) (consent order) (citing deceptive posts on company's Facebook page about purported slimming effect of iPant caffeine-infused undergarments); FTC Warns Marketers of Children's Omega-3 Fatty Acid Supplements That Claims About Brain and Vision Benefits May Be Deceptive (Feb. 16, 2010), *available at* http://www.ftc.gov/opa/2010/02/omega. shtm (Warning Letters to 11 marketers of Omega-3 fatty acid supplements that they should review product packaging and labeling to make sure they do not make unsubstantiated claims about benefits to children's brain and vision function and development); FTC v. Roex, Inc., No. SA-CV-090266 (C.D. Cal. Mar. 6, 2009) (final order) (challenging deceptive claims disseminated primarily through a call-in radio program called "The Truth About Nutrition" for a device sold to treat cancer and supplements advertised to treat or prevent cancer, HIV/AIDS, diabetes, Alzheimer's disease, Parkinson's disease and other conditions); FTC v. D Squared Solutions, LLC, No. AMD 03CV3108 (D. Md. Aug. 9, 2004) (stipulated final order) (challenging use of deceptive pop-up advertisements); Home Shopping Network, Inc., 122 F.T.C. 227 (1996) (consent order) (challenging deceptive claims disseminated via a shopping channel); Zygon Int'l, Inc., 122 F.T.C. 195 (1996) (consent order) (first FTC case challenging deceptive health-related claims disseminated via the Internet); Synchronal Corp., 116 F.T.C. 1189 (1993) (consent order) (challenging deceptive claims disseminated via infomercial); North Am. Philips Corp., 111 F.T.C. 139 (1988) (challenging deceptive claims disseminated via advertisements on television and radio, on product packaging and labeling, and through press releases).

4   *Advertising Substantiation Policy Statement, appended to* Thompson Med. Co., 104 F.T.C. 648, 839 (1984), *aff'd,* 791 F.2d 189 (D.C. Cir. 1986).

5   Pub. L. No. 63-203, 38 Stat. 717 (1914) (codified as amended at 15 U.S.C. §§ 41-58 (2008)).

6   15 U.S.C. § 41.

FTC's two primary law enforcement divisions perform complementary functions in achieving the interrelated goals of protecting consumers and promoting competition. The Bureau of Consumer Protection protects the buying public from fraud and deception by enforcing federal truth-in-advertising laws, other statutes, and trade regulation rules.[7] The Bureau of Competition reviews mergers and acquisitions, and enforces antitrust laws outlawing anticompetitive behavior, such as price fixing and monopolization.[8] A third division, the Bureau of Economics, evaluates the economic impact of FTC actions, and makes recommendations relating to consumer protection and competition.[9]

From FTC's perspective, truthful advertising benefits consumers by encouraging a healthy rivalry among competitors. By ensuring that marketers may truthfully advertise any aspect of their products—superior health benefits, preferred ingredients, lower prices, etc.—FTC's regulatory framework fosters innovation and maximizes consumer choice. When marketers harm consumers and competitors by advertising deceptively, however, FTC's role is to protect consumers and restore fair competition through vigorous law enforcement.

Law Enforcement Authority

The agency's primary law enforcement tool is section 5 of the FTC Act, which provides: "Unfair methods of competition in or affecting commerce, and unfair or deceptive acts or practices in or affecting commerce, are hereby declared unlawful."[10] The reach of section 5 is vast: it covers all but a limited number of "persons, partnerships, or corporations" whose activities are specifically exempt from FTC jurisdiction.[11] Section 5 also provides, however, that any FTC action under it must be "to the interest of the public."[12] As a general rule, FTC

---

[7] The Bureau of Consumer Protection is divided into seven operating units, all of which engage in activities that to some extent affect the marketing of food and drugs: the Division of Advertising Practices, the Division of Enforcement, the Division of Financial Practices, the Division of Marketing Practices, the Division of Privacy and Identity Protection, the Division of Consumer and Business Education, and the Division of Planning and Information.

[8] FTC's Bureau of Competition has taken an active role in challenging allegedly anticompetitive practices by pharmaceutical companies, hospitals, health professionals, and other sellers of health-related products and services. *See, e.g.*, North Carolina State Board of Dental Examiners v. FTC, No. 13-534 (S. Ct. Feb. 25, 2015); FTC v. Actavis, 133 S. Ct. 2223 (2013); FTC v. Indiana Fed'n of Dentists, 476 U.S. 447 (1986); ProMedica Health System v. FTC, 749 F.3d 559 (6th Cir. 2014); Maine Health Alliance, 136 F.T.C. 616 (2003) (consent order); Hoechst Marion Roussel, Inc., 131 F.T.C. 924 (2001) (consent order). The agency's law enforcement in the antitrust arena is beyond the scope of this chapter.

[9] FTC has regional offices in Atlanta, Chicago, Cleveland, Dallas, Los Angeles, San Francisco, and Seattle. The work of the regional offices is identical to the work of staff at FTC headquarters in Washington, D.C.

[10] 15 U.S.C. § 45(a)(1).

[11] The FTC Act expressly exempts banks, savings and loan institutions, federal credit unions, "common carriers subject to the Acts to regulate commerce," and airlines. 15 U.S.C. § 45(a)(2). However, other recent challenges to FTC's jurisdiction have proven unsuccessful. *See, e.g.*, Daniel Chapter One, FTC Dkt. No. D-9329 (Dec. 24, 2009) (Commission Decision) (rejecting defendants' First Amendment claims and holding that FTC's jurisdiction extends to a corporation organized to carry on business for its own profit or that of its members). In addition, although the insurance industry is not specifically included in the list of exceptions under section 45(a)(2), the McCarran-Ferguson Act generally leaves the regulation of the business of insurance to the states. 15 U.S.C. §§ 1011-1015. However, the provisions of the FTC Act apply to the insurance industry "to the extent that such business is not regulated by State law." 15 U.S.C. § 1012(b).

[12] 15 U.S.C. § 45(a)(1).

has interpreted this requirement to mean that individual disputes between a consumer and a company or between competitors are beyond the scope of section 5.[13]

Section 12(a) of the FTC Act specifically prohibits false advertisements likely to induce the purchase of food, drugs, devices, or cosmetics.[14] Section 15 defines the terms "food,"[15] "drug,"[16] "device,"[17] and "cosmetic,"[18] and provides that an advertisement for a drug shall not be deemed false if it is disseminated only to members of the medical profession, contains no false representation of a material fact, and includes a truthful disclosure of the drug's formula.[19]

---

[13]   See 16 C.F.R. § 2.3 (2011) ("The Commission acts only in the public interest and does not initiate an investigation or take other action when the alleged violation of law is merely a matter of private controversy and does not tend adversely to affect the public."). Although FTC's primary mission is the protection of consumers, the agency has on occasion challenged deceptive or unfair practices in business-to-business transactions. See, e.g., FTC and Florida Halt Internet 'Yellow Pages' Scammers (July 17, 2014), available at http://www.ftc.gov/news-events/press-releases/2014/07/ftc-florida-halt-internet-yellow-pages-scammers. In addition, the agency has challenged the acts of manufacturers, wholesalers, distributors, etc., that have provided others with the "means and instrumentalities" to violate the law. See, e.g., FTC v. Applied Food Sciences, Inc., No. 1:14-CV-00851 (W.D. Tex. Sept. 8, 2014) (stipulated order for permanent injunction) ($3.5 million to settle charges that supplier of green coffee extract cited results of flawed study that retailers then used in marketing purported weight loss products to consumers); FTC v. Stella Labs, LLC, No. 2:09-CV-01262-WJM-CCC (D.N.J. Nov. 3, 2011) (stipulated judgment) ($22.5 million judgment against individuals and companies that sold ingredient purporting to be hoodia to others that marketed weight loss products); Oreck Corp., 151 F.T.C. 289 (2011) (consent order) (alleging, among other things, that company making unsubstantiated health claims for vacuums and air filters provided franchised stores with "means and instrumentalities" to disseminate deceptive representations to consumers).

[14]   15 U.S.C. § 52(a).

[15]   The statute defines "food" to mean "(1) articles used for food or drink for man or other animals, (2) chewing gum, and (3) articles used for components of any such article." 15 U.S.C. § 55(b). This definition of "food" is identical to that in section 201(f) of the Federal Food, Drug, and Cosmetic Act (FDCA), 21 U.S.C. § 321(f) (2012).

[16]   The statute defines "drug" to mean "(1) articles recognized in the official United States Pharmacopoeia, official Homoeopathic Pharmacopoeia of the United States, or official National Formulary, or any supplement to any of them; and (2) articles intended for use in the diagnosis, cure, mitigation, treatment, or prevention of disease in man or other animals; and (3) articles (other than food) intended to affect the structure or any function of the body of man or other animals; and (4) articles intended for use as a component of any article specified in clause (1), (2), or (3); but does not include devices or their components, parts, or accessories." 15 U.S.C. § 55(c). This definition is very similar to that in section 201(g) of the FDCA, 21 U.S.C. § 321(g) (2012).

[17]   The statute defines "device" to mean "an instrument, apparatus, implement, machine, contrivance, implant, in vitro reagent, or other similar or related article, including any component, part, or accessory, which is (1) recognized in the official National Formulary, or the United States Pharmacopeia, or any supplement to them, (2) intended for use in the diagnosis of disease or other conditions, or in the cure, mitigation, treatment, or prevention of disease, in man or other animals, or (3) intended to affect the structure or any function of the body of man or other animals, and which does not achieve any of its principal intended purposes through chemical action within or on the body of man or other animals and which is not dependent upon being metabolized for the achievement of any of its principal intended purposes." 15 U.S.C. § 55(d). The definition is identical to that in section 201(h) of the FDCA, 21 U.S.C. § 321(h) (2012).

[18]   The statute defines "cosmetic" to mean "(1) articles to be rubbed, poured, sprinkled, or sprayed on, introduced into, or otherwise applied to the human body or any part thereof intended for cleansing, beautifying, promoting attractiveness, or altering the appearance, and (2) articles intended for use as a component of any such article; except that such term shall not include soap." 15 U.S.C. § 55(e). This definition is identical to that in section 201(i) of the FDCA, 21 U.S.C. § 321(i) (2012).

[19]   15 U.S.C. § 55(a)(1).

Pursuant to section 18 of the FTC Act, FTC may promulgate "general statements of policy with respect to unfair or deceptive acts or practices"[20] and trade regulation rules, "which define with specificity acts or practices which are unfair or deceptive."[21] However, unlike the authority of many administrative agencies, FTC's authority to promulgate regulations independently under the Administrative Procedure Act was substantially altered by the Federal Trade Commission Improvement Act of 1980.[22] Most recent FTC rulemakings have been undertaken at Congress' express direction to promulgate implementing regulations. In addition, Congress has given FTC the authority to enforce a variety of statutes that prohibit specifically defined business practices.[23]

Law Enforcement Procedures

Investigative Procedures

The FTC staff typically begins a law enforcement investigation either by sending a party an "access letter"—an informal request for information—or by asking the commission to authorize the use of compulsory process. Pursuant to its Rules of Practice, the commission may issue Civil Investigative Demands (CIDs) requiring the named recipients to answer questions, provide documents, and/or give testimony.[24] Recipients must either comply with the return date of the CID, negotiate with commission staff authorized by Rule 2.7(c) to modify the terms of the CID, or, pursuant to Rule 2.7(d), file a petition to limit or quash the CID. Although precomplaint investigations are generally nonpublic, petitions to limit or quash CIDs immediately become part of the public record.[25] A commissioner designated by the Chairman is delegated the authority to rule upon petitions to limit or quash.[26] After the commissioner rules, any petitioner may request that the full commission review the ruling.[27] FTC may file an enforcement proceeding in a federal district court against any individual or company that fails or refuses to comply with a CID.[28]

Administrative Litigation

FTC may take law enforcement action to challenge allegedly deceptive or unfair practices either administratively before a commission administrative law judge (ALJ) or in a federal district court. In the administrative process, if the commission has "reason to believe" that a violation of law has occurred, it will issue a complaint setting out its allegations.[29] If the respondent elects to settle the charges, it must sign a consent order (without admitting liability), agree that the order will be made public, and waive all right to judicial review.[30] If the commission accepts the proposed consent order, it places the order on the public record

---

[20] 15 U.S.C. § 57a(a)(1)(A). *See, e.g.,* Guides for the Use of Environmental Marketing Claims, 16 C.F.R. § 260.1-8 (2014); Enforcement Policy Statement on Food Advertising, 59 Fed. Reg. 28,388 (June 1, 1994).

[21] 15 U.S.C. § 57a(a)(1)(B). *See, e.g.,* Ophthalmic Practices Rule (Eyeglass Rule), 16 C.F.R. § 456 (2014); Mail or Telephone Order Merchandise Rule, 16 C.F.R. § 435.1-4 (2014).

[22] 15 U.S.C. § 57a.

[23] *See, e.g.,* Restore Online Shoppers' Confidence Act, 15 U.S.C. § 8401 (2010); Truth in Lending Act, 15 U.S.C. §§ 1601-1667f (2008).

[24] 16 C.F.R. § 2.7(b) (2014).

[25] 16 C.F.R. § 2.7(g) (2014).

[26] 16 C.F.R. § 2.7(d)(4) (2014).

[27] 16 C.F.R. § 2.7(f) (2014).

[28] 16 C.F.R. § 2.13 (2014).

[29] 15 U.S.C. § 45(b).

[30] 16 C.F.R. § 2.32 (2014)

for 30 days so that members of the public may comment on the agency's proposed action.[31] At the end of the comment period, the commission will either make the order final or take other action based on the comments it has received.[32]

If the respondent chooses to contest the charges, the complaint is adjudicated before an ALJ in a trial conducted under the FTC's Rules of Practice.[33] The administrative prosecution of a consumer protection matter is the responsibility of "complaint counsel," i.e., staff from the agency's Bureau of Consumer Protection or one of its seven regional offices.[34] After hearing testimony and considering all admitted evidence, the ALJ issues an initial decision that includes findings of fact and conclusions of law. The initial decision also recommends either the entry of an order to cease and desist or the dismissal of the complaint. Neither the ALJ nor the commission has the authority to assess fines; order refunds, redress, or the disgorgement of profits; or impose other financial remedies.[35] Either complaint counsel or respondent—or both—may appeal the ALJ's initial decision to the commission.

On appeal, the commission receives briefs, hears oral argument, and issues its own decision and order. The commission's decision is appealable to any United States Court of Appeals within whose jurisdiction the respondent "resides or carries on business or where the challenged practice was employed."[36] The party losing in the Court of Appeals may seek review by the Supreme Court.

When an FTC order becomes final either through settlement or adjudication, a respondent that violates an order is liable for civil penalties of up to $16,000 per day for each violation.[37]

---

[31]   16 C.F.R. § 2.34 (2014).

[32]   16 C.F.R. § 2.34(e) (2014).

[33]   16 C.F.R. §§ 3.1-.83 (2014).

[34]   In their capacity as complaint counsel, commission attorneys and investigators may not have contact with members of the commission or their personal staffs. See 16 C.F.R. § 4.7(b) (2014).

[35]   The commission may, however, enter into administrative consent orders that require respondents to pay redress to consumers or to disgorge profits. See, e.g., Wacoal Am., Inc., FTC Dkt. No. 4496 (Sept. 29, 2014) (consent order) ($1.3 million to settle charges that company made false and unsubstantiated slimming claims for caffeine-infused shapewear); Lornamead, Inc., FTC Dkt. No. C-4488 (May 28, 2014) (consent order) ($500,000 to settle charges that company made deceptive efficacy claims for Lice Shield line of lice prevention products); CVS Caremark Corp., FTC Dkt. No. C-4357 (Jan. 12, 2012) (consent order) ($5 million to settle charges that company misrepresented prices of certain Medicare Part D drugs at CVS and Walgreens pharmacies); NBTY, Inc., 151 F.T.C. 201 (2011) (consent order) ($2.1 million redress for deceptive brain and eye development claims for Disney- and Marvel Heroes-licensed children's multivitamin gummies and tablets); Vital Basics, Inc., 137 F.T.C. 254 (2004) (consent order) ($1 million redress for deceptive memory enhancement and sexual performance claims for dietary supplements); ValueVision Int'l, Inc., 132 F.T.C. 338 (2001) (consent order) (requiring home shopping company to offer refunds to all purchasers of weight loss, cellulite, and baldness products).

[36]   15 U.S.C. § 45(c).

[37]   15 U.S.C. § 45(l). See, e.g., United States v. ICON Health & Fitness, Inc., No. 1:14-CV-1578 (D.D.C. Sept. 14, 2014) (stipulated order) ($3 million civil penalty for deceptive weight loss and fitness claims for ab GLIDER, in violation of 1997 FTC order); United States v. Jason Pharms., Inc., No. 12-1476 (D.D.C. Sept. 10, 2012) (consent decree) ($3.5 million civil penalty for deceptive weight loss claims for Medifast, in violation of 1992 FTC order); United States v. QVC, Inc., No. 04-CV-1276 (E.D. Pa. Mar. 19, 2009) (consent decree) ($1.5 million civil penalty for deceptive claims for Lipofactor Cellulite Target Lotion, in violation of 2000 FTC order, and an additional $6 million redress for deceptive claims for For Women Only weight loss pills, Lite Bites weight loss bars and shakes, and Bee-Alive Royal Jelly energy supplements).

The penalty is assessed in a suit brought in United States District Court to enforce the commission's order.[38]

After all judicial review of an administrative proceeding is complete, FTC may file suit in United States District Court to seek consumer redress from the respondent pursuant to section 19(b) of the FTC Act.[39] To prevail, the commission must establish that the respondent "acted in a way that a reasonable [person] would have known under the circumstances was dishonest or fraudulent."[40]

Federal Court Litigation

Section 13(b) of the FTC Act authorizes the commission to file suit in United States District Court to seek preliminary and permanent injunctions to remedy a violation of "any provision of law enforced by the Federal Trade Commission."[41] Pursuant to section 13(b), if the commission has reason to believe that any party "is violating, or is about to violate" any law it enforces, the agency may ask the district court to enjoin the allegedly unlawful conduct, pending completion of an FTC administrative proceeding. Section 13(b) also authorizes federal courts to grant permanent injunctions "in proper cases."[42]

In recent years, FTC has used section 13(b) to take action in federal court challenging allegedly deceptive practices, including misleading advertisements for health-related products.[43] The commission has successfully argued that the broad language of section 13(b) authorizes federal courts not only to enter permanent injunctions barring deceptive practices but also to impose a wide variety of equitable relief, including financial remedies

---

[38]   *Id.*

[39]   15 U.S.C. § 57b.

[40]   15 U.S.C. § 57b(a)(2). *See* FTC v. Figgie Int'l, Inc., 994 F.2d 595 (9th Cir. 1993).

[41]   15 U.S.C. § 53(b).

[42]   *Id.*

[43]   *See, e.g.,* FTC v. Bronson Partners, LLC, 654 F.3d 359 (2d Cir. 2011) (challenging deceptive weight loss claims for Chinese Diet Tea and Bio-Slim Patch); FTC v. Direct Mktg. Concepts, Inc., 624 F.3d 1 (1st Cir. 2010) (challenging deceptive weight loss and disease prevention claims for Coral Calcium and Supreme Greens); FTC v. TriVita, Inc., No. 2:14-CV-01557-DLR (D. Ariz. July 15, 2014) (challenging deceptive claims that cactus-based Nopalea beverage relieves pain, reduces swelling, alleviates respiratory problems, and relieves skin conditions); FTC v. Wellness Support Network, Inc., No. 10-CV-4879 (N.D. Cal. Mar. 7, 2014) (final judgment) (challenging deceptive diabetes prevention and treatment claims for Diabetic Pack and Insulin Resistance Pack); FTC v. Sunny Health Nutrition Technology & Prods., No. 8:06-CV-2193-T-24EAJ (M.D. Fla. Apr. 24, 2007) (stipulated final order) (challenging deceptive claims for HeightMax, a dietary supplement purporting to make teens and young adults taller); FTC v. Seville Mktg., Ltd., No. C04-1181L (W.D. Wash. June 1, 2005) (amended stipulated judgment) (challenging efficacy claims for at-home HIV test kits advertised as 99.4 percent accurate, but with error rates as high as 59.3 percent); FTC v. Media Maverick, Inc., No. 04-3395-SVW (CWx) (C.D. Cal. Oct. 25, 2004) (stipulated final order) (challenging deceptive claims for a purported pain relief bracelet); FTC v. Liverite Prods., Inc., No. SA 01-778 AHS (ANx) (S.D. Cal. Aug. 21, 2001) (stipulated final order) (challenging deceptive claims that dietary supplement was effective in the treatment of hepatitis C, cirrhosis, and hangovers, and could prevent liver damage and other side effects from use of HIV drugs, hepatitis C medications, chemotherapy, interferon, and anabolic steroids). *See also* FTC v. Airborne, Inc., No. CV-08-05300 (C.D. Cal. Aug. 14, 2008) (stipulated judgment); FTC v. Walgreens Co., No.1:10-CV-01813 (N.D. Ill. Mar. 23, 2010) (stipulated final order); FTC v. CVS Pharmacy, Inc., No. CA-09-420 (D.R.I. Sept. 8, 2009) (stipulated final order); and FTC v. Rite Aid Corp., No. 1:09-CV-01333-JEJ (M.D. Pa. July 13, 2009) (stipulated final order) (challenging deceptive cold and flu prevention claims for Airborne and for similar "house brand" products sold in national chain drug stores).

such as redress for consumers or the disgorgement of profits.[44] As a result, much of FTC's consumer protection litigation is now conducted in federal courts, rather than before ALJs.[45]

FTC's choice of forum often presents interesting strategic issues. The most common reason the commission files suit under section 13(b) is that the court may award both injunctive and monetary relief. Nevertheless, administrative adjudication does maintain a role in FTC enforcement. For example, the staff may still try cases administratively when novel legal theories or fact patterns are presented. On judicial review of a matter initially brought administratively, the court is obliged to affirm the commission's findings of fact if they are supported by substantial evidence.[46] A reviewing court must also give substantial deference to constructions of the FTC Act articulated by the commission in an administrative adjudication.[47] In matters brought pursuant to section 13(b), the commission receives no such deference as to a position taken in an individual case.

When Is an Act or Practice "Deceptive" or "Unfair" Under the FTC Act?

Applying FTC's Deception Standard

Over the years, legal decisions by the commission and federal courts have added flesh to the FTC Act's general prohibition of "deceptive acts or practices," which in FTC parlance includes deceptive claims, representations, and omissions of material facts. FTC's 1983

---

[44]   See, e.g., FTC v. Bronson Partners, LLC, 654 F.3d 359 (2d Cir. 2011); FTC v. Freecom Commc'ns, Inc., 401 F.3d 1192, 1202 n.6 (10th Cir. 2005); FTC v. Gem Merch. Corp., 87 F.3d 466, 468 (11th Cir. 1996); FTC v. Pantron I Corp., 33 F.3d 1088, 1102 (9th Cir. 1994); FTC v. Sec. Rare Coin & Bullion Corp., 931 F.2d 1312, 1314-15 (8th Cir. 1991); FTC v. Amy Travel Serv., Inc., 875 F.2d 564, 571-72 (7th Cir. 1989); FTC v. H.N. Singer, Inc., 668 F.2d 1107, 1113 (9th Cir. 1982); FTC v. Southwest Sunsites, Inc., 665 F.2d 711, 718 (5th Cir. 1982).

[45]   See, e.g., FTC v. Nat'l Urological Group, Inc., No. 1:04-CV-3294 (N.D. Ga. Jan. 15, 2009) (final judgment) ($15.8 million redress judgment after trial on FTC charges alleging deceptive advertising claims for Thermalean and Lipodrene, purported weight loss products with ephedra, and Spontane-ES, a purported erectile dysfunction product with yohimbine). See also FTC v. Nat'l Urological Group, Inc., No 1:04:CV-3294 (N.D. Ga. Aug. 20, 2014) (order) ($40 million judgment for failure to comply with terms of 2008 order relating to the advertising and recall of dietary supplements).

[46]   See, e.g., FTC v. Mary Carter Paint Co., 382 U.S. 46 (1965); POM Wonderful, LLC v. FTC, No. 13-1060, slip op. at 15 (D.C. Cir. Jan. 30, 2015) ("On review of an order under the FTC Act, the findings of the Commission as to the facts, if supported by evidence, shall be conclusive. That standard is essentially identical to the familiar substantial evidence test under the Administrative Procedures Act. The Commission is often in a better position than are courts to determine when a practice is deceptive within the meaning of the FTC Act, and that admonition is especially true with respect to allegedly deceptive advertising since the finding of a § 5 violation in this field rests so heavily on inference and pragmatic judgment.") (internal citations omitted); Kraft, Inc. v. FTC, 970 F.2d 311, 317 (7th Cir. 1992) ("While it could be posited that it is counter-intuitive to grant more deference to the Commission than to courts, Commission findings are well-suited to deferential review because they may require resolution of exceedingly complex and technical factual issues. In addition, the determination of whether an ad has a tendency to deceive is an impressionistic one more closely akin to a finding of fact than a conclusion of law.") (citations omitted).

[47]   See Thompson Med. Co. v. FTC, 791 F.2d 189, 197 (D.C. Cir. 1986) ("Although the meaning of the statutory phrase 'deceptive acts or practices' is ultimately a matter for judicial construction, the Commission's conclusion that acts or practices are likely to deceive is due special deference owing to the nature of the inquiry and the Commission's expertise in evaluating deception.").

Deception Policy Statement forms the foundation of the agency's approach to advertising law.[48] According to the Deception Policy Statement, in determining whether an act or practice—for example, the dissemination of an advertising claim—is deceptive under section 5, the commission requires three elements. First, "there must be a representation or an omission of information that is likely to mislead the consumer."[49] Second, the commission examines the representation or omission to ensure that it is misleading "from the perspective of a consumer acting reasonably in the circumstances."[50] Third, the representation, omission, or practice must be "material," defined as "likely to affect the consumer's conduct or decision with regard to a product or service."[51] In the case of allegedly deceptive advertising claims, the commission considers these three elements in evaluating claims for all products, regardless of the media in which advertisers disseminate their claims.

"There Must Be A Representation, Omission, or Practice That Is Likely to Mislead the Consumer."[52]

The first step in the FTC's deception analysis is to identify the representations and omissions made by an advertisement. To determine the "net impression" an advertisement conveys, FTC looks at an advertisement from the point of view of the reasonable consumer.[53] The commission examines "the entire mosaic, rather than each tile separately,"[54] and takes care to judge the advertisement "as a whole, without emphasizing isolated words or phrases apart from their context."[55] The analysis includes an evaluation of "the visual and aural imagery of advertisements" because, "[w]ithout this mode of examination, the Commission would have limited recourse against crafty advertisers whose deceptive messages were conveyed by means other than, or in addition to, spoken words."[56] The commission need not prove that consumers were, in fact, misled. As the Deception Policy Statement makes clear, "[t]he issue is whether the act or practice is likely to mislead, rather than whether it causes actual deceptions."[57]

---

[48]   Deception Policy Statement, appended to Cliffdale Assocs., Inc., 103 F.T.C. 110, 174 (1984). Numerous federal courts evaluating claims of deceptive advertising have cited the Deception Policy Statement with approval. See, e.g., Novartis Corp. v. FTC, 223 F.3d 783 (D.C. Cir. 2000); FTC v. Pantron I Corp., 33 F.3d 1088 (9th Cir. 1994).

[49]   Deception Policy Statement, 103 F.T.C. at 175. Before the commission issued the Deception Policy Statement, the standard was an advertisement's "tendency or capacity to deceive." See Southwest Sunsites, Inc. v. FTC, 785 F.2d 1431, 1435 (9th Cir. 1986).

[50]   Deception Policy Statement, 103 F.T.C. at 175.

[51]   Id.

[52]   Id.

[53]   Id.

[54]   Id. at 179 (citing FTC v. Sterling Drug, 317 F.2d 669, 674 (2d Cir. 1964)).

[55]   Id.

[56]   Id. 181 (quoting Am. Home Prods. Corp. v. FTC, 695 F.2d 681, 688 (3d Cir. 1982)). FTC has long challenged visual depictions that convey deceptive product claims. See, e.g., FTC v. Colgate-Palmolive Co., 380 U.S. 374 (1965) (challenging deceptive on-camera demonstration that purported to show advertiser's shaving cream softening sandpaper when, in fact, the depiction was actually sand sprinkled on glass); Nissan North Am., Inc., FTC Dkt. No. C-4454 (Jan. 23, 2014) (consent order) (challenging deceptive representation of Nissan Frontier truck pushing a dune buggy up a sand dune); United States v. Goodtimes Entm't, Ltd., No. 03 CV 6037 (S.D.N.Y. Aug. 11, 2003) (consent decree) (challenging deceptive before-and-after photos for Copa hair straightening product); Volvo North Am. Corp., 115 F.T.C. 87 (1992) (consent order) (challenging deceptive demonstration depicting monster truck driving over row of cars because Volvo had been reinforced, and roof supports of other cars had been severed).

[57]   Id. at 176. See generally FTC v. Algoma Lumber Co., 291 U.S. 67, 81 (1934).

Claims may be conveyed to consumers expressly or by implication. As defined by the commission, "[a] misrepresentation is an express or implied statement contrary to fact."[58] As one federal appellate court explained the distinction between express and implied claims:

> Suppose a certain automobile gets poor gas mileage, say, 10 miles per gallon. One advertisement boasts that it gets 30 miles per gallon while another identifies the car as the "Miser," depicts it rolling through the countryside past one gas station after another, and proclaims that the car is inexpensive to operate. Both ads make deceptive claims: the first does so expressly, the second does so impliedly.[59]

An advertisement or business practice also may be deceptive by omission. Of course, not all omissions or failures to disclose information are deceptive, even if providing the information would be beneficial to consumers.[60] "In determining whether an omission is deceptive, the Commission will examine the overall impression created by a practice, claim, or representation."[61]

The commission relies on its administrative expertise in determining the claims that reasonable consumers take from an advertisement.[62] In the case of express claims, no evaluation beyond a reading of the advertisement is usually necessary. In the case of implied claims, the commission—exercising its administrative expertise—often can determine the meaning through a close examination of the representation, including an evaluation of the nature of the claim, the nature of the proposed transaction, and the juxtaposition of phrases and imagery within the advertisement.[63] As to both express and implied claims, courts give substantial deference to commission determinations of deception.[64]

If the commission is unable to determine with confidence from an advertisement, itself, what claims are conveyed, it looks to extrinsic evidence.[65] The commission has considered extrinsic evidence in many forms, including consumer testimony, copy testing, expert opinion, consumer surveys, "generally accepted principles drawn from market research," and other reliable evidence.[66] Such extrinsic evidence must be based on methodologically sound procedures.[67]

That an advertiser did not intend to convey a certain claim to consumers is not a defense under section 5. "Advertisers are liable for materially misleading claims or omissions that

---

[58]   *Deception Policy Statement*, 103 F.T.C. at 175 n.4.

[59]   Kraft, Inc. v. FTC, 970 F.2d 311, 318 n.4 (7th Cir. 1992).

[60]   *Deception Policy Statement*, 103 F.T.C. at 175.

[61]   *Id.* at 175 n.4. *See* Simeon Mgmt. Corp. v. FTC, 579 F.2d 1137, 1145 (9th Cir. 1978).

[62]   *Deception Policy Statement*, 103 F.T.C. at 176 ("[I]n cases of express claims, the representation itself establishes the meaning."). *See* Kraft, 970 F.2d at 318.

[63]   *Deception Policy Statement*, 103 F.T.C. at 176.

[64]   *See* Porter & Dietsch, Inc. v. FTC, 605 F.2d 294, 300 (7th Cir. 1979) ("Whether particular advertising has a tendency to deceive or mislead is obviously an impressionistic determination more closely akin to a finding of fact than to a conclusion of law. Giving due regard to the FTC's expertise, we must sustain the FTC's findings if they are supported by substantial evidence on the record viewed as a whole.") (citations omitted).

[65]   *See* Kraft, Inc., 970 F.2d at 318.

[66]   Kraft Inc., 114 F.T.C. 40, 121-22 (1991), *aff'd*, Kraft, Inc. v. FTC, 970 F.2d 311 (7th Cir. 1992).

[67]   Stouffer Foods Corp., 118 F.T.C. 746, 807-08 (1994); Thompson Med. Co., 104 F.T.C. at 790.

their advertisements convey to reasonable consumers, even if this is done inadvertently."[68] As the commission has held, "Although firms are unlikely to possess substantiation for implied claims they do not believe the ad makes, they should generally be aware of reasonable interpretations and will be expected to have prior substantiation for such claims."[69]

"The Act or Practice Must Be Considered from the Perspective of the Reasonable Consumer."[70]

The second factor in the commission's deception analysis is an examination of the advertisement or business practice from the perspective of a consumer acting reasonably in the circumstances. In general, FTC reviews advertisements from the point of view of the "reasonable consumer," often defined as a member of the "general populace"[71] or "the average listener,"[72] as distinguished from the opposite ends of the spectrum—the particularly savvy and sophisticated consumer, and "the ignorant, the unthinking and the credulous."[73]

The commission's approach takes into account that reasonable consumers can take multiple meanings from the same advertisement. A consumer's interpretation may still be reasonable even if it was not what the advertiser meant to convey, and even if the interpretation is not shared by a majority of consumers. "An ad is misleading if at least a significant minority of reasonable consumers are likely to take away the misleading claim."[74] If an advertisement is subject to multiple reasonable interpretations—one of which is deceptive and the rest of which are non-deceptive—the advertiser may be held liable under section 5 for conveying the deceptive claim.[75] Even if the wording of an advertisement is literally truthful, the advertisement may nonetheless violate section 5 if the net impression consumers take from it is deceptive.[76] "The impression created by the advertising, not its literal truth or falsity, is the desideratum."[77]

---

68 Kraft, Inc., 114 F.T.C. at 53 n.33. *See* Telebrands Corp., 140 F.T.C. 278, 304 (2005) ("A showing of an intent to make a particular claim is not required to find liability for violating Section 5 of the FTC Act."), *aff'd*, 457 F.3d 354 (4th Cir. 2006).

69 *Substantiation Policy Statement*, 104 F.T.C. at 840. *See* FTC's Substantiation Doctrine *infra* p. 904.

70 *Deception Policy Statement*, 103 F.T.C. at 175.

71 *Id.* citing Grolier, Inc., 91 F.T.C. 315, 430 (1978), *remanded on other grounds*, 615 F.2d 1215 (9th Cir. 1980), *modified on other grounds*, 98 F.T.C. 882 (1981), *reissued*, 99 F.T.C. 379 (1982) ("In determining the meaning of an advertisement, a piece of promotional material or a sales presentation, the important criterion is the net impression that it is likely to make on the general populace."). *See also* Kraft Inc., 970 F.2d at 314.

72 Warner-Lambert Co., 86 F.T.C. 1398, 1415 n.4 (1975), *aff'd*, 562 F.2d 749 (D.C. Cir. 1977).

73 *See* FTC v. Balme, 23 F.2d 615, 620 (2d Cir. 1928), *citing* Florence Mfg. Co. v. J.C. Dowd & Co., 178 F. 73, 75 (2d Cir. 1910).

74 Telebrands Corp., 140 F.T.C. at 291. *See* Thompson Med. Co., 104 F.T.C. at 837-39 (holding advertiser liable for failure to substantiate claim conveyed to 16-18 percent of consumers). However, "[a]n advertiser cannot be charged with liability in respect of every conceivable misconception, however outlandish, to which his representations might be subject . . . . A representation does not become false and deceptive merely because it will be unreasonably misunderstood by an insignificant and unrepresentative segment of the class of persons to whom the representation is addressed." Heinz W. Kirchner, 63 F.T.C. 1282, 1290 (1963).

75 Sears, Roebuck & Co., 95 F.T.C. 406, 511 (1980), *aff'd*, 676 F.2d 385 (9th Cir. 1982).

76 Grolier, Inc., 91 F.T.C. at 431 (Initial Decision) ("The Commission is not confined to proscribing affirmative misrepresentations. The literal truth employed in a particular context may be used to deceive and deception, moreover, may be accomplished by innuendo, as well as by outright false statements.").

77 FTC v. Cyberspace.com LLC, 453 F.3d 1196, 1200 (9th Cir. 2006), *citing* Am. Home Prods. Corp. v. FTC, 695 F.2d at 687.

In evaluating how reasonable consumers interpret a claim, the commission considers the target market for the advertisement. If the representation or practice affects, or is directed primarily to, members of a particular group, the commission examines reasonableness from the perspective of that population.[78] The commission has shown particular concern when deceptive acts or practices are aimed at vulnerable consumers. For example, in evaluating toy advertisements directed to children, the commission adopted the holding from the initial decision that "[f]alse, misleading and deceptive advertising claims beamed at children tend to exploit unfairly a consumer group unqualified by age or experience to anticipate or appreciate the possibility that representations may be exaggerated or untrue."[79] Similarly, in determining the claims conveyed by advertisements for "psychic surgery," the commission viewed the promotions from the point of view of the target audience: "desperate consumers with terminal illnesses."[80]

With regard to disclosures in advertising, the commission has held that accurate information elsewhere in the text may not remedy a false headline because reasonable consumers may read only the headline.[81] This principle is grounded in the observation that reasonable consumers may spend "[t]ypically a few seconds at most" to evaluate an advertisement.[82] Thus, if a disclosure is necessary to prevent an advertisement from being deceptive, the disclosure must be "clear and conspicuous," i.e., prominent enough to be noticed, read, and understood by reasonable consumers.[83]

As commission caselaw makes clear, a fine-print disclosure at the bottom of a print advertisement, a disclaimer buried in a dense block of text, a fleeting superscript on a television screen, or a vaguely labeled hyperlink on an Internet website is not likely to be considered adequate to cure misleading representations elsewhere in an advertisement.[84]

---

[78]   *Deception Policy Statement*, 103 F.T.C. at 179.

[79]   Ideal Toy Corp., 64 F.T.C. 297, 310 (1964). *See also* Audio Commc'ns, Inc., 114 F.T.C. 414 (1991) (consent order) (challenging under section 5 television advertisements that invited children to make 900-number calls to cartoon characters, and resulted in expensive phone bills for their parents).

[80]   Travel King, Inc., 86 F.T.C. 715 (1975).

[81]   *Deception Policy Statement*, 103 F.T.C. at 180. *See generally* Stouffer Foods Corp., 118 F.T.C. 746 (1994) (holding that sodium-content claims for Lean Cuisine products were false and unsubstantiated, and not cured by a fine-print footnote); Häagen-Dazs Co., 119 F.T.C. 762 (1995) (consent order) (challenging effectiveness of fine-print footnote modifying allegedly deceptive claim that frozen yogurt was "98% fat free").

[82]   *Deception Policy Statement*, 103 F.T.C. at 180 n.33, *citing* Crown Central Petroleum Corp., 84 F.T.C. 1493, 1543 nn.14-15 (1974). *See also* Giant Food, Inc., 61 F.T.C. 326, 348 (1962) ("[V]ery few if any of the persons who would read Giant's advertisements would take the trouble to, or did, read the fine print disclaimer.").

[83]   *See* Thompson Med. Co., 104 F.T.C. at 842-43; Removatron Int'l Corp. v. FTC, 884 F.2d 1489, 1497 (1st Cir. 1989).

[84]   *See* FTC v. Cyberspace.com, 453 F.3d 1196 (9th Cir. 2006) (holding that fine-print statement on purported rebate check was insufficient to clearly disclose that cashing the check would trigger monthly charges for Internet access services); Sears Holdings Mgmt. Corp., FTC Dkt. No. C-4264 (June 4, 2009) (consent order) (alleging that company invited consumers to download software while inadequately disclosing in long, complicated "terms and conditions" page that software would monitor nearly all of Internet behavior on that computer); Palm, Inc., 133 F.T.C. 715 (2002) (consent order) (challenging as ineffective a disclosure in a print advertisement that was in a light color on a white background and oriented perpendicular to the text); Office Depot, Inc., FTC Dkt. No. C-3977 (Sept. 8, 2000) (consent order) (challenging as ineffective a one-sentence disclosure buried in a 15-line block of fine print); Buy.com, Inc., FTC Dkt. No. C-3978 (Sept. 8, 2000) (consent order) (challenging as ineffective a disclosure in a print advertisement that was in four-point type in the upper left corner of a full-page newspaper advertisement). *See generally* Operation "Full Disclosure" Targets More than 60 National Advertisers (Sept. 23, 2014), *available at* http://www.ftc.

To ensure that disclosures are effective, commission cases have directed advertisers to use clear language, avoid small type, place any qualifying information close to the claim being qualified, and avoid making inconsistent statements or adding distracting elements that could undercut, contradict, or divert consumer attention away from the disclosure.[85] For television advertisements, FTC has given substantial weight to consumer research suggesting that dual-modality disclosures (disclosures that simultaneously appear on the screen and are read in voice-over) are most effective for conveying information to consumers.[86] For that reason, FTC orders have routinely required that mandated disclosures in advertising on television appear simultaneously on the screen and in voice-over.[87] Even if the advertiser discloses the truth elsewhere in the transaction, section 5 may still be violated if the first contact between a seller and a buyer occurs through a deceptive practice.[88] As the commission has made clear, "It is well settled that dishonest advertising is not cured or excused by honest labeling."[89]

Because the primary purpose of the FTC Act is to protect the public rather than to punish wrongdoers, the commission need not prove a willful, knowing, or deliberate act or an advertiser's intent to deceive consumers to prevail under section 5. "Neither the lack of intent nor the existence of good faith is a defense to a Section 5 violation."[90] Nor is a company's offer of a money-back guarantee a defense to a charge of deceptive advertising.[91]

The commission has held that certain categories of claims are unlikely to deceive reasonable consumers. For example, subjective claims about a product's taste, feel, appearance, or smell are generally not actionable under section 5 because reasonable consumers would understand that they are grounded in personal opinion.[92] In addition, the commission generally does not pursue cases that involve obviously exaggerated representations, often termed "puffery," which FTC has described as "highly subjective, not capable of measurement, and not taken

---

gov/news-events/press-releases/2014/09/operation-full-disclosure-targets-more-60-national-advertisers. com; .com Disclosures: How to Make Effective Disclosures in Digital Advertising (FTC Staff Report) (March 2013), *available at* http://www.ftc.gov/news-events/press-releases/2013/03/ftc-staff-revises-online-advertising-disclosure-guidelines; Dot.Com Disclosures: Information About Online Advertising (FTC Staff Report) (May 2000), *available at* www.ftc.gov/bcp/conline/pubs/buspubs/dotcom/index.shtml.

[85] *See, e.g.,* Kraft, 114 F.T.C. at 124 (holding that complicated quantitative superscript—"one ¾ ounce slice has 70% of the calcium of five ounces of milk"—did not cure deceptive calcium-content claim for cheese slices).

[86] *Id.* ("Generally recognized marketing principles suggest that, given the distracting visual and audio elements and the brief appearance of the complex superscript in the middle of the commercial, it is unlikely that the visual disclosure is effective as a corrective measure.").

[87] *See* Thompson Med. Co., 104 F.T.C. at 842-43; United States v. Bayer Corp., No. CV 00-132 (NHP) (D.N.J. Jan. 11, 2000) (consent decree) (requiring that mandated television disclosures "be presented simultaneously in both the audio and video portions of the advertisement").

[88] *Deception Policy Statement*, 103 F.T.C. at 180.

[89] *Id.* at n.37, *citing* Am. Home Prods. Corp., 98 F.T.C. 136, 370 (1981), *aff'd & modified on other grounds*, 695 F.2d 681 (3d Cir. 1982), *modified*, 103 F.T.C. 528 (1984).

[90] Kraft, Inc., 114 F.T.C. at 53 n.33. *See* FTC v. Bay Area Bus. Council, 423 F.3d 627, 635 (7th Cir. 2005); FTC v. Amy Travel Servs., Inc., 875 F.2d 564, 573 (7th Cir. 1989); Porter & Dietsch, Inc. v. FTC, 605 F.2d 294, 309 (7th Cir. 1979); Chrysler Corp. v. FTC, 561 F.2d 357, 363 n.5 (D.C. Cir. 1977).

[91] *See* FTC v. Pantron I Corp., 33 F.3d 1088, 1102 (9th Cir. 1994); FTC v. Think Achievement Corp., 312 F.3d 258, 262 (7th Cir. 2002) (money-back guarantee "does not sanitize a fraud").

[92] *Deception Policy Statement*, 103 F.T.C. at 181. Context is critical in this regard. The commission probably would distinguish between a subjective product claim ("ABC Coffee tastes great") and an objective representation ("In a recent survey, 78% of consumers preferred the taste of ABC Coffee over XYZ Coffee.").

seriously."[93] Compared to objective product claims, which "contain affirmative information about a product's attributes, performance or efficacy and require some level of substantiation in support," consumers would not expect puffery to be backed up by evidence.[94] Especially when a product is inexpensive, frequently purchased, and easy for consumers to evaluate on their own, advertisers who depend on repeat business will have little motivation to mislead the buying public. When "market incentives place strong constraints on the likelihood of deception," the commission will be disinclined to take law enforcement action.[95]

"The Representation, Omission, or Practice Must Be Material."[96]

To be actionable, a misleading claim must be material. A misrepresentation is material if it involves information that is important to consumers, and therefore is likely to affect their decision whether to buy or use a product or service.[97] Proof of actual consumer injury, however, is not required.[98]

FTC considers three categories of information to be presumptively material: 1) express claims; 2) implied claims, where there is evidence that the seller intended to make such a claim; and 3) claims that involve health, safety, or other "central characteristics" that would be relevant to reasonable consumers, e.g., the efficacy, purpose, cost, performance, ingredients, or quality of a product or service.[99] Under the FTC Act, the omission of material information may be deceptive. The commission has made clear that an advertisement is actionable under section 5 if it fails to disclose information that is necessary to prevent a claim from misleading consumers.[100]

Applying FTC's Unfairness Standard

In addition to deceptive acts or practices, section 5 of the FTC Act prohibits acts and practices that are "unfair." FTC's 1980 *Policy Statement on Unfairness (Unfairness Policy*

---

93 Removatron Int'l Corp., 111 F.T.C. 206, 296 (1988) ("An advertisement touting a foreign sports car as 'the sexiest European,' for example, fits into this category."), *aff'd*, 884 F.2d 1489 (1st Cir. 1989).

94 *Id.*

95 *Deception Policy Statement*, 103 F.T.C. at 181.

96 *Id.*

97 *Id.* at n.45. *See* Novartis Corp. v. FTC, 223 F.3d 783, 786 (D.C. Cir. 2000).

98 *See* Spiegel, Inc. v. FTC, 494 F.2d 59, 62 (7th Cir. 1974); Cliffdale Assocs., 103 F.T.C. 110, 166 n.11 (1982).

99 *Id.* at 182-83. *See* Novartis Corp. v. FTC, 223 F.3d at 786; Kraft, Inc. v. FTC, 970 F.2d 311, 322 (7th Cir. 1992); Thompson Med. Co., 104 F.T.C. 648, 816-17 (1984), *aff'd*, 791 F.2d 189 (D.C. Cir. 1986); Am. Home Prods. Corp., 98 F.T.C. 136, 368-69 (1981) ("The very fact that AHP sought to distinguish its products from aspirin strongly implies that knowledge of the true ingredients of those products would be material to purchasers."), *aff'd*, 695 F.2d 681 (3d Cir. 1982). *See* e.g., Brain-Pad, Inc., FTC Dkt. No. C-4375 (Aug. 16, 2012) (challenging unsubstantiated claims that company's mouth guards reduced the risk of sports-related concussions); Prince Lionheart, Inc., 138 F.T.C. 403 (2004) (consent order) (challenging unsubstantiated claims for baby stroller accessory advertised to repel mosquitos and protect children from West Nile Virus).

100 *See, e.g.,* Campbell Soup Co., 115 F.T.C. 778 (1992) (consent order) (challenging company's failure to disclose sodium content as a violation of section 5 in light of representations that product was heart-healthy and low in fat and cholesterol); N. Am. Philips Corp., 111 F.T.C. 139 (1988) (challenging company's failure to disclose that a water filter emitted a potentially hazardous chemical into drinking water as a violation of section 5 in light of representations that the device cleaned water).

Statement) outlines the agency's approach to unfairness.[101] According to the *Policy Statement*, an advertisement is unfair if: 1) it causes or is likely to cause substantial consumer injury; 2) that is not reasonably avoidable by consumers, themselves; and 3) that is not outweighed by countervailing benefits to consumers or competition.[102] In 1994, Congress incorporated this three-prong test into the FTC Act.[103]

International Harvester, the first major case to apply the commission's 1980 *Unfairness Policy Statement*, illustrates the narrow, but important, scope of FTC's unfairness authority. There, an ALJ held that the company's failure to disclose the potential risk of explosion from "fuel geysering" on its tractors was deceptive and unfair. The commission reversed the finding that the practice was deceptive. It ruled that the incidence of fuel geysering was so low—of the 1.3 million gasoline-powered tractors manufactured by International Harvester during the relevant period, only 12 episodes of fuel geysering resulted in bodily injury—that it was not a deceptive omission for the company to fail to disclose the hazard.[104] The commission agreed, however, that it was an unfair practice. Applying the first prong of the three-part test for unfairness—that the practice causes or is likely to cause substantial consumer injury—the commission held that, although the risk of fuel geysering was small, the injury caused was substantial. Applying the second prong—that the injury not be reasonably avoidable by consumers, themselves—the agency noted that consumers had no way to learn about the safety risk on their own. Applying the third prong—that the risk of injury to consumers from the practice is not outweighed by countervailing benefits to consumers or competition—FTC held that the cost to the company to warn consumers about the safety risk was insignificant.[105] Thus, the commission agreed that the company had engaged in an unfair practice in violation of section 5, but only after the agency applied the three-part cost-benefit analysis mandated by the *Unfairness Policy Statement*.

The commission rarely uses its unfairness jurisdiction to challenge false and misleading advertising claims, including those relating to FDA-regulated products, but, instead, relies on its authority to prohibit deceptive representations or material omissions. The commission relies on its unfairness authority to challenge practices, other than representations and omissions, that cause substantial consumer injury. FTC has, however, used its unfairness

---

[101] Letter from the FTC to Hon. Wendell Ford and Hon. John Danforth, Committee on Commerce, Science and Transportation, United States Senate, Commission Statement of Policy on the Scope of Consumer Unfairness Jurisdiction (Dec. 17, 1980), reprinted in In re Int'l Harvester Co.,104 F.T.C. 949, 1070, 1074 n.3 (1984) (*Unfairness Policy Statement*).

[102] Before issuing the *Unfairness Policy Statement*, the commission considered the following factors in determining whether a practice was unfair: 1) whether it injured consumers; 2) whether it violated established public policy; and 3) whether it was unethical or unscrupulous. *See Unfairness Policy Statement*, 104 F.T.C. at 1070, 1072 nn. 8-9; FTC v. Sperry & Hutchinson Co., 405 U.S. 223, 244-45 n.5 (1972).

[103] 15 U.S.C. § 45(n) provides:

The Commission shall have no authority under this section or Section 57a of this title to declare unlawful an act or practice on the grounds that such act or practice is unfair unless the act or practice causes or is likely to cause substantial injury to consumers which is not reasonably avoidable by consumers themselves and not outweighed by countervailing benefits to consumers or to competition. In determining whether an act or practice is unfair, the Commission may consider established public policies as evidence to be considered with all other evidence. Such public policy considerations may not serve as a primary basis for such determination.

[104] Int'l Harvester, 104 F.T.C. at 1063.

[105] *Id.* at 1065.

authority to challenge such practices as breach of contract,[106] unauthorized billing,[107] certain deceptive online practices,[108] and the failure to disclose safety risks posed by a product.[109] In addition, the commission has used both its deception and unfairness authorities to challenge companies' deceptive privacy promises and failure to employ reasonable and appropriate security measures to protect personal information, including health-related data.[110]

As FTC noted in *International Harvester*, "The Commission's unfairness jurisdiction provides a more general basis for action against acts or practices which cause significant consumer injury. This part of our jurisdiction is broader than that involving deception, and the standards for its exercise are correspondingly more stringent."[111] In comparing its unfairness and deception authorities, the commission has stated, "[t]o put the point another way, unfairness is the set of general principles of which deception is a particularly well-

---

[106]   *See, e.g.*, Orkin Exterminating Co., 108 F.T.C. 263 (1986), *aff'd*, 849 F. 2d 1354 (11th Cir. 1988) (upholding ruling that Orkin's action in unilaterally raising fees on certain contracts that had provided for a lifetime fixed annual inspection fee met FTC's test for unfairness); FTC v. Certified Merchant Servs., Ltd., No. 4:02CV44 (E.D. Tex. Jan. 15, 2004) (stipulated final order) (challenging as unfair defendant's unilateral breach of contract by insisting on compliance with additional terms that were not part of the original contract).

[107]   *See* e.g., FTC v. AT&T Mobility, LLC, No. 1:14-cv-3227-HLM (N.D. Ga. Oct. 8, 2014) (stipulated order) ($80 million settlement for cramming of unauthorized charges onto mobile phone bills); Google, Inc., FTC Dkt. No. C-4499 (Sept. 11, 2014) (consent order) (at least $19 million settlement for charging consumers for children's in-app purchases without account holder's authorization); Apple, Inc., FTC Dkt. No. C-4444 (Jan. 15, 2014) (consent order) (at least $32.5 million for charging consumers for children's in-app purchases without account holder's authorization).

[108]   *See, e.g.*, Aaron's, Inc., FTC Dkt. No. C-4442 (Oct. 22, 2013) (consent order) (challenging rent-to-own franchisor's role in using undisclosed webcams and location tracking software to monitor users of rented computers); Zango, Inc., FTC Dkt. No. C-4186 (Mar. 9, 2007) (consent order) (alleging that it was an unfair practice for a company to install on consumers' computers, without their knowledge or authorization, adware that consumers could not reasonably identify, locate, or remove); FTC v. Zuccarini, No. 01-CV-4854 (E.D. Pa. May 24, 2002) (stipulated final order) (challenging the unfair practice of "mousetrapping," whereby defendant used consumers' Internet connections to take control of their computers, and forced them to view dozens of websites advertising products such as online gambling, psychic services, and adult entertainment).

[109]   *See, e.g.*, Beck's, N. Am. Inc., 127 F.T.C. 379 (1999) (consent order) (alleging an alcohol company's depictions of unsafe behavior in advertising to be an unfair trade practice); Consumer Direct, Inc., 113 F.T.C. 923 (1990) (consent order) (alleging a company's failure to disclose the substantial risk of physical injury posed by its exercise device to be an unfair trade practice). *See also* FTC Sends Warning Letters to Marketers of Caffeinated Alcohol Drinks (Nov. 17, 2011), *available at* http://www.ftc.gov/opa/2010/11/alcohol.shtm (citing incidents suggesting that alcohol containing added caffeine presents unusual risks to health and safety and warning companies that marketing of such beverages may constitute an unfair or deceptive practice, in violation of the FTC Act).

[110]   *See* GMR Transcription Servs., Inc., C-4482 (Jan. 31, 2014) (consent order) (alleging that inadequate data security measures of medical transcription company unfairly exposed consumers' personal information—including medical histories and examination notes—on the Internet); Accretive Health, Inc., FTC Dkt. No. C-4432 (consent order) (Dec. 31, 2013) (alleging that inadequate data security measures of medical billing services unfairly exposed sensitive consumer information to the risk of theft or misuse); CBR Systems, Inc., 155 F.T.C. 841 (consent order) (2013) (alleging that cord blood company's inadequate security practices contributed to a breach that exposed Social Security, credit, and debit card numbers of nearly 300,000 consumers); Rite Aid Corp., 150 F.T.C. 694 (consent order) (2010) (alleging that company's failure to implement reasonable procedures for securely disposing of personal information was an unfair trade practice); CVS Caremark Corp., FTC Docket No. C-4259 (Feb. 18, 2009) (consent order) (same). *See also* Health Breach Notification Rule, 16 C.F.R. pt. 318 (2014) (requiring vendors of personal health records and related entities not covered by HIPAA to notify consumers and others when the security of individually identifiable health information has been breached).

[111]   *Id.* at 1060.

:stablished and streamlined subset."[112] Thus, one primary difference between unfairness ınalysis and deception analysis is that deception analysis does not require a cost-benefit :alculation, but assumes that, when a material falsehood or omission exists, there are rarely, f ever, any countervailing benefits.

FTC-FDA Law Enforcement Framework

:TC and FDA share jurisdiction over the marketing of food, over-the-counter (OTC) drugs, nedical devices, and cosmetics.[113] The two agencies work closely to ensure that their :nforcement efforts are, to the fullest extent feasible, consistent and efficient. Traditionally, :TC has relied heavily on FDA's scientific expertise; and FDA has looked to FTC's expertise n marketing and consumer behavior.[114] To coordinate their efforts, a 1971 liaison ıgreement governs the division of responsibilities between the two agencies.[115] Pursuant to he agreement, which reflects a voluntary allocation of resources, as opposed to a division :f legal jurisdiction, FDA has primary responsibility for regulating the labeling of food,)TC drugs, devices, and cosmetics, and FTC has primary responsibility for regulating the ıdvertising of those products. An exception to this general division of labor is prescription irugs, over which FDA exercises primary authority over both labeling and advertising.[116] :ven in the area of prescription drug advertising, however, FTC shares with FDA its :xpertise in advertising and marketing.[117]

:or marketers accustomed to FDA's regulatory approach, FTC's law enforcement framework nay seem curious. Whereas FDA has promulgated detailed regulations relating to the ıdvertising of prescription drugs,[118] FTC has promulgated no specific rules on the advertising)f the health-related products for which it has primary responsibility. Unlike FDA, FTC ioes not approve products or pre-clear advertising claims. Whether FDA classifies a product ıs a food, an OTC drug, a device, or a dietary supplement does not legally control the :TC's analysis of the product's advertising. From FTC's perspective, the primary concern is

---

[12]   *Id.*

[13]   FTC also has used section 5 to challenge the unfair or deceptive practices in the marketing of alcoholic beverages. It coordinates those law enforcement activities with other federal and state agencies, including the Treasury Department's Alcohol and Tobacco Tax and Trade Bureau (TTB). *See, e.g.,* Phusion Products, LLC, FTC Dkt. No. C-4382 (Oct. 3, 2011 and July 25, 2015) (consent order).

[14]   An agency of attorneys and economists, FTC does not employ an in-house scientific staff. Rather, it relies on the scientific and medical expertise of FDA, the National Institutes of Health, the Centers for Disease Control and Prevention, and other federal and state agencies, as well as experts in academia and the private sector.

[15]   Working Agreement Between FTC and FDA, 4 Trade Reg. Rep. (CCH) ¶ 9.850.01 (1971) (updating and replacing prior agreements of 1954 and 1958).

[16]   *See* 21 U.S.C. § 352(a).

[17]   *See, e.g.,* In re Request for Comments on Agency Draft Guidance Documents Regarding Consumer-Directed Promotion, FDA Dkt. No. 2004D-0042, Comments of the Staff of the Bureau of Consumer Protection, Bureau of Economics, and Office of Policy Planning of the Federal Trade Commission (May 10, 2004), *available at* http://www.ftc.gov/opa/2004/05/dtcdrugs.shtm; In re Request for Comments on Consumer-Directed Promotion, FDA Dkt. No. 2003N-0344, Comments of the Staff of the Bureau of Consumer Protection, Bureau of Economics, and Office of Policy Planning of the Federal Trade Commission (Dec. 1, 2003), *available at* http://www.ftc.gov/opa/2003/12/fdadtc.shtm.

[18]   21 C.F.R. § 202.1 (2010).

that advertising claims for a product be substantiated by competent and reliable scientific evidence, regardless of the content of the claims or FDA's regulatory classification of the product.[119]

FDA's expertise is still relevant to FTC. The commission accords substantial weight to FDA's scientific determinations, and has specifically held, for example, that FDA final monographs for OTC drugs may form a reasonable basis for health-related advertising claims.[120] In appropriate circumstances, FTC has approved for an OTC drug "safe harbor" provisions expressly permitting companies to make advertising claims that FDA has approved under a final monograph or a new drug application. For example, in settling cases challenging deceptive health claims, commission orders often expressly provide: "Nothing in this order shall prohibit respondents from making any representation for any drug that is permitted in labeling for such drug under any tentative final or final standard promulgated by the [FDA], or under any new drug application approved by the [FDA]."[121] Similarly, FTC has made clear that order provisions shall not be construed to prohibit advertisers from "making any representation for any product that is specifically permitted in labeling for such product by regulations promulgated by the [FDA] pursuant to the Nutrition Labeling and Education Act of 1990."[122] On the basis of more recent monographs, FTC has also modified earlier orders.[123] Conversely, marketers who disseminate claims expressly disallowed by an FDA monograph can expect their advertisements to face careful FTC scrutiny.

A substantial change in FDA's approach to health claims for food resulted principally from the Nutrition Labeling and Education Act of 1990 (NLEA).[124] Soon after FDA issued regulations implementing the NLEA, FTC promulgated its *Enforcement Policy Statement on Food Advertising* (*Food Policy Statement*).[125] An overarching theme of the *Food Policy Statement* is FTC's recognition of the importance of consistent treatment of health claims in advertising and on labels, and its consequent goal of harmonizing its approach with FDA's to the extent feasible under the FTC Act. This policy serves two important interests: 1) making it easier for consumers to make informed purchase decisions by having one consistent set of descriptors on labels and in advertisements; and 2) simplifying compliance for food marketers, who must follow both FDA labeling standards and FTC advertising standards.

---

[119] *See, e.g.,* L'Oreal USA, Inc., FTC Dkt. No. C-4489 (June 30, 2014) (consent order) (alleging that company failed to have appropriate scientific substantiation to support advertising claims for Génifique and Youth Code skin care products); The Dannon Company, Inc., 151 F.T.C. 62 (2011) (consent order) (alleging that company failed to have appropriate scientific substantiation to support advertising claims for Activia yogurt and DanActive dairy drink).

[120] *See* Thompson Med. Co., 104 F.T.C. at 826.

[121] *See, e.g.,* Elation Therapy, Inc., FTC Dkt. No. C-4204 (Nov. 7, 2007) (consent order) (challenging claims that progesterone product was effective in preventing or reducing the risk of osteoporosis and cancer); Hi-Health Supermarket Corp., 139 F.T.C. 319 (2005) (consent order) (challenging claims that vitamin product could restore vision lost from macular degeneration or eliminate floaters).

[122] *See, e.g.,* Interstate Bakeries Corp., 133 F.T.C. 687 (2002) (consent order) (challenging claims that Wonder Bread containing added calcium could improve children's brain function and memory); Conopco, Inc., 123 F.T.C. 135 (1997) (consent order) (challenging claims about the nutritional content and health benefits of margarine and a spread).

[123] *See, e.g.,* Chesebrough-Ponds, Inc., 105 F.T.C. 567 (1985) (modifying, on the basis of FDA's 1983 monograph on skin protectants, a 1963 order against the marketer of Vaseline petroleum jelly).

[124] Pub. L. No. 101-535, 104 Stat. 2353 (1990) (codified in part at 21 U.S.C. § 343(i), (q), and (r)).

[125] 59 Fed. Reg. at 28,388.

Since promulgating the *Food Policy Statement*, FTC has been consistent in applying to advertising the definitions of nutrient content descriptors promulgated by FDA for labeling.[126] The *Food Policy Statement* left open the possibility that, in certain limited instances, FTC might allow in advertising a carefully qualified claim that had not been authorized by FDA for labeling. The commission has made clear, however, that such a claim must be supported by strong scientific evidence, and that an advertiser must take the utmost care in its wording and presentation.[127]

FDA experienced another major change to its enforcement regimen with the enactment of the Dietary Supplement Health and Education Act of 1994 (DSHEA).[128] Under DSHEA, the marketers of dietary supplements are specifically allowed to make two kinds of health-related representations on labeling: 1) "health claims"; and 2) "statements of nutritional support." Health claims—representations about the relationship between a nutrient and a disease or health-related condition—are permitted only if they have been authorized by FDA.[129] In contrast to health claims, "structure/function" claims—a subgroup within the broader category of "statements of nutritional support"—are representations about a dietary supplement's effect on the structure or function of the body for the maintenance of good health and nutrition. Structure/function claims are not subject to FDA pre-authorization, and a marketer may make such a claim in labeling if it notifies FDA and includes an FDA-mandated disclaimer.[130]

FDA's regulatory differentiation between "structure/function" claims and "health" claims, however, is not a legally definitive distinction under section 5 of the FTC Act. FTC has expressly cautioned advertisers that statements intended to convey a representation about a product's effect on a normal structure or function of the body may, in fact, convey to reasonable consumers an implied claim that the product is beneficial for the treatment of a disease. For dietary supplements and any other products, what matters to FTC is how reasonable consumers interpret advertising claims. Thus, DSHEA did not alter FTC's approach to truth in advertising, a conclusion emphasized in FTC's 1998 staff publication, *Dietary Supplements: An Advertising Guide for Industry*.[131] As the *Dietary Supplement Guide*

---

[126] *See, e.g.*, Pizzeria Uno Corp., 123 F.T.C. 1038 (1997) (consent order) (challenging deceptive low-fat representations for Thinzetta pizzas); Mrs. Fields Cookies, Inc., 121 F.T.C. 599 (1996) (consent order) (challenging deceptive low-fat claims for cookies); The Dannon Co., 121 F.T.C. 136 (1996) (consent order) (challenging deceptive low-fat, low-calorie, and "lower in fat than ice cream" claims for Pure Indulgence frozen yogurt); Häagen-Dazs Co., 119 F.T.C. 762 (1995) (consent order) (challenging deceptive low-fat representations for Häagen-Dazs frozen yogurt); Eskimo Pie Corp., 120 F.T.C. 312 (1995) (consent order) (challenging low-calorie claims for Sugar Freedom products).

[127] *See* FTC, *Dietary Supplements: An Advertising Guide for Industry* at 6-7 (1998) (*Dietary Supplement Guide*), *available at* www.ftc.gov/bcp/conline/pubs/buspubs/dietsupp.pdf. This plain-language guide describes basic principles of FTC advertising law, and provides hypothetical examples from the dietary supplement industry to illustrate how these principles apply in practice.

[128] Pub. L. No. 103-417, 108 Stat. 4325 (1994) (codified as amended in scattered sections of 21 U.S.C.).

[129] For a comprehensive discussion of FDA's treatment of health claims, including qualified health claims, *see supra* Chapter 6.

[130] *See* 21 U.S.C. § 343(r)(6). This section of DSHEA also requires that structure/function claims in labeling be substantiated and not misleading. *See also* Certain Types of Statements for Dietary Supplement, 21 C.F.R. § 101.93 (2007); Regulations of Statements Made for Dietary Supplements Concerning the Effect of the Product on the Structure or Function of the Body, 65 Fed. Reg. 1000, 1034-35 (Jan. 6, 2000); Food Labeling: Nutrient Content Claims, Health Claims, and Statements of Nutritional Support for Dietary Supplements, 62 Fed. Reg. 49,859, 49,860, 49,861, & 49,864 (Sept. 23, 1997).

[131] *Dietary Supplement Guide, supra* note 127.

makes clear, marketers remain free to highlight in their advertising virtually any truthful and non-deceptive health claim they wish, as long as they possess what FTC considers to be "competent and reliable scientific evidence" to support their representations.[132]

One area that demonstrates the two agencies' close coordination, but independent legal authority, is the regulation of weight loss products. For example, in 2011, FTC and FDA staff sent joint Warnings Letters to marketers of purportedly homeopathic weight loss products containing human chrorionic gonadotropin (HCG).[133] The letters warned marketers that their products were unapproved new drugs in violation of sections 301 and 505 of the Federal Food, Drug, and Cosmetic Act (FDCA)[134] and misbranded in violation of sections 503 and 301 of the Act.[135] In addition, the letters raised concerns that the companies' advertising claims were unsubstantiated, in violation of the FTC Act. FTC followed up by filing law enforcement actions against marketers that did not heed the joint Warning Letters.[136]

In addition to bringing actions jointly with FDA, FTC has independently brought hundreds of lawsuits challenging false or deceptive weight loss and fitness claims. The agency has challenged weight loss representations for herbal treatments, dietary supplements, and other products ingested by consumers;[137] diet programs;[138] fitness equipment;[139] and purported slimming creams.[140] For example, separate law enforcement actions against

---

[132]   See infra p. 907.

[133]   See FDA, FTC act to remove "homeopathic" HCG weight loss products from the market (Dec. 6, 2011), available at http://www.fda.gov/NewsEvents/Newsroom/PressAnnouncements/ucm282334.htm.

[134]   21 U.S.C. §§ 331 and 355.

[135]   21 U.S.C. §§ 353 and 331.

[136]   See, e.g., FTC v. HCG Platinum LLC, No. 2:14-CV-00258-CW (D. Utah Dec. 11, 2014) (stipulated final judgment) (challenging claims that product marketed as homeopathic HCG drops would cause consumers to rapidly lose substantial weight); FTC v. HCG Diet Direct, LLC, No. 2:14-CV-00015-NVW (D. Ariz. Jan. 7, 2014) (stipulated final judgment) (same).

[137]   See, e.g., FTC v. Applied Food Sciences, Inc., 1-14-CV-00851 (W.D. Tex. Sept. 8, 2014) (stipulated final judgment ($3.5 million monetary judgment for deceptive weight and fat loss claims for dietary supplements containing green coffee extract); FTC v. Sensa Products, LLC, No. 11CV72 (N.D. Ill. Jan. 7, 2014) (stipulated final judgment) ($26.5 million redress for deceptive weight loss claims and misleading endorsements for product sprinkled on food); United States v. Bayer Corp., No. 07-01(HAA) (D.N.J. Jan. 4, 2007) (consent decree) ($3.2 million civil penalty for deceptive weight loss claims for One-A-Day WeightSmart, disseminated in violation of an earlier FTC order); TrimSpa, Inc., FTC Dkt. No. C-4185 (Jan. 4, 2007) (consent order) ($1.5 million redress for deceptive claims that hoodia gordonii enables users to lose substantial weight by suppressing the appetite).

[138]   See, e.g., United States v. Jason Pharms., Inc., No. 1:12-CV-01476 (D.D.C. Sept. 10, 2012) (consent decree) ($3.7 million civil penalty from subsidiary of Medifast for violations of FTC order regarding marketing of weight loss programs).

[139]   See, e.g., United States v. Icon Health & Fitness, Inc., No. 1:14-CV-1578 (D.D.C. Sept. 14, 2014) (stipulated order) ($3 million civil penalty for deceptive reduction and fitness claims for ab GLIDER for violation of 1997 FTC Order); FTC v. v. Fitness Brands, No. 1:12-CV-23065-CMA (S.D. Fla. Aug. 23, 2012) (stipulated final judgment) (between $15 million and $25 million redress for deceptive weight loss and fitness claims for Ab Circle Pro).

[140]   See, e.g., L'Occitane, Inc., FTC Dkt. No. C-4445 (Jan. 7, 2014) (consent order) (challenging deceptive slimming claims for Almond Beautiful Shape and Almond Shaping Delight skin creams); Beiersdorf, Inc., 152 F.T.C. 414 (2011) (challenging deceptive slimming claims for Nivea My Silhouette!).

Reebok International Ltd.[141] and *Skechers U.S.A., Inc.*[142] resulted in settlements totaling $65 million for deceptive muscle strengthening and toning claims for EasyTone and Shape-ups shoes.

FTC's Substantiation Doctrine

The touchstone for FTC's truth-in-advertising enforcement is the requirement of substantiation. According to FTC's *Policy Statement Regarding Advertising Substantiation* (*Substantiation Policy Statement*), advertisers must have substantiation for all objective advertising claims before disseminating them to consumers.[143] This requirement is based on the premise that an objective claim about a product carries with it an express or implied representation that the advertiser possesses a "reasonable basis" for the claim.[144] Reviewing courts apply the "substantial evidence" standard to commission findings of whether companies possess appropriate substantiation for the advertising claims they convey.[145] When conducting that inquiry, courts are "mindful of the Commission's 'special expertise' in determining what sort of substantiation is necessary to assure that advertising is not deceptive."[146]

Unlike the FDCA, FTC law does not differentiate among food, OTC drugs, medical devices, cosmetics, dietary supplements, and other health-related products. The kind of substantiation required under the law depends on the nature of the advertising claim, not on FDA's classification of the product advertised. An evaluation of FTC's approach to claims for cosmetics is illustrative. As a general rule, the agency does not challenge subjective representations related to beauty or appearance. However, marketers are, with increasing frequency, making advertising claims for cosmetics that require scientific substantiation. For example, in *L'Oreal USA, Inc.*,[147] the agency alleged that the company had made false and unsubstantiated claims that Génifique and Youth Code skin creams provided anti-aging benefits by targeting users' genes. Similarly, in *Beiersdorf, Inc.*,[148] FTC challenged claims that Nivea My Silhouette! skin cream can significantly reduce users' body size.

---

[141]   No. 1:11-CV-02046-DCN (N.D. Ohio Sept. 28, 2011) (stipulated final judgment) ($25 million redress for deceptive claims regarding the ability of Reebok EasyTone and RunTone shoes to provide extra toning and strengthening of leg and buttock muscles). *See also* Wacoal Am., Inc., C-4496 (Sept. 29, 2014) (consent order) ($1.3 million for deceptive reduction claims for caffeine-infused shapewear).

[142]   No 1:12-CV-01214-JG (N.D. Ohio May 16, 2012) (stipulated final judgment) ($40 million redress for deceptive claims that Skechers Shape-ups and other shoes would help people lose weight, and strengthen and tone their buttocks, legs, and abdominal muscles).

[143]   *Policy Statement Regarding Advertising Substantiation, appended* to Thompson Med. Co., 104 F.T.C. at 839.

[144]   *Id.* ("[W]e reaffirm our commitment to the underlying legal requirement of advertising substantiation—that advertisers and ad agencies have a reasonable basis for advertising claims before they are disseminated.").

[145]   POM Wonderful, LLC v. FTC, slip op. at 22 (*quoting* Removatron Int'l Corp. v. FTC, 884 F.2d 1489, 1497 (1st Cir. 1989)).

[146]   POM Wonderful, LLC v. FTC, slip op. at 22 (*quoting* Thompson Med. Co., 791 F.2d at 196).

[147]   FTC Dkt. No. C-4489 (June 30, 2014) (consent order). *See also* Foru Int'l Corp., FTC Dkt. No. C-4457 (consent order) (Jan. 7, 2014) (challenging deceptive claims for skin care and other products advertised as customized to each consumer's unique genetic profile based on assessment of DNA obtained from cheek swab); Genelink, Inc., FTC Dkt. C-4456 (Jan. 7, 2014) (consent order) (same).

[148]   152 F.T.C. 414 (consent order).

If an advertiser makes an express or implied representation about the level of substantiation it possesses, the advertiser must, in fact, possess the specified level of substantiation.[14] An express reference to a study conveys to consumers the implied claims that the study is methodologically sound and that the results are statistically significant.[150] In addition marketers who use phrases such as "tests prove," "doctors recommend," and "studies show"—called "establishment" claims, in FTC parlance[151]—must possess at least the advertised level of substantiation."[152] Visual images, such as the prominent display of medical literature scientific charts and graphs, or the depiction of a person in a white lab coat, may convey a claim of scientific foundation by implication.[153]

If an advertisement makes no express claim about the level of underlying scientific support FTC determines the requisite level of substantiation by applying what have come to be known as the "*Pfizer* factors."[154] These six factors, first articulated in the *Pfizer* case but later adopted in the commission's *Substantiation Policy Statement*, are: the type of product, the type of claim, the consequences of a false claim, the benefits of a truthful claim, the cost of developing substantiation for the claim, and the amount of substantiation experts in the field believe is reasonable.[155]

The first two *Pfizer* factors—the type of product and the type of claim—reflect FTC's reasoning that consumers assume that health-related representations are supported by scientific evidence.[156] Furthermore, representations for health-related products are often "credence claims," representations that may be "difficult or impossible for consumers to evaluate for themselves."[157] Consumers are able to judge the accuracy of an advertiser's claim that its product has a pleasing taste or convenient packaging, but they are not in a position to evaluate representations about cardiovascular health or cancer-risk reduction.[158]

---

[149] Removatron Int'l Corp., 884 F.2d at 1492 n.3.

[150] *Dietary Supplement Guide, supra* note 127, Example 1. *See also* Am. Home Prods. Corp., 98 F.T.C. at 377.

[151] Removatron Int'l Corp., 884 F.2d at 1492 n.3 ("'Establishment' claims are statements to the effect that scientific tests establish that a product works.").

[152] *Id. See* Removatron Int'l Corp., 111 F.T.C. at 297; Thompson Med. Co., 104 F.T.C. at 814. "The question whether 'a claim of establishment is in fact made is a question of fact the evaluation of which is within the FTC's peculiar expertise.'" POM Wonderful, LLC v. FTC, slip op. at 18 (quoting Thompson Med. Co., 791 F.2d at 194).

[153] *See* Am. Home Prods. Corp., 98 F.T.C. at 375 n.28; Bristol-Myers Co., 102 F.T.C. 21, 321 (1983), *aff'd*, 738 F.2d 554 (2d Cir. 1984).

[154] The factors are derived from Pfizer, Inc., 81 F.T.C. 23 (1972).

[155] *Substantiation Policy Statement*, 104 F.T.C. at 840.

[156] *Id. See also* Porter & Dietsch, Inc. v. FTC, 605 F.2d at 302 n.5 ("[T]here may be some types of claims for some types of products for which the only reasonable basis, in fairness and in the expectations of consumers, would be a valid scientific or medical basis. The case at bar, in which the representations concern the efficacy of a drug, is such a case.") (citations omitted).

[157] Thompson Med. Co., 104 F.T.C. at 822; Sterling Drug, Inc. v. FTC, 741 F.2d 1146, 1155 (9th Cir. 1984) (observing that "it is difficult for consumers to compare analgesic products effectively, so they are more likely to give credence to advertising claims"); Am. Home Prods. Corp., 695 F.2d at 698 ("Another consideration in favor of holding comparative effectiveness and safety claims for analgesics to high standards of substantiation is the difficulty for the average consumer to evaluate such claims through personal experience, and the consequent tenacity of advertising-induced beliefs about superiority.").

[158] *See, e.g.*, POM Wonderful, LLC v. FTC, slip op. at 18-27 (upholding commission decision that companies deceptively advertised that POM Wonderful 100% Pomegranate Juice and POMx supplements treat heart disease by decreasing arterial plaque, lowering blood pressure, or improving blood flow to the heart, and prevent or reduce the risk of prostate cancer by prolonging prostate-specific antigen doubling time).

The third *Pfizer* factor—the consequences of a false claim—reflects FTC's interest in protecting consumers from the dangers of deceptive health claims. When health claims are false or unsubstantiated, consumer injury can take any of many forms. Often, the primary injury is financial: a company's deceptive claims induce consumers to buy products that do not perform as advertised.[159] In other cases, companies make misleading representations that their products protect consumers from known health hazards, thereby increasing the risk of injury to consumers who are lulled into a false sense of security by the deceptive representations.[160] FTC has taken action against products advertised as providing health benefits when, in fact, the use of the products actually *increased* the risk of consumer injury.[161] Courts have noted that deceptive health representations may injure consumers by inducing them to forgo proven treatments.[162] The agency has also used its unfairness authority to challenge advertisements that caused consumer injury by failing to disclose safety risks.[163]

The fourth and fifth *Pfizer* factors—the benefits of a truthful claim and the cost of developing substantiation for the claim—are often considered together "to ensure that the level of substantiation [the FTC] require[s] is not likely to deter product development or prevent consumers from being told potentially valuable information about product characteristics."[164] With regard to health claims, however, the commission has never exempted advertisers from the legal requirement of substantiation even where the requisite level of research would be expensive to conduct. The cost of developing substantiation may be relevant to the nature and amount of evidence the commission may require, but it does not modify the fundamental requirement that companies substantiate their advertised claims.

The sixth *Pfizer* factor—the amount of substantiation experts in the field believe is reasonable—has been the deciding element in many FTC cases.[165] Where there is an existing standard for substantiation developed by a governmental agency or authoritative nongovernmental body, FTC accords substantial deference to that standard.[166] For objective product representations, the agency typically has required that the advertiser possess

---

[159]   *See, e.g.*, Goen Tech. Corp., Inc., FTC Dkt. C-4185 (Jan. 4, 2007) (consent order) (challenging claims that TrimSpa diet product would cause rapid and substantial weight loss); Telebrands Corp., 140 F.T.C. at 278 (finding that company's claims that Ab Force electronic belt would cause weight loss and give users well-defined abdominal muscles were deceptive).

[160]   *See, e.g.*, FTC v. Vital Living Prods., Inc., No. 3:02CV74-MU (W.D.N.C. Feb. 27, 2002) (stipulated final order) (challenging deceptive efficacy claims for a purported do-it-yourself test kit represented to detect anthrax bacteria and spores); FTC v. Medimax, Inc., No. 99-1485-CIV (M.D. Fla. Mar. 22, 2000) (stipulated final order) (challenging false representation that home HIV test kits could accurately detect HIV virus); FTC v. Cyberlinx Mktg., Inc., No. CV-S-99-1564-PMP-LRL (D. Nev. Nov. 8, 1999) (stipulated final order) (same).

[161]   *See, e.g.*, FTC v. Western Botanicals, Inc., No. CIV.S-01-1332 DFL GGH (E.D. Cal. July 1, 2001) (stipulated final order) (challenging the health risks of product containing comfrey); Panda Herbal Int'l, Inc., 132 F.T.C. 125 (2001) (consent order) (challenging the health risks of a product containing St. John's Wort when advertised to consumers taking prescription drugs for HIV/AIDS).

[162]   *See, e.g.*, FTC v. QT, Inc., 512 F.3d 858, 863 (7th Cir. 2008) ("Deceit such as the tall tales that defendants told about the Q-Ray Ionized Bracelet will lead some consumers to avoid treatments that cost less and do more; the lies will lead others to pay too much for pain relief or otherwise interfere with the matching of remedies to medical conditions.").

[163]   *See* Consumer Direct, Inc, 113 F.T.C. 923 (1990) (challenging as an unfair practice a company's failure to disclose the risk that the spring on the Gut Buster exercise device could break, thereby injuring consumer).

[164]   Removatron, 111 F.T.C. at 306 n.20.

[165]   *See, e.g., id.* at 307 n.20; Thompson Med., 104 F.T.C. at 825.

[166]   *Dietary Supplement Guide* at 9.

"competent and reliable evidence." For representation about a product's "health benefits, safety, performance, or efficacy"—regardless of whether FDA classifies the product as a food, OTC drug, dietary supplement, device, or cosmetic—the FTC standard is "competent and reliable *scientific* evidence."[167]

Substantiating Health Claims Under the FTC Act

Given the broad range of potential advertising claims, FTC has not promulgated a universal testing methodology adequate for substantiating all claims. Of course, when advertisers state expressly or by implication the kind of proof they have, section 5 mandates that they possess that level of substantiation. For example, in its settlement with Kellogg Co., FTC alleged that the company had expressly represented in its ads that eating a bowl of Frosted Mini-Wheats cereal for breakfast was clinically shown to improve children's attentiveness by nearly 20 percent.[168] According to the FTC's complaint, in the clinical study to which Kellogg's ads referred, only about half the children who ate the cereal showed any improvement after three hours as compared to their pre-breakfast baseline. In addition, FTC alleged that only one in seven children who ate the cereal improved in attentiveness 18 percent or more, and only about one in nine improved by 20 percent or more. Consequently, FTC challenged the representations as false.[169]

For health-related claims, FTC caselaw sheds substantial light on the factors the agency will consider in determining what comprises "competent and reliable scientific evidence." Many agency cases define that term to mean "tests, analyses, research, studies, or other evidence based on the expertise of professionals in the relevant area, that has been conducted and evaluated in an objective manner by persons qualified to do so, using procedures generally accepted in the profession to yield accurate and reliable results."[170]

In addition, in 1998, the Commission responded to the passage of DSHEA by issuing the *Dietary Supplements Guide*.[171] The *Guide* outlines a number of considerations to assist advertisers in assessing the adequacy of the scientific support for health-related claims. These considerations include the amount and type of evidence, the quality of evidence, the totality of evidence, and the relevance of the evidence to the specific representation.[172] When read in context with FTC cases, the *Guide* offers advice for all advertisers—not just those marketing dietary supplements—about how the agency will evaluate substantiation for health claims, in light of the requirement that they possess "competent and reliable scientific evidence."

---

167   *Compare* CompUSA Inc., 139 F.T.C. 357 (2005) (consent order) (requiring computer company to possess "competent and reliable evidence" to support representations about when consumers *will* receive requested rebates) with Conopco, Inc., 121 F.T.C. 131 (1997) (consent order) (requiring food company to possess "competent and reliable scientific evidence" to support representations that margarine or any other spread will help to reduce the risk of heart disease").

168   Kellogg Co., FTC Dkt. No. C-4262 (July 31, 2009) (consent order).

169   *Id.* (Compl. ¶¶ 7-10).

170   *See, e.g.*, Telebrands, 140 F.T.C. at 459; United States v. Bayer Corp., No. 07-01 (HAA) (D.N.J. Jan. 4, 2007) (consent decree); KFC Corp., 138 F.T.C. 422 (2004) (consent order); Interstate Bakeries Corp., 133 F.T.C. 687 (2002) (consent order).

171   *See supra* note 127.

172   *Dietary Supplement Guide* at 10-18.

The Amount and Type of Evidence

In evaluating whether an advertiser's substantiation meets the "competent and reliable scientific evidence" standard, FTC has given great weight to the final *Pfizer* factor: the kind of substantiation that experts in the relevant field believe would be necessary to support the representation. Through the *Dietary Supplement Guide*, the commission has made clear that well-controlled clinical studies are the most reliable method of substantiating health claims.[173]

The number of well-controlled studies needed has been an issue of some controversy at the commission. The issue typically has arisen in the context of order provisions against companies alleged to have violated the FTC Act. For certain representations—often related to weight loss, pain relief, or the prevention or treatment of diseases or medical conditions—FTC has defined "competent and reliable scientific evidence" to require "at least two adequate and well-controlled, double-blinded clinical studies that conform to acceptable designs and protocols and are conducted by different persons, independently of each other."[174] The commission's rationale for requiring multiple studies is that the replication of research results adds to the weight of the evidence.[175]

Removatron offers some insight into how FTC determines the number of clinical trials it will require to substantiate a representation. There, an ALJ held that the advertiser needed "two adequate and well-controlled, double-blind clinical studies" to support its claim that a device could remove unwanted hair permanently. The commission upheld most of the ALJ's factual findings and legal conclusions, but substituted the more general requirement that the advertiser possess "adequate and well-controlled, double-blind clinical testing," for the specific mandate of two studies.[176] In reaching that conclusion, the commission conducted a step-by-step application of the *Pfizer* factors. Weighing the benefits of a truthful claim and the cost of developing substantiation for the claim, the commission noted that a second clinical trial would cost the company $40,000 of its annual gross revenue of only $500,000.[177] It also observed that the advertised claim—permanent removal of unwanted hair—did not raise serious health concerns.[178] In addition, the commission gave weight to expert testimony that only one well-controlled clinical test would be sufficient to substantiate the advertised claim.[179]

---

[173]   *Id.* at 10.

[174]   *See, e.g.*, Novartis, 127 F.T.C. at 726 (requiring two well-controlled clinical studies to substantiate certain analgesic claims); Viral Response Sys., Inc., 115 F.T.C. 676, 693 (1992) (consent order) (requiring two well-controlled clinical studies to substantiate cold-prevention or -cure claims); Thompson Med., 104 F.T.C. at 850.

[175]   *See, e.g.*, Thompson Med., 104 F.T.C. at 720-21 (initial decision) ("Replication is necessary because there is a potential for systematic bias and random error in any clinical trial: the methodology may be insensitive, or the wrong conclusion may be reached by sheer chance. Moreover, even an experienced investigator may use an aberrant methodology, or some unexpected flaw or anomaly in the randomized population may bias the test results. Other possible sources of systematic bias include the geographic location of the trial and idiosyncrasies in the way the data are collected.") (citations omitted).

[176]   Removatron, 111 F.T.C. at 318.

[177]   *Id.* at 306-07 n.20.

[178]   *Id.*

[179]   *Id.*

Thus, in consent orders for health-related products, the kind of substantiation required by the commission to substantiate respondents' future claims has often depended on the nature of the claim conveyed to consumers. In some consent orders, the commission has defined "competent and reliable scientific evidence" as "tests, analyses, research, studies, or other evidence based on the expertise of professionals in the relevant area, that has been conducted and evaluated in an objective manner by persons qualified to do so, using procedures generally accepted in the profession to yield accurate and reliable results," without further specificity about the nature or number of clinical trials.[180] In other cases, the commission has defined "competent and reliable scientific evidence" differently for different kinds of claims. For example, in *Natural Innovations, Inc.*,[181] the commission required that pain-relief claims related to migraine headache, diverticulitis, allergies, menstrual cramps and other medical conditions be supported by competent and reliable scientific evidence defined as "adequate and well-controlled clinical testing conforming to acceptable designs and protocols and conducted by a person or persons qualified by training and experience to conduct such testing." In that same order, however, for claims related to the temporary relief of minor aches and pains, the agency defined "competent and reliable scientific evidence" by using the standard definition of "tests, analyses, research, studies, or other evidence based on the expertise of professionals in the relevant area, that has been conducted and evaluated in an objective manner by persons qualified to do so, using procedures generally accepted in the profession to yield accurate and reliable results."[182]

In recent settlements, the commission has been more specific in designating the nature and number of clinical trials required to support future claims. For example, in some cases, the definition of "competent and reliable scientific evidence" has expressly required "evidence that is sufficient in quality and quantity based on standards generally accepted in the relevant scientific fields, when considered in light of the entire body of relevant and reliable scientific evidence, to substantiate that the representation is true."[183] This additional requirement addresses the situation in which the substantiation the company relies upon to support its advertising claims, although conducted according to established protocols, achieved results that were nonetheless inconsistent with the weight of the scientific evidence in the relevant field.

In addition, for companies charged with violations of the FTC Act, the commission has added greater specificity to the amount and type of evidence required to substantiate certain representations in the future. For example, recent settlements have required such companies to possess two well-controlled clinical studies to support weight loss claims[184] and claims that a product will reduce children's sick-day absences or the duration of acute diarrhea in children up to age three.[185]

---

[180] *See, e.g.*, Unither Pharma, Inc., 136 F.T.C. 145 (2003) (consent order) (requiring marketer of nutrition bars to substantiate with competent and reliable scientific evidence claims that the product could treat, cure, or prevent cardiovascular disease or improve cardiovascular or vascular function); FTC v. Blue Stuff, Inc., No. Civ-02-1631W (W.D. Okla. Nov. 18, 2002) (stipulated final order) (requiring marketer of a topical cream to substantiate pain-relief claims with competent and reliable scientific evidence).

[181] 123 F.T.C. 698 (1997) (consent order).

[182] *Id.* at 744.

[183] *See, e.g.*, Nestlé Healthcare Nutrition, Inc., 151 F.T.C. 1 (2011) (consent order) ; FTC v. Iovate Health Sciences USA, Inc., No. 10-CV-587 (W.D.N.Y. July 29, 2010) (stipulated final order).

[184] *See* FTC v. HCG Platinum LLC, No, 2:14-CV-00258-CW (D. Utah Dec. 11, 2014) (stipulated final judgment).

[185] *See* Nestlé Healthcare Nutrition, Inc., FTC Dkt. No. C-4312 (consent order) (July 14, 2010).

In *POM Wonderful, LLC v. FTC*,[186] the United States Court of Appeals for the District of Columbia Circuit addressed the related issue of whether the commission may impose an across-the-board fencing-in requirement that an advertiser possess at least two randomized clinical trials for all health claims conveyed in future advertising. In that case, the defendants, marketers of POM Wonderful 100% Pomegranate Juice and POMx supplements, appealed a commission decision that they had deceptively advertised their products; did not have adequate support for claims that the products could treat, prevent, or reduce the risk of heart disease, prostate cancer, and erectile dysfunction; and did not have appropriate substantiation for their representations that the products were clinically proven to work.[187] As part of the fencing-in remedy, the FTC's order required POM to possess at least two randomized and controlled human clinical trials (RCTs) to support claims that any food, drug, or dietary supplement is "effective in the diagnosis, cure, mitigation, treatment, or prevention of any disease."

The D.C. Circuit upheld the commission's finding that the defendants lacked appropriate substantiation for their claims and thus had violated section 5 of the FTC Act. The court, however, modified the FTC's requirement that POM support all future disease-related claims with two RCTs.[188] The D.C. Circuit examined the order provision under *Central Hudson Gas & Electric Corporation v. Public Service Commission*,[189] the Supreme Court's "general test for commercial speech restrictions."[190] Specifically, the court held that the two-RCT requirement for all disease claims failed the *Central Hudson* test because it did not provide a "reasonable fit" with the goal of preventing deceptive claims, and could harm consumers by denying them useful, truthful information.[191]

Notably, however, the court upheld the order requirement that disease claims must be substantiated by randomized clinical testing: "Here, insofar as the Commission's order imposes a general RCT-substantiation requirement for disease claims—i.e., without regard to any particular number of RCTs—the order satisfies those tailoring components of *Central Hudson* review."[192] The court ruled that the RCT requirement "is justified by petitioners' demonstrated propensity to make deceptive representations about the health benefits of their products, and also by the expert testimony supporting the necessity of RCTs to establish causation for disease-related claims generally."[193] Furthermore, the court explicitly stated that the commission was not barred from imposing a two-RCT requirement under any circumstance, but only that it had failed on the record before the court to justify the across-the-board two-RCT requirement for all future disease claims made by POM.[194]

---

[186]   No. 13-1060 (D.C. Cir. Jan. 30, 2015).

[187]   *Id.*

[188]   *Id.* at 33.

[189]   447 U.S. 557 (1980).

[190]   POM Wonderful, LLC v. FTC, slip op. at 37.

[191]   *Id.* at 38-39 (*citing* Board of Trustees v. Fox, 492 U.S. 469, 480 (1989)).

[192]   *Id.* at 37.

[193]   *Id.* at 38.

[194]   *Id.* at 45.

Fencing-in provisions in other recent commission cases offer insights into how the FTC harmonizes its policies with those of FDA.[195] For example, in *Iovate Health Sciences*, the stipulated final order provides that for cold- and flu-related claims for drugs or dietary supplements, the product must be covered by, and in conformance with, a final or tentative OTC drug monograph promulgated by FDA or must be the subject of a new drug application for such use approved by FDA. Similarly, the order in *Nestlé Healthcare Nutrition* prohibits cold- or flu-related claims unless specifically permitted in FDA food labeling regulations.[196] In a public statement accompanying the release of *Nestlé Healthcare Nutrition*, the commission acknowledged that FDA pre-approval generally is not required to comply with the FTC Act, but noted that, in that case, the requirement was necessary to provide clearer guidance to facilitate the defendants' compliance with the order and to make the order easier to enforce.[197]

The *Iovate* and *Nestlé Healthcare Nutrition* settlements also provide insight into when a company may rely on studies conducted on other products or ingredients to substantiate its own advertising claims. For certain claims, the orders define "competent and reliable scientific evidence" as:

> at least two adequate and well-controlled human clinical studies of the product, or of an *essentially equivalent product*, conducted by different researchers, independently of each other, that conform to acceptable designs and protocols and whose results, when considered in light of the entire body of relevant and reliable scientific evidence, are sufficient to substantiate that the representation is true.[198]

The phrase "essentially equivalent product" is defined as:

---

[195] For example, the then-Director of FTC's Bureau of Consumer Protection stated:

> We are also concerned about health benefit claims for various kinds of so-called "functional foods"—claims that such foods will boost the immune system, assist with memory and brain function, boost metabolism, protect the heart, or afford other physical or mental health benefits. Advertisers need to be very careful when they venture into this realm that they have good scientific research, that they are not overstating what the research shows, *and that they are not making disease prevention or treatment claims not approved by the FDA.*

Remarks of David Vladeck at the 2009 National Advertising Division Annual Conference (Oct. 5, 2009) (emphasis added), *available at* www.ftc.gov/speeches/vladeck/091005vladecknationaladvertising.pdf.

[196] 151 F.T.C. at 12-13.

[197] *See* Analysis of Proposed Consent Order to Aid Public Comment, at 2 (July 14, 2010), *available at* http://www.ftc.gov/sites/default/files/documents/cases/2010/07/100714nestleanal.pdf. In the administrative action that preceded the appeal to the D.C. Circuit in *POM Wonderful, LLC v. FTC*, the FTC staff had urged the commission to require that POM have FDA pre-approval before making disease-related establishment and efficacy claims. The commission held that the staff's intended goal—a bright-line standard that would be easier for the FTC to enforce and would provide certainty for the respondents—was sufficiently accomplished by the requirement of two randomized clinical trials. Although the D.C. Circuit ultimately reversed the across-the-board two-RCT standard as unsupported by the record in that particular case, the question of FDA pre-approval was not before that court. In its administrative opinion in *POM*, however, the commission noted that in an exercise of its "substantial discretion to fashion relief appropriate to the circumstances of a particular case," it "may again conclude, in an appropriate case, that FDA pre-approval would be an appropriate remedy." POM Wonderful LLC, FTC Dkt. No. D-9344, slip op. at 52, n.37 (Jan. 16, 2013) (Commission Decision).

[198] Iovate Health Sciences USA, Inc., Stipulated Final Order at 7; Nestlé Healthcare Nutrition, Inc., 151 F.T.C. at 13.

a product that contains the identical ingredients, except for inactive ingredients (e.g., inactive binders, flavors, preservatives, colors, fillers, excipients), in the same form and dosage, and with the same route of administration (e.g., orally, sublingually), as the covered product; provided that the covered product may contain additional ingredients if reliable scientific evidence generally accepted by experts in the field demonstrates that the amount and combination of additional ingredients is unlikely to impede or inhibit the effectiveness of the ingredients in the essentially equivalent product.[199]

The orders establish that the burden of proving that a product satisfies the definition of "essentially equivalent product" rests with the advertiser.[200]

Another substantiation-related provision that has been included in recent commission orders is the requirement that the respondents retain all the data on which they rely to substantiate any claim covered by the order.[201] If the test was conducted or funded by the company or its affiliates, including suppliers or manufacturers of the product, the company must preserve and secure all underlying or supporting data and documents generally accepted by experts in the field as relevant to an assessment of the test, including:

• All protocols and protocol amendments, reports, articles, write-ups, or other accounts of the results of the test, and including drafts reviewed by the test sponsor or any other person not employed by the research entity;

• All documents relating to recruitment; randomization; instructions (including oral instructions) to participants; and participant compliance;

• Documents sufficient to identify all test participants, including those who did not complete the test; all communications with participants; all raw data collected from participants; source documents for such data; data dictionaries; and any case report forms;

• All documents referring or relating to any statistical analysis of any test data, including pretest analysis, intent-to-treat analysis, or between-group, and

• All documents relating to test sponsorship, including contracts and communications between any sponsor and any researchers.[202]

These record-retention requirements do not apply to tests conducted by unaffiliated third parties and published in a peer-reviewed journal in a form that includes sufficient information for experts to assess the test's reliability.[203]

---

[199] Iovate Health Sciences USA, Inc., Stipulated Final Order at 4; Nestlé Healthcare Nutrition, Inc., 151 F.T.C. at 12.

[200] Iovate Health Sciences USA, Inc., Stipulated Final Order at 7; Nestlé Healthcare Nutrition, Inc., 151 F.T.C. at 13.

[201] I-Health, Inc. & Martek Biosciences Corp., FTC Dkt. No.C-4486 (June 9, 2014) (consent order); FTC v. Applied Food Sciences, Inc., 1-14-CV-00851 (W.D. Tex. Sept. 8, 2014) (stipulated order); Wacoal Am., Inc., FTC Dkt. No. C-4496 (Sept. 29, 2014) (consent order).

[202] I-Health, Inc., and Martek Sciences, FTC Dkt. No. C-4486, Final Consent Order at 5-6; FTC v. Applied Food Sciences, Inc., Stipulated Final Order at 14-16; Wacoal, Inc., FTC Dkt. No. C-4496, Final Consent Order at 6.

[203] Id.

Depending on the circumstances, FTC may consider results of animal and in vitro studies, particularly where they are widely considered to be acceptable substitutes for human research or where human research is infeasible.[204] In addition, epidemiologic evidence will be considered, especially when supported by other evidence, such as research explaining the biological mechanism underlying the claimed effect.[205]

The question of qualified health claims—claims that are qualified to convey the limited or emerging nature of the scientific support—is a topic of ongoing regulatory interest both at FTC and at FDA,[206] and has proven to be a challenge for advertisers.[207] As is the case with all representations, the touchstone is consumer perception. According to its *Food Policy Statement*, FTC will be "especially vigilant in examining whether qualified claims are presented in a manner that ensures that consumers understand both the extent of the support for the claim and the existence of any significant contrary view within the scientific community. In the absence of adequate qualification the Commission will find such claims deceptive."[208] Vague qualifying terms—for example, that the advertised product "may" have the claimed benefit or "helps" achieve the claimed benefit—are unlikely to be adequate under section 5.[209] Similarly, advertisements that make either an express or an implied claim of safety should include information about any significant safety risks.[210] Moreover, the risks posed by some products may be so great as to trigger an affirmative duty to disclose safety concerns about the use of the product even in the absence of an express or implied safety representation.[211]

FTC and the courts have made clear that anecdotal evidence about the individual experience of consumers is not sufficient to substantiate a health claim.[212] As the Ninth Circuit held

---

204   *Compare* FTC v. Enforma Natural Prods., Inc., 362 F.3d 1204, 1217 (9th Cir. 2004), with FTC v. SlimAmerica, Inc., 77 F. Supp. 2d 1263, 1274 (S.D. Fla. 1999).

205   *Dietary Supplement Guide* at 10.

206   *See supra* Chapter 6 for a comprehensive discussion regarding FDA's regulatory framework for qualified health claims.

207   *See, e.g., In re Assessing Consumer Perceptions of Health Claims, Comments of the Staff of the Bureau of Economics, Bureau of Consumer Protection, and Office of Policy Planning of the Federal Trade Commission,* FDA Dkt. No. 2005N-0413 (Jan. 17, 2006), *available at* http://www.ftc.gov/policy/policy-actions/advocacy-filings/2006/01/ftc-staff-comment-food-and-drug-administration-matter; FTC, *Generic Copy Test of Food Health Claims in Advertising: A Joint Staff Report of the Bureaus of Economics and Consumer Protection* (Nov. 1998), *available at* http://www.ftc.gov/reports/generic-copy-test-food-health-claims-advertising.

208   *Food Policy Statement*, 59 Fed Reg. at 28,394.

209   *See* e.g., POM Wonderful LLC v. FTC, slip op. at 21 (citing favorably the commission holding that the "use of one or two adjectives does not alter the net impression," especially "when the chosen adjectives (such as 'promising') provide a positive spin on the studies rather than a substantive disclaimer."); *Dietary Supplement Guide* at 7.

210   *Id.* at 6, Example 7. *See, e.g.,* Indoor Tanning Ass'n, FTC Dkt. No. C-4290 (May 19, 2010) (consent order) (requiring that advertising for sunlamps that make health- or safety-related claims also include a mandatory safety warning); Panda Herbal Int'l, Inc., 132 F.T.C.at 151-52 (requiring that advertising that makes claims regarding the safety or efficacy of products containing St. John's Wort also include a mandatory safety warning).

211   *Dietary Supplement Guide* at 6, Example 8. *See, e.g.,* FTC v. Western Botanicals, Inc., Stipulated Final Order for Permanent Injunction at 5 (challenging the health risks of product containing comfrey).

212   *Dietary Supplement Guide.* at 10 ("Anecdotal evidence about the individual experience of consumers is not sufficient to substantiate claims about the effects of a supplement. Even if those experiences are genuine, they may be attributable to a placebo effect or other factors unrelated to the supplement. Individual experiences are not a substitute for scientific research."). *See also* Removatron, 111 F.T.C. at 302 (testimonials from satisfied customers are not scientific substantiation sufficient to demonstrate a product's effectiveness).

in *Simeon Management*, "Anecdotal evidence, such as testimonials by satisfied patients or statements by doctors that, based on their experience, they believe a drug is effective do not constitute adequate and well-controlled investigations and cannot, therefore, provide substantial evidence of effectiveness."[213] The Ninth Circuit later held in *FTC v. Pantron* that consumer satisfaction surveys similarly are insufficient to satisfy the "competent and reliable scientific evidence" standard.[214]

FTC's *Guides Concerning Use of Endorsements and Testimonials in Advertising* offer marketers substantial advice on the use of endorsements by consumers, celebrities, professional organizations, and experts.[215] The most important lesson for advertisers is that they may not, through the use of an endorsement, make a health claim they cannot otherwise substantiate with the requisite level of competent and reliable scientific evidence.[216] It is not enough that the testimonial represents the honest opinion of the endorser. Under FTC law, advertisers must still have adequate scientific evidence to support the claims they make.[217] As the Seventh Circuit held in rejecting testimonials as a form of proof in *QT, Inc.*, "Most testimonials represent a logical fallacy: *post hoc ergo propter hoc*. (A person who experiences a reduction in pain after donning the bracelet may have enjoyed the same reduction without it. That's why the 'testimonial' of someone who keeps elephants off the streets of a large city by snapping his fingers is the basis of a joke rather than proof of cause and effect.)."[218]

The Quality of Evidence

In addition to the amount and type of evidence supporting a claim, FTC examines the scientific validity of each piece of evidence relied on as substantiation. Study design, implementation, and methodology and the statistical significance of test results are all important in assessing the adequacy of the substantiation.[219] FTC has made it clear, for example, that well-controlled studies, with blinding of subjects and researchers, are likely to yield more reliable results than studies without those features.[220] FTC has also given

---

[213] Simeon Mgt. Corp., 579 F.2d at 1143.

[214] FTC v. Pantron I Corp, 33 F.3d at 1097.

[215] 16 C.F.R. § 255.0-255.5 (2014). After requesting public comment on "the overall costs, benefits, and regulatory and economic impact" of the *Guides*, the commission revised them in 2009. A violation of the *Guides* does not create an independent cause of action; rather "the Guides address the application of Section 5 of the FTC Act (15 U.S.C. 45) to the use of endorsements and testimonials in advertising." 16 C.F.R. § 255.0(a) (2014).

[216] *See* 16 C.F.R. § 255.1(a) (2014) ("[Endorsements] may not contain any representations which would be deceptive, and could not be substantiated if made directly by the advertiser."); *Dietary Supplement Guide* at 18.

[217] *Id.*

[218] QT, Inc., 512 F.3d at 862. *See infra* at p. 916.

[219] *Dietary Supplement Guide* at 12. *See* FTC v. QT, Inc., 448 F. Supp. 2d 908, 932-48 (N.D. Ill. 2006), *aff'd*, 512 F.3d 858, 863 (7th Cir. 2008); FTC v. Cal. Pac. Research, Inc., No. CV-N-88-602 BRT (D. Nev. Aug. 27, 1991) (order granting permanent injunction); Sterling Drug, 102 F.T.C. 395, 429 (1983) ("In a well-controlled clinical test, drugs are tested on real patients having actual symptoms. It is not disputed in this case that the elements of a well-controlled clinical test are the use of an appropriate pain model, replication of results, experienced unbiased investigator and adequately trained personnel, a written protocol, double-blinding, use of a placebo control, use of appropriate predetermined analytical techniques, and statistical and clinical significance of the results.").

[220] *Dietary Supplement Guide* at 12. *See* Schering Corp., 118 F.T.C. at 1030 (Initial Decision) ("Double blinding minimizes bias by withholding knowledge of placebo or treatment group assignments from the subject and the investigator. Double blinding is especially important when subjective measurements are made, for if the

greater weight to studies of longer duration and larger size.[221] Evidence of a dose-response relationship or a documented biological or chemical mechanism to explain the claimed effect are also factors the agency believes lend credibility to a study's results.[222]

The results should also translate into a meaningful benefit for consumers. Some results that are statistically significant may be so small that they would translate into only a *de minimis* benefit to consumer health.[223] The nature and quality of the report of the research may also be relevant. Although FTC will consider unpublished proprietary research, a peer-reviewed study published in a reputable journal carries substantial weight. FTC also considers studies conducted in foreign countries as long as their design and implementation are scientifically sound.[224]

Another important consideration is the statistical significance of the results asserted to support the advertised claim.[225] A study that fails to show a statistically significant difference between the test group and the control group may indicate that any perceived benefit is merely the result of the placebo effect or chance. The commission has expressly cautioned advertisers that results caused by the placebo effect—"the tendency of patients to respond favorably to a treatment regardless of the treatment's medical efficacy"—and the usage effect—"the tendency of users of a product to rate it more highly than non-users of the product"—do not meet the criteria for competent and reliable scientific evidence,[226] and courts have agreed with this conclusion.[227] As the trial court held in *QT, Inc.*, "Where, as here, a product's effectiveness arises solely as a result of the placebo effect, a representation that the product is effective constitutes a false advertisement, even though some consumers may experience positive results."[228] Affirming the decision, the Seventh Circuit added, "If a condition responds to treatment, then selling a placebo as if it had therapeutic effect directly injures the consumer .... Since the placebo effect can be obtained from sugar pills, charging $200 for a device that is represented as a miracle cure but works no better than a dummy pill is a form of fraud."[229]

The Totality of Evidence

Studies cannot be properly evaluated in isolation. Under section 5, marketers must consider all evidence relevant to the advertised claim, and not just the research that supports the

---

investigator knows to which group the subject is assigned, his perception of the treatment's effects may be altered by that knowledge.").

[221]   Schering Corp., 118 F.T.C. at 1030.

[222]   *Id. See also* Am. Home Prods., 98 F.T.C. at 155 (initial decision) ("The dose-response curve is generally accepted by clinical pharmacologists as a useful statistical tool in guessing the efficacy of a drug dosage in terms of its anticipated potency based on clinical data obtained from actual tests of graded dosages.").

[223]   *See* Statement of Chairwoman Edith Ramirez and Commissioner Julie Brill in i-Health, Inc. & Martek Biosciences Corp., FTC Dkt. No. C-4486 at 2 (June 9, 2014) (consent order) (noting that the proffered study "failed to demonstrate that the very small, statistically significant improvement on one of those tasks that it did report correlates with improvements in memory tasks outside of the laboratory," citing *Dietary Supplement Guide* at 12.)

[224]   *Dietary Supplement Guide* at 12.

[225]   *See* Telebrands, 140 F.T.C. at 321 n.40.

[226]   Novartis, 127 F.T.C. at 685 n.20.

[227]   *See, e.g.*, QT, Inc., 512 F.3d at 862-63; Pantron, 33 F.3d at 1100.

[228]   QT, Inc., 467 F. Supp. 2d at 964.

[229]   QT, Inc., 512 F.3d at 862.

claim they intend to disseminate.[230] Inconsistent or conflicting results should raise in an advertiser's mind serious questions about the adequacy of its substantiation.[231] The surrounding body of evidence will significantly affect the type, amount, and quality of additional evidence that will be required to substantiate a claim and how that claim may lawfully be presented in advertising, i.e., how the claim is qualified to reflect accurately the strength of the evidence.[232] If a stronger body of surrounding evidence runs contrary to a claimed effect, even a qualified claim is likely to be deceptive.[233]

FTC's settlement in *The Dannon Company* illustrates this principle.[234] There, FTC challenged as false the advertising claims that eating one daily serving of Activia yogurt relieves temporary irregularity and helps with slow intestinal transit time. According to FTC, two studies of the product used placebo groups, "but that information was withheld from the scientific journal to which the studies were submitted for publication, thereby concealing the fact that there was no statistically significant difference in transit time between the active and placebo groups, and eight of ten scientific studies conducted on Activia showed no statistically significant effect of Activia on transit time when compared to a placebo."[235]

The Relevance of the Evidence to the Advertised Claim

One common mistake in the dissemination of health-related representations is the failure to ensure that the science relied on for substantiation "fits" the advertised claim. In some FTC cases, companies had violated section 5 by relying on consumer testimonials, popular press articles, or other nonscientific material to substantiate health-related claims.[236] An even more common error is to rely on a nugget of information from a scientific study of limited application to substantiate a broad, unqualified advertising claim.[237]

Advertisers must take care to ensure that the composition, dosage, and form of administration of the advertised product are the same as, or substantially similar to, those of the product tested in the studies relied on.[238] Marketers should also consider whether the subjects in

---

230 *Dietary Supplement Guide* at 14.

231 *Id.*

232 In its *Food Policy Statement*, for example, FTC observed that, when a claim is based on science that is inconsistent with the larger body of evidence, it is likely to be misleading, even despite an advertiser's efforts to qualify the claim. 59 Fed. Reg. at 28,393-94.

233 *Dietary Supplement Guide* at 14.

234 151 F.T.C. 62 (2011) (consent order).

235 *Id.* In the same case, FTC also challenged representations that drinking DanActive, a probiotic dairy drink, reduces the likelihood of getting colds or flu.

236 *See, e.g.*, Removatron, 111 F.T.C. at 302; Original Mktg., Inc., 102 F.T.C. 278 (1995) (consent order) (challenging the use of consumer testimonials that did not represent the typical experience of consumers who used weight loss product).

237 For example, in Quigley Corp., FTC Dkt. No. C-3926 (Feb. 10, 2000) (consent order), and QVC, Inc., FTC Dkt. No. C-3955 (June 16, 2000) (consent order), the claim on the product packaging was that use of Cold-Eeze zinc lozenges would "reduce the severity and duration" of colds. The advertised claims, however, went far beyond that qualified representation by promising consumers that, "if you take these on a preventative basis, you might not ever get a cold at all."

238 *See, e.g.*, Valuevision Int'l, Inc., 132 F.T.C. 338 (2001) (consent order) (alleging that company's purported substantiation was based on studies using a formulation different from that of the advertised weight loss product). *See also* NBTY, Inc., FTC Dkt. No. C-4318 (Dec. 13, 2010) (consent order) ($2.1 million redress to settle charges that marketers touted the purported health benefits to children of 100 milligrams of DHA when the daily serving of their vitamins contained only 0.1 milligram of the ingredient).

the study relied on reflect the characteristics of consumers likely to use the advertised product.[239] Advertisers should assess the significance of any differences between the research conditions and the conditions of actual consumer use of the advertised product.[240] If significant discrepancies exist between the research conditions and the conditions of day-to-day use by consumers, advertisers must take care to evaluate whether it is appropriate to extrapolate from the research to the advertised effect when the product is used by consumers.[241]

The Consequences of a Finding of Deceptive or Unfair Advertising Under the FTC Act

When an advertiser is found to have engaged in unfair or deceptive acts or practices, the FTC Act gives the commission the right to seek a wide range of remedies to provide restitution to aggrieved consumers and to deter future violations.[242] At minimum, FTC insists on a cease-and-desist order that requires the advertiser to stop disseminating the deceptive claims, and imposes civil penalties of $16,000 per day per advertisement for any future violation of the order.[243] The fact that the advertiser has already discontinued the advertising campaign or pledges not to disseminate the same deceptive claims in the future is not a defense to an FTC action. "Courts have recognized that discontinuance of an offending practice is neither a defense to liability, nor grounds for omission of an order."[244]

Almost all FTC orders include some measure of "fencing in" relief, i.e., provisions directed not only against the same form of deception that was the subject of the original enforcement action, but also against other types of violations that reasonably relate to the past deception.[245]

---

[239]   *Dietary Supplement Guide* at 16. *See* United States v. Bayer Corp., No. CV 00-132 (NHP) (D.N.J. Jan. 11, 2000) (consent decree) (challenging unqualified heart-health claim for aspirin regimen when studies allegedly supported benefits only for patients who had already had one heart attack); Schering Corp., 118 F.T.C. 1030 (1994) (initial decision) (challenging unqualified weight loss claims when subjects in studies were also on diet and exercise programs).

[240]   *See* Honeywell Inc., 126 F.T.C. 202 (1998) (consent order) (challenging as deceptive the representation that an air filter will remove 99.97 percent of impurities from the air because testing was not conducted in conditions approximating household use).

[241]   *Dietary Supplement Guide* at 16.

[242]   *See, e.g.,* FTC v. H.N. Singer, Inc., 668 F.2d 1107, 1113 (9th Cir. 1982); FTC v. Sec. Rare Coin & Bullion Corp., 931 F.2d 1312, 1316 (8th Cir. 1991).

[243]   *See* Federal Civil Penalties Inflation Adjustment Act, 28 U.S.C. § 2461 (2014). Each dissemination of a deceptive claim is considered a separate violation. Therefore, civil penalties can often total in the millions of dollars. *See, e.g.,* United States v. Bayer Corp., No. 07-01 (HAA) (D.N.J. Jan. 4, 2007) (consent decree) ($3.2 million civil penalty for violating the terms of a 1991 FTC order by making allegedly deceptive weight loss claims for One-A-Day WeightSmart); United States v. NBTY, Inc., No. CV-05-4793 (E.D.N.Y. Oct. 12, 2005) ($2 million civil penalty for violating terms of 1995 FTC order by making allegedly deceptive claims for products advertised to cause weight loss and treat diabetes, cancer, Alzheimer's disease, and other serious conditions); United States v. Nu Skin Int'l, Inc., No. 97-CV-0626G (D. Utah Aug. 6, 1997) (stipulated permanent injunction) ($1.5 million civil penalty against seller of weight loss products for violating 1994 FTC order barring deceptive claims); United States v. Gen. Nutrition Corp., No. 94-686 (W.D. Pa. Apr. 28, 1994) (stipulated permanent injunction) ($2.4 million civil penalty for violating FTC order requiring substantiation for disease, weight loss, and muscle-building claims).

[244]   Sears, Roebuck & Co., 95 F.T.C. at 520, *citing* Fedders Corp. v. FTC, 529 F.2d 1398, 1403 (2d Cir. 1976).

[245]   FTC v. Nat'l Lead Co., 352 U.S. 419, 431 (1957) ("[R]espondents must remember that those caught violating the Act must expect some fencing in."). *See* FTC v. Colgate-Palmolive Co., 380 U.S. 374 (1965).

As the Supreme Court held in *FTC v. Ruberoid Company*, "If the Commission is to attain the objectives Congress envisioned, it cannot be required to confine its road block to the narrow lane the transgressor has traveled; it must be allowed effectively to close all roads to the prohibited goal, so that its order may not be by-passed with impunity."[246]

In many cases involving health-related products, FTC imposes an "all products" order.[247] Under the terms of such an order, any future violation of section 5 will trigger the civil penalties provision. In other cases, the commission may limit its order to include only future health-related claims; only claims made for food, drugs, dietary supplements, cosmetics, or devices; or other relief tailored to the nature of the violation.[248]

Courts will overturn a fencing-in remedy imposed by FTC "only where there is no reasonable relation between the remedy and the violation."[249] FTC and reviewing courts consider three factors in determining whether order coverage bears a "reasonable relation" to the violation it is intended to remedy: "(1) the seriousness and deliberateness of the violation; (2) the ease with which the violative claim may be transferred to other products; and (3) whether the respondent has a history of prior violations."[250]

An essential feature of any administrative cease-and-desist order is a requirement that, for the next 20 years, the company file with FTC periodic compliance reports about its marketing activities and the steps it has taken to prevent future violations of the FTC Act.[251]

---

[246] 343 U.S. 470, 473 (1952).

[247] *See, e.g.,* Synchronal Corp., 116 F.T.C. 1189 (1993) (consent order) (ordering sellers of purported baldness remedy and anti-cellulite cream to cease and desist from "making any representation, directly or by implication, regarding the performance, benefits, efficacy or safety of any product or service . . . unless, at the time of making such representation, respondents possess and rely upon competent and reliable evidence that substantiates the representation"); Zygon Int'l, Inc., 122 F.T.C. 195 (1996) (consent order) (ordering sellers of dietary supplements and "brain tuner" device to cease and desist from "making any representation, in any matter, directly or by implication . . . regarding the performance, benefits, efficacy or safety of any product or service . . . unless, at the time of making such representation, respondents possess and rely upon competent and reliable evidence, which when appropriate must be competent and reliable scientific evidence, that substantiates such representation").

[248] *See, e.g.,* Tropicana Prods., Inc., 140 F.T.C. 176, 185-86 (2005) (consent order) (scope of order includes any future claims that a food will affect cholesterol, folate levels, or homocysteine levels; blood pressure; or the risk of developing heart disease, stroke, or cancer); KFC Corp., 138 F.T.C. 422 (2004) (consent order) (scope of order includes any future claims about the nutrients or health benefits of any product containing chicken).

[249] Telebrands Corp. v. FTC, 457 F.3d 354, 358 (4th Cir. 2006), *citing* Atlantic Ref. Co. v. FTC, 381 U.S. 357, 377 (1965). *See* Southwest Sunsites, 785 F.2d 1431, 1439 (9th Cir. 1985) ("The Commission has broad remedial power and a remedial order should be upheld if reasonably related to the unlawful practices found to exist.").

[250] Telebrands Corp., 457 F.3d at 358. *See also* Sears, Roebuck & Co., 676 F.2d at 392; Kraft, Inc., 970 F.2d at 326; Bristol-Myers, 738 F.2d at 561. The Fourth Circuit in *Telebrands* noted that some courts have applied an additional factor: the extent to which the claim was health-related or the product posed a health risk. 457 F.3d at 358 n. 6. *See, e.g.,* Removatron Int'l Corp., 884 F.2d at 1499. *See also* Am. Home Prods., 695 F.2d at 706. In addition, in reviewing the scope of the fencing-in provision in POM Wonderful, LLC v. FTC, slip op. at 38, the D.C. Circuit applied the Supreme Court's commercial speech test established in *Central Hudson* and its progeny, which requires the government to "demonstrate a 'reasonable fit' between the particular means chosen and the government interest pursued." See Board of Trustees v. Fox, 492 U.S. at 477.

[251] *See, e.g.,* Pfizer, Inc., 126 F.T.C. 847, 861-62 (1998) (consent order) (imposing requirement that "[t]his order will terminate . . . twenty (20) years from the most recent date that the United States or the [FTC] files a complaint (with or without an accompanying consent decree) in federal court alleging any violation of the

It may also require corporate defendants to distribute a copy of the order to current and future employees.[252]

In appropriate cases, the commission may seek full financial restitution directly to consumers. Cases involving deceptive health claims have resulted in multimillion-dollar redress orders against advertisers.[253] In the most serious cases, courts have required violators to post substantial bonds before continuing to market products to consumers, or have banned the violators outright from particular industries.[254]

In addition to financial remedies, the commission occasionally has sought informational remedies from advertisers alleged to have made deceptive claims, including corrective advertising and mandatory disclosures in future advertising and on product labeling. FTC first won the right to seek corrective advertising in the landmark case of *Warner-Lambert Co. v. FTC.*[255] For decades, the marketer of Listerine mouthwash had advertised the product as effective in preventing the common cold, a claim FTC alleged—and the D.C. Circuit agreed—was deceptive. In fashioning a remedy, the commission was concerned that simply ordering the company not to disseminate the deceptive claim in the future would do nothing to correct the misimpression, left with millions of consumers by the decades-long

---

order, whichever comes later . . ."); London Int'l Group, Inc.,125 F.T.C. 726, 734 (1998) (consent order) (same); Johnson & Johnson Consumer Prods., Inc. 121 F.T.C. 22, 31-32 (1996) (consent order) (same).

[252] *See, e.g.,* HealthyLife Sciences, Inc., FTC Dkt. No. 4493 (Sept. 11, 2014) (consent order) (imposing requirement that "respondent and successors shall deliver a copy of this Order to all current and future principals, officers, directors, and other employees having responsibilities with respect to the subject matter of this Order, and shall secure from each such person a signed and dated statement acknowledging receipt of the Order. Respondent shall deliver this Order to current personnel within thirty (30) days after date of service of this Order, and to future personnel within thirty (30) days after the person assumes such position or responsibilities").

[253] Whenever the commission can identify consumers who purchased the product that was deceptively advertised, it uses redress judgments to pay refunds to them. If that is not feasible, any financial restitution won by the agency escheats to the U.S. Treasury. No portion of financial judgments goes to FTC's operating budget. *See, e.g.,* FTC v. Sensa Products, LLC, No. 11CV72 (N.D. Ill. Jan. 7, 2014) (stipulated final judgment) (more than $26 million in consumer redress for deceptive weight loss claims); FTC v. Bronson Partners, LLC, 654 F.3d 359 (2d Cir. 2011) (upholding $1.9 million redress order for deceptive weight loss claims); FTC v. Great Am. Prods., Inc., No. 3:05-CV-00170-RV-MD (N.D. Fla. May 20, 2005) (stipulated final order) (up to $20 million redress for unsubstantiated anti-aging claims for purported human growth hormone product, deceptive format for radio and television infomercials, and violations of the Telemarketing Sales Rule); FTC v. Blue Stuff, Inc., No. Civ-02-1631W (W.D. Okla. Nov. 18, 2002) (stipulated final order) ($3 million in consumer redress for allegedly deceptive claims for Blue Stuff pain reliever and two dietary supplements advertised to reduce cholesterol and reverse bone loss); FTC v. Enforma Natural Prods., Inc., No. 04376JSL(CWx) (C.D. Cal. Apr. 26, 2000) (stipulated final order) ($10 million in consumer redress from marketer of purported weight loss product); FTC v. American Urological Corp., No. 98-CVC-2199-JOD (N.D. Ga. Apr. 29, 1999) (permanent injunction) ($18.5 million judgment against marketers of dietary supplement purporting to treat impotence).

[254] *See, e.g.,* FTC v. 7 Day Marketing, Inc., No. CV08-01094-ER-FFM (C.D. Cal. Feb. 27, 2008) (permanent injunction) (banning individuals who sold "7 Day Miracle Cleanse Program" from marketing any health-related product in any medium); FTC v. Sagee U.S.A. Group, Inc., No. CV04 10560 GPS (CWx) (C.D. Cal. Aug. 10, 2006) (modified stipulated final judgment & order) (imposing lifetime ban from selling health-related products); FTC v. Am. Urological Corp., No. 98-CVC-2199-JOD (N.D. Ga. Apr. 29, 1999) (permanent injunction) (imposing $6 million bond on marketer of "Väegra," a dietary supplement purporting to treat impotence); Synchronal Corp., 116 F.T.C. 1189 (1993) (consent order) (requiring corporate officer who sold baldness, anti-cellulite, and skin care products to establish $500,000 escrow account before future marketing of certain products).

[255] Warner-Lambert Co. v. FTC, 562 F.2d 749 (D.C. Cir. 1977), *aff'g*, 86 F.T.C. 1398 (1975).

campaign, that the product was effective for that purpose. Establishing the use of corrective advertising as a remedy in deceptive advertising cases, the court held:

> If a deceptive advertisement has played a substantial role in creating or reinforcing in the public's mind a false and material belief which lives on after the false advertising ceases, there is clear and continuing injury to competition and to the consuming public as consumers continue to make purchasing decisions based on the false belief. Since this injury cannot be averted by merely requiring respondent to cease disseminating the advertisement, we may appropriately order respondent to take affirmative action designed to terminate the otherwise continuing ill effects of the advertisement.[256]

The D.C. Circuit reached a similar result in *Novartis Corp. v. FTC*. There, the commission challenged the long-standing advertising campaign claiming that Doan's pills contained an ingredient that, for relieving back pain, was superior to the ingredients in competing products.[257] Although the ingredient in Doan's was recognized by FDA as an effective analgesic, the company could not substantiate its representation that the ingredient was superior to other analgesics for the treatment of back pain. Upholding the propriety of corrective advertising, the court held that FTC had carried its burden under *Warner-Lambert* of proving that Novartis' advertisements had played a substantial role in reinforcing in the public's mind a false belief about the product that would linger even after the false advertising ceased.[258]

Informational remedies have been particularly important to FTC to correct consumer misimpressions about the safety or correct use of health-related products. When an advertiser is able to identify the consumers who purchased its product, FTC has required the advertiser to contact consumers directly to warn them of the health or safety problem posed by the deceptively advertised product.[259] In other cases, the commission has required disclosures in future advertisements and on labels to alert consumers to possible risk.[260]

---

[256] *Id.* at 762. The nature of the corrective advertising remedy will depend on the fact of the particular case. For example in *Warner-Lambert*, the commission ordered that for a two-year period, all advertising for Listerine had to include this statement in a clear and conspicuous fashion: "Contrary to prior advertising of Listerine, Listerine will not prevent or cure colds or sore throats, and Listerine will not be beneficial in the treatment of cold symptoms or sore throats." The D.C. Circuit upheld the imposition of the remedy, but struck the "Contrary to prior advertising of Listerine" preamble.

[257] Novartis Corp. v. FTC, 223 F.3d 783 (D.C. Cir. 2000), *aff'g*, 127 F.T.C. 580 (1996).

[258] *Id.* at 788. Specifically, the D.C. Circuit upheld the commission's corrective remedy, which required Novartis to include in future advertising the statement, "Although Doan's is an effective pain reliever, there is no evidence that Doan's is more effective than other pain relievers for back pain." The order required the remedy to continue "for one year and until respondent has expended on Doan's advertising a sum equal to the average spent annually during the eight years of the challenged campaign," subject to an exemption for 15-second radio and television ads.

[259] *See, e.g.*, PhaseOut of Am., Inc., 123 F.T.C. 395 (1997) (consent order) (requiring marketer of device advertised to reduce health risks of smoking to notify purchasers that the product had not been proven to reduce the risk of smoking-related diseases); Consumer Direct, Inc., 113 F.T.C. 923 (1990) (consent order) (requiring marketer of Gut Buster exercise device to mail to purchasers a warning regarding a serious safety hazard posed by the product).

[260] *See, e.g.*, FTC v. Met-Rx USA, Inc., No. 99-WI-2197 (C.D. Cal. Nov. 15, 1999) (stipulated final order) (requiring labeling and advertising for purported body-building supplements containing androgen and other steroid hormones to disclose: "WARNING: This product contains steroid hormones that may cause

The majority of FTC enforcement actions target the company primarily responsible for the advertising at issue. That company may be held strictly liable for violations of the FTC Act, i.e., the commission may find that company legally responsible regardless of whether it intended to violate the law or knew that it was violating the law.[261]

In some circumstances, FTC may take action against not only the corporate entity responsible for deceptive advertising, but also corporate officers and others in their individual capacities.[262] Corporate officers may be held individually liable for violations of the FTC Act if naming them individually is necessary for the order to be effective in preventing the deceptive practices challenged by the commission.[263] FTC and the courts have looked to a number of factors in determining whether individual liability is justified, e.g., "where an executive officer of the respondent company is found to have personally participated in or controlled the challenged acts or practices,"[264] whether the officer held a position of control over employees who committed illegal acts,[265] and whether the individual "had knowledge that the corporation or one of its agents engaged in dishonest or fraudulent conduct, that the misrepresentations were the type upon which a reasonable and prudent person would rely, and that consumer injury resulted."[266]

In *FTC v. Ross*,[267] the Fourth Circuit summarized the legal standard in this way:

> We hold that one may be found individually liable under the Federal Trade Commission Act if she (1) participated directly in the deceptive practices or had authority to control those practices, and (2) had or should have had knowledge of the deceptive practices. The second prong of the analysis may be established by showing that the individual had actual knowledge

---

breast enlargement, testicle shrinkage, and infertility in males, and increased facial and body hair, voice deepening, and clitoral enlargement in females. Higher doses may increase these risks. If you are at risk for prostate or breast cancer, you should not use this product."); FTC v. AST Nutritional Concepts & Research, Inc., No. SAC V-99-1407 (D. Colo. Nov. 15, 1999) (stipulated final order) (same); R.J. Reynolds Tobacco Co., 128 F.T.C. 262 (1999) (consent order) (requiring marketer of Winston "no additives" cigarettes to state in future advertisements: "No additives in our tobacco does NOT mean a safer cigarette.").

[261]   Chrysler Corp. v. FTC, 561 F.2d 357, 363 & n.5 (D.C. Cir. 1977). *See* Regina Corp. v. FTC, 322 F.2d 765, 768 (3d Cir. 1963); Orkin Exterminating Co. v. FTC, 849 F.2d 1354 (11th Cir. 1988) (holding that company's purported good-faith reliance on advice of counsel is not a defense under Section 5).

[262]   *See, e.g.*, POM Wonderful LLC v. FTC, slip op. at 31 (upholding corporate officer's liability for deceptive advertising claims and citing favorably the standard of other circuits that "individuals may be liable for FTC Act violations committed by a corporate entity if the individual participated directly in the deceptive practices or acts or had authority to control them") (citations omitted); FTC v. Ross, 743 F.3d 886 (4th Cir. 2014) (upholding corporate officer's joint and several personal liability for $163 million judgment for role in "scareware" scam); Mark Dreher, 150 F.T.C. 560 (2010) (consent order) (challenging role of then-Vice President of Science and Regulatory Affairs of POM Wonderful pomegranate juice company in making false and unsubstantiated claims that products could prevent or treat heart disease and prostate cancer).

[263]   *See, e.g.*, FTC v. Standard Educ. Soc'y, 302 U.S. 112, 119-20 (1937); Pati-Port, Inc. v. FTC, 313 F.2d 103 (4th Cir. 1963).

[264]   Rentacolor, Inc., 103 F.T.C. 400, 438 (1984).

[265]   Thiret v. FTC, 512 F.2d 176, 181-82 (10th Cir. 1975).

[266]   FTC v. Affordable Media, LLC, 179 F.3d 1228, 1234 (9th Cir. 1999) (*quoting* FTC v. Publ'g Clearing House, Inc., 104 F.3d 1168, 1171 (9th Cir. 1996)). The knowledge requirement can be satisfied by showing that the individuals had actual knowledge of a material misrepresentation, were recklessly indifferent to the falsity of a misrepresentation, or were aware of the probability of fraud and intentionally avoided knowledge of the truth. Affordable Media, 179 F.3d at 1234.

[267]   743 F.2d at 892.

of the deceptive conduct, was recklessly indifferent to its deceptiveness, or had an awareness of a high probability of deceptiveness and intentionally avoided learning the truth.

To hold defendants personally liable, FTC is not required to show that they intended to defraud consumers.[268]

The commission also may take action against other participants in the dissemination of misleading claims, most notably advertising agencies.[269] "In order to be held liable for false advertising, an agency must have been an active participant in preparing the violative advertisements, and it must have known or had reason to know that the advertisements were false or deceptive."[270] Under the "knew or should have known" standard, an advertising agency will not be held strictly liable for false or unsubstantiated claims because an agency cannot be expected to conduct independent clinical testing to determine whether a scientific claim has been substantiated.[271] The commission has held, however, that the disparity between the advertising claims and the underlying proof may be so great "as to preclude a conclusion that the ads in question were conceived through reasonable reliance on the substantiation provided by the manufacturer of the product."[272] Furthermore, given their expertise in fashioning and communicating representations, advertising agencies "will be strictly held to know what claims are made in advertisements."[273]

Over the years, the commission has expanded the scope of liability under section 5 by taking action against other entities involved in facilitating the dissemination of deceptive claims to consumers. For example, FTC has brought lawsuits for deceptive or unfair practices

---

[268]   Id.

[269]   See Deutsch LA, Inc., FTC Dkt. No. 122-253 (Nov. 25, 1014) (proposed consent order issued for public comment) (alleging that advertising agency disseminated favorable comments about client's gaming system on employees' personal Twitter accounts without disclosing their connection to the company; TBWA Worldwide, Inc., FTC Dkt. No. C-4455 (Jan. 23, 2014) (consent order) (challenging advertising agency's role in deceptive on-camera demonstration of Nissan Frontier truck); Campbell Mithun, L.L.C., 133 F.T.C. 702 (2002) (consent order) (challenging advertising agency's role in advertisements claiming that Wonder Bread with added calcium could improve children's brain function and memory); Bozell Worldwide, Inc., 127 F.T.C. 1 (1999) (consent order) (challenging advertising agency's role in advertisements containing deceptive representations of car-leasing terms); Jordan McGrath Case & Taylor, 122 F.T.C. 152 (1996) (consent order) (challenging advertising agency's role in advertisements making deceptive claims for pain-relief superiority of Doan's pills); NW Ayer & Son, Inc., 121 F.T.C. 656 (1996) (consent order) (challenging advertising agency's role in advertisements containing deceptive claims regarding the effect of Eggland's Best eggs on blood cholesterol); BBDO Worldwide, Inc., 121 F.T.C. 33 (1996) (consent order) (challenging advertising agency's role in advertisements containing deceptive claims for nutritional content of Häagen-Dazs frozen yogurt).

[270]   Bristol-Myers Co., 102 F.T.C. at 364, citing Doherty, Clifford, Steers & Shenfield, Inc. v. FTC, 392 F.2d 921, 927 (6th Cir. 1968).

[271]   Bristol-Myers Co., 102 F.T.C. at 364.

[272]   Id.

[273]   Id. at 225, citing Merck & Co., 69 F.T.C. 526, 559 (1966), aff'd, 392 F.2d 921 (6th Cir. 1968).

against infomercial producers,[274] shop-at-home channels,[275] catalogue companies,[276] affiliate marketers,[277] retailers,[278] and others that play a role in the dissemination of deceptive representations.[279]

In addition to suing a broad variety of distributors that market directly to consumers, the commission also used section 5 to challenge the behind-the-scenes roles of companies that provided others the "means and instrumentalities" to advertise deceptively. For example, in *FTC v. Applied Food Sciences, Inc.*,[280] the agency accepted a $3.5 million settlement with the marketer of green coffee extract, an ingredient sold to trade customers as a constituent of diet products. The complaint alleged that Applied Food Sciences used the results of a flawed study to make baseless weight loss claims, which retailers repeated in advertising their products—which contained that ingredient—to consumers.

FTC has also taken enforcement action against what it considers to be deceptive endorsements or testimonials. Through its *Guides Concerning Use of Endorsements and Testimonials in Advertising*, the Commission has made clear that false or deceptive endorsements —whether by experts, groups, celebrities, or consumers—violate section 5.[281] The *Guides* are premised on the principle that, because consumers may rely on the opinions of endorsers in making

---

[274] *See, e.g.*, World Media TV, Inc., C-3717 (Feb. 28, 1997) (consent order) (challenging infomercial producer for role in disseminating claims for a pain-relief device).

[275] *See, e.g.*, Home Shopping Network, Inc., 122 F.T.C. 227 (1995) (consent order) (holding home shopping company liable for deceptive claims for vitamin and stop-smoking sprays); United States v. Home Shopping Network, Inc., No. 99-897-CIV-T-25C (M.D. Fla. Apr. 15, 1999) (consent decree) ($1.1 million civil penalty for violating previous FTC order barring false and unsubstantiated claims for skin care, weight loss, and MS/menopause products); ValueVision Int'l, Inc., 132 F.T.C. 338 (2001) (holding home shopping company liable for deceptive claims for weight loss, cellulite, and baldness products); QVC, Inc., C-3955 (June 16, 2000) (consent order) (holding home shopping company liable for deceptive cold-prevention claims for zinc supplement).

[276] *See, e.g.*, Sharper Image Corp., 116 F.T.C. 606 (1993) (consent order) (holding cataloguer liable for unsubstantiated claims for exercise device and dietary supplement); Lifestyle Fascination, Inc., 118 F.T.C. 171 (1994) (consent order) (holding cataloguer liable for deceptive claims for pain-relief device and a "Brain Tuner" advertised to treat addiction and depression).

[277] Affiliate marketing is a promotional arrangement in which a seller of a product pays others to post hyperlinks directing potential buyers to the seller's site. An affiliate is typically paid a percentage of each sale generated by its link. *See, e.g.*, FTC v. IMM Interactive, Inc. d/b/a COPEAC & Intermark Media, Case No. 1:11-CV-02484 (N.D. Ill. Mar. 21, 2012) (stipulated final judgment) (challenging defendant's role in affiliate marketing promotion that used advertisements deceptively designed to mimic legitimate news reports to promote the sale of acai berry weight loss products).

[278] *See, e.g.*, Walgreens Co., 109 F.T.C. 156 (1987) (consent order) (challenging retail drugstore chain's role in disseminating advertising claims that over-the-counter analgesics had the same medical benefit as prescription drugs).

[279] *See, e.g.*, FTC v. First Am. Payment Processing, Inc., No. CV 04-0074 PHX SRB (D. Ariz. Nov. 3, 2004) (stipulated permanent injunction) ($1.5 million redress for electronic payment processor's role in assisting fraudulent telemarketers by electronically debiting consumers' bank accounts in violation of the Telemarketing Sales Rule and the FTC Act); FTC v. No. 1025798 Ontario, Inc. (W.D.N.Y. Oct. 12, 2004) (stipulated final order) (holding fulfillment company liable for its role in marketing of deceptively advertised weight loss products); FTC v. Lane Labs-USA, Inc., No. 00CV3174 (D.N.J. June 28, 2000) (stipulated final order) (applying common-enterprise theory to hold both the product manufacturer and a company that distributed information about the use of the product liable for deceptive cancer-treatment claims for shark-cartilage product).

[280] No. 1-14-CV-00851 (W.D. Tex. Sept. 8, 2014) (stipulated order).

[281] 16 C.F.R. §§ 255.0-.5 (2014). *See, e.g.*, Norm Thompson Outfitters, Inc., FTC Dkt. No. C-4495 (Sept. 29, 2014) (consent order) (challenging false claim that Dr. Oz had endorsed caffeine-infused shapewear advertised to reduce wearers' hips and thighs).

product decisions, endorsements must be non-deceptive. Endorsements "may not contain any representations which would be deceptive, or could not be substantiated if made directly by the advertiser."[282] That the endorsement represents the bona fide opinion of the endorser is not enough. Under FTC law, an advertiser must still have appropriate evidence to support the underlying efficacy claim conveyed through an endorsement.[283] Endorsements are not, themselves, substantiation for advertising claims; rather, they give rise to the need for the advertiser to possess competent and reliable evidence to support the underlying efficacy representations conveyed by the endorsers to consumers.

Furthermore, as the *Guides* establish, consumer testimonials are generally presumed to represent the results that others will achieve by using the product:

> An advertisement containing an endorsement relating the experience of one or more consumers on a central or key attribute of the product or service also will likely be interpreted as representing that the endorser's experience is representative of what consumers will generally achieve with the advertised product or service in actual, albeit variable, conditions of use.[284]

Thus, endorsements usually carry with them an implied representation of typicality, which advertisers must substantiate.

"If the advertiser does not have substantiation that the endorser's experience is representative of what consumers will generally achieve, the advertisement should clearly and conspicuously disclose the generally expected performance in the depicted circumstances, and the advertiser must possess and rely on adequate substantiation for that representation."[285] Thus, the 2009 revisions to the *Guides* establish that the ubiquitous "Results not typical" or "Your results may vary" disclaimer is probably ineffective to qualify the implied claim that consumers will achieve results similar to those reported by the endorser.[286]

Endorsers represented directly or by implication to be experts must have qualifications sufficient to give them the represented expertise.[287] In addition, they must have performed an examination or testing of the product at least as extensive as someone with the same degree of expertise would normally need to conduct in order to support the conclusions represented in the endorsement.[288] Both the company and the expert endorser are responsible

---

[82] 16 C.F.R. § 255.1(a) (2011).

[83] *See* FTC v. QT, Inc., 512 F.3d at 862.

[84] 16 C.F.R. § 255.2(b) (2011).

[85] 16 C.F.R. § 255.2 (2014).

[86] *Id.* at n.1. Although not ruling out the possibility that "a strong disclaimer of typicality could be effective in the context of a particular advertisement," the agency observed that "an advertiser possessing reliable empirical testing demonstrating that the net impression of its advertisement with such a disclaimer is non-deceptive will avoid the risk of the initiation of such an action in the first instance." *Id.*

[87] 16 C.F.R § 255.3 (2014). *See* FTC v. Kendall, No. 00-09358-AHM (AIJx) (C.D. Cal. Aug. 31, 2000) (stipulated final order) (challenging false representation that person who appeared on an infomercial touting a weight loss product was a nutritionist).

[88] *See* Black & Decker (U.S.) Inc., 113 F.T.C. 63 (1990) (consent order).

for ensuring that the endorsements are substantiated.[289] Given the high level of credence consumers give to the opinions of physicians and other scientific experts, the commission has insisted that advertisers and experts exercise care when using expert endorsements in advertising.[290]

In addition, any material connection between the endorser and the advertiser—i.e., a relationship that is not reasonably expected by a consumer and that might materially affect the weight or credibility of the endorsement—must be disclosed. One of the many examples included in the *Guides* illustrates this principle:

> A drug company commissions research on its product by an outside organization. The drug company determines the overall subject of the research (e.g., to test the efficacy of a newly developed product) and pays a substantial share of the expenses of the research project, but the research organization determines the protocol for the study and is responsible for conducting it. A subsequent advertisement by the drug company mentions the research results as the "findings" of that research organization. Although the design and conduct of the research project are controlled by the outside research organization, the weight consumers place on the reported results could be materially affected by knowing that the advertiser had funded the project. Therefore, the advertiser's payment of expenses to the research organization should be disclosed in this advertisement.[291]

FTC enforcement actions further demonstrate when material connections should be disclosed. For example, the agency alleged in *FTC v. Skechers U.S.A., Inc.*,[292] that the company's failure

---

[289] *See, e.g.*, FTC v. Sensa Products, LLC, No. 11CV72 (N.D. Ill. Jan. 7, 2014) (stipulated final judgment) (alleging that expert endorser failed to have appropriate scientific evidence to support endorsement); Synchronal Corp., 116 F.T.C. 1189 (1993); Steven Victor, M.D., 116 F.T.C. 1189 (1993) (consent orders) (holding company and physician responsible for allegedly deceptive endorsements given by the physician for products advertised as treatments for baldness); Patricia Wexler, M.D., 115 F.T.C. 849 (1992) (consent order) (holding company and physician responsible for allegedly deceptive endorsements given by the physician for products advertised as treatments for cellulite).

[290] *See, e.g.*, FTC v. Terrill Mark Wright, M.D., No. 1:04-CV-3294 (N.D. Ga. Jan. 15, 2009) (final judgment and permanent injunction) ($15,454 redress for doctor's deceptive endorsement of Thermalean weight loss product); FTC v. Mark J. Buchfuhrer, M.D., No. 03CV5002-RNBX (C.D. Cal 2003) (stipulated final order) (challenging deceptive representations made by physician for a purported anti-snoring treatment); Robert M. Currier, D.O., 132 F.T.C. 672 (2002) (consent order) (challenging deceptive representations made by eye doctor for a purported anti-snoring treatment); William S. Gandee, 123 F.T.C. 698 (1997) (consent order) (challenging chiropractor's role in the marketing of a purported pain-relief device); William E. Shell, M.D., 123 F.T.C. 1519 (1997) (consent order) (challenging physician's role in the marketing of a purported weight loss pill). Endorsements by groups perceived by reasonable consumers to be expert organizations must meet the same standards as endorsements by expert individuals, and must be reached by a process sufficient to ensure that the endorsement reflects the collective judgment of the organization. *See* 16 C.F.R. § 255.1, Example 3 (2014) ("An ad for an acne treatment features a dermatologist who claims that the product is 'clinically proven' to work. Before giving the endorsement, she received a write-up of the clinical study in question, which indicates flaws in the design and conduct of the study that are so serious that they preclude any conclusions about the efficacy of the product. The dermatologist is subject to liability for the false statements she made in the advertisement. The advertiser is also liable for misrepresentations made through the endorsement.").

[291] 16 C.F.R. § 255.5, Example 1 (2011).

[292] No 1:12-CV-01214-JG (N.D. Ohio May 16, 2012) (stipulated final judgment).

to disclose that a medical professional endorsing the product was married to the company's senior vice president for marketing was a deceptive practice. In *FTC v. Sensa Products, LLC*,[293] the FTC charged that the company violated section 5 by failing to disclose financial benefits provided by the advertiser to consumer endorsers. In *Creative Health Institute, Inc.*, FTC challenged an advertiser's failure to disclose that endorsers who appeared in advertisements for a dietary supplement that was purported to improve memory and concentration were, in fact, principals in a public relations company that had been retained by the advertiser to promote the product, distributors of the product, and the company's attorney.[294] In *Numex Corp.*, FTC alleged that it was a violation of section 5 for a company not to disclose that a physician and sports figure who endorsed a pain-relief device were also officers of the advertiser.[295] In *TrendMark International, Inc.*, the commission challenged an advertiser's failure to disclose that consumer endorsers of a weight loss product were either distributors of the product or spouses of distributors.[296]

The *Guides* also offer insights into the use of endorsements in new media, including blogs and social networking sites. One example explains the differentiation between the personal use of such media and their integration as part of an advertising campaign:

> A consumer who regularly purchases a particular brand of dog food decides one day to purchase a new, more expensive brand made by the same manufacturer. She writes in her personal blog that the change in diet has made her dog's fur noticeably softer and shinier, and that in her opinion, the new food definitely is worth the extra money. This posting would not be deemed an endorsement under the Guides.
>
> Assume that rather than purchase the dog food with her own money, the consumer gets it for free because the store routinely tracks her purchases and its computer has generated a coupon for a free trial bag of this new brand. Again, her posting would not be deemed an endorsement under the Guides.
>
> Assume now that the consumer joins a network marketing program under which she periodically receives various products about which she can write reviews if she wants to do so. If she receives a free bag of the new dog food through this program, her positive review would be considered an endorsement under the Guides.[297]

---

[293]   No. 11CV72 (N.D. Ill. Jan. 7, 2014) (stipulated final judgment).

[294]   137 F.T.C. 350 (2004) (consent order).

[295]   116 F.T.C. 1078 (1993) (consent order). *See also* James L. McElhaney, M.D., 116 F.T.C. 1137 (1993) (consent order),16 C.F.R. § 255.5, Example 4 ("An ad for an anti-snoring product features a physician who says that he has seen dozens of products come on the market over the years and, in his opinion, this is the best ever. Consumers would expect the physician to be reasonably compensated for his appearance in the ad. Consumers are unlikely, however, to expect that the physician receives a percentage of gross product sales or that he owns part of the company, and either of these facts would likely materially affect the credibility that consumers attach to the endorsement. Accordingly, the advertisement should clearly and conspicuously disclose such a connection between the company and the physician.").

[296]   126 F.T.C. 375 (1998) (consent order).

[297]   16 C.F.R. § 255.0, Example 8 (2011).

The *Guides* make clear that endorsers must be *bona fide* users of the advertised product, and that "[e]ndorsements must always reflect the honest opinions, findings, beliefs, or experience of the endorser."[298] An advertiser may use the endorsement of an expert or celebrity only as long as it has good reason to believe that the endorser continues to subscribe to the views presented.[299] Although celebrity endorsements are governed by the same standards as other endorsements, advertisers need not disclose a material financial connection between the celebrity and the advertiser because the commission believes that "the manner in which celebrities are compensated does not materially affect the weight or credibility of an endorsement."[300]

FTC's first enforcement action under the revised *Endorsement Guides*—although not involving the marketing of a health-related product—nonetheless illustrates how the *Guides* apply in the burgeoning promotional area of social media. In *Reverb Communications, Inc.*, FTC alleged that a public relations company hired by videogame developers directed its staff to post favorable game reviews online without disclosing that the reviews came from employees working on the developers' behalf.[301] The company's fee often included a percentage of the sales of it clients' products. According to FTC's complaint, the company falsely represented that what it posted were independent reviews reflecting the opinions of ordinary consumers who had used the products. Reasoning that knowledge of Reverb's affiliation with the developers probably would have affected the weight consumers would give the reviews, FTC charged that the failure to disclose that material connection was a deceptive practice.[302]

Conclusion

As the nation's general consumer protection agency, FTC acts to prevent fraud, deception, and unfair business practices in the marketplace. An important part of FTC's efforts has focused on the marketing of products and services that purportedly provide health benefits to consumers. As this chapter has illustrated, the broad range of administrative and judicial remedies available to the commission has historically served to complement and enhance FDA's authority to address false and unsubstantiated claims for foods, dietary supplements, OTC drugs and devices, and cosmetics.

---

[298]   16 C.F.R. § 255.1(a). *See* FTC v. Garvey, 383 F.3d 891, 905 (9th Cir. 2004) (holding that baseball player was not liable under section 5 for claims about a weight loss product because his statements reflected his "actual beliefs and experiences"). FTC has also taken law enforcement action against marketers who falsely represented that their products were endorsed by celebrities. *See, e.g.*, FTC v. Central Coast Nutraceuticals, Inc., No. 10C-4931 (N.D. Ill. Jan. 9, 2012) (stipulated order for permanent injunction) (alleging that marketers of purported acai berry diet product and colon cleanser falsely represented that products were endorsed by Oprah Winfrey and Rachael Ray).

[299]   16 C.F.R. § 255.1 (2014).

[300]   Cooga Mooga, Inc., 98 F.T.C. 814, 815 (1981), *modifying* 92 F.T.C. 310 (1978) (consent order).

[301]   Reverb Communications, Inc., 150 F.T.C. 782 (2010) (consent order).

[302]   *See also* Deutsch LA, Inc., FTC File No. 122-3252 (Nov. 25, 2014) (proposed consent order issued for public comment) (alleging that advertising agency disseminated favorable comments about client's gaming system on employees' personal Twitter accounts without disclosing their connection to the company); Legacy Learning Sys., Inc., 151 F.T.C. 383 (2011) (consent order) ($250,000 to settle charges that company deceptively advertised its products through online affiliate marketers who falsely posed as ordinary consumers or independent reviewers).

CHAPTER 25

DEA REGULATION OF CONTROLLED SUBSTANCES AND LISTED CHEMICALS

JOHN A. GILBERT, JR. AND KARLA L. PALMER[*]

....

Introduction

In 1970, Congress passed the Comprehensive Drug Abuse Prevention and Control Act,[1] establishing an all-inclusive scheme to regulate and increase enforcement against the abuse of drugs. The act, popularly known as the Controlled Substances Act (CSA), was enacted to reduce the abuse of both illicit substances and prescription drugs.[2] The scope has expanded over the years to include "designer" and synthetic substances. In particular, a number of amendments to the CSA have focused on preventing the diversion and misuse of precursor or "listed" chemicals that are directly or indirectly used in the illicit manufacture of controlled substances.[3]

The Drug Enforcement Administration (DEA), created three years after enactment of the CSA, is the agency within the U.S. Department of Justice that has been delegated the authority to administer and enforce the CSA.[4] DEA is the primary U.S. law enforcement agency whose mission is to prevent the illicit diversion, distribution, and misuse of controlled substances and listed chemicals.[5] DEA's Drug Diversion Control Program, administered through the Office of Diversion Control,[6] was established "to prevent, detect, and investigate the diversion of controlled pharmaceuticals and listed chemicals from legitimate sources while

---

[*] The co-authors thank Andrew J. Hull, associate at Hyman, Phelps & McNamara, P.C. for his assistance on this chapter.

[1] Pub. L. No. 91-513, tit. I-II, 84 Stat. 1236 (1970) (codified in 21 U.S.C. § 801 *et seq.*).

[2] DEA PRACTITIONER'S MANUAL 4 (2006 ed.), *available at* http://www.deadiversion.usdoj.gov/pubs/manual/pract/pract_manual012508.pdf.

[3] *See, e.g.,* Chemical Diversion and Trafficking Act of 1988 (CDTA), Pub. L. 100-690, 102 Stat. 4312 (1988); Combat Methamphetamine Epidemic Act of 2005 (CMEA), Pub. L. No. 109-177, 120 Stat. 256 (2006).

[4] 21 U.S.C. § 821; 28 C.F.R. § 0.100 (delegation of duties by the U.S. Attorney General to DEA).

[5] *See* DEA Mission Statement, *available at* http://www.usdoj.gov/dea/agency/mission.htm.

[6] Office of Diversion Control, *available at* http://www.deadiversion.usdoj.gov.

ensuring an adequate and uninterrupted supply for legitimate medical, commercial, and scientific needs."[7] Congress has mandated that the entire cost of this program be recovered through the registration fees paid by DEA registrants.[8]

DEA has established regulations to implement the CSA, controlling the import, export, manufacture, distribution, and dispensing of controlled substances.[9] These regulations provide the primary source of guidance on these requirements. The agency has also issued a series of manuals summarizing specific requirements for categories of registrants (e.g., practitioners), but otherwise publishes rather limited policy guidance. These manuals are generally available through DEA's website.[10] DEA has also attempted to regulate through communications with registrants via letters to industry. For example, it has informed distributors about requirements for establishing a suspicious order monitoring program including customer due diligence under 21 C.F.R. § 1301.74(b).[11]

This chapter provides a general overview of the federal regulation of controlled substances and listed chemicals and DEA's enforcement of the CSA and regulations as they pertain to the regulated industry.[12] It focuses on the process for classification of these substances and the primary measures used to maintain a closed chain of distribution from manufacturing to ultimate consumption by the end-user, including imports and exports, in order to minimize the potential for diversion or misuse of these substances.

---

[7]   Program Description, Inside Diversion Control, *available at* http://www.deadiversion.usdoj.gov/prog_dscrpt/index.html.

[8]   21 U.S.C. § 886a.

[9]   *See generally* 21 C.F.R. pt. 1300.

[10]   Office of Diversion Control, *supra* note 6; *see, e.g.,* DEA CHEMICAL HANDLER'S MANUAL (rev. ed. 2013), *available at* http://www.deadiversion.usdoj.gov/pubs/manuals/pharm2/pharm_manual.pdf; DEA NARCOTIC TREATMENT PROGRAMS MANUAL (2000), *available at* http://www.deadiversion.usdoj.gov/pubs/manuals/narcotic/narcotic.pdf; DEA PHARMACIST'S MANUAL (rev. ed. 2010), *available at* http://www.deadiversion.usdoj.gov/pubs/manuals/pharm2/pharm_manual.pdf; DEA PRACTITIONER'S MANUAL, *supra* note 2. DEA states that the "Practitioner's Manual is intended to summarize and explain the basic requirements for prescribing, administering, and dispensing controlled substances under the Controlled Substances Act [ ], 21 U.S.C. § 801-890, and the DEA regulations, Title 21, Code of Federal Regulations [ ], Parts 1300 to 1316." DEA PRACTITIONER'S MANUAL at 1.

[11]   *See infra* note 55.

[12]   Most states have adopted controlled substances statutes and regulations modeled on the CSA that regulate both controlled substances and listed chemicals, especially pseudoephedrine. Congress specifically reserved such jurisdiction to the states, stating that the CSA does not preempt a more strict state law. 21 U.S.C. § 903. Notwithstanding that federal law permits states to apply standards more stringent that federal standards, recent state marijuana initiatives run contrary to this general notion. *See generally* COLO. CONST. art. 18, § 16; WASH. REV. CODE § 69.50. In light of the legalized recreational use of marijuana in some states, the Department of Justice has issued guidance to federal prosecutors recommending use of prosecutorial discretion for enforcing only certain marijuana-related federal crimes. *See, e.g.,* Memorandum from James M. Cole, Dep. Att. Gen., U.S. Dep't of Justice, to All United States Attorneys (Feb. 14, 2014), *available at* http://www.justice.gov/usao/waw/press/newsblog%20pdfs/DAG%20Memo%20-%20Guidance%20Regarding%20Marijuana%20Related%20Financial%20Crimes%202%2014%2014%20(2).pdf. The United States is also a signatory to a number of international drug control treaties administered under the United Nations International Drug Control Program. These treaties obligate the United States to maintain certain standards in the regulation of controlled substances and listed chemicals, especially imports and exports thereof.

Classification of Drugs and Chemicals of Abuse

The CSA classifies drugs of abuse into five schedules of controlled substances.[13] A drug is scheduled pursuant to its relative potential for abuse, including the degree to which it may cause physical or psychological dependence, and whether it has a currently accepted medical use in treatment in the United States.[14] For example, Schedule I includes drugs that have a high potential for abuse and dependence and drugs for which there is *no* accepted medical use in the United States (e.g., PCP, MDMA, heroin).[15] Under federal law, Schedule I drugs may not be prescribed, administered, or dispensed for medical use in the United States.[16] Controlled substances that have a legitimate medical use are classified in Schedules II through V depending on their abuse potential relative to other drugs. For example, drugs in Schedule II have a high potential for abuse and may lead to severe psychological or physical dependence. Narcotics listed in Schedule II include morphine and opium products such as oxycodone, hydromorphone, and fentanyl. As of October 6, 2014, hydrocodone combination products (HCPs) were rescheduled and placed into Schedule II.[17] Schedule II stimulants include amphetamine, cocaine, pentobarbital, methamphetamine, and phenobarbital. Physician prescriptions for Schedule II drugs are subject to the most restrictive requirements; for example, they must be issued in writing and they cannot be refilled. Drugs listed in Schedule III (e.g., acetaminophen with codeine, buprenorphine) have a lower abuse potential than drugs in Schedule II, but a higher abuse potential than drugs in Schedules IV and V.

There is some overlap in drug classifications. For example, combination drug products that contain both controlled and non-controlled substances can sometimes be placed in other schedules. Codeine is controlled in Schedule II because of its high potential for abuse; however, certain codeine formulations that also contain non-controlled drugs (such as acetaminophen) are classified in Schedules III, IV, and V.[18] These combination drugs are considered to have a lower potential for abuse because they tend to have smaller amounts of the controlled substance in the formulation, or the combination of the controlled substance with other substances reduces the drug's abuse potential. The CSA schedules drugs primarily by "substance," although there are a few exceptions. For example, dronabinol (synthetic

---

[13]   21 U.S.C. § 812.

[14]   *Id.* § 812(b).

[15]   *Id.* For a complete list, *see* 21 C.F.R. §1308, *available at* http://www.deadiversion.usdoj.gov/schedules/index. html.

[16]   Despite DEA's current position that there is no evidence of adequate, well-controlled studies demonstrating marijuana's safety and effectiveness as a medicine, and there recently was no consensus among experts on these issues permitting rescheduling from Schedule I, *see Americans for Safe Access v. Drug Enforcement Administration*, No. 11-1265, slip op. at 25 (D.C. Cir. Jan. 22, 2013), several states have legalized the use of marijuana for medicinal purposes. *See, e.g.,* COLO. CONST. art. 18, § 14; ALASKA STAT. § 17.37.030; CONN. GEN. STAT. § 21a-408a; MONT. CODE ANN. § 50-46-301.

[17]   79 Fed. Reg. 49,661 (Aug. 22, 2014). HCPs had been regulated under Schedule III since their original scheduling in 1971. Hydrocodone single-entity products (such as Zohydro™) are included in Schedule II. The rescheduling initiative for combination products began with a petition in 1999; yet in 2008, the U.S. Department of Health and Human Services (DHHS) provided to DEA its recommendation that HCPs remain controlled in Schedule III of the CSA. *Id.* The 2012 Food and Drug Administration Safety and Innovation Act (FDASIA) (Pub. L. No. 112-144, 126 Stat. 993), § 1139, included a provision requiring review, including public meetings, on rescheduling of HCPs. As a result of that required review, FDA recommended rescheduling hydrocodone combination products to Schedule II.

[18]   21 U.S.C. § 812(c)(a)(H), (d)(4).

tetrahydrocannabinol) is in Schedule I,[19] but the specific dosage form of dronabinol contained in a branded product approved by the Food and Drug Administration (FDA) is classified as a Schedule III drug.[20]

Congress retains the authority to schedule drugs as controlled substances by legislative action, and has exercised this authority over the years.[21] The CSA provides, however, that drugs may be scheduled, rescheduled, or descheduled pursuant to administrative notice-and-comment rulemaking, and changes in the scheduling of a drug are most commonly made by rulemaking.[22] Drug scheduling may be initiated by DEA, the U.S. Department of Health and Human Services (DHHS), or upon a petition by any interested party.[23] Although DEA has primary authority for conducting such rulemaking, DHHS also plays a critical role in scheduling actions. The basis for all scheduling decisions derives from a scientific and medical evaluation of either a substance's potential for abuse or its demonstrated abuse based on epidemiological and other relevant data. This process is known as the "eight-factor analysis."[24] DHHS is required to provide DEA with a scientific and medical evaluation of the abuse potential of a drug or substance as part of any scheduling action.[25] DHHS may also recommend when and in what schedule the drug should be listed; however, such a recommendation is not binding on DEA except where DHHS recommends that a new drug approved for marketing not be controlled.[26]

DEA will consider the DHHS evaluation along with its own independent evaluation of a drug's potential for abuse in determining whether to issue a proposed scheduling action.[27] FDA, specifically its Controlled Substance Staff, takes the lead role in preparing the DHHS

---

[19]   *Id.* § 812(c), Schedule I(c)(17).

[20]   21 C.F.R. § 1308.13(g). DEA published a notice of proposed rulemaking to amend the dronabinol Schedule III listing to include other formulations (natural THC and other dosage forms). Listing of Approved Drug Products Containing Dronabinol as Schedule III, 75 Fed. Reg. 67,054 (Nov. 1, 2010) (expressing concern that drug listing based on differences in formulation (rather than the chemical or drug itself) is inconsistent with the purpose of the CSA). However, at the time the regulation was originally promulgated placing the approved form of dronabinol in Schedule III, DEA had not anticipated a generic formulation could be developed that did not fit precisely within the wording of the listing that appeared in Schedule III. As of the date of this publication, DEA has not acted on the proposed rule.

[21]   For example, in February 2000, Congress enacted legislation placing gamma-hydroxybutyric acid (commonly referred to as the "date rape drug") into Schedule I of the CSA. *See* Hillory J. Farias and Samantha Reid Date-Rape Drug Prohibition Act of 2000, Pub. L. No. 106-172, 114 Stat. 7 (2000). More recently, with the passage of the Food and Drug Administration Safety and Innovation Act (FDASIA) in July 2012, Pub. L. No. 112-144, 126 Stat. 993 (2012), Congress added 26 substances to Schedule I of the CSA. These synthetic cannabis and psychedelic/hallucinogenic drugs include those commonly found in products marketed as bath salts, plant food, "K2," and "Spice." The law doubles the length of time a substance may be temporarily placed in Schedule I (from 18 to 36 months). FDASIA also creates a new definition for "cannabamimetic agents," creating criteria by which similar chemical compounds may be controlled.

[22]   21 U.S.C. § 811(a).

[23]   *Id.*

[24]   *Id.* § 811(c). These eight factors are: 1) the drug's actual or relative potential for abuse; 2) the scientific evidence of the drug's pharmacological effect, if known; 3) the state of current scientific knowledge about the drug; 4) the drug's history or current pattern of abuse; 5) scope, duration, and significance of the drug's abuse; 6) the risk, if any, to public health; 7) the drug's physiological or psychic dependence liability; and 8) whether the drug is an immediate precursor of a substance already controlled under this subchapter. *Id.*

[25]   *Id.* § 811(b).

[26]   *Id.*

[27]   *See, e.g.,* Schedules of Controlled Substances: Placement of Pregabalin into Schedule V, 70 Fed. Reg. 43,633 (July 28, 2005); Listing of Approved Drug Products Containing Dronabinol in Schedule III, 75 Fed. Reg. 67,054 (Nov. 1, 2010).

recommendation, in consultation with the National Institute on Drug Abuse. FDA attempts to coordinate with DEA so that DHHS recommendations are forwarded prior to FDA approval of a new drug and so that DEA can initiate a scheduling action prior to approval. DEA's rulemaking is conducted independent of FDA's drug approval process. Thus, the marketing launch of a new drug may be delayed until the final rulemaking by DEA on its scheduling action. When scheduling occurs after approval, the product's launch can be delayed and the applicant can lose some period of marketing exclusivity under the Federal Food, Drug, and Cosmetic Act (FDCA) for the period of time after it has received FDA approval, but DEA has failed to complete its scheduling action.[28]

This occurred most recently in the case of FDA's approval of epilepsy drug FYCOMPA™. Although FDA approved FYCOMPA™ for marketing in October 2012, DEA's inaction in scheduling for almost a year resulted in its manufacturer petitioning a federal appeals court for a Writ of Mandamus that DEA must act to schedule the drug. The D.C. Circuit denied the request in part because DEA promised in response to the petition to issue the scheduling notice within a specified period of time.[29] DEA issued its scheduling notice within three months after drug maker Eisai filed its writ petition.

In extreme cases, as permitted in 21 U.S.C. § 811(b), DEA may temporarily place a substance into Schedule I for a one-year period without complying with the usual scheduling requirements under section 811(b), if the agency determines that such action is necessary to avoid an imminent hazard to the public health.[30]

---

[28] *See* Schedules of Controlled Substances: Placement of Zopiclone into Schedule IV, 70 Fed. Reg. 16,935 (Apr. 4, 2005).

[29] *In re Eisai Inc.*, No. 13-1243, slip op. at 1 (D.C. Cir. Oct. 22, 2013). DEA ultimately placed FYCOMPA™ in Schedule III effective January 2, 2014. Schedules of Controlled Substances: Placement of Perampanel into Schedule III, 78 Fed. Reg. 72,013 (Dec. 2, 2013). Likely as a result of the delay resulting from DEA's scheduling of FYCOMPA™ (and the effect of that delay on the drug's exclusivity period), a bill was introduced in Congress that would significantly streamline the drug scheduling process for new medical therapies and reduce the potential for unnecessary delays in the availability of these needed medicines. Improving Regulatory Transparency for New Medical Therapies Act, H.R. 4299, 113th Cong. (2014). The bill would also require the DEA to make a decision on new registration applications for the manufacturing and distribution of drugs and substances used in clinical trials. *Id.*

[30] DEA used its emergency scheduling powers on multiple occasions since 2011. Most of DEA's recent emergency scheduling actions involved temporary scheduling in Schedule I of synthetic cannabinoids and cathinones. *See, e.g.*, Schedules of Controlled Substances: Temporary Placement of Ten Synthetic Cathinones into Schedule I, 79 Fed. Reg. 12,938 (Mar. 7, 2014); Schedules of Controlled Substances: Temporary Placement of Four Synthetic Cannabinoids into Schedule I, 79 Fed. Reg. 7577 (Feb. 10, 2014); Schedules of Controlled Substances: Temporary Placement of Three Synthetic Cathinones into Schedule I, 76 Fed. Reg. 65,371 (Oct. 21, 2011). These synthetic cathinone substances have no known medical use in the United States, and are being abused. DEA noted there have been reports of emergency room admissions and deaths associated with the abuse of synthetic cathinone substances. Products containing synthetic cathinones have been falsely marketed as "research chemicals," "plant fertilizer," "jewelry cleaner," "stain remover," "plant food or fertilizer," "insect repellants," or "bath salts." *See id.* at 65,372. The products are sold at smoke shops, head shops, convenience stores, adult book stores, and gas stations and can be purchased on the Internet. These substances are in the form of powders, crystals, resins, tablets, and capsules. Schedules of Controlled Substances: Temporary Placement of 10 Synthetic Cathinones into Schedule I, 79 Fed. Reg. 4429 (Jan. 28, 2014). DEA explained that temporary scheduling is necessary to avoid an imminent hazard to public safety because they are not intended for human consumption; there has been a significant increase in their abuse. *Id.* Prior to 2011, the last time that DEA invoked its emergency scheduling authority was in April 2003. *See* 68 Fed. Reg. 16,427 (Apr. 4, 2003) (temporary placement of alpha-methyltryptamine and 5-methoxy-N,N-diisopropyltryptamine in Schedule I).

The CSA's classification of listed chemicals differs from that of controlled substances in that the regulations do not provide a complete closed chain of distribution, although for some chemicals the distinction has narrowed considerably.[31] For example, because of the increased concern with diversion of pseudoephedrine (PSE) in the illicit manufacture of methamphetamine, PSE is now subject to requirements similar to a controlled substance, e.g., quotas, retail restrictions, etc.[32]

Listed chemicals are those chemicals that can be either directly used illicitly to manufacture controlled substances (List I chemicals), such as PSE, or chemicals that are important to the manufacture of controlled substances (List II chemicals), such as phosphorous or toluene.[33] The classification of chemicals in either List I or List II affects the extent of regulation, e.g., registration, recordkeeping, and reporting requirements.[34] Notably, the types of controls that DEA places on chemicals are less stringent than the controls imposed on controlled drugs because most of the listed chemicals have a legitimate industrial application in non-drug-related products such as paints and solvents. Thus, DEA believes that use of the term "regulated" is more appropriate to describe "chemicals," as opposed to the term "controlled," which DEA uses for certain drugs.[35] Listed chemicals are contained in many prescription and over-the-counter (OTC) medicines.[36] Currently, the CSA includes 30 List I chemicals and 11 List II chemicals.[37] In addition to regulations, DEA provides guidance in its recently updated *Chemical Handlers' Manual* concerning the handling of listed chemicals (prepared by the DEA, Office of Diversion Control), to assist those who handle scheduled listed chemical products including List I and II chemicals in understanding the CSA and its implementing regulations as they pertain to regulated chemicals.[38]

Links in the Closed Chain of Distribution

The CSA accomplishes its objective of creating a closed chain of distribution by creating a closed system of registration, recordkeeping, security, and reporting requirements to ensure that controlled substances, and to a lesser extent listed chemicals, are accounted for at each point in the distribution chain where they are handled. These requirements apply to all DEA registrants, but the specific requirements vary depending on the type of registration activity and the schedule of controlled substance or class of listed chemical handled by the registrant.

---

31   CMEA, *supra* note 4.
32   *Id.*
33   21 U.S.C. § 802(34), (35).
34   *Compare, e.g.,* 21 C.F.R. pt. 1304, *with* 21 C.F.R. pt. 1309.
35   *See* DEA, U.S. Chemical Control, http://www.justice.gov/dea/concern/chemical_controlp.html.
36   21 U.S.C. §§ 823(h), 830.
37   21 C.F.R. § 1310.02.
38   DEA CHEMICAL HANDLER'S MANUAL, *supra* note 10.

Registration

Every person or entity, except a patient (i.e., end user), who physically handles a controlled substance must be registered with DEA.[39] This requirement includes manufacturers, distributors, healthcare practitioners, importers, exporters, researchers, and analytical laboratories.[40] A DEA registration is required for each independent activity. For example, a separate DEA registration is necessary to import, export, or manufacture a controlled substance. A separate DEA registration is also required for each separate facility engaged in an activity.[41] DEA's regulation specifically states: "A separate registration is required for each principal place of business or professional practice at one general physical location where controlled substances are manufactured, distributed, imported, exported, or dispensed by a person."[42]

DEA registration periods vary in length: Importers, exporters, manufacturers, and distributors must register and renew their registrations annually; whereas registrations for practitioners such as doctors, dentists and veterinarians, hospitals, and pharmacies are effective for three years.[43] A DEA registration is considered a privilege that DEA grants only if the registration is in the "public interest."[44] The public interest factors that DEA must specifically consider for manufacturers, distributors, and practitioners are set forth in the CSA.[45] The criteria for registration under the public interest standard include whether an applicant can maintain effective controls against diversion, the applicant's history of compliance with applicable laws, past experience in handling controlled substances, and lack of any prior convictions or adverse actions related to controlled substances.[46] A prerequisite for registration that most often affects practitioners, such as physicians and pharmacies, is the requirement that they also be licensed under the applicable state law.[47]

List I chemical handlers are also generally subject to DEA registration requirements, especially for importers, exporters, manufacturers, and distributors.[48] Although physical handling of controlled substances always requires a DEA registration, possessing a List I or II chemical does not automatically require registration. For example, use of a List I chemical in a manufacturing process where the chemical is not further distributed would not require a DEA registration. The DEA registration requirement for a chemical depends on whether it is in List I or List II, the type of chemical involved, and in some cases the quantity of chemical produced or distributed. For example, retail distributors of scheduled listed chemical products (SLCPs) are required to be registered with DEA; the same is not generally true of all other retail sales of List I or II chemicals.[49] DEA applies the same public

---

39   21 U.S.C. § 822.
40   Id. §§ 822, 957.
41   Id. § 822(e).
42   21 C.F.R. § 1301.12(a).
43   Id. § 1301.13(e).
44   21 U.S.C. § 823.
45   Id.
46   See generally id.; see also, e.g., Edmund Chein, M.D., 72 Fed. Reg. 6580 (Feb. 12, 2007); Scott C. Bickman, M.D., Revocation of Registration, 76 Fed. Reg. 17,694 (Mar. 30, 2011) (setting forth analysis of public interest factors considered under practitioner public interest standard with respect to revocation of registration).
47   See, e.g., Karen Joe Smiley, M.D., 68 Fed. Reg. 48,944 (Aug. 15, 2003).
48   21 U.S.C. § 823(h).
49   SLCPs include ephedrine, pseudoephedrine, and phenylpropanolamine.

interest standard in determining whether to grant registrations to those who handle listed chemicals or those who handle controlled substances.

Security

All DEA registrants must maintain effective controls to prevent diversion, including adequate physical security in the storage and handling of controlled substances. Again, the security requirements vary by the type of registrant (e.g., manufacturer, distributor, or practitioner) and the scheduling classification of the drug (e.g., Schedule II or Schedule III).[50] For example, manufacturers and distributors of Schedule II controlled substances are required to store such substances in a vault constructed according to specifications detailed in the DEA regulations.[51] Also, controlled substances in Schedules III-V are subject to security cage and alarm system requirements also specified in DEA regulations.[52] Practitioners, such as physicians and pharmacies, are required to store controlled substances in securely locked cabinets and may employ other measures to maintain security; e.g., pharmacies may mix stock of controlled substances with stock of non-controlled substances to conceal their identity and prevent theft.[53]

Registrants handling listed chemicals must maintain adequate security for the storage and handling of these substances.[54] Neither the CSA nor DEA regulations provide specific security requirements for listed chemicals, in contrast to controlled substances. DEA will evaluate the security of an applicant or registrant on the basis of the type of registration and other factors, such as location, public access, and pattern of potential theft and loss. For both controlled substances and listed chemicals, DEA requires manufacturers and distributors to identify and report suspicious orders and transactions.[55]

Quotas

The CSA requires that DEA establish quotas for certain controlled substances and certain listed chemicals. These quotas effectively limit the amount of such drugs that can be manufactured and distributed in a given calendar year. The CSA establishes quotas to regulate and control the amount of Schedule I and II controlled substances that may be manufactured in the United States in any given year.[56] DEA establishes by rulemaking an

---

[50]   21 C.F.R. §§ 1301.71-1301.77.

[51]   *Id.*

[52]   *Id.*

[53]   *Id.* § 1301.75.

[54]   *See id.* § 1301.71.

[55]   When determining whether the registrant has designed a system to detect and report suspicious orders, DEA relies on case law concerning distributors, which is scant (*see, e.g.,* Southwood Pharmaceuticals, Inc.; Revocation of Registration, 72 Fed. Reg. 36,487 (July 3, 2007) (discussing Internet pharmacy sales of hydrocodone efforts, and insufficient customer due diligence efforts concerning orders of same)), and guidance from DEA to industry through communications including industry letters dealing with Internet pharmacies dated September 2006 and December 2007. The 2006 letter states, for example, that distributors, in addition to reporting suspicious orders, have a "statutory responsibility" not to fill suspicious orders that might be diverted; filling such orders could provide a basis for registration revocation or suspension. Letter to Registrants dated September 27, 2006, from Joseph T. Rannazzisi, Deputy Asst. Administrator, DEA. The letter cautions distributors not to rely on customers holding a DEA registration and against "turn[ing] a blind eye to the suspicious circumstances," that they must confirm the legitimacy of all orders before filling them, and they must consider the totality of the circumstances when evaluating orders. *Id.*

[56]   21 U.S.C. § 826.

annual aggregate quota for the entire United States for each substance in Schedule I or II and some chemicals.[57] DEA then assigns companies individual manufacturing quotas for the manufacture of controlled substances in bulk, such as active pharmaceutical ingredients morphine and codeine.[58] DEA also issues procurement quotas, which authorize companies to procure a basic class of a Schedule I or II drug (i.e., hydrocodone, oxycodone, or codeine base) to make the finished dosage forms (i.e., pills or liquid) of approved drugs.[59] Companies may manufacture quantities only within the limits of their manufacturing quotas and may purchase source materials or conduct dosage form manufacturing only within the limits of their procurement quotas.

A registrant must apply each year to the agency for an annual manufacturing or procurement quota.[60] DEA will consider the registrant's prior sales history, current inventories, estimates of future sales, current market conditions, and other relevant data to assign quotas.[61] A registrant may apply for additional quota throughout the year to the extent that the amount of quota granted by DEA is insufficient to meet manufacturing or sales needs, or to the extent that the registrant needs more quota than it originally anticipated when estimating its annual need and applying for the quota. A registrant may challenge DEA's decision on allocation of quotas or the refusal to increase a quota in a hearing before an administrative law judge (ALJ).[62] The ALJ's recommended opinion is then submitted to DEA's Deputy Administrator for a final ruling on whether to increase the quota. That decision can be appealed to a federal court of appeals. Notwithstanding any court appeal, however, the process of appealing a DEA quota decision often outlives the calendar year for which the DEA granted the original quota, and so many become moot.

Failure of DEA to provide an adequate overall quota for a medicinal controlled substance on a timely basis can adversely affect the nation's drug supply. In at least one case, the failure to provide an adequate quota for methylphenidate was alleged to have created a shortage.[63] This same allegation involving methylphenidate surfaced again in May 2011, when certain drug manufacturers alleged that drug shortages and unavailability of products for the U.S. market resulted from DEA's failure to approve quotas for additional quantities.[64]

For listed chemicals, the CMEA amended the CSA to require DEA to establish production and import quotas for SLCPs.[65] As required by the CMEA, DEA publishes in the *Federal Register* a proposed assessment of annual needs, which represents "those quantities of

---

7   *Id.* § 826(a). DEA, Notice, Established Aggregate Production Quotas for Schedule I and II Controlled Substances and Assessment of Annual Needs for the List I Chemicals Ephedrine, Pseudoephedrine, and Phenylpropanolamine for 2015, 79 Fed. Reg. 53,216 (Sept. 8, 2014).

8   *Id.* § 826(b).

9   *See* 21 C.F.R. § 1303.12.

0   21 C.F.R. §§ 1303.12(a) (procurement), 1303.22 (manufacturing).

1   21 C.F.R. § 1303.11.

2   *Id.* § 1303.31.

3   For example, on September 27, 1994, DEA issued an interim rule to increase the aggregate production quota for methylphenidate. Controlled Substances. Established Revised 1994 Aggregate Production Quotas, 59 Fed. Reg. 49,256 (Sept. 27, 1994). DEA stated at that time that the "increase is immediately required to meet the 1994 year-end medical needs of the United States." *Id.*; *see also* U.S. Department of Justice, DEA, Methylphenidate (A Background Paper) (October 1995), U.S. Government Accountability Office, GAO/GGD-95-52R, Controlled Substance Quotas (1995).

4   *See* Peter Loftus, *Attention Disorder Drug Shortage Prompts Finger-Pointing*, WALL ST. J., May 5, 2011.

5   CMEA § 713, *see supra* note 3; *see also* 21 U.S.C. § 826(a).

ephedrine, PSE and phenylpropanolamine which may be manufactured domestically and, or imported into the United States to provide adequate supplies of each substance to meet the estimated medical, scientific, research, and industrial needs of the United States; lawful export requirements; and the establishment and maintenance of reserve stocks."[66] As with controlled substance quota determinations, DEA is required to consider information contained in applications for import, manufacturing, and procurement, as well as public comments in reaching its final assessment.

Recordkeeping

All registrants who handle controlled substances or listed chemicals must maintain for at least two years complete and accurate records of certain transactions.[67] Complete and accurate records of all controlled substances received, distributed, or otherwise disposed of are critical to maintaining compliance with the CSA and DEA's regulations. Business records, such as purchase orders and invoices, may be sufficient to meet this requirement, but only if those records are complete and contain the required information, such as date shipped and received, quantity, DEA number, and other relevant information about the transaction.

All registrants handling controlled substances must take and monitor an initial inventory of all controlled substances on hand, then take and maintain a biennial inventory.[68] For Schedule II and narcotic drugs, these inventories must be completed by taking actual physical counts. Although many registrants such as pharmacies find it useful to maintain perpetual inventories, the CSA specifically does not require registrants to maintain a perpetual inventory.[69] Inventories of all Schedule I (research drugs) and Schedule II substances must be separate from inventories of all other substances.

The CSA also requires registrants to use DEA Form 222 order form when transferring Schedule I and II drugs.[70] DEA is very particular that these forms be accurately executed and properly maintained. DEA has established a program to automate the DEA Order Form system to improve the efficiency of the process.[71]

Listed chemical registrants are also subject to recordkeeping requirements on transactions involving List I chemicals, although there are no specific inventory requirements except for manufacturers of certain List I chemicals.[72] Also, some recordkeeping requirements for listed chemicals are triggered only by a transaction that is a "regulated transaction," i.e., generally one that involves at least a certain threshold quantity of a listed chemical. In addition, under the CMEA, retail sellers of pseudoephedrine must maintain a logbook that

---

66   *See* Assessment of Annual Needs for the List I Chemicals Ephedrine, Pseudoephedrine, and Phenylpropanolamine for 2011, 75 Fed. Reg. 55,605, 55,606 (Sept. 13, 2010).

67   21 U.S.C. § 827.

68   21 C.F.R. § 1304.11.

69   21 U.S.C. § 827(a)(3).

70   *Id.* § 828; 21 C.F.R. § 1305.03.

71   DEA's Controlled Substances Ordering System (CSOS) provides an alternative electronic method for the transmission and storage of electronic orders and prescriptions. *See* 21 C.F.R. pt. 1311. A practitioner may also utilize this electronic system to issue prescriptions for controlled substances. 21 C.F.R. § 1311.100 (b).

72   *Id.* § 1310.03.

records the quantity and form of PSE sold, the purchaser's name and address, the date and time of sale, and the purchaser's signature.[73]

Given the CSA and DEA's emphasis on accountability, noncompliance with CSA recordkeeping provisions is a serious issue. The CSA provides that it shall be unlawful for any person "to refuse or negligently fail to make, keep, or furnish any record, [or] report" required under the CSA.[74] As discussed more fully below, a failure to make, keep, or furnish to DEA any required, complete record or report can result in violations of the CSA, leading to administrative or civil penalties and fines of up to $10,000 per recordkeeping violation.[75]

Prescribing and Dispensing

The CSA and regulations promulgated by DEA contain specific requirements for prescribing controlled substances.[76] The regulations define "prescription" as "an order for medication which is dispensed to or for an ultimate user . . . ."[77] DEA regulations contain specific provisions that govern the content and format of these prescriptions, as well as rules relating to the purposes for which a prescription is issued.[78] Generally, with some exceptions, prescriptions for Schedule II substances must be written by a practitioner and physically delivered to the pharmacist, and may not be refilled, whereas prescriptions for Schedule III-V substances may be written or oral and may be refilled.[79] In October 2010, DEA announced a Statement of Policy by which a registrant (i.e., a physician) may use an agent, including a nurse in a long-term care facility, to communicate controlled substance prescriptions to a pharmacy. Although DEA recognizes that the core responsibilities of prescribing controlled substances may not be delegated, an individual practitioner may authorize an agent to communicate controlled-substance prescriptions to a pharmacy in order to make the prescription process more efficient.[80]

DEA regulations also require that, for a prescription to be effective, it must "be issued for a legitimate medical purpose by an individual practitioner acting in the usual course of [ ] professional practice."[81] The "legitimate medical purpose" rule can be difficult in its application, in that it refers to the exercise of a practitioner's subjective professional judgment

---

73 CMEA § 711(e); *see also* 21 U.S.C. § 830(e).

74 21 U.S.C. § 842(a)(5).

75 *Id.* § 842(c)(1)(B); *see* 21 C.F.R. §§ 1304.03 (requirement that registrants keep records and file reports); 1304.11 (inventory requirements); 1304.21 (general requirements for continuing records); 1304.22 (requirements for dispensers of controlled substances to maintain certain records).

76 21 U.S.C. § 829; 21 C.F.R. pt. 1306.

77 21 C.F.R. § 1300.01(35).

78 *Id.* § 1306.11. The regulations also allow for the use of electronic prescriptions. 21 C.F.R. pt. 1311. Practitioners utilizing electronic prescriptions must maintain an electronic prescription application (or program) requiring an authentication credential for each practitioner to access the application. *Id.* §§ 1311.100-.130. These applications must also be able to conduct internal audits and reports and maintain records electronically. *Id.* §§ 1311.150-.305. However, pharmacies are not required to accept electronic prescriptions for controlled substances. Whether a practitioner or pharmacy uses electronic prescriptions for controlled substances is voluntary, from DEA's perspective.

79 *Id.*

80 *See* DEA, Statement of Policy: Role of Authorized Agents in Communicating Controlled Substance Prescriptions to Pharmacies, 75 Fed Reg. 61,613 (Oct. 6, 2010).

81 21 C.F.R. § 1306.04; United States v. Moore, 423 U.S. 122 (1975) (physician violates the CSA when he sells illicit drugs to addicts and is acting outside the usual course of practice); *see also* United States v. Collier, 478 F.2d 268 (5th Cir. 1973) (physician abusing drugs is outside the scope of the practice of medicine).

regarding the medical circumstances that may or may not justify the use of a controlled substance to treat a particular patient.

Although prescribing practitioners are responsible for ensuring that prescriptions comply with all CSA and DEA requirements, a corresponding responsibility rests with the prescription-filling pharmacists.[82] DEA regulations impose a corresponding responsibility on a pharmacist to avoid knowingly filling a prescription that was not issued for a legitimate medical purpose as reflected in the circumstances known to the pharmacist. DEA will pursue enforcement action against pharmacists who fail to comply with this requirement.[83]

Appropriate prescribing and dispensing of pain medication has been an ongoing issue between DEA and practitioners since before the CSA was enacted. The need to ensure adequate availability of pain drugs that have a high potential for abuse creates a conflict between DEA and the pain community.[84] This conflict has been exacerbated by DEA concerns about unlawful sales of prescription drugs over the Internet and about increases in the number of clinics devoted exclusively to treatment of pain. Recently, DEA, along with FDA and the Office of National Drug Control Policy, announced an initiative to require greater training and education of practitioners prescribing and dispensing controlled substances.[85] In reaction to DEA's enforcement of pharmacists' corresponding responsibility requirements, and increased scrutiny of controlled substance prescriptions by pharmacists, the American Medical Association considered resolutions at its 2013 meeting to recognize pharmacy "gatekeeper" attempts to verify prescriptions as unwarranted intrusions into the practice of medicine.[86]

---

[82]   21 C.F.R. § 1306.04.

[83]   *See, e.g.,* Trinity Health Care Corp., D/B/A Oviedo Discount Pharmacy, 72 Fed. Reg. 30,849, 30,854 (June 4, 2007). *See also* East Main Street Pharmacy: Affirmation of Suspension Order, 75 Fed. Reg. 66,149 (Oct. 27, 2010) (ALJ's elaboration of pharmacist's corresponding responsibility; when prescriptions are not issued for a legitimate medical purpose, a "pharmacist may not intentionally close his eyes and thereby avoid [actual] knowledge of the real purpose of the prescription."); Holiday CVS, L.L.C., d/b/a CVS/Pharmacy Nos. 219 and 5195: Decision and Order, 77 Fed. Reg. 62,315 (Oct. 12, 2012) (Final Order revoking after immediate suspension and ALJ hearing DEA registrations of two CVS/Pharmacy locations located in Florida; DEA found, *inter alia*, that pharmacists did not appropriately exercise their corresponding responsibility when filling oxycodone and other controlled substances prescriptions, and pharmacists filled prescriptions based on invalid DEA numbers). In 2013, Walgreens also reached the largest DEA civil settlement in history related to several of its Florida pharmacists' violations of DEA's corresponding regulations (21 C.F.R. § 1306.04) and suspicious order monitoring regulations (21 C.F.R. § 1374(b)) at its distribution centers that delivered oxycodone products into Florida. *See* DEA Press Release, Walgreens Agrees to Pay a Record Settlement of $80 Million for Civil Penalties under the Controlled Substances Act, http://www.justice.gov/dea/divisions/mia/2013/mia061113.shtml.

[84]   *See* Pain and Policy Group, Achieving Balance in Federal and State Pain Policy: 2006 Guide to Evaluation, Third Edition, Univ. of Wisconsin Paul P. Carbone Comprehensive Cancer Center, Madison, Wisconsin (2006); *see also* A Joint Statement from 21 Health Organizations and the Drug Enforcement Administration, Promoting Pain Relief and Preventing Abuse of Pain Medications: A Critical Balancing Act (2001), http://www.painpolicy.wisc.edu/consensus2.pdf.

[85]   *See* Press Release, Office of National Drug Control Policy, Obama Administration Releases Action Plan to Address National Prescription Drug Abuse Epidemic; Announces FDA Action Requiring Drug Makers to Develop Education Program for Prescribers About Safe Use of Opioids (Apr. 19, 2011), http://www.whitehousedrugpolicy.gov/news/press11/041911.html.

[86]   *See, e.g.,* AMA Tells Pharmacists: "Don't Call Us We'll Call You," *available at* http://www.fdalawblog.net/fda_law_blog_hyman_phelps/2013/06/ama-tells-pharmacists-dont-call-us-well-call-you-.html.

here are some ongoing issues on how the CSA applies to compounding pharmacies. For example, DEA revoked the DEA registration of a pharmacy because it found that the pharmacy compounded drugs and delivered them to the veterinarian practitioners and not the end-user animal patients in violation of the CSA.[87] The D.C. Circuit vacated that revocation on the ground that the agency had not considered the unique issues relating to dispensing to veterinarians.[88]

Historically, DEA's interpretation of the closed chain of distribution and guidelines concerning the destruction of controlled substances generally prohibits return of a controlled substance from the patient back to a registrant. However, given concerns about prescription drug abuse, and the limited secure controlled substance disposal options for registrants and ultimate users, DEA recently changed this rule.[89] The new regulations implement the Secure and Responsible Drug Disposal Act of 2010[90] by expanding options for the collection from ultimate users to include take-back events,[91] mail-back programs,[92] and collection receptacle locations.[93] The regulations allow authorized manufacturers, distributors, reverse distributors, narcotic treatment programs, hospitals and clinics with an on-site pharmacy, and retail pharmacies to voluntarily administer mail-back programs and maintain collection receptacles (after authorization from DEA).[94] In addition, the final rule also allows retail pharmacies and hospitals and clinics with an on-site pharmacy to maintain collection receptacles at long-term care facilities.[95]

Reporting

All registrants must report any theft or significant loss of controlled substances by: 1) notifying a local DEA field office in writing upon discovery of such a theft or loss within one business day of discovery; and 2) filing a written report (DEA Form 106) of the results of the investigation into the theft or loss.[96] Registrants must also notify the local DEA field office of any suspicious order for controlled substances when discovered by the registrant.[97] Suspicious orders include orders of unusual size, orders deviating from a normal pattern, and orders of unusual frequency.[98] For the past several years, DEA has expended significant resources on educating distributors of controlled substances about suspicious order monitoring and compliance as a critical element in its efforts against diversion. It has also been aggressive in its enforcement of these requirements. DEA has also filed administrative

---

[87] Wedgewood Village Pharmacy, 71 Fed. Reg. 16,593 (Apr. 3, 2006).
[88] Wedgewood Village Pharmacy v. Drug Enforcement Admin., 509 F.3d 541 (D.C. Cir. 2007). DEA and the registrant settled this dispute (which had lasted over eight years), with DEA restoring the right of the registrant to dispense controlled substances subject to certain restrictions set forth in a memorandum of agreement between the parties. *Id.*
[89] DEA, Final Rule, Disposal of Controlled Substances, 79 Fed. Reg. 53,519 (Sept. 9, 2014) (codified at 21 C.F.R. pts. 1300, 1301, 1304, 1305, 1307, and 1317).
[90] Pub. L. No. 111-273.
[91] 21 C.F.R. § 1317.65.
[92] 21 C.F.R. § 1317.70.
[93] 21 C.F.R. § 1317.75.
[94] *See* 21 C.F.R. §§ 1317.70, 1317.75
[95] 21 C.F.R. § 1317.80.
[96] 21 C.F.R. §§ 1301.74(c), 1301.76(b).
[97] *Id.* §§ 1301.74(b), 1301.76(b).
[98] *Id.*

actions and levied fines[99] against distributors that DEA believes are not in compliance with DEA's suspicious order monitoring regulations and guidance documents.[100] Notwithstanding DEA's recent enforcement actions against distributors and pharmacies, DEA can at times be overly aggressive in holding distributors accountable as a controlled substances diversion gatekeeper.[101]

Registrants that manufacture or distribute controlled substances must submit monthly or quarterly transaction reports of Schedule II drugs to account for acquisitions and distributions of Schedule II from inventory.[102]

Reporting requirements for registrants that deal with listed chemicals are specifically set forth in the regulations.[103] These reporting requirements include suspicious transactions involving List I chemicals; that is, any regulated transaction involving an extraordinary quantity of a listed chemical, any uncommon method of payment or delivery, or any other circumstance where the regulated person believes that the chemical may be used in violation of the law. Registrants must also report any unusual or excessive loss or disappearance of a listed chemical. In addition, any regulated person, not just a DEA registrant, must report any domestic regulated transaction involving a tableting machine or an encapsulating machine (including reporting the import or export of such a machine).[104]

Since enactment of the CMEA, retail sellers of nonprescription SLCPs must certify to DEA the following: 1) that consumers purchase no more than 3.6 grams of PSE per 24-hour period or no more than 9 grams of PSE per 30-day period; 2) that PSE-containing products are kept behind a counter or in a locked cabinet; 3) that logbooks record the quantity and form of PSE sold, the purchaser's name and address, the date and time of sale, and the purchaser's signature; 4) that photo identification is provided by all purchasers of PSE-containing products, and the information on an identification is confirmed to be consistent with the information a consumer enters into the logbook; and 5) that all employees involved in providing PSE-containing products to consumers and in collecting money for the purchase of such products have completed DEA-required training.[105]

---

[99]   See KeySource Medical Inc. v. United States, Civ. No. 1:11-cv-00390 (filed June 15, 2011) (alleged violation of suspicious order monitoring and reporting requirements in 21 C.F.R. § 1301.74(b) resulted in immediate suspension of registration); see also DEA, Press Release, DEA Suspends for Two Years Pharmaceutical Wholesale Distributor's Ability to Sell Controlled Substances from Lakeland, Florida Facility (May 15, 2012), http://www.dea.gov/pubs/pressrel/pr051512.html (DEA and Cardinal Health, a distributor headquartered in Dublin, Ohio, entered into a settlement agreement including a two-year suspension of its ability to sell controlled substances from a Florida distribution facility. Other settlement terms applied to all of Cardinal's 28 registered distribution facilities.).

[100]   See U.S. Gov't Accountability Office, GAO-11-744, Prescription Drug Control: DEA Has Enhanced Efforts to Combat Diversion, But Could Better Assess and Report Program Results, at 17 (2011).

[101]   In Re Masters Pharmaceuticals Inc., DEA Docket No. 13-39 (Initial Decision issued July 24, 2014) (Masters Pharmaceuticals' (Cincinnati, Ohio) CEO and others testified that the company complied with DEA's guidance and regulations. Masters prevailed before the ALJ after a full evidentiary hearing, and, as of the date of publication, is awaiting a Final Decision by the Deputy Administrator).

[102]   21 C.F.R. § 1304.33.

[103]   21 C.F.R. pt. 1310.

[104]   Id. § 1310.06.

[105]   Retail Sales of Scheduled Listed Chemical Products; Self-Certification of Regulated Sellers of Scheduled Listed Chemical Products, 71 Fed. Reg. 56,008 (Sept. 26, 2006).

Some state laws regulating PSE sales are stricter than the federal law,[106] and a few states have addressed PSE sales by regulating PSE as a prescription or scheduled drug.[107]

Imports and Exports

Any company seeking to import or export a controlled substance must file an application with DEA for a permit or an import declaration for each shipment. An importer or exporter must apply for a permit in the case of any controlled substance in Schedule I or II and any narcotic drug in Schedules III, IV, or V.[108] The registrant may not import or export the drug until the permit has been issued. An import or export of a Schedule III through V drug requires the filing of an import/export declaration at least 14 days prior to the expected shipment.[109] A registrant may complete the shipment any time after 14 days unless DEA specifically notifies the registrant that it objects to the import or export.

The CSA significantly limits the import of Schedule II drugs, other than narcotic raw materials, to: 1) research; and 2) emergencies or situations where the drug is needed but not available or there is a lack of competition among domestic manufacturers of the drug.[110] Also, the CSA has recently been amended to authorize the export of Schedule I, II, and all narcotic drugs for re-export to other countries.[111] Previously, the export of these substances was restricted to the destination country of the export.

DEA has imposed import requirements for listed chemicals as well. Under the CMEA, DEA added regulations requiring additional reporting for import, export, and international transactions involving all List I and List II chemicals.[112] The rule implements section 716 of the CMEA, which extended current reporting requirements for importations, exportations, and international transactions involving List I and List II chemicals. The numerous changes include:

- a substantially revised DEA Form 486, which must be used by all U.S. importers and exporters of List I and II chemicals to notify DEA of their imports and exports;

- a 15-day advance notice period for such transactions in most circumstances;

- a requirement that an importer provide information regarding the person or persons to whom the importer intends to transfer the chemical;

- provisions concerning what to do if a planned sale falls through; and

---

[106] Office of National Drug Control Policy, Pushing Back Against Meth: A Progress Report on the Fight Against Methamphetamine in the United States (Nov. 30, 2006), https://www.ncjrs.gov/ondcppubs/publications/pdf/pushingback_against_meth.pdf.

[107] Only Oregon (since 2006) and Mississippi (since 2010) require prescriptions for PSE. *See* Or. Rev. Stat. § 475.973 (rulemaking authority regarding products containing pseudoephedrine), Miss. Code Ann. § 41-29-117.

[108] 21 U.S.C. §§ 952, 953; 21 C.F.R. §§ 1312.12, 1312.22.

[109] 21 U.S.C. §§ 952(b), 953(e); *see also* 21 C.F.R. §§ 1312.18, 1312.27.

[110] 21 U.S.C. § 952(a)(2).

[111] Controlled Substances Export Reform Act of 2005, Pub. L. No. 109-57, 119 Stat. 592 (2005).

[112] Implementation of the Combat Methamphetamine Epidemic Act of 2005; Notice of Transfers Following Importation or Exportation, 72 Fed. Reg. 17,401 (Apr. 19, 2007); *see also* 21 C.F.R. pt. 1313.

the requirement of a declaration upon completion of a transaction.[113]

DEA implemented additional regulations in 2010 to clarify certain regulations and to remove the thresholds for importation, exportation, and domestic distributions of the List I chemicals pseudoephedrine and phenylpropanolamine.[114] Elimination of thresholds will trigger reporting requirements, thus permitting DEA to make a more accurate determination of need for these listed chemicals when engaging in its annual quota-setting analysis.

Enforcement of the CSA

The CSA provides the authority for administrative, civil, and criminal enforcement actions for violations. DEA will take action against any manufacturer, distributor, practitioner, importer, exporter, researcher, or analytic laboratory that fails to maintain effective controls against diversion as elaborated in the CSA and DEA regulatory requirements.

Administrative actions include a letter of admonition, an informal administrative hearing, or an order to show cause (OTSC).[115] A letter of admonition is usually issued for minor violations of recordkeeping or reporting requirements. The letter will advise a registrant of the alleged violations and allow for voluntary corrective action. In an informal administrative hearing, DEA provides the registrant an opportunity to discuss potential violations of a more serious nature. These hearings often are resolved with a memorandum of understanding. An OTSC is a formal DEA action to deny or revoke a DEA registration.[116] An OTSC is generally issued as a result of significant violations involving a registrant's failure to maintain effective controls against diversion or a pattern of violations occurring over a prolonged time period, in which the Deputy Administrator has alleged that continued registration is not in the public interest. A registrant has a right to challenge an OTSC through a formal administrative hearing before a DEA ALJ.[117] The ALJ will issue a recommended opinion, which is then submitted to the DEA Deputy Administrator for a final decision.[118] An adverse ruling from the DEA Deputy Administrator can be appealed to a U.S. Court of Appeals. Prior to a final agency action, the administrative OTSC cannot be litigated in federal district court.

DEA may also pursue a civil action in federal district court for monetary penalties for violations of recordkeeping and reporting requirements of the CSA. These civil matters are litigated through the Office of the U.S. Attorney.[119] Civil fines under the CSA can be significant, up to $10,000 for each recordkeeping and reporting violation and up to $25,000 for any other type of violation. The courts have considered four factors in determining the

---

[113]   *Id.*

[114]   Removal of Thresholds for the List I Chemicals Pseudoephedrine and Phenylpropanolamine, 75 Fed. Reg. 38,915 (July 7, 2010).

[115]   21 U.S.C. § 875. A summary of the administrative process in DEA cases is provided in John J. Mulrooney II & Andrew J. Hull, *Drug Diversion Administrative Revocation and Application Hearings for Medical and Pharmacy Practitioners: A Primer for Navigating Murky, Drug-Infested Waters*, 78 Albany L. Rev. 101 (Spring 2014).

[116]   *Id.* § 824; 21 C.F.R. § 1301.37.

[117]   21 C.F.R. §§ 1301.41-.46.

[118]   *Id.* § 1301.46.

[119]   21 U.S.C. § 842.

mount of a fine to be assessed: 1) the willfulness of the violations; 2) the harm to the public; 3) whether the defendant profited from the failure to comply; and 4) the ability to pay.[120] DEA has collected millions of dollars in fines over the years[121] and continues to aggressively pursue civil fines for recordkeeping and reporting violations.

DEA will investigate and the U.S. Attorneys' Offices will prosecute registrants for criminal penalties in federal district court for knowing and intentional acts in the unlawful manufacture and distribution of controlled substances.[122] Such violations can include unlawful prescribing, distributing, and dispensing of controlled substances and listed chemicals, and unlawful use of a DEA registration. DEA has also recently investigated notable non-registrants concerning their alleged conspiratorial involvement with the diversion of controlled substances. For example, United Parcel Service, Inc. (UPS) and the United States Attorney's Office for the Northern District of California entered into a Non-Prosecution Agreement in which UPS agreed to forfeit $40 million in payments from illicit online pharmacies.[123] UPS also agreed to implement a compliance program designed to ensure that illegal online pharmacies will not be able to use the company's services to illegally distribute drugs.[124] The government alleged, among other conduct, that from 2003 through 2010, UPS was on notice, through its employees, that Internet pharmacies were using its transportation services to distribute controlled substances that were not supported by valid prescriptions.[125]

Another significant DEA enforcement authority is the commencement of administrative or criminal forfeiture actions. Pursuant to the Civil Asset Forfeiture Reform Act of 2000 (CAFRA),[126] and Executive Order, the Department of Justice published a final rule in 2012 addressing the seizure and forfeiture of property by DEA, the Bureau of Alcohol, Tobacco, Firearms and Explosives (ATF), and the Federal Bureau of Investigation (FBI). The rule recognizes that, as of 2002, the ATF is part of the Department of Justice, and consolidates the regulations governing the seizure and administrative forfeiture of property by ATF with those of the DEA and the FBI. The rule also conforms the seizure and forfeiture regulations of ATF, DEA, FBI, and the department's Criminal Division to address procedural changes necessitated by the CAFRA. The rule also allows ATF, DEA, and FBI to publish

---

[20] United States v. Poulin, 926 F. Supp. 246, 253 (D. Mass. 1996).

[21] *Statement Before Subcomm. on Commerce, Justice, Science & Related Agencies of the H. Comm. on Appropriations*, 113th Cong. 4 (2014) (statement of Michele M. Leonhart, Administrator, Drug Enforcement Administration).

[22] 21 U.S.C. §§ 841, 843.

[23] *See* DEA Press Release, UPS Agrees to Forfeit $40 Million in Payments from Illicit Online Pharmacies for Shipping Services (Mar. 29, 2013), http://www.justice.gov/dea/divisions/sf/2013/sf032913.shtml.

[24] *Id.*

[25] *Id.* A prescription based solely on a customer's completion of an on-line questionnaire is not valid. Despite being on notice that this type of activity was occurring concerning the products delivered on behalf of the online pharmacies, UPS allegedly did not implement procedures to monitor or close the Internet pharmacy accounts. *See id.* DEA has alleged similar activities occurred at Federal Express, but Federal Express did not settle the matter with the government. Instead, on July 17, 2014, DEA announced a federal grand jury in San Francisco indicted FedEx Corporation, FedEx Express, Inc., and FedEx Corporate Services, Inc., alleging conspiracies to traffic in controlled substances and misbranded prescription drugs involving "its role in distributing controlled substances and prescription drugs for illegal Internet pharmacies." Press Release, FedEx Indicted for Its Role in Distributing Controlled Substances and Prescription Drugs (July 17, 2014), *available at* http://www.justice.gov/dea/divisions/sf/2014/sf071814.shtml. Note that both the UPS and Fed Ex matters have been handled by the same U.S. Attorney's Office in the Northern District of California.

[26] Pub. L. No. 106-185, 114 Stat. 202.

administrative forfeiture notices on an official government website instead of in newspapers. Lastly, the rule updates the regulations to reflect current forfeiture practice and clarifies the existing regulations concerning the return of assets to victims.[127]

Conclusion

The CSA and implementing regulations promulgated by DEA regulate who can handle medicinal controlled substances and the quantity they can manufacture, distribute, or dispense. This regulatory system gives rise to an inherent conflict between the public interest in preventing diversion of drugs with a potential for abuse and the public interest in ensuring that these important medicines remain available for patients in need. The CSA and DEA regulations must continue to evolve to balance these interests, especially given growing concerns over prescription drug abuse. Also, new advances in technology, such as the way prescribers order medication, how medicines are delivered to patients, and the development of new dosage form therapies, will require changes to DEA policy.

---

[127]   Consolidation of Seizure and Forfeiture Regulations, 77 Fed. Reg. 56,093 (Oct. 12, 2012) (codified at 21 C.F.R. pt. 8).

CHAPTER 26

REIMBURSEMENT, FRAUD, AND ABUSE

GAIL L. DAUBERT, JOSEPH W. METRO,
AND GORDON B. SCHATZ*

Introduction

The Food and Drug Administration (FDA) and the Federal Food, Drug, and Cosmetic Act (FDCA) have historically been primary regulatory concerns for product approval, labeling, compliance, product development, and marketing for manufacturers of medical devices, drugs, and biologics. Life-science companies need to look beyond FDA and the FDCA, however, to plan for reimbursement, along with fraud and abuse compliance, as administered through the Centers for Medicare & Medicaid Services (CMS), and the Office of Inspector General (OIG) in the Department of Health and Human Services (DHHS). New payment policies create opportunities for early coverage and higher payment, but enforcement of the anti-kickback and false-claims laws has created heightened risks for companies introducing innovative medical products.

This chapter gives an overview of the reimbursement and fraud-and-abuse issues most important for medical-technology manufacturers. Reimbursement and fraud-and-abuse principles derive from health insurance policies and programs. Although such policies and programs are generally contractual in nature, federal or state laws may also govern payment for items and services furnished to patients, particularly where the payor is a governmental entity.

Because there are many different health insurance programs, reimbursement and fraud-and-abuse policies can vary widely, even for the same product. The primary categories of payors include: 1) governmental payors (e.g., Medicare, Medicaid, the U.S. Department of

*   The authors would like to thank members of Reed Smith's health care team for their assistance: Robert Hill, Katie Pawlitz, Debra McCurdy, and Nancy Sheliga in Reed Smith's Washington, D.C. and Virginia offices, along with Katelyn Mineo, a student at Seton Hall University School of Law, and a 2014 summer intern in Reed Smith's Princeton, New Jersey office.

Veterans Affairs (VA), and TRICARE);[1] 2) private nonprofit insurers (e.g., Blue Cross and Blue Shield plans);[2] 3) commercial insurers; and 4) managed-care organizations (e.g., health maintenance organizations (HMOs)). This chapter concentrates primarily on Medicare and Medicaid. By virtue of their size, these two programs often influence other insurers, and therefore offer an important starting point for any reimbursement analysis.

By understanding the unique data demands of payors, and the regulatory barriers and opportunities in federal and state payment programs, manufacturers can most effectively structure clinical trials and take regulatory approval pathways that support labeling/product claims and appropriate reimbursement. Product success requires companies to navigate an increasingly complex payment environment. Economic and cost-effectiveness studies, along with outcomes data, may become even more important in light of recently enacted health reform legislation.

Basic Reimbursement Components

Key components of reimbursement include:

- Coverage
- Coding
- Payment

Coverage raises the issue whether *any* payment will be made for a product and for what indications, which patients, and in what circumstances. Particularly knotty issues relate to whether payment will be made for products used in clinical trials or for off-label uses. Coding involves the appropriate billing numbers that hospitals and physicians put on a claim form to identify a product or associated procedure when presented to the patient's health insurance company. Payment deals with the amount of payment that an insurer provides to the hospital, physician, supplier, or other provider that uses the product. Often coverage, coding, and payment policies do not address specific devices, drugs, or biologics. Instead, the policies typically deal with the hospital or physician service or test furnished to a patient. The costs of the product are embedded in the costs submitted by the provider to the patient's health insurance company. In some circumstances, however, reimbursement policies deal directly with a drug, a device, or durable medical equipment. When policies are device-specific, they usually do not distinguish one manufacturer's product from another's, but, rather, cover and pay for the device regardless of which company manufactured it.

---

[1]   Medicare is a federally funded health insurance program for persons who are age 65 or older, who have end-stage renal disease, or who otherwise qualify by virtue of a disability. *See* 42 U.S.C. § 1395 (2012). Medicaid is a joint federal-state welfare program to provide health services to the indigent. *See* 42 U.S.C. § 1396 (2012). Medicare and Medicaid are administered by the Secretary of DHHS through CMS (formerly the Health Care Financing Administration (HCFA)). VA provides a variety of medical services to veterans directly and through arrangements with private healthcare providers. The TRICARE program (formerly CHAMPUS) pays for care and services furnished to dependents of members of the armed forces.

[2]   These plans are typically organized under state law, and operate in a single state or part of a state. Traditionally, Blue Cross plans pay for institutional care, and Blue Shield plans pay for physicians' services and outpatient care.

Drug reimbursement, however, is often manufacturer specific. Further, for many insurers, reimbursement for a product can vary depending upon where the product is used (e.g., in a hospital inpatient or outpatient setting, ambulatory surgical center, physician's office, or patient's home).[3]

The Patient Protection and Affordable Care Act (ACA),[4] which was enacted in 2010, has made significant changes in Medicare and Medicaid policies in the following areas:

- Enhanced support for children's health insurance;

- Options for states to cover long-term care;

- Changes in Medicaid coverage for prescription drugs;

- Linking payment to quality outcomes;

- Prevention of chronic disease, and increased access to preventive services;

- Patient-centered outcomes research; and

- Improved access to innovative therapies through price competition.

The ACA has authorized quite broad changes, for example, extending coverage to members of the American public who did not have health insurance. New healthcare insurance and delivery structures, such as accountable care organizations (ACOs), could be vehicles for implementing ACA requirements. There is also heightened attention to comparative-effectiveness and evidence-based reimbursement decision making, using outcomes data. Recent legislation propels a number of reimbursement decisions, as well as actions by CMS, such as the creation of the Council on Technology Innovation. Technology breakthroughs open some new regulatory challenges, for example in the area of personalized medicine.[5]

For manufacturers of drugs and medical devices, the ACA's sections of greatest importance that are now being implemented include:

- Company reporting of financial transactions with physicians under the Sunshine Act

- Establishment of an Independent Payment Advisory Board

- ACOs that meet quality thresholds sharing in cost savings

- Creation of the Innovation Center within CMS

- Quality reporting and provider compare provisions

- Comparative effectiveness research

- Changes in Part D drug pricing

One of the best CMS summaries of reimbursement can be found in Innovators' Guide to Navigating Medicare, v2.0 (2010), *available at* http://cms.hhs.gov/Medicare/Coverage/CouncilonTechInnov/index.html.
Patient Protection and Affordable Care Act, Pub. L. No. 111-148, 124 Stat. 119 (2010) (Affordable Care Act or ACA).
See, e.g., Gail Daubert, Paul Sheives & Joseph Metro, *Reimbursement for Personalized Medicine, in* PERSONALIZED MEDICINE: PRESCRIPTIONS AND PROSPECTS (Joanne Hawana & Deborah Runkle, eds., 2011).

Manufacturer Reporting Under the Sunshine Act

A very high-profile development emerging in 2014, 2015, and beyond is the federal requirement for companies to report payment arrangements with physicians and other providers under section 6002 of ACA, commonly referred to as the Physician Payment Sunshine Act or Sunshine Act.[6] Manufacturers of drugs, devices, biologicals, or medical supplies reimbursed by Medicare, Medicaid, or Children's Health Insurance Program (CHIP) must report annually to CMS on certain payments and other transfers of value furnished to physicians and teaching hospitals. Additionally, manufacturers and group purchasing organizations must report ownership or investment interests held by physicians or their immediate family members.

The underlying purpose of the Physician Payment Sunshine Act and its implementing regulations[7] (known as the Open Payments program) is to provide increased transparency as to the nature and scope of financial and other relationships among manufacturers, physicians, and teaching hospitals, on the theory that such transparency will enable patients to make more informed treatment decisions—and assess possible conflicts of interest.

Manufacturers are required to attest to the accuracy, completeness, and timeliness of submitted data. Physicians, teaching hospitals, and physician owners have an opportunity to review and dispute the information manufacturers submit to CMS, but such information will otherwise be published on a website available to the public. Failure to report accurately, completely, and in a timely manner may subject manufacturers to civil monetary penalties.

In addition to the federal reporting requirements under the Sunshine Act, certain state laws also require annual reporting with respect to the sales and marketing activities of manufacturers.[8] The reporting requirements vary by state, but generally include reporting, with some exclusions and dollar minimums, the value, nature, and purpose of payments, gifts, or anything of value provided to healthcare providers.

Importantly, the Sunshine Act preempts only those state laws that require manufacturers to disclose or report the same type of information required by the federal law; it does not preempt any state laws that require the disclosure of additional or different information.[9] Because certain state reporting requirements are broader than the federal reporting requirements, manufacturers may be required to make annual reports to CMS, as well as to individual states.[10] These reports can vary in form and content.

---

6   Affordable Care Act, Pub. L. No. 111-148, § 6002, 124 Stat. 119 (2010) (codified at 42 U.S.C. § 1320a-7h (2012)).

7   42 C.F.R. § 403.900 (2013).

8   *See, e.g.,* MASS. GEN. LAWS ch. 111N; MINN. STAT. § 151.47; VT. STAT. ANN. tit. 18, § 4632; D.C. CODE §§ 48-833.01; W. VA. CODE § 210-1-3.2.

9   42 U.S.C.A. § 1320a-7h(d)(3) (West 2014).

10   For example, whereas the Sunshine Act applies only to payments and transfers of value provided to physicians and teaching hospitals, some state laws require reporting with respect to a wider range of healthcare professionals and providers (e.g., physician assistants and nurse practitioners).

Separate and apart from reporting requirements, certain state laws also place restrictions on gifts to healthcare providers, including imposing annual limits and/or identifying specific allowable and prohibited expenditures.[11] In addition, various state laws also require manufacturers to adopt compliance programs and codes of conduct.[12] Manufacturers may be required to attest to compliance with the relevant state restrictions and requirements and to pay annual registration fees.[13]

Reimbursement for Medical Devices

Coverage for Medical Devices

Medicare

Medicare is the largest single health insurance program in the United States. Medicare reimbursement policies therefore are significant because of both the potential volume of Medicare-related business and Medicare's potential influence on other payors. The Medicare program is governed by federal statutes and regulations, and by policies issued at both the national and local levels.

The Medicare program is divided into four parts (A, B, C, and D), each of which covers a distinct set of goods and services[14]:

Part A   Hospital, skilled nursing facility, home health agency, renal dialysis, and hospice services;

Part B   Physician services, clinical laboratory and diagnostic tests provided outside a hospital, infused and certain other drugs and vaccines, durable medical equipment and other products provided to patients for use in their home;

Part C   Medicare + Choice programs typically through managed-care programs; and

Part D   The Prescription Drug Benefit program.

---

[11]   *See, e.g.,* CAL. HEALTH & SAFETY CODE §§ 119400-119402; MASS. GEN. LAWS ch. 111N; MINN. STAT. § 151.461; VT. STAT. ANN. tit. 18, § 4631a.

[12]   *See, e.g.,* CAL. HEALTH & SAFETY CODE §§ 119400-119402; CONN. GEN. STAT. § 21a-70e; MASS. GEN. LAWS CH. 111N; NEV. REV. STAT § 639.570.

[13]   *See id.*

[14]   All Medicare beneficiaries are eligible for Part A services. 42 U.S.C. §§ 1811-1821 (2012). Only those Medicare beneficiaries who pay a monthly premium are eligible for Medicare Part B. 42 U.S.C. §§ 1831-1848. The overwhelming majority of Medicare beneficiaries pay the monthly Part B premium. *See also* 42 U.S.C §§ 1851-1859 (Medicare Part C Medicare Advantage managed care programs), §§ 1860D-1 to 1860D-31 (Medicare Part D Prescription Drug Benefit Program).

Coverage Criteria

To analyze whether a product will be covered under Medicare, several types of authorities should be examined, typically: 1) the definitions of covered services and benefits; 2) exclusions; and 3) product or procedure-specific policies.

Under the Medicare statute,[15] covered services include:

- Inpatient hospital services;
- Inpatient psychiatric hospital services;
- Outpatient occupational therapy services;
- Extended-care services;
- Home-health services;
- Durable medical equipment;
- Hospice care;
- Physician services; and
- Medical and other health services, such as:
  - Supplies incident to a physician's services commonly furnished in the office, rendered without charge, or included in the physician's bill;
  - Outpatient hospital services;
  - Outpatient diagnostic services;
  - Outpatient physical therapy and occupational therapy;
  - Home-dialysis supplies and equipment;
  - Antigens prepared by a physician;
  - Diagnostic x-ray tests;
  - X-ray, radium, and radioactive-isotope therapy, including materials and services of technicians;
  - Surgical dressings, splints, casts, and other devices used for reduction of fractures and dislocations;
  - Prosthetic devices (other than dental) that replace all or part of an internal body organ (including colostomy bags and supplies directly related to colostomy care), including replacement of such devices, and one pair of conventional eyeglasses or contact lenses furnished subsequent to each cataract surgery with insertion of an intraocular lens;
  - Leg, arm, back, and neck braces, and artificial legs, arms, and eyes;
  - Pap smears and screening mammography, prostate cancer, colorectal cancer, cardiovascular, diabetes, glaucoma, abdominal aortic aneurysm by ultrasound, and other screening tests;

---

[15]   42 U.S.C. § 1395x -1395y (2012).

- Bone mass measurement

- Intravenous immune globulin

- Cardiac and pulmonary rehabilitation

- Medical-nutrition therapy, kidney disease education; and

- Vaccines for influenza, hepatitis B.

For a product to be covered by Medicare, the product must, among other things, fall within one of these statutorily defined categories of benefits. If a product cannot be so classified, CMS does not have the authority to cover it, as is the case with disposable infusion pumps used in the home, which do not qualify as durable medical equipment.[16]

Even if a product is included in a covered benefit category, it may be excluded from coverage under the general authority that Medicare will not pay for any item or service that is "[n]ot reasonable or necessary for the diagnosis or treatment of illness or injury or to improve the functioning of a malformed body member."[17] Several judicial decisions have addressed the government's application of this concept and generally have upheld the agency's exclusion of coverage.[18]

Coverage for Clinical Trials and Off-Label Uses

CMS has issued a number of policies and a national coverage determination (NCD) on Medicare coverage for research and clinical trials. Historically, coverage was only available for FDA-approved products. The policies provide significant insights into coverage available during early stages of product development and the criteria CMS sees as important in covering devices used in clinical trials.[19] Specifically, under the clinical trial NCD,[20] a device or procedure subject to a clinical trial must meet the following requirements to be considered for coverage:

See HCPCS Public Meeting Agenda Item #5 (May 20, 2014) Attachment # 14.038 (recommending no HCPCS code for a cryopreserved, injectable allograft, because of no Medicare benefit category), *available at* https://www.cms.gov/MedHCPCSGenInfo/08_HCPCSPublicMeetings.asp#TopOfPage.

42 U.S.C. § 1395y(a)(1)(A) (2012). *See* Erringer v. Thompson, 371 F.3d 625, 628 (9th Cir. 2004) (articulating that the "Secretary adopts NCDs to exclude certain items and services from coverage on a national level that are not 'reasonable and necessary'").

See, e.g., Woodfill v. Sebelius, 2013 U.S. Dist. LEXIS 69273 (N.D. Ohio Mar. 25, 2013); C&I Med. Equip. v. Sebelius, 2010 U.S. Dist. LEXIS 56978 (E.D. Mich. June 9, 2010); Almy v. Sebelius, 679 F.3d 297 (4th Cir. 2012); Friedrich v. Secretary of Health & Human Servs., 894 F.2d 829 (6th Cir. 1990); Wilkens v. Sullivan, 889 F.2d 135 (7th Cir. 1989); Goodman v. Sullivan, No. 88 Civ. 4163 (S.D.N.Y. Apr. 17, 1989), *reprinted in* Medicare & Medicaid Guide (CCH) ¶ 37856, Pinneke v. Preisser, 623 F.2d 546 (8th Cir. 1980); Mackenzie Med. Supply, Inc. v. Leavitt, 419 F. Supp. 2d 766, 773 (D. Md. 2006); Gulfcoast Med. Supply, Inc. v. Secretary of Health and Human Servs., 2005 U.S. Dist. LEXIS 41457 (M.D. Fla. Nov. 16, 2005) (noting that courts have "routinely" deferred to the Secretary's judgment regarding what items or services are not reasonable and unnecessary). Judicial challenges of national coverage decisions are quite limited, and cannot be predicated on a violation of the Administrative Procedure Act. *See* 42 U.S.C. § 1395ff(f)(4) (2012).

See generally, Innovators' Guide *supra* note 3, and Gordon Schatz, *Implications of Medicare Clinical Trial Policy Changes for Device Companies,* 1 MEDICAL DEVICES LAW & INDUSTRY REPORT at 193 (May 23, 2007); *see also* Medicare Clinical Trial Policies (June 28, 2013), *available at* http://www.cms.gov/ClinicalTrialPolicies.

MEDICARE NATIONAL COVERAGE DETERMINATIONS MANUAL, CMS Pub. No. 100-03, § 310.1 (May 28, 2014), *available at* http://www.cms.gov/Regulations-and-Guidance/Guidance/Manuals/Internet-Only-Manuals-IOMs-Items/CMS014961.html.

- The subject or purpose of the trial is the evaluation of an item or service that falls within a Medicare benefit category (e.g., physician's service, durable medical equipment diagnostic test), and is not statutorily excluded from coverage (e.g., cosmetic surgery hearing aids);

- The trial is not designed exclusively to test toxicity or disease pathophysiology. It must have therapeutic intent; and

- The trial enrolls patients with diagnosed disease rather than healthy volunteers. Trials of diagnostic interventions may enroll healthy patients in order to have a proper control group.

Satisfaction of these three requirements is insufficient by itself to qualify a clinical trial for Medicare coverage of routine costs. To be covered, a clinical trial also should have the following desirable characteristics (some trials, as described below, are presumed to have these characteristics and are automatically qualified to receive Medicare coverage):

- The principal purpose of the trial is to test whether the intervention potentially improves the participants' health outcomes;

- The trial is well supported by available scientific and medical information or it is intended to clarify or establish the health outcomes of an intervention already in common clinical use;

- The trial does not unjustifiably duplicate existing studies;

- The trial design is appropriate to answer the research question being asked in the trial;

- The trial is sponsored by a credible organization or individual capable of executing it successfully;

- The trial is in compliance with federal regulations relating to the protection of human subjects; and

- All aspects of the trial are conducted according to the appropriate standards of scientific integrity.[21]

Additionally, use of FDA-approved products outside the scope of FDA-approved labeling may be covered if there is credible scientific evidence establishing safety and effectiveness of the use or the use is generally accepted within the medical community as safe and effective.[22] The mere fact of FDA approval, however, may not be a sufficient basis for Medicare to cover a product. For example, CMS denied coverage for the use of single-chamber or dual-chamber cardiac pacemakers in Medicare patients suffering from asymptomatic sinus bradycardia because there was insufficient evidence of the necessity and reasonableness for such use.[23]

In addition to coverage of the routine patient-care costs in a clinical trial, Medicare can cover an investigational device if underlying questions of safety and effectiveness have already

---

21   *Id.*

22   *See, e.g.,* Medicare Benefit Policy Manual; Chapter 15: Covered Medical and Other Health Services, CMS Pub. No. 100-02 (Apr. 16, 2014), *available at* http://www.cms.gov/Regulations-and-Guidance/Guidance/Manuals/Internet-Only-Manuals-IOMs-Items/CMS012673.html.

23   CMS NCD at § 20.8.3, http://www.cms.gov/medicare-coverage-database/details/ncd-details aspx?NCDId=357&ncdver=1&bc=AAAAgAAAAAAAAA%3d%3d& (last visited Sept. 8, 2014).

been resolved.[24] Under the Medicare regulations, FDA will categorize products furnished under an investigation device exemption (IDE) into the following categories:

> Category A—Experimental/investigational. Innovative devices for which absolute risk has not been established and initial questions of safety and effectiveness have not been resolved, including Class III devices.

> Category B—Non-experimental/investigational. Devices in Class I, II, or III for which the incremental risk is the primary risk in question, so that underlying questions of safety and effectiveness of the device type have been resolved, or it is known that the device type can be safe and effective.

Medicare can cover a device under an IDE if the device is in Category B. This possibility offers manufacturers, but more precisely, their hospital customers, an important opportunity to obtain payment for devices and related services in advance of final premarket approval. The opportunity for early coverage, however, turns on the manufacturer's decision to follow an IDE/PMA route, instead of a 510(k) approach.[25]

Pilot Parallel Review Program by FDA and CMS

After several years in development, FDA and CMS have implemented a pilot program enabling concurrent review of certain FDA premarket review submissions and CMS national coverage determinations for medical devices.[26] By reducing the interval between FDA marketing approval and Medicare coverage, the new program could speed development and commercialization of innovative devices.

Parallel review is available for up to five innovative devices per year. Devices must meet one of the following criteria:

(1) The sponsor/requester has a pre-IDE or an approved IDE.

(2) An original or supplemental application for a PMA is required for the device.

(3) The device falls within a Part A or Part B Medicare benefit category and there is no applicable NCD.

Notably, the program does not change the separate and distinct review standards for FDA device approval and CMS coverage determination. It is a voluntary program. By mid-2014, 10 companies had applied, and Exact Sciences' Cologard screening test for colorectal cancer had been approved for parallel review.[27]

---

24   *See* Medicare Program; Criteria and Procedures for Extending Coverage to Certain Devices and Related Services, 60 Fed. Reg. 48,417 (Sept. 19, 1995); 42 C.F.R. § 405.201 (2013).

25   See 42 C.F.R. § 405.203. This may not preclude devices moving initially through the 510(k) if at some point there is a decision to obtain clinical data under an IDE. *Compare* FDCA § 515, 21 U.S.C. § 360e *with* FDCA § 510(k), 21 U.S.C. § 360k.

26   Pilot Program for Parallel Review of Medical Products; Extension of the Duration of the Program, 78 Fed. Reg. 76,628 (Dec. 18, 2013).

27   *See* FDA Approves First Non-invasive DNA Screening Test for Colorectal Cancer (Aug. 11, 2014), *available at* http://www.fda.gov/newsevents/newsroom/pressannouncements/ucm409021.htm.

Example of Medicare Coverage Decision for Positron Emission Tomography (PET) for Dementia

Even though FDA had approved an amyloid beta PET radiopharmaceutical, CMS denied broad coverage for this diagnostic test, and allows only limited coverage with evidence development.[28] CMS determined that there was insufficient evidence to conclude that the use of PET amyloid-beta (Aβ) imaging was reasonable and necessary for the diagnosis or treatment of illness or injury or to improve the functioning of a malformed body member for Medicare beneficiaries with dementia or neurodegenerative disease.

CMS did find, however, sufficient evidence that the use of PET Aβ imaging was "promising" in two scenarios: 1) to exclude Alzheimer's disease (AD) in narrowly defined and clinically difficult differential diagnoses, such as AD versus frontotemporal dementia (FTD); and 2) to enrich clinical trials seeking better treatments or prevention strategies for AD, by allowing for selection of patients on the basis of biological as well as clinical and epidemiological factors.

CMS, therefore, would extend limited coverage for one PET Aβ scan per patient through coverage with evidence development (CED),[29] in clinical studies that meet very specific criteria.[30]

Procedures for Making Medicare Coverage Decisions

Medicare coverage decisions are made nationally and also locally. Medicare administrative contractors (MACs) (formerly fiscal intermediaries for Part A, carriers for Part B, and durable medical equipment regional carriers for home care products) review claims for services or products and determine coverage by applying national policies or by making determinations based on general authority. Often, claims processing is the point of first contact between a new technology and Medicare. For durable medical equipment, prosthetics, orthotics, surgical dressings, and other products used in a patient's home, claims from suppliers are processed by four durable medical equipment Medicare administrative contractors (DME MACs).

The following is a diagram of the coverage process and key Medicare agencies involved in national decisions.[31]

---

[28]   *See* Decision Memo for Beta Amyloid Positron Emission Tomography in Dementia and Neurodegenerative Disease (CAG-00431N) (Sept. 27, 2013), *available at* http://www.cms.gov/medicare-coverage-database/details/nca-decision-memo.aspx?NCAId=265. CMS cited its authority under section 1862(a)(1)(A), 42 U.S.C. § 1395y(a)(1)(A) (2012).

[29]   42 U.S.C. § 1395y(a)(1)(E) (2012), which gives CMS separate authority to cover research aimed at measuring outcomes, effectiveness, and appropriateness under 42 U.S.C. § 1320b-12 (2012).

[30]   *See* Decision Memo for Beta Amyloid Positron Emission Tomography *supra* note 28 at 1.

[31]   *See* Innovators' Guide *supra* note 3 at 16.

NATIONAL MEDICARE COVERAGE PROCESS[32]

Manufacturers seeking coverage for a new technology should consider contacting contractors in the areas where claims will be processed to discuss coverage, especially if there is no applicable national coverage policy.

Medicaid

The federal Medicaid statute gives states substantial latitude with respect to the mix of services they will cover.[33] Although states are required to cover only hospital and physicians' services, most states have adopted plans covering a broad variety of other healthcare goods and services. Once a state elects to cover a particular service, it must furnish assistance in sufficient "amount, duration, and scope" to reasonably achieve its purpose.[34] Aside from these general federal standards, states have broad discretion to make coverage policies; and, for purposes of Medicaid, a new technology will be assessed at the local rather than the national level. Nonetheless, states often adopt some Medicare coverage and reimbursement principles as part of their Medicaid state plan.

Blue Cross and Blue Shield Center for Clinical Effectiveness

Another significant player in technology reimbursement is the Blue Cross and Blue Shield Association (BCBSA) Center for Clinical Effectiveness (CCE), formerly the Technology

---

32   Id.

33   See 42 U.S.C. §§ 1396a(a)(10) (2012); 42 C.F.R. pts. 440 & 441 (2013).

34   See 42 U.S.C. § 1396a(a)(10)(B) (2012); 42 C.F.R. §§ 440.200, 440.230 (2013).

Evaluation Center (TEC).[35] The CCE, which includes participation by Kaiser Permanente, uses five criteria when developing a coverage analysis:

- The technology must have final approval from the appropriate governmental regulatory bodies;
- The scientific evidence must support conclusions concerning the effect of the technology on health outcomes;
- The technology must improve the net health outcome;
- The technology must be as beneficial as any established alternatives; and
- The improvement must be attainable outside the investigational setting.

The CCE/TEC criteria have articulated "outcomes" as a significant consideration in determining coverage, and often look beyond FDA proof of safety and effectiveness for documentation in the peer-reviewed medical literature of the clinical benefits of a new technology.[36]

Local Blue Cross and Blue Shield plans operate independently from BCBSA. They are active in local coverage policies and are not bound to follow CCE assessments. They create coverage policies in the absence of CCE policies and can restrict or withdraw coverage on their own initiative.[37]

Practical Strategies for Coverage

To support favorable coverage, device and drug companies should plan clinical trials that consider the following:

- Configure the product (for example durable vs. disposable) to support inclusion in a coverage category like durable medical equipment used in the home;
- Include patients 65 years of age or older in clinical trials for data specific to Medicare patients;
- Measure improvement in net health outcomes, which may go beyond traditional safety and effectiveness;
- Develop cost-effectiveness and economic analyses (although Medicare says it does not consider these for coverage determinations);

---

[35] *See* Technology Evaluation Center (TEC), Service Through Research, http://www.bcbs.com/blueresources/ tec (last visited Sept. 8, 2014).

[36] *See, e.g.,* Gene Expression Analysis for Prostate Cancer Management, http://www.bcbs.com/blueresources/ tec/vols/28/gene-expression-analysis-prostate-cancer-management.html (last visited Sept. 9, 2014), (finding that evidence on Prolaris and Oncotype Dx Prostate gene tests did not meet TEC criteria (April 2014)), *but see also* Percutaneous Tibial Nerve Stimulation for the Treatment of Voiding Dysfunction, http://www. bcbs.com/blueresources/tec/vols/28/percutaneous-tibial-nerve.html (last visited Sept. 9, 2014) (finding sufficient evidence of improved outcomes with PTNS as treatment for voiding dysfunction (January 2014)).

[37] *See, e.g.,* Arkansas Blue Cross policy on high dose chemotherapy with allogeneic bone marrow, stem cell, or progenitor cell support (Sept. 2014), *available at* http://www.arkansasbluecross.com/members/ report.aspx?policyNumber=2013036&viewIntro=yes, and changing Medicare local coverage for vertebroplasty and kyphoplasty, *available at* https://www.noridianmedicare.com/cgi-bin/coranto/viewnews. cgi?id=EFEuApFFEEbWPfoKxl&tmpl=part_a_viewnews&style=part_ab_viewnews (last visited Sept. 9, 2014).

- Consider clinical trial sites to seek early stage reimbursement through local coverage before national coverage;

- Help clinical trial sites work with local insurers;

- Draft indications for use and labeling consistent with reimbursement requirements; and

- Consider parallel FDA/CMS review or informal ways to work with both agencies at the same time to expedite approvals.

Payment for Medical Devices

Payment for a medical device typically is included in payment for the procedure utilizing the device. Payment methodologies can be complex and can vary depending on whether the product is used in an inpatient or outpatient hospital setting, ambulatory surgical center, skilled nursing facility, or in a patient's home. This section provides an overview of the payment methods most significant for medical devices.[38]

Hospital Inpatient Services

DRGs and Capital

Prior to 1983, Medicare paid hospitals on the basis of "reasonable costs."[39] However, this reasonable-cost system was criticized as lacking sufficient financial controls and as contributing to inflationary medical costs.[40] Consequently, the Medicare inpatient prospective payment system (PPS) was implemented in 1983.[41] Under PPS, when a Medicare patient is admitted to a hospital as an inpatient, most of the costs of the devices and other products, and the services rendered in treating the patient are covered under a fixed payment determined by the Medicare Severity Diagnosis-Related Group (MS-DRG) into which the patient is classified.[42] Therefore, payment to the hospital for services to a patient who receives procedures using, *inter alia*, catheters, clinical laboratory or radiology equipment, or orthopedic or cardiac implants no longer directly reflects the costs of individual products used or services rendered. Instead, payment for the device is part of the fixed amount a hospital receives to cover all items and services used during the patient's inpatient stay. Each

---

[38] Because of the diversity of payment methodologies, we have focused on Medicare policies to illustrate these issues. As noted earlier, Medicaid and private insurers often are influenced by Medicare principles.

[39] *See generally* Medicare Program; Changes to the Inpatient Hospital Prospective Payment   System   and Fiscal Year 1986 Rates, 50 Fed. Reg. 24,459 (June 10, 1985).

[40] *See generally* R. Sutter, M. Philp & B. Williams, *Medicare Prospective Payment System for Inpatient Operating Costs*, 2 HEALTH LAW PRACTICE GUIDE § 21:1 (2014).

[41] Social Security Amendments, Pub. L. No. 98-21, § 601(e), 97 Stat. 65 (1983).

[42] Every year, CMS updates the inpatient PPS system through notice-and-comment rulemaking, which includes detailed descriptions of the existing DRG system and proposed and final changes. *See*, for example, Medicare Program; Hospital Inpatient Prospective Payment Systems for Acute Care Hospitals and the Long-Term Care Hospital Prospective Payment System and Fiscal Year 2014 Rates; Quality Reporting Requirements for Specific Providers; Hospital Conditions of Participation; Payment Policies Related to Patient Status, 78 Fed. Reg. 50,495 (Aug. 19, 2013). Medicare Program; Hospital Inpatient Prospective Payment Systems for Acute Care Hospitals and the Long-Term Care Hospital Prospective Payment System and Fiscal Year 2015 Rates; Quality Reporting Requirements for Specific Providers; Reasonable Compensation Equivalents for Physician Services in Excluded Hospitals and Certain Teaching Hospitals; Provider Administrative Appeals and Judicial Review; Enforcement Provisions for Organ Transplant Centers; and Electronic Health Record (EHR) Incentive Program; Final Rule, 79 Fed. Reg. 49,853 (Aug. 22, 2014). Payment applies to discharges after October 1of each year. *See* Medicare Program; Hospital Inpatient Prospective Payment Systems for Acute Care Hospitals and the Long-Term Care Hospital Prospective Payment System and Proposed Fiscal Year 2015 Rates, 79 Fed. Reg. 27,977 (May 15, 2014).

MS-DRG is assigned a relative weight, and these weights are updated every year. Examples of DRGs, weights, and estimated payment for 2014 include[43]:

MS-DRG	Descriptor	2014 Final Relative Weight*	National Average 2014 Final Payment**	National Average 2015 Final Payment***
246	Percutaneous cardiovascular procedure with drug-eluting stent with major complications or comorbidities (MCC) or 4+ vessels/stents	3.1830	$18,460	$18,985
247	Percutaneous cardiovasc proc w drug-eluting stent w/o MCC	2.0408	$11,840	$12,075
248	Percutaneous cardiovasc proc w non-drug-eluting stent w MCC or 4+ ves/stents	2.9479	$17,100	$17,838
249	Percutaneous cardiovasc proc w non-drug-eluting stent w/o MCC	1.8245	$10,580	$11,032
250	Percutaneous cardiovasc proc w/o coronary artery stent w MCC	2.9881	$17,330	$17,529
251	Percutaneous cardiovasc proc w/o coronary artery stent w/o MCC	1.9737	$11,450	$11,965
435	Malignancy of hepatobiliary system or pancreas w MCC	1.7356	$10,070	$10,279

---

[43]   *See* Prospective Payment System for Inpatient Hospital Capital-Related Costs, 56 Fed. Reg. 43,358 (Aug. 30, 1991). *See generally* Sutter, *Medicare Prospective Payment System for Inpatient Hospital Capital Costs*, 2 HEALTH LAW PRACTICE GUIDE § 22:1 (West 2014). Medicare Program; Hospital Inpatient Prospective Payment Systems for Acute Care Hospitals and the Long-Term Care Hospital Prospective Payment System and Fiscal Year 2013 Rates; Hospitals' Resident Caps for Graduate Medical Education Payment Purposes; Quality Reporting Requirements for Specific Providers and for Ambulatory Surgical Centers, 77 Fed. Reg. 53,257 (Aug. 31, 2012).

MS-DRG	Descriptor	2014 Final Relative Weight*	National Average 2014 Final Payment**	National Average 2015 Final Payment***
436	Malignancy of hepatobiliary system or pancreas w CC	1.1548	$6,700	$6,827
437	Malignancy of hepatobiliary system or pancreas w/o CC/MCC	0.9282	$5,380	$5,262
466	Revision of hip or knee replacement w MCC	5.2748	$30,590	$30,215
467	Revision of hip or knee replacement w CC	3.414	$19,800	$20,078
468	Revision of hip or knee replacement w/o CC/MCC	2.7624	$16,020	$16,219

Per final 2014 figures released by CMS at 78 Fed. Reg. 50,495 (Aug. 19, 2013), https://www.cms.gov/Medicare/Medicare-Fee-for-Service-Payment/AcuteInpatientPPS/FY2014-IPPS-Final-Rule-Home-Page.html.

* Actual payment amounts will vary from hospital to hospital.

** Per final 2015 figures released by CMS at 79 Fed. Reg. 49,853 (Aug. 22, 2014). Actual payment amounts will vary from hospital to hospital.

In addition to the DRG payment by Medicare to a hospital, which covers primarily the hospital's operating costs, Medicare also pays hospitals for certain capital expenses, also on the basis of prospectively determined amounts. For example, for an inpatient receiving a test performed by magnetic resonance imaging (MRI), Medicare would pay the operating costs of the test paid under the DRG and also the capital costs of the MRI (depreciation, lease payments, interest, taxes).[44] The MS-DRG system is important because the fixed nature of the payment may create financial disincentives for hospitals to buy products that add costs to the treatment of a patient. Even a clinically significant technological advance may not be accommodated within existing payment levels. Conversely, products that reduce overall

---

[44] Prospective Payment Systems for Inpatient Hospital Capital-Related Costs, 56 Fed. Reg. 43,499 (Aug. 30, 1991); 42 C.F.R. § 412.300 (2013).

costs of treatment make the hospital more efficient and thereby can enable the hospital to realize financial advantages under the DRG payment system.[45]

New-Technology DRG Add-on

In addition to the DRG and capital payments, Medicare can pay hospitals a new-technology DRG add-on for drugs, devices, and procedures that meet the statutory[46] and regulatory[47] criteria:

- New, i.e., the product has received recent FDA approval and data associated with the cost of the product have not been captured in Medicare DRG payments;

- Inadequate payment, i.e., the existing DRGs that would apply to the related procedure have too low a payment level to reflect the costs of the drug or device; and

- Significant clinical advance that substantially improves the diagnosis or treatment of Medicare beneficiaries compared to alternatives.

The amount of DRG payment add-on is based on 50 percent of the cost of the new technology in excess of the full DRG payment. Examples of products that have qualified for DRG add-on payment in 2013-2014 include: Second Sight Medical Products, Inc.'s Argus II Retinal Prosthesis System (partially restores functional vision in patients who are blind from retinitis pigmentosa), BTG International Inc.'s Glucarpidase (treatment of toxic methotrexate), Cook, Inc.'s Zenith Fenestrated Abdominal Aortic Aneurysm Endovascular Graft, and Cook, Inc.'s Zilver PTX Drug Eluting Peripheral Stent (treatment of peripheral artery disease).[48]

In 2014-2015, CMS approved DRG add-on payments for CardioMEMS, Inc.'s CardioMEMS™ HF Monitoring System (an implantable hemodynamic monitoring system used in the management of heart failure), Abbott Vascular's MitraClip® System (a transcatheter mitral valve repair system for certain high-risk patients), and NeuroPace, Inc.'s Responsive Neurostimulator (RNS®) System (an implantable medical device for treating partial onset seizures in certain persons diagnosed with epilepsy).[49]

---

[45]   Similar incentives exist under managed care delivery systems, under which a fixed *per capita* amount is paid to cover all of a patient's healthcare services.

[46]   42 U.S.C. § 1395ww(d)(5)(K) & (L) (2012).

[47]   42 C.F.R. § 412.87 (2013).

[48]   *See, e.g.,* Medicare Program; Hospital Inpatient Prospective Payment Systems for Acute Care Hospitals and the Long-Term Care Hospital Prospective Payment System and Fiscal Year 2014 Rates; Quality Reporting Requirements for Specific Providers; Hospital Conditions of Participation; Payment Policies Related to Patient Status, 78 Fed. Reg. 50,495 (Aug. 19, 2013); New Medical Services and New Technologies (Feb. 11, 2014), *available at* http://www.cms.gov/Medicare/Medicare-Fee-for-Service-Payment/AcuteInpatientPPS/newtech.html; *see* Publication of Special Fraud Alerts (Dec. 19, 1994), *available at* http://oig.hhs.gov/fraud/docs/alertsandbulletins/121994.html.

[49]   Medicare Program; Hospital Inpatient Prospective Payment Systems for Acute Care Hospitals and the Long-Term Care Hospital Prospective Payment System and Fiscal Year 2015 Rates; Quality Reporting Requirements for Specific Providers; Reasonable Compensation Equivalents for Physician Services in Excluded Hospitals and Certain Teaching Hospitals; Provider Administrative Appeals and Judicial Review; Enforcement Provisions for Organ Transplant Centers; and Electronic Health Record (EHR) Incentive Program, 79 Fed. Reg. 49,918, 49,925 (Aug. 22, 2014).

Hospital Outpatient Services

The hospital outpatient prospective payment systems (HOPPS or OPPS) have been one of the most dynamic of the Medicare payment systems, especially with respect to new drugs and devices.[50] The HOPPS program pays hospitals on the basis of ambulatory payment classifications (APCs), under which a single, prospectively fixed payment is established for groups of clinically similar services requiring comparable resources to provide.[51] When a Medicare patient is treated in a hospital outpatient setting, the hospital can receive payment based on a combination of APCs (surgical, diagnostic radiology, and certain drugs, for example). APC payments only cover hospital outpatient services, compared to the DRG system, which applies to inpatient hospital care.

Examples of APCs include the following:

APC	Title	Payment Rate (2014)
62	Level I Treatment Fracture/Dislocation	$2,012.19
63	Level II Treatment Fracture/Dislocation	$4,124.82
64	Level III Treatment Fracture/Dislocation	$5,383.64
157	Colorectal Cancer Screening, Barium enema	$289.96
158	Colorectal Cancer Screening, Colonoscopy	$646.73
159	Colorectal Cancer Screening, flexible sigmoidoscopy	$461.13

An APC is intended to capture procedures that are clinically comparable (e.g., of similar qualitative "type" and similar with respect to resources consumed). The so-called "two times" rule requires that no procedure be classified in an APC if the mean cost of that procedure is two times higher than the cost of the other procedures in that APC.[52] If the Medicare patient receives multiple surgical procedures during an outpatient encounter, the second or third surgical procedure may be paid for at a reduced rate.[53] Further, payments may be reduced in the case of replacement implanted devices where the device has been replaced without cost to the provider or the beneficiary.[54]

---

[50]   42 U.S.C. § 1395l(t) (2012); 42 C.F.R. pt. 419 (2013).
[51]   The HOPPS rules are updated each year through rulemaking, beginning with a proposed rule generally published in July. Following a 60-day comment period, the final rule is usually released in November and takes effect on January 1 of the new year. *See, e.g.*, Medicare and Medicaid Programs; CY 2015 Home Health Prospective Payment System Rate Update; Home Health Quality Reporting Requirements; and Survey and Enforcement Requirements for Home Health Agencies, 79 Fed. Reg. 38,365 (July 7, 2014).
[52]   42 U.S.C. § 1395l(t)(2) (2012).
[53]   42 C.F.R. § 419.44 (2013).
[54]   *Id.* § 419.45.

Therapeutic drugs with average costs of more than $90 per dose can be paid for separately, on the basis of the manufacturer's reported average sales price plus 6 percent. In addition, new drugs can be paid for under a transitional pass-through payment for two to three years.[55] New devices that represent a new category of medical devices that have not been paid under HOPPS may also qualify for a transitional pass-through payment.[56] Only five devices have been approved for pass-through payment in the past five years.[57]

In its most recent proposed HOPPS rule,[58] CMS proposed to implement a system of comprehensive APCs in 2015. CMS described this policy as "moving the [H]OPPS from what currently resembles a hybrid of a prospective payment system and a fee schedule, to a more complete prospective payment system."[59]

Ambulatory Surgery Centers (ASC)

An ASC payment is based on a percentage of the corresponding HOPPS APC payment. The payment amounts cover an ASC's facility costs, including nursing and technician services, surgical dressings, supplies, splints, casts, diagnostic services directly related to a surgery, and anesthesia materials.[60] Separate payment is available for physician services and laboratory or x-ray services (not directly related to the surgery).[61]

Physician and Certain Diagnostic Services

Medicare pays for physician and certain diagnostic services (such as radiology, electrocardiograms, and ultrasound procedures) according to a resource-based, relative value scale (RBRVS).[62] This methodology is quite important for devices used in a physician's office because payment for such devices may be included in payment for the physician's services.

Payment is calculated according to the following summary formula:

Relative Value Units		Geographic Adjustment Factor		Conversion Factor		Medicare Payment
	x		x		=	

---

55   *Id.* § 419.64.

56   *Id.* § 419.66.

57   *See* Pass-Through Payment Status and New Technology Ambulatory Payment Classification (APC) (Feb. 5, 2014), *available at* http://www.cms.gov/Medicare/Medicare-Fee-for-Service-Payment/ HospitalOutpatientPPS/passthrough_payment.html.

58   Medicare and Medicaid Programs; Hospital Outpatient Prospective Payment and Ambulatory Surgical Center Payment Systems and Quality Reporting Programs; Physician-Owned Hospitals: Data Sources for Expansion Exception; Physician Certification of Inpatient Hospital Services; Medicare Advantage Organizations and Part D Sponsors: Appeals Process for Overpayments Associated With Submitted Data, 79 Fed. Reg. 40,915 (July 14, 2014).

59   *Id.* at 40,922.

60   *See* 42 C.F.R. pt. 416 (2013).

61   42 C.F.R. § 416.61 (2013).

62   *See generally* Medicare Program; Revisions to Payment Policies Under the Physician Fee Schedule, Clinical Laboratory Fee Schedule & Other Revisions to Part B for CY 2014, 78 Fed. Reg. 74,229 (Dec. 10, 2013) (final update to the 2014 Medicare physician fee schedule).

elative value units (RVUs) have been calculated for nearly all physician procedures.[63] The VUs are based on three components: physician work; practice expenses associated with aff and supplies in the physician's office; and malpractice expenses. The conversion factor a mechanism used to update payments for physician services annually in order to comply ith Sustainable Growth Rate (SGR) targets established by Congress to control Medicare ending on physician services. Each year since 2002, expenditures for the previous year ave exceeded target expenditures, and the result has been significant reductions to the onversion factors under the SGR formula. Facing significant payment cuts, physicians have ccessfully advocated for legislative adjustment to the conversion factor virtually every ear.[64]

enerally, any supplies and equipment used in a physician's office will be paid for as part of e practice-expense component of the RBRVS payment.

Clinical Laboratory Tests

When a clinical laboratory test is performed in a hospital outpatient setting, an independent inical laboratory, or a physician's office, Medicare pays the lower of the actual charge or e national limitation amount for the test.[65] National limitation amounts, also known as fee aps, for a number of clinical laboratory tests were determined on the basis of a percentage of e national median charge for the tests.[66] During 2006 and 2007, CMS began to implement gulations for the determination of payment for new clinical laboratory tests, considering ew data, gap filling or cross-walking existing payment amounts for tests similar to the new sts.[67] A pilot program of competitive bidding for clinical laboratory tests was authorized y Congress in 2003 but subsequently repealed in 2008.[68]

he Protecting Access to Medicare Act of 2014 ("the Act"),[69] directs substantial changes in e way clinical laboratories will be paid for diagnostic testing beginning in 2017. Instead f a fee-schedule approach, Medicare will pay laboratories using a market approach, rates that are based on what private payors pay for the test. Specifically, beginning in 016, laboratories will report the rates that private payors paid for each test (reflecting all iscounts, rebates, or other price concessions), and the volume of tests that were billed to e payor, during the applicable reporting period. Using this information, Medicare will alculate Medicare reimbursement rates for each test equal to the median of the rates private ayors paid, weighted by volume. If the rates calculated pursuant to the new methodology e lower than existing rates, the reductions in payment will be phased in over time.

ew tests and new "advanced diagnostic laboratory tests" (defined as tests that analyze ultiple DNA, RNA, or protein biomarkers, or are approved by FDA and are furnished y a single laboratory that developed the test), will be subject to separate reimbursement

---

See id. (listing the RVUs for 2014).

See 42 U.S.C. § 1395w-4(d) (2012).

42 U.S.C. § 1395l(a)(2)(D) (2002).

Id. § 1395l(h) (2002).

See 42 C.F.R. § 414.508 (2013).

See Medicare Prescription Drug, Improvement and Modernization Act of 2003, Pub. L. No. 108-173, § 302(b), 108 Stat. 2066 (2003), *See also*, Medicare Improvements for Patients and Providers Act, Pub. L. No. 110-275, § 145(a), 122 Stat. 2494 (2008).

Protecting Access to Medicare Act of 2014, Pub. L. No. 113-93, 128 Stat. 1040 (2014).

policies. New tests that are not "advanced diagnostic laboratory tests" will initially be paid by either the cross-walking or the gap-filling process that is currently used to establish reimbursement rates for new diagnostic tests. A new advanced diagnostic laboratory test will initially be paid for on the basis of a laboratory's actual list charge for the test. If it turns out that such list charge exceeds the market rate that would have been paid under the new methodology by 30 percent, Medicare must recoup the difference. Finally, the Act requires MACs to follow the local coverage determination process when issuing coverage policies with respect to clinical diagnostic laboratory tests and allows the Secretary to designate up to four MACs to establish coverage policies and process claims for clinical laboratory tests.

Durable Medical Equipment, Prosthetics, Orthotics

Medicare covers and pays for various items of durable medical equipment (DME), prosthetics, orthotics, and supplies (collectively DMEPOS) in accordance with federal statutes, regulations, and guidelines. DME is equipment that:

- Can withstand repeated use;
- Is primarily and customarily used to serve a medical purpose;
- Generally is not useful to a person in the absence of illness or injury; and
- Is appropriate for use in the home.[70]

Except for those items subject to competitive bidding, payment for DME, prosthetic devices, and orthotics is generally based on the lesser of the reasonable charge or the amount determined under a fee schedule, although special payment rules apply for surgical dressings, ostomy products, transcutaneous electrical stimulators, and power wheelchairs.[71] Congress established six classes of products paid for under fee schedules, often referred to as the Six Point Plan.[72]

The six categories are:

- Inexpensive or other routinely purchased DME;
- Items for which frequent and substantial servicing is necessary, such as ventilators, nebulizers, aspirators, and intermittent positive pressure breathing machines;
- Customized items;
- Covered items other than DME, e.g., prosthetic devices, orthotics;
- Other items of DME paid for on the basis of a capped rental amount; and
- Oxygen and oxygen equipment.

A competitive acquisition program is also in place for certain items of DME whereby suppliers must go through a bidding process and meet certain program standards in order to supply covered items within the competitive acquisition area.[73] Items included in

---

[70]   42 C.F.R. § 414.202 (2013).

[71]   42 U.S.C. § 1395m (2012).

[72]   *See id.*

[73]   Medicare Prescription Drug, Improvement and Modernization Act of 2003, Pub. L. No. 108-173, § 302, 108 Stat. 2066 (2003). *See also* Medicare Learning Network fact sheet (Sept. 2, 2014), *available at* http://

competitive acquisition are: 1) DME (including DME used with infusion and drugs, other than inhalation drugs) and supplies used in conjunction with DME; 2) enteral nutrients, equipment, and supplies; and (3) off the shelf orthotics.

As of 2014, there have been two rounds of competitive bidding and a national mail order competition for diabetic testing supplies. Contract prices have averaged significantly below Medicare DMEPOS fee schedule amounts.[74] Under the Affordable Care Act of 2010, all areas of the country will be subject either to DMEPOS competitive bidding or payment rate adjustments using competitively bid rates by 2016.[75]

Coding for Medical Devices and Procedures

Codes are systems of numbers or alpha-numeric combinations that describe diseases, procedures, or products. These coding systems are essential for reimbursement. Codes describing patient conditions, services rendered, or products provided are placed on a claim form by the hospital, physician, or other provider, and are submitted to the patient's insurer. The provider can submit the claim manually or electronically. In turn, the insurer processes the claim by reviewing procedure or product codes, and making coverage and payment decisions.

There are several major coding systems:

- International Classification of Diseases, Ninth Edition, Clinical Modification (ICD-9-CM);[76] International Classification of Diseases, Tenth Edition, Clinical Modification / Procedure Coding System (ICD-10-PCS, or ICD-10);

- Current Procedural Terminology (CPT);

- Healthcare Common Procedure Coding System (HCPCS); and

- American Hospital Association (AHA) Revenue Codes.

These coding systems are used with corresponding payment methodologies:

---

www.cms.gov/Outreach-and-Education/Medicare-Learning-Network-MLN/MLNProducts/downloads/DMEPOS_Competitive_Bidding_Factsheets.pdf.

[74] *See* DMEPOS Competitive Bidding Program, About the Program, www.dmecompetitivebid.com/palmetto/cbicrd2.nsf/DocsCat/Home (last visited Sept. 8, 2014).

[75] *See* DMEPOS Competitive Bidding - Home (July 15, 2014), *available at* www.cms.gov/DMEPOSCompetitiveBid/01_overview.asp.

[76] CMS plans to transition from the ICD-9-CM to a new ICD-10 coding system on October 1, 2015. This is a one-year delay from the agency's previous implementation target, as required by Congress under the Protecting Access to Medicare Act of 2014. The significant transition from ICD-9-CM to ICD-10 is occurring because ICD-9 produces limited data about patients' medical conditions and hospital inpatient procedures. In addition, ICD-9 is 30 years old, has outdated terms, and is inconsistent with current medical practice. Finally, the structure of ICD-9 limits the number of new codes that can be created, and many ICD-9 categories are full. ICD-10 will affect diagnosis and inpatient procedure coding for everyone covered by the Health Insurance Portability and Accountability Act, not just those who submit Medicare or Medicaid claims. The change to ICD-10 does not affect CPT coding for outpatient procedures. *See* Centers for Medicare & Medicaid Services, ICD-10 (Aug. 13, 2014), *available at* http://www.cms.gov/Medicare/Coding/ICD10/index.html *and* ICD-9-CM and ICD-10 (Feb. 6, 2014), *available at* http://www.cms.gov/Medicare/Coding/ICD9ProviderDiagnosticCodes/index.html.

Coding System	Subject	Medicare Payment Method
ICD-9-CM	Patient diseases	
	Inpatient hospital procedures	DRG
CPT	Outpatient hospital procedures	APC
	Physician and diagnostic procedures	RBRVS
	Clinical lab tests	Fee Schedule
HCPCS	Drugs,	Average Sales Price
	DME, prosthetics, orthotics, supplies	Fee Schedule

Coding analysis early in the development of a new product is important because many new products can fall within descriptions in existing codes. If so, coverage and payment levels may already be set on the basis of previously developed products. Creating a new procedure code or product code may open an opportunity for changing a payment amount. A new code, however, may disadvantage a new product by enabling insurers to pinpoint it and deny coverage. Thus, the creation of a new code does not ensure coverage or payment at any particular level.

The agencies responsible for coding include:

Coding System	Responsible Agency
ICD	ICD Coordination and Maintenance Committee – CMS and National Center for Health Statistics
CPT	American Medical Association CPT Editorial Panel
HCPCS	HCPCS Alpha-Numeric Panel – for new codes
	Pricing Data Analysis Contractor (PDAC) – for coding verification*

* www.dmepdac.com/dmecs.

Manufacturers, physicians, specialty societies, and hospitals can submit requests to these agencies to create new or revised codes that will more accurately describe new products or procedures as technology and clinical practice evolve. Coding discussions/meetings have ecome more open to public participation,[77] but they are subject to changing standards, nd the rationale for creating or denying a coding request is often opaque. With respect ɔ standards to create a new CPT code, the AMA has increasingly demanded widespread .se and recognition of a product in peer-reviewed medical journals.[78] HCPCS codes may equire evidence of substantial clinical or therapeutic benefits compared to other products.[79] .xamples of new codes include:

ICD-9-CM (diagnosis)	796.2	Borderline hypertension
ICD-9-CM (procedure)	1.20	Cranial implantation or replacement of neurostimulator pulse generator
ICD-10-CM (diagnosis)	R03.0	Borderline hypertension
ICD-10-CM (procedure)	0NH00NZ	Insertion of Neurostimulator Generator into Skull, Open Approach
CPT	34841	Endovascular repair of visceral aorta (e.g., aneurysm, pseudoaneurysm, dissection, penetrating ulcer, intramural hematoma, or traumatic disruption) by deployment of a fenestrated visceral aortic endograft and all associated radiological supervision and interpretation, including target zone angioplasty, when performed; including one visceral artery endoprosthesis (superior mesenteric, celiac or renal artery)
HCPCS	A4253	Blood glucose test or reagent strips for home blood glucose monitor per 50 strips

[7] See CMS procedures for ICD-9-CM coding (May 15, 2014), available at http://www.cms.gov/Medicare/ Coding/ICD10/ICD-9-CM-Coordination-and-Maintenance-Committee-Meetings.html; see also HCPCS – General Information (July 2, 2014), available at http://www.cms.hhs.gov/MedHCPCSGenInfo; see also Applying for CPT Codes at http://www.ama-assn.org/ama/pub/physician-resources/solutions-managing-your-practice/coding-billing-insurance/cpt/applying-cpt-codes.page.

[8] See AMA website, supra at note 77.

[9] See id. at www.cms.gov/MedHCPCSGenInfo.

Reimbursement for Drugs and Biologics

Coverage

Medicare and Medicaid

Medicare Part A and Part B

Part A of the Medicare program generally provides reimbursement for institutional healthcare services (i.e., inpatient hospital, skilled nursing facility (SNF), home health, hospice, and dialysis services), and Part B generally relates to "outpatient" services (e.g., physicians' services, DME, therapy, laboratory services, and the like).

Under Part A, Medicare covers drugs ordinarily provided by hospitals and SNFs for the care and treatment of inpatients.[80] Drug coverage usually is not provided for home health services (although coverage of a *service* may be provided for visits necessary to administer noncovered drugs). With respect to hospice care, Medicare covers drugs that are used primarily to relieve pain and symptoms of a patient's terminal illness.[81]

Medicare Part B covers drugs for outpatient use that are typically injected by a physician or health professional.[82] Subject to the exceptions discussed below, Part B covers only prescription drugs that are furnished to a patient "incident to" a physician's services. Consequently, an outpatient drug is covered only if it: 1) cannot be self-administered by a patient; 2) is administered by a physician (or under a physician's supervision) on an outpatient basis; 3) is reasonable and necessary for the treatment for which it is administered according to accepted standards of medical practice; and 4) is ordinarily furnished in a physician's office or clinic, and represents a cost to the physician that is not separately charged in the physician's bill.[83] Further, most immunizations are not covered by Medicare.[84]

There are several exceptions to the general rule excluding self-administered drugs and preventive immunizations from coverage under Medicare Part B. including, for example, antigens, pneumococcal pneumonia vaccine, hepatitis B vaccine, blood-clotting factors, immunosuppressive drugs, factors, immunosuppressive drugs, erythropoietin (EPO), drugs used to treat osteoporosis, and certain anticancer drugs.[85] In some instances, drugs needed for the effective use of DME may also be covered under Part B. For example, Part B may cover tumor chemotherapy agents used with an infusion pump, and heparin used with a home dialysis system.[86] Other drugs similarly covered include respiratory medications used with nebulizers and certain pain-management drugs administered through covered DME.

---

[80]   *See* 42 C.F.R. § 409.13 (2013).

[81]   *See* Medicare Claims Processing Manual Ch., 4 § 10 (CMS-Pub. 100-04).

[82]   As part of the Medicare Catastrophic Coverage Act, Pub. L. No. 100-360, 102 Stat. 683 (1988), Congress added a comprehensive outpatient drug benefit to the Medicare program. A year later, in 1989, the benefit was repealed as part of the Medicare Catastrophic Coverage Repeal Act, Pub. L. No. 101-234, 103 Stat. 1979 (1989).

[83]   42 U.S.C. § 1395x(s)(2)(A) (2012).

[84]   *Id.* § 1395y(a)(7).

[85]   *Id.* §§ 1395x(s)(2)(G), (I), (J), (O)-(Q), 1395x(s)(10)(A)-(B).

[86]   *See* MEDICARE CLAIMS PROCESSING MANUAL, Ch.17 § 10 (CMS-Pub. 100-04).

Medicare Part D

The most significant expansion of Medicare drug coverage came through the creation of the Medicare Part D program under the Medicare Prescription Drug Improvement and Modernization Act of 2003,[87] often referred to as the MMA. The central feature of the MMA is the establishment of a new Medicare prescription drug benefit under Part D of the Social Security Act (SSA), which covers certain outpatient prescription drugs starting on January 1, 2006. Participation in the program is voluntary. Those beneficiaries who choose to participate select either: 1) a qualified prescription-drug plan (PDP), which is a stand-alone, drug-only insurance benefit offered by a private entity licensed to offer health insurance under state law; or 2) a Medicare Advantage (MA) managed-care plan,[88] which includes prescription drug coverage along with other Medicare services (MA-PD).

In general, PDPs and MA-PD plans (collectively referred to as Part D plans) offer either "standard coverage" or its actuarial equivalent (with out-of-pocket threshold and deductible amounts that do not exceed those of standard coverage).[89] In 2014, the annual deductible for standard coverage was $310.[90] After a beneficiary meets the annual deductible, a drug plan offering standard coverage covers 75 percent of drug costs incurred between $311 and $2,850, and the beneficiary pays the remaining 25 percent of the costs.[91] Once the $2,850 limit is met, the beneficiary pays 72 percent for generic drugs and 47.5 percent for brand-name drugs until yearly out-of-pocket costs reach $4,550 (the so-called "donut hole").[92] Many plans have adopted other actuarially equivalent cost-sharing arrangements, including tiered co-payment systems. After out-of-pocket costs have exceeded $4,550, the beneficiary pays the greater of 5 percent coinsurance or $2.55 for generic drugs and $6.35 for all other drugs.[93] Premium and cost-sharing subsidies are available for certain low-income beneficiaries.[94] Drug plans also offer supplemental coverage, consisting of reductions in deductibles or cost-sharing amounts, or expanded drug coverage.

The Medicare program periodically updates the particular dollar thresholds associated with these Part D coverage tiers on the basis of anticipated coverage and costs. As part of ACA, however, Congress has sought to close the "donut hole" in part by 2020. This closure would be financed in significant part by manufacturer rebates equal to 50 percent of the negotiated payment amount for prescription drugs dispensed to certain low-income beneficiaries in the donut hole.[95]

Beneficiaries must be provided a choice of at least two qualifying Part D plans offered by at least two different entities in their region.[96] If there are insufficient bids for a given region,

---

87   Medicare Prescription Drug, Improvement, and Modernization Act, Pub. L. No. 108-173, § 101, 107 Stat. 2066 (2003). *See also* 42 U.S.C. §1395w-101; 42 C.F.R. pt. 423 (2013); Prescription Drug Coverage – General Information (July 14, 2014), *available at* http://www.cms.hhs.gov/PrescriptionDrugCovGenIn.

88   Formerly referred to as Medicare+Choice or "M+C" plans.

89   42 U.S.C. § 1395w-102(a) (2012).

90   42 U.S.C. § 1395w-102(b) (2012).

91   *Id.*

92   *See* Understanding Part D Medicare (Sept. 30, 2013), *available at* http://www.ibxmedicare.com/new_to_medicare/part_d_101.html.

93   *Id.*

94   *Id.*§ 1395w-114.

95   Patient Protection and Affordable Care Act, Pub. L. No. 111-148, § 3301, 124 Stat. 119 (2010).

96   42 U.S.C. § 1395w-103 (2012).

the Secretary of Health and Human Services (Secretary) may approve a "limited risk bid" for the region.[97] If access requirements in a region still are not met, the Secretary must establish a process for the solicitation of bids from eligible "fallback entities" that provide standard prescription drug benefits, provide access to negotiated prices, and meet the requirements for PDP sponsors.[98]

Prospective sponsors of Part D plans must comply with a bid process established by the Secretary, and must meet the extensive requirements for drug-plan sponsors.[99] Among other things, drug plans are required to provide a beneficiary with access to negotiated prices for covered drugs (including access to discounts, subsidies, rebates, and other price concessions the plan receives from drug manufacturers), even if the beneficiary directly pays for the drugs (i.e., for deductible expenses or in the "donut hole").[100] Negotiated prices offered to beneficiaries will not be taken into account for purposes of determining a pharmaceutical manufacturer's "best price" under the Medicaid drug rebate program.[101] The MMA also requires drug plans to disclose to the Secretary the aggregate negotiated price concessions made available to the drug plan and passed through to the beneficiaries in the form of greater subsidies, lower monthly premiums, and lower prices for drugs.

PART D "STANDARD" BENEFIT STRUCTURE*

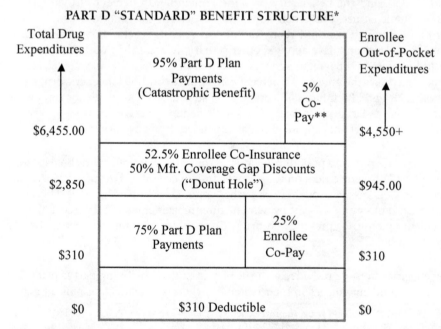

* Numbers shown are for 2014. *See* http://www.q1medicare.com/PartD-The-2014-Medicare-Part-D-Outlook. php.
** Catastrophic benefit cost-sharing is higher of i) 5 percent or ii) $2.55 generic or preferred multi-source drug, or $6.35 for any other drug.

---

97   *Id.* § 1395w-111(f).
98   *Id.* § 1395w-111(g).
99   *Id.* § 1395w-112.
100   *Id.* § 1395w-102.
101   *Id.* § 1396r-8(c).

he MMA includes complex provisions establishing payments to Part D plan sponsors.[102] n short, a plan's bid amount (including administrative costs and assumed profit) generally epresents the payment to the sponsor. However, this payment amount is subject to "risk orridor" adjustments, an additional "re-insurance" subsidy with respect to the catastrophic enefit and cost-sharing subsidies with respect to reduced cost sharing for low-income nrollees.[103] Further, plan amounts are subject to adjustment based on beneficiary health tatus risk factors to be established by CMS.[104] The MMA also requires the Secretary to nake special subsidy payments to sponsors of qualified retiree prescription drug plans in rder to encourage those plans to continue providing prescription drug coverage to their nrollees.[105]

)rug plans that use formularies must establish a pharmaceutical and therapeutic (P&T) ommittee that meets certain standards as to the development and review of the plan's ormulary.[106] Formularies must include drugs from each therapeutic category and class of overed outpatient drugs, but may exclude specific drugs within such categories or classes. he MMA directs the Secretary to request that the United States Pharmacopeia (USP) levelop a list of categories and classes that may be used by drug plans when developing heir formularies.[107] Although the use of formularies is optional, drug plans are required o establish cost-effective utilization-management programs and certain quality-assurance neasures.[108]

Medicaid

'rescription drugs are among the "optional" categories of services that a state may cover nder its Medicaid program.[109] If a state elects to cover prescription drugs, it must meet a umber of specific provisions relating to coverage and utilization of outpatient prescription lrugs, which were adopted as part of the Omnibus Budget Reconciliation Act of 1990[110] and he Veterans Health Care Act of 1992.[111]

Jnder those statutes, a drug manufacturer must enter into a series of agreements with the ecretaries of DHHS and Veterans Affairs. These agreements generally require a manufacturer o provide rebates and discounts to specified purchasers, and are described in greater detail)elow.[112]

f a manufacturer enters into the required discount and pricing agreements, the Medicaid tatute specifically limits the circumstances under which a state Medicaid program may

---

[02] Id. § 1395w-111.
[03] Id. § 1395w-115.
[04] Id.
[05] Id. § 1395w-132.
[06] Id. § 1395w-104.
[07] As discussed below, USP has released final model categories and classes. See USP Medicare Model Guidelines, v6.0 (Feb. 4, 2014), available at http://www.usp.org/usp-healthcare-professionals/usp-medicare-model-guidelines.
[08] 42 U.S.C. § 1395w-104 (2012).
[09] See 42 U.S.C. §§ 1396a(a)(10)(A), 1396d(a)(12) (2012).
[10] Omnibus Budget Reconciliation Act, Pub. L. No. 101-508, 104 Stat. 115 (1990).
[11] Veterans Health Care Act, Pub. L. No. 102-585, 106 Stat. 4961 (1992).
[12] 42 U.S.C. § 1396r-8(a) (2012). See infra Federal Drug Pricing Legislation.

otherwise exclude from coverage or restrict the use of the manufacturer's drugs. First, a state may subject any drug to prior authorization, provided that the state's prior-authorization program furnishes a response within 24 hours and permits reimbursement for a 72-hour supply of the drug in cases of emergency.[113] Second, a state may exclude or restrict coverage of drugs for uses other than those that are medically indicated.[114] Third, a state may exclude or restrict coverage of specifically enumerated classes of drugs.[115] Fourth, a state may exclude or restrict coverage of drugs pursuant to an agreement with the manufacturer.[116] Fifth, a state may provide limits on the quantity or number of refills of drugs if such limits are necessary to discourage waste.[117]

Sixth, a state may restrict coverage of a drug pursuant to a formulary that meets various federal requirements.[118] The formulary must: 1) be developed by a committee of physicians, pharmacists, and "other appropriate individuals appointed by the governor or the state's drug use review board"; 2) include those drugs of a manufacturer that have not been specifically excluded or that are not otherwise subject to exclusion because they belong to one of the classes of drugs subject to exclusion or restriction; 3) exclude a drug from coverage only with respect to a particular disease or condition for an identified population if the drug "does not have a significant, clinically meaningful therapeutic advantage in terms of safety, effectiveness, or clinical outcome" over other drugs in the formulary; 4) not exclude drugs from coverage without a publicly available, written explanation; and 5) allow as to drugs excluded from the formulary coverage under a prior authorization program.[119]

Coverage of Prescription Drugs Under Medicare and Medicaid Managed-Care Programs

Historically, the Medicare and Medicaid programs operated primarily on a fee-for-service basis, and the coverage rules described above have applied. Recently, however, managed-care models have taken on increasing importance in these programs in light of the belief that they can produce cost savings. The coverage standards for outpatient prescription drugs under Medicare and Medicaid are different in the managed care context from what they are in the fee-for-service context.

As noted previously, Medicare Advantage managed-care plans may offer prescription-drug coverage under Medicare Part D, subject to the Part D regulatory standards. Under Medicaid, drugs dispensed through HMOs were historically exempt from the requirements relating

---

[113]   42 U.S.C. § 1396r-8(d)(1)(A) (2012).

[114]   *Id.* § 1396r-8(d)(1)(B)(i).

[115]   *Id.* § 1396r-8(d)(1)(B)(ii). In addition, the Secretary is authorized to name additional classes of drugs subject to restriction because of clinical abuse or inappropriate use. *Id.* § 1396r-8(d)(3).

[116]   *Id.* § 1396r-8(d)(1)(B)(iii).

[117]   *Id.* § 1396r-8(d)(6) (2008).

[118]   *Id.* § 1396r-8(d)(1)(B)(iv).

[119]   *Id.* § 1396r-8(d)(4).

to manufacturer rebate agreements, coverage limits, formulary standards, and the like.[120] In the Medicaid managed-care context, an HMO with a managed-care contract, therefore, has significant latitude to employ restrictive formularies, prior authorization, and other coverage limits. As part of the ACA, however, drugs dispensed through Medicaid managed-care organizations are now subject to Medicaid rebates, and thus it is unclear whether manufacturers will continue to pay rebates to Medicaid managed-care organizations as part of formulary contracting.

Payment
Medicare

Medicare payment for a covered drug varies according to the setting in which the drug is provided, and on whether the covered service falls under Medicare Part A, Part B, or Part D.

Under Part A, payment for a drug depends on the service provider that furnishes the drug to the Medicare beneficiary. For a hospital inpatient, payment for both prescription and nonprescription drugs is included in the DRG payments.[121] Other institutional providers, such as SNFs and home health agencies, generally are reimbursed on the basis of daily or per-visit prospective rates.[122] For hospices, reimbursement is made using a cost-related prospective-payment method, subject to a ceiling.[123]

To the extent that Medicare Part B currently covers drugs furnished "incident to" physician services, they are reimbursed separately from the physician's services. Medicare reimbursement for covered drugs that are incident to a physician's services has transitioned from a methodology based on manufacturer reported average wholesale price (AWP)[124] to one based on manufacturer reported average sales price (ASP).[125]

Finally, insofar as Medicare Part D is implemented through contracts with Part D plans, a pharmacy will generally receive from the Part D plan payment based on a rate negotiated by it under its network pharmacy-participation contract.[126]

Medicaid

The federal Medicaid statute contains relatively limited standards for reimbursement of prescription drugs and related pharmacy services, consistent with states' general flexibility

---

[120] See id. § 1396r-8(j).

[121] See, supra Payment for Medical Devices – Hospital Inpatient Services.

[122] See 42 U.S.C. §§ 1395yy, 1395fff (2012).

[123] 42 C.F.R. § 418.302 (2013).

[124] Id. § 405.517.

[125] 42 C.F.R. §414.800 (2013); Medicaid Drug Price Comparison: Average Sales Price to Average Wholesale Price (June 2005) ("Average sales price is a manufacturer's unit sales of a drug to all purchasers in the United States in a calendar quarter divided by the total number of units of the drug sold by the manufacturer in that same quarter." While, the average wholesale price is "the published price reported in commercial publications."), available at oig.hhs.gov/oei/reports/oei-03-05-00200.pdf.

[126] Comparing Pharmacy Reimbursement: Medicare Part D to Medicaid (Feb. 2009), available at oig.hhs.gov/oei/reports/oei-03-07-00350.pdf.

with respect to the design of their state Medicaid programs.[127] Nonetheless, federal regulations provide some standards for such reimbursement, and the ACA has expanded the federal role in reimbursement for generic drugs.

Specifically, the aggregate state payments for drugs may not exceed certain "upper limits."[128] CMS must establish upper limits for multiple-source drugs (to be applicable except where a prescriber certifies a particular brand as medically necessary) where FDA has rated three or more drug products as therapeutically and pharmaceutically equivalent in its most recent edition of Approved Drug Products with Therapeutic Equivalence Evaluations ("The Orange Book"). For such drugs, pursuant to the ACA, the upper limit must be set at 175 percent of the average manufacturer price (AMP) of the weighted average AMP of the equivalent products, plus a reasonable dispensing fee.[129] For multiple-source drugs certified as "brand medically necessary" and for other drugs, a state's aggregate payments may not exceed the lower of 1) the provider's estimated acquisition costs of the drug plus a reasonable dispensing fee or 2) the provider's usual and customary charge to the general public.[130] CMS has released, for review and comment, draft federal upper limits (FULs) and related data, as well as its draft methodology for calculating such upper limits. CMS has also indicated that it intends to release further detailed implementation guidance for the states. As of October 2014, CMS has not issued a final upper limit calculation methodology.

The ACA also changed certain definitions relating to AMP and other requirements for calculation of AMP and upper limits. CMS has released proposed regulations in this regard and in the same release has proposed that Medicaid reimbursement of drugs to which FULs do not apply be based on an "actual acquisition cost" measure, with new requirements for Medicaid dispensing fees.

Aside from these standards, states have wide latitude in establishing the method and amount of payments for drugs and pharmacy services. In most cases, states reimburse pharmacies an amount to cover drug costs as well as a separate dispensing fee. The amount to cover drug costs typically is expressed in terms of a percentage of published wholesale acquisition costs or average wholesale price, or similar measure. A few states reimburse drug costs on the basis of the pharmacy's actual acquisition cost.[131] A few states have more directly regulated pharmacies' charges by implementing "most favored nation" restrictions. More significantly, CMS has hired a private company to perform a monthly nationwide survey of retail community pharmacy prescription drug prices and to provide states with ongoing pricing files in order to assist them in rate setting. CMS expects that these pricing files will

---

[127]   The only statutory payment standard currently applicable to pharmacy services is the so-called "equal access" requirement of 42 U.S.C. § 1396a(a)(30)(A) (2012), which requires that state payments be "consistent with efficiency, economy, and quality of care and . . . sufficient to enlist enough providers so that care and services are available under the [state Medicaid] plan at least to the extent that such care and services are available to the general population in the geographic area."

[128]   42 C.F.R. §§ 447.512-447.514 (2013).

[129]   42 U.S.C. §1396r-8 (2012).

[130]   42 C.F.R. § 447.512(b) (2013).

[131]   See, e.g., State Prescription Drug Resources: State Medicaid Reimbursement Information (Mar. 8, 2014), available at http://www.medicaid.gov/Medicaid-CHIP-Program-Information/By-Topics/Benefits/Prescription-Drugs/State-Prescription-Drug-Resources.html; Survey of Retail Prices (May 7, 2014), available at http://www.medicaid.gov/Medicaid-CHIP-Program-Information/By-Topics/Benefits/Prescription-Drugs/Survey-of-Retail-Prices.html.

rovide state Medicaid agencies with an array of covered outpatient drug prices concerning cquisition costs and consumer purchase prices, which states can use to compare their ricing methodologies and payments to those derived from these surveys.[132]

Federal Drug Pricing Legislation

n addition to regulating reimbursement to pharmacies for dispensing prescription drugs nder Medicare and Medicaid, federal law mandates rebates and price reductions from rug manufacturers to certain categories of purchasers. These laws can significantly affect he way in which a pharmaceutical manufacturer may choose to market or distribute its roducts. For example, differential pricing, the use of wholesalers, and the provision of iscounts all have implications under these statutes.

The Medicaid Drug Rebate Statute

n 1990, Congress enacted the Medicaid drug rebate statute, which requires a drug nanufacturer to enter into an agreement to pay quarterly rebates for "covered outpatient lrugs" dispensed and paid for under the Medicaid program's outpatient drug benefit, in rder for federal matching funds to be available for the manufacturer's products.[133] The basic oal of the statute is to place state Medicaid programs on cost terms comparable to those njoyed by other large-volume purchasers of drugs.

Covered outpatient drugs subject to rebates include all FDA-approved drugs, biologics, and nsulin.[134] However, a product is not considered to be a "covered outpatient drug" for which rebate is due if it is furnished in connection with, *and its cost is covered as part of the eimbursement for*, certain other Medicaid-covered services.[135]

he amount of a rebate due from a manufacturer depends on whether the product is onsidered to be a single-source, innovator-multiple source, or non-innovator-multiple-ource drug. A single-source drug is one that is produced or distributed under an original lew drug application (NDA).[136] An innovator-multiple-source drug is one that was originally narketed under an original NDA and is one of two or more drug products marketed during rebate period that are 1) therapeutically equivalent and 2) pharmaceutically equivalent nd bioequivalent.[137] Non-innovator-multiple-source drugs include all other multiple-ource drugs, and typically include most drugs marketed under abbreviated new drug pplications.[138]

---

[32] *See* Survey of Retail Prices: Payment and Utilization Rates and Performance Rankings (May 7, 2014), *available at* http://www.medicaid.gov/Medicaid-CHIP-Program-Information/By-Topics/Benefits/Prescription-Drugs/Survey-of-Retail-Prices.html. The collection of information about consumer purchase prices was suspended on July 1, 2013 pending funding decisions. Surveys relating to retail community pharmacy acquisition costs continue to be conducted.

[33] 42 U.S.C. § 1396r-8 (2012).

[34] *Id.* § 1396r-8(k).

[35] *Id.* § 1396r-8(k)(2)-(3).

[36] *Id.* § 1396r-8(k)(7)(A)(iv).

[37] *Id.* § 1396r-8(k)(7)(A)(ii).

[38] *Id.* § 1396r-8(k)(7)(A)(iii).

For single-source drugs and innovator-multiple-source drugs, manufacturers must pay a "basic rebate" for each unit of a drug dispensed. The basic rebate is equal to the greater of: 1) the difference between the AMP for the drug and the "best price" for the drug; or 2) the AMP times a statutory "rebate percentage."[139] In addition to the basic rebate, a manufacturer must pay an "additional rebate" with respect to single-source and innovator-multiple-source drugs. The additional rebate equals the amount by which the AMP for the drug exceeds the AMP for the drug in a "base period" after adjusting for inflation using the consumer price index.[140] The additional rebate is designed to provide a disincentive to drug price increases that exceed the rate of inflation. For a non-innovator-multiple-source drug, the required rebate is equal to 13 percent of the AMP of the drug;[141] and there is no requirement to pay an additional rebate.

The ACA made several adjustments to this scheme. First, it created a new basic rebate level of 17.1 percent of AMP for drugs approved exclusively for pediatric indications and for certain clotting agents. Second, it provided that for a new formulation of an existing oral dosage form of a single-source or innovator-multiple-source drug, the rebate is equal to the greater of 1) the rebate as calculated above, or 2) the greatest additional rebate applicable to any strength of the original formulation of the drug. This provision was intended to discourage manufacturers from avoiding additional rebates by making modest changes to their products. Third, the ACA established a cap on the amount of rebates due for single-source or innovator-multiple-source products equal to 100 percent of the AMP.[142]

The ACA also redefined "AMP" to mean the average price paid to a manufacturer for a drug for direct and indirect sales to "retail community pharmacies." The new definition specifically excludes prompt-pay discounts and certain service fees, such as distribution-service fees, stocking allowances, inventory-management allowances, and returns-management payments.[143] The term "retail community pharmacies" generally includes independent, chain, grocery, and mass-merchandiser pharmacies, but not hospital, mail, long-term care, or other managed-care arrangements.

"Best price" is currently defined as the "lowest price available from the manufacturer . . . to any wholesaler, retailer, provider, health maintenance organization, nonprofit entity, or governmental entity within the United States," excluding 1) prices charged to certain federal agencies, state veterans homes, and entities receiving funding under Public Health Service grants; 2) prices under the Federal Supply Schedule; 3) prices under state pharmaceutical assistance programs; 4) depot prices and single-award contract prices, and 5) price concessions to Medicare Part D PDPs.[144] Nominal prices (i.e., prices less than 10 percent of the AMP) also do not establish a Best Price if they are offered to specified designated providers.[145]

---

139   *Id.* § 1396r-8(c)(1)(A)-(B). The current rebate percentage is 23.1. Social Security Act § 1927(c)(1)(B)(i)(IV).
140   *Id.* § 1396r-8(c)(2).
141   *Id.* § 1396r-8(c)(3).
142   *See* ACA § 2501 (2010).
143   *Id.* § 1396r-8(k)(1). Manufacturers are required to calculate and report their AMP and Best Price to CMS on a monthly basis. Social Security Act § 1927(b)(3)(A).
144   42 U.S.C. § 1396r-8(c)(1)(C) (2012).
145   42 U.S.C. § 1396r-8(c)(1)(C)(i). Further, "best price" is inclusive of cash discounts, free goods that are contingent on any purchase requirement, volume discounts and rebates. *Id.* § 1396r-8(c)(1)(C)(ii).

In July 2007, CMS issued final rules to implement the rebate program.[146] These rules provide significantly greater clarity with respect to the calculation of AMP (particularly the entities that will be deemed to be the "retail pharmacy class of trade")[147] and Best Price.[148] In addition, the rules establish new principles for the treatment of sales of "authorized generic" drugs, which create financial disincentives to such arrangements.[149] However, following the passage of the ACA, CMS withdrew the AMP rules,[150] and the agency has proposed a new rule that is awaiting publication.

Veterans Health Care Act Pricing to Federal Agencies

Section 602 of the Veterans Health Care Act (VHCA) establishes a separate manufacturer drug pricing program as an additional condition to 1) federal Medicaid reimbursement and 2) direct federal purchases by the U.S. Department of Defense (DOD), U.S. Department of Veterans Affairs (DVA), or the Public Health Service (PHS).[151] Whereas the Medicaid rebate statute requires retrospective rebates to Medicaid programs, the VHCA requires prospective discounts to certain federal purchasers. As explained below, these discounts are computed on the basis of data entirely separate from those used under Medicaid.

The VHCA contains three basic requirements. First, a manufacturer must make each of its products available for procurement under the Federal Supply Schedule (FSS).[152] When negotiating an FSS contract with a vendor, the government's goal is to obtain pricing comparable to that of the vendor's most favored customer.[153]

Second, the vendor/manufacturer must enter into an agreement under which the price it charges the DOD, DVA, or PHS for certain products may not exceed a "federal ceiling price."[154] The federal ceiling price is equal to 76 percent of the average manufacturer price for sales to non-federal-government purchasers, plus an "additional discount."[155] The additional discount is comparable to the "additional rebate" under the Medicaid program, insofar as it penalizes manufacturers that increase their prices faster than the rate of inflation on a year-to-year basis. To the extent that a manufacturer's federal ceiling price exceeds its most favored customer price, the government will continue to seek the lower price.

---

[146]   42 C.F.R. § 447.500 (2013); *See* Medicaid Program; Prescription Drugs, 72 Fed. Reg. 39,239 (July 17, 2007).

[147]   42 C.F.R. § 447.504 (2013).

[148]   *Id.* § 447.505.

[149]   *Id.* § 447.506.

[150]   Medicaid Program; Withdrawal of Determination of Average Manufacturer Price, Multiple Source Drug Definition, and Upper Limits for Multiple Source Drugs, 75 Fed. Reg. 69,591 (Nov. 15, 2010).

[151]   Veterans Health Care Act of 1992, Pub. L. No. 102-585, § 602, 106 Stat. 4943 (1992).

[152]   38 U.S.C. § 8126(a)(1) (2012). The FSS is a system under which a vendor enters into a government-wide, indefinite-quantity contract, and is designed to enable the government to aggregate its volume when negotiating purchase prices. Individual federal agencies may then purchase supplies from the vendor at the contract price. The FSS for drugs is administered by the DVA.

[153]   *See generally* Department of Veterans Affairs Federal Supply Schedule Service, http://www.fss.va.gov/ (last visited Sept. 8, 2014).

[154]   38 U.S.C. § 8126(a)(2) (2012).

[155]   *Id.* In calculating the non-federal average manufacturer price, the Department of Veterans Affairs does not employ the definitions or rules used by CMS for calculating AMP under the Medicaid rebate agreement. *See* Prices for Brand-Name Drugs Under Selected Federal Programs, Congressional Budget Office (June 1, 2005), *available at* http://www.cbo.gov/publication/16634.

Third, manufacturers must agree to charge state veterans homes prices that do not exceed the FSS price.[156]

Discounted Pricing to "Covered Entities"

The VHCA also established an additional program under which manufacturers must make their products available at discounted prices to certain specified "covered entities."[157] Most of the classes of covered entities are clinics and similar programs receiving grants under the Public Health Service Act, but certain hospitals serving a disproportionate share of indigent patients are also eligible for PHS discounts, along with children's hospitals, cancer hospitals, rural referral centers and sole community hospitals.[158] The amount of the PHS discount is equal to the AMP (as computed for purposes of the Medicaid rebate statute) times a "rebate percentage." The "rebate percentage" is equal to the average total rebate percentage under Medicaid.[159] The ACA authorized significant new oversight of the program, and it formalized administration in a number of ways, including establishing clearer audit authority, administrative dispute resolution procedures, and civil monetary penalties. As of October 2014, a proposed rule regarding the program had been developed but not yet published.

Fraud and Abuse

Since the late 1990s, pharmaceutical and medical device manufacturers have been subject to increasing scrutiny through fraud-and-abuse investigations. These investigations have focused on four basic types of laws: 1) anti-kickback laws, which address financial incentives to doctors or hospitals for use of products and that may rise to the level of bribery or conflict of interest; 2) false claims laws, which address inappropriate billing; 3) government pricing laws such as those described in the preceding section that address low pricing for government programs; and 4) off-label promotion, which may also result in false-claims issues insofar as government programs may not reimburse for certain off-label uses. This section will discuss the standards in the first two areas, and will use the federal Anti-Kickback Statute and the federal False Claims Act (FCA) to illustrate the general principles. Many states have their own analogous prohibitions.

The Federal Anti-Kickback Statute

The federal Anti-Kickback Statute[160] establishes criminal penalties that apply to any person who knowingly and willfully offers, pays, solicits, or receives any remuneration to induce or in return for 1) referring an individual to a person for the furnishing or arranging for the furnishing of any item or service payable in whole or in part under federal healthcare programs, or 2) purchasing, leasing, ordering, or arranging for or recommending, purchasing, leasing, or ordering any good, facility, service, or item payable under federal

---

[156]   38 U.S.C. § 8126(a)(3) (2012).

[157]   *See* 42 U.S.C. § 256b (2012). A number of these classes of covered entities were added under the ACA.

[158]   *Id.* § 256b(a)(4).

[159]   *Id.* § 256b(a)(2).

[160]   42 U.S.C. § 1320a-7b(b) (2012).

ealthcare programs.[161] In addition, the DHHS OIG may bring an administrative proceeding ɔ exclude a provider from Medicare or Medicaid participation without having to obtain a riminal conviction under the statute. Judicial and administrative decisions have interpreted ne statute broadly.[162] The Affordable Care Act established that a claim that results from a ickback violation is a false claim.[163]

ix of the 11 statutory exceptions to the basic anti-kickback prohibition include properly .isclosed discounts or other reductions in price, payments to bona fide employees, payments ɔ group-purchasing organizations, waiver of coinsurance for Medicare Part B services for ertain individuals who qualify for certain PHS programs, risk-sharing arrangements, nd payment practices set forth in regulations defining conduct that will not be subject to nforcement.[164]

'ursuant to this last exception, the OIG's "safe harbor" regulations define payment practices hat will not run afoul of the statute.[165] The fact that a particular arrangement does not fall ithin a safe harbor does not mean that the arrangement is unlawful. Rather, its facts and ircumstances must be analyzed to determine whether it involves remuneration intended to nduce referrals or recommendations. The safe harbors most pertinent to manufacturers of evices and drugs cover 1) equipment rental; 2) personal services and management contracts;) warranties; 4) discounts; 5) certain payments to group-purchasing organizations; 6) ompensation to employees; and 7) shared-risk arrangements.[166]

n addition to the safe harbor regulations, the OIG has issued a variety of other guidance ɔ manufacturers with respect to the Anti-Kickback Statute. For example, the agency's egulations authorize the issuance of advisory opinions on specific transactions.[167] 'urther, for pharmaceutical manufacturers, the agency has issued "compliance program

---

[61] Historically, the federal anti-kickback statute applied only to goods and services reimbursable under Medicare, Medicaid, or certain other state healthcare programs. The passage of the Health Insurance Portability and Accountability Act of 1996, Pub. L. No. 104-191, 110 Stat. 1936 (1996), however, expanded the statute to apply to all federally funded healthcare programs except the Federal Employees' Health Benefits Program. *Id.* § 1320a-7b(f).

[62] *See, e.g.,* United States v. Mathur, 2012 U.S. Dist. LEXIS 143197, at *14 (D. Nev. Sept. 13, 2012) (the PPACA clarifies that the government need not show a defendant's actual knowledge of the Anti-Kickback Act or a specific intent to violate it in order to prove a violation of the statute); Hanlester Network v. Shalala, 51 F.3d 1390 (9th Cir. 1995) (mandatory requirement of referrals in exchange for remuneration is unnecessary to violate the statute); United States v. Bay State Ambulance & Hosp. Rental Serv., Inc., 874 F.2d 20 (1st Cir. 1989) (giving person an opportunity to earn money may constitute an improper inducement); United States v. Greber, 760 F.2d 68 (3d Cir. 1985), *cert. denied*, 474 U.S. 988 (1985) (payment for actual services rendered may violate statute if "one purpose" of the payment was to induce referrals).

[63] 42 U.S.C. § 1320a-7b(g) (2012).

[64] 42 U.S.C. § 1320a-7b(b)(3) (2012).

[65] 42 C.F.R. § 1001.952 (2013).

[66] To gain the benefit of a safe harbor, one must satisfy every regulatory element. Although a detailed examination of those elements is beyond the scope of this chapter, the discussion will highlight some of the key requirements in various contexts. Nonetheless, when evaluating compliance, it is imperative that the particular elements of a transaction be compared with the applicable regulations.

[67] 42 C.F.R. § 1008.1 (2013). The OIG has issued numerous advisory opinions affecting manufacturer practices. *See* Advisory Opinions, http://oig.hhs.gov/compliance/advisory-opinions/index.asp (last visited Sept. 9, 2014). Recently, the OIG issued a Special Advisory Bulletin that addresses the subsidizing of payments for prescription drugs, and defines the term "disease state" to be reasonably broad. *See* Supplemental Special Advisory Bulletin: Independent Charity Patient Assistance Programs, 79 Fed. Reg. 31,120 (May 30, 2014).

guidance" containing general standards,[168] as well as several "fraud alerts" addressing more specific issues.[169] For example, in 1994, the OIG issued a "Special Fraud Alert" concerning prescription drug marketing practices that potentially run afoul of the Anti-Kickback Statute.[170] The Special Fraud Alert described general conditions that might trigger scrutiny and also identified a number of specific arrangements that OIG viewed as problematical if one purpose of the arrangements was to induce the provision of a specific prescription drug under Medicare or Medicaid. These programs included:

- "Fee per switch" programs, in which a manufacturer offered cash incentives to a pharmacy each time the pharmacy persuaded the prescriber to change the prescription from a competitor's product to the manufacturer's product;

- In-kind bonuses (e.g., frequent flier miles) provided to physicians, suppliers, or managed care organizations in exchange for, or based on, prescribing particular products;

- Bogus research grants for *de minimis* recordkeeping activities that have little scientific value and require little scientific research; and

- Payments for marketing functions in the guise of patient education and counseling programs that are within the scope of pharmacy practice.

OIG also has entered into Corporate Integrity Agreements in connection with global settlements with pharmaceutical and medical device manufacturers, which articulate standards of care and compliance controls that may be appropriate to minimize anti-kickback risks to federal programs.[171]

The Anti-Kickback Statute potentially has far-reaching implications with respect to a broad range of activities in the marketing of pharmaceuticals and medical devices, including product-supply arrangements, research grants, payments for pharmacy services, and educational subsidies. Several of these issues are described generally below.

With respect to product-supply arrangements, manufacturers often provide discounts, rebates, and other incentives to purchasers of their products. The discount safe harbor may protect certain of these arrangements, depending on the nature of the price reduction and the method of reimbursement. Generally, in order for the parties to gain the benefit of the safe harbor, the buyer must report the amount of the discount to the Medicare or Medicaid program, and the seller must disclose the net price and provide the buyer with the information necessary to facilitate the reporting.[172] However, the safe harbor does not protect: 1) a discount on one product in exchange for an agreement to buy another product; 2) discounts not offered to Medicare or Medicaid; or 3) "discounts" in the form of retroactive rebates where the buyer is reimbursed on a basis other than cost reports, as are

---

[168]   OIG Compliance Program Guidance for Pharmaceutical Manufacturers, 68 Fed. Reg. 23,731 (May 5, 2003), *available at* http://oig.hhs.gov/compliance/compliance-guidance/index.asp.

[169]   *See* Publication of OIG Special Fraud Alerts (Dec. 19, 1994), *available at* http://oig.hhs.gov/fraud/docs/alertsandbulletins/121994.html.

[170]   *See* MEDICARE & MEDICAID GUIDE (CCH) ¶ 42,609.

[171]   Corporate Integrity Agreement Documents, http://www.oig.hhs.gov/compliance/corporate-integrity-agreements/cia-documents.asp (last visited July 9, 2014).

[172]   *See* 42 C.F.R.§ 1001.952(h) (2013). The claim forms of state Medicaid programs, however, do not provide a mechanism for pharmacies to report the amount of the discount.

most pharmacies.[173] Recently there have been several challenges and settlements regarding putative arrangements that involve market-share rebates being given to long-term care facilities.[174]

Many manufacturers seek to obtain data concerning their products and patients through pharmacist-patient contacts, and also sponsor other activities involving research. Because such activities involve actual services, the safe harbor for personal services and management contracts may provide protection for them.[175] The most critical element here is whether the compensation is consistent with fair market value, specified in advance, and not tied to the volume or value of business generated. In addition, caution must be exercised because the services must be of a scope reasonably necessary to achieve a commercially reasonable business purpose and must be "actually performed."[176] For example, the government has entered into settlements and deferred prosecution agreements with several major orthopedic implant manufacturers relating primarily to their consulting and service agreements with orthopedic surgeons. The settlements were based on allegations that those relationships were excessive in scope and payment amount, and that the services for which the payments purportedly were made were not actually rendered at times.[177] The area of service agreements also bears close attention as products become more complicated, and subject to detailed risk-evaluation and management-strategy requirements, or are subject to limited-distribution systems. In these contexts, manufacturers may enter into arrangements with healthcare providers to provide patients with product support, and these arrangements may attract the attention of OIG and/or federal prosecutors.

Manufacturers also may provide educational and research grants to prescribers and dispensers. In general, there is no safe harbor that covers such activities. Thus, additional relevant factors to consider when evaluating research-grant programs include: 1) whether the researcher is selected because of special knowledge or previous dispensing history; 2) whether the research data are sought by the manufacturer's medical department or marketing department; 3) whether bona fide scientific research or education is involved; 4) whether the manufacturer actually collects and uses the data for some legitimate purpose; and 5) the degree, if any, of involvement by the manufacturer's sales or marketing forces in the consideration and approval of the requested funding.

As noted, many states have enacted their own anti-kickback laws, many of which contain prohibitions that parallel those of the federal statute. Many of these laws apply only to goods and services furnished under the state's Medicaid program, but a few apply broadly to all healthcare services and payors.[178] In addition, a large number of states have enacted

---

[173]   Id. See Joseph Metro, *Unanswered Questions: A Critical Look at the Discount Safe Harbor and Its Limitations in* HEALTH LAW HANDBOOK § 9:7 (2007).

[174]   For example, recently, Amgen paid $24.9 million to resolve allegations that it used kickbacks to induce long-term care facilities to use more of its drug. The government alleged that the kickbacks took the form of performance-based rebates that were tied to market-share or volume thresholds. See Department of Justice, Office of Public Affairs (Apr. 16, 2013), *available at* http://www.justice.gov/opa/pr/2013/April/13-civ-438. html.

[175]   See 42 C.F.R. § 1001.952(d) (2013).

[176]   Id.

[177]   Department of Justice News Release (Sept. 27, 2007), *available at* www.justice.gov/usao/nj/Press/files/pdffiles/Older/hips0927.rel.pdf.

[178]   See, e.g., MASS. GEN. LAWS, ch. 175H, § 3 (2013).

professional practice statutes that prohibit kickbacks, fee-splitting, and other practices viewed as unprofessional conduct. Although these statutes may be interpreted to be consistent with federal law, they should be analyzed separately to determine the specific parties, programs, and conduct to which they apply.

False Claims Prohibitions

Federal statutes establish criminal, civil, and administrative penalties for false or fraudulent claims for reimbursement.[179] The definition of the term "false claim" is generally broad, and permits prosecutors to make claims where there is no actual government payment. The statute also applies to corporate entities or other individuals who merely caused or conspired to cause a false claim to be filed.[180] For example, in 1995, a manufacturer of lymphedema pumps settled with the U.S. Department of Justice and paid $4.9 million to resolve questions over the manufacturer's recommendations to suppliers as to which HCPCS billing codes to use.[181] Further, the false claim need not be filed intentionally, but merely with "deliberate ignorance" or "reckless disregard" for the truth.[182]

Violations of false claims prohibitions can result in significant penalties, including criminal fines and imprisonment, treble damages, and civil penalties.[183] Perhaps most significantly, the civil false claims statute authorizes "whistleblower" lawsuits, known as "*qui tam*" actions, whereby an individual (known as a "relator") may bring an action for false claims on behalf of the United States and receive a portion of any recovery.[184] This private enforcement, coupled with the breadth of the statute and the significant leverage afforded to the government as a result of the financial penalties, has made the FCA the typical vehicle used by the government to settle healthcare fraud investigations, regardless of whether the "core"

---

[179]   *See* 18 U.S.C. § 287 (2012); 31 U.S.C. § 3729 (2012); 42 U.S.C. § 1320a-7a(a) (2012).

[180]   31 U.S.C. § 3729(a)(1) (2012); United States ex rel. Ruscher v. Omnicare, Inc., 2014 U.S. Dist. LEXIS 79885, at *84 (S.D. Tex. June 12, 2014); United States, ex rel. Woodruff v. Haw. Pacific Health, 560 F. Supp. 2d 988 (D. Haw. 2008); United States ex rel. Reagan v. E. Tex. Med. Ct. Reg'l Healthcare Sys., 274 F. Supp. 2d 824, 839 (S.D. Tex. 2003) (articulating the necessary elements required to establish a violation of the FCA based on a conspiracy).

[181]   Selected Cases (Oct. 27, 1997), *available at* http://www.justice.gov/opa/health/hcf2.htm.

[182]   *See* 31 U.S.C. § 3729 (2012).

[183]   *See* 42 C.F.R. § 1003.102 (2013) (the OIG may seek civil monetary penalties for a wide variety of conduct).

[184]   *See* 31 U.S.C. § 3730 (2012).

rongdoing was "traditional" billing fraud,[185] kickbacks,[186] government pricing errors,[187] or ff-label promotion.[188]

Administrative Remedies

he OIG has independent authority to seek monetary payments and exclusion against an ndividual or entity based on a variety of prohibited activities. Often in lieu of exercising such emedies the OIG will instead negotiate CIAs with healthcare providers, manufacturers, and ther entities as part of the settlement of false claims allegations.[189] CIAs have become the de cto mechanism of enforcement regulations. In large-scale settlements, the manufacturer ften enters into a CIA with the OIG, under which the company agrees to take certain rospective steps to prevent and detect potential future noncompliance. These agreements ypically entail significant training and monitoring expenses, including through external arties.[190] Newer CIAs have more conduct remedies such as requiring the Board of irectors to certify to the government that business units are in compliance and prohibiting ncentive compensation. The OIG has recently issued a notice in the *Federal Register* that it considering revising the criteria for implementing its exclusion authority and is seeking ublic comments.[191]

Conclusion

With changes in Medicare and Medicaid payment, the shift to bundled payment and ACOs nd emphasis on evidence-based decision making, improved outcomes data, and costs of

---

[5] *See* The Department of Health and Human Services and The Department of Justice Health Care Fraud and Abuse Control Program Annual Report for FY 2004 (Sept. 2005), *available at* http://oig.hhs.gov/ publications/docs/hcfac/hcfacreport2004.htm (settlement against nutritional manufacturers based in part on improper coding advice); *see also* FY 2013, *available at* http://oig.hhs.gov/reports-and-publications/ hcfac/ (settlement against Healthpoint Ltd. based in part on the submission of false claims to Medicare and Medicaid for an unapproved new drug that did not qualify for reimbursement).

[6] *See* 42 U.S.C. § 1320a-7b(g) (2012). The Department of Health and Human Services and The Department of Justice Health Care Fraud and Abuse Control Program Annual Report for FY 2013, http://oig.hhs. gov/reports-and-publications/hcfac/ (Amgen Inc. to pay $612 million to in part to resolve FCA allegations that Amgen engaged in off-label promotion, false reporting practices, and offered illegal kickbacks to a wide range of entities in an effort to influence healthcare providers to select its products for use, regardless of whether they were reimbursable by federal healthcare programs or were medically necessary).

[7] Aventis Pharmaceutical to Pay U.S. $95.5 Million to Settle False Claims Act Allegations (May 28, 2009), *available at* http://www.justice.gov/opa/pr/2009/May/09-civ-520.html (settlement based on underpaying drug rebates to the Medicaid program and overcharging for drug products).

[8] *See id., available at* http://oig.hhs.gov/reports-and-publications/hcfac/ (Abbott Laboratories to pay $1.5 billion to resolve criminal & civil liability relating to off-label promotion).

[9] *See* Corporate Integrity Agreements, https://oig.hhs.gov/compliance/corporate-integrity-agreements/ (last visited Sept. 9, 2014).

[0] *See* Corporate Integrity Agreement Documents (Sept. 8, 2014), *available at* https://oig.hhs.gov/compliance/ corporate-integrity-agreements/cia-documents.asp.

[1] *See* Solicitation of Information and Recommendations for Revising OIG's Non-Binding Criteria for Implementing Permissive Exclusion Authority Under Section 1128(b)(7) of the Social Security Act, 79 Fed. Reg. 40,114 (July 11, 2014).

medical technology,[192] manufacturers need to incorporate reimbursement strategies during the early stages of and throughout product development and commercialization.

Manufacturers need to consider the following:

- Planning data points to capture improved net health outcomes and cost-effectiveness;
- Well-designed clinical trials that deliver robust data for FDA along with government and private insurers;
- Reporting of data in peer-reviewed scientific journals;
- Configuring products and labeling to support favorable reimbursement;
- Coordinating with medical specialty societies;
- Obtaining and clarifying product and procedure coding;
- Regular and early communications with key insurers, and consideration of parallel FDA CMS review;
- Seeking new or expanded coverage and payment; and
- Engaging in the yearly updates on payment and periodic changes in codes and coverage to preserve favorable payment.

By understanding and working with customers and insurers on reimbursement issues, manufacturers can better direct the process of medical innovation and contribute to quality and cost-effective care for patients. At the same time, manufacturers must be vigilant that their relationships with physicians and hospitals in clinical trials, promotion, marketing, sales and customer support comply with federal and state fraud-and-abuse provisions, including a comprehensive and fully implemented corporate compliance function. Manufacturers funding of many customer programs are now subject to new reporting requirements that will open new areas of risk and challenge traditional product development and product management practices.

---

[192]   Gilead Sciences Hepatitis C drug Sovaldis, at $900 per pill and $84,000 per treatment, has been a controversial issue, especially comparing U.S. with international pricing (Aug. 8, 2014), *available at* http://www.forbes. com/sites/johnlamattina/2014/08/08/even-at-900-per-cure-sovaldis-cost-could-be-unacceptable-in-india/.

INDEX

CPSIA information can be obtained
at www.ICGtesting.com
Printed in the USA
LVHW051759110123
736941LV00005B/439

9 781935 065739